A GARDEN OF PLEASANT FLOWERS

(Paradisi in Sole: Paradisus Terrestris)

by

JOHN PARKINSON

Dover Publications, Inc.

New York

PUBLISHER'S NOTE

One of the great seventeenth-century English botanists was John Parkinson (1567–1650), apothecary to King James I and, after the publication in 1629 of the *Paradisus Terrestris* (dedicated to Queen Henrietta Maria), "first royal botanist" to Charles I. He is considered as the last Englishman "who belonged to the true lineage of herbalists." His largest work was the 1640 *Theatrum Botanicum. The Theater of Plantes, or An Universall and Complete Herball* (it was the premature announcement of the *Theatrum* that spurred Thomas Johnson's competitive revision of John Gerard's *Herball* in 1633). There has been much controversy over the value of the *Theatrum* and its alleged plagiarisms from Lobelius (Mathias de l'Obel), but no one has disputed the charm of Parkinson's first book, the *Paradisus Terrestris,* and its pioneering importance for English (and, later, American) horticulture, with special emphasis on the flower garden. The original 1629 edition is reprinted here in its entirety; the posthumous 1656 edition, though labeled as "corrected and enlarged," was substantially identical.

The woodcut illustration on the title page depicts Adam and Eve in Paradise (etymologically an Iranian/Greek word for "park" or "garden"). At the top of the page is the chief Hebrew name of God. At the very bottom is a four-line French poem meaning: "Whoever wishes to compare art with nature and our parks with Eden, indiscreetly measures the stride of the elephant by the stride of the mite and the flight of the eagle by that of the gnat." The main cartouche contains the punning Latin title (to be rendered "Park in Sun's [= Parkinson's] Earthly Paradise") and a long, fully descriptive English title. All the woodcuts in the volume, including the title page and the portrait, were done in England by the German artist C. Switzer (either Christoph or his son Christopher).

Following the dedication is Parkinson's epistle to the reader, in which he clearly states the aim, approach and limits of the work, and promises a future fourth part on simples (this eventually developed into the *Theatrum*). The sixteenth-century predecessors he mentions are Clusius (Charles de l'Ecluse) from Artois, William Turner (the "father of English botany"), the Fleming Dodonaeus (Rembert Dodoens) and Gerard.

Next come Latin compliments from friends and colleagues of Parkinson: a prose letter (dated Oct. 1, 1629) by the great physician Sir Theodore Turquet de Mayerne, who served James I, Charles I and Charles II (Mayerne apologizes for his inability to versify); and poems by the physician Othowell Meverall, William Atkins (a printer's error for the court physician Henry Atkins?), William "Brodus" and the above-mentioned Thomas Johnson.

The woodcut portrait of Parkinson bears a Latin legend meaning: "Portrait of John Parkinson, London apothecary, at 62 years of age, 1629 A.D."

Parkinson's main text, in easy, readable English, discusses nearly 1000 plants from all over the world that could then be grown in England. These fall under the three headings announced on his title page: the "garden of pleasure," i.e., flowers and fragrant herbs (this section alone comprises three-fourths of the entire work); the kitchen garden (culinary herbs and vegetables); and the orchard (trees, shrubs and vines that produce edible fruit). Some 812 plants are illustrated on 108 full-page plates. Some of these renderings were original with Switzer; many were adapted from the works of Lobelius (1570) and Clusius (1601), others from the *Hortus Floridus* of Crispin de Passe (Utrecht, 1614) and elsewhere. There are a few other drawings of garden plans and tools. Each of the three divisions of the book begins with an essay on "ordering" (preparing) the respective type of garden, but there are no specific growing instructions in the descriptions of the individual plants (in which the heading "vertues" means "medicinal properties").

The work concludes with an index of Latin plant names, an English plant name index, a table of medicinal properties, a list of errata, and the colophon of the printers.

Published in Canada by General Publishing Company, Ltd., 30 Lesmill Road, Don Mills, Toronto, Ontario. Published in the United Kingdom by Constable and Company, Ltd., 3 The Lanchesters, 162–164 Fulham Palace Road, London W6 9ER.

This Dover edition, first published in 1991, is an unaltered republication of the clothbound Dover edition of 1976 which was an unabridged republication of the work originally printed by Humphrey Lownes and Robert Young, London, in 1629. A new Publisher's Note was added to the 1976 edition and is also reprinted here.

International Standard Book Number: 0-486-26758-X
Library of Congress Catalog Card Number: 76-15697

Manufactured in the United States of America
Dover Publications, Inc.
31 East 2nd Street
Mineola, New York 11501

TO
THE QVEENES
MOST EXCELLENT
MAIESTIE.

Madame,

Knowing your Maieſtie ſo much delighted with all the faire Flowers of a Garden, and furniſhed with them as farre beyond others, as you are eminent before
them; this my VVorke of a Garden, long
before this intended to be publiſhed, and
but now only finiſhed, ſeemed as it were
deſtined, to bee firſt offered into your
Highneſſe hands, as of right challenging the proprietie of
Patronage from all others. Accept, I beſeech your Maieſtie,
this ſpeaking Garden, that may informe you in all the particulars of your ſtore, as well as wants, when you cannot ſee
any of them freſh vpon the ground : and it ſhall further en-
courage him to accompliſh the remainder; who, in praying
that your Highneſſe may enioy the heauenly Paradiſe, after
the many yeares fruition of this earthly, ſubmitteth to be

Your Maieſties

in all

humble deuotion,

IOHN PARKINSON.

TO THE COVRTEOVS
READER.

Lthough the ancient *Heathens* did appropriate the first inuention of the knowledge of *Herbes,* and so consequently of *Physicke,* some vnto *Chiron the Centaure,* and others vnto *Apollo* or *Æculapius his sonne;* yet wee that are *Christians haue* out of a better *Schoole* learned, that *God, the Creator* of *Heauen* and *Earth,* at the beginning when he created *Adam, inspired him* with the knowledge of all naturall things (which successiuely descended to *Noah afterwardes,* and to his *Posterity):* for, as he was able to giue names to all the liuing *Creatures,according* to their seuerall natures ; so no doubt but hee had also the knowledge, both what *Herbes* and *Fruits* were fit,eyther for *Meate* or *Medicine,* for *Vse* or for *Delight. And* that *Adam might exercise* this knowledge, *God planted a Garden* for him to liue in, (wherein euen in his innocency he was to labour and spend his time)which hee stored with the best and choysest *Herbes* and *Fruits* the earth could produce, that he might haue not onely for necessitie whereon to feede, but for pleasure also; the place or garden called *Paradise importing* as much,and more plainly the words set downe in *Genesis the second,which are these ;* Out of the ground the Lord *God* made to grow euerie tree pleasant to the sight and good for meate; and in the *24.* of *Numbers,the Parable of Balaam,mentioning the Aloe trees* that *God planted* ; and in other places if there were neede to recite them. But my purpose is onely to shew you, that *Paradise was a place (whether you will call it a Garden,or Orchard,or both,no doubt of some large extent) wherein Adam was first* placed to abide; that *God was the Planter thereof, hauing furnished it with trees* and *herbes,as well pleasant to the sight, as good for meate, and that hee being* to dresse and keepe this place,must of necessity know all the things that grew therein, and to what vses they serued, or else his labour about them, and knowledge in them,had been in vaine. *And although Adam lost* the place for his transgression, yet he lost not the naturall knowledge,nor vse of them : but that,as *God made the* whole world, and all the *Creatures therein* for *Man,* so hee may *vse* all things as well of pleasure as of necessitie, to bee helpes vnto him to serue his God. *Let men* therefore, according to their first institution, so vse their seruice, that they also in them may remember their seruice to God, and not (like our *Grand-mother Eve)* set their affections so strongly on the pleasure in them,as to deserue the losse of them in this *Paradise,* yea and of *Heauen* also. For truly from all sorts of *Herbes* and *Flowers* we may draw matter at all times not only to magnifie the *Creator* that hath giuen them such diuersities of formes, sents and colours, that the most *cunning*

Worke-

Worke-man cannot imitate, and ſuch vertues and properties, that although wee know many, yet many more lye hidden and vnknowne, but many good inſtructions alſo to our ſelues: That as many herbes and flowers with their fragrant ſweete ſmels doe comfort, and as it were reuiue the ſpirits, and perfume a whole houſe; euen ſo ſuch men as liue vertuouſly, labouring to doe good, and profit the Church of God and the Common wealth by their paines or penne, doe as it were ſend forth a pleaſing ſauour of ſweet inſtructions, not only to that time wherein they liue, and are freſh, but being drye, withered and dead, ceaſe not in all after ages to doe as much or more. Many herbes and flowers that haue ſmall beautie or ſauour to commend them, haue much more good vſe and vertue: ſo many men of excellent rare parts and good qualities doe lye hid vnknown and not reſpected, vntill time and vſe of them doe ſet forth their properties. Againe, many flowers haue a glorious ſhew of beauty and brauery, yet ſtinking in ſmell, or elſe of no other vſe: ſo many doe make a glorious oſtentation, and flouriſh in the world, when as if they ſtinke not horribly before God, and all good men, yet ſurely they haue no other vertue then their outſide to commend them, or leaue behind them. Some alſo riſe vp and appear like a Lilly among Thornes, or as a goodly Flower among many Weedes or Graſſe, eyther by their honourable authoritie, or eminence of learning or riches, whereby they excell others, and thereby may doe good to many. The frailty alſo of Mans life is learned by the ſoone fading of them before their flowring, or in their pride, or ſoone after, being either cropt by the hand of the ſpectator, or by a ſudden blaſt withered and parched, or by the reuolution of time decaying of it owne nature: as alſo that the faireſt flowers or fruits firſt ripe, are ſooneſt and firſt gathered. The mutabilitie alſo of ſtates and perſons, by this, that as where many goodly flowers & fruits did grow this yeare and age, in another they are quite pulled or digged vp, and eyther weedes and graſſe grow in their place, or ſome building erected thereon, and their place is no more known. The Ciuill reſpects to be learned from them are many alſo: for the delight of the varieties both of formes, colours and properties of Herbes and Flowers, hath euer beene powerfull ouer dull, vnnurtured, ruſticke and ſauage people, led only by Natures inſtinct; how much more powerfull is it, or ſhould be in the mindes of generous perſons? for it may well bee ſaid, he is not humane, that is not allured with this obiect. The ſtudy, knowledge, and trauel in them, as they haue been entertained of great Kings, Princes and Potentates, without diſparagement to their Greatneſſe, or hinderance to their more ſerious and weighty Affaires: ſo no doubt vnto all that are capable thereof, it is not onely pleaſant, but profitable, by comforting the minde, ſpirits and ſenſes with an harmeleſſe delight, and by enabling the iudgement to conferre and apply helpe to many dangerous diſeaſes. It is alſo an Inſtructer in the verity of the genuine Plants of the Ancients, and a Correcter of the many errours whereunto the world by continuance hath bin diuerted, and almoſt therein fixed, by eradicating in time, and by degrees, the pertinacious wilfulneſſe of many, who becauſe they were brought vp in their errours, are moſt vnwilling to leaue them without conſideration of the good or euill, the right or wrong, they draw on therewith. And for my ſelfe I may well ſay, that had not mine owne paines and ſtudies by a naturall inclination beene more powerfull in mee then any others helpe (although ſome through an euill diſpoſition and ignorance haue ſo far traduced me as to ſay this was rather another mans worke then mine owne, but I leaue them to their folly) I had neuer done ſo much as I here publiſh; nor been fit or prepared for a larger, as time may ſuddenly (by Gods permiſſion) bring to light, if the maleuolent diſpoſitions of degenerate ſpirits doe not hinder the accompliſhment.

But

But perswading my selfe there is no showre that produceth not some fruit, or no word but worketh some effect, eyther of good to perswade, or of reproofe to euince; I could not but declare my minde herein, let others iudge or say what they please. For I haue alwaies held it a thing vnfit, to conceale or bury that knowledge God hath giuen, and not to impart it, and further others therewith as much as is conuenient, yet without ostentation, which I haue euer hated. Now further to informe the courteous Reader, both of the occasion that led me on to this worke, and the other occurrences to it. First, hauing perused many Herbals in Latine, I obserued that most of them haue eyther neglected or not knowne the many diuersities of the flower Plants, and rare fruits are known to vs at this time, and (except Clusius) haue made mention but of a very few. In English likewise we haue some extant, as Turner and Dodonæus translated, who haue haue said little of Flowers, Gerard who is last, hath no doubt giuen vs the knowledge of as many as he attained vnto in his time, but since his daies we haue had many more varieties, then he or they euer heard of, as may be perceiued by the store I haue here produced. And none of them haue particularly seuered those that are beautifull flower plants, fit to store a garden of delight and pleasure, from the wilde and vnfit: but haue enterlaced many, one among another, whereby many that haue desired to haue faire flowers, haue not known either what to choose, or what to desire. Diuers Bookes of Flowers also haue been set forth, some in our owne Countrey, and more in others, all which are as it were but handfuls snatched from the plentifull Treasury of Nature, none of them being willing or able to open all sorts, and declare them fully ; but the greatest hinderance of all mens delight was, that none of them had giuen any description of them, but the bare name only. To satisfie therefore their desires that are louers of such Delights, I took vpon me this labour and charge, and haue here selected and set forth a Garden of all the chiefest for choyce, and fairest for shew, from among all the seuerall Tribes and Kindreds of Natures beauty, and haue ranked them as neere as I could, or as the worke would permit, in affinity one vnto another. Secondly, and for their sakes that are studious in Authors, I haue set down the names haue bin formerly giuen vnto them, with some of their errours, not intending to cumber this worke with all that might bee said of them, because the deciding of the many controuersies, doubts, and questions that concerne them, pertaine more fitly to a generall History : yet I haue beene in some places more copious and ample then at the first I had intended, the occasion drawing on my desire to informe others with what I thought was fit to be known, reseruing what else might be said to another time & worke; wherein (God willing) I will inlarge my selfe, the subiect matter requiring it at my hands, in what my small ability can effect. Thirdly, I haue also to embellish this Worke set forth the figures of all such plants and flowers as are materiall and different one from another : but not as some others haue done, that is, a number of the figures of one sort of plant that haue nothing to distinguish them but the colour, for that I hold to be superfluous and waste. Fourthly, I haue also set down the Vertues and Properties of them in a briefe manner, rather desiring to giue you the knowledge of a few certaine and true, then to relate, as others haue done, a needlesß and false multiplicitie, that so there might as well profit as pleasure be taken from them, and that nothing might be wanting to accomplish it fully. And so much for this first part, my Garden of pleasant and delightfull Flowers. My next Garden consisteth of Herbes and Rootes, fit to be eaten of the rich and poor as nourishment and food, as sawce or condiment, as sallet or refreshing, for pleasure or profit; where I doe as well play the Gardiner, to shew you (in briefe, but not at large) the times

and

and manner of ſowing, ſetting, planting, replanting, and the like (although all theſe things, and many more then are true, are ſet down very largely in the ſeuerall bookes that others haue written of this ſubiect) as alſo to ſhew ſome of the Kitchen uſes (becauſe they are Kitchen herbes &c.) although I confeſſe but very ſparingly, not intending a treatiſe of cookery, but briefly to giue a touch thereof ; and alſo the Phyſicall properties, to ſhew ſomewhat that others haue not ſet forth ; yet not to play the Empericke, and giue you receipts of medicines for all diſeaſes, but only to ſhew in ſome ſort the qualities of Herbes, to quicken the minds of the ſtudious. And laſtly an Orchard of all ſorts of domeſticke or forraine, rare and good fruits, fit for this our Land and Countrey, which is at this time better ſtored and furniſhed then euer in any age before. I haue herein endeauoured, as in the other Gardens, to ſet forth the varieties of euery ſort in as briefe a manner as poſſibly could be, without ſuperfluous repetitions of deſcriptions, and onely with eſpeciall notes of difference in leaues, flowers and fruits. Some few properties alſo are ſet downe, rather the chiefeſt then the moſt, as the worke did require. And moreouer before euery of theſe parts I haue giuen Treatiſes of the ordering, preparing and keeping the ſeuerall Gardens and Orchard, with whatſoeuer I thought was conuenient to be known for euery of them.

Thus haue I ſhewed you both the occaſion and ſcope of this Worke, and herein haue ſpent my time, paines and charge, which if well accepted, I ſhall thinke well employed, and may the ſooner haſten the fourth Part, A Garden of Simples ; which will be quiet no longer at home, then that it can bring his Maſter newes of faire weather for the iourney.

Thine in what he may,

IOHN PARKINSON.

Ioanni

Ioanni Parkinſono *Pharmacopoeo Londinenſi ſolertiſ-
ſimo Botanico conſummatiſsimo*
T. D. M. S. P. D.

Oema panegyricum Opus tuum indefeſſi laboris, vtili-
tatis eximiæ poſtulat, & meriti iure à me extorqueret
(mi Parkinſone) ſi fauentibus Muſis, & ſecundo Apol-
line in bicipiti ſomniare Parnaſſo, & repentè Poetæ mihi
prodire liceret. In fœtus tui bonis auibus in lucem editi,
& prolixiorem nepotum ſeriem promittentis laudes, alii
Deopleni Enthouſiaſtæ carmine ſuos pangant elenchos;
quos ſub figmentis ampullata hyperbolicarum vocum mulcedine, vates
ferè auribus mentibuſue inſinuant. Veritas nuditatis amans, fuco natiuum
candorem obumbranti non illuſtranti perpetuum indixit bellum : In ſim-
plicitate, quam aſſertionum neruoſa breuitas exprimit, exultat. Audi quid
de te ſentiam, Tu mihi ſis in poſterum Crateuas Brittannus; inter omnes,
quotquot mihi hic innotuerunt, peritiſsimus, exercitatiſsimus, oculatiſ-
ſimus, & emunctiſsimæ naris Botanicus : Cuius opera in fortunata hac
Inſula rem herbariam tractari, emendari, augeri, & popularibus tuis ver-
naculo ſermone ad amuſsim tradi, non decentiæ modo, ſed etiam necesſi-
tatis eſt. Macte tua ſedulitate (Vir optime) neque te laborum tam arduis
lucubrationibus datorum hactenus pœniteat, vel deinceps impendendo-
rum pigeat. Difficilia quæ pulchra. Leniet debitæ laudis dulcedo vigiliarum
acerbitatem, & Olympicum ſtadium cito pede, à carceribus ad metas ala-
criter decurrentem nobile manet βραβεῖον. Sed memento Artem longam,
Vitam eſſe breuem. Μηδὲν ἀναβαλλόμενος. Vide quid ad antiquum illum, cuius
ſi non animam, ſaltem genium induiſti, Crateuam ſcribat Hippocrates,
Τέχνης πάσης ἀλλότριον ἀναβολὴ ἰατρικῆς δὲ κ᾽ πάνυ; ἐν ᾗ ψυχῆς κίνδυνος ἢ ὑπέρθεσις. Nobiliſsimam
Medicinæ partem Botanicam eſſe reputa. Floræ nunc litaſti & Pomonæ,
Apollini vt audio propediem Horto Medico facturus. Amabò integræ
Veſtæ ſacra conficito, eiuſque variegatum multis ſimplicium morbifugo-
rum myriadibus ſinum abſolutè pandito, quem ſine velo nobis exhibeas.
Nulla dies abeat ſine linea. Sic tandem fructus gloriæ referes vberrimos,
quos iuſtè ſudoribus partos, vt in cruda & viridi ſenectute decerpas diu,
iiſque longum fruaris opto. *Vale.* *Datum Londini Calendas Octobris anno*
ſalutis **1 6 2 9.**

Theodorus de Mayerne *Eques aurat. in Aula*
Regum Magnæ Britanniæ Iacobi & Caroli
P. & F. Archiatrorum Comes.

Ad eximium arte & vſu Pharmacopæum & Botanographum *I. Parkinſonum.*

Gu. Turnerus. M. D.

Io. Gerardus Chirurgus.

Erbarum vires, primus te (magne Britannæ)
  Edocuit medicas, inclytus arte ſophus.
Atque cluens herbis alter, Chironis alumnus,
  Deſcripſit plantas, neu cadat vlla ſalus.
Fortunate ſenex, ſis tu nunc tertius Heros
Hortos qui reſeras, deliciaſque ſoli,
Et flores Veneris lætos, herbaſque virentes,
Arboreos fætus, pharmacum & arte potens.
Poſteritas iuſtos poſthac tibi ſolvet honores,
  Laudabitque tuæ dexteritatis opus.

Ottuellus Meuerell. D. M. & Collegiæ
Med. Lond. ſocius.

Amico ſuo *Ioanni Parkinſono.*

Xtollunt alij quos (Parkinſone) labores
  Da mihi iam veniam comminuiſſe tuos.
Extremos poteris credi migraſſe per Indos:
  Cum liber haud aliud quam tuus hortus hic eſt:
Ipſe habitare Indos tecum facis, haud petis Indos
  I nunc, & tua me comminuiſſe refer.
Eſt liber Effigies, tuus hic qui pingitur hortus,
  Digna manu facies hæc, facieque manus !
Vidi ego ſplendentem varigatis vndique gemmis
  Vna fuit Salomon, turba quid ergo fuit?
Vt vario ſplendent Pallacia regia ſumptu,
  Et Procerum turbis Atria tota nitent :
Tunc cum feſta dies veniam dedit eſſe ſuperbis
  Quoſque ficus texit, nunc tria rura tegunt:
Plena tuo pariter ſpectatur Curia in Horto,
  Hic Princeps, Dux hic, Sponſaque pulchra Ducis.
Quæque dies eſt feſta dies, nec parcius vnquam
  Luxuriant, lauta hæc; Quotidiana tamen.
Ecce velut Patriæ Paradiſi haud immemor Exul,
  Hunc naturali pingit amore ſibi.
Pingit & ad vivum ſub eodem nomine, & hic eſt
  Fronticuli ſudor quem cerebrique dedit :
Aſtat Adam medius Paradiſo noſter in iſto
  Et ſpecies nomen cuique dat ipſe ſuum.
Hos cape pro meritis, qui florem nomine donas
  Æternum florens tu tibi Nomen habe.

Guilielmus Atkins.

Ad Amicum *Ioannem Parkinsonum* Pharmacopæum, & Archibotanicum Londinensem.

Frica quas profert Plantas, quas India mittit,
  Quas tua dat tellus, has tuus hortus habet :
Atque harum Species, florendi tempora, vires,
  Et varias formas iste libellus habet :
Nescio plus librum talem mirabor, an hortum
  Totus inest horto mundus ; at iste libro.
Parkinsone tuus liber, & labor, & tua sit laus,
  Herbas dum nobis das ; datur herba tibi.

Guilielmus Brodus Pharmacopæus
ac Philobotanicus Londinensis.

Ad Amicum *Ioannem Parkinsonum* Pharmacopæum & Botanicum insignem. Carmen.

Vam magno pandis Floræ penetralia nixu
  Atque facis cœlo liberiore frui ?
Omnibus vt placeas, ô quam propensa voluntas,
  Solicitusque labor noKte dieque premit ?
Quam magno cultum studio conquirere in hortum
  Herbarum quicquid mundus in orbe tenet,
Immensus sumptus, multosque extensus in annos
  Te labor afficiunt ? & data nulla quies.
Talia quærenti, surgit novus ardor habendi,
  Nec tibi tot soli munera magna petis ;
Descriptos vivâ profers sub imagine flores,
  Tum profers mensæ quicquid & hortus alit,
Laudatos nobis fruKtus & promis honores,
  Profers, quas celebrant nullibi scripta virum,
Herbarum species, quibus est quoque grata venustas :
  Sic nos multiplici munere, Amice, beas.
Hoc cape pro meritis, florum dum gratia floret,
  Suntque herbis vires ; en tibi Nomen erit.
In serum semper tua gloria floreat ævum,
  Gloria quæ in longum non peritura diem.

Thomas Iohnson vtriusque
Societatis consors.

THE ORDERING OF THE
GARDEN OF PLEASVRE.

CHAP. I.

The ſituation of a Garden of pleaſure, with the nature of ſoyles, and how to amend the defeᴄts that are in many ſorts of ſituations and grounds.

HE ſeuerall ſituations of mens dwellings, are for the moſt part vnauoideable and vnremoueable; for moſt men cannot appoint forth ſuch a manner of ſituation for their dwelling, as is moſt fit to auoide all the inconueniences of winde and weather, but muſt bee content with ſuch as the place will afford them; yet all men doe well know, that ſome ſituations are more excellent than o-thers: according therfore to the ſeuerall ſituation of mens dwel-lings, ſo are the ſituations of their gardens alſo for the moſt part. And although diuers doe diuerſly preferre their owne ſeuerall places which they haue choſen, or wherein they dwell; As ſome thoſe places that are neare vnto a riuer or brooke to be beſt for the pleaſantneſſe of the water, the eaſe of tranſportation of them-ſelues, their friends and goods, as alſo for the fertility of the ſoyle, which is ſeldome bad neare vnto a riuers ſide; And others extoll the ſide or top of an hill, bee it ſmall or great, for the proſpeᴄts ſake; And againe, ſome the plaine or champian ground, for the euen leuell thereof: euery one of which, as they haue their commodities accompa-nying them, ſo haue they alſo their diſcommodities belonging vnto them, according to the Latine Prouerbe, *Omne commodum fert ſuum incommodum.* Yet to ſhew you for eue-rie of theſe ſituations which is the fitteſt place to plant your garden in, and how to de-fend it from the iniuries of the cold windes and froſts that may annoy it, will, I hope, be well accepted. And firſt, for the water ſide, I ſuppoſe the North ſide of the water to be the beſt ſide for your garden, that it may haue the comfort of the South Sunne to lye vpon it and face it, and the dwelling houſe to bee aboue it, to defend the cold windes and froſts both from your herbes, and flowers, and early fruits. And ſo likewiſe I iudge for the hill ſide, that it may lye full open to the South Sunne, and the houſe aboue it, both for the comfort the ground ſhall receiue of the water and raine deſcending into it, and of defence from winter and colds. Now for the plaine leuell ground, the buil-dings of the houſe ſhould be on the North ſide of the garden, that ſo they might bee a defence of much ſufficiency to ſafeguard it from many iniurious cold nights and dayes, which elſe might 'ſpoyle the pride thereof in the bud. But becauſe euery one cannot ſo appoint his dwelling, as I here appoint the fitteſt place for it to be, euery ones pleaſure thereof ſhall be according to the ſite, coſt, and endeauours they beſtow, to cauſe it come neareſt to this proportion, by ſuch helpes of bricke or ſtone wals to defend it, or by the helpe of high growne and well ſpread trees, planted on the North ſide thereof, to keepe it the warmer. And euery of theſe three ſituations, hauing the faireſt buildings of the houſe facing the garden in this manner before ſpecified, beſides the benefit of ſhelter it ſhall haue from them, the buildings and roomes abutting thereon, ſhall haue recipro-cally the beautifull proſpeᴄt into it, and haue both ſight and ſent of whatſoeuer is ex-cellent, and worthy to giue content out from it, which is one of the greateſt pleaſures a garden can yeeld his Maſter. Now hauing ſhewed you the beſt place where this your

A garden

garden ſhould be, let me likewiſe aduiſe you where it ſhould not be, at leaſt that it is the worſt place wherein it may be, if it be either on the Weſt or Eaſt ſide of your houſe, or that it ſtand in a mooriſh ground, or other vnwholſome ayre (for many, both fruits, herbes, and flowers that are tender, participate with the ayre, taking in a manner their chiefeſt thriuing from thence) or neare any common Lay-ſtalles, or common Sewers, or elſe neare any great Brew-houſe, Dye-houſe, or any other place where there is much ſmoake, whether it be of ſtraw, wood, or eſpecially of ſea-coales, which of all other is the worſt, as our Citie of London can giue proofe ſufficient, wherein neither herbe nor tree will long proſper, nor hath done euer ſince the vſe of ſea-coales beganne to bee frequent therein. And likewiſe that it is much the worſe, if it bee neare vnto any Barnes or Stackes of corne or hey, becauſe that from thence will continually with the winde bee brought into the garden the ſtrawe and chaffe of the corne, the duſt and ſeede of the hey to choake or peſter it. Next vnto the place or ſituation, let mee ſhew you the grounds or ſoyles for it, eyther naturall or artificiall. No man will deny, but the naturall blacke mould is not only the fatteſt and richeſt, but farre exceedeth any other either naturall or artificiall, as well in goodneſſe as durability. And next thereunto, I hold the ſandy loame (which is light and yet firme, but not looſe as ſand, nor ſtiffe like vnto clay) to be little inferiour for this our Garden of pleaſure; for that it doth cauſe all bulbous and tuberous rooted plants to thriue ſufficiently therein, as likewiſe all other flower-plants, Roſes, Trees, &c. which if it ſhall decay by much turning and working out the heart of it, may ſoone be helped with old ſtable manure of horſes, being well turned in, when it is old and almoſt conuerted to mould. Other grounds, as chalke, ſand, grauell, or clay, are euery of them one more or leſſe fertill or barren than other; and therefore doe require ſuch helpes as is moſt fit for them. And thoſe grounds that are ouer dry, looſe, and duſtie, the manure of ſtall fedde beaſts and cattell being buried or trenched into the earth, and when it is thorough rotten (which will require twice the time that the ſtable ſoyle of horſes will) well turned and mixed with the earth, is the beſt ſoyle to temper both the heate and drineſſe of them. So contrariwiſe the ſtable dung of horſes is the beſt for cold grounds, to giue them heate and life. But of all other ſorts of grounds, the ſtiffe clay is the very worſt for this purpoſe; for that although you ſhould digge out the whole compaſſe of your Garden, carry it away, and bring other good mould in the ſtead thereof, and fill vp the place, yet the nature of that clay is ſo predominant, that in a ſmall time it will eate out the heart of the good mould, and conuert it to its owne nature, or very neare vnto it: ſo that to bring it to any good, there muſt bee continuall labour beſtowed thereon, by bringing into it good ſtore of chalke, lime, or ſand, or elſe aſhes eyther of wood or of ſea-coales (which is the beſt for this ground) well mixed and turned in with it. And as this ſtiffe clay is the worſt, ſo what ground ſoeuer commeth neareſt vnto the nature thereof, is neareſt vnto it in badneſſe, the ſignes whereof are the ouermuch moyſture thereof in Winter, and the much cleauing and chapping thereof in Summer, when the heate of the yeare hath conſumed the moyſture, which tyed and bound it faſt together, as alſo the ſtiffe and hard working therein: but if the nature of the clay bee not too ſtiffe, but as it were tempered and mixed with ſand or other earths, your old ſtable ſoyle of horſes will helpe well the ſmall rifting or chapping thereof, to be plentifully beſtowed therin in a fit ſeaſon. Some alſo do commend the caſting of ponds and ditches, to helpe to manure theſe ſtiffe chapping grounds. Other grounds, that are ouermoiſt by ſprings, that lye too neare the vpper face of the earth, beſides that the beds thereof had need to be laid vp higher, and the allies, as trenches and furrowes, to lye lower, the ground it ſelfe had neede to haue ſome good ſtore of chalke-ſtones beſtowed thereon, ſome certaine yeares, if it may be, before it be laid into a Garden, that the Winter froſts may breake the chalke ſmall, and the Raine diſſolue it into mould, that ſo they may bee well mixed together; than which, there is not any better manure to ſoyle ſuch a moiſt ground, to helpe to dry vp the moyſture, and to giue heate and life to the coldneſſe thereof, which doth alwayes accompany theſe moiſt grounds, and alſo to cauſe it abide longer in heart than any other. For the ſandy and grauelly grounds, although I know the well mollified manure of beaſts and cattell to be excellent good, yet I know alſo, that ſome commend a white Marle, and ſome a clay to be well ſpread thereon, and after turned thereinto: and for the chalkie ground, *è conuerſo*, I commend fatte clay to helpe it. You muſt vnderſtand, that the leſſe rich or more barren that your ground is, there needeth

deth the more care, labour, and cost to bee bestowed thereon, both to order it rightly, & so to preserue it from time to time : for no artificiall or forc't ground can endure good any long time, but that within a few yeares it must be refreshed more or lesse, according as it doth require. Yet you shall likewise vnderstand, that this Garden of pleasure stored with these Out-landish flowers; that is, bulbous and tuberous rooted plants, and other fine flowers, that I haue hereafter described, and assigned vnto it, needeth not so much or so often manuring with soyle, &c. as another Garden planted with the other sorts of English flowers, or a Garden of ordinary Kitchin herbes doth. Your ground likewise for this Garden had neede to bee well cleansed from all annoyances (that may hinder the well doing or prospering of the flowers therein) as stones, weedes, rootes of trees, bushes, &c. and all other things cumbersome or hurtfull; and therefore the earth being not naturally fine enough of it selfe, is vsed to bee sifted to make it the finer, and that either through a hurdle made of sticks, or lathes, or through square or round sieues plated with fine and strong thin stickes, or with wyers in the bottome. Or else the whole earth of the Garden being course, may be cast in the same manner that men vse to try or fine sand from grauell, that is, against a wall; whereby the courser and more stony, falling downe from the fine, is to be taken away from the foote of the heape, the finer sand and ground remaining still aboue, and on the heape. Or else in the want of a wall to cast it against, I haue seene earth fined by it selfe in this manner : Hauing made the floore or vpper part of a large plat of ground cleane from stones, &c. let there a reasonable round heape of fine earth be set in the midst thereof, or in stead thereof a large Garden flower-pot, or other great pot, the bottome turned vpwards, and then poure your course earth or the top or head thereof, one shouell full after another somewhat gently, and thereby all the course stuffe and stones will fall downe to the bottome round about the heape, which must continually be carefully taken away, and thus you may make your earth as fine as if it were cast against a wall, the heape being growne great, seruing in stead thereof. Those that will not prepare their grounds in some of these manners aforesaid, shall soone finde to their losse the neglect thereof : for the trash and stones shall so hinder the encrease of their roots, that they will be halfe lost in the earth among the stones, which else might be saued to serue to plant wheresoeuer they please.

Chap. II.
The frame or forme of a Garden of delight and pleasure, with the seuerall varieties thereof.

ALthough many men must be content with any plat of ground, of what forme or quantity soeuer it bee, more or lesse, for their Garden, because a more large or conuenient cannot bee had to their habitation : Yet I perswade my selfe, that Gentlemen of the better sort and quality, will prouide such a parcell of ground to bee laid out for their Garden, and in such conuenient manner, as may be fit and answerable to the degree they hold. To prescribe one forme for euery man to follow, were too great presumption and folly : for euery man will please his owne fancie, according to the extent he designeth out for that purpose, be it orbicular or round, triangular or three square, quadrangular or foure square, or more long than broad. I will onely shew you here the seuerall formes that many men haue taken and delighted in, let euery man chuse which him liketh best, or may most fitly agree to that proportion of ground hee hath set out for that purpose. The orbicular or round forme is held in it owne proper existence to be the most absolute forme, containing within it all other formes whatsoeuer; but few I thinke will chuse such a proportion to be ioyned to their habitation, being not accepted any where I thinke, but for the generall Garden to the Vniuersity at Padoa. The triangular or three square is such a forme also, as is seldome chosen by any that may make another choise, and as I thinke is onely had where another forme cannot be had, necessitie constraining them to betherewith content. The foure square forme is the most vsually accepted with all, and doth best agree to any mans dwelling, being (as I said before) behinde the house, all the backe windowes thereof opening into it. Yet if it bee longer than the breadth, or broader than the length, the proportion of walkes, squares, and knots may be soon brought to the square forme, and be so cast, as the beauty thereof may

bee no leſſe than the foure ſquare proportion, or any other better forme, if any be. To forme it therfore with walks, croſſe the middle both waies, and round about it alſo with hedges, with ſquares, knots and trayles, or any other worke within the foure ſquare parts, is according as euery mans conceit alloweth of it, and they will be at the charge: For there may be therein walkes eyther open or cloſe, eyther publike, or priuate, a maze or wilderneſſe, a rocke or mount, with a fountaine in the midſt thereof to conuey water to euery part of the Garden, eyther in pipes vnder the ground, or brought by hand, and emptied into large Ciſternes or great Turkie Iarres, placed in conuenient places, to ſerue as an eaſe to water the neareſt parts thereunto. Arbours alſo being both gracefull and neceſſary, may be appointed in ſuch conuenient places, as the corners, or elſe where, as may be moſt fit, to ſerue both for ſhadow and reſt after walking. And becauſe many are deſirous to ſee the formes of trayles, knots, and other compartiments, and becauſe the open knots are more proper for theſe Out-landiſh flowers; I haue here cauſed ſome to be drawne, to ſatisfie their deſires, not intending to cumber this worke with ouer ma-nie, in that it would be almoſt endleſſe, to expreſſe ſo many as might bee conceiued and ſet downe, for that euery man may inuent others farre differing from theſe, or any other can be ſet forth. Let euery man therefore, if hee like of theſe, take what may pleaſe his mind, or out of theſe or his own conceit, frame any other to his fancy, or cauſe others to be done as he liketh beſt, obſeruing this *decorum*, that according to his ground he do caſt out his knots, with conuenient roome for allies and walkes; for the fairer and larger your allies and walkes be, the more grace your Garden ſhall haue, the leſſe harme the herbes and flowers ſhall receiue, by paſſing by them that grow next vnto the allies ſides, and the better ſhall your Weeders cleanſe both the beds and the allies.

CHAP. III.

The many ſorts of herbes and other things, wherewith the beds and parts of knots are bordered to ſet out the forme of them, with their commodities and diſcommodities.

IT is neceſſary alſo, that I ſhew you the ſeuerall materials, wherewith theſe knots and trayles are ſet forth and bordered; which are of two ſorts: The one are liuing herbes, and the other are dead materials; as leade, boords, bones, tyles, &c. Of herbes, there are many ſorts wherewith the knots and beds in a Garden are vſed to bee ſet, to ſhew forth the forme of them, and to preſerue them the longer in their forme, as alſo to be as greene, and ſweete herbes, while they grow, to be cut to perfume the houſe, keeping them in ſuch order and proportion, as may be moſt conuenient for their ſeuerall natures, and euery mans pleaſure and fancy: Of all which, I intend to giue you the knowledge here in this place; and firſt, to begin with that which hath beene moſt anci-ently receiued, which is Thrift. This is an euerliuing greene herbe, which many take to border their beds, and ſet their knots and trayles, and therein much delight, becauſe it will grow thicke and buſhie, and may be kept, being cut with a paire of Garden ſheeres, in ſome good handſome manner and proportion for a time, and beſides, in the Summer time ſend forth many ſhort ſtalkes of pleaſant flowers, to decke vp an houſe among o-ther ſweete herbes: Yet theſe inconueniences doe accompany it; it will not onely in a ſmall time ouergrow the knot or trayle in many places, by growing ſo thicke and buſhie, that it will put out the forme of a knot in many places: but alſo much thereof will dye with the froſts and ſnowes in Winter, and with the drought in Summer, whereby many voide places will be ſeene in the knot, which doth much deforme it, and muſt therefore bee yearely refreſhed: the thickneſſe alſo and buſhing thereof doth hide and ſhelter ſnayles and other ſmall noyſome wormes ſo plentifully, that Gilloflowers, and other fine herbes and flowers being planted therein, are much ſpoyled by them, and cannot be helped without much induſtry, and very great and daily attendance to deſtroy them. Germander is another herbe, in former times alſo much vſed, and yet alſo in many pla-ces; and becauſe it will grow thicke, and may be kept alſo in ſome forme and proportion with cutting, and that the cuttings are much vſed as a ſtrawing herbe for houſes, being pretty and ſweete, is alſo much affected by diuers: but this alſo will often dye and grow out of forme, and beſides that, the ſtalkes will grow too great, hard and ſtubby, the rootes doe ſo farre ſhoote vnder ground, that vpon a little continuance thereof, will spread into many places within the knot, which if continually they be not plucked vp, they will spoile the whole knot it selfe ; and therefore once in three or foure yeares at the most, it must be taken vp and new set, or else it will grow too roynish and cumbersome. Hyssope hath also been vsed to be set about a knot, and being sweet, will serue for strewings, as Germander : But this, although the rootes doe not runne or creep like it, yet the stalkes doe quickly grow great aboue ground, and dye often after the first yeares setting, whereby the grace of the knot will be much lost. Marierome, Sauorie, and Thyme, in the like manner being sweete herbes, are vsed to border vp beds and knots, and will be kept for a little while, with cutting, into some conformity ; but all and euery of them serue most commonly but for one yeares vse, and will soone decay and perish : and therefore none of these, no more than any of the former, doe I commend for a good bordering herbe for this purpose. Lauander Cotton also being finely slipped and set, is of many, and those of the highest respect of late daies, accepted, both for the beauty and forme of the herbe, being of a whitish greene mealy colour, for his sent smelling somewhat strong, and being euerliuing and abiding greene all the Winter, will, by cutting, be kept in as euen proportion as any other herbe may be. This will likewise soone grow great and stubbed, notwithstanding the cutting, and besides will now and then perish in some places, especially if you doe not strike or put off the snow, before the Sunne lying vpon it dissolue it : The rarity & nouelty of this herbe, being for the most part but in the Gardens of great persons, doth cause it to be of the greater regard, it must therfore be renewed wholly euery second or third yeare at the most, because of the great growing therof. Slips of Iuniper or Yew are also receiued of some & planted, because they are alwayes green, and that the Iuniper especially hath not that ill sent that Boxe hath, which I will presently commend vnto you, yet both Iuniper and Yew will soon grow too great and stubbed, and force you to take vp your knot sooner, than if it were planted with Boxe. Which lastly, I chiefly and aboue all other herbes commend vnto you, and being a small, lowe, or dwarfe kinde, is called French or Dutch Boxe, and serueth very well to set out any knot, or border out any beds : for besides that it is euer greene, it being reasonable thicke set, will easily be cut and formed into any fashion one will, according to the nature thereof, which is to grow very slowly, and will not in a long time rise to be of any height, but shooting forth many small branches from the roote, will grow very thicke, and yet not require so great tending, nor so much perish as any of the former, and is onely receiued into the Gardens of those that are curious. This (as I before said) I commend and hold to bee the best and surest herbe to abide faire and greene in all the bitter stormes of the sharpest Winter, and all the great heates and droughts of Summer, and doth recompence the want of a good sweet sent with his fresh verdure, euen proportion, and long lasting continuance. Yet these inconueniences it hath, that besides the vnpleasing sent which many mislike, and yet is but small, the rootes of this Boxe do so much spread themselues into the ground of the knot, and doe draw from thence so much nourishment, that it robbeth all the herbes that grow neare it of their sap and substance, thereby making all the earth about it barren, or at least lesse fertile. Wherefore to shew you the remedy of this inconuenience of spreading, without either taking vp the Boxe of the border, or the herbes and flowers in the knot, is I thinke a secret knowne but vnto a few, which is this : You shall take a broad pointed Iron like vnto a Slise or Chessill, which thrust downe right into the ground a good depth all along the inside of the border of Boxe somewhat close thereunto, you may thereby cut away the spreading rootes thereof, which draw so much moisture from the other herbes on the inside, and by this meanes both preserue your herbes and flowers in the knot, and your Boxe also, for that the Boxe will be nourished sufficiently from the rest of the rootes it shooteth on all the other sides. And thus much for the liuing herbes, that serue to set or border vp any knot. Now for the dead materials, they are also, as I said before diuers : as first, Leade, which some that are curious doe border their knots withall, causing it to be cut of the breadth of foure fingers, bowing the lower edge a little outward, that it may lye vnder the vpper crust of the ground, and that it may stand the faster, and making the vpper edge either plain, or cut out like vnto the battlements of a Church : this fashion hath delighted some, who haue accounted it stately (at the least costly) and fit for their degree, and the rather, because it will be bowed and bended into any round square, angular, or other proportion as one listeth, and is not much to be misliked, in that the Leade

doth

doth not easily breake or spoile without much iniury, and keepeth vp a knot for a very
long time in his due proportion : but in my opinion, the Leade is ouer-hot for Summer, and ouer-cold for Winter. Others doe take Oaken inch boords, and sawing them
foure or fiue inches broad, do hold vp their knot therewith : but in that these boordes
cannot bee drawne compasse into any small scantling, they must serue rather for long
outright beds, or such knots as haue no rounds, halfe rounds, or compassings in them.
And besides, these boordes are not long lasting, because they stand continually in the
weather, especially the ends where they are fastned together will soonest rot and perish, and so the whole forme will be spoyled. To preuent that fault, some others haue
chosen the shanke bones of Sheep, which after they haue beene well cleansed and
boyled, to take out the fat from them, are stucke into the ground the small end downewards, and the knockle head vpwards, and thus being set side to side, or end to end
close together, they set out the whole knot therewith, which heads of bones although
they looke not white the first yeare, yet after they haue abiden some frosts and heates
will become white, and prettily grace out the ground : but this inconuenience is incident to them, that the Winter frosts will raise them out of the ground oftentimes, and
if by chance the knockle head of any doe breake, or be strucke off with any ones foot,
&c. going by, from your store, that lyeth by you of the same sort, set another in the
place, hauing first taken away the broken peece : although these will last long in forme
and order, yet because they are but bones many mislike them, and indeed I know but
few that vse them. Tyles are also vsed by some, which by reason they may bee
brought compasse into any fashion many are pleased with them, who doe not take the
whole Tyle at length, but halfe Tyles, and other broken peeces set somewhat deepe
into the ground, that they may stand fast, and these take vp but little roome, and keepe
vp the edge of the beds and knots in a pretty comely manner, but they are often out of
frame, in that many of them are broken and spoiled, both with mens feete passing by,
the weather and weight of the earth beating them downe and breaking them, but e-
specially the frosts in Winter doe so cracke off their edges, both at the toppes and
sides that stand close one vnto another, that they must bee continually tended and re-
paired, with fresh and sound ones put in the place of them that are broken or decayed.
And lastly (for it is the latest inuention) round whitish or blewish pebble stones, of
some reasonable proportion and bignesse, neither too great nor too little, haue beene
vsed by some to be set, or rather in a manner but laide vpon the ground to fashion out
the traile or knot, or all along by the large grauelly walke sides to set out the walke, and
maketh a pretty handsome shew, and because the stones will not decay with the iniuries of any time or weather, and will be placed in their places againe, if any should be
thrust out by any accident, as also that their sight is so conspicuous vpon the ground,
especially if they be not hid with the store of herbes growing in the knot; is accounted
both for durability, beauty of the sight, handsomnesse in the worke, and ease in the
working and charge, to be of all other dead materials the chiefest. And thus, Gentlemen, I haue shewed you all the varieties that I know are vsed by any in our Countrey, that are worth the reciting (but as for the fashion of Iawe-bones, vsed by some
in the Low-Countries, and other places beyond the Seas, being too grosse and base, I
make no mention of them) among which euery one may take what pleaseth him best,
or may most fitly be had, or may best agree with the ground or knot. Moreouer, all
these herbes that serue for borderings, doe serue as well to be set vpon the ground of a
leuelled knot; that is, where the allies and foot-pathes are of the same leuell with the
knot, as they may serue also for the raised knot, that is, where the beds of the knot are
raised higher than the allies : but both Leade, Boordes, Bones, and Tyles, are only for
the raised ground, be it knot or beds. The pebble stones againe are onely for the leuelled ground, because they are so shallow, that as I said before, they rather lye vpon
the earth than are thrust any way into it. All this that I haue here set downe, you must
vnderstand is proper for the knots alone of a Garden. But for to border the whole
square or knot about, to serue as a hedge thereunto, euery one taketh what liketh him
best; as either Priuet alone, or sweete Bryer, and white Thorne enterlaced together,
and Roses of one, or two, or more sorts placed here and there amongst them. Some
also take Lauander, Rosemary, Sage, Southernwood, Lauander Cotton, or some such
other thing. Some againe plant Cornell Trees, and plash them, or keepe them lowe, to

forme

forme them into an hedge. And some againe take a lowe prickly shrubbe, that abideth alwayes greene, described in the end of this Booke, called in Latine *Pyracantha*, which in time will make an euer greene hedge or border, and when it beareth fruit, which are red berries like vnto Hawthorne berries, make a glorious shew among the greene leaues in the Winter time, when no other shrubbes haue fruit or leaues.

CHAP. IV.

The nature and names of diuers Out-landish flowers, that for their pride, beauty, and earlinesse, are to be planted in Gardens of pleasure for delight.

Hauing thus formed out a Garden, and diuided it into his fit and due proportion, with all the gracefull knots, arbours, walkes, &c. likewise what is fit to keepe it in the same comely order, is appointed vnto it, both for the borders of the squares, and for the knots and beds themselues; let vs now come and furnish the inward parts, and beds with those fine flowers that (being strangers vnto vs, and giuing the beauty and brauery of their colours so early before many of our owne bred flowers, the more to entice vs to their delight) are most beseeming it: and namely, with Daffodils, Fritillarias, Iacinthes, Saffron-flowers, Lillies, Flowerdeluces, Tulipas, Anemones, French Cowslips, or Beares eares, and a number of such other flowers, very beautifull, delightfull, and pleasant, hereafter described at full, whereof although many haue little sweete sent to commend them, yet their earlinesse and exceeding great beautie and varietie doth so farre counteruaile that defect (and yet I must tell you with all, that there is among the many sorts of them some, and that not a few, that doe excell in sweetnesse, being so strong and heady, that they rather offend by too much than by too little sent, and some againe are of so milde and moderate temper, that they scarce come short of your most delicate and dantiest flowers) that they are almost in all places with all persons, especially with the better sort of the Gentry of the Land, as greatly desired and accepted as any other the most choisest, and the rather, for that the most part of these Out-landish flowers, do shew forth their beauty and colours so early in the yeare, that they seeme to make a Garden of delight euen in the Winter time, and doe so giue their flowers one after another, that all their brauery is not fully spent, vntil that Gilliflowers, the pride of our English Gardens, do shew themselues: So that whosoeuer would haue of euery sort of these flowers, may haue for euery moneth seuerall colours and varieties, euen from Christmas vntill Midsommer, or after; and then, after some little respite, vntill Christmas againe, and that in some plenty, with great content and without forcing, so that euery man may haue them in euery place, if they will take any care of them. And because there bee many Gentlewomen and others, that would gladly haue some fine flowers to furnish their Gardens, but know not what the names of those things are that they desire, nor what are the times of their flowring, nor the skill and knowledge of their right ordering, planting, displanting, transplanting, and replanting; I haue here for their sakes set downe the nature, names, times, and manner of ordering in a briefe manner, referring the more ample declaration of them to the worke following. And first of their names and natures: Of Daffodils there are almost an hundred sorts, as they are seuerally described hereafter, euery one to be distinguished from other, both in their times, formes, and colours, some being eyther white, or yellow, or mixt, or else being small or great, single or double, and some hauing but one flower vpon a stalke, others many, whereof many are so exceeding sweete, that a very few are sufficient to perfume a whole chamber, and besides, many of them be so faire and double, eyther one vpon a stalke, or many vpon a stalke, that one or two stalkes of flowers are in stead of a whole nose-gay, or bundell of flowers tyed together. This I doe affirme vpon good kuowledge and certaine experience, and not as a great many others doe, tell of the wonders of another world, which themselues neuer saw nor euer heard of, except some superficiall relation, which themselues haue augmented according to their owne fansie and conceit. Againe, let me here also by the way tell you, that many idle and ignorant Gardiners and others, who get names by stealth, as they doe many other things, doe call

some

some of these Daffodils Narciffes, when as all know that know any Latine, that Narciffus is the Latine name, and Daffodill the Englifh of one and the fame thing; and therefore alone without any other Epithite cannot properly diftinguifh feuerall things. I would willingly therefore that all would grow iudicious, and call euery thing by his proper Englifh name in fpeaking Englifh, or elfe by fuch Latine name as euery thing hath that hath not a proper Englifh name, that thereby they may diftinguifh the feuerall varieties of things and not confound them, as alfo to take away all excufes of miftaking; as for example: The fingle Englifh baftard Daffodill (which groweth wilde in many Woods, Groues, and Orchards in England.) The double Englifh baftard Daffodill. The French fingle white Daffodill many vpon a ftalke. The French double yellow Daffodill. The great, or the little, or the leaft Spanifh yellow baftard Daffodill, or the great or little Spanifh white Daffodill. The Turkie fingle white Daffodill, or, The Turkie fingle or double white Daffodill many vpon a ftalke, &c. Of Fritillaria, or the checkerd Daffodill, there are halfe a fcore feuerall forts, both white and red, both yellow and blacke, which are a wonderfull grace and ornament to a Garden in regard of the Checker like fpots are in the flowers. Of Iacinthes there are aboue halfe an hundred forts, as they are fpecified hereafter; fome like vnto little bells or ftarres, others like vnto little bottles or pearles, both white and blew, sky-coloured and blufh, and fome ftarlike of many pretty various formes, and all to giue delight to them that will be curious to obferue them. Of Crocus or Saffron flowers, there are alfo twenty forts; fome of the Spring time, others flowring onely in the Autume or Fall, earlier or later than another, fome whereof abide but a while; others indure aboue a moneth in their glorious beauty. The Colchicum or Medowe Saffron, which fome call the fonne before the father, but not properly, is of many forts alfo; fome flowring in the Spring of the yeare, but the moft in Autume, whereof fome haue faire double flowers very delightfull to behold, and fome party coloured both fingle and double fo variable, that it would make any one admire the worke of the Creatour in the various fpots and ftripes of thefe flowers. Then haue wee of Lillies twenty feuerall forts and colours, among whom I muft reckon the Crowne Imperiall, that for his ftately forme deferueth fome fpeciall place in this Garden, as alfo the Martagons, both white and red, both blufh and yellow, that require to be fet by themfelues apart, as it were in a fmall round or fquare of a knot, without many other, or tall flowers growing neare them. But to tell you of all the forts of Tulipas (which are the pride of delight) they are fo many, and as I may fay, almoft infinite, doth both paffe my ability, and as I beleeue the skill of any other. They are of two efpeciall forts, fome flowring earlier, and others later than their fellowes, and that naturally in all grounds, wherein there is fuch a wonderfull variety and mixture of colours, that it is almoft impoffible for the wit of man to defcipher them thoroughly, and to giue names that may be true & feuerall diftinctions to euery flower, threefcore feuerall forts of colours fimple and mixed of each kind I can reckon vp that I haue, and of efpeciall note, and yet I doubt not, but for euery one of them there are ten others differing from them, which may be feen at feuerall times, and in feuerall places: & befides this glory of variety in colors that thefe flowers haue, they carry fo ftately & delightfull a forme, & do abide fo long in their brauery (enduring aboue three whole moneths from the firft vnto the laft) that there is no Lady or Gentlewoman of any worth that is not caught with this delight, or not delighted with thefe flowers. The Anemones likewife or Windeflowers are fo full of variety and fo dainty, fo pleafant and fo delightfome flowers, that the fight of them doth enforce an earneft longing defire in the minde of any one to be a poffeffour of fome of them at the leaft: For without all doubt, this one kinde of flower, fo variable in colours, fo differing in forme (being almoft as many forts of them double as fingle) fo plentifull in bearing flowers, and fo durable in lafting, and alfo fo eafie both to preferue and to encreafe, is of it felfe alone almoft fufficient to furnifh a garden with their flowers for almoft halfe the yeare, as I fhall fhew you in a fit and conuenient place. The Beares eares or French Cowflips muft not want their deferued commendations, feeing that their flowers, being many fet together vpon a ftalke, doe feeme euery one of them to bee a Nofegay alone of it felfe: and befides the many differing colours that are to be feene in them, as white, yellow, blufh, purple, red, tawney, murrey, haire colour, &c. which encreafe much delight in all forts of the Gentry of the Land, they are not vnfurnifhed with a pretty fweete fent,
which

which doth adde an encreaſe of pleaſure in thoſe that make them an ornament for their wearing. Flowerdeluces alſo are of many ſorts, but diuided into two eſpeciall kindes; the one bearing a leafe like a flagge, whoſe rootes are tuberous, thicke and ſhort (one kinde of them being the Orris rootes that are ſold at the Apothecaries, whereof ſweete powders are made to lye among garments) the other hauing round rootes like vnto Onions, and narrow long leaues ſomewhat like graſſe: Of both theſe kindes there is much variety, eſpecially in their colours. The greater Flagge kinde is frequent enough and diſperſed in this Land, and well doth ſerue to decke vp both a Garden and Houſe with natures beauties: But the chiefe of all is your Sable flower, ſo fit for a mourning habit, that I thinke in the whole compaſſe of natures ſtore, there is not a more patheticall, or of greater correſpondency, nor yet among all the flowers I know any one comming neare vnto the colour of it. The other kinde which hath bulbous or Onion like rootes, diuerſifieth it ſelfe alſo into ſo many fine colours, being of a more neate ſhape and ſuccinct forme than the former, that it muſt not bee wanting to furniſh this Garden. The Hepatica or Noble Liuerwoort is another flower of account, whereof ſome are white, others red, or blew, or purple, ſomewhat reſembling Violets, but that there are white threads in the middeſt of their flowers, which adde the more grace vnto them; and one kinde of them is ſo double, that it reſembleth a double thicke Daſie or Marigold, but being ſmall and of an excellent blew colour, is like vnto a Button: but that which commendeth the flower as much as the beauty, is the earlineſſe in flowring, for that it is one of the very firſt flowers that open themſelues after Chriſtmas, euen in the midſt of Winter. The Cyclamen or Sowebread is a flower of rare receipt, becauſe it is naturally hard to encreaſe, and that the flowers are like vnto red or bluſh coloured Violets, flowring in the end of Summer or beginning of Autumne: the leaues likewiſe hereof haue no ſmall delight in their pleaſant colour, being ſpotted and circled white vpon greene, and that which moſt preferreth it, is the Phyſicall properties thereof for women, which I will declare when I ſhall ſhew you the ſeuerall deſcriptions of the varieties in his proper place. Many other ſorts of flowers there are fit to furniſh this Garden, as Leucoium or Bulbous Violet, both early and late flowring. Muſcari or Muske Grape flower. Starre flowers of diuers ſorts. Phalangium or Spiderwort, the chiefe of many is that ſort whoſe flowers are like vnto a white Lilly. Winter Crowfoote or Wolfes bane. The Chriſtmas flower like vnto a ſingle white Roſe. Bell flowers of many kindes. Yellow Larkes ſpurre, the prettieſt flower of a ſcore in a Garden. Flower-gentle or Floramour. Flower of the Sunne. The Maruaile of Peru or of the world. Double Marſh Marigold or double yellow Buttons, much differing and farre exceeding your double yellow Crowfoote, which ſome call Batchelours Buttons. Double French Marigolds that ſmell well, and is a greater kinde than the ordinary, and farre ſurpaſſeth it. The double red Ranunculus or Crowfoote (farre excelling the moſt glorious double Anemone) and is like vnto our great yellow double Crowfoote. Thus hauing giuen you the knowledge of ſome of the choiſeſt flowers for the beds of this Garden, let me alſo ſhew you what are fitteſt for your borders, and for your arbours. The Iaſmine white and yellow. The double Honyſockle. The Ladies Bower, both white, and red, and purple ſingle and double, are the fitteſt of Outlandiſh plants to ſet by arbours and banqueting houſes, that are open, both before and aboue to helpe to couer them, and to giue both ſight, ſmell, and delight. The ſorts of Roſes are fitteſt for ſtandards in the hedges or borders. The Cherry Bay or Laurocerasus. The Roſe Bay or Oleander. The white and the blew Syringa or Pipe tree, are all gracefull and delightfull to ſet at ſeuerall diſtances in the borders of knots; for ſome of them giue beautifull and ſweete flowers. The Pyracantha or Prickly Corall tree doth remaine with greene leaues all the yeare, and may be plaſhed, or laid downe, or tyed to make a fine hedge to border the whole knot, as is ſaid before. The Wilde Bay or Laurus Tinus, doth chiefly deſire to be ſheltered vnder a wall, where it will beſt thriue, and giue you his beautifull flowers in Winter for your delight, in recompence of his fenced dwelling. The Dwarfe Bay or Meſereon, is moſt commonly either placed in the midſt of a knot, or at the corners thereof, and ſometimes all along a walke for the more grace. And thus to fit euery ones fancy, I haue ſhewed you the variety of natures ſtore in ſome part for you to diſpoſe of them to your beſt content.

CHAP.

Chap. V.

The nature and names of those that are called vsually English flowers.

THose flowers that haue beene vsually planted in former times in Gardens of this Kingdome (when as our forefathers knew few or none of those that are recited before) haue by time and custome attained the name of English flowers, although the most of them were neuer naturall of this our Land, but brought in from other Countries at one time or other, by those that tooke pleasure in them where they first saw them: and I doubt not, but many other sorts than here are set downe, or now knowne to vs, haue beene brought, which either haue perished by their negligence or want of skill that brought them, or else because they could not abide our cold Winters; those onely remaining with vs that haue endured of themselues, and by their encreasing haue beene distributed ouer the whole Land. If I should make any large discourse of them, being so well knowne to all, I doubt I should make a long tale to small purpose: I will therefore but briefly recite them, that you may haue them together in one place, with some little declaration of the nature and quality of them, and so passe to other matters. And first of Primroses and Cowslips, whereof there are many prettie varieties; some better knowne in the West parts of this Kingdome, others in the North, than in any other, vntill of late being obserued by some curious louers of varieties, they haue been transplanted diuersly, and so made more common: for although we haue had formerly in these parts about London greene Primroses vsually, yet we neuer saw or heard of greene Cowslips both single and double but of late dayes, and so likewise for Primroses to be both single and double from one roote, and diuers vpon one stalke of diuers fashions, I am sure is not vsuall: all which desire rather to bee planted vnder some hedge, or fence, or in the shade, than in the Sunne. Single Rose Campions, both white, red, and blush, and the double red Rose Campion also is knowne sufficiently, and will abide moderate Sunne as well as the shade. The flower of Bristow or None-such is likewise another kinde of Campion, whereof there is both white flowring plants and blush as well as Orange colour, all of them being single flowers require a moderate Sunne and not the shadow: But the Orange colour None-such with double flowers, as it is rare and not common, so for his brauery doth well deserue a Master of account that will take care to keepe and preserue it. Batchelours Buttons both white and red, are kindes of wilde Campions of a very double forme, and will reasonably well like the Sunne but not the shade. Wall flowers are common in euery Garden, as well the ordinary double as the single, and the double kinde desireth no more shade than the single, but the greater kindes both double and single must haue the Sunne. Stock-Gilloflowers likewise are almost as common as Wall-flowers, especially the single kindes in euery womans Garden, but the double kindes are much more rare, and possessed but of a few, and those onely that will bee carefull to preserue them in Winter; for besides that the most of them are more tender, they yeeld no seede as the single kindes doe to preserue them, although one kinde from the sowing of the seed yeeld double flowers: They will all require the comfort of the Sunne, especially the double kindes, and to be defended from cold, yet so as in the Summer they doe not want water wherein they much ioy, and which is as it were their life. Queenes Gilloflowers (which some call Dames Violets, and some Winter Gilloflowers, are a kinde of Stock-Gilloflower) planted in Gardens to serue to fill vp the parts thereof for want of better things, hauing in mine opinion neither sight nor sent much to commend them. Violets are the Springs chiefe flowers for beauty, smell, and vse, both single and double, the more shadie and moist they stand the better. Snapdragon are flowers of much more delight, and in that they are more tender to keep, and will hardly endure the sharpe Winters, vnlesse they stand well defended, are scarce seene in many Gardens. Columbines single and double, of many sorts, fashions, and colours, very variable both speckled and party coloured, are flowers of that respect, as that no Garden would willingly bee without them, that could tell how to haue them, yet the rarer the flowers are, the more trouble to keepe; the ordinary sorts on the contrary

trary

trary part will not be loft, doe what one will. Larkes heeles, or fpurres, or toes, as in feuerall Countries they are called, exceed in the varietie of colours, both fingle and double, any of the former times; for vntill of late dayes none of the moft pleafant colours were feene or heard of: but now the fingle kindes are reafonable well difperft ouer the Land, yet the double kindes of all thofe pleafant colours (and fome other alfo as beautifull) which ftand like little double Rofes, are enioyed but of a few: all of them rife from feed, and muft be fowne euery yeare, the double as well as the fingle. Panfyes or Hartes eafes of diuers colours, and although without fent, yet not without fome refpect and delight. Double Poppies are flowers of a great and goodly proportion, adorning a Garden with their variable colours to the delight of the beholders, wherein there is fome fpeciall care to be taken, left they turne fingle; and that is, if you fee them grow vp too thicke, that you muft pull them vp, and not fuffer them to grow within leffe than halfe a yard diftance, or more one from another. Double Daifies are flowers not to be forgotten, although they be common enough in euery Garden, being both white and red, both blufh and fpeckled, or party coloured, befides that which is called Iacke an Apes on horfebacke, they require a moift and fhadowie place; for they are fcorched away, if they ftand in the Sunne in any dry place. Double Marigolds alfo are the moft common in all Gardens. And fo are the French Marigolds that haue a ftrong heady fent, both fingle and double, whofe glorious fhew for colour would caufe any to beleeue there were fome rare goodneffe or vertue in them. Thefe all are fometimes preferued in the Winter, if they bee well defended from the cold. But what fhall I fay to the Queene of delight and of flowers, Carnations and Gilloflowers, whofe brauery, variety, and fweete fmell ioyned together, tyeth euery ones affection with great earneftneffe, both to like and to haue them? Thofe that were knowne, and enioyed in former times with much acceptation, are now for the moft part leffe accounted of, except a very few: for now there are fo many other varieties of later inuention, that troubleth the other both in number, beauty, and worth: The names of them doe differ very variably, in that names are impofed and altered as euerie ones fancy will haue them, that carryed or fent them into the feuerall Countries from London, where their trueft name is to be had, in mine opinion. I will here but giue you the names of fome, and referre you to the worke enfuing for your further knowledge. The red and the gray Hulo. The old Carnation, differing from them both. The Gran Pere. The Camberfiue. The Sauadge. The Chriftall. The Prince. The white Carnation, or Delicate. The ground Carnation. The French Carnation. The Douer. The Oxford. The Briftow. The Weftminfter. The Daintie. The Granado, and many other Gilloflowers too tedious to recite in this place, becaufe I haue amply declared them in the booke following. But there is another fort of great delight and varietie, called the Orange tawny Gilloflower, which for the moft part hath rifen from feed, and doth giue feed in a more plentifull manner than any of the former forts, and likewife by the fowing of the feed there hath been gained fo many varieties of that excellent worth and refpect, that it can hardly be expreffed or beleeued, and called by diuers names according to the marking of the flowers; as The Infanta. The Stript Tawny. The Speckled Tawny. The Flackt Tawny. The Grifeld Tawny, and many others, euery one to bee diftinguifhed from others: Some alfo haue their flowers more double and large than others, and fome from the fame feed haue fingle flowers like broad fingle Pinkes: the further relation of them, *viz.* their order to fowe, encreafe, and preferue them, you fhall haue in the fubfequent difcourfe in a place by it felfe. Pinkes likewife both fingle and double are of much variety, all of them very fweete, comming neare the Gilloflowers. Sweete Williams and Sweete Iohns, both fingle and double, both white, red, and fpotted, as they are kindes of wilde Pinkes, fo for their grace and beauty helpe to furnifh a Garden, yet defire not to ftand fo open to the Sunne as the former. Double and fingle Peonies are fit flowers to furnifh a Garden, and by reafon of their durability, giue out frefh pleafure euery yeare without any further trouble of fowing. And laftly, Hollihocks both fingle and double, of many and fundry colours, yeeld out their flowers like Rofes on their tall branches, like Trees, to fute you with flowers, when almoft you haue no other to grace out your Garden: the fingle and double doe both yeeld feed, and yet doe after their feeding abide many yeares. Thus haue I fhewed you moft of the Englifh, as well as (I did before) the Out-

landifh

landish flowers, that are fit to furnish the knots, trailes, beds, and borders of this Garden. Roses onely, as I said before, I reserue to circle or encompasse all the rest, because that for the most part they are planted in the outer borders of the quarters, and sometimes by themselues in the middle of long beds, the sorts or kindes whereof are many, as they are declared in their proper place : but the White Rose, the Red, and the Damaske, are the most ancient Standards in England, and therefore accounted naturall.

Chap. VI.

The order and manner to plant and replant all the sorts of Out-landish flowers spoken of before, as well those with bulbous rootes, as others with stringie rootes.

WHereas it is the vsuall custome of most in this Land, to turne vp their Gardens, and to plant them againe in the Spring of the yeare, which is the best time that may bee chosen for all English flowers, yet it is not so for your Out-landish flowers. And herein indeede hath beene not onely the errour of a great many to hinder their rootes from bearing out their flowers as they should, but also to hinder many to take delight in them, because as they say they will not thriue and prosper with them, when as the whole fault is in the want of knowledge of the fit and conuenient time wherein they should bee planted. And beeause our English Gardiners are all or the most of them vtterly ignorant in the ordering of these Out-landish flowers, as not being trained vp to know them, I haue here taken vpon mee the forme of a new Gardiner, to giue instructions to those that will take pleasure in them, that they may be the better enabled with these helpes I shall shew them, both to know how they should be ordered, and to direct their Gardiners that are ignorant thereof, rightly to dispose them according to their naturall qualities. And I doe wish all Gentlemen and Gentlewomen, whom it may concerne for their owne good, to bee as carefull whom they trust with the planting and replanting of these fine flowers, as they would be with so many Iewels ; for the rootes of many of them being small, and of great value, may be soone conueyed away, and a cleanly tale faire told, that such a roote is rotten, or perished in the ground if none be seene where it should be, or else that the flower hath changed his colour, when it hath been taken away, or a counterfeit one hath beene put in the place thereof ; and thus many haue been deceiued of their daintiest flowers, without remedy or true knowledge of the defect. You shall therefore, if you will take the right course that is proper for these kindes of flowers, not set or plant them among your English flowers ; for that when the one may be remoued, the other may not be stirred : but plant those rootes that are bulbous, or round like Onions, eyther in knots or beds by themselues which is the best, or with but very few English or Out-landish flower plants that haue stringie rootes : For you must take this for a generall rule, that all those rootes that are like Lillies or Onions, are to bee planted in the moneths of Iuly or August, or vnto the middle or end of September at the furthest, if you will haue them to prosper as they should, and not in the Spring of the yeare, when other gardening is vsed. Yet I must likewise giue you to vnderstand, that if Tulipas, and Daffodils, and some other that are firme and hard rootes, and not limber or spongie, being taken vp out of the ground in their fit season, that is, in Iune, Iuly, and August, and likewise kept well and dry, may bee reserued out of the ground vntill Christmas or after, and then (if they could not be set sooner) being set, will thriue reasonable well, but not altogether so well as the former, being set long before : but if you shall remoue these bulbous rootes againe, either presently after their planting hauing shot their small fibres vnder the round rootes, and sprung likewise vpwards, or before they be in flower at the soonest (yet Tulipas, Daffodils, and many other bulbous, may be safely remoued being in flower, and transplanted into other places, so as they be not kept too long out of the ground) you shall much endanger them either vtterly to perish, or to be hindered from bearing out their flowers they then would haue

B

borne,

borne, and for two or three years after from bearing flowers againe. For the order of their planting there are diuers wayes, some whereof I will shew you in this place: Your knot or beds being prepared fitly, as before is declared, you may place and order your rootes therein thus, Eyther many rootes of one kind set together in a round or cluster, or longwise crosse a bed one by another, whereby the beauty of many flowers of one kinde being together, may make a faire shew well pleasing to many; Or else you may plant one or two in a place dispersedly ouer the whole knot, or in a proportion or diameter one place answering another of the knot, as your store will suffer you, or your knot permit: Or you may also mingle these rootes in their planting many of diuers sorts together, that they may giue the more glorious shew when they are in flower; and that you may so doe, you must first obserue the seuerall kindes of them, which doe flower at one and the same time, and then to place them in such order and so neare one vnto another, that their flowers appearing together of seuerall colours, will cause the more admiration in the beholders: as thus, The Vernall Crocus or Saffron flowers of the Spring, white, purple, yellow, and stript, with some Vernall Colchicum or Medow Saffron among them, some Deus Caninus or Dogges teeth, and some of the small early Leucoium or Bulbous Violet, all planted in some proportion as neare one vnto another as is fit for them, will giue such a grace to the Garden, that the place will seeme like a peece of tapestry of many glorious colours, to encrease euery ones delight: Or else many of one sort together, as the blew, white and blush Grape flowers in the same manner intermingled, doe make a maruellous delectable shew, especially because all of them rise almost to an equall height, which causeth the greater grace, as well neare hand as farre of. The like order may be kept with many other things, as the Hepatica, white, blew, purple, and red set or sowne together, will make many to beleeue that one roote doth beare all those colours: But aboue and beyond all others, the Tulipas may be so matched, one colour answering and setting of another, that the place where they stand may resemble a peece of curious needle-worke, or peece of painting: and I haue knowne in a Garden, the Master as much commended for this artificiall forme in placing the colours of Tulipas, as for the goodnesse of his flowers, or any other thing. The diuers sorts and colours of Anemones or Winde-flowers may be so ordered likewise, which are very beautifull, to haue the seuerall varieties planted one neare vnto another, that their seuerall colours appearing in one place will be a very great grace in a Garden, or if they be dispersed among the other sorts of flowers, they will make a glorious shew. Another order in planting you may obserue; which is this, That those plants that grow low, as the Aconitum Hyemale or Winter-wolues bane, the Vernall Crocus or Saffron flowers of diuers sorts, the little early Leucoium or Bulbous Violet, and some such other as rise not vp high, as also some Anemones may be very well placed somewhat neare or about your Martagons, Lillies, or Crownes Imperiall, both because these little plants will flower earlier than they, and so will bee gone and past, before the other greater plants will rise vp to any height to hinder them; which is a way may well be admitted in those Gardens that are small, to saue roome, and to place things to the most aduantage. Thus hauing shewed you diuers wayes and orders how to plant your rootes, that your flowers may giue the greater grace in the Garden, let mee shew you likewise how to set these kindes of rootes into the ground; for many know not well eyther which end to set vpwards or downewards, nor yet to what depth they should be placed in the ground. Daffodils if they be great rootes, will require (as must bee obserued in all other great plants) to bee planted somewhat deeper then the smaller of the same kinde, as also that the tops or heads of the rootes be about two or three fingers breadth hid vnder ground. The Tulipas likewise if you set them deepe, they will be the safer from frosts if your ground be cold, which will also cause them to be a little later before they be in flower, yet vsually if the mould be good, they are to be set a good hand breadth deep within the ground, so that there may be three or foure inches of earth at the least aboue the head, which is the smaller end of the roote: for if they shall lye too neare the vpper face or crust of the earth, the colds & frosts will pierce and pinch them the sooner. After the same order and manner must Hyacinthes, whether great or small, and other such great rootes be planted. Your greater rootes, as Martagons, Lillies, and Crownes Imperiall, must be set much deeper then any other bulbous roote, because they are greater rootes then others, and by themselues also, as

is

is moſt vſuall either in ſome ſquare, round, triangle, or other ſmall part in the Garden, becauſe they ſpread and take vp a very great deale of ground. All of them likewiſe are to be ſet with the broad end of the roote downewards, and the ſmall end vpwards, that is, both Lillies, Daffodils, Hyacinthes, and Tulipas, and all other ſorts of round rootes, which ſhew one end to bee ſmaller than another. But the Colchicum or Me-dow-Saffron onely requireth an exception to this generall rule, in regard the roote thereof hath a ſmall eminence or part on the one ſide thereof, which muſt bee ſet or planted downeward, and not vpward ; for you ſhall obſerue, if the roote lye a little moiſt out of the ground, that it will ſhoote fibres out at the ſmall long end thereof, al-though you may perceiue when you take it vp, that the fibres were at the other broad end or ſide of the roote. As for the Crowne Imperiall, which is a broad round roote and flat withall, hauing a hole in the middle, for the moſt part quite thorow, when it is taken vp in his due time out of the ground, you ſhall perceiue the ſcales or cloues of the rootes to bee a little open on the vpperſide, and cloſe and flat on the vnderſide, which will direct you which part to ſet vpward, as alſo that the hole is bigger aboue then it is below. The Perſian Lilly is almoſt like vnto the Crowne Imperiall, but that the roote thereof is not ſo flat, and that it hath a ſmaller head at the one part, whereby it may be diſcerned the plainer how to be ſet. The Fritillaria is a ſmall white root di-uided as it were into two parts, ſo that many haue doubted, as formerly in the Crowne Imperiall, what part to ſet vppermoſt; you ſhall therefore marke, that the two parts of the roote are ioyned together at the bottome, where it ſhooteth out fibres or ſmall ſtringie rootes, as all other ſorts of bulbous rootes doe, and withall you ſhall ſee, that betweene the two parts of the roote a ſmall head will appeare, which is the burgeon that will ſpring vp to beare leaues and flowers. In the rootes of Anemones there are ſmall round ſwelling heads, eaſie enough to be obſerued if you marke it, which muſt be ſet vpwards. All other ſorts of ſtringie rooted plants (and not bulbous or tuberous rooted) that loſe their greene leaues in Winter, will ſhew a head from whence the leaues and flowers will ſpring, and all others that keepe their greene leaues, are to bee planted in the ſame manner that other herbes and flower-plants are accuſtomed to be. But yet for the better thriuing of the ſtringie rooted plants, when you will plant them, let me informe you of the beſt way of planting, and the moſt ſure to cauſe any plant to comprehend in the ground without failing, and is no common way with any Gardiner in this Kingdome, that euer I heard or knew, which is thus : Preſuming that the ſtringie rooted plant is freſh and not old gathered, and a plant that being remoued will grow againe, make a hole in the ground large enough where you meane to ſet this roote, and raiſe the earth within the hole a little higher in the middle then on the ſides, and ſet the roote thereon, ſpreading the ſtrings all abroad about the middle, that they may as it were couer the middle, and then put the earth gently round about it, preſſing it a little cloſe, and afterwards water it well, if it be in Summer, or in a dry time, or o-therwiſe moderately : thus ſhall euery ſeuerall ſtring of the roote haue earth enough to cauſe it to ſhoote forth, and thereby to encreaſe farre better than by the vſuall way, which is without any great care and reſpect to thruſt the rootes together into the ground. Diuers other flower plants are but annuall, to bee new ſowne euery yeare ; as the Maruaile of the world, the Indian Creſſes, or yellow Larkes heeles, the Flower of the Sunne, and diuers other : they therefore that will take pleaſure in them, that they may enioy their flowers the earlier in the yeare, and thereby haue ripe ſeede of them while warme weather laſteth, muſt nurſe vp their ſeedes in a bed of hot dung, as Me-lons and Cowcumbers are, but your bed muſt be prouided earlier for theſe ſeeds, than for Melons, &c. that they may haue the more comfort of the Summer, which are to be carefully tended after they are tranſplanted from the hot bed, and couered with ſtraw from colds, whereby you ſhall not faile to gaine ripe ſeed euery yeare, which other-wiſe if you ſhould miſſe of a very kindly & hot Summer, you ſhould neuer haue. Some of theſe ſeedes neede likewiſe to be tranſplanted from the bed of dung vnder a warme wall, as the Flower of the Sunne, and the Maruaile of the world, and ſome others, and that for a while after their tranſplanting, as alſo in the heate of Summer, you water them at the roote with water that hath ſtood a day or two in the Sunne, hauing firſt laid a round wiſpe of hay or ſuch other thing round about the roote, that ſo all helpes may further their giuing of ripe ſeede. One or two rules more I will giue you concerning

theſe

these dainty flowers, the first whereof is this, That you shall not bee carefull to water any of your bulbous or tuberous rooted plants at any time; for they all of them do better prosper in a dry ground than in a wet, onely all forts of tuberous rooted Flowerdeluces vpon their remouall had neede of a little water, and some will doe so also to such Tulipas and other bulbous rootes as they transplant, when they are in flower, and this is I grant in some fort tolerable, if it bee not too much, and done onely to cause the stalke and flower to abide sometime the longer before they wither, but elfe in no other case to be permitted. The second rule is, That I would aduife you to water none of your dainty flowers or herbes, with any water that hath presently before been drawne out of a well or pumpe, but onely with such water that hath stood open in the Sunne in some cisterne, tubbe, or pot for a day at the least, if more the better: for that water which is presently drawne out of a well, &c. is so cold, that it presently chilleth & killeth any dainty plant be it younger or elder grown, wherof I haue had sufficient proofe: and therfore I giue you this caution by mine own experience. Thus haue I directed you from point to point, in all the particulars of preparing & planting that belong to this Garden, sauing only that yet I would further enforme you, of the time of the flowring of these Out-landish plants, according to the feuerall moneths in the yeare, that euery one may know what flowers euery moneth yeeldeth, and may chufe what them liketh best, in that they may see that there is no moneth, but glorieth in some peculiar forts of rare flowers. I would likewife rather in this place shew you, the true and best manner & order to encreafe and preferue all forts of Gilloflowers & Carnations, then ioyne it with the Chapter of Gilloflowers in the worke following, becaufe it would in that place take vp too much roome. And lastly, I must of necessity oppofe three sundry errours, that haue poffeffed the mindes of many both in former and later times, which are, that any flower may be made to grow double by art, that was but single before by nature: And that one may by art caufe any flower to grow of what colour they will: And that any plants may be forced to flower out of their due feafons, either earlier or later, by an art which some can vfe. All which being declared, I then suppofe enough is spoken for an introduction to this worke, referring many other things to the feuerall directions in the Chapters of the booke.

Chap. VII.

The feuerall times of the flowring of these Out-landish flowers, according to the feuerall moneths of the yeare.

I Intend in this place onely to giue you briefly, the names of some of the chiefeft of these Out-landish flowers, according to the feuerall moneths of the yeare wherein they flower, that euery one seeing what forts of flowers euery moneth yeeldeth, may take of them which they like best. I begin with Ianuary, as the first moneth of the yeare, wherein if the frofts be not extreme, you shall haue thefe flowers of plants; the Christmas flower or Helleborus niger verus, Winter wolues bane or Aconitum hyemale, Hepatica or Noble Liuer wort blew and red, and of shrubbes, the Laurus Tinus or Wilde Bay tree, and Mefereon or the dwarfe Bay: but becaufe Ianuarie is oftentimes too deepe in frofts and snow, I therefore referre the Hepaticas vnto the moneth following, which is February, wherein the weather beginneth to be a little milder, and then they will flower much better, as alfo diuers forts of Crocus or Saffron flower will appeare, the little early Summer foole or Leucoium bulbofum, and towards the latter end thereof the Vernall Colchicum, the Dogges tooth Violet or Deus Caminus, and some Anemones, both single and double, which in some places will flower all the Winter long. March will yeeld more varieties; for befides that it holdeth some of the flowers of the former moneth, it will yeeld you both the double blew Hepatica, and the white and the blufh single: then alfo you shall haue diuers other forts of Crocus or Saffron flowers, Double yellow Daffodils, Orientall Iacinths and others, the Crowne Imperiall, diuers forts of early Tulipas, some forts of French Cowflips, both tawney, murry, yellow, and blufh, the early Fritillaria or checkerd Daffodill,

dill, and some other sorts of early Daffodils, and many sorts of Anemones. In Aprill commeth on the pride of these strangers; for herein you may behold all the sorts of Auricula Vrsi or Beares Eares, many sorts of Anemones, both single and double, both the sorts of Tulipas, the earlier vntill the middle of the moneth, and the later then beginning, which are of so many different colours, that it is almost impossible to expresse them, the white, red, blacke, and yellow Fritillarias, the Muscari or Muske Grape flower, both ash colour and yellow. Diuers other sorts of Iacinths and Daffodils, both single and double, the smaller sorts of Flowerdeluces, the Veluet Flowerdeluce and double Honysuckles, with diuers others. May likewise at the beginning seemeth as glorious as Aprill, although toward the end it doth decline, in regard the heate of the Sunne hath by this time drawne forth all the store of natures tenderest dainties, which are vsually spent by the end of this moneth, and then those of stronger constitution come forward. Herein are to bee seene at the beginning the middle flowring Tulipas, and at the end the later sort : some kindes of Daffodils, the Day Lillies, the great white Starre flower, the Flowerdeluce of Constantinople or the mourning Sable flower, the other sorts of Flowerdeluces. Single and double white Crowfoote, and single and double red Crowfoot, the glory of a Garden : the early red Martagon, the Persian Lilly, the yellow Martagon, the Gladiolus or Corne flagge, both white, red, and blush : the double yellow Rose, and some other sorts of Roses. In Iune doe flower the white and the blush Martagon, the Martagon Imperiall, the mountaine Lillies, and the other sorts of white and red Lillies, the bulbous Flowerdeluces of diuers sorts, the red flowred Ladies bower, the single and double purple flowred Ladies bower, the white Syringa or Pipe tree, for the blew Pipe tree flowreth earlier, the white and the yellow Iasmin. Iuly holdeth in flower some of the Ladies bowers and Iasmines, and besides doth glory in the Female Balsame apple, the Indian Cresses or yellow Larkes spurres, the purple Flower-gentle and the Rose Bay. In August begin some of the Autumne bulbous flowers to appeare, as the white and the purple Colchicum or Medow Saffron, the purple mountaine Crocus or Saffron flower, the little Autumne Leucoium and Autumne Iacinth, the Italian Starrewort, called of some the purple Marigold, the Meruaile of Peru or of the world, the Flower of the Sunne, the great blew Bell-flower, the great double French Marigold. September flourisheth with the Flower of the Sunne, the Meruaile of the world, the purple Marigold, and blew Bell-flower spoken of before, and likewise the other sorts of Medow Saffron, and the double kinde likewise, the siluer Crocus, the Autumne yellow Daffodill, Cyclamen also or Sowbread shew their flowers in the end of this moneth. October also will shew the flowers of Cyclamen, and some of the Medow Saffrons. In Nouember, as also sometimes in the moneth before, the party coloured Medow Saffron may bee seene, that will longest hold his flower, because it is the latest that sheweth it selfe, and the ash coloured mountaine Crocus. And euen December it selfe will not want the true blacke Hellebor or Christmas flower, and the glorious shew of the Laurus Tinus or wilde Bay tree. Thus haue I shewed you some of the flowers for euery moneth, but I referre you to the more ample declarion of them and all the others, vnto the work following.

Chap. VIII.

The true manner and order to encrease and preserue all sorts of Gilloflowers, as well by slippes as seedes.

Ecause that Carnations and Gilloflowers bee the chiefest flowers of account in all our English Gardens, I haue thought good to entreate somewhat amply of them, and that a part by it selfe, as I said a little before, in regard there is so much to be said concerning them, and that if all the matters to be entreated of should haue beene inserted in the Chapter of Gilloflowers, it would haue made it too tedious and large, and taken vp too much roome. The particular matters whereof I mean in this place to entreate are these : How to encrease Gilloflowers by planting and by

sowing,

sowing, and how to preserue them being encreased, both in Summer from noysome and hurtfull vermine that destroy them, and in Winter from frosts, snowes, and windes, that spoile them. There are two wayes of planting, whereby to encrease these faire flowers; the one is by slipping, which is the old and ready vsuall way, best knowne in this Kingdome; the other is more sure, perfect, ready, and of later inuention, *videlicet*, by laying downe the branches. The way to encrease Gilloflowers by slipping, is so common with all that euer kept any of them, that I thinke most persons may thinke me idle, to spend time to set downe in writing that which is so well known vnto all : Yet giue me leaue to tell them that so might imagine, that (when they haue heard or read what I haue written thereof, if they did know fully as much before) what I here write, was not to informe them, but such as did not know the best, or so good a way as I teach them : For I am assured, the greatest number doe vse, and follow the most vsuall way, and that is not alwaies the best, especially when by good experience a better way is found, and may be learned; and therefore if some can doe a thing better than others, I thinke it is no shame to learne it of them. You shall not then (to take the surest course) take any long spindled branches, nor those branches that haue any young shootes from the ioynts on them, nor yet sliue or teare any slippe or branch from the roote ; for all these waies are vsuall and common with most, which causeth so many good rootes to rot and perish, and also so many slippes to be lost, when as for the most part, not the one halfe, or with some, not a third part doth grow and thriue of those slippes they set. And although many that haue store of plants, doe not so much care what hauocke they make to gaine some, yet to saue both labour and plants, I doe wish them to obserue these orders : Take from those rootes from whence you intend to make your encrease, those shootes onely that are reasonable strong, but yet young, and not either too small and slender, or hauing any shootes from the ioynts vpon them; cut these slippes or shootes off from the stemme or roote with a knife, as conueniently as the shoote or branch will permit, that is, either close vnto the maine branch, if it be short, or leauing a ioynt or two behinde you, if it be long enough, at which it may shoote anew : When you haue cut off your slippes, you may either set them by and by, or else as the best Gardiners vse to doe, cast them into a tubbe or pot with water for a day or two, and then hauing prepared a place conuenient to set them in, which had neede to bee of the finest, richest, and best mould you can prouide, that they may thriue therein the better, cut off your slippe close at the ioynt, and hauing cut away the lowest leaues close to the stalke, and the vppermost euen at the top, with a little sticke make a little hole in the earth, and put your slippe therein so deep, as that the vpper leaues may be wholly aboue the ground, (some vse to cleaue the stalke in the middle, and put a little earth or clay within the cleft, but many good and skilfull Gardiners doe not vse it) ; put the earth a little close to the slippe with your finger and thumbe, and there let it rest, and in this manner doe with as many slippes as you haue, setting them somewhat close together, and not too farre in sunder, both to saue ground and cost thereon, in that a small compasse will serue for the first planting, and also the better to giue them shadow : For you must remember in any case, that these slippes new set, haue no sight of the Sunne, vntill they be well taken in the ground, and shot aboue ground, and also that they want not water, both vpon the new planting and after. When these slippes are well growne vp, they must be transplanted into such other places as you thinke meete; that is, either into the ground in beds, or otherwise, or into pots, which that you may the more safely doe, after you haue well watered the ground, for halfe a day before you intend to transplant them, you shall separate them seuerally, by putting down a broad pointed knife on each side of the slippe, so cutting it out, take euery one by it selfe, with the earth cleauing close vnto the root, which by reason of the moisture it had formerly, and that which you gaue presently before, will be sufficient with any care had, to cause it to hold fast vnto the roote for the transplanting of it : for if the earth were dry, and that it should fall away from the roote in the transplanting, it would hazzard and endanger the roote very much, if it did thriue at all. You must remember also, that vpon the remouing of these slips, you shadow them from the heate of the Sunne for a while with some straw or other thing, vntill they haue taken hold in their new place. Thus although it bee a little more labour and care than the ordinary way is, yet it is surer, and will giue you plants that

will

will be ſo ſtrongly growne before Winter, that with the care hereafter ſpecified, you ſhall haue them beare flowers the next yeare after, and yeeld you encreaſe of ſlippes alſo. To giue you any ſet time, wherein theſe ſlippes will take roote, and begin to ſhoote aboue ground, is very hard to doe; for that euery ſlip, or yet euery kinde of Gilloflower is not alike apt to grow; nor is euery earth in like manner fit to produce and bring forward the ſlippes that are ſet therein : but if both the ſlippe be apt to grow, and the earth of the beſt, fit to produce, I thinke within a fortnight or three weekes, you ſhall ſee them begin to put forth young leaues in the middle, or elſe it may be a moneth and more before you ſhall ſee any ſpringing. The beſt time likewiſe when to plant, is a ſpeciall thing to be knowne, and of as great conſequence as any thing elſe : For if you ſlippe and ſet in September, as many vſe to doe, or yet in Auguſt, as ſome may thinke will doe well, yet (vnleſſe they be the moſt ordinary ſorts, which are likely to grow at any time, and in any place) the moſt of them, if not all, will either aſſuredly periſh, or neuer proſper well : for the more excellent and dainty the Gilloflower is, the more tender for the moſt part, and hard to nurſe vp will the ſlippes be. The beſt time therefore is, that you cut off ſuch ſlippes as are likely, and ſuch as your rootes may ſpare, from the beginning of May vntill the middle of Iune at the furtheſt, and order them as I haue ſhewed you before, that ſo you may haue faire plants, plenty of flowers, and encreaſe ſufficient for new ſupply, without offence or loſſe of your ſtore. For the enriching likewiſe of your earth, wherein you ſhall plant your ſlippes, that they may the better thriue and proſper, diuers haue vſed diuers ſorts of manure; as ſtable ſoyle of horſe, beaſts or kine, of ſheepe, and pigeons, all which are very good when they are thoroughly turned to mould, to mixe with your other earth, or being ſteeped in water, may ſerue to water the earth at times, and turned in with it. And ſome haue likewiſe proued Tanners earth, that is, their barke, which after they haue vſed, doth lye on heapes and rot in their yards, or the like mould from wood-ſtackes or yards; but eſpecially, and beyond all other is commended the Willow earth, that is, that mould which is found in the hollow of old Willow trees, to be the moſt principall to mixe with other good earth for this purpoſe. And as I haue now giuen you directions for the firſt way to encreaſe them by ſlipping, ſo before I come to the other way, let mee giue you a caueat or two for the preſeruing of them, when they are beginning to runne vtterly to decay and periſh : The one is, that whereas many are ouer greedy to haue their plants to giue them flowers, and therefore let them runne all to flower, ſo farre ſpending themſelues thereby, that after they haue done flowring, they grow ſo weake, hauing out ſpent themſelues, that they cannot poſſibly be preſerued from the iniuries of the ſucceeding Winter; you ſhall therefore keepe the kinde of any ſort you are delighted withall, if you carefully looke that too many branches doe not runne vp and ſpindle for flowers, but rather either cut ſome of them downe, before they are run vp too high, within two or three ioynts of the rootes; or elſe plucke away the innermoſt leaues where it ſpringeth forwards, which you ſee in the middle of euery branch, before it be runne vp too high, which will cauſe them to breake out the faſter into ſlips and ſuckers at the ioynts, to hinder their forward luxurie, and to preſerue them the longer : The other is, If you ſhall perceiue any of your Gilloflower leaues to change their naturall freſh verdure, and turne yellowiſh, or begin to wither in anie part or branch thereof, it is a ſure ſigne that the roote is infected with ſome cancker or rottenneſſe, and will ſoone ſhew it ſelfe in all the reſt of the branches, whereby the plant will quickly be loſt : to preſerue it therefore, you ſhall betime, before it be runne too farre, (for otherwiſe it is impoſſible to ſaue it) either couer all or moſt of the branches with freſh earth, or elſe take the faireſt ſlippes from it, as many as you can poſſibly, and caſt them into a pot or tubbe with water, and let them there abide for two or three daies at the leaſt : the firſt way hath recouered many, being taken in time. Thus you ſhall ſee them recouer their former ſtiffeneſſe and colour, and then you may plant them as you haue beene heretofore directed; and although many of them may periſh, yet ſhall you haue ſome of them that will grow to continue the kinde againe. The other or ſecond way to encreaſe Gilloflowers by planting, is, as I ſaid before, by in-laying or laying downe the branches of them, and is a way of later inuention, and as frequently vſed, not onely for the tawney or yellow Gilloflower, and all the varieties therof, but with the other kinds of Gilloflowers, whereof experience hath ſhewed

that

that they will likewife take if they be fo vfed ; the manner whereof is thus : You muft choofe out the youngeft, likelieft, and loweft branches that are neareft the ground (for the vpper branches will fooner breake at the ioynt, than bend downe fo low into the earth, without fome pot with earth raifed vp vnto them) and cut it on the vnderfide thereof vpwards at the fecond ioynt next vnto the roote, to the middle of the branch, and no more, and not quite thorough in any cafe, and then from that fecond ioynt vnto the third, flit or cut the branch in the middle longwife, that fo it may be the more eafily bended into the ground, the cut ioynt feeming like the end of a flippe, when you haue bended downe the branch where it is cut into the ground (which muft bee done very gently for feare of breaking) with a little fticke or two thruft flopewife, croffe ouer it, keepe it downe within the earth, and raife vp fufficient earth ouer it, that there it may lye and take roote, which commonly will be effected within fixe weekes or two moneths in the Summer time, and then (or longer if you doubt the time too fhort for it to take fufficient roote) you may take or cut it away, and tranfplant it where you thinke good, yet fo as in any cafe you fhadow it from the heate of the Sunne, vntill it haue taken good hold in the ground.   The other way to encreafe Gilloflowers, is by fowing the feede : It is not vfuall with all forts of Gilloflowers to giue feede, but fuch of them as doe yeeld feede may be encreafed thereby, in the fame manner as is here fet downe. The Orange tawney Gilloflower and the varieties thereof is the moft vfuall kinde, (and it is a kinde by it felfe, how various foeuer the plants be that rife from the feede) that doth giue feede, and is fowne, and from thence arifeth fo many varieties of colours, both plaine and mixt, both fingle and double, that one can hardly fet them downe in writing : yet fuch as I haue obferued and marked, you fhall finde expreffed in the Chapter of Gilloflowers in the worke following.   Firft therefore make choife of your feede that you intend to fowe (if you doe not defire to haue as many more fingle flowers as double) that it bee taken from double flowers, and not from fingle, and from the beft colours, howfoeuer fome may boaft to haue had double and ftript flowers from the feede of a fingle one · which if it were fo, yet one Swallow (as we fay) maketh no Summer, nor a thing comming by chance cannot bee reckoned for a certaine and conftant rule ; you may be affured they will not vfually doe fo : but the beft, faireft, and moft double flowers come alwaies, or for the moft part, from the feede of thofe flowers that were beft, faireft, and moft double ; and I doe aduife you to take the beft and moft double : for euen from them you fhall haue fingle ones enow, you neede not to fowe any worfer fort. And againe, fee that your feede bee new, of the laft yeares gathering, and alfo that it was full ripe before it was gathered, left you lofe your labour, or miffe of your purpofe, which is, to haue faire and double flowers. Hauing now made choife of your feede, and prepared you a bedde to fowe them on, the earth whereof muft be rich and good, and likewife fifted to make it the finer ; for the better it is, the better fhall your profit and pleafure bee : hereon, being firft made leuell, plaine, and fmooth, fowe your feede fomewhat thinne, and not too thicke in any cafe, and as euenly as you can, that they be not too many in one place, and too few in another, which afterwards couer with fine fifted earth ouer them about one fingers thickneffe ; let this be done in the middle of Aprill, if the time of the yeare be temperate, and not too cold, or elfe ftay vntill the end of the moneth : after they are fprung vp and growne to be fomewhat bigge, let them bee drawne forth that are too clofe and neare one vnto another, and plant them in fuch place where they fhall continue, fo that they ftand halfe a yard of ground diftance afunder, which after the planting, let be fhadowed for a time, as is before fpecified ; and this may bee done in the end of Iuly, or fooner if there be caufe. I haue not fet downe in all this difcourfe of planting, tranfplanting, fowing, fetting, &c. any mention of watering thofe flips or plants, not doubting but that euery ones reafon will induce them to thinke, that they cannot profper without watering: But let this Caueat be a fufficient remembrance vnto you, that you neuer water any of thefe Gilloflowers, nor yet indeede any other fine herbe or plant with cold water, fuch as you haue prefently before drawne out from a pumpe or Well, &c. but with fuch water as hath ftood open in the aire in a cifterne, tubbe, or pot, for one whole day at the leaft ; if it be two or three daies it will be neuer the worfe, but rather the better, as I haue related before : yet take efpeciall heede that you doe not giue them too much to ouer-glut them at any time, but temperately to ir-

rorate

rorate, bedew or fprinkle them often. From the feedes of thefe Gilloflowers hath rifen both white, red, blufh, ftamell, tawny lighter and fadder, marbled, fpeckled, ftriped, flaked, and that in diuers manners, both fingle and double flowers, as you fhall
fee them fet downe in a more ample manner in the Chapter of Gilloflowers. And
thus much for their encreafe by the two wayes of planting and fowing : For as for a
third way, by grafting one into or vpon another, I know none fuch to be true, nor to
be of any more worth than an old Wiues tale, both nature, reafon, and experience, all
contefting againft fuch an idle fancy, let men make what oftentation they pleafe. It
now refteth, that we alfo fhew you the manner how to preferue them, as well in Summer from all noyfome and hurtfull things, as in the Winter and Spring from the fharp
and chilling colds, and the fharpe and bitter killing windes in March. The hurtfull
things in the Summer are efpecially thefe, too much heate of the Sunne which fcorch-
eth them, which you muft be carefull to preuent, by placing boughes, boords, clothes
or mats, &c. before them, if they bee in the ground; or elfe if they bee in pots, to
remoue into them into the fhadow, to giue them refrefhing from the heate, and giue
them water alfo for their life : too much water, or too little is another annoyance,
which you muft order as you fee there is iuft caufe, by withholding or giuing them water gently out of a watering pot, and not caft on by difhfuls : Some alfo to water their
Gilloflowers, vfe to fet their pots into tubbes or pots halfe full of water, that fo the
water may foake in at the lower holes in each flower pot, to giue moifture to the roots
of the Gilloflowers onely, without cafting any water vpon the leaues, and affuredly it
is an excellent way to moiften the rootes fo fufficiently at one time, that it doth faue a
great deale of paines many other times. Earwickes are a moft infeftuous vermine, to
fpoyle the whole beauty of your flowers, and that in one night or day; for thefe creatures delighting to creepe into any hollow or fhadowie place, doe creepe into the
long greene pods of the Gilloflowers, and doe eate away the white bottomes of their
leaues, which are fweete, whereby the leaues of the flowers being loofe, doe either
fall away of themfelues before, or when they are gathered, or handled, or prefently
wither within the pods before they are gathered, and blowne away with the winde.
To auoide which inconuenience, many haue deuifed many waies and inuentions to
deftroy them, as pots with double verges or brimmes, containing a hollow gutter betweene them, which being filled with water, will not fuffer thefe fmall vermine to
paffe ouer it to the Gilloflowers to fpoile them. Others haue vfed old fhooes, and fuch
like hollow things to bee fet by them to take them in : but the beft and moft vfuall
things now vfed, are eyther long hollow canes, or elfe beafts hoofes, which being
turned downe vpon ftickes ends fet into the ground, or into the pots of earth, will
foone draw into them many Earwickes, lying hid therein from funne, winde, and
raine, and by care and diligence may foone bee deftroyed, if euery morning and euening one take the hoofes gently off from the ftickes, and knocking them againft the
ground in a plain allie, fhake out all the Earwicks that are crept into them, which quickly with ones foot may be trode to peeces. For fodain blafting with thunder and lighte-
ning, or fierce fharpe windes, &c. I know no other remedy, vnleffe you can couer
them therefrom when you firft forefee the danger, but patiently to abide the loffe,
whatfoeuer fome haue aduifed, to lay litter about them to auoide blafting; for if any
fhall make tryall thereof, I am in doubt, he fhall more endanger his rootes thereby, being the Summer time, when any fuch feare of blafting is, than any wife faue them from
it, or doe them any good. For the Winter preferuation of them, fome haue aduifed to
couer them with Bee-hiues, or elfe with fmall Willow ftickes, prickt croffewife into
the ground ouer your flowers, and bowed archwife, and with litter laid thereon,
to couer the Gilloflowers quite ouer, after they haue beene fprinkled with fope afhes
and lyme mixt together: and this way is commended by fome that haue written thereof, to be fuch an admirable defence vnto them in Winter, that neither Ants, nor
Snailes, nor Earwickes fhall touch them, becaufe of the fope afhes and lyme, and neyther frofts nor ftormes fhall hurt them, becaufe of the litter which fo well will defend
them; and hereby alfo your Gilloflowers will bee ready to flower, not onely in the
Spring very early, but euen all the Winter. But whofoeuer fhall follow thefe directions, may peraduenture finde them in fome part true, as they are there fet downe for
the Winter time, and while they are kept clofe and couered; but let them bee affured,

that

that all such plants, or the most part of them, will certainely perish and dye before the Summer be at an end : for the sope ashes and lyme will burne vp and spoile any herbe; and againe, it is impossible for any plant that is kept so warme in Winter, to abide eyther the cold or the winde in the Spring following, or any heate of the Sun, but that both of them will scorch them, and carry them quite away. One great hurt vnto them, and to all other herbes that wee preserue in Winter, is to suffer the snow to lye vpon them any time after it is fallen, for that it doth so chill them, that the Sunne afterward, although in Winter, doth scorch them and burne them vp : looke therefore vnto your Gilloflowers in those times, and shake or strike off the snow gently off from them, not suffering it to abide on them any day or night if you can ; for assure your selfe, if it doth not abide on them, the better they will be. The frosts likewise is another great annoyance vnto them, to corrupt the rootes, and to cause them to swell, rot, and breake : to preuent which inconuenience, I would aduise you to take the straw or litter of your horse stable, and lay some thereof about euery roote of your Gilloflowers (especially those of the best account) close vnto them vpon the ground, but be as carefull as you can, that none thereof lye vpon the greene leaues, or as little as may be, and by this onely way haue they been better defended from the frosts that spoile them in Winter, then by any other that I haue seen or knowne. The windes in March, and Sunneshine dayes then, are one of the greatest inconueniences that happeneth vnto them : for they that haue had hundreds of plants, that haue kept faire and greene all the Winter vntill the beginning or middle of March, before the end thereof, haue had scarce one of many, that either hath not vtterly perished, or been so tainted, that quickly after haue not been lost; which hath happened chiefly by the neglect of these cautions before specified, or in not defending them from the bitter sharpe windes and sunne in this moneth of March. You shall therefore for their better preseruation, besides the litter laid about the rootes, which I aduise you not to remoue as yet, shelter them somewhat from the windes, with eyther bottomlesse pots, pales, or such like things, to keep away the violent force both of windes and sun for that moneth, and for some time before & after it also : yet so, that they be not couered close aboue, but open to receiue ayre & raine. Some also vse to wind withes of hey or straw about the rootes of their Gilloflowers, and fasten them with stickes thrust into the ground, which serue very well in the stead of the other. Thus haue I shewed you the whole preseruation of these worthy and dainty flowers, with the whole manner of ordering them for their encrease : if any one haue any other better way, I shall be as willing to learne it of them, as I haue beene to giue them or any others the knowledge of that I haue here set downe.

CHAP. IX.

That there is not any art whereby any flower may be made to grow double, that was naturally single, nor of any other sent or colour than it first had by nature ; nor that the sowing or planting of herbes one deeper than other, will cause them to be in flower one after another, euery moneth in the yeare.

THe wonderfull desire that many haue to see faire, double, and sweete flowers, hath transported them beyond both reason and nature, feigning and boasting often of what they would haue, as if they had it. And I thinke, from this desire and boasting hath risen all the false tales and reports, of making flowers double as they list, and of giuing them colour and sent as they please, and to flower likewise at what time they will, I doubt not, but that some of these errours are ancient, and continued long by tradition, and others are of later inuention : and therefore the more to be condemned, that men of wit and iudgement in these dayes should expose themselues in their writings, to be rather laughed at, then beleeued for such idle tales. And although in the contradiction of them, I know I shall vndergoe many calumnies, yet notwithstanding, I will endeauour to set downe and declare so much, as I hope may by reason

perswade

perſwade many in the truth, although I cannot hope of all, ſome being ſo ſtrongly wedded to their owne will, and the errours they haue beene bred in, that no reaſon may alter them. Firſt therefore I ſay, that if there were any art to make ſome flowers to grow double, that naturally were ſingle, by the ſame art, all ſorts of flowers that are ſingle by nature, may be made to grow double : but the ſorts of flowers that are ſingle by nature, whereof ſome are double, were neuer made double by art ; for many ſorts abide ſtill ſingle, whereof there was neuer ſeene double : and therefore there is no ſuch art in any mans knowledge to bring it to paſſe. If any man ſhall ſay, that becauſe there are many flowers double, whereof there are ſingle alſo of the ſame kinde, as for example, Violets, Marigolds, Daiſyes, Daffodils, Anemones, and many other, that therefore thoſe double flowers were ſo made by the art of man : *viz.* by the obſeruati-on of the change of the Moone, the conſtellations or coniunctions of Planets, or ſome other Starres or celeſtiall bodies. Although I doe confeſſe and acknowledge, that I thinke ſome conſtellations, and peraduenture changes of the Moone, &c. were appointed by the God of nature, as conducing and helping to the making of thoſe flowers double, that nature hath ſo produced ; yet I doe deny, that any man hath or ſhall euer be able to proue, that it was done by any art of man, or that any man can tell the true cauſes and ſeaſons, what changes of the Moone, or conſtellations of the Pla-nets, wrought together for the producing of thoſe double flowers, or can imitate na-ture, or rather the God of nature, to doe the like. If it ſhall bee demanded, From whence then came theſe double flowers that we haue, if they were not ſo made by art? I anſwer, that aſſuredly all ſuch flowers did firſt grow wilde, and were ſo found dou-ble, as they doe now grow in Gardens, but for how long before they were found they became double, no man can tell ; we onely haue them as nature hath produced them, and ſo they remaine. Againe, if any ſhall ſay, that it is likely that theſe double flowers were forced ſo to be, by the often planting and tranſplanting of them, becauſe it is ob-ſerued in moſt of them, that if they ſtand long in any one place, and not be often re-moued, they will grow ſtill leſſe double, and in the end turne ſingle. I doe confeſſe, that *Facilior eſt deſcenſus quàm aſcenſus,* and that the vnfruitfulneſſe of the ground they are planted in, or the neglect or little care had of them, or the growing of them too thicke or too long, are oftentimes a cauſe of the diminiſhing of the flowers doubleneſſe ; but withall you ſhall obſerue, that the ſame rootes that did beare double flowers (and not any other that neuer were double before) haue returned to their for-mer doubleneſſe againe, by good ordering and looking vnto : ſingle flowers haue only beene made ſomewhat fairer or larger, by being planted in the richer and more fruit-full ground of the Garden, than they were found wilde by nature ; but neuer made to grow double, as that which is naturally ſo found of it ſelfe : For I will ſhew you mine owne experience in the matter. I haue been as inquiſitiue as any man might be, with euery one I knew, that made any ſuch report, or that I thought could ſay any thing therein, but I neuer could finde any one, that could aſſuredly reſolue me, that he knew certainly any ſuch thing to be done : all that they could ſay was but report, for the ob-ſeruation of the Moone, to remoue plants before the change, that is, as ſome ſay, the full of the Moone, others the new Moone, whereupon I haue made tryall at many times, and in many ſorts of plants, accordingly, and as I thought fit, by planting & tran-ſplanting them, but I could neuer ſee the effect deſired, but rather in many of them the loſſe of my plants. And were there indeed ſuch a certaine art, to make ſingle flowers to grow double, it would haue beene knowne certainly to ſome that would practiſe it, and there are ſo many ſingle flowers, whereof there were neuer any of the kinde ſeene double, that to produce ſuch of them to be double, would procure both credit and coyne enough to him that ſhould vſe it ; but *Vltra poſſe non eſt eſſe* : and therefore let no man beleeue any ſuch reports, bee they neuer ſo ancient ; for they are but meere tales and fables. Concerning colours and ſents, the many rules and directions extant in ma-nie mens writings, to cauſe flowers to grow yellow, red, greene, or white, that neuer were ſo naturally, as alſo to be of the ſent of Cinamon, Muske, &c. would almoſt per-ſwade any, that the matters thus ſet downe by ſuch perſons, and with ſome ſhew of probability, were conſtant and aſſured proofes thereof : but when they come to the triall, they all vaniſh away like ſmoake. I will in a few words ſhew you the matters and manners of their proceedings to effect this purpoſe : Firſt (they ſay) if you ſhall ſteepe

your

your seedes in the lees of red Wine, you shall haue the flowers of those plants to be of a purple colour. If you will haue Lillies or Gilloflowers to be of a Scarlet red colour, you shall put Vermillion or Cynaber betweene the rinde and the small heads growing about the roote : if you will haue them blew, you shall dissolue Azur or Byse between the rinde and the heads : if yellow, Orpiment : if greene, Vardigrease, and thus of any other colour. Others doe aduise to open the head of the roote, and poure into it any colour dissolued, so that there be no fretting or corroding thing therein for feare of hurting the roote, and looke what colour you put in, iust such or neare vnto it shall the colour of the flower bee. Some againe doe aduise to water the plants you would haue changed, with such coloured liquor as you desire the flower to be of, and they shall grow to be so. Also to make Roses to bee yellow, that you should graft a white Rose (some say a Damaske) vpon a Broome stalke, and the flower will be yellow, supposing because the Broome flower is yellow, therefore the Rose will be yellow. Some affirme the like, if a Rose be grafted on a Barbery bush, because both the blossome and the barke of the Barbery is yellow, &c. In the like manner for sents, they haue set downe in their writings, that by putting Cloues, Muske, Cinamon, Benzoin, or any other such sweete thing, bruised with Rose water, between the barke and the body of trees, the fruit of them will smell and taste of the same that is put vnto them ; and if they bee put vnto the toppe of the rootes, or else bound vnto the head of the roote, they will cause the flowers to smell of that sent the matter put vnto them is of : as also to steep the seeds of Roses, and other plants in the water of such like sweet things, and then to sowe them, and water them morning and euening with such like liquor, vntill they be growne vp ; besides a number of such like rules and directions set downe in bookes, so confidently, as if the matters were without all doubt or question : when-as without all doubt and question I will assure you, that they are all but meere idle tales & fancies, without all reason or truth, or shadow of reason or truth : For sents and colours are both such qualities as follow the essence of plants, euen as formes are also, and one may as well make any plant to grow of what forme you will, as to make it of what sent or colour you will; and if any man can forme plants at his will and pleasure, he can doe as much as God himselfe that created them. For the things they would adde vnto the plants to giue them colour, are all corporeall, or of a bodily substance, and whatsoeuer should giue any colour vnto a liuing and growing plant, must be spirituall : for no solide corporeall substance can ioyne it selfe with the life and essence of an herbe or tree, and the spirituall part of the colour thereof is not the same with the bodily substance, but is a meere vapour that riseth from the substance, and feedeth the plant, whereby it groweth, so that there is no ground or colour of reason, that a substantiall colour should giue colour to a growing herbe or tree : but for sent (which is a meere vapour) you will say there is more probability. Yet consider also, that what sweete sent soeuer you binde or put vnto the rootes of herbes or trees, must be either buried, or as good as buried in the earth, or barke of the tree, whereby the substance will in a small time corrupt and rot, and before it can ioyne it selfe with the life, spirit, and essence of the plant, the sent also will perish with the substance : For no heterogeneall things can bee mixed naturally together, as Iron and Clay; and no other thing but homogeneall, can be nourishment or conuertible into the substance of man or beast : And as the stomach of man or beast altereth both formes, sents, and colours of all digestible things ; so whatsoeuer sent or colour is wholsome, and not poysonfull to nature, being receiued into the body of man or beast, doth neither change the bloud or skinne into that colour or sent was receiued : no more doth any colour or sent to any plant ; for the plants are onely nourished by the moisture they draw naturally vnto them, be it of wine or any other liquor is put vnto them, and not by any corporeall substance, or heterogeneall vapour or sent, because the earth like vnto the stomach doth soone alter them, before they are conuerted into the nature and substance of the plant. Now for the last part I vndertooke to confute, that no man can by art make all flowers to spring at what time of the yeare hee will ; although, as I haue here before shewed, there are flowers for euery moneth of the yeare, yet I hope there is not any one, that hath any knowledge in flowers and gardening, but knoweth that the flowers that appeare and shew themselues in the seuerall moneths of the yeare, are not one and the same, and so made to flower by art ; but that they are seuerall sorts of plants, which

will

will flower naturally and constantly in the same moneths one yeare, that they vse to doe in another, or with but little alteration, if the yeares proue not alike kindly: As for example, those plants that doe flower in Ianuary and February, will by no art or industry of man be caused to flower in Summer or in Autumne; and those that flower in Aprill and May, will not flower in Ianuary or February; or those in Iuly, August, &c. either in the Winter or Spring: but euery one knoweth their owne appointed naturall times, which they constantly obserue and keepe, according to the temperature of the yeare, or the temper of the climate, being further North or South, to bring them on earlier or later, as it doth with all other fruits, flowers, and growing greene herbes, &c. except that by chance, some one or other extraordinarily may be hindered in their due season of flowring, and so giue their flowers out of time, or else to giue their flowers twice in the yeare, by the superaboundance of nourishment, or the mildnesse of the season, by moderate showers of raine, &c. as it sometimes also happeneth with fruits, which chance, as it is seldome, and not constant, so we then terme it but *Lusus naturæ*: or else by forcing them in hot stoues, which then will perish, when they haue giuen their flowers or fruits. It is not then, as some haue written, the sowing of the seedes of Lillies, or any other plants a foote deepe, or halfe a foote deepe, or two inches deepe, that will cause them to be in flower one after another, as they are sowne euery moneth of the yeare; for it were too grosse to thinke, that any man of reason and iudgement would so beleeue. Nor is it likewise in the power of any man, to make the same plants to abide a moneth, two, or three, or longer in their beauty of flowring, then naturally they vse to doe; for I thinke that were no humane art, but a supernaturall worke. For nature still bendeth and tendeth to perfection, that is, after flowring to giue fruit or seede; nor can it bee hindered in the course thereof without manifest danger of destruction, euen as it is in all other fruit-bearing creatures, which stay no longer, then their appointed time is naturall vnto them, without apparent damage. Some things I grant may be so ordered in the planting, that according to that order and time which is obserued in their planting, they shall shew forth their faire flowers, and they are Anemones, which will in that manner, that I haue shewed in the worke following, flower in seuerall moneths of the yeare; which thing as it is incident to none or very few other plants, and is found out but of late, so likewise is it knowne but vnto a very few. Thus haue I shewed you the true solution of these doubts: And although they haue not beene amplified with such Philosophicall arguments and reasons, as one of greater learning might haue done, yet are they truely and sincerely set downe, that they may serue *tanquam galeatum*, against all the calumnies and obiections of wilfull and obdurate persons, that will not be reformed. As first, that all double flowers were so found wilde, being the worke of nature alone, and not the art of any man, by planting or transplanting, at or before the new or full Moone, or any other obseruation of time, that hath caused the flower to grow double, that naturally was single: Secondly, that the rules and directions, to cause flowers to bee of contrary or different colours or sents, from that they were or would be naturally, are meere fancies of men, without any ground of reason or truth. And thirdly, that there is no power or art in man, to cause flowers to shew their beauty diuers moneths before their naturall time, nor to abide in their beauty longer then the appointed naturall time for euery one of them.

THE

THE GARDEN
OF
PLEASANT FLOWERS.

CHAP. I.

Corona Imperialis. The Crowne Imperiall.

Ecause the Lilly is the more stately flower among manie : and amongst the wonderfull varietie of Lillies, knowne to vs in these daies, much more then in former times, whereof some are white, others blush, some purple, others red or yellow, some spotted, others without spots, some standing vpright, others hanging or turning downewards, The Crowne Imperiall for his stately beautifulnesse, deserueth the first place in this our Garden of delight, to be here entreated of before all other Lillies : but because it is so well knowne to most persons, being in a manner euery where common, I shall neede onely to giue you a relation of the chiefe parts thereof (as I intend in such other things) which are these : The roote is yellowish on the outside, composed of fewer, but much thicker scales, then any other Lilly but the Persian, and doth grow sometimes to be as great as a pretty bigge childes head, but somewhat flat withall, from the sides whereof, and not from the bottome, it shooteth forth thicke long fibres, which perish euery yeare, hauing a hole in the midst thereof, at the end of the yeare, when the old stalke is dry and withered, and out of the which a new stalke doth spring againe (from a bud or head to be seen within the hollownesse on the one side) the yeare following : the stalke then filling vp the hollownesse, riseth vp three or foure foote high, being great, round, and of a purplish colour at the bottome, but greene aboue, beset from thence to the middle thereof with many long and broad greene leaues, very like to the leaues of our ordinary white Lilly, but somewhat shorter and narrower, confusedly without order, and from the middle is bare or naked without leaues, for a certaine space vpwards, and then beareth foure, sixe, or tenne flowers, more or lesse, according to the age of the plant, and the fertility of the soyle where it groweth : The buddes at the first appearing are whitish, standing vpright among a bush or tuft of greene leaues, smaller then those below, and standing aboue the flowers, after a while they turne themselues, and hang downewards euerie one vpon his owne footestalke, round about the great stemme or stalke, sometimes of an euen depth, and other while one lower or higher than another, which flowers are neare the forme of an ordinary Lilly, yet somewhat lesser and closer, consisting of sixe leaues of an Orange colour, striped with purplish lines and veines, which adde a great grace to the flowers : At the bottome of the flower next vnto the stalke, euery

leafe

leafe thereof hath on the outfide a certaine bunch or eminence, of a darke purplifh colour, and on the infide there lyeth in thofe hollow bunched places, certaine cleare drops of water like vnto pearles, of a very fweete tafte almoft like fugar : in the midft of each flower is a long white ftile or pointell, forked or diuided at the end, and fixe white chiues tipt with yellowifh pendents, ftanding clofe about it : after the flowers are paft, appeare fixe fquare feede veffels ftanding vpright, winged as it were or welted on the edges, yet feeming but three fquare, becaufe each couple of thofe welted edges are ioyned clofer together, wherein are contained broad, flat, and thinne feedes, of a pale brownifh colour, like vnto other Lillies, but much greater and thicker alfo. The ftalke of this plant doth oftentimes grow flat, two, three, or foure fingers broad, and then beareth many more flowers, but for the moft part fmaller then when it beareth round ftalkes. And fometimes it happeneth the ftalke to be diuided at the top, carrying two or three tufts of greene leaues, without any flowers on them. And fometimes likewife, to beare two or three rowes or crownes of flowers one aboue another vpon one ftalke, which is feldome and fcarce feene, and befides, is but meere accidentall : the whole plant and euery part thereof, as well rootes, as leaues and flowers, doe fmell fomewhat ftrong as it were the fauour of a Foxe, fo that if any doe but come neare it, he cannot but fmell it, which yet is not vnwholfome.

I haue not obferued any variety in the colour of this flower, more then that it will be fairer in a cleare open ayre, and paler, or as it were blafted in a muddy or fmoakie ayre. And although fome haue boafted of one with white flowers, yet I could neuer heare that any fuch hath endured in one vniforme colour.

The Place.

This plant was firft brought from Conftantinople into thefe Chriftian Countries, and by the relation of fome that fent it, groweth naturally in Perfia.

The Time.

It flowreth moft commonly in the end of March, if the weather be milde, and fpringeth not out of the ground vntill the end of February, or beginning of March, fo quicke it is in the fpringing : the heads with feed are ripe in the end of May.

The Names.

It is of fome called *Lilium Perficum*, the Perfian Lilly : but becaufe wee haue another, which is more vfually called by that name, as fhall be fhewed in the next Chapter, I had rather with Alphonfus Pancius the Duke of Florence his Phyfitian, (who firft fent the figure thereof vnto Mr. Iohn de Brancion) call it *Corona Imperialis*, The Crowne Imperiall, then by any other name, as alfo for that this name is now more generally receiued. It hath been fent alfo by the name *Tufai*, and *Tufchai*, and *Turfani*, or *Turfanda*, being, as it is like, the Turkifh names.

The Vertues.

For any Phyficall Vertues that are in it, I know of none, nor haue heard that any hath been found out : notwithftanding the ftrong fent would perfwade it might be applyed to good purpofe.

Chap. II.
Lilium Perficum. The Perfian Lilly.

THe roote of the Perfian Lilly is very like vnto the root of the Crowne Imperiall, and lofing his fibres in like maner euery yeare, hauing a hole therin likewife where the old ftalke grew, but whiter, rounder, and a little longer, fmaller, and not ftinking at all like it, from whence fpringeth vp a round whitifh greene ftalke, not
much

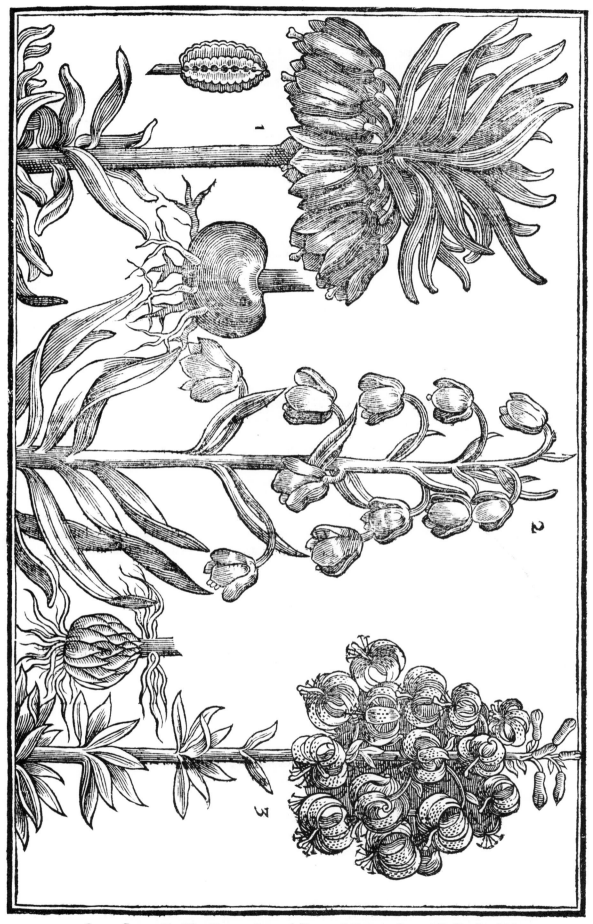

1 *Corona Imperialis.* The Crowne Imperiall.   2 *Lilium Perficum.* The Perfian Lilly.
3 *Martagon Imperiale.* The Martagon Imperiall.

much

much lower than the Crowne Imperiall, but much smaller, beset from the bottome to the middle thereof, with many long and narrow leaues, of a whitish or blewish greene colour, almost like to the leafe of a Tulipa : from the middle vpwards, to the toppe of the stalke, stand many flowers one aboue another round about it, with leaues at the foote of euery one of them, each whereof is pendulous or hanging downe the head, like vnto the Crowne Imperiall, and not turning vp any of the flowers againe, but smaller than in any other kinde of Lilly, yea not so bigge as the flower of a Fritillaria, consisting of sixe leaues a peece, of a dead or ouerworne purplish colour, hauing in the midst a small long pointell, with certaine chiues tipt with yellow pendents : after the flowers are past (which abide open a long time, and for the most part flower by degrees, the lowest first, and so vpwards) if the weather be temperate, come sixe square heads or seede vessels, seeming to be but three square, by reason of the wings, very like to the heads of the Crowne Imperiall, but smaller and shorter, wherein are contained such like flat seed, but smaller also, and of a darker colour.

The Place.

This was, as it is thought, first brought from Persia vnto Constantinople, and from thence, sent vnto vs by the meanes of diuers Turkie Merchants, and in especiall, by the procurement of M^r. Nicholas Lete, a worthy Merchant, and a louer of all faire flowers.

The Time.

It springeth out of the ground very neare a moneth before the Crowne Imperiall, but doth not flower till it bee quite past (that is to say) not vntill the latter end of Aprill, or beginning of May : the seed (when it doth come to perfection, as it seldome doth) is not ripe vntill Iuly.

The Names.

It hath been sent by the name of *Pennachio Persiano*, and wee thereupon doe most vsually call it *Lilium Persicum*, The Persian Lilly. Clusius saith it hath been sent into the Low-Countries vnder the name of Susam giul, and he thereupon thinking it came from Susis in Persia, called it *Lilium Susianum*, The Lilly of Susis.

The Vertues.

Wee haue not yet heard, that this hath beene applyed for any Physicall respect.

Chap. III.

Martagon Imperiale, siue Lilium Montanum maius,
The Martagon Imperiall.

VNder this title of *Lilium Montanum*, or *Lilium Siluestre*, I do comprenend only those kindes of Lillies, which carry diuers circles of greene leaues set together at certaine distances, round about the stalke, and not sparsedly as the two former, and as other kindes that follow, doe. And although there bee many of this sort, yet because their chiefest difference is in the colour of the flower, wee will containe them all in one Chapter, and begin with the most stately of them all, because of the number of flowers it beareth vpon one stalke. The Imperiall Lilly hath a scaly roote, like vnto all the rest of the Lillies, but of a paler yellow colour, closely compact or set together, being short and small oftentimes, in comparison of the greatnesse of the stemme

stemme growing from it. The stalke is brownish and round at the bottome, and some-times flat from the middle vpwards, three foote high or more, beset at certaine distan-ces with rondles or circles of many broad leaues, larger and broader for the most part than any other of this kinde, and of a darke green colour: It hath two or three, and sometimes foure of these rondles or circles of leaues, and bare without any leafe be-tweene; but aboue toward the tops of the stalkes, it hath here and there some leaues vpon it, but smaller than any of the other leaues: at the toppe of the stalke come forth many flowers, sometime three or foure score, thicke thrust, or confusedly set together, and not thinne or sparsedly one aboue another, as in the lesser of this kinde of Moun-taine Lilly. It hath been sometimes also obserued in this kinde, that it hath borne ma-nie flowers at three seuerall spaces of the stalke, one aboue another, which hath made a goodly shew; each flower whereof is pendulous, hanging downe, and each leafe of the flower turning vp againe, being thicke or fleshy, of a fine delayed purple colour, spotted with many blackish or brownish spots, of a very pleasant sweet sent, which ma-keth it the more acceptable: in the middle of the flower hangeth downe a stile or pointell, knobbed or buttoned at the end with sixe yellow chiues, tipt with loose pen-dents of an Orient red or Vermillion colour, which will easily sticke like dust vpon any thing that toucheth them: the heads or seede vessels are small and round, with small edges about them, wherein is contained flat browne seede like other Lillies, but lesser. The root is very apt to encrease or set of, as we call it, wherby the plant seldome commeth to so great a head of flowers, but riseth vp with many stalkes, and then carry fewer flowers.

Of this kinde there is sometimes one found, that beareth flowers without any spots: *Martagon* the leaues whereof and stalke likewise are paler, but not else differing. *Imperiale flore non pun-ctato.*

Martagon flore albo. The White Martagon.

We haue also some other of this kind, the first wherof hath his stalke & leafe greener than the former, the stalke is a little higher, but not bearing so thicke a head of flowers, although much more plentifull than the lesser Mountaine Lilly, being altogether of a fine white colour, without any spots, or but very few, and that but sometimes also: the pendents in the middle of this flower are not red, as the former, but yellow; the roote of this, and of the other two that follow, are of a pale yellow colour, the cloues or scales of them being brittle, and not closely compact, yet so as if two, and sometimes three scales or cloues grew one vpon the head or vpperpart of another; which diffe-rence is a speciall note to know these three kindes, from any other kinde of Mountaine Lilly, as in all old rootes that I haue seene, I haue obserued, as also in them that are rea-sonably well growne, but in the young rootes it is not yet so manifest.

Martagon flore albo maculato. The White spotted Martagon.

The second is like vnto the first in all things, saue in this, that the flowers hereof are not altogether so white, and besides hath many reddish spots on the inside of the leaues of the flower, and the stalke also is not so greene but brownish.

Martagon flore carneo. The blush Martagon.

A third sort there is of this kinde, whose flowers are wholly of a delayed flesh co-lour, with many spots on the flowers, and this is the difference hereof from the former.

Lilium Montanum siue siluestre minus. The lesser Mountaine Lilly.

The lesser Mountaine Lilly is so like in root vnto the greater that is first described, that it is hard to distinguish them asunder; but when this is sprung vp out of the ground, which is a moneth after the first: it also carrieth his leaues in rondles about the stalke, although not altogether so great nor so many. The flowers are more thinly set on the stalkes one aboue another, with more distance betweene each flower than the former, and are of a little deeper flesh colour or purple, spotted in the same manner. The buds

1 *Martagon flore albo.* The white Martagon.   2 *Martagon siue Lilium Canadense maculatum,* The spotted Martagon, or Lilly of Canada,   3 *Martagon Pomponeum.* The Martagon Pompony, or early red Martagon.

or heads of flowers, in some of these before they be blowne, are hoary white, or hairie, whereas in others, there is no hoarinesse at all, but the buddes are smooth and purplish : in other things this differeth not from the former.

Of this sort also there is one that hath but few spots on the flowers, whose colour is somewhat paler than the other. *Lilium Montanum non maculatum.*

Martagon Canadense maculatum. The spotted Martagon of Canada.

Although this strange Lilly hath not his flowers hanging downe, and turning vp again, as the former kinds set forth in this Chapter; yet because the green leaues stand at seuerall ioynts as they do, I must needs insert it here, not knowing where more fitly to place it. It hath a small scaly roote, with many small long fibres thereat, from whence riseth vp a reasonable great stalke, almost as high as any of the former, bearing at three or foure distances many long and narrow greene leaues, but not so many or so broad as the former, with diuers ribbes in them: from among the vppermost rundle of leaues breake forth foure or fiue flowers together, euery one standing on a long slender foote stalke, being almost as large as a red Lilly, but a little bending downewards, and of a faire yellow colour, spotted on the inside with diuers blackish purple spots or strakes, hauing a middle pointell, and sixe chiues, with pendents on them.

The Place.

All these Lillies haue been found in the diuers Countries of Germany, as Austria, Hungaria, Pannonia, Stiria, &c. and are all made Denisons in our London Gardens, where they flourish as in their owne naturall places. The last was was brought into France from Canada by the French Colonie, and from thence vnto vs.

The Time.

They flower about the later end of Iune for the most part, yet the first springeth out of the ground a moneth at the least before the other, which are most vsually in flower before it, like vnto the Serotine Tulipas, all of them being early vp, and neuer the neere.

The Names.

The first is vsually called *Martagon Imperiale*, the Imperiall Martagon, and is *Lilium Montanum maius*, the greatest Mountaine Lilly; for so it deserueth the name, because of the number of flowers vpon a head or stalke. Some haue called it *Lilium Sarasenicum*, and some *Hemerocallis*, but neither of them doth so fitly agree vnto it.

The second is *Lilium Montanum maius flore albo*, and of some *Martagon Imperiale flore albo*, but most vsually *Martagon flore albo*, the white Martagon. The second sort of this second kinde, is called *Martagon flore albo maculato*, the spotted white Martagon. And the third, *Martagon flore carneo*, the blush Martagon.

The third kinde is called *Lilium Montanum*, the Mountaine Lilly, and some adde the title *minus*, the lesser, to know it more distinctly from the other. Some also *Lilium Siluestre*, as Clusius, and some others, and of Matthiolus *Martagon*. Of diuers women here in England, from the Dutch name, Lilly of Nazareth. The last hath his title *Americanum & Canadense*, and in English accordingly.

CHAP. IV.

CHAP. IV.

1. Martagon Pomponeum siue Lilium rubrum præcox, vel Lilium Macedonicum.
The early red Martagon, or Martagon Pompony.

AS in the former Chapter we described vnto you such Lillies, whose flowers being pendulous, turne their leaues backe againe, and haue their greene leaues, set by spaces about the stalke: so in this wee will set downe those sorts, which carry their greene leaues more sparsedly, and all along the stalke, their flowers hanging downe, and turning vp againe as the former, and begin with that which is of greatest beauty, or at least of most rarity.

1. Martagon Pomponeum angusti folium præcox.

1. This rare Martagon hath a scaly root closely compact, with broader and thinner scales than others, in time growing very great, and of a more deepe yellow colour then the former, from whence doth spring vp a round greene stalke in some plants, and flat in others, two or three foote high, bearing a number of small, long, and narrow greene leaues, very like vnto the leaues of Pinkes, but greener, set very thicke together, and without order about the stalke, vp almost vnto the toppe, and lesser by degrees vpwards, where stand many flowers, according to the age of the plant, and thriuing in the place where it groweth; in those that are young, but a few, and more sparsedly, and in others that are old many more, and thicker set: for I haue reckoned threescore flowers and more, growing thicke together on one plant with mee, and an hundred flowers on another: these flowers are of a pale or yellowish red colour, and not so deep red as the red Martagon of Constantinople, hereafter set down, nor fully so large: yet of the same fashion, that is, euery flower hanging downe, and turning vp his leaues againe. It is not so plentifull in bearing of seede as the other Lillies, but when it doth, it differeth not but in being lesse.

2. Martagon angusti folium magis serotinum.
3. Martagon Pomponeum latifolium præcox.

There is another, whose greene leaues are not so thicke set on the stalke, but else differeth not but in flowring a fortnight later.

There is another also of this kind, so like vnto the former in root, stalk, flower, & maner of growing, that the difference is hardly discerned; but consisteth chiefly in these two points: First, that the leaues of this are a little broader and shorter then the former; and secondly, that it beareth his flowers a fortnight earlier than the first. In the colour or forme of the flower, there can no difference bee discerned, nor (as I said) in any other thing. All these Lillies doe spring very late out of the ground, euen as the yellow Martagons doe, but are sooner in flower then any others.

4. Martagon flore phœniceo.

A fourth kinde hereof hath of late been knowne to vs, whose leaues are broader and shorter then the last, and the flowers of a paler red, tending to yellow, of some called a golden red colour: but flowreth not so early as they.

2. Lilium rubrum Byzantinum, siue Martagon Constantinopolitanum.
The red Martagon of Constantinople.

1. The red Martagon of Constantinople is become so common euery where, and so well knowne to all louers of these delights, that I shall seeme vnto them to lose time, to bestow many lines vpon it; yet because it is so faire a flower, and was at the first so highly esteemed, it deserueth his place and commendations, howsoeuer encreasing the plenty hath not made it dainty. It riseth out of the ground early in the spring, before many other Lillies, from a great thicke yellow scaly root, bearing a round brownish stalke, beset with many faire greene leaues confusedly thereon, but not so broad as the common white Lilly, vpon the toppe whereof stand one, two, or three, or more flowers, vpon long footestalkes, which hang downe their heads, and turne vp their leaues againe, of an excellent red crimson colour, and sometimes paler, hauing a long pointell in the middle, compassed with sixe whitish chiues, tipt with loose yellow pendents, of a reasonable good sent, but somewhat faint. It likewise beareth seede in heads, like vnto the other, but greater.

Martagon Constantinopolitanum maculatum.
The red spotted Martagon of Constantinople.

We haue another of this kinde, that groweth somewhat greater and higher, with a larger flower, and of a deeper colour, spotted with diuers blacke spots, or strakes and lines, as is to be seene in the Mountaine Lillies, and in some other hereafter to be described; but is not so in the former of this kinde, which hath no shew of spots at all. The whole plant as it is rare, so it is of much more beauty then the former.

2. *Martagon Pannonicum, siue Exoticum flore spadicee.*
The bright red Martagon of Hungarie.

Although this Martagon or Lilly bee of another Countrey, yet by reason of the neerenesse both in leafe and flower vnto the former, may more fitly be placed next vnto them, then in any other place. It hath his roote very like the other, but the leaues are somewhat larger, and more sparsedly set vpon the stalke, else not much vnlike: the flowers bend downe, and turne vp their leaues againe, but somewhat larger, and of a bright red, tending to an Orenge colour, that is, somewhat yellowish, and not crimson, like the other.

3. *Martagon Luteum punctatum.* The Yellow spotted Martagon.

1. This Yellow Martagon hath a great scaly or cloued roote, and yellow, like vnto all these sorts of turning Lillies, from whence springeth vp a round greene strong stalke, three foote high at the least, confusedly set with narrow long greene leaues, white on the edges vp to the very toppe thereof almost, hauing diuers flowers on the head, turning vp againe as the former doe, of a faint yellowish, or greenish yellow colour, with many blacke spots or strakes about the middle of the leafe of euery flower, and a forked pointell, with sixe chiues about it, tipt with reddish pendents, of a heauie strong smell, not very pleasant to many. It beareth seede very plentifully, in great heads, like vnto the other former Lillies, but a little paler.

2. *Martagon Luteum non maculatum.* The Yellow Martagon without spots.

The other yellow Martagon differeth in no other thing from the former, but onely that it hath no spots at all vpon any of the leaues of the flowers; agreeing with the former, in colour, forme, height, and all things else.

3. *Martagon Luteum serotinum.* The late flowring Yellow Martagon.

There is yet another yellow Martagon, that hath no other difference then the time of his flowring, which is not vntill Iuly, vnlesse in this, that the flower is of a deeper yellow colour.

The Place.

The knowledge of the first kindes of these early Martagons hath come from Italy, from whence they haue bin sent into the Low-Countries, and to vs, and, as it seemeth by the name, whereby they haue bin sent by some into these parts, his originall should be from the mountaines in Macedonia.

The second sort is sufficiently knowne by his name, being first brought from Constantinople, his naturall place being not farre from thence, as it is likely. But the next sort of this second kinde, doth plainly tell vs his place of birth to be the mountaines of Pannonia or Hungarie.

The third kindes grow on the Pyrenæan mountaines, where they haue been searched out, and found by diuers louers of plants, as also in the Kingdome of Naples.

The

The Time.

The firſt early Martagons flower in the end of May, or beginning of Iune, and that is a moneth at the leaſt before thoſe that come from Conſtantinople, which is the ſecond kinde. The two firſt yellow Martagons flower ſomewhat more early, then the early red Martagons, and ſometimes at the ſame time with them. But the third yellow Martagon, as is ſaid, flowreth a moneth later or more, and is in flower when the red Martagon of Conſtantinople flowreth. And although the early red and yellow Martagons, ſpring later then the other Martagons or Lillies, yet they are in flower before them.

The Names.

The firſt early red Lillies or Martagons haue beene ſent vnto vs by ſeuerall names, as *Martagon Pomponeum*, and thereafter are called Martagon of Pompony, and alſo *Lilium* or *Martagon Macedonicum*, the Lilly or Martagon of Macedonia. They are alſo called by Cluſius *Lilium rubrum præcox*, the one *anguſtiore folio*, the other *latiore folio*. And the laſt of this kinde hath the title *flore phæniceo* added or giuen vnto it, that is, the Martagon or Lilly of Macedonia with gold red flowers.

The Martagons of Conſtantinople haue beene ſent by the Turkiſh name *Zuſiniare*, and is called *Martagon*, or *Lilium Byzantinum* by ſome, and *Hemerocallis Chalcedonica* by others; but by the name of the Martagon of Conſtantinople they are moſt commonly receiued with vs, with the diſtinction of *maculatum* to the one, to diſtinguiſh the ſorts. The laſt kinde in this *claſsis*, hath his name in his title, as it hath been ſent vnto vs.

The Yellow Martagons are diſtinguiſhed in their ſeuerall titles, as much as is conuenient for them.

CHAP. V.

Lilium Aureum & Lilium Rubrum. The Gold and Red Lillies.

THere are yet ſome other kindes of red Lillies to bee deſcribed, which differ from all the former, and remaine to be ſpoken of in this place. Some of them grow high, and ſome lowe, ſome haue ſmall knots, which wee call bulbes, growing vpon the ſtalkes, at the ioynts of the leaues or flowers, and ſome haue none: all which ſhall be intreated of in their ſeuerall orders.

Lilium pumilum cruentum. The dwarfe red Lilly.

The dwarfe red Lilly hath a ſcaly roote, ſomewhat like vnto other Lillies, but white, and not yellow at all, and the cloues or ſcales thicker, ſhorter, and fewer in number, then in moſt of the former: the ſtalke hereof is not aboue a foote and a halfe high, round and greene, ſet confuſedly with many faire and ſhort greene leaues, on the toppe of which doe ſtand ſometimes but a few flowers, and ſometimes many of a faire purpliſh red colour, and a little paler in the middle, euery flower ſtanding vpright, and not hanging downe, as in the former, on the leaues whereof here and there are ſome blacke ſpots, lines or markes, and in the middle of the flower a long pointell, with ſome chiues about it, as is in the reſt of theſe Lillies.

Lilium rubrum multiplici flore. This kinde is ſometimes found to yeeld double flowers, as if all the ſingle flowers ſhould grow into one, and ſo make it conſiſt of many leaues, which notwithſtanding his

his

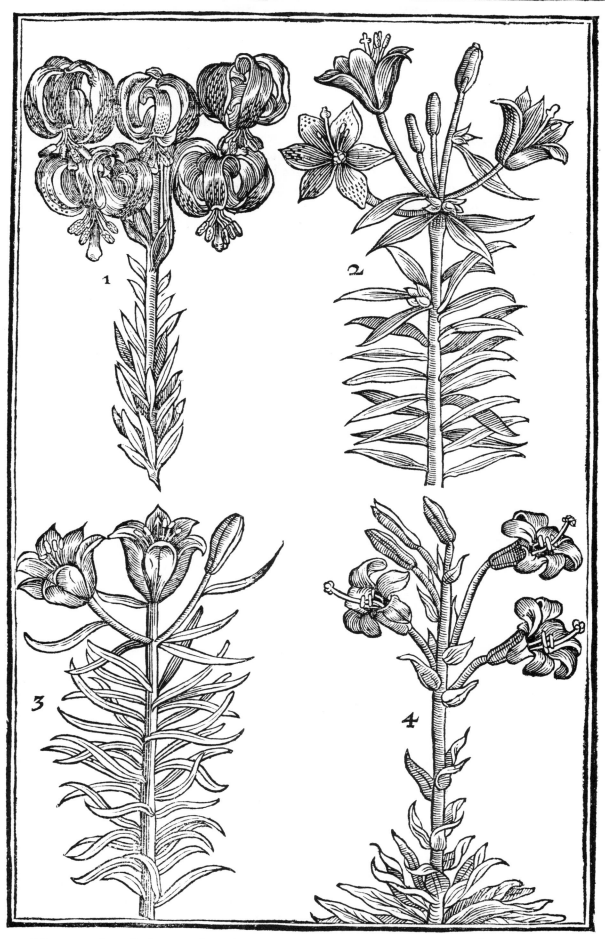

1 *Martagon rubrum siue luteum.* The red or the yellow Martagon.   2 *Lilium Bulbiferum.* The red bulbed Lilly.   3 *Lilium aureum.* The gold red Lilly.   4 *Lilium album.* The white Lilly.

his so continuing sundry yeares, vpon transplanting, will *redire ad ingenium*, that is, quickly come againe to his old byas or forme.

Lilium Aureum. The Gold red Lilly.

The second red Lilly without bulbes groweth much higher then the first, and almost as high as any other Lilly : the roote hereof is white and scaly, the leaues are somewhat longer, and of a darke or sad greene colour ; the flowers are many and large, standing vpright as all these sorts of red Lillies doe, of a paler red colour tending to an Orenge on the inside, with many blacke spots, and lines on them, as in the former, and more yellow on the outside : the seede vessels are like vnto the roundish heads of other Lillies, and so are the seedes in them likewise.

1. *Lilium minus bulbiferum.* The dwarfe bulbed Lilly.

The first of the Lillies that carrieth bulbes on the stalke, hath a white scaly roote like the former ; from whence riseth vp a small round stalke, not much higher then the first dwarfe Lilly, seeming to be edged, hauing many leaues thereon of a sad green colour set about it, close thrust together : the greene heads for flowers, will haue a kind of woollinesse on them, before the flowers begin to open, and betweene these heads of flowers, as also vnder them, and among the vppermost leaues, appeare small bulbes or heads, which being ripe if they be put into the ground, or if they fall of themselues, will shoote forth leaues, and beare flowers within two or three yeares like the mother plant, and so will the bulbes of the other hereafter described : the flowers of this Lilly are of a faire gold yellow colour, shadowed ouer with a shew of purple, but not so red as the first, or the next to bee described. This Lilly will shoote strings vnder ground, like as the last red Lilly will doe also, whereat will grow white bulbed roots, like the rootes of the mother plant, thereby quickly encreasing it selfe.

2. *Lilium Cruentum bulbiferum.* The Fierie red bulbed Lilly.

The second bulbed Lilly riseth vp with his stalke as high as any of these Lillies, carrying many long and narrow darke greene leaues about it, and at the toppe many faire red flowers, as large or larger then any of the former, and of a deeper red colour, with spots on them likewise, hauing greater bulbes growing about the toppe of the stalke and among the flowers, then any else.

Lilium Cruentum flore pleno. The Fierie red double Lilly.

The difference of this doth chiefly consist in the flower, which is composed of manie leaues, as if many flowers went to make one, spotted with black spots, and without any bulbes when it thus beareth, which is but accidentall, as the former double Lilly is said to be.

3. *Lilium maius bulbiferum.* The greater bulbed red Lilly.

The third red Lilly with bulbes, riseth vp almost as high as the last, and is the most common kinde we haue bearing bulbes. It hath many leaues about the stalke, but not of so sad a greene colour as the former : the flowers are of as pale a reddish yellow colour as any of the former, and comming neerest vnto the colour of the Gold red Lilly. This is more plentifull in bulbes, and in shooting strings, to encrease rootes vnder ground, then the others.

The Place.

These Lillies doe all grow in Gardens, but their naturall places of growing is the Mountaines and the Vallies neere them in Italy, as Matthiolus saith faith : and in many Countries of Germany, as Hungarie, Auſtria, Stiria, and Bohemia, as Cluſius and other doe report.

The Time.

They flower for the moſt part in Iune, yet the firſt of theſe is the earlieſt of all the reſt.

The Names.

All theſe Lillies are called *Lilia Rubra*, Red Lillies : Some call them *Lilium Aureum, Lilium Purpureum, Lilium Puniceum, & Lilium Cruentum.* Some alſo call them *Martagon Chimiſtarum.* Cluſius calleth theſe bulbed Lillies *Martagon Bulbiferum.* It is thought to be *Hyacinthus Poetarum*, but I referre the diſcuſſing thereof to a fitter time. Wee haue, to diſtinguiſh them moſt fitly (as I take it) giuen their proper names in their ſeuerall titles.

CHAP. VI.

Lilium Album. The White Lilly.

NOw remaineth onely the White Lilly, of all the whole family or ſtocke of the Lillies, to bee ſpoken of, which is of two ſorts. The one is our common or vulgar White Lilly ; and the other, that which was brought from Conſtantinople.

Lilium Album vulgare. The ordinary White Lilly.

The ordinary White Lilly ſcarce needeth any deſcription, it is ſo well knowne, and ſo frequent in euery Garden ; but to ſay ſomewhat thereof, as I vſe to doe of euery thing, be it neuer ſo common and knowne ; it hath a cloued or ſcaly roote, yellower and bigger then any of the red Lillies : the ſtalke is of a blackiſh greene colour, and riſeth as high as moſt of the Lillies, hauing many faire, broad, and long greene leaues thereon, larger and longer beneath, and ſmaller vpon the ſtalke vpwards ; the flowers are many or few, according to the age of the plant, fertility of the ſoile, and time of ſtanding where it groweth : and ſtand vpon long greene footſtalkes, of a faire white colour, with a long pointell in the middle, and white chiues tipt with yellow pendents about it ; the ſmell is ſomewhat heady and ſtrong.

Lilium Album Byzantinum. The White Lilly of Conſtantinople.

The other White Lilly, differeth but little from the former White Lilly, either in roote, leafe, or flower, but only that this vſually groweth with more number of flowers, then euer we ſaw in our ordinary White Lilly : for I haue ſeene the ſtalke of this Lilly turne flat, of the breadth of an hand, bearing neere two hundred flowers vpon a head, yet moſt commonly it beareth not aboue a dozen, or twenty flowers, but ſmaller then the ordinary, as the greene leaues are likewiſe.

The Place.

The firſt groweth onely in Gardens, and hath not beene declared where it is found wilde, by any that I can heare of. The other hath beene ſent from Conſtantinople, among other rootes, and therefore is likely to grow in ſome parts neere thereunto.

The Time.

They flower in Iune or thereabouts, but ſhoote forth greene leaues in

Autumne,

Autumne, which abide greene all the Winter, the ſtalke ſpringing vp betweene the lower leaues in the Spring.

The Names.

It is called *Lilium Album*, the White Lilly, by moſt Writers; but by Poets *Roſa Iunonis*, Iuno's Roſe. The other hath his name in his title.

The Vertues.

This Lilly aboue all the reſt, yea, and I thinke this onely, and none of
the reſt is vſed in medicines now adayes, although in former times Empe-
ricks vſed the red; and therefore I haue ſpoken nothing of them in the end
of their Chapters, reſeruing what is to be ſaid in this. This hath a mollifying, digeſting, and cleanſing quality, helping to ſuppurate tumours, and to
digeſt them, for which purpoſe the roote is much vſed. The water of the
flowers diſtilled, is of excellent vertue for women in trauell of childe bearing, to procure an eaſie deliuery, as Matthiolus and Camerarius report. It
is vſed alſo of diuers women outwardly, for their faces to cleanſe the skin,
and make it white and freſh. Diuers other properties there are in theſe
Lillies, which my purpoſe is not to declare in this place. Nor is it the ſcope
of this worke; this that hath been ſaid is ſufficient: for were it not, that I
would giue you ſome taſte of the qualities of plants (as I ſaid in my Preface)
as I goe along with them, a generall worke were fitter to declare them
then this.

Chap. VII.

Fritillaria. The checkerd Daffodill.

ALthough diuers learned men do by the name giuen vnto this delightfull plant,
thinke it doth in ſome things partake with a Tulipa or Daffodill, and haue
therefore placed it betweene them; yet I, finding it moſt like vnto a little Lilly,
both in roote, ſtalke, leafe, flower, and ſeede, haue (as you ſee here) placed it next
vnto the Lillies, and before them. Hereof there are many ſorts found out of late, as
white, red, blacke, and yellow, beſides the purple, which was firſt knowne; and of
each of them there are alſo diuers ſorts: and firſt of that which is moſt frequent, and
then of the reſt, euery one in his place and order.

1. *Fritillaria vulgaris.* The common checkerd Daffodill.

The ordinary checkerd Daffodill (as it is vſually called, but might more properly
be called the ſmall checkerd Lilly) hath a ſmall round white roote, and ſomewhat
flat, made as it were of two cloues, and diuided in a maner into two parts, yet ioyning
together at the bottome or ſeate of the roote, which holdeth them both together:
from betweene this cleft or diuiſion, the budde for the ſtalke &c. appeareth, which in
time riſeth vp a foote, or a foote and a halfe high, being round and of a browniſh
greene colour, eſpecially neere vnto the ground, whereon there ſtandeth diſperſedly
foure or fiue narrow long and greene leaues, being a little hollow: at the toppe of the
ſtalke, betweene the vpper leaues (which are ſmaller then the loweſt) the flower ſheweth it ſelfe, hanging or turning downe the head, but not turning vp againe any of his
leaues, as ſome of the Lillies before deſcribed doe; (ſometimes this ſtalke beareth
two flowers, and very ſeldome three) conſiſting of ſixe leaues, of a reddiſh purple colour, ſpotted diuerſly with great ſpots, appearing like vnto ſquare checkers, of a deeper colour; the inſide of the flower is of a brighter colour then the outſide, which
hath ſome greenneſſe at the bottome of euery leafe: within the flower there appeare
ſixe

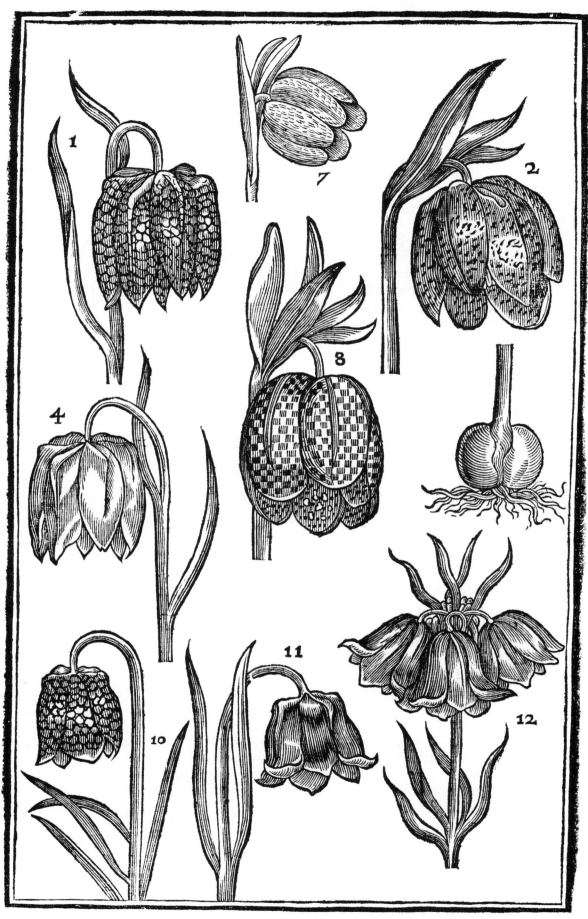

1 *Fritillaria vulgaris.* The common Fritillaria. 2 *Fritillaria flore atrorubente.* The darke red Fritillaria. 4 *Fritillaria alba.* The white Fritillaria. 7 *Fritillaria lutea punctata.* The yellow checkerd Fritillaria. 8 *Fritillaria lutea Italica.* The great yellow Italian Fritillaria. 10 *Fritillaria lutea Lusitanica.* The small yellow Fritillaria of Portugall. 11 *Fritillaria Pyrenæa.* The blacke Fritillaria. 12 *Fritillaria umbellifera.* The Spanish blacke Fritillaria.

sixe chiues tipt with yellow pendents, and a three-forked ftile or pointell compaffing a greene head, which when the flower is paft, rifeth vpright againe, and becommeth the feede veffell, being fomewhat long and round, yet hauing a fmall fhew of edges, flat at the head, like the head of a Lilly, and without any crowne as the Tulipa hath, wherein is contained pale coloured flat feede, like vnto a Lilly, but fmaller.

*Fritillaria vul-
garis pallidior,
præcox, & fe-
rotina.*
There is fome variety to be feene in this flower ; for in fome the colour is paler, and in others againe of a very high or deepe colour: fometimes alfo they haue eight leaues, and fometimes ten or twelue, as if two flowers were made one, which fome thereupon haue called a Double Fritillaria. Some of them likewife doe flower very early, euen with or before the early flowring Tulipas ; and fome againe flower not vntill a moneth or more after the former.

2. *Fritillaria flore atrorubente.* The bloud red Fritillaria.

The roote of this Fritillaria is fomewhat rounder and clofer then the former, from whence the ftalke rifeth vp, being fhorter and lower then in any other of thefe kindes, hauing one or two leaues thereon, and at the top thereof two or three more fet clofer together, which are broader, fhorter, and whiter then any of them before, almoft like vnto the leaues of the yellow Fritillaria, from among which toppe leaues commeth forth the flower, fomewhat bending downe, or rather ftanding forth, being larger then any of the former, and almoft equall in bigneffe vnto the yellow Fritillaria, of a duskie gray colour all ouer on the outfide, and of a very darke red colour on the infide, diuerfly fpotted or ftraked : this very hardly encreafeth by the roote, and as feldome giueth ripe feede, but flowreth with the other firft forts, and before the blacke, and a-bideth leffe time in flower then any.

3. *Fritillaria maxima purpurea fiue rubra.* The great purple or red Fritillaria.

This great Fritillaria hath his roote equall to the bigneffe of the reft of his parts, from whence rifeth vp one, & oftentimes two ftalks, hauing one, two or three flowers a peece on them, as nature and the feafons are fitting : euery one of thefe flowers are larger and greater then any of the former defcribed, and pendulous as they are, of a fad red or purplifh colour, with many thwart lines on them, and fmall long markes, which hardly feeme checkerwife, nor are fo eminent or confpicuous as in the former : the ftalke is ftrong and high, whereon are fet diuers long whitifh greene leaues, larger and broader then thofe of the former.

4. *Fritillaria alba.* The white Fritillaria.

The white Fritillaria is fo like vnto the firft, that I fhall not neede to make another defcription of this : it fhall (I hope) be fufficient to fhew the chiefe differences, and fo proceed to the reft. The ftalke and leaues of this are wholly greene, whereby it may eafily be knowne from the former, which, as is faid, is brownifh at the bottome. The flower is white, without almoft any fhew of fpot or marke in it, yet in fome the markes are fomewhat more plainly to be feene, and in fome againe there is a fhew of a faint kinde of blufh colour to be feene in the flower, efpecially in the infide, the bottomes of the leaues of euery flower fometimes are greenifh, hauing alfo a fmall lift of greene, comming downe towards the middle of each leafe : the head or feede veffell, as alfo the feede and the roote, are fo like vnto the former, that the moft cunning cannot di-ftinguifh them.

5. *Fritillaria flore duplici albicante.* The double blufh Fritillaria.

This Fritillaria hath a round flattifh white roote, very like vnto the laft Fritillaria, bearing a ftalke with long greene leaues thereon, little differing from it, or the firft or-dinary Fritillaria : the flower is faid to be conftant, compofed of many leaues, being ten at the leaft, and moft vfually twelue, of a pale whitifh purple colour, fpotted like vnto the paler ordinary Fritillaria that is early, fo that one would verily thinke it were

but

but an accidentall kinde thereof, whereas it is (as is said before) held to bee conſtant, continuing in this manner.

6. *Fritillaria flore luteo puro.* The pure yellow Fritillaria.

The pure yellow Fritillaria hath a more round, and not ſo flat a whitiſh roote as the former kindes, and of a meane bigneſſe; from the middle riſeth vp a ſtalke a foote and a halfe high, and ſometimes higher, whereon are ſet without order diuers long and ſomewhat broad leaues of a whitiſh greene colour, like vnto the leaues of the blacke Fritillaria, but not aboue halfe ſo broad: the flower is ſomewhat ſmall and long, nor much vnlike to the blacke for ſhape and faſhion, but that the leaues are ſmaller and rounder pointed, of a faint yellowiſh colour, without any ſhew of ſpots or checkers at all, eyther within or without the flower, hauing ſome chiues and yellow pendents in the middle, as is to be ſeene in all of them: the ſeede is like the firſt kinde.

7. *Fritillaria flore luteo vario ſiue punctato.* The checkerd yellow Fritillaria.

This Fritillaria groweth not much lower then the former, and browniſh at the riſing vp, hauing his leaues whiter, broader, and ſhorter then it, and almoſt round pointed. The flower is greater, and larger ſpread then any other before, of a faire pale yellow colour, ſpotted in very good order, with fine ſmall checkers, which adde a wonderfull pleaſing beauty thereunto: it hath alſo ſome liſts of greene running downe the backe of euery leafe. It ſeldome giueth ſeede; the roote alſo is like the other, but not ſo flat.

8. *Fritillaria lutea maxima Italica.* The great yellow Italian Fritillaria.

This kinde of Fritillaria riſeth vp with a round and browne greene ſtalke, whereon are ſet diuers leaues ſomewhat broad and ſhort, which compaſſe the ſtalke at the bottome of them, of a darke greene colour; at the toppe of the ſtalke, which bendeth a little downewards, doe moſt vſually ſtand three or foure leaues, betweene which commeth forth moſt vſually but one flower, which is longer then the laſt, hanging downe the head as all the others doe, conſiſting of ſixe leaues, of a darke yellowiſh purple colour, ſpotted with ſome ſmall red checkers. This kinde flowreth late, and not vntill all the reſt are paſt.

9. *Fritillaria Italorum polyanthos flore paruo.* The ſmall Italian Fritillaria.

This ſmall Italian Fritillaria carrieth more ſtore of flowers on the ſtalke, but they are much ſmaller, and of a yellowiſh greene colour, ſpotted with long and ſmall darke red checkers or markes: the ſtalke hath diuers ſmall ſhort greene leaues thereon, vnto the very toppe.

10. *Fritillaria lutea Iuncifolia Luſitanica.* The ſmall yellow Fritillaria of Portugall.

The leaues of this Fritillaria are ſo ſmall, narrow and long, that it hath cauſed them to take the name of ruſhes, as if you ſhould call it, The ruſh leafed Fritillaria, which ſtand on a long weake round ſtalke, ſet without order: the flower is ſmall and yellow, but thicker checkerd with red ſpots then any of the other yellow Fritillaria's; the ſtalk of the flower, at the head thereof, being alſo of a yellowiſh colour.

11. *Fritillaria Pyrenæa ſiue Apenninea.* The blacke Fritillaria.

The roote of this kinde doth often grow ſo great, that it ſeemeth like vnto the roote of a ſmall Crowne Imperiall: the ſtalke is ſtrong, round, and high, ſet without order, with broader and whiter greene leaues then any of the former, bearing one, two, or three flowers; ſometimes at the toppe, being not ſo large as thoſe of the ordinary purple Fritillaria, but ſmaller, longer, and rounder, ſometimes a little turning vp the brims or edges of the leaues againe, and are of a yellowiſh ſhining greene colour on

the

the infide, fometimes fpotted with red fpots almoft through the whole infide of the flower, vnto the very edge, which abideth of a pale yellow colour, and fometimes there are very few fpots to be feene, and thofe from the middle onely on the infide (for on the outfide there neuer appeareth any fpots at all in this kinde) and fometimes with no fhew of fpots at all, fometimes alfo of a more pale greene, and fometime of a more yellow colour: the outfide of the flowers doe likewife vary, for in fome the out-fide of the leaues are of a darke fullen yellow, &c. elfe more pale yellow, and in other of a darke purplifh yellow colour, which in fome is fo deepe, and fo much, that it ra-ther feemeth blacke then purple or yellow, and this efpecially about the bottome of the flower, next vnto the ftalke, but the edges are ftill of a yellowifh greene: the head of feede, and the feede likewife is like vnto the former, but bigger in all refpects.

12. *Fritillaria Hiſpanica vmbelliſera.* The Spanifh blacke Fritillaria.

This Fritillaria is no doubt of kindred to the laft recited, it is fo like, but greater in all parts thereof, as if growing in a more fruitfull foile, it were the ftronger and luftier to beare more ftore of flowers: the flowers grow foure or fiue from the head together, hanging downe round about the ftalke, like vnto a Crowne Imperiall, and are of a yellowifh greene colour on the infide, fpotted with a few red fpots, the outfide being blackifh as the former.

The Place.

The firft of thefe plants was firft brought to our knowledge from France, where it groweth plentifully about Orleance; the other forts grow in di-uers other Countries, as fome in Portugall, Spaine, Italy, &c. as their names doe import, and as in time they haue been obferued by thofe that were cu-rious fearchers of thefe rarities, haue been fent to vs.

The Time.

The early kindes doe flower in the beginning of Aprill or thereabouts, according to the mildeneffe or fharpeneffe of the precedent Winter. The other doe flower after the firft are paft, for a moneths fpace one after ano-ther, and the great yellow is very late, not flowring vntill about the middle or end of May.

The Names.

This hath receiued diuers names: fome calling it *Flos Meleagridis*, the Ginny Hen Flower, of the variety of the colours in the flower, agreeing with the feathers of that Bird. Some call it *Narciſſus Caparonius*, of the name of the firft inuentor or finder thereof, called Noel Caperon, an Apothecary dwelling in Orleance, at the time he firft found it, and was fhortly after the finding thereof taken away in the Maffacre in France. It is now generally called *Fritillaria*, of the word *Fritillus*, which diuers doe take for the Cheffe borde or table whereon they play, whereunto, by reafon of the refemblance of the great fquares or fpots fo like it, they did prefently referre it. It is called by Lobel *Lilionarciſſus purpureus variegatus*, *&* *teſſulatus*, making it a kinde of Tulipa; but as I faid in the beginniug of the Chapter, it doth moft neerely refemble a fmall pendulous Lilly, and might therefore rightly hold the name of *Lilium variegatum*, or in Englifh, the checkerd Lilly. But be-caufe the errour which firft referred it to a Daffodill, is growne ftrong by cuftome of continuance, I leaue to euery one their owne will, to call it in Englifh eyther Fritillaria, as it is called of moft, or the checkerd Daffodill, or the Ginnie Hen flower, or, as I doe, the checkerd Lilly. I fhall not neede in this place further to explaine the feuerall names of euery of them, hauing giuen you them in their titles.

The

The Vertues.

I haue not found or heard by any others of any property peculiar in this plant, to be applied either inwardly or outwardly for any difease : the chiefe or onely vfe thereof is, to be an ornament for the Gardens of the curious louers of thefe delights, and to be worne of them abroad, which for the gallant beauty of many of them, deferueth their courteous entertainment, among many other the like pleafures.

Chap. VIII.

Tulipa. The Turkes Cap.

NExt vnto the Lillies, and before the Narcisfi or Daffodils, the difcourfe of Tulipas deferueth his place, for that it partaketh of both their natures; agreeing with the Lillies in leaues, flowers, and feede, and fomewhat with the Daffodils in rootes. There are not onely diuers kindes of Tulipas, but fundry diuerfities of colours in them, found out in thefe later dayes by many the fearchers of natures varieties, which haue not formerly been obferued : our age being more delighted in the fearch, curiofity, and rarities of thefe pleafant delights, then any age I thinke before. But indeede, this flower, aboue many other, deferueth his true commendations and acceptance with all louers of thefe beauties, both for the ftately afpect, and for the admirable varietie of colours, that daily doe arife in them, farre beyond all other plants that grow, in fo much, that I doubt, although I fhall in this Chapter fet downe the varieties of a great many, I fhall leaue more vnfpoken of, then I fhall defcribe; for I may well fay, there is in this one plant no end of diuerfity to be expected, euery yeare yeelding a mixture and variety that hath not before been obferued, and all this arifing from the fowing of the feede. The chiefe diuifion of Tulipas, is into two forts : *Præcoces*, early flowring Tulipas, and *Serotinæ*, late flowring Tulipas. For that fort which is called *Media* or *Dubia*, that is, which flower in the middle time betweene them both, and may be thought to be a kinde or fort by it felfe, as well as any of the other two : yet becaufe they doe neerer participate with the *Serotinæ* then with the *Præcoces*, not onely in the colour of the leafe, being of the fame greenneffe with the *Serotinæ*, and moft vfually alfo, for that it beareth his ftalke and flower, high and large like as the *Serotinæ* doe; but efpecially, for that the feede of a *Media Tulipa* did neuer bring forth a *Præcox* flower (although I know Clufius, an induftrious, learned, and painfull fearcher and publifher of thefe rarities, faith otherwife) fo farre as euer I could, by mine owne care or knowledge, in fowing their feede apart, or the affurance of any others, the louers and fowers of Tulipa feede, obferue, learne, or know : and becaufe alfo that the feede of the *Serotinæ* bringeth forth *Medias*, and the feede of *Medias Serotinæ*, they may well bee comprehended vnder the generall title of *Serotinæ* : But becaufe they haue generally receiued the name of *Media*, or middle flowring Tulipas, to diftinguifh betweene them, and thofe that vfually doe flower after them; I am content to fet them downe, and fpeake of them feuerally, as of three forts. Vnto the place and ranke likewife of the *Præcoces*, or early flowring Tulipas, there are fome other feuerall kinds of Tulipas to be added, which are notably differing, not onely from the former *Præcox Tulipa*, but euery one of them, one from another, in fome fpeciall note or other : as the *Tulipa Bolonienfis flore rubro*, the red Bolonia Tulipa. *Tulipa Bolonienfis flore luteo*, the yellow Bolonia Tulipa. *Tulipa Perfica*, the Perfian Tulipa. *Tulipa Cretica*, the Candie Tulipa, and others : all which fhall bee defcribed and entreated of, euery one apart by it felfe, in the end of the ranke of the *Præcoces*, becaufe all of them flower much about their time. To begin then with the *Præcox*, or early flowring Tulipas, and after them with the *Medias* and *Serotines*, I fhall for the better method, diuide their flowers into foure primary or principall colours, that is to fay, White, Purple, Red, and Yellow, and vnder euery one of thefe colours, fet downe the feuerall varieties

ties of mixtures we haue seene and obserued in them, that so they may be both the better described by me, and the better conceiued by others, and euery one placed in their proper ranke. Yet I shall in this, as I intend to doe in diuers other plants that are variable, giue but one description in generall of the plant, and then set downe the varietie of forme or colour afterwards briefly by themselues.

Tulipa præcox. The early flowring Tulipa.

The early Tulipa (and so all other Tulipas) springeth out of the ground with his leaues folded one within another, the first or lowest leafe riseth vp first, sharpe pointed, and folded round together, vntill it be an inch or two aboue the ground, which then openeth it selfe, shewing another leafe folded also in the bosome or belly of the first, which in time likewise opening it selfe, sheweth forth a third, and sometimes a fourth and a fifth : the lower leaues are larger then the vpper, and are faire, thicke, broad, long, and hollow like a gutter, and sometimes crumpled on the edges, which will hold water that falleth thereon a long time, of a pale or whitish greene colour, (and the *Mediæ* and *Serotinæ* more greene) couered ouer as it were with a mealinesse or hoarinesse, with an eye or shew of rednesse towards the bottome of the leaues, and the edges in this kinde being more notable white, which are two principall notes to know a *Præcox Tulipa* from a *Media* or *Serotina :* the stalke with the flower riseth vp in the middle, as it were through these leaues, which in time stand one aboue another, compassing it at certaine vnequall distances, and is often obserued to bend it selfe crookedly downe to the ground, as if it would thrust his head thereinto, but turning vp his head (which will be the flower) againe, afterwards standeth vpright, sometimes but three or foure fingers or inches high, but more often halfe a foote, and a foot high, but the *Mediæ,* and *Serotinas* much higher, carrying (for the most part) but one flower on the toppe thereof, like vnto a Lilly for the forme, consisting of sixe leaues, greene at the first, and afterwards changing into diuers and sundry seuerall colours and varieties, the bottomes likewise of the leaues of these sometimes, but most especially of the *Mediæ,* being as variable as the flower, which are in some yellow, or green, or blacke, in others white, blew, purple, or tawnie ; and sometimes one colour circling another : some of them haue little or no sent at all, and some haue a better then others. After it hath been blowne open three or foure dayes or more, it will in the heate of the Sunne spread it selfe open, and lay it selfe almost flat to the stalke : in the middle of the flower standeth a greene long head (which will be the seed vessell) compassed about with sixe chiues, which doe much vary, in being sometimes of one, and sometimes of another colour, tipt with pendents diuersly varied likewise : the head in the middle of the flower groweth after the flower is fallen, to be long, round, and edged, as it were three square, the edges meeting at the toppe, where it is smallest, and making as it were a crowne (which is not seen in the head of any Lilly) and when it is ripe, diuideth it selfe on the inside into sixe rowes, of flat, thinne, brownish, gristly seede, very like vnto the seede of the Lillies, but brighter, stiffer, and more transparent : the roote being well growne is round, and somewhat great, small and pointed at the toppe, and broader, yet roundish at the bottome, with a certaine eminence or seate on the one side, as the roote of the Colchicum hath ; but not so long, or great, it hath also an hollownesse on the one side (if it haue borne a flower) where the stalke grew, (for although in the time of the first springing vp, vntill it shew the budde for flower, the stalke with the leaues thereon rise vp out of the middle of the roote ; yet when the stalke is risen vp, and sheweth the budde for flower, it commeth to one side, making an impression therein) couered ouer with a brownish thin coate or skin, like an Onion, hauing a little woollinesse at the bottome ; but white within, and firme, yet composed of many coates, one folding within another, as the roote of the Daffodils be, of a reasonable good taste, neyther very sweete, nor yet vnpleasant. This description may well serue for the other Tulipas, being *Mediæ* or *Serotinas,* concerning their springing and bearing, which haue not any other great variety therein worth the note, which is not expressed here ; the chiefe difference resting in the variety of the colours of the flower, and their seuerall mixtures and markes, as I said before : sauing onely, that the flowers of some are great and large, and of others smaller, and the leaues of some long

and

1   *Tulipa præcox alba siue rubra, &c. vnius coloris.* The early white or red Tulipa, &c. being of one colour.
2   *Tulipa præcox purpurea oris albis.* The early purple Tulipa with white edges, or the Prince.   3 *Tulipa præcox variegata.* The early stript Tulipa.   4 *Tulipa præcox rubra oris luteis.* The early red Tulipa with yellow edges, or the Duke.

and pointed, and of others broad and round, or bluntly pointed, as shall bee shewed in the end of the Chapter: I shall therefore onely expresse the colours, with the mixture or composure of them, and giue you withall the names of some of them, (for it is impossible I thinke to any man, to giue seuerall names to all varieties) as they are called by those that chiefly delight in them with vs.

Tulipa præcox Alba.	The early White Tulipa.
1 *Niuea tota interdum purpureis staminibus, vel saltem luteis, fundo puro flaua luteo.*	1 The flower whereof is either pure snow white, with purple sometimes, or at least with yellow chiues, without any yellow bottome.
2 *Alba siue niuea fundo luteo.*	2 Or pure white with a yellow bottome.
3 *Albida.*	3 Or milk white that is not so pure white.
4 *Alba, venis cæruleis in dorso.*	4 White with blew veines on the outside.
5 *Alba purpureis oris.* ⎫ *Harum flores vel*	5 White with purple edges. ⎫ Some of these abiding constant,
6 *Alba carneis oris.* ⎬ *constantes, vel*	6 White with blush edges. ⎬ & others spreading or running.
7 *Alba sanguineis oris.* ⎭ *dispergentes.*	7 White with red edges. ⎭
8 *Alba oris magnis carneis, & venis intro respicientibus.*	8 White with great blush edges, and some strakes running from the edge inward.
9 *Alba extra, carnei vero coloris intus, oras habens carneas saturatiores.*	9 White without, and somewhat blush within, with edges of a deeper blush.
10 *Albida, oris rubris, vel oris purpureis.*	10 Whitish, or pale white with red or purple edges.
11 *Albida purpurascentibus maculis extra, intus vero carnei vinacissimi.*	11 Whitish without, with some purplish veins & spots, & of a liuely blush within.
12 *Alba, purpureis maculis aspersa extra, intus vero alba purpurantibus oris.*	12 White without, spotted with small purple spots, and white within with purple edges.
13 *Dux Alba, i. e. coccineis & albis variata flammis, à medio ad oras intercursantibus.*	13 A white Duke, that is, parted with white & crimson flames, from the middle of each leafe to the edge.
14 *Princessa, i.e. argentei coloris maculis purpurascentibus.*	14 The Princesse, that is, a siluer colour spotted with fine deepe blush spots.
15 *Regina pulcherrima, albis & sanguineis aspersa radijs & punctis.*	15 The Queen, that is, a fine white sprinkled with bloud red spots, and greater strakes.

Tulipa præcox purpurea.	The early purple Tulipa.
1 *Purpurea satura rubescens, vel violacea.*	1 A deep reddish purple, or more violet.
2 *Purpurea pallida, Columbina dicta.*	2 A pale purple, called a Doue colour.
3 *Persici coloris saturi.*	3 A deep Peach colour.
4 *Persici coloris pallidioris.*	4 A paler Peach colour.
5 *Paoniæ floris coloris.*	5 A Peony flower colour.
6 *Rosea.*	6 A Rose colour.
7 *Chermesina peramæna.*	7 A Crimson very bright.
8 *Chermesina parum striata.*	8 A Crimson stript with a little white.
	9 Princeps,

9 *Princeps, i.e. purpurea saturatior vel dilutior, oris albis magnis vel paruis, fundo luteo, vel albo orbe, quæ multum variatur, & colore, & oris, ita vt purpurea elegans oris magnis albis, dicta est, Princeps excellens, &*

10 *Princeps Columbina, purpurea dilutior.*

11 *Purpurea Chermesina, rubicundioris coloris, albidis vel albis oris.*

12 *Purpurea, vel obsoleta albidis oris Princeps Brancion.*

13 *Purpurea diluta, oris dilutioris purpurei coloris.*

14 *Purpurea in exterioribus, carnei vero ad medium intus, oris albis, fundo luteo.*

15 *Purpurea albo plumata extra, oris albis, purpurascens intus, fundo luteo, vel orbe albo.*

16 *Aliæ, minus elegans plumata, minoribusq́; oris albidis.*

9 A Prince or Bracklar, that is, a deepe or pale purple, with white edges, greater or smaller, and a yellow bottome, or circled with white, which varieth much, both in the purple & edges, so that a faire deep purple, with great white edges, is called, The best or chiefe Prince, and

10 A paler purple with white edges, called a Doue coloured Prince.

11 A Crimson Prince or Bracklar.

12 A Brancion Prince, or purple Brancion.

13 A purple with more pale purple edges.

14 Purple without, and blush halfe way within, with white edges, and a yellow bottome.

15 Purple feathered with white on the out side, with white edges, and pale purple within, the ground being a little yellow, or circled with white.

16 Another very neere vnto it, but not so fairely feathered, being more obscure, and the edges not so great or whitish.

Tulipa præcox rubra.

The early red Tulipa.

1 *Rubra vulgaris fundo luteo, & aliquando nigro.*

2 *Rubra satura oris luteis paruis, dicta Roan.*

3 *Baro, i.e. rubra magis intensa, oris luteis paruis.*

4 *Dux maior & minor, i.e. rubra magis aut minus elegans satura, oris luteis maximis vel minoribus, & fundo luteo magno. Alia alijs est magis amœna, in alijs etiam fundo nigro vel obscuro viridi.*

5 *Ducissa, i.e. Duci similis, at plus lutei quàm rubri, oris magnis luteis, & rubore magis aut minus intus in gyrum acto, fundo item luteo magno.*

6 *Testamentum Brancion, i.e. rubra sanguinea satura, aut minus rubra, oris pallidis, magnis vel paruis: alia alijs magis aut minus elegans diuersimodo.*

1 An ordinary red, with a yellow, & sometimes a blacke bottome.

2 A deep red, with a small edge of yellow, called a Roane.

3 A Baron, that is, a faire red with a small yellow edge.

4 A Duke, a greater and a lesser, that is, a more or less faire deep red, with greater or lesser yellow edges, and a great yellow bottome. Some of this sort are much more or lesse faire then others, some also haue a blacke or darke greene bottome.

5 A Dutchesse, that is like vnto the Duke, but more yellow then red, with greater yellow edges, and the red more or lesse circling the middle of the flower on the inside, with a large yellow bottome.

6 A Testament Brancion, or a Brancion Duke,

E

7 *Flambans, ex rubore & flauedine radiata, vel striata fundo luteo.*

8 *Mali Aurantij coloris, ex rubore, & flauedine integrè, non separatim mixta, oris luteis paruis, vel absq̃ oris.*

9 *Minij, siue Cinabaris coloris, i.e. ex purpurea, rubedine, & flauedine radiata, vnguibus luteis, & aliquando oris.*

10 *Rex Tuliparum, i.e. ex sanguineo & aureo radiatim mixta, à flammea diuersa, fundo luteo, orbe rubro.*

11 *Tunica Morionis, i.e. ex rubore & aureo separatim diuisa.*

Duke, that is, a faire deepe red, or lesse red, with a pale yellow or butter coloured edge, some larger others smaller: and some more pleasing then others, in a very variable manner.

7 A Flambant, differing from the Dutchesse; for this hath no such great yellow edge, but streaks of yellow through the leafe vnto the very edge.

8 An Orenge colour, that is, a reddish yellow, or a red and yellow equally mixed, with small yellow edges, and sometimes without.

9 A Vermillion, that is, a purplish red, streamed with yellow, the bottome yellow, and sometimes the edges.

10 The Kings flower, that is, a crimson or bloud red, streamed with a gold yellow, differing from the Flambant, the bottome yellow, circled with red.

11 A Fooles coate, parted with red and yellow guardes.

Tulipa præcox lutea.

1 *Lutea siue flaua.*
2 *Pallida lutea siue straminea.*
3 *Aurea, oris rubicundis.*
4 *Straminea, oris rubris.*
5 *Aurea, rubore perfusa extra.*
6 *Aurea, vel magis pallida, rubore in gyrum acta simillima Ducissa, nisi minus rubedinis habet.*
7 *Aurea, extremitatibus rubris, dici potest, Morionis Pilæus præcox.*

The early yellow Tulipa.

1 A faire gold yellow without mixture.
2 A strawe colour.
3 A faire yellow with reddish edges.
4 A strawe colour, with red edges.
5 A faire yellow, reddish on the out side onely.
6 A gold or paler yellow, circled on the inside a little with red, very like the Dutchesse, but that it hath lesse red therein.
7 A gold yellow with red toppes, and may be called, The early Fooles Cap.

Tulipa de Caffa. The Tulipa of Caffa.

There is another fort or kinde of early Tulipa, differing from the former, whofe pale greene leaues being as broad and large as they, and fometimes crumpled or wa-ued at the edges, in fome haue the edges onely of the faid leaues for a good breadth, of a whitifh or whitifh yellow colour, and in others, the leaues are lifted or parted with whitifh yellow and greene : the ftalke rifeth not vp fo high as the former, and beareth a flower at the toppe like vnto the former, in fome of a reddifh yellow colour, with a ruffet coloured ground or bottome, and in others, of other feuerall colours : the feede and roote is fo like vnto others of this kinde, that they cannot be diftinguifhed.

There is (as I doe heare) of this kinde, both *Præcoces*, and *Serotina*, early flowring, and late flowring, whereof although wee haue not fo exact knowledge, as of the reft, yet I thought good to fpeake fo much, as I could hitherto vnderftand of them, and giue others leaue (if I doe not) hereafter to amplifie it.

Tulipa Bolonienfis, fiue Bombycina flore rubro major. The greater red Bolonia Tulipa.

There are likewife other kindes of early Tulipas to bee fpoken of, and firft of the red Bolonia Tulipa ; the roote whereof is plainly difcerned, to be differing from all o-thers : for that it is longer, and not hauing fo plaine an eminence at the bottome there-of, as the former and later Tulipas, but more efpecially becaufe the toppe is plenti-fully ftored with a yellowifh filke-like woollineffe : the outfide likewife or skinne is of a brighter or paler red, not fo eafie to be pilled away, and runneth vnder ground both downeright and fidewife (efpecially in the Countrey ground and ayre, where it will encreafe aboundantly, but not either in our London ayre, or fore't grounds) fomewhat like vnto the yellow Bolonia Tulipa next following. It fhooteth out of the ground with broad and long leaues, like the former ; but neither fo broad, nor of fo white or mealy a greene colour as the former, but more darke then the late flowring Tulipa, fo that this may bee eafily difcerned by his leafe from any other Tulipa aboue the ground, by one that is skilfull. It beareth likewife three or foure leaues vpon the ftalke, like the former, and a flower alfo at the toppe of the fame fafhion, but that the leaues hereof are alwayes long, and fomewhat narrow ; hauing a large blacke bot-tome, made like vnto a cheuerne, the point whereof rifeth vp vnto the middle of the leafe, higher then any other Tulipa ; the flower is of a pale red colour, nothing fo liuely as in the early or late red Tulipas, yet fweeter for the moft part then any of them, and neereft vnto the yellow Bolonia Tulipa, which is much about the fame fent.

Tulipa pumilio rubra, fiue Bergomenfis rubra media & minor. The dwarfe red Bergomo Tulipa, a bigger and a leffer.

There are two other forts hereof, and becaufe they were found about Bergomo, do carry that name, the one bigger or leffer then another, yet neither fo great as the for-mer, hauing very little other difference to bee obferued in them, then that they are fmaller in all parts of them.

Tulipa Bolonienfis flore luteo. The yellow Bolonia Tulipa.

The roote of this Tulipa may likewife bee knowne from the former red (or any o-ther Tulipa) in that it feldome commeth to bee fo bigge, and is not fo woolly at the toppe, and the skinne or outfide is fomewhat paler, harder, and fharper pointed : but the bottome is like the former red, and not fo eminent as the early or late Tulipas. This beareth much longer and narrower leaues then any (except the Perfian & dwarfe yellow Tulipas) and of a whitifh greene colour : it beareth fometimes but one flower on a ftalke, and fometimes two or three wholly yellow, but fmaller, & more open then the other kinds, and (as I faid) fmelleth fweete, the head for feede is fmaller then in o-thers, and hath not that crowne at the head thereof, yet the feed is like, but fmaller.

E 3 *Tulipa*

Tulipa Narbonensis, siue Monspeliensis vel pumilio.
The French or dwarfe yellow Tulipa.

This Tulipa is very like vnto the yellow Bolonia Tulipa, both in roote, leafe, and flower, as also in the colour thereof, being yellow : the onely difference is, that it is in all things lesser and lower, and is not so apt to beare, nor so plentifull to encrease by the roote.

Tulipa Italica maior & minor. The Italian Tulipa the greater and the lesser.

Both these kindes of Tulipas doe so neere resemble the last kinde, that I might almost say they were the same, but that some difference which I saw in them, maketh mee set them apart ; and consisteth in these things, the stalkes of neither of both these rise so high, as of the first yellow Bolonia Tulipa: the leaues of both sorts are writhed in and out at the edges, or made like a waue of the sea, lying neerer the ground, and the flower being yellow within, is brownish or reddish on the backe, in the middle of the three outer leaues the edges appearing yellow. Both these kindes doe differ one from the other in nothing, but in that one is bigger, and the other smaller then the other which I saw with Iohn Tradescante, my very good friend often remembred.

Tulipa Lusitanica, siue pumilio versicolor. The dwarfe stript Tulipa.

This dwarfe Tulipa is also of the same kindred with the three last described ; for there is no other difference in this from them, then that the flower hath some red veins running in the leaues thereof.
There are two other sorts of dwarfe Tulipas with white flowers, whereof Lobel hath made mention in the Appendix to his *Aduersaria* ; the one whereof is the same that Clusius setteth forth, vnder the title of *Pumilio altera* : but because I haue not seen either of them both, I speake no further of them.

Tulipa pumilio alba. The white dwarfe Tulipa.

But that white flower that Iohn Tradescante shewed me, and as hee saith, was deliuered him for a white Pumilio, had a stalke longer then they set out theirs to haue, and the flower also larger, but yet had narrower leaues then other sorts of white Tulipas haue.

Tulipa Bicolor. The small party coloured Tulipa.

Vnto these kindes, I may well adde this kinde of Tulipa also, which was sent out of Italy, whose leaues are small, long, and narrow, and of a darke greene colour, somewhat like vnto the leaues of an Hyacinth : the flower is small also, consisting of sixe leaues, as all other Tulipas doe, three whereof are wholly of a red colour, and the other three wholly of a yellow.

Tulipa Persica. The Persian Tulipa.

This rare Tulipa, wherewith we haue beene but lately acquainted, doth most fitly deserue to be described in this place, because it doth so neerely participate with the Bolonia and Italian Tulipas, in roote, leafe, and flower : the roote hereof is small, couered with a thicke hard blackish shell or skinne, with a yellowish woollinesse both at the toppe, and vnder the shell. It riseth out of the ground at the first, with one very long and small round leafe, which when it is three or foure inches high, doth open it selfe, and shew forth another small leafe (as long almost as the former) breaking out of the one side thereat, and after it a third, and sometimes a fourth, and a fift ; but each shorter then other, which afterwards be of the breadth of the dwarfe yellow Tulipa, or somewhat broader, but much longer then any other, and abiding more hollow, and of the colour of the early Tulipas on the inside : the stalke riseth vp a foot and a halfe
high

Tulipa Bombycina flore rubro. The red Bolonia Tulipa.   2 Tulipa Boloniensis flore luteo. The yellow Bolonia Tulipa.   3 Tulipa pumilio rubra sive lutea. The red or yellow dwarfe Tulipa.   4 Folium Tulipæ de Caffa per totum striatum. The leafe of the Tulipa of Caffa striped throughout the whole leafe.   5 Folium Tulipæ de Caffa per oras striatum. The leafe of the Tulipa of Caffa striped at the edges onely.   6 Tulipa Persica. The Persian Tulipa.   7 Tulipa Cretica. The Tulipa of Candie.   8 Tulipa Armeniaca. The Tulipa of Armenia.

E 3

high sometimes, bearing one flower thereon, composed of sixe long and pointed leaues of the forme of other small Tulipas, and not shewing much bigger then the yellow Italian Tulipa, and is wholly white, both inside and outside of all the leaues, except the three outtermost, which haue on the backe of them, from the middle toward the edges, a shew of a brownish blush, or pale red colour, yet deeper in the midst, and the edges remaining wholly white : the bottomes of all these leaues are of a darke or dun tawnie colour, and the chiues and tippes of a darkish purple or tawnie also. This doth beare seed but seldome in our Country, that euer I could vnderstand, but when it doth, it is small like vnto the Bolonia or dwarfe yellow Tulipas, being not so plentifull also in parting, or setting of by the roote as they, and neuer groweth nor abideth so great as it is brought vnto vs, and seldome likewise flowreth after the first yeare : for the rootes for the most part with euery one grow lesse and lesse, decaying euery yeare, and so perish for the most part by reason of the frosts and cold, and yet they haue been set deepe to defend them, although of their owne nature they will runne downe deep into the ground.

Tulipa Byzantina duobus floribus Clusij.   The small Tulipa of Constantinople.

The small Tulipa of Constantinople, beareth for the most part but two leaues on the stalke, which are faire and broad, almost like vnto the Candy Tulipa, next hereunto to be described : the stalke it selfe riseth not aboue a foote high, bearing sometimes but one flower, but most commonly two thereon, one below another, and are no bigger then the flowers of the yellow Bolonia Tulipa, but differing in colour ; for this is on the outside of a purplish colour, mixed with white and greene, and on the inside of a faire blush colour, the bottome and chiues being yellow, and the tippes or pendents blackish : the roote is very like the yellow Bolonia Tulipa.

Tulipa Cretica.   The Tulipa of Candie.

This Tulipa is of later knowledge with vs then the Persian, but doth more hardly thriue, in regard of our cold climate ; the description whereof, for so much as wee haue knowledge, by the sight of the roote and leafe, and relation from others of the flower, (for I haue not yet heard that it hath very often flowred in our Country) is as followeth. It beareth faire broad leaues, resembling the leaues of a Lilly, of a greenish colour, and not very whitish : the stalke beareth thereon one flower, larger and more open then many other, which is eyther wholly white, or of a deepe red colour, or else is variably mixed, white with a fine reddish purple, the bottomes being yellow, with purplish chiues tipt with blackish pendents : the roote is small, and somewhat like the dwarfe yellow Tulipa, but somewhat bigger.

Tulipa Armeniaca.   The Tulipa of Armenia.

This small Tulipa is much differing from all the former (except the small or dwarfe white Tulipas remembred by Lobel and Clusius, as is before set downe) in that it beareth three or foure small, long, and somewhat narrow greene leaues, altogether at one ioynt or place ; the stalke being not high, and naked or without leaues from them to the toppe, where it beareth one small flower like vnto an ordinary red Tulipa, but somewhat more yellow, tending to an Orenge colour with a blacke bottome : the roote is not much bigger then the ordinary yellow Bolonia Tulipa, before set downe.

And these are the sorts of this first *Classis* of early Tulipas.

Tulipa media.   The meaner or middle flowring Tulipa.

For any other, or further description of this kinde of Tulipa, it shall not neede, hauing giuen it sufficiently in the former early Tulipa, the maine difference consisting first in the time of flowring, which is about a moneth after the early Tulipas, yet some more some lesse : for euen in the *Præcoces*, or early ones, some flower a little earlier, and later then others, and then in the colours of the flowers ; for wee haue obserued many

colours,

colours, and mixtures, or varieties of colours in the *Medias*, which we could neuer see in the *Præcoces*, and so also some in the *Præcoces*, which are not in the *Medias* : yet there is farre greater varieties of mixture of colours in these *Medias*, then hath been obserued in all the *Præcoces*, (although Clusius saith otherwise) eyther by my selfe, or by any other that I haue conuersed with about this matter, and all this hath happened by the sowing of the seede, as I said before. I will therefore in this place not trouble you with any further circumstance, then to distinguish them, as I haue done in the former early Tulipas, into their foure primary colours, and vnder them, giue you their seuerall varieties and names, for so much as hath come to my knowledge, not doubting, but that many that haue trauelled in the sowing of the seed of Tulipas many yeares, may obserue each of them to haue some variety that others haue not: and therefore I thinke no one man can come to the knowledge of all particular distinctions.

Tulipa media alba.	The white meane flowring Tulipa.

Tulipa media alba.

1 *Niuea, fundo albo vel luteo.*

2 *Argentea, quasi alba cineracea fundo lutescente, purpureis staminibus.*

3 *Margaritina alba, carneo dilutissima.*

4 *Alba, fundo cæruleo vel nigro.*

5 *Albida.*

6 *Alba, oris rubris.*

7 *Alba, purpureis oris.*

8 *Alba, oris coccineis.*

> *Hæc tria genera in aliquibus constanter tenent oras, in aliis dispergunt.*

9 *Albida primum, deinde albidior, oris purpureis, & venis intrò respicientibus, dicta nobis Hackquenay.*

10 *Alba, sanguineo colore variata, fundo vel albissimo, vel alio.*

11 *Alba, radiatim disposita flammis, & maculis coccineis.*

12 *Alba, purpurea rubedine plumata, diuersarum specierum, quæ cum superiore, vel albo, vel luteo, vel paruo cæruleo constant fundo, quæ constanter tenent punctatos colores, & non dispergunt, sed post trium aut quatuor dierum spatium pulchriores apparent.*

13 *Panni argentei coloris, i.e. alba, plumata, punctata, striata, vel diuersimodè variata, rubedine dilutiore, vel saturatiore purpurea, interius vel exterius, vel vtrinq́, diuersarum specierum.*

14 *Tunica morionis alba varia, i.e. ex albo & purpureo striata diuersimodè, fundo albo vel alio.*

15 *Holias alba vel albida, absq́ fundo, vel fundo purpureo cæruleo, vel cæruleo albo circundato, diuersè signata, vel variata intus ad medietatem foliorum, sursum in orbem vt plurimum, vel ad oras pertingens amplas & albas. Hæ species tantoperè multiplicantur, vt vix sint explicabiles.*

The white meane flowring Tulipa.

1 A snow white, with a white or yellow bottome.

2 A siluer colour, that is, a very pale or whitish ashe colour, with a yellowish bottome and purple chiues.

3 A Pearle colour, that is, white, with a wash or shew of blush.

4 A white, with a blew or black bottome.

5 A Creame colour.

6 A white, with red edges.

7 A white, with purple edges.

8 A white, with crimson edges.

> These three sorts doe hold their edges constant in some, but well spread in others.

9 A pale or whitish yellow, which after a few dayes groweth more white, with purplish red edges, and some streakes running inward from the edge, which we call an Hackney.

10 A white mixed with a bloud red very variably, and with a pure white, or other coloured bottome.

11 A white, streamed with crimson flames, and spots through the whole flower.

12 A white, speckled with a reddish purple, more or lesse, of diuers sorts, with white, yellow, or blew bottomes, all which doe hold their markes constant, and doe not spread their colours, but shew fairer after they haue stood blown three or foure dayes.

13 A cloth of siluer of diuers sorts, that is, a white spotted, striped, or otherwise marked with red or purple, in some paler, in some deeper, either on the inside, or on the outside, or on both.

14 A white Fooles coate of diuers sorts, that is, purple or pale crimson, and white, as it were empaled together, eyther with a white ground or other, whereof there is great variety.

15 A white Holias, that is, a faire white, or paler white, eyther without a bottome, or with a blewish purple bottome, or blew and white circling the bottome,

and

and from the middle vpwards, speckled and straked on the inside for the most part, with bloud red or purplish spots and lines vnto the very edges, which abide large and white. Of this kinde there are found very great varieties, not to be expressed.

Of this sort there is so much variety, some being larger or fairer marked then others, their bottomes also varying, that it is almost impossible to expresse them.

Tanta est huius varietas, vel multitudine, vel striarum paucitate & distinctione, vel fundis variantibus, vt ad tædium esset perscribere.

Tulipa media purpurea.

The meane flowring purple Tulipa.

1 *Purpurea satura.*
2 *Purpurea dilutior, diuersarum specierum, quarum Rosea vna, Carnea sit altera.*
3 *Persici coloris, duarum aut trium specierum.*
4 *Chermesina, obscura, aut pallida.*
5 *Stamela, intensior aut remissior.*
6 *Xerampelina.*
7 *Purpurea, striata.*
8 *Persici saturi, vel diluti coloris, vndulata, vel radiata.*
9 *Columbina, oris & radijs albis.*
10 *Purpurea rubra, oris albis, similis Præcoci, dicta Princeps.*
11 *Chermesina, vel Heluola, lineis albis in medio, & versus oras, fundo cæruleo, vel albo, itemq́; albo orbe.*
12 *Purpurea remissior, aut intensior, oris albis, paruis aut magnis, vt in Principe præcoci, fundo vel cæruleo orbe albo, vel albo orbe cæruleo amplo.*
13 *Holias Heluola, sanguineis guttis intus à medio sursum in orbem, fundo cæruleo.*
14 *Tunica Morionis purpurea rubra satura, albido striata, quam in alba saturatior, fundo ex cæruleo & albo.*
15 *Purpurea rubra satura vel diluta, albo vel albedine, punctata vel striata diuersimodè, dicta Cariophyllata.*

1 A faire deep purple.
2 A paler purple, of many sorts, whereof a Rose colour is one, a Blush another.
3 A Peach colour of two or three sorts.
4 A Crimson, deepe, or pale.
5 A Stamell, darke or light.
6 A Murrey.
7 A purple, stript and spotted.
8 A Peach colour, higher or paler, waued or stript.
9 A Doue colour, edged and straked with white.
10 A faire red purple, with white edges, like vnto the early Tulipa, called a Prince
11 A faire Crimson, or Claret wine colour, with white lines both in the middle, and towards the edges, most haue a blew bottome, yet some are white, or circled with white.
12 A light or deepe purple, with white edges, greater or smaller, like the early Prince, the bottomes eyther blew circled with white, or white circled with a large blew.
13 A purple Holias, the colour of a pale Claret wine, marked and spotted with bloud red spots, round about the middle of each leafe vpward on the inside onely, the bottome being blew.
14 A Crimson Fooles Coate, a darke crimson, and pale white empaled together, differing from the white Fooles Coate, the bottome blew and white.
15 A deeper or paler reddish purple, spotted or striped with a paler or purer white, of diuers sorts, called the Gilloflower Tulipa.

Tulipa

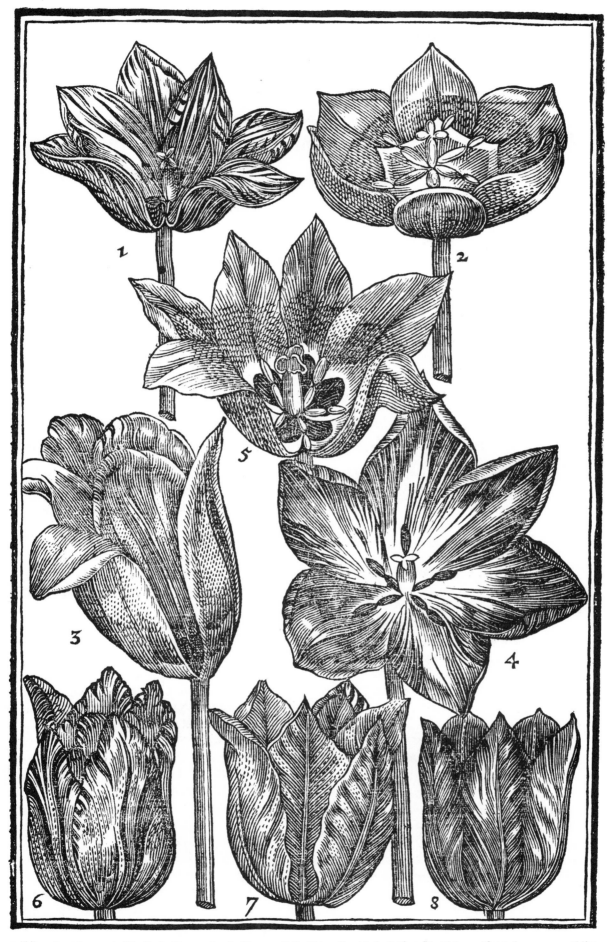

1 *Tulipa rubra & lutea varia* The Fooles Coate red and yellow. 2 *Tulipa Holeas alba absq; fundo.* The white Holeas without a bottome. 3 *Tulipa argentea, vel punctata, &c.* The cloth of filuer, or other fpotted Tulipa. 4 *Tulipa alba flammis coccineis.* The white Fooles Coate. 5 *Tulipa Holeas alba, &c. fundo purpureo, &c.* A white Holeas, &c. with a purple bottome, &c. 6 *Tulipa rubra & lutea flammea, &c.* A red and yellow flamed Tulipa, &c. 7 *Tulipa alba striata & punctata.* A white striped and spotted Tulipa. 8 *Tulipa altera variata, &c.* Another variable Tulipa.

Tulipa media rubra.	The meane flowring red Tulipa.
1 *Rubra communis, fundo luteo, vel nigro.*	1 A faire red which is ordinary, with a yellow or blacke bottome.
2 *Mali Aurantij coloris.*	2 A deepe Orenge colour.
3 *Cinabaris coloris.*	3 A Vermillion.
4 *Lateritij coloris.*	4 A pale red, or Bricke colour.
5 *Rubra, luteo aspersa.*	5 A Gingeline colour.
6 *Rubra, oris luteis.*	6 A red with small yellow edges.
7 *Testamentum Brancion rubra satura, oris pallidis, diversarum specierum, rubore variantium, & orarum amplitudine.*	7 A Testament Brancion of diuers sorts, differing both in the deepnesse of the red, and largenesse of the pale coloured edges.
8 *Cinabaris radiata, magis aut minus serotina.*	8 A Vermillion flamed, flowring later or earlier.
9 *Rubra purpurascens obsoleta, exterioribus folijs, perfusa luteo intus, oris pallidis luteis.*	9 A dead purplish red without, and of a yellowish red within, with pale yellow edges.
10 *Rubra purpurascens elegans extra, & intus lutescens, oris pallidis luteis, fundo luteo vel viridi.*	10 A bright Crimson red on the outside, more yellowish on the inside, with pale yellow edges, and a bottome yellow or greene.
11 *Rubra flambans coccinea, crebris maculis luteis absq́, fundo.*	11 A red Flambant, spotted thicke with yellow spots without any bottome.
12 *Flambans elegantior rubra, i.e. radijs luteis intercursantibus ruborem*	12 A more excellent red Flambant, with flames of yellow running through the red.
13 *Flambans remissior vtroq́, colore.*	13 A pale coloured Flambant.
14 *Panni aurei coloris.*	14 A cloth of gold colour.
15 *Tunica Morionis verior, seu Palto du Sot. optima, tenijs amplis amœnis & crebris, ex rubro & flauo separatim diuisis & excurrentibus, flos constans.*	15 A true Fooles Coate, the best is a faire red & a faire yellow, parted into guards euery one apart, varied through euery leafe to the very edge, yet in most abiding constant.
16 *Tunica Morionis altera, tenijs minoribus & minus frequentibus, magis aut minus alia alijs inconstans.*	16 Another Fooles Coate, not so fairely marked, nor so much, some of these are more or lesse constant in their marks, & some more variable then others.
17 *Tunica Morionis pallida, i.e. tenijs vel strijs frequentioribus in vtroq́, colore pallidis, flos est constans & elegans.*	17 A pale Fooles Coate, that is, with pale red, and pale yellow guardes or stripes very faire and constant.
18 *Pileus Morionis, radijs luteis, in medio foliorum latis, per ruborem excurrentibus, fundo luteo, apicibus luteis, & tribus exterioribus folijs luteis oris rubris, vel absq́, oris.*	18 A Fooles Cappe, that is, with lists or stripes of yellow running through the middle of euery leafe of the red, broader at the bottome then aboue, the bottome being yellow, the three outer leaues being yellow with red edges, or without.

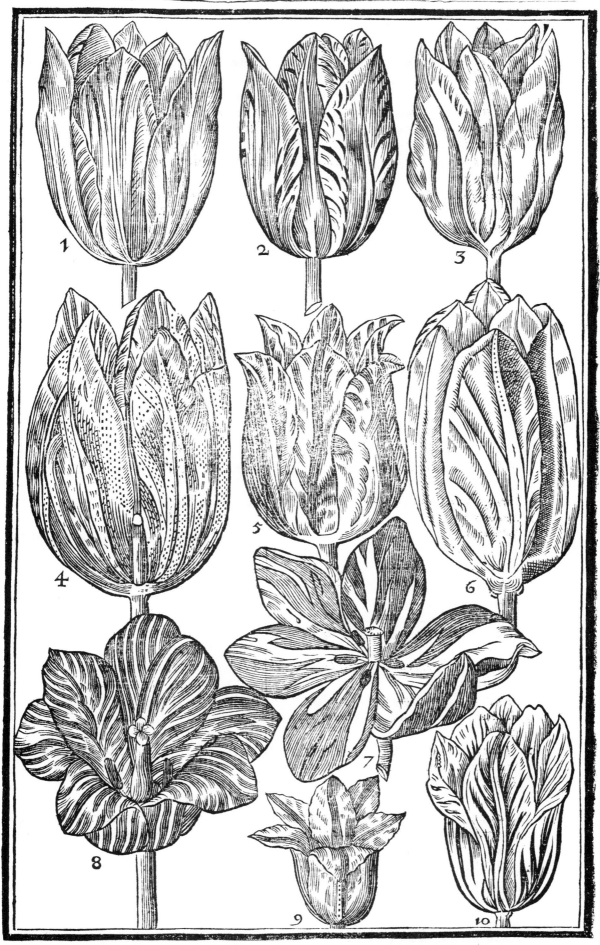

1 *Tulipa tricolor.* A Tulipa of three colours. 2 *Tulipa Macedonica, siue de Caffa varia.* The Tulipa of Caffa purple, with pale white stripes. 3 *Tulipa Heluola charmesina versicolor.* A pure Claret wine colour variable. 4 *Tulipa Caryophyllata Wilmeri.* Mr. Wilmers Gilloflower Tulipa. 5 *Tulipa Chermesina flammis albis.* A Crimson with white flames. 6 *Tulipa Goliah.* A kind of Zwitter called Goliah. 7 *Tulipa le Zwisse.* A Tulipa called the Zwitter. 8 *Tulipa alba flammis coccineis.* Another white Flambant or Fooles Coate. 9 *Tulipa Cinnabarina albo flammata.* The Vermillion flamed. 10 *Tulipa plumata rubra & lutea.* The feathered Tulipa red and yellow.

19 *Le Suiſſe, tenijs radiata magnis ex rubore & pallore.*

19 A Swiſſe, paned with a faire red and pale white or ſtrawe colour.

20 *Altera dicta Goliab à floris magnitudine, tenijs radiata ſimillima le Suiſſe, niſi rubor & albedo ſint elegantiores.*

20 A Goliah, ſo called of the bigneſſe of the flower, moſt like to the Swiſſe in the marks and guardes, but that the red and white is more liuely.

21 *Holias rubra, i.e. ſanguinea argenteis radijs, & guttis in orbem diſpoſitis, præſertim interiùs, fundo viridi ſaturo.*

21 A red Holias. A bloud red ſtript with ſiluer white veines and ſpots, with a darke green bottome.

22 *Holias coccinea, rubra coccinea, albo radiata in orbem, circa medium foliorum interiùs, fundo albo.*

22 A Crimſon red Holias, that is, a faire purpliſh red, ſpotted with white circlewiſe about the middle of the inner leaues, and a white bottome.

23 *Alia huic ſimilis, fundo albo & cæruleo.*

23 Another like thereunto, with a blew and white bottome.

Tulipa media lutea.

The meane flowring yellow Tulipa.

1 *Lutea, ſiue Aurea vulgaris.*

1 A faire gold yellow.

2 *Straminea.*

2 A Strawe colour.

3 *Sulphurea.*

3 A Brimſtone colour pale yellowiſh greene.

4 *Mali Aurantij pallidi coloris.*

4 A pale Orenge colour.

5 *Lutea dilutè purpurea ſtriata, aurei panni pallidi inſtar,*

5 A pale cloth of gold colour.

6 *Pallidè lutea fuſcedine adumbrata.*

6 A Cuſtard colour a pale yellow ſhadowed ouer with a browne.

7 *Flaua, oris rubris magnis, aut paruis.*

7 A gold yellow with red edges, greater or ſmaller.

8 *Straminea oris rubris magnis intenſis, vel paruis remiſſis.*

8 A Strawe colour with red edges, deeper or paler, greater or ſmaller.

9 *Obſcura & fuliginoſa lutea, inſtar Folij decidui, ideoq́; Folium mortuum appellatur.*

9 A ſullen or ſmoakie yellow, like a dead leafe that is fallen, and therefore called, *Fueille mort.*

10 *Flaua, rubore perfuſa, etiamque ſtriata per totum, dorſo coccineo, oris pallidis.*

10 A yellow ſhadowed with red, and ſtriped alſo through all the leaues, the backſide of them being of a red crimſon, and the edges pale.

11 *Pallidè lutea, perfuſa & magis aut minus rubore ſtriata, fundo vel luteo, vel viridi.*

11 A pale yellow, ſhadowed and ſtriped with red, in ſome more in ſome leſſe, the bottomes being either yellow or green.

12 *Teſtamentum Cluſij, i.e. lutea pallida fuligine obfuſca, exteriùs & interiùs ad oras vſq́; pallidas, per totum vero floris medium, maculis interiùs aſperſa inſtar omnium aliarum Holias, dorſo obſcuriore, fundo viridi.*

12 A *Teſtamentum Cluſij*, that is, a ſhadowed pale yellow, both within & without, ſpotted round about the middle on the inſide, as all other Holias are, the backe of the leaues being more obſcure or ſhadowed with pale yellow edges, and a greene bottome.

13 *Flambans lutea, diuersimode intus magis aut minus striata, vel in alijs extra maculata rubore, fundo vt plurimum nigro, vel in alijs luteo.*

14 *Flambans pallidior & elegantior.*

15 *Holias lutea intensior vel remissior diuersimode, in orbem radiata interius, rubris maculis ad supremas vsq; oras, aliquoties crebrè, aliàs parcè, fundo viridi, vel tanctto obscuro.*

16 *Holias straminea rubore striata & punctata, instar alba Holias.*

17 *Tunica Morionis lutea, alijs dicta Flammea, in qua color flavius magis & conspicuus rubore, diuersimodè radiata.*

Huc reddenda esset viridium Tuliparum classis, quæ diuersarum etiam constat specierum. Vna viridis intensior, cuius flos semper ferè semiclausus manet staminibus fimbriatis. Altera remissior, instar Psittaci pennarum viridium, luteo variata oris albis. Tertia adhuc dilutiori viriditate oris purpureis. Quarta, cujus folia æqualiter purpura diluta, & viriditate diuisa sunt. Quinta, folijs longissimis stellæ modo expansis, ex rubore & viriditate coacta.

13 A yellow Flambant of diuers sorts, that is, the whole flower more or lesse streamed or spotted on the inside, and in some on the outside with red, the bottome in most being blacke, yet in some yellow.

14 A paler yellow Flambant more beautifull.

15 A yellow Holias, paler or deeper yellow very variable, spotted on the inside round about the middle, with red sometimes plentifully, or else sparingly, with a green or dark tawny bottome.

16 A strawe coloured Holias, spotted and streamed with red, as is to bee seene in the white Holias.

17 A yellow Fooles coate, of some called a flame colour, wherein the yellow is more then the red, diuersly streamed.

Vnto these may be added the greene Tulipa, which is also of diuers sorts. One hauing a great flower of a deepe green colour, seldome opening it selfe, but abiding alwaies as it were halfe shut vp and closed, the chiues being as it were feathered. Another of a paler or yellowish green, paned with yellow, and is called, The Parret, &c. with white edges. A third of a more yellowish gieen, with red or purplish edges. A fourth, hath the leaues of the flower equally almost parted, with greene and a light purple colour, which abiding a long time in flower, groweth in time to be fairer marked: for at the first it doth not shew it selfe so plainely diuided. Some call this a greene Swisser. A fifth hath the longest leaues standing like a starre, consisting of greene and purple.

Tulipa Serotina. The late flowring Tulipa.

The late flowring Tulipa hath had his description expressed in the precedent discourse, so that I shall not neede to make a repetition of what hath already beene set downe. The greatest matter of knowledge in this kinde is this, That it hath no such plentifull variety of colours or mixtures in his flowers, as are in the two former sorts, but is confined within these limits here expressed, as farre as hath come to our knowledge.

Tulipa Serotina.	The late flowring Tulipa.
Rosea intensior, aut remissior.	A Rose colour deeper or paler.
Rubra vulgaris, aut saturatior, & quasi nigricans, fundo luteo vel nigro, vel nigro orbe, aureo incluso, dicta Oculus Solis.	An ordinary red, or else a deeper red like blacke bloud, with a blacke or yellow bottome, or blacke circled with yellow, called the Suns eye.
Lutea communis.	An ordinary yellow.
Lutea oris rubris.	A yellow with red edges.
Lutea guttis sanguineis, fundo nigro vel vario.	A yellow with red spots and veines, the bottome blacke or discoloured.

F

There

There yet remaine many obſeruations, concerning theſe beautifull flowers, fit to be knowne, which could not, without too much prolixity, be comprehended within the body of the deſcription of them ; but are reſerued to bee intreated of a part by themſelues.

All ſorts of Tulipas beare vſually but one ſtalke, and that without any branches : but ſometimes nature is ſo plentifull in bearing, that it hath two or three ſtalkes, and ſometimes two, or more branches out of one ſtalke (euery ſtalke or branch bearing one flower at the toppe) but this is but ſeldome ſeene ; and when it doth happen once, it is hardly ſeene againe in the ſame roote, but is a great ſigne, that the roote that doth thus, being an old roote, will the ſame yeare part into diuers rootes, whereof euery one, being of a reaſonable greatneſſe, will beare both his ſtalke and flower the next yeare, agreeing with the mother plant in colour, as all the of-ſets of Tulipas doe for the moſt part : for although the young of-ſets of ſome doe vary from the maine roote, euen while it groweth with them, yet being ſeparated, it will bee of the ſame colour with the mother plant.

There groweth oftentimes in the *Mediæ*, and ſometimes alſo in the *Præcoces*, but more ſeldome, a ſmall bulbe or roote, hard aboue the ground, at the bottome of the ſtalke, and betweene it and the lower leafe, which when the ſtalke is dry, and it ripe, being put into the ground, will bring forth in time a flower like vnto the mother plant, from whence it was taken.

The flowers alſo of Tulipas conſiſt moſt commonly of ſixe leaues, but ſometimes they are ſeene to haue eight or tenne, or more leaues ; but vſually, thoſe rootes beare but their ordinary number of ſixe leaues the next yeare : the head for ſeede then, is for the moſt part foure ſquare, which at all other times is but three ſquare, or when the flower wanteth a leafe or two, as ſometimes alſo it doth, it then is flat, hauing but two ſides.

The forme of the flower is alſo very variable ; for the leaues of ſome Tulipas are all ſharpe pointed, or all blunt and round pointed, and many haue the three outer leaues ſharpe pointed, and the three inner round or pointed, and ſome contrariwiſe, the three outermoſt round pointed, and the three inner ſharpe pointed. Againe, ſome haue all the leaues of the flowers long and narrow, and ſome haue them broader and ſhorter. Some *Præcoces* alſo haue their flowers very large and great, equall vnto eyther the *Mediæ*, or *Serotina*, which moſt commonly are the largeſt, and others haue them as ſmall as the Bolonia Tulipa.

The bottomes of the leaues of the flowers are alſo variably diuerſified, and ſo are both the chiues or threeds that ſtand vp about the head, and the tips or pendents that are hanging looſe on the toppes of them ; and by the difference of the bottomes or chiues, many flowers are diſtinguiſhed, which elſe are very like in colour, and alike alſo marked.

For the ſmell alſo there is ſome diuerſity ; for that the flowers of ſome are very ſweete, of others nothing at all, and ſome betweene both, of a ſmall ſent, but not offenſiue : and yet ſome I haue obſerued haue had a ſtrong ill ſent ; but how to ſhew you to diſtinguiſh them, more then by your owne ſenſe, I cannot : for the ſeedes of ſweete ſmelling Tulipas doe not follow their mother plant, no more then they doe in the colour.

And laſtly, take this, which is not the leaſt obſeruation, worth the noting, that I haue obſerued in many : When they haue beene of one entire colour for diuers yeares, yet in ſome yeare they haue altered very much, as if it had not beene the ſame, *viz.* from a purple or ſtamell, it hath beene variably either parted, or mixed, or ſtriped with white, eyther in part, or through the whole flower, and ſo in a red or yellow flower, that it hath had eyther red or yellow edges, or yellow or red ſpots, lines, veines, or flames, running through the red or yellow colour, and ſometimes it hath happened, that three leaues haue been equally parted in the middle with red and yellow, the other three abiding of one colour, and in ſome the red had ſome yellow in it, and the yellow ſome red ſpots in it alſo ; whereof I haue obſerued, that all ſuch flowers, not hauing their originall in that manner, (for ſome that haue ſuch or the like markes from the beginning, that is, from the firſt and ſecond yeares flowring, are conſtant, and doe not change) but as I ſaid, were of one colour at the firſt, doe ſhew the

weakneſſe

weakneſſe and decay of the roote, and that this extraordinary beauty in the flower, is but as the brightneſſe of a light, vpon the very extinguiſhing thereof, and doth plainly declare, that it can doe his Maſter no more ſeruice, and therefore with this iollity doth bid him good night. I know there is a common opinion among many (and very conſidently maintained) that a Tulipa with a white flower, hath changed to beare a red or yellow, and ſo of the red or yellow, and other colours, that they are likewiſe inconſtant, as though no flowers were certaine : but I could neuer either ſee or heare for certaine any ſuch alteration, nor any other variation, but what is formerly expreſſed. Let not therefore any iudicious be carried away with any ſuch idle conceit, but rather ſuſpect ſome deceit in their Gardeners or others, by taking vp one, and putting in another in the place, or elſe their owne miſtaking.

Now for the ſowing, planting, tranſplanting, choiſe, and ordering of Tulipas, which is not the leaſt of regard, concerning this ſubiect in hand, but (as I think) would be willingly entertained ; What I haue by my beſt endeauours learned, by mine owne paines in almoſt forty yeares trauell, or from others informations, I am willing here to ſet downe ; not doubting, but that ſome may adde what hath not come to my knowledge.

Firſt, in the ſowing of ſeedes of Tulipas, I haue not obſerued (whatſoeuer others haue written) nor could of certainty learne of others, that there doth ariſe from the ſeedes of *Præcoces* any *Medias* or *Serotine* Tulipas, (or but very ſeldome) nor am certainly aſſured of any : but that the ſeedes of all *Præcoces* (ſo they be not doubtfull, or of the laſt flowring ſorts) will bring *Præcoces* : And I am out of doubt, that I neuer ſaw, nor could learne, that euer the ſeede of the *Medias* or *Serotines* haue giuen *Præcoces* ; but *Medias* or *Serotines*, according to their naturall kinde. But if there ſhould bee any degeneration, I rather incline to thinke, that it ſooner commeth to paſſe *(à meliore ad peius*, for *facilis eſt deſcenſus*, that is) that *Præcoces* may giue *Medias*, then that *Medias* or *Serotines* ſhould giue *Præcoces*.

For the choiſe of your ſeede to ſowe. Firſt, for the *Præcoces*, Cluſius ſaith, that the *Præcox Tulipa*, that beareth a white flower, is the beſt to giue the greateſt variety of colours. Some among vs haue reported, that they haue found great variety riſe from the ſeede of the red *Præcox*, which I can more hardly beleeue : but Cluſius his experience hath the greater probability, but eſpecially if it haue ſome mixture of red or purple in it. The purple I haue found to be the beſt, next thereunto is the purple with white edges, and ſo likewiſe the red with yellow edges, each of them will bring moſt of their owne colours. Then the choiſe of the beſt *Medias*, is to take thoſe colours that are light, rather white then yellow, and purple then red ; yea white, not yellow, purple, not red : but theſe againe to be ſpotted is the beſt, and the more the better ; but withall, or aboue all in theſe, reſpect the ground or bottome of the flower, (which in the *Præcox Tulipa* cannot, becauſe you ſhall ſeldome ſee any other ground in them but yellow) for if the flower be white, or whitiſh, ſpotted, or edged, and ſtraked, and the bottome blew or purple (ſuch as is found in the Holias, and in the Cloth of ſiluer, this is beyond all other the moſt excellent, and out of queſtion the choiſeſt of an hundred, to haue the greateſt and moſt pleaſant variety and rarity. And ſo in degree, the meaner in beauty you ſowe, the leſſer ſhall your pleaſure in rarities be. Beſtowe not your time in ſowing red or yellow Tulipa ſeede, or the diuers mixtures of them ; for they will (as I haue found by experience) ſeldome be worth your paines. The *Serotina*, or late flowring Tulipa, becauſe it is ſeldome ſeene, with any eſpeciall beautifull variety, you may eaſily your ſelues gheſſe that it can bring forth (euen as I haue alſo learned) no raritie, and little or no diuerſity at all.

The time and manner to ſowe theſe ſeedes is next to be conſidered. You may not ſowe them in the ſpring of the yeare, if you hope to haue any good of them ; but in the Autumne, or preſently after they be thorough ripe and dry : yet if you ſowe them not vntill the end of October, they will come forward neuer the worſe, but rather the better ; for it is often ſeene, that ouer early ſowing cauſeth them to ſpring out of the ground ouer early, ſo that if a ſharpe ſpring chance to follow, it may goe neere to ſpoile all, or the moſt of your ſeede. Wee vſually ſowe the ſame yeares ſeede, yet if you chance to keepe of your owne, or haue from others ſuch ſeed, as is two years old, they will thriue and doe well enough, eſpecially if they were ripe and well gathered :

You muſt not ſowe them too thicke, for ſo doing hath loſt many a pecke of good ſeede, as I can tell; for if the ſeede lye one vpon another, that it hath not roome vpon the ſprouting, to enter and take roote in the earth, it periſheth by and by. Some vſe to tread downe the ground, where they meane to ſowe their ſeede, and hauing ſowne them thereon, doe couer them ouer the thickneſſe of a mans thumbe with fine ſifted earth, and they thinke they doe well, and haue good reaſon for it: for conſidering the nature of the young Tulipa rootes, is to runne downe deeper into the ground, euery yeare more then other, they thinke to hinder their quicke deſcent by the faſtneſſe of the ground, that ſo they may encreaſe the better. This way may pleaſe ſome, but I doe not vſe it, nor can finde the reaſon ſufficient; for they doe not conſider, that the ſtiffeneſſe of the earth, doth cauſe the rootes of the young Tulipas to bee long before they grow great, in that a ſtiffe ground doth more hinder the well thriuing of the rootes, then a looſe doth, and although the rootes doe runne downe deeper in a looſe earth, yet they may eaſily by tranſplanting be holpen, and raiſed vp high enough. I haue alſo ſeene ſome Tulipas not once remoued from their ſowing to their flowring; but if you will not loſe them, you muſt take them vp while their leafe or ſtalke is freſh, and not withered: for if you doe not follow the ſtalke downe to the roote, be it neuer ſo deepe, you will leaue them behinde you. The ground alſo muſt be reſpected; for the finer, ſofter, and richer the mould is, wherein you ſowe your ſeede, the greater ſhall be your encreaſe and varietie: Sift it therefore from all ſtones and rubbiſh, and let it be either fat naturall ground of it ſelfe, or being muckt, that it bee thoroughly rotten: but ſome I know, to mend their ground, doe make ſuch a mixture of grounds, that they marre it in the making.

After the ſeede is thus ſowne, the firſt yeares ſpringing bringeth forth leaues, little bigger then the ordinary graſſe leaues; the ſecond yeare bigger, and ſo by degrees euery yeare bigger then other. The leaues of the *Præcoces* while they are young, may be diſcerned from the *Medias* by this note, which I haue obſerued. The leaues of them doe wholly ſtand vp aboue the ground, ſhewing the ſmall footſtalkes, whereby euerie leafe doth ſtand, but the leaues of the *Medias* or *Serotines* doe neuer wholly appeare out of the ground, but the lower part which is broad, abideth vnder the vpper face of the earth. Thoſe Tulipas now growing to bee three yeares old, (yet ſome at the ſecond, if the ground and ayre be correſpondent) are to bee taken vp out of the ground, wherein yee ſhall finde they haue runne deepe, and to be anew planted, after they haue been a little dryed and cleanſed, eyther in the ſame, or another ground againe, placing them reaſonable neare one vnto another, according to their greatneſſe, which being planted and couered ouer with earth againe, of about an inch or two thickneſſe, may be left vntaken vp againe for two yeare longer, if you will, or elſe remoued euery yeare after, as you pleaſe; and thus by tranſplanting them in their due ſeaſon (which is ſtill in the end of Iuly, or beginning of Auguſt, or thereabouts) you ſhall according to your ſeede and ſoyle, haue ſome come to bearing, in the fifth yeare after the flowring, (and ſome haue had them in the fourth, but that hath beene but few, and none of the beſt, or in a rich ground) ſome in the ſixth and ſeuenth, and ſome peraduenture, not vntill the eighth or tenth yeare: but ſtill remember, that as your rootes growe greater, that in re-planting you giue them the more roome to be diſtant one from another, or elſe the one will hinder, if not rot the other.

The ſeede of the *Præcoces*, doe not thriue and come forward ſo faſt as the *Medias* or *Serotines*, nor doe giue any of-ſets in their running downe as the *Medias* doe, which vſually leaue a ſmall roote at the head of the other that is runne downe euery yeare; and beſides, are more tender, and require more care and attendance then the *Medias*, and therefore they are the more reſpected.

This is a generall and certaine rule in all Tulipas, that all the while they beare but one leafe, they will not beare flower, whether they bee ſeedlings, or the of-ſets of elder rootes, or the rootes themſelues, that haue heretofore borne flowers; but when they ſhew a ſecond leafe, breaking out of the firſt, it is a certaine ſigne, that it will then beare a flower, vnleſſe ſome caſualty hinder it, as froſt or raine, to nip or ſpoile the bud, or other vntimely accident befall it.

To ſet or plant your beſt and bearing Tulipas ſomewhat deeper then other rootes, I hold it the beſt way; for if the ground bee either cold, or lye too open to the cold
Northerne

Northerne ayre, they will be the better defended therein, and not suffer the frosts or cold to pierce them so soone: for the deepe frosts and snowes doe pinch the *Præcoces* chiefly, if they bee too neare the vppermost crust of the earth; and therefore many, with good successe, couer ouer their ground before Winter, with either fresh or old rotten dung, and that will maruelloufly preserue them. The like course you may hold with seedlings, to cause them to come on the forwarder, so it bee after the first yeares sowing, and not till then.

To remoue Tulipas after they haue shot forth their fibres or small strings, which grow vnder the great round rootes, (that is, from September vntill they bee in flower) is very dangerous; for by remouing them when they haue taken fast hold in the ground, you doe both hinder them in the bearing out their flower, and besides, put them in hazzard to perish, at least to bee put backe from bearing for a while after, as oftentimes I haue proued by experience: But when they are now risen to flower, and so for any time after, you may safely take them vp if you will, and remoue them without danger, if you haue any good regard vnto them, vnlesse it be a young bearing roote, which you shall in so doing much hinder, because it is yet tender, by reason it now beareth his first flower. But all Tulipa roots when their stalke and leaues are dry, may most safely then be taken vp out of the ground, and be so kept (so that they lye in a dry, and not in a moist place) for sixe moneths, without any great harme: yea I haue knowne them that haue had them nine moneths out of the ground, and haue done reasonable well, but this you must vnderstand withall, that they haue not been young but elder rootes, and they haue been orderly taken vp and preserued. The dryer you keep a Tulipa roote the better, so as you let it not lye in the sunne or winde, which will pierce it and spoile it.

Thus Gentlewomen for your delights, (for these pleasures are the delights of leasure, which hath bred your loue & liking to them, and although you are herein predominant, yet cannot they be barred from your beloued, who I doubt not, wil share with you in the delight as much as is fit) haue I taken this paines, to set downe, and bring to your knowledge such rules of art, as my small skill hath enabled mee withall concerning this subiect, which of all other, seemed fittest in this manner to be enlarged, both for the varietie of matter, and excellency of beautie herein, and also that these rules set forth together in one place, might saue many repetitions in other places, so that for the planting and ordering of all other bulbous rootes, and the sowing the seedes of them, you may haue recourse vnto these rules, *(tanquam ad normam & examen)* which may serue in generall for all other, little diuersitie of particulars needing exception.

The Place.

The greater Tulipas haue first beene sent vs from Conſtantinople, and other parts of Turkie, where it is said they grow naturally wilde in the Fields, Woods, and Mountaines; as Thracia, Macedonia, Pontus about the Euxine Sea, Cappadocia, Bithynia, and about Tripolis and Aleppo in Syria also: the lesser haue come from other seuerall places, as their names doe descipher it out vnto vs; as Armenia, Persia, Candye, Portugall, Spaine, Italy, and France. They are all now made Denizens in our Gardens, where they yeeld vs more delight, and more encrease for their proportion, by reason of the culture, then they did vnto their owne naturals.

The Time.

These doe flower some earlier, some later, for three whole moneths together at the least, therein adorning out a Garden most glorioufly, in that being but one kinde of flower, it is so full of variety, as no other (except the Daffodils, which yet are not comparable, in that they yeeld not that alluring pleasant variety) doe the like besides. Some of the *Præcoces* haue beene in flower with vs, (for I speake not of their owne naturall places, where the Winters are milder, and the Spring earlier then ours) in the moneth of Ianuary, when the Winter before hath beene milde, but many in February,

and

and all the *Præcoces*, from the beginning to the end of March, if the yeare be kindly : at what time the *Medias* doe begin, and abide all Aprill, and part of May, when the *Serotines* flower and fade ; but this, as I said, if the yeare be kindly, or else each kinde will be a moneth later. The seede is ripe in Iune and Iuly, according to their early or late flowring.

The Names.

There haue beene diuers opinions among our moderne Writers, by what name this plant was knowne to the ancient Authors. Some would haue it be *Cosmosandalos*, of the Ancient. Dodonæus referreth it to πυπῶν of Theophraftus, in his seuenth Booke and thirteenth Chapter : but thereof he is so briefe, that besides the bare name, wee cannot finde him to make any further relation of forme, or quality. And Bauhinus, vpon Matthiolus Commentaries of Dioscorides, and in his Pinax also, followeth his opinion. Camerarius in his Hortus Medicus is of opinion, it may be referred to the Helychrysum of Crateua. Gesner, as I thinke, first of all, and after him Lobel, Camerarius, Clusius and many others, referre it to the Satyrium of Dioscorides : and surely this opinion is the most probable for many reasons. First, for that this plant doth grow very frequent in many places of Greece, and the lesser Asia, which were no doubt sufficiently knowne both to Theophraftus, and Dioscorides, and was accounted among bulbous rootes, although by sundry names. And secondly, as Dioscorides setteth forth his Satyrium, so this most commonly beareth three leaues vpon a stalke (although sometimes with vs it hath foure or fiue) like vnto a Lilly, whereof some are often seen to be both red, in the first springing, and also vpon the decaying, especially in a dry time, and in a dry ground : the flower likewise of some is white, and like a Lilly ; the roote is round, and as white within as the white of an egge, couered with a browne coate, hauing a sweetish, but not vnpleasant taste, as any man without danger many try. This description doth so liuely set forth this plant, that I thinke wee shall not neede to be any longer in doubt, where to finde Dioscorides his Satyrium Triphyllum, seeing wee haue such plenty growing with vs. And thirdly, there is no doubt, but that it hath the same qualities, as you shall hereafter heare further. And lastly, that plant likewise that beareth a red flower, may very well agree with his Erythronium ; for the descriptions in Dioscorides are both alike, as are their qualities, the greatest doubt may be in the seede, which yet may agree vnto Lin or Flaxe as fitly, or rather more then many other plants doe, in many of his comparisons, which yet wee receiue for currant. For the seede of Tulipas are flat, hard, and shining as the seede of *Linum* or Flaxe, although of another colour, and bigger, as Dioscorides himselfe setteth it downe. But if there should be a mistaking in the writing of λίνε for λέα, in the Greeke Text, as the slippe is both easie and likely, it were then out of all question the same : for the seede is very like vnto the seede of Lillies, as any man may easily discerne that know them, or will compare them. It is generally called by all the late Writers, *Tulipa*, which is deriued from the name *Tulpan*, whereby the Turkes of *Dalmatia* doe entitle their head Tyres, or Caps ; and this flower being blowne, laide open, and inuerted, doth very well resemble them. We haue receiued the early kinde from Constantinople, by the name of *Casa lale*, and the other by the name of *Cauala lale*. Lobel and others doe call it *Lilio-narcissus*, because it doth resemble a Lilly in the leafe, flower, and seede, and a Daffodill in the roote. We call it in English the Turkes Cap, but most vsually Tulipa, as most other Christian Countries that delight therein doe. Daleschampius calleth it Oulada.

The Vertues.

Dioscorides writeth, that his first Satyrium is profitable for them that
haue

haue a convulsion in their necke, (which wee call a cricke in the necke) if it be drunke in harsh (which we call red) wine.

That the roots of Tulipas are nourishing, there is no doubt, the pleasant, or at least the no vnpleasant taste, may hereunto perswade ; for diuers haue had them sent by their friends from beyond Sea, and mistaking them to bee Onions, haue vsed them as Onions in their pottage or broth, and neuer found any cause of mislike, or any sense of euill quality produced by them, but accounted them sweete Onions.

Further, I haue made tryall of them my selfe in this manner. I haue preserued the rootes of these Tulipas in Sugar, as I haue done the rootes of E-ringus, Orchis, or any other such like, and haue found them to be almost as pleasant as the Eringus rootes, being firme and sound, fit to be presented to the curious; but for force of Venereous quality, I cannot say, either from my selfe, not hauing eaten many, or from any other, on whom I haue bestowed them : but surely, if there be any speciall propertie in the rootes of Orchis, or some other tending to that purpose , I thinke this may as well haue it as they. It should seeme, that Dioscorides doth attribute a great Venereous faculty to the seede , whereof I know not any hath made any especiall experiment with vs as yet.

Chap. IX.

Narcissus. The Daffodill.

THere hath beene great confusion among many of our moderne Writers of plants, in not distinguishing the manifold varieties of Daffodils ; for euery one almost, without consideration of kinde or forme, or other speciall note, giueth names so diuersly one from another, that if any one shall receiue from seuerall places the Catalogues of their names (as I haue had many) as they set them down, and compare the one Catalogue with the other, he shall scarce haue three names in a dozen to agree together, one calling that by one name, which another calleth by another, that very few can tell what they meane. And this their confusion, in not distinguishing the name of *Narcissus* from *Pseudonarcissus*, is of all other in this kinde the greatest and grossest errour. To auoide therefore that gulfe, whereof I complaine that so manie haue bin endrenched ; and to reduce the Daffodils into such a methodicall order, that euery one may know, to what *Classis* or forme any one doth appertaine, I will first diuide them into two principall or primary kindes : that is, into *Narcissos*, true Daffodils, and *Pseudonarcissos*, bastard Daffodils: which distinction I hold to be most necessarie to be set downe first of all, that euery one may be named without confusion vnder his owne primary kind, and then to let the other parts of the subdiuision follow, as is proper to them, and fittest to expresse them. Now to cause you to vnderstand the difference betweene a true Daffodill and a false, is this ; it consisteth onely in the flower, (when as in all other parts they cannot bee distinguished) and chiefly in the middle cup or chalice ; for that we doe in a manner onely account those to bee *Pseudonarcissos*, bastard Daffodils, whose middle cup is altogether as long, and sometime a little longer then the outter leaues that doe encompasse it, so that it seemeth rather like a trunke or long nose, then a cup or chalice, such as almost all the *Narcissi*, or true Daffodils haue; I say almost, because I know that some of them haue their middle cup so small, that we rather call it a crowne then a cup ; and againe, some of them haue them so long, that they may seem to be of the number of the *Pseudonarcissi*, or bastard Daffodils: but yet may easily be knowne from them, in that, although the cup of some of the true Daffodils be great, yet it is wider open at the brim or edge, and not so long and narrow all alike as the bastard kindes are ; and this is the chiefe and onely way to know how to seuer these kindes, which rule holdeth certaine in all, except that kinde which is called *Narcissus Iuncifolius reflexo flore*, whose cup is narrow, and as long as the leaues that turne vp againe.

Secondly,

Secondly, I will subdiuide each of these again apart by themselues, into foure sorts ; and first the *Narciffos*, or true Daffodils into

Latifolios, broad leafed Daffodils.

Angustifolios, narrow leafed Daffodils.

Iuncifolios, Rushe Daffodils, and

Marinos, Sea Daffodils.

These sorts againe doe comprehend vnder them some other diuisions, whereby they may the better be distinguished, and yet still bee referred to one of those foure former sorts : as

Monanthos, that is, Daffodils that beare but one flower, or two at the most vpon a stalke, and

Polyanthos, those that beare many flowers together vpon a stalke : as also

Simplici flore, those that beare single flowers, and

Multiplici flore, or *flore pleno*, that is, haue double flowers.

Vernales, those that flower in the Spring, and among them some that are earlier; and therefore called

Præcoces, early flowring Daffodils, and

Autumnales, those that flower in Autumne onely.

And lastly, with the *Pfeudonarciffos*, or bastard Daffodils, I will keepe the same order, to distinguish them likewise into their foure seuerall sorts ; and as with the true Daffodils, so with these false, describe vnder euery sort : first, those that beare single flowers, whether one or many vpon a stalke ; and then those that beare double flowers, one or many also. As for the distinctions of *maior* and *minor*, greater and lesser, and of *maximus* and *minimus*, greatest and least, they doe not onely belong to these Daffodils ; and therefore must be vsed as occasion permitteth, but vnto all other sort of plants. To begin therefore, I thinke fittest with that stately Daffodill, which for his excellency carrieth the name of None such.

1. *Narciffus latifolius omnium maximus, amplo calice flauo, siue Nompareille.* The great None such Daffodill, or Incomparable Daffodill.

This *Narciffus Nompareille* hath three or foure long and broad leaues, of a grayish greene colour, among which riseth vp a stalke two foote high at the least, at the toppe whereof, out of a thinne skinnie huske, as all Daffodils haue, commeth forth one large single flower, and no more vsually, consisting of sixe very pale yellow large leaues, almost round at the point, with a large cuppe in the middle, somewhat yellower then the leaues, the bottome whereof next vnto the stalke is narrow and round, rising wider to the mouth, which is very large and open, and vneuenly cut in or indented about the edges. The cup doth very well resemble the chalice, that in former dayes with vs, and beyond the Seas is still vsed to hold the Sacramentall Wine, that is with a narrower bottome, and a wide mouth. After the flower is past, sometimes there commeth (for it doth not often) a round greene head, and blacke round seede therein, like vnto other Daffodils, but greater. The roote is great, as other Daffodils that beare large flowers, and is couered ouer with a brownish coate or skinne. The flower hath little or no sent at all.

Flore geminato   This doth sometimes bring forth a flower with ten or twelue leaues, and a cup much larger, as if it would be two, euen as the flower seemeth.

2. *Narciffus omnium maximus flore & calice flauo.* The great yellow Incomparable Daffodill.

This other kinde differeth neither in forme, nor bignesse of leafe or flower from the former, but in the colour of the circling leaues of the flower, which are of the same yellow colour with the cup.

Flore geminato.   This doth sometimes degenerate and grow luxurious also, bringing forth two flowers vpon a stalke, each distinct from other, and sometimes two flowers thrust together, as if they were but one, although it be but seldome ; for it is not a peculiar kinde that is constant, yearly abiding in the same forme.

3. *Narciffus*

3. *Narciſſus maximus griſeus calice flauo.* The gray Peerleſſe Daffodill.

This Peerleſſe Daffodill well deſerueth his place among theſe kindes, for that it doth much reſemble them, and peraduenture is but a difference raiſed from the ſeede of the former, it is ſo like in leafe and flower, but that the leaues ſeeme to be ſomewhat greater, and the ſixe outer leaues of the flower to be of a gliſtering whitiſh gray colour, and the cup yellow, as the former, but larger.

4. *Narciſſus latifolius flauo flore amplo calice, ſiue Matteneſſe.*
The leſſer yellow Nompareille, or the Lady Matteneſſes Daffodill.

The leaues of this Daffodill, are ſomewhat like vnto the leaues of the firſt kind, but not altogether ſo long or broad : the ſtalke likewiſe riſeth not vp fully ſo high, and beareth one flower like the former, but leſſer, and both the cuppe and the leaues are of one colour, that is, of a pale yellow, yet more yellow then in the former : the cup of this alſo is leſſer, and a little differing ; for it is neither fully ſo ſmall in the bottome, nor ſo large at the edges, nor ſo crumpled at the brimmes, ſo that all theſe differences doe plainly ſhew it to be another kinde, quite from the former.

The Place.

The places of none of theſe are certainly knowne to vs where they grow naturally, but we haue them onely in our Gardens, and haue beene ſent, and procured from diuers places.

The Time.

They flower ſometimes in the end of March, but chiefly in Aprill.

The Names.

The firſt and ſecond haue been ſent vs by the name of *Narciſſe Nompareille*, as it is called in French ; and in Latine, *Narciſſus omnium maximus amplo calice flauo*, and *Narciſſus Incomparabilis*, that is, the Incomparable Daffodill, or the greateſt Daffodill of all other, with a large yellow cuppe : but aſſuredly, although this Daffodill doth exceed many other, both in length and bigneſſe, yet the great Spaniſh baſtard Daffodill, which ſhall be ſpoken of hereafter, is in my perſwaſion oftentimes a farre higher and larger flower ; and therefore this name was giuen but relatiuely, we may call it in Engliſh, The great None ſuch Daffodill, or the Incomparable Daffodill, or the great Peerleſſe Daffodill, or the Nompareille Daffodill, which you will : for they all doe anſwer either the French or the Latine name ; and becauſe this name *Nompareille* is growne currant by cuſtome, I know not well how to alter it. The third kinde may paſſe with the title giuen it, without controule. The laſt is very well knowne beyond the Seas, eſpecially in the Low Countries, and thoſe parts, by the Lady Matteneſſe Daffodill, becauſe Cluſius receiued it from her. We may call it in Engliſh, for the correſpondency with the former, The leſſer yellow Nompareille, or Peerleſſe Daffodill, or the Lady Matteneſſe Daffodill, which you will.

Narciſſus Indicus flore rubro, dictus Iacobæus.
The Indian Daffodill with a red flower.

This Indian Daffodill is ſo differing, both in forme, not hauing a cuppe, and in colour, being red, from the whole Family of the Daffodils (except the next that followeth, and the Autumne Daffodils) that ſome might iuſtly queſtion the fitneſſe of his place here. But becauſe as all the plants, whether bulbous or other, that come from the

the Indies, either Eaſt or Weſt (although they differ very notably, from thoſe that grow in theſe parts of the world) muſt in a generall ſuruey and muſter be ranked euery one, as neere as the ſurueiours wit will direct him, vnder ſome other growing with vs, that is of neereſt likeneſſe ; Euen ſo vntill ſome other can direct his place more fitly, I ſhall require you to accept of him in this, with this deſcription that followeth, which I muſt tell you alſo, is more by relation then knowledge, or ſight of the plant it ſelfe. This Daffodill hath diuers broad leaues, ſomewhat like vnto the common or ordinary white Daffodill, of a grayiſh greene colour ; from the ſides whereof, as alſo from the middle of them, riſe vp ſometimes two ſtalkes together, but moſt vſually one after another (for very often it flowreth twice in a Summer) and often alſo but one ſtalke alone, which is of a faint reddiſh colour, about a foote high or more, at the toppe whereof, out of a deepe red skinne or huske, commeth forth one flower bending downewards, conſiſting of ſixe long leaues without any cup in the middle, of an excellent red colour, tending to a crimſon; three of theſe leaues that turne vpwards, are ſomewhat larger then thoſe three that hang downewards, hauing ſixe threads or chiues in the middle, tipt with yellow pendents, and a three forked ſtile longer then the reſt, and turning vp the end thereof againe : the roote is round and bigge, of a browniſh colour on the outſide, and white within. This is ſet forth by Aldinus, Cardinall Farneſius his Phyſitian, that at Rome it roſe vp with ſtalkes of flowers, before any leaues appeared.

The Place, Time, and Names.

This naturally groweth in the Weſt Indies, from whence it was brought into Spaine, where it bore both in Iune and Iuly, and by the Indians in their tongue named AZCAL XOCHITL, and hath beene ſent from Spaine, vnto diuers louers of plants, into ſeuerall parts of Chriſtendome, but haue not thriued long in theſe tranſalpine colder Countries, ſo far as I can heare.

Narciſſus Trapezunticus flore luteo præcociſsimus.
The early Daffodill of Trebizond.

Becauſe this Daffodill is ſo like in flower vnto the former, although differing in colour, I thought it the fitteſt place to ioyne it the next thereunto. This early Daffodill hath three or foure ſhort very greene leaues, ſo like vnto the leaues of the Autumne Daffodill, that many may eaſily bee deceiued in miſtaking one for another, the difference conſiſting chiefly in this, that the leaues of this are not ſo broad or ſo long, nor riſe vp in Autumne : in the midſt of theſe leaues riſeth vp a ſhort green ſtalke, an handfull high, or not much higher vſually, (I ſpeake of it as it hath often flowred with mee, whether the cauſe be the coldneſſe of the time wherein it flowreth, or the nature of the plant, or of our climate, I am in ſome doubt ; but I doe well remember, that the ſtalkes of ſome plants, that haue flowred later with me then the firſt, haue by the greater ſtrength, and comfort of the Sunne, riſen a good deale higher then the firſt) bearing at the top, out of a whitiſh thinne skinne ſtriped with greene, one flower a little bending downewards, conſiſting of ſixe leaues, laid open almoſt in the ſame manner with the former Indian Daffodill, whereof ſome doe a little turne vp their points againe, of a faire pale yellow colour, hauing ſixe white chiues within it, tipt with yellow pendents, and a longer pointell : the roote is not very great, but blackiſh on the outſide, ſo like vnto the Autumne Daffodill, but that it is yellow vnder the firſt or outermoſt coate, that one may eaſily miſtake one for another.

The Place.

It was ſent vs from Conſtantinople among other rootes, but as wee may gheſſe by the name, it ſhould come thither from Trapezunte or Trebizond

The Time.

It flowreth ſometimes in December, if the former part of the Winter haue

1 *Narciſſus Nonpareille*. The incomparable Daffodill. 2 *Narciſſus Mattaneſe*. The leſſer yellow Nomparelle Daffodill. 3 *Narciſſus Iacobæus flore rubro*. The red Indian Daffodill. 4 *Narciſſus Trapezunticus*. The early Daffodill of Trabeſond. 5 *Narciſſus Montanus albus apophyſibus præditus*. The white winged Daffodill. 6 *Narciſſus Montanus, ſiue Nompareille totus albus*. The white Nompareille, or Peerleſſe Daffodill. 7 *Narciſſus albus oblongo calice*. The white Daffodill with a long cup.

haue been milde; but most vsually about the end of Ianuary, or else in Februarie the beginning or the end.

The Names.

Wee doe vsually call it from the Turkish name, *Narciʃʃus Trapezunticus*, and some also call it *Narciʃʃus vernus præcox*, as Clusius doth, in English, The early Daffodill of Trebizond.

Narciʃʃus Montanus albus apophyʃibus præditus.
The white Mountaine Daffodill with eares, or
The white winged Daffodill.

This Mountaine Daffodill riseth vp with three or foure broad leaues, somewhat long, of a whitish greene colour, among which riseth vp a stalke a foote and a halfe high, whereon standeth one large flower, and sometimes two, consisting of sixe white leaues a peece, not very broad, and without any shew of yellowneʃʃe in them, three whereof haue vsually each of them on the backe part, at the bottome vpon the one side of them, and not on both, a little small white peece of a leafe like an eare, the other three hauing none at all: the cup is almost as large, or not much leʃʃe then the small Nompareille, small at the bottome, and very large, open at the brimme, of a faire yellow colour, and sometimes the edges or brimmes of the cup will haue a deeper yellow colour about it, like as if it were discoloured with Saffron: the flower is verie sweete, the roote is great and white, couered with a pale coate or skinne, not verie blacke, and is not very apt to encrease, seldome giuing of-sets; neither haue I euer gathered seede thereof, becauʃe it paʃʃeth away without bearing any with me.

Narciʃʃus Montanus, ʃiue Nompareille totus albus amplo calice.
The white Nompareille Daffodill.

This white Nompareille Daffodill, is in roote and leafe very like vnto the former mountain or winged Daffodill, but that they are a little larger: the stalke from among the leaues riseth vp not much higher then it, bearing at the top one large flower, composed of sixe long white leaues, each whereof is as it were folded halfe way together, in the middle whereof standeth forth a large white cup, broader at the mouth or brims then at the bottome, very like vnto the leʃʃer Nompareille Daffodill before remembred, which hath caused it to be so entituled: the sent whereof is no leʃʃe sweete then the former.

The Place.

The naturall places of these Daffodils are not certainly knowne to vs; but by the names they carry, they should seeme to bee bred in the Mountaines.

The Time.

These flower not so early as many other kindes doe, but rather are to bee accounted among the late flowring Daffodils; for they shew not their flowers vntill the beginning of May, or the latter end of Aprill, with the soonest.

The Names.

The names set downe ouer the heads of either of them be such, whereby they are knowne to vs: yet some doe call the first *Narciʃʃus auriculatus*, that is to say, The Daffodill with eares: and the other, *Narciʃʃus Nompareille totus albus*, that is to say, The white Nompareille, or Peerleʃʃe Daffodill.

1. *Narciʃʃus*

1. *Narciſſus albus oblongo calice luteo præcox minor.*
The ſmall early white Daffodill with a long cup.

The leaues of this early Daffodill are broad, very greene, and not whitiſh as others, three or foure ſtanding together, about a foote long or better, among which riſeth vp a greene ſtalke, not full ſo high as the leaues, bearing one flower at the toppe thereof of a reaſonable bigneſſe, but not ſo great as the later kindes that follow are, conſiſting of ſix whitiſh leaues, but not perfect white, hauing a ſhew of a Creame colour appearing in them; in the middle is a long round yellow cup, about halfe an inch long or better. The ſmell of this flower is reaſonable ſweete, the roote is of a reaſonable bigneſſe, yet leſſer then the rootes of the later kindes.

2. *Narciſſus pallidus oblongo calice flauo præcox.*
The early Strawe coloured Daffodill with a long cup.

The leaues of this Daffodill are as greene as the former, but much narrower; and the leaues of the flower are more enclining to yellow, but yet very pale, as if it were a light ſtrawe colour, and ſeeme to bee a little more narrow and pointed then the former : the cup of this, is as long and yellow as the precedent. The ſmell whereof is very like the former, yet neither of them being ſo ſweete as thoſe that follow.

3. *Narciſſus albus oblongo calice luteo ſerotinus maior.*
The great late flowring white Daffodill with a long cup.

This later flowring Daffodill hath his leaues ſomewhat narrow & long, of a grayiſh or whitiſh greene colour, among which the ſtalke riſeth vp a foote and a halfe high, bearing one flower at the toppe, made of ſix white leaues, hauing the cup in the middle thereof as long as the former, and of a deepe yellow : the edges of this cuppe are ſometimes plaine, and ſometimes a little crumpled; they are often alſo circled at the brimmes with a Saffron colour, and often alſo without it, the ſmell whereof is very pleaſant, and not heady : the roote hereof is reaſonable bigge, and couered ouer rather with a pale then blackiſh skinne. This flower doth ſometimes alter his forme into eight leaues, which being narrow and long, ſeeme like a white ſtarre, compaſſing a yellow trunke.

4. *Narciſſus totus pallidus oblongo calice ſerotinus minor.*
The late pale coloured Daffodill with a long cup.

There is another of this kinde, whoſe flower is wholly of a pale white, or yellowiſh colour, differing neither in leafe nor roote from the former.

5. *Narciſſus pallidus oblongo calice flauo ſerotinus.*
The Strawe coloured late flowring Daffodill with a long yellow cup.

The chiefe difference of this Daffodill from the former, conſiſteth in the colour of the top of the flower, which is of a more yellow colour, and a little larger then the former, and the brimmes or edges of the cup of a deeper yellow, or Saffron colour. The ſmell of this is no leſſe ſweete then in the former.

6. *Narciſſus albus oblongo calice flauo ſerotinus, duobus floribus in caule.*
The late white Daffodill with a long cup, and two flowers on a ſtalke.

This Daffodill is ſurely a kinde of it ſelfe, although it be ſo like the former, abiding conſtant in his forme and manner of flowring, vſually bearing without miſſing two flowers vpon a ſtalke, very like vnto the former great white kinde, that one cannot know any greater matter of difference betweene them, then that it beareth two flowers on a ſtalke : the cuppes whereof are ſeldome touched with any ſhew of Saffron colour on them at the brimmes or edges, as ſome of the former haue.

G   The

The Place.

All thefe Daffodils doe grow on the Pyrenæan mountaines, and haue been fought out, and brought into thefe parts, by thofe curious or couetous fearchers of thefe delights, that haue made vs partakers of them.

The Time.

The former kindes flower earlier by a fortnight then the later, the one in the later end of March, and the other not vntill the middle of Aprill.

The Names.

Their names are giuen to euery one of them in their feuerall titles, as fitly as may beft agree with their natures ; and therefore I fhall not neede to fpeake any further of them.

Narciffus medioluteus vulgaris.
The common white Daffodill called Primrofe Peerleffe.

This Daffodill is fo common in euery Countrey Garden almoft through England, that I doubt I fhall but fpend my time in vaine, to defcribe that which is fo well knowne, yet for their fakes that know it not, I will fet downe the defcription of it in this manner. It hath long limber and broad leaues, of a grayifh greene colour, among which rifeth vp a ftalke, bearing at the toppe out of a skinnie huske fometimes but one flower, but moft commonly two flowers, and feldome three or more, but larger for the moft part, then any that beare many flowers vpon a ftalke, of a pale whitifh Creame colour, tending fomewhat neare vnto the colour of a pale Primrofe (which hath caufed our Countrey Gentlewomen, I thinke, to entitle it Primrofe Peerleffe) with a fmall round flat Crowne, rather then a cup in the middle, of a pale yellow colour, with fome pale chiues ftanding therein, being of a fweete, but ftuffing fent : the roote is reafonable great, and encreafing more then a better plant.

Narciffus mediocroceus ferotinus. The late flowring white Daffodill.

This Daffodill hath much fmaller leaues, and fhorter then the laft, the ftalke alfo rifeth not fo high by much, and beareth but one flower thereon, of a pure white colour, made of fix fmall leaues, and fomewhat narrow, ftanding feuerally one from another, and not fo clofe together as the former, but appearing like a ftarre : the cup is fmall and round, of a pale yellow colour, but faffrony about the brims, hauing fix fmall pale chiues in the middle, the fmell whereof is much fweeter then in the former.

The Place.

The firft is thought to grow naturally in England, but I could neuer heare of his naturall place. I am fure it is plentifull enough in all Country Gardens, fo that wee fcarce giue it place in our more curious parkes. The fecond liueth onely with them that delight in varieties.

The Time.

The firft Daffodill flowreth in the middle time, being neither of the earlieft, nor of the lateft ; but about the middle, or end of Aprill. The other flowreth with the lateft in May.

The Names.

I fhall not neede to trouble you with further repetitions of names, they hauing been fet downe in their titles, which are proper to them.

1. *Narciffus*

1 *Narciſſus vulgaris medio luteus.* The common white Daffodill, or Primrose Peerleſſe. 2 *Narciſſus medio purpureus maximus.* The great white purple ringed Daffodill. 3 *Narciſſus medio purpureus præcox.* The early purple ringed Daffodill. 4 *Narciſſus medio purpureus ſtellatus.* The ſtarry purple ringed Daffodill. 5 *Narciſſus Perſicus.* The Perſian Daffodill. 6 *Narciſſus Autumnalis minor.* The leſſer Winter Daffodill. 7 *Narciſſus Autumnalis maior.* The greater Winter Daffodill.

1. *Narcissus medio purpureus præcox.* The early purple ringed Daffodill.

This early Daffodill hath many long grayish greene leaues, somewhat narrower and stiffer then the former common white Daffodill, among which riseth vp a long naked hollow stalke (as all other Daffodils haue) bearing at the toppe one flower, and seldome two, made of sixe long white leaues, standing close together about the stalke; the cup is yellow, and so flat, that it might rather bee called a crowne : for it standeth very close to the middle, and very open at the brimmes, circled with a reddish or purple coloured ring, hauing certaine chiues in the middle of it also. The smell hereof is very sweete, exceeding many other.

2. *Narcissus medio purpureus serotinus.* The late purple ringed Daffodill.

The leaues of this Daffodill are alwayes broader then the former early one, and some are very neare twice as broad : the flower is very like the former, being large, and his leaues standing close one to the side of another; the ring likewise that compasseth the yellow coronet, is sometimes of a paler reddish purple, and sometimes as deepe a red as the former : so that it differeth not in any other materiall point, then that it flowreth not vntill the other is past and gone. The sent of this is like the former, the roote hereof is greater, as well as the leafe and flower.

3. *Narcissus medio purpureus maximus.*
The great white purple ringed Daffodill.

There is another kinde, whose flower (as well as leaues and rootes) is larger then any other of this kinde, which onely maketh it a distinct sort from the other : it flowreth also with the later sort of these purple ringed Daffodils.

4. *Narcissus medio purpureus stellaris.* The starry purple ringed Daffodill.

This Daffodill hath his leaues a little narrower and greener then the former sorts, the flower also of this hath his sixe white leaues not so broad, but narrower, and seeming longer then they, not closing together, but standing apart one from another, making it seeme like a white starre : it hath also a yellow coronet in the middle, circled about with purple, like the former. This doth smell nothing so sweete as the first, but yet hath a good sent.

The Place.

The first, third, and fourth of these Daffodils, haue alwayes beene sent vs from Constantinople among other bulbous rootes, so that wee know no further of their naturall places.

The second groweth in many places of Europe, both in Germany, France, and Italy, as Clusius hath noted.

The Time.

The first flowreth very early in March, euen with the first Daffodils. The second, third, and fourth, about a moneth after.

The Names.

The early and starre Daffodils, haue been sent vs by the Turkish name of *Deuebohini,* and *Serincade.* But their names, they haue receiued since, to bee endenizond with vs, are set downe in their seuerall titles.

Narcissus Persicus. The Persian Daffodill.

This Persian Daffodill differeth from all other kindes of Daffodils in his manner of
growing,

growing, for it neuer hath leaues and flowers at one time together, wherein it is like vnto a Colchicum, yet in roote and leafe it is a Daffodill. The roote is a little blackish on the outside, somewhat like the roote of the Autumne Daffodill, from whence riseth vp a naked foote stalke, bearing one pale yellow flower, breaking through a thinne skinne, which first enclosed it, composed of six leaues, the three outermost being a little larger then the rest, in the middle of the flower there are six small chiues, and a longer pointell. The whole flower is of an vnpleasant sent : After the flower is past, come vp the leaues, sometimes before Winter, but most vsually after the deepe of Winter is past with vs, in the beginning of the yeare, which are broad, long, and of a pale greene colour, like the leaues of other Daffodils, but not greene as the Autumne Daffodill is, and besides they doe a little twine themselues, as some of the Pancratium, or bastard Sea Daffodils doe.

Narcissus Autumnalis maior. The greater Autumne or Winter Daffodill.

The greater Autumne Daffodill riseth vp with three or foure faire broad and short leaues at the first, but afterwards grow longer, of a very deepe or darke greene colour, in the middle of which riseth vp a short, stiffe, round footestalke, bearing one faire yellow flower on the head thereof (inclosed at the first in a thinne skinne, or huske) and consisteth of six leaues as the former, with certaine chiues in the middle, as all or most other Daffodils haue, which passeth away without shew of any seed, or head for seed, although vnder the head there is a little greene knot, which peraduenture would beare seede, if our sharpe Winters did not hinder it. The roote is great and round, couered ouer with a blackish skinne or coate.

Narcissus Autumnalis minor. The lesser Autumne or Winter Daffodill.

Clusius setteth downe, that the manner of the flowring of this lesser Daffodill, is more like vnto the Persian Daffodill, then vnto the former greater Autumne kind; but I doe finde that it doth in the same sort, as the greater kinde, rise vp with his leaues first, and the flowers a while after : the flower of this is lesser, and a little paler then the flower of the greater kinde, but consisting in like sort of six leaues, narrow and sharpe pointed; the greene leaues also are almost of as deepe a greene colour, as the greater kinde, but smaller and narrower, and a little hollow in the middle. The roote is also alike, but lesser, and couered with a blackish skinne as the former. This hath sometimes borne blacke round seede in three square heads.

The Place.

The Persian Daffodill hath beene sent sometimes, but very seldome, among other rootes from Constantinople, and it is probable by the name whereby it was sent, that it should naturally grow in Persia.

The other two haue likewise beene sent from Constantinople, and as it is thought, grow in Thracia, or thereabouts.

The Time.

They all doe flower much about one time, that is, about the end of September, and in October.

The Names.

The first hath been sent by the name of *Serincade Persiana*, and thereupon is called *Narcissus Persicus*, The Persian Daffodill.

The other two haue been thought by diuers to be Colchica, and so haue they called them, vpon no other ground, but that their flower is in forme and time somewhat like Colchicum, when as if they had marked them better, they might plainly discerne, that in all other things they did resemble Daffodils; but now the names of *Colchicum luteum maius, & minus*, is quite

lost,

loft, time hauing worne them out, and they are called by moſt Herbariſts now adayes, *Narciſſus Autumnalis maior & minor*, The greater and the leſſer Autumne Daffodill.

Thus farre haue I proceeded with thoſe Daffodils, that hauing broad leaues, beare but one ſingle flower, or two at the moſt vpon a ſtalke: And now to proceed with the reſt, that haue broad leaues, and beare ſingle flowers, but many vpon a ſtalke.

Narciſſus Africanus aureus maior. The great yellow Daffodill of Africa.

This braue and ſtately Daffodill hath many very long and broad leaues, of a better greene colour, then many others that are grayiſh, among which appeareth a ſtalke, not riſing to the height of the leaues, bearing at the toppe out of a skinnie hoſe many faire, goodly, and large flowers, to the number of ten or twelue, if the roote bee well growne, and ſtand in a warme place, euery one being larger then any of the French, Spaniſh, or Turkie Daffodils, that beare many ſingle flowers vpon a ſtalke, and commeth neere vnto the bigneſſe of the Engliſh Daffodill, called Primroſe Peerleſſe, before deſcribed, or that French kinde hereafter deſcribed, that beareth the largeſt flowers, many vpon a ſtalke (which ſome would make to bee a kinde of that Engliſh Daffodill, but bearing more flowers) and of a faire ſhining yellow colour, hauing large, round, and open cups or boules, yellower then the outer leaues; and is of ſo exceeding ſweete a ſent, that it doth rather offend the ſenſes by the aboundance thereof: the roote is great, and couered with a blackiſh browne coate or skinne.

Narciſſus Africanus aureus minor. The leſſer Barbary Daffodill.

This leſſer kinde is very neere the ſame with the former, but that it lacketh ſomewhat of his ſtatelineſſe of height, largeneſſe of flower and cup (being of a paler yellow) and beauty of colour, for it beareth neither of theſe equall vnto the former, but is in them all inferiour. And thus by this priuatiue, you may vnderſtand his poſitiue, and that ſhall be ſufficient at this time.

Narciſſus Byzantinus totus luteus. The yellow Turkie Daffodill.

Whereas the laſt deſcribed, came ſhort of the beauty of the former, ſo this lacketh of that beauty is in the laſt; for this, although it haue very long leaues, and a high ſtalke, yet the flowers are neither ſo many, as not being aboue foure or fiue, nor ſo large, being not much greater then the ordinary French Daffodill hereafter deſcribed, nor the colour ſo faire, but much paler, and the cup alſo ſmaller; and herein conſiſteth the chiefeſt differences betweene this, and both the other, but that the ſent of this is alſo weaker.

The Place.

The firſt and the ſecond grow in Barbary, about Argier, and Fez, as by the relation of them, that haue brought them into theſe parts, wee haue been enformed.

The laſt hath been often brought from Conſtantinople among other varieties of Daffodils, but from whence they receiued them, I could neuer learne.

The Time.

Theſe Daffodils do flower very early, euen with the firſt ſort of Daffodils, I meane after they haue been accuſtomed vnto our climate: for oftentimes vpon their firſt bringing ouer, they flower in Ianuary or February, eſpecially if they be preſerued from the froſts, and kept in any warme place; for they are very tender, and will ſoone periſh, being left abroad.

The Names.

The firſt is called by diuers in French, *Narciſſe d'Algiers*, and in many

places

places of the Low Countries, *Narciffen van Heck*, or *Narciffus Heckius* ; by diuers others *Narciffus Africanus aureus maior*, we may call it in Englifh, The great African Daffodill, or the great Barbary Daffodill, or the great yellow Daffodill of Argiers, which you pleafe.

The fecond hath no other variation of name, then a diminutiue of the former, as is fet downe in the title.

The third is no doubt the fame, that Clufius fetteth downe in the twelfth Chapter of his fecond Booke of the Hiftory of more rare plants, and maketh the fourth fort, which came from Conftantinople, and may alfo be the fame, which he maketh his fifth, which (as he faith) he receiued from Doctour *Simor Touar* of Seuill in Spaine. Wee call it, from the place from whence we receiued it, *Narciffus Byzantinus*, with the addition of *totus luteus*, to put a diffrence from other forts that come from thence alfo : in Englifh, The yellow fingle Daffodill of Turkie.

Narciffus Sulphureus maior. The greater Lemon coloured Daffodill.

The greater of thefe Daffodils, beareth three or foure greene and very long leaues, a foote and a halfe long at the leaft, among which rifeth vp a round, yet crefted ftalke, not fo high as the leaues, bearing fiue or fixe fingle flowers thereon, euery one of them being greater then the ordinary French or Italian Daffodils, with many flowers vpon a ftalke ; of a faint, but yet pleafant yellow colour at the firft, which after they haue been in flower a fortnight or thereabouts, change into a deeper, or more fullen yellow colour : the cup in the middle is likewife larger, then in thofe formerly named, and of a deeper yellow colour then the outer leaues, hauing onely three chiues within it. The fmell is very pleafant.

Narciffus Sulphureus minor. The leffer Lemon coloured Daffodill.

This leffer Daffodill hath broader and fhorter leaues then the former, of the colour of other Daffodils, and not greene like the former : the ftalke of this rifeth vp higher then the leaues, bearing foure or fiue flowers vpon fhorter footeftalkes, and no bigger then the French Daffodill, of a pale yellow, which moft doe call a Brimftone colour, the cup or rather crowne in the middle, is fmall, and broad open, of a little deeper yellow, hauing many chiues within it, and is as it were fprinkled ouer with a kinde of mealineffe. The fmell of this is not full fo pleafant as the former.

The Place.

Both thefe haue been gathered on the Pyrenæan Mountaines, and both likewife haue been fent out of Italy.

The Time.

They both flower in the middle time of the Daffodils flowring, that is, in Aprill.

The Names.

They haue their Latine names expreffed in their titles, and fo are their Englifh alfo, if you pleafe fo to let them paffe ; or elfe according to the Latine, you may call them, The greater and the leffer Brimftone coloured Daffodils ; fome haue called them *Narciffus Italicus*, but the Italians themfelues haue fent them by the name of *Narciffo Solfarigno*.

Narciffus totus albus polyanthos. The milke white Daffodill many vpon a ftalke.

The leaues of this Daffodill are of a meane fize, both for length and breadth, yet fomewhat greener then in the ordinary forts, that haue fome whiteneffe in them : the flowers are many vpon the ftalke, as fmall for the moft part, as any of thefe kindes that beare many together, being wholly of a milke, or rather fnow white colour, both the cuppe, which is fmall, and the outer leaues that compaffe it; after which come fmall heads, wherein is contained round blacke feede, as all other Daffodils doe, although fome greater, and others leffer, according to the proportion of the plants: the roote is couered ouer with a blackifh skinne or coate; the fmell is very fweete.

There are two other forts more of this kinde, the differences whereof are, that the one hath his leaues fomewhat broader, and the flowers greater then the former: And the other fmaller leaues and flowers alfo, whofe cups being fmall, are neuer feene fully open, but as it were halfe clofed at the brimmes.

Narciffus latifolius totus albus, mediocri calice reflexus.
The milke white Daffodill with the great cup.

There is yet another fort of thefe milke white Daffodils, whofe leaues are as broad as any of the former, and whofe cup in the middle of the flower, is fomewhat larger then in any of the leffer forts, and leffer then in the greater kinde: but the leaues of the flowers doe a little turne themfelues vpwards, which maketh a chiefe difference.

The Place.

Thefe Daffodils grow in Spaine, from whence I receiued many that flourifhed a while, but perifhed by fome fierce cold Winters: they likewife grow in France, from whence many alfo haue been brought vnto vs. They haue likewife been fent from Conftantinople to vs, among other kindes of Daffodils.

The Time.

They that come from Conftantinople, for the moft part doe flower earlier then the other, euen after they are accuftomed to our ayre. Some of them flower notwithftanding in the end of March, the reft in Aprill.

The Names.

They are vfually called *Narciffus totus albus polyanthos*, adding thereunto the differences of *maior, medius*, and *minor*, that is, The milke white Daffodill, the greater, the middle, and the leffer; for fo fome doe diftinguifh them. The laft, for diftinction, hath his name in his title fufficient to expreffe him.

1. Narciffus Narbonenfis, fiue medio luteus præcox,
The early French Daffodill.

The leaues of this Daffodill, fpring vp out of the ground a moneth or two fometimes before the other of this kinde, that follow; being alfo fhorter, and narrower: the ftalke likewife is not very high, bearing diuers flowers at the top, breaking through a thinne skinne, as is vfuall with all the Daffodils, euery one whereof is fmall, confifting of fix white leaues, and a fmall yellow cup in the middle, which is of a prettie fmall fent, nothing fo ftrong as many others: the roote is great and round, and feldome parteth into of-fets, euen as all the other that follow, bearing many fingle flowers, doe.

2. Narciffus Narbonenfis vulgaris. The ordinary French Daffodill.

This Daffodill hath long and broad greene leaues, a little hollowifh in the middle, and edged on both fides; the ftalke is a foote and a halfe high, bearing at the toppe diuers flowers, fomewhat larger then the former, confifting of fix white leaues, fomewhat round; the cup is yellow in the middle, fmall and round, like vnto an Acorne cuppe, or a little fuller in the middle: this is the forme of that fort which was firft
brought

1 *Narciſſus Africanus aureus maior.* The great yellow Daffodill of Africa.   2 *Narciſſus Africanus luteus minor.* The leſſer yellow Daffodill of Africa.   3 *Narciſſus Narbonenſis medio luteus.* The French Daffodill.   4 *Narciſſus Piſanus, vel totus albus.* The Italian Daffodill, or the all white Daffodill.   5 *Narciſſus Muſſart.* Muſſart his Daffodill.   6 *Narciſſus Anglicus polyanthos.* The great Engliſh Daffodill.

brought vnto vs : But since there is found out some, whose cup is shorter, others flatter, some of a paler, others of a deeper yellow colour, and some that haue their cuppe longer then the rest. The rootes of them all are couered with a blackish skin or coate.

3. *Narcissus Narbonensis maior amplo flore.*
The French Daffodill with great flowers.

The leaues of this Daffodill are somewhat like vnto the last, but not so broad, yet full as long, and spring sooner out of the ground, yet not so early as the first of these kindes: the stalke hereof is flatter, and riseth higher, bearing foure or fiue flowers, much larger then any of this kinde ; for euery one of them doth equall the English Daffodill, before described, but whiter then it, and the yellow cup larger, and more open then in any of the rest. The roote of this is not so great, or round, as the former, but is more plentifull in of-sets, then any other of these French, or Italian kindes.

4. *Narcissus Pisanus.* The Italian Daffodill.

This Italian Daffodill hath his leaues as large, or larger then the second French Daffodill, and his stalke somewhat higher, bearing many white flowers, very like vnto the common French Daffodill, but somewhat larger also; and the yellow cup in the middle likewise is larger, and rounder, then is vsually seen in any of the French kinds, except the last with the greatest flowers.

5. *Narcissus mediocroceus polyanthos.*
The French Daffodill with Saffron coloured cups.

This French Daffodill hath diuers leaues of a grayish greene colour, not so broad or long as the last recited Daffodill, but comming neerer vnto the second French kinde, the flowers likewise are white, and many vpon a stalke, like thereunto, but the yellow cup is somewhat large, and circled with a Saffron like brimme or edge, which maketh the chiefest difference.

6. *Narcissus mediocroceus alter, dictus Mussart.* Mussart his Daffodill.

The affinity between this & the last, (for it is not the same to be expressed vnder one title) hath made me ioyne it next vnto it, yet because it hath a notable difference, it deserueth a place by himselfe. The leaues are large and long, and the flowers, being white, are larger also then in any other, except the greatest, but the cup hereof is small and short, rather seeming a coronet then a cup, of a deepe Saffron colour all about the brimmes or edges.

7. *Narcissus Anglicus polyanthos.* The great English Daffodill.

This Daffodill hath his leaues not much broader or longer, then the French kinde with great flowers, before described, the stalke with flowers riseth not fully so high as it, bearing many flowers thereon, not altogether so white, yet whiter then the former English Daffodill, called Primrose Peerlesse, but nothing so large, and with short, broad, and almost round leaues, standing close one vnto another : the yellow cup in the middle is bowle fashion, being somewhat deeper then in any of the former kinds, but not much greater : the smell hereof is very sweete and pleasant.

8. *Narcissus Narbonensis, siue medio luteus serotinus maior.*
The greater late flowring French Daffodill.

The roote as well as the leaues of this Daffodill, are greater, larger, broader, and longer then in any other of the former French, or Italian kindes ; the stalke is as high as any of them, bearing at the toppe fiue or sixe white flowers, standing open spread like a starre, and not close together, euery one whereof is large, and round pointed,

the

the cup is yellow, fmall and fhort, yet not lying flat to the flower, but a little ftanding out with fome threads in the middle, as all the former Daffodils haue. This is not fo fweete as the earlier kindes.

9. Narciffus medioluteus alter ferotinus calice breui.
The leffer late flowring French Daffodill.

This Daffodill is of the fame kinde with the laft defcribed, the onely difference is, that it is leffer, and the yellow cuppe in the middle of the flower, is fomewhat fhorter then the former, although the former be fhorter then many others, otherwife it differeth not, no not in time; for it flowreth late as the former doth.

The Place.

Thefe Daffodils haue been brought vs from diuers places: The firft and fecond grow naturally in many places of Spaine, that are open to the Sea: they grow likewife about Mompelier, and thofe parts in France. They haue been likewife fent among many other forts of Daffodils from Conftantinople, fo that I may thinke, they grow in fome places neere thereunto.

The fourth groweth plentifully in Italy, about Pifa in Tufcane, from whence we haue had plants to furnifh our Gardens.

The feuenth is accounted beyond Sea to be naturall of our Country, but I know not any with vs that haue it, but they haue had it from them.

The reft haue been brought at diuers times, but wee know no further of their naturall places.

The Time.

The firft flowreth earlier then any of the reft by a moneth, euen in the beginning of March, or earlier, if the weather be milde. The other in Aprill, fome a little before or after another. The late kinds flower not vntill May.

The Names.

There can be no more faid of the names of any of them, then hath beene fet out in their titles; for they diftinguifh euery fort as fitly as we can: onely fome doe call the firft two forts, by the name of *Donax Narbonenfis.*

After all thefe Daffodils, that hauing broad leaues beare fingle flowers, either one or many vpon a ftalke, I fhall now goe on to fet forth thofe broad leafed Daffodils, that carry double flowers, either one or many vpon a ftalke together, in the fame order that we haue vfed before.

1. Narciffus albus multiplex. The double white Daffodill.

The leaues of this Daffodill are not very broad, but rather of a meane fize, being of the fame largeneffe with the leaues of the purple ringed Daffodill, the ftalke rifeth vp to be a foote and a halfe high, bearing out of a thinne white skinne or hofe, one flower and no more, confifting of many leaues, of a faire white colour, the flower is larger then any other double white Daffodill, hauing euery leafe, efpecially the outermoft, as large almoft as any leafe of the fingle Daffodill with the yellow cup, or purple ring. Sometimes it happeneth, that the flower is very little double, and almoft fingle, but that is either in a bad ground, or for that it hath ftood long in a place without remouing; for then it hath fuch a great encreafe of rootes about it, that it draweth away into many parts, the nourifhment that fhould be for a few: but if you doe tranfplant it, taking away the of-fets, and fet his rootes fingle, it will then thriue, and beare his flower as goodly and double, as I haue before defcribed it: and is very fweete.

2. Narciffus mediopurpureus multiplex. The double purple ringed Daffodill.

There is little difference in the leaues of this kinde, from the leaues of the fingle purple

ple ringed Daffodill; for it is probable it is of the same kinde, but by natures gift (and not by any humane art) made more plentifull, which abideth constant, and hath not that dalliance, which oftentimes nature sheweth, to recreate the senses of men for the present, and appeareth not againe in the same forme : the chiefest difference is, that the flower (being but sometimes one on a stalke, and sometimes two) consisteth of six white outer leaues, as large as the leaues of the single kinde, hauing many small yellow peeces, edged with purple circles round about them, instead of a cup ; and in the middle of these peeces, stand other six white leaues, lesser then the former, and a yellow cup edged with a purple circle likewise, parted into peeces, and they comprehend a few other white leaues, smaller then any of the other, hauing among them some broken peeces of the cup, with a few chiues also in the middle of the flower. The flower is very sweete.

There is of this kinde another, whose flower hath not so plaine a distinction, of a triple rowe of leaues in it : but the whole flower is confusedly set together, the outer leaues being not so large, and the inner leaues larger then the former ; the broken yellow cuppe, which is tipt with purple, running diuersly among the leaues ; so that it sheweth a fairer, and more double flower then the former, as it is indeed.

3. *Narcissus medioluteus corona duplici.*
The Turkie Daffodill with a double crowne.

This Daffodill hath three or foure leaues, as large and long almost, as the great double Daffodill of Constantinople next following hath : the stalke likewise is very neere as great, but as high altogether, bearing at the toppe foure or fiue flowers, the leaues whereof are as large, as of the first or second kinde of French Daffodils, before described, but not altogether of so pure a white colour ; and being six in number, stand like the former single French Daffodils, but that the yellow cup in the middle of this is thicke and double, or as it were crumpled together, not standing very high to be conspicuous, but abiding lowe and short, so that it is not presently marked, vnlesse one looke vpon it precisely ; yet is exceeding sweete. The roote is like vnto the roote of the purple ringed Daffodill, or somewhat bigger.

4. *Narcissus Chalcedonicus flore pleno albo polyanthos.*
The double white Daffodill of Constantinople.

This beautifull and goodly Daffodill (wherewith all Florists greatly desire to bee acquainted, as well for the beauty of his double flowers, as also for his superabounding sweete smell, one stalke with flowers being instead of a nosegay) hath many very broad, and very long leaues, somewhat greener then gray, among which riseth vp a strong round stalke, being sometimes almost flat, and ribbed, bearing foure or fiue, or more white flowers at the toppe, euery one being very great, large, and double, the leaues being confusedly set together, hauing little peeces of a yellow cup running among them, without any shew of that purple ring that is in the former, and fall away without bearing seed, euen as all, or most other double flowers doe : the smell is so exceeding sweet and strong, that it will soone offend the senses of any, that shall smell much vnto it : the roote is great and thicke, couered with a blackish coate.

5. *Narcissus Chalcedonicus fimbriatus multiplex polyanthos.*
The great double purple ringed Daffodill of Constantinople.

This Daffodill differeth very little or nothing in leafe from the former, the onely difference is in the flowers, which although they bee double, and beare many vpon a stalke, like vnto them, yet this hath the peeces of the yellow cuppes tipt with purple, as if they were shred or scattered among the white leaues, whereas the other hath only the yellow, without any shew of purple tips vpon them : the smell of this is as strong as of the other.

6. *Narcissus*

1 *Narcissus albus multiplex.* The double white Daffodill. 2 *Narcissus medioluteus corona duplici.* The Turkie Daffodill with a double crowne. 3 *Narcissus mediopurpureus multiplex.* The double purple ringed Daffodill. 4 *Narcissus Chalcedonicus flore pleno albo polyanthos.* The double white Daffodill of Constantinople.

6. *Narcissus Cyprius flore pleno luteo polyanthos.*
The double yellow Daffodill of Cyprus.

The leaues of this Daffodill are almost as broad and long as the former, the stalke is a foot high and more, bearing foure or fiue flowers on the top, euery one very double, and of a fine pale yellow colour, of a strong heady sent. The root of this is also like the former.

The Place.

The first of these Daffodils, was first brought into England by M^r. Iohn de Franqueuille the elder, who gathered it in his owne Countrey of Cambray, where it groweth wilde, from whose sonne, M^r. Iohn de Franqueuille, now liuing, we all haue had it. The rest haue come from Constantinople at seuerall times ; and the last is thought to come from Cyprus. Wee haue it credibly affirmed also, that it groweth in Barbary about Fez and Argiers. Some of the double white kindes grow in Candy , and about Aleppo also.

The Time.

The Turkie kindes doe for the most part all flower early, in the end of March, or beginning of Aprill at the furthest, and the first double, about the middle or end of Aprill.

The Names.

All these Daffodils , except the first , haue had diuers Turkish names set vpon the packets, wherein they haue been sent, but there is small regard of certainty to be expected from them ; for that the name *Serincade*, without any more addition, which is a single Daffodill , hath beene imposed vpon that parcell of rootes, that haue borne most of them double flowers of diuers sorts ; and the name *Serincade Catamer lale*, which signifieth a double flowred Daffodill, hath had many single white flowers, with yellow cups, and some whose flowers haue been wholly white, cuppe and all, and some purple ringed, and double also among them.   Their names, whereby they are knowne and called with vs, are, as fitly as may be, imposed in their titles: And this I hope shall suffice, to haue spoken of these sorts of Daffodils.

Hauing finished the discourse of the former sort of broad leafed Daffodils, it is fit to proceede to the next , which are *Angustifolios Narcissos*, those Daffodils that haue narrow leaues, and first to set downe those that beare single flowers , whether one or many flowers vpon a stalke, and then those that beare double flowers in the same manner.

Narcissus Virgineus. The Virginia Daffodill.

This plant I thought fittest to place here in the beginning of this *Classis*, not finding where better to shroud it. It hath two or three long, and very narrow leaues, as greene as the leaues of the great *Leucoium bulbosum*, and shining withall , which grow sometimes reddish, especially at the edges : the stalke riseth vp a spanne high , bearing one flower and no more on the head thereof, standing vpright like a little Lilly or Tulipa, made of six leaues, wholly white, both within and without, except that at the bottome next to the stalke, and a little on the backside of the three outer leaues , it hath a small dash or shew of a reddish purple colour : it hath in the middle a few chiues , standing about a small head pointed ; which head groweth to bee small and long , containing small blackish flat seede : the roote is small, long , and round, a little blackish on the outside, and white on the inside.

The

The Place.

This bulbous plant was brought vs from Virginia, where they grow a-boundantly ; but they hardly thriue and abide in our Gardens to beare flowers.

The Time.

It flowreth in May, and feldome before.

The Names.

The Indians in Virginia do call it *Attamufco,* fome among vs do call it *Lilionarciffus Virginianus,* of the likeneffe of the flower to a Lilly, and the leaues and roote to a Daffodill. Wee for breuity doe call it *Narciffus Virgineus,* that is, The Daffodill of Virginia, or elfe you may call it according to the former Latine name, The Lilly Daffodill of Virginia, which you will ; for both names may ferue well to expreffe the plant.

Narciffus anguftifolius albidus præcox oblongo calice.
The early white narrow leafed Daffodill with a long cup.

This Daffodill hath three or foure narrow, long, and very greene leaues, a foote long for the moft part : the ftalke rifeth not vp fo high as the leaues, whereon ftandeth one flower, not altogether fo great as the late flowring Daffodill, with a long cuppe, defcribed before among the broad leafed ones, which confifteth of fix pale coloured leaues, not pure white, but hauing a wafh of light yellow among the white : the cuppe in the middle is round and long, yet not fo long as to bee accounted a baftard Daffodill, within which is a middle pointell, compaffed with fix chiues, hauing yellow mealy pendents.

The Place.

This Daffodill groweth with the other forts of broad leafed ones, on the Pyrenæan Mountaines, from whence they haue beene brought vnto vs, to furnifh our Gardens.

The Time.

It flowreth early, a moneth before the other forts of the fame fafhion, that is, in the beginning of March, if the time be milde, which the other before fpoken of doe not.

The Names.

It hath no other name that I know, then is expreffed in the title.

2. *Narciffus mediocroceus tenuifolius.* The fmall Daffodill with a Saffron crown.

This fmall Daffodill hath foure or fiue narrow leaues about a fpanne long, among which rifeth vp a ftalke fome nine inches high, bearing at the toppe one fmall white flower, made of fix leaues, with a fmall yellow cup in the middle, fhadowed ouer at the brimmes with a Saffron colour : the roote is fmall, round, and little long withall, couered with a blackifh skinne or coate.

3. *Narciffus minimus mediopurpureus.* The leaft purple ringed Daffodill.

This little Daffodill hath fmall narrow leaues, fhorter by much then any of the purple ringed Daffodils, before defcribed : the ftalke and flower keepe an equall proportion to the reft of the plant, being in forme and colour of the flower, like vnto the

H 2   Starre

Starre Daffodill before recited , but vnlike in the greatnesse : this also is to bee obserued, that the purple colour that circleth the brimmes of the cuppe , is so small , that
sometimes it is not well perceiued.

4. *Narcissus minimus Iuncifolij flore*. The least Daffodill of all.

This least Daffodill hath two or three whitish greene leaues, narrower then the two
last recited Daffodils, and shorter by halfe, being not aboue two or three inches long,
the stalke likewise is not aboue three or foure inches high, bearing one single flower at
the toppe , somewhat bigger then the smalnesse of the plant should seeme to beare,
very like vnto the least Rush Daffodill, and of the same bignesse , or rather somewhat
bigger, being of a faint yellow colour, both leaues, and cup, or crowne, (if you please
so to call it) ; for the middle part is spread very much, euen to the middle of the leaues
almost, and lyeth flat open vpon the flower : the roote is small, euen the smallest of any
Daffodill, and couered with a blackish skinne or coate.

The Place.

The first of these Daffodils haue beene brought vs from the Pyrenæan
Mountaines, among a number of other rare plants, and the last by a French
man, called Francis le Veau, the honestest roote-gatherer that euer came o-
uer to vs. The second was sent to Mʳ.Iohn de Franqueuille,before remembred , who imparted it to mee , as hee hath done many other good things;
but his naturall place wee know not.

The Time.

They all flower about the latter end of Aprill.

The Names.

Being brought without names, wee haue giuen them their names according to their face and fashion, as they are set downe in their titles.

Narcissus Autumnalis minor albus. The little white Autumne Daffodill.

This little Autumne Daffodill riseth with his flowers first out of the ground,without
any leaues at all. It springeth vp with one or two stalkes about a finger long, euery one
bearing out of a small huske one small white flower , laid open abroad like vnto the
Starre white Daffodill , before spoken of : in the middle of the flower is a small yellow cup of a meane size, and after the flower is past, there commeth in the same place
a small head, containing small, round, blacke seede, like vnto the Autumne Hyacinth:
the leaues come vp after the seede is ripe and gone, being small and narrow, not much
bigger then the Autumne Hyacinth : the roote is small and blackish on the outside.

The Place.

This Daffodill groweth in Spaine, where Clusius saw it , and brought it
into these parts.

The Time.

It flowreth in the beginning of Autumne, and his seede is ripe in the end
of October in those hot Countries, but in ours it will scarce abide to shew a
flower.

The Names.

The Spaniards, as Clusius reporteth, call it *Tonada,* and he vpon the sight
thereof,

1 *Narcissus Virgineus.* The Virginian Daffodill. 2 *Narcissus minimus luncifolij flore.* The least Daffodill of all. 3 *Narcissus Autumnalis minor albus.* The little white Autumne Daffodill. 4 *Narcissus albus Autumnalis medio obsoletus.* The white Autumne Daffodill with a sullen crown. 5 *Narcissus luncifolius maximus amplo calice.* The great Iunquilia with the largest flower or cup. 6 *Narcissus totus albus flore plano Virginianus.* The double white Daffodill of Virginia.

thereof, *Narciſſus Autumnalis minor albus*, and wee in Engliſh thereafter, The little white Autumne Daffodill.

Narciſſus albus Autumnalis medio obſoletus.
The white Autumne Daffodill with a ſullen crowne.

This Autumne Daffodill hath two or three leaues at the moſt, and very narrow, ſo that ſome doe reckon it among the Ruſh Daffodils, being ſomewhat broad at the bottome, and more pointed at the toppe, betweene theſe leaues commeth vp the ſtalke, bearing vſually two flowers and no more at the toppe, made of ſixe white leaues a peece, pointed and not round : the cup is ſmall and round, like vnto the cup or crowne of the leaſt Ruſh Daffodill, of a yellow colour at the bottome, but toward the edge of a dunne or ſullen colour.

Narciſſus anguſtifolius luteus ſemper florens Caccini.
The yellow Italian Daffodill of Caccini.

This Daffodill beareth a number of ſmall, long, narrow, and very greene leaues, broader then the leaues of any Ruſh Daffodill, among which riſe vp diuers ſtalkes, bearing at the head two or three flowers a peece, each of them being ſmall and yellow, the cup or crowne is ſmall alſo, of a deeper yellow then the flower. The Nobleman of Florence, who firſt ſent this plant to Chriſtian Porret at Leyden, after the death of Carolus Cluſius, writeth that euery ſtalke doth beare with him more ſtore of flowers, then are formerly ſet downe, and that it neuer ceaſeth to beare flowers, but that after one or moe ſtalkes haue been in flower together, and are paſt, there ſucceed other in their places.

The Place.

The firſt is naturall of Spain, the naturall place of the other is not known to vs.

The Time.

The times of the flowring, are ſet downe both in the title and in the deſcriptions ; the one to be in Autumne, the other to be all the Summer long.

The Names.

The Latine names are impoſed on them, as are fitteſt for them, and the laſt by that honourable man that ſent it, which is moſt fit to continue, and not to bee changed. But wee, to let it bee knowne by an Engliſh name to Engliſh people, haue entituled it, The yellow Italian Daffodill of Caccini: if any man can giue it a more proper name, I ſhall bee therewith right well content.

Narciſſus anguſtifolius, ſiue Iuncifolius maximus amplo calice.
The great Iunquilia with the large flower or cup.

Although this Daffodill importeth by his name, not to be of this family, but of the next, conſidering it is ſo like vnto them, but bigger ; yet I haue thought good to place it in the end of theſe narrow leafed Daffodils, as being indifferent, whether it ſhould bee referred to this or to that. For this carrieth diuers long greene leaues, like vnto the other Ruſh Daffodils, but thicker and broader, ſo that it may without any great errour, bee reckoned among theſe narrow leafed Daffodils, bearing at the toppe two or three very faire large flowers, with a large and more open cuppe, then in any other of the Ruſh Daffodils, both of them of a faire yellow colour, yet the cuppe a little deeper then the flower, and a little crumpled about the edges, and hath a pretty ſharpe ſent : the roote is greater and longer then the other Ruſh Daffodill, and couered likewiſe with a blackiſh coate.

The

The Place.

We haue this in Gardens onely, and haue not heard of his naturall place.

The Time.

It flowreth in Aprill.

The Names.

I leaue it indifferent, as I said, whether you will call it *Narciſſus anguſtifolius*, or *Iuncifolius magno calice*, or *maximus*, becauſe it is the greateſt of all the reſt of that kinde.

Narciſſus totus albus flore pleno Virginianus.
The double white Daffodill of Virginia.

The roote of this Daffodill, is very like vnto the former ſingle Virginia Daffodill, ſet forth in the firſt place of this ranke of narrow leafed Daffodils, but that it is a little bigger and rounder, being a little long withall, and blackiſh alſo on the outſide, as that is: from whence riſeth vp two leaues, ſomewhat broader then the former: but of a like greenneſſe: the ſtalke riſeth vp betweene theſe two leaues, about a ſpan high, or not much higher, bearing one faire double ſnow white flower, very like in the faſhion vnto the pale yellow double Daffodill, or baſtard Daffodill of Robinus, hereafter deſcribed: For it is in the like manner laid open flat, and compoſed of ſix rowes of leaues, euery rowe lying in order iuſt oppoſite, or one before another, whereof thoſe ſix leaues that make the firſt or outermoſt courſe, are the greateſt, and all the reſt lying, as I ſaid, one vpon or before another, are euery rowe ſmaller then others from the middle of this flower, thruſteth forth a ſmall long pointed forke or horne, white as the flower is.

The Place.

The place is named to be Virginia, but in what part it is not known to vs.

The Time.

It flowreth in the end of Aprill.

The Names.

It may be that this doth grow among the former ſingle kinde, and called by the ſame name Attamuſco, for that the plant is not much differing, yet hereof I am not certaine: But we, from the forme and countenance of the plant, doe call it *Narciſſus Virginianus*, The Virginian Daffodill, and becauſe it beareth a double flower, it hath the title of double added vnto it.

The third order of Daffodils, I ſaid in the beginning, was of *Iuncifolios*, Ruſh Daffodils, which are now next to be entreated of, I ſhall herein keepe the ſame order I vſed in the former; but becauſe I finde none of this order, that beare but one flower vpon a ſtalke, I muſt begin with thoſe that beare many.

1. *Narciſſus Iuncifolius albus.* The white Iunquilia.

This white Ruſh Daffodill hath ſmall long leaues, a little broader, and of a whiter greene colour then the ordinary yellow Ruſh Daffodils: the ſtalke riſeth vp halfe a foote high or more, bearing two or three ſmall white flowers vpon a ſtalke, yet ſomewhat bigger then the common yellow Ruſh Daffodill, hauing a ſmall round cuppe in the middle, white alſo as the leaues are. The ſeede is ſmall, blacke,

blacke, and round, as other feedes of Daffodils are : the roote is fmall and round, couered with a blackifh coate.

*Narciffus Iuncifolius albus magno calice.*The white Iunquilia with a great cup.

There is of this kinde another fort, that hath the cup in the middle of the flower, a
little larger then the other, but in all other things alike.

2. *Narciffus Iuncifolius flore albo reflexo.*
The white turning Iunquilia, or Rufh Daffodill.

This turning white Daffodill hath foure or fiue long greene leaues, yet fhorter and
broader then the ordinary yellow Iunquilia, and fully as greene alfo, from among
which rifeth vp a flender greene ftalke, a foote high, bearing out of a thinne skinnie
huske, three or foure, or more fnow white flowers, ftanding vpon long greene foot-
ftalkes, euery flower hanging downe his head, and turning vp his fix narrow and long
leaues, euen to the very foot-ftalke againe : from the middle of the flower hangeth
downe a long round cuppe, as white as the leaues, within which are contained three
fmall white chiues, tipt with yellow, and a fmall long pointell, thrufting out beyond
the brimmes of the cup : after the flowers are paft, there come vp in their places fmall
three fquare heads, wherein is contained very fmall, round, and blacke fhining feede :
the roote is fmall, round, and a little long withall, couered with a blackifh browne
coate or skin. The flower is quite without any good fent, or indeed rather none at all.

3. *Narciffus Iuncifolius flore Inteareflexo.*
The yellow turning Iunquilia, or Rufh Daffodill.

The leaues of this Rufh Daffodill are greater and longer then the former, and of a
paler greene colour : the ftalke rifeth fomewhat higher, bearing two or three flowers
thereon wholly of a gold yellow colour, both the cuppe and the leaues that turne vp
againe.

4. *Narciffus Iuncifolius calice albo reflexis folÿs luteis.*
The yellow turning Iunquilia with a white cup.

This Daffodill hath his long rufh-like leaues ftanding vpright as the former, betweene which rifeth vp a greene ftalke, about a foote high or more, bearing two or
three flowers thereon, whofe turning leaues are of a faire pale yellow, and the cuppe
pale white, and not fo pure a white as the former.

5. *Narciffus Iuncifolius calice luteo reflexis folÿs albidis.*
The white turning Iunquilia with a yellow cup.

As the laft had the leaues of the flower that turne vp againe yellow, and the cuppe
whitifh, fo this hath contrariwife the turning leaues of a whitifh yellow, and the long
cup yellower, elfe in his long green leaues, or any other thing, there is fmall difference.

6. *Narciffus Iuncifolius luteus magno calice.*
The Iunquilia, or Rufh Daffodill with a great cup.

This Rufh Daffodill hath bigger leaues, and longer then the ordinary yellow Rufh
Daffodill, being a little flat on the one fide, and round on the other, but of the fame
greenneffe with all the reft : the ftalke rifeth vp two foote high, bearing two, and
fometimes three flowers thereon, being of a faire yellow colour, with a large open
cup in the middle, of a little deeper yellow colour, like vnto the great Iunquilia with
the large flower, before fet downe, whereof this is a kinde, no doubt; but that is larger
and greater then this, both in leafe, flower, cup, &c. and this onely fomewhat leffe in
all parts then that.

7. *Narciffus*

1 *Narcissus Iuncifolius albus.* The white Iunquilia. 2 *Narcissus Iuncifolius flore albo reflexo.* The white turning Iunquilia. 3 *Narcissus Iuncifolius calice luteo reflexis folijs albis.* The yellow turning Iunquilia. 4 *Narcissus Iuncifolius luteus magno calice.* The yellow Iunquilia with a great cuppe. 5 *Narcissus iuncifolius luteus maior vulgaris.* The ordinary yellow Iunquilia. 6 *Narcissus iuncifolius Autumnalis flore viridi.* The greene Autumne Iunquilia. 7 *Narcissus angustifolius aureus multiplex.* The golden double narrow leafed Daffodill. 8 *Narcissus Iuncifolius flore plene.* The double Iunquilia.

7. *Narcissus Iuncifolius luteus vulgaris maior.*
The ordinary Iunquilia, or Ruſh Daffodill.

This ordinary Ruſh Daffodill hath foure or fiue long greene round leaues, like vnto Ruſhes, whereof it tooke the name : among theſe leaues riſeth vp the ſtalke, round and greene, a foote and a halfe high very often, bearing at the toppe three or foure flowers all yellow, but much ſmaller then the laſt, and ſo is the cup alſo : the ſeede is ſmall and blacke, incloſed in ſmall cornered heads; the roote is blackiſh on the outſide. The ſmell of the flower is very ſweete in all theſe ſorts of Ruſh Daffodils.

8. *Narcissus Iuncifolius luteus medius.* The ſmaller Iunquilia, or Ruſh Daffodill.

The leaues of this Daffodill are like vnto the former, but ſmaller and rounder, the ſtalke riſeth not vp ſo high, nor are the flowers ſo great, but the leaues of the flower are a little rounder, and not ſo pointed as in the former, in all things elſe alike, ſauing leſſer.

9. *Narcissus Iuncifolius luteus minor.* The leaſt Iunquilia, or Ruſh Daffodill.

This leaſt Daffodill hath fiue or ſix ſmall greene leaues, a little broader, and not ſo long as the laſt, among which riſeth vp a ſtalke almoſt a foote high, bearing one or two ſmall flowers at the toppe, of a paler yellow colour then the former, with a yellow open cuppe, or crowne rather in the middle, bigger then in either of the laſt two : the roote is very ſmall and blacke, like vnto the laſt in roundneſſe and colour.

10. *Narcissus Iuncifolius luteus albicantibus lineis diſtinctus.*
The yellow Iunquilia, or Ruſh Daffodill with white lines.

This Ruſh Daffodill hath round, greene, and long leaues, like vnto the ordinary Ruſh Daffodill, with a ſtalke bearing two or three yellow flowers, hauing leaues ſome-what round at the point or end, with a line or ſtrake of white in the middle of euerie one of them, the cup is ſhort, and crowne faſhion, a little crumpled about the brims : the ſeede, roote, or any thing elſe differeth not.

11. *Narcissus Iuncifolius Autumnalis flore viridi.*
The Autumne Ruſh Daffodill with a greene flower.

This ſtrange Ruſh Daffodill (I call it ſtrange, not onely becauſe it differeth from all others of this kinde, but alſo becauſe there are but few in theſe parts that haue had it, and fewer that doe ſtill enioy it, in that it is periſhed withall that had it) hath but one onely leafe, very long, round, and greene, in all that euer I ſaw growing, which bea-reth no flower while that greene leafe is freſh, and to bee ſeene : but afterwards the ſtalke riſeth vp, being like vnto the former greene leafe, round, naked, and greene vp to the toppe, where two or three flowers breake forth out of a ſmall thin ſkinne, euery one conſiſting of ſix ſmall and narrow greene leaues, very ſharpe pointed at the end, and as it were ending in a ſmall pricke or thorne : in the middle whereof is a ſmall round cup, or rather crowne, of the ſame colour with the leaues and ſtalke, which flower ſmelleth very ſweete, ſomewhat like vnto the reſt of the Ruſh Daffodils : this ſheweth not his flower vntill October, and the froſts quickly following after their flowring, cauſe them ſoone to periſh.

12. *Narcissus anguſtifolius aureus multiplex.*
The golden double narrow leafed Daffodill.

The leaues of this Daffodill are very narrow, and of a whitiſh greene colour, not aboue foure or fiue inches long, from among which riſeth vp a ſtalke about a foote high, bearing at the top one flower, conſiſting of ſome outer leaues, which are of a yellow

low colour, and of many other leaues in the middle being smaller, and set thicke and round together of a more yellow gold colour, but with some whiter leaues among them, the middle part a little pointing forth : the flower standeth long before it doth perfect his colour, and abideth long in flower before the colour decay : the roote is in fashion almost like the ordinary Iunquilia, or Rush Daffodill. I acknowledge this Daffodill hath not his proper place ; but because the figure is set in this table, let it thus passe at this time.

13. *Narcissus Iuncifolius luteus flore pleno.* The double Iunquilia, or Rush Daffodill.

The double Rush Daffodill hath his long greene leaues round, like the leaues of the common or ordinary Rush Daffodill, and of the same bignesse, among which riseth vp a long slender greene stalke, bearing two or three, seldome more small flowers, yellow and double, that is, with diuers rowes of leaues, hauing the yellow cup such as is in the single flower, broken into small shreads or peeces, running among the leaues of the flower, which peeces in some flowers are not so easily seene, being smaller then in others, this beareth no button or head vnder the flower for seede, his roote is round and blackish, browne on the outside, so like vnto the common Rush Daffodill, that it is almost impossible to know the one from the other.

There is another of this kinde, whose flowers are smaller, and not so double, one, *Alter minori* two, or three at the most vpon a stalke, and of lesse beauty by much. *flore.*

The Place.

All these Rush Daffodils, doe for the most part grow in Spaine and France, and on the Pyrenæan Mountaines, which are betweene Spaine and France, which Mountains are the Nourseries of many of the finest flowers, that doe adorne the Gardens of these louers of natures pride, and gathered in part by industrious, learned, generous men, inhabiting neare thereunto, and in part by such as make a gaine of their labours, bestowed vpon these things. Onely that with the greene flower was gathered in Barbary, and imparted vnto vs from France.

The Time.

They flower in the Spring, that is, in March and Aprill, except such whose time is set downe to be in Autumne.

The Names.

Their names are specified in their titles, and therefore I shall not need to set downe any further repetitions.

To conclude therefore this discourse of true Daffodils, there remaineth to speake of the Sea Daffodils, which (as I said in the beginning) is but one, that is frequent, and doth abide with vs. But there bee some others found about the Cape of good Hope, and in the West Indies, and brought into these parts rather for ostentation, then continuance, where they haue flowred only once (if peraduenture so often) so that being such strangers, of so remote Countries, and of so diuers natures, I shall but shew you some of them, rather cursorily then curiously; and but onely for your satisfaction, giue you knowledge of two or three of them, that there haue beene seene such in flower, and that they are scarce to bee seene againe, except they bee fetcht a new euery yeare that they be seene.

Narcissus Marinus, siue tertius Matthioli.
The great white Sea Daffodill, or Matthiolus his third Daffodill.

The roote of this Daffodill by long continuance, standing in one place without being remoued, groweth to be much greater and larger, then any other Daffodill whatsoeuer,

soeuer, and as bigge as any meane Squilla or Sea Onion roote, hauing many long, thicke, and white fibres, or long rootes, diuersly branched, and spread vnder the vpper part of the earth, beside some others that grow downward, and perish not euery yeare, as the fibres of all, or most of the other Daffodils doe; and therefore this plant will not thriue, and beare flowers, if it be often transplanted, but rather desire to abide in one place without remouing, as I said, and that not to be ouershadowed, or couered with other herbes standing too neare it, which then will flourish, and beare aboundantly: from this roote, which is couered with many blackish coates, ariseth six or seuen, or more leaues, twice so broad almost, as any of the former Daffodils, but not so long by halfe as many of them, being but short, in comparison of the breadth, and of a white greene colour; from the middle of which leaues, as also from the sides sometimes, springeth vp one or two, or more stalkes, roundish and thicke, and sometimes a little flat and cornered, a foote high or somewhat more, bearing at the toppe, out of a skinnie huske, eight, ten, twelue, or more very large flowers, consisting of six white leaues a peece, spread or laid open, with a white short cuppe or crowne in the middle, lying flat vpon the leaues, cut or diuided into six corners (and not whole, as the cuppe or crowne of any other single Daffodill) from euery of which edges, or corners of this cup or crowne, standeth one white long thread, a little crooked or turning vp at the end, tipt with a yellow pendent, and some other white threads tipt with yellow pendents, standing also in the middle: after the flower is past, there come vp great three square heads, wherein the seede is contained, which is great, blacke, and round, like vnto the seede of other Daffodils, but greater: the flower hath a reasonable good sent, but not very strong.

The Place.

It was first found by the Sea side, in the Isle of Sardinia, and on the high Mountaines also of the same Isle, where it hath borne by report, thirty fiue flowers vpon a stalke: it groweth likewise about Illyricum, and in diuers other places.

The Time.

It springeth later out of the ground then any other Daffodill, that is to say, not vntill the later end of March, or beginning of Aprill, and flowreth in the end of May, or the beginning of Iune: the seede is ripe in the end of Iuly, or beginning of August.

The Names.

The first that hath made mention of this Daffodill, was Matthiolus, who placed it in the third place among his Daffodils, and is most vsually now a-dayes called, *Narcissus tertius Matthioli*, Matthiolus his third Daffodill, the rather, because Clusius vpon a more mature deliberation, first referred it thereunto, but called it at the first, *Lilionarcissus Hemerocallidis facie*, and, as hee saith, Iacobus Plateau (who first sent him the figure hereof, with the description) called it *Lilionarcissus Orientalis*, but Clusius vpon certaine information, that it grew in the places aforesaid, misliked the name of *Orientalis,* and added *Hemerocallis*, which yet is not fit, for that his *Hemerocallis Valentina*, is a plaine Pancration or Sea bastard Daffodill, whose middle cup is longer then the cup of any true Daffodill, which (as I said in the beginning of this Chapter) is the chiefest note of difference, betweene a true and a bastard Daffodill. I receiued the seede of this Daffodill among many other seedes of rare plants, from the liberality of Mr. Doctor Flud, one of the Physitians of the Colledge in London, who gathered them in the Vniuersity Garden at Pisa in Italy, and brought them with him, returning home from his trauailes into those parts, by the name of *Martagon rarissimum,* (and hauing sowne them, expected fourteene yeares, before I saw them beare a flower, which the first yeare that it did flower, bore foure stalkes of flowers,

1 *Narciſſus tertius Matthioli.* The great white Sea Daffodill. 2 *Narciſſus Indicus Autumnalis.* The nd an
Autumne Daffodill. 3 *Narciſſus marinus Africanus.* The Sea Daffodill of Africa. 4 *Narciſſus marinus exo-*
ticus. The ſtrange Sea Daffodill.

flowers, with euery one of them eight or ten flowers on them) which of all other names, doth leaft anfwer the forme or qualities of this plant. It may moft fitly be called *Narciffus marinus maximus*, in Englifh, The great Sea Daffodill, both becaufe it is a true Daffodill, and the greateft of all other, and alfo becaufe it hath not been found, but in Iflands, or elfe in other places neare the Sea. Lobelius entituleth it *Pancratium Indicum alterum vernum, fiue Narciffus Indicus alter facie Pancratij Monfpeliaci*, but all this is wide from the matter, as may eafily be known, by that that hath been faid before. It is generally (as I faid before) called of all *Narciffus tertius Matthioli*, Matthiolus his third Daffodill, which may either fo paffe with vs, or as I called it, The great Sea Daffodill, which you will, & fo Clufius doth laftly entitle it.

1. *Pancratium Indicum, aut Narciffus Indicus Autumnalis quorundam Lobelij.*
The Indian Autumne Daffodill of Lobel.

This plant hath in my opinion, a farre nearer refemblance vnto an Hyacinthus, then vnto any Daffodill: But becaufe Lobel hath fo fet it forth, I will fo publifh it vnto you, leauing it to iudgement. The roote is, as he faith, a fpan long, and of the thickneffe of a mans arme, couered with many white fhells, whereof the outermoft are of a darke red or Chefnut colour: the flowers rife vp in September, and October, being eight or ten in number, euery one by it felfe vpon a fmall footftalke, made of fix leaues a peece, fomewhat long, narrow, and pointed, like vnto the flowers of the Englifh Colchicum, or Medowe Saffron, of a whitifh yellow dunne colour, with fix long threads in the middle: the greene leaues are long and broad, and broad pointed.

2. *Narciffus Marinus Africanus, fiue Exoticus Lobelij.*
The Sea Daffodill of Africa.

The roote of this ftrange plant (which of fome likeneffe is called a Daffodill) is very great, made as it were of many fcaly cloues, from whence rifeth vp a fmall fhort ftalke, bearing hard aboue the ground two faire broad greene pointed leaues, more long then broad, fo compaffing the ftalke at the bottome, that it feemeth to run through them: the ftalke is fpotted with diuers difcoloured fpots, and is bare or naked from thefe two leaues vnto the toppe, where it beareth one faire double flower, like vnto a double Auemone, of a delayed reddifh colour, tending to a blufh, with many threads fet about the middle head.

3. *Narciffus Marinus Exoticus.* The ftrange Sea Daffodill

This ftrange Sea Daffodill, hath fiue or fix large and long leaues of a pale greene colour, from among which rifeth vp a ftrong and bigge ftalke, bearing at the toppe, out of a thinne hofe or skinne, many very large flowers, made of fix long and pointed leaues apeece, of a blewifh purple colour, with a large round open cup in the middle, of a fadder colour then the leaues: the roote is very great, yet like vnto other great Daffodils, the outer skins whereof are of a darke browne colour.

The Place.

The Indian Daffodils grew in the vpper part of Hifpaniola in the Weft Indies, and brought hither, where they all foone perifhed.
The other grew neare the Cape of good Hope, and was brought into the parts of Holland and thereabouts, from whence we had it, & perifhed alfo.
The laft is vnknowne where it was gathered.

The Time.

The firft flowred in Autumne, as it is faid.
The other in the firft Summer of their bringing.
And fo did the laft, but the fame rootes will not flower with vs againe.
The

The Names.

So much hath been said of their names in their titles, as hath come to our knowledge; and therefore let that suffice.

Thus hauing gone through the whole Family of the true Daffodils, (for so much as hath come to our knowledge) and set them downe euery one by his name, and in his order; it is fit that we speake of their bastard brethren, and shew you them also, in the same order held with the former, as neare as the plenty of variety herein, which is not the like with the former, will giue leaue, that when you know them both by face and name, you may the better know to place or distinguish of others, that haue not passed vnder this rod.

Pseudonarcissus aureus Hispanicus maximus.
The great yellow Spanish bastard Daffodill.

The roote of this kinde of Daffodill is reasonable great, and blackish on the out-side, desiring to be deepe in the ground; and therefore will runne downe, where it will then encrease into many of-sets, from whence rise vp many thicke, long, and stiffe leaues, of a grayish greene colour, among which riseth vp a round strong stalke, some-times three foote high or better, bearing at the toppe one onely faire great yellow flower, standing forth right, and not pendulous, consisting of six short and somewhat broad leaues, with a very great, large, and long trunke, of an equall largenesse, but open at the mouth, and turning vp the brimmes a little, which are somewhat crum-pled: after the flower is past, there commeth in the place a three square head, contai-ning round blacke seede, like vnto other Daffodils.

Pseudonarcissus Pyrenæus Hispanico & Anglico similis.
The Mountaine bastard Daffodill of diuers kindes.

There is much variety in this kinde of bastard Daffodill: For one sort hath verie broad and whitish greene leaues, somewhat short in comparison of others, that are of that breadth: the flower is wholly yellow, but a little paler then the former Spanish kinde, hauing the leaues of his flower long, and somewhat narrow, standing like wings about the middle trunke, which is as long as the leaues, and smaller then in many other of this kinde, but a little yellower then the wings. Another sort hath narrower green leaues then this last, and longer, the flower is all yellow, but the trunke is larger, wider, and more open at the mouth then the former, and almost as large as the former Spa-nish, but not so high as the last. A third hath the wings of the flower of a Strawe co-lour, but the trunke is long and narrow, of a faire yellow. A fourth hath such like flowers, but that it is shorter, both the wings and the trunke: Some likewise haue the wings of the flower longer, then the long trunke, and some shorter. Some also are all yellow, and some haue their wings onely a little more pale or white, like the English kinde: Some againe haue their trunkes long and narrow, others haue them larger and wider open, and crumpled at the brimmes; so that it is needlesse, to spend a great deale of time and labour vpon such smally respected flowers, but that in the beholding of them, we may therein admire the worke of the Creatour, who can frame such diuersity in one thing: But this is beside the text, yet not impertinent.

Pseudonarcissus pallidus præcox. The early Strawe coloured bastard Daffodill.

The leaues of this Daffodill are of a meane size, betweene the broadest and the nar-rower kindes, of a grayish greene colour, and not very long: the stalke riseth vp a foot high or more, whereon standeth one large great flower, equalling the greatest Spanish bastard Daffodill, before described, in the largenesse of his trunke, and hauing the brimmes turned vp a little, which maketh it seeme the larger: the wings or outer leaues are in a maner as short, as they are in the greatest Spanish kinde, (and not long flagging down, like vnto the Mountain kinds) and stand straight outright: all the whole flower is

of

of one euen colour, that is, of a fine pale yellow, somewhat like vnto the colour of a Lemon peele or rinde, but somewhat whiter, which vsually we call a Strawe colour: the greatnesse of the flower, the earlinesse of the flowring, and the difference of colour from all the rest of this kinde, hath made me entreate of it apart by it selfe, as being no lesse worthy.

Pseudonarcissus Hispanicus flore albo maior.
The great white Spanish bastard Daffodill.

This bastard Daffodill hath diuers leaues rising vp together, long and broad, somewhat like vnto the first Spanish kinde, but a little broader, and of a whiter greene colour, yet not so white, as in the lesser Spanish white kindes, hereafter described: among these leaues riseth vp a round strong stalke, about two foote high, bearing one white flower at the toppe, bending downe the head, as all these white kindes doe, but is not of so pure a white, as the lesser kindes that follow, yet whiter then the greatest white Spanish kinde, next of all to be described: the whole flower, as well trunke as wings, is much larger then the lesser white kindes, and almost equalling the first Spanish yellow, but a little longer and narrower, a little crumpled and turning vp at the brimmes: the head and seede are like the first; the roote is greater and thicker then the first Spanish, and doth not encrease so much, nor is couered with a blacke, but rather with a whitish coate.

Pseudonarcissus Hispanicus maximus albidus.
The greatest Spanish white bastard Daffodill.

This kinde of bastard Daffodill is very like the last mentioned Daffodill, both in leaues and flowers, but larger in both: the flower of this is not full so white, but hath some shew of palenesse therein, and more vpon the first opening of the flower then afterwards, and is as great altogether, as the great Spanish yellow, at the least with a longer, and somewhat narrower trunke: the seede is like vnto the former, and so is the roote also, but greater, being white on the outside, and not blacke.

Pseudonarcissus Hispanicus flore albo medius & minor.
The two lesser white Spanish bastard Daffodils.

There are two other of these kindes of white Spanish Daffodils, one greater or lesser then the other, but neither of them so great as the former. The leaues of both are of a whitish greene colour, one a little broader then the other: the flowers of both are pure white, and bending downe the heads, that they almost touch the stalke againe, the greater flower hath the longer and narrower trunke; and the lesser flower, the shorter and wider open, yet both a little crumpled at the edges or brimmes: the rootes of both are like one vnto another, but differ in the greatnesse. From the seede of these haue sprung much variety, few or none keeping either colour or height with the mother plants.

Pseudonarcissus Anglicus vulgaris. Our common English wilde bastard Daffodill.

This bastard Daffodill is so common in all England, both in Copses, Woods, and Orchards, that I might well forbeare the description thereof, and especially, in that growing wilde, it is of little respect in our Garden: but yet, left I bee challenged of ignorance in common plants, and in regard of some variety therein worth the marking, I will set downe his description and variety as briefly as I may: It hath three or foure grayish greene leaues, long and somewhat narrow, among which riseth vp the stalke, about a span high or little higher, bearing at the toppe, out of a skinnie huske, as all other Daffodils haue, one flower (although sometimes I haue seene two together) somewhat large, hauing the six leaues that stand like wings, of a pale yellow colour, and the long trunke in the middle of a faire yellow, with the edges or brimmes a little crumpled or vneuen: after the flower is past, it beareth a round head, seeming three square, containing round blacke seede; the roote is somewhat blackish on the outside.

But

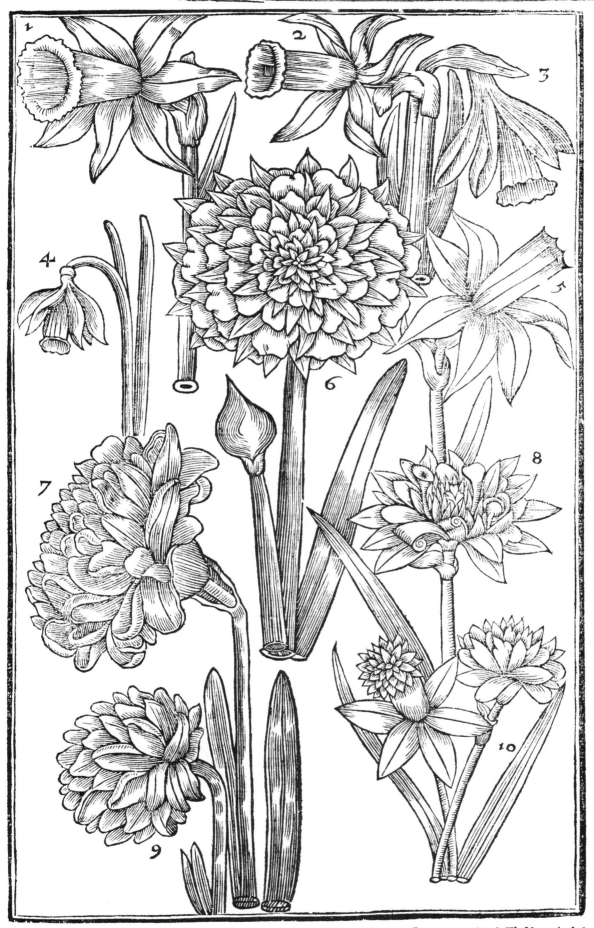

1 *Pseudonarcissus Hispanicus maximus aureus.* The great yellow Spanish bastard Daffodill. 2 *Pseudonarcissus Pyreneus variformis.* The Mountaine bastard Daffodill of divers kindes. 3 *Pseudonarcissus Hispanicus maior albus* The greater white Spanish bastard Daffodill. 4 *Pseudonarcissus Hispanicus minor albus.* The lesser Spanish white bastard Daffodill 5 *Pseudonarcissus tubo sexangulari.* The six cornered bastard Daffodill. 6 *Pseudonarcissus maximus aureus, sive Roseus Tradescanti.* John Tradescants great Rose Daffodill 7 *Pseudonarcissus aureus Anglicus maximus.* Master Wilmers great double Daffodill. 8 *Pseudonarcissus Hispanicus aureus flore pleno.* The double Spanish Daffodill, or Parkinsons double Daffodill. 9 *Pseudonarcissus Gallicus maior flore pleno.* The greater double French Daffodill. 10 *Pseudonarcissus Anglicus flore pleno.* The double English Daffodill, or Gerrards double Daffodill.

But there is another of this kinde like vnto the former, whose further description you haue here before ; the wings of which flower are much more white then the former, and in a manner of a milke white colour, the trunke remaining almost as yellow as the former, and not differing in any thing else.

Pseudonarcissus tubo sexangulari. The six cornered bastard Daffodill.

This kinde of Daffodill hath two or three long, and somewhat broader leaues then the last, between which commeth forth a stalke, bearing one flower somewhat large, hauing the six outer leaues of a pale yellow colour, and the long trunke plaited or cornered all along vnto the very edge into six parts, of a little deeper yellow then the wings.

The Place.

The first great Spanish kinde was brought out of Spaine. The rest from the Pyrenæan Mountaines, onely the last sauing one is plentifull in our owne Countrey, but the white sort of that kinde came with the rest from the same Mountaines.

The Time.

The pale or third kinde, and the English bee the most early, all the rest flower in Aprill, and the greatest yellow somewhat earlier, then the other greater or lesser white.

The Names.

Their seuerall names are expressed in their titles sufficient to distinguish them, and therefore there needeth no more to be said of them.

1. *Pseudonarcissus aureus maximus flore pleno, siue Roseus Tradescanti.*
The greatest double yellow bastard Daffodill, or
Iohn Tradescant his great Rose Daffodill.

This Prince of Daffodils (belongeth primarily to Iohn Tradescant, as the first founder thereof, that we know, and may well bee entituled the Glory of Daffodils) hath a great round roote, like vnto other Daffodils, couered with a brownish outer skinne or peeling, from whence riseth vp foure or fiue somewhat large and broad leaues, of a grayish greene colour, yet not fully so long and large as the next following Daffodill: from the middle whereof riseth vp a stalke almost as high and great as it, bearing at the toppe (out of a skinnie huske) one faire large great flower (the budde, before it breake open, being shorter and thicker in the middle, and ending in a longer and sharper point then any of the other Daffodils) very much spread open, consisting of smaller and shorter leaues then the next, but more in number, and thicker and rounder set together, making it seeme as great and double as any Prouince Rose, and intermixt with diuers yellow and pale leaues, as it were in rowes one vnder another. It abideth long in flower, and spreadeth, by standing long, to be the broadest in compasse of any of the Daffodils, but falleth away at the last without giuing any seede, as all double Daffodils doe.

2. *Pseudonarcissus aureus Anglicus maximus.* Mr. Wilmers great double Daffodill.

The other great double Daffodill doth so neare resemble our ordinary English double kinde, that I doe not finde therein any greater difference, then the largenesse both of leaues and flowers, &c. and the statelinesse of growth. It beareth three or foure large, long, and broad leaues, somewhat longer and broader then the former, and of a whitish greene colour : the stalke riseth to bee two foote high, growing (in a fruitfull and fat soyle) strong, and somewhat round, bearing at the toppe, out of a thin skinne, one great and faire double flower, each leafe whereof is twice as large and

broad

broad as the former, diuerfly intermixt with a rowe of paler, and a rowe of deeper yellow leaues, wholly difperfed throughout the flower, the pale colour as well as the deeper yellow, in this as in the other fmall Englifh kinde, growing deeper by ftanding: fometimes the leaues hereof are fcattered, and fpread wholly, making it fhew a faire, broad, open flower: and fometimes the outer leaues ftand feparate from the middle trunke, which is whole and vnbroken, and very thicke of leaues: and fometimes the middle trunke will bee halfe broken, neither expreffing a full open double flower, nor a clofe double trunke, as it is likewife feene in the fmall Englifh kinde, as fhall bee declared in his place: this beareth no feede; the roote hereof is thicke and great, and encreafeth as well as any other Daffodill.

3. *Pfeudonarciffus aureus Hifpanicus flore pleno.*
The great double yellow Spanifh baftard Daffodill, or Parkinfons Daffodill.

This double Spanifh Daffodill hath diuers leaues rifing from the roote, ftiffer, narrower, and not of fo whitifh a greene colour as the former, but more fullen or grayifh, plainely refembling the leaues of the fingle great kinde, from whence this hath rifen: the ftalke hereof likewife rifeth almoft as high as it, and neare the height of the laft recited double, bearing one double flower at the toppe, alwayes fpread open, and neuer forming a double trunke like the former, yet not fo faire and large as it, the outermoft leaues whereof being of a greenifh colour at the firft, and afterward more yellow, doe a little turne themfelues backe againe to the ftalke, the other leaues are fome of a pale yellow, and others of a more gold yellow colour, thofe that ftand in the middle are fmaller, and fome of them fhew as if they were hollow trunked, fo that they feeme to be greenifh, whitifh, yellow, and gold yellow, all mixed one among another: the root is great, round, and whitifh on the infide, couered with darke coloured skinnes or peelings. I thinke none euer had this kinde before my felfe, nor did I my felfe euer fee it before the yeare 1618. for it is of mine own raifing and flowring firft in my Garden.

4. *Pfeudonarciffus Gallicus maior flore pleno.*
The greater double French baftard Daffodill.

This greater double Daffodill, hath his whitifh greene leaues longer and broader then the fmaller French kinde, hereafter following, to bee defcribed, and broader, longer, and more limber then the double Englifh kinde: the ftalke rifeth vp not much higher, then the fmaller French kinde, but a little bigger, bearing at the top one great double flower, which when it is fully and perfectly blowne open (which is but feldome; for that it is very tender, the leaues being much thinner, and thereby continually fubiect, vpon any little diftemperature of the time, to cleaue fo faft one vnto another, that the flower cannot blow open faire) is a faire and a goodly flower, larger by halfe then the fmaller kinde, and fuller of leaues, of the fame pale whitifh yellow, or Lemon colour, with the leffer, or rather a little whiter, and not fet in the fame order of rowes as it is, but more confufedly together, and turning backe the ends of the outermoft leaues to the ftalke againe, and hauing the bottome of the flower on the backfide fomewhat greene, neither of which is found in the leffer kinde: the roote is very like vnto the leffer kinde, but a little bigger and longer.

5. *Pfeudonarciffus Anglicus flore pleno.*
The double Englifh baftard Daffodill, or Gerrards double Daffodill.

The leaues of this double Daffodill are very like vnto the fingle kinde, being of a whitifh greene colour, and fomewhat broad, a little fhorter and narrower, yet ftiffer then the former French kinde: the ftalke rifeth vp about a foote high, bearing at the toppe one very double flower, the outermoft leaues being of the fame pale colour, that is to bee feene in the wings of the fingle kinde; thofe that ftand next them, are fome as deepe a yellow as the trunke of the fingle, and others of the fame pale colour, with fome greene ftripes on the backe of diuers of the leaues: thus is the whole flower variably intermixt with pale and deepe yellow, and fome greene ftripes among them,
when

when it is fully open, and the leaues difperfed and broken. For fometimes the flower
fheweth a clofe and round yellow trunke in the middle, feparate from the pale outer
wings, which trunke is very double, fhewing fome pale leaues within it, difperfed
among the yellow : And fometimes the trunke is more open, or in part broken, fhewing forth the fame colours intermixt within it : the flower paffeth away without giuing any feede, as all other bulbous rootes doe that beare double flowers : the roote is
fmall, very like vnto the French double kindes, efpecially the leffer, that it is verie
hard to know the one from the other.

The Place.

The firft and greateft kinde, we had firft from Iohn Tradefcante (as I faid
before) whether raifed from feed, or gained from beyond Sea, I know not.

The fecond we firft had from Vincent Sion, borne in Flanders, dwelling
on the Banke fide, in his liues time, but now dead ; an induftrious and worthy louer of faire flowers, who cherifhed it in his Garden for many yeares,
without bearing of any flowers vntill the yeare 1620. that hauing flowred
with him, (and hee not knowing of whom hee receiued it, nor hauing euer
feene the like flower before) he fheweth it to Mr. Iohn de Franqueuille, of
whom he fuppofed he had receiued it, (for from beyond Sea he neuer receiued any) who finding it to bee a kinde neuer feene or knowne to vs before,
caufed him to refpect it the more, as it is well worthy. And Mr. George
Wilmer of Stratford Bowe Efquire, in his liues time hauing likewife receiued it of him (as my felfe did alfo) would needes appropriate it to himfelfe,
as if he were the firft founder thereof, and call it by his owne name Wilmers double Daffodill, which fince hath fo continued.

The third is of mine owne foftering or raifing, as I faid before ; for affuredly, it is rifen from the feede of the great Spanifh fingle kinde, which I
fowed in mine owne Garden, and cherifhed it, vntill it gaue fuch a flower
as is defcribed.

The fourth is not certainly knowne where his originall fhould be : Some
thinke it to be ot France, and others of Germany.

The laft is affuredly firft naturall of our owne Countrey, for Mr. Gerrard
firft difcouered it to the world, finding it in a poore womans Garden in the
Weft parts of England, where it grew before the woman came to dwell
there, and, as I haue heard fince, is naturall of the Ifle of Wight.

The Time.

They doe all flower much about one time, that is, from the middle or
end of March, as the yeare is forward, vnto the middle of Aprill.

The Names.

Vpon the three firft I haue impofed the names in Latine, as they are expreffed in their titles : and for the Englifh names, if you pleafe, you may let
them paffe likewife as they are expreffed there alfo, that thereby euery one
may be truely diftinguifhed, and not confounded. The fourth, befides the
name in the title, is called of fome *Narciffus Germanicus*, which whether it
be of Germany, or no, I know not ; but that the name fhould import fo much.
The laft doth vfually carry Mr. Gerrards name, and called Gerrards double
Daffodill.

1. *Pfeudonarciffus anguftifolius flore flauefcente tubo quafi abfciffo.*
The narrow leafed baftard Daffodill with the clipt trunke.

This kinde of Daffodill hath long and narrow grayifh greene leaues, bearing one
fingle flower at the toppe of his ftalke, like vnto the former fingle baftard kindes, before

fore fpecified, hauing his outer leaues of a pale yellow colour, and his trunke of a deeper yellow : the chiefe differences in this from the former, is in the leaues, being narrow, and then in the trunke of the flower, which is not crumpled or turned vp, as moft of the other are ; and that the brimmes or edges of the flower is as if it had beene clipt off, or cut euen.

2. *Pfeudonarciffus Hifpanicus medius & minor luteus.*
The two leffer Spanifh yellow baftard Daffodils.

Thefe two leffer kindes of Spanifh Daffodils, doe but differ in greatneffe the one from the other, and not in any thing elfe ; fo that in declaring the one, you may vnderftand the other to bee a little greater. The leffer then hath three or foure narrow fhort whitifh greene leaues, from among which commeth forth a fhort ftalke, not aboue an hand breadth, or halfe a foote high, bearing one fingle flower, not fully ftanding outright, but a little bending downe, confifting of fix fmall leaues, ftanding as wings about a fmall, but long trunke, a little crumpled at the brimmes : the whole flower, as well leaues as trunke, are of one deepe yellow colour, like vnto the great Spanifh kinde : the roote is but fmall, and couered with a darkifh coate. The other is in all parts greater, and (as I faid) differeth not elfe.

3. *Pfeudonarciffus Hifpanicus luteus minimus.*
The leaft Spanifh yellow baftard Daffodill.

The leaues of this fmall kinde are fmaller and fhorter then the former, feldome exceeding the length of three inches, and very narrow withall, but of the fame grayifh greene colour with the former : euery flower ftandeth vpon a fmall and fhort footeftalke, fcarce rifing aboue the ground; fo that his nofe, for the moft part, doth lye or touch the ground, and is made after the fame fafhion, and of the fame colour with the former, but much fmaller, as his roote is fo likewife.

4. *Pfeudonarciffus Gallicus minor flore pleno.*
The leffer French double baftard Daffodill.

The rootes of this leffer French kinde (if I may lawfully call it, or the greater kinde before fpecified, a baftard Daffodill ; for I fomewhat doubt thereof, in that the flower of either is not made after the fafhion of any of the other baftard Daffodils, but doth more nearely refemble the forme of the double white Daffodill, expreffed before among the true Daffodils) are like vnto the double Englifh kinde, as alfo to the former double greater French kinde, and the leaues are of the fame whitifh greene colour alfo, but narrower and not longer : the ftalke rifeth a little higher then the Englifh, and not fully fo high as the greater French, bearing one faire double flower thereon, of a pale yellow or Lemon colour, confifting of fix rowes of leaues, euery rowe growing fmaller then other vnto the middle, and fo fet and placed, that euery leafe of the flower doth ftand directly almoft in all, one vpon or before another vnto the middle, where the leaues are fmalleft, the outermoft being the greateft, which maketh the flower feeme the more beautifull : this and the greater kinde hath no trunke, or fhew of any other thing in the middle, as all or moft of the other former double baftard Daffodils haue, but are flowers wholly compofed of leaues, ftanding double euen to the middle.

The Place.

The firft is vndoubtedly a naturall of the Pyrenæan Mountaines.
The Spanifh kindes grew in Spaine, and
The French double kinde about Orleance in France, where it is faid to grow plentifully.

The Time.

The firft flowreth at the end of March.

The

The Spanish kindes are the most early, flowring betimes in March. The French double doth flower presently after.

The Names.

More cannot bee said or added, concerning the names of any of these Daffodils, then hath been set downe in their titles : onely the French kinde is most vsually called Robinus his Daffodill.

Pseudonarcissus Iuncifolius albus. The white bastard Rush Daffodill, or Iunquilia.

This bastard Rush Daffodill hath two or three long and very greene leaues, very like vnto the small yellow Rush Daffodill, formerly described, but not altogether so round, among which riseth vp a short stalke, seldome halfe a foote high, bearing at the toppe, out of a small skinnie huske, one small white flower, sometime declining to a pale colour, hauing six small and short leaues, standing about the middle of the trunke, which is long, and much wider open at the mouth, then at the bottome : the small outer leaues or wings are a little tending to greene, and the trunke (as I said) is either white, or whitish, hauing the brimmes a little vneuen : the seede is small, blacke, and round, like vnto other Rush Daffodils, but smaller.

Pseudonarcissus Iuncifolius luteus maior.
The greater yellow Iunquilia, or bastard Daffodill.

The leaues of this greater kinde are longer, greater, and a little broader then the former ; the stalke also is higher, and the flower larger, more open at the mouth and crumpled, then the white, but wholly of a yellow colour : the seede and the roots are bigger, according to the proportion of the plant.

Pseudonarcissus Iuncifolius luteus minor. The lesser yellow bastard Iunquilia.

This is so like vnto the last in all things, that I shall not neede to trouble you with repetitions of the same things formerly spoken ; the chiefest difference is the smalnesse of the plant in all parts.

Pseudonarcissus Iuncifolius luteus serotinus. The late yellow bastard Iunquilia.

There is likewise a third kinde, as great as the greater yellow, and in all his parts expressing and equalling it, but is accounted the fairer, and flowreth somewhat later.

The Place.

The Pyrenæan Hils haue afforded vs all these varieties, and wee preserue them carefully ; for they are all tender.

The Time.

All these flower in Aprill, except the last, which is a moneth later.

The Names.

The French and Lowe-Countrey men call them *Trompettes*, that is, Trumpets, from the forme of the trunke ; wee sometimes call them also by that name, but more vsually bastard Iunquilia's.

Pseudonarcissus marinus albus, Pancratium vulgo.
The white Sea bastard Daffodill.

The Sea bastard Daffodill (to conclude this Chapter, and the discourse of Daffodils)

1 *Pseudonarcissus tubo quasi abscisso.* The baltard Daffodill with the clipt trunke. 2 *Pseudonarcissus Hispanicus minor.* The lesser Spanish bastard Daffodill.
3 *Pseudonarcissus Hispanicus minimus.* The least Spanish bastard Daffodill. 4 *Pseudonarcissus Gallicus minor flore pleno.* The lesser double French bastard Daffodill. 5 *Pancratium flore albo* The white Sea bastard Daffodill. 6 *Pseudonarcissus iuncifolius luteus maior.* The greater yellow bastard Iunquilia. 7 *Pseudonarcissus iunciolius luteus minor.* The lesser yellow bastard Iunquilia 8 *Pseudonarcissus iuncifolius luteus serotinus.* The late yellow bastard
Iunquilia 9 *Leucoium bulbosum praecox maius.* The great early bulbous Violet. † *Leucoium bulbosum praecox minus.* The lesser early bulbous Violet.
10 *Leucoium bulbosum autumnale.* The small Autumne bulbous Violet. 11 *Leucoium bulbosum maius serotinum.* The great late flowring bulbous Violet.

dils) hath diuers broad whitith greene leaues , but not very long, among which riseth vp a stiffe round stalke, at the top whereof breaketh out of a great round skinny huske, fiue or six flowers, euery one made somewhat of the fashion of the great bastard Rush Daffodill, but greater, and wholly white ; the six leaues, being larger and longer then in the Rush kinde, and extending beyond the trunke, are tipt with greene at the point of each leafe, and downe the middle likewise on the backside. The trunke is longer, larger, and wider open at the mouth, cut in or indented at the brims or edges, and small at the bottome, with diuers white threeds in the middle, and is very sweet : vnder the flower is a round greene head, which groweth very great, hauing within it, when it is ripe, flat and blacke seede : the roote is great and white.

Flore luteo, & flore rubro. It is reported, that there are found other sorts ; some that beare yellow flowers, and others that beare red: but we haue seene none such, and therefore I can say no more of them.

The Place.

This kinde groweth neare the Sea side, both in Spaine, Italy, and France, within the Straights, and for the most part, vpon all the Leuant shoare and Islands also, but will seldome either flower, or abide with vs in these colder Countries, as I haue both seene by those that I receiued from a friend, and heard by others.

The Time.

It flowreth in the end of Summer, that is, in August and September.

The Name.

Diuers doe call it *Pancratium,* as the learned of Mompeher, and others, with the addition of *flore Lilij,* after they had left their old errour, in taking it to be *Scylla,* and vsing it for *Scylla,* in the *Trochisces* that go into Andromachus Treakle. The learned of Valentia in Spaine, as Clusius saith, doe call it *Hemerocallis,* thinking it to be a Lilly ; and Clusius doth thereupon call it, *Hemerocallis Valentina :* but in my opinion, all these are deceiued in this plant ; for it is neither a Lilly, to haue the name of *Hemerocallis* giuen vnto it, nor *Scylla,* nor *Pancratium,* as many doe yet call it : for certainly this is a kinde of Daffodill, the forme both of roote, leafe, and flower, doth assure me that haue seene it, and not *Pancratium,* which (as Dioscorides testifieth) is a kinde of *Scylla,* and in his time called *Scylla,* with a red roote, and a leafe like a Lilly, but longer, and was vsed both with the same preparation and quantity, and for the same diseases that *Scylla* was vsed, but that his force was weaker : all which doth plainly shew the errours that many learned men haue been conuersant in, and that all may see how necessary the knowledge of Herbarisme is to the practice of Physicke ; And lest the roote of this Sea bastard Daffodill bee vsed in the stead of an wholsome remedy, which (as Clusius maketh mention) was deadly to him that did but cut his meate with that knife, which had immediately before cut this roote, and done in malice by him, that knew the force thereof, to kill his fellow, it working the more forceably by the euill attracting quality of the iron.

The Vertues of Daffodils in generall.

Howsoeuer Dioscorides and others, doe giue vnto some of them speciall properties, both for inward and outward diseases, yet know I not any in these dayes with vs, that apply any of them as a remedy for any griefe, whatsoeuer Gerrard or others haue written.

CHAP.

Chap. X.

Leucoium bulbosum. The bulbous Violet.

HAuing thus set downe the whole family, both of the true and bastard Daffo-dils, I should next set in hand with the Hyacinths; but because *Leucoium bul-bosum*, The bulbous Violet is a plant that doth challenge a place next vnto the Daffodils, as most nearly partaking with them, and a little with the Hyacinthes, I must of necessity interpose them, and shew their descriptions and differences, whereof some are early, of the first Spring, others later, and some of the Autumne.

Leucoium bulbosum præcox maius. The greater early bulbous Violet.

This bulbous Violet hath three or foure very greene, broad, flat, and short leaues, among which riseth vp a naked greene stalke, bearing out of a small skinny hose (as the former Daffodils doe) one white flower, hanging downe his head by a very small foot-stalke, made of six leaues, of an equall length, euery one whereof is tipt at the end with a small greenish yellow spot: after the flower is past, the head or seed-vessell groweth to be reasonable great, somewhat long and round, wherein is contained hard round seede, which being dry, is cleare, and of a whitish yellow colour: the roote is somewhat like a Daffodill roote, and couered with a blackish outside or skinne.

Leucoium bulbosum præcox minus. The lesser early bulbous Violet.

This lesser kinde riseth vp with two narrow grayish greene leaues, between which commeth forth the stalke, fiue or six inches high, bearing one small pendulous flower, consisting of three white leaues, which are small and pointed, standing on the out-side, and hauing three other shorter leaues, which seeme like a cup in the middle, being each of them round at the ends, and cut in the middle, making the forme of an heart, with a greene tippe or spot at the broad end or edge: the seede is whitish, inclosed in long and round heads, like the former, but lesser: the roote is like a small Daffodill, with a blackish gray coate, and quickly diuideth into many of-sets.

There is another of this kinde, that came among other bulbous rootes from Con-stantinople, and differeth in nothing from it, but that it is a little greater, both in root, leafe, and flower. *Minus Byzan-tinum.*

The Place.

The two first are found in many places of Germany, and Hungary. The third, as I said, was brought from Constantinople.

The Time.

The two lesser sorts doe most commonly flower in February, if the wea-ther be any thing milde, or at the furthest in the beginning of March, but the first is seldome in flower, before the other be well neare past, or altoge-ther.

The Names.

Lobel and Dodonæus call the lesser kinde *Leucoium triphyllum*, and *Leu-conarcissolirion triphyllum*, of the three leaues in the flower. Some doe call it *Viola bulbosa alba*. The first or greater kinde is called by Lobel, *Leuconar-cissolirion paucioribus floribus*; and by Dodonæus, *Leucoium bulbosum hexa-phyllum*. We doe most vsually call them, *Leucoium bulbosum præcox maius, & minus*, The greater, or the lesser early bulbous Violet. In Dutch, *Somer Sottekens*, and not *Druifkens*, which are Grape-flowers, as some haue thought.

K *Leucoium*

1. *Leucoium bulbosum Vernum minimum.*
The small bulbous Violet of the Spring.

This small *Leucoium* sendeth forth his small and long greene leaues, like haires in Autumne, and before Winter, which abide greene vntill Aprill, and then wither away quite, and about May there ariseth vp a naked slender stalke, at the toppe whereof breake forth two small white flowers, made of six leaues a peece, hanging downe their heads, the three inner leaues being a little larger then the three outward, a little reddish neare the stalke, and very sweet : the root is small and round, and couered with a darke coate.

2. *Leucoium bulbosum Autumnale.* The small Autumne bulbous Violet.

As the former small *Leucoium* sprang vp with his leaues without flowers in Autumne, so this contrariwise, riseth vp with his slender brownish stalke of flowers in Autumne, before any greene leaues appeare, whereon stand two or three very small snow white pendulous flowers, consisting of six leaues a peece, and a little reddish at the bottome of the flower next vnto the stalke, so like vnto the former, that one would take them to be both one : after which, there grow small browne heads, containing small, blacke, round seed ; after the flower is past, and the seede is ripening, and sometimes after the heads are ripe, the leaues begin to spring vp, which when they are full growne, are long, greene, and as small, or smaller then the leaues of the Autumne Hyacinth, which abide all the Winter, and Spring following, and wither away in the beginning of Summer : the roote is small, long, and white.

3. *Leucoium maius bulbosum serotinum.*
The great late flowring bulbous Violet.

The late bulbous Violet hath three or foure broad flat greene leaues, very like vnto the first, but longer, among which riseth vp a flattish stalke, being thicker in the middle then at both edges, on the toppe whereof stand three or foure flowers, hanging downe their heads, consisting of six leaues a peece, all of an equall length and bignesse, wholly white, except that each leafe hath a greene tippe at the end of them : the seede hereof is blacke and round ; the roote is reasonable great and white.

The Place.

The two former small ones were first found in Spaine, and Portugall, and sent to me by Guillaume Boel ; but the first was so tender, that scarce one of a score sprang with me, or would abide. The greatest haue beene found wilde in Germany and Austria.

The Time.

The small ones haue their times expressed in their titles and descriptions, the last flowreth not vntill May.

The Names.

These names that are set downe in their titles, doe passe with all Herbarists in these daies.

The Vertues.

Wee haue not knowne these plants vsed Physically, either inwardly or outwardly, to any purposes in these dayes.

CHAP.

Chap. XI.

Hyacinthus. The Hyacinth or Iacinth.

THe Iacinths are next to be entreated of, whereof there are many more kindes found out in thefe later times, then formerly were knowne, which for order and method fake, I will digeft vnder feuerall forts, as neare as I can, that a-uoiding confufion, by enterlacing one among another, I may the better put euery fort vnder his owne kinde.

Hyacinthus Indicus maior tuberofa radice.
The greater Indian knobbed Iacinth.

I haue thought fitteft to begin with this Iacinth, both becaufe it is the greateft and higheft, and alfo becaufe the flowers hereof are in fome likeneffe neare vnto a Daffo-dill, although his roote be tuberous, and not bulbous as all the reft are. This Indian Iacinth hath a thicke knobbed roote (yet formed into feuerall heads, fomewhat like vnto bulbous rootes) with many thicke fibres at the bottome of them ; from the di-uers heads of this roote arife diuers ftrong and very tall ftalkes, befet with diuers faire, long, and broad leaues, ioyned at the bottome clofe vnto the ftalke, where they are greateft, and grow fmaller to the very end, and thofe that grow higher to the toppe, being fmaller and fmaller, which being broken, there appeare many threeds like wooll in them : the toppes of the ftalkes are garnifhed with many faire large white flowers, each whereof is compofed of fix leaues, lying fpread open, as the flowers of the white Daffodill, with fome fhort threeds in the middle, and of a very fweete fent, or rather ftrong and headie.

Hyacinthus Indicus minor tuberofa radice.
The fmaller Indian knobbed Iacinth.

The roote of this Iacinth is knobbed, like the roote of Arum or Wake Robin, from whence doe fpring many leaues, lying vpon the ground, and compaffing one another at the bottome, being long and narrow, and hollow guttered to the end, which is fmall and pointed, no leffe woolly, or full of threeds then the former : from the middle of thefe leaues rifeth vp the ftalke, being very long and flender, three or foure foot long, fo that without it be propped vp, it will bend downe, and lye vpon the ground, where-on are fet at certaine diftances many fhort leaues, being broad at the bottome, where they doe almoft compaffe the ftalke, and are fmaller toward the end where it is fharpe pointed: at the top of the ftalke ftand many flowers, with a fmall peece of a green leafe at the bottome of euery foot-ftalke, which feeme to bee like fo many white Orientall Iacinths, being compofed of fix leaues, which are much thicker then the former, with fix chiues or threeds in the middle, tipt with pale yellow pendents.

The Place.

They both grow naturally in the Weft Indies, from whence being firft brought into Spaine, haue from thence been difperfed vnto diuers louers of plants.

The Time.

They flower not in thefe cold Countries vntill the middle of Auguft, or not at all, if they bee not carefully preferued from the iniury of our cold Winters ; and then if the precedent Summer be hot, it may be flower a mo-neth fooner.

The Names.

Clufius calleth the leffer (for I thinke hee neuer faw the firft) *Hyacinthus Indicus*

K 2

Indicus tuberosa radice, that is in English, The Indian Iacinth with a tuberous roote : Some would call these *Hyacinthus Eriophorus Indicus*, that is, The Indian woolly Iacinth, because they haue much wooll in them when they are broken ; yet some doe doubt that they are not two plants seuerall, as of greater and lesser, but that the greatnesse is caused by the fertility of the soyle wherein it grew.

1. *Hyacinthus Botroides maior Moschatus, siue Muscari flore flauo.*
The great yellow Muske Grape-flower, or yellow Muscari.

This Muske Iacinth or Grape-flower, hath fiue or six leaues spread vpon the ground in two or three heads, which at the first budding or shooting forth out of the ground, are of a reddish purple colour, and after become long, thicke, hollow, or guttered on the vpperside, of a whitish greene colour, and round and darke coloured vnderneath : in the middle of these heads of leaues, rise vp one or two hollow weake brownish stalkes, sometimes lying on the ground with the weight of the flowers, (but especially of the seede) yet for the most part standing vpright, when they are laden towards the toppe, with many bottle-like flowers, which at their first appearing, and vntill the flowers begin to blow open, are of a browne red colour, and when they are blowne, of a faire yellow colour, flowring first below, and so vpwards by degrees, euery one of these flowers is made like vnto a little pitcher or bottle, being bigge in the belly, and small at the mouth, which is round, and a little turned vp, very sweete in smell, like vnto Muske, whereof it tooke the name *Muscari* ; after the flowers are past, there come three square thicke heads, puffed vp as if it were bladders, made of a spongie substance, wherein are here and there placed blacke round seed : the roote is long, round, and very thicke, and white on the outside, with a little woollinesse on them, being broken, and full of a slimie iuice, whereunto are annexed thicke, fat, and long fibres, which perish not as most of the other Iacinths ; and therefore desireth not to bee often remoued, as the other sorts may.

2. *Hyacinthus Botroides maior Moschatus, seu Muscari flore cineritio.*
The Ashcoloured Muske Grape-flower, or Muscari.

This Muscari differeth not in rootes, or forme of leaues or flowers from the former, the chiefe differences are these : the leaues hereof do not appeare so red at the first budding out of the ground, nor are so darke when they are fully growne ; the stalke also most vsually hath more store of flowers thereon, the colour whereof at the first budding is a little duskie, and when they are full blowne, are of a bleake, yet bright ashcolour, with a little shew of purple in them, and by long standing change a little more gray ; being as sweete, or as some thinke, more sweete then the former : the roote (as I said) is like the former, yet yeeldeth more encrease, and will better endure our cold clymate, although it doth more seldome giue ripe seede.

3. *Hyacinthus Botroides maior Moschatus, siue Muscari flore rubro.*
The red Muske Grape-flower.

This kinde (if there be any such, for I am in some doubt thereof) doth chiefly differ in the colour of the flower from the first, in that this should beare flowers when they are blowne, of a red colour tending to yellownesse.

4. *Hyacinthus Botroides maior Moschatus, siue Muscari flore albo.*
The white Muske Grape-flower.

This also is said to haue (if there bee such an one) his leaues like vnto the second kinde, but of a little whiter greene, and the flowers pale, tending to a white : the roots of these two last are said vsually not to grow to be so great as of the former two.

The Place.

The rootes of the two first sorts, haue been often sent from Constantinople,

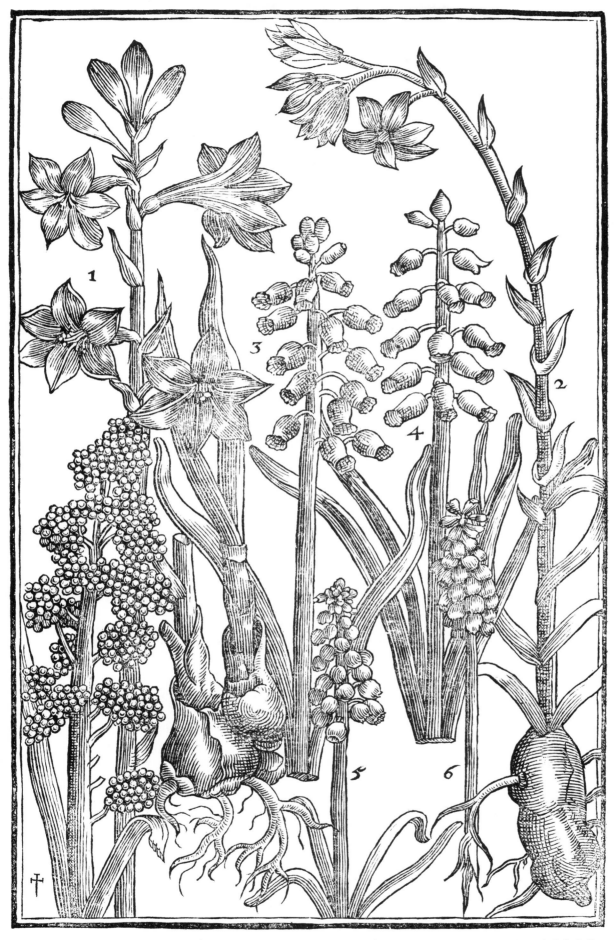

1 *Hyacinthus Indicus maior tuberosa radice.* The greater Indian knobbed Iacinth. 2 *Hyacinthus Indicus minor tuberosa radice.* The lesser Indian knobbed Iacinth. 3 *Muscari flore flauo.* The yellow Muscari. 4 *Muscari flore cineritio.* The ashcoloured Muscari. 5 *Hyacinthus Botroides caeruleus amoenus.* The skie coloured Grape-flower. 6 *Hyacinthus Botroides flore albo.* The white Grape flower. † *Hyacinthus Botroides ramosus.* The branched Grape-flower.

ple, among many other forts of rootes, and it may be come thither from beyond the Bofphorus in Afia; we haue them in our Gardens.

The other two forts are fprung (it is probable, if they be *in rerum natura*) from the feede of the two former; for we could neuer get fuch from Conftantinople, as if the Turkes had neuer knowledge of any fuch.

The Time.

They flower in March or Aprill, as the yeare is temperate, but the firft is fooneft vp out of the ground.

The Names.

The two former haue beene fent from Turkie by the name of *Mufchoromi* and *Dipcadi*. Matthiolus calleth it *Bulbus vomitorius*, faying that no root doth more prouoke vomit then it. Cafpar Bauhinus doth moft properly call it *Hyacinthus Mofchatus*. It is moft generally called *Mufcari*, by all Herbarifts and Florifts, yet becaufe it doth fo neerely refemble the Grapeflower, I haue named it *Hyacinthus Botroides maior Mufchatus*, to put a difference from the leffer Grape-flowers that follow; in Englifh, The great Muske Grape-flower, or Mufcari.

Hyacinthus Botroides minor cæruleus obfcurus.
The darke blew Grape-flower.

This Grape-flower hath many fmall, fat, and weake leaues lying vpon the ground, which are fomewhat brownifh at their firft comming vp, and of a fad greene afterwards, hollow on the vpperfide, and round vnderneath, among which rife vp round, fmooth, weake ftalkes, bearing at the toppe many fmall heauie bottle-like flowers, in fhape like the former Mufcari, but very thicke thruft together, fmaller, and of a very darke or blackifh blew colour, of a very ftrong fmell, like vnto Starch when it is new made, and hot: the root is round, and blackifh without, being compaffed with a number of fmall rootes, or of-fets round about it, fo that it will quickly choke a ground, if it be fuffered long in it. For which caufe, moft men doe caft it into fome by-corner, if they meane to preferue it, or caft it out of the Garden quite.

Alter maior. There is another of this kinde that is greater, both in leafe and flower, and differeth not in colour or any thing elfe.

Hyacinthus Botroides cæruleus amœnus. The skie coloured Grape-flower.

This Iacinth fpringeth vp with fewer leaues then the firft, and not reddifh, but green at his firft appearing; the leaues, when they are full growne, are long and hollow, like the former, but greener, fhorter, and broader, ftanding vpright, and not lying along vpon the ground as they doe: the flowers grow at the toppe of the ftalke, more fparfedly fet thereon, and not fo thicke together, but like a thinne bunch of grapes, and bottle-like as the former, of a perfect blew or skie-colour, euery flower hauing fome white fpots about the brimmes of them: this hath a very fweet fmell, nothing like the former: this roote is whiter, and doth not fo much encreafe as the former, yet plentifull enough.

Hyacinthus Botroides ramofus. The branched Grape-flower.

Of this kinde, there is another found to grow with many branches of flowers, breaking out from the fides of the greater ftalkes or branches: the leaues as all the reft of the plant is greater then the former.

Hyacinthus Botroides flore albo. The white Grape-flower.

The white Grape-flower hath his greene leaues a little whiter, then the blew or

skie

skie coloured Grape-flower, his flowers are very pure white, alike sparsedly set on the stalkes, but a little lower and smaller then it, in all other things there is no difference.

Hyacinthus Botroides flore albo rubente. The blush Grape-flower.

The roote of this Grape-flower groweth greater, then either the skie coloured, or white Grape-flower, and seldome hath any small rootes or of-sets, as the other haue: his leaues also are larger, and somewhat broader; the flowers are of a pale, or bleake blush colour out of a white, and are a little larger, and grow a little higher and fuller of flowers then the white.

The Place.

They naturally grow in many places both of Germany and Hungary; in Spaine likewise, and on Mount Baldus in Italy, and Narbone in France, about the borders of the fields: we haue them in our Gardens for delight.

The Time.

These flower from the beginning of March, or sooner sometimes, vntill the beginning of May.

The Names.

They are most commonly called *Botroides*, but more truely *Botryodes*, of Βότρυς the Greeke word, which signifieth a bunch or cluster of grapes: Lobelius calleth the white one, *Dipcadi flore albo*, transferring the name *Dipcadi*, whereby the *Muscari* is called to this Iacinth, as if they were both one. Their seuerall names, whereby they are knowne and called, are set downe in their titles. The Dutchmen call them *Driuekens*, as I said before. Some English Gentlewomen call the white Grape-flower Pearles of Spaine.

1. *Hyacinthus Comosus albus.* The white haired Iacinth.

This Iacinth doth more neerly resemble the Grape-flowers, then the faire haired Iacinths that follow, whereof it beareth the name, in that it hath no haire or threeds at the toppe of the stalke or sides, as they: and therefore I haue placed it next vnto them, and the other to follow it, as being of another kinde. The root hereof is blackish, a little long and round, from whence rise vp three or foure leaues, being smooth and whitish, long, narrow, and hollow, like a trough or gutter on the vpperside: among which the stalke riseth vp a foote high or more, bearing at the toppe diuers small flowers, somewhat like the former, but not so thicke set together, being a little longer, and larger, and wider at the mouth, and as it were diuided into six edges, of a darke whitish colour, with some blacker spots about the brimmes on the inside: the heads or seede-vessels are three square, and somewhat larger, then the heads of any of the former lesser Grape-flowers, wherein is contained round blacke seede.

2. *Hyacinthus Comosus Byzantinus.* The Turkie faire haired Iacinth.

This other Iacinth which came from Constantinople, is somewhat like the former, but that it is bigger, both in roote, and leafe, and flower, and bearing greater store of flowers on the head of the stalke: the lower flowers, although they haue short stalkes at their first flowring, yet afterwards the stalkes grow longer, and those that are lower, stand out further then those that are highest, whose foot-stalkes are short, and almost close to the stemme, and of a more perfect purple then any below, which are of a duskie greenish purple colour: the whole stalke of flowers seem like a Pyramis, broad belowe, and small aboue, or as other compare it, to a water sprinkle; yet neither of both these Iacinths haue any threeds at the tops of the stalkes, as the other following haue.

3. *Hyacinthus*

3. *Hyacinthus Comosus maior purpureus.*
The great purple faire haired Iacinth.

This faire haired Iacinth hath his leaues softer, longer, broader, and lesse hollow then the former, lying for the most part vpon the ground : the stalke riseth vp in the midst of the leaues, being stronger, higher, and bearing a greater and longer head of flowers also then they : the flowers of this stand not vpon such long foote-stalkes, but are shorter below, and close almost to the stalke aboue, hauing many bright purplish blew threeds, growing highest aboue the flowers, as it were in a bush together, euery one of these threeds hauing a little head at the end of them, somewhat like vnto one of the flowers, but much smaller : the rest of the flowers below this bush, are of a sadder or deader purple, and not so bright a colour, and the lowest worst of all, rather encli-ning to a greene, like vnto the last Turkie kinde : the whole stalke with the flowers vp-on it, doth somewhat resemble a long Purse tassell, and thereupon diuers Gentlewo-men haue so named it : the heads and seede are like vnto the former, but greater : the roote is great and white, with some rednesse on the outside.

4. *Hyacinthus Comosus ramosus purpureus.*
The faire haired branched Iacinth.

The leaues of this Iacinth are broader, shorter, and greener then of the last, not lying so weakly on the ground, but standing somewhat more vpright : the stalke riseth vp as high as the former, but branched out on euery side into many tufts of threeds, with knappes, as it were heads of flowers, at the ends of them, like vnto the head of threeds at the toppe of the former Iacinth, but of a little darker, and not so faire a blewish purple colour : this Iacinth doth somewhat resemble the next Curld haire Ia-cinth, but that the branches are not so fairely composed altogether of curled threeds, nor of so excellent a faire purple or Doue colour, but more duskie by much : the roote is greater and shorter then of the next, and encreaseth faster.

5. *Hyacinthus Pennatus, siue Comosus ramosus elegantior.*
The faire Curld-haire Iacinth.

This admirable Iacinth riseth vp with three or foure leaues, somewhat like vnto the leaues of the Muske Grape-flower, but lesser ; betweene which riseth vp the stalke a-bout a foote high, or somewhat more, bearing at the toppe a bush or tuft of flowers, which at the first appearing, is like vnto a Cone or Pineapple, and afterwards opening it selfe, spreadeth into many branches, yet still retaining the forme of a Pyramis, be-ing broad spread below, and narrow vp aboue : each of these branches is againe diui-ded into many tufts of threeds or strings, twisted or curled at the ends, and of an ex-cellent purple or Doue colour, both stalkes and haires. This abideth a great while in his beauty, but afterwards all these flowers (if you will so call them) do fall away with-out any seede at all, spending it selfe as it should seeme in the aboundance of the flow-ers : the roote is not so great as the last, but white on the outside.

The Place.

The two first haue been sent diuers times from Constantinople, the third is found wilde in many places of Europe, and as well in Germany, as in Italy. The two last are onely with vs in Gardens, and their naturall pla-ces are not knowne vnto vs.

The Time.
The three former kindes doe flower in Aprill, the two last in May.

The Names.
The first and second haue no other names then are expressed in their ti-tles.

1 *Hyacinthus Comosus albus.* The white haired Iacinth. 2 *Hyacinthus Comosus Byzantinus.* The Turkie faire haired Iacinth. 3 *Hyacinthus Comosus maior purpureus.* The purple faire haired Iacinth, or Purse tassels. 4 *Hyacinthus Comosus ramosus, siue Calamistratus.* The faire haired branched Iacinth. 5 *Hyacinthus Pennatus, siue Comosus elegantior.* The faire curld haire Iacinth.

tles. The third is called of some onely *Hyacinthus maior*, and of others *Hyacinthus comosus maior*: We call it in English, The purple faire haired Iacinth, because of his tuft of purple threeds, like haires at the toppe, and (as I said) of diuers Gentlewomen, purple tassels. The fourth is called by some as it is in the title, *Hyacinthus comosus ramosus*, and of others *Hyacinthus Calamistratus*. And the last or fifth is diuersly called by diuers, Fabius Columna in his *Phytobasanos* the second part, calleth it *Hyacinthus Sannesius*, because hee first saw it in that Cardinals Garden at Rome. Robin of Paris sent to vs the former of the two last, by the name of *Hyacinthus Pennatus*, and *Hyacinthus Calamistratus*, when as others sent the last by the name *Pennatus*, and the other by the name of *Calamistratus*; but I thinke the name *Cincinnatus* is more fit and proper for it, in that the curled threeds which seeme like haires, are better expressed by the word *Cincinnus*, then *Calamistrum*, this signifying but the bodkin or instrument wherewith they vse to frisle or curle the haire, and that the bush of haire it selfe being curled. Some also haue giuen to both these last the names of *Hyacinthus Comosus Parnassi*, the one fairer then the other. Of all these names you may vse which you please; but for the last kinde, the name *Cincinnatus*, as I said, is the more proper, but *Pennatus* is the more common, and *Calamistratus* for the former of the two last.

1. *Hyacinthus Orientalis Brumalis, siue præcox flore albo.*
The white Winter Orientall Iacinth.

This early Iacinth riseth vp with his greene leaues (which are in all respects like to the ordinary Orientall Iacinths, but somewhat narrower) before Winter, and sometimes it is in flower also before Winter, and is in forme and colour a plaine white Orientall Iacinth, but somewhat lesser, differing onely in no other thing, then the time of his flowring, which is alwayes certaine to be long before the other sorts.

2. *Hyacinthus Orientalis Brumalis, siue præcox flore purpureo.*
The purple Winter Orientall Iacinth.

The difference of colour in this flower causeth it to bee distinguished, for else it is of the kindred of the Orientall Iacinths, and is, as the former, more early then the rest that follow: Vnderstand then, that this is the same with the former, but hauing fine blewish purple flowers.

3. *Hyacinthus Orientalis maior præcox, dictus Zumbul Indi.*
The greatest Orientall Iacinth, or Zumbul Indi.

The roote of this Orientall Iacinth, is vsually greater then any other of his kinde, and most commonly white on the outside, from whence rise vp one or two great round stalkes, spotted from within the ground, with the lower part of the leaues also vpward to the middle of the stalkes, or rather higher, like vnto the stalkes of Dragons, but darker; being set among a number of broad, long, and somewhat hollow greene leaues, almost as large as the leaues of the white Lilly: at the toppe of the stalkes stand more store of flowers, then in any other of this kinde, euery flower being as great as the greatest sort of Orientall Iacinths, ending in six leaues, which turne at the points, of a faire blewish purple colour, and all standing many times on one side of the stalkes, and many times on both sides.

4. *Hyacinthus Orientalis vulgaris diuersorum colorum.*
The ordinary Orientall Iacinth.

The common Orientall Iacinth (I call it common, because it is now so plentifull in all Gardens, that it is almost not esteemed) hath many greene leaues, long, somewhat broad and hollow, among which riseth vp a long greene round stalke, beset from the middle thereof almost, with diuers flowers, standing on both sides

of

of the stalkes, one aboue another vnto the toppe, each whereof next vnto the foote-stalke is long, hollow, round, and close, ending in six small leaues laid open, and a little turning at the points, of a very sweete smell : the colours of these flowers are diuers, for some are pure white, without any shew of other colour in them : another is almost white, but hauing a shew of blewnesse, especially at the brims and bottomes of the flowers. Others againe are of a very faint blush, tending towards a white : Some are of as deepe a purple as a Violet ; others of a purple tending to red-nesse, and some of a paler purple. Some againe are of a faire blew, others more wat-chet, and some so pale a blew, as if it were more white then blew : after the flowers are past, there rise vp great three square heads, bearing round blacke seede, great and shining : the roote is great, and white on the outside, and oftentimes purplish also, flat at the bottome, and small at the head.

There is a kinde of these Iacinths, whose flowers are of a deepe purplish Violet co- *Flore purpureo uiolaceo lineis albicantis in dorso.* lour, hauing whitish lines downe the backe of euery leafe of the flower, which turne themselues a little backwards at the points.

There is another, whose flowers stand all opening one way, and not on all sides, but *Floribus antrorsum respicienti-bus.* are herein like the great Zumbul Indi, before set out.

There is againe another kinde which flowreth later then all the rest, and the flow- *Serotinus erectis floribus diuersorum colorum.* ers are smaller, standing more vpright, which are either white or blew, or mixt with white and purple.

5. *Hyacinthus Orientalis folioso caule.* The bushy stalked Orientall Iacinth.

This strange Iacinth hath his rootes, leaues, and flowers, like vnto the former Ori-entall Iacinths : the onely difference in this is, that his stalke is not bare or naked, but hath very narrow long leaues, growing dispersedly, and without order, with the flow-ers thereon, which are blew, and hauing for the most part one leafe, and sometimes two at the foote, or setting on of euery flower, yet sometimes it happeneth, some flow-ers to be without any leafe at the bottome, as nature, that is very variable in this plant, listeth to play : the heads and seede are blacke and round, like the other also.

6. *Hyacinthus Orientalis flore duplici.* The bleake Orientall Iacinth once double.

This double Iacinth hath diuers long leaues, like vnto the other Orientall Iacinths, almost standing vpright, among which riseth vp a stalke, brownish at the first, but growing greene afterwards, bearing many flowers at the toppe, made like the flowers of the former Iacinths, and ending in six leaues, greene at the first, and of a blewish white when they are open, yet retaining some shew of greennesse in them, the brims of the leaues being white ; from the middle of each flower standeth forth another small flower, consisting of three leaues, of the same colour with the other flower, but with a greene line on the backe of each of these inner leaues : in the middle of this lit-tle flower, there stand some threeds tipt with blacke : the smell of this flower is not so sweete as of the forme ; the heads, seede, and rootes are like the former.

7. *Hyacinthus Orientalis flore pleno cæruleo, vel purpuro violaceo.* The faire double blew, or purple Orientall Iacinth.

The leaues of these Iacinths are smaller, then the leaues of most of the other for-mer sorts ; the stalkes are shorter, and smaller, bearing but three or foure flowers on the heads of them for the most part, which are not composed like the last, but are more faire, full, and double of leaues, where they shew out their full beauties, and of a faire blew colour in some, and purple in others, smelling pretty sweete ; but these doe sel-dome beare out their flowers faire ; and besides, haue diuers other flowers that will be either single, or very little double vpon the same stalke.

8. *Hyacinthus Orientalis candidissimus flore pleno.* The pure white double Orientall Iacinth.

This double white Iacinth hath his leaues like vnto the single white Orientall Ia-cinth ;

cinth; his stalke is likewise long, slender, and greene, bearing at the toppe two or three flowers at the most, very double and full of leaues, of a pure white colour, without any other mixture therein, hanging downe their heads a little, and are reasonable sweete. I haue this but by relation, not by sight, and therefore I can giue no further assurance as yet.

The Place.

All these Orientall Iacinths, except the last, haue beene brought out of Turkie, and from Constantinople: but where their true originall place is, is not as yet vnderstood.

The Time.

The two first (as is said) flower the earliest, sometimes before Christmas, but more vsually after, and abide a great while in flower, in great beauty, especially if the weather be milde, when as few or no other flowers at that time are able to match them. The other greatest kinde flowreth also earlier then the rest that follow, for the most part. The ordinary kindes flower some in March, and some in Aprill, and some sooner also; and so doe the double ones likewise. The bushy stalked Iacinth flowreth much about the same time.

The Names.

The former two sorts are called *Hyacinthus Orientalis Brumalis*, and *Hyacinthus Orientalis praecox flore albo*, or *caruleo.* The third is called of many *Zumbul Indicum*, or *Zumbul Indi*, and corruptly *Simboline*; of others, and that more properly, *Hyacinthus Orientalis maior praecox.* The Turkes doe call all Iacinths *Zumbul*, and by adding the name of *Indi*, or *Arabi*, do shew from what place they are receiued. In English, The greatest Orientall Iacinth; yet some doe call it after the Turkish name *Zumbul Indi*, or *Simboline*, as is said before. The rest haue their names set downe in their titles, which are most fit for them.

Hyacinthus Hispanicus minor Orientalis facie.
The little Summer Orientall Iacinth.

This little Iacinth hath foure or fiue long narrow greene leaues, lying vpon the ground, among which riseth vp a slender smooth stalke, about a spanne high or more,
Flore caruleo. bearing at the toppe many slender bleake blew flowers, with some white stripes and edges to be seene in most of them, fashioned very like vnto the flowers of the Orientall Iacinth, but much smaller: the flower hath no sent at all; the seede is like the seede of the English Iacinth, or Hares bels: the roote is small and white.
Flore albo. There is another of this kinde, differing in nothing but in the colour of the flower, which is pure white.
Flore rubente. There is also another, whose flowers are of a fine delayed red colour, with some deeper coloured veines, running along the three outer leaues of the flower, differing in no other thing from the former.

The Place.

These plants haue been gathered on the Pyrenæan Mountaines, which are next vnto Spaine, from whence, as is often said, many rare plants haue likewise been gathered.

The Time.

They flower very late, euen after all or most of the Iacinths, in May for the most part.

The

1 *Hyacinthus Orientalis brumalis.* The Winter Orientall Iacinth. 2 *Zumbul Indi.* The greateſt Orientall Iacinth. 3 *Hyacinthus Orientalis vulgaris.* The ordinary Orientall Iacinth. 4 *Hyacinthus Orientalis folioſo caule.* The buſhy ſtalked Orientall Iacinth. 5 *Hyacinthus Orientalis flore duplici.* The Orientall Iacinth once double. 6 *Hyacinthus Orientalis flore pleno qæruleo.* The faire double blew Orientall Iacinth.

L

The Names.

They are called eyther *Hyacinthus Hispanicus minor Orientalis facie*, as it is in the title, or *Hyacinthus Orientalis facie*, that is to say, The lesser Spanish Iacinth, like vnto the Orientall : yet some haue called them, *Hyacinthus Orientalis serotinus minor*, The lesser late Orientall Iacinth, that thereby they may be knowne from the rest.

Hyacinthus Hispanicus obsoletus. The Spanish dunne coloured Iacinth.

This Spanish Iacinth springeth very late out of the ground, bearing foure or fiue short, hollow, and soft whitish greene leaues, with a white line in the middle of euery one of them, among which rise vp one or more stalkes, bearing diuers flowers at the toppes of them, all looking one way, or standing on the one side, hanging downe their heads, consisting of six leaues, three whereof being the outermost, lay open their leaues, and turne back the ends a little again : the other three which are innermost, do as it were close together in the middle of the flower, without laying themselues open at all, being a little whitish at the edges : the whole flower is of a purplish yellow colour, with some white and green as it were mixed among it, of no sent at all : it beareth blacke and flat seede in three square, great, and bunched out heads : the roote is reasonable great, and white on the outside, with many strong white fibres at it, which perish not yearely, as the fibres of many other Iacinths doe, and as it springeth late, so it holdeth his greene leaues almost vntill Winter.

Mauritanicus. There hath been another hereof brought from about Fez and Marocco in Barbary, which in all respects was greater, but else differed little.

Maximus Æthiopicus. There was another also brought from the Cape of good Hope, whose leaues were stronger and greener then the former, the stalke also thicker, bearing diuers flowers, confusedly standing vpon longer foote-stalkes, yet made after the same fashion, but that the three inner leaues were whitish, and dented about the edges, otherwise the flowers were yellow and greenish on the inside.

The Place.

These plants grow in Spaine, Barbary, and Ethiopia, according as their names and descriptions doe declare.

The Time.

The first flowreth not vntill Iune ; for, as I said, it is very late before it springeth vp out of the ground, and holdeth his leaues as is said, vntill September, in the meane time the seede thereof ripeneth.

The Names.

They haue their names according to the place of their growing ; for one is called *Hyacinthus Hispanicus obsoletioris coloris.* The other is called also *Hyacinthus Mauritanicus.* And the last, *Hyacinthus Æthiopicus obsoletus.* In English, The Spanish, Barbary, or Ethiopian Iacinth, of a dunne or duskie colour.

Hyacinthus Anglicus Belgicus, vel Hispanicus.
English Haref-bels, or Spanish Iacinth.

Our English Iacinth or Haref-bels is so common euery where, that it scarce needeth any description. It beareth diuers long and narrow greene leaues, not standing vpright, nor yet fully lying vpon the ground, among which springeth vp the stalke, bearing at the toppe many long and hollow flowers, hanging downe their heads all forwards

forwards for the moſt part, parted at the brimmes into ſix parts, turning vp their points a little againe, of a ſweetiſh, but heady ſent, ſomewhat like vnto the Grape-flower: the heads for ſeede are long and ſquare, wherein is much blacke ſeede: the colour of the flowers are in ſome of a deeper blew, tending to a purple; in others of a paler blew, or of a bleake blew, tending to an aſh colour: Some are pure white, and ſome are party coloured, blew and white; and ſome are of a fine delayed purpliſh red or bluſh colour, which ſome call a peach colour. The rootes of all ſorts agree, and are alike, being white and very ſlimie; ſome whereof will be great and round, others long and ſlender, and thoſe that lye neare the toppe of the earth bare, will be greene.

Hyacinthus Hiſpanicus maior flore campanulæ inſtar.
The greater Spaniſh bell-flowred Iacinth.

This Spaniſh bell-flowred Iacinth, is very like the former Engliſh or Spaniſh Ia-cinth, but greater in all parts, as well of leaues as flowers, many growing together at the toppe of the ſtalke, with many ſhort greene leaues among them, hanging downe their heads, with larger, greater, and wider open mouths, like vnto bels, of a darke blew colour, and no good ſent.

The Place.

The firſt groweth in many places of England, the Lowe-Countries, as we call them, and Spaine, but the laſt chiefly in Spaine.

The Time.

They flower in Aprill for the moſt part, and ſometimes in May.

The Names.

Becauſe the firſt is more frequent in England, then in Spain, or the Lowe-Countries, it is called with vs *Hyacinthus Anglicus*, The Engliſh Iacinth; but it is alſo called as well *Belgicus*, as *Hiſpanicus*: yet Dodonæus calleth it *Hyacinthus non ſcriptus*, becauſe it was not written of by any Authour be-fore himſelfe. It is generally knowne in England by the name of Hare-bels. The other Spaniſh Iacinth beareth his name in his title.

Hyacinthus Eriophorus. The Woolly Iacinth.

This Woolly Iacinth hath many broad, long, and faire greene leaues, very like vn-to ſome of the Iacinths, but ſtiffer, or ſtanding more vpright, which being broken, doe yeeld many threeds, as if a little fine cotton wooll were drawne out: among theſe leaues riſeth vp a long greene round ſtalke, a foote and a halfe high or more, whereon is ſet a great long buſh of flowers, which blowing open by degrees, firſt below, and ſo vpwards, are very long in flowring: the toppe of the ſtalke, with the flowers, and their little footſtalkes, are all blew, euery flower ſtanding outright with his ſtalke, and ſpreading like a ſtarre, diuided into ſix leaues, hauing many ſmall blew threeds, ſtan-ding about the middle head, which neuer gaue ripe ſeede, as farre as I can heare of: the root is white, ſomewhat like the root of a Muſcari, but as full of wooll or threeds, or rather more, then the leaues, or any other part of it.

The Place.

This hath been ſent diuers times out of Turkie into England, where it continued a long time as well in my Garden as in others, but ſome hard froſty Winters cauſed it to periſh with me, and diuers others, yet I haue had it againe from a friend, and doth abide freſh and greene euery yeare in my Garden.

The

The Time.

This flowred in the Garden of M.^r.Richard Barnesley at Lambeth, onely once in the moneth of May, in the yeare 1606. after hee had there preserued it a long time : but neither he, nor any else in England that I know, but those that saw it at that time, euer saw it beare flower, either before or since.

The Names.

It is called by diuers *Bulbus Eriophorus*, or *Laniferus*, that is, Woolly Bulbous ; but becauſe it is a Iacinth, both in roote, leafe, and flower, and not a *Narciſſus*, or Daffodill, it is called *Hyacinthus Eriophorus*, or *Laniferus*, The Woolly Iacinth. It is very likely, that Theophraſtus in his ſeuenth Book & thirteenth Chapter, did meane this plant, where hee declareth, that garments were made of the woolly ſubſtance of a bulbous roote, that was taken from between the core or heart of the roote (which, as hee ſaith, was vſed to be eaten) and the outermoſt ſhels or peelings ; yet Cluſius ſeemeth to faſten this woolly bulbous of Theophraſtus, vpon the next Iacinth of Spaine.

Hyacinthus Stellatus Bæticus maior, vulgò Perüanus.
The great Spaniſh Starry Iacinth, or of Peru.

This Iacinth (the greateſt of thoſe, whoſe flowers are ſpread like a ſtarre, except the two firſt Indians) hath fiue or ſix, or more, very broad, and long greene leaues, ſpread vpon the ground, round about the roote, which being broken are woolly, or full of threeds, like the former : in the middle of theſe leaues riſeth vp a round ſhort ſtalke, in compariſon of the greatneſſe of the plant (for the ſtalke of the Orientall Iacinth is ſometimes twice ſo high, whoſe roote is not ſo great) bearing at the toppe a great head or buſh of flowers, faſhioned in the beginning, before they bee blowne or ſeparated, very like to a Cone or Pineapple, and begin to flower belowe, and ſo vpwards by degrees, euery flower ſtanding vpon a long blackiſh blew foote-ſtalke, which when they are blowne open, are of a perfect blew colour, tending to a Violet, and made of ſix ſmall leaues, laid open like a ſtarre ; the threeds likewiſe are blewiſh, tipt with yellow pendents, ſtanding about the middle head, which is of a deeper blew, not hauing any good ſent to be perceiued in it, but commendable only for the beauty of the flowers : after the flowers are paſt, there come three ſquare heads, containing round blacke ſeede : the roote is great, and ſomewhat yellowiſh on the outſide, with a knobbe or bunch at the lower end of the roote, (which is called the ſeate of the roote) like vnto the Muſcari, Scylla, and many other bulbous rootes, at which hang diuers white, thicke, and long fibres, whereby it is faſtened in the ground, which periſh not euery yeare, but abide continually, and therefore doth not deſire much remouing.

Hyacinthus Stellatus Bæticus, ſiue Perüanus flore albo.
The great white Spaniſh ſtarry Iacinth.

This other Spaniſh Iacinth is in moſt parts like vnto the former, but that his leaues are not ſo large, nor ſo deep a greene : the ſtalks of flowers likewiſe hath not ſo thicke a head, or buſh on it, but fewer and thinner ſet : the flowers themſelues alſo are whitiſh, yet hauing a ſmall daſh of bluſh in them : the threeds are whitiſh, tipt with yellow pendents : the ſeede and rootes are like vnto the former, and herein conſiſteth the difference betweene this and the other ſorts.

Hyacinthus Stellatus Bæticus, ſiue Perüanus flore carneo.
The great bluſh coloured Spaniſh Starry Iacinth.

This likewiſe differeth little from the two former, but onely in the colour of the
flowers;

1 *Hyacinthus Orientalis faciè.* The little Summer Orientall Iacinth.　2 *Hyacinthus Mauritanicus.* The Barbary Iacinth.　3 *Hyacinthus obsoletus Hispanicus.* The Spanish duskie Iacinth.　4 *Hyacinthus Hispanicus flore campanula.* The greater Spanish bel-flowred Iacinth.　5 *Hyacinthus Anglicus.* The English Iacinth or Harebels.　6 *Hyacinthus Eriophorus.* The Woolly Iacinth　7 *Hyacinthus Stellaris Baticus maior, sine Peruanus.* The great Spanish Starry Iacinth, or of Peru.

flowers ; for this being found growing among both the other , hath h is head of flow ers as great and large as the firſt, but the buds of his flowers, before they are open, are of a deepe bluſh colour, which being open, are more delayed , and of a pleaſant pale purple , or bluſh colour , ſtanding vpon purpliſh ſtalkes : the heads in the middle are whitiſh, and ſo are the threeds compaſſing it, tipt with yellow.

The Place.

Theſe doe naturally grew in Spaine, in the Medowes a little off from the Sea, as well in the Iſland Gades , vſually called Cales , as likewiſe in other parts along the Sea ſide , as one goeth from thence to Porto Santa Maria, which when they be in flower, growing ſo thicke together , ſeeme to couer the ground, like vnto a tapiſtry of diuers colours , as I haue beene credibly enformed by Guillaume Boel , a Freeze-lander borne , often before and hereafter remembred , who being in ſearch of rare plants in Spaine, in the yeare of our Lord 1607. after that moſt violent froſty Winter, which peri- ſhed both the rootes of this , and many other fine plants with vs , ſent mee ouer ſome of theſe rootes for my Garden, and affirmed this for a truth, which is here formerly ſet downe, and that himſelfe gathered thoſe he ſent mee, and many others in the places named , with his owne hands ; but hee ſaith, that both that with the white , and with the bluſh flowers , are farre more rare then the other.

The Time.

They flower in May, the ſeede is ripe in Iuly.

The Names.

This hath beene formerly named *Eriophorus Peruanus* , and *Hyacinthus Stellatus Peruanus*, The Starry Iacinth of Peru, being thought to haue grown in Peru, a Prouince of the Weſt Indies ; but he that gaue that name firſt vn- to it, eyther knew not his naturall place, or willingly impoſed that name, to conceale it , or to make it the better eſteemed. It is moſt generally recei- ued by the name *Hyacinthus Peruanus*, from the firſt impoſer thereof , that is, the Iacinth of Peru : but I had rather giue the name agreeing moſt fitly vnto it, and call it as it is indeede *Hyacinthus Stellatus Bæticus*, The Spaniſh Starry Iacinth ; and becauſe it is the greateſt that I know hath come from thence, I call it, The great Starry Iacinth of Spaine, or Spaniſh Iacinth.

Hyacinthus Stellatus vulgaris, ſiue Biſolius Fuchſij.
The common blew Starry Iacinth.

This Starry Iacinth (being longeſt knowne, and therefore moſt common) riſeth out of the ground, vſually but with two browne leaues, yet ſometimes with three, inclo- ſing within them the ſtalke of flowers , the buds appearing of a darke whitiſh colour, as ſoone as the leaues open themſelues, which leaues being growne, are long, and hol- low , of a whitiſh greene on the vpper ſide , and browne on the vnder ſide , and halfe round, the browne ſtalke riſing vp higher , beareth fiue or ſixe ſmall ſtarre-like flowers thereon, conſiſting of ſix leaues , of a faire deepe blew, tending to a purple. The ſeede is yellowiſh, and round, contained in round pointed heads , which by rea- ſon of their heauineſſe, and the weakneſſe of the ſtalke, lye vpon the ground, and often periſh with wet and froſts, &c. The roote is ſomewhat long , and couered with a yel- lowiſh coate.

Hyacinthus ſtellatus flore albo. The white Starry Iacinth.

The white Starry Iacinth hath his leaues like the former, but greene and freſh, not browne , and a little narrower alſo : the buddes for flowers at the firſt appeare a little bluſh, which when they are blowne, are white, but yet retaine in them a ſmall ſhew of that bluſh colour.
We

We haue another, whose flowers are pure white, and smaller then the other, the *Flore niueo.* leaues whereof are of a pale fresh greene, and somewhat narrower.

Hyacinthus Stellatus flore rubente. The blush coloured Starry Iacinth.

The difference in this from the former, is onely in the flowers, which are of a faire blush colour, much more eminent then in the others, in all things else alike.

Hyacinthus Stellatus Martius, siue præcox cæruleus. The early blew Starry Iacinth.

This Iacinth hath his leaues a little broader, of a fresher greene, and not browne at all, as the first blew Iacinth of Fuchsius last remembred: the buds of the flowers, while they are enclosed within the leaues, and after, when the stalke is gowne vp, doe remaine more blew then the buds of the former: the flowers, when they are blowne open, are like the former, but somewhat larger, and of a more liuely blew colour: the roote also is a little whiter on the outside. This doth more seldome beare seede then the former.

Hyacinthus Stellatus præcox flore albo. The white early Starry Iacinth.

There is also one other of this kinde, that beareth pure white flowers, the green leafe thereof being a little narrower then the former, and no other difference.

Hyacinthus Stellatus præcox flore suaue rubente. The early blush coloured Starry Iacinth.

This blush coloured Iacinth is very rare, but very pleasant, his flowers being as large as the first of this last kinde, and somewhat larger then the blush of the other kinde: the leaues and rootes differ not from the last recited Iacinth.

The Place.

All these Iacinths haue beene found in the Woods and Mountaines of Germany, Bohemia, and Austria, as Fuchsius and Gesner doe report, and in Naples, as Imperatus and others doe testifie. Wee cherish them all with great care in our Gardens, but especially the white and the blush of both kindes, for that they are more tender, and often perish for want of due regard.

The Time.

The common kindes, which are first expressed, flower about the middle of February, if the weather bee milde, and the other kindes sometimes a fortnight after, that is, in March, but ordinarily much about the same time with the former.

The Names.

The first is called in Latine *Hyacinthus Stellatus vulgaris*, and *Hyacinthus Stellatus bifolius*, and *Hyacinthus Stellaris Fuchsij*, and of some *Hyacinthus Stellatus Germanicus*; wee might very well call the other kinde, *Hyacinthus Stellatus vulgaris alter*, but diuers call it *Præcox*, and some *Martius*, as it is in the title. In English they may bee seuerally called: the first, The common; and the other, The early Starry Iacinth (notwithstanding the first flowreth before the other) for distinction sake.

The *Hyacinthus* seemeth to be called *Vacinium* of Virgil in his Eclogues; for hee alwayes reckoneth it among the flowers that were vsed to decke Garlands, and neuer among fruits, as some would haue it. But in that hee calleth it *Vacinium nigrum*, in seuerall places, that doth very fitly answer the

common

common receiued cuſtome of thoſe times, that called all deepe blew colours, ſuch as are purples, and the like, blacke; for the Violet it ſelfe is likewiſe called blacke in the ſame place, where he calleth the *Vacinium* blacke;
ſo that it ſeemeth thereby, that he reckoned them to be both of one colour,
and we know the colour of the Violet is not blacke, as we doe diſtinguiſh of
blacke in theſe dayes. But the colour of this Starry Iacinth, being both of
ſo deepe a purple ſometimes, ſo neare vnto a Violet colour, and alſo more
frequent, then any other Iacinth with them, in thoſe places where Virgil
liued, perſwadeth me to thinke, that Virgil vnderſtood this Starry Iacinth
by *Vacinium*: Let others iudge otherwiſe, if they can ſhew greater probabi-
litie.

1. *Hyacinthus Stellatus Byzantinus nigra radice.*
The Starry Iacinth of Turkie with the blacke roote.

This Starry Iacinth of Conſtantinople hath three or foure freſh greene, thinne, and
long leaues, of the bigneſſe of the Engliſh Iacinth, but not ſo long, betweene which riſeth vp a ſlender lowe ſtalke, bearing fiue or ſix ſmall flowers, diſperſedly ſet thereon,
ſpreading open like a ſtarre, of a pale or bleake blew colour : the leaues of the flowers
are ſomewhat long, and ſtand as it were ſomewhat looſly, one off from another, and
not ſo compactly together, as the flowers of other kindes : it ſeldome beareth ripe
ſeede with vs, becauſe the heads are ſo heauie, that lying vpon the ground, they rotte
with the wet, or are bitten with the froſts, or both, ſo that they ſeldome come to good :
the roote is ſmall in ſome, and reaſonable bigge in others, round, and long, white
within, but couered with deepe reddiſh or purpliſh peelings, next vnto it, and darker
and blacker purple on the outſide, with ſome long and thicke white fibres, like fingers
hanging at the bottome of them, as is to be ſeene in many other Iacinths : the roote it
ſelfe for the moſt part doth runne downewards, ſomewhat deep into the ground.

2. *Hyacinthus Stellatus Byzantinus maior.*
The greater Starry Iacinth of Conſtantinople.

This Iacinth may rightly be referred to the former Iacinth of Conſtantinople, and
called the greater, it is ſo like thereunto, that any one that knoweth that, will ſoone
ſay, that this is another of that ſort, but greater as it is in all his parts, bearing larger
leaues by much, and more ſtore, lying vpon the ground round about the roote : it
beareth many lowe ſtalkes of flowers, as bleake, and ſtanding as looſly as the former :
onely the roote of this, is not black on the outſide, as the other, but three times bigger.

3. *Hyacinthus Stellatus Byzantinus alter, ſiue flore boraginis.*
The other Starry Iacinth of Conſtantinople.

This other Iacinth hath for the moſt part onely foure leaues, broader and greener
then the firſt, but not ſo large or long as the ſecond : the ſtalke hath fiue or ſix flowers
vpon it, bigger and rounder ſet, like other ſtarry Iacinths, of a more perfect or deeper
blew then either of the former, hauing a whitiſh greene head or vmbone in the middle, beſet with ſix blew chiues or threeds, tipt with blacke, ſo cloſly compaſſing the
vmbone, that the threeds ſeeme ſo many prickes ſtucke into a clubbe or head ; ſome
therefore haue likened it to the flower of Borage, and ſo haue called it : after the flowers are paſt, come vp round white heads, wherein is contained round and white ſeede :
the roote is of a darke whitiſh colour on the outſide, and ſometimes a little reddiſh
withall.

The Place.

The firſt and the laſt haue beene brought from Conſtantinople ; the
firſt among many other rootes, and the laſt by the Lord Zouch, as Lobel
witneſſeth. The ſecond hath been ſent vs out of the Lowe-Countries, but
from whence they had it, we do not certainly know. They growe with vs in
our Gardens ſufficiently.   The

The Time.

These flower in Aprill, but the first is the earliest of the rest, and is in flower presently after the early Starry Iacinth, before described.

The Names.

The former haue their names in their titles, and are not knowne vnto vs by any other names that I know; but as I said before, the last is called by some, *Hyacinthus Boraginis flore.* The first was sent out of Turkie, by the name of *Susam giul*, by which name likewise diuers other things haue beene sent, so barren and barbarous is the Turkish tongue.

Hyacinthus Stellatus Æstivus maior. The greater Summer Starry Iacinth.

This late Iacinth hath diuers narrow greene leaues, lying vpon the ground, somewhat like the leaues of the English Iacinth, but stiffer and stronger; among which riseth vp a round stiffe stalke, bearing many flowers at the toppe thereof, and at euery foote-stalke of the flowers a small short leafe, of a purplish colour: the flowers are starre-like, of a fine delayed purplish colour, tending to a pale blew or ash colour, striped on the backe of euery leafe, and hauing a pointed vmbone in the middle, with some whitish purple threeds about it, tipt with blew: the seede is blacke, round, and shining, like vnto the seede of the English Iacinth, but not so bigge: the roote is round and white, hauing some long thicke rootes vnder it, besides the fibres, as is vsuall in many other Iacinths.

Hyacinthus Stellatus Æstivus minor. The lesser Summer Starry Iacinth.

This lesser Iacinth hath diuers very long, narrow, and shining greene leaues, spread vpon the ground round about the roote, among which riseth vp a very short round stalke, not aboue two inches high, carrying six or seuen small flowers thereon, on each side of the stalke, like both in forme and colour vnto the greater before described, but lesser by farre: the seede is blacke, contained in three square heads: the roote is small and white, couered with a browne coate, and hauing some such thicke rootes among the fibres, as are among the other.

The Place.

Both these Iacinths grow naturally in Portugall, and from thence haue been brought, by such as seeke out for rare plants, to make a gaine and profit by them.

The Time.

They both flower in May, and not before: and their seed is ripe in Iuly.

The Names.

Some doe call these *Hyacinthus Lusitanicus*, The Portugall Iacinth. Clufius, who first set out the descriptions of them, called them as is expressed in their titles; and therefore we haue after the Latine name giuen their English, according as is set downe. Or if you please, you may call them, The greater and the lesser Portugall Iacinth.

Hyacinthus Stellaris flore cinereo. The ash coloured Starry Iacinth.

This ash coloured Iacinth, hath his leaues very like vnto the leaues of the English Iacinth, and spreading vpon the ground in the same manner, among which rise vp one or two stalkes, set at the toppe with a number of small starre-like flowers, bushing bigger

ger below then aboue, of a very pale or white blew, tending to an ash colour, and very sweete in smell : the seede is blacke and round, like vnto the seede of the English Iacinth, and so is the roote, being great, round, and white; so like, I say, that it is hard to know the one from the other.

The Place.

The certaine originall place of growing thereof, is not knowne to vs.

The Time.

It flowreth in Aprill.

The Names.

Some doe call this *Hyacinthus Someri*, Somers Iacinth, becaufe as Lobel saith, he brought it first into the Lowe-Countries, eyther from Constantinople, or out of Italy.

Hyacinthus Stellatus Lilifolio & radice cæruleo. The blew Lilly leafed Starre Iacinth.

This Iacinth hath six or seuen broad greene leaues, somewhat like vnto Lilly leaues, but shorter (whereof it tooke his name as well as from the roote) spread vpon the ground, and lying close and round : before the stalke riseth out from the middle of these leaues, there doth appeare a deepe hollow place, like a hole, to bee seene a good while, which at length is filled vp with the stalke, rising thence vnto a foote or more high, bearing many starre-like flowers at the toppe, of a perfect blew colour, neare vnto a Violet, and sometimes of paler or bleake blew colour, hauing as it were a small cuppe in the middle, diuided into six peeces, without any threeds therein : the seede is blacke and round, but not shining : the roote is somewhat long, bigge belowe, and small aboue, like vnto the small roote of a Lilly, and composed of yellow scales, as a Lilly, but the scales are greater, and fewer in number.

Hyacinthus Stellatus Lilifolius albus. The white Lilly leafed Starre Iacinth.

The likenesse of this Iacinth with the former, causeth me to be briefe, and not to repeate the same things againe, that haue already been expressed : You may therefore vnderstand, that except in the colour of the flower, which in this is white, there is no difference betweene them.

Flore carneo, I heare of one that should beare blush coloured flowers, but I haue not yet seene any such.

The Place.

These Iacinths haue been gathered on the Pyrenæan Hils, in that part of France that is called Aquitaine, and in some other places.

The Time.

These flower in Aprill, and sometimes later.

The Names.

Becaufe the roote is so like vnto a Lilly, as the leafe is also, it hath most properly beene called *Hyacinthus Stellatus Lilifolio & radice*, or for breuity *Lilifolius*, that is, The Starry Lilly leafed Iacinth. It is called *Sarahug* by the Inhabitants where it groweth, as Clusius maketh the report from Venerius, who further saith, that by experience they haue found the cattell to swell and dye, that haue eaten of the leaues thereof.

Hyacinthus

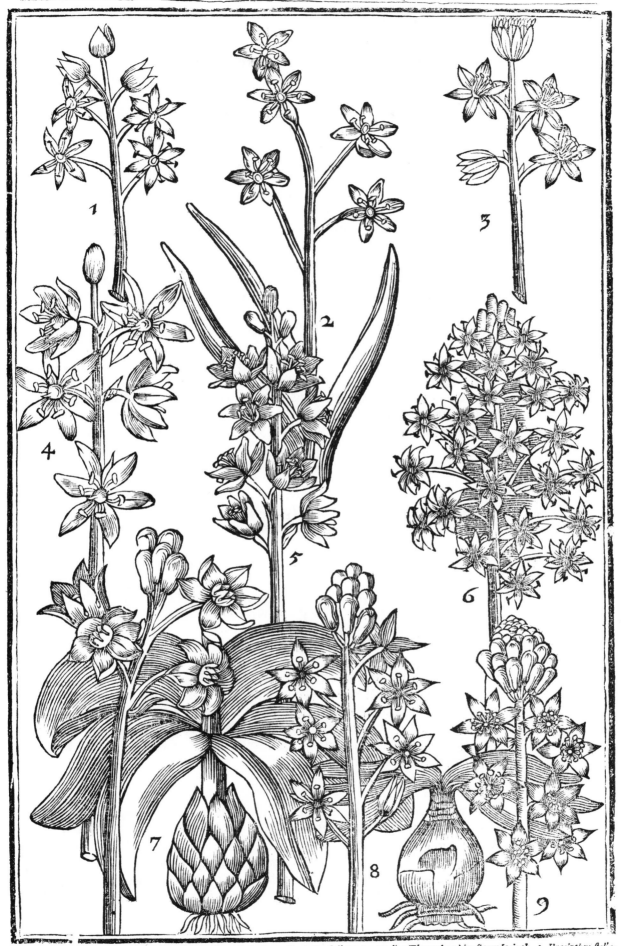

1 *Hyacinthus ſtellatus præcox cærnleus.* The early blew ſtarry Iacinth. 2 *Hyacinthus ſtellatus præcox albus.* The early white ſtarry Iacinth. 3 *Hyacinthus ſtellatus Byzantinus nigra radice.* The Turkie ſtarry Iacinth with a blacke roote. 4 *Hyacinthus Byzantinus altar ſiue flore Boraginis.* The other ſtarry Iacinth of Conſtantinople. 5 *Hyacinthus æſtivus maior.* The greater Summer ſtarry Iacinth. 6 *Hyacinthus ſtellatus flore cinereo.* The aſh coloured ſtarry Iacinth. 7 *Hyacinthus ſtellatus Liliſolius.* The Lilly leafed ſtarre Iacinth. 8 *Hyacinthus Autumnalis.* The Autumne Iacinth. 9 *Scilla alba ſiue Hyacinthus marinus.* The Sea Onion or Squill.

Hyacinthus Autumnalis maior. The greater Autumne Iacinth.

The greater Autumne Iacinth hath fiue or six very long and narrow greene leaues, lying vpon the ground; the stalkes are set at the toppe with many starre-like flowers, of a pale blewish purple colour, with some pale coloured threeds, tipt with blew, standing about the head in the middle, which in time growing ripe, containeth therein small blacke seede, and roundish: the roote is great and white on the outside.

Hyacinthus Autumnalis minor. The lesser Autumne Iacinth.

This lesser Iacinth hath such like long and small leaues, but narrower then the former: the stalke is not full so high, but beareth as many flowers on it as the other, which are of a pale or bleake purple colour, very like vnto it also: the roote and seed are like the former, but smaller. These both for the most part, beare their flowers and seede before the greene leaues rise vp much aboue the ground.

Flore albo. There is a kinde hereof found that beareth white flowers, not differing in any other thing from the smaller purple kinde last mentioned.

The Place.

The first and last are onely kept in Gardens, and not knowne to vs where their naturall place of growing wilde may be.

The second groweth wilde in many places of England. I gathered diuers rootes for my Garden, from the foote of a high banke by the Thames side, at the hither end of Cheltey, before you come at the Kings Barge-house.

The Time.

The greatest flowreth in the end of Iuly, and in August.

The other in August and September, you shall seldome see this plant with flowers and greene leaues at one time together.

The Names.

They haue their names giuen them, as they are expressed in their titles, by all former Writers, except Daleschampius, or hee that set forth that great worke printed at Lyons; for hee contendeth with many words, that these plants can bee no Iacinths, because their flowers appeare before their leaues in Autumne, contrary to the true Iacinth, as he saith: and therefore he would faine haue it referred to *Theophrastus bulbus in libro primo cap.* 12. and calleth it his *Tiphyum* mentioned in that place, as also *Bulbus æstiuus Dalechampij.* Howsoeuer these things may carry some probability in them, yet the likenesse both of rootes, and flowers especially, hath caused very learned Writers to entitle them as is set downe, and therefore I may not but let them passe in the like manner.

The Vertues.

Both the rootes and the leaues of the Iacinths are somewhat cold and drying, but the seede much more. It stayeth the loosnesse of the belly. It is likewise said to hinder young persons from growing ripe too soone, the roote being drunke in wine. It helpeth them also whose vrine is stopt, and is auaileable for the yellow Iaundise; but as you heare some are deadly to cattell, I therefore wish all to bee well aduised which of these they will vse in any inward physicke.

Scilla alba. The Sea Onion or Squill.

As I ended the discourse of both the true and the bastard Daffodils, with the Sea
kindes

kindes of both forts ; fo I thinke it not amiffe, to finifh this of the Iacinths with the defcription of a Sea Iacinth, which (as you fee) I take to be the *Scilla*, or Sea Onion, all his parts fo nearely refembling a Iacinth, that I know not where to ranke him better then in this place, or rather not any where but here. You fhall haue the defcription thereof, and then let the iudicious paffe their fentence, as they thinke meeteft.

The Squill or Sea Onion (as many doe call it) hath diuers thicke leaues, broad, long, greene, and hollo vifh in the middle, and with an eminent or fwelling ribbe all along the backe of the leafe, (I relate it as I haue feene it, hauing fhot forth his leaues in the fhip by the way, as the Mariners that brought diuers rootes from out of the Straights, did fell them to mee and others for our vfe) lying vpon the ground, fomewhat like vnto the leaues of a Lilly : thefe fpring vp after the flowers are paft, and the feed ripe, they abiding all the Winter, and the next Spring, vntill the heate of the Summer hath fpeat and confumed them, and then about the end of Auguft, or beginning of September, the ftalke with flowers arifeth out of the ground a foote and a halfe high, bearing many ftarre-like flowers on the toppe, in a long fpike one aboue another, flowring by degrees, the loweft firft, and fo vpwards, whereby it is long in flowring, very like, as well in forme as bigneffe, to the flowers of the great Starre of Bethlehem (thefe flowers I haue likewife feene fhooting out of fome of the rootes, that haue been brought in the like manner:) after the flowers are paft, there come vp in their places thicke and three fquare heads, wherin is contained fuch like flat, black, and round feed, as the Spanifh duskie Iacinth before defcribed did beare, but greater : the root is great & white, couered with many peelings or couerings, as is plainly enough feen to any that know them, and that fometimes wee haue had rootes, that haue beene as bigge as a pretty childes head, and fometimes two growing together, each whereof was no leffe then is faid of the other.

Scilla rubra fiue Pancratium verum. The red Sea Onion.

The roote of this Squill, is greater oftentimes then of the former, the outer coates or peelings being reddifh, bearing greater, longer, ftiffer, and more hollow leaues, in a manner vpright : this bringeth fuch a like ftalke and flowers, as the former doth, as Fabianus Ilges, Apothecary to the Duke of Briga, did fignifie by the figure thereof drawne and fent to Clufius.

The Place.

They grow alwayes neare the Sea, and neuer farre off from it, but often on the very baich of the Sea, where it wafheth ouer them all along the coafts of Spaine, Portugal, and Italy, and within the Straights in many places : it will not abide in any Garden farre from the Sea, no not in Italy, as it is related.

The Time.

The time wherein they flower, is expreffed to be in Auguft and September : the feede to be ripe in October and Nouember, and the greene leaues to fpring vp in Nouember and December.

The Names.

Thefe are certainly the true kindes of *Scilla* that fhould bee vfed in medicines, although (as Clufius reporteth) the Spaniards forbade him to tafte of the red Squill, as of a moft ftrong and prefent poifon. Pliny hath made more forts then can be found out yet to this day with vs : that *Scilla* that is called *Epimenidia*, becaufe it might be eaten, is thought to be the great *Ornithogalum*, or Starre of Bethlehem. *Pancratium* is, I know, and as I faid before, referred to that kinde of baftard Sea Daffodill, which is fet forth before in the end of the hiftory of the baftard Daffodils ; and diuers alfo would make the *Narciffus tertius Matthioli*, which I call the true Sea Daffodill, to be a *Pancratium*; but feeing Diofcorides (and no other is againft him)

M   maketh

maketh *Pancratium* to be a kinde of Squill with reddifh rootes, I dare not vphold their opinion againft fuch manifeft truth.

The Vertues.

The Squill or Sea Onion is wholly vfed phyfically with vs, becaufe wee can receiue no pleafure from the fight of the flowers. Pliny writeth, that Pithagoras wrote a volume or booke of the properties thereof, for the fingular effects it wrought; which booke is loft, yet the diuers vertues it hath is recorded by others, to be effectuall for the fpleene, lungs, ftomach, liuer, head and heart; and for dropfies, old coughs, Iaundife, and the wormes; that it cleareth the fight, helpeth the tooth-ache, cleanfeth the head of fcurfe, and running fores; and is an efpeciall Antidote againft poifon : and therefore is vfed as a principall ingredient into the *Theriaca Andromachi,* which we vfually call Venice Treakle. The Apothecaries prepare hereof, both Wine, Vinegar, and Oxymel or Syrupe, which is fingular to extenuate and expectorate tough flegme, which is the caufe of much difquiet in the body, and an hinderer of concoction, or difgeftion in the ftomach, befides diuers other wayes, wherein the fcales of the rootes, being dryed, are vfed. And Galen hath fufficiently explained the qualities and properties thereof, in his eight Booke of Simples.

CHAP. XII.

Ornithogalum. Starre of Bethlehem.

AFter the Family of the Iacinths, muft needes follow the kindes of Starre-flowers, or Starres of Bethlehem, as they are called, for that they doe fo nearely refemble them, that diuers haue named fome of them Iacinths, and referred them to that kindred : all of them, both in roote, leafe, and flower, come nearer vnto the Iacinths, then vnto any other plant. They fhall therefore bee next defcribed, euery one in their order, the greateft firft, and the reft following.

Ornithogalum Arabicum. The great Starre-flower of Arabia.

This Arabian Starre-flower hath many broad, and long greene leaues, very like vnto the leaues of the Orientall Iacinth, but lying for the moft part vpon the ground, among which rifeth vp a round greene ftalke, almoft two foote high, bearing at the toppe diuers large flowers, ftanding vpon long foote-ftalkes, and at the bottome of euery one of them a fmall fhort pointed greene leafe : thefe flowers are made of fix pure white leaues a peece, laid open as large as an ordinary Daffodill, but of the forme of a Starre Iacinth, or Starre of Bethlehem, which clofe as they doe euery night, and open themfelues in the day time, efpecially in the Sunne, the fmell whereof is pretty fweete, but weake : in the middle of the flower is a blackifh head, compofed with fix white threeds, tipt with yellow pendents : the feede hath not beene obferued with vs : the roote is great and white, with a flat bottome, very impatient of our cold Winters, fo that it feldome profpereth or abideth with vs; for although fometimes it doe abide a Winter in the ground, yet it often lyeth without fpringing blade, or any thing elfe a whole yeare, and then perifheth : or if it doe fpring, yet many doe not beare, and moft after their firft bearing doe decay and perifh. But if any be defirous, to know how to preferue the roote of this plant, or of many other bulbous rootes that are tender, fuch as the great double white Daffodill of Conftantinople, and other fine Daffodils, that come from hot Countries; let them keepe this rule : Let either the roote be planted in a large pot, or tubbe of earth, and houfed all the Winter, that fo it may bee defended from the frofts; Or elfe (which is the eafier way) keepe the roote out of the ground euery yeare, from September, after the leaues and ftalkes are paft, vntill February, in

some

some dry, but not hot or windy place, and then plant it in the ground vnder a South wall, or such like defended place, which will spring, and no doubt prosper well there, in regard the greatest and deepest frosts are past after February, so that seldome any great frosts come after, to pierce so deepe as the roote is to be set, or thereby to doe any great harme to it in such a place.

The Place.

This hath been often sent out of Turkie, and likewise out of Italy; I had likewise two rootes sent mee out of Spaine by Guillaume Boel before remembred, which (as hee said) hee gathered there, but they prospered not with me, for want of the knowledge of the former rule. It may be likely that Arabia is the place, from whence they of Constantinople receiue it.

The Time.

It flowreth in May, if it be of the first yeares bringing; or in Iune, if it haue been ordered after the manner before set downe.

The Names.

It hath been sent out of Italy by the name of *Lilium Alexandrinum*, The Lilly of Alexandria, but it hath no affinity with any Lilly. Others call it *Hyacinthus Arabicus*; and the Italians, *Iacintho del pater nostro*: but it is no Iacinth neither, although the flowers be like some of them. Some also would referre it to a *Narcissus* or Daffodill, and it doth as little agree with it, as with a Lilly, although his flowers in largenesse and whitenesse resemble a Daffodill. Clusius hath most fitly referred it to the stocke or kindred of *Ornithogala*, or Starres of Bethlehem, as wee call them in English, and from the Turkish name, *Zumbul Arabi*, entituled it *Ornithogalum Arabicum*, although *Zumbul*, as I haue before declared, is with them, a Iacinth, wee may call it in English, The Arabian Starre-flower, or Starre of Bethlehem, or the great Starre-flower of Arabia.

1. *Ornithogalum maximum album.*
The greatest white Starre-flower, or Starre of Bethlehem.

This great Starre-flower hath many faire, broad, long, and very fresh green leaues, rising vp very early, and are greater, longer, and greener then the leaues of any Orientall Iacinth, which doe abide greene, from the beginning or middle of Ianuary, or before sometimes, vntill the end of May, at which time they begin to fade, and the stalke with the head of flowers beginneth to rise, so that it will haue either few or no leaues at all, when the flowers are blowne: the stalke is strong, round, and firme, rising two foote high or more, bearing at the toppe a great bush of flowers, seeming at the first to be a great greene eare of corne, for it is made spike-fashion, which when the flowers are blowne, doth rise to be very high, slender or small at the head aboue, and broad spread and bushing below, so that it is long in flowring; for they flower below first, and so vpwards by degrees: these flowers are snow white, without any line on the backside, and is therein like vnto the former, as also in whitenesse, but nothing so large, with a white vmbone or head in the middle, beset with many white threeds, tipt with yellow: the seede is blacke and round, contained in three square heads: the roote is great, thicke, and short, and somewhat yellowish on the outside, with a flat bottome, both like the former, and the next that followeth.

2. *Ornithogalum maius spicatum album.*
The great white spiked Starre-flower.

This spiked Starre-flower in his growing, is somewhat like vnto the last described,

M 2 but

but fpringeth not vp fo early, nor hath his leaues fo greene, or large, but hath broad, long, whitifh greene hollow leaues, pointed at the end, among which rifeth vp the ftalke, which is ftrong and high, as the former, hauing a great bufh of flowers at the toppe, ftanding fpike-fafhion, fomewhat like the former, flowring in the fame maner by degrees, firft below, and fo vpwards; but it is not fo thicke fet with flowers, nor fo farre fpread at the bottome as it, the flowers alfo are not fo white, and each of the leaues of them haue a greene line downe the backe, leauing the edges on both fides white: after the flowers are paft, the heads for feede grow three fquare, like the other, bearing fuch like blacke feede therein: the roote hereof is vfually bigger then the laft, and whiter on the outfide.

3. *Ornithogalum Pannonicum.* The Hungarian Starre-flower.

This Hungarian Starre-flower fhooteth out diuers narrow, long, whitifh greene leaues, fpread vpon the ground before Winter, which are very like vnto the leaues of Gilloflowers, and fo abide aboue ground, hauing a ftalke rifing in the middle of them the next Spring, about halfe a foote high or thereabouts, bearing many white flowers at the toppe, with greene lines downe the backe of them, very like vnto the ordinary Starres of Bethlehem: the roote is greater, thicker, and longer then the ordinary Starres, and for the moft part, two ioyned together, fomewhat grayifh on the out fide.

4. *Ornithogalum vulgare.* The Starre of Bethlehem.

The ordinary Starre of Bethlehem is fo common, and well knowne in all countries and places, that it is almoft needleffe to defcribe it, hauing many greene leaues with white lines therein, and a few white flowers fet about the toppe of the ftalke, with greenifh lines downe the backe: the roote is whitifh, and encreafeth aboundantly.

5. *Afphodelus bulbofus Galeni, fiue Ornithogalum maius flore fubnirefcente.* The bulbous Afphodill, or greene Starre-flower.

Diuers haue referred this plant vnto the Afphodils, becaufe (as I thinke) the flowers hereof are ftraked on the backe, and the leaues long and narrow, like vnto the Afphodils; but the roote of this being bulbous, I rather (as fome others doe) ioyne it with the *Ornithogala*, for they alfo haue ftrakes on the backe of the flowers. It hath many whitifh greene leaues, long and narrow, fpread vpon the ground, which fpring vp in the beginning of the yeare, and abide vntill May, and then they withering, the ftalke fpringeth vp almoft as high as the firft, hauing many pale yellowifh greene flowers, but fmaller, and growing more fparfedly about the ftalke vpon fhort foot-ftalkes, but in a reafonable long head fpike-fafhion: the feede is like vnto the fecond kinde, but fmaller: the roote is fomewhat yellowifh, like the firft great white kinde.

The Place.

The firft is onely nurfed in Gardens, his originall being not well knowne, yet fome attribute it vnto *Pannonia* or Hungary. The fecond hath been found neare vnto Barcinone, and Toledo in Spaine. The third was found in Hungary by Clufius. Our ordinary euery where in the fields of Italy and France, and (as it is faid) in England alfo. And the laft groweth likewife by the corne fields in the vpper Hungary.

The Time.

They flower in Aprill and May, and fometimes in Iune.

The Names.

The firft is called by Clufius *Ornithogalum maximum album*, becaufe it is
greater

1 *Ornithogalum Arabicum.* The great ftarre-flower of Arabia. 2 *Ornithogalum maximum album* The greateft white ftarre flower. 3 *Ornithogalum maius fpi-*
catum album. The great white fpiked ftarre flower. 4 *Ornithogalum Pannonicum album.* The Hungarian ftarre flower. 5 *Afphodelus bulbofus Galeni, fiue Or-*
nithogalum maius fubuirefcente flore The bulbed Afphodill, or greene ftarre flower. 6 *Ornithogalum Hifpanicum minus.* The little ftarre-flower of Spaine.
7 *Ornithogalum luteum.* The yellow ftarre-flower of Bethlehem. 8 *Ornithogalum Neapolitanum.* The ftarre-flower of Naples.

M 3

greater then the next, which hee tooke formerly for the greateſt : but it might more fitly,in my iudgement,bee called *Aſphodelus bulboſus albus* (if there be any *Aſphodelus bulboſus* at all) becauſe this doth ſo nearly reſemble that, both in the early ſpringing, and the decay of the greene leaues , when the ſtalkes of flowers doe riſe vp. Diuers alſo doe call it *Ornithogalum Pannonicum maximum album.*

The ſecond hath his name in his title , as moſt authors doe ſet it downe, yet in the great Herball referred to Dalechampius,it is called *Ornithogalum magnum Myconi.*

The third hath his name from the place of his birth, and the other from his popularity, yet Dodonæus calleth it *Bulbus Leucanthemos.*

The laſt is called by diuers *Aſphodelo-hyacinthinus* , and *Hyacintho-aſphodelus Galeni.* Dodonæus calleth it *Aſphodelus fæmina* , and *Aſphodelus bulboſus.* But Lobel, and Gerrard from him, and Dodonæus, doe make this to haue white flowers, whereas all that I haue ſeene, both in mine owne, and in others Gardens , bore greeniſh flowers, as Cluſius ſetteth it truely downe. Lobel ſeemeth in the deſcription of this , to confound the *Ornithogalum* of Mompelier with it, and calleth it *Aſphodelus hyacinthinus forte Galeni,* and ſaith that ſome would call it *Pancratium Monſpelienſe,*and *Aſphodelus Galeni.* But as I haue ſhewed, the *Ornithogalum ſpicatum* and this, doe plainly differ the one from the other, and are not both to be called by one name , nor to be reckoned one, but two diſtinᵭ plants.

*Ornithogalum Æthiopicum.*The Starre-flower of Æthiopia.

The leaues of this plant are a foote long, and at the leaſt an inch broad, which being broken,are no leſſe woolly then the woolly Iacinth : the ſtalke is a cubit high , ſtrong and greene ; from the middle whereof vnto the toppe , ſtand large ſnow white flowers, vpon long, greene, thicke foot-ſtalkes,and yellowiſh at the bottome of the flower; in the middle whereof ſtand ſix white threeds, tipt with yellow chiues, compaſſing the head, which is three ſquare, and long containing the ſeede : the roote is thicke and round, ſomewhat like the *Aſphodelus Galeni.*

The Place.

This plant was gathered by ſome Hollanders, on the Weſt ſide of the Cape of good Hope.

The Time.

It flowred about the end of Auguſt with thoſe that had it.

The Names.

Becauſe it came from that part of the continent beyond the line, which is reckoned a part of Æthiopia, it is thereupon ſo called as it is ſet downe.

Ornithogalum Neopolitanum. The Starre-flower of Naples.

This beautifull plant riſeth out of the ground very early, with foure or fiue hollow pointed leaues, ſtanding round together, of a whitiſh greene colour, with a white line downe the middle of euery leafe on the inſide, ſomewhat narrow , but long, (Fabius Columna ſaith,three foot long in Italy, but it is not ſo with vs) in the middle of theſe leaues riſeth vp the ſtalke, a foote and a halfe high, bearing diuers flowers at the toppe, euery one ſtanding in a little cuppe or huſke , which is diuided into three or foure parts, hanging downe very long about the heads for ſeede : after the flower is paſt, theſe flowers doe all hang downe their heads,and open one way, although their little foot-ſtalkes come forth on all ſides of the greater ſtalke, being large, and compoſed of ſix long leaues, of a pure white on the inſide, and of a blewiſh or whitiſh greene colour

on

on the outſide, leauing the edges of euery leafe white on both ſides : in the middle of theſe flowers ſtand other ſmall flowers, each of them alſo made of ſix ſmall white leaues a peece, which meeting together, ſeeme to make the ſhew of a cuppe, within which are contained ſix white threeds, tipt with yellow, and a long white pointell in the middle of them, being without any ſent at all : after the flowers are paſt, come vp great round heads, which are too heauie for the ſtalke to beare ; and therefore lye downe vpon the leaues or ground, hauing certaine lines or ſtripes on the outſide, wherein is contained round, blacke, rough ſeede : the roote is great and white, and ſomewhat flat at the bottome, as diuers of theſe kindes are, and doe multiply as plentifully into ſmall bulbes as the common or any other.

The Place.

This Starre-flower groweth in the Medowes in diuers places of Naples, as Fabius Columna, and Ferrantes Imperatus doe teſtifie, from whence they haue been ſent. And Matthiolus, who ſetteth out the figure thereof among his Daffodils, had (it ſhould ſeeme) ſeene it grow with him.

The Time.

It flowreth in May, although it begin to ſpring out of the ground oftentimes in Nouember, but moſt vſually in Ianuary : the ſeede is ripe in Iuly.

The Names.

Matthiolus reckoneth this (as is ſaid) among the Daffodils, for no other reſpect, as i conceiue, then that he accounted the middle flower to bee the cuppe or trunke of a Daffodill, which it doth ſomewhat reſemble, and ſetteth it forth in the fourth place, whereupon many doe call it *Narciſſus quartus Matthioli*, The fourth Daffodill of Matthiolus. Fabius Columna calleth it *Hyacinthus aruorum Ornithogali flore.* Cluſius (to whom Imperatus ſent it, in ſtead of the Arabian which hee deſired) calleth it of the place from whence he receiued it, *Ornithogalum Neopolitanum,* and we thereafter call it in Engliſh, The Starre-flower of Naples.

*Ornithogalum Hiſpanicum minus.*The little Starre-flower of Spaine.

Cluſius hath ſet forth this plant among his *Ornithogala* or Starre-flowers, and although it doth in my minde come nearer to a *Hyacinthus,* then to *Ornithogalum,* yet pardon it, and let it paſſe as he doth. From a little round whitiſh roote, ſpringeth vp in the beginning of the yeare, fiue or ſix ſmall long green leaues, without any white line in the middle of them, among which riſe vp one or two ſmall ſtalkes, an hand length high or better, bearing ſeuen or eight, or more flowers, growing as it were in a tuft or vmbell, with ſmall long leaues at the foote of euery ſtalke, the lower flowers being equall in length with the vppermoſt, of a pale whitiſh blew or aſh colour, with a ſtrake or line downe the backe of euery leafe of them, with ſome white threeds ſtanding about a blewiſh head in the middle : theſe flowers paſſe away quickly, and giue no ſeed, ſo that it is not knowne what ſeede it beareth.

The Place.

This groweth in Spaine, and from thence hath been brought to vs.

The Time.

It flowreth in May.

The Names.

It hath no other name then is ſet down in the title, being but lately found out.

1.*Ornithogalum album vnifolium.*The white starre-flower with one blade.

This little starre-flower I bring into this place, as the fittest in my opinion where to place it, vntill my minde change to alter it. It hath a very small round white roote, from whence springeth vp one very long and round greene leafe, like vnto a rush, but that for about two or three inches aboue the ground, it is a little flat, and from thence springeth forth a small stalke not aboue three or foure inches high, bearing at the top thereof three or foure small white flowers, consisting of six leaues a peece, within which are six white chiues, tipt with yellow-pendents, standing about a small three square head, that hath a white pointell sticking as it were in the middest thereof : the flower is pretty and sweete, but not heady.

Ornithogalum luteum. The yellow Starre of Bethlehem.

This yellow Starre-flower riseth vp at the first, with one long, round, greenish leafe, which openeth it selfe somewhat aboue the ground, and giueth out another small leafe, lesser and shorter then the first, and afterward the stalke riseth from thence also, being foure or fiue inches high, bearing at the toppe three or foure small green leaues, and among them foure or fiue small yellow starre-like flowers, with a greenish line or streake downe the backe of euery leafe, and some small reddish yellow threeds in the middle : it seldome giueth seede : the roote is round, whitish, and somewhat cleare, very apt to perish, if it bee any little while kept dry out of the ground, as I haue twice tryed to my losse.

The Place.

The first grew in Portugall, and Clusius first of all others desciphers it.
The other is found in many places both of Germany and Hungary, in the moister grounds.

The Time.

The first flowreth in May : the other in Aprill, and sometimes in March.

The Names.

Carolus Clusius calleth the first *Bulbus vnifolius,* or *Bolbine,* but referreth it not to the stocke or kindred of any plant ; but (as you see) I haue ranked it with the small sorts of *Ornithogalum,* and giue it the name accordingly.
The other is referred for likenesse of forme, and not for colour, vnto the *Ornithogala,* or Starres of Bethlehem. It is called by Tragus and Fuchsius *Bulbus siluestris,* because of the obuiousnesse. Cordus taketh it to be *Sisyrinchium.* Lacuna calleth it *Bulbus esculentus.* Lobel and others in these dayes generally, *Ornithogalum luteum,* and wee thereafter in English, The yellow Starre-flower, or Starre of Bethlehem.

The Vertues.

The first kinde being but lately found out, is not knowne to be vsed. The rootes of the common or vulgar, are (as Matthiolus saith) much eaten by poore people in Italy, either rawe or roasted, being sweeter in taste then any Chesnut, and seruing as well for a necessary food as for delight. It is doubtfull whether any of the rest may be so vsed ; for I know not any in our Land hath made any experience.

There are many other sorts of Starre-flowers, which are fitter for a generall then this History ; and therefore I referre them thereunto.

CHAP.

Chap. XIII.

Moly. Wilde Garlicke.

VNto the former Starre-flowers, muſt needes bee ioyned another tribe or kindred, which carry their ſtraked flowers Starre-faſhion, not ſpikewiſe, but in a tuft or vmbell thicke thruſt or ſet together. And although diuers of them ſmell not as the former, but moſt of their firſt Grandfathers houſe, yet all doe not ſo; for ſome of them are of an excellent ſent. Of the whole Family, there are a great many which I muſt leaue, I will onely ſelect out a few for this our Garden, whoſe flowers for their beauty of ſtatelineſſe, forme, or colour, are fit to bee entertained, and take place therein, euery one according to his worth, and are accepted of with the louers of theſe delights.

1. *Moly Homericum, vel potius Theophraſti.*
The greateſt Moly of Homer.

Homers Moly (for ſo it is moſt vſually called with vs) riſeth vp moſt commonly with two, and ſometimes with three great, thicke, long, and hollow guttured leaues, of a whitiſh greene colour, very neare the colour of the Tulipa leafe, hauing ſometimes at the end of ſome of the leaues, and ſometimes apart by it ſelfe, a whitiſh round ſmall button, like vnto a ſmall bulbe, the like whereof alſo, but greater, doth grow betweene the bottome of the leaues and the ſtalke neare the ground, which being planted when it is ripe, will grow into a roote of the ſame kinde : among theſe leaues riſeth vp a round, ſtrong, and tall ſtalke, a yard high or better, bare or naked vnto the toppe, where it beareth a great tuft or vmbell of pale purpliſh flowers, all of them almoſt ſtanding vpon equall foot-ſtalkes, or not one much higher then another, conſiſting of fiue leaues a peece, ſtriped downe the backe with a ſmall pale line, hauing a round head or vmbone with ſome threeds about it in the midſt : Theſe flowers doe abide a great while blowne before they vade, which ſmell not very ſtrong, like any Onion or Garlicke, but of a faint ſmell : and after they are paſt come the ſeede, which is blacke, wrapped in white cloſe huskes : the roote groweth very great, ſometimes bigger then any mans cloſed fiſt, ſmelling ſtrong like Garlicke, whitiſh on the outſide, and greene at the toppe, if it be but a while bare from the earth about it.

2. *Moly Indicum ſiue Caucaſon.* The Indian Moly.

The Indian Moly hath ſuch like thicke large leaues, as the Homers Moly hath, but ſhorter and broader, in the middle whereof riſeth vp a ſhort weake ſtalke, almoſt flat, not hauing any flowers vpon it, but a head or cluſter of greeniſh ſcaly bulbes, incloſed at the firſt in a large thinne skinne, which being open, euery bulbe ſheweth it ſelfe, ſtanding cloſe one vnto another vpon his foot-ſtalke, of the bigneſſe of an Acorne, which being planted, will grow to bee a plant of his owne kinde : the roote is white and great, couered with a darke coate or skinne, which encreaſeth but little vnder ground; but beſides that head, it beareth ſmall bulbes aboue the ground, at the bottome of the leaues next vnto the ſtalke, like vnto the former.

The Place.

Both theſe doe grow in diuers places of Spaine, Italy, and Greece; for the laſt hath been ſent out of Turkie among other rootes. Ferrantes Imperatus a learned Apothecary of Naples, ſent it to diuers of his friends in theſe parts, and hath deſcribed it in his naturall hiſtory among other plants, printed in the Italian tongue. It grew alſo with Iohn Tradeſcante at Canterbury, who ſent me the head of bulbes to ſee, and afterwards a roote, to plant it in my Garden.

The

The Time.

The first flowreth in the end of May, and abideth vnto the midst of Iuly, and sometimes longer. The other beareth his head of bulbes in Iune and Iuly.

The Names.

We haue receiued them by their names expressed in their titles, yet the last hath also been sent by the name of *Ornithogalum Italicum*, but as all may easily see, it is not of that kindred.

1. *Moly montanum Pannonicum bulbiferum primum.* The first bulbed Moly of Hungary.

This first Hungarian Moly hath three or foure broad and long greene leaues, folded together at the first, which after open themselues, and are carried vp with the stalke, standing thereon one aboue another, which is a foote high; at the toppe whereof doe grow a few sad reddish bulbes, and betweene them long footstalkes, bearing flowers of a pale purplish colour; after which followeth blacke seede, inclosed in roundish heads: the roote is not great, but white on the outside, very like vnto the roote of Serpents Moly, hereafter described, encreasing much vnder ground, & smelling strong.

2. *Moly montanum Pannonicum bulbiferum secundum.* The second bulbed Moly of Hungary.

The second Moly hath narrower greene leaues then the former: the stalke is about the same height, and beareth at the toppe a great cluster of small greene bulbes, which after turne of a darker colour; from among which come forth long foot-stalks, whereon stand purplish flowers: the roote is couered with a blackish purple coate or skinne.

3. *Moly Serpentinum.* Serpents Moly.

This Moly must also be ioyned vnto the bulbous Molyes, as of kindred with them, yet of greater beauty and delight, because the bulbes on the heads of the small stalkes are redder, and more pleasant to behold: the stalke is lower, and his grassie winding leaues, which turne themselues (whereof it tooke the name) are smaller, and of a whiter greene colour: it beareth among the bulbes purplish flowers also, but more beautifull, the sent whereof is nothing so strong: the roote is small, round, and whitish, encreasing into a number of small rootes, no bigger then pease round about the greater roote.

4. *Moly caule & folijs triangularibus.* The three cornered Moly.

This three square Moly hath foure or fiue long, and somewhat broad pale greene leaues, flat on the vpper side, and with a ridge downe the backe of the leafe, which maketh it seeme three square: the stalke which riseth vp a foote and a halfe high or better, is three square or three cornered also, bearing at the toppe out of a skinnie huske diuers white flowers, somewhat large and long, almost bell-fashion, with stripes of greene downe the middle of euery leafe, and a few chiues tipt with yellow in the middle about the head, wherein when it is ripe, is inclosed small blacke seede: the roote is white on the outside, and very like the yellow Moly; both roote, leafe, and flower hath a smacke, but not very strong of Garlicke.

5. *Moly Narcissinis folijs.* Daffodill leafed Moly.

This Moly hath many long, narrow, and flat greene leaues, very like vnto the leaues of a Daffodill, from whence it tooke his name (or rather of the early greater *Leucoium bulbosum,*

1 *Moly Homericum vel potius Theophrasti.* The greatest Moly of Homer. 2 *Moly Indicum sive Caucason.* The Indian Moly. 3 *Moly Pannonicum bulbiferum.*
The bulbed Moly of Hungary. 4 *Moly Serpentinum.* Serpents Moly. 5 *Moly purpureum Neapolitanum* The purplish Moly of Naples. 6 *Moly caule &*
folijs triangularibus. The three cornered Moly. 7 *Moly latifolium flore luteo.* The yellow Moly. 8 *Moly Dioscorideum Hispanicum.* The Spanish Moly of
Dioscorides. 9 *Moly Zibettinum vel Moscharinum.* The sweete smelling Moly of Mompelier. 10 *Moly serotinum Coniferum.* The late Pineapple Moly.

bulbosam, or bulbed Violet before described, ioyned next vnto the Daffodils, becaufe it is fo like them) among which rifeth vp two or three ftalkes fometimes, each of a foot and a halfe high, bearing at the toppe, inclofed in a skinny hofe, as all the Molyes haue, a number of fmall purplifh flowers, which doe not long abide, but quickly fade: the feede is blacke as others are; the roote is fometimes knobbed, and more often bulbed, hauing in the knobs fome markes of the old ftalkes to be feene in them, and fmelleth fomewhat like Garlicke, whereby it may be knowne.

6. *Moly montanum latifolium luteo flore.* The yellow Moly.

The yellow Moly hath but one long and broad leafe when it doth not beare flower, but when it will beare flower, it hath two long and broad leaues, yet one alwaies longer and broader then the other, which are both of the fame colour, and neare the bigneffe of a reafonable Tulipa leafe : betweene thefe leaues groweth a flender ftalke, bearing at the toppe a tuft or vmbell of yellow flowers out of a skinnie hofe, which parteth three wayes, made of fix leaues a peece, laid open like a Starre, with a greenifh backe or outfide, and with fome yellow threeds in the middle : the feede is blacke, like vnto others : the roote is whitifh, two for the moft part ioyned together, which encreafeth quickly, and fmelleth very ftrong of Garlicke, as both flowers and leaues doe alfo.

7. *Moly Pyrenæum purpureum.* The purple mountaine Moly.

This purple Moly hath two or three leaues, fomewhat like the former yellow Moly, but not fo broad, nor fo white : the ftalke hath not fo many flowers thereon, but more fparingly, and of an vnpleafant purple colour : the roote is whitifh, fmelling fomewhat ftrongly of Garlicke, but quickly perifheth with the extremity of our cold Winters, which it will not abide vnleffe it be defended.

8. *Moly montanum latifolium purpureum Hifpanicum.* The purple Spanifh Moly.

This Moly hath two broad and very long greene leaues, like vnto the yellow Moly, in this, that they doe compaffe one another at the bottome of them, between which rifeth vp a ftrong round ftalke, two foote high or more, bearing at the toppe, out of a thinne huske, a number of faire large flowers vpon long foot-ftalkes, confifting of fix leaues a peece, fpread open like a Starre, of a fine delayed purple or blufh colour, with diuers threeds of the fame colour, tipt with yellow, ftanding about the middle head : betweene the ftalke and the bottome of the leaues it hath fome fmall bulbes growing, which being planted, will foone fpring and encreafe : the roote alfo being fmall and round, with many fibres thereat, hath many fmall bulbes fhooting from them; but neither roote, leafe, nor flower, hath any ill fent of Garlicke at all.

9. *Moly purpureum Neapolitanum.* The purple Moly of Naples.

The Neapolitane Moly hath three or foure fmall long greene leaues fet vpon the ftalke after it is rifen vp, which beareth a round head of very fine purple flowers, made of fix leaues a peece, but fo clofing together at the edge, that they feeme like vnto fmall cuppes, neuer laying themfelues open, as the other doe; this hath fome fent of his originall, but the roote more then any part elfe, which is white and round, quickly encreafing as moft of the Molyes doe.

10. *Moly pyxidatum argenteum Hifpanicum.* The Spanifh filuer cupped Moly.

This Spanifh Moly hath two or three very long rufh like leaues, which rife vp with the ftalke, or rather vanifh away when the ftalke is rifen vp to bee three foote high or more, bearing a great head of flowers, ftanding clofe at the firft, but afterwards fprea-ding much one from another, euery flower vpon a long foote-ftalke, being of a white

filuer

filuer colour, with ftripes or lines on euery fide, and fafhioned fmall and hollow, like a cuppe or boxe : the feede I could neuer obferue, becaufe it flowreth fo late, that the Winter hindereth it from bearing feede with vs : the roote is fmall and round, white, and in a manner tranfparent, at leaft fo fhining, as if it were fo, and encreafeth nothing fo much, as many of the other forts : this hath no ill fent at all, but rather a pretty fmell, not to bee mifliked.

11. *Moly ferotinum Coniferum.* The late Pineapple Moly.

This late Moly that was fent me with the laft defcribed, and others alfo from Spain, rifeth vp with one long greene leafe, hollow and round vnto the end, towards this end on the one fide, breaketh out a head of flowers, enclofed in a thinne skinne, which after it hath fo ftood a good while, (the leafe in the meane time rifing higher, and growing harder, becommeth the ftalke) breaketh, and fheweth a great bufh or head of buds for flowers, thicke thruft together, fafhioned very like vnto the forme of a Pineapple (from whence I gaue it the name) of the bignefs of a Walnut: after this head hath ftood in this manner a moneth or thereabouts, the flowers fhew themfelues to bee of a fine delayed or whitifh purple colour, with diuers ftripes in euery of them, of the fame cup-fafhion with the former, but not opening fo plainly, fo that they cannot bee difcerned to bee open, without good heede and obferuation. It flowreth fo late in Autumne, that the early frofts doe quickly fpoile the beauty of it, and foone caufe it to rotte : the roote is fmall and round, and fhining like the laft, very tender alfo, as not able to abide our fharpe Winters, which hath caufed it vtterly to perifh with me.

12. *Moly Diofcorideum.* Diofcorides his Moly.

The roote of this fmall Moly is tranfparent within, but couered with a thicke yellowifh skinne, of the bigneffe of an Hafell Nut, or fomewhat bigger, which fendeth forth three or foure narrow graffie leaues, long and hollow, and a little bending downwards, of a whitifh greene colour, among which rifeth vp a flender weake ftalke, a foot and a halfe high, bearing at the toppe, out of a thinne skinne, a tuft of milke white flowers, very like vnto thofe of Ramfons, which ftand a pretty while in their beauty, and then paffe away for the moft part without giuing any feede : this hath little or no fent of Garlicke.

We haue another of this fort that is leffer, and the flowers rounder pointed.

13. *Moly Diofcorideum Hifpanicum.* The Spanifh Moly of Diofcorides.

This Moly came vnto me among other Molyes from Spaine, and is in all things like vnto the laft defcribed, but fairer, larger, and of much more beauty, as hauing his white flowers twice as great as the former ; but (as it feemeth) very impatient of our Winters, which it could not at any hand endure, but quickly perifhed, as fome others that came with it alfo.

14. *Moly Mofchatinum vel Zibettinum Monfpelienfe.* The fweete fmelling Moly of Mompelier.

This fweete Moly, which I haue kept for the laft, to clofe vp your fenfes, is the fmalleft, and the fineft of all the reft, hauing foure or fiue fmall greene leaues, almoft as fine as haires, or like the leaues of the Feather-graffe : the ftalke is about a foote high, bearing fiue or fix or more fmall white flowers, laid open like Starres, made of fix leaues a peece, of an excellent fweete fent, refembling Muske or Ciuet ; for diuers haue diuerfly cenfured of it. It flowreth late in the yeare, fo that if the precedent Summer bee either ouer moift, or the Autumne ouer early cold, this will not haue that fweete fent, that it will haue in a hot drie time, and befides muft be carefully refpected : for it will hardly abide the extremity of our fharpe Winters.

The

The Place.

The places of thefe Molyes, are for the moſt part expreſſed in their titles, or in their deſcriptions.

The Time.

The time is ſet downe, for the moſt part to bee in Iune and Iuly, the reſt later.

The Names.

To make further relation of names then are expreſſed in their tiles, were needleſſe; let theſe therefore ſuffice.

The Vertues.

All theſe ſorts of Molyes are ſmall kindes of wilde Garlicke., and are to be vſed for the ſame purpoſes that the great Garden Garlicke is, although much weaker in their effects. For any other eſpeciall property is in any of theſe, more than to furniſh a Garden of variety, I haue not heard at all.

And thus much may ſuffice of theſe kindes for our Garden, reſeruing manie others that might be ſpoken of, to a generall worke, or to my Garden of Simples, which as God ſhall enable me, and time giue leaue, may ſhew it ſelfe to the world, to abide the iudicious and criticke cenſures of all.

CHAP. XIIII.

Aſphodelus. The Aſphodill.

THere remaine ſome other flowers, like vnto the laſt deſcribed, to be ſpecified, which although they haue no bulbous rootes, yet I thinke them fitteſt to bee here mentioned, that ſo I may ioyne thoſe of neereſt ſimilitude together, vntill I haue finiſhed the reſt that are to follow.

1. Aſphodelus maior albus ramoſus. The great white branched Aſphodill.

The great white Aſphodill hath many long, and narrow, hollow three ſquare leaues, ſharpe pointed, lying vpon the ground round about the roote: the ſtalke is ſmooth, round, and naked without leaues, which riſeth from the midſt of them, diuided at the toppe into diuers branches, if the plant bee of any long continuance, or elſe but into two or three ſmall branches, from the ſides of the maine great one, whereon doe ſtand many large flowers Starre-faſhion, made of ſix leaues a peece, whitiſh on the inſide, and ſtraked with a purpliſh line downe the backſide of euery leafe, hauing in the middle of the flowers ſome ſmall yellow threeds: the ſeede is blacke, and three ſquare, greater then the ſeede of Bucke wheate, contained in roundiſh heads, which open into three parts: the roote is compoſed of many tuberous long clogges, thickeſt in the middle, and ſmaller at both ends, faſtened together at the head, of a darke grayiſh colour on the outſide, and yellow within.

2. Aſphodelus albus non ramoſus. The white vnbranched Aſpodill.

The vnbranched Aſphodill is like vnto the former, both in leaues and flowers, but that the flowers of this are whiter, and without any line or ſtrake on the backe ſide,

and

and the ftalkes are without branches : the rootes likewife are fmaller, and fewer, but made after the fame fafhion.

3. *Afphodelus maior flore carneo.* The blufh coloured Afphodill.

This Afphodill is like to the laft in forme of leaues and branches, and differeth in this, that his leaues are marked with fome fpots, and the flowers are of a blufh or flefh colour, in all other things alike.

4. *Afphodelus minimus albus.* The leaft white Afphodill.

This leaft Afphodill hath foure or fiue very narrow long leaues, yet feeming three fquare like the greateft, bearing a fmall ftalke, of about a foote high among them, without any branches, and at the toppe a few white flowers, ftraked both within and without, with a purplifh line in the middle of euery leafe. The rootes are fuch like tuberous clogges as are in the former, but much leffer.

5. *Afphodelus albus minor fiue Fiftulofus.* The little hollow white Afpnodill.

This little white Afphodill hath a number of leaues growing thicke together, thicker and greener then thofe of the fmall yellow Afphodill, or Kings Speare next following, among which rifeth vp diuers round ftalkes, bearing flowers from the middle to the toppe, Starre-fafhion, with fmall greene leaues among them, which are white on the infide, and ftriped on the backe with purple lines, like vnto the firft defcribed : the feede, and heads containing them, are three fquare, like the feede of the little yellow Afphodill : the rootes of this kinde are not glandulous, as the former, but ftringie, long and white : the whole plant is very impatient of our cold Winters, and quickly perifheth, if it be not carefully preferued, both from the cold, and much wet in the Winter, by houfing it ; and then it will abide many yeares : for it is not an annuall plant, as many haue thought.

6. *Afphodelus luteus minor, fiue Haftula regia.* The fmall yellow Afphodill, or Kings fpeare.

This fmall yellow Afphodill, which is vfually called the Kings fpeare, hath many long narrow edged leaues, which make them feeme three fquare, of a blewifh or whitifh greene colour : the ftalke rifeth vp three foote high oftentimes, befet with fmall long leaues vp vnto the very flowers, which grow thicke together fpike-fafhion one aboue another, for a great length, and wholly yellow, laid open like a Starre, fomewhat greater then the laft white Afphodill, and fmaller then the firft, which when they are paft yeeld round heads, containing blacke cornered feede, almoft three fquare : the rootes are many long yellow ftrings, which fpreading in the ground, doe much encreafe.

The Place.

All thefe Afphodils doe grow naturally in Spaine and France, and from thence were firft brought vnto vs, to furnifh our Gardens.

The Time.

All the glandulous rooted Afphodils doe flower fome in May, and fome in Iune ; but the two laft doe flower, the yellow or laft of them in Iuly, and the former white one in Auguft and September, and vntill the cold and winter hinder it.

The Names.

Their feuerall names are giuen them in their titles, as much as is fit for

this

this difcourfe. For to fhew you that the Greekes doe call the ftalke of the great Afphodill ἈϭϖελⱪⒼ, and the Latines *Albucum*, or what elfe belongeth to them, is fitter for another worke, vnto which I leaue them.

The baftard Afphodils fhould follow next in place, if this worke were fit for them ; but becaufe I haue tyed my felfe to expreffe onely thofe flowers and plants, that for their beauty, or fent, or both, doe furnifh a Garden of Pleafure, and they haue none, I leaue them to a generall Hiftory of plants, or that Garden of Simples before fpoken of, and will defcribe the Lilly Afphodils, and the *Phalangia* or Spider-worts, which are remaining of thofe, that ioyne in name or fafhion, and are to be here inferted, before I paffe to the reft of the bulbous rootes.

1. *Liliafphodelus phaniceus.* The gold red Day Lilly.

Becaufe the rootes of this and the next, doe fo nearely agree with the two laft recited Afphodils, I haue fet them in this place, although fome doe place them next after the Lillies, becaufe their flowers doe come neareft in forme vnto Lillies ; but whether you will call them Afphodils with Lilly flowers, as I thinke it fitteft, or Lillies with Afphodill rootes, or Lillies without bulbous rootes, as others doe, I will not contend. The red Day Lilly hath diuers broad and long frefh greene leaues, folded at the firft as it were double, which after open, and remaine a little hollow in the middle ; among which rifeth vp a naked ftalke three foot high, bearing at the toppe many flowers, one not much diftant from another, and flowring one after another, not hauing lightly aboue one flower blown open in a day, & that but for a day, not lafting longer, but clofing at night, and not opening againe ; whereupon it had his Englifh name, The Lilly for a day : thefe flowers are almoft as large as the flowers of the white Lilly, and made after the fame fafhion, but of a faire gold red, or Orange tawny colour. I could neuer obferue any feede to follow thefe flowers ; for they feeme the next day after they haue flowred, (except the time be faire and dry) to bee fo rotten, as if they had lyen in wet to rotte them, whereby I thinke no feede can follow : the rootes are many thicke and long yellow knobbed ftrings, like vnto the fmall yellow Afphodill rootes, but fomewhat greater, running vnder ground in like fort, and fhooting young heads round about.

2. *Liliafphodelus luteus.* The yellow Day Lilly.

I fhall not neede to make a repetition of the defcription of this Day Lilly, hauing giuen you one fo amply before, becaufe this doth agree thereunto fo nearely, as that it might feeme the fame ; thefe differences onely it hath, the leaues are not fully fo large, nor the flower fo great or fpread open, and the colour thereof is of a faire yellow wholly, and very fweet, which abideth blowne many daies before it fade, and hath giuen blacke round feede, growing in round heads, like the heads of the fmall yellow Afphodill, but not fo great. Clufius hath fet downe, that it was reported, that there fhould be another Liliafphodill with a white flower, but we can heare of none fuch as yet ; but I rather thinke, that they that gaue that report might be miftaken, in thinking the Sauoye Spider-wort to be a white Liliafphodill, which indeede is fo like, that one not well experienced, or not well regarding it, may foone take one for another.

The Place.

Their originall is many moift places in Germany.

The Time.

They flower in May and Iune.

The Names.

They are called by fome *Liliago*, and *Lilium non bulbofum*, and *Liliafpho-*
delus,

1 *Asphodelus maior albus ramosus.* The great white branched Asphodill. 2 *Asphodelus minor albus seu fistulosus.* The little hollow white Asphodill. 3 *Asphodelus minor luteus, siue Hastula regia.* The small yellow Asphodill, or Kings speare. 4 *Liliasphodelus luteus.* The yellow Day Lilly. 5 *Liliasphodelus phœniceus.* The gold red Day Lilly.

delus. In Englifh we call them both Day Lillies, but the name doth not fo well agree with the laft, as with the firft, for the caufes aboue fpecified.

The Vertues.

The rootes of Afphodill hath formerly beene had in great account, but now is vtterly neglected; yet by reafon of their fharpeneffe they open and cleanfe, and therefore fome haue of late vfed them for the yellow Iaundife. The Day Lillies haue no phyficall vfe that I know, or haue heard.

Chap. XV.

Phalangium. Spider-wort.

THefe plants doe fo nearely refemble thofe that are laft fet forth, that I thinke none that knowes them, will doubt, but that they muft follow next vnto them, being fo like vnto them, and therefore of the faireft of this kinde firft.

1. *Phalangium Allobrogicum.* The Sauoye Spider-wort.

The Sauoye Spider-wort fpringeth vp with foure or fiue greene leaues, long and narrow, yet broader at the bottome, narrower pointed at the end, and a little hollow in the middle; among which rifeth vp a round ftiffe ftalke, a foote and a halfe high, bearing at the toppe one aboue another, feuen or eight, or more flowers, euery one as large almoft as the yellow Day Lilly laft defcribed, but much greater then in any other of the Spider-worts, of a pure white colour, with fome threeds in the middle, tipt with yellow, and a fmall forked pointell: after the flowers are paft, the heads or feede veffels grow almoft three fquare, yet fomewhat round, wherein is contained blackifh feede: the rootes are many white, round, thicke, brittle ftrings, ioyned together at the head, but are nothing fo long, as the rootes of the other *Phalangia* or Spider-worts.

2. *Phalangium maius Italicum album.* The great Italian Spider-wort.

This great Spider-wort hath diuers long and narrow leaues fpread vpon the ground, and not rifing vp as the former, and not fo broad alfo as the former, but fomewhat larger then thofe that follow: the ftalke is bigger, but feldome rifeth vp fo high as the next, whereof this is a larger kinde, hauing a long vnbranched ftalke of white flowers, laid open like ftarres as it hath, but fomewhat greater: the rootes are long and white, like the next, but fomewhat larger.

3. *Phalangium non ramofum vulgare.* Vnbranched Spider-wort.

The leaues of this Spider-wort doe feeme to bee little bigger or longer then the leaues of graffe, but of a more grayifh green colour, rifing immediately from the head or tuft of rootes; among which rife vp one or two ftalkes, fometimes two or three foote long, befet toward the toppe with many white Starre-like flowers, which after they are paft turne into fmall round heads, containing blacke feede, like vnto the feed of the little yellow Afphodill, but leffer: the rootes are long white ftrings, running vnder ground.

4. *Phalangium ramefum.* Branched Spider-wort.

The branched Spider-wort hath his leaues fomewhat broader then the former, and of a more yellowifh greene colour: the ftalke hereof is diuerfly branched at the top, bearing many white flowers, like vnto the former, but fmaller: the feedes and rootes are like the former in all things.

The

1 *Phalangium Allobrogicum.* The Sauoye Spider-wort.   2 *Phalangium non ramosum.* Vnbranched Spider-wort.   3 *Phalangium ramosum.* branched Spider-wort.   4 *Phalangium
Ephemerum Virginianum.* Iohn Tradescante's Spider-wort.

The Place.

The firſt groweth on the Hils neare vnto Sauoye, from whence diuers, allured with the beauty of the flower, haue brought it into theſe parts.

The ſecond came vp in my Garden, from the ſeede receiued out of Italy. The others grow in Spaine, France, &c.

The Time.

The vnbranched Spider-wort moſt commonly flowreth before all the other, and the branched a moneth after it : the other two about one time, that is, towards the end of May, and not much after the vnbranched kinde.

The Names.

The firſt (as I ſaid before) hath beene taken to be a white Lilliaſphodill, and called *Liliaſphodelus flore albo*; but Cluſius hath more properly entituled it a *Phalangium*, and from the place of his originall, gaue him his other denomination, and ſo is called of moſt, as is ſet downe in the title.

The other haue no other names then are expreſſed in their titles, but only that Cordus calleth them *Liliago*; and Dodonæus, *lib. 4. hiſt. plant.* would make the branched kinde to bee *Moly alterum Pliny*, but without any good ground.

The Vertues.

The names *Phalangium* and *Phalangites* were impoſed on theſe plants, becauſe they were found effectuall, to cure the poyſon of that kinde of Spider, called *Phalangium*, as alſo of Scorpions and other Serpents. Wee doe not know, that any Phyſitian hath vſed them to any ſuch, or any other purpoſe in our dayes.

5. *Phalangium Ephemerum Virginianum Ioannis Tradeſcant.*
The ſoon fading Spider-wort of Virginia, or Tradeſcant his Spider-wort.

This Spider-wort is of late knowledge, and for it the Chriſtian world is indebted vnto that painfull induſtrious ſearcher, and louer of all natures varieties, Iohn Tradeſcant (ſometimes belonging to the right Honourable Lord Robert Earle of Salisbury, Lord Treaſurer of England in his time, and then vnto the right Honourable the Lord Wotton at Canterbury in Kent, and laſtly vnto the late Duke of Buckingham) who firſt receiued it of a friend, that brought it out of Virginia, thinking it to bee the Silke Graſſe that groweth there, and hath imparted hereof, as of many other things, both to me and others ; the deſcription whereof is as followeth :

From a ſtringie roote, creeping farre vnder ground, and riſing vp againe in many places, ſpringeth vp diuers heads of long folded leaues, of a grayiſh ouer-worne greene colour, two or three for the moſt part together, and not aboue, compaſſing one another at the bottome, and abiding greene in many places all the Winter ; other-where periſhing, and riſing anew in the Spring, which leaues riſe vp with the great round ſtalke, being ſet thereon at the ioynts, vſually but one at a ioynt, broad at the bottome where they compaſſe the ſtalke, and ſmaller and ſmaller to the end : at the vpper ioynt, which is the toppe of the ſtalke, there ſtand two or three ſuch like leaues, but ſmaller, from among which breaketh out a dozen, ſixteene, or twenty, or more round green heads, hanging downe their heads by little foot-ſtalkes, which when the flower beginneth to blow open, groweth longer, and ſtandeth vpright, hauing three ſmall pale greene leaues for a huſke, and three other leaues within them for the flower, which lay themſelues open flat, of a deepe blew purple colour, hauing an vmbone or ſmall head in the middle, cloſely ſet about with ſix reddiſh, hairy, or feathered threeds, tipt with yellow pendents : this flower openeth it ſelfe in the day, & ſhutteth vſually at
night,

night, and neuer openeth againe, but perisheth, and then hangeth downe his head a-gaine; the greene huske of three leaues, closing it selfe againe into the forme of a head, but greater, as it was before, the middle vmbone growing to bee the seede vessell, wherein is contained small, blackish, long seede: Seldome shall any man see aboue one, or two at the most of these flowers blowne open at one time vpon the stalke, whereby it standeth in flowring a long time, before all the heads haue giuen out their flowers.

The Place.

This plant groweth in some parts of Virginia, and was deliuered to Iohn Tradescant.

The Time.

It flowreth from the end of May vntill Iuly, if it haue had greene leaues all the Winter, or otherwise, vntill the Winter checke his luxuriousnesse.

The Names.

Vnto this plant I confesse I first imposed the name, by considering duely all the parts thereof, which vntill some can finde a more proper, I desire may still continue, and to call it *Ephemerum Virginianum Tradescanti*, Iohn Tradescante's Spider-wort of Virginia, or *Phalangium Ephemerum Virginianum*, The soone fading or Day Spider-wort of Virginia.

The Vertues.

There hath not beene any tryall made of the properties since wee had it, nor doe we know whether the Indians haue any vse thereof.

Chap. XVI.

Colchicum. Medowe Saffron.

TO returne to the rest of the bulbous and tuberous rooted plants, that remaine to bee entreated of, the *Colchica* or Medowe Saffrons are first to bee handled, whereof these later dayes haue found out more varieties, then formerly were knowne; some flowring in the Spring, but the most in Autumne, and some bearing double, but the greatest part single flowers: whereof euery one in their order, and first of our owne Country kindes.

1. *Colchicum Anglicum album.* The white English Medowe Saffron.

It is common to all the Medowe Saffrons, except that of the Spring, and one other, to beare their flowers alone in Autumne or later, without any green leaues with them, and afterwards in February, their greene leaues: So that I shall not neede to make ma-nie descriptions, but to shew you the differences that consist in the leaues, and colours of the flowers; and briefly to passe (after I haue giuen you a full description of the first) from one vnto another, touching onely those things that are note worthy. The white English Medowe Saffron then doth beare in Autumne three or foure flowers at the most, standing seuerally vpon weake foote-stalkes, a fingers length or more aboue the ground, made of six white leaues, somewhat long and narrow, and not so large as most of the other kindes, with some threeds or chiues in the middle, like vnto the Saffron flowers of the Spring, wherein there is no colour of Saffron, or vertue to that effect: after the flowers are past and gone, the leaues doe not presently follow, but the roote remaineth in the ground without shew of leafe aboue ground, most part of the Winter, and then in February there spring vp three or foure large and long greene leaues,

leaues, when they are fully growne vp, ſtanding on the toppe of a round, weake, green, and ſhort foote-ſtalke, ſomewhat like the leaues of white Lillies, but not ſo large, and in the middeſt of theſe leaues, after they haue been vp ſome time, appeare two or three looſe skinny heads, ſtanding in the middle of the leaues vpon ſhort, thicke, greene ſtalkes, and being ripe, conteine in them round ſmall browniſh ſeede, that lye as it were looſe therein, and when the head is dry, may bee heard to rattle being ſhaken: the roote is white within, but couered with a thicke blackiſh skinne or coate, hauing one ſide thereof at the bottome longer then the other, with an hollowneſſe alſo on the one ſide of that long eminence, where the flowers riſe from the bottome, and ſhooting downe from thence a number of white fibres, whereby it is faſtened in the ground: the greene leaues afterwards riſing from the top or head of the roote.

2. *Colchicum Anglicum purpureum.* The purple Engliſh Medowe Saffron.

There is no difference at all in this Medowe Saffron from the former, but only in the colour of the flowers, which as they were wholly white in the former, ſo in this they are of a delayed purple colour, with a ſmall ſhew of veines therein.

3. *Colchicum Pannonicum album.* The white Hungary Medowe Saffron.

The greateſt difference in this *Colchicum* from the former Engliſh white one, is, that it is larger both in roote, leaſe, and flower, and beſides, hath more ſtore of flowers together, and continuing longer in beauty, without fading ſo ſoone as the former, and are alſo ſomewhat of a fairer white colour.

4. *Colchicum Pannonicum purpureum.* The purple Hungary Medowe Saffron.

This purple Medowe Saffron is ſomewhat like vnto the white of this kinde, but that it beareth not ſo plentifully as the white, nor doth the roote grow ſo great; but the flowers are in a manner as large as they, and of the like pale delayed purple colour, or ſomewhat deeper, as is in the purple Engliſh, with ſome veines or markes vpon the flowers, making ſome ſhew of a checker on the out ſide, but not ſo conſpicuous, as in the true checkerd kindes. Wee haue a kinde hereof is party coloured with white ſtreakes and edges, which abide conſtant, and hath been raiſed from the ſeede of the former.

5. *Colchicum Byzantinum.* Medowe Saffron of Conſtantinople.

This Medowe Saffron of Conſtantinople hath his leaues ſo broad and large, that hardly could any that neuer ſaw it before, iudge it to be a *Colchicum*; for they are much larger then any Lilly leaues, and of a darke greene colour: the flowers are correſpondent to the leaues, larger and more in number then in any of the former purple kindes, of the ſame colour with the laſt purple kinde, but of a little deeper purple on the inſide, with diuers markes running through the flowers, like vnto it, or vnto checkers, but yet ſomewhat more apparantly: the roote is in the middle greater and rounder then the others, with a longer eminence, whereby it may eaſily bee knowne from all other ſorts.

6. *Colchicum Laſitanicum Fritillaricum.*
The checkerd Medowe Saffron of Portugall.

The flowers of this Medowe Saffron are larger and longer then the flowers of either the Engliſh or Hungarian, and almoſt as large as the laſt before mentioned, and of the ſame colour, but a little deeper, the ſpots and markes whereof are ſomewhat more eaſie to be ſeene euen a farre off, like vnto the flower of a Fritillaria, from whence it tooke his ſignificatiue name: the leaues of this Medowe Saffron doe riſe vp ſooner then in any other of the Autumne kindes; for they are alwayes vp before Winter, and are foure or fiue in number, ſhort rather then long, broad belowe, and pointed at the end, canaled or hollow, and ſtanding round aboue the ground, one encompaſſing another at the bottome, like the great Spaniſh Starre Iacinth, called the Iacinth of Peru,

but

but ſhorter, and of a pale or grayiſh greene colour, differing from the colour of all the other Medowe Saffrons : the roote is like the roote of the Engliſh or Hungarian without any difference, but that it groweth ſomewhat greater. It is one of the firſt Medowe Saffrons that flower in the Autumne.

7. *Colchicum Neapolitanum Fritillaricum.*
The checkerd Medowe Saffron of Naples.

This checkerd Medowe Saffron of Naples, is very like vnto the laſt recited checkerd Saffron of Portugall, but that the flower is ſomewhat larger, yet ſometimes very little, or not at all : the greateſt marke to diſtinguiſh them is, that the flowers of this are of a deeper colour, and ſo are the ſpots on the flowers likewiſe, which are ſo conſpicuous, that they are diſcerned a great way off, more like vnto the flowers of a deepe Fritillaria, then the former, and make a goodlier and a more glorious ſhew : the leaues of this doe riſe vp early after the flowers, and are ſomewhat longer, of a darker greene colour, yet bending to a grayiſh colour as the other, not lying ſo neatly or round, but ſtand vp one by another, being as it were folded together : neither of both theſe laſt named checkerd Medowe Saffrons haue giuen any ſeede in this Countrey, that euer I could learne or heare of, but are encreaſed by the roote, which in this is like the former, but a little bigger.

8. *Colchicum Fritillaricum Chienſe.*
The checkerd Medowe Saffron of Chio or Sio.

This moſt beautifull Saffron flower riſeth vp with his flowers in the Autumne, as the others before ſpecified doe, although not of ſo large a ſize, yet farre more pleaſant and delightfull in the thicke, deepe blew, or purple coloured beautifull ſpots therein, which make it excell all others whatſoeuer : the leaues riſe vp in the Spring, being ſmaller then the former, for the moſt part three in number, and of a paler or freſher greene colour, lying cloſe vpon the ground, broad at the bottome, a little pointed at the end, and twining or folding themſelues in and out at the edges, as if they were indented. I haue not ſeene any ſeede it hath borne : the roote is like vnto the others of this kinde, but ſmall and long, and not ſo great : it flowreth later for the moſt part then any of the other, euen not vntill Nouember, and is very hard to be preſerued with vs, in that for the moſt part the roote waxeth leſſe and leſſe euery yeare, our cold Country being ſo contrary vnto his naturall, that it will ſcarce ſhew his flower ; yet when it flowreth any thing early, that it may haue any comfort of a warme Sunne, it is the glorie of all theſe kindes.

9. *Colchicum verſicolor.* The party coloured Medowe Saffron.

The flowers of this Medowe Saffron moſt vſually doe not appeare, vntill moſt of the other Autumne ſorts are paſt, except the laſt, which are very lowe, ſcarce riſing with their ſtalkes three fingers breadth aboue the ground, but oftentimes halfe hid within the ground : the leaues whereof are ſmaller, ſhorter, and rounder, then in any of the other before ſpecified, ſome being altogether white, and others wholly of a very pale purple, or fleſh colour ; and ſome againe parted, the one halfe of a leafe white, and the other halfe of the ſame purple, and ſometimes ſtriped purple and white, in diuers leaues of one and the ſame flower : and againe, ſome will be the moſt part of the leafe white, and the bottome purple, thus varying as nature liſt, that many times from one roote may be ſeene to ariſe all theſe varieties before mentioned : theſe flowers doe ſtand long before they fade and paſſe away ; for I haue obſerued in my Garden ſome that haue kept their flower faire vntill the beginning of Ianuary, vntill the extremitie of the Winter froſts and ſnowes haue made them hide their heads : the leaues therefore accordingly doe riſe vp after all other, and are of a browniſh or darke greene colour at their firſt ſpringing vp, which after grow to be of a deepe greene colour : the roote is like the former Engliſh or Hungarian kindes, but thicker and greater for the moſt part, and ſhorter alſo.

10. *Colchicum*

10. *Colchicum variegatum alterum.* Another party coloured Medowe Saffron.

There is another, whose party coloured flowers rise a little higher, diuersly striped and marked, with a deeper purple colour, and a pale or whitish blush throughout all the leaues of the flower.

11. *Colchicum montanum Hispanicum minus.* The little Spanish Medowe Saffron.

The flowers of this little Medowe Saffron are narrower and smaller then any of the former, and of a deeper reddish purple colour then either the English or Hungarian kindes: the greene leaues also are smaller then any other, lying on the ground, of a deepe or sad greene colour, rising vp within a while after the flowers are past, and doe abide greene all the Winter long: the roote is small and long, according to the rest of the plant, and like in forme to the others.

12. *Colchicum montanum minus versicolore flore.*
The small party coloured Medowe Saffron.

This little kinde differeth not from the Spanish kinde last set forth, but in the varietie of the flower, which is as small as the former; the three inner leaues being almost all white, and the three outer leaues some of them pale or blush, and some party coloured, with a little greene on the backe of some of them.

13. *Colchicum Hermodactilum.* Physicall Medowe Saffron.

This Physicall Medowe Saffron springeth vp with his leaues in Autumne, before his flowers appeare beyond the nature of all the former kindes, yet the flower doth, after they are vp, shew it selfe in the middle of the greene leaues, consisting of six white leaues, with diuers chiues in the middle, and passeth away without giuing any seede that euer I could obserue: the greene leaues abide all the Winter and Spring following, decaying about May, and appeare not vntill September, when (as I said) the flowers shew themselues presently after the leaues are sprung vp.

14. *Colchicum atropurpureum.* The darke purple Medowe Saffron.

The greatest difference in this kinde consisteth in the flower, which at the first appearing is as pale a purple, as the flower of the former Hungarian kinde: but after it hath stood in flower two or three dayes, it beginneth to change, and will after a while become to bee of a very deepe reddish purple colour, as also the little foote-stalke whereon it doth stand: the flower is of the bignesse of the Hungarian purple, and so is the greene leafe: the seede and roote is like the English purple kinde.

15. *Colchicum atropurpureum variegatum.*
The party coloured darke purple Medowe Saffron.

We haue of late gained another sort of this kinde, differing chiefly in the flower, which is diuersly striped thorough euery leafe of the flower, with a paler purple colour, whereby the flower is of great beauty: this might seeme to bee a degeneration from the former, yet it hath abiden constant with me diuers yeares, and giueth seede as plentifully as the former.

16. *Colchicum flore pleno.* Double flowred Medowe Saffron.

The double Medowe Saffron is in roote and leafe very like vnto the English kinde: the flowers are of a fine pale or delayed purple colour, consisting of many leaues set thicke together, which are somewhat smaller, as in the English flower, being narrow and long, and as it were round at the points, which make a very double flower, hauing

O   some

some chiues with their yellow tips, difperfed as it were among the leaues in the middle: it flowreth in September, a little after the firft fhew of the earlier Medowe Saffrons are paft.

17. Colchicum variegatum pleno flore.
The party coloured double Medowe Saffron.

We haue another of thefe double kinds (if it be not the very fame with the former, varying in the flower as nature pleafeth oftentimes; for I haue this flower in my garden, as I here fet it forth, euery yeare) whofe flowers are diuerfified in the partition of the colours, as is to be feene in the fingle party coloured Medowe Saffron before defcribed, hauing fome leaues white, and others pale purple, and fome leaues halfe white and halfe purple, diuerfly fet or placed in the double flower, which doth confift of as many leaues as the former, yet fometime this party coloured flower doth not fhew it felfe double like the former, but hath two flowers, one rifing out of another, making each of them to be almoft but fingle flowers, confifting of eight or ten leaues a peece: but this diuerfity is not conftant; for the fame roote that this yeare appeareth in that manner, the next yeare will returne to his former kinde of double flowers againe.

18. Colchicum Vernum. Medowe Saffron of the Spring.

This Medowe Saffron rifeth vp very early in the yeare, that is, in the end of Ianuarie fometimes, or beginning, or at the furtheft the middle of February, prefently after the deepe Frofts and Snowes are paft, with his flowers inclofed within three greene leaues, which opening themfelues as foone almoft as they are out of the ground, fhew their buds for flowers within them very white oftentimes, before they open farre, and fometimes alfo purplifh at their firft appearing, which neuer fhew aboue two at the moft vpon one roote, and neuer rife aboue the leaues, nor the leaues much higher then they, while they laft: the flower confifteth of fix leaues, long and narrow, euery leafe being diuided, both at the bottome and toppe, each from other, and ioyned together onely in the middle, hauing alfo fix chiues, tipt with yellow in the middle, euery chiue being ioyned to a leafe, of a pale red or deepe blufh colour, when it hath ftood a while blowne, and is a fmaller flower then any Medowe Saffron, except the fmall Spanifh kindes onely, but continueth in his beauty a good while, if the extremity of fharpe Frofts and Windes doe not fpoile it: the leaues wherein thefe flowers are enclofed, at their firft comming vp, are of a brownifh greene colour, which fo abide for a while, efpecially on the outfide, but on the infide they are hollow, and of a whitifh or grayifh greene colour, which after the flowers are paft, grow to bee of the length of a mans longeft finger, and narrow withall: there rifeth vp likewife in the middle of them the head or feede veffell, which is fmaller and fhorter, and harder then any of the former, wherein is contained fmall round browne feede: the roote is fmall, fomewhat like vnto the rootes of the former, but fhorter, and not hauing fo long an eminence on the one fide of the bottome.

19. Colchicum Vernum atropurpureum. Purple Medowe Saffron of the Spring.

The flower of this Medowe Saffron, is in the rifing vp of his leaues and flowers together, and in all things elfe, like vnto the former, onely the flowers of this fort are at their firft appearing of a deeper purple colour, and when they are blowne alfo are much deeper then the former, diuided in like manner, both at the bottome and toppe as the other, fo that they feeme, like as if fix loofe leaues were ioyned in the middle part, to make one flower, and hath his fmall chiues tipt with yellow, cleauing in like manner to euery leafe.

The Place.

All thefe Medowe Saffrons, or the moft part of them, haue their places expreffed in their titles; for fome grow in the fields and medowes of the champion grounds, others on the mountaines and hilly grounds. The Englifh kindes grow in the Weft parts, as about Bathe, Briftow, Warmifter,

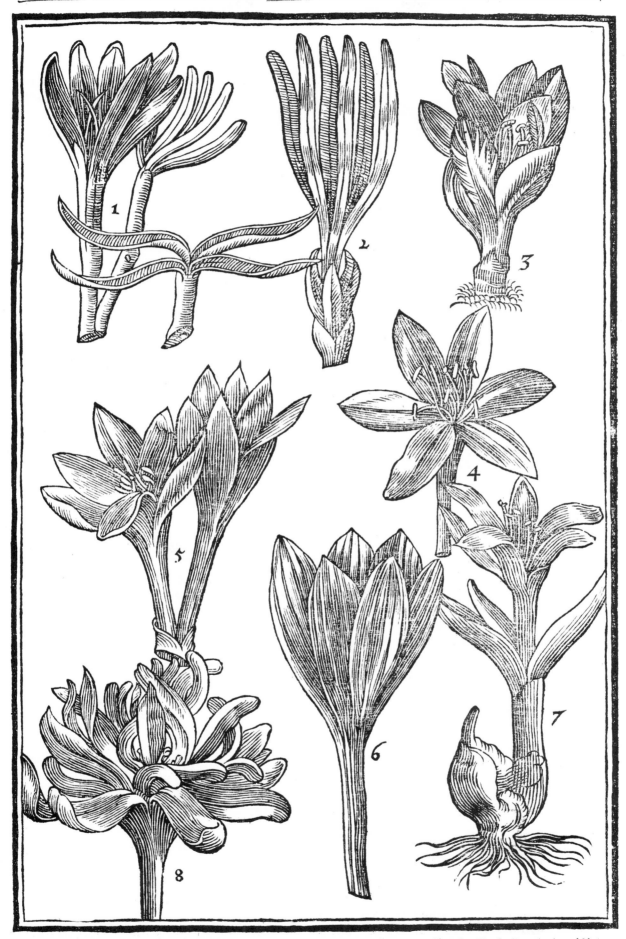

1 *Colchicum montanum Hispanicum.* The little Spanish Medowe Saffron. 2 *Colchicum montanum minus versicolore flore.* The small party coloured Medowe Saffron. 3 *Colchicum versicolor.* The party coloured Medowe Saffron. 4 *Colchicum variegatum alterum.* Another party coloured Medowe Saffron. 5 *Colchicum atropurpureum.* The darke purple Medowe Saffron. 6 *Colchicum atropurpureum variegatum.* The variable darke purple Medowe Saffron. 7 *Colchicum vernum,* Medowe Saffron of the spring. 8 *Colchicum flore pleno,* Double Medowe Saffron.

ster, and other places alſo.   The double kindes are thought to come out of Germany.

The Time.

Their times likewiſe are declared in their ſeuerall deſcriptions : thoſe that are earlieſt in Autumne, flower in Auguſt and September, the later in October, and the lateſt in the end of October, and in Nouember. The other are ſaid to bee of the Spring, in regard they come after the deepe of Winter (which is moſt vſually in December and Ianuary) is paſt.

The Names.

The generall name to all theſe plants is *Colchicum*, whereunto ſome haue added *Ephemerum*, becauſe it killeth within one dayes ſpace ; and ſome *Strangulatorium*. Some haue called them alſo *Bulbus agreſtis*, and *Filius ante Patrem*, The Sonne before the Father, becauſe (as they thinke) it giueth ſeede before the flower : but that is without due conſideration ; for the root of this (as of moſt other bulbous plants) after the ſtalke of leaues and ſeede are dry, and paſt, may be tranſplanted, and then it beginneth to ſpring and giue flowers before leaues, (and therein onely it is differing from other plants) but the leaues and ſeede follow ſucceſſiuely after the flowers, before it may be remoued againe ; ſo that here is not ſeede before flowers, but contrarily flowers vpon the firſt planting or ſpringing, and ſeede after, as in all other plants, though in a diuers manner.

The *Colchicum Hermodactilum* may ſeeme very likely to bee the *Colchicum Orientale* of Matthiolus, or the *Colchicum Alexandrinum* of Lobelius : And ſome thinke it to be the true *Hermodactilus*, and ſo call it, but it is not ſo. We doe generally call them all in Engliſh Medowe Saffrons, or *Colchicum*, according to the Latine, giuing to euery one his other adiunct to know it by.

The Vertues.

None of theſe are vſed for any Phyſicall reſpect, being generally held to be deadly, or dangerous at the leaſt. Only the true Hermodactile (if it be of this tribe, and not this which is here expreſſed) is of great vſe, for paines in the ioynts, and of the hippes, as the *Sciatica*, and the like, to be taken inwardly. Coſtæus in his Booke of the nature of plants, ſaith, that the rootes of our common kindes are very bitter in the Spring of the yeare, and ſweet in Autumne, which Camerarius contradicteth, ſaying, that he found them bitter in Autumne, which were (as he ſaith) giuen by ſome impoſters to diuers, as an antidote againſt the Plague.

CHAP. XVII.

Crocus. Saffron.

THere are diuers ſorts of Saffrons, whereof many doe flower in the Spring time, and ſome in Autumne, among whom there is but one onely kinde, that is called tame or of the Garden, which yeeldeth thoſe blades or chiues that are vſed in meates and medicines, and many wayes profitable for other reſpects, none of the reſt, which are all wilde kindes, giuing any blade equall vnto thoſe of the tame kinde, or for any other vſe, then in regard of their beautifull flowers of ſeuerall varieties, and as they haue been carefully ſought out, and preſerued by diuers, to furniſh a Garden of dainty curioſity.   To entreate therefore of theſe, I muſt, to obſerue an orderly declaration, diuide them into two primary families: the former ſhall be of thoſe that yeeld their pleaſant flowers in the Spring of the yeare, and the other that ſend out

their

their colours in the Autumne, among whom that *Rex pomary* (as I may so call it) the tame or manured kinde, properly called of the Garden, is to be comprehended, for that it giueth his pleasant flowers at that time among others. I shall againe distribute those of the Spring time into three chiefe colours, that is, into white, purple, and yellow, and vnder euery one of them, comprehend the seuerall varieties that doe belong vnto them ; which course I will also hold with those of the Autumne, that thus being rightly ranked, they may the more orderly be described.

1. *Crocus Vernus albus purus minor.*
The smaller pure white Saffron flower of the Spring.

This small Saffron flower springeth vp in the beginning of the yeare, with three or foure small greene leaues, somewhat broader, but much shorter then the true Saffron leaues, with a white line downe the middle of euery leafe : betweene these leaues, out of a white skinne, riseth vp one or two small flowers, made of six leaues a peece, as all the rest in generall are, of a pure white colour, without any mixture in it, which abide not in flower aboue a weeke, or rather lesse, so sodainly is the pleasure of this, and the purple lost : it flowreth not for the most part, vntill a moneth after the yellow Crocus appeareth in flower, and the ordinary stript Crocus is past : the seede is small, round, and reddish, yet not so red as the seede of the yellow, contained in three square heads, yet seldome beareth, but encreaseth by the roote plentifully enough, which is small, round, and flat at the bottome, somewhat white on the outside, but whiter within, shooting out small sprouts on euery side of the roote, which is the best note to know this kinde and the lesser purple, which are both alike, from all other rootes of Saffron flowers.

2. *Crocus albus maior multiflorus.* The great snow white Crocus.

This greater Saffron flower riseth vp vsually with three or foure greene leaues, larger then the former, with a white line in euery one of them : the flowers are greater, and more in number, rising together, but flowring one after another, of a pure snow white colour, and abiding but little longer in flower then the former.

3. *Crocus albus maior alter dictus Masiacus.*
The great white Saffron flower or Crocus of Mesia.

This great white Crocus of Mesia, riseth vp out of the ground, almost as early as the first sort of the yellow, with foure or fiue leaues, being very like vnto the leaues of the yellow Crocus, and as large, with white lines in them : the flowers also are as large as the flowers of the yellow, and many also rising one after another like vnto it, but not of so pure a white colour, as the former or last described, but rather tending to a Milky or Creame colour : the roote is not couered with any reddish, but rather pale skinnes or coates.

4. *Crocus albus Masiacus fundo violaceo.*
The great white Crocus of Mesia with a blew bottome.

There is another of this kinde, like vnto the former in all things, sauing that the bottomes of the flowers of this kinde, with some part of the stalke next the flower, are of a pale shining purple colour, and rising vp a pretty way into the flower; whereas another also of this kind, hath a little shew or marke of blew, and not purple, at the bottome of the flower onely, which maketh a difference.

5. *Crocus albus fundo purpureo.* The white Crocus with a purple bottome.

This Saffron flower is of the same kinde with the first, both in roote, leafe, and flower, in none of them differing from it, but in that the bottome of this flower, with that part of the short foote-stalke next vnto it, is of a violet or purple colour, and sometimes hauing here and there some purple small lines, or spots on the white leaues : it flowreth also with the first white, or somewhat later.

6. *Crocus*

6. *Crocus vernus albus striatus*. The white stript Crocus.

This stript Saffron flower is likewise neare the same first kind, or first white Crocus, hauing the like leaues and flowers, somewhat larger, but as soone fading almost as it : but herein this flower differeth, that it hath pale blewish lines and spots in all the leaues thereof, and more principally in the three outer leaues: the root is also white on the outside, like the first white, but greater, with young ones growing round about it.

7. *Crocus vernus albus polyanthos versicolor.*
The greater party coloured white Crocus.

The greater party coloured Saffron flower, hath his greene leaues like vnto the second great white Crocus before mentioned, hauing more flowers then any of the former, except the first great white, the leaues whereof haue greater stripes then the last recited Crocus, but of a purple Violet colour, making each leafe seeme oftentimes to haue as much purple as white in them : the roote hereof is somewhat like the second white, but of a little more duskie colour on the outside, and not budding out on the sides at all, or very little.

8. *Crocus vernus albus versicolor*. The lesser party coloured white Crocus.

The leaues and flowers of this other party coloured Crocus, are for bignesse in a manner equall with the last, but hath not so many flowers rising together from the roote : the flower is finely marked with blew strakes on the white flower, but nothing so much as in the former : the roote also is like the last.

9. *Crocus Episcopalis*. The Bishops Crocus.

This party coloured or Bishops Saffron flower, is very like both in leaues and rootes vnto the Neapolitane blew Crocus, but somewhat greater : the flowers doe abide not so long time blowne, and hath all the leaues either wholly white, with blew stripes on both sides of them, or wholly of a fine delayed blew Violet colour, and the three innermost more blew and finely striped, both on the inside and outside of them, and sometimes it hath been seen to haue three leaues white, and three leaues of a pale blew.

10. *Crocus vernus striatus vulgaris*. The ordinary stript Crocus.

There is another sort of stript Saffron flower, which is most common and plentifull in most Gardens, which I must needes bring vnder the ranke of these white kinds, although it differre very notably, both in roote, leafe, and flower, from all of them : the leaues of this rise vp sooner then the yellow or white Crocus, lying spread vpon the ground for the most part, but narrower then any of the former: among these leaues spring vp diuers flowers, almost as large as the former great white Crocus, of a very bleake or pale purple colour, tending to white on the inside, and in many almost white, with some small whitish chiues tipt with yellow in the middle : the three outer leaues are of a yellowish white colour on the backe side of them, stript euery one of them with three broad stripes, of a darke murrey or purple colour, and a little sprinkled with some small purple lines, on both sides of those stripes ; but on the inside, of the same pale purple or white colour with the rest : the seede hereof is somewhat darker coloured then of the white, and is more liberall in bearing : the roote is differing from all the former, being rounder and bigger then any of them, except the kindes of Misia, yet somewhat flat withall, not hauing any shootes from the sides, but setting off into rootes plentifully, hauing a round circle compassing the bottome of the roote, which easily falleth away, when it is taken vp out of the ground, and couered with a browne coate, somewhat neare the colour of the yellow Crocus, but not altogether so bright : it flowreth vsually the first of all these sorts, or with the first of the early yellowes.

1 *Crocus vernus albus minor.* The small white Saffron flower of the spring. 2 *Crocus vernus Maßacus albus.* The great white Crocus of Misia. 3 *Crocus vernus albus striatus.* The white stript Crocus. 4 *Crocus vernus albus polyanthos versicolor* The party coloured white Crocus. 5 *Crocus albus fundo purpureo.* The white Crocus with a purple bottome. 6 *Crocus vernus Neapolitanus.* The great blew Crocus of Naples. 7 *Crocus vernus purpureus maximus.* The great purple Crocus. 8 *Crocus vernus purpureus striatus.* The purple stript Crocus. 9 *Crocus vernus purpureus Capillarifolio.* The purple Crocus with small leaues. 10 *Crocus vernus flauus striatus.* The yellow stript Crocus. 11 *Crocus vernus luteus versicolor.* The cloth of gold Crocus.

11. *Crocus vernus striatus Turcicus.* The Turkie stript Crocus.

There is another of this kinde, whose flower is a little larger, and of a deeper purple colour, both on the inside and outside ; the greene leafe also is bigger, and of a more whitish colour.

12. *Crocus vernus Capillarifolio albus.* The white Crocus with small leaues.

This white Crocus is in all things like vnto the purple of the same kinde, but that the flower of this is wholly white: the full description therefore hereof, you shall haue in that purple with small leaues, of this kinde hereafter set downe, whereunto I referre you.

13. *Crocus vernus purpureus minor.* The smaller purple Crocus.

The smaller purple Saffron flower of the Spring, hath his greene leaues so like vnto the first white flowred Saffron, that they can hardly be distinguished, onely they seem to bee a little narrower : the flower is also much about the same bignesse, or a little bigger, and seldome beareth aboue one flower from a roote, euen as the first doth, of a deepe purple Violet colour, the bottome of the flower, with the vpper part of the stalke next thereunto, being of a deeper or blacker purple ; in the middle of the flower are some pale chiues tipt with yellow pendents, and a longer pointell, diuided or forked at the toppe : the roote of this is in all things so like vnto the first white, that it is impossible for the most cunning and conuersant in them, to know the one from the other. This beareth seede very sparingly, as the white doth, and is reddish like vnto it, but recompenseth that defect with a plentifull encrease by the roote : it likewise flowreth at the very same time with the white, and endureth as small a time.

14. *Crocus vernus purpureus maximus.* The greatest purple Crocus.

This great purple Crocus is of the same kinde with the next described, as well in roote as leafe, but greater ; for the greene leaues hereof are the greatest and broadest of all other Crocus, with a large white line in the middle of euery one : it springeth vp much later then the former, and doth not shew his flower vntill the other bee past a good while : the flowers also are the largest of all these Crocus of the Spring time, and equalling, if not surpassing that purple kinde that flowreth in Autumne, hereafter set forth, of a very faire and deepe Violet colour, almost as deepe as the former : the seed vessels are large also and white, wherein is contained pale reddish seede, like vnto the next blew kinde, but somewhat greater : the roote is (as I said before) like vnto the next, that is, flat and round, with a duskie coloured outside, whose head for springing in it is as hardly discerned.

Alter Apicibus albidis.　　We haue one of this kinde, the toppes onely of whose purple flower are whitish, for the breadth of halfe the naile of a mans hand, which abideth constant euery yeare in that manner, and therefore is a difference fit to be remembred.

15. *Crocus vernus Neapolitanus siue caruleus maior.*
The greater blew Crocus of Naples.

This great blew Crocus riseth vp with diuers greene leaues, broader then any of the former (except the last) with a white line running downe the inside of euery leafe, as in the former, among which riseth vp, out of diuers great long white skinnes, diuers large flowers, but not fully so great as the former, consisting of six leaues, of a paler blew or Violet colour then in the former, hauing in the middle of the flowers a few pale threeds, tipt with yellow, and a longer pointell of a gold yellow colour, forked or diuided at the toppe, smelling sweeter then in the former, and abiding a great while longer, being in flower vsually euen with the stript yellow Crocus, or before the former purple, and yeelding more plenty of seede : the roote hereof is not very great, but a little darke on the outside, being round and flat withall, that one can hardly know which is the vpperside thereof.　　　　　　　　　　　　　　　This

This kinde differeth very little from the former, either in roote, leafe, or flower, for the bigneſſe or colour, but that it ſeemeth to be a little bleaker or paler blew, becauſe it flowreth a little earlier. *Crocus Neapo-litanus præco-cior.*

16. *Crocus vernus purpureus ſtriatus.* The ſtript purple Crocus.

The leaues of this ſtript purple Saffron flower, are as large and broad as the laſt, or rather a little longer : the flowers alſo are as plentifull, and as large, of a fine delayed purple colour on the outſide, with three broad ſtrakes or lines downe the backe of the three outer leaues, and of a little deeper purple on the inſide, as the other three leaues are alſo of a deeper purple colour, and are ſtriped with the ſame deepe purple about the ground, or bottome of the leaues : this ſometimes yeeldeth three ſquare heads, containing in them browniſh ſeede : the roote is like vnto the laſt, and flowreth much about the time of the former.

17. *Crocus vernus purpureus verſicolor.* The ſiluer ſtript purple Crocus.

This ſtript Saffron flower, is in leaues and flowers ſomewhat like vnto the laſt ſtript purple, but a little ſmaller : the flowers are of a little deeper purple through the whole leaues, ſtriped with white lines, both on the leaues, and towards the edges, which maketh a peculiar difference from all the reſt : the roote of this is not ſo flat, though like it, and couered with a darke aſh coloured ſkinne : it flowreth about the ſame time.

18. *Crocus purpureus flammeus maior.* The greater purple flame coloured Crocus.

The greene leaues of this Crocus or Saffron flower, are of a reaſonable breadth and length, and of a pleaſant freſh greenneſſe, with a faire broad white line downe the middle of them, but riſing not out of the ground ſo early as the next deſcribed Crocus : the flowers are likewiſe of a meane bigneſſe, of a pale purple on the outſide, ſomewhat whitiſh, eſpecially the three outer leaues ; but on the inſide of a deeper purple, and ſtriped with great ſtripes like flames, hauing ſome chiues in the middle, and a longer one alſo feathered a little at the toppe : the roote is white on the outſide, ſomewhat flat and round, but not ſo flat as the Neapolitane Crocus before deſcribed.

19. *Crocus purpureus flammeus minor.* The leſſer purple flame coloured Crocus.

This Crocus hath almoſt as broad and long greene leaues as the former, and of the ſame verdure, which riſe vp earlier then it, and is in flower likewiſe ſomewhat before it, being ſmaller for ſize by a little, but of as deepe a purple on the outſide, as on the inſide, flamed with faire broad ſtripes from the middle of the leaues, or ſomewhat lower vnto the edges : each of theſe giue ſeed that is of a pale reddiſh colour : the root is very like vnto the former, but a little leſſer.

20. *Crocus vernus purpureus Capillarifolio.* The purple Crocus with ſmall leaues.

This ſmall kinde of Saffron flower riſeth out of the ground, with two or three long and ſmall green leaues, very like vnto the leaues of the fine Fether-Graſſe hereafter deſcribed, ſtanding vpright at the firſt, but afterwards lying vpon the ground ; among which come the flowers, ſometimes three, but moſt vſually two vpon one ſtalke, if the roote be not young, which then will beare but one on a ſtalke, which is very ſhort, ſo that the flowers ſcarce ariſe aboue the ground, yet laying themſelues open in the day time, if it be faire, and the Sunne doe ſhine, otherwiſe they keepe cloſe, and doe not open at all : and after one flower is paſt, which doth not laſt aboue three or foure dayes at the moſt, the others follow, which are of a bleake blewiſh purple in the middle of the flower, and of a deeper purple towards the ends or points of the leaues, but of a more ſullen or darke purple on the outſide of them, and yellowiſh at the bottome, with ſome yellow chiues in the middle : the ſeede is ſmall and darker coloured then any of the former Crocus, contained alſo in ſmaller heads, ſtanding one by another
vpon

vpon the fame fhort foote-ftalke, which then rifeth vp a little higher, fhewing the maner of the ftanding of the flowers, which in their flowring time could not fo eafily bee
difcerned : the roote is very fmall and round, hauing one fide at the bottome lower
then the other, very like the roote of a *Colchicum* or Medowe Saffron, and fomewhat
neare refembling alfo the hoofe of an horfe foote, couered with a very thicke skinne,
of a darke or blackifh browne colour : this flowreth the laft of all the former forts of
Saffron flowers, euen when they are all paft.

21. *Crocus vernus purpureus ftriatus Capillarifolio.*
The ftript purple Crocus with fmall leaues.

This fmall ftript purple Saffron flower hath fuch like leaues, as the laft defcribed
hath, betweene which rifeth the flower vpon as fhort a foote-ftalke, confifting of fix
leaues like the former, of a faire purple colour on the outfide of the three outer leaues,
with three lines or ftrakes downe euery leafe, of a deeper purple colour, and on the infide of a paler purple, as the other three leaues are alfo, with fome chiues tipt with yellow pendents, and a forked pointell in the middle : the roote of this is fomewhat
bigger then the former, and rounder, but couered with as thicke and as browne a
skinne : it flowreth about the fame time with the former.

22. *Crocus vernus luteus fiue Mafiacus.* The yellow Crocus.

The yellow Crocus or Saffron flower, rifeth vp with three or foure leaues out of
the ground, being fomewhat neare the breadth of the great purple kindes, with a white
line in them, as in moft of the reft : the flowers ftand in the middle of thefe leaues, and
are very large, of a gold yellow colour, with fome chiues, and a forked point in the
middle : the feede hereof is of a brighter colour then in any of the other : the roote is
great and round, as great or greater then a Wall Nut fometimes, and couered with reddifh skinnes or coates, yeelding more ftore of flowers then moft of the former, and beginning to blowe with the firft forts, or prefently after, but outlaft many of them, and
are of a pleafant good fent.

Flore aureo.　Of this kinde we haue fome, whofe flowers are of a deeper gold yellow colour then
others, fo that they appeare reddifh withall.

Flore pallido.　And we haue alfo another fort, whofe flowers are very pale, betweene a white and a
yellow, not differing in any thing elfe.

Flore viridante luteo.　And another fmaller, whofe flower hath a fhew of greennefle in the yellow, and
more greene at the bottome.

23. *Crocus vernus flauus ftriatus.* The yellow ftript Crocus.

This kinde of yellow ftript Crocus or Saffron flower, rifeth vp with more ftore of
narrower and greener leaues then the former, and after the leaues are fpread, there rife
vp many yellow flowers from among them, which are not of fo faire and bright a yellow colour, but more dead and fu len, hauing on the backfide of each of the three outtermoft leaues, three fmall ftripes, of an ouer-worne or dull purple colour, with fome
chiues and a pointell in the middle : the roote of this kinde, is very like the roote of
the former yellow, but fomewhat fmaller and fhorter, and couered with the like reddifh skinnes, but a little fadder : it flowreth not fo early as the former yellow, but abideth almoft as long as it.

24. *Crocus vernus luteus verficolor primus.* The beft cloth of gold Crocus.

The faireft cloth of gold Crocus or Saffron flower, rifeth vp very early, euen with
the firft, or the firft of all other Crocus, with three or foure very narrow and fhort
leaues, of a whiter colour then any of the former, which by and by after doe fhew
forth the flowers, rifing from among them out of the fame white skinne, which in-
cludeth the leaues, but are not fo plentifull as the former yellow, being but two or
three at the moft, of a faire gold yellow colour, yet fomewhat paler then the firft, hauing

uing on the backe of euery of the three outer leaues, three faire and great stripes, of a faire deepe purple colour, with some small lines at the sides or edges of those purple stripes; on the inside of these flowers, there is no signe or shew of any line or spot, but wholly of a faire gold yellow, with chiues and a fethertopt pointell in the middle: the seede hereof is like the former, but not so red: the roote of this kinde is easily knowne from the roote of any other Saffron flower, because the outer peelings or shels being hard, are as it were netted on the outside, hauing certaine ribbes, rising vp higher then the rest of the skinnes, diuided in the forme of a net-worke, of a darke browne colour, and is smaller and rounder then the former yellow, and not encreasing so plentifully by the roote.

25. *Crocus vernus luteus versicolor alter*.
The second cloth of gold, or Duke Crocus.

There is no difference either in roote, leafe, or colour of flower, or time of flowring in this sort from the last before mentioned; for the flower of this is of the same bignesse and colour, the only note of difference is in the marking of the three outer leaues, which haue not three stripes like the former, but are wholly of the same deepe purple colour on the backe of them, sauing that the edges of them are yellow, which is the forme of a Duke Tulipa, and from thence it tooke the name of a Duke Crocus.

26. *Crocus vernus versicolor pallideluteus*. The pale cloth of gold Crocus.

We haue a third sort of this kinde of cloth of gold Crocus, which hath leaues and flowers like the former, but differeth in this, that the colour of the flower is of a paler yellow by much, but stript in the same manner as the first, but with a fainter purple colour: the roote also is netted like them, to shew that this is but a variation of the same kinde.

27. *Crocus vernus versicolor albideluteus*. The cloth of siluer Crocus.

The chiefest note of difference in this Saffron flower is, that being as large a flower as any of the former of this kinde, it is of so pale a yellowish white, that it is more white then yellow, which some doe call a butter colour: the three outer leaues are striped on the backe of them, with a paler purple blew shining colour, the bottome of the flower, and the vpper part of the stalke, being of the same purple blew colour: the roote of this is also netted as the other, to shew it is a variety of the same kinde.

And thus much for those Saffron flowers that come in the Spring time; now to those that flower in Autumne onely: and first of the true Saffron.

1. *Crocus vernus satiuus Autumnalis*. The true Saffron.

The true Saffron that is vsed in meates and medicines, shooteth out his narrow long greene leaues first, and after a while the flowers in the middle of them appeare about the end of August, in September and October, according to the soile, and climate where they growe; these flowers are as large as any of the other former or later sorts, composed of six leaues a peece, of a murrey or reddish purple colour, hauing a shew of blew in them: in the middle of these flowers there are some small yellow chiues standing vpright, which are as vnprofitable, as the chiues in any other of the wilde Saffrons, before or hereafter specified; but besides these, each flower hath two, three, or foure greater and longer chiues, hanging downe vpon or betweene the leaues, which are of a fierie red colour, and are the true blades of Saffron, which are vsed physically or otherwise, and no other: All these blades being pickt from the seuerall flowers, are laid and pressed together into cakes, and afterwards dryed very warily on a Kill to preserue them; as they are to be seene in the shops where they are sold. I neuer heard that euer it gaue seede with any: the roote groweth often to be as great, or greater then a green Wall Nut, with the outer shell on it, couered with a grayish or ash-coloured skin, which breaketh into long hairie threeds, otherwise then in any other roote of Crocus.

2. *Crocus*

2. *Crocus Byzantinus argenteus.* The siluer coloured Autumne Crocus.

This Saffron flower springeth vp in October, and seldome before, with three or foure short greene leaues at the first, but growing longer afterwards, and in the midst of them, presently after they haue appeared, one flower for the most part, and seldome two, consisting of six leaues, the three outermost whereof are somewhat larger then the other three within, and are of a pale bleake blew colour, almost white, which many call a siluer colour, the three innermost being of a purer white, with some yellow chiues in the middle, and a longer pointell ragged or fethered at the toppe : this very seldome beareth seede, but when the yeare falleth out to bee very milde ; it is small, round, and of a darke colour : the roote is pretty bigge, and rounder then any other Crocus, without any flat bottome, and couered with a darke russet skinne.

3. *Crocus Pyrenaus purpureus.* The purple mountaine Crocus.

This purple Saffron flower of the Autumne, riseth vp but with one flower vsually, yet sometimes with two one after another, without any leaues at all, in September, or sometimes in August, standing vpon a longer foote-stalke then any kinde of Saffron flower, either of the Spring or Autumne, and is as large as the flower of the greatest purple Saffron flower of the Spring, of a very deepe Violet purple colour, which decayeth after it hath stood blowne three or foure dayes, and becommeth more pale, hauing in the middle some yellow chiues, and a long fether topt pointell, branched, and rising sometimes aboue the edges of the flowers : about a moneth after the flowers are past, and sometimes not vntill the first of the Spring, there riseth vp three or foure long and broad greene leaues, with a white line in euery one of them, like vnto the first purple Vernall kindes, which abide vntill the end of May or Iune : the roote is small and white on the outside, so like vnto the roote of the lesser Vernall purple or white Crocus, that it cannot be distinguished, vntill about the end of August, when it doth begin to shoot, and then by the early shooting vp a long white sprout for flower, it may be knowne. I neuer could obserue it to giue any seede, the Winter (as I thinke) comming on it so quickly after the flowring, being the cause to hinder it.

4. *Crocus montanus Autumnalis.* The Autumne mountaine Crocus.

The mountaine Saffron flower springeth vp later then any of the former, and doth not appeare vntill the middle or end of October, when all the flowers of the former are past, appearing first with three or foure short greene leaues, like vnto the Byzantine Crocus, and afterwards the flowers betweene them, which are of a pale or bleake blew tending to a purple, the foote-stalkes of them being so short, that they scarce appeare aboue ground at the first, but after two or three dayes they grow a little higher : the roote is very great and flat bottomed, couered with a grayish duskie coate or skinne, and encreaseth very little or seldome.

The Place.

The seuerall places of these Saffron flowers, are in part set downe in their titles ; the others haue beene found out, some in one Countrey, and some in another, as the small purple and white, and stript white in Spaine : the yellow in Mesia about Belgrade, the great purple in Italy ; and now by such friends helpes as haue sent them, they prosper as well in our Gardens, as in their naturall places. Yet I must giue you this to vnderstand, that some of these formerly expressed, haue been raised vp vnto vs by the sowing of their seede.

The Time.

Their seuerall times are likewise expressed in their descriptions ; for some shew forth their pleasant flowers in the Spring, wherein for the three first moneths,

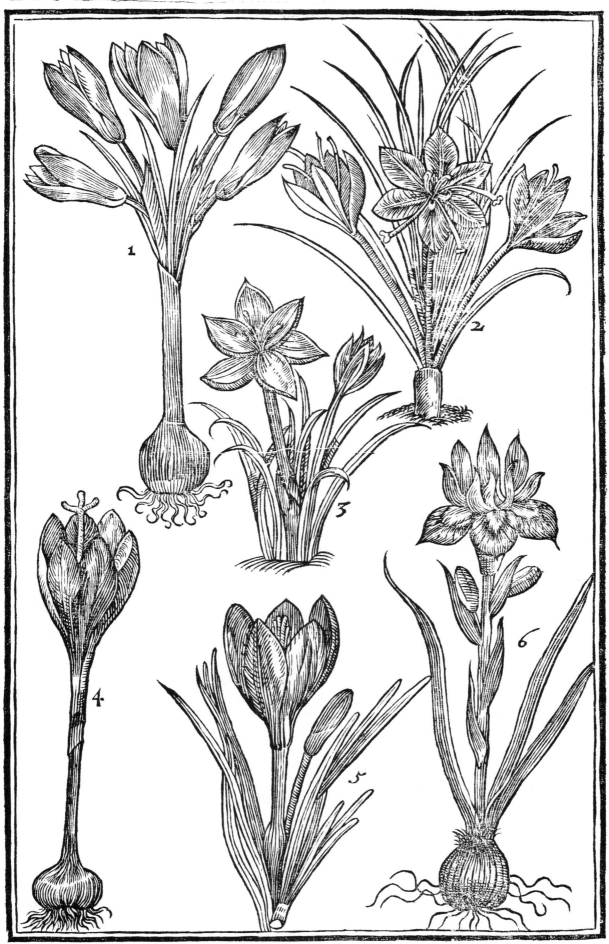

1 *Crocus vernus luteus vulgaris.* The common yellow spring Crocus. 2 *Crocus vernus sativus Autumnalis.* The true Saffron 3 *Crocus Byzantinus argenteus.* The siluer coloured Autumne Crocus. 4 *Crocus Pyrenæus purpureus.* The purple mountaine Crocus. 5 *Crocus montanus Autumnalis.* The Autumne mountaine Crocus. 6 *Sisyrinchium maius.* The greater Spanish Nut.

moneths, our Gardens are furnished with the varietie of one fort or another: the reft in Autumne, that fo they might procure the more delight, in
yeelding their beauty both early and late, when fcarce any other flowers
are found to adorne them.

The Names.

I fhall not neede to trouble you with an idle tale of the name of Crocus,
which were to little purpofe, nor to reiterate the former names impofed
vpon them; let it fuffice that the fitteft names are giuen them, that may diftinguifh them one from another; onely this I muft giue you to vnderftand,
that the gold yellow *Crocus* or Saffron flower, is the true *Crocus Mæfiacus*, as
I fhewed before; and that neither the yellow ftript, or cloth of gold (which
wee fo call after the Dutch name *Gaud Laken*) is the true *Mæfiacus*, as fome
fuppofe; and that the great white Saffron flower, by reafon of his likeneffe
vnto the gold yellow, is called *Crocus albus Mæfiaci facie*, or *facie lutei*, that
is, The white Saffron flower that is like the *Mæfiacus* or yellow.

The Vertues.

The true Saffron (for the others are of no vfe) which wee call Englifh
Saffron, is of very great vfe both for inward and outward difeafes, and is
very cordiall, vfed to expell any hurtfull or venemous vapours from the
heart, both in the fmall Pockes, Meafels, Plague, Iaundife, and many other
difeafes, as alfo to ftrengthen and comfort any cold or weake members.

Chap. XVIII.

Sifyrinchium. The Spanifh Nut.

I Can doe no otherwife then make a peculiar Chapter of this plant, becaufe it is
neither a *Crocus*, although in the roote it come fomewhat neare vnto that kinde that
is netted; but in no other part agreeing with any the delineaments of a Saffron
flower, and therefore could not be thruft into the Chapter amongft them: neither can
I place it in the forefront of the Chapter of the *Iris bulbofa*, or bulbous Flowerdeluces,
becaufe it doth not belong to that Family: and although the flower thereof doth moft
refemble a Flowerdeluce, yet in that no other parts thereof doe fitly agree thereunto,
I haue rather chofen to feate it by it felfe betweene them both, as partaking of both
natures, and fo may ferue in ftead of a bridge, to paffe from the one to the other, that
is, from the *Crocus* or Saffron flower, to the *Iris bulbofa* or bulbous rooted Flowerdeluce, which fhall follow in the next Chapter by themfelues.
    The Spanifh Nut hath two long and narrow, foft and fmooth greene leaues, lying
for the moft part vpon the ground, and fometimes ftanding vp, yet bending downewards; betweene thefe leaues rifeth vp a fmall ftalke, halfe a foote high, hauing diuers
fmooth foft greene leaues vpon it, as if they were skinnes, through which the ftalke
paffeth; at the toppe whereof ftand diuers flowers, rifing one after another, and not
all flowring at once: for feldome fhall you haue aboue one flower blowne at a time,
each whereof doth fo quickly paffe and fade away, that one may well fay, that it is but
one dayes flower, or rather the flower of a few houres: the flower it felfe hath nine
leaues, like vnto a Flowerdeluce, whereof the three that fall downe, haue in each of
them a yellow fpot: the other three, which in the Flowerdeluces are hollow and
ridged, couering the other three that fall downe, in this ftand vpright, and are parted
at the ends: the three that ftand vp in the middle are fmall and fhort: the whole flower
is fmaller then any Flowerdeluce, but of fundry colours; for fome are of an excellent
skie colour blew, others of a Violet purple, others of a darker purple colour, and fome
white, and many others mixed, either pale blew and deepe purple, or white and blew
mixed

mixed or ftriped together very variably, quickly fading as I faid before : the feede is enclofed in fmall cods, fo thinne and tranfparent, that one may eafily fee, and tell the feeds as they lye, which are of a brownifh red colour : the roote is fmall, blackifh and round, wrapped in a thicke fkinne or huske, made like vnto a net, or fomewhat like vnto the roote of the cloth of gold Crocus : when the plant is in flower, it is found to haue two rootes one aboue another, whereof the vppermoft is firme and found, and the vndermoft loofe and fpongie, in like manner as is found in the rootes of diuers Orchides or Satyrions, Bee-flowers and the like, and without any good tafte, or fweet-neffe at all, although Clufius faith otherwife.

Sifyrinchium Mauritanicum. The Barbary Nut.

There is another of this kinde, not differing from the former in any other notable part, but in the flower, which in this is of a delayed purplifh red colour, hauing in each of the three lower leaues a white fpot, in ftead of the yellow in the former, but are as foone fading as they.

The Place.

The former doe grow very plentifully in many parts both of Spaine and Portugall, where Guillaume Boel, a Dutch man heretofore remembred often in this Booke, found them ; of the fundry colours fpecified, whereas Clufius maketh mention but of one colour that he found.

The other was found in that part of Barbary, where Fez and Morocco do ftand, and brought firft into the Lowe-Countries : but they are both very tender, and will hardly abide the hard Winters of thefe colder regions.

The Time.

The firft flowreth in May and Iune, the laft not vntill Auguft.

The Names.

The name *Sifyrinchium* is generally impofed vpon this plant, by all authors that haue written thereof, thinking it to bee the right *Sifyrinchium* of Theophraftus : but concerning the Spanifh name *Nozelha*, which Clufius faith it is called by in Spaine, I haue beene credibly enformed by the aforenamed Boel, that this roote is not fo called in thofe parts ; but that the fmall or common ftript Crocus is called *Nozelha*, which is fweete in tafte, and defired very greedily by the Shepheards and Children, and that the roote of this *Sifyrinchium* or Spanifh Nut, is without any tafte, and is not eaten. And againe, that there is not two kindes, although it grow greater, and with more flowers, in thofe places that are neare the Sea, where both the wafhing of the Sea water, and the moifture and ayre of the Sea, caufeth the ground to bee more fertile. This I thought good, from the true relation of a friend, to giue the world to vnderftand, that truth might expell errour.

The Vertues.

Thefe haue not been knowne to bee vfed to any Phyficall purpofe, but wholly neglected, vnleffe fome may eate them, as Clufius reporteth.

CHAP. XIX.

Iris bulbosa. The bulbous Flowerdeluce.

THe Flowerdeluces that haue bulbous rootes are of two sorts, the one greater then the other : the greater bearing larger and broader leaues and flowers, and the lesser narrower. But before I giue you the descriptions of the vsuall greater kindes, I must needes place one or two in the fore-front that haue no fellowes ; the one is called of Clusius, his broad leafed Flowerdeluce, and the other a Persian, somewhat like vnto it, which although they differ notably from the rest, yet they haue the nearest resemblance vnto those greater kindes, that come next after them.

Iris bulbosa prima latifolia Clusij.
Clusius his first great bulbous Flowerdeluce.

This Flowerdeluce hath diuers long and broad leaues, not stiffe, like all the other, but soft and greenish on the vpperside, and whitish vnderneath ; among which rise vp sometimes seuerall small, short, slender stalkes, and sometimes but one, not aboue halfe a foote high, bearing at the top one flower a peece, somewhat like vnto a Flowerdeluce, consisting of nine leaues, whereof those three that stand vpright, are shorter and more closed together, then in other sorts of Flowerdeluces ; the other three that fall downe, turne vp their ends a little, and those three, that in other Flowerdeluces doe couer them at the bottome, stand like the vpright leaues of other Flowerdeluces, but are parted into two ends, like vnto two small eares : the whole flower is of a faire blew, or pale skie colour in most, with a long stripe in the middle of each of the three falling leaues, and in some white, but more seldome : the roote is reasonable great, round and white, vnder the blackish coates wherewith it is couered, hauing many long thicke white rootes in stead of fibres, which make them seeme to be Asphodill rootes. The flower is very sweete.

Iris bulbosa Persica. The Persian bulbous Flowerdeluce.

This Persian Flowerdeluce is somewhat like vnto the former, both in roote and in leafe, but that the leaues are shorter and narrower, and the flower being much about the same fashion, is of a pale blew russetish colour, each of the three lower falling leaues are almost wholly of a browne purple colour, with a yellow spot in the middle of them : this as it is very rare, so it seldome beareth flowers with vs.

The Place.

The first groweth in many places of Spaine and Portugall, from whence I and others haue often had it for our Gardens, but by reason of the tendernesse thereof, it doth hardly endure the sharpnesse of our cold Winters, vnlesse it be carefully preserued.

The other is said to come from Persia, and therefore it is so entituled, and is as tender to be kept as the other.

The Time.

The first flowreth most vsually not vntill May with vs, yet many times sooner : but in Ianuary and February, as Clusius saith, in the naturall places thereof.

The other is as early oftentimes when it doth flower with vs.

The Names.

Because Clusius by good iudgement referreth the first to the greater
kindes

kindes of Flowerdeluces, and placeth it in the fore ranke, calling it *Iris bulbosa latifolia prima*, that is, The first broad leafed Flowerdeluce, and all others doe the like, I haue (as you see) in the like manner put it before all the other, and keepe the same name. The Spaniards, as he faith, called it *Lirio espadanal*, and they of Corduba, *Lirios azules*.

The other hath no other name then as it is in the title.

1. *Iris bulbofa maior fiue Anglica cærulea.*
The blew English bulbous Flowerdeluce.

This bulbous Flowerdeluce rifeth vp early, euen in Ianuary oftentimes, with fiue or fix long and (narrow, in comparifon of any great breadth, but in regard of the other kinde) broad whitifh green leaues, crefted or ftraked on the backfide, and halfe round, the infide being hollow like a trough or gutter, white all along the infide of the leafe, and blunt at the end ; among which rifeth vp a ftiffe round ftalke, a cubit or two foot high, at the toppe whereof, out of a skinnie huske, commeth forth one or two flowers, confifting of nine leaues a peece, three whereof that are turned downewards, are larger and broader then the other, hauing in each of them a yellow fpot, about the middle of the leafe, other three are fmall, hollow, ridged or arched, couering the lower part next the ftalke of thofe falling leaues, turning vp their ends, which are diuided into two parts, other three ftand vpright, and are very fmall at the bottome of them, and broader toward the toppe : the whole flower is of a faire blew colour ; after the flowers are paft, come vp three fquare heads, fomewhat long, and lanke, or loofe, containing in them round yellowifh feede, which when it is ripe, will rattle by the fhaking of the winde in the dry huskes : the roote of this kinde is greater and longer then any of the fmaller kindes with narrow leaues, couered with diuers browne skinnes, which feeme to be fraught with long threeds like haires, efpecially at the fmall or vpper end of the roote, which thing you fhall not finde in any of the fmaller kindes.

2. *Iris bulbofa maior purpurea & purpuro violacea.*
The paler or deeper purple great bulbous Flowerdeluce.

Thefe purple Flowerdeluces differ not from the laft defcribed, either in roote or leafe : the chiefeft difference confifteth in the flowers, which in thefe are fomewhat larger then in the former, and in the one of a deepe blew or Violet purple colour, and in the other of a deepe purple colour, in all other things alike.

There is alfo another, in all other things like vnto the former, but only in the flower, *Flore cinerea.* which is of a pale or bleake blew, which we call an afh-colour.

3. *Iris bulbofa maior purpurea variegata fiue ftriata.*
The great purple ftript bulbous Flowerdeluce.

There is another of the purple kinde, whofe flower is purple, but with fome veines or ftripes of a deeper Violet colour, diuerfly running through the whole leaues of the flower.

And another of that bleake blew or afh-colour, with lines and veines of purple in the leaues of the flowers, fome more or leffe then other. *Flore cinereo ftriata purpureo.*

And againe another, whofe flower is of a purple colour like vnto the fecond, but that round about that yellow fpot, in the middle of each of the three falling leaues (as is vfuall in all the bulbous Flowerdeluces) there is a circle of a pale blew or afh-colour, the reft of the leafe remaining purple, as the other parts of the flower is. *Flore purpureo orbe cinereo.*

4. *Iris bulbofa maior flore rubente.*
The great peach coloured bulbous Flowerdeluce.

There is another of thefe greater kindes, more rare then any of the former, not differing in roote, leafe, or flower, from the former, but onely that the flower in this is of a pale reddifh purple colour, comming fomewhat neare vnto the colour of a peach bloffome.

5. *Iris bulbosa maior siue latifolia alba.*
The great white bulbous Flowerdeluce.

The great white bulbous Flowerdeluce, riseth not vp so early out of the ground as the blew or purple doth, but about a moneth or more after, whose leaues are somewhat larger, and broader then of the others: the stalke is thicker and shorter, bearing vsually two very large and great flowers, one flowring a little before the other, yet oftentimes both in flower together in the end, of a bleake blewish white colour, which wee call a siluer colour, while they are in the budde, and before they be blowne open, but then of a purer white, yet with an eye or shew of that siluer colour remaining in them, the three falling leaues being very large, and hauing that yellow spot in the middle of each of them: the seedes are likewise inclosed in heads, like vnto the blew or purple kindes, but larger, and are of a reddish yellow colour like them: the roote likewise is not differing, but greater.

6. *Iris bulbosa maior alba variegata.*
The great white stript bulbous Flowerdeluce.

This white stript Flowerdeluce, is in roote, leafe, and flower, and in manner of growing, like vnto the former white Flowerdeluce; the onely difference is in the marking of the flower, being diuers from it: for this hath in the white flower great veines, stripes, or markes, of a Violet blew colour, dispersed through the leaues of the flower very variably, which addeth a superexcellent beauty to the flower.

7. *Iris bulbosa maior siue latifolia versicolor.*
The great party coloured bulbous Flowerdeluce.

There is no difference in this from the former, but in the flower, which is of a whitish colour in the three falling leaues, hauing a circle of ash-colour about the yellow spot, the three rigged leaues being likewise whitish, but ridged and edged with that ash-colour, and the three vpright leaues of a pale blewish white colour, with some veines therein of a blewish purple.

Varietas. There hath beene brought vnto vs diuers rootes of these kindes, with the dryed flowers remaining on them, wherein there hath beene seene more varieties, then I can well remember to expresse, which variety it is very probable, hath risen by the sowing of the seeds, as is truely obserued in the narrower leafed kinde of Flowerdeluce, in the Tulipa, and in some other plants.

Flore luteo. Wee haue heard of one of this kinde of broad leafed Flowerdeluces, that should beare a yellow flower, in the like manner as is to be seene in the narrow leafed ones: but I haue not seene any such, and therefore I dare report no further of it, vntill time hath discouered the truth or falshood of the report.

The Place.

Lobelius is the first reporter, that the blew Flowerdeluce or first kinde of these broad leafed Flowerdeluces, groweth naturally in the West parts of England; but I am in some doubt of the truth of that report: for I rather thinke, that some in their trauels through Spaine, or other parts where it groweth, being delighted with the beauty of the flower, did gather the rootes, and bring them ouer with them, and dwelling in some of the West parts of England, planted them, and there encreasing so plentifully as they doe, they were imparted to many, thereby in time growing common in all Countrey folkes Gardens thereabouts. They grow also, and all the other, and many more varieties, about Tholouse, from whence Plantinianus Gassanus both sent and brought vs them, with many other bulbous rootes, and rare plants gathered thereabouts.

The

1 *Iris bulbosa latifolia prima Clusii.* Clusius his first great bulbous Flowerdeluce. 2 *Iris bulbosa maior cærulea siue Anglica.* The great view of his with bulbous Flowerdeluce. 3 *Iris bulbosa maior purpurea variegata.* The great purple stript bulbous Flowerdeluce. 4 *Iris bulbosa angustifolia maior alba.* The greater white narrow leafed bulbous Flowerdeluce. 5 *Iris bulbosa angustifolia versicolor.* The party coloured narrow leated bulbous Flowerdeluce. 6 *Iris bulbosa angustifolia Africana.* The purple African bulbous narrow leafed Flowerdeluce.

The Time.

Thefe doe flower vfually in the end of May, or beginning of Iune, and their feede is ripe in the end of Iuly or Auguft.

The Names.

Lobel calleth the firft Englifh blew Flowerdeluce, *Hyacinthus Poetarum flore Iridis, & propter Hyacinthinum colorem,id eft violaceum dictus*: but I know not any great good ground for it, more then the very colour; for it is neither of the forme of a Lilly, neither hath it thofe mourning markes imprinted in it, which the Poet faineth to bee in his Hyacinth. It is moft truely called an *Iris*, or Flowerdeluce (and there is great difference betweene a Lilly and a Flowerdeluce, for the formes of their flowers) becaufe it anfwereth thereunto very exactly, for the flower, and is therefore called vfually by moft, either *Iris bulbofa Anglica*, or *Iris bulbofa maior fiue latifolia*, for a difference betweene it, and the leffer with narrow leaues: In Englifh, eyther The great Englifh bulbous Flowerdeluce, or the great broad leafed bulbous Flowerdeluce, which you will, adding the other name, according to the colour.

And thus much for thefe broad leafed bulbous Flowerdeluces, fo much as hath come to our knowledge. Now to the feuerall varieties of the narrow leafed bulbous Flowerdeluces, fo much likewife as we haue been acquainted with.

Iris bulbofa minor fiue angulifolia alba.
The fmaller white or narrow leafed bulbous Flowerdeluce.

This firft Flowerdeluce, which beareth the fmaller flower of the two white ones, that are here to bee defcribed, fpringeth out of the ground alwaies before Winter, which after breaketh forth into foure or fiue fmall and narrow leaues, a foote long or more, of a whitifh greene on the infide, which is hollow and chanalled, and of a blewifh greene colour on the outfide, and round withall : the ftalke of this kinde is longer and flenderer then the former, with fome fhorter leaues vpon it, at the toppe whereof, out of fhort skinny leaues, ftand one or two flowers, fmaller, fhorter, and rounder then the flowers of the former broad leafed Flowerdeluces, but made after the fame proportion with nine leaues, three falling downewards, with a yellow fpot in the middle, other three are made like a long arch, which couer the lower part next the ftalke of thofe falling leaues, and turne vp at the ends of them, where they are diuided into two parts : the other three ftand vpright, betweene each of the three falling leaues, being fomewhat long and narrow : the flower is wholly (fauing the yellow fpot) of a pure white colour, yet in fome hauing a fhew of fome blew throughout, and in others towards the bottome of the three vpright leaues : after the flowers are paft, there rife vp fo many long cods or feede veffels, as there were flowers, which are longer and fmaller then in the former, and a little bending like a Cornet, with three round fquares, and round pointed alfo, which diuiding it felfe when the feede is ripe into three parts, doe fhew fix feuerall cells or places, wherein is contained fuch like round reddifh yellow feedes, but fmaller then the former : the iroote is fmaller and fhorter then the former, and without any haires or threeds, couered with browne thin skinnes, and more plentifull in giuing encreafe.

Iris bulbofa angulifolia alba flore maiore.
The greater white narrow leafed bulbous Flowerdeluce.

I fhall not neede to make a feuerall defcription to euery one of thefe Flowerdeluces that follow, for that were but to make often repetition of one thing, which being once done, as it is, may well ferue to expreffe all the reft, and but onely to adde the efpeciall

ciall differences, either in leafe or flower, for bignesse, colour, or forme, as is expedient to expresse and diftinguish them feuerally. This greater white bulbous Flowerdeluce is like vnto the laft defcribed in all parts, fauing that it is a little larger and higher, both in leafe, ftalke, and flower, and much whiter then any of thefe mixed forts that follow, yet not fo white as the former : the roote hereof is likewife a little bigger and rounder in the middle.

Albefcent. **Milke white.** There is another, whofe falling leaues haue a little fhew of yellownefle in them, and fo are the middle ridges of the arched leaues, but the vpright leaues are more white, not differing in roote or leafe from the firft white.

Argentea. **Siluer colour.** And another, whofe falls are of a yellowifh white, like the laft, the arched leaues are whiter, and the vpright leaues of a blewifh white, which we call a filuer colour.

Albida. **Whitifh.** Another hath the fals yellowifh, and fometimes with a little edge of white about them, and fometimes without; the vpright leaues are whitifh, as the arched leaues are, yet the ridge yellower.

Albida labris luteis. **White with yellow fals.** Another hath his fals yellow, and the vpright leaues white, all thefe flowers are about the fame bignefle with the firft.

Albida angaftior. **The narrow white.** But we haue another, whofe flower is fmaller, and almoft as white as the fecond, the lower leaues are fmall, and doe as it were ftand outright, not hauing almoft any fal at all, fo that the yellow fpot feemeth to be the whole leafe, the arched leaues are not halfe fo large as in the former, and the vpright leaues bowe themfelues in the middle, fo that the tops doe as it were meete together.

And another of the fame, whofe falling leaues are a little more eminent and yellow, with a yellower fpot.

Aurea fiue lutea Hifpanica. **The Spanifh yellow.** We haue another kinde that is called the Spanifh yellow, which rifeth not vp fo high, as ordinarily moft of the reft doe, and is wholly of a gold yellow colour.

Pallide lutea. **Straw colour.** There is another, that vfually rifeth higher then the former yellow, and is wholly of a pale yellow, but deeper at the fpot.

Albida lutea. **Pale Straw colour.** There is alfo another like vnto the pale yellow, but that the falling leaues are whiter then all the reft of the flower.

Mauritanica flaua ferotina minor. **The fmall Barbary yellow.** There is a fmaller or dwarfe kinde, brought from the backe parts of Barbary, neare the Sea, like vnto the yellow, but fmaller and lower, and in ftead of vpright leaues, hath fmall fhort leaues like haires : it flowreth very late, after all others haue almoft giuen their feede.

Verficolor Hifpanica cærulea labris albis. **The party coloured Spanifh** We haue another fort is called the party coloured Spanifh bulbous Flowerdeluce, whofe falling leaues are white, the arched leaues of a whitifh filuer colour, and the vpright leaues of a fine blewifh purple.

Diuerfitas. **The diuerfity or variation of this flower.** Yet fometimes this doth vary; for the falling leaues will haue either an edge of blew, circling the white leaues, the arched leaues being a little blewer, and the vpright leaues more purple.

Or the fals will be almoft wholly blew, edged with a blewer colour, the arched leaues pale blew, and the vpright leaues of a purplifh blew Violet colour.

Or the fals white, the arched leaues pale white, as the vpright leaues are. Or not of fo faire a blewifh purple, as the firft fort is.

Some of them alfo will haue larger flowers then others, and be more liberall in bearing flowers : for the firft fort, which is the moft ordinary, feldome beareth aboue one flower on a ftalke, yet fometimes two. And of the others there are fome that wil beare vfually two and three flowers, yet fome againe will beare but one. All thefe kindes fmell fweeter then many of the other, although the moft part be without fent.

Cærulea fiue purpurea minor *Lufitanica præcox.* **The fmall early purple Portugall.** There is another kinde, that is fmaller in all the parts thereof then the former, the ftalke is flender, and not fo high, bearing at the toppe one or two fmall flowers, all wholly of a faire blewifh purple, with a yellow fpot

in

in euery one of the three falling leaues, this vſually flowreth early , euen with the firſt bulbous Flowerdeluces.

Purpurea ma-
ior.
The greater
purple.

We haue another purple, whoſe flower is larger, and ſtalke higher, and is of a very reddiſh purple colour, a little aboue the ground, at the foote or bottome of the leaues and ſtalke : this flowreth with the later ſort of Flowerdeluces.

Purpurea ſerotina
The late purple.

There is another , whoſe flower is wholly purple , except the yellow ſpot, and flowreth later then any of the other purples.

Purpura rubeſcens
labris cæruleis.
A reddiſh purple
with blew fals.
Purpura rubeſcens
labris albido caru-
leis.
A reddiſh purple
with whitiſh
blew fals.
Purpurea labris
luteis.
Party coloured
purple & yellow
Purpurea labris
ex albido cæruleo
& luteo mixtis.
Party coloured
purple with ſtript
yellow fals.
Subpurpurea labris
luteis.
Pale purple with
yellow fals.
A paler purple-
Subcærulea labris
luteis.
Party coloured
blew and yellow
Crinis coloris ele-
gantioris.
A faire haire co-
lour.
Altera obſoletior.
A dull haire co-
lour.

There is yet another purple , whoſe vpright leaues are of a reddiſh purple, and the falling leaues of a blew colour.

And another of a reddiſh purple, whoſe falling leaues are of a whitiſh blew colour, in nothing elſe differing from the laſt.

Another hath his falling leaues of a faire gold yellow, without any ſtripe, yet in ſome there are veines running through the yellow leaues , and ſome haue an edge of a ſullen darke colour about them : the vpright leaues in euery of theſe, are of a Violet purple.

Another is altogether like this laſt, but that the falling leaues are of a pale blew and yellow, trauerſing one the other, and the arched leaues of a pale purpliſh colour.

Another hath his vpright leaues of a paler purple, and the falling leaues yellow.

And another little differing from it, but that the arched leaues are whitiſh.

Another whoſe vpright leaues are of a pale blew , and the falling leaues yellow.

And another of the ſame ſort, but of a little paler blew.

We haue another ſort, whoſe vpright leaues are of a faire browniſh yellow colour, which ſome call a *Fuille mort*, and others an haire colour ; the falling leaues yellow.

And another of the ſame colour, but ſomewhat deader.

Iris bulboſa Africana ſerpentariæ caule.
The purple or murrey bulbous Barbary Flowerdeluce.

This Flowerdeluce as it is more ſtrange (that is , but lately knowne and poſſeſſed by a few) ſo it is both more deſired , and of more beauty then others. It is in all reſpects, of roote, leafe, and flower , for the forme like vnto the middle ſort of theſe Flowerdeluces, onely the loweſt part of the leaues and ſtalke , for an inch or thereabouts, next vnto the ground, are of a reddiſh colour, ſpotted with many ſpots, and the flower, being of a meane ſize, is of a deepe purpliſh red or murrey colour the whole flower throughout, except the yellow ſpot in the middle of the three lower or falling leaues, as is in all others.

Purpura ceru-
lea obſoleta la-
bris fuſcis.
The duskie
party coloured
purple.

And laſtly , there is another ſort , which is the greateſt of all theſe narrow leafed Flowerdeluces, in all the parts of it ; for the roote is greater then any of the other , being thicke and ſhort : the leaues are broader and longer, but of the ſame colour: the ſtalke is ſtronger and higher then any of them, bearing two or three flowers, larger alſo then any of the reſt, whoſe falling leaues are of a duskie yellow , and ſometimes with veines and borders about the brimmes, of another dunne colour, yet hauing that yellow ſpot that is in all : the arched leaues are of a ſullen pale purpliſh yellow, and the vpright leaues of a dull or duskie blewiſh purple colour : the heads or hornes for ſeede are likewiſe greater, and ſo is the ſeede alſo a little.

The Place.

Theſe Flowerdeluces haue had their originall out of Spaine and Portugall, as it is thought , except thoſe that haue riſen by the ſowing, and thoſe which are named of Africa.

The

The Time.

Thefe flower in Iune, and fometimes abide vnto Iuly, but vfually not fo early as the former broad leafed kindes, and are foone fpoiled with wet in their flowring.

The Names.

The feuerall names, both in Latine and Englifh, are fufficient for them as they are fet downe; for we know no better.

The Vertues.

There is not any thing extant or to be heard, that any of thefe kindes of Flowerdeluces hath been vfed to any Phyficall purpofes, and ferue onely to decke vp the Gardens of the curious.

And thus much for thefe forts of bulbous Flowerdeluces, and yet I doubt not, but that there are many differences, which haue rifen by the fowing of the feede, as many may obferue from their owne labours, for that euery yeare doth fhew forth fome variety that is not feene before. And now I will conuert my difcourfe a while likewife, to paffe through the feuerall rankes of the other kindes of tuberous rooted Flowerdeluces, called Flagges.

Chap. XX.

Iris latifolia tuberofa. The Flagge or Flowerdeluce.

THere are two principall kindes of tuberous or knobby rooted Flowerdeluces, that is, the tall and the dwarfe, or the greater and the leffer; the former called *Iris maior* or *latifolia*, and the other *Iris minor*, or rather *Chamæiris*; and each of thefe haue their leffer or narrow leafed kindes to bee comprehended vnder them: Of all which in their order. And firft of that Flowerdeluce, which for his excellent beautie and raritie, deferueth the firft place.

Iris Chalcedonica fiue Sufiana maior. The great Turkie Flowerdeluce.

The great Turkie Flowerdeluce, hath diuers heads of long and broad frefh greene leaues, yet not fo broad as many other of thofe that follow, one folded within another at the bottome, as all other of thefe Flowerdeluces are: from the middle of fome one of thofe heads (for euery head of leaues beareth not a flower) rifeth vp a round ftiffe ftalke, two foote high, at the toppe whereof ftandeth one flower (for I neuer obferued it to beare two) the largeft almoft, but rareft of all the reft, confifting of nine leaues, like the others that follow, but of the colour almoft of a Snakes skinne, it is fo diuerfly fpotted; for the three lower falling leaues are very large, of a deepe or darke purple colour, almoft blacke, full of grayifh fpots, ftrakes, and lines through the whole leaues, with a blacke thrume or freeze in the middle of each of them: the three arched leaues that couer them, are of the fame darke purple colour, yet a little paler at the fides, the three vpper leaues are very large alfo, and of the fame colour with the lower leaues, but a little more liuely and frefh, being fpeckled and ftraked with whiter fpots and lines; which leaues being laid in water, will colour the water into a Violet colour, but if a little Allome be put therein, and then wrung or preffed, and the iuice of thefe leaues dryed in the fhadow, will giue a colour almoft as deepe as Indico, and may ferue for fhadowes in limming excellent well: the flower hath no fent that can be perceiued, but is onely commendable for the beauty and rarity thereof: it feldome beareth feedes in thefe cold Countries, but when it doth, it is contained in great heads,

being

being brownish and round, but not so flat as in other sorts, the roots are more browne on the outside, and growing tuberous thicke, as all other that are kept in Gardens.

Iris Chalcedonica siue Susiana minor. The lesser Turkie Flowerdeluce.

There is another hereof little differing, but that the leafe is of a more yellowish greene colour, and the flower neither so large or faire, nor of so perspicuous markes and spots, nor the colour of that liuely (though darke) lustre.

The Place.

These haue been sent out of Turkie diuers times among other things, and it should seeme, that they haue had their originall from about Susis, a chiefe Citie of Persia.

The Time.

They flower in May most vsually, before any of the other kindes.

The Names.

They haue been sent vnto vs, and vnto diuers other in other parts, from Constantinople vnder the name of *Alaia Susiana,* and thereupon it hath been called, both of them and vs, either *Iris Chalcedonica,* or *Susiana,* and for distinction *maior* or *minor* : In English, The Turkie Flowerdeluce, or the Ginnie Hen Flowerdeluce, the greater or the lesser.

Iris alba Florentina. The white Flowerdeluce.

The great white Flowerdeluce, hath many heads of very broad and flat long leaues, enclosing or folding one within another at the bottome, and after a little diuided one from another toward the top, thin edged, like a sword on both sides, and thicker in the middle: from the middle of some of these heads of leaues, riseth vp a round stiffe stalk, two or three foot high, bearing at the top one, two, or three large flowers, out of seuerall huskes or skins, consisting of nine leaues, as all the other do, of a faire white colour, hauing in the middle of each of the three falling leaues, a small long yellow frize or thrume, as is most vsuall in all the sorts of the following Flowerdeluces, both of the greater and smaller kindes : after the flowers are past, come the seed, inclosed in thicke short pods, full fraught or stored with red roundish and flat seede, lying close one vpon another : the roote is tuberous or knobby, shooting out from euery side such like tuberous heads, lying for the most part vpon or aboue the ground, and fastened within the ground with long white strings or fibres, which hold them strongly, and encreaseth *Flore pallido.* fast. There is another like vnto this last in all things, sauing that the colour of the flower is of a more yellowish white, which we vsually call a Straw colour.

Iris alba maior Versicolor. The white party coloured Flowerdeluce.

This variable Flowerdeluce is like vnto the former, but that the leaues are not so large and broad, the flower hereof is as large almost, and as white as the former, but it hath a faire list or line of a blewish purple downe the backe of euery one of the three vpright leaues, and likewise round about the edges, both of the vpper and lower leaues, and also a little more purplish vpon the ridge of the arched leaues, that couer the falling leaues : the roote hereof is not so great as of the former white, but a little slenderer and browner.

Iris Dalmatica maior. The great Dalmatian Flowerdeluce.

This greater Flowerdeluce of Dalmatia, hath his leaues as large and broad as any of the Flowerdeluces whatsoeuer, his stalke and flower doe equall his other proportion,

tion, onely the colour of the flower is differing, being of a faire watchet or bleake blew colour wholly, with the yellow frize or thrum downe the middle of the lower or falling leaues, as before is said to be common to all these sorts of Flowerdeluces; in all other parts it little differeth, sauing onely this is obserued to haue a small shew of a purplish red about the bottome of the greene leaues.

Iris purpurea siue vulgaris. The common purple Flowerdeluce.

This Flowerdeluce, which is most common in Gardens, differeth nothing at all from those that are formerly described, either in roote, leafe, or flower for the forme of them, but onely that the leaues of this are not so large as the last, and the flower it selfe is of a deep purple or Violet colour, and sometimes a little declining to rednesse, especially in some places.

Sometimes this kinde of Flowerdeluce will haue flowers of a paler purple colour, *Purpurea pallidior versicolor.* comming neare vnto a blew, and sometimes it will haue veines or stripes of a deeper blew, or purple, or ash colour, running through all the vpper and lower leaues.

There is another like vnto this, but more purple in the fals, and more pale in the *Cærulea labris purpureis.* vpright leaues.

Iris Asiatica cærulea. The blew Flowerdeluce of Asia.

This Flowerdeluce of Asia, is in largenesse of leaues like vnto the Dalmatian, but beareth more store of flowers on seuerall branches, which are of a deeper blew colour, and the arched leaues whitish on the side, and purplish on the ridges, but in other things like vnto it.

There is another neare vnto this, but that his leaues are a little narrower, and his *Purpurea* flowers a little more purple, especially the vpper leaues.

Iris Damascena. The Flowerdeluce of Damasco.

This is likewise altogether like the Flowerdeluce of Asia, but that it hath some white veines in the vpright leaues.

Iris Lusitanica biflora. The Portugall Flowerdeluce.

This Portugall Flowerdeluce is very like the common purple Flowerdeluce, but that this is not so large in leaues, or flowers, and that it doth often flower twice in a yeare, that is, both in the Spring, and in the Autumne againe, and besides, the flowers haue a better or sweeter sent, but of the like purple or Violet colour as it is, and comming forth out of purplish skins or huskes.

Iris Camerarij siue purpurea versicolor maior. The greater variable coloured purple Flowerdeluce.

The greater of the variable purple Flowerdeluces, hath very broad leaues, like vnto the leaues of the common purple Flowerdeluce, and so is the flower also, but differing in colour, for the three lower leaues are of a deepe purple colour tending to rednesse, the three arched leaues are of the colour with the vpper leaues, which are of a pale or bleake colour tending to yellownesse, shadowed ouer with a smoakie purplish colour, except the ridges of the arched leaues, which are of a more liuely purple colour.

Iris purpurea versicolor minor. The lesser variable purple Flowerdeluce.

This Flowerdeluce differeth not in any thing from the last, but onely that it hath narrower greene leaues, and smaller and narrower flowers, else if they be both conferred together, the colours will not seeme to varie the one from the other any whit at all.

There is another somewhat neare vnto these two last kindes, whose huskes from *Altera minus fuliginea.* whence

Q

whence the flowers doe shoote forth, haue purple veines in them, and so haue the falling purplish leaues, and the three vpright leaues are not so smoakie, yet of a dun purple colour.

Iris cærulea versicolor. The blew party coloured Flowerdeluce.

This party coloured Flowerdeluce hath his leaues of the same largenesse, with the lesser variable purple Flowerdeluce last described, and his flowers diuersly marked : for some haue the tals blew at the edges, and whitish at the bottome, the arched leaues of a yellowish white, and the vpright leaues of a whitish blew, with yellowish edges. Some againe are of a darker blew, with brownish spots in them. And some are so pale a blew, that we may well call it an ash-colour: And lastly, there is another of this sort, whose vpright leaues are of a faire pale blew, with yellowish edges, and the falling leaues parted into two colours, sometimes equally in the halfe, each side sutable to the other in colour : And sometimes hauing the one leafe in that manner : And sometimes but with a diuers coloured list in them ; in the other parts both of flower and leafe, like vnto the other.

Iris lutea variegata. The yellow variable Flowerdeluce.

This yellow variable Flowerdeluce loseth his leaues in Winter, contrary to all the former Flowerdeluces, so that his roote remaineth vnder ground without any shew of leafe vpon it : but in the beginning of the Spring it shooteth out faire broad leaues, falling downwards at the points or ends, but shorter many times then any of the former, and so is the stalke likewise, not rising much aboue a foote high, whereon are set two or three large flowers, whose falling leaues are of a reddish purple colour, the three that stand vpright of a smoakie yellow, the arched leaues hauing their ridges of a bleake colour tending to purple, the sides being of the former smoakie yellow colour, with some purplish veines at the foote or bottome of all the leaues : the roote groweth somewhat more slender and long vnder ground, and of a darker colour then manie of the other.

Varietas. Another sort hath the vpright leaues of a reasonable faire yellow, and stand more vpright, not bowing downe as most of the other, and the purple fals haue pale edges. Some haue their greene leaues party coloured, white and greene, more or lesse, and so are the huskes of the flowers, the arched leaues yellow, as the vpright leaues are, with purplish veines at the bottome. And some haue both the arched and vpright leaues of so pale a yellow, that we may almost call it a straw colour, but yellower at the bottome, with purple veines, and the falling leaues purple, with two purple spots in them.

And these are the sorts of the greater tuberous or Flagge Flowerdeluces that haue come to our knowledge : the next hereunto are the lesser or narrow leafed kindes to be described ; and first of the greatest of them.

1. *Iris angustifolia Tripolitana aurea.* The yellow Flowerdeluce of Tripoly.

This Flowerdeluce I place in the forefront of the narrow leafed Flowerdeluces, for the length of the leaues, compared with the breadth of them ; it may fitly bee called a narrow leafed Flowerdeluce, although they be an inch broad, which is broader then any of them that follow, or some of those are set downe before, but as I said, the length make them seem narrow, and therfore let it take vp his roome in this place, with the description that followeth. It beareth leaues a yard long, or not much lesse, and an inch broad, as is said before, or more, of a sad greene colour, but not shining : the stalke riseth vp to be foure or fiue foote high, being strong and round, but not very great, bearing at the toppe two or three long and narrow gold yellow flowers, of the fashion of the bulbous Flowerdeluces, as the next to bee described is, without any mixture or variation therein : the heads for seede are three square, containing within them many flat cornered seedes : the roote is long and blackish, like vnto the rest that follow, but greater and fuller.

1 *Iris Chalcedonica ſiue Suſiana maior.* The great Turkie Flowerdeluce. 2 *Iris alba Florentina.* The white Flowerdeluce. 3 *Iris lati folia variegata.* The variable Flowerdeluce. 4 *Chamæiris latifolia maior.* The greater dwarfe Flowerdeluce.

2. *Iris angustifolia maior cærulea.*
The greater blew Flowerdeluce with narrow leaues.

This kinde of Flowerdeluce hath his leaues very long and narrow, of a whitiſh greene colour, but neither ſo long or broad as the laſt, yet broader, thicker and ſtiffer then any of the reſt with narrow leaues that follow: the ſtalke riſeth ſometimes no higher then the leaues, and ſometimes a little higher, bearing diuers flowers at the top, ſucceſſiuely flowring one after another, and are like vnto the flowers of the bulbous Flowerdeluces, but of a light blew colour, and ſometimes deeper: after the flowers are paſt, riſe vp ſix cornered heads, which open into three parts, wherein is contained browne ſeede, almoſt round: the roote is ſmall, blackiſh and hard, ſpreading into many long heads, and more cloſely growing or matting together.

3. *Iris angustifolia purpurea marina.* The purple narrow leafed Sea Flowerdeluce.

This Sea Flowerdeluce hath many narrow hard leaues as long as the former, and of a darke greene colour, which doe ſmell a little ſtrong: the ſtalke beareth two or three flowers like the former, but ſomewhat leſſe, and of a darke purple or Violet colour: in ſeede and roote it is like the former.

4. *Iris angustifolia purpurea versicolor.*
The variable purple narrow leafed Flowerdeluce.

The leaues of this Flowerdeluce are very like the former Sea Flowerdeluce, and do a little ſtinke like them; the flowers are differing, in that the vpper leaues are wholly purple or violet, and the lower leaues haue white veines, and purple running one among another: the ſeede and rootes differ not from the former purple Sea kinde.

5. *Iris angustifolia minor Pannonica ſiue versicolor Cluſij.*
The ſmall variable Hungarian Flowerdeluce of Cluſius.

This Hungarian Flowerdeluce (firſt found out by Cluſius, by him deſcribed, and of him tooke the name) riſeth vp with diuers ſmall tufts of leaues, very long, narrow, and greene, growing thicke together, eſpecially if it abide any time in a place; among which riſeth vp many long round ſtalkes, higher then the leaues, bearing two or three, or foure ſmall flowers, one aboue another, like the former, but ſmaller and of greater beauty: for the lower leaues are variably ſtriped with white and purple, without any thrume or fringe at all; the vpper leaues are of a blewiſh fine purple or Violet colour, & ſo are the arched leaues, yet hauing the edges a little paler: the heads for ſeede are ſmaller, and not ſo cornered as the other, containing ſeedes much like the former, but ſmaller: the roote is blacke and ſmall, growing thicker and cloſer together then any other, and ſtrongly faſtened in the ground, with a number of hard ſtringie rootes: the flowers are of a reaſonable good ſent.

6. *Iris angustifolia maior flore duplici.* The greater double blew Flowerdeluce.

This Flowerdeluce, differeth not either in roote or leafe from the firſt great blew Flowerdeluce of Cluſius, but onely in that the leaues grow thicker together, and that the flowers of this kinde are as it were double with many leaues confuſedly ſet together, without any diſtinct parts of a Flowerdeluce, and of a faire blew colour with many white veines and lines running in the leaues; yet oftentimes the ſtalke of flowers hath but two or three ſmall flowers diſtinctly ſet together, riſing as it were out of one huſke.

7. *Iris angustifolia minor alba Cluſij.*
The ſmall white Flowerdeluce of Hungary.

This likewiſe differeth little from the former Hungarian Flowerdeluce of Cluſius,

1 *Iris angustifolia Tripolitana.* The yellow Flowerdeluce of Tripoli. 2 *Iris angustifolia maior cærulea.* The greater blew Flowerdeluce with narrow leaues. 3 *Iris angustifolia minor Pannonica siue versicolor Clusii.* The small variable Hungarian Flowerdeluce of Clusius. 4 *Iris angustifolia maior flore duplici.* The greater double blew Flowerdeluce. 5 *Chamæiris angustifolia minor.* The lesser Grasse Flowerdeluce. 6 *Iris tuberosa.* The veluet Flowerdeluce.

but that the leafe is of a little paler greene colour, and the flower is of a faire whitish colour, with some purple at the bottome of the leaues.

Next after these narrow leafed Flowerdeluces, are the greater and smaller sorts of dwarfe kindes to follow; and lastly, the narrow or grasse leafed dwarfe kindes, which will finish this Chapter of Flowerdeluces.

1. *Chamæiris latifolia maior alba.* The greater white dwarfe Flowerdeluce.

This dwarfe Flowerdeluce hath his leaues as broad as some of the lesser kindes last mentioned, but not shorter; the stalke is very short, not aboue halfe a foote high or thereabouts, bearing most commonly but one flower, seldome two, which are in some of a pure white, in others paler, or somewhat yellowish through the whole flower, except the yellow frize or thrume in the middle of euery one of the falling leaues: after the flowers are past, come forth great heads, containing within them round pale seed: the roote is small, according to the proportion of the plant aboue ground, but made after the fashion of the greater kindes, with tuberous peeces spreading from the sides, and strong fibres or strings, whereby they are fastened in the ground.

2. *Chamæiris latifolia maior purpurea.* The greater purple dwarfe Flowerdeluce.

There is no difference either in roote, leafe, or forme of flower in this from the former dwarfe kinde, but onely in the colour of the flower, which in some is of a very deepe or blacke Violet purple, both the toppes and the fals: in others the Violet purple is more liuely, and in some the vpper leaues are blew, and the lower leaues purple, yet all of them haue that yellow frize or thrume in the middle of the falling leaues, that the other kindes haue.

There is another that beareth purple flowers, that might be reckoned, for the smalnesse and shortnesse of his stalke, to the next kinde, but that the flowers and leaues of this are as large as any of the former kindes of the smaller Flowerdeluces.

3. *Chamæiris latifolia minor alba.* The lesser white dwarfe Flowerdeluce.

There is also another sort of these Flowerdeluces, whose leaues and flowers are lesse, and wherein there is much variety. The leaues of this kinde, are all for the most part somewhat smaller, narrower, and shorter then the former: the stalke with the flower vpon it scarce riseth aboue the leaues, so that in most of them it may be rather called a foote-stalke, such as the Saffron flowers haue, and are therefore called of manie ἄκαυλοι, without stalkes; the flowers are like vnto the first described of the dwarfe kindes, and of a whitish colour, with a few purplish lines at the bottome of the vpper leaues, and a list of greene in the falling leaues.

Another hath the flowers of a pale yellow, called a Straw colour, with whitish stripes and veines in the fals, and purplish lines at the bottome of the vpper leaues.

4. *Chamæiris latifolia minor purpurea.* The lesser purple dwarfe Flowerdeluce.

The difference of this from the former, consisteth more in the colour then forme of the flower, which is of a deep Violet purple, sometimes paler, and sometimes so deep, that it almost seemeth blacke: And sometimes the fals purplish, and the vpper leaues blew. Some of these haue a sweete sent, and some none.

There is another of a fine pale or delayed blew colour throughout the whole flower.

5. *Chamæiris latifolia minor suauerubens.* The lesser blush coloured dwarfe Flowerdeluce.

This Flowerdeluce hath the falling leaues of the flower of a reddish colour, and the thrumes blew: the vpper and arched leaues of a fine pale red or flesh colour, called a blush colour; in all other things it differeth not, and smelleth little or nothing at all.

6. *Chamæiris*

6. *Chamæiris latifolia minor lutea verficolor.*
The leffer yellow variable dwarfe Flowerdeluce.

The falling leaues of this Flowerdeluce are yellowifh, with purple lines from the middle downewards, fometimes of a deeper, and fometimes of a paler colour, and white thrumes in the middle, the vpper leaues are likewife of a yellowifh colour, with purple lines in them : And fometimes the yellow colour is paler, and the lines both in the vpper and lower leaues of a dull or dead purple colour.

3. *Chamæiris latifolia minor cærulea verficolor.*
The leffer blew variable dwarfe Flowerdeluce.

The vpper leaues of this flower are of a blewifh yellow colour, fpotted with purple in the broad part, and at the bottome very narrow : the falling leaues are fpread ouer with pale purplifh lines, and a fmall fhew of blew about the brimmes : the thrume is yellow at the bottome, and blewifh aboue: the arched leaues are of a blewifh white, being a little deeper on the ridge.
And fometimes the vpper leaues are of a paler blew rather whitifh, with the yellow: both thefe haue no fent at all.

8. *Chamæiris marina purpurea.* The purple dwarfe Sea Flowerdeluce.

This fmall Flowerdeluce is like vnto the narrow leafed Sea Flowerdeluce before defcribed, both in roote, leafe, and flower, hauing no other difference, but in the fmalneffe and lowneffe of the growing, being of the fame purple colour with it.

9. *Chamæiris anguftifolia maior.* The greater Graffe Flowerdeluce.

This Graffe Flowerdeluce hath many long and narrow darke greene leaues, not fo ftiffe as the former, but lither, and bending their ends downe againe, among which rife vp diuers ftalkes, bearing at the toppe two or three fweete flowers, as fmall as any of them fet downe before, of a reddifh purple colour, with whitifh yellow and purple ftrakes downe the middle of the falling leaues : the arched leaues are of a horfe flefh colour all along the edges, and purple vpon the ridges and tips that turne vp againe : vnder thefe appeare three browne aglets, like vnto birds tongues : the three vpper leaues are fmall and narrow, of a perfect purple or Violet colour : the heads for feede haue fharper and harder cornered edges then the former: the feedes are fomewhat grayifh like the former, and fo are the rootes, being fmall, blacke, and hard, growing thicke together, faftened in the ground with fmall blackifh hard ftrings, which hardly fhoote againe if the roote be remoued.

10. *Chamæiris anguftifolia minor.* The leffer Graffe Flowerdeluce.

This Flowerdeluce is in leaues, flowers, and rootes fo like the laft defcribed, that but onely it is fmaller and lower, it is not to be diftinguifhed from the other. And this may fuffice for thefe forts of Flowerdeluces, that furnifh the Gardens of the curious louers of thefe varieties of nature, fo farre forth as hath paffed vnder our knowledge. There are fome other that may be referred hereunto, but they belong to another hiftory ; and therefore I make no mention of them in this place.

The Place.

The places of moft of thefe are fet downe in their feuerall titles ; for fome are out of Turkie, others out of Hungaria, Dalmatia, Illyria, &c. as their names doe import. Thofe that grow by the Sea, are found in Spaine and France.

The

The Time.

Some of thefe do flower in Aprill, fome in May, and fome not vntill Iune.

The Names.

The names expreffed are the fitteft agreeing vnto them, and therefore it is needleffe againe to repeate them.   Many of the rootes of the former or greater kindes, being dryed are fweete, yet fome more then other, and fome haue no fent at all : but aboue all the reft, that with the white flower, called of Florence, is accounted of all to be the fweeteft root, fit to be vfed to make fweete powders, &c. calling it by the name of *Orris* rootes.

Iris tuberofa. The Veluet Flowerdeluce.

Vnto the Family of Flowerdeluces, I muft needes ioyne this peculiar kinde, becaufe of the neare refemblance of the flower, although it differ both in roote and leafe ; leſt therefore it fhould haue no place, let it take vp a roome here in the end of the Flowerdeluces, with this defcription following. It hath many fmall and foure fquare leaues, two foote long and aboue fometimes, of a grayifh greene colour, ſtiffe at the firft, but afterwards growing to their full length, they are weak and bend downe to the ground: out of the middle, as it were of one of thefe leaues, breaketh out the ftalke, a foot high and better, with fome leaues thereon, at the toppe whereof, out of a huske rifeth one flower, (I neuer faw more on a ftalke) confifting of nine leaues, whereof the three that fall downe are of a yellowifh greene colour round about the edges, and in the middle of fo deepe a purple, that it feemeth to be blacke, refembling blacke Veluet : the three arched leaues, that couer the lower leaues to the halfe, are of the fame greenifh colour that the edges and backfide of the lower leaues are : the three vppermoft leaues, if they may be called leaues, or rather fhort peeces like eares, are green alfo, but wherein a glimpfe of purple may be feene in them : after the flower is paft, there followeth a round knob or whitifh feede veffell, hanging downe by a fmall foote-ftalke, from betweene the huske, which is diuided as it were into two leaues, wherein is contained round white feede.   The roote is bunched or knobbed out into long round rootes, like vnto fingers, two or three from one peece, one diftant from another, and one longer then another, for the moft part of a darkifh gray colour, and reddifh withall on the outfide, and fomewhat yellowifh within.

The Place.

It hath beene fent out of Turkie oftentimes (as growing naturally thereabouts) and not knowne to grow naturally any where elfe.

The Time.

It flowreth in Aprill or May, fometimes earlier or later, as the Spring falleth out to be milde or fharpe.

The Names.

Matthiolus contendeth to make it the true *Hermodactylus*, rather from the fhew of the rootes, which (as is faid) are like vnto fingers, then from any other good reafon : for the rootes hereof eyther dry or greene, do nothing refemble the true *Hermodactyli* that are vfed in Phyficke, as any that knoweth them may eafily perceiue, either in forme or vertue. It is more truely referred to the Flowerdeluces, and becaufe of the tuberous rootes, called *Iris tuberofa,* although all the Flowerdeluces in this Chapter haue tuberous rootes,

rootes, yet this much differing from them all. In Englifh it is vfually called, The Veluet Flowerdeluce, becaufe the three falling leaues feeme to be like fmooth blacke Veluet.

The Vertues.

Both the rootes and the flowers of the great Flowerdeluces, are of great vfe for the purging and cleanfing of many inward, as well as outward difeafes, as all Authors in Phyficke doe record. Some haue vfed alfo the greene rootes to cleanfe the skinne, but they had neede to be carefull that vfe them, left they take more harme then good by the vfe of them. The dryed rootes called *Orris* (as is faid) is of much vfe to make fweete powders, or other things to perfume apparrell or linnen. The iuice or decoction of the green roots doth procure both neezing to be fnuft vp into the noftrils, and vomiting very ftrongly being taken inwardly.

Chap. XXI.

Gladiolus. Corne Flagge.

NExt vnto the Flagges or Flowerdeluces, come the *Gladioli* or Corne Flagges to bee entreated of, for fome refemblance of the leaues with them. There are hereof diuers forts, fome bigger and fome leffer, but the chiefeft difference is in the colour of the flowers, and one in the order of the flowers. Of them all in their feuerall orders.

Gladiolus Narbonenfis. The French Corne Flagge.

The French Corne Flagge rifeth vp with three or foure broad, long, and ftiffe greene leaues, one as it were out of the fide of another, being ioyned together at the bottome, fomewhat like vnto the leaues of Flowerdeluces, but ftiffer, more full of ribbes, and longer then many of them, and fharper pointed: the ftalke rifeth vp from among the leaues, bearing them on it as it rifeth, hauing at the toppe diuers huskes, out of which come the flowers one aboue another, all of them turning and opening themfelues one way, which are long and gaping, like vnto the flowers of Foxegloue, a little arched or bunching vp in the middle, of a faire reddifh purple colour, with two white fpots within the mouth thereof, one on each fide, made like vnto a Lozenge that is fquare and long pointed: after the flowers are paft, come vp round heads or feede veffels, wherein is contained reddifh flat feede, like vnto the feede of the Fritillaria, but thicker and fuller: the roote is fomewhat great, round, flat, and hard, with a fhew as if it were netted, hauing another fhort fpongie one vnder it, which when it hath done bearing, and the ftalke dry, that the roote may be taken vp, fticketh clofe to the bottome, but may be eafily taken away, hauing vfually a number of fmall rootes encreafed about it, the leaft whereof will quickly grow, fo that if it be fuffered any long time in a Garden, it will rather choake and pefter it, then be an ornament vnto it.

Gladiolus Italicus binis floribus ordinibus. The Italian Corne Flagge.

The Italian Corne Flagge is like vnto the French in roote, leafe, and flower, without any other difference, then that the roote is fmaller and browner, the leafe and ftalke of a darker colour, and the flowers (being of a little darker colour like the former, and fomewhat fmaller) ftand out on both fides of the ftalke.

Gladiolus Byzantinus. Corne Flagge of Conftantinople.

This Corne Flagge that came firft from Conftantinople, is in all things like vnto the French Corne Flagge laft defcribed, but that it is larger, both in rootes, leaues, and flowers,

flowers, and likewise that the Flowers of this, which stand not on both sides, are of a deeper red colour, and flower later, after all the rest are past : the roote hereof being netted as plainly as any of the former, is as plentifull also to giue encrease, but is more tender and lesse able to abide our sharpe cold Winters.

Gladiolus flore rubente. Blush Corne Flagge.

This blush kinde is like vnto the French Corne Flagge in all respects, sauing onely that the flowers are of a pale red colour, tending to whitenesse, which wee visually call a blush colour.

Gladiolus flore albo. White Corne Flagge.

This white Corne Flagge also differeth not from the last, but onely that the rootes are whiter on the outside, the leaues are greener, without any brownnesse or darknesse as in the former, and the flowers are snow white.

Gladiolus purpureus minor. The small purple Corne Flagge.

This also differeth not from any of the former, but onely in the smalnesse both of leafe, stalke, and flowers, which stand all on the one side, like vnto the French kinde, and of the same colour : the roote of this kinde is netted more then any other.

The Place.

They grow in France and Italy, the least in Spaine, and the Byzantine, as it is thought, about Constantinople, being (as is said) first sent from thence. Iohn Tradescante assured mee, that hee saw many acres of ground in Barbary spread ouer with them.

The Time.

They all flower in Iune and Iuly, and the Byzantine latest, as is said before.

The Names.

It hath diuers names; for the Latines call it *Gladiolus*, of the forme of a sword, which the leafe doth resemble. The Romanes *Segetalis*, because it groweth in the Corne fields. Some call it *Victorialis rotunda*, to put a difference between it, and the *longa*, which is a kinde of Garlicke. Plinie saith, that *Gladiolus* is *Cypirus*, but to decide that controuersie, and many others, belongeth to another discourse, this being intended only for pleasure. Gerrard mistaketh the French kinde for the Italian.

The Vertues.

The roote being bruised, and applyed with Frankinsense (and often of it selfe without it) in the manner of a pultis or plaister, is held of diuers to be singular good to draw out splinters, thornes, and broken bones out of the flesh. Some take it to be effectuall to stirre vp Venerie, but I somewhat doubt thereof : For Galen in his eighth Booke of Simples, giueth vnto it a drawing, digesting, and drying faculty.

CHAP.

1 *Gladiolus Narbonensis* The French Corne Flagge. 2 *Gladiolus Italicus.* The Italian Corne Flagge. 3 *Gladiolus Byzantinus.* Corne Flagge of Constantinople. 4 *Palma Christi mas* The great male handed Satyrion. 5 *Orchis Hermaphroditica candida.* The white Butterflie Orchis. 6 *Orchis Melitias siue apifera.* The Bee flower or Bee Orchis. 7 *Dens Caninus flore purpurante.* Dogges tooth Violet with a pale purplish flower. 8 *Dens Caninus flore albo.* Dogges tooth Violet with a white flower.

Chap. XXII.

Orchis siue Satyrium. Bee flowers.

ALthough it is not my purpose in this place, to giue a generall history of all the sorts of Orchides, Satyrions, and the rest of that kinde ; yet because many of them are very pleasant to behold, and, if they be planted in a conuenient place, will abide some time in Gardens, so that there is much pleasure taken in them : I shall intrude some of them for curiosities sake, to make vp the prospect of natures beautifull variety, and only entreate of a few, leauing the rest to a more ample declaration.

1. *Satyrium Basilicum siue Palma Christi mas.*
The greater male handed Satyrion.

This handed Satyrion hath for the most part but three faire large greene leaues, neare vnto the ground, spotted with small blackish markes : from among which riseth vp a stalke, with some smaller leaues thereon, bearing at the toppe a bush or spike of flowers, thicke set together, euery one whereof is made like a body, with the belly broader belowe then aboue, where it hath small peeces adioyned vnto it : the flower is of a faire purple colour, spotted with deeper purple spots, and hauing small peeces like hornes hanging at the backes of the flowers, and a small leafe at the bottome of the foote-stalke of euery flower : the rootes are not round, like the other Orchides, but somewhat long and flat, like a hand, with small diuisions belowe, hanging downe like the fingers of a hand, cut short off by the knockles, two alwayes growing together, with some small fibres or strings aboue the heads of these rootes, at the bottome of the stalke.

2. *Satyrium Basilicum siue Palma Christi femina.*
The female handed Satyrion.

This female Satyrion hath longer and narrower leaues then the former, and spotted with more and greater spots, compassing the stalke at the bottome like the other : this beareth likewise a bush of flowers, like vnto the other, but that each of these haue heads like hoods, whereas the former haue none : in some they are white with purple spots, and in others of a reddish purple, with deep or darke coloured spots: the roots are alike.

3. *Orchis Hermaphroditica candida.* The white Butterflie Orchis.

The rootes of this kinde take part with both the sorts of *Orchis* and *Satyrium*, being neither altogether round, nor fully handed, and thereupon it tooke the name, to signifie both kindes : the leaues are two in number, seldome more, being faire and broad, like vnto the leaues of Lillies, without any spot at all in them : at the toppe of the stalke stand many white flowers, not so thicke set as the first or second, euery one being fashioned like vnto a white Butterflie, with the wings spread abroad.

4. *Orchis Melitias siue apifera.* The Bee flower or Bee Orchis.

This is a small and lowe plant for the most part, with three or foure small narrow leaues at the bottome : the stalke is seldome aboue halfe a foote high, with foure or fiue flowers thereon one aboue another, hauing round bodies, and somewhat flat, of a kind of yellowish colour, with purple wings aboue them, so like vnto an honey Bee, that it might soone deceiue one that neuer had seene such a flower before : the roots are two together, round and white, hauing a certaine *muccilaginesse* or clamminesse within them, without any taste almost at all, as all or the most part of these kindes haue.

5. *Orchis Sphegodes.* Gnats Satyrion.

The leaues of this Orchis are somewhat larger then of the Bee flower, the stalke also
somewhat

somewhat higher : the flowers are fewer on the toppe, but somewhat larger then of the Bee flowers, made to the resemblance of a Gnat or great long Flie : the rootes are two round bulbes, as the other are.

6. *Orchis Myodes.* Flie Orchis.

The Flie Orchis is like vnto the last described, both in leafe and roote, the difference is in the flower, which is neither so long as the Gnat Satyrion, nor so great as the Bee Orchis, but the neather part of the Flie is blacke, with a list of ash-colour crossing the backe, with a shew of legges hanging at it : the naturall Flie seemeth so to bee in loue with it, that you shall seldome come in the heate of the day, but you shall finde one sitting close thereon.

The Place.

These grow in many places of England, some in the Woods, as the Butterflie, and the two former handed Satyrions : others on dry bankes and barren balkes in Kent, and many other places.

The Time.

They flower for the most part in the beginning or middle of May, or thereabouts.

The Names.

Their seuerall names are expressed in their titles, so much as may suffice for this discourse.

The Vertues.

All the kindes of Orchis are accounted to procure bodily lust, as well the flowers distilled, as the rootes prepared.

The rootes boyled in red Wine, and afterwards dryed, are held to bee a singular good remedie against the bloody Flixe.

Chap. XXIII.

Dens Caninus. Dogs tooth Violet.

VNto the kindes of Orchides, may fitly be ioyned another plant, which by many is reckoned to be a *Satyrium*, both from the forme of roote and leafe, and from the efficacy or vertue correspondent thereunto. And although it cannot be the *Satyrium Erythronium* of Dioscorides, as some would entitle it, for that as I haue shewed before, his *Satyrium tryphillum* is the Tulipa without all doubt ; yet becaufe it differeth very notably, and carrieth more beauty and respect in his flower then they, I shall entreate thereof in a Chapter by it selfe, and set it next vnto them.

Dens Caninus flore albo. Dogs tooth Violet with a white flower.

The white Dogs tooth hath for his roote a white bulbe, long and small, yet vsually greater then either of the other that follow, bigger belowe then aboue, with a small peece adioyning to the bottome of it, from whence rise vp in the beginning of the Spring, after the Winter frosts are past, two leaues for the most part (when it will flower, or else but one, and neuer three together that euer I saw) closed together when they first come vp out of the ground, which inclose the flower betweene them : the leaues when they are opened do lay themselues flat on the ground, or not much aboue it, one opposite vnto the other, with the stalke and the flower on it standing betweene them, which leaues are of a whitish greene colour, long and narrow, yet broader in the
R   middle

middle then at both ends, growing leſſe by degrees each way, ſpotted and ſtriped all ouer the leaues with white lines and ſpots : the ſtalke riſeth vp halfe a foote high or more, bearing at the toppe one flower and no more, hanging downe the head, larger then any of the other of this kinde that follow, made or conſiſting of ſix white long and narrow leaues, turning themſelues vp againe, after it hath felt the comfort of the Sunne, that they doe almoſt touch the ſtalke againe, very like vnto the flowers of *Cyclamen* or Sowebread : it hath in the middle of the flower ſix white chiues, tipt with darke purple pendents, and a white three forked ſtile in the middle of them: the flower hath no ſent at all, but commendable onely for the beauty and forme thereof : after the flower is paſt, commeth in the place a round head ſeeming three ſquare, containing therein ſmall and yellowiſh ſeede.

Dens Caninus flore purpuraſcente. Dogs tooth with a pale purple flower.

This other Dogs tooth is like vnto the former, but leſſer in all parts, the leafe whereof is not ſo long, but broad and ſhort, ſpotted with darker lines and ſpots : the flower is like the other, but ſmaller, and of a delayed purple colour, very pale ſometimes, and ſometimes a little deeper, turning it ſelfe as the other, with a circle round about the vmbone or middle, the chiues hereof are not white, but declining to purple: the roote is white, and like vnto the former, but leſſer, as is ſaid before.

Dens Caninus flore rubro. Dogs tooth with a red flower.

This is in all things like vnto the laſt, both for forme and bigneſſe of flower and leafe : the chiefe difference conſiſteth in this, that the leaues hereof are of a yellowiſh mealy greene colour, ſpotted and ſtreaked with redder ſpots and ſtripes, and the flower of a deeper reddiſh purple colour, and the chiues alſo more purpliſh then the laſt, in all other things it is alike.

The Place.

The ſorts of *Dens Caninus* doe growe in diuers places ; ſome in Italy on the Euganean Hils, others on the Apenine, and ſome about Gratz, the chiefe Citie of Stiria, and alſo about Bayonne, and in other places.

The Time.

They flower in March moſt vſually, and many times in Aprill, according to the ſeaſonableneſſe of the yeare.

The Names.

Cluſius did call it firſt *Dentali,* and Lobel, and from him ſome others *Satyrium,* and *Erythronium,* but I haue ſaid enough hereof in the beginning of the Chapter. It is moſt commonly called *Dens Caninus,* and we in Engliſh, either Dogs tooth, or Dogs tooth Violet. Geſner called it *Hermodactylus,* and Matthiolus *Pſeudohermodactylus.*

The Vertues.

The roote hereof is held to bee of more efficacy for venereous effects, then any of the Orchides and Satyrions.

They of Stiria vſe the rootes for the falling ſickneſſe.

Wee haue had from Virginia a roote ſent vnto vs, that wee might well Iudge, by the forme and colour thereof being dry, to be either the roote of this, or of an Orchis, which the naturall people hold not onely to be ſingular to procure luſt, but hold it as a ſecret, loth to reueale it.

CHAP.

CHAP. XXIIII.

Cyclamen. Sowebread.

THe likenesse of the flowers, and the spotting of the leaues of the *Dens Caninus*, with these of the *Cyclamen* or Sowebread, maketh mee ioyne it next thereunto : as also that after the bulbous rooted plants I might begin with the tuberous that remaine, and make this plant the beginning of them. Of this kinde there are diuers sorts, differing both in forme of leaues and time of flowring : for some doe flower in the Spring of the yeare, others afterwards in the beginning of Summer : but the most number in the end of Summer, or beginning of Autumne or Harueft, whereof some haue round leaues, others cornered like vnto Iuie, longer or shorter, greater or smaller. Of them all in order, and first of those that come in the Spring.

1. *Cyclamen Vernum flore purpureo.* Purple flowred Sowebread of the Spring.

This Sowebread hath a smaller roote then most of the others, yet round and blackish on the outside, as all or most of the rest are (I speake of them that I haue seene ; for Clusius and others doe report to haue had very great ones) from whence rise vp diuers round, yet pointed leaues, and somewhat cornered withall, greene aboue, and spotted with white spots circlewise about the leafe, and reddish vnderneath, which at their first comming vp are folded together ; among which come the flowers, of a reddish purple colour and very sweete, euery one vpon a small, long, and slender reddish foote-stalke, which hanging downe their heads, turne vp their leaues againe : after the flowers are past, the head or seede vessell shrinketh downe, winding his footestalke, and coyling it selfe like a cable, which when it toucheth the ground, there abideth hid among the leaues, till it be growne great and ripe, wherein are contained a few small round seedes, which being presently sowne, will growe first into round rootes, and afterwards from them shoote forth leaues.

2. *Cyclamen Vernum flore albo.* White flowred Sowebread of the Spring.

The white flowring Sowebread hath his leaues like the former, but not fully so much cornered, bearing small snow white flowers, as sweete as the other : and herein consisteth the chiefest difference, in all other things it is alike.

3. *Cyclamen Vernum Creticum flore albo.* White Candy Sowebread of the Spring.

This Sowebread is somewhat like the former white kinde, but that the leaues grow much larger and longer, with more corners at the edges, and more eminent spots on them : the flowers also somewhat longer and larger, and herein consisteth the whole difference.

4. *Cyclamen Æstivum.* Summer Sowebread.

Summer Sowebread hath round leaues like vnto the Romane Sowebread, but somewhat cornered, yet with shorter corners then the Iuie leafed Sowebread, full of white spots on the vpperside of the leaues, and very purple vnderneath, sometimes they haue fewer spots, and little or no purple vnderneath : the flowers hereof are as small, as purple, and as sweete, as the purple Sowebread of the Spring time : the roote hereof is likewise small, blacke, and round.

5. *Cyclamen Romanum rotundifolium.* Romane Sowebread with round leaues.

The Romane Sowebread hath round leaues, somewhat like vnto the common Sowebread, but not fully so round pointed at the ends, a little cornered sometimes also, or as it were indented, with white spots round about the middle of the leaues,

R 2   and

and very conspicuous, which make it seeme the more beautifull : the flowers appeare in Autumne, and are shorter, and of a deeper purplish red colour then the Iuie Sowebread, rising vp before the leaues for the most part, or at least with them, and little or nothing sweete : the roote is round and blacke, vsually not so flat as it, but growing sometimes to bee greater then any other kinde of Sowebread.   There is sometimes some variety to be seene, both in the leaues and flowers of this kinde ; for that sometime the leaues haue more corners, and either more or lesse spotted with white : the flowers likewise of some are larger or lesser, longer or rounder, paler or deeper coloured one then another.   This happeneth most likely from the sowing of the seede, causing the like variety as is seene in the Iuie leafed Sowebread.   It doth also many times happen from the diuersity of soyles and countries where they grow : the seed of this, as of all the rest, is small and round, contained in such like heads as the former, standing almost like the head of a Snake that is twined or folded within the body thereof. This and the other Autumnall kindes, presently after their sowing in Autumne, shoote forth leaues, and so abide all the Winter, according to their kinde.

Varietas.

6. *Cyclamen folio hederæ autumnale.* Iuie leafed Sowebread.

The Iuie leafed Sowebread groweth in the same manner that the former doth, that is, bringeth forth flowers with the leaues sometimes, or most commonly before them, whose flowers are greater then the common round leafed Sowebread, somewhat longer then the former Romane or Italian Sowebreads, and of a paler purple colour, almost blush, without that sweete sent as is in the first kinde of the Spring : the greene leaues hereof are more long then round, pointed at the ends, and hauing also one or two corners on each side, sometimes much spotted on the vpperside with white spots and marks, and sometimes but a little or not at all ; and so likewise sometimes more or lesse purple vnderneath : all the leaues and flowers doe stand vsually euery one seuerally by themselues, vpon their owne slender foote-stalkes, as most of all the other kindes doe : but sometimes it happeneth, that both leaues and flowers are found growing from one and the same stalke, which I rather take to be accidentall, then naturall so to continue : the seede hereof is like the former kindes, which being sowne produceth variety, both in the forme of the leaues, and colour and smell of the flowers : some being paler or deeper, and some more or lesse sweete then others : the leaues also, some more or lesse cornered then others : the root groweth to be great, being round and flat, and of a blackish browne colour on the outside.

Varietas.

7. *Cyclamen autumnale hederæfolio flore albo.*
Iuie leafed Sowebread with white flowers.

There is one of this kinde, whose leaues are rounder, and not so much cornered as the former, flowring in Autumne as the last doth, and whose flowers are wholly white, not hauing any other notable difference therein.

8. *Cyclamen autumnale angustifolium.* Long leafed Sowebread.

This kinde of Sowebread may easily be knowne from all the other kindes, because his leafe is longer and narrower then others, fashioned at the bottome thereof with points, somewhat like vnto *Arum* or Wake Robin leaues : the flowers are like the former sorts for forme, but of a purple colour.   There is also another of this kinde in all things like the former, but that the flowers are white.

9. *Cyclamen Antiochenum Autumnale flore purpureo duplici.*
Double flowred Sowebread of Antioch.

This Sowebread of Antioch with double flowers, hath his leaues somewhat round, like vnto the leaues of the Summer Sowbread, but with lesse notches or corners, & full of white spots on them : it beareth flowers on stalks, like vnto others, & likewise some stalks that haue two or three flowers on them, which are very large, with ten or twelue

leaues

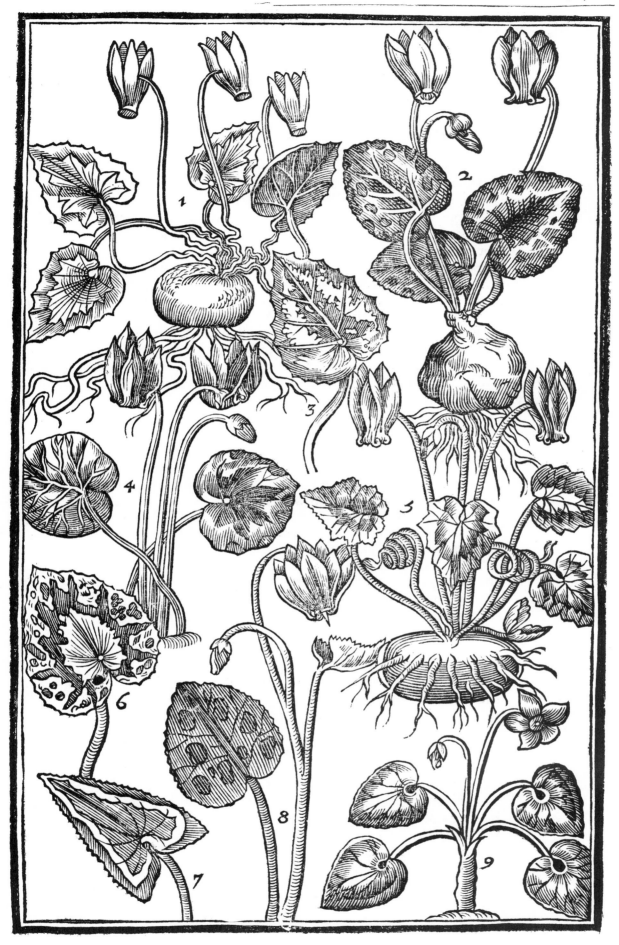

1 *Cyclamen Vernum flore purpureo* Purple flowred Sowebread of the Spring. 2 *Cyclamen aestivum.* Summer Sowebread. 3 *Folium Cyclaminis Cretici ver-*
nalis flore candido. A leafe of Candie Sowebread. 4 *Cyclamen Romanum Autumnale.* Romane Sowebread of the Autumne. 5 *Cyclamen hederæfolio*
Autumnale. Iuie leafed Autumne Sowebread. 6 *Folium Cyclaminis Autumnalis flore albo.* A leafe of the Autumne Sowebread with a white flower.
7 *Folium Cyclaminis angustifolij Autumnalis.* A leafe of the long leafed Sowebread. 8 *Cyclamen Antiochenum Autumnale flore amplo purpureo duplici*
The double flowred Sowebread of Antioch. 9 *Cyclamen vulgare folio rotundo.* The common round leafed Sowebread.

leaues a peece, of a faire Peach colour, like vnto the flowers of purple Sowebread of the Spring, and deeper at the bottome.

There are of this kinde some, whose flowers appeare in the Spring, and are as large and double as the former, but of a pure white colour.

There are of these Sowebreads of Antioch, that haue but single flowers, some appearing in the Spring, and others in Autumne.

10. *Cyclamen vulgare folio rotundo.* The common Sowebread.

The common Sowebread (which is most vsed in the Apothecaries Shops) hath many leaues spread vpon the ground, rising from certaine small long heads, that are on the greater round rootes, as vsually most of the former sorts doe, being in the like manner folded together, and after spread themselues into round greene leaues, somewhat like vnto the leaues of *Asarum*, but not shining, without any white spots on the vpperside for the most part, or but very seldome, and reddish or purplish vnderneath, and very seldome greener : the flowers stand vpon small foot-stalkes, and shew themselues open for the most part, before any leaues doe appeare, being smaller and shorter then those with Iuie leaues, and of a pale purple colour, yet sometimes deeper, hanging downe their heads, and turning vp their leaues againe, as all others doe, but more sweete then many other of the Autumne flowers : after the flowers are past, come the heads turning or winding themselues downe in like manner as the other do, hauing such like seede, but somewhat larger, and more vneuen, or not so round at the least : the roote is round, and not flat, of a browner colour, and not so blacke on the outside as many of the others.

The Place.

The Sowebreads of the Spring doe both grow on the Pyrenæan Mountaines in Italy, and in Candy, and about Mompelier in France; Antioch in Syria also hath yeelded some both of the Spring and Autumne. Those with round and Iuie leaues grow in diuers places both of France and Italy : and the common in Germany, and the Lowe-Countries. But that Autumne Sowebread with white flowers, is reported to grow in the Kingdome of Naples. I haue very curiously enquired of many, if euer they found them in any parts of England, neare or farther off from the places where they dwell : but they haue all affirmed, that they neuer found, or euer heard of any that haue found of any of them. This onely they haue assured, that there groweth none in the places, where some haue reported them to grow.

The Time.

Those of the Spring doe flower about the end of Aprill, or beginning of May. The other of the Summer, about the end of Iune or in Iuly. The rest some in August, and September, others in October.

The Names.

The Common Sowebread is called by most Writers in Latine, *Panis Porcinus*, and by that name it is knowne in the Apothecaries shops, as also by the name *Arthanita*, according to which name, they haue an ointment so called, which is to be made with the iuice hereof. It is also called by diuers other names, not pertinent for this discourse. The most vsuall name, whereby it is knowne to most Herbarists, is *Cyclamen* (which is the Greeke word) or as some call it *Cyclaminus*, adding thereunto their other seuerall titles. In English, Sowebread.

The Vertues.

The leaues and rootes are very effectuall for the spleene, as the Ointment before remembred plainly proueth, being vsed for the same purpose,

and

and that to good effect. It is vsed also for women in long and hard trauels, where there is danger, to accelerate the birth, either the roote or the leafe being applyed. But for any amorous effects, I hold it meere fabulous.

Chap. XXV.

Anemone. Windeflower and his kindes.

THe next tuberous rooted plants that are to follow (of right in my opinion) are the *Anemones* or Windeflowers, and although some tuberous rooted plants, that is, the Asphodils, Spiderworts, and Flowerdeluces haue beene before inferted, it was, both becaufe they were in name or forme of flowers futable to them whom they were ioyned vnto, and also that they fhould not be feuered and entreated of in two feuerall places : the reft are now to follow, at the leaft fo many of them as be beautifull flowers, fit to furnifh a Florifts Garden, for natures delightfome varieties and excellencies. To diftinguifh the Family of *Anemones* I may, that is, into the wilde kindes, and into the tame or mannured, as they are called, and both of them nourfed vp in Gardens ; and of them into thofe that haue broader leaues, and into thofe that haue thinner or more iagged leaues : and of each of them, into thofe that beare fingle flowers, and thofe that beare double flowers. But to defcribe the infinite (as I may fo fay) variety of the colours of the flowers, and to giue to each his true diftinction and denomination, *Hic labor, hoc opus eft,* it farre paffeth my ability I confeffe, and I thinke would grauell the beft experienced this day in Europe (and the like I faid concerning Tulipas, it being as contingent to this plant, as is before faid of the Tulipa, to be without end in yeelding varieties:) for who can fee all the varieties that haue fprung from the fowing of the feede in all places, feeing the variety of colours rifen from thence, is according to the variety of ayres & grounds wherein they are fowne, skill alfo helping nature in ordering them aright. For the feede of one and the fame plant fowne in diuers ayres and grounds, doe produce that variety of colours that is much differing one from another ; who then can difplay all the mixtures of colours in them, to fet them downe in fo fmall a roome as this Book ? Yet as I haue done (in the former part of this Treatife) my good will, to expreffe as many of each kinde haue come to my knowledge, fo if I endeauour the like in this, I hope the courteous wil accept it, and hold me excufed for the reft: otherwife, if I were or could be abfolute, I fhould take from my felf and others the hope of future augmentation, or addition of any new, which neuer will be wanting. To begin therefore with the wilde kinds (as they are fo accounted) I fhall firft entreate of the *Pulfatillas* or Pafque flowers, which are certainly kindes of wilde *Anemones,* both in leafe and flower, as may well be difcerned by them that are iudicious (although fome learned men haue not fo thought, as appeareth by their writings) the rootes of them making one fpeciall note of difference, from the other forts of wilde *Anemones.*

1. *Pulfatilla Anglica purpurea.* The purple Pafque flower.

The Pafque or Paffe flower which is of our owne Country, hath many leaues lying on the ground, fomewhat rough or hairie, hard in feeling, and finely cut into many fmall leaues, of a darke greene colour, almoft like the leaues of Carrets, but finer and fmaller, from among which rife vp naked ftalkes, rough or hairie alfo, fet about the middle thereof with fome fmall diuided leaues compaffing them, and rifing aboue thefe leaues about a fpanne, bearing euery one of them one pendulous flower, made of fix leaues, of a fine Violet purple colour, but fomewhat deepe withall, in the middle whereof ftand many yellow threeds, fet about a middle purple pointell : after the flower is paft, there commeth vp in the ftead thereof a bufhie head of long feedes, which are fmall and hoarie, hauing at the end of euery one a fmall haire, which is gray likewife : the roote is fmall and long, growing downewards into the ground, with a tuft of haire at the head thereof, and not lying or running vnder the vpper cruft thereof, as the other wilde *Anemones* doe.

2. *Pulfa-*

2. *Pulsatilla Danica*. The Passe flower of Denmarke.

There is another that was brought out of Denmarke, very like vnto the former, but that it is larger both in roote and leafe, and flower also, which is of a fairer purple colour, not so deepe, and besides, will better abide to bee mannured then our English kinde will, as my selfe haue often proued.

Vtriusque flore albo & flore duplici.

Of both these sorts it is said, that some plants haue bin found, that haue borne white flowers. And likewise one that bore double flowers, that is, with two rowes of leaues.

3. *Pulsatilla flore rubro*. The red Passe flower.

Lobel, as I take it, did first set forth this kinde, being brought him from Syria, the leaues whereof are finer cut, the flower smaller, and with longer leaues, and of a red colour.

4. *Pulsatilla flore luteo*. The yellow Passe flower.

The yellow Passe flower hath his leaues cut and diuided, very like vnto the leaues of the first kinde, but somewhat more hairie, greene on the vpperside, and hairie vnderneath : the stalke is round and hoary, the middle whereof is beset with some small leaues, as in the other, from among which riseth vp the stalke of the flower, consisting of six leaues of a very faire yellow colour on the inside, and of a hoary pale yellow on the outside ; after which followeth such an head of hairie thrummes as in the former : the roote is of the bignesse of a mans finger.

5. *Pulsatilla flore albo*. The white Passe flower.

The white Passe flower (which Clusius maketh a kinde of *Anemone*, and yet as hee saith himselfe, doth more nearely resemble the *Pulsatilla*) hath, from amongst a tuft or head of haires, which grow at the toppe of a long blacke roote, many leaues standing vpon long stalkes, which are diuided as it were into three wings or parts, and each part finely cut and diuided, like vnto the Passe flower of Denmarke, but somewhat harder in handling, greenish on the vpperside, and somewhat gray vnderneath, and very hairie all ouer : among these leaues rise vp the stalkes, beset at the middle of them with three leaues, as finely cut and diuided as those belowe, from aboue which standeth the flower, being smaller, and not so pendulous as the former, but in the like manner consisting of six leaues, of a snow white colour on the inside, and a little browner on the outside, with many yellow thrums in the middle : after the flower is past, riseth vp such a like hoary head, composed as it were of many haires, each whereof hath a small seede fastened vnto it, like as the former Passe flowers haue.

The Place.

The first is found in many places of England, vpon dry bankes that lye open to the Sunne.

The second was first brought, as I take it, by Doctor Lobel from Denmarke, & is one of the two kinds, that Clusius saith are common in Germanie, this bearing a paler purple flower, and more early then the other, which is the same with our English, whose flower is so darke, that it almost seemeth blacke.

The red kinde, as Lobel saith, came from Syria.

The yellow Passe flower, which Clusius maketh his third wilde *Anemone*, was found very plentifully growing at the foote of St. Bernards Hill, neare vnto the Cantons of the Switzers.

The white one groweth on the Alpes neare Austria, in France likewise, and other places.

The

1 *Pulsatilla purpurea cum folio, semine, & radice.* The purple Pasque flower with leafe, seed, and root. 2 *Pulsatilla luteo flore.* The yellow Pasque flower. 3 *Pulsatilla rubra Syriaca Lobelij.* Red Pasque flower of Lobel. 4 *Pulsatilla rubra Swertij.* Swertz his red Pasque flower. 5 *Pulsatilla flore albo.* White Pasque flower. 6 *Anemone siluestris alba Matthioli.* The wilde white broad leafed Windflower. 7 *Anemone siluestris tenuisfolia alba.* The wilde single white Windflower. 8 *Anemone siluestris tenuisfolia lutea.* The yellow wilde thin leafed Windflower. 9 *Anemone siluestris trifolia Dodonei.* The three leafed wilde Windflower. 10 *Anemone siluestris flore pleno albo.* The double white wilde Windflower. 11 *Anemone siluestris flore pleno purpureo.* The double purple wilde Windflower. ✶ *Semen separatim divulsum.* The seed separated. ✝ *Radix cum folio inferiore.* The roote with a lower leafe.

The Time.

All of them doe flower early in the yeare, that is, in the beginning of Aprill, about which time moſt commonly Eaſter doth fall.

The Names.

Their proper names are giuen to each in their ſeuerall titles, being all of them kindes of wilde *Anemones,* as I ſaid in the beginning of the Chapter, and ſo for the moſt part all Authors doe acknowledge them. We call them in Engliſh, becauſe they flower about Eaſter, Paſque Flower, which is the French name for Eaſter, or *Euphoniæ gratia,* Paſſe Flower, which may paſſe currant, without any further deſcant on the name, or elſe *Pulſatilla,* if you will, being growne old by cuſtome.

The Vertues.

The ſharpe biting and exulcerating quality of this plant, cauſeth it to be of little vſe, notwithſtanding Ioachimus Camerarius ſaith in his *Hortus Medicus,* that in Boruſſia, which is a place in Italy, as I take it, the diſtilled water hereof is vſed with good ſucceſſe, to be giuen to them that are troubled with a Tertian Ague ; for he ſaith that it is *medicamentum* ἐκφρακτικὸν, that is, a medicine of force to helpe obſtructions.

Anemone ſilueſtris latifolia alba ſiue tertia Matthioli.
The white wilde broad leafed Windflower.

This Windflower hath diuers broad greene leaues, cut into diuiſions, and dented about, very like vnto a broad leafed Crowfoote, among which riſeth vp a ſtalke, hauing ſome ſuch like cut leaues in the middle thereof, as growe below, but ſmaller ; on the toppe whereof ſtandeth one large white flower, conſiſting of fiue leaues for the moſt part, with ſome yellow threads in the middle, ſtanding about ſuch a greene head as is in the tame or garden *Anemones,* which growing greater after the flower is paſt, is compoſed of many ſmall ſeedes, wrapped in white wooll, which as ſoone as they are ripe, raiſe themſelues vp from the bottome of the head, and flye away with the winde, as the other tame or garden kindes doe : the roote is made of a number of long blacke ſtrings, encreaſing very much by running vnder ground, and ſhooting vp in diuers places.

Anemone ſilueſtris tenuifolia lutea. The yellow wilde thin leafed Windflower.

The yellow wilde *Anemone* riſeth vp with one or two ſmall round naked ſtalkes, bearing about the middle of them, ſmall, ſoft, and tender iagged leaues, deeply cut in and indented on the edges about, from aboue which doth grow the ſtalke, bearing ſmall yellow flowers, ſtanding vpon weake foote-ſtalkes, like vnto a ſmall Crowfoot, with ſome threads in the middle : the roote is long and ſmall, ſomewhat like vnto the roote of Pollipodie, creeping vnder the vpper cruſt of the earth : this kinde is lower, and ſpringeth ſomewhat earlier then the other wilde kindes that follow.

Anemone ſilueſtris tenuifolia alba ſimplex.
The ſingle white thin leafed wilde Windflower.

This white wilde *Anemone* riſeth vp with diuers leaues vpon ſeuerall long ſtalkes; which are ſomewhat like vnto the former, but that they are ſomewhat harder, and not ſo long, nor the diuiſions of the leaues ſo finely ſnipt about the edges, but a little broader, and deeper cut in on euery ſide : the flowers hereof are larger and broader then the former, white on the inſide, and a little purpliſh on the outſide, eſpecially at

the

the bottome of the flower next vnto the stalke : the roote of this is very like vnto the last.

There is another of this kinde, whose flowers are purple, in all other things it is like *Purpurea.* vnto the white.

And likewise another, with a blush or carnation coloured flower. *Coccinea siue suaue rubens.*

There is one that is onely nursed vp with vs in Gardens, that is somewhat like vnto *Peregrina alba.* these former wilde *Anemones* in roote and leafe, but that the flower of this, being pure white within, and a little purplish without, consisting of eight or nine small round pointed leaues, hath sometimes some leaues vnder the flower, party coloured white and greene : the flower hath likewise a greene head, like a Strawberry, compassed about with white threads, tipt with yellow pendents.

And another of the same kinde with the last, whose flower consisting of eight or *Peregrina viridis.* nine leaues, is of a greenish colour, except the foure outermost leaues, which are a little purplish, and diuided at the points into three parts; the middle part is of a greenish white colour, with a greene head in the middle as the other.

Anemone siluestris trifolia Dodonai. The three leafed wilde Windflower.

This wilde *Anemone* hath his rootes very like vnto the former kindes; the leaues are alwaies three set together at the toppe of slender stalkes, being small and indented about, very like vnto a three leafed Grasse, but smaller : the flower consisteth of eight small leaues, somewhat like vnto a Crowfoote, but of a whitish purple or blush colour, with some white threads, and a greene rough head in the middle.

Anemone siluestris flore pleno albo. The double white wilde Windflower.

This double kinde is very like vnto the single white kinde before described, both in his long running rootes, and thin leaues, but somewhat larger : the flowers hereof are very thicke and double, although they be small, and of a faint sweete sent, very white after it is full blowne for fiue or six dayes, but afterwards it becommeth a little purplish on the inside, but more on the outside : this neuer giueth seede (although it haue a small head in the middle) like as many other double flowers doe.

Anemone siluestris flore pleno purpureo. The double purple wilde Windflower.

This double purple kinde hath such like iagged leaues as the last described hath, but more hoarie vnderneath : the flower is of a fine light purple toward the points of the leaues, the bottomes being of a deeper purple, but as thicke, and full of leaues as the former, with a greene head in the middle, like vnto the former : this kinde hath small greene leaues on the stalkes vnder the flowers, cut and diuided like the lower leaues.

The Place.

The first broad leafed *Anemone* groweth in diuers places of Austria and Hungary. The yellow in diuers woods in Germany, but not in this Countrey that euer I could learne. The other single wilde kindes, some of them are very frequent throughout the most places of England, in Woods, Groues, and Orchards. The double kindes were found, as Clusius saith, in the Lowe-Countries, in a Wood neare Louaine.

The Time.

They flower from the end of March (that is the earliest) and the beginning of Aprill, vntill May, and the double kindes begin within a while after the single kinds are past.

The Names.

They are called *Ranunculi siluarum*, and *Ranunculi nemorum*, and as Clusius

sius would haue them, *Leimonia* of Theophraſtus; they are generally called of moſt Herbariſts *Anemones ſilueſtres*, Wilde *Anemones* or Windflowers. The Italians call them *Gengeuo ſalnatico*, that is, Wilde Ginger, becauſe the rootes are, beſides the forme, being ſomewhat like ſmall Ginger, of a biting hot and ſharpe taſte.

Anemone Luſitanica ſiue hortenſis latifolia flore ſimplici luteo.
The ſingle Garden yellow Windflower or Anemone.

This ſingle yellow Anemone or Windflower hath diuers broad round leaues, ſomewhat diuided and endented withall on the edges, browniſh at the firſt riſing vp out of the ground, and almoſt folded together, and after of a ſad greene on the vpperſide, and reddiſh vnderneath; among which riſe vp ſmall ſlender ſtalkes, beſet at the middle of them with two or three leaues, more cut and diuided then thoſe belowe, with ſmall yellow flowers at the toppe of them, conſiſting of ten or twelue leaues a peece, hauing a few yellow threads in the middle of them, ſtanding about a ſmall greene head, which in time growing ripe hath ſmall flat ſeede, incloſed within a ſoft wooll or downe, which is eaſily blowne away with the winde : the roote groweth downeward into the ground, diuerſly ſpread with branches here and there, of a browniſh yellow on the outſide, and whitiſh within, ſo brittle, that it can hardly bee touched without breaking.

Anemone latifolia flore luteo duplici. The double yellow Anemone or Windflower.

This double yellow Anemone hath ſuch broad round leaues as the ſingle kinde hath, but ſomewhat larger or ranker : the ſtalkes are beſet with larger leaues, more deeply cut in on the edges : the flowers are of a more pale yellow, with ſome purpliſh veines on the outſide, and a little round pointed; but they are all on the inſide of a faire yellow colour, conſiſting of two rowes of leaues, whereof the innermoſt is the narrower, with a ſmall greene head in the middle, compaſſed with yellow threads as in the former : the roote is like the roote of the ſingle; neither of theſe haue any good ſent, and this ſpringeth vp and flowreth later then the ſingle kinde.

Anemone latifolia purpurea ſtellata ſiue papaveracea.
The purple Starre Anemone or Windflower.

The firſt leaues of this purple Anemone, which alwayes ſpring vp before Winter, (if the roote be not kept too long out of the ground,) are ſomewhat like the leaues of *Sanicle* or Selfe-heale, but the reſt that follow are more deeply cut in and iagged; among which riſe vp diuers round ſtalkes, beſet with iagged leaues as all other Anemones are, aboue which leaues, the ſtalkes riſing two or three inches high, beare one flower a peece, compoſed of twelue leaues or more, narrow and pointed, of a bleake purple or whitiſh aſh-colour, ſomewhat ſhining on the outſide, and of a fine purple colour tending to a murrey on the inſide, with many blackiſh blew threads or thrummes in the middle of the flower, ſet about a head, whereon groweth the ſeede, which is ſmall and blacke, incloſed in ſoft wooll or downe, which flieth away with the winde, carrying the ſeede with it, if it be not carefully gathered : the roote is blackiſh on the outſide, and white within, tuberous or knobby, with many fibres growing at it.

Anemone purpurea Stellata altera. Another purple Starre Anemone.

There is ſo great diuerſity in the colours of the flowers of theſe broad leafed kinds of Anemones or Windflowers, that they can very hardly be expreſſed, although in their leaues there is but little or no difference. I ſhall not neede therefore to make ſeuerall deſcriptions of euery one that ſhall be ſet downe; but it will be ſufficient, I thinke, to giue you the diſtinctions of the flowers : for as I ſaid, therein is the greateſt and chiefeſt difference. This other Starre Anemone differeth not from the former in leafe or flower, but onely that this is of a more pale ſullen colour on the outſide, and of a paler purple colour on the inſide.

There

1 *Anemone latifolia flore luteo simplici.* The single yellow Anemone. 2 *Anemone latifolia flore luteo duplici.* The double yellow Anemone. 3 *Anemone latifolia flore purpureo Stellato.* The purple Starre Anemone. 4 *Anemone latifolia purpurea dilutior.* The pale purple Starre Anemone. 5 *Anemone latifolia flore miniato diluto.* The pale red Anemone. 6 *Anemone latifolia coccinea Cardinalis dicta.* The Cardinall Anemone. 7 *Anemone latifolia incarnata Hispanica.* The Spanish incarnate Anemone. 8 *Anemone latifolia Pauo simplex dicta.* The lesser Orenge tawney Anemone. 9 *Anemone latifolia flore carneo.* The carnation Anemone. 10 *Anemone latifolia Arantiaca siue Pauo maior.* The double Orenge tawney Anemone. 11 *Anemone Superitica siue Cyparissia.* The double Anemone of Cyprus. 12 *Anemone latifolia flore pleno albicante.* The double pale blush Anemone. 13 *Anemone Chalcedonica maxima.* The great Spanish Marigold Anemone. 14 *Anemone Casumeni siue Persica.* The double Persian Anemone ✝ *Anemonis latifolia radix.* The roote of a great Anemone.

Viola purpurea
There is another, whose flower hath eight leaues, as many of them that follow haue (although diuers sorts haue but six leaues in a flower) and is of a Violet purple, and therefore is called, The Violet purple Anemone.

Varietas.
Of all these three sorts last described, there be other that differ only in hauing white bottomes, some smaller and some larger.

Purpurea striata.
There is also another of the same Violet purple colour with the former, but a little paler, tending more to rednesse, whose flowers haue many white lines and stripes through the leaues, and is called, The purple stript Anemone.

Carnea vivacissima simplex.
There is another, whose greene leaues are somewhat larger, and so is the flower likewise, consisting of eight leaues, and sometimes of more, of the colour of Carnation silke, sometimes pale and sometimes deeper, with a whitish circle about the bottome of the leaues, which circle in some is larger, and more to be seene then in others, when the flower layeth it selfe open with the heate of the Sunne, hauing blewish threads in the middle. This may be called, the Carnation Anemone.

Persciniolacea.
We haue another, whose flower is betweene a Peach colour and a Violet, which is vsually called a Gredeline colour.

Cochenille.
And another of a fine reddish Violet or purple, which we call, The Cochenille Anemone.

Cardinalis.
And another of a rich crimson red colour, and may be called, The Cardinall Anemone.

Sanguinea.
Another of a deeper, but not so liuely a red, called, The bloud red Anemone.

Cramesina.
Another of an ordinary crimson colour, called, The crimson Anemone.

Coccinea.
Another of a Stamell colour, neere vnto a Scarlet.

Incarnata.
Another of a fine delayed red or flesh colour, and may bee called, The Incarnadine Anemone.

Incarnata Hispanica.
Another whose flower is of a liuely flesh colour, shadowed with yellow, and may be called, The Spanish Incarnate Anemone.

Rubescens.
Another of a faire whitish red, which we call, The Blush Anemone.

Moschutella.
Another whose flower consisteth of eight leaues, of a darke whitish colour, stript all ouer with veines of a fine blush colour, the bottomes being white, this may be called, The Nutmegge Anemone.

Enfumata.
Another whose flower is of a pale whitish colour, tending to a gray, such as the Monkes and Friers were wont to weare with vs, and is called, A Monkes gray.

Pauo maior simplici flore.
There is another, whose leafe is somewhat broader then many or most of the Anemones, comming neare vnto the leafe of the great double Orenge coloured Anemone; the flower whereof is single, consisting of eight large or broad leaues, very neare vnto the same Orenge colour, that is in the double flower hereafter described, but somewhat deeper. This is vsually called in Latine, *Pauo maior simplici flore*, and we in English, The great single Orenge tawnie Anemone.

Pauo minor.
There is likewise of this kinde another, whose flower is lesser, and called, The lesser Orenge tawnie Anemone.

Varietas magna ex seminio.
There is besides these expressed, so great a variety of mixt colours in the flowers of this kinde of Anemone with broad leaues, arising euery yeare from the sowing of the seede of some of the choisest and fittest for that purpose, that it is wonderfull to obserue, not onely the variety of single colours, but the mixture of two or three colours in one flower, besides the diuersity of the bottomes of the flowers, some hauing white or yellowish bottomes, and some none, and yet both of the same colour; and likewise in the thrums or threads in the middle: But the greatest wonder of beauty is in variety of double flowers, that arise from among the other single ones, some hauing two or three rowes of leaues in the flowers, and some so thicke of leaues as a double Marigold, or double Crowfoote, and of the same seuerall colours that are in the single flowers, that it is almost impossible to expresse them seuerally, and (as is said before) some falling out to bee double in one yeare, which will proue single or lesse double in another,

other, yet very many abiding conftant double as at the firft; and therefore let this briefe recitall be fufficient in ftead of a particular of all the colours.

Anemone Chalcedonica maxima verficolor.
The great double Windflower of Conftantinople.

This great Anemone of Conftantinople hath broader and greener leaues then any of the former kindes, and not fo much diuided or cut in at the edges, among which rife vp one or two ftalkes, (feldome more from one roote) hauing fome leaues about the middle of the ftalke, as other Anemones haue, and bearing at the toppes of the ftalkes one large flower a peece, very double, whofe outermoft leaues being broadeft, are greenifh at the firft, but afterwards red, hauing fometimes fome greene abiding ftill in the leaues, and the red ftriped through it: the other leaues which are within thefe are fmaller, and of a perfect red colour; the innermoft being fmalleft, are of the fame red colour, but turned fomewhat inward, hauing no thrummes or threads in the middle, as the former haue, and bearing no feede: the roote is blackifh on the outfide, and white within, thicke and tuberous as the other kindes, but thicker fet and clofe together, not fhooting any long flender rootes as others doe. Some Gentlewomen call this Anemone, The Spanifh Marigold.

Anemone Chalcedonica altera fiue Pauo maior flore duplici.
The great double Orenge tawney Anemone.

This other great Anemone of Conftantinople hath his large leaues fo like vnto the laft, that one can hardly diftinguifh them afunder; the ftalke hath alfo fuch like leaues fet vpon it, bearing at the toppe a faire large flower, confifting of many leaues fet in two or three rowes at the moft, but not fo thicke or double as the laft, yet feeming to be but one thicke rowe of many fmall and long leaues, of an excellent red or crimfon colour, wherein fome yellow is mixed, which maketh that colour is called an Orenge tawney; the bottomes of the leaues are red, compaffed with a whitifh circle, the thrummie head in the middle being befet with many darke blackifh threads: the roote is like the former.

Anemone Superitica fiue Cyparissia. The double Anemone of Cyprus.

This Anemone (which the Dutchmen call Superitz, and as I haue beene enformed, came from the Ifle of Cyprus) hath leaues very like the laft double Anemone, but not altogether fo large: the flower confifteth of fmaller leaues, of colour very neare vnto the laft double Orenge coloured Anemone, but more thicke of leaues, and as double as the firft, although not fo great a flower, without any head in the middle, or thrums about it as is in the laft, and differeth not in the roote from either of them both.

Somewhat like vnto this kinde, or as it were betweene this and the firft kinde of thefe great double Anemones, we haue diuers other forts, bearing flowers very thicke and double; fome of them being white, or whitifh, or purple, deeper or paler, and fome of a reddifh colour tending to Scarlet or a Carnation colour, and fome alfo of a blufh or flefh colour, and diuers other colours, and all of them continue conftant in their colours.

Anemone Cacumeni Maringi fiue Perfica. The double Perfian Anemone.

This rare Anemone, which is faid to come out of Perfia to Conftantinople, and from thence to vs, is in leafe and roote very like vnto the former double Anemones before defcribed; onely the flower hereof is rather like vnto the fecond great double Orenge coloured Anemone, vfually called Pauo maior flore pleno, being compofed of three rowes of leaues, the outtermoft rowe confifting of ten or twelue larger leaues, and thofe more inward leffer and more in number, but all of them variably mixed with white, red, and yellow, hauing the bottomes of the leaues white: but inftead of a middle head with thrums about it, as the other hath, this hath a few narrow leaues, of a deepe yellow colour in the middle of the flower, ftanding vpright.

Hauing

Hauing thus farre proceeded in the two parts of the kindes of Anemones or Wind-flowers, it remaineth to entreate of the rest, which is those Anemones which haue thin cut leaues, whereof some haue reckoned vp thirty sorts with single flowers, which I confesse I haue not seene; but so many as haue come to my knowledge, I shall here set downe.

Anemone tenuifolia siue Geranifolia cærulea.
The Watchet Anemone or Storkes bill leafed Windflower.

This first Windflower with thin cut leaues, riseth not out of the ground vntil the great Winter frosts be past, that is, about the middle or end of February, and are somewhat brownish at their first appearing, but afterwards spread into wings of greene leaues, somewhat broader then the rest that follow, diuided into three parts, & each part into three leaues, euery one cut in about the edges, one standing against another vpon a long slender foote-stalke, and the end leafe by it selfe : among these riseth vp two or three greene stalkes, garnished with such like thin leaues as are at the bottome, from aboue which rise the flowers, but one vpon a stalke, consisting of fourteene or fifteene small pale blew or watchet leaues, lesser then any of the single kindes that follow, compassing many whitish threads, and a small greene head in the middle, somewhat like the head of the wilde Crowfoote, wherein is contained such like seede : the roote is blackish without, thrusting out into long tuberous peeces, somewhat like vnto some of the broad leafed Anemones.

Alba.   Of this kinde there is another, whose leaues are not browne at their first rising, but greene, and the flowers are white, in other things not differing.

Anemone tenuifolia purpurea vulgaris.
The ordinary purple Anemone with thin leaues.

This purple Anemone which is most common, and therefore the lesse regarded, hath many winged leaues standing vpon seuerall stalkes, cut and diuided into diuers leaues, much like vnto the leaues of a Carrot ; among which rise vp stalkes with some leaues thereon (as is vsuall to the whole Family of Anemones, both wilde and tame, as is before said;) at the toppes whereof stand the flowers, made of six leaues most vsu-ally, but sometimes they will haue seuen or eight, being very large, and of a perfect purple Violet colour, very faire and liuely : the middle head hath many blackish thrums or threads about it, which I could neuer obserue in my Gardens to beare seed : the roote is smaller, and more spreading euery way into small long flat tuberous parts, then any other kindes of single or double Anemones.

Carnea pallida.   There is another very like in leafe and roote vnto the former, but the flower is nothing so large, and is whitish, tending to a blush colour, and of a deeper blush colour toward the bottome of the flower, with blackish blew thrums in the middle, and giueth no seede that I could euer obserue.

Carnea viuida vnguibus albis.   There is likewisewise another like vnto the last in leafe and flower, but that the flower is larger then it, and is of a liuely blush colour, the leaues hauing white bottomes.

Alba venis pur-pureis.   And another, whose flower is white, with purple coloured veines and stripes through euery leafe, and is a lesser flower then the other.

Anemone tenuifolia coccinea simplex. The single Scarlet Anemone with thin leaues.

The leaues of this Scarlet Windflower are somewhat like vnto the former, but a lit-tle broader, and not so finely cut and diuided : the flower consisteth of six reasonable large leaues, of an excellent red colour, which we call a Scarlet ; the bottomes of the leaues are large and white, and the thrums or threads in the middle of a blackish pur-ple colour : the roote is tuberous, but consisting of thicker peeces, somewhat like vnto the rootes of the broad leafed Anemones, but somewhat browne, and not so blacke, and most like vnto the roote of the double Scarlet Anemone.

Coccinea absq; vnguibus.   There is another of this kinde, whose flower is neare vnto the same co-lour, but this hath no white bottomes at all in his leaues.

We

*Flore holose-
riceo.* We haue another which hath as large a flower as any single, and is of an Orient deepe red crimson Veluet colour.

Sanguinea. There is another of a deeper red colour, and is called, The bloud red single Anemone.

*Rubra fundo
luteo.* And another, whose flower is red with the bottomes yellow.

*Coccinea dilu-
tior.* Another of a perfect crimson colour, whereof some haue round pointed leaues, and others sharpe pointed, and some a little lighter or deeper then others.

*Alba stamini-
bus purpureis.* There is also one, whose flower is pure white with blewish purple thrums in the middle.

*Carnea Hispa-
nica.* And another, whose flower is very great, of a kinde of sullen blush colour, but yet pleasant, with blewish threads in the middle.

*Alba carneis
venis.* And another with blush veines in euery leafe of the white flower.

*Alba purpureis
vnguibus.* And another, the flower whereof is white, the bottomes of the leaues being purple.

Purpurascens. Another whose flower consisteth of many small narrow leaues, of a pale purple or blush colour on the outside, and somewhat deeper within.

*Facie florum
pomi simplex.* There is another like in leafe and roote vnto the first Scarlet Anemone, but the flower hereof consisteth of seuen large leaues without any bottomes, of a white colour, hauing edges, and some large stripes also of a carnation or flesh colour to bee seene in them, marked somewhat like an Apple blossome, and thereupon it is called in Latine, *Anemone tenuifolia simplex alba instar florum pomi*, or *facie florum pomi*, that is to say in English, The single thin leafed Anemone with Apple blossome flowers.

Multiplex. I haue heard that there is one of this kinde with double flowers.

1. *Anemone tenuifolia flore coccineo pleno vulgaris.*
The common double red or Scarlet Anemone.

The leaues of this double Anemone are very like vnto the leaues of the single Scarlet Anemone, but not so thin cut and diuided as that with the purple flower: the flower hereof when it first openeth it selfe, consisteth of six and sometimes of seuen or eight broad leaues, of a deepe red, or excellent Scarlet colour, the middle head being thick closed, and of a greenish colour, which after the flower hath stood blowne some time, doth gather colour, and openeth it selfe into many small leaues, very thicke, of a more pale red colour, and more Stamell like then the outer leaues : the root of this is thicke and tuberous, very like vnto the root of the single Scarlet Anemone.

2. *Anemone tenuifolia flore coccineo pleno variegata.*
The party coloured double Crimson Anemone.

We haue a kinde hereof, varying neither in roote, leafe, or forme of flower from the former, but in the colour, in that this will haue sometimes the outer broad leaues party coloured, with whitish or blush coloured great streakes in the red leaues both inside and outside ; as also diuers of the middle or inner leaues striped in the same manner : the roote hereof giueth fairer flowers in some yeares then in others, and sometimes giue flowers all red againe.

3. *Anemone tenuifolia flore coccineo saturo pleno.*
The double crimson Veluet Anemone.

Wee haue another also, whose flower is of a deepe Orenge tawny crimson colour, neare vnto the colour of the outer leaues, of the lesser French Marigold, and not differing from the former in any thing else.

4. *Anemone tenuifolia flore pleno suauerubente.* The greater double blush Anemone.

There is small difference to be discerned, either in the roote or leaues of this from the

the former double Scarlet Anemone, sauing that the leaues hereof are a little broader, and seeme to bee of a little fresher greene colour : the flower of this is as large almost, and as double as the former, and the inner leaues likewise almost as large as they, being of a whitish or flesh colour at the first opening of them, but afterwards become of a most liuely blush colour; the bottomes of the leaues abiding of a deeper blush, and with long standing, the tops of the leaues will turne almost wholly white againe.

5. *Anemone tenuifolia flore albo pleno.* The double white Anemone.

This double white Anemone differeth little from the former blush Anemone, but in that it is smaller in all the parts thereof, and also that the flower hereof being wholly of a pure white colour, without any shew of blush therein, hath the middle thrummes much smaller and shorter then it, and not rising vp so high, but seeme as if they were chipped off euen at the toppes.

6. *Anemone tenuifolia flore pleno albicante.* The lesser double blush Anemone.

This small double blush Anemone differeth very little from the double white last recited, but onely in the colour of the flower : for they are both much about the bignesse one of another, the middle thrums likewise being as small and short, and as euen aboue, onely the flower at the first opening is almost white, but afterwards the outer leaues haue a more shew of blush in them, and the middle part a little deeper then they.

7. *Anemone tenuifolia flore pleno purpureo violaceo.* The double purple Anemone.

This double purple Anemone is also of the same kindred with the first double red or Scarlet Anemone for the form or doublenesse of the flower, consisting but of six or seuen leaues at the most in this our Country, although in the hotter it hath ten or twelue, or more as large leaues for the outer border, and as large small leaues for the inner middle also, and almost is double, but of a deepe purple tending toward a Violet colour, the outer leaues being not so deepe as the inner : the roote and leafe commeth neare vnto the single purple Anemone before described, but that the roote spreadeth not so small and so much.

8. *Anemone tenuifolia flore pleno purpureo cæruleo.* The double blew Anemone.

This Anemone differeth not in any thing from the former double purple, but onely that the flower is paler, and more tending to a blew colour.

9. *Anemone tenuifolia flore pleno roseo.* The double Rose coloured Anemone.

The double Rose coloured Anemone differeth also in nothing from the former double purple, but onely in the flower, which is somewhat smaller, and not so thicke and double, and that it is of a reddish colour, neare vnto the colour of a pale red Rose, or of a deepe coloured Damaske.

10. *Anemone tenuifolia flore pleno carneo viuacissimo.* The double Carnation Anemone.

This Anemone, both in roote, leafe, and flower, commeth nearest vnto the former double white Anemone, for the largenesse and doublenesse of the flower, and in the smalnesse of the middle thrums, and euennesse at the toppes of them, being not so large and great a flower as the double purple, either in the inner or outter leaues, but yet is very faire, thicke and double, and of a most liuely Carnation silke colour, very deepe, both the outer leaues and middle thrums also so bright, that it doth as it were amaze, and yet delight the minde of the beholder, but by long standing in the Sun, waxe a little paler, and so passe away as all the most beautifull flowers doe.

Anemone tenuifolia simplex purpurea. The single purple Anemone with thin cut leaues. 2 *Anemone tenuifolia simplex alba pura.* The single pure white Anemone. 3 *Anemone tenuifolia simplex chermesina.* The single bright Crimson Anemone. 4 *Anemone tenuifolia simplex sanguinea.* The single blood red Anemone. 5 *Anemone tenuifolia simplex facie florum pomi.* The single Apple bloome Anemone. 6 *Anemone tenuifolia simplex purpurascens.* The single purplish blush Anemone. 7 *Anemone tenuifolia simplex alba vnguibus carneis.* The single white Anemone with blush bottomes. 8 *Anemone tenuifolia flore pleno coccineo.* The double red or ordinary Scarlet Anemone. 9 *Anemone tenuifolia flore pleno rubrofusca come Amarantina.* The double purple Veluet Anemone. 10 *Anemone tenuifolia flore pleno purpuro violaceo.* The double blewish purple Anemone. 11 *Anemone tenuifolia flore pleno incarnedini coloris sericei vivacissimi.* The double Carnation Anemone, or of a liuely Carnation silke colour.

11. *Anemone tenuifolia flore rubrofusco pleno coma Amarantina.*
The double purple Veluet Anemone.

This double Veluet Anemone is in all things like the laſt deſcribed Carnation A-nemone, but ſomewhat larger, the difference conſiſteth in the colour of the flower, which in this is of a deep or ſad crimſon red colour for the outer leaues, and of a deep purple Veluet colour in the middle thrums, reſembling the colour of the leſſer *Amaranthus purpureus*, or Purple flower gentle hereafter deſcribed, whereof it tooke the name, which middle thrums are as fine and ſmall, and as euen at the toppes as the white or laſt Carnation Anemones.

12. *Anemone tenuifolia flore pleno tricolor.*
The double purple Veluet Anemone of three colours.

This double Anemone alſo is very like the laſt deſcribed Anemone, but that in the middle of the purple thrums, there thruſteth forth a tuft of threads or leaues of a more light crimſon colour.

And thus much for the kindes of Anemones or Windflowers, ſo farre forth as haue hitherto come to our knowledge ; yet I doubt not, but that more varieties haue beene elſewhere collected, and will be alſo in our Countrey daily and yearly obſerued by diuers, that raiſe them vp from ſowing the ſeede, wherein lyeth a pretty art, not yet familiarly knowne to our Nation, although it be very frequent in the Lowe-Countries, where their induſtry hath bred and nouriſhed vp ſuch diuerſities and varieties, that they haue valued ſome Anemones at ſuch high rates, as moſt would wonder at, and none of our Nation would purchaſe, as I thinke. And I doubt not, if wee would be as curious as they, but that both our ayre and ſoyle would produce as great variety, as euer hath been ſeene in the Lowe-Countries ; which to procure, if any of our Nation will take ſo much paines in ſowing the ſeedes of Anemones, as diuers haue done of Tulipas: I will ſet them downe the beſt directions for that purpoſe that I haue learned, or could by much ſearch and tryall attaine vnto ; yet I muſt let them vnderſtand thus much alſo, that there is not ſo great variety of double flowers raiſed from the ſeede of the thin leafed Anemones, as from the broad leafed ones.

Firſt therefore (as I ſaid before) concerning Tulipas, there is ſome ſpeciall choice to be made of ſuch flowers, whoſe ſeed is fitteſt to be taken. Of the *Latifolias*, the double Orenge tawney ſeede being ſowne, yeeldeth pretty varieties, but the purples, and reds, or crimſons, either *Latifolias* or *Tenuifolias*, yeeld ſmall variety, but ſuch as draw neareſt to their originall, although ſome be a little deeper or lighter then others. But the light colours be they which are the chiefe for choice, as white, aſh-colour, bluſh or carnation, light orenge, ſimple or party coloured, ſingle or double, if they beare ſeede, which muſt bee carefully gathered, and that not before it bee thorough ripe, which you ſhall know by the head ; for when the ſeede with the wollineſſe beginneth to riſe a little of it ſelfe at the lower end, it muſt bee then quickly gathered, leſt the winde carry it all away. After it is thus carefully gathered, it muſt be laid to dry for a weeke or more, which then being gently rubbed with a little dry ſand or earth, will cauſe the ſeede to be ſomewhat better ſeparated, although not thoroughly from the woollineſſe or downe that compaſſeth it.

Within a moneth at the moſt after the ſeede is thus gathered and prepared, it muſt be ſowne ; for by that meanes you ſhall gaine a yeare in the growing, ouer that you ſhould doe if you ſowed it in the next Spring.

If there remaine any woollineſſe in the ſeede, pull it in ſunder as well as you can, and then ſowe your ſeede reaſonable thin, and not too thicke, vpon a plaine ſmooth bed of fine earth, or rather in pots or tubbes, and after the ſowing, ſift or gently ſtraw ouer them ſome fine good freſh mould, about one fingers thickneſſe at the moſt for the firſt time : And about a moneth after their firſt ſpringing vp, ſift or ſtraw ouer them in like manner another fingers thickneſſe of fine earth, and in the meane time if the weather proue dry, you muſt water them gently and often, but not to ouerglut them with moiſture ; and thus doing, you ſhall haue them ſpring vp before Winter, and

grow

grow pretty ſtrong, able to abide the ſharpe Winter in their nonage, in vſing ſome little care to couer them looſely with ſome fearne, or furſe, or beane hame, or ſtraw, or any ſuch, which yet muſt not lye cloſe vpon them, nor too farre from them neither.

The next Spring after the ſowing, if you will, but it is better if you ſtay vntill Auguſt, you may then remoue them, and ſet them in order by rowes, with ſufficient diſtance one from another, where they may abide, vntill you ſee what manner of flower each plant will beare, which you may diſpoſe of according to your minde.

Many of them being thus ordered (if your mould be fine, looſe, and freſh, not ſtonie, clayiſh, or from a middin) will beare flowers the ſecond yeare after the ſowing, and moſt or all of them the third yeare, if the place where you ſowe them, be not annoyed with the ſmoake of Brewers, Dyers, or Maultkils, which if it be, then will they neuer thriue well.

Thus much haue I thought good to ſet downe, to incite ſome of our owne Nation to be induſtrious; and to helpe them forward, haue giuen ſuch rules of directions, that I doubt not, but they will vpon the tryall and view of the variety, proceede as well in the ſowing of Anemones as of Tulipas.

I cannot (Gentlewomen) withhold one other ſecret from you, which is to informe you how you may ſo order Anemones, that after all others ordinarily are paſt, you may haue them in flower for two or three moneths longer then are to be ſeene with any other, that vſeth not this courſe I direct you.

The ordinary time to plant Anemones, is moſt commonly in Auguſt, which will beare flower ſome peraduenture before Winter, but moſt vſually in February, March, and Aprill, few or none of them abiding vntill May; but if you will keepe ſome roots out of the ground vnplanted, vntill February, March, and Aprill, and plant ſome at one time, and ſome at another, you ſhall haue them beare flower according to their planting, thoſe that ſhall be planted in February, will flower about the middle or end of May, and ſo the reſt accordingly after that manner: And thus may you haue the pleaſure of theſe plants out of their naturall ſeaſons, which is not permitted to be enioyed in any other that I know, Nature being not ſo prone to bee furthered by art in other things as in this. Yet regard, that in keeping your Anemone rootes out of the ground for this purpoſe, you neither keep them too dry, nor yet too moiſt, for ſprouting or rotting; and in planting them, that you ſet them not in too open a ſunny place, but where they may be ſomewhat ſhadowed.

The Place.

I ſhall not need to ſpend much time in relating the ſeuerall places of theſe Anemones, but onely to declare that the moſt of them that haue not beene raiſed from ſeed, haue come from Conſtantinople to vs; yet the firſt broad leafed or yellow Anemone, was firſt found in Portugall, and from thence brought into theſe parts. And the firſt purple Starre Anemone in Germanie, yet was the ſame ſent among others from Conſtantinople alſo. And the firſt thin cut leafed Anemone came firſt out of Italy, although many of that ſort haue come likewiſe from Conſtantinople. And ſo haue the double red or Scarlet Anemones, and the great double bluſh, which I firſt had by the gift of Mr. Humfrey Packington of Worceſterſhire Eſquire, at Haruington.

The Time.

The times of their flowring are ſufficiently expreſſed in the deſcriptions, or in the rules for planting.

The Names.

The Turkiſh names whereby the great double broad leafed kindes haue beene ſent vnto vs, were *Giul Catamer*, and *Giul Catamer lale*; And *Binizade*, *Binizante*, and *Galipoli lale* for the thinne cut leafed Anemones. All Authors haue called them *Anemones*, and are the true *Herba venti*.

We

Wee call them in Englifh eyther Anemones, after the Greeke name, or Windflowers, after the Latine.

The Vertues.

There is little vfe of thefe in Phyficke in our dayes, eyther for inward or outward difeafes; onely the leaues are vfed in the Ointment called *Marcia-tum*, which is compofed of many other hot herbes, and is vfed in cold griefes, to warme and comfort the parts. The roote, by reafon of the fharpeneffe, is apt to drawe downe rheume, if it be tafted or chewed in the mouth.

Chap. XXVI.

Aconitum. Wolfebane.

THere be diuers forts of Wolfebanes which are not fit for this booke, but are referued for a generall Hiftory or Garden of Simples, yet among them there are fome, that notwithftanding their euill quality, may for the beauty of their flowers take vp a roome in this Garden, of whom I meane to entreate in this place: And firft of the Winter Wolfesbane, which for the beauty, as well as the earlineffe of his flowers, being the firft of all other, that fhew themfelues after Chriftmas, defer-ueth a prime place; and therefore for the likeneffe of the rootes vnto the Anemones, I ioyne it next vnto them.

1. *Aconitum Hyemale.* The Winters Wolfesbane.

This little plant thrufteth vp diuers leaues out of the ground, in the deepe of Win-ter oftentimes, if there be any milde weather in Ianuary, but moft commonly after the deepe frofts, bearing vp many times the fnow vpon the heads of the leaues, which like vnto the Anemone, doe euery leafe rife from the roote vpon feuerall fhort foote-ftalkes, not aboue foure fingers high, fome hauing flowers in the middle of them, (which come vp firft moft vfually) and fome none, which leaues ftand as it were round, the ftalke rifing vp vnder the middle of the leafe, deeply cut in and gafhed to the middle ftalke almoft, of a very faire deepe greene colour, in the middle whereof, clofe vnto the leafe, ftandeth a fmall yellow flower, made of fix leaues, very like a Crowfoote, with yellow threads in the middle: after the flower is fallen, there rife vp diuers fmall hornes or cods fet together, wherein are contained whitifh yellow round feede. The roote is tuberous, fo like both for fhape and colour vnto the rootes of A-nemones, that they will eafily deceiue one not well experienced, but that it is browner and fmoother without, and yellow within, if it be broken.

2. *Aconitum flore albido, fiue Aconitum luteum Ponticum.* The whitifh yellow Wolfesbane.

This Wolfesbane fhooteth not out of the ground vntill the Spring be well begun, and then it fendeth forth great broad greene leaues, deeply cut in about the edges, not much vnlike the leaues of the great wilde Crowfoote, but much greater; from a-mong which leaues rifeth vp a ftrong ftiffe ftalke, three foote high, hauing here and there leaues fet vpon it, like vnto the loweft, but fmaller; the toppe of the ftalke is di-uided into three or foure branches, whereon are fet diuers pale yellow flowers, which turne at the laft to be almoft white, in fafhion like almoft vnto the flowers of the Hel-met flower, but much fmaller, and not gaping fo wide open: after the flowers are paft come vp diuers fhort poddes, wherein is contained blacke feede: the roote is made of a number of darke browne ftrings, which fpread and faften themfelues ftrongly in the ground.

3. *Napellus*

3. *Napellus verus flore cæruleo.* Blew Helmet flower or Monkes hood.

The Helmet flower hath diuers leaues of a fresh greene colour on the vpperside, and grayish vnderneath, much spread abroad and cut into many slits and notches, more then any of the Wolfebanes; the stalke riseth vp two or three foot high, beset to the top with the like leaues, but smaller : the toppe is sometimes diuided into two or three branches, but more vsually without, whereon stand many large flowers one a-boue another, in forme very like vnto a Hood or open Helmet, being composed of fiue leaues, the vppermost of which and the greatest, is hollow, like vnto an Helmet or Headpeece, two other small leaues are at the sides of the Helmet, closing it like cheekes, and come somewhat vnder, and two other which are the smallest hang down like labels, or as if a close Helmet were opened, and some peeces hung by, of a perfect or faire blew colour, (but grow darker, hauing stood long) which causeth it be so nou-rished vp in Gardens, that their flowers, as was vsuall in former times, and yet is in many Countrey places, may be laid among greene herbes in windowes and roomes for the Summer time : but although their beauty may be entertained for the vses afore-said, yet beware they come not neare your tongue or lippes, lest they tell you to your cost, they are not so good as they seeme to be : in the middest of the flower, when it is open and gapeth wide, are seene certaine small threads like beards, standing about a middle head, which when the flower is past, groweth into three or foure, or more small blackish pods, containing in them blacke seede : the rootes are brownish on the out-side, and white within, somewhat bigge and round aboue, and small downewards, somewhat like vnto a small short Carrot roote, sometimes two being ioyned at the head together. But the name *Napellus* anciently giuen vnto it, doth shew they referred the forme of the roote vnto a small Turnep.

Anthora. The wholsome Helmet flower, or counterpoison Monkes hood.

This wholsome plant I thought good to insert, not onely for the forme of the flow-er, but also for the excellent properties thereof, as you shall haue them related here-after. The rootes hereof are small and tuberous, round and somewhat long, ending for the most part in a long fibre, and with some other small threads from the head downeward : from the head whereof riseth vp diuers greene leaues, euery one seue-rally vpon a stalke, very much diuided, as finely almost as the leaues of Larkes heeles or spurres : among which riseth vp a hard round stalke, a foote high and better, with some such leaues thereon as grow belowe, at the toppe whereof stand many small yellowish flowers, formed very like vnto the former whitish Wolfesbane, bearing many blacke seedes in pods afterwards in the like manner.

Many more sorts of varieties of these kindes there are, but these onely, as the most specious, are noursed vp in Florists Gardens for pleasure ; the other are kept by such as are Catholicke obseruers of all natures store.

The Place.

All these grow naturally on Mountaines, in many shadowie places of the Alpes, in Germany, and elsewhere.

The Time.

The first flowreth (as is said) in Ianuary, and February, and sometimes vntill March be well spent, and the seede is soone ripe after.
The other three flower not vntill Iune and Iuly.

The Names.

The first is vsually called *Aconitum hyemale Belgarum.* Lobelius calleth it
Bulbosus

Bulbosus vnifolius Batrachoides, Aconitum Elleboraceum, and *Ranunculus Monophyllos*, and some by other names. Most Herbarists call it *Aconitum hyemale*, and we in English thereafter, Winters Wolfesbane; and of some, Yellow Aconite.

The second is called by most Writers, *Aconitum luteum Ponticum*: Some also *Lupicida*, *Luparia*, and *Canicida*, of the effect in killing Wolues and Dogs: And some, because the flower is more white then yellow, doe call it *Aconitum flore albido*, we call it in English, The whitish yellow Aconite, or Wolfesbane, but some after the Latine name, The yellow Wolfesbane.

The third is called generally *Napellus*, and *Verus*, because it is the true *Napellus* of the ancient Writers, which they so termed from the forme of a Turnep, called *Napus* in Latine.

The fourth is called *Aconitum Salutiferum, Napellus Moysis, Antora* and *Anthora, quasi Antithora*, that is, the remedy against the poisonfull herbe *Thora*, in English according to the title, eyther wholsome Helmet flower, or counterpoison Monkes hood.

The Vertues.

Although the first three sorts of plants be very poisonfull and deadly, yet there may bee very good vse made of them for sore eyes (being carefully applyed, yet not to all sorts of sore eyes neither without discretion) if the distilled water be dropped therein.

The rootes of the counterpoison Monkes hood are effectuall not onely against the poison of the poisonfull Helmet flower, and all others of that kinde, but also against the poison of all venemous beasts, the plague or pestilence, and other infectious diseases, which raise spots, pockes, or markes in the outward skinne, by expelling the poison from within, and defending the heart as a most soueraigne Cordiall. It is vsed also with good successe against the wormes of the belly, and against the paines of the Wind collick.

Chap. XXVII.
Ranunculus. The Crowfoote.

Next vnto the Aconites, of right are to follow the *Ranunculi*, or Crowfeete, for the nearenesse both of forme, of leaues, and nature of the plants, although lesse hurtfull, yet all of them for the most part being sharpe and exulcerating, and not without some danger, if any would be too bold with them. The whole Family of the *Ranunculi* is of a very large extent, and I am constrained within the limits of a Garden of Pleasure; I must therefore select out onely such as are fit for this purpose, and set them here downe for your knowledge, leauing the rest for that other generall worke, which time may perfect and bring to light, if the couetous mindes of some that should be most affected towards it, doe not hinder it: or if the helpe of generous spirits would forward it.

1. *Ranunculus montanus albus humilior*. The lowe white mountaine Crowfoot.

This lowe Crowfoote hath three or foure broad and thicke leaues, almost round, yet a little cut in and notched about the edges, of a fine greene and shining colour on the vpperside, and not so green vnderneath, among which riseth a small short stalke, bearing one snow white flower on the toppe, made of fiue round pointed leaues, with diuers yellow threads in the middle, standing about a greene head, which in time groweth to be full of seede, in forme like vnto a small greene Strawberry: the roote is composed of many white strings.

Duplici flore. There is another of this lowe kinde, whose leaues are somewhat more deeply cut in on the edges, and the flower larger, and sometimes a little double, as it were with two rowes of leaues, in other things not differing from the former.

2. *Ranunculus*

2. *Ranunculus montanus albus maior vel elatior.*
The great single white mountaine Crowfoote.

The leaues of this Crowfoote are large and greene, cut into three, and fometimes into fiue fpeciall diuifions, and each of them befides cut or notched about the edges, fomewhat refembling the leaues of the Globe Crowfoote, but larger : the ftalke is two foote and a halfe high, hauing three fmall leaues fet at the ioynt of the ftalke, where it brancheth out into flowers, which ftand foure or fiue together vpon long foote-ftalkes, made of fiue white leaues a peece, very fweete, and fomewhat larger then the next white Crowfoote, with fome yellow threads in the middle compaffing a greene head, which bringeth feede like vnto other wilde Crowfeete : the roote hath many long thicke whitifh ftrings, comming from a thicke head.

3. *Ranunculus montanus albus minor.* The leffer fingle white Crowfoote.

This Crowefoote hath faire large fpread leaues, cut into fiue diuifions, and fome-what notched about the edges, greene on the vpperfide, and paler vnderneath, hauing many veines running through the leaues : the ftalke of this rifeth not fo high as the former, although this be reafonable tall, as being neare two foote high, fpread into many branches, bearing fuch like white flowers, as in the former, but fmaller : the feede of this is like the former, and fo are the rootes likewife.

4. *Ranunculus albus flore pleno.* The double white Crowfoot.

The double white Crowfoote is of the fame kinde with the laft fingle white Crow-foote, hauing fuch like leaues in all refpects : the onely difference is in the flowers, which in this are very thicke and double. Some doe make mention of two forts of double white Crowfeete, one fomewhat lower then another, and the lower like-wife bearing more ftore of flowers, and more double then the higher : but I con-feffe, I haue neuer feene but one fort of double, which is the fame here expreffed, not growing very high, and reafonably well ftored with flowers.

5. *Ranunculus præcox Rutæfolio fiue Coriandrifolio.*
The early Coriander leafed Crowfoote.

This Crowfoote hath three or foure very greene leaues, cut and diuided into many fmall peeces, like vnto the wing of leaues of Rue, or rather like the lower leaues of the Coriander(for they well refemble either of them)euery of them ftanding vpon a long purplifh ftalke, at the toppe whereof groweth the flower alone, being compofed or made of twelue fmall white leaues, broad pointed, and a little endented at the ends, fomewhat purplifh on the outfide, and white on the infide, fuftained by diuers fmall greene leaues, which are in ftead of a cup or huske : in the middle of the flower are many fmall white threads, tipt with yellow pendents, ftanding about a fmall greene head, which after groweth to bee full of feedes like a Strawberry, which knobs giue fmall blackifh feede : the roote is white and fibrous.

6. *Ranunculus Thalictrifolio maior.* The great colombine leafed Crowfoot.

The lower leaues of this Crowfoote haue long ftalkes, and are very like vnto the fmaller leaues of Colombines, or the great Spanifh *Thalictrum,* which hath his leaues very like vnto a Colombine, foure or fiue rifing from the roote : the ftalke rifeth a-bout a foote and a halfe high, fomewhat reddifh, befet here and there with the like leaues, at the toppe whereof ftand diuers fmall white flowers, made of fiue leaues a peece, with fome pale white threads in the middle : the feede is round and reddifh, contained in fmall huskes or hornes : the roote is made of a bufh or tuft of white ftrings.

T

7. *Ranunculus*

7. *Ranunculus Thalictrifolio minor Asphodeli radice.*
The small white Colombine leafed Crowfoote.

This small Crowfoote hath three or foure winged leaues spread vpon the ground, standing vpon long stalkes, and consisting of many small leaues set together, spreading from the middle ribbe, euery leafe somewhat resembling both in shape and colour the smallest and youngest leaues of Colombines : the flowers are white, standing at the toppe of the stalkes, made of fiue round leaues : the root hath three or foure thick, short, and round yellowish clogs hanging at the head, like vnto the Asphodill roote. The great Herball of Lyons, that goeth vnder the name of *Dalschampius,* saith, that Dr. Myconus found it in Spaine, and sent it vnder the name of Oenanthe; and therefore Ioannes Molineus who is thought to haue composed that booke, set it among the vmbelliferous plants, because the Oenanthes beare vmbels of flowers and seede, and haue tuberous or cloggy rootes ; but with what iudgement, let others say, when they haue compared the vmbels of flowers and seede of the Oenanthes, with the flowers and seede of this plant, and whether I haue not more properly placed it among the *Ranunculi* or Crowfeete, and giuen it a denomination agreeable to his forme.

8. *Ranunculus Globosus.* The Globe Crowfoot.

This Crowfoote (which in the Northerne countries of England where it groweth plentifully, is called Locker goulous) hath many faire, broad, darke greene leaues next the ground, cut into fiue, sixe, or seuen diuisions, and iagged besides at the edges; among which riseth vp a stalke, whereon are set such like leaues as are belowe, but smaller, diuided toward the toppe into some branches, on the which stand seuerall large yellow flowers, alwayes folded inward, or as a close flower neuer blowing open, as other flowers doe, consisting of eleuen leaues for the most part, set or placed in three rowes, with many yellow threads in the middle, standing about a greene rough head, which in time groweth to be small knops, wherein are contained blacke seede : the roote is composed of many blackish strings.

9. *Ranunculus pratensis flore multiplici.* The double yellow field Crowfoot.

There is little or no difference in the leaues of this double Crowfoot, from those of the single kindes that growe in euery medowe, being large and diuided into foure or fiue parts, and indented about the edges, but they are somewhat smaller, and of a fresher greene : the flowers stand on many branches, much diuided or separated, being not very great, but very thicke and double : the roote runneth and creepeth vnder ground like as the single doth.

10. *Ranunculus Anglicus maximus multiplex.*
The Garden double yellow Crowfoot or Batchelours buttons.

This great double Crowfoote, which is common in euery Garden through England, hath many great blackish greene leaues, iagged and cut into three diuisions, each to the middle ribbe : the stalkes haue some smaller leaues on them, and those next vnder the branches long and narrow : the flowers are of a greenish yellow colour, very thicke and double of leaues, in the middle whereof riseth vp a small stalke, bearing another double flower, like to the other, but smaller : the roote is round, like vnto a small white Turnep, with diuers other fibres annexed vnto it.

11. *Ranunculus Gramineus.* Grasse leafed Crowfoot.

The leaues of this Crowfoote are long and narrow, somewhat like vnto Grasse, or rather like the leaues of single Gilloflowers or Pinckes, being small and sharpe pointed, a little hollow, and of a whitish greene colour : among these leaues rise vp diuers slender stalkes, bearing one small flower at the toppe of each, consisting of fiue yellow leaues,

1 *Aconitum hyemale.* Winter Wolfesbane. 2 *Aconitum flore albido siue luteum Ponticum.* The whitish yellow Wolfesbane. 3 *Napellus verus.*
Blew Helmets or Monkeshood. 4 *Anthora.* The counterpoison Monkeshood. 5 *Ranunculus humilis albus simplex.* The single white low Crowfoot.
6 *Ranunculus humilis albus duplici flore.* The double lowe white Crowfoot. 7 *Ranunculus Coriandrifolio* The early Corianderleafed Crowfoot.
8 *Ranunculus montanus elatior albus.* The great single white mountain Crowfoot. 9 *Ranunculus montanus albus flore pleno* The double white mountain
Crowfoot. 10 *Ranunculus Thalictrifolio minor.* The lesser Colombine leafed Crowfoot. 11 *Ranunculus globosus.* The globe Crowfoot.

leaues, with some threads in the middle : the roote is compoſed of many thicke, long, round white ſtrings.

There is another of this kinde that beareth flowers with two rowes of leaues, as if it were double, differing in nothing elſe.

12. *Ranunculus Luſitanicus Autumnalis.* The Portugall Autumne Crowfoot.

This Autumne Crowfoote hath diuers broad round leaues lying on the ground, ſet vpon ſhort foote-ſtalkes, of a faire greene colour aboue, and grayiſh vnderneath, ſnipt all about the edges, hauing many veines in them, and ſometimes ſwelling as with bliſters or bladders on them; from among which riſe vp two or three ſlender and hairy ſtalkes, bearing but one ſmall yellow flower a peece, conſiſting of fiue and ſometimes of ſix leaues, and ſometimes of ſeuen or eight, hauing a few threads in the middle, ſet about a ſmall greene head, like vnto many of the former Crowfeete, which bringeth ſmall blacke ſeede : the roote is made of many thicke ſhort white ſtrings, which ſeeme to be grumous or kernelly rootes, but that they are ſomewhat ſmaller, and longer then any other of that kinde.

13. *Ranunculus Creticus latifolius.* The broad leafed Candy Crowfoot.

This Crowfoote of Candy, hath the greateſt and broadeſt leaues of all the ſorts of Crowfeete, being almoſt round, and without any great diuiſions, but onely a few notches about the edges here and there, as large or larger ſometimes then the palme of a mans hand; among which riſeth vp the ſtalke, not very high when it doth firſt flower, but afterwards, as the other flowers doe open themſelues, the ſtalke groweth to be a foote and a halfe high, or thereabouts, hauing ſome leaues on it, deeply cut in or diuided, and bearing many faire yellow flowers, conſiſting of fiue leaues a peece, being ſomewhat whitiſh in the middle, when the flower hath ſtood blowne a little time : the roote is compoſed of a number of ſmall kernelly knobs, or long graines, ſet thicke together. This flowreth very early, being vſually in flower before the end of March, and oftentimes about the middle thereof.

14. *Ranunculus Creticus albus.* The white Candy Crowfoote.

The leaues of this Crowfoote are very like vnto the leaues of the red Crowfoote of Tripoli or Aſia, hereafter ſet downe, being ſomewhat broad and indented about the edges, ſome of the leaues being alſo cut in or gaſhed, thereby making it as it were three diuiſions, of a pale greene colour, with many white ſpots in them : the ſtalke riſeth vp a foote high, with ſome leaues on it, more diuided then the lower, and diuided at the toppe into two and ſometimes into three branches, each of them bearing a faire ſnow white flower, ſomewhat large, included at the firſt in a browniſh huske or cup of leaues, which afterwards ſtand vnder the flowers, conſiſting of fiue white large round pointed leaues, in the middle whereof is ſet many blackiſh purple thrums, compaſſing a ſmall long greene head, compoſed of many ſcales or chaffie whitiſh huskes, when they are ripe, which are the ſeede, but vnprofitable in all that euer I could obſerue : the rootes are many ſmall graines or kernels, ſet together as in the former, and much about the ſame colour, that is, of a darke or duskie grayiſh colour, but much ſmaller.

Alba purpureis oris & venis.   There is another of this kinde, whoſe flowers haue purple edges, and ſometimes ſome veines of the ſame purple in the leaues of the flowers, not differing in any other thing from the former.

Alba oris rubris.   And another, whoſe edges of the flowers are of a bright red colour.

15. *Ranunculus Creticus flore argenteo.* The Argentine, or cloth of ſiluer Crowfoot.

The greene leaues of this Crowfoote are as ſmall and thinne, cut in or diuided on the edges, as the laſt two ſorts; the ſtalke riſeth vp ſomewhat higher, and diuided into ſome branches, bearing at the toppe of euery of them one flower, ſomewhat ſmaller then the former, compoſed of ſix, ſeuen, and ſometimes of eight ſmall round pointed

leaues,

1 *Ranunculus gramineus flore simplici & duplici.* The single and the double grasse Crowfoot. 2 *Ranunculus Lusitanicus Autumnalis.* The Portugall Autumne Crowfoot. 3 *Ranunculus Creticus latifolius.* The broad leafed Candy Crowfoot. 4 *Ranunculus Anglicus maximus multiplex.* The double English Crowfoot. 5 *Ranunculus pratensis flore multiplici.* The double yellow field Crowfoot. 6 *Ranunculus Creticus albus.* The white Candy Crowfoot. 7 *Ranunculus Asiaticus flore albo vel pallido vario.* The white or the straw coloured Crowfoot with red tops or edges. 8 *Ranunculus Tripolitanus flore rubro simplici.* The single red Crowfoot of Tripoli. 9 *Ranunculus Asiaticus flore rubro amplo.* The large single red Crowfoot of Asia. 10 *Ranunculus Asiaticus flore rubro pleno.* The double red Crowfoot of Asia. 11 *Caltha palustris flore pleno.* Double Marsh Marigold or Batchelours buttons.

leaues, of a whitish yellow blush colour on the inside wholly, except sometimes a little stript about the edges : but the outside of euery leafe is finely stript with crimson stripes, very thicke, somewhat like vnto a Gilloflower : in the middle riseth vp a small blacke head, compassed about with blackish blew threads or thrums, which head is as vnfruitfull for seede in our Countrey as the former. This flower hath no such greene leaues vnder it, or to enclose it before it be blowne open as the former : the rootes are in all things like the former.

16. *Ranunculus Asiaticus siue Tripolitanus flore rubro.*
The single red Crowfoote of Asia or Tripoli.

The lower leaues of this red Crowfoote are alwayes whole without diuisions, being onely somewhat deeply indented about the edges, but the other that rise after them are more cut in, sometimes into three, and sometimes into fiue diuisions, and notched also about the edges : the stalke riseth higher then any of the former, and hath on it two or three smaller leaues, more cut in and diuided then those belowe : at the toppe whereof standeth one large flower, made of fiue leaues, euery one being narrower at the bottome then at the toppe, and not standing close and round one to another, but with a certaine distance betweene, of a duskie yellowish red colour on the outside, and of a deepe red on the inside, the middle being set with many thrums of a darke purple colour : the head for seede is long, and scaly or chaffie, and idle in like manner as the rest : the roote is made of many graines or small kernels set together, and closing at the head, but spreading it selfe, if it like the ground, vnder the vpper crust of the earth into many rootes, encreasing from long strings, that runne from the middle of the small head of graines, as well as at the head it selfe.

17. *Ranunculus Asiaticus flore amplo rubro.* The large single red Crowfoot of Asia.

There hath come to vs out of Turkie, together with the former, among many other rootes, vnder the same title, a differing sort of this Crowfoote, whose leaues weare broader, and much goaler; the flower also larger, and the leaues thereof broader, sometimes eight in a flower, standing round and close one to another, which maketh the fairer shew : in all other things it is like the former.

18. *Ranunculus Asiaticus flore rubro vario simplici.*
The red stript single Crowfoote of Asia.

This party coloured Crowfoote differeth not eyther in roote or leafe from the former, the chiefest difference is in the flower, which being red, somewhat like the former, hath yet some yellow stripes or veines through euery leafe, sometimes but little, and sometimes so much, that it seemeth to bee party coloured red and yellow : this sort is very tender; for we haue twice had it, and yet perished with vs.

19. *Ranunculus Asiaticus flore luteo vario simplici.*
The yellow stript single Crowfoote of Asia.

There is little difference in the roote of this Crowfoote from the last described, but the leaues are much different, being very much diuided, and the flower is large, of a fine pale greenish yellow colour, consisting of six and seuen, and sometimes of eight or nine round leaues; the toppes whereof haue reddish spots, and the edges sometimes also, with such purplish thrums in the middle that the other haue. None of these former Crowfeete with kernelly rootes, haue euer beene found to haue giuen so good seed in England, as that being sowne, any of them would spring vp; for hereof tryall hath been often made, but all they haue lost their labour, that haue bestowed their paines therein, as farre as I know.

20. *Ranunculus Asiaticus flore rubro pleno.*
The double red Crowfoote of Asia.

The double red Crowfoote hath his rootes and leaues so like vnto the single red kinde, that none can perceiue any difference, or know the one from the other, vntill the budde of the flower doe appeare, which after it is any thing forward, may be perceiued to be greater and fuller then the budde of the single kinde. This kinde beareth most vsually but one faire large double flower on the toppe of the stalke, composed of many leaues, set close together in three or foure rowes, of an excellent crimson colour, declining to Scarlet, the outter leaues being larger then the inner ; and in stead of thrummes, hath many small leaues set together : it hath likewise six small narrow greene leaues on the backside of the flower, where the stalke is fastened to the flower.

There is of this double kinde another sort, whose flower is of the same colour with *Polifero flore*. the former, but out of the middle of the flower ariseth another double flower, but smaller.

The Place.

These plants grow naturally in diuers Countries ; some in France, and Germany, and some in England, some in Spaine, Portugall, and Italy, and some haue been sent out of Turkie from Constantinople, and some from other parts, their titles for the most part descrying their Countries.

The Time.

Some of them flower early, as is set downe in their descriptions, or titles. The others in Aprill and May. The white Candy Crowfoote, and the other single and double sorts of Asia, about the same time, or somewhat later, and one in Autumne, as it is set downe.

The Names.

The names that are giuen seuerally to them may well serue this worke, that thereby they may bee distinguished one from another : For to set downe any further controuersie of names, how fitly or vnfitly they haue beene called, and how variably by diuers former Writers, is fitter for a generall History, vnto which I leaue what may be said, both concerning these and the rest : Onely this I would giue you to vnderstand, that the Turkie kindes haue been sent to vs vnder the names of *Teroboles* for the single, and *Teroboles Catamer lale* for the double, and yet oftentimes, those that haue been sent for double, haue proued single, so little fidelity is to bee found among them.

The Vertues.

All or most of these plants are very sharpe and exulcerating, yet the care and industry of diuers learned men haue found many good effects in many of them. For the rootes and leaues both of the wilde kindes, and of some of these of the Garden, stamped and applyed to the wrists, haue driuen away the fits in Feuers. The roote likewise of the double English kinde is applyed for pestilent sores, to helpe to breake them, by drawing the venome to the place. They helpe likewise to take away scarres and markes in diuers places of the body.

CHAP.

Chap. XXVIII.

Caltha palustris flore pleno. Double Marsh Marigold.

AS an appendix to the Crowfeete, I must needes adde this plant, yet seuerally by it selfe, because both it and his single kinde are by most adioyned thereunto, for the neare resemblance both in shape and sharpenesse of quality. The single kinde I leaue to the Ditch sides, and moist grounds about them, as the fittest places for it, and onely bring the double kinde into my Garden, as fittest for his goodly proportion and beauty to be entertained, and haue place therein.

The double Marsh Marigold hath many broad and round greene leaues, a little endented about the edges, like vnto the single kinde, but not altogether so large, especially in a Garden where it standeth not very moist: the stalkes are weake, round, hollow, and greene, diuided into three or foure branches at the toppe, with leaues at the seuerall ioynts, whereon stand very double flowers, of a gold yellow colour: the fiue outer leaues being larger then any of the rest that are encompassed by them, which fall away after they haue stood blowne a great while (for it endureth in flower a moneth or more, especially if it stand in a shadowie place) without bearing any seed: the rootes are composed of many thicke, long, and round whitish strings, which runne downe deep into the ground, and there are fastened very strongly.

The Place.

This plant groweth naturally in diuers Marshes, and moist grounds in Germany, yet in some more double then in others; it hath long agoe beene cherished in our Gardens.

The Time.

It flowreth in Aprill or May, as the yeare proueth earlier or later: all his leaues doe in a manner quite perish in Winter, and spring anew in the end of February, or thereabouts.

The Names.

There is great controuersie among the learned about the single kinde, but thereof I shall not neede to speake in this place; if God permit I may in a fitter. This is called generally in Latine, *Caltha palustris multiplex*, or *flore pleno*. And wee in English (after the Latine, which take *Caltha* to be that which wee vsually call *Calendula*, a Marigold) The double Marsh Marigold.

The Vertues.

The roote hereof is sharpe, comming neare vnto the quality of the Crowfeete, but for any speciall property, I haue not heard or found any.

Chap. XXIX.

Hepatica nobilis siue trifolia. Noble Liuerwort.

Next vnto the Crowfeete are to follow the Hepaticas, becaufe of the likeneffe with them, feeming to be fmall Crowfeete in all their parts, but of another and more wholfome kinde. Their diuerfity among themfelues confifteth chiefly in the colour of the flowers, all of them being fingle, except one which is very thicke and double.

1. *Hepatica flore cæruleo fimplici maior.*
The great fingle blew Hepatica or noble Liuerwort.

The flowers of this Hepatica doe fpring vp, blow open, and fometimes fhed and fall away, before any leaues appeare or fpread open. The rootes are compofed of a bufh of blackifh ftrings, from the feuerall heads or buttons whereof, after the flowers are rifen and blowne, arife many frefh greene leaues, each feuerally ftanding vpon his foot-ftalke, folded together, and fomewhat browne and hairy at their firft comming, which after are broad, and diuided at the edges into three parts : the flowers likewife ftand euery one vpon his owne feuerall foote-ftalke, of the fame height with the leaues for the moft part, which is about foure or fiue fingers breadth high, made of fix leaues moft vfually, but fometimes it will haue feuen or eight, of a faire blew colour, with many white chiues or threads in the middle, ftanding about a middle green head or vmbone, which after the flower is fallen groweth greater, and fheweth many fmall graines or feede fet clofe together (with three fmall greene leaues compaffing them vnderneath, as they did the flower at the bottome) very like the head of feed of manie Crowfeete.

2. *Hepatica minor flore pallido cæruleo.* The fmall blew Hepatica.

The leaues of this Hepatica are fmaller by the halfe then the former, and grow more aboundantly, or bufhing thicke together : the flowers (when it fheweth them, for I haue had the plant halfe a fcore yeares, and yet neuer faw it beare flower aboue once or twice) are of a pale or bleake blew colour, not fo large as the flowers of the former.

3. *Hepatica flore purpureo.* Purple Hepatica or noble Liuerwort.

This Hepatica is in all things like vnto the firft, but onely the flowers are of a deeper blew tending to a Violet purple : and therefore I fhall not neede to reiterate the former defcription.

4. *Hepatica flore albo minor.* The leffer white Hepatica.

The flowers of this Hepatica are wholly white, of the bigneffe of the red or purple, and the leaues fomewhat fmaller, and of a little whiter or paler greene colour, elfe in all other things agreeing with the former.

5. *Hepatica alba magno flore.* The great white Hepatica.

There is no other difference herein from the laft, but that the flower being as white, is as large as the next.

6. *Hepatica albida siue argentea.* Afh-coloured or Argentine Hepatica.

Both the leaues and the flowers of this Hepatica are larger then any of the former, except the laft : the flowers hereof at the firft opening feeme to bee a of blufh afh-colour, which doe fo abide three or foure dayes, decaying ftill vntill it turne almoft white,

white, hauing yet still a shew of that blush ash-colour in them, till the very last.

7. *Hepatica alba straminibus rubris.* White Hepatica with red threads.

There is no difference between this Hepatica and the first white one, sauing that the threads in the middle of the flower, being white, as in the former, are tipt at the ends with a pale reddish colour, which adde a great beauty to the flowers.

8. *Hepatica flore rubro.* Red Hepatica or noble Liuerwort.

The leaues of this Hepatica are of a little browner red colour, both at their first comming vp, and afterwards, especially in the middle of the leafe more then any of the former : the flowers are in forme like vnto the rest, but of a bright blush, or pale red colour, very pleasant to behold, with white threads or chiues in the middle of them.

9. *Hepatica flore purpureo multiplici siue pleno.*
The double purple Hepatica.

The double Hepatica is in all things like vnto the single purple kinde, sauing onely that the leaues are larger, and stand vpon longer foote-stalkes, and that the flowers are small buttons, but very thicke of leaues, and as double as a flower can be, like vnto the double white Crowfoote before described, but not so bigge, of a deepe blew or purple colour, without any threads or head in the middle, which fall away without giuing any seede.

10. *Hepatica flore caruleo pleno.* The double blew Hepatica.

In the colour of this flower, consisteth the chiefest difference from the last, except one may say it is a little lesse in the bignesse of the flower, but not in doublenesse of leaues.

The Place.

All these plants with single flowers grow naturally in the Woods, and shadowie Mountaines of Germany in many places, and some of them in Italy also. The double kinde likewise hath been sent from Alphonsus Pantius out of Italy, as Clusius reporteth, and was also found in the Woods, neare the Castle of Starnbeg in Austria, the Lady Heusenstains possession, as the same Clusius reporteth also.

The Time.

These plants doe flower very early, and are of the first flowers that shew themselues presently after the deepe frosts in Ianuary, so that next vnto the Winter Wolfesbane, these making their pride appeare in Winter, are the more welcome early guests. The double kinde flowreth not altogether so early, but sheweth his flower, and abideth when the others are past.

The Names.

They haue obtained diuers names ; some calling them *Hepatica, Hepatica nobilis, Hepaticum trifolium, Trifolium nobile, Trifolium aureum,* and some *Trinitas,* and *Herba Trinitatis.* In English you may call them either Hepatica, after the Latine name, as most doe, or Noble Liuerwort, which you please.

The Vertues.

These are thought to coole and strengthen the liuer, the name importing as much ; but I neuer saw any great vse of them by any the Physitians of our London Colledge, or effect by them that haue vsed them in Physicke in our Country.

C H A P.

1 *Hepatica flore albo amplo simplici.* The large white Hepatica. 2 *Hepatica flore rubro simplici.* The red Hepatica. 3 *Hepatica flore purpureo pleno.* The double purple Hepatica. 4 *Geranium tuberosum.* Knobbed Cranes bill. 5 *Geranium Batrachoides flore albo vel cæruleo.* The blew or white Crowfoote Cranes bill. 6 *Geranium Hematodes.* The red Rose Cranes bill. 7 *Geranium Romanum striatum.* The variable stript Cranes bill. 8 *Geranium Creticum.* Candy Cranes bill.

Chap. XXX.

Geranium. Storkes bill or Cranes bill.

AS was said before concerning the Crowfeet, of their large extent and reftraint, the like may be faid of the Storkes bils or Cranes bils; for euen of thefe as of them, I muft for this worke fet forth the defcriptions but of a few, and leaue the reft to a generall worke.

1. *Geranium tuberofum vel bulbofum.* Bulbous or knobbed Cranes bill.

The knobbed Cranes hath three or foure large leaues fpread vpon the ground, of a grayifh or rather dufty greene colour, euery one of them being as it were of a round forme, but diuided or cut into fix or feuen long parts or diuifions, euen vnto the middle, which maketh it feeme to be fo many leaues, each of the cuts or diuifions being deeply notched or indented on both fides; among which rifeth vp a ftalke a foote high or better, bearing thereon diuers pale but bright purple flowers, made of fiue leaues a peece, after which come fmall heads with long pointed beakes, refembling the long bill of a Storke or Crane, or fuch like bird, which after it is ripe, parteth at the bottome where it is biggeft, into foure or fiue feedes, euery one whereof hath a peece of the beake head faftened vnto it, and falleth away if it bee not gathered: the roote is tuberous and round, like vnto the roote of the *Cyclamen* or ordinary Sowbread almoft, but fmaller, and of a darke ruffet colour on the outfide, and white within, which doth encreafe vnder ground, by certaine ftrings running from the mother root into fmall round bulbes, like vnto the rootes of the earth Chefnut, and will prefently fhoote leaues, and quickly grow to beare flowers, but will not abide to be kept long dry out of the ground, without danger to be vtterly fpoiled.

Geranium Batrachoides flore caruleo. The blew Crowfoote Cranes bill.

This Crowfoote Cranes bill hath many large leaues, cut into fiue or fix parts or diuifions, euen to the bottome, and iagged befides on the edges, fet vpon very long flender foote-ftalkes, very like the leaues of the wilde Crowfoot; from among which rife vp diuers ftalkes with great ioynts, fomewhat reddifh, fet with leaues like the former: the toppes of the ftalkes are fpread into many branches, whereon ftand diuers flowers, made of fiue leaues a peece, as large as any of the wilde or field Crowfeete, round pointed, of a faire blew or watchet colour, which being paft, there doe arife fuch heads or bils, as other of the Cranes bils haue: the roote is compofed of many reddifh ftrings, fpreading in the ground, from a head made of diuers red heads, which lye oftentimes eminent aboue the ground.

Geranium Batrachoides flore albo. The white Crowfoote Cranes bill.

This Cranes bill is in leafe and flower altogether like the former, the onely difference betweene them confifteth in the colour of the flower, which in this is wholly white, and as large as the former: but the roote of this hath not fuch red heads as the other hath.

Geranium Batrachoides flore albo & caruleo vario. The party coloured Crowfoote Cranes bill.

The flowers of this Cranes bill are variably ftriped and fpotted, and fometimes diuided, the one halfe of euery leafe being white, and the other halfe blew, fometimes with leffer or greater fpots of blew in the white leafe, very variably, and more in fome years then in others, that it is very hard to expreffe all the varieties that may be obferued in the flowers, that blow at one time. In all other parts of the plant, it is fo like vnto the former, that vntill it be in flower, the one cannot be knowne from the other.

Geranium

5. *Geranium Batrachoides alterum flore purpureo.*
Purple Crowfoote Cranes bill.

This purple Cranes bill hath many leaues rifing from the roote, fet vpon long foot-
ftalkes, fomewhat like vnto the other, yet not fo broad, but more diuided or cut, that
is, into feuen or more flits, euen to the middle, each whereof is likewife cut in on the
edges more deeply then the former; the ftalkes are fomewhat knobbed at the ioynts,
fet with leaues like vnto the lower, and bearing a great tuft of buds at the toppes of the
branches, which breake out into faire large flowers, made of fiue purple leaues, which
doe fomewhat refemble the flower of a Mallow, before it be too full blowne, each
whereof hath a reddifh pointell in the middle, and many fmall threads compaffing it,
this vmbell or tuft of buds doe flower by degrees, and not all at once, and euery flower
abideth open little more then one day, and then fheddeth, fo that euery day yeeldeth
frefh flowers, which becaufe they are fo many, are a long while before they are all
paft or fpent: after the flowers are paft, there arife fmall beake heads or bils, like vnto
the other Cranes bils, with fmall turning feede: the roote is compofed of a great tuft
of ftrings, faftened to a knobby head.

6. *Geranium Romanum verficolor fiue ftriatum.* The variable ftript Cranes bill.

This beautifull Cranes bill hath many broad yellowifh greene leaues arifing from
the roote, diuided into fiue or fix parts, but not vnto the middle as the firft kindes are:
each of thefe leaues hath a blackifh fpot at the bottome corners of the diuifions, the
whole leafe as well in forme as colour and fpots, is very like vnto the leafe of the *Ge-*
ranium fufcum, or fpotted Cranes bill, next following to be defcribed, but that the
leaues of this are not fo large as the other: from among thefe leaues fpring vp fundry
ftalkes a foote high and better, ioynted and knobbed here and there, bearing at the
tops two or three fmall white flowers, confifting of fiue leaues a peece, fo thickly & variably ftriped with fine fmall reddifh veines, that no green leafe that is of that bigneffe
can fhew fo many veines in it, nor fo thick running as euery leafe of this flower doth: in
the middle of the flower ftandeth a fmall pointell, which when the flower is paft doth
grow to be the feed veffell, wheron is fet diuers fmall feeds, like vnto the fmall feedes
of other Cranes bils: the root is made of many fmall yellow threads or ftrings.

7. *Geranium fufcum fiue maculatum.* Swart tawny or fpotted Cranes bill.

The leaues of this Cranes bill are in all points like the laft defcribed, as well in the
forme and diuifions as colour of the leaues, being of a yellowifh greene colour, but
larger and ftronger by much: the ftalkes of this rife much higher, and are ioynted or
knobbed with reddifh knees or ioynts, on the tops whereof ftand not many although
large flowers, confifting of fiue leaues a peece, each whereof is round at the end, and a
little fnipt round about, and doe bend or turne themfelues backe to the ftalkewards,
making the middle to be higheft or moft eminent; the colour of the flower is of a darke
or deepe blackifh purple, the bottome of euery leafe being whiter then the reft; it hath
alfo a middle pointell ftanding out, which afterwards bring forth feede like vnto o-
thers of his kinde: the roote confifteth of diuers great ftrings, ioyned to a knobby
head.

8. *Geranium Hematodes.* The red Rofe Cranes bill.

This Cranes bill hath diuers leaues fpread vpon the ground, very much cut in or
diuided into many parts, and each of them againe flit or cut into two or three peeces,
ftanding vpon flender long foote-ftalkes, of a faire greene colour all the Spring and
Summer, but reddifh in Autumne: among thefe leaues fpring vp flender and weake
ftalkes, befet at euery ioynt (which is fomewhat reddifh) with two leaues for the moft
part, like vnto the lower: the flowers grow feuerally on the toppe of the ftalkes, and
not many together in bunches or branches, as in all other of the Cranes bils, euery
flower being as large as a fingle Rofe Campion flower, confifting of fiue large leaues,

of a deeper red colour then in any other Cranes bill at the first opening, and will change more blewish afterwards : when the flower is past, there doth arise such like beakes as are in others of the same kinde, but small : the roote is hard, long, and thicke, with diuers branches spreading from it, of a reddish yellow colour on the outside, and whitish within, which abideth and perisheth not, but shooteth forth some new greene leaues, which abide all the Winter, although those that turne red doe fall away.

Geranium Creticum. Candy Cranes bill.

Candy Cranes bill beareth long and tender stalkes, whereon growe diuers broad and long leaues, cut in or iagged on the edges : the toppes of the stalkes are branched into many flowers, made of fiue leaues of a reasonable bignesse, and of a faire blew or watchet colour, with a purplish pointell in the middle, which being past, there follow beake heads like other Cranes bils, but greater, containing larger, greater, and sharper pointed seede, able to pierce the skinne, if one be not warie of it : the roote is white and long, with some fibres at it, and perisheth when it hath perfected his seede, and will spring of it owne sowing many times, if the Winter be not too sharpe, otherwise (being annuall) it must be sowne in the Spring of the yeare.

The Place.

Most of these Cranes bils are strangers vnto vs by nature, but endenizond in our English Gardens. It hath beene reported vnto mee by some of good credit, that the second or Crowfoot Cranes bill hath been found naturally growing in England, but yet I neuer saw it, although I haue seen many sorts of wilde kindes in many places. Matthiolus saith that the first groweth in Dalmatia and Illyria very plentifully. Camerarius, Clusius, and others, that most of the rest grow in Germany, Bohemia, Austria, &c. The last hath his place recorded in his title.

The Time.

All these Cranes bils doe for the most part flower in Aprill, and May, and vntill the middle of Iune. The variable or stript Cranes bill is vsually the latest of all the rest.

The Names.

The first is vsually called *Geranium tuberosum*, of some *Geranium bulbosum*, of the likenesse of the roote vnto a bulbe : It is without controuersie *Geranium primum* of Dioscorides. The second is called *Geranium Gratia Dei*, of others, *Geranium cæruleum.* The blew Cranes bill Lobel calleth it *Batrachoides*, because both leafe and flower are like vnto a Crowfoote; and the affinity with the Cranes bils in the seede causeth it rather to be referred to them then to the Crowfeete. The stript Cranes bill is called by some *Geranium Romanum.* The last sauing one is called *Geranium Hæmatodes*, or *Sanguineum*, of Lobel *Geranium Gruinale Hæmatodes supinum radice repente.* In English it may be called after the Greek and Latine, The bloudy Cranes bill, but I rather call it, The Rose Cranes bill, because the flowers are as large as single Roses, or as the Rose Campion. Some of them are called in many places of England Bassinets.

The Vertues.

All the kindes of Cranes bils are accounted great wound herbes, and effectuall to stay bleedings, yet some more then others. The Emperickes of Germanie, as Camerarius saith, extoll it wonderfully, for a singular remedie against the Stone, both in the reines and bladder.

CHAP.

Chap. XXXI.

Sanicula guttata maior. Spotted Sanicle.

Auing long debated with my selfe, where to place this & the other plants that follow in the two next Chapters, I haue thought it not amiſſe for this worke to set them downe here, both before the Beares eares, which are kindes of Sanicle, as the beſt Authors doe hold, and after the Cranes bils, both for ſome qualities ſomewhat reſembling them, and for ſome affinity of the flowers with the former.

The ſpotted Sanicle hath many ſmall round leaues, bluntly endented about the edges, ſomewhat like vnto the leaues of our white Saxifrage, of a full greene colour aboue, and whitiſh hairy, and ſomewhat reddiſh withall vnderneath: the ſtalkes are ſet here and there with the like leaues, riſing a foote and a halfe high or more, very much diuided at the toppe into ſundry ſmall branches, bearing many very ſmall white flowers, conſiſting of fiue ſmall leaues, wherein are many ſmall red ſpots to be ſeene, as ſmall as pins points, of a pretty ſweete ſent, almoſt like Hawthorne flowers, in the middle whereof are many ſmall threads compaſſing a head, which when it is ripe containeth ſmall blacke ſeede: the roote is ſcaly, or couered with a chaffie matter, hauing many ſmall white fibres vnderneath, whereby it is faſtened in the ground.

There is another of this kinde, like both in roote, leafe, and flower to the former, *Minor non guttata.* the onely difference is, that this is leſſer then the former, and hath no ſpots in the flower, as the other hath.

We haue alſo another ſmaller kinde then the laſt, both in leafe and flower, the leaues *Minus guttata.* whereof are ſmaller, but rounder, and more finely ſnipt or indented about the edges, like the teeth of a fine ſawe: the ſtalke is little aboue a ſpan high, hauing many ſmall white flowers ſpotted as the firſt, but with fewer ſpots.

The Place.

Theſe growe in the ſhadowie Woods of the Alpes, in diuers places, and with vs they more delight in the ſhade then the ſunne.

The Time.

All theſe Sanicles doe flower in May, and continue flowring vntill Iune, and the ſeede ſoone ripeneth after: the rootes abide all the Winter, with ſome leaues on them, ſpringing afreſh in the beginning of the yeare.

The Names.

The former two are called by Cluſius *Sanicula montana*, and by others *Sanicula guttata*: by Lobel *Geum Alpinum.* The third or laſt hath been ſent vs vnder the name of *Sanicula montana altera minor.*

The Vertues.

The name impoſed on theſe plants doe certainly aſſure vs of their vertues, from the firſt founders, that they are great healers, and from their taſte, that they are great binders.

V 2 Chap.

Chap. XXXII.

Cotyledon altera Matthioli. Spotted Nauelwort.

THis spotted Nauelwort, as many doe call it, hath many thicke small leaues, not so broad as long, of a whitish greene colour, lying on the ground in circles, after the manner of the heads of Houseleeke, and dented about the edges; from the middle whereof sometimes (for it doth not flower euery yeare in many places) ariseth vp a stalke, scarce a foote high, beset with such like leaues as are belowe, but somewhat longer : from the middle of the stalke vp to the top it brancheth forth diuersly, with a leafe at euery ioynt, bearing three or foure flowers on euery branch, consisting of fiue white leaues, spotted with small red spots, like vnto the spotted Sanicle, but with fewer and greater spots, hauing a yellowish circle or eye in the bottome of euery flower, and many whitish threads with yellowish tips in it : the seede is small and blacke, contained in small round heads : the roote is small, long, and threadie, shooting out such heads of leaues, which abide all the Winter, those that beare flower perishing.

Cotyledon altera minor. Small dented Nauelwort.

There is another like vnto that before described in most things, the differences be these : It hath shorter leaues then the former, and dented about the edges in the like manner : the flowers hereof are white, but greater, made of six leaues, and most vsually without any spots at all in them, some are seene to haue spots also : the heads or seede vessels are more cornered then the former.

Cotyledon altera flore rubro stellato. Small red flowred Nauelwort.

This hath also many heads of leaues, but more open, which are longer, greener, and sharper pointed then eyther of the former, somewhat reddish also, and not dented about the edges, but yet a little rough in handling : the stalke ariseth from among the leaues, being somewhat reddish, and the leaues thereon are reddish pointed, diuided at the toppe into many branches, with diuers flowers thereon, made of twelue small long leaues, standing like a starre, of a reddish purple colour, with many threads therein, set about the middle head, which is diuided at the toppe into many small ends, like pods or hornes, containing therein very small seede : the root is small like the former.

Sedum serratum flore rubente maculato. The Princes Feather.

This kinde of Sengreene is composed of heads of larger, broader, and thinner leaues then any of the former, of a sadder greene colour, somewhat vneuenly endented about the edges, and not so close set together, but spreading forth into seuerall heads like as the former sorts doe, although not so plentifully; from the middle of diuers of which heads rise vp brownish or reddish stalkes, set with smaller leaues thereon to the middle thereof, and then brancheth forth into seuerall sprigs, set with diuers small reddish flowers consisting of fiue leaues a peece, the innerside of which are of a pale red, somewhat whitish, spotted with many small bloud red spots, as small almost as pins points, with some small threads in the middle, standing about a small greene head, which turneth into the seede vessell, parted foure wayes at the head, wherein is contained small blackish seede : the rootes are small threads, which spread vnder the ground, and shoote vp seuerall heads round about it.

The Place.

All these growe in Germany, Hungarie, Austria, the Alpes, and other such like places, where they cleaue to the rocke it selfe, that hath but a crust of earth on it to nourish them. They will abide in Gardens reasonable well, if they be planted in shadowie places, and not in the sun.

The

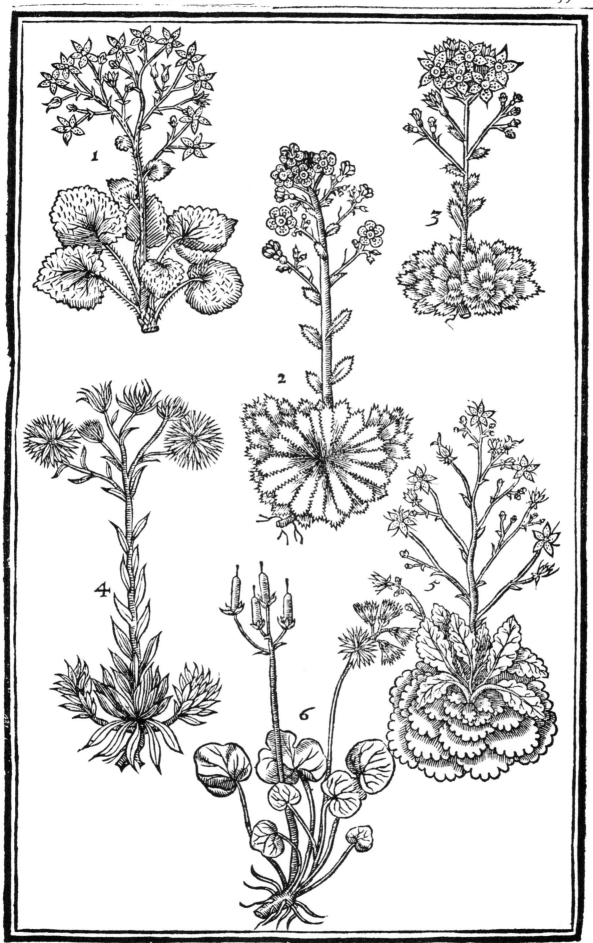

1 *Sanicula guttata.* Spotted Sanicle. 2 *Cotyledon altera Matthioli.* Spotted Nauelwort. 3 *Cotyledon altera minor.* Small dented Nauelwort. 4 *Cotyledon altera flore rubro stellato.* Small red flowred Nauelwort. 5 *Sedum serratum flore rubente maculato.* The Princes Feather. 6 *Soldanella Alpina.* Blew Moonwort.

The Time.

They flower for the moft part in the end of May, and fometimes fooner or later, as the yeare falleth out.

The Names.

The firft is called by Matthiolus, *Cotyledon altera Diofcoridis*, and *Vmbilicus alter*, but it is not the true *Cotyledon altera* of Diofcorides ; for *Sedum vulgare maius*, Our common Houfeleeke, by the confent of the beft moderne Writers, is the true *Cotyledon altera* of Diofcorides, or *Vmbilicus Veneris alter*. I hold it rather to bee a kinde of fmall Houfeleeke, as the other two likewife are. The fecond is called by fome *Aizoum* or *Sedum minus ferratum*. The third hath his name in his title. Wee doe call them Nauelworts in Englifh rather then Houfeleekes, *Euphoniæ gratia*. The laft may be called dented Sengreene with reddifh fpotted flowers, but fome of our Englifh Gentlewomen haue called it, The Princes Feather, which although it be but a by-name, may well ferue for this plant to diftinguifh it, and whereby to be knowne.

The Vertues.

They are all held to be cold and moift, like vnto other Houfeleekes.

Chap. XXXIII.

Soldanella Alpina. Mountaine Soldanella or blew Moonewort.

THis beautifull plant hath many round and hard leaues, fet vpon long footeftalkes, a little vneuenly cut about the edges, greene on the vpperfide, and of a grayifh greene vnderneath, and fometime reddifh like the leaues of Sowbread, which becaufe they doe fomewhat refemble the leaues of *Soldanella marina*, which is the Sea Bindweede, tooke the name thereof : the ftalkes are flender, fmall, round, and reddifh, about a fpan high, bearing foure or fiue flowers at the toppe, euery one hanging downe their heads, like vnto a Bell flower, confifting but of one leafe (as moft of the Bindweeds doe) plated into fiue folds, each of them ending in a long point, which maketh the flower feem to haue fiue leaues, each whereof is deeply cut in on the edges, and hauing a round greene head in the middle, with a pricke or pointell at the end thereof : the flower is of a faire blew colour, fometimes deeper or paler, or white, as nature lifteth without any fmell at all : the middle head, after the flower is fallen, rifeth to be a long round pod, bearing that pricke it had at the end thereof, wherein is contained fmall greenifh feede : the roote hath many fibres fhooting from a long round head or roote.

The Place.

This groweth on the Alpes, which are couered with fnow the greateft part of the yeare, and will hardly abide tranfplanting.

The Time.

In the naturall places it flowreth not vntill the Summer moneths, Iune, Iuly, and Auguft, after the fnow is melted from the Hils, but being brought into Gardens, it flowreth in the beginning of Aprill, or thereabouts.

The

The Names.

This plant, by reafon of the likeneffe of leaues with *Soldanella*, as was before faid, is called by many *Soldanella*, but yet is no Bindweede ; and therefore I rather call it in Englifh a Mountaine Soldanella, then as Gerrard doth, Mountaine Bindweede. It is likewife called by fome, *Lunaria minor cærulea*, The leffer blew Lunary or Moonwort, and fo I would rather haue it called.

The Vertues.

They that impofed the name of *Lunaria* vpon this plant, feeme to referre it to the wound or confolidating herbes, but becaufe I haue no further relation or experience, I can fay no more thereof vntill tryall hath taught it. Some alfo from the name *Soldanella*, which is giuen it, becaufe of the likeneffe of the leaues, haue vfed it to help the Dropfie, for which the Sea plant is thought to be effectuall.

Chap. XXXIIII.

Auricula Vrfi. Beares eares.

THere are fo many fundry and feuerall forts of Beares eares, the variety confifting as well in the differing colours of the flowers, as the forme and colour of the leaues, that I fhall not comprehend and fet downe vnto you all the diuerfities by many, that are rifen vp to thofe that haue beene induftrious in the fowing of the feedes of the feuerall forts of them ; yet If you accept of thefe that I doe here offer vnto you, I fhall giue you the knowledge of others, as time, occafion, and the view of them fhall enable me. And becaufe they are without all queftion kinds of Cowflips, I haue fet them downe before them in the firft place, as being of more beautie and greater refpect, or at the leaft of more rarity vntovs. To difpofe them therefore into order, I fhall ranke them vnder three principall colours, that is to fay, Red or Purple, White, and Yellow, and fhew you the varieties of each of them (for fo many as are come to my knowledge) apart by themfelues, and not promifcuoufly as many others haue done.

1. *Auricula Vrfi flore purpureo.* Purple Beares eare, or The Murrey Cowflip.

This purple Beares eare or Cowflip hath many greene leaues, fomewhat long and fmooth, narrow from the bottome of the leafe to the middle, and broad from thence to the end, being round pointed, and fomewhat fnipt or endented about the edges ; in the middle of thefe leaues, and fometimes at the fides alfo, doe fpring round greene ftalkes foure or fiue fingers high, bearing at the top many flowers, the buds whereof, before they are blowne, are of a very deepe purple colour, and being open, are of a bright, but deepe purple, vfually called a Murrey colour, confifting of fiue leaues a peece, cut in at the end as it were into two, with a whitifh ring or circle at the bottome of each flower, ftanding in fmall greene cups, wherein after the flowers are fallen, are contained very fmall heads, not rifing to the height of the cups, bearing a fmall pricke or pointell at the toppe of them, wherein is little blackifh feede : the roote hath many whitifh ftrings faftened to the maine long roote, which is very like vnto a Primrofe or Cowflip roote, as it is in all other parts befides.

2. *Auricula Vrfi purpurea abfq; orbe.* The murrey Cowflip without eyes.

There is another of this kinde, whofe leafe is fomewhat leffe, as the flower is alfo,
but

but of the same colour, and sometimes somewhat redder, tending to a Scarlet, without any circle at the bottome of the flower, in no other things differing from it.

3. *Auricula Vrsi minor flore tannetto.* Tawney Beares eares.

The leaues of this kinde haue a greater shew of mealinesse to be seene in them, and not much smaller then the former, yet snipt or endented about the ends like vnto them : the flowers are many, of the same fashion with the former, but smaller, each whereof is of as deepe a murrey or tawnie colour when it is blowne, as the buds of the former are before they are blowne, hauing a white circle at the bottome of the flower, and yellowish in the middle belowe the circle.

4. *Auricula Vrsi flore rubro saturo orbe luteo.*
Deepe or bloud red Beares eares with eyes.

This kinde hath small and long greene leaues, nothing mealy, but snipt about the edges, from the middle of the leaues forwards to the ends : the flowers hereof are of a deepe red colour, tending to a bloud red, with a deepe yellow circle, or rather bottome in the middle.

Auricula Vrsi flore rubro saturo absque orbe.

There is another of this kinde, whose leaues are somewhat mealy, and smaller then any (that I haue seene) that haue mealy leaues : the flowers are of the same deepe red colour with the last described, yet hath no circle or bottome of any other colour at all.

5. *Auricula Vrsi flore purpuro caruleo.* The Violet coloured Beares eare.

We haue another, whose leaues are somewhat mealy and large ; the flowers whereof are of a paler purple then the first, somewhat tending to a blew.

6. *Auricula Vrsi flore obsoleto magno.* The Spaniards blush Beares eare.

This great Beares eare hath as large leaues as any other of this kindred whatsoeuer, and whitish or mealy withall, somewhat snipt about the edges, as many other of them are : the flowers stand at the toppe of a strong and tall stalke, larger then any of the other that I haue seene, being of a duskie blush colour, resembling the blush of a Spaniard, whose tawney skinne cannot declare so pure a blush as the English can ; and therefore I haue called it the Spaniards blush.

7. *Auricula Vrsi flore rubello.* Scarlet or light red Beares eares.

The leaues of this kinde are very like the leaues of the first purple kinde, but that they are not so thicke ; of a little paler greene colour, and little or nothing snipt about the edges : the flowers are of a bright, but pale reddish colour, not halfe so deepe as the two last with white circles in the bottomes of them, in other things this differeth not from others.

8. *Auricula Vrsi Roseo colore.* The Rose coloured Beares eare.

We haue another, whose leafe is a little mealy, almost as large as any of the former, whose flowers are of a light red colour, very neare the colour of an ordinary Damaske Rose, with a white eye at the bottome.

9. *Auricula Vrsi flore caruleo folio Boraginis.*
Blew Beares eares with Borage leaues.

This plant is referred to the kindred or family of the Beares eares, onely for the forme of the flower sake, which euen therein it doth not assimilate to the halfe ; but because it hath passed others with that title, I am content to insert it here, to giue you the

1 *Auricula Vrsi flore purpureo.* Purple Cowflips or Beares eares. 2 *Auricula Vrsi flore tannetto.* Tawney Beares eare. 3 *Auricula Vrsi flore & folio Boraginis.* Blew Beares eares with Borage leaues. 4 *Auricula Vrsi flore carneo* Blufh Beares eare. 5 *Auricula Vrsi maxima lutea flore eleganti.* The greateſt faire yellow Beares eares with eyes. 6 *Auricula Vrsi altera flore luteo.* The yellow Beares eare. 7 *Auricula Vrsi crinis coloris ſiue flore ſuſco.* The haire coloured Beares eare. 8 *Cortuſa Mattbioli.* Beares eare Sanicle.

the knowledge thereof, and rather to satisfie others then my selfe with the place there-of : the description whereof is as followeth : It hath diuers broad rough hairy leaues spread vpon the ground, somewhat like vnto the leaues of Borage for the roughnesse, but not for the largenesse; the leaues hereof being somewhat rent in some places at the edges : from among these leaues rise vp one, or two, or more brownish, round, and hairy stalkes, a span high or thereabouts, bearing at the toppes three or foure flowers a peece, consisting of fiue large pointed leaues, of a faire blew or light azur colour, with some small yellow threads in the middle, standing in small greene cups : the roote is long and brownish, hauing many small fibres annexed vnto it.

10. *Auricula Vrsi maior flore albo.* The great white Beares eare.

This white Beares eare hath many faire whitish greene leaues, somewhat paler then the leaues of any of the kindes of Beares eares, and a little snipt about the ends, as ma-nie other are : among these leaues rise vp stalkes foure or fiue inches high, bearing at the toppe many flowers like vnto the small yellow Beares eare hereafter set downe, of a pale whitish colour, tending to yellow at the first opening of the flower, which after two or three dayes change into a faire white colour, and so continue all the while it flowreth : the roote is like the purple kinde, as all or most of the rest are, or very little differing.

11. *Auricula Vrsi minor flore albo.* The lesser white Beares eare.

The lesser Beares eare hath smaller leaues, of a little darker green colour : the stalke and flowers are likewise lesser then the former, and haue no shew of yellownesse at all, eyther in budde or flower, but is pure white, differing not in other things from the rest.

12. *Auricula Vrsi maxima lutea flore eleganti.*
The greatest faire yellow Beares eare with eyes.

This yellow Beares eare hath many faire large thicke leaues, somewhat mealy or hoary vpon the greennesse, being larger then any other kinde, except the sixth, and the next yellow that followeth, smooth about the edges, and without any endenting at all : the stalke is great, round, and not higher then in other of the former, but bearing ma-nie more flowers thereon then in any other kinde, to the number of thirty many times, standing so round and close together, that they seeme to be a Nosegay alone, of the same fashion with the former, but that the leaues are shorter and rounder, yet with a notch in the middle like the rest, of a faire yellow colour, neither very pale nor deepe, with a white eye or circle in the bottome, about the middle of euery flower, which giueth it the greater grace : the seede is of a blackish browne colour, like vnto others, but contained in greater round heads then any other, with a small pointell sticking in the middle : the roote is greater and thicker then any other, with long strings or fibres like vnto the other sorts, but greater.

13. *Auricula Vrsi maior lutea folio in cauo.* The greater yellow Beares eare.

This greater yellow Beares eare hath his leaues larger, and more mealy or hoarie then the last, or any other of these kindes : the flowers are not so many, but longer, and not so thicke thrusting together as the first, but of a deeper yellow colour, without any eye or circle in the middle.

14. *Auricula Vrsi maior flore pallido.* The great Straw coloured Beares eare.

This hath almost as mealy leaues as the last, but nothing so large ; the flowers are of a faire strawe colour, with a white circle at the bottome of them, these three last haue no shew or shadow of any other colour in any part of the edge, as some others that follow haue.

15. *Auricula Vrsi minor flore pallente.* The lesser straw coloured Beares eare.

We haue another, whose leafe is lesse mealy, or rather pale green, and a little mealy withall; the flowers whereof are of a paler yellow colour then the last, and beareth almost as many vpon a stalke as the first g eat yellow.

16. *Auricula Vrsi minor lutea.* The lesser yellow Beares eares.

The leaues of this Beares eare are nothing so large as either of the three former yellow kindes, but rather of the bignesse of the first white kinde, but yet a little larger, thicker, and longer then it, hauing vnder the greennesse a small shew of mealinesse, and somewhat snipt about the edges : the flowers are of a pale yellow colour, with a little white bottome in them : the seed and rootes are like vnto the other kindes.

17. *Auricula Vrsi flore flauo.* The deepe yellow or Cowslip Beares eare.

This kinde hath somewhat larger leaues then the last, of a yellowish greene colour, without any mealinesse on them, or endenting about the edges, but smooth and whole: the flowers are not larger but longer, and not laide open so fully as the former, but of as deepe a yellow colour as any Cowslip almost, without any circle in the bottome : neither of these two last haue any shew of other colour then yellow in them, sauing the white in the eye.

18. *Auricula Vrsi versicolor prima siue flore rubescente.* The blush Beares eare.

The blush Beares eare hath his leaues as large, and as hoary or mealy as the third greater yellow, or straw coloured Beares eare; among which riseth vp a stalke about foure inches high, bearing from six to twelue, or more faire flowers, somewhat larger then the smaller yellow Beares eare before described, hauing the ground of the flower of a darke or dunne yellow colour, shadowed ouer a little with a shew of light purple, which therefore we call a blush colour, the edges of the flower being tipt with a little deeper shew of that purple colour, the bottome of the flower abiding wholly yellow, without any circle, and is of very great beauty, which hath caused me to place it in the forefront of the variable coloured Beares eares. And although some might thinke it should be placed among the first ranke of Beares eares, because it is of a blush colour, yet seeing it is assuredly gained from some of the yellow kindes by sowing the seede, as many other sorts are, as may be seene plainly in the ground of the flower, which is yellow, and but shadowed ouer with purple, yet more then any of the rest that follow; I thinke I haue giuen it his right place: let others of skill & experience be iudges herein.

19. *Auricula Vrsi crinis coloris.* Haire coloured Beares eares.

The leaues of this kinde are more mealy like then the last blush kinde, but somewhat longer and larger, and snipt about the edges in the same manner, from the middle of the leafe forwards : the flower is vsually of a fine light browne yellow colour, which wee doe vsually call an Haire colour, and sometimes browner, the edges of the flower haue a shew or shadow of a light purple or blush about them, but more on the outside then on the inside.

20. *Auricula Vrsi versicolor lutea.* The yellow variable Beares eare.

This variable Beares eare hath his greene leaues somewhat like vnto the deepe yellow, or Cowslip Beares eare before described, but somewhat of a fresher greene, more shining and smaller, and snipt about the edges towards the ends, as many of those before are : the flowers are of a faire yellow colour, much laid open when it is full blowne, that it seemeth almost flat, dasht about the edges onely with purple, being more yellow in the bottome of the flower, then in any other part.

21. *Auricula*

21. *Auricula Vrsi versicolor lutescente viridi flore.* The variable green Beares eare.

This kinde of Beares eare hath greene leaues, very like vnto the laft defcribed, and fnipt in the like manner about the edges, but in this it differeth, that his leaues do turne or fold themfelues a little backwards : the flowers are of a yellowifh greene colour, more clofed then the former, hauing purplifh edges, efpecially after they haue ftood blowne fome time, and haue little or none at the firft opening : thefe haue no circles at all in them.

Many other varieties are to be found, with thofe that are curious conferuers of thefe delights of nature, either naturally growing on the mountaines in feuerall places, from whence they (being fearched out by diuers) haue been taken and brought, or elfe raifed from the feede of fome of them, as it is more probable : for feuerall varieties haue beene obferued (and no doubt many of thefe before fpecified) to bee gotten by fowing of the feedes, euery yeare lightly fhewing a diuerfity, not obferued before, either in the leafe, diuers from that from whence it was taken, or in the flowers. I haue onely fet downe thofe that haue come vnder mine owne view and not any by relation, euen as I doe with all or moft of the things contained in this worke.

The Place.

Many of thefe goodly plants growe naturally on mountaines, efpecially the Alpes, in diuers places ; for fome kindes that growe in fome places, doe not in others, but farre diftant one from the other. There hath likewife fome beene found on the Pyrenæan mountaines, but that kinde with the blew flower and Borage leafe, hath beene gathered on the mountaines in Spaine, and on the Pyrenæans next vnto Spaine.

The Time.

They all flower in Aprill and May, and the feede is ripe in the end of Iune, or beginning of Iuly, and fometimes they will flower againe in the end of Summer, or in Autumne, if the yeare proue temperate, moift, and rainie.

The Names.

It is very probable, that none of thefe plants were euer knowne vnto the ancient Writers, becaufe we cannot be affured, that they may be truely referred vnto any plant that they name, vnleffe we beleeue Fabius Columna, that it fhould be *Alfma* of Diofcorides, for thereunto hee doth referre it. Diuers of the later Writers haue giuen vnto them diuers names, euery one according to his owne conceit. For Gefner calleth it *Lunaria arthritica,* and *Paralytica Alpina.* Matthiolus accounteth it to bee of the kindred of the Sanicles, and faith, that in his time it was called by diuers Herbarifts, *Auricula Vrfi,* which name hath fince bin receiued as moft vfuall. We in Englifh call them Beares eares, according to the Latine, or as they are called by diuers women, French Cowflips ; they may be called Mountaine Cowflips, if you will, for to diftinguifh betweene them and other Cowflips, whereof thefe are feuerall kindes.

Sanicula Alpina fiue Cortufa Matthioli. Beares eare Sanicle.

I cannot chufe but infert this delicate plant in the end of the Beares eares, for that it is of fo neare affinity, although it differ much in the forme of the leaues, the defcription whereof is in this manner : The leaues that fpring vp firft are much crumpled, and as it were folded together, which afterwards open themfelues into faire, broad, and roundifh leaues, fomewhat rough or hairy, not onely cut into fine diuifions, but fomewhat notched alfo about the edges, of a darke greene colour on the vpperfide, and

more

more whitish greene vnderneath ; amongst these leaues riseth vp one or two naked round stalkes, fiue or six inches high, bearing at the toppes diuers small flowers, somewhat sweete, like vnto the first purple Beares eare, hanging downe their heads, consisting of fiue small pointed leaues a peece, of a darke reddish purple colour, with a white circle or bottome in the middle, and some small threads therein : after the flowers are past, there come small round heads, somewhat longer then any of the Beares eares, standing vpright vpon their small foot-stalkes, wherein is contained small round and blackish seede : the roote consisteth of a thicke tuft of small whitish threads, rather then rootes, much enterlaced one among another : the leaues of this plant dye downe euery yeare, and spring vp a new in the beginning of the yeare, whereas all the Beares eares doe hold their leaues greene all the Winter, especially the middlemost, which stand like a close head, the outermost for the most part perishing after seed time.

The Place.

This groweth in many shadowie Woods both of Italy and Germany ; for both Clusius hath described it, finding it in the Woods of Austria and Stiria; and Matthiolus setteth it downe, hauing receiued it from Anthonius Cortusus, who was President of the Garden at Padua, and found it in the woody mountaines of Vicenza, neare vnto Villestagna, whereon (as Matthiolus saith) there is found both with white flowers as well as with blew, but such with white flowers or blew we neuer could see or heare further of.

The Time.

It flowreth much about the time of the Beares eares, or rather a little later, and the seede is ripe with them.

The Names.

Clusius calleth it *Sanicula montana*, and *Sanicula Alpina*, and referreth it to the *Auricula Vrsi*, or Beares eare, which it doth most nearly resemble : but Matthiolus referreth it to the *Cariophyllata* or *Auens*, making it to be of that tribe or family, and calleth it *Cortusa* of him that first sent it him. Wee may call it eyther *Cortusa*, as for the most part all Herbarists doe, or Beares eare Sanicle as Gerrard doth.

The Vertues.

All the sorts of Beares eares are Cephalicall, that is, conducing helpe for the paines in the head, and for the giddinesse thereof, which may happen, eyther by the sight of steepe places subiect to danger, or otherwise. They are accounted also to be helping for the Palsey, and shaking of the ioynts ; and also as a Sanicle or wound-herbe. The leaues of the *Cortusa* taste a little hot, and if one of them bee laide whole, without bruising, on the cheeke of any tender skind woman, it will raise an orient red colour, as if some *fucus* had beene laide thereon, which will passe away without any manner of harme, or marke where it lay : This is Cortusus his obseruation. Camerarius in his *Hortus Medicus* saith, that an oyle is made thereof, that is admirable for to cure wounds.

X   Chap.

Chap. XXXV.

Primula veris & Paralysis. Primroses and Cowslips.

WE haue so great variety of Primroses and Cowslips of our owne Country breeding, that strangers being much delighted with them, haue beene often furnished into diuers Countries, to their good content : And that I may set them downe in some methodicall manner, as I haue done other things, I will first set downe all the sorts of those we call Primroses, both single and double, and afterwards the Cowslips with their diuersities, in as ample manner as my knowledge can direct me. And yet I know, that the name of *Primula veris* or Primrose, is indifferently conferred vpon those that I distinguish for *Paralyses* or Cowslips. I doe therefore for your better vnderstanding of my distinction betweene Primroses and Cowslips, call those onely Primroses that carry but one flower vpon a stalke, be they single or double, except that of Master Hesket, and that with double flowers many vpon a stalke, set out in Gerards Herball, which is his onely, not found (as I thinke) *in rerum natura*, I am sure, such a one I could neuer heare of : And those Cowslips, that beare many flowers vpon a stalke together constantly, be they single or double also. I might otherwise distinguish them also by the leafe ; that all the Primroses beare their long and large broad yellowish greene leaues, without stalkes most vsually ; and all the Cowslips haue small stalkes vnder the leaues, which are smaller, and of a darker greene, as vsually, but that this distinction is neither so certaine and generall, nor so well knowne.

1. *Primula veris flore albo.* The single white Primrose.

The Primrose that groweth vnder euery bush or hedge, in all or most of the Woods, Groues, and Orchards of this Kingdome, I may well leaue to his wilde habitation, being not so fit for a Garden, and so well knowne, that I meane not to giue you any further relation thereof : But we haue a kinde hereof which is somewhat smaller, and beareth milke white flowers, without any shew of yellownesse in them, and is more vsually brought into Gardens for the rarity, and differeth not from the wilde or ordinary kinde, either in roote or leafe, or any thing else, yet hauing those yellow spots, but smaller, and not so deepe, as are in the other wilde kinde.

2. *Primula veris flore viridi simplici.* The single greene Primrose.

The single greene Primrose hath his leaues very like vnto the greater double Primrose, but smaller, and of a sadder greene colour: the flowers stand seuerally vpon long foot stalkes, as the first single kinde doth, but larger then they, and more laide open, of the same, or very neare the same yellowish greene colour that the huske is of, so that at the first opening, the huske and the flower seeme to make one double greene flower, which afterwards separating themselues, the single flower groweth aboue the huske, and spreadeth it selfe open much more then any other single Primrose doth, growing in the end to be of a paler greene colour.

3. *Primula veris flore viridante & albo simplici.*
The single greene and white Primrose.

The leaues of this differ in a manner nothing from the former, neither doth the flower but only in this, that out of the large yellowish green huskes, which containe the flowers of the former, there commeth forth out of the middle of each of them either a small peece of a whitish flower, or else a larger, sometimes making vp a whole flower, like an ordinary Primrose.

4. *Primula veris flore viridi duplici.* The double greene Primrose.

This double Primrose is in his leaues so like the former single greene kindes, that
the

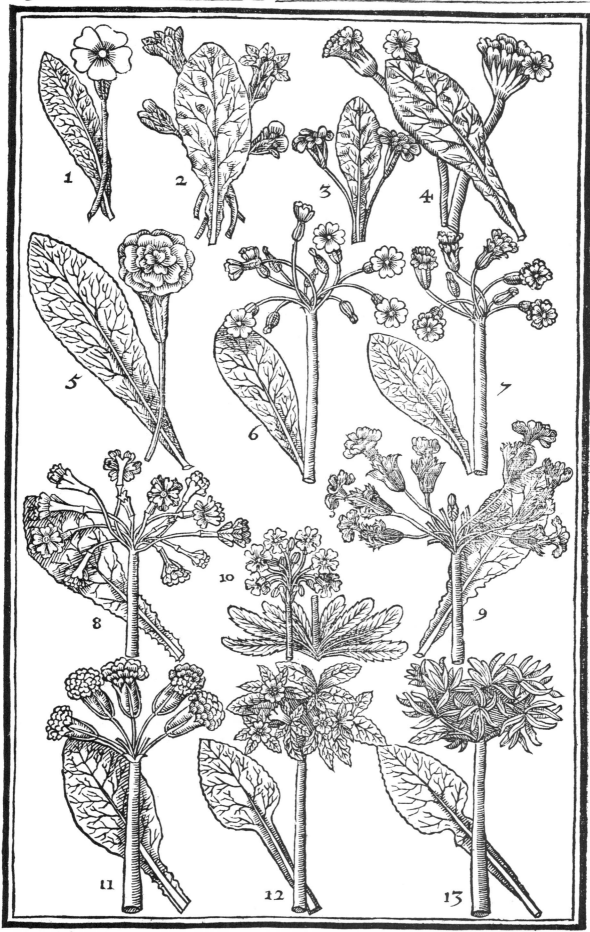

1 *Primula veris flore albo.* The white Primrose. 2 *Primula veris flore viridi & albo simplici.* The green and white Primrose. 3 *Primula veris flore viridi duplici.* The double green Primrose. 4 *Primula veris Hesketi.* Master Heskets double Primrose. 5 *Primula veris flore pleno vulgaris.* The ordinary double Primrose. 6 *Paralysis veris flore viridante simplici* The single green Cowslip. 7 *Paralysis flore geminato odorato* Double Cowslips or hose in hose. 8 *Paralysis inodora flore geminato.* Double Oxelips hose in hose. 9 *Paralysis flore & calice crispo.* Curld Cowslips or Gaskins. 10 *Paralysis minor angustifolia flore rubro.* Red Birds eyen. 11 *Paralysis hortensis flore pleno vulgaris.* Double Paigles. 12 *Paralysis fatua.* The foolish Cowslips or Jacke an Apes on horse backe. 13 *Paralysis flore viridi roseo calamistrato.* The double greene feathered Cowslip.

the one cannot be knowne from the other vntill it come to flower, and then it beareth vpon euery stalke a double green flower, of a little deeper green colour then the flower of the former single kinde consisting but of two rowes of short leaues most vsually, and both of an equall height aboue the huske, abiding a pretty time in flower, especially if it stand in any shadowed place, or where the Sun may come but a while vnto it.

5. *Primula veris Hesketi flore multiplici separatim diuiso.*
Master Heskets double Primrose.

Master Heskets double Primrose is very like vnto the small double Primrose, both in leafe, roote, and heigth of growing, the stalke not rising much higher then it, but bearing flowers in a farre different manner; for this beareth not only single flowers vpon seuerall stalkes, but somtimes two or three single flowers vpon one staik, and also at the same time a bigger stalke, and somewhat higher, hauing one greene huske at the toppe thereof, sometimes broken on the one side, and sometimes whole, in the middle whereof standeth sometimes diuers single flowers, thrust together, euery flower to be seene in his proper forme, and sometimes there appeare with some whole flowers others that are but parts of flowers, as if the flowers were broken in peeces, and thrust into one huske, the leaues of the flowers (being of a white or pale Primrose colour, but a little deeper) seldome rising aboue the height of the very huske it selfe; and sometimes as I haue obserued in this plant, it will haue vpon the same stalke, that beareth such flowers as I haue here described vnto you, a small flower or two, making the stalke seeme branched into many flowers, whereby you may perceiue, that it will vary into many formes, not abiding constant in any yeare, as all the other sorts doe.

6. *Primula hortensis flore pleno vulgaris.* The ordinary double Primrose.

The leaues of this Primrose are very large, and like vnto the single kind, but somewhat larger, because it groweth in gardens: the flowers doe stand euery one seuerally vpon slender long footestalkes, as the single kinde doth, in greenish huskes of a pale yellow colour, like vnto the field Primrose, but very thicke and double, and of the same sweete sent with them.

7. *Primula veris flore duplici.* The small double Primrose.

This Primrose is both in leafe, roote, and flower, altogether like vnto the last double Primrose, but that it is smaller in all things; for the flower riseth not aboue two or three fingers high, and but twice double, that is, with two rowes of leaues, yet of the very same Primrose colour that the former is of.

8. *Paralysis vulgaris pratensis flore flauo simplici odorato.*
The Common field Cowslip.

The common fielde Cowslip I might well forbeare to set downe, being so plentifull in the fields: but because many rake delight in it, and plant it in their gardens, I will giue you the description of it here. It hath diuers green leaues, very like vnto the wilde Primrose, but shorter, rounder, stiffer, rougher, more crumpled about the edges, and of a sadder greene colour, euery one standing vpon his stalke, which is an inch or two long: among the leaues rise vp diuers round stalkes, a foote or more high, bearing at the toppe many faire yellow single flowers, with spots of a deeper yellow, at the buttome of each leafe, smelling very sweete. The rootes are like to the other Primroses, hauing many fibres annexed to the great roote.

9. *Paralysis altera odorata flore pallido polyanthos.* The Primrose Cowslip.

The leaues of this Cowslip are larger then the ordinary fielde Cowslip, and of a darke yellowish greene colour: the flowers are many standing together, vpon the toppes of the stalkes, to the number of thirty sometimes vpon one stalke, as I haue counted them in mine owne Garden, and sometimes more, euery one hauing a longer

foote

foote ftalke then the former, and of as pale a yellowifh colour almoft as the fielde Primrofe, with yellow fpots at the bottome of the leaues, as the ordinary hath, and of as fweet a fent.

10. *Paralyfis flore viridante fimplici.* The fingle greene Cowflip.

There is little difference in leafe or roote of this from the firft Cowflip, the chiefeft varietie in this kinde is this, that the leaues are fomewhat greener, and the flowers being in all refpects like in forme vnto the firft kinde, but fomewhat larger, are of the fame colour with the greene huskes, or rather a little yellower, and of a very fmall fent; in all other things I finde no diuerfitie, but that it ftandeth much longer in flower before it fadeth, efpecially if it ftand out of the Sunne.

11. *Paralyfis flore & calice crifpo.* Curl'd Cowflips or Gallegaskins.

There is another kinde, whofe flowers are folded or crumpled at the edges, and the huskes of the flowers bigger than any of the former, more fwelling out in the middle, as it were ribbes, and crumpled on the fides of the huskes, which doe fomewhat refemble mens hofe that they did weare, and tooke the name of Gallegaskins from thence.

12. *Paralyfis flore geminato odorato.*
Double Cowflips one within another, or Hofe in Hofe.

The only difference of this kinde from the ordinary field Cowflip is, that it beareth one fingle flower out of another, which is as a greene huske, of the like fent that the firft hath, or fomewhat weaker

13. *Paralyfis flore flauo fimplici inodoro abfque calicibus.* Single Oxe lippes.

This kinde of Cowflip hath leaues much like the ordinary kinde, but fomewhat fmaller: the flowers are yellow like the Cowflip, but fmaller, ftanding many vpon a ftalke, but bare or naked, that is, without any huske to containe them, hauing but little or no fent at all; not differing in any thing elfe from the ordinary Cowflip.

14. *Paralyfis flore geminato inodora.* Double Oxelips Hofe in Hofe.

As the former double Cowflip had his flowers one within another, in the very like manner hath this kinde of Cowflip or Oxelippe, fauing that this hath no huske to containe them, no more then the former fingle Oxelippe hath, ftanding bare or naked, of the very fame bigneffe each of them, and of the fame deepe yellow colour with it, hauing as fmall a fent as the former likewife.

Wee haue another of this kinde, whofe leaues are fomewhat larger, and fo are the *Flore pallidiore* flowers alfo, but of a paler yellow colour.

15. *Paralyfis inodora calicibus diffectis.* Oxelips with iagged huskes.

This kinde differeth not from the firft Oxelip in the fmalneffe of the greene leaues, but in the flower, which ftanding many together on a reafonable high ftalke, and being very fmall and yellow, fcarce opening themfelues or layde abroade as it, hath a greene huske vnder each flower, but diuided into fixe feuerall fmall long peeces.

16. *Paralyfis flore fatuo.* The Franticke, or Foolifh Cowflip:
Or Iacke an apes on horfe backe.

Wee haue in our gardens another kinde, not much differing in leaues from the former Cowflip, and is called Fantafticke or Foolifh, becaufe it beareth at the toppe of the ftalke a bufh or tuft of fmall long greene leaues, with fome yellow leaues, as it were peeces of flowers broken, and ftanding among the greene leaues. And fometimes

X 3   fome some stalkes among those greene leaues at the toppe (which are a little larger then when it hath but broken peeces of flowers) doe carry whole flowers in huskes like the single kinde.

17. *Paralysis minor flore rubro.* Red Birds eyes.

This little Cowslippe(which will hardly endure in our gardens, for all the care and industrie we can vse to keepe it) hath all the Winter long, and vntill the Spring begin to come on, his leaues so closed together, that it seemeth a small white head of leaues, which afterwards opening it selfe, spreadeth round vpon the ground, and hath small long and narrow leaues, snipt about the edges, of a pale greene colour on the vpper-side,& very white or mealy vnderneath, among these leaues rise vp one or two stalks, small & hoary,halfe a foot high,bearing at the top a bush or tuft of much smaller flow-ers,standing vpon short foot stalkes, somewhat like vnto Cowslips,but more like vnto the Beares eares,of a fine reddish purple colour, in some deeper,in others paler, with a yellowish circle in the bottomes of the flowers,like vnto many of the Beares eares, of a faint or small sent : the seede is smaller than in any of the former kindes, and so are the rootes likewise,being small,white and thready.

18. *Paralysis minor flore albo.* White Birds eyes.

This kinde differeth very little or nothing from the former, sauing that it seemeth a little larger both in leafe and flower, and that the flowers hereof are wholly white, without any great appearance of any circle in the bottome of them, vnlesse it be well obserued, or at least being nothing so conspicuous, as in the former.

Flore geminato. These two kindes haue sometimes, but very seldome, from among the middle of the flowers on the stalke,sent out another small stalke,bearing flowers theron likewise.

19. *Paralysis hortensis flore pleno.* Double Paigles or Cowslips.

The double Paigle or Cowslip hath smaller and darker greene leaues then the sin-gle kinde hath, and longer stalkes also whereon the leaues doe stand : it beareth diuers flowers vpon a stalke, but not so many as the single kinde, euery one whereof is of a deeper and fairer yellow colour then any of the former, standing not much aboue the brimmes of the huskes that hold them, consisting of two or three rowes of leaues set round together, which maketh it shew very thicke and double, of a prettie small sent, but not heady.

20. *Paralysis flore viridante pleno.* Double greene Cowslips.

This double greene Cowslip is so like vnto the single greene kinde formerly ex-pressed, that vntill they be neare flowring, they can hardly be distinguished: but when it is in flower, it hath large double flowers, of the same yellowish greene colour with the single, and more laid open then the former double Paigle.

21. *Paralysis flore viridante siue calamistrato.*
The greene Rose Cowslip, or double greene feathered Cowslip.

There is small difference in the leaues of this double kinde from the last, but that they are not of so darke a greene : the chiefest difference consisteth in the flowers, which are many, standing together at the toppes of the stalkes, but farre differing from all other of these kindes : for euery flower standing vpon his owne stalke, is composed of many very small and narrow leaues, without any huske to containe them, but spreading open like a little Rose,of a pale yellowish greene colour , and without any sent at all, abiding in flower, especially if it stand in a shadowie place out of the sunne, aboue two moneths, almost in as perfect beauty, as in the first weeke.

The Place.
All these kindes as they haue beene found wilde, growing in diuers places
in

in England, so they haue been transplanted into Gardens, to be there nourished for the delight of their louers, where they all abide, and grow fairer
then in their naturall places, except the small Birds eyes, which will (as I
said) hardly abide any culture, but groweth plentifully in all the North
Countries, in their squally or wet grounds.

The Time.

These doe all flower in the Spring of the yeare, some earlier and some
later, and some in the midst of Winter, as they are defended from the colds
and frosts, and the mildnesse of the time will permit : yet the Cowslips doe
alwayes flower later then the Primroses, and both the single and double
greene Cowslips latest, as I said in their descriptions, and abide much after
all the rest.

The Names.

All these plants are called most vsually in Latine, *Primula veris, Primula
pratenses,* and *Primula siluarum,* because they shew by their flowring the new
Spring to bee comming on, they being as it were the first Embassadours
thereof. They haue also diuers other names, as *Herba Paralysis, Arthritica,
Herba Sancti Petri, Claues Sancti Petri, Verbasculum odoratum, Lunaria arthritica, Phlomis, Alisma siluarum,* and *Alismatis alterum genus,* as Fabius Columna calleth them. The Birds eyes are called of Lobel in Latine, *Paralytica Alpina, Sanicula angustifolia,* making a greater and a lesser. Others call
them *Sanicula angustifolia,* but generally they are called *Primula veris minor.*
I haue (as you see) placed them with the Cowslips, putting a difference betweene Primroses and Cowslips. And some haue distinguished them, by
calling the Cowslips, *Primula veris Elatior,* that is, the Taller Primrose, and
the other *Humilis,* Lowe or Dwarfe Primroses. In English they haue in like
manner diuers names, according to seuerall Countries, as Primroses, Cowslips, Oxelips, Palsieworts, and Petty Mulleins. The first kindes, which are
lower then the rest, are generally called by the name of Primroses (as I
thinke) throughout England. The other are diuersly named ; for in some
Countries they call them Paigles, or Palsieworts, or Petty Mulleins, which
are called Cowslips in others. Those are vsually called Oxelips, whose
flowers are naked, or bare without huskes to containe them, being not so
sweete as the Cowslip, yet haue they some little sent, although the Latine
name doth make them to haue none. The Franticke, Fantasticke, or Foolish
Cowslip, in some places is called by Country people, Iacke an Apes on
horse-backe, which is an vsuall name with them, giuen to many other
plants, as Daisies, Marigolds, &c. if they be strange or fantasticall, differing in the forme from the ordinary kinde of the single ones. The smallest
are vsually called through all the North Country, Birds eyen, because of
the small yellow circle in the bottomes of the flowers, resembling the eye
of a bird.

The Vertues.

Primroses and Cowslips are in a manner wholly vsed in Cephalicall diseases, either among other herbes or flowers, or of themselues alone, to ease
paines in the head, and is accounted next vnto Betony, the best for that purpose. Experience likewise hath shewed, that they are profitable both for
the Palsie, and paines of the ioynts, euen as the Beares eares are, which
hath caused the names of *Arthritica, Paralysis,* and *Paralytica,* to bee giuen
them. The iuice of the flowers is commended to cleanse the spots or marks
of the face, whereof some Gentlewomen haue found good experience.

CHAP.

Chap. XXXVI.

Pulmonaria. Lungwort, or Cowslips of Ierusalem.

ALthough these plants are generally more vsed as Pot-herbes for the Kitchen, then as flowers for delight, yet because they are both called Cowslips, and are of like forme, but of much lesse beauty, I haue ioyned them next vnto them, in a distinct Chapter by themselues, and so may passe at this time.

1. *Pulmonaria maculosa.* Common spotted Cowslips of Ierusalem.

The Cowslip of Ierusalem hath many rough, large, and round leaues, but pointed at the ends, standing vpon long foot stalkes, spotted with many round white spots on the vppersides of the sad greene or browne leaues, and of a grayer greene vnderneath : among the leaues spring vp diuers browne stalkes, a foote high, bearing many flowers at the toppe, very neare resembling the flowers of Cowslips, being of a purple or reddish colour while they are buds, and of a darke blewish colour when they are blowne, standing in brownish greene huskes, and sometimes it hath beene found with white flowers : when the flowers are past, there come vp small round heads, containing blacke seed : the roote is composed of many long and thicke blacke strings.

2. *Pulmonaria altera non maculosa.* Vnspotted Cowslips of Ierusalem.

The leaues of this other kinde are not much vnlike the former, being rough as they are, but smaller, of a fairer greene colour aboue, and of a whiter greene vnderneath, without any spots at all vpon the leaues : the flowers also are like the former, and of the same colour, but a little more branched vpon the stalkes then the former : the rootes also are blacke like vnto them.

3. *Pulmonaria angustifolia.* Narrow leafed Cowslips of Ierusalem.

The leaues hereof are somewhat longer, but not so broad, and spotted with whitish spots also as the former : the stalke hereof is set with the like long hairy leaues, but smaller, being a foote high or better, bearing at the toppe many flowers, standing in huskes like the first, being somewhat reddish in the bud, and of a darke purplish blew colour when they are blowne open : the seede is like the former, all of them doe well resemble Buglosse and Comfrey in most parts, except the roote, which is not like them, but stringie, like vnto Cowslips, yet blacke.

The Place.

The Cowslips of Ierusalem grow naturally in the Woods of Germany, in diuers places, and the first kinde in England also, found out by Iohn Goodier, a great searcher and louer of plants, dwelling at Maple-durham in Hampshire.

The Time.

They flower for the most part very early, that is, in the beginning of Aprill.

The Names.

They are generally called in Latine, *Pulmonaria*, and *maculosa*, or *non maculosa*, is added for distinctions sake. Of some it is called *Symphitum maculosum*, that is, spotted Comfrey. In English it is diuersly called ; as spotted Cowslips of Ierusalem, Sage of Ierusalem, Sage of Bethlehem, Lungwort,
and

and spotted Comfrey, and it might bee as fitly called spotted Buglosse, whereunto it is as like as vnto Comfrey, as I said before.

The Vertues.

It is much commended of some, to bee singular good for vlcered lungs, that are full of rotten matter. As also for them that spit bloud, being boyled and drunke. It is of greatest vse for the pot, being generally held to be good, both for the lungs and the heart.

Chap. XXXVII.

1. *Buglossum & Borrago*. Buglosse and Borage.

Lthough Borage and Buglosse might as fitly haue been placed, I confesse, in the Kitchen Garden, in regard they are wholly in a manner spent for Physicall properties, or for the Pot, yet because anciently they haue been entertained into Gardens of pleasure, their flowers hauing been in some respect, in that they haue alwaies been enterposed among the flowers of womens needle-worke, I am more willing to giue them place here, then thrust them into obscurity, and take such of their tribe with them also as may fit for this place, either for beauty or rarity.

The Garden Buglosse and Borage are so well knowne vnto all, that I shall (I doubt) but spend time in waste to describe them; yet not vsing to passe ouer any thing I name and appropriate to this Garden so sleightly, they are thus to bee knowne : Buglosse hath many long, narrow, hairy, or rough sad greene leaues, among which rise vp two or three very high stalks, branched at the top, whereon stand many blew flowers, consisting of fiue small round pointed leaues, with a small pointell in the middle, which are very smooth, shining, and of a reddish purple while they are buds, and not blowne open, which being fallen, there groweth in the greene huske, wherein the flower stood, three or foure roundish blacke seedes, hauing that thread or pointell standing still in the middle of them : the roote is blacke without, and whitish within, long, thicke, and full of slimie iuice (as the leaues are also) and perisheth not euery yeare, as the roote of Borage doth.

2. *Borrago*. Borage.

Borage hath broader, shorter, greener, and rougher leaues then Buglosse, the stalkes hereof are not so high, but branched into many parts, whereon stand larger flowers, and more pointed at the end then Buglosse, and of a paler blew colour for the most part (yet sometimes the flowers are reddish, and sometimes pure white) each of the flowers consisting of fiue leaues, standing in a round hairy whitish huske, diuided into fiue parts, and haue a small vmbone of fiue blackish threads in the middle, standing out pointed at the end, and broad at the bottome : the seed is like the other : the root is thicker and shorter then the roote of Buglosse, somewhat blackish without also, and whitish within, and perisheth after seede time, but riseth of it owne seede fallen, and springeth in the beginning of the yeare.

3. *Borrago semper virens*. Euerliuing Borage.

Euerliuing Borage hath many broad greene leaues, and somewhat rough, more resembling Comfrey then Borage, yet not so large as either ; the stalkes are not so high as Borage, and haue many small blew flowers on them, very like to the flowers of Buglosse for the forme, and Borage for the colour : the rootes are blacke, thicker then either of them, somewhat more spreading, and not perishing, hauing greene leaues all the Winter long, and thereupon tooke his name.

4. *Anchusa.*

4. *Anchusa.* Sea Buglosse or Alkanet.

The Sea Buglosse or Alkanet hath many long, rough, narrow, and darke greene leaues, spread vpon the ground (yet some that growe by the Sea side are rather hoarie and whitish) among these leaues riseth vp a stalke, spread at the toppe into many branches, whereon stand the flowers in tufts, like vnto the Garden Buglosse, or rather Comfrey, but lesser; in some plants of a reddish blew colour, and in others more red or purplish, and in others of a yellowish colour: after which come the seedes, very like vnto Buglosse, but somewhat longer and paler: the roote of most of them being transplanted, are somewhat blackish on the outside, vntill the later end of Summer, and then become more red: for those that grow wilde, will be then so red, that they will giue a very deepe red colour to those that handle them, which being dryed keepe that red colour, which is vsed to many purposes; the roote within being white, and hauing no red colour at all.

5. *Limonium Rauwolfy.* Marsh Buglosse.

This Limonium (which I referre here to the kindes of Buglosse, as presuming it is the fittest place where to insert it)hath many long, narrow, and somewhat rough leaues lying vpon the ground, waued or cut in on both sides, like an Indenture, somewhat like the leaues of Ceterach or Miltwast, among which rise vp two or three stalkes, somewhat rough also, and with thin skinnes like wings, indented on both sides thereof also, like the leaues, hauing three small, long, rough, and three square leaues at euery ioynt where it brancheth forth; at the toppe whereof stand many flowers vpon their foote stalkes, in such a manner, as is not seene in any other plant, that I know : for although that some of the small winged foot stalkes are shorter, and some longer, standing as it were flatwise, or all on one side, and not round like an vmbell, yet are they euen at the toppe, and not one higher than another ; each of which small foote stalkes doe beare foure or fiue greenish heads or huskes, ioyned together, out of each of which doe arise other pale or bleake blew stiffe huskes, as if they were flowers, made as it were of parchment, which hold their colour after they are dry a long time ; and out of these huskes likewise, doe come (at seuerall times one after another, and not all at one time or together) white flowers, consisting of fiue small round leaues, with some white threds in the middle : after these flowers are past, there come in their places small long seede, inclosed in many huskes, many of those heads being idle, not yeelding any good seede, but chaffe, especially in our Countrey, for the want of sufficient heate of the Sunne, as I take it : the roote is small, long, and blackish on the outside, and perisheth at the first approach of Winter.

The Place.

Borage and Buglosse grow onely in Gardens with vs, and so doth the *Semper virens*, his originall being vnknowne vnto vs. Alkanet or Sea Buglosse groweth neare the Sea, in many places of France, and Spaine, and some of the kindes also in England. But the Limonium or Marshe Buglosse groweth in Cales, and Malacca in Spaine, and is found also in Syria, as Rauwolfius relateth : and in other places also no doubt ; for it hath beene sent vs out of Italie, many yeares before eyther Guillaume Boel found it in Cales, or Clusius in Malacca.

The Time.

Borage and Buglosse doe flower in Iune, and Iuly, and sometimes sooner, and so doth the euer-liuing or neuer dying Borage, but not as Gerrard saith, flowring Winter and Summer, whereupon it should take his name, but leaueth flowring in Autumne, and abideth greene with his leaues all the Winter,

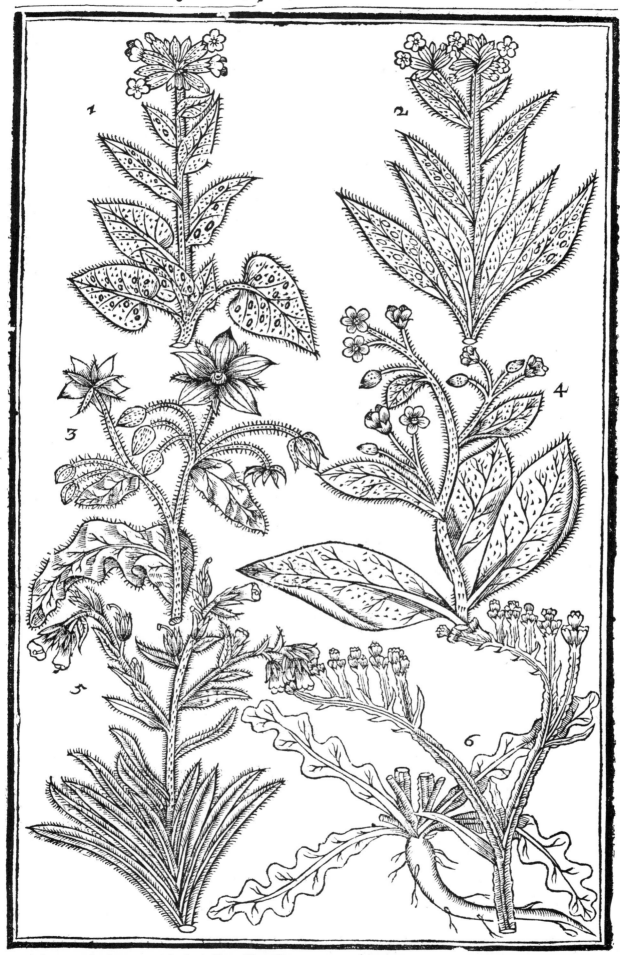

1 *Pulmonaria latifolia maculosa.* Cowslips of Ierusalem. 2 *Pulmonaria angustifolia.* Narrow leafed Cowslips of Ierusalem. 3 *Borrago.* Borage. 4 *Borrago semper virens.* Euerliuing Borage. 5 *Anchusa.* Sea Buglosse or Alkanet. 6 *Limonium Rauwolsij.* Marsh Buglosse.

ter, flowring the next Spring following. The other flower not vntill Iuly, and so continue, especially the Marshe Buglosse vntill September bee well spent, and then giueth seede, if early frosts ouertake it not; for it seldome commeth to be ripe.

The Names.

Our ordinary Borage by the consent of all the best moderne Writers, is the true *Buglossum* of Dioscorides, and that our Buglosse was vnknowne to the ancients. The *Borago semper virens*, Lobel calleth *Buglossum semper virens*, that is, Euer-liuing, or greene Buglosse : but it more resembleth Borage then Buglosse ; yet because Buglosse abideth greene, to auoyde that there should not be two *Buglossa semper virentia*, I had rather call it Borage then Buglosse. Anchusa hath diuers names, as Dioscorides setteth downe. And some doe call it *Fucus herba*, from the Greeke word, because the roote giuing so deepe a colour, was vsed to dye or paint the skinne. Others call it *Buglossum Hispanicum*, in English Alkanet, and of some Orchanet, after the French. Limonium was found by Leonhartus Rauwolfius, neere vnto Ioppa, which he setteth downe in the second Chapter of the third booke of his trauayles, and from him first knowne to these parts : I haue, as you see, referred it to the kindes of Buglosse, for that the flowers haue some resemblance vnto them, although I know that *Limonium genuinum* is referred to the Beetes. Let it therefore here finde a place of residence, vntill you or I can finde a fitter ; and call it as you thinke best, eyther Limonium as Rauwolfius doth, or Marshe Buglosse as I doe, or if you can adde a more proper name, I shall not be offended.

The Vertues.

Borage and Buglosse are held to bee both temperate herbes, beeing vsed both in the pot and in drinkes that are cordiall, especially the flowers, which of Gentlewomen are candid for comfitts. The Alkanet is drying, and held to be good for wounds, and if a peece of the roote be put into a little oyle of Peter or Petroleum, it giueth as deepe a colour to the oyle, as the Hypericon doth or can to his oyle, and accounted to be singular good for a cut or greene wound.

The Limonium hath no vse that wee know, more then for a Garden; yet as Rauwolfius saith, the Syrians vse the leaues as sallats at the Table.

Chap. XXXVIII.

Lychnis. Campions.

THere bee diuers sorts of Campions, as well tame as wilde, and although some of them that I shall here entreate of, may peraduenture be found wilde in our owne Countrey, yet in regard of their beautifull flowers, they are to bee respected, and noursed vp with the rest, to furnish a garden of pleasure; as for the wilde kindes, I will leaue them for another discourse.

1. *Lychnis Coronaria rubra simplex.* The single red Rose Campion.

The single red Rose Campion hath diuers thicke, hoary, or woolly long greene leaues, abiding greene all the winter, and in the end of the spring or beginning of summer, shooteth forth two or three hard round woolly stalkes, with some ioynts thereon, and at euery ioynt two such like hoary greene leaues as those below, but smaller, diuersly branched at the toppe, hauing one flower vpon each seuerall long foot stalke, consisting confifting of fiue leaues, fomewhat broade and round pointed, of a perfect red crimfon colour, ftanding out of a hard long round huske, ridged or crefted in foure or fiue places ; after the flowers are fallen there come vp round hard heads, wherein is contained fmall blackifh feed : the roote is fmall, long and wooddy, with many fibres annexed vnto it, and fhooteth forth anew oftentimes, yet perifheth often alfo.

2. *Lychnis Coronaria alba fimplex.* The white Rofe Campion.

The white Rofe Campion is in all things like the red, but in the colour of the flower, which in this is of a pure white colour.

3. *Lichnis Coronaria albefcens fiue incarnata maculata & non maculata.* The blufh Rofe Campion fpotted and not fpotted.

Like vnto the former alfo are thefe other forts, hauing no other difference to diftinguifh them, but the flowers, which are of a pale or bleake whitifh blufh colour, efpecially about the brims, as if a very little red were mixed with a great deale of white, the middle of the flower being more white ; the one being fpotted all ouer the flower, with fmall fpots and ftreakes, the other not hauing any fpot at all.

4. *Lychnis Coronaria rubra multiplex.* The double red Rofe Campion.

The double red Rofe Campion is in all refpects like vnto the fingle red kinde, but that this beareth double flowers, confifting of two or three rowes of leaues at the moft, which are not fo large as the fingle, and the whole plant is more tender, that is, more apt to perifh, then any of the fingle kindes.

5. *Lychnis Chalcedonica flore fimplici miniato.* Single Nonefuch, or Flower of Briftow, or Conftantinople.

This Campion of Conftantinople hath many broad and long greene leaues, among which rife vp fundry ftiffe round hairy ioynted ftalks three foot high, with two leaues euery ioynt : the flowers ftand at the toppes of them, very many together, in a large tuft or vmbell, confifting of fiue fmall long leaues, broade pointed, and notched-in in the middle, of a bright red orenge colour, which being paft, there come in their places fmall hard whitifh heads or feede veffels, containing blacke feede, like vnto the feede of fweet Williams, and hauing but a fmall fent ; the roote is very ftringie, faftening it felfe very ftrongly in the ground, whereby it is much encreafed.

Of the fingle kinde there is alfo two or three other forts, differing chiefly in the co- *Flore albo.* lour of the flowers. The one is pure white. Another is of a blufh colour wholly, *Et carneo.* without variation. And a third is very variable ; for at the firft it is of a pale red, and *Verficolor.* after a while groweth paler, vntill in the end it become almoft fully white ; and all thefe diuerfities of the flowers are fometimes to bee feene on one ftalke at one and the fame time.

6. *Lychnis Chalcedonica flore miniato pleno.* Double Flower of Briftow, or Nonefuch.

This glorious flower being as rare as it is beautifull, is for rootes beeing ftringie, for leaues and ftalkes being hairy and high, and for the flowers growing in tufts, altogether like the firft fingle kinde : but herein confifteth the chiefeft difference, that this beareth a larger vmbell or tuft of flowers at the toppe of the ftalke, euery flower confifting of three or foure rowes of leaues, of a deeper orenge colour then it, which addeth the more grace vnto it, but paffeth away without bearing feede, as moft other double flowers doe, yet recompenceth that defect with encreafe from the roote.

7. *Lychnis plumaria filuefiris fimplex & multiplex.* The featherd wilde Campion fingle and double.

The leaues of this wilde Campion are fomewhat like the ordinary white wilde

Campion, but not fo large, or rather refembling the leaues of fweete Williams, but that they grow not fo clofe, nor fo many together : the ftalkes haue fmaller leaues at the ioynts then thofe belowe, and branched at the toppe, with many pale, but bright red flowers, iagged or cut in on the edges, like the feathered Pinke, whereof fome haue taken it to be a kinde, and fome for a kinde of wilde William, but yet is but a wilde Campion, as may be obferued, both by his huske that beareth the flowers, and by the grayifh roundifh feede, being not of the Family of Pinkes and Gillowers, but (as I faid) of the Campions : the roote is full of ftrings or fibres.

flore pleno　　The double kinde is very like vnto the fingle kinde, but that it is lower and fmaller, and the flowers very double.

8. *Lychnis filueftris flore pleno rubro.* Red Batchelours buttons.

The double wilde Campion (which of our Countrey Gentlewomen is called Batchelours buttons) is very like both in rootes, leaues, ftalkes, and flowers vnto the ordinary wilde red Campion, but fomewhat leffer, his flowers are not iagged, but fmooth, and very thicke and double, fo that moft commonly it breaketh his fhort huske, wherein the flower ftandeth on the one fide, feldome hauing a whole huske, and are of a reddifh colour.

9. *Lychnis filueftris flore albo pleno.* White Batchelours buttons.

As the leaues of the former double Campion was like vnto the fingle kinde that had red flowers, fo this hath his leaues like vnto the fingle white kinde, differing in no other thing from it, but in the doubleneffe of the flowers, which by reafon of the multiplicity of leaues in them thrufting forth together, breaketh his huskes wherein the flowers doe ftand, as the other doth, and hath fcarce one flower in many that is whole.

10. *Ocymoides arborea femper virens.* Strange Baffil Campion.

This Strange Campion (for thereunto it muft bee referred) fhooteth forth many round, whitifh, wooddy, but brittle ftalkes, whereon ftand diuers long, and fomewhat thicke leaues, fet by couples, narrow at the bottome, and broader toward the point, of a very faire greene and fhining colour, fo that there is more beauty in the greene leaues, which doe fo alwaies abide, then in the flowers, which are of a pale red or blufh colour, confifting of fiue fmall long broad pointed leaues, notched in the middle, which doe not lye clofe, but loofly as it were hanging ouer the huskes : after the flowers are paft, there come heads that containe blackifh feede : the roote is fmall, hard, white, and threadie.

11. *Mufcipula Lobely fiue Ben rubrum Monfpelienfium.* Lobels Catch Flie.

I muft needes infert this fmall plant, to finifh this part of the Campions, whereunto it belongeth, being a pretty toye to furnifh and decke out a Garden. It fpringeth vp (if it haue beene once fowne and fuffered to fhed) in the later end of the yeare moft commonly, or elfe in the Spring with fiue or fix fmall leaues, very like vnto the leaues of Pinkes, and of the fame grayifh colour, but a little broader and fhorter, and when it beginneth to fhoote vp for flower, it beareth fmaller leaues on the clammy or vifcous ftalkes (fit to hold any fmall thing that lighteth on it) being broad at the bottome compaffing them, and ftanding two at a ioynt one againft another : the toppes of the ftalkes are diuerfly branched into feuerall parts, euery branch hauing diuers fmall red flowers, not notched, but fmooth, ftanding out of fmall, long, round, ftript huskes, which after the flowers are paft, containe fmall grayifh feede : the roote is fmall, and perifheth after it hath giuen feede; but rifeth (as is before faid) of its owne feede, if it be fuffered to fhed.

The Place.

The Rofe Campions, Flowers of Briftow, or None fuch, the Baffil Campion,

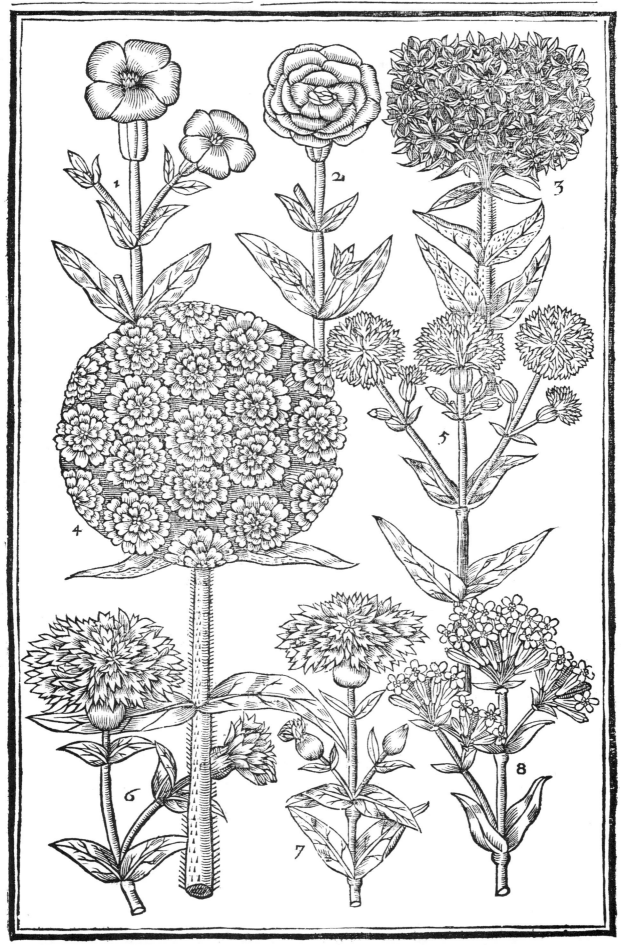

1 *Lychnis Coronaria simplex.* Single Rose Campion. 2 *Lychnis Coronaria rubra multiplex.* The double red Rose Campion. 3 *Lychnis Chalcedonica simplex.* Single None such, or flower of Bristow. 4 *Lychnis Chalcedonica flore pleno* Double None such, or flower of Bristow. 5 *Lychnis plumaria multiplex.* Pleasant in sight. 6 *Lychnis silvestris flore pleno rubro.* Red Batchelours Buttons. 7 *Lychnis silvestris flore pleno albo.* White Batchelours Buttons. 8 *Muscipula Lobelij.* Lobels Catch Flie.

pion, and the Catch Flie, haue been sent vs from beyond the Seas, and are onely noursed vp in Gardens with vs; the other Campions that are double, haue been naturally so found double wilde (for no art or industry of man, that euer I could be assured of to be true, be it by neuer so many repetitions of transplantations, and planeticall obseruations (as I haue said in he beginning of this worke) could bring any flower, single by nature, to become double, notwithstanding many affirmations to that purpose, but whatsoeuer hath been found wilde to be double, nature her selfe, and not art hath so produced it) and being brought into Gardens, are there encreased by slipping, and parting the roote, because they giue no seede.

The Time.

All of them doe flower in the Summer, yet none before May.

The Names.

The first kindes are called *Lychnides satiuæ*, and *coronariæ*, in English generally Rose Campions. The next is called *Lychnis Chalcedonica*, and *Byzantina*; in English, of some Nonesuch, and of others Flower of Bristow, and after the Latine, Flower of Constantinople, because it is thought the seede was first brought from thence; but from whence the double of this kinde came, we cannot tell. The names of the others of this kinde, both single and double, are set downe with their descriptions. The feathered Campions are called *Armoraria pratensis*, and *Flos Cuculi*, and of Clusius and others thought to be *Odontitis Plinij*. Some call them in English Crowflowers, and Cuckowe-Flowers; and some call the double hereof, The faire Maide of France. The Bassil Campions were sent ouer among many other seedes out of Italy, by the name of *Ocimoides arborea semper virens*. *Arborea*, because the stalke is more wooddy and durable then other Campions: And *semper virens*, because the leaues abide greene Winter and Summer. Clusius calleth it *Lychnis semper virens*, because it is certainly a Campion. The last is diuersly called of Authors; Lobel calleth it *Muscipula*: Others *Armoraria altera*: Dodonæus *Armerius flos quartus*. Clusius *Lychnis silaestris altera*, in his Spanish obseruations, and *prima* in his History of plants, and saith, the learned of Salmantica in Spaine called it, *Ben rubrum*, as Lobel saith, they of Mompelier doe also: and by that name I receiued it first out of Italy. It hath the name of Catch Flie, of *Muscipula* the Latine word, because the stalkes in the hot Summer dayes haue a certaine viscous or clammy humour vpon them, whereby it easily holdeth (as I said before) whatsoeuer small thing, as Flies, &c. lighteth vpon it.

The Vertues.

We know none in these dayes, that putteth any of these to any Physicall vse, although some haue in former times.

Chap. XXXIX.

Keiri siue Leucoium luteum. Wall-flowers, or Wall Gilloflowers.

There are two sorts of Wall-flowers, the one single, the other double, and of each of them there is likewise some differences, as shall be shewed in their descriptions.

1. *Keiri ſiue Leucoium luteum ſimplex vulgare.* Common ſingle Wall-flowers.

The common ſingle Wall-flower which groweth wilde abroad, and yet is brought into Gardens, hath ſundry ſmall, narrow, long, and darke greene leaues, ſet without order vpon ſmall round whitiſh wooddy ſtalkes, which beare at the tops diuers ſingle yellow flowers one aboue another, euery one hauing foure leaues a peece, and of a very ſweete ſent: after which come long pods, containing reddiſh ſeede: the roote is white, hard and thready.

2. *Keiri ſiue Leucoium luteum ſimplex maius.* The great ſingle Wall flower.

There is another ſort of ſingle Wall flower, whoſe leaues as well as flowers are much larger then the former: the leaues being of a darker and ſhining greene colour, and the flowers of a very deepe gold yellow colour, and vſually broader then a twentie ſhilling peece of gold can couer: the ſpike or toppe of flowers alſo much longer, and abiding longer in flower, and much ſweeter likewiſe in ſent: the pods for ſeede are thicker and ſhorter, with a ſmall point at the end: this is flower to encreaſe into branches, as alſo to be encreaſed by the branches, and more tender to be preſerued; for the hard froſts doe cauſe it to periſh, if it be not defended from them

3. *Keiri ſimplex flore albo.* White Wall-flower.

This Wall-flower hath his leaues as greene as the great kinde, but nothing ſo large: the flowers ſtand at the toppe, but not in ſo long a ſpike, and conſiſteth of foure leaues, of a very white colour, not much larger then the common kinde, and of a faint or weaker ſent: the pods are nothing ſo great as the former great one: this is more eaſie to be propagated and encreaſed alſo, but yet will require ſome care in defending it from the colds of the Winter.

4. *Keiri ſiue Leucoium luteum vulgare flore pleno.* Common double Wall-flowers.

This ordinary double Wall-flower is in leaues and ſtalke very like vnto the firſt ſingle kinde, but that the leaues hereof are not of ſo deepe a greene colour: the flowers ſtand at the top of the ſtalkes one aboue another, as it were a long ſpike, which flower by degrees, the loweſt firſt, and ſo vpwards, by which it is a long time in flowring, and is very double, of a gold yellow colour, and very ſweete.

5. *Keiri ſiue Leucoium luteum alterum flore pleno.* Pale double Wall-flowers.

Wee haue another ſort of this kinde of double Wall-flower, whoſe double flowers ſtand not ſpike-faſhion as the former, but more open ſpread, and doe all of them blowe open at one time almoſt, and not by degrees as the other doth, and is of a paler yellow colour, not differing in any thing elſe, except that the greene leaues hereof are of a little paler greene then it.

6. *Keiri ſiue Leucoium luteum maius flore pleno ferrugineo.*
Double red Wall-flowers.

We haue alſo another ſort of double Wall-flower, whoſe leaues are as greene, and almoſt as large as the great ſingle yellow kinde, or full as bigge as the leaues of the white Wall-flower: the flowers hereof are not much larger then the ordinary, but are of a darker yellow colour then the great ſingle kinde, and of a more browniſh or red colour on the vnderſide of the leaues, and is as it were ſtriped.

7. *Keiri ſiue Leucoium maximum luteum flore pleno.*
The greateſt double yellow Wall-flower.

This great double Wall-flower is as yet a ſtranger in England, and therefore what I
Y 3
here

here write is more vpon relation (which yet I beleeue to be moſt true) then vpon ſight and ſpeculation. The leaues of this Wall flower are as greene and as large, if not larger then the great ſingle kinde : the flowers alſo are of the ſame deepe gold yellow colour with it, but much larger then any of the former double kindes, and of as ſweet a ſent as any, which addeth delight vnto beauty.

The Place.

The firſt ſingle kind is often found growing vpon old wals of Churches, and other houſes in many places of England, and alſo among rubbiſh and ſtones. The ſingle white and great yellow, as well as all the other double kindes, are nourſed vp in Gardens onely with vs.

The Time.

All the ſingle kindes doe flower many times in the end of Autumne, and if the Winter be milde all the Winter long, but eſpecially in the moneths of February, March, and Aprill, and vntill the heate of the Spring doe ſpend them : but the other double kindes doe not continue flowring in that manner the yeare throughout, although very early ſometimes, and very late alſo in ſome places.

The Names.

They are called by diuers names, as _Viola lutea_, _Leucoium luteum_, and _Keiri_, or _Cheiri_, by which name it is chiefly knowne in our Apothecaries ſhops, becauſe there is an oyle made thereof called _Cheirinum :_ In Engliſh they are vſually called in theſe parts, Wall-flowers : Others doe call them Bee-flowers ; others Wall-Gilloflowers, Winter Gilloflowers, and yellow Stocke-Gilloflowers ; but we haue a kinde of Stocke-Gilloflower that more fitly deſerueth that name, as ſhall be ſhewed in the Chapter following

The Vertues.

The ſweetneſſe of the flowers cauſeth them to be generally vſed in Noſegayes, and to decke vp houſes ; but phyſically they are vſed in diuers manners : As a Conſerue made of the flowers, is vſed for a remedy both for the Appoplexie and Palſie. The diſtilled water helpeth well in the like manner. The oyle made of the flowers is heating and reſoluing, good to eaſe paines of ſtrained and pained ſinewes.

Chap. XL.

Leucoium. Stocke-Gilloflower.

THere are very many ſorts of Stocke-Gilloflowers both ſingle and double, ſome of the fields and mountaines, others of the Sea marſhes and medowes ; and ſome nourſed vp in Gardens, and there preſerued by ſeede or ſlippe, as each kinde is apteſt to bee ordered. But becauſe ſome of theſe are fitter for a generall Hiſtory then for this our Garden of Pleaſure, both for that diuers haue no good ſent, others little or no beauty, and to be entreated of onely for the variety, I ſhall ſpare ſo many of them as are not fit for this worke, and onely ſet downe the reſt.

1. _Leucoium ſimplex ſativum diuerſorum colorum._
Garden Stocke-Gilloflowers ſingle of diuers colours.

Theſe ſingle Stocke-Gilloflowers, although they differ in the colour of their flowers,

1 *Keiri ſiue Leucoium luteum vulgare.* Common Wall-flowers. 2 *Keiri ſiue Leucoium luteum maius ſimplex.* The great ſingle Wall flower. 3 *Keiri ſiue Leucoium luteum flore pleno vulgare.* Ordinary double Wall-flowers. 4 *Keiri maius flore pleno ferrugineo* The great double red Wall-flower. 5 *Leucoium ſativum ſimplex.* Single Stocke-Gilloflowers. 6 *Leucoium ſativum ſimplex flore ſtriato.* Single ſtript Stocke-Gilloflowers.

ers, yet are in leafe and manner of growing, one so like vnto another, that vntill they come to flower, the one cannot be well knowne that beareth red flowers, from another that beareth purple ; and therfore one defcription of the plant fhall ferue, with a declaration of the fundry colours of the flowers. It rifeth vp with round whitifh woody ftalkes, two, three, or foure foot high, whereon are fet many long, and not very broad, foft, and whitifh or grayifh greene leaues, fomewhat round pointed, and parted into diuers branches, at the toppes whereof grow many flowers, one aboue another, fmelling very fweet, confifting of foure fmall, long, and round pointed leaues, ftanding in fmall long huskes, which turne into long and flat pods, fometimes halfe a foote long, wherein is contained fl.t, round, reddifh feedes, with grayifh ringes or circles about them, lying flat all along the middle rib of the pod on both fides : the roote is long, white, and woody, fpreading diuers wayes. There is great variety in the colours of the flowers : for fome are wholly of a pure white colour, others of a moft excellent crimfon red colour, others againe of a faire red colour, but not fo bright or liuely as the other, fome alfo of a purplifh or violet colour, without any fpot, marke, or line in them at all. There are againe of all thefe colours, mixed very variably, as white mixed with fmall or great fpottes, ftrakes or lines of pure or bright red, or darke red, and white with purple fpots and lines ; and of eyther of them whofe flowers are almoft halfe white, and halfe red, or halfe white, and halfe purple. The red of both forts, and the purple alfo, in the like manner fpotted, ftriped, and marked with white, differing neyther in forme, nor fubftance, in any other point.

2. *Leucoium fatiuum albido luteum fimplex.*
The fingle pale yellow Stocke-Gilloflower.

There is very little difference in this kind from the former, for the manner of growing, or forme of leaues or flower. Only this hath greener leaues, and pale yellow almoft white flowers, in all other things alike : this is of no great regard, but only for rarity, and diuerfity from the reft.

3. *Leucoium Melancholicum.* The Melancholick Gentleman.

This wilde kinde of ftocke gilloflower hath larger, longer and greener leaues then any of the former kindes, vneuenly gafhed or finuated on both edges lying on the ground, and a little rough or hairy withall : from among which rife vp the ftalks, a yard high or more, and hairy likewife, bearing theron here and there fome fuch like leaues as are below, but fmaller, and at the top a great number of flowers, as large or larger then any of the former fingle kindes, made of 4. large leaues a peece alfo, ftanding in fuch like long huskes, but of a darke or fullen yellowifh colour : after which come long roundifh pods, wherein lye fomewhat long but rounder and greater feede then any ftocke gilloflower, and nearer both in pod and feede vnto the *Hefperis* or Dames Violet : this perifheth not vfually after feede bearing, although fometimes it doth.

4. *Leucoium marinum Syriacum.* Leuant ftocke gilloflowers.

This kind of ftocke gilloflower rifeth vp at the firft with diuers long and fomewhat broad leaues, a little vneuenly dented or waued on the edges, which fo continue the firft yeare after the fowing : the ftalke rifeth vp the next yeare to bee two foot high or more, bearing all thofe leaues on it that it firft had, which then do grow leffe finuated or waued then before : at the top whereof ftand many flowers, made of foure leaues a peece, of a delayed purple colour, but of a fmall fent which turne into very long and narrow flat pods, wherein are contained flat feed like the ordinary ftocke gilloflowers, but much larger and of a darke or blackifh browne colour : the root is white, and groweth deepe, fpreading in the ground, but growing woody when it is in feede, and perifheth afterwards.

5. *Leucoij alterum genus, flore tam multiplici quam simplici ex seminio oriundum.*
Another fort of Stocke gilloflowers bearing as well double
as fingle flowers from feede.

This kinde of Stocke gilloflower differeth neyther in forme of leaues, ftalkes, nor flowers from the former, but that it oftentimes groweth much larger and taller ; fo that whofoeuer fhall fee both thefe growing together, fhall fcarce difcerne the difference, onely it beareth flowers, eyther white, red or purple, wholly or entire, that is, of one colour, without mixture of other colour in them (for fo much as euer I haue obferued, or could vnderftand by others) which are eyther fingle, like vnto the former, or very thicke and double, like vnto the next that followeth ; but larger, and growing with more ftore of flowers on the long ftalke. But this you muft vnderftand withall, that thofe plants that beare double flowers, doe beare no feede at all, and is very feldome encreafed by flipping or cutting, as the next kinde of double is : but the onely way to haue double flowers any yeare, (for this kinde dyeth euery winter, for the moft part, after it hath borne flowers, and feldome is preferued) is to faue the feedes of thofe plants of this kinde that beare fingle flowers, for from that feede will rife, fome that will beare fingle, and fome double flowers, which cannot bee diftinguifhed one from another, I meane which will be fingle and which double, vntill you fee them in flower, or budde at the leaft. And this is the only way to preferue this kinde : but of the feed of the former kinde was neuer known any double flowers to arife, and therefore you muft be carefull to marke this kinde from the former.

6. *Leucoium flore pleno diuerforum colorum.*
Double Stocke Gillowflowers of diuers colours.

This other kinde of Stock gilloflower that beareth onely double flowers, groweth not fo great, nor fpreadeth his branches fo farre, nor are his leaues fo large, but is in all things fmaller, and lower, and yet is woody, or fhrubby, like the former, bearing his flowers in the like manner, many vpon a long ftalke, one aboue another, and very double, but not fo large as the former double, although it grow in fertile foyle, which are eyther white, or red, or purple wholly, without any mixture, or elfe mixed with fpots and ftripes, as the fingle flowers of the firft kinde, but more variably, and not in all places alike, neuer bearing feede, but muft be encreafed, only by the cutting of the young fproutes or branches, taken in a fit feafon : this kinde perifheth not, as the former double kinde doth, fo as it bee defended in the winter from the extreame frofts, but efpecially from the fnow falling, or at the leaft remaining vpon it.

7. *Leucoium fatiuum luteum flore pleno.*
The double yellow Stocke Gilloflower.

This double yellow Stock gilloflower is a ftranger in England, as far as I can learne, neyther haue I any further familiaritie with him, then by relation from Germany, where it is affirmed to grow only in fome of their gardens, that are curious louers of thefe delights, bearing long leaues fomewhat hoary or white, (and not greene like vnto the Wallflower, whereunto elfe it might be thought to be referred) like vnto the Stock gilloflowers, as the ftalkes and branches alfo are, and bearing faire double flowers, of a faire, but pale yellow colour. The whole plant is tender, as the double Stock gilloflowers are, and muft be carefully preferued in the winter from the coldes, or rather more then the laft double, left it perifh.

The Place.

The fingle kindes, efpecially fome of them, grow in Italie, and fome in Greece, Candy, and the Ifles adiacent, as may be gathered out of the verfes in Plutarches Booke *De Amore fraterno:*

Inter

Inter Echinopodas velut, asperam & inter Ononim,
Interdum crescunt mollia Leucoia.

Which sheweth, that the soft or gentle stocke gilloflowers doe sometimes grow among rough or prickely Furse and Cammocke. The other sorts are only to be found in gardens.

The Time.

They flower in a manner all the yeare throughout in some places, especially some of the single kindes, if they stand warme, and defended from the windes and cold : the double kindes flower sometimes in Aprill, and more plentifully in May, and Iune ; but the double of seed, flowreth vsually late, and keepeth flowring vnto the winter, that the frostes and colde mistes doe pull it downe.

The Names.

It is called *Leucoium, & Viola alba* : but the name Leucoium (which is in English the white Violet) is referred to diuers plants ; we call it in English generally, Stocke gilloflower, (or as others doe, Stocke gillouer) to put a difference betweene them, and the Gilloflowers and Carnations, which are quite of another kindred, as shall be shewne in place conuenient.

The Vertues.

These haue no great vse in Physick that I know : only some haue vsed the leaues of the single white flowred kinde with salt, to be laid to the wrests of them that haue agues, but with what good successe I cannot say, if it happen well I thinke in one (as many such things else will) it will fayle in a number.

Chap. XLI.

1. *Hesperis, siue Viola Matronalis.* Dames Violets,
or Queenes Gilloflowers.

THe ordinary Dames Violets, or Queene Gilloflowers, hath his leaues broader, greener, and sharper pointed, then the Stock gilloflowers, and a little endented about the edges : the stalkes grow two foot high, bearing many greene leaues vpon them, smaller then those at the bottome, and branched at the toppe, bearing many flowers, in fashion much like the flowers of stocke gilloflowers, consisting of foure leaues in like manner, but not so large, of a faint purplish colour in some, and in others white, and of a pretty sweet sent, especially towards night, but in the day time little or none at all : after the flowers are past, there doe come small long and round pods, wherein is contained, in two rowes, small and long blacke seede : the roote is wholly composed of stringes or fibres, which abide many yeares, and springeth fresh stalks euery yeare, the leaues abiding all the Winter.

2. *Hesperis Pannonica.* Dames Violets of Hungary.

The leaues of this Violet are very like the former, but smoother and thicker, and not at all indented, or cut in on the edges : the flowers are like the former, but of a sullen pale colour, turning themselues, and seldome lying plaine open, hauing many purple veines, and streakes running through the leaues of the flowers, of little or no sent in the day time, but of a very sweete sent in the euening and morning ; the seedes are alike also, but a little browner.

3 *Lysimachia*

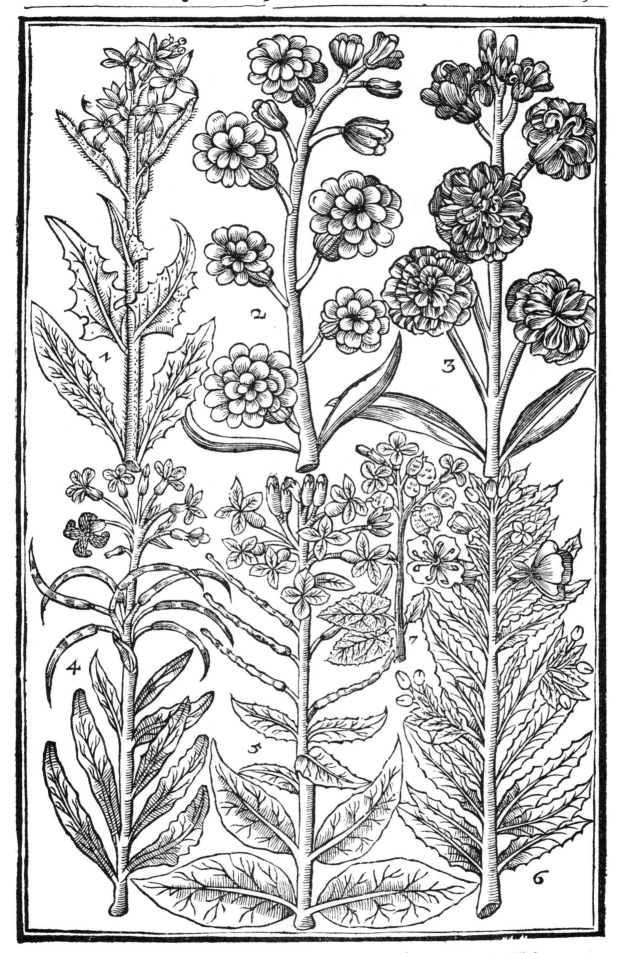

1 *Leucoium Melancholicum.* Sullen Stocke-Gilloflowers. 2 *Leucoium sativum flore pleno.* Double Stocke-Gilloflowers. 3 *Leucoium sativum flore pleno vario.* Party coloured Stocke-Gilloflowers. 4 *Leucoium marinum Syriacum.* Leuant Stocke-Gilloflowers. 5 *Hesperis vulgaris.* Dames Violets or Winter Gilloflowers. 6 *Lysimachia lutea siliquosa Virginiana.* The tree Primrose of Virginia. 7 *Viola Lunaris sive Bolbonach.* The white Sattin flower.

3. *Lysimachia lutea siliquosa Virgiana.* The tree Primrose of Virginia.

Vnto what tribe or kindred I might referre this plant, I haue stood long in suspence, in regard I make no mention of any other *Lysimachia* in this work : lest therfore it should lose all place, let me ranke it here next vnto the Dames Violets, although I confesse it hath little affinity with them.   The first yeare of the sowing the seede it abideth without any stalke or flowers lying vpon the ground, with diuers long and narrow pale greene leaues, spread oftentimes round almost like a Rose, the largest leaues being outermost, and very small in the middle : about May the next yeare the stalke riseth, which will be in Summer of the height of a man, and of a strong bigge size almost to a mans thumbe, round from the bottome to the middle, where it groweth crested vp to the toppe, into as many parts as there are branches of flowers, euery one hauing a small leafe at the foote thereof : the flowers stand in order one aboue another, round about the tops of the stalks, euery one vpon a short foot-stalke, consisting of foure pale yellow leaues, smelling somewhat like vnto a Primrose, as the colour is also (which hath caused the name) and standing in a greene huske, which parteth it selfe at the toppe into foure parts or leaues, and turne themselues downewards, lying close to the stalke : the flower hath some chiues in the middle, which being past, there come in their places long and cornered pods, sharpe pointed at the vpper end, and round belowe, opening at the toppe when it is ripe into fiue parts, wherein is contained small brownish seed : the roote is somewhat great at the head, and wooddy, and branched forth diuersly, which perisheth after it hath borne seede.

The Place.

The two first grow for the most part on Hils and in Woods, but with vs in Gardens onely.

The last, as may be well vnderstood by the title, came out of Virginia.

The Time.

They flower in May, Iune, and Iuly.

The Names.

The name of *Hesperis* is imposed by most Herbarists vpon the two first plants, although it is not certainly knowne to be the same that Theophrastus doth make mention of, in his sixth Booke and twenty fiue Chapter *de caufis plantarum* : but because this hath the like effects to smell best in the euening, it is (as I said) imposed vpon it.   It is also called *Viola Marina Matronalis, Hyemalis, Damascena* and *Muschatella* : In English, Dames Violets, Queens Gilloflowers, and Winter Gilloflowers.

The last hath his Latine name in the title as is best agreeing with it, and for the English, although it be too foolish I confesse, yet it may passe for this time till a fitter be giuen, vnlesse you please to follow the Latine, and call it Virginia Loose-strife.

The Vertues.

I neuer knew any among vs to vse these kindes of Violets in Physicke, although by reason of the sharpe biting taste, Dodonæus accounteth the ordinary sort to be a kinde of Rocket, and saith it prouoketh sweating, and vrine : and others affirme it to cut, digest, and cleanse tough flegme.   The Virginian hath not beene vsed by any that I know, either inwardly or outwardly.

CHAP.

CHAP. XLII.

Viola Lunaris siue Bolbonach. The Sattin flower.

VNto the kindes of Stocke-Gilloflowers I thinke fittest to adioyne these kindes of Sattin-flowers, whereof there are two sorts, one frequent enough in all our Countrie, the other is not so common.

1. *Viola Lunaris vulgaris.* The common white Sattin flower.

The first of these Sattin flowers, which is the most common, hath his leaues broad belowe, and pointed at the end, snipt about the edges, and of a darke greene colour: the stalkes are round and hard, two foot high, or higher, diuided into many branches, set with the like leaues, but smaller: the tops of the branches are beset with many purplish flowers, like vnto Dames Violets, or Stocke-Gilloflowers, but larger, being of little sent: after the flowers are past, there come in their places round flat thin cods, of a darke colour on the outside, but hauing a thinne middle skinne, that is white and cleare shining, like vnto very pure white Sattin it selfe, whereon lye flat and round brownish seede, somewhat thicke and great: the rootes perish when they haue giuen their seede, and are somewhat round, long, and thicke, resembling the rootes of *Lilium non bulbosum,* or Day Lilly, which are eaten (as diuers other rootes are) for Sallets, both in our owne Country, and in many places beside.

2. *Viola Lunaris altera seu peregrina.* Long liuing Sattin flower.

This second kinde hath broader and longer leaues then the former, the stalkes also are greener and higher, branching into flowers, of a paler purple colour, almost white, consisting of foure leaues in like manner, and smelling pretty sweete, bearing such like pods, but longer and slenderer then they: the rootes are composed of many long strings, which dye not as the former, but abide, and shoot out new stalkes euery yeare.

The Place.

The first is (as is said) frequent enough in Gardens, and is found wilde in some places of our owne Country, as Master Gerard reporteth, whereof I neuer could be certainly assured, but I haue had it often sent mee among other seedes from Italy, and other places. The other is not so common in Gardens, but found about Watford, as he saith also.

The Time.

They flower in Aprill or May, and sometimes more early.

The Names.

It hath diuers names, as well in English as in Latine; for it is called most vsually *Bolbonach,* and *Viola Lunaris:* Of some *Viola latifolia,* and of others *Viola Peregrina,* and *Lunaria Greca, Lunaria maior,* and *Lunaria odorata,* and is thought to be *Thlaspi Crateua:* In English, White Satten, or Satten flower: Of some it is called Honesty, and Penny-flower.

The Vertues.

Some doe vse to eate the young rootes hereof, before they runne vp to flower, as Rampions are eaten with Vinegar and Oyle; but wee know no Physicall vse they haue.

Z

CHAP.

Chap. XLIII.

Linum siluestre & Linaria. Wilde Flaxe and Tode Flaxe.

Lthough neither the manured Line or Flaxe is a plant fit for our Garden, nor many of the wilde forts, yet there are fome, whofe pleafant and delightfull afpect doth entertaine the beholders eyes with good content, and thofe I will fet downe here for varietie, and adioyne vnto them fome of the *Linarias*, or Tode Flaxe, for the neare affinity with them.

1. *Linum siluestre flore albo.* Wilde Flaxe with a white flower.

This kinde of wilde Flaxe rifeth vp with diuers flende branches, a foote high or better, full of leaues, ftanding without order, being broader and longer then the manured Flaxe : the tops of the branches haue diuers faire white flowers on them, compofed of fiue large leaues a peece, with many purple lines or ftrikes in them : the feede veffell as well as the feede, is like vnto the heads and feede of the manured Flaxe: the rootes are white ftrings, and abide diuers yeares, fpringing frefh branches and leaues euery yeare, but not vntill the Spring of the yeare.

2. *Linum siluestre luteum.* Wilde Flaxe with a yellow flower.

This wilde Flaxe doth fo well refemble a kinde of St. Iohns wort, that it will foone deceiue one that doth not aduifedly regard it : For it hath many reddifh ftalkes, and fmall leaues on them, broader then the former wilde Flaxe, but not fo long, which are well ftored with yellow flowers, as large as the former, made of fiue leaues a peece, which being paft, there come fmall flattifh heads, containing blackifh feede, but not fhining like the former : the rootes hereof dye not euery yeare, as many other of the wilde kindes doe, but abide and fhoote out euery yeare.

3. *Linaria purpurea.* Purple Tode Flaxe.

This purple Tode Flaxe hath diuers thicke, fmall, long, and fomewhat narrowifh leaues, fnipt about the edges, of a whitifh greene colour, from among which rife vp diuers ftalkes, replenifhed at the tops with many fmall flowers, ftanding together one aboue another fpike-fafhion, which are fmall and fomewhat fweete, while they are frefh, fafhioned fomewhat like the common Tode flaxe that groweth wilde abroad almoft euery where, but much fmaller, with a gaping mouth, but without any crooked fpurre behinde, like vnto them, fometimes of a fad purple neare vnto a Violet, and fometimes of a paler blew colour, hauing a yellow fpot in the middle or gaping place: after the flowers are paft, there come fmall, hard, round heads, wherein are contained fmall, flat, and grayifh feede : the roote is fmall, and perifheth for the moft part euery yeare, and will fpring againe of it owne fowing, if it be fuffered to fhed it felfe, yet fome hard Winters haue killed the feede it fhould feeme, in that fometimes it faileth to fpring againe, and therefore had neede to be fowne anew in the Spring.

4. *Linaria purpurea odorata.* Sweete purple Tode Flaxe.

The lower leaues of this purple Tode Flaxe are nothing like any of the reft, but are long and broad, endented about the edges, fomewhat refembling the leaues of the greater wilde white Daifie : the ftalke is fet at the bottome with fuch like leaues, but a little more diuided and cut in, and ftill fmaller and fmaller vpward, fo that the vppermoft leaues are very like the common Tode Flaxe, the toppe whereof is branched, hauing diuers fmall flowers growing along vpon them, in fafhion and colour almoft like the laft defcribed Tode Flaxe, but not altogether fo deepe a purple : the heads and feedes are very like the former, but that the feede of this is reddifh : the flowers

in

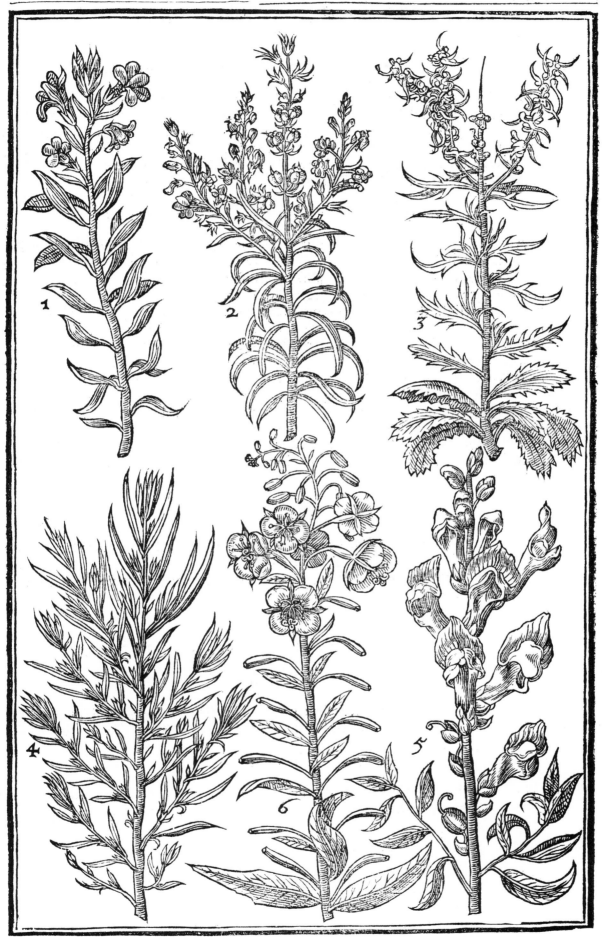

1 *Linum siluestre flore albo.* Wilde Flaxe with a white flower. 2 *Linaria purpurea siue cærulea.* Purple Tode Flaxe. 3 *Linaria purpurea odorata.* Sweete purple Tode Flaxe. 4 *Scoparia siue Beluidere Italorum* Broome Tode Flaxe. 5 *Antirrhinum maius.* The greater Snapdragon. 6 *Chamænerium flore delphinij.* The willowe flower.

in their naturall hot Countries haue a fine fent, but in thefe colder, little or none at all: the rootes are fmall and threadie, and perifh after they haue flowred and feeded.

5. *Linaria Valentina.* Tode Flaxe of Valentia.

This Spanifh Tode Flaxe hath three or fonre thicker and bigger ftalkes then the former, bearing fmall broad leaues, like vnto the fmall Centory, two or three together at a ioynt, round about the lower end of the ftalkes, but without any order vpwards, at the toppes whereof ftand many flowers, in fafhion like vnto the common kinde, and almoft as large, of a faire yellow colour, but the gaping mouth is downie, and the fpurre behinde of a purplifh colour.

6. *Scoparia fiue Beluidere Italorum.* Broome Tode Flaxe.

Although this plant haue no beautifull flowers, yet becaufe the greene plant full of leaues is fo delightfull to behold, being in Italy and other places planted not onely in their Gardens, but fet likewife in pots to furnifh their Windowes, and euen with vs alfo hath growne to be fo dainty a greene bufh, that I haue thought it worthy to be among the delights of my Garden; the defcription whereof is as followeth: This pleafant Broome Flaxe rifeth vp moft vfually with one ftraight vpright fquare ftalke, three foote and a halfe high or better in our Gardens, branching it felfe out diuers waies, bearing thereon many long narrow leaues, like the Garden Line or Flaxe, very thicke fet together, like vnto a bufh, or rather like vnto a faire greene Cypreffe tree, growing broad belowe, and fpire-fafhion vpwards, of a very faire greene colour: at the feuerall ioynts of the branches, towards the tops, and among the leaues, there come forth fmall reddifh flowers, not eafily feene nor much regarded, being of no beauty, which turne into fmall round blackifh gray feede: the rootes are a number of blackifh ftrings fet together, and the whole plant perifheth euery yeare at the firft approach of any cold ayre, as if it neuer had beene fo faire a greene bufh.

The Place.

Thefe kindes of wilde Flaxe doe growe naturally in diuers places, fome in Germany, fome in Spaine, and fome in Italy. Thofe that delight in the beauty of natures variety, doe preferue them, to furnifh vp the number of pleafant afpects.

The Time.

They all flower in the Summer moneths, and foone after perfect their feede.

The Names.

Their names are fufficiently expreffed in their titles, yet I muft giue you to vnderftand, that the laft is called of fome *Linaria magna*, and of others *Ofyris*.

The Vertues.

The wilde Flaxe hath no medecinable vertue appropriate vnto it that is knowne. The Tode Flaxe is accounted to be good, to caufe one to make water.

CHAP.

Chap. XLIIII.

Antirrhinum. Snapdragon.

THere is fome diuerfity in the Snapdragons, fome being of a larger, and others of a leffer ftature and bigneffe; and of the larger, fome of one, and fome of another colour, but becaufe the fmall kindes are of no beautie, I fhall at this time onely entreate of the greater forts.

1. *Antirrhinum album.* White Snapdragon.

The leaues of thefe Snapdragons (for I doe vnder one defcription comprehend the reft) are broader, longer, and greener then the leaues of the Garden Flaxe, or of the wilde Flaxe fet confufedly vpon the tender greene branches, which are fpread on all fides, from the very bottome, bearing at the toppes many flowers, fomewhat refembling the former Tode Flaxe, but much larger, and without any heele or fpurre, of a faire white colour, with a yellow fpot in the mouth or gaping place: after the flowers are paft, there come vp in their places hard round feede veffels, fafhioned fomewhat like vnto a Calues head, the fnout being cut off, wherein is contained fmall blacke feede: the rootes are many white ftrings, which perifh in moft places after they haue giuen feede, notwithftanding any care or paines taken with them to preferue them a-liue, and yet they will abide in fome places where they are defended in the Winter.

2. *Antirrhinum purpureum fiue rofeum.* Purple Snapdragon.

The purple Snapdragon is in ftalkes, leaues, and flowers altogether like the former, and as large and great in euery part, or greater; the only difference is, that this beareth pale Stammell or Rofe coloured flowers, with a yellow fpot in the mouth, and fometimes of a paler colour, almoft blufh.

3. *Antirrhinum variegatum.* Variable Snapdragon.

This variable kinde is fomewhat leffe, and tenderer then the laft defcribed, hauing alfo a reddifh or blufh coloured flower, leffer then the former, but much bigger then the middle kinde of Snapdragon (which is not fet downe in this worke) the yellow fpot in the mouth of it hath fome white about it, and extending to both fides of the fpot: the heads and feede are like the former: the rootes are fmaller, but neuer will abide after they haue giuen flowers and feede.

4. *Antirrhinum luteum.* Yellow Snapdragon.

There is likewife another of thefe kindes, that beareth leaues as large as any of the former, & very faire yellow flowers, as large likewife as they, not differing in any thing elfe from the firft; let not any therefore imagine this to be a *Linaria* or Tode Flaxe: for all parts are anfwerable vnto the Snapdragons.

The Place.

All thefe are nourifhed with vs in our Gardens, although in Spaine and Italy they are found growing wilde.

The Time.

They flower for the moft part the fecond yeare after the fowing, from A-prill vntill Iuly, and the feede is quickly ripe after.

Z 3
The

The Names.

The name *Antirrhinum* is vsually giuen to this plant, although it fully agreeth not eyther with the description of Dioscorides, or Theophrastus: It hath also diuers other names in Latine, as *Orontium*, *Canis cerebrum Os Leonis, Leo herba*, &c. In English Calues snout, from the forme of the seede veffels, and Snapdragon, or Lyons mouth, from the forme of the flowers.

The Vertues.

They are seldome or neuer vsed in Physicke by any in our dayes.

Chap. XLV.

Chamænerium flore delphinÿ. The Willowe flower.

THis plant riseth vp with many strong, woddy, round, brownish great stalkes, three or foure foote high, beset here and there without order, with one broad and long whitish greene leafe at a ioynt, somewhat like vnto a *Lysimachia*, or Willow herbe, as also vnto a Peach leafe, but larger and longer: at the toppe of the branches stand many flowers one aboue another, of a pale reddish purple colour, consisting of fiue leaues, spread open with an heele or spurre behinde them, with many yellow threads in the middle, much larger then any flower of the Larkes spurres, and smelling somewhat sweete withall; it beareth a shew of long pods with seede, but I could neuer obserue the seede: the rootes are like the rootes of *Lysimachia*, or the ordinary yellow Loose-strife, or Willowe herbe, but greater: running and spreading vnder ground, and shooting vp in many places, whereby it filleth a ground that it likes quickly: the stalkes dye downe euery yeare, and spring againe in many places farre asunder.

The Place.

Wee haue not knowne where this Willowe flower groweth naturally, but we haue it standing in an out corner of our Gardens, to fill vp the number of delightfull flowers.

The Time.

It flowreth not vntill May, and abideth a long while flowring.

The Names.

It may seeme to diuers, that this is that plant that Dodonæus called *Pseudolysimachium purpureum minus*, and Lobel seemeth by the name of *Delphinium buccinum* to aime at this plant, but withall calleth it *Chamænerium Gesneri*, and giueth the same figure that Dodonæus hath for his *Pseudolysimachium*: But that is one kinde of plant (which hath smaller and shorter stalkes, and very narrow long leaues, whose flowers stand vpon long slender cods, full of downe, with reddish seede, like vnto the *Lysimachia siliquosa siluestris*, and rootes that abide many yeares, but creepe not) and this is another, much greater, whose true figure is not extant in any Author that I know. It is vsually called *Chamænerium flore delphinÿ*; but the name of *Delphinium buccinum* in my minde may not so conueniently be applyed vnto it. It is called in English, The Willowe flower, for the likenesse of the leaues, and the beauty and respect of the flowers.

The

The Vertues.

There is no vfe hereof in Phyficke that euer I could learne, but is onely cherifhed among other forts of flowers, that ferue to decke and fet forth a Garden of varieties.

CHAP. XLVI.

Aquilegia. Colombines.

THere are many forts of Colombines, as well differing in forme as colour of the flowers, and of them both fingle and double carefully nourfed vp in our Gardens, for the delight both of their forme and colours.

1. *Aquilegia vulgaris flore fimplici.* Single Colombines.

Becaufe the whole difference of thefe Colombines ftandeth in the varieties of the forme, and colour of the flowers, and little in the leaues, I fhall not neede to make anie repetitions of the defcription of them, feeing one onely fhall fuffice for each peculiar kinde. The Colombine hath diuers large fpread leaues, ftanding on long ftalkes: euery one diuided in feuerall partitions, and roundly endented about the edges, in colour fomewhat like the leaues of Celondine, that is, of a darke blewifh greene colonr : the ftalkes rife vp fometimes two or three foote high, diuided vfually into many branches, bearing one long diuided leafe at the lower ioynt, aboue which the flowers growe, euery one ftanding on a long ftalke, confifting of fiue hollow leaues, crooked or horned at the ends, turning backward, the open flower fhewing almoft like vnto a Cinquefoile, but more hollow : after the flowers are paft, there arife fmall long cods, foure or fiue together, wherein are contained blacke fhining feede : the rootes are thicke and round, for a little fpace within the ground, and then diuided into branches, ending in many fmall fibres, abiding many yeares, and fhooting a frefh euery Spring from the round heads, that abide all the Winter. The variety of the colours of thefe flowers are very much, for fome are wholly white, fome of a blew or violet colour, others of a blufh or flefh colour, or deepe or pale red, or of a dead purple, or dead murrey colour, as nature lifteth to fhew it felfe.

2. *Aquilegia vulgaris flore pleno.* Double Colombines.

The double Colombines differ not in leafe or manner of growing from the fingle, fo that vntill they come to flower, they cannot bee difcerned one from another ; the onely difference is, it beareth very thicke and double flowers, that is, many horned or crooked hollow leaues fet together, and are not fo large as the leaues of the fingle flowers. The variety of colours in this double kinde is as plentifull, or rather more then in the fingle ; for of thefe there is party coloured, blew and white, and fpotted very variably, which are not in the fingle kinde, and alfo a very deepe red, very thicke and double, but a fmaller flower, and leffe plentifull in bearing then many of the other double forts. Thefe double kindes doe giue as good feede as the fingle kindes doe, which is not obferued in many other plants.

3. *Aquilegia innerfis corniculis.* Double inuerted Colombines.

Thefe Colombines are not to be diftinguifhed eyther in roote, leaues, or feed from the former, the flowers onely make the difference, which are as double as the former, but that the heeles or hornes of thefe are turned inward, and ftand out in the middle of the flowers together : there is not that plentifull variety of colours in this kinde, as there is in the former : for I neuer faw aboue three or foure feuerall colours in this kinde,

kinde, that is, white, purpliſh, reddiſh, and a dun or darke ouerworne purpliſh colour. Theſe double flowers doe likewiſe turne into pods, bearing ſeede, continuing his kind, and not varying into the former.

4. *Aquilegia Roſea.* Roſe Colombines.

The leaues and other parts of this kinde of Colombine, differ little or nothing from the former, the diuerſitie conſiſteth likewiſe in the flowers, which although they ſtand in the ſame manner ſeuerally vpon their ſmall ſtalkes, ſomewhat more ſparingly then the former doe, yet they haue no heeles or hornes, eyther inward or outward, or very ſeldome, but ſtand ſometimes but with eight or tenne ſmooth ſmall plaine leaues, ſet in order one by one in a compaſſe, in a double rowe, and ſometimes with foure or fiue rowes of them, euery one directly before the other, like vnto a ſmall thick double Roſe layd open, or a ſpread Marigold : yet ſometimes it happeneth, that ſome of theſe flowers will haue two or three of the firſt rowes of leaues without any heele, and the reſt that are inward with each of them a peece of a ſmall horne at them, as the former haue : the colours of theſe flowers are almoſt as variable, and as variably mixed as the former double kindes. This likewiſe giueth ſeede, preſeruing his owne kinde for the moſt part.

5. *Aquilegia degener.* Degenerate Colombines.

This kinde of Colombine might ſeeme to ſome, to bee but a caſuall degeneration, and no true naturall kinde, happening by ſome cauſe of tranſplanting, or otherwiſe by the art of man : but I haue not ſo found it, in that it keepeth, and holdeth his own proper forme, which is like vnto the double Roſe Colombine, but that the outermoſt row of leaues are larger then any of the reſt inwardes, and is of a greeniſh, or elſe of a purpliſh greene colour, and is not altogether ſo apt to giue good ſeed like the former.

The Place.

The ſingle kindes haue beene often found in ſome of the wooddy mountaines of Germany, as Cluſius ſaith, but the double kindes are chiefly cheriſhed in gardens.

The Time.

They flower not vntill May, and abide not for the moſt part when Iune is paſt, and in the meane time perfecteth their ſeede.

The Names.

Coſtæus doth call this plant *Pothos* of Theophraſtus, which Gaza tranſlateth *Deſiderium.* Dalechampius vpon Athenæus, calleth it *Dioſanthos,* or *Iouis flos* of Theophraſtus, who in his ſixth Booke and ſeuenth Chapter reckoneth them both, that is, *Dioſanthos* and *Pathos,* to be Summer flowers, but ſeuerally. Dodonæus *Leoherba,* and Geſner *Leontoſtomium.* Fabius Columna in his Phytobaſanos, vnto whom Cluſius giueth the greateſt approbation, referreth it to the *Iſopyrum* of Dioſcorides. All later Writers doe generally call it, eyther *Aquileia, Aquilina,* or *Aquilegia ;* and we in Engliſh, generally (I thinke) through the whole Countrey, Colombines. Some doe call the *Aquilegia roſea, Aquilegia ſtellata,* The ſtarre Colombine ; becauſe the leaues of the flowers doe ſtand ſo directly one by another, beſides the doubleneſſe, that they ſomewhat repreſent eyther a Roſe or a Starre, and thereupon they giue it the name eyther of a Starre or Roſe.

The Vertues.

Some in Spaine, as Camerarius ſaith, vſe to eate a peece of the roote hereof

1 *Aquilegia simplex.* The single Colombine. 2 *Aquilegia flore multiplici.* The double Colombine. 3 *Aquilegia versicolor.* The party coloured Colombine. 4 *Aquilegia inuersis corniculis.* The double inuerted Colombine. 5 *Aquilegia Rosea siue Stellata.* The Rose or the Starre Colombine. 6 *Thalictrum Hispanicum album.* White Spanish tufts.

of fasting, many dayes together, to helpe them that are troubled with the stone in the kidneyes. Others vse the decoction, of both herbe and roote in wine, with a little Ambargrise, against those kinds of swounings, which the Greekes call ἀδυναμία. The seede is vsed for the iaundise, and other obstructions of the liuer. Clusius writeth from the experience of Franciscus Rapard, a chiefe Physician of Bruges in Flanders, that the seede beaten and drunke is effectuall to women in trauell of childe, to procure a speedy deliuerie, and aduiseth a second draught thereof should be taken if the first succeede not sufficiently.

Chap. XLVII.

Thalictrum Hispanicum. Spanish Tufts, or Tufted Colombines.

FRom among the diuersities of this plant, I haue selected out two sorts for this my garden, as hauing more beautie then all the rest; leauing the other to be entreated of, where all in generall may be included. I haue in this place inserted them, for the likenesse of the leaues only, being in no other part correspondent, and in a Chapter by themselues, as it is most fit.

Thalictrum Hispanicum album. White Spanish tufted Colombines.

These plants haue both one forme, in roote, leafe and flower, and therefore neede but one description. The leaues are both for colour and forme so like vnto Colombines leaues (although lesser and darker, yet more spread, and on larger stalkes) that they may easily deceiue one, that doth not marke them aduisedly ; for the leaues are much more diuided, and in smaller parts, and not so round at the ends : the stalkes are round, strong, and three foote high at the least, branching out into two or three parts, with leaues at the seuerall ioynts of them, at the toppes whereof stand many flowers, which are nothing but a number of threads, made like vnto a small round tuft, breaking out of a white skinne, or leafe, which incloseth them, and being vnblowne, shew like vnto little buttons : the colour of these threds or tufts in this are whitish with yellow tips on them, and somewhat purplish at the bottome, hauing a strong but no good sent, and abiding in their beautie (especially if they grow in the shade, and not too hot in the sun) a great while, and then fall away, like short downe or threds : the seed vessels are three square, containing small, long, and round seede ; the rootes are many long yellow stringes, which endure and encrease much.

Thalictrum Montanum purpureum. Purple tufted Colombines.

This purple tufted Colombine differeth onely from the former, in that it is not so high nor so large, and that the colour of the flower or tuft is of a blewish purple colour with yellow tips, and is much more rare then the other.

The Place.

These grow both in Spaine and Italie.

The Time.

They flower in the end of May, or in Iune, and sometime later.

The Names.

Some doe call them *Thalietrum*, and some *Thalictrum*. Others *Ruta palustris*, and *Ruta pratensis*, and some *Rhabarbarum Monachorum*, or *Pseudorhabarbarum*,

rhabarbarum, by reaʃon that the rootes being yellow, haue an opening qualitie, and drying as Rubarbe. In Engliʃh what other fit Names to giue theʃe then I haue expreʃʃed in the titles, I know not.

The Vertues.

The are a little hot and drying withall, good for old Vlcers, as Dioʃcorides ʃaith, to bring them to cicatriʃing : in Italy they are vʃed againʃt the Plague, and in Saxonye againʃt the Iaundiʃe, as Camerarius ʃaith.

Chap. XLVIII.

Radix caua. Hollow roote.

THe likeneʃʃe of the leaues likewiʃe of this plant with Colombines, hath cauʃed mee to inʃert it next the other, and although ʃome of this kinde bee of ʃmall reʃpect, being accounted but fooliʃh, yet let it fill vp a waʃte corner, that ʃo no place be vnfurniʃhed.

1. *Radix Caua maior flore albo.* The white Hollow roote.

The leaues of this hollow roote breake not out of the ground, vntill the end of March, or ʃeldome before, and are both for proportion and colour ʃomewhat like vnto the leaues of Colombines, diuided into fiue parts, indented about the edges, ʃtanding on ʃmall long footeʃtalkes of a whitiʃh greene colour, among which riʃe vp the ʃtalkes, without any leaues from the bottome to the middle, where the flowers ʃhoote forth one aboue another, with euery one a ʃmall ʃhort leafe at the foote thereof, which are long and hollow, with a ʃpurre behinde it, ʃomewhat like vnto the flowers of Larckes ʃpurres, but hauing their bellies ʃomwhat bigger, and the mouth not ʃo open, being all of a pure white colour : after the flowers are paʃt, ariʃe ʃmall long and round cods, wherein are contained round blackiʃh ʃeede : the roote is round and great, of a yellowiʃh browne colour on the outʃide, and more yellow within, and hollow vnderneath, ʃo that it ʃeemeth but a ʃhell : yet being broken, euery part will grow : it abideth greene aboue ground but a ʃmall time.

2. *Radix Caua maior flore carneo.* Bluʃh colourd Hollow roote.

The bluʃh Hollow roote is in all things like vnto the former, but onely that the flowers hereof are of a delayed red or purple colour, which we call bluʃh : and ʃometimes of a very deepe red or purple colour ; but very rare to meete with.

3. *Radix Caua minor, ʃeu Capnos fabacea radice.* Small hollow roote.

This ʃmall kinde hath his leaues of a blewiʃh greene colour, yet greener and ʃmaller then the former, growing more thicke together : the flowers are like in proportion vnto the former in all reʃpects, but leʃʃer, hauing purpliʃh backes, and white bellyes : ʃtanding cloʃer and thicker together vpon the ʃhort ʃtalkes : the roote is ʃolid or firme, round and a little long withall, two being vʃually ioyned together, yellowiʃh both within and without : but I haue ʃeene the dry roots that came from beyond Sea hither, that haue beene as ʃmall as haʃell nuts, and ʃomewhat flat with the roundneʃʃe, differing from thoʃe that growe with vs, whether the nature thereof is to alter by manuring, I know not.

The Place.

The greater kindes Cluʃius reporteth he found in many places of Hungarie,

rie, and the other parts neere thereunto : the leffer in the lower Germany, or Low Countries, as we call them.

The Time.

Thefe are moft truely to bee reckoned Vernall plants, for that they rife not out of the ground vntill the Spring bee come in, and are gone likewife before it be paft, remaining vnder ground all the reft of the yeare, yet the leffer abideth longer aboue ground then the greater.

The Names.

Concerning the former of thefe, there is a controuerfie among diuers, whether it fhould be *Thefium* of Theophraftus, or *Eriphium* of Galen, but here is no fit place to trauerfe thofe opinions. Some would haue it to bee *Corydalis*, and fome referre it to Plinie his *Capnos Cheledonia*, for the likeneffe it hath both with Fumeterie and Celandine. It is generally called of all moderne Writers, *Radix Caua*, and we in Englifh thereafter, Hollow roote. The leffer for the firmeneffe of his round roote, is vfually called, *Capnos fabacea radice*, and the Dutch men thereafter, 𝔅𝔬𝔬𝔫𝔨𝔢𝔫𝔰 𝔥𝔬𝔩𝔩𝔴𝔬𝔯𝔱𝔢𝔩𝔩: we of the likeneffe with the former, doe call it the leffe Hollow roote.

The Vertues.

Some by the bitterneffe doe coniecture (for little proofe hath beene had thereof, but in outward cafes) that it clenfeth, purgeth, and dryeth withall.

Chap. XLIX.

Delphinium. Larkes heeles.

OF Larkes heeles there are two principall kindes, the wilde kinde, and the tame or garden ; the wilde kinde is of two forts, one which is with vs nourfed vp chiefly in gardens, and is the greateft ; the other which is fmaller and lower, often found in our plowed landes, and elfewhere : of the former of thefe wilde forts, there are double as well as fingle : and of the tame or more vpright, double alfo and fingle : and of each of diuers colours, as fhall be fet downe.

1. *Delphinium maius fiue vulgare.* The ordinary Larkes heeles.

The common Larkes heele fpreadeth with many branches much more ground then the other, rather leaning or bending downe to the ground, then ftanding vpright, whereon are fet many fmall long greene leaues, finely cut, almoft like Fennell leaues : the branches end in a long fpike of hollow flowers, with a long fpurre behinde them, very like vnto the flowers of the Hollow roote laft defcribed, and are of *Varietas.* diuers feuerall colours, as of a blewifh purple colour, or white, or afh colour or red, paler or deeper, as alfo party coloured of two colours in a flower : after the flowers are paft, (which in this kinde abide longer then in the other) there come long round cods, containing very blacke feede : the root is hard after it groweth vp to feede, fpreading both abroad and deepe, and perifheth euery yeare, vfually raifing it felfe from it own fowing, as well as from the feede fowen in the fpring time.

2. *Delphinium vulgare flore pleno.* Double common Larkes heeles.

Of this vulgar kinde there is fome difference in the flower, although in nothing elfe: the flowers ftand many vpon a ftalke like the former, but euery one of them are as if
three

three or foure fmall flowers were ioyned together, with euery one his fpurre behinde, the greateft flower being outermoft, and as it were containing the reft, which are of a pale red, or deepe blufh colour : Another of this kinde will beare his flowers with three or foure rowes of leaues in the middle, making a double flower with one fpurre behinde onely : and of this kinde there is both with purple, blew, blufh, and white flowers, and party coloured alfo, thefe doe all beare feed like the fingle, wherby it is encreafed euery yeare.

3. *Delphinium aruenfe.* Wilde Larkes fpurres.

This wilde Larkes fpurre hath fmaller and fhorter leaues, fmaller and lower branches, and more thinly or fparfedly growing vpon them, then any of the former : the flowers likewife are neyther fo large as any of the former, nor fo many growing together, the cods likewife haue fmaller feede, and is harder to grow in gardens then any of the former; the moft vfuall colour hereof is a pale reddifh or blufh colour, yet fometimes they are found both white and blew, and fometimes mixt of blew and blufh, variably difpofed, as nature can when fhe lifteth ; but are much more rare.

4. *Diphinium elatius flore fimplici diuerforum colorum.* Single vpright bearing Larkes heeles of many colours.

The difference betweene this and the laft is, that the leaues of this are not fully fo greene, nor fo large; the ftalkes grow vpright, to the height of a man, and fometimes higher, hauing fome branches thereon, but fewer then the former, and ftanding likewife vpright, and not leaning downe as the former : the toppes of the ftalkes are better ftored with flowers then the other, being fometimes two foote long and aboue, of the fame fafhion, but not altogether fo large, but of more diuers and feueral colours, as white, pale, blufh, redde deeper or paler, afhcoloured, purple or violet, and of an ouerworne blewifh purple, or iron colour : for all thefe we haue fimple, without any mixture or fpot : but we haue other forts, among the fimple colours, that rife from the fame feede, and will haue flowers that wil be halfe white, and halfe blufh or purple, or one leafe white, and another blufh or purple, or elfe variably mixed and fpotted : the feede and feede veffels are like the former but larger and harder.

5. *Delphinium elatius flore pleno diuerforum colorum.* Double vpright Larkes heeles of many colours.

Thefe double Larkes heeles cannot bee knowne from the fingle of the fame kinde, vntill they come towards flowring; for there appeare many flowers vpon the ftalkes, in the fame manner, and of as many colours almoft as of the fingle, except the party coloured, which ftand like little double Rofes, layd or fpread broade open, as the Rofe Colombine without any heeles behinde them, very delightfull to behold, confifting of many fmall leaues growing together, and after they are fallen there come vp in their places three or foure fmall cods fet together, wherein is contained here and there (for all are not full of feede, as the fingle kindes) blacke feede, like vnto all the reft, but fmaller, which being fowen will bring plants that will beare both fingle and double flowers againe, and it often happeneth, that it variably altereth in colours from it owne fowing : for none of them hold conftantly his owne colour, (fo farre as euer I could obferue) but fall into others as nature pleafeth.

6. *Delphinium Hifpanicum paruum.* Spanifh wilde Larkes fpurres.

This fmall Larkes fpurre of Spaine, hath diuers long and broad leaues next the ground, cut-in on both fides, fomewhat like vnto the leafe of a Scabious, or rather that kinde of Stœbe, which Lobel calleth *Crupina*, for it doth fomewhat neerly refemble the fame, but that this is fmooth on the edges, and not indented befides the cuts, as the *Crupina* is, being of a whitifh greene colour, and fomewhat fmooth and foft in handling : among the leaues rifeth vp a whitifh greene ftalke, hauing many fmaller

A a   leaues

leaues vpon it that grow belowe, but not diuided, branching out into many small stalkes, bearing flowers like vnto the wilde Larkes heeles, but smaller, and of a bleake blewish colour, which being past, there come vp two or three small cods ioyned together, wherein is blacke seede, smaller and rounder then any of the former: the roote is small and thready, quickly perishing with the first cold that ouertaketh the plant.

The Place.

The greatest or first wilde kindes growe among corne in many countries beyond the Seas, and where corne hath beene sowne, and for his beauty brought and nourished in our Gardens: the lesser wilde kinde in some fields of our owne Country. The Spanish kinde likewise in the like places, which I had among many seedes that Guillaume boel brought mee out of Spaine. The first double and single haue been common for many yeares in all countries of this Land, but the tall or vpright single kindes haue been entertained but of late yeares. The double kindes are more rare.

The Time.

These flower in the Summer onely, but the Spanish wilde kinde flowreth very late, so that oftentimes in our Country, the Winter taketh it before it can giue ripe seede: the double kindes, as well the vpright as the ordinary or wilde, are very choise and dainty many times, not yeelding good seede.

The Names.

They are called diuersly by diuers Writers, as *Consolida regalis*, *Calcaris flos*; *Flos regius*, *Buccinum Romanorum*, and of Matthiolus, *Cuminum siluestre alterum Dioscoridis*: but the most vsuall name with vs is *Delphinium*: but whether it be the true *Delphinium* of Dioscorides, or the Poets Hyacinth, or the flower of Aiax, another place is fitter to discusse then this. Wee call them in English Larkes heeles, Larkes spurres, Larkes toes or clawes, and Monkes hoods. The last or Spanish kinde came to mee vnder the name of *Delphinium latifolium trigonum*, so stiled eyther from the diuision of the leaues, or from the pods, which come vsually three together. Bauhinus vpon Matthiolus calleth it, *Consolida regalis peregrina paruo flore*.

The Vertues.

There is no vse of any of these in Physicke in these dayes that I know, but are wholly spent for their flowers sake.

Chap. L.

Balsamina faemina. The Female Balsam Apple.

I Haue set this plant in this place, for some likenesse of the flower, rather then for any other comparison, euen as I must also with the next that followeth. This plant riseth vp with a thicke round reddish stalke, with great and bunched ioynts, being tender and full of iuice, much like to the stalke of Purslane, but much greater, which brancheth it selfe forth from the very ground, into many stalkes, bearing thereon manie long greene leaues, snipt about the edges, very like vnto the Almond or Peach tree leaues; among which from the middle of the stalkes vpwards round about them, come forth vpon seuerall small short foot-stalkes many faire purplish flowers, of two or three colours in them, fashioned somewhat like the former Larkes heeles, or Monks hoods, but that they are larger open at the mouth, and the spurres behinde crooke or bend downewards: after the flowers are past, there come in their places round rough heads,

1 *Radix Caua maior flore albo.* The white flowred Hollow roote. 2 *Capnos fabacea radice.* The small Hollow roote. 3 *Delphinium flore simplici.* Single Larkes spurs. 4 *Delphinium vulgare flore medio duplici.* Larkes spurs double in the middle. 5 *Delphinium vulgare flore pleno.* Common Larks spurs double. 6 *Delphinium elatius flore pleno.* Double vpright Larkes spurs. 7 *Delphinium Hispanicum parvum,* Small Spanish Larkes spurs. 8 *Balsamina faemina.* The Female Balsam apple. 9 *Nasturtium Indicum.* Indian Cresses, or yellow Larkes spurs.

heads, pointed at the end, greene at the firſt, and a little yellower when they bee ripe, containing within them ſmall round blackiſh ſeede, which will ſoone skippe out of the heads, if they be but a little hardly preſſed betweene the fingers : the rootes ſpread themſelues vnder ground very much from the toppe, with a number of ſmall fibres annexed thereunto : this is a very tender plant, dying euery yeare, and muſt bee ſowne carefully in a pot of earth, and tended and watered in the heate of Summer, and all little enough to bring it to perfection.

The Place.

Wee haue alwaies had the ſeede of this plant ſent vs out of Italy, not knowing his originall place.

The Time.

It flowreth from the middle of Iuly, to the end of Auguſt : the ſeed doth ſeldome ripen with vs, eſpecially if the Summer be backward, ſo that wee are oftentimes to ſeeke for new and good ſeede from our friends againe.

The Names.

Some vſe to call it *Charantia fœmina, Balſamina fœmina, Balſamella,* and *Anguillara, Herba Sancta Katharina.* We haue no other Engliſh name to call it by, then the Female Balſame Apple, or *Balſamina.*

The Vertues.

Some by reaſon of the name, would attribute the property of Balme vnto this plant, but it is not ſufficiently knowne to haue any ſuch ; yet I am well perſwaded, there may bee ſome extradinary quality in ſo beautifull a plant, which yet lyeth hid from vs.

Chap. LI.

Naſturtium Indicum. Indian Creſſes, or yellow Larkes heeles.

THe likeneſſe (as I ſaid before) of this flower likewiſe, hauing ſpurres or heeles maketh me ioyne it with the reſt, which is of ſo great beauty and ſweetneſſe withall, that my Garden of delight cannot bee vnfurniſhed of it. This faire plant ſpreadeth it ſelfe into very many long trayling branches, enterlaced one within another very confuſedly (yet doth it not winde it ſelfe with any claſpers about either pole or any other thing, but if you will haue it abide cloſe thereunto, you muſt tye it, or elſe it will lye vpon the ground) foure or fiue foot in length at the leaſt, wherby it taketh vp a great deale of ground : the leaues are ſmooth, greene, and as round as the Penniwort that groweth on the ground, without any cut or inciſure therein at all in any part, the ſtalkes whereof ſtand in the middle of each leafe, and ſtand at euery ioynt of the ſtalke, where they are a little reddiſh, and knobbed or bunched out : the flowers are of an excellent gold yellow colour, and grow all along theſe ſtalkes, almoſt at euery ioynt with the leaues, vpon pretty long foote-ſtalkes, which are compoſed of fiue leaues, not hollow or gaping, but ſtanding open each leafe apart by it ſelfe, two of them, that be larger and longer then the other, ſtand aboue, and the other two that are leſſer belowe, which are a little iagged or bearded on both ſides, and the fift loweſt : in the middle of each of the three lower leaues (yet ſometimes it is but in two of them) there is a little long ſpot or ſtreake, of an excellent crimſon colour, with a long heele or ſpurre behinde hanging downe : the whole flower hath a fine ſmall ſent, very pleaſing, which being placed in the middle of ſome Carnations or Gilloflowers

flowers (for they are in flower at the fame time) make a delicate Tuffimuffie, as they call it, or Nofegay, both for fight and fent : After the flower is paft, come the feede, which are rough or vneuen, round, greenifh yellow heads, fometimes but one, and fometimes two or three ftanding together vpon one ftalke, bare or naked of themfelues, without any huske, containing a white pulpy kernell : the rootes are fmall, and fpreading vnder ground, which perifh with the firft frofts, and muft be fowne a new euery yeare ; yet there needeth no bed of horfe-dung for the matter : the naturall ground will be fufficient, fo as you defend it a little from thofe frofts, that may fpoile it when it is newly fprung vp, or being yet tender.

The Place.

This goodly plant was firft found in the Weft Indies, and from thence fent into Spaine vnto Monardus and others, from whence all other parts haue receiued it. It is now very familiar in moft Gardens of any curiofity, where it yearly giueth ripe feed, except the yeare be very vnkindly.

The Time.

It flowreth fometimes in Iune, but vfually in Iuly (if it be well defended and in any good ground) and fo continueth flowring, vntill the cold frofts and miftes in the middle or end of October, doe checke the luxurious nature thereof, and in the meane time the feede is ripe, which will quickly fall downe on the ground, where for the moft part the beft is gathered.

The Names.

Some doe reckon this plant among the *Clematides* or *Convolvuli*, the Clamberers or Bindweedes ; but (as I faid) it hath no clafpers, neither doth it winde it felfe : but by reafon of the number of his branches, that run one within another, it may feeme to climbe vp by a pole or fticke, which yet doth but onely clofe it, as hauing fomething whereon to leane or reft his branches. Monardus and others call it *Flos fanguineus*, of the red fpots in the flowers, as alfo *Maftnerzo de las Indias*, which is *Nafturtium Indicum*, by which name it is now generally knowne and called, and wee thereafter in Englifh, Indian Creffes, yet it may bee called from the forme of the flowers onely, Yellow Larkes heeles.

The Vertues.

The Spaniards and others vfe the leaues hereof in ftead of ordinary Creffes, becaufe the tafte is fomewhat fharpe agreeing thereunto, but other Phyficall properties I haue heard of none attributed to it.

Chap. LII.

Viola. Violets.

THe Garden Violets (for the Wilde I leaue to their owne place) are fo well knowne vnto all, that either keepe a Garden, or hath but once come into it, that I fhall (I thinke) but lofe labour and time to defcribe that which is fo common. Yet becaufe it is not onely a choife flower of delight, notwitftftanding the popularity, and that I let not paffe any thing without his particular defcription, I muft alfo doe fo by this. And hereunto I muft adde that kinde of Violet, which, although it wantthat fmell of the other, goeth beyond it in variety of dainty colours, called *Viola tricolor & flammea*, or Harts eafes.

1. *Viola simplex Martia.* Single March Violets.

The single Garden Violet hath many round greene leaues, finely fnipt or dented about the edges, ftanding vpon feuerall fmall ftalkes, fet at diuers places of the many creeping branches, which as they runne, doe here and there take roote in the ground, bearing thereon many flowers feuerally at the ioynts of the leaues, which confift of fiue fmall leaues, with a fhort round tayle or fpurre behinde, of a perfect blew purple colour, and of a very fweete fent, it bringeth forth round feede veffels, ftanding likewife vpon their feuerall fmall ftalkes, wherein is contained round white feede: but thefe heads rife not from where the flowers grew, as in all other plants that I know, but apart by themfelues, and being fowne, will produce others like vnto it felfe, whereby there may be made a more fpeedy encreafe to plant a Garden(as I haue done) or any other place, then by flipping, as is the vfuall manner: the rootes fpread both deepe and wide, taking ftrong hold in the ground.

Flore albo. Of this kinde there is another that beareth white flowers, not differing in fmell or any thing elfe from the former.

Flore obfoleto. And alfo another, that beareth flowers of a dead or fad reddifh colour, in all other things alike, fauing that this hath not altogether fo good a fent as the other.

2. *Viola Martia flore multiplici.* Double March Violets.

There is no difference betweene this Violet and the former, in any other thing then in the doublenefle of the flowers, which haue fo many leaues fet and thruft together, that they are like vnto hard buttons. There is of this double kinde both white and purple, as in the fingle; but the white fort is feldome fo thicke and double as the purple: but of the red colour to be double I neuer heard.

3. *Viola flammea fiue tricolor.* Harts eafes or Panfies.

The Harts eafe hath his leaues longer, and more endented or cut in on the edges then the Violet hath, and fomewhat round withall: the ftalkes are vpright, yet weake, and ready to fall downe, and lye vpon the ground, fet here and there with the like leaues, from whence come forth the flowers, of little or no fent at all, made like vnto a Violet, yet more open, and with larger leaues; but fo variably mixed with blew or purple, white and yellow, that it is hard to fet downe all the varieties: For fome flowers will be more white, and but fome fpots of purple or blew in the two vpper leaues, and the lower leaues with fome ftripes of yellow in the middle: others will haue more purple in them then any other colour, both in the vpper and lower leaues, the fide leaues blew, and the middle yellow, and others white and blew with yellow ftripes, as nature lifteth to diftribute their colours: the feede is fmall, whitifh, and round, contained in fmall round heads: the roote perifheth euery yeare, and raifeth it felfe vp plentifully by it owne fowing, if it be fuffered.

4. *Viola tricolor flore duplici.* Double Harts eafe.

We haue in our Gardens another fort, that beareth flowers with more leaues then the former, making it feeme to be twice double, and that onely in Autumne; for the firft flowers are fingle that come in Summer: This is of that fort that beareth purple flowers: And it is to be obferued, that the feed of this kinde will not all bring double flowers, but only fome, if the ground be fit and liking, fo that if you haue once had of this double kinde, you fhall feldome miffe to haue double flowers againe euery yeare of it owne growing or fowing.

5. *Viola flammea lutea maxima.* The great yellow Panfie.

There is one other kinde of Harts eafe, that decketh vp our Gardens not to be forgotten, whofe leaues and flowers are like the former, but more plentifull in ftalkes and branches, and better abideth our Winters: the flowers are larger then any of the former,

former, of a faire pale yellow colour, with some yellower stripes now and then about the middle ; for it is sometimes without any stripes, and also of a little deeper yellow colour : this is to bee encreafed by flips, which will soone comprehend in a moift or moiftened ground, for that I neuer could obferue that it bore feede.

The Place.

Thefe plants were firft wilde, and by manuring brought to be both fairer in colour, and peraduenture of a better fent then when they grew wilde.

The Time.

The Violets flower in March, and fometimes earlier, and if the yeare be temperate and milde, in Autumne againe. The double Violets, as they are later before they flower then the fingle, fo they hold their flowers longer. The Harts eafe flowreth feldome vntill May ; but then fome will abide to flower vntill the end of Autumne almoft, efpecially if the frofts be not early.

The Names.

The Violet is called *Viola nigra, purpurea*, and *Martia*: In Englifh, Violets, March Violets, and purple Violets. The Harts eafe is called *Viola flammea, Viola tricolor, Viola multicolor*, and of fome, *Iacea, Flos trinitatis,* and *Herba clauellata* : In Englifh, Harts eafe, and Panfies, of the French name *Penfees*. Some giue it foolifh names, as Loue in idleneffe, Cull mee to you, and Three faces in a hood. The great yellow Harts eafe is fo called, becaufe it is like in forme, and is the greateft of all other, although it haue not that diuerfity of colours in it that the other haue.

The Vertues.

The properties of Violets are fufficiently knowne to all, to coole and moiften : I fhall forbeare to recite the many vertues that may be fet downe, and onely let you know, that they haue in them an opening or purging quality, being taken either frefh and greene, or dryed, and made into powder, efpecially the flowers ; the dryed leaues will doe the like, but in greater quantity. Coftæus in his booke of the nature of all plants faith, that the diftilled water of Harts eafe, is commended in the French difeafe, to be profitable, being taken for nine dayes or more, and fweating vpon it, which how true it is, I know not, and wifh fome better experience were made of it, before we put any great confidence in that affertion.

Chap. LIII.

Epimedium. Barrenwort.

THis pretty plant rifeth vp out of the ground with vpright, hard, round, fmall ftalkes, a foote and a halfe high, or not two foote high at the higheft, diuided into three branches for the moft part, each branch whereof is againe diuided for the moft part into three other branches, and each of them beare three leaues (feldome either more or leffe) fet together, yet each vpon his owne foote-ftalke, each leafe being broad, round, and pointed at the end, fomewhat hard or dry in feeling, hayrie, or as it were prickly about the edges, but very tenderly, without harme, of a light greene colour on the vpperfide, and a little whiter vnderneath : from the middle of the ftemme or ftalke of leaues doth likewife come forth another long ftalke, not much higher then thofe with the leaues on them, diuided into other branches, each
whereof

whereof hath likewife three flowers, each vpon his owne footeftalke, confifting of eight fmall leaues a peece, yet feeming to be but of foure leaus fpread or layd open flat, for that the foure vppermoft, which are the fmaller and being yellow, doe lye fo clofe on the foure vndermoft, wᶜʰ are a little broader and red, that they fhew as if they were yellow flowers with red edges, hauing yellow threds tipt with greene, ftanding in the middle of the flowers: the vnderfide of the lower leaues are of a pale yellowifh red, ftriped with white lines: after the flowers are paft, there come fmall long pods, wherin are contained flat reddifh feede: the rootes are fmall, reddifh and hard, fpreading, branching and enterlacing themfelues very much, and is fit to be placed on fome fhady fide of a garden: the whole plant is rather of a ftrong then any good fent, yet is cherifhed for the pleafant varietie of the flowers.

The Place.

Cæfalpinus faith it groweth on the mountaines of Liguria, that is nigh vnto Ligorne, in the Florentine Dominion. Camerarius faith, nigh vnto Vicenzo in Italie. Bauhinus on the Euganian hils, nigh vnto Padoa, and in Romania in fhadowie wet grounds.

The Time.

It flowreth from Iune vntill the end of Iuly, and to the middle of Auguft, if it ftand, as I faid it is fitteft, in a fhadowie place.

The Names.

It is of moft Writers accepted for the true *Epimedium* of Diofcorides, though he faith it is without flower or feede, being therein eyther miftaken, or mif-informed, as he was alfo in *Dictamnus* of Candy, and diuers other plants. From the triple triplicitie of the ftanding of the ftalkes and leaues, and quadriplicitie of the flowers, it might receiue another name in Englifh then is already impofed vpon it: but left I might be thought to be fingular or full of noueltie, let it paffe with the name Barrenwort, as it is in the title.

The Vertues.

It is thought of diuers to agree in the propertie of caufing barrenneffe, as the ancients doe record of *Epimedium*.

CHAP. LIIII.

Papauer fatiuum. Garden Poppies.

OF Poppies there are a great many forts, both wilde and tame, but becaufe our Garden doth entertaine none, but thofe of beautie and refpect, I wil onely giue you here a few double ones, and leaue the reft to a general furuey.

1. *Papauer multiplex album*. Double white Poppies.

The double white Poppy hath diuers broade, and long whitifh greene leaues, giuing milke (as all the reft of the plant aboue ground doth, wherefoeuer it is broken) very much rent or torne in on the fides, and notched or indented befides, compaffing at the bottome of them a hard round brittle whitifh greene ftalke, branched towards the toppe, bearing one faire large great flower on the head of euery branch, which before it breaketh out, is contained within a thin skinne, and being blowne open is very thick of leaues, and double, fomewhat iagged at the ends, and of a white colour; in the

middle

1 *Viola Martia simplex.* Single March Violets. 2 *Viola Martia multiplex.* Double March Violets. 3 *Viola flammea sive tricolor.* Ordinary garden Pansies or Hartsease. 4 *Viola flammea lutea magna.* Great yellow Pansies. 5 *Viola tricolor duplex.* Double Pansies or Hartseases. 6 *Epimedium.* Barrenwort. 7 *Papauer satiuum flore pleno.* Double garden Poppies. 8 *Papauer satiuum flore pleno laciniato.* Double feathered Poppies. 9 *Nigella Hispanica flore amplo.* Spanish Nigella or Fenell flower. 10 *Nigella multiplex cærulea* Double blew Nigella or Fenell flower. 11 *Nigella duplex flore albo.* Double white Nigella. 12 *Ptarmica flore pleno.* Double wilde Pelletory.

middle whereof ſtandeth a round head or bowle, with a ſtriped crowne on the heade of it, very like a ſtarre, compaſſed about with ſome threds, wherein when it is ripe, is contained ſmall, round, white ſeede, diſpoſed into ſeuerall cels : the roote is hard, wooddy, and long, periſhing euery yeare, and muſt bee new ſowne euery Spring, if they doe not ſpring of their own ſowing, which if it doe, the flowers are ſeldome ſo faire and double as they that are ſowne in the Spring : the whole plant is of a ſtrong heady ſmell.

2. *Papauer multiplex rubeſcens.* Double red or bluſh Poppies.

This other kind of double Poppy differeth not in any other thing from the former, but only in the colour of the flowers, which are of a bright red, tending to a bluſh colour, parted, paned or ſtriped in many places with white, and exceedingly more iagged then the former, almoſt like a feather at the ends, the bottomes of all the leaues being white : the ſeede hereof is white as the former, which is not ſo in any other Poppie, that beareth not a full white flower.

3. *Papauer multiplex nigrum ſiue purpureum.* Double purple or murry Poppies.

This kinde varyeth both in flowers and ſeede, although neyther in leaues or any other thing from the firſt : the flowers are thicke and double, and ſomewhat iagged at the ends, in ſome more, in ſome leſſe, eyther red or bluſh, or purpliſh red, more or leſſe, or of a ſad murrey or tawney, with browne, or blacke, or tawny bottomes : the ſeede is eyther of a grayiſh blew colour, or in others more blackiſh.

4. *Papauer Rhœas flore multiplici.* The double red field Poppie.

This double Poppie is like the wilde or fielde Poppie, which is well knowne to all to haue longer, narrower, and more iagged greene leaues then the former, the ſtalkes more hairy, and the flower of a deepe yellowiſh red colour, knowne to all. Now this differeth in nothing from it, but in the doubleneſſe of the flower, which is very thicke and double, but not ſo large as the former. This riſeth of ſeede in the like manner as they doe, and ſo to bee preſerued.

The Place.

From what place they haue beene firſt gathered naturally I cannot aſſure you, but we haue had them often and long time in our gardens, being ſent from Italie and other places. The double wilde kindes came from Conſtantinople, which whether it groweth neere vnto it or further off, we cannot tell as yet.

The Time.

They flower in the beginning or middle of Iune at the furtheſt, the ſeede is ripe within a ſmall while after.

The Names.

The generall knowne name to all, is *Papauer*, Poppie : the ſeuerall diſtinctions are according to their colours. Yet our Engliſh Gentlewomen in ſome places, call it by a by-name, Ione ſiluer pinne : *ſubanditur*, Faire without and fowle within.

The Vertues.

It is not vnknowne, I ſuppoſe to any, that Poppie procureth ſleepe, for which cauſe it is wholly and onely vſed, as I thinke : but the water of the
wilde

wilde Poppies, besides that it is of great vse in Pleuresies, and Rheumatick-or thinne Distillations, is found by daily experience, to bee a soueraigne remedy against surfeits ; yet some doe attribute this propertie to the water of the wilde Poppies.

Chap. LV.

Nigella. The Fenell flower, or Nigella.

AMong the many sorts of Nigella, both wilde and tame, both single and double, I will onely set downe three sorts, to be nourled vp in this garden, referring the rest to a Physicke garden, or a generall Historie, which may comprehend all.

1. *Nigella Hispanica flore simplici.* The great Spanish Nigella.

Spanish Nigella riseth vp with diuers greene leaues, so finely cut, and into so many parts, that they are finer then Fenell, and diuided somewhat like the leaues of Larkes heeles, among which rise vp stalkes, with many such like leaues vpon them, branched into three or foure parts, at the toppe of each whereof standeth one faire large flower, like vnto other single Nigella's, consisting of fiue or six leaues sometimes, of a bleake blew, or of a purplish blew colour, with a greene head in the middle, compassed about with seuen or eight small blewish greene flowers, or peeces of flowers rather, made like gaping hoodes, with euery of them a yellowish line thwart or crosse the middle of them, with some threds also standing by them : after the flower is past the head groweth greater, hauing sixe, seuen or eight hornes as it were at the toppe, greater and longer, and standing closer together then any other Nigella, spreading very like a starre, or the crowne of the Poppy head, but larger and longer, each whereof being folded together, openeth a little when the head is ripe, which is greater aboue, and smaller below, and not so round as the others are, containing within them small yellowish greene seede, or not so blacke as the other sorts : the rootes are small and yellow, perishing euery yeare as the others likewise doe.

2. *Nigella Damascena flore multiplici.* Double blew Nigella, or The Fenell flower.

The double Nigella is in leaues, stalkes and rootes, very like vnto the former Nigella, so that the one can very hardly bee discerned from the other before this rise vp to flower, except it be that the leaues hereof are not fully so large as they : the flower consisteth of three or foure rowes of leaues, layde one vpon another, of a pale blew colour, with a greene round head compassed with diuers short threads in the middle, and hauing fiue or sixe such small greene Fenell-like leaues vnder the flower, to beare it vp (as it were) below, which adde a greater grace to the flowers, which at the first sheweth sometimes white, but changeth quickely after : the horned heads hereof are like vnto the heads of the other wilde kinde, which are somewhat rounder and greater, hauing within them blacke vneuen seedes, but without any sent.

3. *Nigella Catrina flore albo multiplici.* Double white Nigella.

This double white Nigella hath such like leaues as the last hath, but somewhat larger, of a yellower greene colour, and not so finely cut and iagged : the flowers are somewhat lesse, and lesser double then the former, and in colour white, hauing no greene leaues vnder the flower, as the former hath, the head whereof in the middle is very like the head of the last double kinde, but not so great, wherein is contained black seede for the most part, and sweete like the Romane Nigella, which only is sweet besides this : yet sometimes it is not so blacke, but rather a little more white or yellowish: the roote is yellow, and perisheth as the others euery yeare.

The

The Place.

All thefe, and the reft be found wilde in diuers Countreyes, as France, Spaine, Italie, &c. but wee onely cherifh them in our Gardens for our delight.

The Time.

They flower in the end of Iune, and in Iuly, or thereabouts.

The Names.

They are called *Melanthium*, *Gith*, and *Nigella*, and of fome *Flos Diuæ Catherinæ*. We may either call them *Nigella* according to the Latine name, or the Fenell flower, as fome doe, becaufe the double blew Nigella hath fmall Fenell-like leaues bearing vp the flower, as I fhewed before in the defcription.

The Vertues.

Thefe Nigella's are nothing fo hot in qualitie as the fingle Romane kind is, as may well be knowne by the fmell of the feede thereof, and therefore are not fit to be vfed in the fteed of it, as many ignorant perfons vfe to doe: for the fingle Romane feede is vfed to helpe paines, and cold diftillations in the head, and to dry vp the rheume. Pena faith, that the preffed oyle of the feede as well taken inwardly as vfed outwardly is an excellent remedy for the hardneffe and fwelling of the fpleene.

Chap. LVI.

Ptarmica filueftris flore pleno. Double wilde Pelletory.

THe double wilde Pelletorie hath ftraight and flender ftalkes, befet with long and narrow leaues, fnipt round about the edges, in all points like vnto the fingle wilde kinde, that groweth common with vs almoft euery where : on the toppes of the ftalkes ftand foure or fiue, or more white flowers, one aboue another, with a greene leafe at the bottome of the footeftalke of euery one of them, beeing fmall, thicke, and very double, with a little yellowifhneffe in the middle of euery flower, like both for forme and colour vnto the flower of the double Featherfew, but fmaller : the rootes are many long ftrings, running here and there in the ground : this hath no fmell at all, but is delightfome only for the double white flowers.

The Place.

It is only cherifhed in fome few Gardens, for it is very rare.

The Time.

It flowreth in the end of Iune or thereabouts.

The Names.

It is called of moft *Ptarmica*, or *Sternutamentoria*, of his qualitie to prouoke neefing ; and of fome *Pyrethrum*, of the hot biting tafte. We vfually call it Double wilde Pelletorie, and fome Sneefewort, but *Elleborus albus* is vfually fo called, and I would not two things fhould be called by one name, for the miftaking and mif-ufing of them.

The

The Vertues.

The properties hereof, no doubt, may well bee referred to the single kinde, beeing of the same qualitie, yet as I take it, a little more milde and temperate.

Chap. LVII.

Parthenium flore pleno. Double Featherfew.

FEatherfew that beareth double flowers is so like vnto the single kinde, that the one cannot be discerned from the other, vntill it come to flower, bearing broad, pale or fresh greene leaues, much cut in on the sides : the stalkes haue such like leaues on them as grow below, from the toppes whereof come forth many double white flowers, like vnto the flowers of the former wilde Pelletory, but larger, and like also vnto the flowers of the double Camomill : the sent whereof is as strong as of the single.

The Place.

We haue this kinde only in Gardens, and as it is thought by others, is peculiar only to our owne Countrey.

The Time.

It flowreth in the end of May, and in Iune and Iuly.

The Names.

It is called diuersly by diuers : Some thinke it to be *Parthenium* of Dioscorides, but not of Galen; for his *Parthenium* is a sweet herbe, and is thought to bee *Amaracus*, that is Marierome : others call it *Matricaria*; and some *Amarella*. Gaza translateth it *Muraleum, Theoph. lib. 7. cap. 7.* It is generally in these parts of our Country called Double Feauerfew, or Featherfew.

The Vertues.

It is answerable to all the properties of the single kinde which is vsed for womens diseases, to procure their monthly courses chiefly. It is held to bee a speciall remedy to helpe those that haue taken *Opium* too liberally. In Italy some vse to eate the single kinde among other greene herbes, as Camerarius saith, but especially fryed with egges, and so it wholly loseth his strong and bitter taste.

Chap. LVIII.

Chamæmelum. Camomill.

OVr ordinary Camomill is well knowne to all, to haue many smal trayling branches, set with very fine smal leaues, bushing and spreading thicke ouer the ground, taking roote still as it spreadeth : the toppes of the branches haue white flowers, with yellow thrummes in the middle, very like vnto the Featherfew, before described, but somewhat greater, not so hard, but more soft and gentle in handling, and the whole herbe to be of a very sweet sent.

Bb x. Cha-

1. *Chamæmelum nudum.* Naked Camomill.

We haue another fort of Camomill in fome Gardens, but very rare, like vnto the former, but that it is whiter, finer, and fmaller, and raifeth it felfe vp a little higher, and beareth naked flowers; that is, without that border of white leaues that is in the former, and confifteth onely of a yellow round thrummie head, fmelling almoft as fweete as the former.

2. *Chamæmelum flore pleno.* Double flowred Camomill.

The double Camomill groweth with his leaues vpon the ground, as the other fingle kinde doth, but of a little frefher greene colour, and larger withall: the ftalkes with the flowers on them, doe raife themfelues vp a little higher then the ordinary, and bearing one or two flowers vpon a ftalk, which are compofed of many white leaues fet together in diuers rowes, which make a fine double flower, with a little yellow fpot in the middle for the moft part of euery one, and are much larger then any fingle kinde, fmelling better, and more pleafing then the ordinary: this doth creepe vpon the ground as the other, but is more tender to be kept in the Winter. Yet if you faue the flowers hereof (and fo will the double Featherfew alfo) when they haue ftood long, and ready to fade, and keepe them dry vntill the Spring, and then breaking them or pulling them to peeces, fowe them, there will fpring vp from them Camomill, and alfo Featherfew, that will againe beare double flowers.

The Place.

Our ordinary Camomill groweth wilde in many places of our Country, and as well neare London as in other places. The others are onely found in our Gardens, where they are cherifhed. Bauhinus faith, that the double flowred Camomill is found wilde about Orleance in France.

The Time.

The double kinde is vfually in flower in Iune, before the ordinary kinde, and moft commonly paft before it flowreth, which is not vntill Iuly or Auguft. The naked Camomill flowreth betweene them both, or later.

The Names.

Camomill is called *Anthemis, Leucanthemis,* and *Leucanthemum,* of the whiteneffe of the flowers; and *Chamæmelum* of the corrupted Italian name *Camomilla.* Some call the naked Camomill, *Chryfanthemum odoratum.* The double Camomill is called by fome *Chamæmelum Romanum flore multiplici.*

The Vertues.

Camomill is put to diuers and fundry vfes, both for pleafure and profit, both for inward and outward difeafes, both for the ficke and the found, in bathings to comfort and ftrengthen the found, and to eafe paines in the difeafed, as alfo in many other formes applyed outwardly. The flowers boyled in Poffet drinke prouoketh fweat, and helpeth to expell colds, aches, and other griefes. A Syrupe made of the iuice of the double Camomill, with the flowers and white wine, as Bauhinus faith, is vfed by fome againft the Iaundife and Dropfie, caufed by the euill difpofition of the fplene.

CHAP.

1 *Parthenium flore pleno.* Double Featherfew. 2 *Chamæmelum nudum.* Naked Camomill. 3 *Chamæmelum flore pleno.* Double Camomill. 4 *Pyrethrum officinarum.* Pelletory of Spaine. 5 *Flos Adonis flore rubro & flore luteo.* Adonis flower both red & yellow.
6 *Helleborus niger ferulaceus siue Buphthalmum.* The great Oxe eye or the great yellow Anemone. 7 *Buphthalmum vulgare.* The
common yellow Oxe eye.

CHAP. LIX.

Pyrethrum officinarum. Pelletory of Spaine.

I Muft needes adioyne vnto the Camomils this fine and tender plant, for fome neare refemblance it hath with them in face, though not in quality. It is a fmall and lowe plant, bearing many fine greene leaues vpon his flender branches, which leane or lye down vpon the ground, diuided into many parts, yet fomewhat larger and broader then Camomill, the ftalkes whereof are bigger, and more iuicie then it : the flowers that ftand at the toppes of the ftalkes are fingle, but much larger then any Camomill flower, hauing a pale or border of many leaues, white on the vpperfide, and reddifh vnderneath, fet about the yellow middle thrumme ; but not ftanding fo clofe together ioyning at the bottome, as the Camomill flowers doe, but more feuered one from another : it beareth fmall whitifh feede, which is hardly found and difcerned from the chaffe : the roote is long, and growing downe right, of the bignefſe of a mans finger or thumbe in our Countrey, but not halfe fo great where it groweth naturally, with fome fibres and branches from the fides thereof, of a very hot, fharpe, and biting tafte, drawing much water into the mouth, after it hath been chewed a while : the plant with vs is very tender, and will hardly or not at all endure the hardnefſe and extremities of our Winters, vnlefſe it be very carefully preferued.

The Place.

It groweth in Spaine wilde in many places, and in other hot Countries, where it may feele no frofts to caufe it perifh.

The Time.

It flowreth fo late with vs, that it is not vntill Auguft, that oftentimes we cannot gather ripe feedes from it, before it perifh.

The Names.

The name *Pyrethrum* (taken from πῦρ, that is, *ignis*, fire) is giuen to this plant, becaufe of the heate thereof, and that the roote is fomewhat like in fhew, but fpecially in property vnto the true *Pyrethrum* of Diofcorides, which is an vmbelliferous plant, whofe rootes are greater, and more feruent a great deale, and haue a hayrie bufh or toppe as *Meum*, and many other vmbelliferous plants haue. It is alfo called in Latine, *Salinaris*, of the effect in drawing much moifture into the mouth, to be fpit out. We doe vfually call it Pelletory of Spaine.

The Vertues.

It is in a manner wholly fpent to draw rheume from the teeth, by chewing it in the mouth, thereby to eafe the tooth-ach, and likewife from the head, in the paines thereof.

Chap. LX.

Flos Adonis flore rubro. Red Adonis flower.

ADonis flower may well be accounted a kinde of Camomill, although it hath some especiall differences, hauing many long branches of leaues lying vpon the ground, and some rising vp with the stalke, so finely cut and iagged, that they much resemble the leaues of Mayweed, or of the former *Nigella:* at the top of the stalkes, which rise a foote high or better, stand small red flowers, consisting of six or eight round leaues, hauing a greene head in the middle, set about with many blackish threads, without any smell at all : after the flowers are past, there grow vp heads with many roundish white seedes at the toppes of them, set close together, very like vnto the heads of seede of the great Oxe eye, set downe in the next Chapter, but smaller : the rootes are small and thready, perishing euery yeare, but rising of his owne seede againe, many times before Winter, which will abide vntill the next yeare.

Yellow Adonis flower is like vnto the red, but that the flower is somewhat larger, *Flore luteo,* and of a faire yellow colour.

The Place.

The first groweth wilde in the corn fields in many places of our own country, as well as in others, and is brought into Gardens for the beauties sake of the flower. The yellow is a stranger, but nourised in our Gardens with other rarities.

The Time.

They flower in May or Iune, as the yeare falleth out to be early or late : the seed is soone ripe after, and will quickly fall away, if it be not gathered.

The Names.

Some haue taken the red kinde to be a kinde of Anemone ; other to be *Eranthemum* of Dioscorides : the most vsuall name now with vs is *Flos Adonis,* and *Flos Adonidis:* In English, where it groweth wilde, they call it red Maythes, as they call the Mayweede, white Maythes ; and some of our English Gentlewomen call it Rosarubie : we vsually call it Adonis flower.

The Vertues.

It hath been certainly tryed by experience, that the seed of red Adonis flower drunke in wine, is good to ease the paines of the Collicke and Stone.

Chap. LXI.

Buphthalmum. Oxe eye.

VNder the name *Buphthalmum,* or Oxe eye, are comprehended two or three seuerall plants, each differing from other, both in face and property, yet because they all beare one generall name, I thinke fittest to comprise them all in one Chapter, and first of that which in leafe & seed commeth nearest to the Adonis flower.

1. *Buphthalmum maius siue Helleborus niger ferulaceus.* Great Oxe eye, or the yellow Anemone.

This great Oxe eye is a beautifull plant, hauing many branches of greene leaues

leaning

leaning or lying vpon the ground for the moſt part, yet ſome ſtanding vpright, which are as fine, but ſhorter then Fenell, ſome of them ending in a ſmall tuft of green leaues, and ſome hauing at the toppes of them one large flower apeece, ſomewhat reddiſh or browniſh on the outſide, while they are in bud, and a while after, and being open, ſhew themſelues to conſiſt of twelue or fourteene long leaues, of a faire ſhining yellow colour, ſet in order round about a greene head, with yellow thrums in the middle, laying themſelues open in the ſunne, or a faire day, but elſe remaining cloſe : after the flower is paſt, the head growing greater, ſheweth it ſelfe compact of many round whitiſh ſeede, very like vnto the head of ſeede of the Adonis flower laſt deſcribed, but much greater : the rootes are many long blackiſh fibres or ſtrings, ſet together at the head, very like vnto the rootes of the leſſer blacke Hellebor or Bearefoote, but ſomewhat harder, ſtiffer, or more brittle, and ſeeming without moiſture in them, which abide and encreaſe euery yeare.

2. *Buphthalmum minus, ſeu Anthemis flore luteo.* Small Oxe eye.

This plant might ſeeme to be referred to the Camomils, but that it is not ſweete, or to the Corne-Marigolds, but that the ſtalkes and leaues are not edible : it is therefore put vnder the Oxe eyes, and ſo we will deſcribe it ; hauing many weake branches lying vpon the ground, beſet with winged leaues, very finely cut and iagged, ſomewhat like vnto Mayweede, but a little larger : the flowers are like vnto the Corne Marigold, and larger then any Camomill, being wholly yellow, as well the pale or border of leaues, as the middle thrummes : the rootes are ſomewhat tough and long.

3. *Buphthalmum vulgare.* Common Oxe eye.

This Oxe eye riſeth vp with hard round ſtalkes, a foote and a halfe high, hauing many winged leaues vpon them, made of diuers long and ſomething broad leaues, ſnipt about the edges, ſet together ſomewhat like vnto Tanſie, but ſmaller, and not ſo much winged : the flowers ſtand at the toppes of the ſtalkes, of a full yellow colour, both the outer leaues and the middle thrum, and not altogether ſo large as the laſt : the rootes of this kinde periſh euery yeare, and require a new ſowing againe.

The Place.

The firſt groweth in diuers places of Auſtria, Bohemia, and thoſe parts, it hath beene likewiſe brought out of Spaine. The ſecond in Prouence, a country in France. The laſt in diuers places, as well of Auſtria as Morauia, and about Mentz and Norimberg, as Cluſius ſetteth downe. We haue them in our Gardens, but the firſt is of the greateſt reſpect and beauty.

The Time.

The firſt flowreth betimes, oftentimes in March, or at the furtheſt in Apill ; the ſeede is ripe in May, and muſt be quickly gathered, leſt it bee loſt. The other two flower not vntill Iune.

The Names.

The firſt is called *Buphthalmum* of Dodonæus, *Pſeudohelleborus* of Matthiolus, *Helleborus niger ferulaceus Theophraſti* by Lobel, of ſome others *Elleborus niger verus,* vſing it for the true blacke Ellebor, but it is much differing, as well in face as properties. Of others *Seſamoides minus.* Some haue thought it to be a yellow Anemone, that haue looked on it without further iudgement, and by that name is moſt vſually knowne to moſt of our Engliſh Gentlewomen that know it. But it may moſt fitly be called a *Buphthalmum,* as Dodonæus doth, and *Hiſpanicum* or *Auſtriacum,* for diſtinctions ſake. We doe moſt vſually call it *Helleborus niger ferulaceus,* as Lobel doth : Bauhinus
calleth

calleth it *Helleborus niger tenuifolius Buphthalmi flore.* The second is called *Buphthalmum Narbonense* : In English, The French, or lesser Oxe eye, as the first is called, The great Oxe eye. The last, The common Oxe eye.

The Vertues.

The first hath been vsed in diuers places for the true blacke Ellebor, but now is sufficiently knowne to haue been an errour ; but what Physicall property it hath, other then Matthiolus hath expressed, to be vsed as Setterwort for cattell, when they rowell them, to put or draw the rootes hereof through the hole they make in the dewe lappe, or other places, for their coughes or other diseases, I know not, or haue heard or read of any. The others likewise haue little or no vse in Physicke now a dayes that I know.

Chap. LXII.

Chrysanthemum. Corne Marigold.

ALthough the sorts of Corne Marigolds, which are many, are fitter for another then this worke, and for a Catholicke Garden of Simples, then this of Pleasure and Delight for faire Flowers ; yet giue me leaue to bring in a couple : the one for a corner or by-place, the other for your choisest, or vnder a defenced wall, in regard of his statelinesse.

1. *Chrysanthemum Creticum.* Corne Marigold of Candy.

This faire Corne Marigold hath for the most part one vpright stalke, two foote high, whereon are set many winged leaues, at euery ioynt one, diuided and cut into diuers parts, and they againe parted into seuerall peeces or leaues : the flowers growe at the toppes of the stalkes, rising out of a scaly head, composed of ten or twelue large leaues, of a faire, but pale yellow colour, and more pale almost white at the bottome of the leaues, round about the yellow thrumme in the middle, being both larger and sweeter then any of the other Corne Marigolds : the seede is whitish and chaffie : the roote perisheth euery yeare.

2. *Chrysanthemum Peruuianum, siue Flos Solis.*
The golden flower of Peru, or the Flower of the Sunne.

This goodly and stately plant, wherewith euery one is now adayes familiar, being of many sorts, both higher and lower (with one stalke, without branches, or with many branches, with a blacke, or with a white seede, yet differing not in forme of leaues or flowers one from another, but in the greatnesse or smalnesse) riseth vp at the first like vnto a Pompion with two leaues, and after two, or foure more leaues are come forth, it riseth vp into a great stalke, bearing the leaues on it at seuerall distances on all sides thereof, one aboue another vnto the very toppe, being sometimes, and in some places, seuen, eight, or ten foote high, which leaues standing out from the stemme or stalke vpon their seuerall great ribbed foote-stalkes, are very large, broad belowe, and pointed at the end, round, hard, rough, of a sad greene colour, and bending downewards : at the toppe of the stalke standeth one great, large, and broad flower, bowing downe the head vnto the Sunne, and breaking forth from a great head, made of scaly greene leaues, like vnto a great single Marigold, hauing a border of manie long yellow leaues, set about a great round yellow thrumme, as it were in the middle, which are very like vnto short heads of flowers, vnder euery one whereof there is a seede, larger then any seede of the Thistles, yet somewhat like, and lesser, and rounder then any Gourd seede, set in so close and curious a manner, that when the seede is taken out, the head with the hollow places or cels thereof, seemeth very like vnto an hony combe ; which seede is in some plants very blacke, in the hotter countries, or very

white,

white, and great, or large, but with vs is neither fo large, blacke, or white; but fome-times blackifh or grayifh. Some fort rifeth not vp halfe the height that others doe, and fome againe beare but one ftemme or ftalke, with a flower at the toppe thereof; and others two or three, or more fmall branches, with euery one his flower at the end; and fome fo full of branches from the very ground almoft, that I haue accounted threefcore branches round about the middle ftalke of one plant, the loweft neare two yards long, others aboue them a yard and a halfe, or a yard long, with euery one his flower thereon; but all fmaller then thofe that beare but one or two flowers, and leffer alfo for the moft part then the flower on the middle ftalke it felfe. The whole plant, and euery part thereof aboue ground hath a ftrong refinous fent of Turpentine, and the heads and middle parts of the flowers doe oftentimes (and fometimes the ioynts of the ftalke where the leaues ftand) fweat out a moft fine thin & cleare Roffin or Turpen-tine, but in fmall quantity, and as it were in drops, in the heate and dry time of the year, fo like both in colour, fmell, and tafte vnto cleare Venice Turpentine, that it cannot be knowne from it: the roote is ftrongly faftened in the ground by fome greater roots branching out, and a number of fmall ftrings, which growe not deepe, but keepe vn-der the vpper cruft of the earth, and defireth much moifture, yet dyeth euery yeare with the firft frofts, and muft be new fowne in the beginning of the Spring.

The Place.

Their places are fet downe in their titles, the one to come out of Candy, the other out of Peru, a Prouince in the Weft Indies.

The Time.

The firft flowreth in Iune, the other later, as not vntill Auguft, and fome-times fo late, that the early frofts taking it, neuer fuffer it to come to ripenefs.

The Names.

The firft hath his name in his title. The fecond, befides the names fet downe, is called of fome *Planta maxima, Flos maximus, Sol Indianus,* but the moft vfuall with vs is, *Flos Solis*: In Englifh, The Sunne Flower, or Flower of the Sunne.

The Vertues.

There is no vfe of either in Phyficke with vs, but that fometimes the heads of the Sunne Flower are dreffed, and eaten as Hartichokes are, and are accounted of fome to be good meate, but they are too ftrong for my tafte.

Chap. LXIII.

Calendula. Marigolds.

SOme haue reckoned vp many forts of Marigolds, I had rather make but two, the fingle and the double; for doubtleffe, thofe that be moft double, rife from the beft feede, which are the middlemoft of the great double, and fome will be leffe double, whofe feede is greater then the reft, according to the ground where it grow-eth; as alfo thofe that be of a paler colour, doe come of the feed of the yellower fort.

1. *Calendula maxima.* The great Garden Marigold.

The Garden Marigold hath round greene ftalkes, branching out from the ground into many parts, whereon are fet long flat greene leaues, broader and rounder at the

point

1 *Chrysanthemum Creticum.* Corne Marigolds of Candy. 2 *Flos Solis.* The Flower of the Sunne. 3 *Calendula.* Marigolds. 4 *Aster Atticus sine Italorum.* The purple Marigold. 5 *Pilosella maior.* Golden Mouse-eare. 6 *Scorsonera Hispanica.* Spanish Vipers grasse. 7 *Tragopogon.* Goates beard, or goe to bed at noone.

point then any where elſe, and ſmaller alſo at the ſetting to of the ſtalke, where it compaſſeth it about : the flowers are ſometimes very thicke and double (breaking out of a
ſcaly clammy greene head) compoſed of many rowes of leaues, ſet ſo cloſe together
one within another, that no middle thrume can bee ſeene, and ſometimes leſſe double;
hauing a ſmall browne ſpot of a thrume in the middle : and ſometimes but of two or
three rowes of leaues, with a large browne thrume in the middle; euery one whereof is ſomewhat broader at the point, and nicked into two or three corners, of an excellent faire deepe gold yellow colour in ſome, and paler in others, and of a pretty
ſtrong and reſinous ſweete ſent : after the flowers are paſt, there ſucceede heads of
crooked ſeede, turning inward, the outermoſt biggeſt, and the innermoſt leaſt : the
roote is white, and ſpreadeth in the ground, and in ſome places will abide after the
ſeeding, but for the moſt part periſheth, and riſeth againe of his owne ſeede. Sometimes this Marigold doth degenerate, and beareth many ſmall flowers vpon ſhort
ſtalkes, compaſſing the middle flower : but this happeneth but ſeldome, and therefore accounted but *luſus naturæ*, a play of nature, which ſhe worketh in diuers other
plants beſides.

2. *Calendula ſimplex.* The ſingle Marigold.

There is no difference betweene this and the former, but that the flowers are ſingle,
conſiſting of one rowe of leaues, of the ſame colour; eyther paler or deeper yellow,
ſtanding about a great browne thrumme in the middle : the ſeed likewiſe is alike, but
for the moſt part greater then in the double kindes.

The Place.

Our Gardens are the chiefe places for the double flowers to grow in; for
we know not of any other naturall place : but the ſingle kinde hath beene
found wilde in Spaine, from whence I receiued ſeede, gathered by Guillaume Boel, in his time a very curious, and cunning ſearcher of ſimples.

The Time.

They flower all the Summer long, and ſometimes euen in winter, if it be
milde, and chiefly at the beginning of thoſe monethes, as it is thought.

The Names.

They are called *Caltha* of diuers, and taken to be that *Caltha*, wherof both
Virgil and Columella haue written. Others doe call them *Calendula*, of the
Kalendes, that is the firſt day of the monthes, wherein they are thought
chiefly to flower; and thereupon the Italians call them, *Fiori di ogni meſe*,
that is, The Flowers of euery moneth : We cal them in Engliſh generally,
eyther Golds, or Marigolds.

The Vertues.

The herbe and flowers are of great vſe with vs among other pot-herbes
and the flowers eyther greene or dryed, are often vſed in poſſets, broths, and
drinkes, as a comforter of the heart and ſpirits, and to expel any malignant
or peſtilential quality, gathered neere thereunto. The Syrupe and Conſerue
made of the freſh flowers, are vſed for the ſame purpoſes to good effect.

Chap. LXIIII.

Aster. Starre-wort.

Dioſcorides and other of the ancient Writers, haue ſet forth but one kinde of Starre-wort, which they call *Aſter Atticus,* of the place no doubt, where the greateſt plentie was found, which was the Countrey of Athens : the later Writers haue found out many other plants which they referre to this kinde, calling them by the ſame name. It is not my purpoſe to entreate of them all, neyther doth this garden fitly agree with them : I ſhall therefore ſelect out one or two from the reſt, and giue you the knowledge of them, leauing the reſt to their proper place.

1. *Aſter Atticus flore luteo.* Yellow Starre-wort.

This Starre-wort riſeth vp with two or three rough hairy ſtalkes, a foote and a halfe high, with long, rough or hairie, browniſh, darke greene leaues on them, diuided into two or three branches · at the toppe of euery one whereof ſtandeth a flat ſcaly head, compaſſed vnderneath with fiue or ſixe long, browne, rough greene leaues, ſtanding like a Starre, the flower it ſelfe ſtanding in the middle thereof, made as a border of narrow, long, pale yellow leaues, ſet with a browniſh yellow thrume : the roote dyeth euery yeare, hauing giuen his flower.

2. *Aſter Atticus Italorum flore purpureo.* Purple Italian Starre-wort.

This Italian Starre-wort hath many wooddy, round brittle ſtalkes, riſing from the roote, ſomewhat higher then the former, ſometimes ſtanding vpright, and other-whiles leaning downewards, whereon are ſet many ſomewhat hard, and rough long leaues, round pointed, without order vp to the toppe, where it is diuided into ſeuerall branches, whereon ſtand the flowers, made like vnto a ſingle Marigold, with a border of blewiſh purple leaues, ſet about a browne middle thrume, the heads ſuſtaining the flowers, are compoſed of diuers ſcaly greene leaues, as is to be ſeene in the Knap-weedes or Matfelons, which after the flowers are paſt yeelde a certaine downe, wherein lye ſmall blacke and flat ſeedes, ſomewhat like vnto Lettice ſeede, which are carried away with the winde : the roote is compoſed of many white ſtrings, which periſheth not as the former, but abideth, and ſpringeth afreſh euery yeare.

The Place.

The firſt is found in Spaine, as Cluſius, and in France, as Lobel ſay. The other hath beene found in many places in Germany, and Auſtria : in Italie alſo, and other places ; we haue it plentifully in our Gardens.

The Time.

The firſt flowreth in Summer. And the other not vntill Auguſt or September.

The Names.

The firſt is called *Aſter Atticus flore luteo, Bubonium, & Inguinalis,* and of many is taken to be the true *Aſter Atticus* of Dioſcorides : yet Matthiolus thinketh not ſo, for diuers good reaſons, which hee ſetteth downe in the Chapter of *Aſter Atticus,* as any man may vnderſtand, if they will but reade the place, which is too long to bee inſerted here. The other is thought by Matthiolus, to bee the truer *Aſter Atticus,* (vnto whom I muſt alſo conſent) and conſtantly alſo affirmed to be the *Amellus Virgilij,* as may be ſeene in the ſame place : but it is vſually called at this day, *Aſter Italorum flore cæruleo* or *purpureo,*

purpureo. Their English names are sufficiently expressed in their titles, yet some call the last, The purple Marigold, because it is so like vnto one in form.

The Vertues.

They are held, if they bee the right, to bee good for the biting of a mad dogge, the greene herbe being beaten with old hogs greafe, and applyed, as also for swolne throats : It is likewise vsed for botches that happen in the groine, as the name doth import.

Chap. LXV.

Pilosella maior. Golden Mouse-eare.

SOme resemblance that the flowers of this plant hath with the former Golds, maketh me to insert it in this place, although I know it agreeth not in any other part, yet for the pleasant aspect thereof, it must bee in this my garden, whose description is as followeth : It hath many broade greene leaues spread vpon the ground, spotted with pale spots, yet more conspicuous at sometimes then at other ; somewhat hairy both on the vpper and vnderside, in the middle of these leaues rise vp one, two or more blackish hairy stalkes, two foote high at the least, bare or naked vp to the top, where it beareth an vmbell, or short tuft of flowers, set close together vpon short stalkes, of the forme or fashion of the Haukeweedes, or common Mouse-eare, but somewhat smaller, of a deep gold yellow, or orenge tawney colour, with some yellow threds in the middle, of little or no sent at all: after the flowers are past, the heads carry small, short, blacke seede, with a light downie matter on them, ready to bee carried away with the winde, as many other plants are, when they be ripe : the rootes spread vnder ground, and shoote vp in diuers other places, whereby it much encreaseth, especially if it be set in any moist or shadowie place.

The Place.

It groweth in the shadowie woods of France, by Lions, and Mompelier, as Lobell testifieth : we keepe it in our gardens, and rather in a shadowie then sunnie place.

The Time.

It flowreth in Somer, and sometimes againe in September.

The Names.

It is called by Lobell, *Pulmonaria Gallorum Hieratij facie* : and the Herbarists of France take it to be the true *Pulmonaria* of Tragus. Others call it *Hieratium flore aureo.* Pelleterius *Hieratium Indicum.* Some *Pilosella,* or *Auricula muris maior flore aureo.* And some *Chondrilla flore aureo.* Dalechamptus would haue it to bee *Corchorus,* but farre vnfitly. The fittest English name we can giue it, is Golden Mouse-eare, which may endure vntill a fitter bee imposed on it : for the name of Grim the Collier, whereby it is called of many, is both idle and foolish.

The Vertues.

The French according to the name vse it for the defects of the lunges, but with what good successe I know not.

Chap.

CHAP. LXVI.

Scorsonera. Vipers grasse.

ALthough there be foure or fiue sorts of *Scorsonera*, yet I shall here desire you to be content with the knowledge only of a couple.

1. *Scorsonera Hispanica maior.* The greater Spanish Vipers grasse.

This Spanish Vipers grasse hath diuers long, and somewhat broad leaues, hard and crumpled on the edges, and sometimes vneuenly cut in or indented also, of a blewish greene colour : among which riseth vp one stalke, and no more for the most part, two foote high or thereabouts, hauing here and there some narrower long leaues thereon then those below : the toppe of the stalke brancheth it selfe forth into other parts, euery one bearing a long scaly head, from out of the toppe whereof riseth a faire large double flower, of a pale yellow colour, much like vnto the flower of yellow Goates-beard, but a little lesser, which being past, the seede succeedeth, being long, whitish and rough, inclosed with much downe, and among them many other long smooth seedes, which are limber and idle, and are carryed away at the will of the winde : the roote is long, thicke and round, brittle and blacke, with a certaine roughnesse on the outside : but very white within, yeelding a milkie liquor being broken, as euery other part of the plant doth besides, yet the roote more then any other part, and abideth many yeares without perishing.

2. *Scorsonera Pannonica purpurea.* Purple flowred Vipers grasse.

This purple flowred Vipers grasse hath long and narrow leaues, of the same blewish greene colour with the former : the stalke riseth vp a foote and a halfe high, with a few such like leaues, but shorter thereon, breaking at the toppe into two or three parts, bearing on each of them one flower, fashioned like the former, and standing in the like scaly knoppe or head, but of a blewish purple colour, not fully so large, of the sweetest sent of any of this kinde, comming neerest vnto the smell of a delicate perfume.

The Place.

The first is of Spaine. The other of Hungarie and Austrich : which now furnish our gardens.

The Time.

They flower in the beginning of May : the seede is soone ripe after, and then perishing downe to the roote for that yeare, springeth afresh before Winter againe.

The Names.

They are called after the Spanish name *Scorsonera*, which is in Latine *Viperaria*, of some *Viperina*, and *Serpentina* : Wee call them in English Vipers grasse, or *Scorsonera*.

The Vertues.

Manardus as I thinke first wrote hereof, and saith that it hath been found to cure them that are bitten of a Viper, or other such like venemous Creature. The rootes hereof being preserued with sugar, as I haue done often, doe eate almost as delicate as the Eringus roote, and no doubt is good to comforr and strengthen the heart, and vitall spirits. Some that haue vsed the preserued roote haue found it effectuall to expelling winde out of the stomacke, and to helpe swounings and faintnesse of the heart.

Cc

CHAP.

Chap. LXVII.

Tragopogon. Goates beard.

I Must in this place set downe but two sorts of Goates beards; the one blew or ash-colour, the other red or purple, and leaue the other kindes : some to bee spoken of in the Kitchin Garden, and others in a Physicall Garden.

1. *Tragopogon flore cæruleo.* Blew Goates beard.

All the Goates beards haue long, narrow, and somewhat hollow whitish greene leaues, with a white line downe the middle of euery one on the vpperside : the stalke riseth vp greater and stronger then the Vipers grasse, bearing at the toppe a great long head or huske, composed of nine or ten long narrow leaues, the sharpe points or ends whereof rise vp aboue the flower in the middle, which is thicke and double, somewhat broad and large spread, of a blewish ash-colour, with some whitish threads among them, shutting or closing it selfe within the greene huske euery day, that it abideth blowing, vntill about noone, and opening not it selfe againe vntill the next morning : the head or huske, after the flower is past, and the seede neare ripe, openeth it selfe; the long leaues thereof, which closed not before now, falling downe round about the stalke, and shewing the seede, standing at the first close together, and the doune at the toppe of them : but after they haue stood a while, it spreadeth it selfe round, and is ready to be carried away with the winde, if it be not gathered : the seede it selfe is long, round, and rough, like the seede of the Vipers grasse, but greater and blacker : the roote is long, and not very great, but perisheth as soone as it hath borne seede, and springeth of the fallen seede, that yeare remaining greene all Winter, and flowring the next yeare following : the whole yeeldeth milke as the former, but somewhat more bitter and binding.

2. *Tragopogon purpureum.* Purple Goates beard.

There is little difference in this kind from the former, but that it is a little larger, both in the leafe, and head that beareth the seed: the flowers also are a little larger, and spread more, of a darke reddish purple colour, with some yellow dust as it were cast vpon it, especially about the ends : the roote perisheth in the like manner as the other.

The Place.

Both these haue been sent vs from the parts beyond the Seas, I haue had them from Italy, where no doubt they grow naturally wilde, as the yellow doth with vs : they are kept in our Gardens for their pleasant flowers.

The Time.

They flower in May and Iune : the seede is ripe in Iuly.

The Names.

Their generall name is after the Greeke word *Tragopogon*, which is in Latine, *Barba hirci* : In English, Goates beard ; the head of seede when it is readie to bee carried away with the winde, causing that name for the resemblance : and because the flower doth euery day close it selfe at noone (as I said before) and openeth not againe vntill the next Sunne, some haue fitly called it, Goe to bed at noone.

The Vertues.

The rootes of these kindes are a little more bitter and more binding also then

then the yellow kinde expreſſed in the Kitchin Garden ; and therefore fitter for medicine then for meate, but yet is vſed as the yellow kinde is, which is more fit for meate then medicine. The diſtilled water is good to waſh old ſores and wounds.

CHAP. LXVIII.

Flos Africanus. The French Marigold.

OF the French or African Marigolds there are three kindes as principall, and of each of them both with ſingle and double flowers : of theſe, ſome diuerſity is obſerued in the colour of the flowers, as well as in the forme or largeneſſe, ſo that as you may here ſee, I haue expreſſed eight differences, and Fabius Columna nine or ten, in regard hee maketh a diuerſity of the paler and deeper yellow colour : and although the leſſer kinde, becauſe of its euill ſent, is held dangerous, yet for the beauty of the flower it findeth roome in Gardens.

1. *Flos Africanus maior ſiue maximus multiplex.* The great double French Marigold.

This goodly double flower, which is the grace and glory of a Garden in the time of his beauty, riſeth vp with a ſtraight and hard round greene ſtalke, hauing ſome creſts or edges all along the ſtalke, beſet with long winged leaues, euery one whereof is like vnto the leafe of an Aſh, being compoſed of many long and narrow leaues, ſnipt about the edges, ſtanding by couples one againſt another, with an odde one at the end, of a darke or full greene colour : the ſtalke riſeth to be three or foure foote high, and diuideth it ſelfe from the middle thereof into many branches, ſet with ſuch like leaues to the toppes of them, euery one bearing one great double flower, of a gold yellow colour aboue, and paler vnderneath, yet ſome are of a pale yellow, and ſome betweene both, and all theſe riſing from one and the ſame ſeede : the flower, before it be blowne open, hath all the leaues hollow ; but when it is full blowne open, it ſpreadeth it ſelfe larger then any Prouince Roſe, or equall vnto it at the leaſt, if it be in good earth, and riſeth out of a long greene huske, ſtriped or furrowed, wherein after the flower is paſt, (which ſtandeth in his full beauty a moneth, and oftentimes more, and being gathered, may be preſerued in his full beauty for two moneths after, if it be ſet in water) ſtandeth the ſeede, ſet thicke and cloſe together vpright, which is blacke, ſomewhat flat and long : the roote is full of ſmall ſtrings, whereby it ſtrongly comprehendeth in the ground : the flower of this, as well as the ſingle, is of the very ſmell of new waxe, or of an honie combe, and not of that poiſonfull ſent of the ſmaller kindes.

2. *Flos Africanus maior ſimplex.* The great ſingle French Marigold.

This ſingle Marigold is in all things ſo like vnto the former, that it is hard to diſcerne it from the double, but by the flowers, onely the ſtalke will be browner then the double ; and to my beſt obſeruation, hath and doth euery yeare riſe from the ſeede of the double flower : ſo that when they are in flower, you may ſee the difference (or not much before, when they are in bud) this ſingle flower euer appearing with thrums in the middle, and the leaues, which are the border or pale ſtanding about them, ſhewing hollow or fiſtulous, which after lay themſelues flat and open (and the double flower appearing with all his leaues folded cloſe together, without any thrum at all) and are of a deeper or paler colour, as in the double.

3. *Flos Africanus fiſtuloſo flore ſimplex & multiplex.* Single and double French Marigolds with hollow leafed flowers.

As the former two greateſt ſorts haue riſen from the ſeede of one and the ſame (I

meane

meane the pod of double flowers) fo doe thefe alfo, not differing from it in any thing, but that they are lower, and haue fmaller greene leaues, and that the flower alfo being fmaller, hath euery leafe abiding hollow, like vnto an hollow pipe, broad open at the mouth, and is of as deepe a yellow colour for the moft part as the deepeft of the former, yet fometimes pale alfo.

4. *Flos Africanus minor multiplex.* The leffer double French Marigold.

The leffer double French Marigold hath his leaues in all things like vnto the former, but fomewhat leffer, which are fet vpon round browne ftalkes, not fo ftiffe or vpright, but bowing and bending diuers wayes, and fometimes leaning or lying vpon the ground : the ftalkes are branched out diuerfly, whereon are fet very faire double flowers like the former, and in the like greene huskes, but fmaller, and in fome the outermoft leaues will be larger then any of the reft, and of a deeper Orenge colour, almoft crimfon, the innermoft being of a deepe gold yellow colour, tending to crimfon : the whole flower is fmaller, and of a ftronger and more vnpleafant fauour, fo that but for the beautifull colour, and doubleneffe of the flower, pleafant to the eye, and not to any other fenfe, this kinde would finde roome in few Gardens : the rootes and feedes are like the former, but leffer.

5. *Flos Africanus minor simplex.* The fmall fingle French Marigold.

This fingle kinde doth follow after the laft in all manner of proportion, both of ftalkes, leaues, feedes, and rootes : the flowers onely of this are fingle, hauing fiue or fix broad leaues, of a deepe yellow crimfon colour, with deepe yellow thrummes in the middle, and of as ftrong a ftinking fent, or more then the laft.

The Place.

They growe naturally in Africa, and efpecially in the parts about Tunis, and where old Carthage ftood, from whence long agoe they were brought into Europe, where they are onely kept in Gardens, being fowne for the moft part euery yeare, vnleffe in fome milde Winters. The laft fingle and double kindes (as being more hardy) haue fometimes endured : but that kinde with hollow leafed flowers, as Fabius Columna fetteth it downe, is accounted to come from Mexico in America.

The Time.

They flower not vntill the end of Summer, efpecially the greater kindes: but the leffer, if they abide all the Winter, doe flower more early.

The Names.

They haue been diuerfly named by diuers men : Some calling them *Caryophyllus Indicus,* that is, Indian Gilloflowers, and *Tanacetum Peruvianum,* Tanfie of Peru, as if it grew in Peru, a Prouince of America ; and *Flos Indicus,* as a flower of the Indies ; but it hath not beene knowne to haue beene brought from thence. Others would haue it to be *Othonna* of Plinie, and others ; fome to be *Lycoperficum* of Galen. It is called, and that more truely, *Flos Tunetenfis, Flos Africanus,* and *Caltha Africana,* that is, the flower of Tunis, the flower of Africa, the Marigold of Africa, and peraduenture *Pedna Panorum.* We in Englifh moft vfually call them, French Marigolds, with their feuerall diftinctions of greater or fmaller, double or fingle. To that with hollow leafed flowers, Fabius Columna giueth the name of *Fiftilufo flore,* and I fo continue it.

The

1 *Flos Africanus maximus multiplex.* The greatest double French Marigold. 2 *Flos Africanus maior multiplex.* The greater double French Marigold.
3 *Flos Africanus maximus simplex* The greatest single French Marigold. 4 *Flos Africanus multiplex fistulosus.* The doule hollow French Marigold.
5 *Flos Africanus simplex fistulosus.* The single hollow French Marigold. 6 *Flos Africanus minor multiplex.* The smaller double French Marigold. 7 *Flos*
Africanus minor multiplex alter. Another sort of the lesser double French Marigold. 8 *Flos Africanus minor simplex,* The lesser single French Marigold.

The Vertues.

We know no vfe they haue in Phyficke, but are cherifhed in Gardens for their beautifull flowers fake.

CHAP. LXIX.

Caryophyllus hortenfis. Carnations and Gilloflowers.

TO auoide confufion, I muft diuide Gilloflowers from Pinkes, and intreate of them in feuerall Chapters. Of thofe that are called Carnations or Gilloflowers, as of the greater kinde, in this Chapter; and of Pinkes, as well double as fingle, in the nexr. But the number of them is fo great, that to giue feuerall defcriptions to them all were endleffe, at the leaft needleffe: I will therefore fet downe onely the defcriptions of three (for vnto thefe three may be referred all the other forts) for their fafhion and manner of growing, and giue you the feuerall names (as they are vfually called with vs) of the reft, with their variety and mixture of colours in the flowers, wherein confifteth a chiefe difference. I account thofe that are called Carnations to be the greateft, both for leafe and flower, and Gilloflowers for the moft part to bee leffer in both; and therefore will giue you each defcription apart, and the Orenge tawnie or yellow Gilloflower likewife by it felfe, as differing very notably from all the reft.

1. *Caryophyllus maximus Harwicenfis fiue Anglicus.* The great Harwich or old Englifh Carnation.

I take this goodly great old Englifh Carnation, as a prefident for the defcription of all the reft of the greateft forts, which for his beauty and ftatelineffe is worthy of a prime place, hauing beene alwayes very hardly preferued in the Winter; and therefore not fo frequent as the other Carnations or Gilloflowers. It rifeth vp with a great thicke round ftalke, diuided into feuerall branches, fomewhat thickly fet with ioynts, and at euery ioynt two long greene rather then whitifh leaues, fomewhat broader then Gilloflower leaues, turning or winding two or three times round (in fome other forts of Carnations they are plaine, but bending the points downewards, and in fome alfo of a darke reddifh greene colour, and in others not fo darke, but rather of a whitifh greene colour:) the flowers ftand at the toppes of the ftalkes in long, great, and round greene huskes, which are diuided into fiue points, out of which rife many long and broad pointed leaues, deeply iagged at the ends, fet in order round and comely, making a gallant great double flower, of a deepe Carnation colour, almoft red, fpotted with many blufh fpots and ftrakes, fome greater and fome leffer, of an excellent foft fweete fent, neither too quicke as many others of thefe kinds are, nor yet too dull, and with two whitifh crooked threads like hornes in the middle: this kinde neuer beareth many flowers, but as it is flow in growing, fo in bearing, not to be often handled, which fheweth a kinde of ftatelineffe, fit to preferue the opinion of magnificence: the roote is branched into diuers great, long, wooddy rootes, with many fmall fibres annexed vnto them.

2. *Caryophyllus hortenfis flore pleno rubro.* The red or Cloue Gilloflower.

The red Cloue Gilloflower, which I take as a prefident for the fecond fort, which are Gilloflowers, grow like vnto the Carnations, but not fo thicke fet with ioynts and leaues: the ftalkes are more, the leaues are narrower and whiter for the moft part, and in fome doe as well a little turne: the flowers are fmaller, yet very thicke and double in moft, and the greene huskes wherein they ftand are fmaller likewife then the former: the ends of the leaues in this flower, as in all the reft, are dented or iagged, yet in fome more then in others; fome alfo hauing two fmall white threads, crooked at the ends like hornes, in the middle of the flower, when as diuers other haue none. Thefe

kindes,

1 *Caryophyllus maximus rubro varius.* The great old Carnation or gray Hulo. 2 *Caryophyllus maior rubro & albo varius.* The white Carnation. 3 *Caryophyllus albo rubeus.* The Camberline or the Poole flower. 4 *Caryophyllus Cantij striatus.* The faire mad of Kent. 5 *Caryophyllus Sabaudieus carneus.* The blush Sauadge. 6 *Caryophyllus Xerampelinus.* The Gredeline Carnation. 7 *Caryophyllus dictus Grimelo.* The Grimelo or Prince. 8 *Caryophyllus albus maior.* The great white Gilloflower. 6 *Elegans Heroina Bradshawy.* Master Bradshawes dainty Lady.

kindes, and especially this that hath a deepe red crimson coloured flower, doe endure the cold of our winters, and with lesse care is preserued : these sorts as well as the former doe very seldome giue any seede, as far as I could euer obserue or learne.

3. *Caryophyllus Silesiacus flore pleno miniato.*
The yellow or Orenge tawny Gilloflower.

This Gilloflower hath his stalkes next vnto the ground, thicker set, and with smaller or narrower leaues then the former for the most part : the flowers are like vnto the Cloue Gilloflowers, and about the same bignesse and doublenesse most vsually, yet in some much greater then in others ; but of a pale yellowish Carnation colour, tending to an Orenge, with two small white threds, crooked at the ends in the middle, yet some haue none, of a weaker sent then the Cloue Gilloflower : this kinde is more apt to beare seede then any other, which is small, black, flat, and long, and being sowen, yeelde wonderfull varieties both of single and double flowers : some being of a lighter or deeper colour then the mother plants : some with stripes in most of the leaues : Others are striped or spotted, like a speckled Carnation or Gilloflower, in diuers sorts, both single and double : Some againe are wholly of the same colour, like the mother plant, and are eyther more or lesse double then it, or else are single with one row of leaues, like vnto a Pinck ; and some of these likewise eyther wholly of a crimson red, deeper or lighter, or variably spotted, double or single as a Pinck, or blush eyther single or double, and but very seldome white : yet all of them in their greene leaues little or nothing varying or differing.

Cariophylli maximi.

CARNATIONS.

Caryophyllus maximus dictus Hulo rubro-varius.

THe gray *Hulo* hath as large leaues as the former old Carnation, and as deepely iagged on the edges : it hath a great high stalke, whereon stand the flowers, of a deepe red colour, striped and speckled very close together with a darkish white colour.

Caryophyllus maximus dictus Hulo ruber non variatus.

The red *Hulo* is also a faire great flower, of a stamell colour, deeply iagged as the former, and groweth very comely without any spot at all in it, so that it seemeth to bee but a stamell Gilloflower, saue that it is much greater.

Caryophyllus maximus dictus Hulo caruleo purpureus.

The blew *Hulo* is a goodly faire flower, being of a faire purplish murrey colour, curiously marbled with white, but so smally to be discerned, that it seemeth only purple, it hath so much the Mastrie in it ; it resembleth the Brassill, but that it is much bigger.

Caryophyllus maximus dictus Grimelo siue Prinsep.

The *Grimelo* or Prince is a faire flower also, as large as any Chrystall or larger, being of a faire crimson colour, equally for the most part striped with white, or rather more white then red, thorough euery leafe from the bottome, and standeth comely.

Caryophyllus maximus Incarnadinus albus.

The white Carnation or Delicate, is a goodly delightfull faire flower in his pride and perfection, that is, when it is both marbled and flaked, or striped and speckled with white vpon an incarnate crimson colour, beeing a very comely flower, but abideth not constant, changing oftentimes to haue no flakes or strakes of white, but marbled or speckled wholly.

Caryophyllus maximus Incarnadinus Gallicus.

The French Carnation is very like vnto the white Carnation, but that it hath more specks, and fewer stripes or flakes of white in the red, which hath the mastrie of the white.

Caryophyllus maximus Incarnadinus grandis.

The ground Carnation (if it be not the same with the graund or great old Carnation first set downe, as the alteration but of one letter giueth the coniecture) is a thicke flower, but spreadeth not his leaues abroade as others doe, hauing the middle standing higher then the outer leaues, and turning vp their brimmes or edges; it is a sad flower,with few stripes or spots in it : it is very subiect to breake the pod, that the flower seldome commeth faire and right ; the greene leaues are as great as the *Hulo* or Lombard red.

Caryophyllus maximus Chrystallinus. The Chrystall or Chrystalline(for they are both one,howsoeuer some would make them differ) is a very delicate flower when it is well marked, but it is inconstant in the markes, being sometimes more striped with white and crimson red, and sometimes lesse or little or nothing at all, and changing also sometimes to be wholly red, or wholly blush.

Caryophyllus maximus flore rubro. The red Chrystall, which is the red hereof changed, is the most orient flower of all other red Gilloflowers, because it is both the greatest, as comming from the Chrystall, as also that the red hereof is a most excellent crimson.

Caryophyllus maximus dictus Fragrans. The Fragrant is a faire flower, and thought to come from the Chrystall, being as large, but of a blush red colour,spotted with small speckes, no bigger then pinnes points, but not so thicke as in the Pageant.

Caryophyllus maximus Sabaudicus varius. The stript Sauadge is for forme and bignesse equall with the Chrystall or White Carnation, but as inconstant as eyther of them, changing into red or blush; so that few branches with flowers containe their true mixtures, which are a whitish blush, fairely striped with a crimson red colour,thicke and short, with some spots also among.

Caryophyllus maximus Sabaudicus carneus. The blush Sauadge is the same with the former, the same root of the stript Sauadge, as I said before, yeelding one side or part whose flowers will be eyther wholly blush,or hauing some small spots, or sometimes few or none in them.

Caryophyllus maximus Sabaudicus ruber. The red Sauadge is as the blush,when the colour of the flower is wholly red without any stripes or spots in them, and so abideth long ; yet it is sometimes seene,that the same side,or part, or roote being separate from the first or mother plant, will giue striped and well marked flowers againe.

Caryophyllus maximus Oxoniensis. The Oxeford Carnation is very like vnto the French Carnation, both for forme,largenesse and colour : but that this is of a sadder red colour, so finely marbled with white thereon, that the red hauing the maistry,sheweth a very sad flower,not hauing any flakes or stripes at all in it.

Caryophyllus maximus Regius, siue Bristoliensis maior. The Kings Carnation or ordinary Bristow, is a reasonable great flower, deepely iagged, of a sad red, very smally striped and speckled with white : some of the leaues of the flower on the one side will turne vp their brimmes or edges : the greene leafe is very large.

Caryophyllus maximus Granatensis. The greatest *Granado* is a very faire large flower, bigger then the Chrystall,and almost as bigge as the blew *Hulo* : it is almost equally diuided and stript with purple and white, but the purple is sadder then in the ordinary *Granado* Gilloflower, else it might bee said it were the same,but greater. Diuers haue taken this flower to bee the *Gran Pere*, but you shall haue the difference shewed you in the next ensuing flower.

Caryophyllus maximus Gran Pere dictus. The *Gran Pere* is a fair great flower,and comely for the forme, but of no great beautie for colour, because although it be stript red and white like the Queenes Gilloflower, yet the red is so sad that it taketh away all the delight to the flower.

Caryophyllus maximus Cambersine dictus. The Cambersine is a great flower and a faire, beeing a redde flower, well marked or striped with white, somewhat like vnto a

Sauadge

Sauadge, ſay ſome, but that the red is not crimſon as the Sauadge; others ſay the Daintie, but not ſo comely : the leaues of the flowers are many, and thruſt together, without any due forme of ſpreading.

Caryophyllus maximus Longo-bardicus ruber.

The great Lombard red is a great ſad red flower, ſo double and thick of leaues, that it moſt vſually breaketh the pod, and ſeldome ſheweth one flower among twenty perfect : the blades or greene leaues are as large as the *Hulo.*

Caryophylli majores.

GILLOFLOWERS.

Caryophyllus maior Weſtmin-ſterienſis.

THe luſtie Gallant or Weſtminſter (ſome make them to be one flower, and others to bee two, one bigger then the other) at the firſt blowing open of the flower ſheweth to be of a reaſonable ſize and comelineſſe, but after it hath ſtood blowen ſome time it ſheweth ſmaller and thinner : it is of a bright red colour, much ſtriped and ſpeckled with white.

Caryophyllus maior Briſtolien-ſis purpureus.

The Briſtow blew hath greene leaues, ſo large, that it would ſeeme to bring a greater flower then it doth, yet the flower is of a reaſonable ſize, and very like vnto the ordinary *Granado* Gillo-flower, ſtriped and fluked in the ſame manner, but that the white of this is purer then that, and the purple is more light, and tending to a blew : this doth not abide conſtant, but changeth into purple or bluſh.

Caryophyllus maior Briſtolien-ſis carneus.

The Briſtow bluſh is very like the laſt both in leafe and flower, the colour only ſheweth the difference, which ſeldome varyeth to be ſpotted, or change colour.

Caryophyllus maior Doroborni-enſis ruber.

The red Douer is a reaſonable great Gilloflower and conſtant, being of a faire red thicke poudered with white ſpots, and ſeemeth ſomewhat like vnto the ground Carnation.

Caryophyllus maior Doroborni-enſis dilutus ſiue albus.

The light or white Douer is for forme and all other things more comely then the former, the colour of the flower is bluſh, thicke ſpotted with very ſmall ſpots, that it ſeemeth all gray, and is very delightfull.

Caryophyllus maior Cantii.

The faire maide of Kent, or Ruffling Robin is a very beautiful flower, and as large as the white Carnation almoſt : the flower is white, thicke poudered with purple, wherein the white hath the maſtrie by much, which maketh it the more pleaſant.

Caryophyllus maior Reginæus.

The Queenes Gilloflower is a reaſonable faire Gilloflower although very common, ſtriped red and white, ſome great and ſome ſmall with long ſtripes.

Caryophyllus maior elegans.

The Daintie is a comely fine flower, although it be not great, and for the ſmallneſſe and thinneſſe of the flower being red ſo finely marked, ſtriped and ſpeckled, that for the liuelineſſe of the colours it is much deſired, beeing inferiour to very few Gillo-flowers.

Caryophyllus maior Braſilienſis.

The Braſſill Gilloflower is but of a meane ſize, being of a ſad purple colour, thicke poudered and ſpeckled with white, the purple herein hath the maſtrie, which maketh it ſhew the ſadder, it is vnconſtant, varying much and often to bee all purple : the greene leaues lye matting on the ground.

Caryophyllus maior Grana-tenſis.

The *Granado* Gilloflower is purple and white, fluked and ſtriped very much: this is alſo much ſubiect to change purple. There is a greater and a leſſer of this kinde, beſides the greateſt that is formerly deſcribed.

The

Caryophyllus Turcicus. The Turkie Gilloflower is but a small flower, but of great delight, by reason of the well marking of the flower, being most vsually equally striped with red and white.

Caryophyllus Cambrensis Poole. The Poole flower, growing naturally vpon the rockes neare Cogshot Castle in the Isle of Wight, is a small flower, but very pleasant to the eye, by reason of the comely proportion thereof; it is of a bright pale red, thicke speckled, and very small with white, that it seemeth to bee but one colour, the leaues of the flower are but smally iagged about : it is constant.

Caryophyllus Pegma dilutior. The light or pale Pageant is a flower of a middle size, very pleasant to behold, and is both constant and comely, and but that it is so common, would be of much more respect then it is : the flower is of a pale bright purple, thicke poudered, and very euenly with white, which hath the mastery, and maketh it the more gracefull.

Caryophyllus Pegma saturatior. The sad Pageant is the same with the former in forme and bignesse, the difference in colour is, that the purple hath the mastery, which maketh it so sad, that it doth resemble the Brassill for colour, but is not so bigge by halfe.

Caryophyllus Heroina dictus elegans Magistri Bradshawy. Master Bradshawe his dainty Lady may bee well reckoned among these sorts of Gilloflowers, and compare for neatenesse with most of them : the flower is very neate, though small, with a fine small iagge, and of a fine white colour on the vnderside of all the leaues, as also all the whole iagge for a pretty compasse, and the bottome or middle part of the flower on the vpperside also : but each leafe is of a fine bright pale red colour on the vpperside, from the edge to the middle, which mixture is of wonderfull great delight.

Caryophyllus albus optimus maior Londinensis & alius. The best white Gilloflower groweth vpright, and very double, the blades growe vpright also, and crawle not on the ground.

The London white is greater and whiter then the other ordinary white, being wholly of one colour.

Caryophyllus maior rubens & minor. The stamell Gilloflower is well knowne to all, not to differ from the ordinary red or cloue Gilloflower, but only in being of a brighter or light red colour : there is both a greater and a lesser of this kinde.

Caryophyllus purpureus maior & minor. The purple Gilloflower a greater and a lesse : the stalke is so slender, and the leaues vpon them so many and thicke, that they lye and traile on the ground : the greatest is almost as bigge as a Chrystall, but not so double : the lesse hath a smaller flower.

Caryophyllus Persico violaceus. The Gredeline Gilloflower is a very neate and handsome flower, of the bignesse of the Cloue red Gilloflower, of a fine pale reddish purple or peach colour, enclining to a blew or violet, which is that colour is vsually called a gredeline colour : it hath no affinity with eyther Purple, Granado, or Pageant.

Caryophyllus purpuro caeruleus. The blew Gilloflower is neither very double nor great, yet round and handsome, with a deepe iagge at the edge, and is of an exceeding deepe purple colour, tending to a tawnie : this differeth from all other sorts, in that the leafe is as greene as grasse, and the stalkes many times red or purple : by the greene leaues it may be knowne in the Winter, as well as in the Summer.

Caryophyllus carneus. The blush Gilloflower differeth not from the red or stamell, but only in the colour of the flower, which is blush.

Caryophyllus Silesiacus maximus Wittie. Iohn Wittie his great tawny Gilloflower is for forme of growing, in leafe and flower altogether like vnto the ordinary tawny, the flower onely, because it is the fairest and greatest that any other

ther

ther hath nourled vp, maketh the difference, as also that it is of a faire deepe scarlet colour.

There are also diuers other Tawnies, either lighter or sadder, either lesse or more double, that they cannot be numbered, and all rising (as I said before) from sowing the seede of some of them : besides the diuersities of other colours both simple and mixed, euery yeare and place yeelding some variety was not seen with them before : I shall neede but onely to giue you the names of some of them we haue abiding with vs, I meane such as haue receiued names, and leaue the rest to euery ones particular denomination.

Of Blushes there are many sorts, as the deepe blush, the pale blush, the Infanta blush, a blush enclining to a red, a great blush, the fairest and most double of all the other blushes, and many others both single and double.

Of Reds likewise there are some varieties, but not so many as of the other colours ; for they are most dead or deepe reds, and few of a bright red or stamell colour ; and they are single like Pinkes, either striped or speckled, or more double striped and speckled variably, or else

There are neither purple nor white that rise from this seede that I haue obserued, except one white in one place.

Caryophyllus Silesiacus striatus.

The striped Tawny are either greater or lesser, deeper or lighter flowers twenty sorts and aboue, and all striped with smaller or larger stripes, or equally diuided, of a deeper or lighter colour : and some also for the very shape or forme will bee more neate, close, and round ; others more loose, vnequall, and sparsed.

Caryophyllus Silesiacus marmor-amulus.

The marbled Tawny hath not so many varieties as the striped, but is of as great beauty and delight as it, or more : the flowers are greater or smaller, deeper or lighter coloured one then another, and the veines or markes more conspicuous, or more frequent in some then in others : but the most beautifull that euer I did see was with Master Ralph Truggie, which I must needes therefore call

Heroina Rodolphi florum Imperatoris.

Master Tuggies Princesse, which is the greatest and fairest of all these sorts of variable tawnies, or seed flowers, being as large fully as the Prince or Chrystall, or something greater, standing comely and round, not loose or shaken, or breaking the pod as some other sorts will ; the marking of the flower is in this manner : It is of a stamell colour, striped and marbled with white stripes and veines quite through euery leafe, which are as deeply iagged as the Hulo : sometimes it hath more red then white, and sometimes more white then red, and sometimes so equally marked, that you cannot discerne which hath the mastery; yet which of these hath the predominance, still the flower is very beautifull, and exceeding delightsome.

Caryophyllus Silesiacus assulosus

The Flaked Tawny is another diuersity of these variable or mixt coloured flowers, being of a pale reddish colour, flaked with white, not alwaies downeright, but often thwart the leaues, some more or lesse then others ; the marking of them is much like vnto the Chrystall : these also as well as others will be greater or smaller, and of greater or lesse beauty then others.

Caryophyllus Silesiacus plumatus.

The Feathered Tawny is more rare to meete with then many of the other; for most vsually it is a faire large flower and double, equalling the Lumbard red in his perfection : the colour hereof is vsually a scarlet, little deeper or paler, most curiously feathered and streamed with white through the whole leafe.

Caryophyllus Silesiacus punctatus.

The Speckled Tawny is of diuers sorts, some bigger, some lesse,

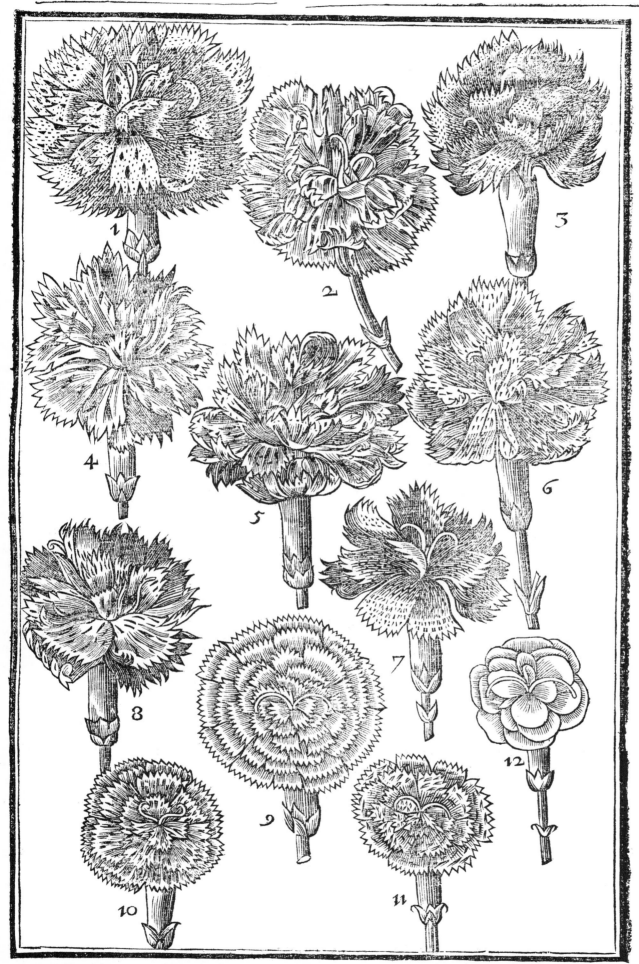

1 *Heroina Radolphi florum Imperatoris Princessa dictus*. Mafter Tuggie his Princeffe. 2 *Caryophyllus Oxoniensis*. The French or Oxford Carnation. 3 *Caryophyllus Westmonasteriensis*. The Gallant or Weftminfter Gilloflower. 4 *Caryophyllus Bristoliensis*. The Briftow. 5 *Caryophyllus Chrystallinus*. The Chryftall or Chryftalline. 6 *Caryophyllus Sabaudicus striatus*. The ftript Sauadge. 7 *Caryophyllus Granatensis maximus*. The Granpere or greateft Granado. 8 *Caryophyllus peramœnus*. The Dainty. 9 *Caryophyllus Silesiacus maximus Iagonij Ioanni*. Iohn Witty his great tawny Gilloflower. 10 *Caryophyllus Silesiacus striatus*. The ftript Tawny. 11 *Caryophyllus marmor œmulus*. The marbled Tawny. 12 *Caryophyllus roseus rotundus magistri Tuggie*. Mafter Tuggie his Rofe Gilloflower.

leffe, fome more, and fome leffe fpotted then others : Vfually it is a deepe fcarlet, fpeckled or fpotted with white, hauing alfo fome ftripes among the leaues.

Caryophyllus rofeus rotundus Magiftri Tuggie.

Mafter Tuggie his Rofe Gilloflower is of the kindred of thefe Tawnies, being raifed from the feede of fome of them, and onely poffeffed by him that is the moft induftrious pr eferuer of all natures beauties, being a different fort from all other, in that it hath round leaues, without any iagge at all on the edges, of a fine ftamell full colour, without any fpot or ftrake therin, very like vnto a fmall Rofe, or rather much like vnto the red Rofe Campion, both for forme, colour, and roundneffe, but larger for fize.

The Place.

All thefe are nourifhed with vs in Gardens, none of their naturall places being knowne, except one before recited, and the yellow which is *Silefia*; many of them being hardly preferued and encreafed.

The Time.

They flower not vntill the heate of the yeare, which is in Iuly (vnleffe it be an extraordinary occafion) and continue flowring, vntill the colds of the Autumne checke them, or vntill they haue wholly out fpent themfelues, and are vfually encreafed by the flips.

The Names.

Moft of our later Writers doe call them by one generall name, *Caryophyllus fativus*, and *flos Caryophylleus*, adding thereunto *maximus*, when wee meane Carnations, and *maior* when we would expreffe Gilloflowers, which name is taken from Cloues, in that the fent of the ordinary red Gilloflower efpecially doth refemble them. Diuers other feuerall names haue beene formerly giuen them, as *Vetonica*, or *Betonica altera*, or *Vetonica altilis*, and *coronaria. Herba Tunica, Viola Damafcena, Ocellus Damafcenus*, and *Barbaricus.* Of fome *Cantabrica Pliny.* Some thinke they were vnknowne to the Ancients, and fome would haue them to be *Iphium* of Theophraftus, wherof he maketh mention in his fixth and feuenth Chapters of his fixth booke, among Garland and Summer flowers; others to be his *Dios anthos*, or *Iouis flos*, mentioned in the former, and in other places. We call them in Englifh (as I faid before) the greateft kindes, Carnations, and the others Gilloflowers (*quafi* Iuly flowers) as they are feuerally expreffed.

The Vertues.

The red or Cloue Gilloflower is moft vfed in Phyficke in our Apothecaries fhops, none of the other being accepted of or vfed (and yet I doubt not, but all of them might ferue, and to good purpofe, although not to giue fo gallant a tincture to a Syrupe as the ordinary red will doe) and is accounted to be very Cordiall.

Chap. LXX.

Caryophylli filueftres. Pinkes.

There remaine diuers forts of wilde or fmall Gilloflowers (which wee vfually call Pinkes) to be entreated of, fome bearing fingle, and fome double flowers, fome fmooth, almoft without any deepe dents on the edges, and fome iagged, or as it were feathered. Some growing vpright like vnto Gilloflowers, others creeping

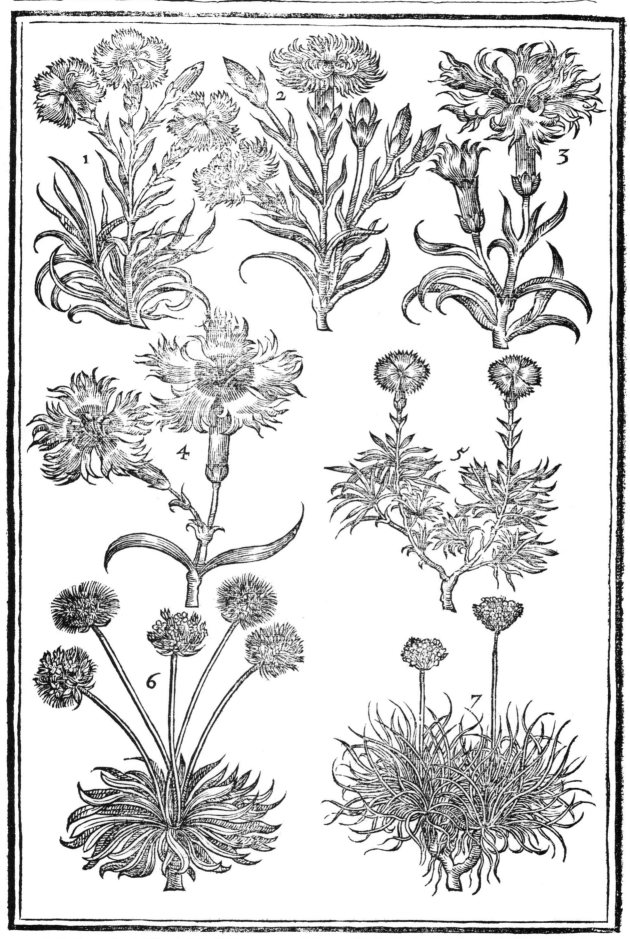

1 *Caryophyllus siluestris simplex.* The vsuall single Pinke. 2 *Caryophyllus multiplex siluestris.* Double Pinkes. 3 *Cariophyllus siluestris pluma-marius.* Feathered or iagged Pinkes. 4 *Caryophyllus Stellatus.* Starre Pinkes. 5 *Caryophyllus repens.* Matted Pinkes. 6 *Caryophyllus me-diterraneus.* The great Thistle or Sea Gilloflower. 7 *Caryophyllus marinus.* The ordinary Thistle or Sea Cushion.

ping or spreading vnder the toppe or crust of the ground, some of one colour, some of another, and many of diuers colours : As I haue formerly done with the Gilloflowers, so must I doe with these that are entertained in our Gardens, onely giue you the descriptions of some three or foure of them, according to their variety, and the names of the rest, with their distinctions.

1. *Caryophyllus minor siluestris multiplex & simplex.*
Double and single Pinkes.

The single and double Pinkes are for forme and manner of growing, in all parts like vnto the Gilloflowers before described, sauing onely that their leaues are smaller and shorter, in some more or lesse then in others, and so are the flowers also : the single kindes consisting of fiue leaues vsually (seldome six) round pointed, and a little snipt for the most part about the edges, with some threads in the middle, either crooked or straight : the double kindes being lesser, and lesse double then the Gilloflowers, hauing their leaues a little snipt or endented about the edges, and of diuers seuerall colours, as shall hereafter be set downe, and of as fragrant a sent, especially some of them as they : the rootes are long and spreading, somewhat hard and wooddy.

2. *Caryophyllus plumarius.* Feathered or iagged Pinkes.

The iagged Pinkes haue such like stalkes and leaues as the former haue, but somewhat shorter and smaller, or grasse-like, and of a whitish or grayish greene colour likewise : the flowers stand in the like manner at the toppes of the stalkes, in long, round, slender, greene huskes, consisting of fiue leaues, very much cut in on the edges, and iagged almost like a feather, of a light red, or bright purple colour, with two white threads standing in the middle, crooked like a horne at the end, and are of a very good sent. Some of these haue not those two crooked threads or hornes in the middle, but haue in their stead many small threads, not crooked at all : the seedes of them all are like vnto the seedes of Gilloflowers, or the other Pinkes, that is, small, blacke, long, and flat : the rootes are small and wooddy likewise.

3. *Caryophyllus plumarius albus orbe rubro siue Stellatus.* Starre Pinkes.

Of this kinde there is another sort, bearing flowers almost as deeply cut or iagged as the former, of a faire white colour, hauing a ring or circle of red about the bottome or lower part of the leaues, and are as sweete as the former : this being sowne of seede doth not giue the starre of so bright a red colour, but becommeth more dunne.

4. *Caryophyllus plumarius Austriacus siue Superba Austriaca.*
The feathered Pinke of Austria.

This kinde of Pinke hath his first or lower leaues, somewhat broader and greener then any of the former Pinkes, being both for breadth and greennesse more like vnto the Sweete Iohns, which shall bee described in the next Chapter : the leaues on the stalkes are smaller, standing by couples at euery ioynt, at the toppes whereof stand such like iagged flowers as the last described, and as large, but more deeply cut in or iagged round about, some of them of a purplish colour, but the most ordinary with vs are pure white, and of a most fragrant sent, comforting the spirits and senses afarre off : the seedes and rootes are like vnto the former. Some haue mistaken a kinde of wilde Campion, growing in our Woods, and by the paths sides in Hornsie Parke, and other places, to be this feathered Pinke : but the flowers declare the difference sufficiently.

5. *Caryophyllus minor repens simplex & multiplex.*
Single and double matted Pinkes.

The matted Pinke is the smallest, both for leafe and flower of all other Pinkes that are nourished in Gardens, hauing many short and small grassie greene leaues vpon the

stalkes,

stalkes, which as they grow and lye vpon the ground (and not standing so vpright as the former) doe take roote againe, whereby it quickly spreadeth, and couereth a great deale of ground in a little space: the flowers are small and round, a little snipt about the edges, whereof some are white, and some red, and some are white spotted with red, and some red spotted with white, all of them being single flowers. But there is another of this kinde, not differing in leafe, but in flower: for that the first flowers are but once double, or of two rowes of leaues, of a fine reddish colour, spotted with siluer spots: but those that follow, are so thicke and double, that they oftentimes doe breake the pod or huske; being not altogether of so deepe a red colour, but more pale.

6. *Caryophyllus Mediterraneus siue Marinus maior.*
Great Sea Gilloflower or Great Thrift.

Vnto these kindes of Pinkes I must needs adde, not only our ordinary Thrift (which is more frequent in gardens, to empale or border a knot, because it abideth greene Winter and Summer, and that by cutting, it may grow thick, and be kept in what form one list, rather then for any beautie or the flowers) but another greater kinde, which is of as great beautie and delight almost as any of the former Pinkes, as well for that the leaues are like vnto Gilloflowers, being longer and larger then any Pinkes, and of a whitish greene colour like vnto them, not growing long or by couples vpon the stalkes as Pinkes and Gilloflowers doe, but tufting close vpon the ground, like vnto the common Thrift: as also that the stalkes, rising from among the leaues (being sometimes two foote high (as I haue obserued in my garden) are yet so slender and weake, that they are scarce able to beare the heads of flowers, naked or bare, both of leaues and ioynts, sauing only in one place, where at the ioynt each stalke hath two small and very short leaues, not rising vpwards as in all other Gilloflowers, Pinkes, and other herbes, but growing downewards) and doe beare each of them a tuft or vmbell of small purplish, or blush coloured flowers, at the toppes of them standing somewhat like vnto sweete Williams, but more roundly together, each flower consisting of fiue small, round, stiffe or hardish leaues, as if they were made of paper, the bottome or middle being hollow, not blowing all at once as the ordinary Thrift, but for the most part one after another, not shewing vsually aboue foure or fiue flowers open at one time (so farre as I could obserue in the plants that I kept) so that it was long before the whole tuft of flowers were past; but yet the hoter and dryer the time was, the sooner it would be gone: the seede I haue not perfectly obserued, but as I remember, it was somewhat like vnto the seede of Scabious; I am sure nothing like vnto Gilloflowers or Pinkes: the roote is somewhat great, long and hard, and not so much spreading in the ground as Gilloflowers or Pinkes.

Caryophyllus Marinus. Thrift, or Sea Cushion.

Our common Thrift is well knowne vnto all, to haue many short and hard greene leaues, smaller then many of the grasses, growing thicke together, and spreading vpon the ground: the stalkes are naked of leaues a spanne high, bearing a small tuft of light purple, or blush coloured flowers, standing round and close thrusting together.

Double Pinkes.

THe double white Pinke is onely with more leaues in it then the single, which maketh the difference.
The double red Pinke is in the same manner double, differing from the single of the same colour.
The double purple Pinke differeth not

Single Pinkes.

THe single white ordinary Pinke hath a single white flower of fiue leaues, finely iagged about the edges.
The single red Pink is like the white, but that the leaues are not so much iagged, and the flower is of a pale purplish red colour,

from

from the single purple for colour, but only in the doublenesse of the flower.

The *Granado* Pinke differeth not from the Gilloflower of the same name, but in the smalnesse both of leaues and flower.

The double Matted Pinke is before described.

The double blush Pinke is almost as great as the ordinary blush Gilloflower, and some haue taken it for one, but the greene leaues are almost as small as Pinks, and therefore I referre it to them.

The single purple Pinke is of a faire purple colour, like almost vnto the purple Gilloflower.

The great blush Pinke hath broader and larger leaues in the flower then any other Pinke, and of a faire blush colour.

The white Featherd Pinke hath the edges of the flower more finely and deeply cut in then the former.

The red or light purple Featherd Pinke is like the former featherd Pinke, but only differeth in colour.

The Starre Pinke is a faire flower, finely iagged on the edges, with a faire red circle at the lower end of the leaues on the inside.

The white featherd Pinke of Austria is described before. The purple featherd Pinke of Austria is so likewise. The single matted Pinke is before described. The speckled Pinke is a small flower hauing small spots of red here and there dispersed ouer the white flower.

Those single flowers being like vnto Pinkes that rise from the sowing of the orenge tawney, I bring not into this *classis*, hauing already spoken of them in the precedent Chapter.

The Place.

These are all like as the former, nourished in Gardens with vs, although many of them are found wilde in many places of Austria, Hungarie, and Germany, on the mountaines, and in many other places, as Clusius recordeth. The ordinary Thrift groweth in the salt Marshes at Chattam by Rochester, and in many other places in England : but the great kinde was gathered in Spaine, by Guillaume Boel that painefull searcher of simples, and the seede thereof imparted to me, from whence I had diuers plants, but one yeare after another they all perished,

The Time.

Many of these Pinkes both single and double, doe flower before any Gilloflower, and so continue vntill August, and some, most of the Summer and Autumne.

The Names.

The seuerall titles that are giuen to these Pinkes, may suffice for their particular names : and for their generall they haue beene expressed in the former Chapter, beeing of the same kindred, but that they are smaller, and more frequently found wilde. The two sorts of Thrift are called *Caryophyllus Marinus*. The greater, *Maior & Mediterraneus* ; In English, The greater or Leuant Thrift, or Sea Gilloflower. The lesser *Minimus*, and is accounted of some to be a grasse, and therefore called *Gramen Marinum & Polyanthemum* ; In English, Thrift, Sea grasse, and our Ladies Cushion, or Sea Cushion.

The Vertues.

It is thought by diuers, that their vertues are answerable to the Gilloflowers, yet as they are of little vse with vs, so I thinke of as small effect.

CHAP.

Chap. LXXI.

Armerius. Sweet Iohns, and sweet Williams.

THese kindes of flowers as they come neerest vnto Pinkes and Gilloflowers, though manifestly differing, so it is fittest to place them next vnto them in a peculiar Chapter.

1. *Armerius angustifolius rubens simplex.* Single red sweete Iohns.

The sweete Iohn hath his leaues broader, shorter and greener then any of the former Gilloflowers, but narrower then sweete Williams, set by couples, at the ioynts of the stalkes, which are shorter then most of the former, and not aboue a foote and a halfe high, at the tops whereof stand many small flowers, like vnto small Pinkes, but standing closer together, and in shorter huskes, made of fiue leaues, smaller then most of them, and more deeeply iagged then the Williams, of a red colour in the middle, and white at the edges, but of a small or soft sent, and not all flowring at once, but by degrees : the seede is blacke, somewhat like vnto the seede of Pinkes, the roote is dispersed diuersly, with many small fibres annexed vnto it.

2. *Armerius angustifolius albus simplex.* Single white sweet Iohns.

This white Iohn differeth not in any thing from the former, but onely that the leafe doth neuer change brownish, and that the flower is of a faire white colour, without any mixture.

3. *Armerius angustifolius duplex.* Double sweet Iohns.

There is of both those former kindes, some whose flowers are once double, that is, consisting of two or three rowes of leaues, and the edges not so deepely iagged ; not differing in any thing else.

4. *Armerius latifolius simplex flore rubro.* Single red sweet Williams.

The sweet Williams doe all of them spread into many very long trayling branches, with leaues lying on the ground, in the very like manner that the sweete Iohns doe : the chiefe differences betweene them are, that these haue broader, and darker greene leaues, somewhat brownish, especially towards the points, and that the flowers stand thicker and closer, and more in number together, in the head or tuft, hauing many small pointed leaues among them, but harmlesse, as all men know; the colour of the flower is of a deep red, without any mixture or spot at all.

5. *Armerius latifolius flore rubro multiplici.* Double red sweete Williams.

The double kinde differeth not from the single kinde of the same colour, but only in the doublenesse of the flowers, which are with two rowes of leaues in euery flower.

6. *Armerius latifolius variegatus siue versicolor.* Speckled sweete Williams, or London pride.

These spotted Williams are very like the first red Williams, in the forme or maner of growing, hauing leaues as broade, and browne sometimes as they, the flowers stand as thicke or thicker, clustring together, but of very variable colours : for some flowers will be of a fine delayed red, with few markes or spots vpon them, and others
will

will bee full peckled or sprinkled with white or siluer spots, circlewise about the middle of the flowers, and some will haue many specks or spots vpon them dispersed: all these flowers are not blowne at one time, but some are flowring, when others are decaying, so that abiding long in their pride, they become of the more respect: The seede is blacke, as all the rest, and not to be distinguished one from another: the roots are some long, and some small and threddy, running vnder the vpper crust of the earth.

7. *Armerius latifolius flore rubro saturo holosericeo.*
Sweet Williams of a deepe red or murrey colour.

The leaues of this kinde seeme to be a little larger, and the ioints a little redder then the former, but in the flower consisteth the chiefest difference, which is of a deepe red, or murrey purple colour, like vnto veluet of that colour, without any spots, but smooth, and as it were soft in handling, hauing an eye or circle in the middle, at the bottome of the leaues.

8. *Armerius latifolius simplex flore albo.*
Single white sweete Williams.

The white kinde differeth not in forme, but in colour from the former, the leaues are not browne at all, but of a fresh greene colour, and the flowers are wholly white, or else they are all one.

The Place.

These for the most part grow wilde in Italie, and other places: we haue them in our Gardens, where they are cherished for their beautifull varietie.

The Time.

They all generally doe flower before the Gilloflowers or Pinkes, or with the first of them: their seede is ripe in Iune and Iuly, and doe all well abide the extremitie of our coldest winters.

The Names.

They all generally are called *Armerius*, or *Armeria*, as some doe write, and distinguished as they are in their titles: Yet some haue called them *Vetonica agrestis*, and others *Herba Tunica, Scarlatea, & Caryophyllus siluestris*: Wee doe in English in most places, call the first or narrower leafed kindes, Sweet Iohns, and all the rest Sweete Williams; yet in some places they call the broader leafed kindes that are not spotted, Tolmeiners, and London tufts: but the speckled kinde is termed by our English Gentlewomen, for the most part, London pride.

The Vertues.

We haue not knowne any of these vsed in Physicke.

Chap. LXXII.

Bellis. Daisie.

THere be diuers sorts of Daisies, both great and small, both single and double, both wilde growing abroade in the fieldes, and elsewhere, and manured growing only in Gardens: of all which I intend not to entreate, but of those that are of most beautie and respect, and leaue the rest to their proper place.

1. *Bellis*

1 *Armeriæ angustifolius simplex.* Single sweete Iohns. 2 *Armeriæ angustifolius multiplex* Double sweet Iohns. 3 *Armeriæ latifolius simplex.* Single sweete
Williams. 4 *Armeriæ latifolius versicolor.* Spotted sweet Williams or pride of London. 5 *Armeriæ latifolius multiplex* Double sweet Williars. 6 *Bellis
hortensis minor multiplex.* Double Garden Daisies. 7 *Bellis minor hortensis flore vario.* Double-red Daisies stript 8 *Bellis minor hortensis prolifera.* Double
fruitfull Daisies or Iacke an Apes on horsebacke. 9 *Bellis cærulea siue Globularia.* Double blew Daisies or blew Globeflower. 10 *Bellis lutea montana
siue Globularia lutea montana,* Double yellow Daisies or yellow Globeflower,

1. *Bellis maior flore albo pleno.* The great double white Daisie.

The great Daisie with the double white flower, is in all things so like vnto the great single kinde, that groweth by the high wayes, and in diuers medowes and fields, that there is no difference but in the flower, which is double. It hath many long, and somewhat broad leaues lying vpon the ground, deeply cut in on both sides, somewhat like vnto an oaken leafe; but those that are on the stalkes are shorter, narrower, and not so deeply cut in, but onely notched on the edges: the flowers at the toppe are (as I said) white and double, consisting of diuers rowes of leaues, being greater in compasse then any of the double Daisies that follow, but nothing so double of leaues.

2. *Bellis minor flore rubro simplici.* Single red Daisies.

This single Daisie (like as all the rest of the small Daisies) hath many smooth, greene, round pointed leaues lying on the ground, a little snipt about the edges; from among which rise many slender round foote-stalkes, rather then stalkes or stems, about an hand breadth high at the most, and oftentimes not halfe so high, bearing one flower a peece, consisting of many small leaues, as a pale or border set about a middle thrumme: the leaues of this kinde are almost wholly red, whereas in the wilde they are white or whitish, enclining to red on the edges, the middle being yellow in both sorts: the rootes are many small white threads or strings.

3. *Bellis minor hortensis flore pleno variorum colorum.* Double Garden Daisies of diuers colours.

The leaues of all the double Daisies are in forme like vnto the single ones, but that they are smaller, and little or nothing snipt or notched about the edges: the small stalkes likewise are smaller and lower, but bearing as double flowers as any that growe on the ground, being composed of many small leaues, thicke thrust together, of diuers colours; for some are wholly of a pure white, others haue a little red, either dispersed vpon the white leaues, or on the edges, and sometimes on the backes of the leaues: some againe seeme to be of a whitish red, or more red then white, when as indeede they are white leaues dispersed among the red; others of a deepe or darke red colour, and some are speckled or striped with white and red through the whole flower: and some the leaues will bee red on the vpperside, and white vnderneath; and some also (but those are very rare) are of a greenish colour.

4. *Bellis minor hortensis prolifera.* Double double Daisies or childing Daisies.

There is no difference either in leafe or roote in this kinde from the former double Daisies: the chiefest variety consisteth in this, that it beareth many small double flowers, standing vpon very short stalkes round about the middle flower, which is vsually as great and double as any of the other double kindes, and is either wholly of a deepe red colour, or speckled white and red as in some of the former kindes, or else greenish, all the small flowers about it being of the same colour with the middlemost.

5. *Bellis cærulea siue Globularia.* Blew Daisies.

The likenesse and affinity that this plant hath with the former, both in the forme of leafe and flower, as also in the name, hath caused me to insert it, and another rare plant of the same kinde, in this place, although they be very rare to be met with in our English Gardens. This beareth many narrower, shorter, and blacker greene leaues then the former, lying round about vpon the ground; among which rise vp slender but stiffe and hard stalks, halfe a foot high or more, set here and there with small leaues, and at the top a small round head, composed of many small blew leaues, somewhat like vnto the head of a Scabious: It hath bin found likewise with a white head of flowers: the roote is hard and stringie: the whole plant is of a bitter taste.

6. *Globularia*

6. *Globularia lutea montana.* Yellow Daisies.

This mountaine yellow Daisie or Globe-flower hath many thicke, smooth, round pointed leaues, spread vpon the gronnd like the former; among which spring diuers small round rushie stalkes, a foote high, bearing about the middle of them two small leaues at the ioynts, and at the toppes round heads of flowers thrust thicke together, standing in purplish huskes, euery of which flowers do blow or spread into fiue leaues, starre-fashion, and of a faire yellow colour, smelling like vnto broome flowers, with many small threads in the middle compassing a flat pointell, horned or bended two wayes: after the flowers are past rise vp the seede vessels, which are round, swelling out in the middle, and diuided into foure parts at the toppes, containing within them round, flat, blacke seede, with a small cut or notch in them : the roote is a finger long, round and hard, with a thicke barke, and a woddy pith in the middle, of a sharpe drying taste and strong sent : the leaues are also sharpe, but bitter.

The Place.

The small Daisies are all planted, and found onely in Gardens, and will require to be replanted often, lest they degenerate into single flowers, or at least into lesse double. The blew Daisie is naturall of Mompelier in France, and on the mountaines in many places of Italy, as also the yellow kinde in the Kingdome of Naples.

The Time.

The Daisies flower betimes in the Spring, and last vntill May, but the last two flower not vntill August or September.

The Names.

They are vsually called in Latine *Bellides*, and in English Daisies. Some call them *Herba Margarita*, and *Primula veris*, as it is likely after the Italian names, of *Marguerite*, and *Fior di prima vera gentile*. The French call them *Pasquettes*, and *Marguerites*, and the Fruitfull sort, or those that beare small flowers about the middle one, *Margueritons* : our English women call them Iacke an Apes on horse-backe, as they doe Marigolds before recited, or childing Daisies : but the Physitians and Apothecaries doe in generall call them, especially the single or Field kindes, *Consolida minor*. The blew Daisie is called *Bellis carulea*, and *Globularia*, of some *Scabiosa pumilum genus*. The Italians call it *Botanaria*, because the heads are found like buttons. The yellow, *Globularia montana*, is onely described by Fabius Columna, in his last part of *Phytobasanos*, and by him referred vnto the former *Globularia*, although it differ in some notable points from it.

The Vertues.

The properties of Daisies are certainly to binde, and the roote especially being dryed, they are vsed in medicines to that purpose. They are also of speciall account among those herbes, that are vsed for wounds in the head.

CHAP,

CHAP. LXXIII.

Scabiosa. Scabious.

THe sorts of Scabious being many, yeeld not flowers of beauty or respect, fit to bee cherished in this our Garden of delight; and therefore I leaue them to the Fields and Woods, there to abide. I haue onely two or three strangers to bring to your acquaintance, which are worthy this place.

1. *Scabiosa flore albo.* White flowred Scabious.

This white Scabious hath many long leaues, very much iagged or gasht in on both sides, of a meane bignesse, being neither so large as many of the field, nor so small as any of the small kindes : the stalkes rise about a foote and a halfe high, or somewhat higher, at the tops whereof grow round heads, thicke set with flowers, like in all points vnto the field Scabious, but of a milke white colour.

2. *Scabiosa rubra Austriaca.* Red Scabious of Austria.

This red Scabious hath many leaues lying vpon the ground, very like vnto Deuils bit, but not so large, being shorter and snipt, not gashed about the edges, of a light greene colour; yet (there is another of a darker greene colour, whose flower is of a deeper red) the stalkes haue diuers such leaues on them, set by couples at the ioynts as grow belowe, and at the tops small heads of flowers, each consisting of fiue leaues, the biggest flowers standing round about in the outer compasse, as is vsuall almost in all the kinds of Scabious, of a fine light purple or red colour : after the flowers are past, come the seede, which is somewhat long and round, set with certaine haires at the head thereof, like vnto a Starre : the roote is composed of a number of slender strings, fastened at the head.

3. *Scabiosa rubra Indica.* Red flowred Indian Scabious.

This (reputed Indian) Scabious hath many large faire greene leaues lying on the ground, iagged or cut in on both sides to the middle ribbe, euery peece whereof is narrower then that at the end, which is the broadest : among these leaues rise vp sundry slender and weake stalkes, yet standing vpright for the most part, set with smaller and more iagged leaues at certaine distances, two or three at euery ioynt, branching forth at the toppe into other smaller branches, bearing euery one head of flowers, like in forme vnto other Scabiouses, but of an excellent deepe red crimson colour (and sometimes more pale or delayed) of no sent at all : after which doe come small roundish seede, like vnto the field Scabious : the roote is long and round, compassed with a great many small strings, and perisheth vsually as soone as it hath borne out his flowers and seede : otherwise if it doe not flower the first yeare of the sowing, if it be carefully defended from the extremity of Winter, it will flower the sooner the next yeare, as I my selfe haue often found by experience.

The Place.

The first is sometimes found wilde in our owne Countrey, but it is very geason, and hath been sent among other rare seedes from Italy.

The second was first found and written of by Clusius, in Pannonia and Austria, where it is very plentifull.

The third hath been sent both from Spaine & Italy, and is verily thought to grow naturally in both those parts.

The

1 *Scabiosa flore albo.* White flowred Scabious. 2 *Scabiosa rubra Austriaca.* Red Scabious of Austria. 3 *Scabiosa rubra Indica.* Red flowred Indian Scabious. 4 *Cyanus vulgaris minor.* Corn-flower of diuers colours. 5 *Cyanus Baticus.* Spanish Corn-flower. 6 *Cyanus floridus Turcicus.* The braue Sultans flower. 7 *Carthamus sativus.* Spanish Saffron.

Ee

The Time.

The firſt and ſecond flower earlier thenthe laſt, for that it flowreth not vntill September or October, (vnleſſe it be not apt to beare the firſt yeare as I before ſaid) ſo that many times (if none be more forward) it periſheth without bearing ripe ſeede, whereby we are oftentimes to ſeeke new ſeede from our friends in other parts.

The Names.

They haue all one generall name of Scabious, diſtinguiſhed eyther by their flower, or place of growing, as in their titles : yet the laſt is called of diuers *Scabioſa exotica*, becauſe they thinke the name *Indica*, is not truely impoſed vpon it.

The Vertues.

Whether theſe kindes haue any of the vertues of the other wilde kinds, I know none haue made any experience, and therefore I can ſay no more of them.

Chap. LXXIIII.

Cyanus. Corne flower, or blew Bottles.

VNder the name of *Cyanus* are comprehended, not onely thoſe plants which from the excellent blew colour of their flowers (furniſhing or rather peſtering the Corne fieldes) haue peculiarly obtained that name, and which doth much vary alſo, in the colour of the flowers, as ſhallbe ſhewed; but ſome other plants alſo for their neere reſemblance, but with ſeuerall diſtinctions. The *Cyanus maior, Ptarmica Auſtriaca, Ptarmica Imperati*, and many others which may be adioyned vnto them, do more fitly belong to the Garden of Simples, whereunto I leaue them, and will here only entreate of thoſe that may moſt pleaſe the delight of our Gentle Floriſts, in that I labour and ſtriue, to furniſh this our garden, with the chiefeſt choyſe of natures beauties and delights.

1. *Cyanus vulgaris diuerſorum colorum.* Corne flower of diuers colours.

All theſe ſorts of Corne flowers are for the moſt part alike, both in leaues and flowers one vnto another for the forme : the difference betweene them conſiſteth in the varying colour of the flowers : For the leaues are long, and of a whitiſh greene colour, deeply cut in on the edges in ſome places, ſomewhat like vntothe leaues of a Scabious : the ſtalkes are two foote high or better, beſet with ſuch like leaues but ſmaller, and little or nothing ſlit on the edges : the toppes are branched, bearing many ſmal greene ſcaly heads, out of which riſe flowers, conſiſting of fiue or ſixe, or more long and hollow leaues, ſmall at the bottome, and opening wider and greater at the brims, notched or cut in on the edges, and ſtanding round about many ſmall threds in the middle : the colours of theſe flowers are diuers, and very variable ; for ſome are wholly blew, or white, or bluſh, or of a ſad, or light purple, or of a light or dead red, or of an ouerworne purple colour, or elſe mixed of theſe colours, as ſome, the edges white, and the reſt blew or purple, or the edges blew or purple, and the reſt of the flower white, or ſtriped, ſpotted, or halfed, the one part of one colour, and the other of another, the threds likewiſe in the middle varying in many of them ; for ſome will haue the middle thrume of a deeper purple then the outer leaues, and ſome haue white or bluſh leaues, the middle thrume being reddiſh, deeper or paler : After the flowers are paſt, there come ſmall, hard, white and ſhining ſeede in thoſe heads, wrapped

ped or fet among a deale of flockie matter, as is moft vfuall, in all plants that beare fcaly heads: the rootes are long and hard, perifhing euery yeare when it hath giuen feede.

2. *Cyanus floridus Turcicus*. The Sultans flower.

As a kinde of thefe Corne flowers, I muft needes adioyne another ftranger, of much beautie, and but lately obtained from Conftantinople, where, becaufe (as it is faid) the great Turke, as we call him, faw it abroade, liked it, and wore it himfelfe; all his vaffals haue had it in great regard, and hath been obtained from them, by fome that haue fent it into thefe parts. The leaues whereof are greener, and not only gafhed, but finely fnipt on the edges: the ftalkes are three foote high, garnifhed with the like leaues as are below, and branched as the former, bearing large fcaly heads, and fuch like flowers but larger, hauing eight or nine of thofe hollow gaping leaues in euery flower, ftanding about the middle threds (if it be planted in good and fertile ground and be well watered, for it foone ftarueth and perifheth with drought) the circling leaues are of a fine delayed purple or blufh colour, very beautifull to behold; the feede of this is fmaller and blacker, and not enclofed in fo much dounie fubftance, as the former (yet in our Countrey the feede is not fo blacke, as it came vnto vs, but more gray) the roote perifheth likewife euery yeere.

3. *Cyanus Bæticus fupinus*. The Spanifh Corne-flower.

This Spanifh kinde hath many fquare low bending or creeping ftalkes, not ftanding fo vpright as the former, but branching out more diuerfly; fo that one plant will take vp a great deale of ground: the leaues are broader then any of the reft, fofter alfo, of a pale or whitifh greene colour, and not much gafhed on the edges: the flowers ftand in bigger heads, with foure or fiue leaues vnder euery head, and are of a light pale purple or blufh colour; after which come feede, but not fo plentifully, yet wrapped in a great deale of flockie matter, more then any: the roote groweth downe deepe into the ground, but perifheth euery yeare as they doe.

The Place.

The firft or former kindes, grow many times in the Corne fields of our own Countrey, as well as of others, efpecially that fort with a blew flower: but the other forts or colours are not fo frequent, but are nourifhed in gardens, where they will vary wonderfully.

The fecond as is before fet downe, groweth in Turkie: and the laft in Spaine, found out and firft fent to vs by that induftrious fearcher of fimples, Guillaume Boel before remembred.

The Time.

The firft doe flower in the end of Iune, and in Iuly, and fomtimes fooner. The other two later, and not vntill Auguft moft commonly, and the feede is foone ripe after.

The Names.

The firft is generally called *Cyanus*, and fome following the Ditch name, call it *Flos frumenti*. The olde Writers gaue it the name of *Bapti fecuba*, which is almoft worne out. We doe call them in Englifh, Blew Bottles, and in fome places, Corne flowers, after the Ditch names. The fecond hath beene fent by the name of *Ambreboi*, which whether it be a Turkie or Arabian name, I know not. I haue called it from the place, from whence we had it, *Turcicus*, and for his beauty, *Floridus*. The Turkes themfelues as I vnderftand, doe call it The Sultans flower, and I haue done fo likewife, that it may bee diftinguifhed from all the other kindes, or elfe you may call it,

The Turkey blush Corne flower, which you please. The last was sent by the name of *Iacea Batica*, but I had rather to referre it to the *Cyanus*, or Corne flowers, because the flowers are like vnto the Corne flowers, and not vnto the Iaceas or Knapweedes.

The Vertues.

These had no vse in Physicke in Galen and Dioscorides time, in that (as it is thought) they haue made no mention of them : We in these dayes doe chiefly vse the first kindes (as also the greater sort) as a cooling Cordiall, and commended by some to be a remedy, not onely against the plague and pestilentiall diseases, but against the poison of Scorpions and Spiders.

Chap. LXXV.

Iacea Marina Batica. Spanish Sea Knapweede.

THere are a great many sorts of Knapweedes, yet none of them all fit for this our Garden, but this only stranger, which I haue beene bold to thrust in here, for that it hath such like gaping or open flowers, as the former Corne flowers haue, but notably differing, and therefore deserueth a peculiar Chapter, as partaking both with *Cyanus* and *Iacea*. It hath many long and narrow leaues vneuenly dented or waued on both edges (and not notched, gashed or indented, as many other herbes are) being thicke, fleshie and brittle, a little hairy, and of an ouerworne darke greene colour, among which rise lowe weake stalkes, with such like leaues as grow at the bottome, but smaller, bearing but here and there a flower, of a bright reddish purple colour, like in forme vnto the Corne flowers, but much larger, with many threds or thrumes in the middle of the same colour, standing vp higher then any of the former: this flower riseth out of a large scaly head, all set ouer with small sharpe (but harmelesse) white prickles : the seedes are blackish, like vnto the Knapweedes, and larger then any of the former Corne flowers : the roote is great and thicke, growing deepe into the ground, fleshie and full of a slimie or clammy iuice, and easie to bee broken, blackish on the outside, and whitish within, enduring many yeares, like as the other Knapweedes, or Matfelons doe, growing in time to be very thicke and great.

The Place.

It groweth naturally by the Sea side in Spaine, from whence I receiued the seedes of Guillaume Boel, and did abide well in my garden a long time, but is now perished.

The Time.

It flowreth in the beginning of Iuly, or thereabouts, and continueth not long in flower : but the head abideth a great while, and is of some beauty after the flower is past; yet seldome giueth good seed with vs.

The Names.

It hath no other name then is set down in the title, being altogether a Neuelist, and not now to be seene with any sauing my selfe.

The Vertues.

We haue not yet known any vse hereof in Physick.

Chap.

Chap. LXXVI.

Cnicus siue Carthamus sativus. Bastard or Spanish Saffron.

THere are two or three sorts of *Cnicus* or bastard Saffrons which I passe ouer, as not fit for this Garden, and onely set downe this kinde, whose flowers are of a fairer and more liuely colour in our Country, then any hath come ouer from Spaine, where they manure it for the profit they make thereof, seruing for the dying of Silke especially, and transporting great quantities to diuers Countries. It hath large broad leaues, without any prickes at all vpon them in our Country, growing vpon the stalke, which is strong, hard, and round, with shorter leaues thereon vp to the toppe, where they are a little sharpe pointed, and prickly about the edges sometimes, which stalke riseth three or foure foote high, and brancheth it selfe toward the toppe, bearing at the end of euery branch one great open scaly head, out of which thrusteth out many gold yellow threads, of a most orient shining colour, which being gathered in a dry time, and kept dry, will abide in the same delicate colour that it bare when it was fresh, for a very long time after: when the flowers are past, the seede when it is come to maturity, which is very seldome with vs, is white and hard, somewhat long, round, and a little cornered: the roote is long, great, and wooddy, and perisheth quickly with the first frosts.

The Place.

It groweth in Spaine, and other hot Countries, but not wilde, for that it is accounted of the old Writers, Theophrastus and Dioscorides, to be a manured plant.

The Time.

It flowreth with vs not vntill August, or September sometimes, so that it hardly giueth ripe seede (as I said) neither is it of that force to purge, which groweth in these colder Countries, as that which commeth from Spaine, and other places.

The Names.

The name *Cnicus* is deriued from the Greekes, and *Carthamus* from the Arabians, yet still *sativus* is added vnto it, to shew it is no wilde, but a manured plant, and sowne euery where that wee know. Of some it is called *Crocus hortensis*, and *Sarasenicus*, from the Italians which so call it. We call it in English Bastard Saffron, Spanish Saffron, and Catalonia Saffron.

The Vertues.

The flowers are vsed in colouring meates, where it groweth beyond Sea, and also for the dying of Silkes: the kernels of the seede are onely vsed in Physicke with vs, and serueth well to purge melancholicke humours.

Chap. LXXVII.

Carduus. Thistles.

YOu may somewhat maruaile, to see mee curious to plant Thistles in my Garden, when as you might well say, they are rather plagues then pleasures, and more trouble to weede them out, then to cherish them vp, if I made therein no distinction or choise; but when you haue viewed them well which I bring in, I will

Ee 3 then

then abide your cenfure, if they be not worthy of fome place, although it be but a corner or the Garden, where fomething muft needes be to fill vp roome. Some of them are fmooth, and without prickes at all, fome at the heads onely, and fome all ouer; but yet not without fome efpeciall note or marke worthy of refpect : Out of this difcourfe I leaue the Artichoke, with all his kindes, and referue them for our Kitchin Garden, becaufe (as all know) they are for the pleafure of the tafte, and not of the fmell or fight.

1. *Acanthus fativus.* Garden Beares breech.

The leaues of this kinde of fmooth thiftle (as it is accounted) are almoft as large as the leaues of the Artichoke, but not fo fharp pointed, very deeply cut in and gafhed on both edges, of a fad green & fhining colour on the vpperfide, and of a yellowifh green vnderneath, with a great thicke rib in the middle, which fpread themfelues about the root, taking vp a great deale of ground. After this plant hath ftood long in one place, and well defended from the iniury of the cold, it fendeth forth from among the leaues one or more great and ftrong ftalkes, three or foure foote high, without any branch at all, bearing from the middle to the top many flowers one aboue another, fpike-fafhion round about the ftalke, with fmaller but not diuided greene leaues at euery flower, which is white, and fafhioned fomewhat like vnto a gaping mouth; after which come broad, flat, thicke, round, brownifh yellow feede (as I haue well obferued by them haue beene fent me out of Spaine, and which haue fprung vp, and doe grow with me; for in our Countrey I could neuer obferue any feede to haue growne ripe) the rootes are compofed of many great and thicke long ftrings, which fpread farre in and vnder the ground, fomewhat darkifh on the outfide, and whitifh within, full of a clammy moifture (whereby it fheweth to haue much life) and doe endure our Winters, if they be not too much expofed to the fharpe violence thereof, which then it will not endure, as I haue often found by experience.

2. *Acanthus filueftris.* Wilde or prickly Beares breech.

This prickly Thiftle hath diuers long greenifh leaues lying on the ground, much narrower then the former, but cut in on both fides, thicke fet with many white prickes and thornes on the edges : the ftalke rifeth not vp fo high, bearing diuers fuch like thornie leaues on them, with fuch a like head of flowers on it as the former hath : but the feede hereof (as it hath come to vs from Italy and other places, for I neuer faw it beare feed here in this Country) is blacke and round, of the bigneffe of a fmall peafe : the roote abideth reafonable well, if it be defended fomewhat from the extremity of our Winters, or elfe it will perifh.

3. *Eringium Pannonicum fiue Montanum.* Hungary Sea Holly.

The lower leaues of this Thiftle that lye on the ground, are fomewhat large, round, and broad, hard in handling, and a little fnipt about the edges, euery one ftanding vpon a long foote-ftalke : but thofe that growe vpon the ftalke, which is ftiffe, two or three foote high, haue no foote-ftalke, but encompaffe it, two being fet at euery ioynt, the toppe whereof is diuided into diuers branches, bearing fmall round rough heads, with fmaller and more prickly leaues vnder them, and more cut in on the fides then thofe belowe : out of thefe heads rife many blew flowers, the foote-ftalkes of the flowers, together with the toppes of the branches, are likewife blew and tranfparent, or fhining.

Flore albo. We haue another of this kinde, the whole toppes of the ftalkes, with the heads and branches, are more white then blew : the feede contained in thefe heads are white, flat, and as it were chaffie : the roote is great and whitifh, fpreading farre into many branches, and fomewhat fweete in tafte, like the ordinary Sea Holly rootes.

4. *Carduus mollis.* The gentle Thiftle.

The leaues of this foft and gentle Thiftle that are next vnto the ground, are greene

1 *Acanthus sativus,* Garden Beares breech. 2 *Acanthus siluestris.* Wilde Beares breech. 3 *Eringium Pannonicum* Mountaine Sea Holly. 4 *Carlina humilis.* The lowe Carline Thistle. 5 *Carduus sphærocephalus maior.* The greater Globe-Thistle 6 *Carduus sphærocephalus minor.* The lesser Globe-Thistle. 7 *Carduus Eriocephalus.* The Friers crowne. 8 *Fraxinella,* Bastard Dittanie.

on the vpperside, and hoary vnderneath, broad at the bottome, somewhat long pointed, and vneuenly notched about the edges, with some soft hairie prickles, not hurting
the handler, euery one standing vpon a short foote-stalke; those that growe about the
middle stalke are like the former, but smaller and narrower, and those next the toppe
smallest, where it diuideth it selfe into small branches, bearing long and scaly heads,
out of which breake many reddish purple threads: the seede is whitish and hard, almost as great as the seede of the greater Centory: the roote is blackish, spreading vnder the ground, with many small fibres fastened vnto it, and abideth a great while.

5. *Carlina humilis*. The lowe Carline Thistle.

This lowe Thistle hath many iagged leaues, of a whitish greene colour, armed with
small sharp white prickles round about the edges, lying round about the root vpon the
ground, in the middle whereof riseth vp a large head, without any stalke vnder it, compassed about with many small and long prickly leaues, from among which the flower
sheweth it selfe, composed of many thin, long, whitish, hard shining leaues, standing
about the middle, which is flat and yellow, made of many thrums or threads like small
flowers, wherein lye small long seede, of a whitish or siluer colour: the roote is somewhat aromaticall, blackish on the outside, small and long, growing downewards into
the ground. There is another of this kinde that beareth a higher stalke, and a redder
flower, but there is a manifest difference betweene them.

6. *Carduus Sphærocephalus siue Globosus maior*. The greater Globe Thistle.

The greatest of these beautifull Thistles, hath at the first many large and long leaues
lying on the ground, very much cut in and diuided in many places, euen to the middle
ribbe, set with small sharpe (but not very strong) thornes or prickles at euery corner of
the edges, greene on the vpperside, and whitish vnderneath: from the middle of these
leaues riseth vp a round stiffe stalke, three foote and a halfe high, or more, set without
order with such like leaues, bearing at the toppe of euery branch a round hard great
head, consisting of a number of sharpe bearded huskes, compact or set close together,
of a blewish greene colour, out of euery one of which huskes start small whitish blew
flowers, with white threads in the middle of them, and rising aboue them, so that the
heads when they are in full flower, make a fine shew, much delighting the spectators:
after the flowers are past, the seede encreaseth in euery one, or the most part of the
bearded huskes, which doe still hold their round forme, vntill that being ripe it openeth it selfe, and the huskes easily fall away one from another, containing within
them a long whitish kernell: the roote is great and long, blackish on the outside, and
dyeth euery yeare when it hath borne seede.

7. *Carduus Globosus minor*. The lesser Globe Thistle.

The lesser kinde hath long narrow leaues, whiter then the former, but cut in and
gashed on the edges very much with some small prickes on them; the stalke is not
halfe so long, nor the heads halfe so great, but as round, and with as blew flowers as the
greater: this seldome giueth ripe seede, but recompenseth that fault, in that the roote
perisheth not as the former, but abideth many yeares.

8. *Carduus Eriocephalus siue Tomentosus*. The Friers Crowne.

This woolly Thistle hath many large and long leaues lying on the ground, cut in on
both sides into many diuisions, which are likewise somewhat vnequally cut in or diuided againe, hauing sharpe white prickles at euery corner of the diuisions, of a dead
or sad greene colour on the vpperside, and somewhat woolly withall, and grayish vnderneath: the stalke is strong and tall, foure or fiue foote high at the least, branching
out into diuers parts, euery where beset with such like leaues as growe below; at the
toppe of euery branch there breaketh out a great whitish round prickly head, flattish at
the toppe, so thicke set with wooll, that the prickles seeme but small spots or haires,
and

and doth fo well refemble the bald crowne of a Frier, not onely before it be in flower, but efpecially after it hath done flowring, that thereupon it deferuedly receiued the name of the Friers Crowne Thiftle : out of thefe heads rifeth forth a purple thrumme, fuch as is to be feene in many other wilde Thiftles, which when they are ripe, are full of a flockie or woolly fubftance, which breake at the toppe fhedding it, and the feede which is blackifh, flat, and fmooth : the roote is great and thicke, enduring for fome yeares, yet fometimes perifhing, if it be too much expofed to the violence of the frofts in Winter.

The Place.

The firft groweth naturally in Spaine, Italy, and France, and in many other hot Countries, and growe onely in Gardens in thefe colder climates, and there cherifhed for the beautifull afpect both of the greene plants, and of the ftalkes when they are in flower. The Carline Thiftle is found both in Germany and Italy in many places, and as it is reported, in fome places of the Weft parts in England. The others are found fome in France, fome in Hungary, and on the Alpes, and the laft in Spaine.

The Time.

They doe all flower in the Summer moneths, fome a little earlier or later then others.

The Names.

The firft is called *Acanthus fativus* (becaufe the other that is prickly, is called *filueftris* or *fpinofus*) and *Branca vrfina* ; In Englifh, Branck vrfine, and Beares breech. The third is called *Eryngium montanum, Alpinum*, and *Pannonicum latifolium* : In Englifh, Mountaine or Hungary Sea Holly. The fourth is called *Carduus mollis*, The gentle Thiftle, becaufe it hath no harmfull prickles, although it feeme at the firft fhew to be a Thiftle. The fifth is called of diuers *Chamæleo albus*, and *Carlina*, as if they were both but one plant ; but Fabius Columna hath in my iudgement very learnedly defcided that controuerfie, making *Carlina* to be *Ixine* of Theophraftus, and *Chamæleo* another differing Thiftle, which Gaza tranflateth *Vernilago*. We call it in Englifh, The Carline Thiftle. The other haue their names in their titles, as much as is conuenient for this difcourfe.

The Vertues.

The firft hath alwaies been vfed Phyfically, as a mollifying herbe among others of the like flimie matter in Glifters, to open the body ; yet Lobel feemeth to make no difference in the vfe of them both (that is, the prickly as well as the fmooth.) The Carline Thiftle is thought to bee good againft poyfons and infection. The reft are not vfed by any that I know.

Chap. LXXVIII.

Fraxinella. Baftard Dittany.

Hauing finifhed thofe pleafing Thiftles, I come to other plants of more gentle handling, and firft bring to your confideration this baftard Dittany, whereof there are found out two efpeciall kindes, the one with a reddifh, the other with a whitifh flower, and each of thefe hath his diuerfity, as fhall be prefently declared.

1. *Fraxinella flore rubente.* Baftard Dittany with a reddifh flower.

This goodly plant rifeth vp with diuers round, hard, brownifh ftalkes, neare two
foote

foote high, the lower parts whereof are furnished with many winged leaues, somewhat like vnto Liquerice, or a small young Ashe tree, consisting of seuen, nine, or eleuen leaues set together, which are somewhat large and long, hard and rough in handling, of a darkish greene colour, and of an vnpleasant strong resinous sent: the vpper parts of the stalkes are furnished with many flowers, growing spike fashion, at certaine distances one aboue another, consisting of fiue long leaues a peece, whereof foure that stand on the two sides, are somewhat bending vpwards, and the fift hanging downe, but turning vp the end of the leafe a little againe, of a faint or pale red colour, striped through euery leafe with a deeper red colour, and hauing in the middle a tassell of fiue or six long purplish threds, that bowe downe with the lower leafe, and turne vp also the ends againe, with a little freese or thrume at the ends of euery one: after the flowers are past, arise hard, stiffe, rough, clammy huskes, horned or pointed at the end, foure or fiue standing together, somewhat like the seede vessels of the Wolfes-banes, or Colombines, but greater, thicker and harder, wherein is contained round shining blacke seede, greater then any Colombine seede by much, and smaller then Peony seede: the roote is white, large, and spreading many wayes vnder ground, if it stand long: the whole plant, as well roots as leaues and flowers, are of a strong sent, not so pleasing for the smell, as the flowers are beautifull to the sight.

2. *Fraxinella flore rubro.* Bastard Dittaine with a red flower.

This differeth not from the former eyther in roote, leafe or flower for the forme, but that the stalkes and leaues are of a darker greene colour, and that the flowers are of a deeper red colour, (and growing in a little longer spike) wherein the difference chiefly consisteth, which is sufficient to distinguish them.

3. *Fraxinella flore albo.* Bastard Dittanie with a white flower.

The white flowred *Fraxinella* hath his leaues and stalkes of a fresher greene colour then any of the former; and the flowers are of a pure white colour, in forme differing nothing at all from the other.

4. *Fraxinella flore albo cæruleo.*
Bastard Dittanie with an ash coloured flower.

The colour of the flower of this *Fraxinella* onely putteth the difference betweene this, and the last recited with a white flower: for this beareth a very pale, or whitish blew flower, tending to an ash colour.

The Place.

All these kindes are found growing naturally, in many places both of Germany, and Italie: and that with the white flower, about Franckford, which being sent me, perished by the way by long and euill carriage.

The Time.

They flower in Iune and Iuly, and the seede is ripe in August.

The Names.

The name *Fraxinella* is most generally imposed on those plants, because of the resemblance of them vnto young Ashes, in their winged leaues. Yet some doe call them *Dictamus albus*, or *Dictamnus albus*, and *Diptamus albus*, as a difference from the *Dictamnus Creticus*, which is a farre differing plant. Some would haue it to be *Tragium* of Dioscorides, but beside other things wherein this differeth from *Tragium*, this yeeldeth no milkie iuice, as Dioscorides saith *Tragium* doth: We in English doe eyther call it *Fraxinella*, or after the other corrupted name of *Dictamus*, Bastard Dittanie.

The

The Vertues.

It is held to be profitable againſt the ſtingings of Serpents, againſt contagious and peſtilent diſeaſes, to bring downe the feminine courſes, for the paines of the belly and the ſtone, and in Epilepticall diſeaſes, and other cold paines of the braines : the roote is the moſt effectuall for all theſe, yet the ſeede is ſometimes vſed.

Chap. LXXIX.

Legumina. Pulſe.

IF I ſhould deſcribe vnto you all the kindes of Pulſe, I ſhould vnfold a little world of varieties therein, more knowne and found out in theſe dayes, then at any time before, but that muſt bee a part of a greater worke, which will abide a longer time before it ſee the light. I ſhall only ſelect thoſe that are fit for this garden, and ſet them downe for your conſideration. All ſorts of Pulſe may be reduced vnder two generall heads, that is, of Beanes and Peaſe, of each whereof there is both tame and wilde : Of Beanes, beſides the tame or vſuall garden Beane, and the French or Kidney Beane, (whereof I meane to entreate in my Kitchen garden, as pertinent thereto) there is the Lupine or flat Beane, whereof I meane to entreate here, and the blacke Beane and others which muſt bee reſerued for the Phyſicke Garden. And of the kindes of Peaſe ſome are fit for this Garden, (whereunto I will adioyne two or three other plants as neereſt of affinitie, the flowers of ſome, and the fruit of others being delightfull to many, and therefore fit for this garden) ſome for the Kitchen, the reſt for the Phyſicke garden. And firſt of Lupines or flat Beanes, accepted as delightfull to many, and therefore fit for this garden.

1. *Lupinus ſativus albus.* The white garden Lupine.

The garden Lupine riſeth vp with a great round ſtalke, hollow and ſomewhat woolly, with diuers branches, whereon grow vpon long footeſtalkes many broade leaues, diuided into ſeuen or nine parts, or ſmaller leaues, equally ſtanding round about, as it were in a circle, of a whitiſh greene colour on the vpperſide, and more woolly vnderneath : the flowers ſtand many together at ſeuerall ioynts, both of the greater ſtalke, and the branches, like vnto beanes, and of a white colour in ſome places, and in others of a very bleake blew tending to white : after the flowers are paſt, there come in their places, long, broade, and flat rough cods, wherein are contained round and flat ſeede, yellowiſh on the inſide, and couered with a tough white skin, and very bitter in taſte : the rootes are not very great, but full of ſmall fibres, whereby it faſteneth it ſelfe ſtrongly in the ground, yet periſheth euery yeare, as all the reſt of theſe kindes doe.

2. *Lupinus caruleus maximus.* The greater blew Lupine.

The Stemme or ſtalke of this Lupine is greater then the laſt before recited, as alſo the leaues more ſoft and woolly, and the flowers are of a moſt perfect blew colour, with ſome white ſpots in the middle : the long rough greeniſh cods are very great and large, wherein are contained hard, flat and round ſeede, not ſo white on the outſide as the former, but ſomewhat yellower, greater alſo, and more rough or hard in handling.

3. *Lupinus caruleus minor.* The leſſer blew Lupine.

This kinde of wilde Lupine differeth not in the forme of leafe or flower from the former, but only that it is much ſmaller, the leaues are greener, and haue fewer diuiſions in them : the flower is of as deepe a blew colour as the laſt ; the cods likewiſe are ſmall and long, containing ſmall round ſeede, not ſo flat as the former, but more
difcoloured

Minimus. difcoloured or fpotted on the outfide, then the greater kinde is. There is a leſſer kind then this, not differing in any thing from this, but that it is leſſer.

4. *Lupinus flore luteo.* The yellow Lupine.

The yellow Lupine groweth not vſually ſo high, but with larger leaues then the ſmall blew Lupine ; the flowers grow in two or three rundles or tufts, round about the ſtalke and the branches at the ioynts, of a delicate fine yellow colour, like in faſhion vnto the other kindes, being larger then the laſt, but nothing ſo large as the greater kindes, and of a fine ſmall ſent : the ſeede is round, and not flat, but much about the forme and bigneſſe of the ſmall blew, or ſomewhat bigger, of a whitiſh colour on the outſide, ſpotted with many ſpots.

The Place.

The firſt groweth in many places of Greece, and the Eaſterne Countries beyond it, where it hath beene anciently cheriſhed for their foode, being often watered to take away the bitterneſſe. It groweth alſo in theſe Weſtern parts, but ſtill where it is planted. The great blew Lupine is thought to come from beyond the parts of Perſia, in Caramania. The leſſer blew is found very plentifully wilde, in many places both of Spaine and Italy. The laſt hath beene brought vs likewiſe out of Spaine, whereas it is thought it groweth naturally. They all grow now in the gardens of thoſe, that are curious louers of theſe delights.

The Time.

They flower in Summer, and their ſeede is ripe quickly after.

The Names.

They are generally called *Lupini.* Plautus in his time ſaith, they were vſed in Comedies in ſtead of money, when in any Scene thereof there was any ſhew of payment, and therefore he calleth them *Aurum Comicum.* And Horace hath this Verſe,

Nec tamen ignorant, quid diſtent æra Lupinis,

to ſhew that counterfeit money (ſuch as counters are with vs, or as theſe Lupines were vſed in thoſe times) was eaſily knowne from true and currant coine. In Engliſh wee vſually call them after the Latine name, Lupines ; and ſome after the Dutch name, Figge-beanes, becauſe they are flat and round as a Figge that is preſſed ; and ſome Flat-beanes for the ſame reaſon. Some haue called the yellow Lupine, Spaniſh Violets : but other fooliſh names haue beene giuen it, as Virginia Roſes, and the like, by knauiſh Gardiners and others, to deceiue men, and make them beleeue they were the finders out, or great preſeruers of rarities, of no other purpoſe, but to cheate men of their money : as you would therefore auoyde knaues and deceiuers, beware of theſe manner of people, whereof the skirts of our towne are too pitifully peſtered.

The Vertues.

The firſt or ordinary Lupine doth ſcoure and cleanſe the skin from ſpots, morphew, blew markes, and other diſcolourings thereof, beeing vſed eyther in a decoction or ponther. Wee ſeldome vſe it in inward medicines, not that it is dangerous, but of neglect, for formerly it hath beene much vſed for the wormes, &c.

1 *Lupinus maior*. The great Lupine. 2 *Lupinus luteus*. The yellow Lupine. 3 *Lathyrus latifolius seu Pisum perenne*. Peafe euerlafting. 4 *Pisum quadratum*. The crimfon bloffomd or fquare Peafe. 5 *Medica cochleata vulgaris* Snailes or Barbary buttons. 6 *Medica spinosa*. Prickly Snailes. 7 *Medica spinosa altera*. Another fort of prickly Snailes. 8 *Medica folliculo lato*. Broad buttons or Snailes. 9 *Medica Lunata*. Halfe Moons. 10 *Hedysarum clypeatum*. The red Sattin flower, or French Honyfuckle. 11 *Scorpioides minus*. The leffer Caterpiller. 12 *Scorpioides maius*. The greater Caterpiller. 13 *Orobus Venetus*. Blew vpright Peafe euerlafting.

1. *Lathyrus latifolius, siue Pisum perenne.* Pease euerlasting.

This kinde of wilde Pease that abideth long, and groweth euery yeare greater then other, springeth vp with many broade trayling branches, winged as it were on both the sides, diuersly diuided into other smaller branches, at the seuerall ioynts whereof stand two hard, not broad, but somewhat long greene leaues, and diuers twining claspers, in sundry places with the leaues, from betweene the branches and the leaues, at the ioynts towards the toppes, come forth diuers purplish pease like blossomes, standing on a long stemme or stalke, very beautifull to behold, and of a pretty sent or smell: after which come small, long, thin, flat, hard skind cods, containing small round blackish seede: the roote is great and thicke, growing downe deepe into the ground, of the thicknesse sometimes of a mans arme, blackish on the outside, and whitish within, with some branches and a few fibres annexed thereunto.

2. *Orobus Venetus.* Blew vpright euerlasting Pease.

This pretty kinde of Pease blossome beareth diuers slender, but vpright greene branches somewhat cornered, two foote high or thereabouts, hauing at seuerall distances on both sides of them certaine winged leaues, set together vpon long footestalkes one against another, consisting of six or eight leaues, somewhat broade and pointed, and without any odde one at the end: at the ioynts toward the toppes, betweene the leaues and the stalkes, come forth many flowers set together at the end of a pretty long footestalke, of the fashion of the former Pease blossome, but somewhat smaller, and of a purplish violet colour: after which come slender and long pointed pods rounder then they, wherein is contained small round grayish pease: the roote is blacke, hard or woody, abiding after seede bearing as the former doth, and shooting afresh euery yeare.

3. *Lathyrus annuus siliquis orobi.* Partie coloured Cichelings.

This small Pulse or wild Pease, hath two or three long slender winged branches, with smaller leaues theron then the former, and without any claspers at all on them: the flowers stand single, euery one by it selfe, or two at the most together, the middle leaues whereof that close together are white, and the vpper leaues of a reddish purple colour: after which come long round flattish cods, bunched out in the seuerall places where the seedes lye, like vnto the cods of *Orobus* or the bitter Vetch, but greater: the roote is small and dyeth euery yeare.

4. *Pisum quadratum.* The crimson blossomd or square codded Pease.

This pretty kinde of Pulse might very well for the forme of the leaues, be referred to the kindes of *Lotus* or Trefoiles: but because I haue none of that kindred to entreate of in this Worke, I haue thought fittest to place it here before the Medica's, because both pods and seedes are like also. It hath three or foure small weake stalkes, diuided into many branches, hauing two stalkes of leaues at euery ioynt, and three small soft leaues standing on a very small stalke, comming from the ioynts: the flowers stand for the most part two together, of a perfect red or crimson colour, like in forme almost vnto a Pease blossome; after which come long thicke and round cods, with two skinnes or filmes, running all along the cod at the backe or vpperside, and two other such like filmes, all along the belly or vnder side, which make it seeme foure square, wherein there lye round discoloured Pease, somewhat smaller and harder then ordinary Pease: the roote is small and perisheth euery yeare.

5. *Medica Cochleata vulgaris.* Snailes or Barbary buttons.

The plant that beareth these pretty toyes for Gentlewomen, is somewhat like vnto a Threeleafed grasse or Trefoile, hauing many long trayling branches lying vpon the ground, whereon at diuers places are three small greene leaues, set together at the end of a little footestalke, each of them a little snipt about the edges: at seuerall distances,

from

from the middle of thefe branches to the ends of them, come forth the flowers, two for the moft part ftanding together vpon a little footftalke, which are of a pale yellow colour, very fmall, and of the forme of a Peafe bloffome : after which come fmooth heads, which are turned or writhen round, almoft like a Snaile, hard and greene at the firft, fomewhat like a greene button (from the formes of both which came their names) but afterwards growing whiter, more foft and open, wherein lyeth yellowifh round and flat feede, fomewhat like vnto the Kidney beane : the roote is fmall and ftringie, dying downe euery yeare, and muft be new fowne in the fpring, if you defire to haue it.

6. *Medica fpinofa maior.* Prickly or thorny Snailes, or Buttons.

This kinde of *Medica* is in all things very like vnto the former, both in the long trayling branches, & three leaues alwaies growing together, but a little greater pale yellow flowers, and crooked or winding heads : but herein chiefly confifteth the difference, that this kinde hath his heads or buttons harder, a little greater, more clofed together, and fet with fhort and fomewhat hard prickles, all the head ouer, which being pulled open, haue thofe prickles ftanding on each fide of the filme or skinne, whereof the head confifteth, fomewhat like vnto a fifh bone, and in this kinde goeth all one way; in which are contained fuch like feedes for the forme, as are in the former, but great and blacke, and fhining withall.

7. *Medica fpinofa altera.* Small thorney Buttons, or Snailes.

This other kinde is alfo like vnto the laft defcribed in all other things, except in the heads or buttons, which are a little fmaller, but fet with longer and fofter prickes vpon the filmes, and may eafily bee difcerned to goe both forwards and backewards, one enterlacing within another, wherein are contained fuch like flat and blacke fhining feede, made after the fafhion of a kidney, as are in the former, but fomewhat fmaller : the roote perifheth in like manner euery yeare.

8. *Medica lata.* Broade Buttons.

This kinde differeth not from the firft in leafe or flower, the fruite onely hereof is broade and flat, and not fo much twined as it.

9. *Medica Lunata.* Halfe Moones.

This is alfo a kinde of thefe Medicke fodders, hauing a trefoyle leafe and yellow flowers like the former forts, but both fomewhat larger, the chiefeft difference confifteth in the head or fruite, which is broade and flat, and not twined like the reft, but abideth halfe clofed, refembling a halfe Moone (and thereupon hath affumed both the Latine and Englifh name) wherein is contained flat feede, kidney fafhion like the former.

10. *Hedyfarum clypeatum.* The red Sattin flower.

This red flowred Fitchling, hath many ftalkes of winged faire greene leaues, that is, of many fet on both fides a middle ribbe, whereof that at the end is the greateft of the reft : from the ioynts where the leaues ftand, come forth pretty long fmall ftalkes, bearing on them very many flowers, vp to the toppe one aboue another, of an excellent fhining red or crimfon colour, very like vnto Sattin of that colour, and fometimes of a white colour, (as Mafter William Coys, a Gentleman of good refpect in Effex, a great and ancient louer and cherifher of thefe delights, and of all other rare plants, in his life time affured me, he had growing in his garden at Stubbers by North Okenden) which are fomewhat large, and more clofed together, almoft flat and not open, as in moft of the other forts : after the flowers are paft, there come rough, flat, round huskes, fomewhat like vnto the old fafhioned round bucklers without pikes, three or foure ftanding one vpon or aboue another, wherein are contained small brownish seede : the roote perisheth the same yeare it beareth seede, for oftentimes it flowreth not the first yeare it is sowne.

11. *Scorpioides maius & minus.*
Great and small Caterpillers.

Vnder one description I comprehend both these sorts of Scorpions grasse, or Caterpillers, or Wormes, as they are called by many, whereof the greater hath been known but of late yeares ; and ioyne them to these pulses, not hauing a fitter place where to insert them. It is but a small low plant, with branches lying vpon the ground, and somewhat long, broad, and hard leaues theron, among which come forth small stalkes, bearing at the end for the most part, two small pale yellowish flowers, like vnto Tares or Vetches, but smaller, which turne into writhed or crooked tough cods; in the greater sort they are much thicker, rounder and whiter, and lesser wound or turned together then in the smaller, which are slenderer, more winding, yet not closing like vnto the Snailes, and blacker more like vnto a Caterpiller then the other, wherein are contained brownish yellow seede, much like vnto a *Medica* : the rootes of both are small and fibrous, perishing euery yeare.

The Place.

These are found seuerally in diuers and seuerall places, but wee sow and plant them vsually to furnish our gardens.

The Time.

They doe all flower about the moneths of Iune and Iuly, and their seede is ripe soone after : but the second is earlier then the rest.

The Names.

The first is called *Clymenum* of Matthiolus, and *Lathyris* of Lobel and others : but *Lathyris* in Greeke is *Cataputia* in Latine, which is our Spurge, farre differing from this Pulse ; and therefore *Lathyrus* is more proper to distinguish them asunder, that two plants so farre vnlike should not bee called by one name : this is also called *Lathyrus latifolius*, because there is another called *angustifolius*, that differeth from it also : It is most vsually called with vs, *Pisum perenne*, and in English Pease blossome, or Pease euerlasting. The second is called by Clusius, *Orobus venetus*, because it was sent him from Venice, with another of the same kinde that bore white flowers ; yet differeth but little or nothing from that kinde he found in Hungary, that I thinke the seuerall places of their growing only cause them to beare seuerall names, and to be the same in deede. Although I yeeld vnto Clusius the Latine name which doth not sufficiently content mee ; yet I haue thought good to giue it a differing English name, according as it is in the title. The third, because I first receiued it among other seeds from Spaine, I haue giuen it the name, as it is entituled. The fourth is called of some *Sandalida Cretica*, & *Lotus siliquosus flore rubello*, *Lotus tetragonolobus*, *Pisum rubrum*, & *Pisum quadratum* : We vsually call it in English, Crimson Pease, or square Pease. The *Medica Cochleata* is called of Dodonæus *Trifolium Cochleatum*, but not iudged to be the true *Medica*. Wee call it in English, Medick fodder, Snailes Clauer, or as it is in the title, and so the rest of the Medica's accordingly. The *Hedysarum clypeatum* or *Securidaca* is called of Dodonæus *Onobrichis altera*, and we in English for the likenesse, The red Sattin flower, although some foolishly call it, the red or French Honysuckle. The last is called by Lobel, *Scorpioides bupleurifolio*, I haue called it *minus*, because the greatest sort which came to me out of Spaine was not knowne vnto him: in English they are generally called Caterpillers.

The

The Vertues.

The Medica's are generally thought to feede cattell fat much more then the Medow Trefoile, or Clauer graffe, and therefore I haue known diuers Gentlemen that haue plowed vp fome of their pafture grounds, and fowen them with the feedes of fome Medica's to make the experience. All the other forts are pleafures to delight the curious, and not any way profitable in Phyficke that I know.

Chap. LXXX.

Pæonia. Peonie.

There are two principall kindes of Peonie, that is to fay, the Male and the Female. Of the male kinde, I haue onely known one fort, but of the Female a great many; which are thus to be diftinguifhed. The Male his leafe is whole, without any particular diuifion, notch or dent on the edge, & his rootes long & round, diuided into many branches, fomewhat like to the rootes of Gentian or Elecampane, and not tuberous at all. The Female of all forts hath the leaues diuided or cut in on the edges, more or leffe, and hath alwaies tuberous rootes, that is, like clogs or Afphodill rootes, with many great thick round peeces hanging, or growing at the end of fmaller ftrings, and all ioyned to the toppe of the maine roote.

1. *Pæonia mas.* The Male Peonie.

The Male Peonie rifeth vp with many brownifh ftalkes, whereon doe grow winged leaues, that is, many faire greene, and fometimes reddifh leaues, one fet againft another vpon a ftalke, without any particular diuifion in the leafe at all : the flowers ftand at the toppes of the ftalkes, confifting of fiue or fix broade leaues, of a faire purplifh red colour, with many yellow threds in the middle, ftanding about the head, which after rifeth to be the feede veffels, diuided into two, three or foure rough crooked pods like hornes, which when they are ful ripe, open and turn themfelues down one edge to another backeward, fhewing within them diuers round black fhining feede, which are the true feede, being full and good, and hauing alfo many red or crimfon graines. which are lancke and idle, intermixed among the blacke, as if they were good feede, whereby it maketh a very pretty fhew: the roots are great, thick and long, fpreading in the ground, and running downe reafonable deepe.

2. *Pæonia fæmina vulgaris flore fimplici.*
The ordinary fingle Female Peonie.

This ordinary Female Peonie hath many ftalkes, with more ftore of leaues on them then the Male kinde hath, the leaues alfo are not fo large, but diuided or nicked diuerfly on the edges, fome with great and deepe, and others with fmaller cuts or diuifions, and of a darke or dead greene colour : the flowers are of a ftrong heady fent, moft vfually fmaller then the male, and of a more purple tending to a murrey colour, with yellow thrumes about the head in the middle, as the male kinde hath : the heads or hornes with feed are like alfo but fmaller, the feede alfo is blacke, but leffe fhining: the rootes confift, as I faid, of many thicke and fhort tuberous clogs, faftened at the ends of long ftrings, and all from the head of the roote, which is thicke and fhort, and tuberous alfo, of the fame or the like fent with the male.

3. *Pæonia fæmina vulgaris flore pleno rubro.*
The double red Peonie.

This double Peonie as well as the former fingle, is fo frequent in euerie Garden of note, through euery Countrey, that it is almoft labour in vaine

to defcribe it : but yet becaufe I vfe not to paffe ouer any plant fo flightly, I will fet
down the defcription briefly, in regard it is fo common.It is very like vnto the former
fingle female Peony, both in ftalkes and leaues, but that it groweth fomewhat higher,
and the leaues are of a frefher greene colour : the flowers at the tops of the ftalkes are
very large, thicke, and double (no flower that I know fo faire, great, and double ; but
not abiding blowne aboue eight or ten daies) of a more reddifh purple colour then
the former female kinde, and of a fweeter fent : after thefe flowers are paft, fometimes
come good feed, which being fowne, bring forth fome fingle flowers, and fome double : the rootes are tuberous, like vnto the former female.

4. *Paonia famina flore carneo fimplici*. The fingle blufh Peony.

The fingle blufh Peony hath his ftalkes higher, and his leaues of a paler or whiter
greene colour then the double blufh, and more white vnderneath (fo that it is very probable it is of another kinde, and not rifen from the feede of the double blufh, as fome
might thinke) with many veines, that are fomewhat difcoloured from the colour of
the leafe running through them : the flowers are very large and fingle, confifting of
fiue leaues for the moft part, of a pale flefh or blufh colour, with an eye of yellow difperfed or mixed therewith, hauing many whitifh threads, tipt with yellow pendents
ftanding about the middle head : the rootes are like the other female Peonies.

5. *Paonia famina flore pleno albicante*. The double blufh Peony.

The double blufh Peony hath not his ftalkes fo high as the double red, but fomewhat lower and ftiffer, bearing fuch like winged leaues, cut in or diuided here and there
in the edges, as all thefe female kindes are, but not fo large as the laft : the flowers are
fmaller, and leffe double by a good deale then the former double red, of a faint fhining
crimfon colour at the firft opening, but decaying or waxing paler euery day : fo that
after it hath ftood long (for this flower fheddeth not his leaues in a great while) it will
change fomewhat whitifh ; and therefore diuers haue ignorantly called it, the double
white Peony : the feedes, which fometimes it beareth, and rootes, are like vnto the
former female kindes, but fomewhat longer, and of a brighter colour on the outfide.

6. *Paonia famina Byzantina*. The fingle red Peony of Conftantinople.

This red Peony of Conftantinople is very like in all things vnto the double red Peonie, but that the flowers hereof are fingle, and as large as the laft, and that is larger
then either the fingle female, or the male kinde, confifting of eight leaues, of a deeper
red colour then either the fingle or double Peonies, and not purplifh at all, but rather
of the colour of an ordinary red Tulipa, ftanding clofe and round together : the roots
of this kinde haue longer clogs, and not fo fhort as of the ordinary female kinde, and
of a paler colour on the outfide.

The Place.

All thefe Peonies haue beene fent or brought from diuers parts beyond
the Seas ; they are endenized in our Gardens, where wee cherifh them for
the beauty and delight of their goodly flowers, as well as for their Phyficall
vertues.

The Time.

They all flower in May, but fome (as I faid) abide a fmall time, and o-
thers many weekes.

The Names.

The name *Paonia* is of all the later Writers generally giuen to thefe
plants, although they haue had diuers other names giuen by the elder Writers, as *Rofa fatuina, Idaus dactylus, Aglaophotis*, and others, whereof to fet
downe

1 *Pæonia mas tum femine*. The male Peony & the feed. 2 *Pæonia femina Byzantina*. The female red Peony of Constantinople. 3 *Pæonia femina flore pleno vulgaris*. The ordinary double Peony. 4 *Pæonia flore pleno albicante*. The double white Peony. 5 *Helleborus vernus atrorubente flore*. The early white Ellebor with a darke red flower. 6 *Helleborus niger verus*. The Christmas flower. 7 *Calceolus Mariæ*. Our Ladies Slipper.

downe the caufes, reafons, and errours, were to fpend more time then I intend for this worke. Wee call them in Englifh, Peonie, and diftinguifh them according to their titles.

The Vertues.

The male Peony roote is farre aboue all the reft a moft fingular approued remedy for all Epilepticall difeafes, in Englifh, The falling ficknefle (and more efpecially the greene roote then the dry) if the difeafe be not too inueterate, to be boyled and drunke, as alfo to hang about the neckes of the younger fort that are troubled herewith, as I haue found it fufficiently experimented on many by diuers. The feede likewife is of efpeciall vfe for women, for the rifing of the mother. The feede of the female kinde, as well as the rootes, are moft vfually fold, and may in want of the other be (and fo are generally) vfed.

Chap. LXXXI.

Helleborus niger. Beares foote.

THere are three forts of blacke Hellebor or Beares foote, one that is the true and right kinde, whofe flowers haue the moft beautifull afpect, and the time of his flowring moft rare, that is, in the deepe of Winter about Chriftmas, when no other can bee feene vpon the ground : and two other that are wilde or baftard kindes, brought into many Gardens for their Phyficall properties ; but I will only ioyne one of them with the true kinde in this worke, and leaue the other for another.

1. *Helleborus niger verus.* The true blacke Hellebor, or Chriftmas flower.

The true blacke Hellebor (or Beare foote as fome would call it, but that name doth more fitly agree with the other two baftard kindes) hath many faire greene leaues rifing from the roote, each of them ftanding on a thicke round flefhly ftiffe green ftalke, about an hand breadth high from the ground, diuided into feuen, eight, or nine parts or leaues, and each of them nicked or dented, from the middle of the leafe to the pointward on both fides, abiding all the Winter, at which time the flowers rife vp on fuch fhort thicke ftalkes as the leaues ftand on, euery one by it felfe, without any leafe thereon for the moft part, or very feldome hauing one fmall fhort leafe not much vnder the flower, and very little higher then the leaues themfelues, confifting of fiue broad white leaues, like vnto a great white fingle Rofe (which fometimes change to be either leffe or more purple about the edges, as the weather or time of continuance doth effect) with many pale yellow thrummes in the middle, ftanding about a greene head, which after groweth to haue diuers cods fet together, pointed at the ends like hornes, fomewhat like the feede veffels of the *Aconitum hyemale,* but greater & thicker, wherein is contained long, round, and blackifh feede, like the feede of the baftard kindes : the rootes are a number of brownifh ftrings running downe deepe into the ground, and faftened to a thicke head, of the bigneffe of a finger at the toppe manie times, and fmaller ftill downewards.

2. *Helleborafter minor.* The leffer baftard blacke Hellebor, or Beare foote.

The fmaller Beare foote is in moft things like vnto the former true blacke Hellebor; for it beareth alfo many leaues vpon fhort ftalkes, diuided into many leaues alfo, but each of them are long and narrow, of a blacker greene colour, fnipt or dented on both edges, which feele fomewhat hard or fharpe like prickes, and perifh euery yeare, but rife againe the next Spring : the flowers hereof ftand on higher ftalkes, with fome leaues on them alfo, although but very few, and are of a pale greene colour, like in

forme

forme vnto the flowers of the former, but ſmaller, hauing alſo many greeniſh yellow threads or thrums in the middle, and ſuch like heads or ſeede veſſels, and blackiſh ſeed: the rootes are ſtringie and blackiſh like the former.

The Place.

The firſt groweth onely in the Gardens of thoſe that are curious, and delight in all ſorts of beautifull flowers in our Countrey, but wilde in many places of Germany, Italy, Greece, &c.

The other groweth wilde in many places of England, as well as the other greater ſort, which is not here deſcribed; for beſides diuers places within eight or ten miles from London, I haue ſeen it in the Woods of Northamptonſhire, and in other places.

The Time.

The firſt of theſe plants doth flower in the end of December, and beginning of Ianuary moſt vſually, and the other a moneth or two after, and ſometime more.

The Names.

The firſt is called *Helleborus*, or *Elleborus niger verus*, and is the ſame that both Theophraſtus and Dioſcorides haue written of, and which was called *Melampodion*, of Melampus the Goateheard, that purged and cured the mad or melancholicke daughters of Prætus with the rootes thereof. Dodonæus calleth it *Veratrum nigrum primum*, and the other *ſecundum*: Wee call it in Engliſh, The true blacke Hellebor, or the Chriſtmas flower, becauſe (as I ſaid) it is moſt commonly in flower at or before Chriſtmas. The ſecond is a baſtard or wilde kinde thereof, it ſo nearely reſembleth the true, and is called of moſt of the later Writers, *Pſeudoelleborus niger minor*, or *Helleboraſter minor*, for a diſtinction betweene it and the greater, which is not here deſcribed: and is called in Engliſh, The ſmaller or leſſer Beare foote, and moſt vſed in Phyſicke, becauſe it is more plentifull, yet is more churliſh and ſtrong in operation then the true or former kinde.

The Vertues.

The rootes of both theſe kindes are ſafe medecines, being rightly prepared, to be vſed for all Melancholicke diſeaſes, whatſoeuer others may feare or write, and may be without danger applied, ſo as care and skill, and not temerary raſhneſſe doe order and diſpoſe of them.

The powder of the dryed leaues, eſpecially of the baſtard kinde, is a ſure remedy to kill the wormes in children, moderately taken.

Chap. LXXXII.

Elleborus albus. White Ellebor or Neeſewort.

THere are two ſorts of great white Ellebors or Neeſeworts, whereas there was but one kinde knowne to the Ancients; the other being found out of later dayes: And although neither of both theſe haue any beauty in their flowers, yet becauſe their leaues, being faire and large, haue a goodly proſpect, I haue inſerted them in this place, that this Garden ſhould not be vnfurniſhed of them, and you not vnacquainted with them.

1. Elleborus

1. *Elleborus albus vulgaris.* White Ellebor or Neesing roote.

The first great white Ellebor riseth at the first out of the ground, with a whitish greene great round head, which growing vp, opencth it selfe into many goodly faire large greene leaues, plaited or ribbed with eminent ribbes all along the leaues, compassing one another at the bottome, in the middle whereof riseth vp a stalke three foot high or better, with diuers such like leaues thereon, but smaller to the middle thereof; from whence to the toppe it is diuided into many branches, hauing many small yellowish, or whitish greene starre-like flowers all along vpon them, which after turne into small, long, three square whitish seede, standing naked, without any huske to containe them, although some haue written otherwise: the roote is thicke and reasonable great at the head, hauing a number of great white strings running downe deepe into the ground, whereby it is strongly fastened.

2. *Elleborus albus præcox siue atrorubente flore.*
The early white Ellebor with reddish flowers.

This other Ellebor is very like the former, but that it springeth vp a moneth at the least before it, and that the leaues are not fully so thicke or so much plaited, but as large or larger, and doe sooner perish and fall away from the plant: the stalke hereof is as high as the former, bearing such like starry flowers, but of a darke or blackish red colour: the seede is like the other: the roote hath no such head as the other (so farre as I haue obserued, both by mine own and others plants) but hath many long white strings fastened to the top, which is as it were a long bulbous scaly head, out of which spring the leaues.

The Place.

The first groweth in many places of Germany, as also in some parts of Russia, in that aboundance, by the relation of that worthy, curious, and diligent searcher and preseruer of all natures rarities and varieties, my very good friend, Iohn Tradescante, often heretofore remembred, that, as hee said, a good ship might be loaden with the rootes hereof, which hee saw in an Island there.

The other likewise groweth in the vpland wooddy grounds of Germanie, and other the parts thereabouts.

The Time.

The first springeth vp in the end or middle of March, and flowreth in Iune. The second springeth in February, but flowreth not vntill Iune.

The Names.

The first is called *Elleborus albus*, or *Helleborus albus*, the letter *H*, as all Schollers know, being but *aspirationis nota*: and *Veratrum album flore viridante*, of some *Sanguis Herculis*. The other is called *Elleborus albus præcox*, and *flore atrorubente*, or *atropurpurante*. We call the first in English, White Ellebor, Neesewort, or Neesing roote, because the powder of the roote is vsed to procure neesing; and I call it the greater, in regard of those in the next Chapter. The other hath his name according to the Latine title, most proper for it.

The Vertues.

The force of purging is farre greater in the roote of this Ellebor, then in the former; and therefore is not carelesly to bee vsed, without extreame danger; yet in contumatious and stubborne diseases it may bee vsed with
good

good caution and aduice. There is a Syrupe or Oxymelmade hereof in the Apothecaries shops, which as it is dangerous for gentle and tender bodies, so it may be very effectuall in stronger constitutions. Pausanias *in Phocicis*, recordeth a notable stratagem that Solon vsed in besieging the Citie of Cirrheus, *viz.* That hauing cut off the riuer Plistus from running into the Citie, he caused a great many of these rootes to be put into a quantity thereof, which after they had steeped long enough therein, and was sufficiently infected therewith, he let passe into the Citie againe : whereof when they had greedily drunke, they grew so weake and feeble by the superpurgation thereof, that they were forced to leaue their wals vnmand, and not guarded, whereby the Amphyctions their enemies became masters of their Citie. The like stratagems are set downe by diuers other Authors, performed by the helpe of other herbes.

CHAP. LXXXIII.

Elleborine. Small or wilde white Ellebor.

THe likenesse of the leaues of these plants, rather then any other faculty with the former white Ellebor, hath caused them to be called *Elleborine*, as if they were smaller white Ellebors. And I for the same cause haue ioyned them next, whereof there are found many sorts : One which is the greater kinde, is of greatest beauty ; the other which are lesser differ not much one from another, more then in the colour of the flowers, whereof I will onely take three, being of the most beautie, and leaue the rest to another worke.

1. *Helleborine vel Elleborine maior, siue Calceolus Mariæ.*
Our Ladies Slipper.

This most beautifull plant of all these kindes, riseth vp with diuers stalkes, a foote and a halfe high at the most, bearing on each side of them broad greene leaues, somewhat like in forme vnto the leaues of the white Ellebor, but smaller and not so ribbed, compassing the stalke at the lower end ; at the tops of the stalkes come forth one, or two, or three flowers at the most, one aboue another, vpon small short foote-stalkes, with a small leafe at the foote of euery stalke : each of these flowers are of a long ouall forme, that is, more long then round, and hollow withall, especially at the vpper part, the lower being round and swelling like a belly : at the hollow part there are two small peeces like eares or flippets, that at the first doe couer the hollow part, and after stand apart one from another, all which are of a fine pale yellow colour, in all that I haue seene (yet it is said there are some found, that are more browne or tending to purple) there are likewise foure long, narrow, darke coloured leaues at the setting on of the flower vnto the stalke, wherein as it were the flower at the first standeth : the whole flower is of a pretty small sent : the seede is very small, very like vnto the seede of the *Orchides* or Satyrions, and contained in such like long pods, but bigger : the roots are composed of a number of strings enterlacing themselues one within another, lying within the vpper crust of the earth, & not spreading deep, of a darke brownish colour.

2. *Elleborine minor flore albo.*
The small or wilde white Ellebor with a white flower.

This smaller wilde white Ellebor riseth vp in the like manner vnto the former, and not much lower, bearing such like leaues, but smaller, and of a whiter greene colour, almost of the colour and fashion of the leaues of Lilly Conually ; the top of the stalke hath many more flowers, but lesser, growing together, spike-fashion, with small short leaues at the stalke of euery flower, which consisteth of fiue small white leaues, with a small close hood in the middle, without any sent at all : the seede and seede vessels are
like

like vnto the former, but smaller : the rootes are many small strings , dispersing them-selues in the ground.

3. *Elleborine minor flore purpurante.*
The small or wilde white Ellebor with blush flowers.

The leaues of this kinde are like vnto the last described , but somewhat narrower : the stalkes and flowers are alike , but smaller also, and of a pale purplish or blush colour, which causeth the difference.

The Place.

The first groweth in very many places of Germany, and in other Countries also. it groweth likewise in Lancashire, neare vpon the border of Yorkeshire, in a wood or place called the Helkes, which is three miles from Ingleborough, the highest Hill in England, and not farre from Ingleton, as I am enformed by a courteous Gentlewoman, a great louer of these delights, called Mistris Thomasin Tunstall, who dwelleth at Bull-banke, neare Hornby Castle in those parts, and who hath often sent mee vp the rootes to London, which haue borne faire flowers in my Garden. The second groweth in many places of England, and with the same Gentlewoman also before remembred, who sent me one plant of this kinde with the other. The last I haue not yet knowne to growe in England; but no doubt many things doe lye hid, and not obserued, which in time may bee discouered, if our Country Gentlemen and women, and others, in their seuerall places where they dwell, would be more carefull and diligent, and be aduertised either by themselues, or by others capable and fit to be imployed, as occasion and time might serue, to finde out such plants as growe in any the circuits or limits of their habitations, or in their trauels, as their pleasures or affaires leade them. And because ignorance is the chiefe cause of neglect of many rare things, which happen to their view at sometimes, which are not to be seene againe peraduenture, or not in many yeares after, I would heartily aduise all men of meanes, to be stirred vp to bend their mindes, and spend a little more time and trauell in these delights of herbes and flowers, then they haue formerly done, which are not onely harmlesse, but pleasurable in their time, and profitable in their vse. And if any would be better enformed, and certified of such things they know not, I would be willing and ready to my best skill to aduertise them, that shall send any thing vp to me where I dwell in London. Thus farre I haue digressed from the matter in hand, and yet not without some good vse I hope, that others may make of it.

The Time.

The two first flower earlier then the last, and both the first about one time, that is, in the end of Aprill, or beginning of May. The last in the end of May, or in Iune.

The Names.

The first is called *Elleborine recentiorum maior*, and *Calceolus Mariæ* : Of some thought to be *Cosmosandalos*, because it is *Sandali forma*. In English we call it our Ladies Slipper, after the Dutch name. The other two lesser kinds haue their names in their titles: I haue thought it fit to adde the title of small white Ellebors vnto these, for the forme sake, as is before said.

The Vertues.

There is no vse of these in Physicke in our dayes that I know.

Chap.

Chap. LXXXIIII.

Lilium Conuallium. Lilly Conually.

THe remembrance of the Conuall Lilly, spoken of in the precedent Chapter, hath caused me to insert these plants among the rest, although differing both in face and properties; but lest it should lose all place, let it keepe this. It is of two sorts, differing chiefly in the colour of the flowers, the one being white, and the other reddish, as shall be shewed in their descriptions following.

1. *Lilium Conuallium flore albo.* The white Lilly Conually.

The white Conuall or May Lilly, hath three or foure leaues rising together from the roote, one enclosed within another, each whereof when it is open is long and broad, of a grayish shining greene colour, somewhat resembling the leaues of the former wilde Neesewort, at the side whereof, and sometime from the middle of them, riseth vp a small short naked foote-stalke, an hand breadth high or somewhat more, bearing at the toppe one aboue another many small white flowers, like little hollow bottles with open mouths, nicked or cut into fiue or six notches, turning all downewards one way, or on one side of the stalke, of a very strong sweete sent, and comfortable for the memory and senses, which turne into small red berries, like vnto Asparagus, wherein is contained hard white seede: the rootes runne vnder ground, creeping euery way, consisting of many small white strings.

2. *Lilium Conuallium flore rubente.* May Lillies with red flowers.

This other May Lilly differeth neither in roote, leafe, nor forme of flower from that before, but onely in the colour of the flower, which is of a fine pale red colour, being in my iudgement not altogether so sweet as the former.

The Place.

The first groweth abundantly in many places of England. The other is a stranger, and groweth only in the Gardens of those that are curious louers of rarities.

The Time.

They both flower in May, and the berries are ripe in August.

The Names.

The Latines haue no other name for this plant but *Lilium Conuallium*, although some would haue it to be *Lilium vernum* of Theophrastus, and others *Oenanthe* of the same Author. Gesner thinketh it to be *Callionymus*. Lonicerus to be *Cacalia*, and Fuchsius to be *Ephemerum non lethale*: but they are all for the most part mistaken. We call it in English Lilly Conually, May Lilly, and of some Liriconfancie.

The Vertues.

The flowers of the white kinde are often vsed with those things that help to strengthen the memory, and to procure ease to Apoplecticke persons. Camerarius setteth downe the manner of making an oyle of the flowers hereof, which he saith is very effectuall to ease the paines of the Goute, and such like diseases, to be vsed outwardly, which is thus: Hauing filled a glasse with the flowers, and being well stopped, set it for a moneths space in an Ants hill, and after being drayned cleare, set it by to vse.

Gg　　　　　　　　　　　　　　　　　　　　　Chap.

Chap. LXXXV.

Gentiana. Gentian or Fell-wort.

THere are diuers forts of Gentians or Fell-wortes, fome greater, others leffer, and fome very fmall ; many of them haue very beautifull flowers, but becaufe fome are very fuddenly paft, before one would thinke they were blowne open, and others will abide no culture and manuring, I will onely fet forth vnto you two of the greater forts, and three of the leffer kindes, as fitteft, and more familiarly furnifhing our gardens, leauing the reft to their wilde habitations, and to bee comprehended in a generall Worke.

1. *Gentiana maior flore flauo.* The great Gentian.

The great Gentian rifeth vp at the firft, with a long, round and pointed head of leaues, clofing one another, which after opening themfelues, lye vpon the ground, and are faire, long and broad, fomewhat plaited or ribbed like vnto the leaues of white Ellebor or Neefeworte, but not fo fairely or eminently plaited, neyther fo ftiffe, but rather refembling the leaues of a great Plantane : from among which rifeth vp a ftiffe round ftalke, three foote high or better, full of ioynts, hauing two fuch leaues, but narrower and fmaller at euery ioynt, fo compaffing about the ftalke at the lower end of them, that they will almoft hold water that falleth into them : from the middle of the ftalke to the toppe, it is garnifhed with many coronets or rundles of flowers, with two fuch greene leaues likewife at euery ioynt, and wherein the flowers doe ftand, which are yellow, layd open like ftarres, and rifing out of fmall greenifh huskes, with fome threds in the middle of them, but of no fent at all, yet ftately to behold, both for the order, height and proportion of the plant : the feede is browne and flat, contained in round heads, fomewhat like vnto the feede of the *Fritillaria*, or checkerd Daffodill, but browner : the rootes are great, thicke and long, yellow, and exceeding bitter.

2. *Gentiana maior folio Afclepiadis.* Swallow-wort Gentian.

This kinde of Gentian hath many ftalkes rifing from the roote, neere two foote high, whereon grow many faire pale greene leaues, fet by couples, with three ribs in euery one of them, and doe fomewhat refemble the leaues of *Afclepias* or Swallow-wort, that is, broade at the bottome, and fharpe at the point : the flowers grow at the feuerall ioynts of the ftalkes, from the middle vpwards, two or three together, which are long and hollow, like vnto a bell flower, ending in fiue corners, or pointed leaues, and folded before they are open, as the flowers of the Bindeweedes are, of a faire blew colour, fometimes deeper, and fometimes paler : the heads or feede veffels haue two points or hornes at the toppes, and containe within them flat grayifh feed, like vnto the former, but leffe : the rootes hereof are nothing fo great as the former, but are yellow, fmall and long, of the bigneffe of a mans thumbe.

3. *Gentiana minor Cruciata.* Croffe-wort Gentian.

This fmall Gentian hath many branches lying vpon the ground, fcarce lifting themfelues vpright, and full of ioynts, whereat grow vfually foure leaues, one oppofite vnto another, in manner of a Croffe, from whence it tooke his name, in fhape very like vnto *Saponaria* or Sopewort, but fhorter, and of a darker greene colour: at the tops of the ftalkes ftand many flowers, thick thrufting together, and likewife at the next ioynt vnderneath, euery one of them ftanding in a darke blewifh greene huske, and confifting of fiue fmall leaues, the points or ends whereof only appeare aboue the huskes wherein they ftand, and are hardly to be feene, but that they are of a fine pale blew colour, and that many grow together : the feed is fmall and brown, hard, and fomewhat like

1. *Lilium Conuallium.* Liriconfancy or Lilly Conually. 2 *Gentiana maior.* The great Gentian. 3 *Gentianella verna.* Small Gentian of the Spring. 4 *Gentiana Cruciata.* Croſſewort Gentian. 5 *Pneumonanthe ſeu Gentiana Autumnalis.* Autumne Gentian. 6 *Saponaria flore duplici.* Double flowred Sopewort. 7 *Plantago Roſea.* Roſe Platane.

like vnto the feed of the Marian Violets, or Couentry bels: the roots are fmall and whitifh, difperfing themfelues diuerfly in the ground, of as bitter a tafte almoft as the reft.

4. *Gentianella Verna.* Small Gentian of the Spring.

The fmall Gentian of the Spring hath diuers fmall hard greene leaues, lying vpon the ground, as it were in heads or tufts, fomewhat broade below, and pointed at the end, with fiue ribs or veines therein, as confpicuous as in the former Gentians, among which rifeth vp a fmall fhort ftalke, with fome fmaller leaues thereon, at the toppe whereof ftandeth one faire, large, hollow flower, made bell fafhion, with wide open brimmes, ending in fiue corners or diuifions, of the moft excellent deepe blew colour that can be feene in any flower, with fome white fpots in the bottome on the infide: after the flower is paft, there appeare long and round pods, wherein are contained fmall blackifh feede: the rootes are fmall, long, pale yellow ftrings, which fhoot forth here and there diuers heads of leaues, and thereby encreafe reafonable well, if it finde a fit place, and ground to grow, or elfe will not be nourfed vp, with all the care and diligence can be vfed: the whole plant is bitter, but not fo ftrong as the former.

5. *Gentiana Autumnalis fiue Pneumonanthe.* Calathian Violet or Autumne Gentian.

This Gentian that flowreth in Autumne, hath in fome places higher ftalkes then in others, with many leaues thereon, fet by couples as in other Gentians, but long and narrow, yet fhewing the three ribbes or veines that are in each of them: the toppes of the ftalkes are furnifhed euery one with a flower or two, of an excellent blew purple colour, ending in fiue corners, and ftanding in long huskes: the rootes are fomewhat great at the top, and fpreading into many fmall yellow ftrings, bitter as the reft are.

6. *Saponaria flore duplici.* Double flowred Sopeworte.

Vnto thefe kindes of Gentians, I muft needes adde thefe following plants, for that the former is of fome neere refemblance in leafe with fome of the former. And becaufe the ordinary Sopeworte or Bruifeworte with fingle flowers is often planted in Gardens, and the flowers ferue to decke both the garden and the houfe; I may vnder the one defcribe them both: for this with double flowers is farre more rare, and of greater beautie. It hath many long and flender round ftalkes, fcarce able to fuftaine themfelues, and ftand vpright, being ful of ioynts and ribbed leaues at them, euery one fomewhat like a fmall Gentian or Plantane leafe: at the toppes of the ftalkes ftand many flowers, confifting of two or three rowes of leaues, of a whitifh or pale purple colour, and of a ftrong fweet fent, fomewhat like the fmell of Iafmin flowers, ftanding in long and thicke pale greene huskes, which fall away without giuing any feede, as moft other double flowers doe that encreafe by the roote, which fpreadeth within the ground, and rifeth vp in fundry diftant places like the fingle.

7 *Plantago Rofea.* Rofe Plantane.

This other plant is in all things like vnto the ordinary Plantane or Ribworte, that groweth wilde abroade in many places, whofe leaues are very large: but in ftead of the long flender fpike, or eare that the ordinary hath, this hath eyther a thicke long fpike of fmall greene leaues vpon fhort ftalkes, or elfe a number of fuch fmall greene leaues layd round-wife like vnto a Rofe, and fometimes both thefe may be feene vpon one and the fame roote, at one and the fame time, which abide a great while frefh vpon the roote, and fometimes alfo giueth feede, efpecially from the more long and flender fpikes.

The Place.

Some of thefe Gentians grow on the toppes of hils, and fome on the fides and foote of them in Germany and other Countreyes: fome of them alfo vpon barren heaths in thofe places, as alfo in our owne Countrey, efpecial-

ly

ly the Autumne Gentian, and as it is reported, the Vernall likewife. The fingle or ordinary Sopeworte is found wilde in many places with vs, but the double came to vs from beyond the Sea, and is fcarce known or heard of in England. The Rofe Plantaine hath beene long in England, but whether naturall thereof or no, I am not affured.

The Time.

They flower for the moft part in Iune and Iuly, but the fmall Gentian of the Spring flowreth fomewhat earlier, and that of the Autumne in Auguft and September.

The Names.

Gentiana is the generall name giuen to the Gentians. We call them in Englifh Gentian, Fellworte, Bitterwort, and Baldmoney. *Saponaria* taketh his name from the fcouring qualitie it hath : Wee call it in Englifh Sopewort, and in fome places Bruifewort. Some haue thought it to bee *Struthium* of Diofcorides, or at leaft haue vfed it for the fame caufes, but therein they are greatly deceiued, as Matthiolus hath very well obferued thereon, and fo is Dodonæus, that thought it to be *Alifma*. The Rofe Plantaine is fo called of the double fpikes it carrieth.

The Vertues.

The wonderfull wholfomneffe of Gentian cannot bee eafily knowne to vs, by reafon our daintie taftes refufe to take thereof, for the bitterneffe fake : but otherwife it would vndoubtedly worke admirable cures, both for the liuer, ftomacke and lunges. It is alfo a fpeciall counterpoifon againft any infection, as alfo againft the violence of a mad dogges tooth : wilde Sopewort is vfed in many places, to fcoure the countrey womens treen, and pewter veffels, and phyfically fome make great boaft to performe admirable cures in Hydropicall difeafes, becaufe it is diureticall, and in *Lue Veneria*, when other Mercuriall medicines haue failed. The Rofe Plantaine no doubt hath the fame qualities that the ordinary hath.

Chap. LXXXVI.

Campanula. Bell-flowers.

Vnder the title of Bell-flowers are to bee comprehended in this Chapter, not only thofe that are ordinarily called *Campanula*, but *Viola Mariana*, and *Tracheliumm* alfo, whereof the one is called Couentry, the other Canterbury Bells.

1. *Campanula Perficifolio alba, vel cærulea.* Peach-leafed Bell-flowers white or blew.

The Peach-leafed Bell-flower hath many tufts, or branches of leaues lying vpon the ground, which are long and narrow, fomewhat like vnto the leafe of an Almond or Peach tree, being finely nicked about the edges, and of a fad greene colour, from among which rife vp diuers ftalkes, two foote high or more, fet with leaues to the middle, and from thence vpwards, with many flowers ftanding on feuerall fmall footeftalkes, one aboue another, with a fmall leafe at the foote of euery one : the flowers ftand in fmall greene huskes, being fmall and round at the bottome, but wider open at the brimme, and ending in fiue corners, with a three forked clapper in the middle, fet about with fome fmall threds tipt with yellow, which flowers in fome plants are pure

white

white, and in others of a pale blew or watchet colour, hauing little or no sent at all : the seede is small, and contained in round flat heads, or seede vessels : the roote is very small, white and threddy, creeping vnder the vpper crust of the ground, so that often-times the heat and drought of the Summer wil goe near to parch and wither it vtterly: it requireth therefore to be planted in some shadowie place.

2. *Campanula maior, siue Pyramidalis.*
The great or steeple Bell-flower.

This great Bell-flower hath diuers stalkes, three foote high or better, whereon grow diuers smooth, darke, greene leaues, broade at the bottome, and small at the point, somewhat vneuenly notched about the edges, and standing vpon longer footestalkes below then those aboue : the flowers are blew, and in some white, not so great or large as the former, but neare of the same fashion, growing thicker and more plenti-fully together, with smaller leaues among them, bushing thicke below, and rising smal-ler and thinner vp to the toppe, in fashion of a *Pyramis* or speere Steeple : the roote is thicke and whitish, yeelding more store of milke being broken (as the leaues and stalks also doe) then any other of the Bell-flowers, euery one whereof doe yeelde milke, some more and some lesse.

3. *Viola Mariana flore albido vel purpureo.*
Couentry Bels white or purple.

The leaues of Couentry Bels are of a pale or fresh greene colour, long, and narrow next vnto the bottome, and broader from the middle to the end, and somewhat round pointed, a little hairy all ouer, and snipt about the edges : the stalkes rise vp the yeare after the sowing, being somewhat hairy also, and branching forth from the roote, into diuers parts, whereon stand diuers leaues, smaller then the former, and of a darker greene colour : at the end of euery branch stand the flowers, in greene huskes, from whence come large, round, hollow Bels, swelling out in the middle, and rising some-what aboue it, like the necke of a pot, and then ending in fiue corners, which are either of a faire or faint white, or of a pale blew purplish colour, and sometimes of a deeper purple or violet: after the flowers are past, there rise vp great square, or cornered seede vessels, wherein is contained in diuers diuisions, small, hard, shining, browne, flat seeds: the roote is white, and being young as in the first yeares sowing, is tender, and often eaten as other Rampions are; but the next yeare, when it runneth vp to seede, it grow-eth hard, and perisheth : so that it is to be continued by euery other yeares sowing.

4. *Trachelium maius flore albo vel purpureo.*
Great Canterbury Bels white or purple.

The greater Canterbury Bels, or Throateworte, hath many large rough leaues, somewhat like vnto Nettle leaues, being broad and round at the bottome, and pointed at the end, notched or dented on the edges, and euery one standing on a long footstalk: among these leaues rise vp diuers square rough stalkes, diuided at the toppe into diuers branches, whereon grow the like leaues as grow below, but lesser; toward the ends of the branches stand the flowers, mixed with some longer leaues, euery one in his seuerall huske, which are hollow, long and round, like a bell or cup, wide open at the mouth, and cut at the brimme into fiue corners, or diuisions, somewhat lesser then the Co-uentry Bels, in some of a pure white, and others of a faire deepe purple violet colour, and sometimes paler : after the flowers are past, come smaller and rounder heades then in the former, containing flat seede, but blacker, and not so redde as the last : the roote is hard and white, dispersing it selfe into many branches vnder ground, not perishing euery yeare as the former (although it loseth all the leaues in winter) but abiding many yeares, and encreasing into diuers heades or knobs, from whence spring new leaues and branches.

5. *Trache-*

1 *Campanula persicifolia*. Peach leafed Bell-flower. 2 *Trachelium maius simplex*. Canterbury Bels. * *Trachelium flore duplici*. Double Canterbury Bels. 3 *Viola Mariana*. Couentry Bels. 4 *Trachelium Giganteum*. Giants Throatewort 5 *Trachelium minus*. The lesser Throatewort. 6 *Trachelium Americanum siue Cardinalis planta*. The rich crimson Cardinals flower.

5. *Trachelium maius flore duplici albo & cæruleo.*
Canterbury Bels with double flowers both white and blew.

Of this kinde of Throateworte or Canterbury Bels, there is another fort, not differing in any thing from the former, but in the doubleneffe of the flower : For there is of both the kindes, one that beareth double white flowers, and the other blew : Of each whereof I receiued plants from friends beyond the Sea, which grow well with me.

6. *Trachelium Giganteum flore purpurante.*
Pale purple Giants Throateworte.

This Bell-flower, although it hath a Gigantine name, yet did I neuer perceiue it in my Garden, to rife vp h gher then the former, the epithite beeing in my perfwafion, only giuen for difference fake : the leaues whereof are not fo rough, but as large, and dented about the edges, fomewhat larger pointed, and of a frefher greene colour : the ftalkes beare fuch like leaues on them, but more thinly or difperfedly fet, hauing a flower at the fetting on of euery one of the leaues, from the middle vpwards, and are fomewhat like the great Throateworte in forme, but of a pale or bleake reddifh purple colour, turning the brims or corners a little backwards, with a forked clapper in the middle, fufficient eminent and yellow : the feede hereof is white, and plentifull in the heads, which will abide all the winter vpon the ftalkes, vntill all the feede being fhed, the heads remaining feeme like torne rags, or like thin pecces of skin, eaten with wormes : the roote is great, thicke and white, abiding long without perifhing.

Flore albo. There is another which differeth not any thing but in the flower, which is white.

7. *Trachelium minus flore albo & purpureo.*
Small Throateworte or Canterbury Bells both white and purple.

The leffer Throateworte hath fmaller leaues, nothing fo broade or hard as the former great kinde, but long, and little or nothing dented about the edges : the ftalkes are fquare and brownifh, if it beare purple flowers, and greene if it beare white flowers, which in forme are alike, and grow in a bufh or tuft, thicke fet together, more then any of the former, and fmaller alfo, being not much bigger then the flowers of the fielde, or garden Rampions : the roote is lafting, and fhooteth afrefh euery yeare.

8. *Trachelium Americarum flore ruberrimo, fiue Planta Cardinalis.*
The rich crimfon Cardinals flower.

This braue plant, from a white roote fpreading diuers wayes vnder ground, fendeth forth many greene leaues, fpread round about the head thereof, each whereof is fomewhat broade and long, and pointed at the end, finely alfo fnipt about the edges : from the middle whereof arifeth vp a round hollow ftalke, two foote high at the leaft, befet with diuers fuch leaues as grow below, but longer below then aboue, and branching out at the toppe aboundantly, euery branch bearing diuers greene leaues on them, and one at the foote of euery of them alfo, the toppes whereof doe end in a great large tuft of flowers, with a fmall greene leafe at the foote of the ftalke of euery flower, each footeftalke being about an inch long, bearing a round greene huske, diuided into fiue long leaues or points turned downwards, and in the midft of euery of them a moft rich crimfon coloured flower, ending in fiue long narrow leaues, ftanding all of them foreright, but three of them falling downe, with a long vmbone fet as it were at the backe of them, bigger below, and fmaller aboue, and at the toppe a fmall head, being of a little paler colour then the flower, but of no fent or fmell at all, commendable only for the great bufh of fo orient red crimfon flowers : after the flowers are paft, the feede commeth in fmall heads, clofed within thofe greene husks that held the flowers, which is very like vnto the feede veffels of the *Viola Mariana,* or Couentry Bels, and is fmall and brownifh.

The

The Place.

All thefe Bell-flowers do grow in our Gardens, where they are cherifhed for the beautie of their flowers. The Couentry Bels doe not grow wilde in any of the parts about Couentry, as I am credibly informed by a faithfull Apothecary dwelling there, called Mafter Brian Ball, but are nourfed in Gardens with them, as they are in other places. The laft groweth neere the riuer of Canada, where the French plantation in America is feated.

The Time.

They flower from May vntill the end of Iuly or Auguft, and in the mean time the feed is ripe : But the Peache-leafed Bell-flowers, for the moft part, flower earlier then the other.

The Names.

The firft is generally called *Campanula Perficifolia,* in Englifh Peach-leafed Bell-flower. The fecond is called *Campanula maior, Campanula lactefcens Pyramidalis,* and *Pyramidalis Lutetiana* of Lobel, in Englifh, Great or Steeple Bell-flower. The third is vfually called *Viola Mariana,* and of fome *Viola Marina.* Lobel putteth a doubt whether it be not *Medium* of Diofcorides, as Matthiolus and others doe thinke ; but in my opinion the thickneffe of the roote, as the text hath it, contradicteth all the reft. We call it generally in Englifh Couentry Bels. Some call it Marian, and fome Mercuries Violets. The fourth and fift are called *Trachelium* or *Ceruicaria,* of fome *Vuularia,* becaufe many haue vfed it to good purpofe, for the paines of the *Vuula,* or Throate : Yet there is another plant, called alfo by fome *Vuularia,* which is *Hippogloffum,* Horfe tongue, or Double tongue. The fixt hath his title to defcipher it out fufficiently, as is declared. The feuenth is called *Trachelium minus,* and *Ceruiaria minor,* of fome *Saponaria altera* ; in Englifh, Small Throateworte, or Small Canterbury Bels. The laft hath his name in the title, as it is called in France, from whence I receiued plants for my Garden with the Latine name : but I haue giuen it in Englifh.

The Vertues.

The Peach-Bels as well as the others may fafely bee vfed in gargles and lotions for the mouth, throate, or other parts, as occafion ferueth. The rootes of many of them, while they are young, are often eaten in fallets by diuers beyond the Seas.

CHAP. LXXXVII.

Campana Cærulea fiue Convolvulus Cæruleus.
Blew Bell flowers, or blew Bindeweede.

THere are two other kindes of Bell-flowers, much differing from the Tribe or Familie of the former, becaufe of their climbing or winding qualitie, which I muft needes place next them, for the likeneffe of the flowers, although otherwife they might haue beene placed with the other clamberers that follow. Of thefe there is a greater, and a leffer, and of each likewife fome difference, as fhall be declared.

1. *Convolvulus cæruleus maior rotundifolius.*
The greater blew Bindweede, or Bell-flower with round leaues.

This goodly plant riseth vp with many long and winding branches, whereby it climbeth and windeth vpon any poles, herbes, or trees, that stand neare it within a great compasse, alwaies winding it selfe contrary to the course of the Sunne: on these branches doe growe many faire great round leaues, and pointed at the end, like vnto a Violet leafe in shape, but much greater, of a sad greene colour: at the ioynts of the branches, where the leaues are set, come forth flowers on pretty long stalkes, two or three together at a place, which are long, and pointed almost like a finger, while they are buds, and not blowne open, and of a pale whitish blew colour, but being blowne open, are great and large bels, with broad open mouths or brims ending in fiue corners, and small at the bottome, standing in small greene huskes of fine leaues: these flowers are of a very deepe azure or blew colour, tending to a purple, very glorious to behold, opening for the most part in the euening, abiding so all the night and the next morning, vntill the Sunne begin to growe somewhat hot vpon them, and then doe close, neuer opening more: the plant carrieth so many flowers, if it stand in a warme place, that it will be replenished plentifully, vntill the cold ayres and euenings stay the luxury thereof: after the flowers are past, the stalkes whereon the flowers did stand, bend downwards, and beare within the huskes three or foure blacke seedes, of the bignesse of a Tare or thereabouts: the rootes are stringy, and perish euery yeare.

2. *Convolvulus trifolius siue hederaceus purpureus.*
The greater purple Bindeweede, or Bell flower with cornered leaues.

The growing and forme of this Bindeweede or Bell flower, is all one with the former, the chiefest differences consisting in the forme of the leafe, which in this is three cornered, like vnto an Iuie leafe with corners; and in the flower, which is of a deeper blew, tending more to a deepe purple Violet, and somewhat more reddish in the fiue plaites of each flower, as also in the bottomes of the flowers.

3. *Convolvulus tennifolius Americanus.* The red Bell-flower of America.

Although this rare plant (because wee seldome haue it, and can as hardly keepe it) be scarce knowne in these cold Countries, yet I could not but make mention of it, to incite those that haue conueniencie to keepe it, to be furnished of it. It springeth vp at the first from the seede with two leaues, with two long forked ends, which abide a long time before they perish, betweene which riseth vp the stalke or stemme, branching forth diuers waies, being of a brownish colour, which windeth it selfe as the former great Bell-flower doth, whereon are set at seuerall ioynts diuers winged leaues, that is to say, many small narrow and long leaues set on both sides of the middle ribbe, and one at the end: from these ioynts arise long stalkes, at the ends whereof stand two or three small, long, hollow flowers, fashioned very like vnto the flowers of a Bindeweede, or the flowers of Tabacco, and ending in the like manner in fiue points, but not so much laide open, being of a bright red colour, plaited as the Bindeweedes or Bell-flowers before they be open, with some few threads in the middle, which turne into long pointed cods, wherein is contained long and blacke seede, tasting hot like Pepper: the roote is small and stringy, perishing euery yeare, and with vs will seldome come to flower, because our cold nights and frosts come so soone, before it cannot haue comfort enough of the Sun to ripen it.

4. *Convolvulus cæruleus minor Hispanicus.*
The Spanish small blew Bindeweede.

This small Bindeweede hath small long leaues, somewhat broader then the next that followeth, and not so broad as the common small Bindeweede (that groweth
euery

euery where wilde on the bankes of fields abroad) fet vpon the fmall trayling branches, which growe aboue two or three foote high : from the middle of thefe branches, and fo vnto the toppes of them, come forth the flowers at the ioynts with the
leaues, folded together at the firft into fiue plaites, which open into fo many corners,
of a moft excellent faire skie coloured blew (fo pleafant to behold, that often it ama-
zeth the fpectator) with white bottomes, and yellowifh in the middle, which turne
into fmall round white heads, wherein are contained fmall blackifh cornered feede,
fomewhat like the former, but fmaller : the roote is fmall and threddy, perifhing as
the former euery yeare : this neuer windeth it felfe about any thing, but leaneth by
reafon of the weakneffe of the branches, and dyeth euery yeare after feede time, and
not to be fowne againe vntill the next Spring.

5. *Convolvulus purpureus Spicæfolius.* Lauander leafed Bindeweede.

This fmall purple Bindeweede, where it naturally groweth, is rather a plague then
a pleafure, to whatfoeuer groweth with it in the fields ; yet the beauty of the flower
hath caufed it to be receiued into Gardens, bearing longer and fmaller leaues then the
laft, and fuch like fmall Bell-flowers, but of a fad purple colour : the roote is liuing,
as the common kinds are, and fpringeth againe where it hath been once fowne, without feare of perifhing.

The Place.

The firft two greater kindes haue beene fent vs out of Italy, but whether
they had them from the Eaft Indies, or from fome of the Eafterne Countries on this fide, wee know not : but they thriue reafonable well in our
Country, if the yeare be any thing kindly. The next came out of America,
as his name teftifieth. The leffer blew kinde groweth naturally in many
places both of Spaine and Portugall (from whence I firft receiued feedes
from Guillaume Boel, heretofore remembred.) The laft groweth wilde in
the fields, about Dunmowe in Effex, and in many other places of our
owne Countrey likewife.

The Time.

The three firft greater kindes flower not vntill the end of Auguft, or
thereabouts, and the feede ripeneth in September, if the colds and frofts
come not on too fpeedily. The leffer kindes flower in Iune and Iuly.

The Names.

The firft is called of fome *Campana Lazura,* as the Italians doe call it, or
Campana cærulea, of others *Convolvulus cæruleus maior, fiue Indicus,* and *Flos
noctis.* Of fome *Nil Auicenne.* The fecond is called *Convolvulus trifolius,*
or *hæderaceus,* for the diftinction of the leaues. In Englifh wee call them eyther Great blew Bell-flowers, or more vfually, Great blew Bindeweedes.
That of America is diuerfly called by diuers. It is called *Quamoclit* of the
Indians, and by that name it was fent to Ioachinus Camerarius out of Italy,
where it is fo called ftill, as Fabius Columna fetteth it downe, and as my
felfe alfo can witneffe it, from thence being fo fent vnto mee : but Andræas
Cæfalpinus calleth it, *Iafminum folio Millefolij,* fuppofing it to be a Iafmine.
Camerarius faith, it may not vnfitly be called *Convolvulus tenuifolius,* accounting it a kinde of Bindeweede. Columna entituleth it *Convolvulus pennatus exoticus rarior,* and faith it cannot bee referred to any other kinde of
plant then to the Bindeweedes. Hee that publifhed the *Curæ pofteriores* of
Clufius, giueth it the name of *Iafminum Americanum,* which I would doe
alfo, if I thought it might belong to that Family ; but feeing the face and
forme of the plant better agreeing with the Bindeweedes or Bell-flowers,
I haue

I haue (as you see) inferted it among them , and giuen it that name may bee moft fit for it, efpecially becaufe it is but an annuall plant. The leffer kindes haue their names fufficiently expreffed in their titles.

The Vertues.

We know of no vfe thefe haue in Phyficke with vs , although if the firft be *Nil* of Auicen, both he and Serapio fay it purgeth ftrongly.

Chap. LXXXVIII.

Stramonium. Thorne-Apple.

VNto the Bell-flowers, I muft adioyne three other plants , in the three feuerall Chapters following, for fome affinity of the flowers : and firft of the Thorne-Apples, whereof there are two efpeciall kindes , that is, a greater and a leffer, and of each fome diuerfity, as fhall be fet downe.

1. *Stramonium maius album.* The great white flowred Thorne-Apple.

The greater Thorne-Apple hath a great, ftrong, round greene ftalke, as high as any man, if it be planted in good ground, and of the bigneffe of a mans wreft almoft at the bottome, fpreading out at the toppe into many branches , whereon ftand many very large and broad darke greene leaues, cut in very deeply on the edges, and hauing manie points or corners therein : the flowers come forth at the ioynts, betweene two branches towards the toppe of them, being very large, long, and wide open , ending in fiue points or corners, longer and larger then any other Bell-flowers whatfoeuer : after the flowers are paft, come the fruit, which are thorny long heads, more prickly and greene then the leffer kindes, which being ripe openeth it felfe into three or foure parts , hauing a number of flat blackifh feede within them : the roote is aboundant in fibres , whereby it ftrongly taketh hold in the ground , but perifheth with the firft frofts ; yet the feede that is fhed when the fruit is ripe, commeth vp the next yeare.

2. *Stramonium maius purpureum.* The great purple flowred Thorne-Apple.

This purple Thorne-Apple is in largeneffe of leaues, thickneffe and height of ftalke, greatneffe and forme of flowers and fruit , euery way equall and correfpondent vnto the former, the chiefe differences be thefe : the ftalke is of a darke purple colour ; the leaues are of a darker greene, fomewhat purplifh, and the flowers are of light purple or pale Doue colour, enclining to white; and whiter at the bottome.

3. *Stramonium minus feu Nux Metel flore albo.* The fmaller Thorne-Apple with a white flower.

The fmaller Thorne-Apple rifeth vp with one round ftalke , of the bigneffe of a mans finger, and neuer much aboue two foote high with vs, bearing a few large, broad, fmooth leaues thereon, without any branches at all, which are vneuenly rent or torne about the edges, with many ribs, and fmaller veines running through them, yet leffer by much then the greater kinde : at the ioynts where the leaues ftand, come forth long and large white flowers, with broad or wide open brims, folded together before their opening, as the other former Bell-flowers or Bindeweedes, but hauing their fiue corners more pointed or horned then either they, or the former Thorne-Apples : after the flowers are paft, fucceed fmall fruit, rounder and harder, fet with harder, but blunt prickes then the former, wherein is contained brownifh yellow flat feede,

sticking

1 *Convolvulus maior cæruleus.* The greater blew Bindweed or Bell flower. 2 *Convolvulus trifolius seu hederaceus.* The great purple Bindweed. 3 *Convolvulus minor cæruleus Hispanicus.* The Spanish small blew Bindweed. 4 *Stramonium maius seu Pomum spinosum.* The great Thorne Apple. 5 *Datura seu Stramonium minus.* The small Thorne Apple. 6 *Stramonium flore duplici.* The double flowred Thorne-Apple. 7 *Stramonium flore geminato.* Double Thorne-Apple one out of another 8 *Tabacco latifolium.* Broad leafed Tabacco. 9 *Mirabilia Peruana.* The Meruaile of the world.

sticking to the inward pulpe : the roote is not very great, but full of strings, and quickly perisheth with the first frosts.

4. *Stramonium minus flore geminato purpurante.*
The small double flowred purple Thorne-Apple.

In the flower of this plant, consisteth the chiefest difference from the former, which is as large as the last, pointed into more hornes or corners, and beareth two flowers, standing in one huske, one of them rising out from the middle of the other, like vnto those kindes of Cowslips and Oxelips, called double, or Hose in hose, before described, which are of a pale purplish colour on the outside, and almost white within : the fruit is round like the last, and beareth such like seede, so that vntill it bee in flower, their difference can hardly bee discerned : this is more tender then the last, although euen it is so tender, that it seldome beareth ripe seede with vs.

Flore duplici. Sometimes (for I think it is not another kind) the flower will haue as it were double rowes of leaues, close set together, and not consisting of two, rising so distinctly one aboue another.

The Place.

All these kindes haue been brought or sent vs out of Turkie and Egypt; but Garcias, and Christopherus Acosta, with others, affirme that they grow in the East Indies. The lesser kindes are very rare with vs, because they seldome come to maturity ; and therefore we are still to seeke of new seede to sowe. The greater kindes are plentifull enough in our Gardens, and will well abide, and giue ripe fruit.

The Time.

The smaller kindes flower later then the greater ; and therefore their fruit are the sooner spoiled with the cold ayres, dewes, and frosts, that come at the latter end of the yeare : but the greater kinds neuer misse lightly to ripen.

The Names.

Both the greater and smaller kindes are generally called *Stramonium*, *Stramonia*, *Pomum spinosum*, and *Datura*. Bauhinus vpon Matthiolus his Comentaries on Dioscorides, calleth it *Solanum fœtidum spinosum*. Some learned men haue referred it to *Nux Metel*, of the Arabian Authors. Wee call them generally in English, Thorne-Apples, and distinguish them by their titles of greater and lesser, single and double.

The Vertues.

The East Indian lasciuious women performe strange acts with the seed (of the smaller kinde, as I suppose, or it may be of either) giuing it their husbands to drinke. The whole plant, but especially the seed, is of a very cold and soporiferous quality, procuring sleep and distraction of senses. A few of the seeds steeped and giuen in drinke, will cause them that take it to seem starke drunke or dead drunke, which fit will within a few houres weare away, and they recouer their senses againe, as a drunken man raysed after sleep from his wine. It may therefore (in my opinion) be of safe and good vse to one, that is to haue a legge or an arme cut off, or to be cut for the stone, or some other such like cure to be performed, to take away the sense of paine for the time of doing it ; otherwise I hold it not fit to be vsed without great caution. But the greene leaues of the greater kindes (as also of the lesser, but that with vs they are not so plentifull) are by tryed experience, found to be excellent good for any scalded or burned part, as also to take away any hot inflammations, being made vp into a salue or ointment with suet, waxe, and rossin, &c. or with *Axungia*, that is, Hogs larde.

CHAP.

Chap. LXXXIX.

Tabacco. Indian Henbane, or Tabacco.

THere hath beene formerly but three kindes of Tabacco knowne vnto vs, two of them called Indian, and the third Englifh Tabacco. In thefe later yeares, we haue had in our gardens about London (before the fuppreffing of the planting) three or foure other forts at the leaft, and all of the Indian kinde, hauing fome efpeciall difference, eyther in leafe, or flower, or both : And in regard the flowers of fome of thefe carry a pretty fhew, I fhall only entreate of them, and not of the Englifh kind.

Tabacco latifolium. Broade leafed Tabacco.

The great Indian Tabacco hath many very large, long, thicke, fat and faire greene leaues, ftanding foreright for the moft part, and compaffing the ftalkes at the bottome of them, being fomewhat pointed at the end : the ftalke is greene and round, fixe or feuen foote high at fometimes, and in fome places, in others not paft three or foure foote high, diuided towards the toppe into many branches, with leaues at euery ioynt, and at the toppes of the branches many flowers, the bottomes hereof are long and hollow, and the toppes plaited or folded before they are open, but being open, are diuided fometimes into foure, or more vfually into fiue corners, fomewhat like vnto other of the Bell-flowers, but lying a little flatter open, of a light carnation colour. The feede is very fmall and browne, contained in round heads, that are clammy while they are greene, and pointed at the end : the roote is great, whitifh, and woody at the head, difperfing many long branches, and fmall fibres vnder the ground, whereby it is ftrongly faftened, but perifheth with our violent frofts in the winter, if it be left abroad in the garden, but if it be houfed, or fafely prouided for againft the froftes, the rootes will liue, and fpring afrefh the next yeare.

There is of this kinde another fort, whofe leaues are as large and long as the former, but thicker, and of a more dead greene colour, hanging downe to the ground-ward, and fcarce any ftanding forth-right, as the former, vnleffe they bee very young : the flowers of this kinde are almoft whole, without any great fhew of corners at the brims or edges, in all other things there is no difference.

There is another, whofe large and thicke flat leaues doe compaffe the ftalke at the bottome, and are as it were folded together one fide vnto another : the flowers are of a deeper blufh, or carnation colour, and with longer points and corners then in any of the former ; and in thefe two things confifteth the difference from the others, and is called Verines Tabacco.

Another hath his leaues not fo large and long as the firft, and thefe haue fhort footeftalkes, whereon they ftand, and doe not compaffe the ftalke as the other doe : the flower hereof is like the firft, but fmaller, and of a little paler colour.

Tabacco anguftifolium. Narrow leafed Tabacco.

This kinde of Tabacco hath fomewhat lower, and fmaller ftalkes, then any of the former : the leaues hereof are fmaller and narrower, and not altogether fo thicke, but more pointed, and euery one ftanding vpon a footftalke, an inch and a halfe long at the leaft : the flowers hereof ftand thicker together, vpon the fmall branches, fomewhat larger, of a deeper blufh colour, and more eminent corners then in any the former : the feed and roots are alike, and perifh in like manner, vnleffe it be brought into a cellar, or other fuch couert, to defend it from the extremitie of the Winter.

The Place.

America or the Weft Indies is the place where all thefe kindes doe grow naturally, fome in one place, and fome in another, as in Peru, Trinidado,

Hifpani-

Hiſpaniola, and almoſt in euery Iland and Countrey of the continent thereof : with vs they are cheriſhed in gardens, as well for the medicinable qualities, as for the beauty of the flowers.

The Time.

It flowreth in Auguſt, ſeldome before, and the ſeede is ripe quickly after; If it once ſowe it ſelfe in a Garden, it will giue next year after young plants: but for the moſt part they will ſpring vp late, and therefore they that would haue them more early, haue ſowen the ſeede vpon a bed of dung, and tranſplanted them afterwards.

The Names.

This plant hath gotten many names. The Indians call it in ſome places *Petum*, in others *Picielt*, and *Perebecenuc*, as Ouiedus and others doe relate. The Spaniards in the Indies firſt called it *Tabacco*, of an Iland where plenty of it grew. It hath in Chriſtendome receiued diuers other names, as *Nicotiana*, of one Nicot a French man, who ſeeing it in Portugall, ſent it to the French Queene, from whom it receiued the name of *Herba Regina*. Lobel calleth it *Sancta herba, & Sana ſancta Indorum*. Some haue adiudged it to be an *Hioſcyamus*, and therefore call it *Peruvianus*. The moſt vſuall name wherby we call it in Engliſh, is Tabacco.

The Vertues.

The herbe is, out of queſtion, an excellent helpe and remedy for diuers diſeaſes, if it were rightly ordered and applyed, but the continuall abuſe thereof in ſo many, doth almoſt aboliſh all good vſe in any. Notwithſtanding if men would apply their wits to the finding out of the vertues, I make no doubt but many ſtrange cures would bee performed by it, both inward and outward. For outward application, a Salue made hereof (as is before recited of the Thorne apple leaues) cureth vlcers, and wounds of hard curation : And for inward helpes, a Syrupe made of the iuice and ſugar, or honey, procureth a gentle vomit (but the dryed leafe infuſed in wine much more) and is effectuall in aſtmaticall diſeaſes, if it bee carefully giuen. And likewiſe cleanſeth cankers and fiſtulaes admirably, as hath beene found by late experience. The aſhes of Tabacco is often vſed, and with good ſucceſſe, for cuts in the hands, or other places, and for other ſmall greene wounds.

Chap. XC.

Mirabilia Peruviana. The Meruaile of Peru.

THis plant yeeldeth in our Gardens fiue or ſixe ſeuerall varieties of beautifull flowers, as pure white, pure yellow, pure red, white and red ſpotted, and red and yellow ſpotted. But beſides theſe, I haue had ſome other ſorts, among which was one, of a pale purple or peach colour : all which, comming vnto mee out of Spaine with many other, ſeedes in an vnkindly yeare (an early winter following a cold ſummer) periſhed with mee ; yet I plainely might diſcerne by their leaues, and manner of growing, to be diuers from them that we now haue and keepe. I ſhall need therefore (becauſe the chiefeſt difference conſiſteth almoſt in the flowers) to giue only one deſcription of the plant, and therein ſhew the varieties as is before declared.

Admirabilis. The Meruaile of the World.

The ſtalke of this meruellous plant is great and thick, bigger then any mans thumbe, bunched

bunched out or swelling at euery ioynt, in some the stalkes will bee of a faire greene colour, and those will bring white, or white and red flowers : in others they will bee reddish, and more at the ioynts, and those giue red flowers ; and in some of a darker greene colour, which giue yellow flowers ; the stalkes and ioynts of those that will giue red and yellow flowers (spotted, are somewhat brownish, but not so red as those that giue wholly red flowers : vpon these stalkes that spread into many branches, doe grow at the ioynts vpon seuerall footestalkes, faire greene leaues, broad at the stalke, and pointed at the end : at the ioynts likewise toward the vpper part of the branches, at the foote of the leaues, come forth seuerall flowers vpon short footestalkes, euery one being small, long and hollow from the bottome to the brimme, which is broade spread open, and round, and consist but of one leafe without diuision, like vnto a Bell flower, but not cornered at all : which flowers, as I said, are of diuers colours, and diuersly marked and spotted, some being wholly white, without any spot in them for the most part, through all the flowers of the plant ; so likewise some being yellow, and some wholly red ; some plants againe being mixed and spotted, so variably either white and red, or purple, (except here and there some may chance to be wholly white, or red or purple among the rest) or red and yellow through the whole plant, (except as before some may chance in this kinde to be eyther wholly red, or wholly yellow) that you shall hardly finde two or three flowers in a hundred, that will bee alike spotted and marked, without some diuersitie, and so likewise euery day, as long as they blow, which is vntill the winters, or rather autumnes cold blastes do stay their willing pronenesse to flower : And I haue often also obserued, that one side of a plant will giue fairer varieties then another, which is most commonly the Easterne, as the more temperate and shadowie side. All these flowers doe open for the most part, in the euening, or in the night time, and so stand blowne open, vntill the next mornings sun beginne to grow warme vpon them, which then close themselues together, all the brims of the flowers shrinking into the middle of the long necke, much like vnto the blew Bindeweede, which in a manner doth so close vp at the sunnes warme heate : or else if the day be temperate and milde, without any sunne shining vpon them, the flowers will not close vp for the most part of that day, or vntill toward night : after the flowers are past, come seuerall seedes, that is, but one at a place as the flowers stood before, of the bignesse (sometimes) of small pease, but not so round, standing within the greene huskes, wherein the flowers stood before, being a little flat at the toppe, like a crowne or head, and round where it is fastened in the cup, of a blacke colour when it is ripe, but else greene all the while it groweth on the stalke, and being ripe is soone shaken downe with the wind, or any other light shaking : the roote is long and round, greater at the head, and smaller downwards to the end, like vnto a Reddish, spreading into two or three, or more branches, blackish on the outside and whitish within. These rootes I haue often preserued by art a winter, two or three (for they will perish if they be left out in the garden, vnlesse it be vnder a house side) because many times, the yeare not falling out kindely, the plants giue not ripe seede, and so we should be to seeke both of seede to sow, and of rootes to set, if this or the like art to keep them, were not vsed ; which is in this manner : Within a while after the first frosts haue taken the plants, that the leaues wither and fall, digge vp the rootes whole, and lay them in a dry place for three or foure dayes, that the superfluous moysture on the outside, may be spent and dryed, which done, wrap them vp seuerally in two or three browne papers, and lay them by in a boxe, chest or tub, in some conuenient place of the house all the winter time, where no winde or moist ayre may come vnto them; and thus you shall haue these rootes to spring afresh the next yeare, if you plant them in the beginning of March, as I haue sufficiently tryed. But some haue tryed to put them vp into a barrell or firkin of sand, or ashes, which is also good if the sand and ashes be thorough dry, but if it bee any thing moist, or if they giue againe in the winter, as it is vsuall, they haue found the moisture of the rootes, or of the sand, or both, to putrefie the rootes, that they haue beene nothing worth, when they haue taken them forth. Take this note also for the sowing of your seede, that if you would haue variable flowers, and not all of one colour, you must choose out such flowers as be variable while they grow, that you may haue the seede of them : for if the flowers bee of one entire co-lour, you shall haue for the most part from those seedes, plants that will bring flowers all of that colour, whether it be white, red or yellow.

The

The Place.

These plants grow naturally in the West Indies, where there is a perpetuall summer, or at the least no cold frosty winters, from whence the seede hath been sent into these parts of Europe, and are dispersed into euery garden almost of note.

The Time.

These plants flower from the end of Iuly sometimes, or August, vntill the frosts, and cold ayres of the euenings in October, pull them down, and in the meane time the seed is ripe.

The Names.

Wee haue not receiued the seedes of this plant vnder any other name, then *Mirabilia Peruviana*, or *Admirabilis planta*. In English wee call them, The meruaile of Peru, or the meruaile of the world : yet some Authors haue called it *Gelseminum*, or *Iasminum rubrum, & Indicum* : and Bauhinus *Solanum Mexiocanum flore magno.*

The Vertues.

We haue not knowne any vse hereof in Physicke.

Chap. XCI.

Malua. Mallowes.

OF the kindred of Mallowes there are a great number, some of the gardens, others wilde, some with single flowers, others with double, some with whole leaues, others with cut or diuided : to entreate of them all is not my purpose, nor the scope of this worke, but onely of such whose flowers, hauing beautie and respect, are fit to furnish this garden, as ornaments thereunto. And first of those single kindes, whose flowers come neerest vnto the fashion of the former Bell-flowers, and after to the double ones, which for their brauery, are entertained euery wheie into euery Countrey womans garden.

1. *Malua Hispanica flore carneo amplo.*
The Spanish blush Mallow.

The Spanish Mallow is in forme and manner of growing, very like vnto our common fielde Mallow, hauing vpright stalkes two or three foote high, spread into diuers branches, and from the bottome to the toppe, beset with round leaues, like vnto our Mallowes, but somewhat smaller, rounder, and lesse diuided, yet larger below then aboue : the flowers are plentifully growing vpon the small branches, folding or writhing their leaues one about another before they bee blowne, and being open consist of fiue leaues, with a long forked clapper therein, of the same colour with the flower : the chiefest difference from the common consisteth in this, that the leaues of these flowers are longer, and more wide open at the brimmes (almost like a Bell-flower) and of a faire blush or light carnation colour, closing at night, and opening all the day : after the flowers are past, there come such like round heads, with small blacke seede, like vnto the common kinde, but somewhat smaller: the roote is small and long, and perisheth euery yeare.

2. *Alcea vulgaris flore carneo.* Vervaine Mallow with blush flowers.

There is a Mallow that hath long stalkes, and flowers like vnto the common wilde
Mal-

1 *Malua Hispanica flore carneo amplo.* The Spanish Mallow. 2 *Alcea Veneta.* The Venice Mallow. 3 *Alcea Americana.* Thorney Mallow. 4 *Alcea Ægyptia.* The Mallow of Egypt. 5 *Althæa frutex.* The shrubbe Mallow. 6 *Malua hortensis simplex.* Single Hollihockes. 7 *Malua rosea multiplex.* Double Hollihockes.

Mallow, and of the same deepe colour with it, so that you can hardly know it from the ordinary kinde, which is found growing wilde together with it, but onely by the leafe, which is as round and as large as the former, but cut into many fine diuisions, euen to the stalke that vpholdeth it, that it seemeth to consist onely of ragges, or peeces of leaues : Of this kinde I take a plante for this garden, growing in all respects like vnto it, but differing onely in the colour of the flowers, which are of the same blush or light carnation colour, or not much differing from the former Spanish kinde, with some veines therein of a deeper colour: the root hereof liueth, as the root of the common wilde kinde doth.

3. *Alcea peregrina siue vesicaria.*
Venice Mallow, or Good night at noone.

The Venice Mallow hath long and weake stalkes, most vsually lying or leaning vpon the ground, hauing here and there vpon them long leaues and somewhat broad, cut in or gashed very deepely on both edges, that it seemeth as if they were diuers leaues set together, euery one standing on a long footestalke : at the ioynts of these stalkes, where the leaues are set, come forth seuerall flowers, standing vpon long foot-stalkes, which are somewhat larger then any of the former flowers, consisting of fiue leaues, small at the bottome, and wide at the brimmes, of a whitish colour tending to a blush, and sometimes all white, with spots at the bottomes of the leaues on the inside, of a very deepe purple or murrey colour, which addeth a great grace to the flower, and hauing also a long pestle or clapper in the middle, as yellow as gold : these flowers are so quickly faded and gone, that you shall hardly see any of them blowne open, vnlesse it bee betimes in the morning before the Sunne doe grow warme vpon them, for as soone as it feeleth the Sunnes warme heate, it closeth vp and neuer openeth againe, so that you shall very seldome see a flower blowne open in the day time, after nine a clocke in the morning : after these flowers are past, there rise vp in their places thinne, round, shining or transparent bladders, pointed at the toppe, and ribbed down all along, wherein are contained small, round, blackish seede : the roote is long and small, and perisheth euery yeare.

4. *Alcea fruticosa pentaphyllea.* Cinquefoile Mallow.

The stalkes of this Mallow are very long, hard or wooddy, more then of any of the other Mallowes : at the lower part whereof, and vp to the middle, stand diuers leaues vpon long footestalkes, parted or diuided into fiue parts or leaues, and dented about the edges ; but vpwards from the middle to the toppe, the leaues haue but three diuisions : among these leaues stand large wide open flowers, of the colour of the common Mallow : the seede is smaller then in any other Mallow, but the rootes are great and long, spreading in the ground like vnto the roots of Marsh Mallowes, springing vp afresh euery yeare from the roote.

5. *Sabdarifa seu Alcea Americana.* Thorney Mallowe.

This Thorney Mallowe hath greene leaues next vnto the ground, that are almost round, but pointed at the end, and dented very much about the edges; the other leaues that growe vpon the stalke are diuided into three parts, like vnto a trefoile, and some of them into fiue diuisions, all of them dented about the edges : the stalke is reddish, with some harmelesse prickles in sundry places thereon, and riseth vp three or foure foote high in a good ground, a fit place, and a kindly yeare, bearing plenty of flowers vpon the stalkes, one at the foote of euery leafe, the toppe it selfe ending in a long spike, as it were of buddes and leaues together : the flowers are of a very pale yellow, tending to a white colour, spotted in the bottome of each of the fiue leaues, with a deepe purple spot, broad at the lower part, and ending in a point about the middle of the leafe, which are quickly fading, and not abiding aboue one day, with a long pestle in the middle diuided at the toppe : after the flower is past, commeth vp a short prickly podde, set within a small greene huske or cup that bore the flower. wherein is contained

ned whitish, or rather brownish yellow feede, flat and fomewhat round, like vnto the feedes of Hollyhocke: the roote is ftringie, and quickly perifheth ; for it will hardly endure in our cold Country to giue flowers, much leffe feede, vnleffe (as I faid before) it happen in a kindly yeare, and be well planted and tended.

6. *Bamia feu Alcea Ægyptia.* The Mallow of Egypt.

This Mallow is alfo as tender to nourfe vp as the laft, hauing the lower leaues broad like a Marfh Mallow, and of a frefh greene colour ; but thofe that growe vpon the ftalke, and vp to the toppe, are diuided into fiue parts or points, but are not cut in to the middle ribbe, like the former Thorney Mallow, yet dented about the edges like vnto them : the flowers growe at the fetting to of the leaues, like vnto a Mallow for forme, but of a whitifh colour ; after which come long fiue fquare pointed pods, with hard fhels, wherein are contained round blackifh gray feede, as bigge as a Vetch or bigger : the roote perifheth quickly with vs, euen with the firft frofts.

7. *Althæa frutex flore albo vel purpureo.*
Shrubbe Mallow with a white or purple flower.

There are diuers forts of fhrubbe Mallowes, whereof fome that haue their ftemmes or ftalkes leffe wooddy, dye downe to the ground euery yeare, and others that abide alwayes, are more wooddy: Of the former forts I intend not to fpeake, referring them to a fitter place ; and of the other, I will onely giue you the knowledge of one or two in this place, although I doe acknowledge their fitteft place had been to be among the fhrubbes ; but becaufe they are Mallowes, I pray let them paffe with the reft of their kindred, and their defcriptions in this manner : Thefe wooddy kindes of fhrub Mallowes haue fomewhat large, long, and diuided leaues, of a whitifh greene colour, foft alfo, and as it were woolly in handling, fet difperfedly on the whitifh hard or wooddy ftalkes : their flowers are large, like vnto a fingle Rofe or Hollyhocke, in the one being white with purple fpots in the bottome ; in the other either of a deepe red colour, or elfe of a paler purple, with a deeper bottome, and with veines running in euery leafe: they are fomewhat tender, and would not be fuffered to be vncouered in the Winter time, or yet abroad in the Garden, but kept in a large pot or tubbe, in the houfe or in a warme cellar, if you would haue them to thriue.

8. *Malua hortenfis rofea fimplex & multiplex diuerforum colorum.*
Hollihockes fingle and double of feuerall colours.

I fhall not neede to make many defcriptions of Hollihockes, in regard the greateft difference confifteth in the flowers, which are in fome fingle, in fome double, in fome of one colour, and in others of other colours : for the loweft leaues of Hollihockes are all round, and fomewhat large, with many corners, but not cut in or diuided, foft in handling; but thofe that growe vp higher are much more diuided into many corners : the ftalkes fometimes growe like a tree, at the leaft higher then any man, with diuers fuch diuided leaues on them, and flowers from the middle to the toppe, where they ftand as it were a long fpike of leaues and buds for flowers together : the flowers are of diuers colours, both fingle and double, as pure white, and pale blufh, almoft like a white, and more blufh, frefh and liuely, of a Rofe colour, Scarlet, and a deeper red like a crimfon, and of a darke red like blacke bloud; thefe are the moft efpeciall colours both of fingle and double flowers that I haue feene : the fingle flowers confift of fiue broad and round leaues, ftanding round like vnto fingle Rofes, with a middle long ftile, and fome chiues aboue them : the double flowers are like vnto double Rofes, very thicke, fo that no ftile or vmbone is feene in the middle, and the outermoft rowe of leaues in the flowers are largeft, the innermoft being fmaller and thicke fet together : after the flowers are paft, there come vp as well in the double as fingle, flat round heads, like flat cakes, round about the bottomes whereof growe flat whitifh feede : the roote is long and great at the head, white and tough, like the roote of the common Mallowes, but greater, and will reafonably well abide the Winter.

The

The Place.

The first groweth wilde in Spaine. The second in our owne Countrey. The third is thought to growe in Italy and Venice; but Lobel denieth it, saying, that it is there onely in Gardens, and is more plentifull in these parts then with them. The fourth Clusius saith he found in many places of Germany. The fifth is supposed to be first brought out of the West Indies, but an Arabicke name being giuen it, maketh me somewhat doubtfull how to beleeue it. The sixth groweth in Egypt, where it is of great vse, as Prosper Alpinus hath set downe in his Booke of Egyptian plants. The seuenth groweth in some parts both of Spaine and France. The last is not found but in Gardens euery where.

The Time.

The first, second, third, fourth, and last, doe flower from Iune vntill the end of Iuly and August. The rest flower very late, many times not vntill September or October.

The Names.

The first and second haue their names sufficiently expressed in their titles. The third is diuersly called, as *Malua boraria*, *Alcea vesicaria*, *Alcea Veneta*, *Alcea Peregrina*, and of Matthiolus, *Hypecoum*. The most vsuall English name is Venice Mallow. The fourth is called *Alcea fruticosa pentaphyllea*, and *Cannabinifolio*, or *Pentaphyllifolio*: In English, Cinquefoile Mallow. The fifth hath been sent vnder the name of *Sabdarifa*, and *Sabdariffa*, and (as I said) is thought to be brought from America, and therefore it beareth the name of that Country. The sixth is called in Egypt, *Bamia*, or *Bammia*, and by that name sent with the addition *del Cayro* vnto it: In English, Egyptian Mallow, or Mallow of Egypt. The seuenth is called *Althea frutex*, and of some *Althea arborea*: In English, Shrubbe Mallow, because his stemme is wooddie, and abideth as shrubbes and trees doe. The eight and last is called *Malua hortensis*, *Malua Rosea*, and of some *Rosa vltra marina*: In English, of some Hockes, and vsually Hollihockes.

The Vertues.

All forts of Mallowes, by reason of their viscous or slimie quality, doe helpe to make the body soluble, being vsed inwardly, and thereby helpe also to ease the paines of the stone and grauell, causing them to be the more easily voided: being outwardly applyed, they mollifie hard tumors, and helpe to ease paines in diuers parts of the body; yet those that are of most vse, are most common. The rest are but taken vpon credit.

Chap. XCII.

Amaranthus. Flower-gentle.

WE haue foure or fiue sorts of Flower-gentle to trimme vp this our Garden withall, which doe differ very notably one from another, as shall be declared in their seuerall descriptions; some of which are very tender, and must be carefully regarded, and all little enough to cause them beare seede with vs, or else wee shall bee to seeke euery yeare: others are hardy enough, and will hardly be lost out of the Garden.

1. *Amaranthus purpureus minor.* The small purple Flower-gentle.

This gallant purple Veluet flower, or Flower-gentle, hath a crested stalke two foote high or more, purplish at the bottome, but greene to the toppe, whereout groweth many small branches, the leaues on the stalkes and branches are somewhat broad at the bottome, and sharpe pointed, of a full greene colour, and often somewhat reddish withall, like in forme vnto the leaues of Blites (whereof this and the rest are accounted *species*, or sorts) or small Beetes : the flowers are long, spikie, soft, and gentle tufts of haires, many as it were growing together, broad at the bottome, and small vp at the toppe, pyramis or steeple-fashion, of so excellent a shining deepe purple colour, tending to a murrey, that in the most excellent coloured Veluet, cannot be seene a more orient colour, (and I thinke from this respect, the French call it *Passe velours*, that is to say, passing Veluet in colour) without any smell at all, which being bruised giueth the same excellent purple colour on paper, and being gathered in his full strength and beauty, will abide a great time (if it be kept out of the winde and sunne in a dry place) in the same grace and colour : among these tufts lye the seede scattered, which is small, very blacke, and shining : the rootes are a few threddy strings, which quickly perish, as the whole plant doth, at the first approach of Winter weather.

2. *Amaranthus Coccineus.* Scarlet Flower-gentle.

The leaues of this Flower-gentle are longer, and somewhat narrower then the former ; the stalke groweth somewhat higher, bearing his long tufts at seuerall leaues, as also at the toppe of the stalkes, many being set together, but separate one from another, and each bowing or bending downe his head, like vnto a Feather, such as is worn in our Gallants and Gentlewomens heads, of an excellent bloudy Scarlet colour : the seede is blacke, like vnto the former : the roote perisheth quicklier, because it is more tender.

3. *Amaranthus tricolor.* Spotted or variable Flower-gentle.

The chiefest beauty of this plant consisteth in the leaues, and not in the flowers ; for they are small tufts growing all along the stalke, which is nothing so high as the former, especially with vs, and at the ioynts with the leaues : the leaues hereof are of the same fashion that the former are, and pointed also ; but euery leafe is to be seene parted into greene, red, and yellow, very orient and fresh (especially if it come to his full perfection, which is in hot and dry weather) diuided not all alike, but in some leaues, where the red or yellow is, there will be greene, and so varying, that it is very pleasant to behold : the seede hereof is blacke and shining, not to bee knowne from the former.

4. *Amaranthus Carnea spica.* Carnation Flower-gentle.

There is another more rare then all the rest, whose leaues are somewhat longer, and narrower then the first, and like vnto the second kinde : the spikes are short, many set together, like branches full of heads or eares of corne, euery one whereof hath some long haires sticking out from them, of a deep blush, tending to a carnation colour.

5. *Amaranthus purpureus maior panniculis sparsis.*
Great Floramour, or purple Flower-gentle.

The great Floramour hath one thicke, tall, crested, browne red stalke, fiue or six foote high, from whence spring many great broad leaues, like vnto the former for the forme, but much larger & redder for the most part, especially the lowest, which brancheth forth into diuers parts, & from between these leaues, & the stalks or branches, as also at the tops of them, stand long spikie, round, & somewhat flat tufts, of a more reddish purple colour then the first, and diuided also into seuerall parts, wherin when they

are

are full ripe, are to be seen an innumerable company of white seed, standing out among the short thrums, and do then easily fall away with a little touching; euery one of these white seed hath as it were an hole halfe bored through therin: the root is a great bush of strings, spreading in the ground, whereby it is strongly fastened, yet perisheth euery yeare, after it hath giuen his seede.

The Place.

All these plants growe in the Easterne Countries, as Persia, Syria, Arabia, &c. except the greatest, which hath been brought out of the West Indies, where it is much vsed, especially the seede : they are all, except it, noursed vp with much care in our Gardens, and yet in a backward or cold yeare they will not thriue, for that they desire much heate : but the greatest doth alwayes giue ripe seede euery yeare.

The Time.

They beare their gallant tufts or spikes for the most part in August, and some not vntill September.

The Names.

The name *Amaranthus* is giuen to all these plants, taken from the Greeke word *ἀμαράντινος*, *non marcescens*, or *non senescens*, that is, neuer waxing old, and is often also imposed on other plants, who haue the same property, that is, that their flowers being gathered in a fit season, will retaine their natiue colour a long time, as shall be shewed in the Chapter following. Diuers do thinke the first to be *Phlox*, or *Flamma* of Theophrastus. The third is called *Gelosia*, or *Celosia* of Tragus. Spigelius in his *Isagoges* saith, it is generally taken to be *Sophonia*, whereof Plinie maketh mention; and Lobel, to bee the Persians *Theombroton* of Plinie. The Italians, from whom I had it (by the meanes of Mr. Doctor Iohn More, as I haue had many other rare simples) call it, *Blito di tre colori*, A three coloured Blite. The fifth, which is the greatest, hath been sent from the West Indies by the name of *Quinua*, as Clusius reporteth. The name Flower-gentle in English, and *Floramour*, which is the French, of *Flos amoris*, and *Passe velours*, as is before said, or Veluet flower, according to the Italian, *Fior veluto*, are equally giuen to all these plants, with their seuerall distinctions, as they are expressed in their titles.

The Vertues.

Diuers suppose the flowers of these plants doe helpe to stay the fluxe of bloud in man or woman, because that other things that are red or purple doe performe the same. But Galen disproueth that opinion very notably, *in lib.2. & 4. de simpl. medicament. facultatibus.*

Chap. XCIII.

Helichrysum, siue Amaranthus luteus.
Golden Flower-gentle, Goldilockes, or Gold-flower.

THe propinquity of property (as I before said) hath caused the affinity in name, and so in neighbourhood in these plants, wherein there are some diuersity; and although they differ from them before in many notable points, yet they all agree with themselues in the golden, or siluer heads or tufts they beare; and therefore I
haue

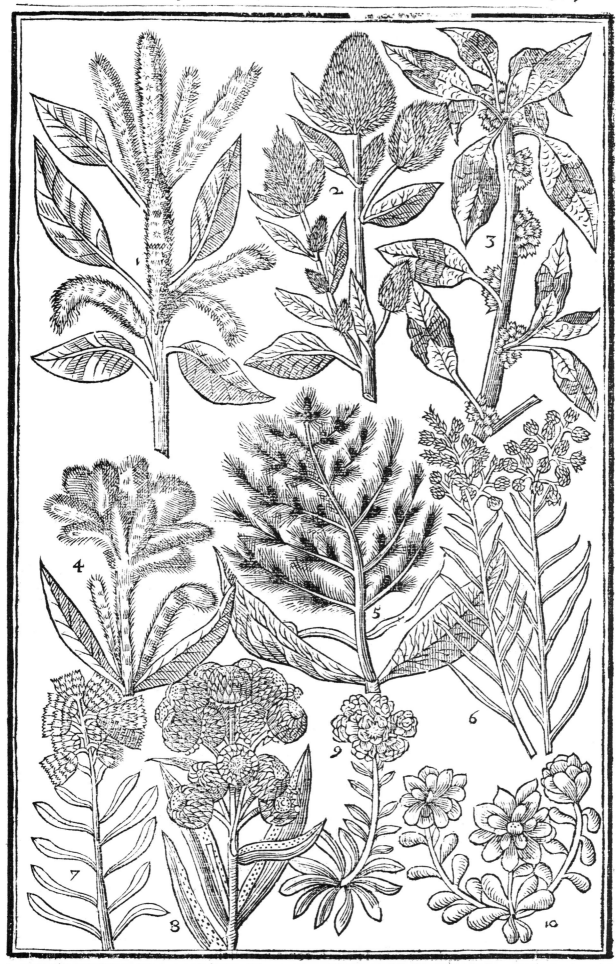

haue comprifed them in one Chapter, and will begin with that which commeth neareſt vnto the *Helichryſum* of Dioſcorides, or *Aurelia* (as Gaza tranſlateth it) of Theophraſtus.

1. *Heliochryſum.* The Golden flower of life.

This firſt Golden tuft riſeth vp with many hard, round, white ſtalkes, a foote and a
halfe high, whereon at certaine diſtances ſtand many fine cut leaues, or rather one leafe
cut into many ſmall fine parts, almoſt as ſmall as Fenell, but grayiſh, like vnto the Cud-
weedes or Cotton-weedes (whereof certainly theſe are ſpeciall kindes) at the toppes
of the ſtalkes ſtand many round flowers, of a pale gold colour, in an vmbell cloſe together, yet euery flower vpon his owne ſtalke, and all of an euen height, which will
keepe the colour, being gathered, and kept dry for a long time after, and are of a hot
and quicke ſent : the roote is ſmall and wooddy, ſpreading vnder the vpper cruſt of
the earth, and liueth long in his owne naturall place, but very hardly endureth the
cold of our Winters, vnleſſe they be milde, or it be well defended.

2. *Helichryſum Creticum.* Candy Goldilockes.

Candy Goldilockes hath two or three ſmall ſlender white branches, ſet here and
there very ſcatteringly, with ſmall, long, and narrow hoary leaues, hauing yellow
heads of flowers at the tops made into vmbels or tufts, not ſo round and euen as the
former, but longwiſe one aboue another, the heads being made as it were of ſcales,
loofly, and not ſo cloſely ſet together, as in the next following, which when they are
full ripe, doe paſſe into doune, and are blowne away with the winde, hauing a ſmall
reddiſh ſeede at the end ; but will abide a long time, as the other in his beauty, being
gathered in time, as the reſt will doe.

3. *Helichryſum Orientale ſiue Amaranthus luteus.*
Golden Flower-gentle.

This moſt beautifull plant is very like vnto the former Candy Goldilockes laſt deſcribed, but growing vp higher, with many more branches, and more hoary, white,
and woolly, hauing alſo long and narrow white leaues, but ſomewhat broader, and
thicker ſet on the branches : the tufts of flowers or vmbels likewiſe doe conſiſt of
longer and larger heads, more ſcaly, and cloſer compact together, of an excellent
pale gold yellow colour, and ſhining, with ſome yellow threads or thrummes in the
middle : the roote dyeth not euery yeare, but liueth long, eſpecially in the South and
Eaſt Countries, where no colds or froſts are felt ; but will require extraordinary care
and keeping, and yet ſcarce ſufficient to preſerue it in theſe cold Countries.

4. *Chryſocome ſiue Stœchas Citrina.* Golden tufts or Golden Caſſidony.

This Golden flower is ſomewhat like the former of theſe two laſt deſcribed, hauing
hoary ſtalkes and leaues, ſtanding confuſedly on them, being long, and narrower then
any of the former : the tops of the ſtalkes are diuided into many parts, each bearing a
ſmall long yellow head or flower at the toppe, with ſome yellow thrummes in them,
which heads being many, are diffuſedly ſet together, like a looſe or ſparſed vmbell,
keeping their colour long before they wither, and when they are ripe, haue thinne
ſmall reddiſh ſeede, like Mariorome ſeede, but ſmaller ; the roote is ſmall and blacke :
the whole plant, as well leaues and flowers, as rootes, are of a ſtrong ſharpe ſent, yet
pleaſant.

5. *Argyrocome ſiue Gnaphalium Americanum.*
Liue long or Life euerlaſting.

This ſiluer tuft or Indian Cotton weede, hath many white heads of leafes at their
firſt ſpringing out of the ground, couered with a hoary woollineſſe like cotton, which
riſing into hard, thicke round ſtalkes, containe ſtill the ſame hoarineſſe vpon them, as
alſo vpon the long and narrow leaues which are ſet thereon, eſpecially on the vnder
ſide,

side, for the vpper sides are of a darke shining greene colour : the stalkes are diuided at the toppe into many small branches, each whereof haue many scaly tufted heads set together, couered ouer with cotton before their opening, and then disseuering one from another, abiding very white on the outside, when they are fully growne, but with a small yellow thrume in the midde of euery flower, which in time turne into yellow doune, apt to be blowne away with euery winde : the roots are long and black on the outside, creeping vnder ground very much.

6. *Gnaphalium montanum flore albo & flore purpureo.* White and purple Cats foote.

This small Cudweede or Cottonweede, hath many small white woolly leaues growing from the roote, which is composed of a few small blackish threds, and lying vpon the ground somewhat like vnto the leaues of a small Mouse-eare, but smaller; from among which riseth vp a small stalke of halfe a foote high or thereabouts, beset here and there with some few leaues, at the top whereof commeth forth a tuft of small flowers, set close together, in some of a pure white, in others of a purple or reddish colour, in some of a pale red or blush, and in others of a white and purple mixt together, which for the beauty is much commended and desired, but will hardly abide to be kept in Gardens, so vnwilling they are to leaue their naturall abiding.

7. *Gnaphalium Roseum.* The Cotton Rose.

This little rose Cotton weede hath many such like woolly leaues, growing as the former from the roote vpon small short branches, not full an hand breadth high, in fashion somewhat like vnto Daysie leaues, but lesser, and round pointed : at the toppe of euery stalke or branch, standeth one flower, composed of two rowes of small white leaues, layd open like a Starre or a Rose, as it beareth the name, hauing a round head in the middle made of many yellow threds or thrumes, which falling away, there riseth vp a small round head, full of small seedes : the root is small, long and threddy.

The Place.

The foure first plants doe grow naturally in many of the hot Countries of Europe, as Spaine, Italie, and Prouince in France ; as also in Candy, Barbary, and other places, and must be carefully kept with vs in the winter time. The Liue long was brought out of the West Indies, and groweth plentifully in our gardens. The two last doe grow as well in the colder Countries of Germany, as in France and other places.

The Time.

They all flower in the end of September, if they will shew out their beauty at all with vs, for sometimes it is so late, that they haue no faire colour at all, especially the foure first sorts.

The Names.

Variable and many are the names that seuerall Writers do call these foure first sorts of plants, as *Helichrysum, Heliochrysum,* or *Elichrylum. Eliochrysum, Chrysocome, Coma aurea, Amaranthus luteus, Stoechas Citrina,* and *Aurelia,* with others, needlesse here to be recited : it is sufficient for this worke, to giue you knowledge that their names are sufficient as they are expressed in their titles : The fift is called *Gnaphalium* by Carolus Clusius, from the likenesse of the vmbels or tufts of heads, though greater and white : for as I said before, the Cotton weedes are of kindred with the golden tufts : It hath been called by our English Gentlewomen, Liue long, and Life euerlasting, because of the durabilitie of the flowers in their beautie. The two last are called *Gnaphalium*, according to their titles ; and in Englifh they may paffe vnder thofe names are fet downe with them.

The Vertues.

The foure firft are accounted to bee hot and dry, and the three laft to bee cold and dry : yet all of them may to fome good purpofe bee applyed to rheumaticke heads. The former foure are likewife vfed to caufe vrine, and in baths to comfort and heate cold parts. They are alfo layd in chefts and wardrobes, to keepe garments from moths ; and are worne in the heads and armes of Gentiles and others, for their beautifull afpect.

CHAP. XCIIII.

Canna Indica. The Indian flowring Reede.

THere are two kindes or forts of this beautifull plant, the one with a red flower, the other with a yellow, fpotted with reddifh fpots, both which in fome kindly yeares haue borne their braue flowers, but neuer any ripe feede, and doth not abide the extremities of our winters, eyther abroade or vnder couert, vnleffe it meete with a ftoue or hot-houfe, fuch as are vfed in Germany, or fuch other like place: For neyther houfe nor cellar will preferue it, for want of heate.

Canna Indica flore rubro. Red flowred Indian Reede.

This beautifull plant rifeth vp with faire greene, large, broade leaues, euery one rifing out of the middle of the other, and are folded together, or writhed like vnto a paper Coffin (as they call it) fuch as Comfitmakers and Grocers vfe, to put in their Comfits and Spices, and being fpread open, another rifeth from the bottome thereof, folded in the fame manner, which are fet at the ioynts of the ftalke when it is rifen vp, like vnto our water Reede, and growing (if it runne vp for flower) to be three or foure foote high, as I haue obferued in mine owne garden : the flowers grow at the toppe of the ftalke one aboue another, which before their opening are long, fmall, round, and pointed at the end, very like vnto the claw of a Crauife or Sea-Crab, and of the fame red or crimfon colour, but being open, are very like vnto the flower of *Gladiolus* or Corne-flagge, but of a more orient colour then at the firft, and ftanding in a rough huske, wherein afterwards ftandeth a three fquare head, containing therein round blacke feede, of the bigneffe of a peafe : the roote is white and tuberous, growing into many knobs, from whence arife fuch other leaues and ftalkes, whereby it encreafeth very much, if it be righrly kept and defended.

Canna Indica flore flauo punctato.
Yellow fpotted Indian Reede.

This Reede groweth vp with leaues and flowers, in all points fo like vnto the former, that it cannot bee knowne from it, vntill it come to flower, which is of a yellow colour, fpotted with reddifh fpots, without any other difference.

The Place.

Thefe plants grow naturally in the Weft Indies, from whence they were firft fent into Spaine, and Portugall, where Clufius faith he faw them planted by the houfes fides, flowring in winter, which might be in thofe warme Countreyes. We preferue them with great care in our gardens, for the beautifull afpect of their flowers.

The

The Time.

They flower not with vs vntill the end, or middle of Auguſt, at the ſooneſt.

The Names.

They are called of ſome *Canna Indica*, and *Arundo Indica*, of others *Cannacorus*, and of ſome *Flos Cancri*, becauſe the colour of the flowers, as well as the forme of the buds, are ſo like vnto a Sea-Crabs cle, or claw.

The Vertues.

There is not any vſe of theſe in Phyſicke that I know.

CHAP. XCV.

Mandragoras. Mandrake.

THe Mandrake is diſtinguiſhed into two kindes, the male and the female ; the male hath two ſorts, the one differing from the other, as ſhall be ſhewed; but of the female I know but one : The male is frequent in many gardens, but the female, in that it is more tender and rare, is nourſed vp but in a few.

Manadrgoras mas. The male Mandrake.

The male Mandrake thruſteth vp many leaues together out of the ground, which being full growne, are faire, large and greene, lying round about the roote, and are larger and longer then the greateſt leaues of any Lettice, whereunto it is likened by Dioſcorides and others : from the middle, among theſe leaues, riſe vp many flowers, euery one vpon a long ſlender ſtalke, ſtanding in a whitiſh greene huske, conſiſting of fiue pretty large round pointed leaues, of a greeniſh white colour, which turne into ſmall round apples, greene at the firſt, and of a pale red colour when they are ripe, very ſmooth and ſhining on the outſide, and of a heady or ſtrong ſtuffing ſmell, wherein is contained round whitiſh flat ſeede : the roote is long and thicke, blackiſh on the outſide, and white within, conſiſting many times but of one long roote, and ſometimes diuided into two branches a little below the head, and ſometimes into three or more, as nature liſteth to beſtow vpon it, as my ſelfe haue often ſeene, by the tranſplanting of many, as alſo by breaking and cutting off of many parts of the rootes, but neuer found harme by ſo doing, as many idle tales haue beene ſet downe in writing, and deliuered alſo by report, of much danger to happen to ſuch, as ſhould digge them vp or breake them ; neyther haue I euer ſeene any forme of man like or woman-like parts, in the rootes of any : but as I ſaid, it hath oftentimes two maine rootes running down-right into the ground, and ſometimes three, and ſometimes but one, as it likewiſe often happeneth to Parſneps, Carrots, or the like. But many cunning counterfeit rootes haue bin ſhaped to ſuch formes, and publickly expoſed to the view of all that would ſee them, and haue been tolerated by the chiefe Magiſtrates of the Citie, notwithſtanding that they haue beene informed that ſuch practices were meere deceit, and vnſufferable; whether this happened through their ouer-credulitie of the thing, or of the perſons, or through an opinion that the information of the truth roſe vpon enuy, I know not, I leaue that to the ſearcher of all hearts : But this you may bee bold to reſt vpon, and aſſure your ſelues, that ſuch formes as haue bin publickly expoſed to be ſeene, were neuer ſo formed by nature, but only by the art and cunning of knaues and deceiuers. and let this be your *Galeatum* againſt all ſuch vaine, idle and ridiculous toyes of mens inuentions.

There

There is likewise another sort of these male Mandrakes, which I first saw at Canterbury, with my very louing and kinde friende Iohn Tradescante, in the garden of the Lord Wotton, whose gardiner he was at that time ; the leaues whereof were of a more grayish greene colour, and somewhat folded together, when as the former kind that grew hard by it, was of the same forme that is before described, and ordinary in all others : but whether the apples were differing from the other, I know not, nor did they remember that euer it had borne any.

Mandragoras femina. The female Mandrake.

The female Mandrake doth likewise put vp many leaues together, from the head of the roote, but they are nothing so large, and are of a darker greene colour, narrower also and shining, more crumpled, and of a stronger sent : the flowers are many, rising vp in the middle of the leaues, vpon slender stalkes, as in the male kind, but of a blewish purple colour, which turne into small round fruite or apples, and not long like a peare (as Clusius reporteth that saw them naturally growing in Spaine) greene at the first, and of a pale yellowish colour, when they are full ripe; of a more pleasing, or if you will, of a lesse heady sent then the apples of the male, wherein is contained such like seede, but smaller and blacker : the rootes are like the former, blacke without and white within, and diuided in the same manner as the male is, sometimes with more, and sometimes with fewer parts or branches.

The Place.

They grow in many places of Italie, as Matthiolus reporteth, but especially on Mount Garganus in Apulia. Clusius saith hee found the female in many wet grounds of Spaine, as also in the borders of those medowes that lye neere vnto riuers and water courses. The male is cherished in many Gardens, for pleasure as well as for vse : but the female as is said, is both very rare, and farre more tender.

The Time.

The Male flowreth in March, and the fruit is ripe in Iuly. The Female, if it be well preserued, flowreth not vntill August, or September; so that without extraordinary care, we neuer see the fruite thereof in our gardens.

The Names.

Mandragoras mas is called *albus,* as the *Femina* is called *niger,* which titles of blacke and white, are referred vnto the colour of the leaues : the female is called also *Thridacias,* from the likenesse of Lettice, whereunto they say in forme it doth carry some similitude. Dioscorides saith, that in his time the male was called *Morion,* and both of them *Antimelum,* and *Circea.* Wee call them in English, The male, and the female Mandrake.

The Vertues.

The leaues haue a cooling and drying qualitie, fit for the oyntment *Populeon,* wherein it is put. But the Apples haue a soporiferous propertie, as Leuinus Lemnius maketh mention in his Herball to the Bible, of an experiment of his owne. Besides, as Dioscorides first, and then Serapio, Auicen, Paulus Ægineta, and others also do declare, they conduce much to the cooling and cleansing of an hot *matrix.* And it is probable, that Rachel knowing that they might be profitable for her hot and dry body, was the more earnest with Leah for her Sonne Rubens Apples, as it is set downe *Genesis* 30.*verse* 14. The strong sent of these apples is remembred also, *Cant.* 7. 13. although some would diuert the signification of the Hebrew word, דודאים,
vnto

vnto Violets, or fome other fweet flowers, in the former place of *Genefis*, and the fruit of *Mufa*, or Adams Apples in this place of the *Canticles*. Hamilcar the Carthaginian Captaine is faid to haue infected the wine of the Lybians (his enemies againft whom he fought) with the apples of Mandrake, whereby they being made exceeding drowfie, he obtained a famous victory ouer them.

CHAP. XCVI.

Pomum Amoris. Loue Apples.

ALthough the beautie of this plant confifteth not in the flower, but fruit, yet giue me leaue to infert it here, left otherwife it haue no place : whereof there are two efpeciall forts, which wee comprehend in one Chapter, and diftinguifh them by *maius* and *minus*, greater and fmaller : yet of the greater kinde, we haue nourfed vp in our Gardens two forts, that differ only in the colour of the fruite, and in nothing elfe.

Pomum Amoris maius fructu rubro. Great Apple of Loue the ordinary red fort.

This greater kinde of Loue Apples, which hath beene moft frequently cherifhed with vs, hath diuers long and trayling branches, leaning or fpreading vpon the ground, not able to fuftaine themfelues, whereon doe grow many long winged leaues, that is, many leaues fet on both fides, and all along a middle ribbe, fome being greater, and others leffe, iagged alfo and dented about the edges, of a grayifh ouer-worne greene colour, fomewhat rough or hairy in handling; from among the leaues and the branches come forth long ftalkes, with diuers flowers fet thereon, vpon feuerall fhort footftalks, confifting of fixe, and fometimes of eight fmall long yellow leaues, with a middle pricke or vmbone, which after the flowers are fallen, rifeth to be the fruite, which are of the bigneffe of a fmall or meane Pippin, vneuenly bunched out in diuers places, and fcarce any full round without bunches, of a faire pale reddifh colour, or fomewhat deeper, like vnto an Orenge, full of a flimie iuice and watery pulpe, wherein the feede lyeth, which is white, flat and fomewhat rough : the roote fhooteth with many fmall ftrings and bigger branches vnder ground, but perifheth at the firft feeling of our winter weather. The fruite hereof by often fowing it in our Land, is become much fmaller then I haue here defcribed it : but was at the firft, and fo for two or three yeares after, as bigge as I haue related it.

Pomum Amoris maius fructu luteo. Yellow Amorous Apples.

Of the fame kinde is this other fort of Amorous Apples, differing in nothing but the colour of the fruite, which is of a pale yellow colour, hauing bunches or lobes in the fame manner, and feede alfo like the former.

Pomum Amoris minus, fiue Mala Ethiopica parua. Small Loue Apples.

The fmall Apples of Loue in the very like manner, haue long weake trayling branches, befet with fuch like leaues as the greater kinde hath, but fmaller in euery part : the flowers alfo ftand many together on a long ftalke, and yellow as the former, but much fmaller : the fruite are fmall, round, yellowifh red berries, not much bigger then great grapes, wherein are contained white flat feede, like the other, but fmaller : the roote perifheth in like manner euery yeare. and therefore muft bee new fowen euery fpring, if you will haue the pleafure of their fight in the garden ; yet fome yeares I haue known them rife of their owne fowing in my garden.

The

The Place.

They growe naturally in the hot **Countries** of **Barbary**, and **Ethiopia**; yet some report them to be first brought from **Peru**, a **Prouince** of the **West Indies**. Wee onely haue them for curiosity in our Gardens, and for the amorous aspect or beauty of the fruit.

The Time.

They flower in Iuly and August, and their fruit is ripe in the middle or end of September for the most part.

The Names.

The first is named diuersly by diuers Authors; for Lobel, Camerarius, and others, call them *Poma amoris*. Dodonæus *Aurea Mala*. Gesnerus first, and Bauhinus after him, make it to be a kinde of *Solanum Pomiferum*. Anguillara taketh it to be *Lycopersicum* of Galen. Others thinke it to bee *Glaucium* of Dioscorides. The last is called *Mala Æthiopica parua*, and by that title was first sent vnto vs, as if the former were of the same kinde and country. We call them in English, Apples of Loue, Loue-Apples, Golden Apples, or Amorous Apples, and all as much to one purpose as another, more then for their beautifull aspect.

The Vertues.

In the hot Countries where they naturally growe, they are much eaten of the people, to coole and quench the heate and thirst of their hot stomaches. The Apples also boyled, or infused in oyle in the sunne, is thought to be good to cure the itch, assuredly it will allay the heate thereof.

CHAP. XCVII.

Digitalis. Foxegloue.

THere are three principall sorts of Foxegloues, a greater, a middle or meane sort, and a lesser, and of them, three especiall colours, that is, purple, white, and yellow; the common purple kinde that groweth abroad in the fields, I leaue to his wilde habitation: and of the rest as followeth.

1. *Digitalis maxima ferruginea.* Dun coloured Foxegloues.

The leaues of this Foxegloue are long and large, of a grayish green colour, finely cut or dented about the edges, like the teeth of a fine sawe; among which commeth vp a strong tall stalke, which when it was full growne, and with ripe seede thereon, I haue measured to be seuen foot high at the least, wheron grow an innumerable company (as I may so say, in respect of the aboundance) of flowers, nothing so large as the common purple kinde, that groweth wilde euery where in our owne Countrey, and of a kinde of browne or yellowish dunne colour, with a long lippe at euery flower; after them come seede, like the common kinde, but in smaller heads: the rootes are stringie like the ordinary, but doe vsually perish, or seldome abide after it hath giuen seed.

2. *Digitalis maior flore carneo.* Blush coloured Foxegloues.

This kinde of Foxegloues hath reasonable large leaues, yet not altogether so large

as

1 *Canna Indica.* The Indian Reed. 2 *Mandragoras mas.* The male Mandrake. 3 *Pomum amoris maius.* Great Apples of loue. 4 *Digitalis maior flore luteo amplo.* The great yellow Foxegloue. 5 *Digitalis media flore luteo rubente.* Orenge tawny Foxegloues. 6 *Digitalis maxima ferruginea.* Dun coloured Foxegloues.

as the common field kinde : the flowers are also smaller then the common sort, but of a blush colour.

3. *Digitalis media flore luteo rubente*. Orenge tawnie Foxegloue.

As this Foxegloue is none of the greatest, so also is it none of the smallest; but a sort betweene both, hauing leaues in some proportion correspondent to the lesser yellow Foxegloue, but not so large as the lesser white : the flowers are long and narrow, almost as large as the last white, but nothing so large as the first white, of a faire yellowish browne colour, as if the yellow were ouershadowed with a reddish colour, and is that colour wee vsually call an Orenge tawnie colour : the seede is like the former : the rootes perish euery yeare that they beare seede, which is vsually the second yeare of the springing.

4. *Digitalis maior alba*. The greater white Foxegloue.

This white Foxegloue is in all things so like vnto the purple wilde kinde, that it can hardly be distinguished from it, vnlesse it be in the fresher greennesse and largenesse of the leaues : the flowers are as great in a manner as the purple, but wholly white, without any spot in them : the seed and other things agree in all points.

5. *Digitalis alba altera seu minor*. The lesser white Foxegloue.

We haue in our Gardens another sort of white Foxegloue, whose leaues are like vnto the last described, but not altogether so long or large, and of a darker greene colour : the stalke groweth not so high, as not full three foote : the flowers are pure white, fashioned like vnto the former, but not so great or large, in all other things alike : the rootes hereof did abide sometime in our Gardens, but since perished, and the seede also, since when we neuer could obtaine from any our friends of that kinde againe.

6. *Digitalis maior lutea flore amplo*. The great yellow Foxegloue.

The leaues of this greater yellow Foxegloue, are in forme somewhat like vnto the common purple kinde, but not altogether so large : the stalke groweth to bee three or foure foote high, whereon stand many long hollow pendulous flowers, in shape like the ordinary purple : but somewhat shorter, and more large and open at the brimmes, of a faire yellow colour, wherein are long threads, like as in the others : the roote hereof is greater at the head, and more wooddy then any of the rest, with many smaller fibres, spreading themselues in the ground, and abideth almost as well as our common purple kinde.

7. *Digitalis minor lutea siue pallida*. The small pale yellow Foxegloue.

This small pale yellow Foxegloue hath somewhat short, broad, smooth and darke greene leaues, snipt or dented about the edges very finely : the stalke is two foot high, beset with such like leaues, but lesser : the flowers are moe in number then in any of the rest, except the first and greatest, and growe along the vpper part of the stalke, being long and hollow, like the other, but very small, and of a pale yellow colour almost white : the seede vessels are small like the former, wherein are contained seede like the rest, but smaller : the rootes are stringy, but durable, and seldome perish with any iniury of the extreamest frosts.

The Place.

The great white kinde hath been often, and in many places found wilde in our owne Country, among or hard by the common purple kinde. All the rest are strangers, but cherished in our Gardens.

The

The Time.

They flower in Iune and Iuly, and some in August, their seede becomming ripe quickly after.

The Names.

Onely the name *Digitalis*, is of all Writers giuen vnto these plants ; for it is not knowne to bee remembred of any of the old Authors. Wee call them generally in English, Foxegloue ; but some (as thinking it to bee too foolish a name) doe call them Finger-flowers, because they are like vnto the fingers of a gloue, the ends cut off.

The Vertues.

Foxegloues are not vsed in Physicke by any iudicious man that I know ; yet some Italians of Bononia, as Camerarius saith, in his time vsed it as a wound herbe.

CHAP. XCVIII.

Verbascum. Mullein.

THere be diuers kindes of Mullein, as white Mullein, blacke Mullein, wooddy Mullein, base Mullein, Moth Mullein, and Ethiopian Mullein, all which to distinguish or to descríbe, is neither my purpose, nor the intent of this worke, which is to store a Garden with flowers of delight, and sequester others not worthy of that honour. Those that are fit to bee brought to your consideration in this place, are first, the *Blattarias,* or Moth Mulleins, and then the wooddy Mullein, which otherwise is called French Sage, and lastly, the Ethiopian Mullein, whose beauty consisteth not in the flower, but in the whole plant ; yet if it please you not, take it according to his Country for a Moore, an Infidell, a Slaue, and so vse it.

1. *Blattaria lutea odorata.* Sweete yellow Moth Mullein.

The yellow Moth Mullein whose flower is sweete, hath many hard grayish greene leaues lying on the ground, somewhat long and broad, and pointed at the end : the stalks are two or three foot high, with some leaues on them, & branching out from the middle vpwards into many long branches, stored with many small pale yellow flowers, of a pretty sweete sent, somewhat stronger then in the other sorts, which seldome giueth seede, but abideth in the roote, liuing many yeares, which few or none of the others doe.

2. *Blattaria lutea maior siue Hispanica.* The great yellow Moth Mullein.

This Spanish kinde hath larger and greener leaues then the former, and rounder and larger then the next that followeth : the stalke is higher then in any of the Moth Mulleins, being for the most part foure or fiue foote high, whereon toward the toppe growe many goodly yellow flowers, consisting of fiue leaues, as all the rest doe, not so thicke set as the former, but much larger, with some small purplish threads in the middle : the ends whereof are fashioned somewhat like as if a Flie were creeping vp the flower, which turne into round heads, sometimes two or three or more standing together, but vsually one, wherein lye small duskie seed : the roote is not great nor full of threads, and doth perish most vsually hauing giuen seede, except the Winter bee very milde.

3. *Blattaria*

3. *Blattaria lutea altera vulgatior.* The ordinary yellow Moth Mullein.

This yellow Moth Mullein (which is the moſt frequent in our Gardens) hath longer, and narrower leaues then any of the former, and roundly notched or dented on the edges, of a darke greene colour : the ſtalke is ſometimes branched, but moſt vſually ſingle, whereon ſtand many gold yellow flowers, not fully ſo large as the Spaniſh kinde, but with the like purple threads in the middle : the ſeede is ſmall, and contained in the like round heads, but alwaies euery one ſingle by it ſelfe : the roote periſheth euery yeare that it beareth ſeede.

4. *Blattaria flore luteo purpuraſcente.* Cloth of gold Moth Mullein.

The greateſt point of difference betweene this and the laſt deſcribed, conſiſteth chiefly in the colour of the flower, which in this is of the colour of cloth of gold, that is, the ground yellow, and ouerſhadowed with a bright crimſon colour, which is a fine colour of much delight : the threads in the middle are not ſo purple red as in the former, but much about the colour of the flower : this is not ſo willing to giue ſeede, and will as hardly abide in the roote, and hath out of queſtion riſen from the ſeede of the former.

5. *Blattaria flore albo.* White Moth Mullein.

The leaues of the white Moth Mullein are ſomewhat like vnto the yellow, yet not altogether ſo much roundly notched about the edges, but rather a little dented, with ſharper notches : the ſtalke riſeth as high as the yellow, and hath now and then ſome branches about it : the flowers hereof are pure white, as large and great as the ordinary yellow, or ſomewhat larger, with the like purple threads in the middle, as are in the yellow : the ſeed is like the other; the root periſheth in like maner, and will not endure.

6. *Blattaria flore purpureo.* Purple Moth Mullein.

The Purple Moth Mullein hath his leaues lying on the ground, broader and ſhorter then any of the other, of a more grayiſh greene colour, and without any denting for the moſt part about the edges, ſharpe pointed alſo at the end of the leafe ; among the leaues riſeth vp the ſtalke, not ſo high as either the white or the yellow, and many times branched, bearing many flowers thereon, of the ſame faſhion, and no whit ſmaller, of a faire deepe blewiſh colour tending to redneſſe, the threads in the middle of the flowers being yellow : the ſeede veſſels hereof are ſomewhat ſmaller then any of the former, except the firſt ſweete yellow kinde : the roote hereof is long, thicke, and blackiſh on the outſide, abiding very well from yeare to yeare, and riſeth well alſo from the ſowing of the ſeede.

7. *Blattaria flore cæruleo.* Blew Moth Mullein.

This blew Moth Mullein is in all reſpects like vnto the former purple kinde, ſauing onely in the colour of the flower, which is of a blewiſh violet colour, and is not much inferiour either in greatneſſe of the plant, or in the largeneſſe of the flower, vnto the former purple kinde, and endureth many yeares in the like manner. And theſe be all the ſorts of this kinde of Moth Mullein, that I haue ſeene and nourſed vp for this my Garden, without interpoſing any vnknowne, not ſeene, or vnworthy.

8. *Verbaſcum ſilueſtre ſiue quartum Matthioli.*
Wooddy Mullein or French Sage.

Wooddy Mullein or French Sage, hath diuers wooddy branches two or three foot high, very hoary or white, whereon at ſeuerall ioynts ſtand diuers thicke leaues, white alſo and hoary, long, ſomewhat broad, round pointed, and rough, ſomewhat reſembling the leaues of Sage in the forme and roughneſſe, but not in the ſent, whereof our
people

people gaue it the name of Sage, calling it French Sage (when as it is as great a ftranger in France as in England, yet they doe with this as with many other things, calling them French, which come from beyond the Seas; as for example, all or moft of our bulbous flowers, they call French flowers, &c.) at the toppes of the ftalkes and branches, at certaine diftances, are placed round about them many gaping flowers, like vnto the flowers of Sage, but yellow : after which now and then come feede, fomewhat bigger then the Moth Mulleins, and leffe then the next Mullein of Ethiopia: the roote is wooddy at the toppe, with diuers blackifh ftrings growing from it, and endureth as well aboue ground with his leaues, as vnder it with his rootes.

9. *Æthiopis.* Ethiopian Mullein.

This Mullein of Ethiopia hath many great, broad, and large leaues lying on the ground, rent or torne in diuers of them very much on the fides, of fo hoary a white greene colour, that it farre paffeth any of the white Mulleins, that growe wilde abroad in our owne Country; for they are of a yellowifh white hoarineffe, nothing fo pleafant to looke on as this : in the middle of thefe leaues rifeth vp a fquare ftrong ftalke, foure or fiue foote high, fet full of fuch like leaues as growe belowe, but much leffer, and leffer ftill vp to the toppe, all hoary and woolly, as the reft, and diuided into manie branches, fpreading farre, and taking vp a great compaffe of ground, more then any one roote of Garden Clary, or other fuch like plant : at each of the ftalkes and branches are fet two fmall leaues, and with them, round about the ftalkes, ftand many fmall gaping flowers, of a pale bleake blew colour : the feede is almoft as large as Garden Clary feede, and of the fame forme and colour : the roote is wooddy, and perifheth as foone as it hath borne feede, which is vfually the fecond yeare after the fowing; for the firft yeare it feldome runneth vp to flower.

10. *Lamium Pannonicum fiue Galeopfis Pannonica.* Hungary dead Nettle or the Dragon flower.

Let mee thruft this plant into this place, rather then make a peculiar Chapter, becaufe I haue no other of the fame ftocke or kindred to be ioyned with it, and is a pretty ornament in a Garden. The leaues whereof are very large, round, and great, rough or full of veines, which make it feeme crumpled, dented or deepely notched about the edges, and of a very darke greene colour, and fometimes brownifh, or of a darke reddifh colour withall, euery one ftanding on a long foote-ftalke, very like in forme vnto the great white Arch-Angell leaues, but farre larger and blacker : the ftalkes are great and foure fquare, hauing leaues and flowers ftanding round about them at the ioynts like coronets, which flowers are very great, long, and wide gaping open, of a darke red or purple colour, with fome whiteneffe or fpots in the iawes, and fome hairineffe alfo on the fides, which ftand in full flower two or three moneths moft vfually, and fometimes longer, after which come brownifh feede : the roote is a great tuft or bufh of long whitifh ftrings, and encreafeth euery yeare, not fearing the greateft iniuries of our coldeft and extreameft Winters.

The Place.

All thefe plants are ftrangers in our Countrey, and onely preferued in Gardens, to furnifh them with variety; but (as I faid) the cloth of gold Moth Mullein hath been raifed from feed in our owne Country.

The Time.

The laft flowreth firft, before all the reft, beginning in Aprill. The Moth Mulleins in May and Iune. The French Sage in Iuly.

The Names.

All the forts of *Blattaria* may bee comprehended vnder the kindes of

K k   *Verbafcum*

Verbascum nigrum, as any one but meanely exercised in the knowledge of plants, may discerne. And although Plinie saith, that Moths doe most frequently haunt where *Blattaria* either groweth, or is laid, yet it is not observed sufficiently in our Country so to doe, notwithstanding the name of Moth Mullein is generally giuen them. The last is generally called with vs *Lamium Pannonicum*, but certainely it is the *Galeosis maxima Pannonica* of Clusius.

The Vertues.

Other qualities I haue not found hath been allotted vnto the *Blattaria* or Moth Mullein, then those of Plinie, to engender Moths. Wee vse none of these plants in Physicke in these daies.

Chap. XCIX.

Valeriana. Valerian.

THe many sorts of Valerian (or Set-wall as many doe call them) are fitter for a generall worke, or a generall Physicall Garden of Simples, then this of delightfull flowers. I will therefore select out a few, worthy of the place, and offer them to your considerations.

1. *Valeriana rubra Dodonæi*. Red Valerian.

This Valerian hath diuers hard, but brittle whitish greene stalkes, rising from the roote, full of tuberous or swelling ioynts, whereat stand two leaues, on each side one, and now and then some small leaues from betweene them, which are somewhat long and narrow, broadest in the middle, and small at both ends, without either diuision or incisure on the edges, of a pale greene colour : the stalkes are branched at the top into diuers parts, at the ends whereof stand many flowers together, as it were in an vmbell or tuft, somewhat like vnto the flowers of our ordinary Valerian, but with longer neckes, and of a fine red colour, very pleasant to behold, but of no sent of any Valerian : after these flowers haue stood blowne a very great while, they sodainely fall away, and the seede is ripe very quickly after, which is whitish, standing vpon the branches naked, as the Valerians doe, and very like vnto them, with a little white doune at the end of euery one of them, whereby they are soone carried away with the winde : the roote is great, thicke, and white, continuing long, and shooting out new branches euery yeare, and smelling somewhat like a Valerian.

2. *Nardus Montana tuberosa*. Knobbed Mountaine Valerian.

This kinde of Valerian or Spiknard, if you will so call it, hath his first leaues lying on the ground, without any diuision in them at all, being smooth, and of a dark greene colour, which so abide all the winter ; but those that spring vp after, and when it runneth vp to flower, are cut in on the edges, very like vnto the iagged leaues of the great garden Valerian, and so the elder they grow, the more cut and iagged they are : the stalke and flowers are very like the stalke with flowers of the garden Valerian, but of a darke or deepe red colour, and more store of them thrust together, by double the number almost : the seede is like the seede of the great Valerian : the root is tuberous, or knobbed in many parts, round about, aboue and below also, with some fibres shooting from them, whereby it is encreased, and smelleth very like the roote of the garden Setwall, or not altogether so strong.

3. *Valeriana*

1 *Blattaria flore albo.* Moth Mullein with a white flower. 2 *Blattaria flore purpureo.* Moth Mullein with a purple flower. 3 *Verbascum quartum Matthioli.* French Sage. 4 *Æthiopis.* Ethiopian Mullein. 5 *Valeriana rubra Dodonæi.* Red Valerian. 6 *Valeriana Græca.* Greek Valerian. 7 *Lamium Pannonicum.* Hungary dead Nettle. 8 *Cardamine flore pleno.* Double Cuckowe flower or Ladies smocks.

3. *Valeriana Graca.* Greeke Valerian.

The Greek Valerian hath many winged leaues lying vpon the ground, that is, many small leaues set on both sides of a middle ribbe, very like vnto the wilde Valerian, that groweth by the ditch sides, but much smaller and tenderer, among which rise vp one or two round brittle stalkes, two foote high or thereabouts, whereon are set at the ioynts, such like leaues as grow below, but smaller : the toppes of the stalkes are diuided into many small branches, thicke set together, full with flowers, consisting of fiue small round leaues a peece, layd open like vnto the Cinquefoile flower, with some white threds in the middle, tipt with yellow pendents : the colour of these flowers in some plants, is of a faire bleake blew colour, and in others pure white : And I doe heare of one beyond the Seas (if the report bee true, for I haue not seene such a one) which should beare red flowers : after the flowers are past, there come vp in their places small hard huskes or heads, containing small blackish seedes : the roote is composed of a number of small long blackish threds, fastened together at the head, without any sent at all of a Valerian, eyther in roote or leafe ; and why it should bee called a Valerian I see no great reason, for it agreeth with none of them, in flower or seede, and but onely with the wilde Valerian in leafe, as I said before : but as it is, we so giue it you, and for the flowers sake is receiued into our gardens, to helpe to fill vp the number of natures rarities and varieties.

The Place.

All these Valerians are strangers, but endenizond for their beauties sake in our Gardens. The Mountaine Valerian I had of the liberalitie of my louing friend Iohn Tradescante, who in his trauaile, and search of natures varieties, met with it, and imparted thereof vnto me.

The Time.

They flower in the Summer moneths, and seed quickly after.

The Names.

The first is generally called of most, *Valeriana rubra Dodonæi*, who saith also that some would haue it to be *Behen rubrum.* Some call it *Valerianthon*, others make it a kinde of *Ocimastrum*, and some *Saponaria altera*, with other names, which are to no great purpose to set downe in this place, it beeing fitter for a generall worke to discusse of names, wherein both reading, knowledge and iudgement must bee shewen, to correct errours, and set downe the truth, that one may rest thereon. The others haue their names in their titles sufficient to distinguish them.

The Vertues.

The Mountaine Valerian is of all the the rest here set downe of most vse in Physicke, the rest hauing little or none that I know, although it be much weaker then the great garden kinde, or the Indian Nardus, in whose steed anciently it was vsed, in oyles, oyntments, &c.

Chap. C.

Cardamine. Cuckow flowers, or Ladies smockes.

OF the common sorts of Cuckow flowers that grow by ditch-sides, or in moist medowes, & wet grounds, it is not my purpose here to write, but of one or two other, the most specious or faire of all the tribe, that doe best besit this garden.

1. *Cardamine*

1. *Cardamine flore pleno.* Double Cuckow flowers.

The double *Cardamine* hath a few winged leaues, weake and tender, lying on the ground, very like vnto the single medow kinde ; from among which riseth vp a round greene stalke, set here and there, with the like leaues that grow below, the top wherof hath a few branches, whereon stand diuers flowers, euery one vpon a small footestalk, consisting of many small whitish round leaues, a little dasht ouer with a shew of blush, set round together, which make a double flower : the roote creepeth vnder ground, sending forth small white fibres, and shooteth vp in diuers places.

2. *Cardamine trifolia.* Trefoile Ladies smockes.

This small plant hath diuers hard, darke round greene leaues, somewhat vneuen about the edges, alwayes three set together on a blackish small footstalke, among which rise vp small round blackish stalkes, halfe a foote high, with three small leaues at the ioynts, where they branch forth; at the toppes whereof stand many flowers, consisting of foure leaues a peece, of a whitish or blush colour very pale : after which come vp small, thicke and long pods, wherein is contained small round seede : the root is composed of many white threds, from the heads whereof runne out small strings, of a dark purple colour, whereby it encreaseth.

The Place.

The first with the double flower is found in diuers places of our owne Countrey, as neere Micham about eight miles from London ; also in Lancashire, from whence I receiued a plant, which perished, but was found by the industrie of a worthy Gentlewoman, dwelling in those parts heretofore remembred, called Mistresse Thomasin Tunstall, a great louer of these delights. The other was sent me by my especial good friend Iohn Tradescante, who brought it among other dainty plants from beyond the Seas, and imparted thereof a roote to me.

The Time.

The last most vsually floweth before the former, yet not much differing, that is, in the end of Aprill or in May.

The Names.

The first is a double kinde of that plant, that growing wilde abroade, is vsually called *Cardamine altera*, and *Sisymbrium alterum* of Dioscorides, and of some *Flos cuculi*, but not fitly ; for that name is more vsually giuen vnto the wilde featherd Campions, both single and double, as is before expressed : yet for want of a fitter name, wee may call it in English, eyther Cuckowe flower, or Ladyes smockes, which you will. The second hath beene sent vnder the name of *Sanicula trifolia*, but the most frequent name now receiued, is *Cardamine trifolia*, and in English Trefoile Ladies spockes.

The Vertues.

The double Ladies smockes are of the same qualitie with the single, and is thought to be as effectuall as Watercresses. The propertie of the other I thinke is not much knowne, although some would make it a wound herbe.

CHAP. CI.

Thlaspi Creticum. Candy Tufts.

OF the many forts of *Thlaspi* it is not the scope of this worke to relate, I will se-lect but onely two or three, which for their beautie are fit to bee inserted into this garden.

Thlaspi Creticum vmbellatum flore albo & purpureo.
Candy Tufts white and purple.

This small plant riseth seldome aboue a foote and a halfe high, hauing small, narrow, long and whitish greene leaues, notched or dented with three or foure notches on each side, from the middle to the point-wards ; from among which rise vp the stalkes, branched from the bottome almost into diuers small branches, at the toppes whereof stand many small flowers, thick thrust together in an vmbell or tuft, making them seeme to be small, round, double flowers of many leaues, when as euery flower is single, and standeth a part by it selfe, of a faire white colour in some plants, without any spot, and in others with a purplish spot in the centre or middle, as if some of the middle leaues were purple, in others againe the whole flower is purplish all ouer, which make a pretty shew in a garden : the seede is contained in many small and flat seed vessels, which stand together in an vmbell, as the flowers did, in which are contained somewhat reddish seede, like vnto some other sorts of *Thlaspi*, called Treakle Muftards : the roote is small and hard, and perisheth euery yeare hauing giuen seede.

Thlaspi Mari-num Baticum. We haue another sort, whose leaues before it sendeth forth any stalke, are a little toothed, or finely dented about the edges, and brancheth not so much out, but carryeth an vmbell of purplish flowers like vnto the former, and paler yellow seede.

The Place.

These doe grow in Spaine and Candie, not farre from the Sea side.

The Time.

These *Thlaspi* giue not their flowers vntill the end of Iune, or beginning of Iuly, and the seed is ripe soone after.

The Names.

The first is named by some, *Draba*, or *Arabis*, as Dodonæus, but *Draba* is another plant differing much from this. Wee call one fort, *Thlaspi Creti-cum*, and the other *Thlaspi Baticum marinum*, because the one came from Spaine, and the other from Candy ; we giue it in English, the name of Tufts, because it doth fit the forme of the flowers best, although ordinarily all the *Thlaspi* are Englished Wilde Muftardes.

The Vertues.

Candy, or Spanish Tufts, is not so sharpe biting in taste, as some other of the Thlaspies are, and therefore is not to be vsed in medicines, where *Thlaspi* should be in the stead thereof.

CHAP.

Chap. CII.

Clematis. Clamberers, or Creepers.

HAuing shewed you all my store of herbes bearing fine flowers, let mee now bring to your consideration the rest of those plants, be they Shrubs or Trees, that are cherished in our garden, for the beauty of their flowers chiefly, or for some other beautifull respect: and first I will begin with such as creepe on the ground, without climing, and then such as clime vp by poles, or other things, that are set or grow neere them, fit to make Bowers, and Arbours, or else are like them in forme, in name, or some other such qualitie or propertie.

1. *Clematis Daphnoides, siue Vinca peruinca simplex minor diuersorum colorum.*
Single Perwinkle of diuers colours.

The smaller Perwinkle which not onely groweth wilde in many places, but is most vsuall in our Gardens, hath diuers creeping branches, trayling or running vpon the ground, shooting out small fibres at the ioynts, as it creepeth, taking thereby hold in the ground, and rooteth in diuers places : at the ioynts of these branches stand two small darke greene shining leaues, somewhat like vnto small Baye leaues, but smaller, and at the ioynts likewise with the leaues, come forth the flowers, one at a ioynt, standing vpon a tender footestalke, being somewhat long and hollow, parted at the brims, sometimes into foure leaues, and sometimes into fiue, the most ordinary sort is of a pale or bleake blew colour, but some are pure white, and some of a darke reddish purple colour: the root is in the body of it, little bigger then a rush, bushing in the ground, and creeping with his branches farre about, taking roote in many places, whereby it quickely possesseth a great compasse ; and is therefore most vsually planted vnder hedges, or where it may haue roome to runne.

2. *Vinca peruinca flore duplici purpureo.*
Double purple Perwinkle.

The double Perwinkle is like vnto the former single kinde, in all things except in the flower, which is of that darke reddish purple colour that is in one of the single kindes ; but this hath another row of leaues within the flower, so that the two rowes of leaues causeth it to be called double, but the leaues of these are lesser then the single. I haue heard of one with a double white flower, but I haue not yet seene it.

3. *Clematis Daphnoides siue Peruinca maior.*
The greater Perwinkle.

This greater Perwinkle is somewhat like the former, but greater, yet his branches creepe not in that manner, but stand more vpright, or lesse creeping at the least : the leaues also hereof stand by couples at the ioynts, but they are broader and larger by the halfe : the flowers are larger, consisting of fiue leaues that are blew, a little deeper then the former blew : this plant is farre tenderer to keepe then the other, and therefore would stand warme, as well as in a moist shadowie place.

4. *Clematis altera siue vrens flore albo.*
Burning Clamberer, or Virgins Bower.

This Causticke or burning Climer, hath very long and climing tender branches, yet somewhat woody below, which winde about those things that stand neere it, couered with a brownish greene barke, from the ioynts whereof shoote forth many winged leaues, consisting for the most part of fiue single leaues, that is, two and two together, and one at the end, which are a little cut in or notched on the edges here and
there,

there, but euery part of them is lesser then the leaues of the next following Climer, without any clasping tendrels to winde about any thing at all : towards the vpper part of the branches, with the said leaues, come forth long stalks, wheron stand many white flowers clustering together, opening the brims into sixe or eight small leaues, sprea-ding like a starre, very sweet of smell, or rather of a strong heady sent, which after turne into flattish and blackish seede, plumed at the head, which plume or feather fly-eth away with the winde after it hath stood long, and leaueth the seede naked or bare : the roote is white and thicke, fleshie and tender, or easie to be broken, as my selfe can well testifie, in that desiring to take a sucker from the roote, I could not handle it so tenderly, but that it broke notwithstanding all my care. Master Gerard in his Herball maketh mention of one of this kinde with double white flowers, which hee saith he recouered from the seede was sent him from Argentine, that is Strasborough, whereof hee setteth forth the figure with double flowers : but I neuer saw any such with him, neither did I euer heare of any of this kinde with double flowers. Clusius indeed saith, that hee receiued from a friend some seede vnder the name of *Clematis flore albo pleno* : but he doubteth whether there bee any such : the plants that sprang with him from that seede, were like vnto the vpright kinde called *Flammula Matthioli,* or *Iouis cresta,* as he there saith : but assuredly I haue beene informed from some of my especiall friends beyond Sea, that they haue a double white *Clematis,* and haue promi-sed to send it; but whether it will be of the climing or vpright sort, I cannot tell vntill I see it : but surely I doe much doubt whether the double will giue any good seede.

5. *Clematis altera siue peregrina flore rubro.* Red Ladies Bower.

This Climer hath many limber and weake climing branches like the former, coue-red with a browne thin outer barke, and greene vnderneath : the leaues stand at the ioynts, consisting but of three leaues or parts, whereof some are notched on one side, and some on both, without any clasping tendrels also, but winding with his branches about any thing standeth next vnto it : the flowers in like manner come from the same ioynts with the leaues, but not so many together as the former vpon long footstalkes, consisting of foure leaues a peece, standing like a crosse, of a darke red colour ; the seed is flat and round, and pointed at the end, three or foure or more standing close to-gether vpon one stalk, without any doune vpon them at all, as in the former : the roots are a bundell of brownish yellow strong strings, running down deep into the ground, from a bigge head aboue.

6. *Clematis peregrina flore purpureo simplici.* Single purple Ladies Bower.

This Ladies Bower differeth in nothing from the last described, but onely in the colour of the flower, which is of a sad blewish purple colour ; so that the one is not possible to be known from the other, vntill they be in flower.

7. *Clematis peregrina flore purpureo pleno.* Double flowred purple Ladies Bower.

This double *Clematis* hath branches and leaues so neere resembling the single kinds, that there can be knowne no difference, vnlesse it be, that this groweth more goale and great, and yeeldeth both more store of branches from the ground, and more spreading aboue : the chiefest marke to distinguish it is the flower, which in this is very thicke and double, consisting of a number of smaller leaues, set close together in order in the middle, the foure outermost leaues that encompasse them, being much broader and larger then any of the inward, but all of a dull or sad blewish purple colour, the points or ends of the leaues seeming a little darker then the middle of them : this beareth no seede that euer I could see, heare of, or learne by any of credit, that haue nourfed it a great while ; and therefore the tales of false deceitfull gardiners, and others, that diliuer such for truth, to deceiue persons ignorant thereof, must not bee credulously entertained.

In

In the great booke of the Garden of the Biſhop of Eyſtot (which place is neere *clematis pere-* vnto Noremberg) in Germany, I reade of a *Clematis* of this former kinde, whoſe fi- *grina flore car-* gure is thereto alſo annexed, with double flowers of an incarnate, or pale purple ten- *neceruleo.* ding to a bluſh colour, whereof I haue not heard from any other place.

8. *Flammula Iouis erecta.* Vpright Virgins Bower.

This kinde of *Clematis* hath diuers more vpright ſtalkes then any of the foure laſt deſcribed, ſometimes foure or fiue foote high, or more; yet leaning or bending a lit-tle, ſo that it had ſome neede of ſuſtaining, couered with a browniſh barke; from whence come forth on all ſides diuers winged leaues, conſiſting of fiue or ſeuen leaues, ſet on both ſides of a middle ribbe, whereof one is at the end: the tops of the ſtalkes are diuided into many branches, bearing many white ſweet ſmelling flowers on them, like in faſhion vnto the white Virgins Bower; after which come ſuch like feather topt ſeede, which remaine and ſhew themſelues, being flat like the other, when the plumes are blowne abroad: the roote ſpreadeth in the ground from a thicke head, into many long ſtrings, and faſteneth it ſelfe ſtrongly in the earth; but all the ſtalkes dye downe euery yeare, and ſpring afreſh in the beginning of the next.

9. *Clematis cærulea Pannonica.* The Hungarian Climer.

The ſtalks of this plant ſtand vpright, & are foure ſquare, bearing at euery ioynt two leaues, which at the firſt are cloſed together, and after they are open, are ſomewhat like vnto the leaues of *Aſclepias*, or Swallow-wort: from the tops of the ſtalks, and ſome-times alſo from the ſides by the leaues commeth forth one flower, bending the head downward, conſiſting of foure leaues, ſomewhat long & narrow, ſtanding like a croſſe, and turning vp their ends a little againe, of a faire blew or skie colour, with a thicke pale yellow ſhort thrumme, made like a head in the middle: after the flower is paſt, the head turneth into ſuch a like round feather topt ball, as is to be ſeene in the Tra-uellers ioy, or *Viorna* (as it is called) that groweth plentifully in Kent, and in other places by the way ſides, and in the hedges, wherein is included ſuch like flat ſeede. Theſe ſtalkes (like as the laſt) dye downe to the ground euery yeare, and riſe againe in the Spring following, ſhooting out new branches, and therby encreaſeth in the root.

10. *Maracoc ſiue Clematis Virginiana.* The Virginia Climer.

Becauſe this braue and too much deſired plant doth in ſome things reſemble the former Climers, ſo that vnto what other family or kindred I might better conioyne it I know not; let me I pray inſert it in the end of their Chapter, with this deſcription. It riſeth out of the ground (very late in the yeare, about the beginning of May, if it be a plant hath riſen from the ſeed of our owne ſowing, and if it be an old one, ſuch as hath been brought to vs from Virginia, not till the end thereof) with a round ſtalke, not a-boue a yard and a halfe high (in any that I haue ſeene) but in hotter Countries, as ſome Authors haue ſet it downe, much higher, bearing one leafe at euery ioynt, which from the ground to the middle thereof hath no claſpers, but from thence vpwards hath at the ſame ioynt with the leafe both a ſmall twining claſper, like vnto a Vine, and a flower alſo: euery leafe is broad at the ſtalke thereof, and diuided about the middle on both ſides, making it ſomewhat reſemble a Figge leafe, ending in three points, whereof the middlemoſt is longeſt: the bud of the flower, before it doe open, is very like vnto the head or ſeede veſſell of the ordinary ſingle *Nigella*, hauing at the head or top fiue ſmall crooked hornes, which when this bud openeth, are the ends or points of fiue leaues, that are white on the inſide, and lay themſelues flat, like vnto an Anemone, and are a little hollow like a ſcoope at the end, with fiue other ſmaller leaues, and whiter then they lying betweene them, which were hid in the bud before it opened, ſo that this flower being full blowne open, conſiſteth of ten white leaues, laide in or-der round one by another: from the bottome of theſe leaues on the inſide, riſe diuers twined threads, which ſpread and lay themſelues all ouer theſe white leaues, reaching beyond the points of them a little, and are of a reddiſh peach colour: towards the bot-
tomes

tomes likewife of thefe white leaues there are two red circles, about the breadth of
an Oten ftrawe, one diftant from another (and in fome flowers there is but one circle
feen) which adde a great grace vnto the flower, for the white leaues fhew their colour
through the peach coloured threads, and thefe red circles or rings vpon them being

alfo perfpicuous, make a tripartite fhew
of colours moft delightfull : the middle
part of this flower is hollow, and yellowifh, in the bottome whereof rifeth vp an
vmbone, or round ftile, fomewhat bigge,
of a whitifh greene colour, fpotted with
reddifh fpots like the ftalkes of Dragons,
with fiue round threads or chiues, fpotted in the like manner, and tipt at the
ends with yellow pendents, ftanding a-
bout the middle part of the faid vmbone, and from thence rifing higher, en-
deth in three long crooked hornes moft
vfually (but fometimes in foure, as hath
beene obferued in Rome by Dr. Aldine,
that fet forth fome principall things of
Cardinall Farnefius his Garden) fpotted
like the reft, hauing three round greene
buttons at their ends : thefe flowers are
of a comfortable fweete fent, very acceptable, which perifh without yeelding
fruit with vs, becaufe it flowreth fo late :
but in the naturall place, and in hot
Countries, it beareth a fmall round whitifh fruit, with a crowne at the toppe
thereof, wherein is contained (while it is
frefh, and before it be ouer dried) a fweet

The Iefuites Figure of the Maracoc.

GRANADILLVS FRVTEX INDICVS
CHRISTI PASSIONIS IMAGO.

liquor, but when it is dry, the feede within it, which is fmall, flat, fomewhat rough
and blacke, will make a ratling noife : the rootes are compofed of a number of exceeding long and round yellowifh browne ftrings, fpreading farre abroad vnder the
ground (I haue feene fome rootes that haue beene brought ouer, that were as long as
any rootes of *Sarfa parilla*, and a great deale bigger, which to be handfomely laid into
the ground, were faine to be coyled like a cable) and fhooting vp in feuerall places a
good diftance one from another, whereby it may be well encreafed.

The Place.

The firft blew Perwinkle groweth in many Woods and Orchards, by
the hedge fides in England, and fo doth the white here and there, but the
other fingle and double purple are in our Gardens onely. The great Perwinkle groweth in Prouence of France, in Spaine, and Italy, and other
hot Countries, where alfo growe all the twining Clamberers, as well fingle
as double : but both the vpright ones doe growe in Hungary and thereabouts. The furpaffing delight of all flowers came from Virginia. Wee
preferue them all in our Gardens.

The Time.

The Perwinkles doe flower in March and Aprill. The Climers not vntill the end of Iune, or in Iuly, and fometimes in Auguft. The Virginian
fomewhat later in Auguft ; yet fometimes I haue knowne the flower to fhew
it felfe in Iuly.

The Names.

The firft is out of queftion the firft *Clematis* of Diofcorides, and called of
many

1 *Thlaspi Creticum.* Candy tufts. 2 *Vinca peruinca flore simplici.* Single Perwinkle. 3 *Vinca peruinca flore duplici.* Double Perwinkle.
4 *Flammula Matthioli.* Vpright Virgins Bower. 5 *Clematis peregrina flore simplici.* The single Ladies Bower. 6 *Clematis peregrina flore*
pleno purpureo. Double flowred Ladies Bower. 7 *Maracoc siue Clematis Virginiana.* The Virginian Climer.

many *Clematis Daphnoides* (but not that plant that is simply called *Daphnoides*, for that is *Laureola*) and is vsually called *Vinca pervinca*: but it is not *Chamædaphne*, for that is another plant, as shall be shewed in his place; some call it *Centunculus*: In English wee call it Perwinkle. The other is *Clematis altera* of Dioscorides, and is called also *Clematis peregrina*, whose distinctions are set downe in their titles: In English, Ladies Bower, or Virgins Bower, because they are fit to growe by Arbours, to couer them. The first vpright Clamberer is called, and that rightly of some, *Clematis erecta*, or *surrecta*. Of others, *Flammula frutex*, and *Flammula Iouis*, or *surrecta*: In English, Vpright Virgins Bower. The next is called by Clusius, *Clematis Pannonica cærulea*, who thought it to be *Climeni species*, by the relation of others, at the first, but after entituled it, *Clematis*: In English, the Hungarian Climer. The last may be called in Latine, *Clematis Virginiana*: In English, The Virgin or Virginian Climer; of the Virginians, *Maracoc*: of the Spaniards in the West Indies *Granadillo*, because the fruit (as is before said) is in some fashion like a small Pomegranate on the outside; yet the seede within is flattish, round, and blackish. Some superstitious Iesu-ite would faine make men beleeue, that in the flower of this plant are to be seene all the markes of our Sauiours Passion; and therefore call it *Flos Passionis*: and to that end haue caused figures to be drawne, and printed, with all the parts proportioned out, as thornes, nailes, speare, whippe, pillar, &c. in it, and all as true as the Sea burnes, which you may well perceiue by the true figure, taken to the life of the plant, compared with the figures set forth by the Iesuites, which I haue placed here likewise for euery one to see: but these bee their aduantagious lies (which with them are tolerable, or rather pious and meritorious) wherewith they vse to instruct their people; but I dare say, God neuer willed his Priests to instruct his people with lyes: for they come from the Diuell, the author of them. But you may say I am beside my Text, and I am in doubt you will thinke, I am in this besides my selfe, and so nothing to be beleeued herein that I say. For, for the most part, it is an inherent errour in all of that side, to beleeue nothing, be it neuer so true, that any of our side shall affirme, that contrarieth the assertions of any of their Fathers, as they call them: but I must referre them to God, and hee knoweth the truth, and will reforme or deforme them in his time. In regard whereof I could not but speake (the occasion being thus offered) against such an erroneous opinion (which euen D^r. Aldine at Rome, before remembred, disproued, and contraried both the said figures and name) and seek to disproue it, as doth (I say not almost, but I am affraid altogether) leade many to adore the very picture of such things, as are but the fictions of superstitious brains: for the flower it selfe is farre differing from their figure, as both Aldine in the aforesaid booke, and Robinus at Paris in his *Theatrum Floræ*, doe set forth; the flowers and leaues being drawne to the life, and there exhibited, which I hope may satisfie all men, that will not be perpetually obstinate and contentious.

The Vertues.

Costæus saith hee hath often seene, that the leaues of Perwinkle held in the mouth, hath stayed the bleeding at the nose. The French doe vse it to stay the menstruall fluxes. The other are causticke plants, that is, fiery hot, and blistering the skinne; and therefore (as Dioscorides saith) is profitable to take away the scurfe, leprye, or such like deformities of the skin. What property that of Virginia hath, is not knowne to any with vs I thinke, more then that the liquor in the greene fruit is pleasant in taste; but assuredly it cannot be without some speciall properties, if they were knowne.

CHAP.

Chap. CIII.

Chamælæa. Dwarfe Spurge Oliue, or Dwarfe Baye.

I Haue three forts of *Chamælæa* to bring to your confideration, euery one differing notably from other; two of them of great beauty in their flowers, as well as in the whole plant: the third abiding with greene leaues, although it haue no beauty in the flower, yet worthy of the place it holds. And vnto thefe I muft adioyne another plant, as comming nearest vnto them in the brauery of the flowers.

1. *Chamælæa Germanica fiue Mezereon floribus dilutioris coloris & faturatioris.* Dwarfe Baye, or flowring Spurge Oliue.

We haue two forts of this Spurge Oliue or Dwafe Baye, differing onely in the colour of the flowers. They both rife vp with a thicke wooddy ftemme, fiue or fix foot high fometimes, or more, and of the thickneffe (if they be very old) of a mans wreft at the ground, fpreading into many flexible long branches, couered with a tough grayifh barke, befet with fmall long leaues, fomewhat like vnto Priuet leaues, but fmaller and paler, and in a manner round pointed: the flowers are fmall, confifting of foure leaues, many growing together fometimes, and breaking out of the branches by themfelues: in the one fort of a pale red at the firft blowing, and more white afterwards; the other of a deeper red in the bloffome, and continuing of a deeper red colour all the time of the flowring, both of them very fweete in fmell: after the flowers are paft, come the berries, which are greene at the firft, and very red afterwards, turning blackifh red, if they ftand too long vpon the branches: the rootes fpread into many tough long branches, couered with a yellowifh barke.

2. *Chamælæa Alpina.* Mountaine Spurge Oliue.

This Mountaine Laurell rifeth vp with a fmall wooddy ftemme, three or foure foot high, or more, branching forth towards the vpper parts into many flender and tough branches, couered with a rough hoary greene barke, befet at the ends thereof with flatter, fuller, and fmaller round pointed leaues then the former, of a grayifh greene colour on the vpperfide, and hoary vnderneath, which abide on the branches in Winter, and fall not away as the former: the flowers are many fet together at the ends of the branches, greater then the former, and confifting of foure leaues a peece, of a light blufh colour, ftanding in fmall grayifh huskes, of little or no fent at all: the fruit followeth, which are fmall long graines or berries, of an excellent red colour, which afterwards turne blacke: the roote is long, and fpreadeth about vnder the vpper part of the earth.

3. *Chamælæa tricoccos.* Widowe Wayle.

This three berried Spurge Oliue hath no great ftemme at all, but the whole plant fpreadeth from the ground into many flexible tough greene branches, whereon are fet diuers narrow, long, darke greene leaues all along the branches, which abide greene all the Winter: the flowers are very fmall, fcarce to be feene, and come forth between the leaues and the ftalke, of a pale yellow colour, made of three leaues; after which come fmall blackifh berries, three vfually fet together: the roote fpreadeth it felfe in the ground not very farre, being hard and wooddy, and often dyeth, if it bee not well defended from the extremity of our fharpe Winters.

4. *Cneorum Matthioli.* Small Rocke Rofes.

I was long in doubt in what place I fhould difpofe of this plant, whether among the Campions, as Bauhinus, or among thefe, as Clufius doth; but left my Gorden fhould want it wholly, let it take vp roome for this time here. This gallant plant hath diuers

L l   long.

long, weake, ſlender, but yet tough branches lying vpon the ground, diuided vſually into other ſmaller branches, whereon growe many, ſmall, long, and ſomewhat thicke leaues, ſomewhat like vnto the leaues of the former *Mezereon*, ſet without any order to the very tops, from whence doe come forth a tuft of many ſmall flowers together, made or conſiſting of foure leaues a peece, of a bright red or carnation colour, and very ſweete withall, which turne into ſmall round whitiſh berries, wherein is contained ſmall round ſeede, couered with a grayiſh coate or skinne : the roote is long and yellowiſh, ſpreading diuers wayes vnder the ground, and abideth many yeares ſhooting forth new branches.

Flore albo.　　It hath beene obſerued in ſome of theſe plants, to bring forth white flowers, not differing in any thing elſe.

The Place.

The firſt ſorts growe plentifully in many places of Germany. The ſecond in the mountaines by Sauoye. The third in Prouence and Spaine. The laſt in diuers parts of Germany, Bohemia, and Auſtria, and about Franckford.

The Time.

The two firſt ſorts are moſt vſually in flower about Chriſtmas, or in Ianuary, if the weather be not violent, and ſometimes not vntill February. The ſecond flowreth not vntill Aprill. The third in May. The berries of them ripen ſome in Iune and Iuly ; ſome in Auguſt and September, as their flowring is earlier or later. The laſt flowreth as well in the Spring as in Autumne, ſo apt and plentifull it is in bearing, and the ſeede at both times doth ripen ſoone after.

The Names.

The firſt is called of ſome *Chamælæa*, with this addition *Germanica*, that it may differ from the third, which is the true *Chamælæa* of Dioſcorides, as all the beſt Authors doe agree, and is alſo called *Piper montanum* of the Italians. It is generally called *Mezereon*, and is indeede the true *Mezereon* of the Arabians, and ſo vſed in our Apothecaries ſhops, whereſoeuer the Arabians *Mezereon* is appointed, although the Arabians are ſo intricate and vncertaine in the deſcriptions of their plants, confounding *Chamælæa* and *Thymelæa* together. Matthiolus maketh it to be *Daphnoides* of Dioſcorides ; but in my opinion he is therein miſtaken : for all our beſt moderne Writers doe account our *Laureola*, which hath blacke berries, to bee the true *Daphnoides* : the errour of his Countrey might peraduenture drawe him thereunto ; but if hee had better conſidered the text of Dioſcorides, that giueth black berries to *Daphnoides*, and red to *Chamædaphne*, he would not ſo haue written ; and truly, I ſhould thinke (as Lobel doth) with better reaſon, that this *Chamælæa* were Dioſcorides *Chamædaphne*, then hee to ſay it were *Daphnoides* : for the deſcription of *Chamædaphne*, may in all parts be very fitly applyed to this *Chamælæa* : and euen theſe words, *Semen annexum folÿs*, wherein may be the greateſt doubt in the deſcription, may not vnfitly bee conſtrued, that as is ſeene in the plant, the berries growe at the foote of the leaues, about the branches : the faculties indeede that Dioſcorides giueth to *Chamædaphne*, are (if any repugnancie be) the greateſt let or hinderance, that this *Chamælæa* ſhould not be it : but I leaue the diſcuſſing of theſe and others of the like nature, to our learned Phyſitians ; for I deale not ſo much with vertues as with deſcriptions. The ſecond is called of Lobel *Chamælæa Alpina incana*, of Cluſius *Chamælæa ſecunda*, and ſaith hee had it out of Italy. Wee may call it in Engliſh, Mountaine Spurge Oliue, as it is in the deſcription, or Mountaine Laurell, which you will. The laſt hath the name of *Cneorum*, firſt giuen it by Matthiolus, which ſince is continued by all others. Bauhinus (as I ſaid) referreth it to the Mountaine Campions, but Cluſius

(as

1 *Chamælea Germanica seu Mezereon.* Mezereon or Dwarfe Bay. 2 *Chamælea Alpina.* Mountain Spurge Oliue. 3 *Cneorum Matthioli.* Small Rocke Roses. 4 *Laurus Tinus siue siluestris.* The wild Bay tree. 5 *Oleander siue Laurus Rosea.* The Rose Bay tree. 6 *Laurocerasus.* The Bay Cherrie tree.

(as I doe)to the kindes of *Chamælæa* or *Thymelæa*. For want of an English name I haue (as you see,and that is according to the name the Germane women, as Clusius saith, doe call it) entituled it the Small Rocke Rose; which may abide vntill a fitter may be conferred vpon it.

The Vertues.

All these plants except the last, as well leaues as berries, are violent purgers, and therefore great caution is to bee had in the vse of them. The last hath not beene applyed for any disease that I know.

Chap. CIII.

Laurus. The Bay Tree.

MY meaning is not to make any description of our ordinary Bayes in this place (for as all may very well know,they may be for an Orchard or Courtyard,and not for this Garden)but of two or three other kindes,whose beautifull aspect haue caused them to be worthy of a place therein : the one is called *Laurus Tinus*,The wilde Baye : the other *Laurus Rosea* or *Oleander*, The Rose Bay : and a third is *Laurocerasus*, The Cherry Bay ; which may haue not onely some respect for his long bush of sweet smelling flowers, but especially for the comely statelinesse of his gallant euer fresh greene leaues ; and the rather, because with vs in most places, it doth but *frutescere*, vse to bee Shrub high, not *arborescere*, Tree high, which is the more fit for this Garden.

1. *Laurus Tinus siue siluestris*. The wilde Bay tree.

This wilde Baye groweth seldome to bee a tree of any height, but abideth for the most part low, shooting forth diuers slender branches, whereon at euery ioynt stand two leaues, long, smooth, and of a darke greene colour, somewhat like vnto the leaues of the Female Cornell tree, or between that and Baye leaues : at the toppes of the branches stand many small white sweete smelling flowers, thrusting together, as it were in an vmbell or tuft, consisting of fiue leaues a peece, the edges whereof haue a shew of a wash purple,or light blush in them, which for the most part fall away without bearing any perfect ripe fruit in our Countrey : Yet sometimes it hath small black berries,as if they were good, but are not. In his naturall place it beareth small,round, hard and pointed berries, of a shining blacke colour, for such haue come often to my hands (yet Clusius writeth they are blew) ; but I could neuer see any spring that I put into the ground. This that I here describe, seemeth to me to be neither of both those that Clusius saw growing in Spain and Potugall,but that other,that(as he saith)sprang in the low Countreyes of Italian seede.

2. *Laurus Rosea siue Oleander*. The Rose Bay.

Of the Rose Bay there are two sorts, one bearing crimson coloured flowers, which is more frequent, and the other white, which is more rare. They are so like in all other things, that they neede but one description for both. The stemme or trunke is many times with vs as bigge at the bottome as a good mans thumbe,but growing vp smaller, it diuideth it selfe into branches, three for the most part comming from one ioynt or place, and those branches againe doe likewise diuide themselues into three other,and so by degrees from three to three, as long as it groweth : the lowest of these are bare of leaues, hauing shed or lost them by the cold of winters, keeping onely leaues on the vppermost branches, which are long, and somewhat narrow, like in forme vnto Peach leaues, but thicker, harder, and of a darke greene colour on the vpperside, and
yellowish

yellowifh greene vnderneath : at the tops of the young branches come forth the flowers, which in the one fort before they are open, are of an excellent bright crimfon colour, and being blowen, confift of foure long and narrow leaues, round pointed, fomewhat twining themfelues, of a paler red colour, almoft tending to blufh, and in the other are white, the greene leaues alfo being of a little frefher colour : after the flowers are paft, in the hot countries, but neuer in ours, there come vp long bending or crooked flat pods, whofe outward fhell is hard, almoft woody, and of a browne colour, wherein is contained fmall flat brownifh feede, wrapped in a great deale of a brownifh yellow doune, as fine almoft as filke, fomewhat like vnto the huskes of *Afclepias*, or *Periploca*, but larger, flatter and harder ; as my felfe can teftifie, who had fome of the pods of this Rofe bay, brought mee out of Spaine, by Mafter Doctor Iohn More, the feedes whereof I fowed, and had diuers plants that I raifed vp vnto a reafonable height, but they require, as well old as young, to bee defended from the colde of our winters.

3. *Laurocerafus.* The Bay Cherry.

This beautifull Bay in his naturall place of growing, groweth to bee a tree of a reafonable bigneffe and height, and oftentimes with vs alfo if it bee pruined from the lower branches ; but more vfually in thefe colder Countries, it groweth as a fhrub or hedge bufh, fhooting forth many branches, whereof the greater and lower are couered with a darke grayifh greene barke, but the young ones are very greene, whereon are fet many goodly, faire, large, thicke and long leaues, a little dented about the edges, of a more excellent frefh fhining greene colour, and farre larger then any Bay leafe, and compared by many to the leaues of the *Pomeritron* tree (which becaufe wee haue none in our Countrey, cannot be fo well known) both for colour and largeneffe, which yeeld a moft gracefull afpect : it beareth long ftalkes of whitifh flowers, at the ioynts of the leaues both along the branches and towards the ends of them alfo, like vnto the Birds Cherry or *Padus Theophrafti,* which the French men call *Putier & Cerifier blanc,* but larger and greater, confifting of fiue leaues with many threds in the middle: after which commeth the fruite or berries, as large or great as Flanders Cherries, many growing together one by another on a long ftalke, as the flowers did, which are very blacke and fhining on the outfide, with a little point at the end, and reafonable fweete in tafte, wherein is contained a hard round ftone, very like vnto a Cherry ftone, as I haue obferued as well by thofe I receiued out of Italie, as by them I had of Mafter Iames Cole a Merchant of London lately deceafed, which grew at his houfe in Highgate, where there is a faire tree which hee defended from the bitterneffe of the weather in winter by cafting a blanket ouer the toppe thereof euery yeare, thereby the better to preferue it.

The Place.

The firft is not certainly knowne from whence it came, and is communicated by the fuckers it yeeldeth. The fecond groweth in Spaine, Italie, Grece, and many other places : that with white flowers is recorded by Bellonius, to grow in Candy. The laft, as Matthiolus, and after him Clufius report, came firft from Conftantinople : I had a plant hereof by the friendly gift of Mafter Iames Cole, the Merchant before remembred, a great louer of all rarities, who had it growing with him at his countrey houfe in Highgate aforefaid, where it hath flowred diuers times, and borne ripe fruit alfo.

The Time.

The firft flowreth many times in the end of the yeare before Chriftmas, and often alfo in Ianuary, but the moft kindly time is in March and Aprill, when the flowers are fweeteft. The fecond flowreth not vntill Iuly. The laft in May, and the fruit is ripe in Auguft and September.

The

The Names.

The firſt is called *Laurus ſilueſtris*, and *Laurus Tinus* : in Engliſh Wilde Bay, or Sweete flowring Bay. The ſecond is called *Laurus Roſea, Oleander, Nerium,* and *Rhododendros* : in Engliſh The Roſe Bay, and Oleander. The laſt was ſent by the name of *Trebezon Curmaſi,* that is to ſay, *Dactylus Trapezuntina,* but not hauing any affinitie with any kinde of Date, Bellonius as I thinke firſt named it *Laurocerasus,* and *Ceraſus Trapezuntina.* Dalechampius thinketh it to bee *Lotus Aphricana,* but Cluſius refuteth it. Thoſe ſtones or kernels that were ſent me out of Italie, came by the name of *Laurus Regia,* The Kings Bay. Wee may moſt properly call it according to the Latine name in the title, The Cherry bay, or Bay Cherry, becauſe his leaues are like vnto Bay-leaues, and both flowers and fruit like vnto the Birdes Cherry or Cluſter Cherry, for the manner of the growing ; and therfore I might more fitly I confeſſe haue placed it in my Orchard among the ſorts of Cherries : but the beautifulneſſe of the plant cauſed mee rather to inſert it here.

The Vertues.

The wilde Bay hath no propertie allotted vnto it in Phyſicke, for that it is not to be endured, the berries being chewed declare it to be ſo violent hot and choking. The Roſe Bay is ſaid by Dioſcorides, to be death to all foure footed beaſts, but contrariwiſe to man it is a remedie againſt the poiſon of Serpents, but eſpecially if Rue bee added vnto it. The Cherry Bay is not knowne with vs to what phyſicke vſe it may be applyed.

CHAP. CIIII.

Ceraſus flore multiplici. The Roſe or double bloſſomd Cherry.
Malus flore multiplici. The double bloſſomd Apple tree. And
Malus Perſica flore multiplici. The double bloſſomd Peach tree.

THe beautifull ſhew of theſe three ſorts of flowers, hath made me to inſert them into this garden, in that for their worthineſſe I am vnwilling to bee without them, although the reſt of their kindes I haue tranſferred into the Orchard, where among other fruit trees, they ſhall be remembred : for all theſe here ſet downe, ſeldome or neuer beare any fruite, and therefore more fit for a Garden of flowers, then an Orchard of fruite.

Ceraſus flore pleno vel multiplici.
The Roſe Cherry, or double bloſſomd Cherry.

The double bloſſomed Cherry tree is of two ſorts for the flower, but not differing in any other part, from the ordinary Engliſh or Flanders Cherry tree, growing in the very like manner : the difference conſiſteth in this, that the one of theſe two ſorts hath white flowers leſſe double, that is, of two rowes or more of leaues, and the other more double, or with more rowes of leaues, and beſides I haue obſerued in this greater double bloſſomd Cherry, that ſome yeares moſt of the flowers haue had another ſmaller and double flower, riſing vp out of the middle of the other, like as is to bee ſeene in the double Engliſh Crow-foote, and double redde *Ranunculus* or Crowfoote, before deſcribed : this I ſay doth not happen euery yeare, but ſometimes. Sometimes alſo theſe trees will giue a few berries, here and there ſcattered, and that with leſſe double flowers more often, which are like vnto our Engliſh Cherries both for taſte and bigneſſe. Theſe be very fit to be ſet by Arbours.

Malus

1 *Cerasus flore pleno.* The double blossomd Cherry tree. 2 *Malus flore multiplici* The double blossomd Apple tree. 3 *Malus Perfica flore pleno.* The double blossomd Peach tree. 4 *Periclymenum perfoliatum.* Double Honisuckle. 5 *Periclymenum rectum.* Vpright Honisuckle.

Malus flore multiplici. The double bloſſomd Apple tree.

This double bloſſomd Apple tree is altogether like vnto our ordinary Pippin tree in body, branch and leafe, the only difference is in the flower, which is altogether whitiſh, ſauing that the inner leaues towards the middle are more reddiſh, but as double and thicke as our double Damaske Roſes, which fall away without bearing fruit.

Malus Perſica flore multiplici. The double bloſſomd Peach tree.

This Peach tree for the manner of growing, is ſo like vnto an ordinary Peach tree, that vntill you ſee it in bloſſome you can perceiue no difference : the flower is of the ſame colour with the bloſſomes of the Peach, but conſiſting of three or foure, or more rowes of leaues, which fall often away likewiſe without bearing any fruite ; but after it hath abiden ſome yeares in a place doth forme into fruite, eſpecially being planted againſt a wall.

The Place.

Both the Cherry trees are frequent in many places of England, nourſed for their pleaſant flowers. The Apple is as yet a ſtranger. And the Peach hath not been ſeen or knowne, long before the writing hereof.

The Time.

They all flower in April & May, which are the times of their other kinds.

The Names.

Their names are alſo ſufficiently expreſſed to know them by.

The Vertues.

Cherries, Peaches and Apples, are recorded in our Orchard, and there you ſhall finde the properties of their fruit : for in that theſe beare none or very few, their bloſſomes are of moſt vſe to grace and decke the perſons of thoſe that will weare or beare them.

Chap. CV.

Periclymenum. Honyſuckles.

THe Honiſuckle that groweth wilde in euery hedge, although it be very ſweete, yet doe I not bring into my garden, but let it reſt in his owne place, to ſerue their ſenſes that trauell by it, or haue no garden. I haue three other that furniſh my Garden, one that is called double, whoſe branches ſpreade far, and being very fit for an arbour will ſoone couer it : the other two ſtand vpright, and ſpreade not any way far, yet their flowers declaring them to be Honiſuckles, but of leſſe delight, I conſort them with the other.

Periclymenum perfoliatum ſiue Italicum. The double Honiſuckle.

The truncke or body of the double Honiſuckle, is oftentimes of the bigneſſe of a good ſtaffe, running out into many long ſpreading branches, couered with a whitiſh barke, which had neede of ſome thing to ſuſtaine them, or elſe they will fall down to the ground (and therefore it is vſually planted at an arbour, that it may run thereon, or againſt a houſe wall,and faſtened thereto in diuers places with nailes)from whence ſpring forth at ſeuerall diſtances, and at the ioynts, two leaues, being like in forme vnto the wilde Honiſuckles, and round pointed for the moſt part; theſe branches diuiding themſelues diuers wayes, haue at the toppes of them many flowers,ſet at certaine diſtances one aboue another, with two greene leaues at euery place; where the flowers doe ſtand, ioyned ſo cloſe at the bottome, and ſo round and hollow in the middle,that it ſeemeth like a hollow cuppe or ſawcer of flowers : the flowers ſtand round about the middle of theſe cuppes or ſawcers, being long, hollow, and of a whitiſh yellow colour, with open mouthes daſht ouer with a light ſhew of purple, and ſome threds within them, very ſweet in ſmell,like both in forme and colour vnto the common Honiſuckles, but that theſe cuppes with the flowers in them are two or three ſtanding one aboue another(which make a far better ſhew then the common, which come forth all at the heade of the branches, without any greene leaues or cuppes vnder them) and therefore theſe were called double Honiſuckles.

Periclymenum rectum fructu rubro. Red Honiſuckles.

This vpright Woodbinde hath a ſtraight woody ſtemme, diuided into ſeuerall branches, about three or foure foote high, couered with a very thinne whitiſh barke, whereon ſtand two leaues together at the ioynts, being leſſer then the former, ſmooth and pleine, and a little pointed : the flowers come forth vpon ſlender long footſtalks at the ioynts where the leaues ſtand, alwayes two ſet together, and neuer more, but ſeldome one alone, which are much ſmaller then the former, but of the ſame faſhion, with a little button at the foote of the flower; the buds of the flowers before they are open are very reddiſh, but being open are not ſo red,but tending to a kinde of yellowiſh bluſh colour : after which come in their places two ſmall red berries, the one withered for the moſt part, or at leaſt ſmaller then the other, but (as Cluſius ſaith) in their naturall places they are both full and of one bigneſſe.

Periclymenum rectum fructu cæruleo. Blew berried Honiſuckles.

This other vpright Woodbinde groweth vp as high as the former, or rather ſomewhat higher, couered with a blackiſh rugged barke, chapping in diuers places, the younger branches whereof are ſomewhat reddiſh, and couered with an hoary doune : the leaues ſtand two together at the ioints,ſomewhat larger then the former, and more whitiſh vnderneath : the flowers are likewiſe two ſtanding together, at the end of a ſlender footeſtalke, of a pale yellowiſh colour when they are blowne, but more reddiſh in the bud : the berries ſtand two together as the former, of a darke blewiſh colour when they are fully ripe, and full of a red liquour or iuice, of a pleaſant taſte, which doth not only dye the hands of them that gather them, but ſerueth for a dying colour to the inhabitants where they grow plentifully, wherein are contained many flat ſeede : The roote is woody as the former is.

The Place.

The firw groweth in Italie, Spaine,and Prouence of France, but not in the colder countreyes, vnleſſe it be there planted, as is moſt frequent in our countrey. The others grow in Auſtria, and Stiria, as Cluſius ſaith, and are entertained into their gardens onely that are curious.

The Time.

The firſt flowreth vſually in Aprill, the reſt in May.

The Names.

The firſt is called *Periclymenum, Caprifolium perfoliatum,* and *Italicum,* as a difference from the common kinde : In Engliſh Double Woodbinde,

or

or double Honisuckles. The others, as they are rare, and little knowne, so are their names also : yet according to their Latine, I haue giuen them English names.

The Vertues.

The double Honisuckle is as effectuall in all things, as the single wilde kinde, and besides, is an especiall good wound herbe for the head or other parts. I haue not knowne the vpright kindes vsed in Physicke.

Chap. CVI.

Iasminum siue Gelseminum. Iasmine or Gesmine.

WE haue but one sort of true Iasmine ordinarily in our Gardens through-out the whole Land ; but there is another greater sort, which is farre more tender, brought out of Spaine, and will hardly endure any long time with vs, vnlesse it be very carefully preserued. Wee haue a third kinde called a yellow Iasmine, but differeth much from their tribe in many notable points : but be-cause the flowers haue some likenesse with the flowers of the true Iasmine, it hath been vsually called a Iasmine ; and therefore I am content for this Garden to conioyne them in one Chapter.

1. *Iasminum album.* The white Iasmine.

The white Iasmine hath many twiggy flexible greene branches, comming forth of the sundry bigger boughes or stems, that rise from the roote, which are couered with a grayish darke coloured barke, hauing a white pith within it like the Elder, but not so much : the winged leaues stand alwaies two together at the ioynts, being made of ma-nie small and pointed leaues, set on each side of a middle ribbe, six most vsually on both sides, with one at the end, which is larger, more pointed then any of the rest, and of a darke greene colour : at the toppes of the young branches stand diuers flow-ers together, as it were in an vmbell or tuft, each whereof standeth on a long greene stalke, comming out of a small huske, being small, long, and hollow belowe, ope-ning into fiue white small, pointed leaues, of a very strong sweete smell, which fall away without bearing any fruit at all, that euer I could learne in our Country ; but in the hot Countries where it is naturall, it is said to beare flat fruit, like Lupines : the rootes spread farre and deepe, and are long and hard to growe, vntill they haue taken strong hold in the ground.

2. *Iasminum Catalonicum.* The Spanish Iasmine.

This Catalonia Iasmine groweth lower then the former, neuer rising halfe so high, and hath slender long greene branches, rising from the toppe of the wooddy stemme, with such like leaues set on them as the former, but somewhat shorter and larger : the flowers also are like vnto the former, and stand in the same manner at the end of the branches, but are much larger, being of a blush colour before they are blowne, and white with blush edges when they are open, exceeding sweete of smell, more strong then the former.

3. *Iasminum luteum, siue Trifolium fruticans alijs Polemonium.* The yellow Iasmine.

This that is called the yellow Iasmine, hath many long slender twiggy branches ri-sing from the roote, greene at the first, and couered with a darke grayish barke after-wards, whereon are set at certaine distances, three small darke greene leaues together, the end leafe being alwaies the biggest : at the ioynts where the leaues come forth,

stand

stand long stalkes, bearing long hollow flowers, ending in fiue, and some in six leaues, very like vnto the flowers of the first Iasmine, but yellow, whereupon it is vsually called the Yellow Iasmine : after the flowers are past, there come in their places round blacke shining berries, of the bignesse of a great Pease, or bigger, full of a purplish iuyce, which will dye ones fingers that bruise them but a little : the roote is tough, and white, creeping farre about vnder the ground, shooting forth plentifully, whereby it greatly encreaseth.

The Place.

The first is verily thought to haue been first brought to Spaine out of Syria, or thereabouts, and from Spaine to vs, and is to be seene very often, and in many of our Country Gardens. The second hath his breeding in Spaine also, but whether it be his originall place we know not, and is scarce yet made well acquainted with our English ayre. The third groweth plentifully about Mompelier, and will well abide in our London Gardens, and any where else.

The Time.

The first flowreth not vntill the end of Iuly. The second somewhat earlier. The third in Iuly also.

The Names.

The first is generally called *Iasminum album*, and *Gelseminum album* : In English, The white Iasmine. The second hath his name in his title, as much as may be said of it. The third hath been taken of some to be a *Cytisus*, others iudge it to be *Polemonium*, but the truest name is *Trifolium fruticans*, although many call it *Iasminum luteum*: In English most vsually, The yellow Iasmine, for the reasons aforesaid ; or else after the Latine name, Shrubbie Trefoile, or Make-bate.

The Vertues.

The white Iasmines haue beene in all times accepted into outward medicines, eyther for the pleasure of the sweete sent, or profit of the warming properties. And is in these dayes onely vsed as an ornament in Gardens, or for sent of the flowers in the house, &c. The yellow Iasmine, although some haue adiudged it to be the *Polemonium* of Dioscorides, yet it is not vsed to those purposes by any that I know.

Chap. CVII.

Syringa. The Pipe tree.

Vnder the name of *Syringa*, is contained two speciall kinds of Shrubs or Trees, differing one from another ; namely, the *Lilac* of Matthiolus, which is called *Syringa cærulea*, and is of two or three sorts : And the *Syringa alba*, which also is of two sorts, as shall bee declared.

1. *Lilac siue Syringa cærulea*. The blew Pipe tree.

The blew Pipe tree riseth sometimes to be a great tree, as high and bigge in the bodie as a reasonable Apple tree (as I haue in some places seene and obserued) but most vsually groweth lower, with many twigs or branches rising from the roote, hauing as much pith in the middle of them as the Elder hath, couered with a grayish greene
barke,

barke, but darker in the elder branches, with ioynts set at a good distance one from another, and two leaues at euery ioynt, which are large, broad, and pointed at the ends, many of them turning or folding both the sides inward, and standing on long foote stalkes : at the toppes of the branches come forth many flowers, growing spike-fashion, that is, a long branch of flowers vpon a stalke, each of these flowers are small, long, and hollow belowe, ending aboue in a pale blewish flower, consisting of foure small leaues, of a pretty small sent : after the flowers are past, there come sometimes (but it is not often in our Country, vnlesse the tree haue stood long, and is grown great, the suckers being continually taken away, that it may growe the better) long and flat cods, consisting as it were of two sides, a thin skinne being in the midst, wherein are contained two long flattish red seede : the rootes are strong, and growe deepe in the ground.

2. *Syringa flore lacteo siue argenteo.*
The siluer coloured Pipe tree.

This Pipe tree differeth not from the former blew Pipe tree, either in stemme or branches, either in leaues or flowers, or manner of growing, but onely in the colour of the flower, which in this is of a milke, or siluer colour, which is a kinde of white, wherein there is a thinne wash, or light shew of blew shed therein, comming somewhat neare vnto an ash-colour.

3. *Lilac lacimatis folijs.* The blew Pipe tree with cut leaues.

This Pipe tree should not differ from the first in any other thing then in the leaues, which are said to be cut in on the edges into seuerall parts, as the relation is giuen *à viris fide dignis* ; for as yet I neuer saw any such; but I here am bold to set it downe, to induce and prouoke some louer of plants to obtaine it for his pleasure, and others also.

4. *Syringa flore albo simplici.* The single white Pipe tree.

The single white Pipe tree or bush, neuer commeth to that height of the former, but abideth alwaies like a hedge tree or bush, full of shootes or suckers from the roote, much more then the former : the young shootes hereof are reddish on the outside, and afterward reddish at the ioynts, and grayish all the rest ouer : the young as well as the old branches, haue some pith in the middle of them, like as the Elder hath : the leaues stand two at a ioynt, somewhat like the former, but more rugged or crumpled, as also a little pointed, and dented about the edges : the flowers growe at the toppes of the branches, diuers standing together, consisting of foure white leaues, like vnto small Muske Roses, and of the same creame colour, as I may call it, with many small yellowish threads in the middle, and are of a strong, full, or heady sent, not pleasing to a great many, by reason of the strange quicknesse of the sent : the fruit followeth, being flat at the head, with many leafie shels or scales compassing it, wherein is enclosed small long seede : the rootes runne not deepe, but spread vnder the ground, with many fibres annexed vnto them.

5. *Syringa Arabica flore albo duplici.*
The double white Pipe tree.

This Pipe tree hath diuers long and slender branches, whereon growe large leaues, somewhat like vnto the leaues of the former single white kinde, but not so rough or hard, and not at all dented about the edges, two alwaies standing one against another at euery ioynt of the stalke, but set or disposed on contrary sides, and not all vpon one side; at the ends whereof come forth diuers flowers, euery one standing on his owne foote-stalke, the hose or huske being long and hollow, like vnto the white Iasmine, and the flowers therin consisting of a double rowe of white and round pointed leaues, fiue or six in a rowe, with some yellownesse in the middle, which is hollow, of a very strong and heady sweet sent, and abiding a long time flowring, especially in the hotter Countries, but is very tender, and not able to abide any the least cold weather with vs;

for

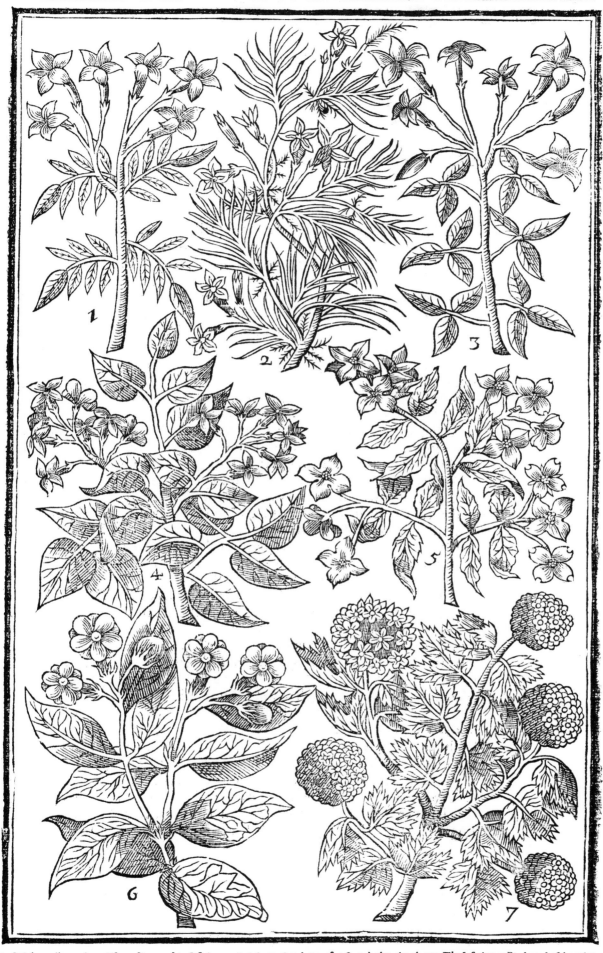

1 *Iasminum album vulgare.* The ordinary white Iasmine. 2 *Iasminum Americanum siue Convolvulus Americanus.* The Iasmine or Bindweed of America.
3 *Iasminum luteum vulgare.* The yellow Iasmine. 4 *Lilac seu Syringa cærulea.* The blew Pipe tree. 5 *Syringa alba vulgaris.* The single white Syringa or
Pipe tree. 6 *Syringa flore albe duplici.* The double white Syringa. 7 *Sambucus rosea.* The Elder or Gelder Rose.

for the cold windes will (as I vnderſtand) greatly moleſt it : and therefore muſt as charily be kept as Orenge trees with vs, if wee will haue it to abide.

The Place.

The firſt groweth in Arabia (as Matthiolus thinketh, that had it from Conſtantinople.) We haue it plentifully in our Gardens. The ſecond and third are ſtrangers with vs as yet. The fourth is as frequent as the firſt, or rather more, but his originall is not knowne. The laſt hath his originall from Arabia, as his name importeth.

The Time.

The firſt, ſecond, and third flower in Aprill, the other two not vntill May.

The Names.

The firſt is called of Matthiolus *Lilac*, and by that name is moſt vſually called in all parts. It is alſo called *Syringa cærulea*, becauſe it commeth neareſt vnto thoſe woods, which for their pithy ſubſtance, were made hollow into pipes. It is called of all in Engliſh, The blew Pipe tree. It ſeemeth likely, that Petrus Bellonius in his third Booke and fiftieth Chapter of his obſeruations (making mention of a ſhrubbe that the Turkes haue, with Iuie leaues alwaies greene, bearing blew or violet coloured flowers on a long ſtalke, of the bigneſſe and faſhion of a Foxe taile, and thereupon called in their language a Foxe taile) doth vnderſtand this plant here expreſſed. The certainty whereof might eaſily be knowne, if any of our Merchants there reſiding, would but call for ſuch a ſhrubbe, by the name of a Foxe taile in the Turkiſh tongue, and take care to ſend a young roote, in a ſmall tubbe or basket with earth by Sea, vnto vs here at London, which would be performed with a very little paines and coſt. The ſecond and third, as kindes thereof, haue their names in their titles. The fourth is called by Cluſius and others, *Frutex Coronarius*; ſome doe call it *Lilac flore albo*, but that name is not proper, in that it doth confound both kindes together. Lobel calleth it *Syringa Italica*. It is now generally called of all *Syringa alba*, that is in Engliſh, The white Pipe tree. Some would haue it to bee *Oſtrys* of Theophraſtus, but Cluſius hath ſufficiently cleared that doubt. Of others *Liguſtrum Orientale*, which it cannot be neither ; for the *Cyprus* of Plinie is Dioſcorides his *Liguſtrum*, which may be called *Orientale*, in that it is moſt proper to the Eaſterne Countries, and is very ſweete, whoſe ſeede is like vnto Coriander ſeede. The laſt is called by diuers *Syringa Arabica flore albo duplici*, as moſt fitly agreeing thereunto. Of Baſilius Beſlerus that ſet forth the great booke of the Biſhop of Eyſtot in Germany his Garden, *Syringa Italica flore albo pleno*, becauſe, as it is likely, hee had it from Italy. It is very likely, that Proſper Alpinus in his booke of Egyptian plants, doth meane this plant, which hee there calleth *Sambach, ſiue Iaſminum Arabicum*. Matthæus Caccini of Florence in his letter to Cluſius entituleth it *Syringa Arabica, ſiue Iaſminum Arabicum, ſiue Iaſminum ex Gine*, whereby hee declareth that it may not vnfitly be referred to either of them both. We may call it in Engliſh as it is in the title, The double white Pipe tree.

The Vertues.

We haue no vſe of theſe in Phyſicke that I know, although Proſper Alpinus ſaith, the double white Pipe tree is much vſed in Egypt, to help women in their trauailes of childbirth.

CHAP.

Chap. CVIII.

Sambucus Rosea. The Elder or Gelder Rose.

Lthough there be diuers kindes of Elders, yet there is but one kinde of Elder Rose, whereof I meane to intreate in this Chapter, being of neare affinity in some things vnto the former Pipe trees, and which for the beauty of it deserueth to be remembred among the delights of a Garden.

Sambucus Rosea. The Gelder Rose.

The Gelder Rose (as it is called) groweth to a reasonable height, standing like a tree, with a trunke as bigge as any mans arme, couered with a darke grayish barke, somewhat rugged and very knotty : the younger branches are smooth and white, with a pithy substance in the middle, as the Elders haue, to shew that it is a kind thereof, whereon are set broad leaues, diuided into three parts or diuisions, somewhat like vnto a Vine leafe, but smaller, and more rugged or crumpled, iagged or cut also about the edges : at the toppes of euery one of the young branches, most vsually commeth forth a great tuft, or ball as it were, of many white flowers, set so close together, that there can be no distinction of any seuerall flower seene, nor doth it seeme like the double flower of any other plant, that hath many rowes of leaues set together, but is a cluster of white leaued flowers set together vpon the stalke that vpholdeth them, of a small sent, which fall away without bearing any fruit in our Country, that euer I could obserue or learne : The roote spreadeth neither farre nor deepe, but shooteth many small rootes and fibres, whereby it is fastened in the ground, and draweth nourishment to it, and sometimes yeeldeth suckers from it.

The Place.

It should seeme, that the naturall place of this Elder is wet and moist grounds, because it is so like vnto the Marsh Elder, which is the single kind hereof. It is onely noursed vp in Gardens in all our Country.

The Time.

It flowreth in May, much about the time of the double Peony flower, both which being set together, make a pleasant variety, to decke vp the windowes of a house.

The Names.

It is generally called *Sambucus Rosea* : In English, The Elder Rose, and more commonly after the Dutch name, the Gelder Rose. Dalechampius seemeth to make it *Thraupalus* of Theophrastus, or rather the single Marsh Elder ; for I thinke this double kinde was not knowne in Theophrastus his time.

The Vertues.

It is not applyed to any Physicall vse that I know.

Chap.

Chap. CIX.

Rosa. The Rose tree or bush.

THe great varietie of Roses is much to be admired, beeing more then is to bee seene in any other shrubby plant that I know, both for colour, forme and smell. I haue to furnish this garden thirty sorts at the least, euery one notably differing from the other, and all fit to be here entertained : for there are some other, that being wilde and of no beautie or smell, we forbeare, and leaue to their wilde habitations. To distinguish them by their colours, as white, red, incarnate, and yellow, were a way that many might take, but I hold it not so conuenient for diuers respects : for so I should confound those of diuers sorts one among another, and I should not keepe that methode which to me seemeth most conuenient, which is, to place and ranke euery kinde, whether single or double, one next vnto the other, that so you may the better vnderstand their varieties and differences : I will therefore beginne with the most ancient, and knowne Roses to our Countrey, whether naturall or no I know not, but assumed by our precedent Kings of all others, to bee cognisances of their dignitie, the white Rose and the red, whom shall follow the damaske, of the finest sent, and most vse of all the other sorts, and the rest in their order.

1. *Rosa Anglica alba.* The English white Rose.

The white Rose is of two kindes, the one more thicke and double then the other : The one riseth vp in some shadowie places, vnto eight or ten foote high, with a stocke of a great bignesse for a Rose. The other growing seldome higher then a Damaske Rose. Some doe iudge both these to be but one kinde, the diuersitie happening by the ayre, or ground, or both. Both these Roses haue somewhat smaller and whiter greene leaues then in many other Roses, fiue most visually set on a stalke, and more white vnderneath, as also a whiter greene barke, armed with sharpe thornes or prickles, whereby they are soone knowne from other Roses, although the one not so easily from the other : the flowers in the one are whitish, with an eye or shew of a blush, especially towards the ground or bottome of the flower, very thicke double, and close set together, and for the most part not opening it selfe so largely and fully as eyther the Red or Damaske Rose. The other more white, lesse thicke and double, and opening it selfe more, and some so little double as but of two or three rowes, that they might be held to be single, yet all of little or no smell at all. To describe you all the seuerall parts of the Rose, as the bud, the beards, the threds &c. were needlesse, they are so conuersant in euery ones hand, that I shall not neede but to touch the most speciall parts of the varieties of them, and leaue a more exact relation of all things incident vnto them, vnto a generall worke.

2. *Rosa Incarnata.* The Carnation Rose.

The Carnation Rose is in most things like vnto the lesser white rose, both for the growing of the stocke, and bignesse of the flower, but that it is more spreade abroad when it is blown then the white is, and is of a pale blush colour all the flower throughout, of as small a sent as the white one is almost.

Rosa Belgica siue Vitrea. This kinde of Rose is not very great, but very thicke and double, and is very variable in the flowers, in that they will be so different one from another : some being paler then others, and some as it were blasted, which commeth not casually, but naturally to this rose : but the best flowers (whereof there will bee still some) will be of a bright pale murrey colour, neere vnto the Veluet rose, but nothing so darke a colour.

3. *Rosa Anglica rubra.* The English red Rose.

The red Rose (which I call English, not only for the reason before expressed, but because

cause (as I take it) this Rose is more frequent and vsed in England, then in other places) neuer groweth so high as the damaske Rose bush, but most vsually abideth low, and shooteth forth many branches from the roote (and is but seldome suffered to grow vp as the damaske Rose into standards) with a greene barke, thinner set with prickles, and larger and greener leaues on the vpperside then in the white, yet with an eye of white vpon them, fiue likewise most vsually set vpon a stalke, and grayish or whitish vnderneath. The Roses or Flowers doe very much vary, according to their site and abiding ; for some are of an orient, red or deepe crimson colour, and very double (although neuer so double as the white) which when it is full blowne hath the largest leaues of any other Rose ; some of them againe are paler, tending somewhat to a damaske ; and some are of so pale a red, as that it is rather of the colour of the canker Rose, yet all for the most part with larger leaues then the damaske, and with many more yellow threds in the middle : the sent hereof is much better then in the white, but not comparable to the excellencie of the damaske Rose, yet this Rose being well dryed and well kept, will hold both colour and sent longer then the damaske, bee it neuer so well kept.

4. *Rosa Damascena.* The Damaske Rose.

The Damaske Rose bush is more vsually nourced vp to a competent height to stand alone, (which we call Standards) then any other Rose : the barke both of the stocke and branches, is not fully so greene as the red or white Rose : the leaues are greene with an eye of white vpon them, so like vnto the red Rose, that there is no great difference betweene them, but that the leaues of the red Rose seeme to bee of a darker greene. The flowers are of a fine deepe blush colour, as all know, with some pale yellow threds in the middle, and are not so thicke and double as the white, nor being blowne, with so large and great leaues as the red, but of the most excellent sweet pleasant sent, far surpassing all other Roses or Flowers, being neyther heady nor too strong, nor stuffing or vnpleasant sweet, as many other flowers.

5. *Rosa Prouincialis siue Hollandica Damascena.* The great double Damaske Prouince or Holland Rose.

This Rose (that some call *Centifolia Batauica incarnata*) hath his barke of a reddish or browne colour, whereby it is soone discerned from other Roses. The leaues are likewise more reddish then in others, and somewhat larger, it vsually groweth very like the Damaske rose, and much to the same height : the flowers or roses are of the same deepe blush colour that the damaske roses are, or rather somewhat deeper, but much thicker, broader, and more double, or fuller of leaues by three parts almost, the outer leaues turning themselues backe, when the flower hath stood long blowne, the middle part it selfe (which in all other roses almost haue some yellow threds in them to be seene) being folded hard with small leaues, without any yellow almost at all to be seene, the sent whereof commeth neerest vnto the damaske rose, but yet is short of it by much, howsoeuer many doe thinke it as good as the damask, and to that end I haue known some Gentlewomen haue caused all their damaske stockes to bee grafted with prouince Roses, hoping to haue as good water, and more store of them then of damask Roses ; but in my opinion it is not of halfe so good a sent as the water of damaske Roses: let euery one follow their own fancie.

6. *Rosa Prouincialis rubra.* The red Prouince Rose.

As the former was called *incarnata*, so this is called *Batauica centifolia rubra*, the difference being not very great : the stemme or stocke, and the branches also in this, seeming not to be so great but greener, the barke being not so red ; the leaues of the same largenesse with the former damaske Prouince. The flowers are not altogether so large, thicke and double, and of a little deeper damaske or blush colour, turning to a red Rose, but not comming neere the full colour of the best red Rose, of a sent not so sweete as the damaske Prouince, but comming somewhat neere the sent of the or-

dinary

dinary red rofe, yet exceeding it. This rofe is not fo plentifull in bearing as the damaske Prouince.

7. *Rofa Prouincialis alba.* The white Prouince Rofe.

It is faid of diuers, that there is a white Prouince Rofe, whereof I am not *oculatus teftis*, and therfore I dare not giue it you for a certaintie, and indeed I haue fome doubt, that it is the greater and more double white rofe, whereof I gaue you the knowledge in the beginning: when I am my felfe better fatisfied, I fhall bee ready to fatisfie others.

8. *Rofa verficolor.* The party coloured Rofe, of fome Yorke and Lancafter.

This Rofe in the forme and order of the growing, is neereft vnto the ordinary damaske rofe, both for ftemme, branch, leafe and flower: the difference confifting in this, that the flower (being of the fame largeneffe and doubleneffe as the damask rofe) hath the one halfe of it, fometimes of a pale whitifh colour, and the other halfe, of a paler damaske colour then the ordinary; this happeneth fo many times, and fometimes alfo the flower hath diuers ftripes, and markes in it, as one leafe white, or ftriped with white, and the other halfe blufh, or ftriped with blufh, fometimes alfo all ftriped, or fpotted ouer, and other times little or no ftripes or markes at all, as nature lifteth to play with varieties, in this as in other flowers: yet this I haue obferued, that the longer it abideth blowen open in the fun, the paler and the fewer ftripes, markes or fpots will be feene in it: the fmell whereof is of a weake damaske rofe fent.

9. *Rofea Chryftallina.* The Chryftall Rofe.

This Rofe is very like vnto the laft defcribed, both for ftocke, branch and leafe: the flower hereof is not much different from it, being no great large or double Rofe, it of a meane fize, ftriped and marked with a deeper blufh or red, vpon the pale co-oured leafe, that it feemeth in the marking and beauty thereof, to bee of as much de-light as the Chryftall Gilloflower: this, euen like the former, foone fadeth and paffeth away, not yeelding any great ftore of flowers any yeare.

10. *Rofa rubra humilis fiue pumilio.* The dwarfe red Rofe, or Gilloflower Rofe.

This Rofe groweth alwayes low and fmall, otherwife in moft refpects like vnto the ordinary redde Rofe, and with few or no thornes vpon it: the Flowers or Rofes are double, thicke, fmall and clofe, not fo much fpread open as the ordinary red, but fomewhat like vnto the firft double white Rofe before expreffed; yet in fome places I haue feene them more layde open then thefe, as they grew in my garden, being fo e-uen at the toppes of the leaues, as if they had been clipt off with a paire of fheeres, and are not fully of fo red a colour as the red Prouince Rofe, and of as fmall or weak fent as the ordinary red Rofe, or not fo much.

11. *Rofa Francafurtenfis.* The Franckford Rofe.

The young fhootes of this Rofe are couered with a pale purplifh barke, fet with a number of fmall prickes like haires, and the elder haue but very few thornes: the flower or rofe it felfe hath a very great bud or button vnder it, more then in any other rofe, and is thicke and double as a red rofe, but fo ftrongly fwelling in the bud, that ma-ny of them breake before they can be full blowen, and then they are of a pale red rofe colour, that is, betweene a red and a damaske, with a very thicke broade and hard vm-bone of fhort yellow threds or thrumes in the middle, the huske of the flower hauing long ends, which are called the beards of the rofe, which in all other are iagged in fome of them, in this hath no iagge at all: the fmell is neereft vnto a red Rofe.

1 *Rosa Damascena.* The Damaske Rose. 2 *Rosa Prouincialis siue Hollandica.* The great Prouince Rose. 3 *Rosa Francafurtensis.* The Franckford Rose. 4 *Rosa rubra humilis.* The dwarfe red Rose. 5 *Rosa Hungarica.* The Hungarian Rose. 6 *Rosa lutea multiplex.* The great double yellow Rose.

12. *Rosa Hungarica.* The Hungarian Rose.

The Hungarian Rose hath greene shootes slenderly set with prickes, and seldome groweth higher then ordinarily the red Rose doth; the stemme or stocke being much about that bignesse : the flower or rose is as great, thicke and double, as the ordinary red Rose, and of the same fashion, of a paler red colour, and beeing neerely looked vpon is finely spotted with faint spots, as it were spreade ouer the red; the smell wherof is somewhat better then the smell of the ordinary red Rose of the best kinde.

13. *Rosa Holoserica simplex & multiplex.* The Veluet Rose single and double.

The old stemme or stock of the veluet Rose is couered with a dark coloured barke, and the young shootes of a sad greene with very few or no thornes at all vpon them : the leaues are of a sadder greene colour then in most sorts of Roses, and very often seuen on a stalke, many of the rest hauing but fiue: the Rose is eyther single or double : the single is a broade spread flower, consisting of fiue or sixe broade leaues with many yellow threds in the middle : the double hath two rowes of leaues, the one large, which are outermost, the other smaller within, of a very deepe red crimson colour like vnto crimson veluet, with many yellow threds also in the middle; and yet for all the double rowe of leaues, these Roses stand but like single flowers : but there is another double kinde that is more double then this last, consisting oftentimes of sixteene leaues or more in a flower, and most of them of an equall bignesse, of the colour of the first single rose of this kinde, or somewhat fresher; but all of them of a smaller sent then the ordinary red Rose.

14. *Rosa sine spinis simplex & multiplex.* The Rose without thornes single and double.

The Rose without thornes hath diuers greene smooth shootes, rising from the root, without any pricke or thorne at all vpon them, eyther young or old: the leaues are not fully so large as of the red rose : the flowers or roses are not much bigger then those of the double Cinamon Rose, thicke set together and short, of a pale red Rose colour, with diuers pale coloured veines through euery leafe of the flower, which hath caused some to call it The marbled Rose, and is of a small sent, not fully equall to the red Rose. The single of this kinde differeth not in any other thing from the former, then in the doublenesse or singlenesse of the flowers, which in this are not halfe so double, nor yet fully single, and are of a paler red colour.

Rosa sine spina flore albo. I haue heard likewise of a white Rose of this kinde, but I haue seene none such as yet, and therefore I can say no more thereof.

15. *Rosa Cinamomea simplex & multiplex.* The Cinamon Rose single and double.

The single Cinamon Rose hath his shootes somewhat red, yet not so red as the double kinde, armed with great thornes, like almost vnto the Eglantine bush, thereby showing, as well by the multiplicitie of his shootes, as the quicknesse and height of his shooting, his wilde nature : On the stemme and branches stand winged leaues, sometimes seuen or more together, which are small and greene, yet like vnto other Roses. The Roses are single, of fiue leaues a peece, somewhat large, and of a pale red colour, like vnto the double kinde, which is in shootes redder, and in all other things like vnto the single, but bearing small, short, thicke and double Roses, somewhat like vnto the Rose without thornes, but a little lesser, of a paler red colour at the end of the leaues, and somewhat redder and brighter toward the middle of them, with many yellow short thrumes; the small sent of Cinamon that is found in the flowers hath caused it to beare the name.

16. *Rosa lutea simplex.* The single yellow Rose.

This single yellow Rose is planted rather for variety then any other good vse. It often groweth to a good height, his ftemme being great and wooddy, with few or no prickes vpon the old wood, but with a number of fmall prickes like haires, thicke fet, vpon the younger branches, of a darke colour fomewhat reddifh, the barke of the young fhootes being of a fad greene reddifh colour : the leaues of this Rofe bufh are fmaller, rounder pointed, of a paler greene colour, yet finely fnipt about the edges, and more in number, that is, feuen or nine on a ftalke or ribbe, then in any other Garden kinde, except the double of the fame kinde that followeth next : the flower is a fmall fingle Rofe, confifting of fiue leaues, not fo large as the fingle Spanifh Muske Rofe, but fomewhat bigger then the Eglantine or fweete Briar Rofe, of a fine pale yellow colour, without any great fent at all while it is frefh, but a little more, yet fmall and weake when it is dryed.

17. *Rosa lutea multiplex fiue flore pleno.*
The double yellow Rose.

The double yellow Rofe is of great account, both for the rarity, and doublenefe of the flower, and had it fent to the reft, would of all other be of higheft efteeme. The ftemme or ftocke, the young fhoots or branches, the fmall hairy prickes, and the fmall winged leaues, are in all parts like vnto the former fingle kinde ; the chiefeft difference confifteth in the doublenefe of the flower or Rofe, which is fo thicke and double, that very often it breaketh out on one fide or another, and but a few of them abiding whole and faire in our Countrey, the caufe whereof wee doe imagine to bee the much moifture of our Countrey, and the time of flowring being fubiect to much raine and fhowers ; many therefore doe either plant it againft a wall, or other wayes defend it by couering : againe, it is fo plentifull in young fhootes or branches, as alfo in flowers at the toppe of euery branch, which are fmall and weake for the moft part, that they are not able to bring all the flowers to ripenefe ; and therefore moft of them fall or wither away without comming to perfection (the remedy that many doe vfe for this inconuenience laft recited is, that they nippe away moft of the buds, leauing but fome few vpon it, that fo the vigour of the plant may be collected into a few flowers, whereby they may the better come to perfection, and yet euen thus it is hardly effected) which are of a yellowifh greene colour in the bud, and before they be blowne open, but then are of a faire yellow colour, very full of leaues, with many fhort haires rather then leaues in the middle, and hauing fhort, round, greene, fmooth buttons, almoft flat vnder them : the flower being faire blowne open, doth fcarce giue place for largenefe, thicknefe, and doublenefe, vnto the great Prouence or Holland Rofe. This Rofe bufh or plant is very tender with vs here about London, and will require fome more care and keeping then the fingle of this kinde, which is hardy enough ; for I haue loft many my felfe, and I know but a few about this towne that can nourfe it vp kindly, to beare or fcarce to abide without perifhing ; but abideth well in euery free aire of all or the moft parts of this Kingdome : but (as I heare) not fo well in the North.

18. *Rosa Mofchata fimplex & multiplex.*
The Muske Rose single and double.

The Muske Rofe both fingle and double, rife vp oftentimes to a very great height, that it ouergroweth any arbour in a Garden, or being fet by an houfe fide, to bee ten or twelue foote high, or more, but more efpecially the fingle kinde, with many green farre fpread branches, armed with a few fharpe great thornes, as the wilder forts of Rofes are, whereof thefe are accounted to be kindes, hauing fmall darke greene leaues on them, not much bigger then the leaues of Eglantine : the flowers come forth at the toppes of the branches, many together as it were in an vmbell or tuft, which for the moft part doe flower all at a time, or not long one after another, euery one ftanding on a pretty long ftalke, and are of a pale whitifh or creame colour, both the fingle and

the

the double ; the single being small flowers , consisting of fiue leaues, with many yellow threads in the middle : and the double bearing more double flowers, as if they were once or twice more double then the single , with yellow thrummes also in the middle, both of them of a very sweete and pleasing smell, resembling Muske : some there be that haue auouched, that the chiefest sent of these Roses consisteth not in the leaues, but in the threads of the flowers.

19. *Rosa Moschata multiplex altera : alijs Damascena alba, vel verisimilior Cinamomea flore pleno albo.* The double white Damaske Muske Rose.

This other kinde of Muske Rose (which with some is called the white Damaske Muske, but more truely the double white Cinamon Rose) hath his stemme and branches also shorter then the former, but as greene : the leaues are somewhat larger, and of a whiter greene colour ; the flowers also are somewhat larger then the former double kinde, but standing in vmbels after the same manner, or somewhat thicker, and of the same whitish colour, or a little whiter, and somewhat, although but a little , neare the smell of the other, but nothing so strong.   This flowreth at the time of other Roses, or somewhat later, yet much before the former two sorts of Muske Roses, which flower not vntill the end of Summer, and in Autumne ; both which things, that is, the time of the flowring , and the sent being both different, shew plainly it cannot be of the tribe of Muske Roses.

20. *Rosa Hispanica Moschata simplex.* The Spanish Muske Rose.

This Spanish Rose riseth to the height of the Eglantine, and sometimes higher, with diuers great greene branches, the leaues whereof are larger and greener then of the former kindes : the flowers are single Roses, consisting of fiue whiter leaues then in any of the former Muske Roses, and much larger, hauing sometimes an eye of a blush in the white, of a very sweete smell, comming nearest vnto the last recited Muske Rose, as also for the time of the flowring.

21. *Rosa Pomifera maior.* The great Apple Rose.

The stemme or stocke of this Rose is great, couered with a darke grayish barke, but the younger branches are somewhat reddish, armed here and there with great and sharpe thornes, but nothing so great or plentifull as in the Eglantine , although it be a wilde kinde : the leaues are of a whitish greene colour, almost like vnto the first white Rose, and fiue alwaies set together, but seldome seuen : the flowers are small and single , consisting of fiue leaues, without any sent, or very little, and little bigger then those of the Eglantine bush, and of the very same deepe blush colour, euery one standing vpon a rough or prickly button, bearded in the manner of other Roses, which when the flowers are fallen growe great, somewhat long and round, peare-fashion, bearing the beards on the tops of them ; and being full ripe are very red, keeping the small prickles still on them, wherein are many white, hard, and roundish seedes, very like vnto the seede of the Heppes or Eglantine berries, lying in a soft pulpe, like vnto the Hawthorne berries or Hawes : the whole beauty of this plant consisteth more in the gracefull aspect of the red apples or fruit hanging vpon the bushes, then in the flowers, or any other thing. It seemeth to be the same that Clusius calleth *Rosa Pumila,* but that with me it groweth much higher and greater then he saith his doth.

22. *Rosa siluestris odora siue Eglenteria simplex.* The single Eglantine or sweete Briar bush.

The sweete Briar or Eglantine Rose is so well knowne , being not onely planted in Gardens, for the sweetenesse of the leaues , but growing wilde in many woods and hedges, that I thinke it lost time to describe it ; for that all know it hath exceeding long greene shootes, armed with the cruellest sharpe and strong thornes, and thicker set
then

1 *Rosa sine spinis multiplex.* The double Rose without thorns. 2 *Rosa Cinamomea flore pleno.* The double Cinamon Rose. 3 *Rosa Holoserica simplex.* The single Veluet Rose. 4 *Rosa Holoserica duplex.* The double Veluet Rose. 5 *Rosa Moschata multiplex.* The double Muske Rose. 6 *Rosa Moschata Hispanica simplex.* The single Spanish Muske Rose. 7 *Rosa Pomifera maior.* The great Apple Rose. 8 *Rosa siluestris siue Eglanteria duplex.* The double Eglantine Rose.

then is in any Rofe either wilde or tame : the leaues are fmaller then in moft of thofe that are nourfed vp in Gardens, feuen or nine moft vfually fet together on a ribbe or ftalke, very greene and fweete in fmell, aboue the leaues of any other kinde of Rofe : the flowers are fmall fingle blufh Rofes, of little or no fent at all, which turne into reddifh berries, ftuffed within with a dounie or flocky matter or fubftance, wherein doth lye white hard feede.

23. *Rofa filueftris odora fiue Eglenteria flore duplici.*
The double Eglantine.

The double Eglantine is in all the places that I haue feene it a grafted Rofe, (but I doubt not, but that his originall was naturall, and that it may be made naturall againe, as diuers other Rofes are.) It groweth and fpreadeth very well, and with a great head of branches, whereon ftand fuch like leaues as are in the fingle kinde, but a little larger, not fmelling fully fo fweete as it : the flowers are fomewhat bigger then the fingle, but not much, hauing but one other rowe of leaues onely more then the former, which are fmaller, and the outer leaues larger, but of the fame pale reddifh purple colour, and fmelleth fomewhat better then the fingle.

24. *Rofa femper virens.* The euer greene Rofe bufh.

This Rofe or bufh is very like vnto a wilde fingle Eglantine bufh in many refpects, hauing many very long greene branches, but more flender and weake, fo that many times they bend downe againe, not able to fuftaine themfelues without fome helpe, and armed with hooked thornes as other Rofes be; the winged leaues confift of feuen for the moft part, whereof thofe two that are loweft and oppofite, are fmalleft, the next two bigger then they, the third couple bigger then any of the reft belowe, and the end leafe biggeft of all : this proportion generally it holdeth in euery winged leafe through the whole plant, which at the firft comming forth are fomewhat reddifh, with the young branch that fhooteth out with them, but being full growne, are of a deepe greene colour, and fomewhat fhining, dented about the edges, and fall not away from the branches as other Rofes doe, but abide thereon for the moft part all the Winter : the flowers ftand foure or fiue together at the tops of the branches, being fingle Rofes, made of fiue leaues a peece, of a pure white colour, much larger then the ordinary Muske Rofe, and of a fine fent, comming neareft thereunto, with many yellow chiues or threads in the middle.

The Place.

Some of thefe Rofes had their originall, as is thought in England, as the firft and fecond; for thefe dryed red Rofes that come ouer to vs from beyond the Seas, are not of the kinde of our red Rofe, as may well be perceiued by them that will compare our Englifh dryed leaues with thofe. Some in Germany, Spaine, and Italy. Some againe in Turkie, as the double yellow Rofe, which firft was procured to be brought into England, by Mafter Nicholas Lete, a worthy Merchant of London, and a great louer of flowers, from Conftantinople, which (as wee heare) was firft brought thither from Syria; but perifhed quickly both with him, and with all other to whom hee imparted it : yet afterwards it was fent to Mafter Iohn de Franqueuille, a Merchant alfo of London, and a great louer of all rare plants, as well as flowers, from which isfprung the greateft ftore, that is now flourifhing in this Kingdome.

The Time.

The Cinamon Rofe is the earlieft for the moft part, which flowreth with vs about the middle of May, and fometimes in the beginning. The ordinary Muske Rofes both fingle and double flower lateft, as is faid. All the other flower much about one time, in the beginning of Iune, or thereabouts, and continue flowring all that moneth, and the next throughout for the moft part, and the red vntill Auguft be halfe paft.

The

The Names.

The feuerall names, whereby they are moft commonly knowne vnto vs in this Countrey, are expreffed in their titles; but they are much differing from what they are called in other Countries neare vnto vs, which to compare, conferre, and agree together, were a worke of more paines then vfe: But to proportion them vnto the names fet downe by Theophraftus, Pliny, and the reft of the ancient Authors, were a worke, wherein I might be fure not to efcape without falling into errour, as I verily beleeue many others haue done, that haue vndertaken to doe it: I will therefore for this worke defire that you will reft contented, with fo much as hath already been deliuered, and expect an exact definition and complete fatisfaction by fuch a methodicall courfe as a generall Hiftory will require, to be performed by them that fhall publifh it.

The Vertues.

The Rofe is of exceeding great vfe with vs; for the Damaske Rofe (befides the fuperexcellent fweete water it yeeldeth being diftilled, or the perfume of the leaues being dryed, feruing to fill fweete bags) ferueth to caufe folublenelfe of the body, made into a Syrupe, or preferued with Sugar moift or dry candid. The Damaske Prouince Rofe, is not onely for fent neareft of all other Rofes vnto the Damaske, but in the operation of folubility alfo. The red Rofe hath many Phyficall vfes much more then any other, feruing for many forts of compofitions, both cordiall and cooling, both binding and loofing. The white Rofe is much vfed for the cooling of heate in the eyes: diuers doe make an excellent yellow colour of the iuyce of white Rofes, wherein fome Allome is diffolued, to paint or colour flowers or pictures, or any other fuch things. There is little vfe of any other fort of Rofes; yet fome affirme, that the Muske Rofes are as ftrong in operation to open or loofen the belly as the Damaske Rofe or Prouince.

CHAP. CXI.

Ciftus. The Holly Rofe or Sage Rofe.

THere are three principall kindes of *Ciftus*, the male, the female, and the gumme or fweete fmelling *Ciftus* bearing *Ladanum*, called *Ledon*. Of each of thefe three there are alfo diuers forts: Of them all to intreate in this worke is not my minde, I will onely felect out of the multitude fome few that are fit for this our Garden, and leaue the reft to a greater.

1. *Ciftus mas.* The male Holly Rofe or Sage Rofe.

The male *Ciftus* that is moft familiar vnto our Countrey, I meane that will beft abide, is a fmall fhrubby plant, growing feldome aboue three or foure foote high with vs, hauing many flender brittle wooddy branches, couered with a whitifh barke, whereon are fet many whitifh greene leaues, long and fomewhat narrow, crumpled or wrinckled as it were with veines, and fomewhat hard in handling, efpecially the old ones; for the young ones are fofter, fomewhat like vnto Sage leaues for the forme and colour, but much fmaller, two alwaies fet together at a ioynt: the flowers ftand at the toppe of the branches, three or foure together vpon feuerall flender footftalkes, confifting of fiue fmall round leaues a peece, fomewhat like vnto a fmall fingle Rofe, of a fine reddifh purple colour, with many yellow threads in the middle, with-

out

out any sent at all, and quickly fading or falling away, abiding seldome one whole day blowne at the most: after the flowers are past, there come vp round hard hairie heads in their places, containing small brownish seede: the roote is wooddy, and will abide some yeares with vs, if there be some care had to keepe it from the extreamity of our Winters frostes, which both this, and many of the other sorts and kinds, will not abide doe what we can.

2. *Cistus femina.* The female Holly Rose.

The female Holly Rose groweth lower, and smaller then the former male kinde, hauing blackish branches, lesse woody, but not lesse brittle then it: the leaues are somewhat rounder and greener, but a little hard or rough withall, growing in the same manner vpon the branches by couples: the flowers grow at the toppes of the branches, like vnto the former, consisting of fiue leaues, but somewhat lesser, and wholly white, with yellow threds in the middle, as quickly fading, and of as little sent as the former: the heads and seede are somewhat bigger then in the former.

3. *Chamæcistus Frisicus.* The dwarfe Holly Rose of Friseland.

This dwarfe Cistus is a small low plant, hauing diuers shootes from the rootes, full of leaues that are long and narrow, very like vnto the leaues of the French Spikenard or *Spica Celtica*; from among which leaues shoote forth short stalkes, not aboue a span high, with a few smaller leaues thereon; and at the toppes diuers small flowers one aboue another, consisting of six small round leaues, of a yellow colour, hauing two circles of reddish spots round about the bottome of the leaues, a little distant one from another, which adde much grace to the flower: after the flowers are past, there come in their places small round heads, being two forked at the end, containing within them small brownish chaffie seede: the roote is small and slender, with many fibres thereat creeping vnder ground, and shooting forth in diuers places, whereby it much encreaseth: the whole plant, and euery part of it, smelleth strong without any pleasant sent.

4. *Cistus annuus.* The Holly Rose of a yeare.

This small Cistus that endureth but a year (and will require to be sowne euery year, if ye will haue it) riseth vp with straight, but slender hard stalkes, set here and there confusedly with long and narrow greenish leaues, very like vnto the leaues of the Gum Cistus or Ledon, being a little clammy withall: at the toppe of the stalkes, and at the ioynts with the leaues, stand two or three pale yellow flowers, consisting of fiue leaues a peece, with a reddish spot neere the bottome of euery leafe of the flower, as quickely fading as any of the former: after which follow small three square heades, containing small seede, like vnto the first female kinde, but somewhat paler or yellower: the root is small and woody, and perisheth as soone as it hath borne seede.

5. *Cistus Ledon.* The Gum Cistus, or Sweete Holly Rose.

This sweete Holly Rose or Gum Cistus, riseth higher, and spreadeth larger then the former male kind doth, with many blackish woody branches, whereon are set diuers long and narrow darke greene leaues, but whitish vnderneath, two alwayes standing together at a ioint, both stalks and leaues bedeawed as it were continually with a clammy sweete moisture (which in the hot Countries is both more plentifull, and more sweet then in ours) almost transparent, and which being gathered by the inhabitants, with certaine instruments for that purpose (which in some places are leather thongs, drawne ouer the bushes, and after scraped off from the thongs againe, and put together) is that kind of blacke sweet gum, which is called *Ladanum* in the Apothecaries shops: at the tops of the branches stand single white flowers, like vnto single Roses, being larger then in any of the former kindes, consisting of fiue leaues, whereof euery one hath at the bottome a dark purplish spot, broad below, and small pointed vpwards, with some yellow threds in the middle: after which are past, there arise cornered heads,

1 *Ciſtus mas* The male Holly Roſe. 2 *Chamæciſtus Friſucus.* The dwarfe Holly Roſe of Friſia. 3 *Ciſtus Ledon.* The ſweet Holly Roſe or gumme Ciſtus. 4 *Ledum Alpinum.* The mountaine Holly Roſe. 5 *Ledum Sileſiacum.* The ſweet Mary Roſe of Sileſia. 6 *Roſmarinum aureum.* Gilded Roſemary.

heads, containing such small brownish seede as is in the former male kinde : the roote is woody, and spreadeth vnder ground, abiding some yeares, if it be placed vnder a wall, where it may bee defended from the windes that often breake it, and from the extremitie of our winters, and especially the snow, if it lye vpon it, which quickly causeth it to perish.

6. *Ledum Alpinum seu Rosa Alpina.* The Mountaine sweet Holly Rose.

The fragrant smell with properties correspondent of two other plants, causeth me to insert them in this Chapter, and to bring them to your knowledge, as well worthy a fit place in our Garden. The first of them hath diuers slender woody branches, two foote high or thereabouts, couered with a grayish coloured barke, and many times leaning downe to the ground, whereby it taketh roote againe : vpon these branches grow many thicke, short, hard greene leaues, thicke set together, confusedly without order, sometimes whitish vnderneath, and sometimes yellowish : the toppes of the branches are loden with many flowers, which cause them to bend downwards, being long, hollow and reddish, opening into fiue corners, spotted on the outside with many white spots, and of a paler red colour on the inside, of a fine sweet sent : after the flowers are past, there follow small heads, containing small brownish seede : the root is long, hard and woody, abiding better if it comprehend in the ground, then some of the former, because his originall is out of a colder country.

7. *Ledum Silesiacum.* The sweete Mary Rose, or Rosemary of Silesia.

This other sweete plante riseth vp with woody ash-coloured branches two foote high or more, which shoote forth other branches, of a reddish or purplish colour, co-uered with a brownish yellow hoarinesse, on which are set many narrow long greene leaues, like vnto Rosemary leaues, but couered with the like hoarinesse as the stalks are (especially in the naturall places, but not so much being transplanted) and folding the sides of the leaues so close together, that they seeme nothing but ribbes, or stalkes, of an excellent sweet and pleasant sent ; at the ends of the branches there grow certaine brownish scaly heads, made of many small leaues set thicke together, out of which breake forth many flowers, standing in a tuft together, yet seuerally euery one vpon his owne footstalke, consisting of fiue white leaues, with certaine white threds in the middle, smelling very sweete : after which rise small greene heads, spotted with brownish spots, wherein is contained very small, long, yellowish seede : the roote is hard and woodie.

The Place.

The first, second, fourth and fifth, grow in the hot Countries, as Italie, Spaine, &c. The third, and the two last in the colder Countries, as Frise-land, Germanie, Bohemia.

The Time.

They do all flower in the Summer moneths of Iune, Iuly and August, and their seede is ripe quickly after.

The Names.

The first, second, fourth and fift, baue their names sufficiently expressed in their desctiptions. The third was sent vnto Clusius, vnder the name of *Herculus Frisicus*, because of the strong sent : but he referreth it to the kinds of *Chamæcistus*, that is, dwarfe or low *Cistus*, both for the low growth, and for the flowers and seede sake. The sixt is diuersly called; for Clusius calleth it *Ledum Alpinum* : others, *Nerium Alpinum*, making it to bee a Rose Bay.

Gesner

Gefner according to the Countrey peoples name, *Rosa Alpina*, and *Rosa Montana*. Lobel calleth it *Balsamum Alpinum*, of the fragrant smell it hath, and *Chamærhododendros Chamaelææ folio*. And some haue called it *Euonymus*, without all manner of iudgement. In Engiifh wee may call it, The Mountaine Rofe, vntill a fitter name be giuen it. The laft is called of Matthiolus, *Rofmarinum filuestre*, but of Clufius *Ledum*, referring it to their kindred ; and *Silefiacum*, becaufe he found it in that Countrey ; or for diftinction fake, as he faith, it may bee called, *Ledum folys Rofmarini*, or *Ledum Bohemicum*. Cordus, as it feemeth in his Hiftory of Plants, calleth it *Chamæpeuce*, as though he did account it a kinde of low Pine, or Pitch tree.

The Vertues.

The firft, fecond, and fift, are very aftringent, effectuall for all forts of fluxes of humours. The fweet Gum called *Ladanum*, made artificially into oyle, is of fingular vfe for *Alopecia*, or falling of the haire. The feed of the fourth is much commended againft the ftone of the Kidneyes. The fweete Rofemary of Silefia is vfed of the inhabitants, where it naturally groweth, againft the fhrinking of finewes, crampes, or other fuch like difeafes, wherof their daily experience makes it familiar, being vfed in bathing or otherwife.

Chap. CXII.

Rofmarinum. Rofemary.

THere hath beene vfually knowne but one fort of Rofemary, which is frequent through all this Country : but there are fome other forts not fo well knowne; the one is called Gilded Rofemary ; the other broade leafed Rofemary ; a third I will adioyne, as more rare then all the other, called Double flowred Rofmary, becaufe few haue heard thereof, much leffe feene it, and my felfe am not well acquainted with it, but am bold to deliuer it vpon credit.

1. *Libanotis Coronaria fiue Rofmarinum vulgare.*
Our Common Rofmary.

This common Rofemary is fo well knowne through all our Land, being in euery womans garden, that it were fufficient but to name it as an ornament among other fweete herbes and flowers in our Garden, feeing euery one can defcribe it : but that I may fay fomething of it, It is well obferued, as well in this our Land (where it hath been planted in Noblemens, and great mens gardens againft bricke wals, and there continued long) as beyond the Seas, in the naturall places where it groweth, that it rifeth vp in time vnto a very great height, with a great and woody ftemme (of that compaffe, that (being clouen out into thin boards) it hath ferued to make lutes, or fuch like inftruments, and here with vs Carpenters rules, and to diuers other purpofes) branching out into diuers and fundry armes that extend a great way, and from them againe into many other fmaller branches, wheron are fet at feuerall diftances, at the ioynts, many very narrow long leaues, greene aboue, and whitifh vnderneath ; among which come forth towards the toppes of the ftalkes, diuers fweet gaping flowers, of a pale or bleake blewifh colour, many fet together, ftanding in whitifh huskes ; the feed is fmall and red, but thereof feldome doth any plants arife that will abide without extraordinary care ; for although it will fpring of the feede reafonable well, yet it is fo fmall and tender the firft yeare, that a fharpe winter killeth it quickly, vnleffe it be very well defended : the whole plant as well leaues as flowers, fmelleth exceeding fweete.

2. *Rofmarinum ftriatum, fiue aureum.* Gilded Rofemary.

This Rofemary differeth not from the former, in forme or manner of growing, nor in the forme or colour of the flower, but only in the leaues, which are edged, or striped, or pointed with a faire gold yellow colour, which so continueth all the yeare throughout, yet fresher and fairer in Summer then in Winter ; for then it will looke of a deader colour, yet so, that it may be discerned to be of two colours, green & yellow.

3. *Rosmarinum latifolium.* Broade leafed Rosemary.

This broad leafed Rosemary groweth in the same manner that the former doth, but that we haue not seene it in our Countrey since we had it to grow so great, or with such woody stemmes : the leaues stand together vpon the long branches after the same fashion, but larger, broader and greener then the other, and little or nothing whitish vnderneath : the flowers likewise are of the same forme and colour with the ordinary, but larger, and herein consisteth the difference.

4. *Rosmarinum flore duplici.* Double flowred Rosmary.

The double flowred Rosmary thus far differeth from the former, that it hath stronger stalkes, not so easie to breake, fairer, bigger and larger leaues, of a faire greene colour, and the flowers are double, as the Larkes heele or spurre : This I haue onely by relation, which I pray you accept, vntill I may by sight better enforme you.

The Place.

Our ordinary Rosmary groweth in Spaine, and Prouence of France, and in others of those hot Countryes, neere the Sea side. It will not abide (vnlesse kept in stoues) in many places of Germany, Denmarke, and those colder Countries. And in some extreame hard winters, it hath well neere perished here in England with vs, at the least in many places: but by slipping it is vsually, and yearly encreased, to replenish any garden.

The Time.

It flowreth oftentimes twice in the yeare ; in the Spring first, from April vntill the end of May or Iune, and in August and September after, if the yeare before haue been temperate.

The Names.

Rosmary is called of the ancient Writers, *Libanotis,* but with this distinction, *Stephanomatica,* that is, *Coronaria,* because there were other plants called *Libanotis,* that were for other vses, as this for garlands, where flowers and sweete herbes were put together. The Latines call it *Rosmarinum.* Some would make it to be *Cneorum nigrum* of Theophrastus, as they would make Lauander to bee his *Cneorum album,* but Matthiolus hath sufficiently confuted that errour.

The Vertues.

Rosmary is almost of as great vse as Bayes, or any other herbe both for inward and outward remedies, and as well for ciuill as physicall purposes. Inwardly for the head and heart ; outwardly for the sinewes and ioynts : for ciuill vses, as all doe know, at weddings, funerals, &c. to bestow among friends : and the physicall are so many, that you might bee as well tyred in the reading, as I in the writing, if I should set down all that might be said of it. I will therefore onely giue you a taste of some, desiring you will be content therewith. There is an excellent oyle drawne from the flowers alone by the heate of the Sunne, auaileable for many diseases both inward and outward, and accounted a soueraigne Balsame: it is also good to helpe dimnesse

nesse of sight, and to take away spots, markes and scarres from the skin; and is made in this manner. Take a quantitie of the flowers of Rosemary, according to your owne will eyther more or lesse, put them into a strong glasse close stopped, set them in hot horse dung to digest for fourteene dayes, which then being taken forth of the dung, and vnstopped, tye a fine linnen cloth ouer the mouth, and turne downe the mouth thereof into the mouth of another strong glasse, which being set in the hot Sun, an oyle will distill downe into the lower glasse; which preserue as precious for the vses before recited, and many more, as experience by practice may enforme diuers.

There is another oyle Chymically drawne, auaileable in the like manner for many the same inward and outward diseases, *viz.* for the heart, rheumaticke braines, and to strengthen the memory, outwardly to warme and comfort cold benummed sinewes, whereof many of good iudgement haue had much experience.

Chap. CXIII.

Myrtus. The Mirtle tree or bush.

IN the hot Countreyes, there haue been many sorts of Mirtles found out, naturally growing there, which will not fructifie in this of ours, nor yet abide without extraordinary care, and conueniencie withall, to preserue them from the sharpenesse of our winters. I shall only bring you to view three sorts in this my Garden, the one with a greater, the other two with lesser leaues, as the remainder of others which wee haue had, and which are preserued from time to time, not without much paine and trouble.

1. *Myrtus latifolia.* The greater leafed Mirtle.

The broader leafed Mirtle riseth vp to the height of foure or fiue foote at the most with vs, full of branches and leaues growing like a small bush, the stemme and elder branches whereof are couered with a dark coloured bark, but the young with a green, and some with a red, especially vpon the first shooting forth, whereon are set many fresh greene leaues, very sweet in smell, and very pleasant to behold, so neer resembling the leaues of the Pomegranate tree that groweth with vs, that they soone deceiue many that are not expert therein, being somewhat broade and long, and pointed at the ends, abiding alwaies green: at the ioynts of the branches where the leaues stand, come forth the flowers vpon small footestalkes, euery one by it selfe consisting of fiue small white leaues, with white threds in the middle, smelling also very sweet: after the flowers are past, there doe arise in the hot Countries, where they are naturall, round blacke berries, when they are ripe, wherein are contained many hard white crooked seedes, but neuer in this Countrey, as I said before: the roote disperseth it selfe into many branches, with many fibres annexed thereto.

2. *Myrtus minor, seu minore folio.* The smaller leafed Mirtle.

The smaller leafed Mirtle is a low shrub or bush, like vnto the former, but scarce rising so high, with branches spreading about the stemme, much thicker set with leaues then the former, smaller also, and pointed at the ends, of a little deeper greene colour, abiding greene also winter and summer, and very sweete likewise: the flowers are white like vnto the former, and as sweete, but shew not themselues so plentifull on the branches: the fruit is blacke in his naturall places, with seedes therein as the former.

3. *Myrtus minor rotundiore folio.* Boxe Mirtle.

Wee haue another sort of this small kinde of Mirtle, so like vnto the former both for smalnesse, deepe greene colour of the leaues, and thicke growing of the branches, that

that it will be thought of most, without good heede, and comparing the one with the other, to be the very same with the former: but if it bee well viewed, it will shew, by the roundnesse at the ends of the leaues very like vnto the small Boxe leaues, to be another differing kinde, although in nothing else. Wee nourse them with great care, for the beautifull aspect, sweete sent and raritie, as delights and ornaments for a garden of pleasure, wherein nothing should be wanting that art, care and cost might produce and preserue : as also to set among other euer greene plants to sort with them.

The Place.

These and many other sorts of Mirtles grow in Spaine, Portugall, Italie, and other hot Countries in great aboundance, where they make their hedges of them : wee (as I said) keepe them in this Countrey, with very great care and diligence.

The Time.

The Mirtles doe flower very late with vs, not vntill August at the soonest, which is the cause of their not fructifying.

The Names.

They are called in Latine *Myrtus*, and in English Mirtle tree, without any other diuersitie of names, for the generall title. Yet the seuerall kindes haue had seuerall denominations, in Plinies time, and others, as *Romana, Coningala, Terentina, Egyptia, alba, nigra, &c.* which haue noted the differences, euen then well obserued.

The Vertues.

The Mirtle is of an astringent qualitie, and wholly vsed for such purposes.

Chap. CXIIII.

Malus Punica siue Granata. The Pomegranet tree.

THere are two kindes of Pomegranet trees, The one tame or manured, bearing fruit, which is distinguished of some into two sorts, of others into three, that is, into sower, and sweet, and into sower sweete. The other wilde, which beareth no fruite, because it beareth double flowers, like as the Cherry, Apple, and Peach tree with double blossomes, before described, and is also distinguished into two sorts, the one bearing larger, the other lesser flowers. Of the manured kinde wee haue onely one sort (so farre as we know) for it neuer beareth ripe fruit in this our Countrey) which for the beautifull aspect, both of the greene verdure of the leaues, and faire proportion and colour of the flowers, as also for the raritie, are nourfed in some few of their gardens that delight in such rarities : for in regard of the tendernesse, there is neede of diligent care, that is, to plant it against a brick wall, and defend it conueniently from the sharpenesse of our winters, to giue his Master some pleasure in seeing it beare flowers : And of the double kinde we haue as yet obtained but one sort, although I shall giue you the knowledge and description of another.

1. *Malus Punica satina.* The tame Pomegranet tree.

This Pomegranet tree groweth not very high in his naturall places, and with vs sometimes it shooteth forth from the roote many brownish twigges or branches, or if it bee pruned from them, and suffered to grow vp, it riseth to bee seuen or eight foote high,

spreading

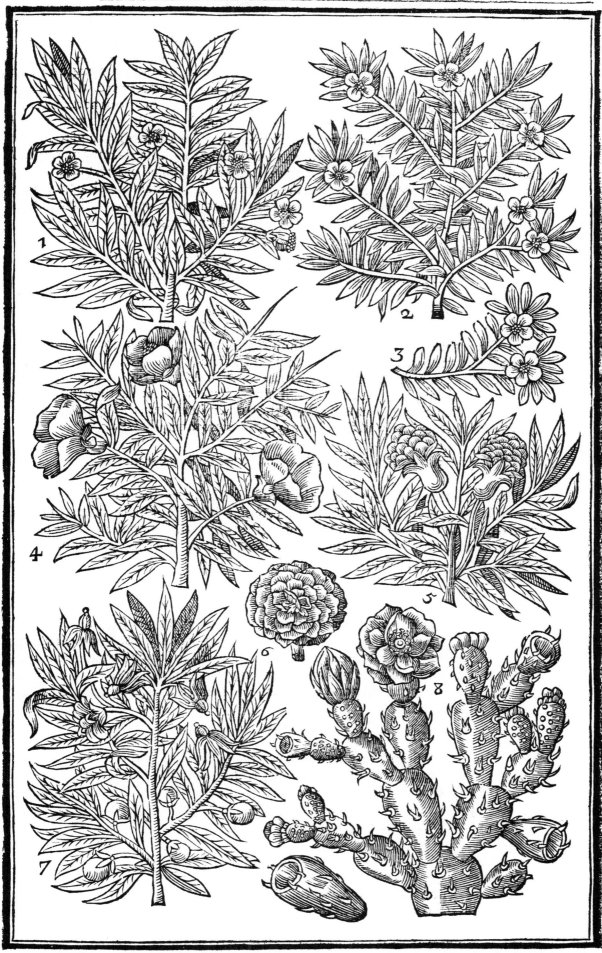

1 *Myrtus latifolia maior.* The broad leafed Myrtle. 2 *Myrtus angustifolia minor.* The small leafed Myrtle. 3 *Myrtus buxifolia minor.* The Boxe leafed Myrtle. 4 *Malus Granatus simplici flore.* The ordinary Pomegranet tree. 5 *Balaustium Romanum seu minus.* The lesser double flowred Pomegranet tree. 6 *Balaustium maius siue Cyprium.* The greater double flowred Pomegranet. 7 *Pseudocapsicum seu Amomum Plinij.* The Winter Cherry tree. 8 *Ficus Indica cum suo fructu.* The Indian Figgetree and his fruit.

spreading into many small and slender branches, here and there set with thornes, and with many very faire greene shining leaues, like in forme and bignesse vnto the leaues of the larger Myrtle before described, euery one hauing a small reddish foote-stalke vpon these branches : among the leaues come forth here and there, long, hard, and hollow reddish cups, diuided at the brimmes, wherein doe stand large single flowers, euery one consisting of one whole leafe, smaller at the bottome then at the brimme, like bels, diuided as it were at the edges into fiue or six parts, of an orient red or crimson colour in the hotter Countries; but in this it is much more delayed, and tendeth neare vnto a blush, with diuers threads in the middle. The fruit is great and round, hauing as it were a crowne on the head of it, with a thicke tough hard skinne or rinde, of a brownish red colour on the outside, and yellow within, stuffed or packt full of small graines, euery one encompast with a thin skin, wherein is contained a cleare red iuyce or liquor, either of a sweet (as I said before) or sower taste, or betweene them both of a winie taste : the roote disperseth it selfe very much vnder ground.

2. *Balaustium maius siue Malus Punica siluestris maior.*
The greater wilde or double blossomd Pomegranet tree.

The wilde Pomegranet is like vnto the tame in the number of purplish branches, hauing thornes, and shining faire greene leaues, somewhat larger then the former : from the branches likewise shoote forth flowers, farre more beautifull then those of the tame or manured sort, because they are double, and as large as a double Prouince Rose, or rather more double, of an excellent bright crimson colour, tending to a silken carnation, standing in brownish cups or huskes, diuided at the brims vsually into foure or fiue seuerall points, like vnto the former, but that in this kinde there neuer followeth any fruit, no not in the Country, where it is naturally wilde.

3. *Balaustium minus.* The smaller wilde Pomegranet tree.

This smaller kinde differeth from the former in his leaues, being of a darker greene colour, but not in the height of the stemme, or purplishnesse of his branches, or thorns vpon them; for this doth shew it selfe more like vnto a wilde kind then it : the flowers hereof are much smaller, and not so thicke and double, of a deeper or sadder red Orenge tawny colour, set also in such like cups or huskes.

The Place.

The tame or manured kinde groweth plentifully in Spaine, Portugall, and Italy, and other in other warme and hot countries. Wee (as I said before) preserue it with great care. The wilde I thinke was neuer seene in England, before Iohn Tradescante my very louing good friend brought it from the parts beyond the Seas, and planted it in his Lords Garden at Canterbury.

The Time.

They flower very late with vs, that is, not vntill the middle or end of August, and the cold euenings or frosts comming so soone vpon it, doth not onely hinder it from bearing, but many times the sharpe winters so pinch it, that it withereth it downe to the ground, so that oftentimes it hardly springeth againe.

The Names.

The name *Malus Punica* for the tree, and *Malum Punicum* for the fruit, or *Malus Granata*, and *Malum Granatum*, is the common name giuen vnto this tree, which is called in English the Pomegarnet or Pomegranet tree. The flowers of the tame kinde are called *Cytini*, as Dioscorides saith, although Plinie seemeth either to make *Cytinus* to be the flower of the wilde kinde, or

Balaustium

Balaustium to be the flower of both tame and wilde kinde : but properly, as I take it, *Cytinus* is the cup wherein the flower as well of the tame as wilde kinde doth stand ; for vnto the similitude of them, both the flowers of *Asarum*, and the seede vessels of *Hyosciamus* are compared and resembled, and not vnto the whole flower : the barke or rinde of the fruit is called of diuers *Sidion*, and in the Apothecaries shops *Psidium*, and *cortex Granatorum*. The wilde kinde is called *Malus Punica siluestris* : In English, The wilde Pomegranet tree ; the flower thereof is properly called *Balaustium*. The lesser kind is vsually called *Balaustium Romanum*, as the greater is called *Creticum* and *Cyprinum*, because they growe in Candy and Cyprus.

The Vertues.

The vse of all these Pomegranets is very much in Physicke, to coole and binde all fluxibility both of body and humours : they are also of singular effect in all vlcers of the mouth, and other parts of the body, both of man and woman. There is no part of them but is applyed for some of these respects. The rinde also of the Pomegranet is vsed of diuers in stead of Gaules, to make the best sort of writing Inke, which is durable to the worlds end.

Chap. CXV.

Amomum Plinij seu Pseudocapsicum.
Tree Night shade or the Winter Cherry tree.

IHaue adioyned this plant, for the pleasurable beauty of the greene leaues, and red berries. It groweth vp to be a yard or foure foote high at the most, hauing a small wooddy stemme or stocke, as bigge as ones finger or thumbe, couered with a whitish greene barke, set full of greene branches, and faire greene leaues, somewhat vneuen sometimes on the edges, narrower then any Night shade leaues, and very neare resembling the leaues of the *Capsicum*, or Ginny pepper, but smaller and narrower, falling away in the Winter, and shooting fresh in the Spring of the yeare : the flowers growe often two or three together, at the ioynts of the branches with the leaues, being white, opening starre-fashion, and sometimes turning themselues backe, with a yellow pointell in the middle, very like vnto the flowers of Night shade : after the flowers are past, come forth in their stead small greene buttons, which after turne to be pleasant round red berries, of the bignesse of small Cherries when they are ripe, which with vs vsually ripen not vntill the Winter, or about Christmas, wherein are contained many small whitish seede that are flat : all the whole plant, as well leaues and flowers as seede, are without either smell or taste : the roote hath many yellowish strings and fibres annexed vnto it.

The Place.

The originall place hereof is not well knowne, but is thought to bee the West Indies. It hath been planted of long time in most of these Countries, where it abideth reasonable well, so that some care bee had thereof in the extreamity of the Winter.

The Time.

It flowreth sometimes in Iune, but vsually in Iuly and August, and the fruit is not ripe (as is said) vntill the Winter.

The

The Names.

This plant hath diuers names ; for it is thought to be that kinde of *Amomum* that Plinie setteth downe.   Dodonæus calleth it *Pseudocapsicum*, for some likenesse in the leafe and fruit vnto the small *Capsicum* or Ginnie Pepper, although much vnlike in the taste and property.   Others doe call it *Strichnodendron*, that is, *Solanum arborescens*, and wee in English according thereunto, Tree Night shade.   But some Latine asses corrupting the Latine word *Amomum*, doe call it the Mumme tree. Dalechampius calleth it *Solanum Americum, seu Indicum*, and saith the Spaniards call it in their tongue, *Guindas de las Indias*, that is, *Cerasa Indiana*, Indian Cherries, which if any would follow, I would not bee much against it : but many Gentlewomen doe call them Winter Cherries, because the fruit is not throughly ripe vntill Winter.

The Vertues.

I finde no Physicall property allotted vnto it, more then that by reason of the insipidity, it is held to be cooling.

Chap. CXVI.

Ficus Indica minor. The smaller Indian Figge tree.

THis Indian Figge tree, if you will call it a tree (because in our Country it is not so, although it groweth in the naturall hot Countries from a wooddy stemme or body into leaues) is a plant consisting only of leaues, one springing out of another, into many branches of leaues, and all of them growing out of one leafe, put into the ground halfe way, which taking roote, all the rest rise out thereof, those belowe for the most part being larger then those aboue ; yet all of them somewhat long, flat, and round pointed, of the thicknesse of a finger vsually, and smallest at the lower end, where they are ioyned or spring out of the other leaues, hauing at their first breaking out a shew of small, red, or browne prickes, thicke set ouer all the vpper side of the leaues, but with vs falling away quickly, leauing onely the markes where they stood : but they haue besides this shew of great prickes, a few very fine, and small, hard, white, and sharpe, almost insensible prickes, being not so bigge as haires on the vnderside, which will often sticke in their fingers that handle them vnaduisedly, neither are they to be discerned vnlesse one look precisely for them: the leaues on the vnderside hauing none of those other great pricks or marks at all, being of a faire fresh pale green colour: out of the vppermost leaues breake forth certaine greene heads, very like vnto leaues (so that many are deceiued, thinking them to be leaues, vntill they marke them better, and be better experienced in them) but that they growe round and not flat, and are broad at the toppe ; for that out of the tops of euery of them shooteth out a pale yellow flower, consisting of two rowes of leaues, each containing fiue leaues a peece, laid open with certaine yellow threads, tipt with red in the middle : this greene head, vntill the flower be past, is not of halfe that bignesse that it attaineth vnto after, yet seldome or neuer commeth vnto perfection with vs, being long and round, like vnto a Figge, small belowe, and greater aboue, bearing vpon the flat or broad head the marke of the flower ; some holding still on them the dryed leaues, and others hauing lost them, shew the hollownesse which they haue in the toppe or middle of the head, the sides round about being raised or standing vp higher : this head or figge in our Country abideth greene on the outside, and little or nothing reddish within (although it abide all the Winter, and the Summer following, as sometimes it doth) for want of that heate and comfort of the Sunne it hath in his naturall place, where it groweth
reddish

reddiſh on the outſide, and containing within it a bloudy red clammy iuyce, making the vrine of them that eate of them as red as bloud, which many ſeeing, were in doubt of themſelues, leſt their vrine were not very bloud; of what ſweetneſſe, like a figge, in the naturall places, I am not well aſſured, yet affirmed: but thoſe that haue beene brought vnto me, whoſe colour on the outſide was greeniſh, were of a reddiſh purple within, and contained within them round, ſmall, hard ſeede, the taſte was flat, wateriſh, or inſipide: the roote is neither great, nor diſperſeth it ſelfe very deepe or farre, but ſhooteth many ſmall rootes vnder the vpper cruſt of the earth.

There is a greater kinde hereof, whoſe leaues are twice or thrice as bigge, which hauing been often brought vs, will ſeldome abide more then one Summer with vs, our Winters alwaies rotting the leaues, that it could not be longer kept.

The Place.

This Indian Figge tree groweth diſperſedly in many places of America, generally called the Weſt Indies: The greater kinde in the more remote and hot Countries, as Mexico, Florida, &c. and in the Bermudas or Summer Iſlands, from whence wee haue often had it. The leſſer in Virginia, and thoſe other Countries that are nearer vnto vs, which better endureth with vs.

The Time.

It flowreth with vs ſometimes in May, or Iune; but (as I ſaid) the fruit neuer commeth to perfection in this Country.

The Names.

Diuers doe take it to bee *Opuntia Pliny*, whereof hee ſpeaketh in the 21. Booke and 17. Chapter of his Naturall Hiſtory: but he there ſaith, *Opuntia* is an herbe, ſweete and pleaſant to be eaten, and that it is a wonder that the roote ſhould come from the leafe, and ſo to growe; which words although they deſcipher out the manner of the growing of this plant, yet becauſe this is a kinde of tree, and not an herbe, nor to be eaten, it cannot bee the ſame: but eſpecially becauſe there is an herbe which groweth in the ſame manner, or very neare vnto it, one leafe ſtanding on the toppe or ſide of another, being a Sea plant, fit to be eaten with vinegar and oyle (as many other herbes are that growe in the ſalt marſhes, or neare the Sea, whereof Sea Purſlane is one) which Cluſius calleth *Lychen Marinus*, and (as Cluſius ſaith) Cortuſus very fitly called *Opuntia marina*, and out of doubt is the verie ſame *Opuntia* that Theophraſtus maketh mention of, and Plinie out of him. Our Engliſh people in Virginia, and the Bermuda Iſland, where it groweth plentifully, becauſe of the form of the fruit, which is ſomewhat like to a Peare, & not being ſo familiarly acquainted with the growing of Figs, ſent it vnto vs by the name of the prickly Peare, from which name many haue ſuppoſed it to be a Peare indeede, but were therein deceiued.

The Vertues.

There is no other eſpeciall property giuen hereunto, by any that haue written of the Weſt Indies, then of the colouring of the vrine, as is before ſaid.

Chap. CXVII.

Yuca sine Iucca. The supposed Indian Iucca.

THis rare Indian plant hath a great thicke tuberous roote (spreading in time into many tuberous heads) from the head whereof shooteth forth many long, hard, and guttured leaues, very sharpe pointed, compassing as it were one another at the bottome, of a grayish greene colour, which doe not fall away, but abide euer greene on the plant; from the middle whereof springeth forth (now and then, but not euery yeare) a strong round stalke, diuided into diuers branches, whereon stand diuers white, and somewhat large flowers, hanging downe their heads, consisting of six leaues, with diuers veines, of a weake reddish or blush colour, spread on the backe of the three outer leaues, especially from the middle of the leaues to the bottome, and not rising to the edge of the leafe of any flower, which fall away without bearing any seede in our Country, as farre as euer could be obserued either in the plant that Master Gerard kept a long time by him, or by Robinus at Paris his plant, which Master Gerard sent vnto him, or yet by that plant, that Vespasian Robin the sonne of old Robin sent vnto Master Iohn de Franqueuille, and now abideth and flourisheth in my Garden.

The Place.

It was first brought into England (as Master Gerard saith) from the West Indies, by a seruant of Master Thomas Edwards, an Apothecary of Exeter, and imparted to him, who kept it vnto his death: but perished with him that got it from his widow, intending to send it to his Country house.

The Time.

It flowreth not vntill Iuly, and the flowers fall away sodainely, after they haue beene blowne open a while.

The Names.

Master Gerard first as I thinke called it *Iucca*, supposing it to bee the true *Yuca* of *Theuet*, wherewith the Indians make bread, called *Cassaua*: but the true *Iucca* is described to haue a leafe diuided into seuen or nine parts, which this hath not: Yet not knowing by what better name to call it, let it hold still his first imposition, vntill a fitter may be giuen it.

The Vertues.

Wee haue not heard of any, that hath either read, heard, or experimented the faculties hereof, nor yet whether it hath good or euill taste; for being rare, and possessed but by a few, they that haue it are loth to cut any thereof, for feare of spoiling and losing the whole roote.
Some haue affirmed, that in some parts of Turkie, where as they say this plant groweth, they make a kinde of cloth from the threads are found running through the leaues; but I finde the threads are so strong and hard, that this cannot be that plant the relators meane is vsed in that manner.

1 *Yuca siue Iucca.* The Indian Iucca. 2 *Arbor vitæ.* The tree of life. 3 *Arbor Iudæ.* Iudas tree. 4 *Laburnum.* Beane Trefoile.
5 *Cytisus.* Tree Trefoile.

Chap. CXVIII.

Arbor vitæ. The tree of life.

THe tree of life riseth vp in some places where it hath stood long, to be a tree of a reasonable great bignesse and height, couered with a redder barke then any other tree in our Country that I know, the wood whereof is firme and hard, and spreadeth abroad many armes and branches, which againe send forth many smaller twigges, bending downewards; from which twiggy or slender branches, being flat themselues like the leaues, come forth on both sides many flat winged leaues, somewhat like vnto Sauine, being short and small, but not pricking, seeming as if they were brayded or folded like vnto a lace or point, of a darke yellowish greene colour, abiding greene on the branches Winter and Summer, of a strong resinous taste, not pleasing to most, but in some ready to procure casting, yet very cordiall and pectorall also to them that can endure it: at the toppes of the branches stand small yellowish dounie flowers, set in small scaly heads, wherein lye small, long, brownish seede, which ripen well in many places, and being sowne, doe spring and bring forth plants, which with some small care will abide the extreamest Winters we haue.

The Place.

The first or originall place where it naturally groweth, as farre as I can learne or vnderstand, is that part of America which the French doe inhabite, about the riuer of Canada, which is at the backe of Virginia Northward, and as it seemeth, first brought by them from thence into Europe, in the time of Francis the first French King, where it hath so plentifully encreased, and so largely beene distributed, that now few Gardens of respect, either in France, Germany, the Lowe-Countries, or England, are without it.

The Time.

It flowreth in the end of May, and in Iune; the fruit is ripe in the end of August and Sptember.

The Names.

All the Writers that haue written of it, since it was first knowne, haue made it to be *Thuyæ genus,* a kinde of Thuya, which Theophrastus compareth vnto a Cypresse tree, in his fifth Book and fifth Chapter: but *Omne simile non est idem,* and although it haue some likenesse, yet I verily beleeue it is *proprium sui genus,* a proper kinde of it owne, not to bee paralleld with any other. For wee finde but very few trees, herbes, or plants in America, like vnto those that growe in Europe, the hither part of Africa, or in the lesser Asia, as experience testifieth. Some would make it to be *Cedrus Lycia,* but so it cannot be. The French that first brought it, called it *Arbor vitæ,* with what reason or vpon what ground I know not: but euer since it hath continued vnder the title of the Tree of life.

The Vertues.

It hath beene found by often experience, that the leaues hereof chewed in the morning fasting, for some few dayes together, haue done much good to diuers, that haue beene troubled with shortnesse of breath, and to helpe to expectorate thinne purulentous matter stuffing the lungs. Other properties I haue not heard that it hath; but doubtlesse, the hot resinous smell and taste tafte it hath, both while it is frefh, and after it hath beene long kept dry, doth euidently declare his tenuity of parts, a digefting and cleanfing quality it is poffeffed with, which if any induftrious would make tryall, hee fhould finde the effects.

CHAP. CXIX.

Arbor Iudæ. Iudas tree.

IVdas tree rifeth vp in fome places, where it ftandeth open from a wall, and alone free from other trees (as in a Garden at Battherfey, which fometimes agoe belonged to Mafter Morgan, Apothecary to the late Queene Elizabeth of famous memory) to be a very great and tall tree, exceeding any Apple tree in height, and equall in bigneffe of body thereunto (as my felfe can teftifie, being an eye witneffe thereof) when as it had many ftalkes of flowers, being in the bud, breaking out of the body of the tree through the barke in diuers places, when as there was no bough or branch near them by a yard at the leaft, or yet any leafe vpon the tree, which they gathered to put among other flowers, for Nofegayes) and in other places it groweth to bee but an hedge bufh, or plant, with many fuckers and fhootes from belowe, couered with a darke reddifh barke, the young branches being more red or purplifh: the flowers on the branches come forth before any fhew or budding of leaues, three or foure ftanding together vpon a fmall foote-ftalke, which are in fafhion like vnto Peafe bloffomes, but of an excellent deepe purplifh crimfon colour: after which come in their places fo many long, flat, large, and thinne cods, of a brownifh colour, wherein are contained fmall, blackifh browne, flat, and hard feede: the roote is great, and runneth both deepe, and farre fpreading in the earth: the leaues come forth by themfelues, euery one ftanding on a long ftalke, being hard & very round, like vnto the leafe of the largeft *Afarum,* but not fo thick, of a whitifh green on the vpper fide, and grayifh vnderneath, which fall away euery yeare, and fpring afrefh after the Spring is well come in, and the buds of flowers are fprung.

There is another of this kinde, growing in fome places very high, fomewhat like the former, and in other places alfo full of twiggy branches, which are greener then the former, as the leaues are likewife: the flowers of this kinde are wholly white, and the cods nothing fo red or browne, in all other things agreeing together. *Flore albo.*

The Place.

The former groweth plentifully in many places of Spaine, Italy, Prouence in France, and in many other places. The other hath beene fent vs out of Italy many times, and the feede hath fprung very well with vs, but it is fomewhat tender to keepe in the Winter.

The Time.

The flowers (as I faid) appeare before the leaues, and come forth in Aprill and May, and often fooner alfo, the leaues following fhortly after; but neither of them beareth perfect feede in our Country, that euer I could learne, or know by mine owne or others experience.

The Names.

Some would referre this to *Cercis,* whereof Theophraftus maketh mention in his firft Booke and eighteenth Chapter, among thofe trees that beare their fruit in cods, like as Pulfe doe: and hee remembreth it againe in the fourteenth Chapter of his third Booke, and maketh it not vnlike the white

Poplar tree, both in greatneffe and whiteneffe of the branches, with the leafe of an Iuie, without corners on the one part, cornered on the other, and fharpe pointed, greene on both fides almoft alike, hauing fo flender long footeftalkes that the leaues cannot ftand forthright, but bend downwards, with a more rugged barke then the white Poplar tree. Clufius thinketh this large defcription is but an ample defcription of the third kinde of Poplar, called *Lybica*, the Afpen tree, which Gaza tranflateth *Alpina* : but who fo will well confider it, fhall finde it neyther anfwerable to any Poplar tree, in that it beareth not cods as *Cercu* doth ; nor vnto this *Arbor Iudæ*, becaufe it beareth not white branches. Clufius faith alfo, that the learned of Mompelier in his time, referred it to *Colytea* of Theophraftus in his third booke and feuenteenth chapter, where he doth liken it to the leaues of the broadeft leafed Bay tree, but larger and rounder, green on the vpperfide, and whitifh vnderneath, and whereunto (as he faith) Theophraftus giueth cods in the fourteenth chapter of the fame third booke: and by the contracting of their defcriptions both together, faith, they agree vnto this Iudas tree. But I find fome doubts and differences in thefe places : for the *Colutæa* that Diofcorides mentioneth in the faid fourteenth chapter of his third booke, hath (as he faith there) a leafe like vnto the Willow, and therefore cannot bee the fame *Colutæa* mentioned in the feuenteenth chapter of the fame third book, which hath a broade Bay leafe : indeede hee giueth feede in cods : but that with broade Bay leaues is (as he faith) without eyther flower or fruite ; and befides all this, he faith the rootes are very yellow, which is not to bee found in this *Arbor Iudæ*, or Iudas tree: let others now iudge if thefe things can bee well reconciled together. Some haue for the likeneffe of the cods vnto Beane cods, called it *Fabago*. And Clufius called it *Siliqua filueftris*. It is generally in thefe dayes called *Arbor Iudæ*, and in Englifh after the Latine name, vntill a fitter may be had, Iudas tree.

The Vertues.

There is nothing extant in any Author of any Phyficall vfe it hath, neyther hath any later experience found out any.

Chap. CXX.

Laburnum. Beane Trefoile.

THere be three forts of thefe codded trees or plants, one neere refembling another, whereof *Anagyris* of Diofcorides is one. The other two are called *Laburnum* ; the larger whereof Matthiolus calleth *Anagyris altera*, and fo doe fome others alfo : the third is of the fame kinde with the fecond, but fmaller. I fhall not for this our Garden trouble you or my felfe with any more of them then one, which is the leffer of the two *Liburnum*, in that it is more frequent, and that it will far better abide then the *Anagyris*, which is fo tender, that it will hardly endure the winters of our Countrey : and the greater *Laburnum* is not fo eafily to be had.

Laburnum. Beane Trefoile.

This codded tree rifeth vp with vs like vnto a tall tree, with a reafonable great body, if it abide any long time in a place, couered with a fmooth greene barke; the branches are very long, greene, pliant, and bending any way, whereon are fet here and there diuers leaues, three alwaies ftanding together vpon a long ftalk, being fomwhat long, and not very narrow, pointed at the ends, greene on the vpperfide, and of a filuer fhining colour vnderneath, without any fmell at all : at the ioynts of thefe branches, where the leaues ftand, come forth many flowers, much like vnto broome flowers, but not fo

large

large or open, growing about a very long branch or ftalke, fometimes a good fpan or more in length, and of a faire yellow colour, but not very deepe ; after which come flat thin cods, not very long or broade, but as tough and hard as the cods of Broome; wherein are contained blackifh feede, like, but much leffe then the feede of *Anagyris vera* (which are as big as a kidney beane, purplifh and fpotted) : the roote thrufteth down deepe into the ground, fpreading alfo farre, and is of a yellowifh colour.

The Place.

This tree groweth naturally in many of the woods of Italie, and vpon the Alpes alfo, and is therefore ftill accounted to be that *Laburnum* that Plinie calleth *Arbor Alpina*. It groweth in many gardens with vs.

The Time.

It flowreth in May, the fruit or cods, and the feedes therein are ripe in the end of Auguft, or in September.

The Names.

This tree (as I faid before) is called of Matthiolus *Anagyris altera, fiue fecunda,* of Cordus, Gefner and others, efpecially of moft now adayes, *Laburnum*. It is probable in my opinion, that this fhould bee that *Colutea* of Theophraftus, mentioned in the fourteenth Chapter of his third book with the leafe of a Willow ; for if you take any one leafe by it felfe, it may well refemble a Willow leafe both for forme and colour, and beareth fmall feed in cods like vnto pulfe as that doth. Of fome it hath beene taken for a kinde of *Cytifus*, but not truely. We call it in Englifh, Beane Trefoile, in regard of his cods and feede therein, fomewhat like vnto Kidney Beanes, and of the leaues, three alwayes ftanding together, vntill a more proper name may bee giuen it.

The Vertues.

There is no vfe hereof in Phyficke with vs, nor in the naturall place of the growing, faue only to prouoke a vomit, which it will doe very ftrongly.

Chap. CXXI.

Cytifus. Tree Trefoile.

THere are fo many forts of *Cytifus* or Tree trefoiles, that if I fhould relate them all, I fhould weary the Reader to ouerlooke them, whereof the moft part pertaine rather to a generall worke then to this abftract. I fhall not therefore trouble you with any fuperfluous, but only with two, which we haue nourfed vp to furnifh wafte places in a garden.

Cytifus Marantha. Horned Tree Trefoile.

This Tree Trefoile which is held of moft Herbarifts to bee the true *Cytifus* of Diofcorides, rifeth vp to the height of a man at the moft, with a body of the bigneffe of a mans thumbe, couered with a whitifh bark, breaking forth into many whitifh branches fpreading farre, befet in many places with fmall leaues, three alwayes fet together vpon a fmall fhort footeftalke, which are rounder, and whiter then the leaues of Beane Trefoile : at the ends of the branches for the moft part, come forth the flowers three or foure togethers, of a fine gold colour, and of the fafhion of Broome flowers, but

not

not so large : after the flowers are past, there come in their places crooked flat thinne cods, of the fashion of a halfe moone, or crooked horne, whitish when they are ripe, wherein are contained blackish seede : the roote is hard and woody, spreading diuers wayes vnder the ground : the whole plant hath a pretty small hot sent.

Cytisus vulgatior. The common Tree Trefoile.

This *Cytisus* is the most common in this Land, of any the other sorts of tree trefoiles, hauing a blackish colourd barke, the stemme or body whereof is larger then the former, both for height and spreading, bearing also three leaues together, but smaller and greener then the former : the flowers are smaller, but of the same fashion and colour: the cods blackish and thin, and not very long, or great, but lesser then Broome cods, wherein there lyeth small blackish hard seede : the roote is diuersly dispersed in the ground.

The Place.

The first groweth in the kingdome of Naples, and no doubt in many other places of Italie, as Matthiolus saith. The other groweth in diuers places of France.

The Time.

They flower for the most part in May or Iune : the seede is ripe in August or September.

The Names.

The first (as I said) is thought of most to be the true *Cytisus* of Dioscorides, and as is thought, was in these later dayes first found by Bartholomæus Maranta of Naples, who sent it first to Matthiolus, and thereupon hath euer since beene called after his name, *Cytisus Maranthæ.* Some doe call it *Cytisus Lunatus,* because the cods are made somewhat like vnto an halfe Moone. We call it in English, Horned Tree Trefoile. The other is called *Cytisus vulgaris* or *vulgatior;* in English, The common Tree Trefoile, because we haue not any other so common.

The Vertues.

The chiefest vertues that are appropriate to these plants, are to procure milke in womens breasts, to fatten pullen, sheep &c. and to be good for bees.

CHAP. CXXII.

Colutea. The Bastard Sena Tree.

WEe haue in our Gardens two or three sorts of the Bastard Sena tree ; a greater as I may so call it, and two lesser : the one with round thin transparent skins like bladders, wherein are the seede : the others with long round cods, the one bunched out or swelling in diuers places, like vnto a Scorpions tale, wherein is the seede, and the other very like vnto it, but smaller.

1. *Colutea Vesicaria.* The greater Bastard Sena with bladders.

This shrub or tree, or shrubby tree, which you please to call it riseth vnto the height of a pretty tree, the stemme or stock being sometimes of the bignesse of a mans arme, couered with a blackish greene rugged barke, the wood whereof is harder then of an
Elder,

Elder, but with an hollowneſſe like a pith in the heart or middle of the branches, which are diuided many wayes, and whereon are ſet at ſeuerall diſtances, diuers winged leaues, compoſed of many ſmall round pointed, or rather flat pointed leaues, one ſet againſt another, like vnto Licoris, or the Hatchet Fitch ; among theſe leaues come forth the flowers, in faſhion like vnto Broome flowers, and as large, of a very yellow colour : after which appeare cleare thinne ſwelling cods like vnto thinne tranſparent bladders, wherein are contained blacke ſeede, ſet vpon a middle ribbe or ſinew in the middle of the bladder, which if it be a little cruſhed betweene the fingers, will giue a cracke, like as a bladder full of winde. The roote groweth branched and woody.

2. *Colutæa Scorpioides maior.* The greater Scorpion podded Baſtard Sena.

This Baſtard Sena groweth nothing ſo great or tall, but ſhooteth out diuerſly, like vnto a ſhrub, with many ſhoots ſpringing from the root : the branches are greener, but more rugged, hauing a white barke on the beſt part of the elder growne branches ; for the young are greene, and haue ſuch like winged leaues ſet on them as are to be ſeen in the former, but ſmaller, greener, and more pointed : the flowers are yellow, but much ſmaller, faſhioned ſomewhat like vnto the former, with a reddiſh ſtripe downe the backe of the vppermoſt leafe : the long cods that follow are ſmall, long and round, diſtinguiſhed into many diuiſions or dents, like vnto a Scorpions tayle, from whence hath riſen the name : in theſe ſeuerall diuiſions lye ſeuerall blacke ſeede, like vnto the ſeede of Fenigrecke : the roote is white and long, but not ſo woody as the former.

3. *Colutæa Scorpioides minor.* The leſſer Scorpion Baſtard Sena.

This leſſer Baſtard Sena is in all things like the former, but ſomewhat lower, and ſmaller both in leafe, flower, and cods of ſeede, which haue not ſuch eminent bunches on the cods to be ſeene as the former.

The Place.

They grow as Matthiolus ſaith about Trent in Italie, and in other places : the former is frequent enough through all our Countrey, but the others are more rare.

The Time.

They flower about the middle or end of May, and their ſeede is ripe in Auguſt. The bladders of the firſt will abide a great while on the tree, if they be ſuffered, and vntill the winde cauſe them to rattle, and afterwards the skins opening, the ſeed will fall away.

The Names.

The name *Colutæa* is impoſed on them, and by the iudgement of moſt writers, the firſt is taken to bee that *Colutæa* of *Lipara* that Theophraſtus maketh mention of, in the ſeuenteenth chapter of his third booke. But I ſhould rather thinke that the *Scorpioides* were the truer *Colutæa* of Theophraſtus, becauſe the long pods thereof are more properly to bee accounted *ſiliquæ*, then the former which are *veſicæ tumentes*, windy bladders, and not *ſiliquæ* : and no doubt but Theophraſtus would haue giuen ſome peculiar note of difference if he had meant thoſe bladders, and not theſe cods. Let others of iudgement be vmpeeres in this caſe ; although I know the currant of writers ſince Matthiolus, doe all hold the former *Colutæa veſicaria* to be the true *Colutæa Liparæ* of Theophraſtus. Wee call it in Engliſh, Baſtard Sena, from Ruellius, who as I thinke firſt called it Sena, from the forme of the leaues. The ſecond and third (as I ſaid before) from the forme of the cods receiued their names, as it is in the titles and deſcriptions ; yet they may as properly be called *Siliquoſæ*, for that their fruite are long cods.

The

The Vertues.

Theophraſtus ſaith it doth wonderfully helpe to fatten ſheepe : But ſure it is found by experience,that if it be giuen to man it cauſeth ſtrong caſtings both vpwards and downwards ; and therefore let euery one beware that they vſe not this in ſteede of good Sena, leſt they feele to their coſt the force thereof.

CHAP. CXII.

Spartum Hiſpanicum frutex. Spaniſh Broome.

ALthough Cluſius and others haue found diuers ſorts of this ſhrubby Spartum or Spaniſh Broome, yet becauſe our Climate will nourſe vp none of them,and euen this very hardly, I ſhall leaue all others, and deſcribe vnto you this one only in this manner : Spaniſh Broome groweth to bee fiue or ſixe foote high, with a woody ſtemme below, couered with a darke gray,or aſh-coloured barke, and hauing aboue many pliant, long and ſlender greene twigs, whereon in the beginning of the yeare are ſet many ſmall long greene leaues,which fall away quickly,not abiding long on ; towards the tops of theſe branches grow the flowers, faſhioned like vnto Broom flowers,but larger, as yellow as they,and ſmelling very well ; after which come ſmall long cods, creſted at the backe, wherein is contained blackiſh flat ſeede, faſhioned very like vnto the Kidney beanes: the roote is woody,diſperſing it ſelfe diuers waies.

The Place.

This groweth naturally in many places of France, Spaine and Italie,wee haue it as an ornament in our Gardens, among other delightfull plants, to pleaſe the ſenſes of ſight and ſmelling.

The Time.

It flowreth in the end of May,or beginning of Iune, and beareth ſeede, which ripeneth not with vs vntill it be late.

The Names.

It is called *Spartium Græcorum,* and *Spartum frutex,* to diſtinguiſh it from the ſedge or ruſh, that is ſo called alſo. Of ſome it is called *Geniſta,* and thought not to differ from the other *Geniſta,* but they are much deceiued ; for euen in Spaine and Italie,the ordinary *Ganiſta* or Broome groweth with it, which is not pliant, and fit to binde Vínes, or ſuch like things withall as this is.

The Vertues.

There is little vſe hereof in Phyſicke, by reaſon of the dangerous quali-tie of vomiting, which it doth procure to them that take it inwardly : but being applyed outwardly, it is found to helpe the *Sciatica,* or paine of the hippes.

1 *Colutea vulgaris.* Ordinary baſtard Sene. 2 *Periploca recta Virginiana.* Virginian Silke. 3 *Colutea Scorpioides.* Scorpion baſtard
Sene. 4 *Spartum Hiſpanicum.* Spaniſh Broome. 5 *Liguſtrum.* Priuet. 6 *Saluia variegata.* Party coloured Sage. 7 *Maiorana aurea.*
Guilded Maierome.

Chap. CXXIIII.

Periploca recta Virginiana. Virginian Silke.

LEft this stranger should finde no hospitality with vs, being so beautifull a plant, or not finde place in this Garden, let him be here receiued, although with the last, rather then not at all. It riseth vp with one or more strong and round stalkes, three or foure foote high, whereon are set at the seuerall ioynts thereof two faire, long, and broad leaues, round pointed, with many veines therein, growing close to the stemme, without any foote-stalke: at the tops of the stalkes, and sometimes at the ioynts of the leaues, groweth forth a great bush of flowers out of a thinne skinne, to the number of twenty, and sometimes thirty or forty, euery one with a long foote-stalke, hanging downe their heads for the most part, especially those that are outermost, euery one standing within a small huske of greene leaues, turned to the stalkeward, like vnto the Lysimachia flower of Virginia before described, and each of them consisting of fiue small leaues a peece, of a pale purplish colour on the vpperside, and of a pale yellowish purple vnderneath, both sides of each leafe being as it were folded together, making them seeme hollow and pointed, with a few short chiues in the middle: after which come long and crooked pointed cods standing vpright, wherein are contained flat brownish seede, dispersedly lying within a great deale of fine, soft, and whitish browne silke, very like vnto the cods, seede, and silke of *Asclepias,* or Swallow-wort, but that the cods are greater and more crooked, and harder also in the outer shell: the roote is long and white, of the bignesse of a mans thumbe, running vnder ground very far, and shooting vp in diuers places, the heads being set full of small white grumes or knots, yeelding forth many branches, if it stand any time in a place: the whole plant, as well leaues as stalkes, being broken, yeeld a pale milke.

The Place.

It came to me from Virginia, where it groweth aboundantly, being raised vp from the seede I receiued.

The Time.

It flowreth in Iuly, and the seede is ripe in August.

The Names.

It may seeme very probable to many, that this plant is the same that Prosper Alpinus in the twenty fift Chapter of his Booke of Egyptian plants, nameth *Beidelsar;* and Honorius Bellus in his third and fourth Epistles vnto Clusius (which are at the end of his History of plants) calleth *Ossar frutex:* And Clusius himselfe in the same Booke calleth *Apocynum Syriacum, Palastinum,* and *Ægyptiacum,* because this agreeth with theirs in very many and notable parts; yet verily I thinke this plant is not the same, but rather another kinde of it selfe: First, because it is not *frutex,* a shrub or wooddy plant, nor keepeth his leaues all the yeare, but loseth both leaues and stalks, dying downe to the ground euery yeare: Secondly, the milke is not causticke or violent, as Alpinus and Bellus say *Ossar* is: Thirdly, the cods are more crooked then those of Clusius, or of Alpinus, which Honorius Bellus acknowledgeth to be right, although greater then those he had out of Egypt: And lastly, the rootes of these doe runne, whereof none of them make any mention. Gerard in his Herball giueth a rude figure of the plant, but a very true figure of the cods with seede, and saith the Virginians call it *wisanck,* and referreth it to the *Asclepias,* for the likenesse of the cods stuffed with

silken

filken doune. But what reafon Cafpar Bauhinus in his *Pinax Theatri Botanici* had, to call it (for it is Clufius his *Apocynum Syriacum*) by the name of *Lapathum Ægyptiacum lactefcens filiqua Afclepiadis*, I know none in the world: for but that he would fhew an extreame fingularity in giuing names to plants, contrary to all others (which is very frequent with him) how could he thinke, that this plant could haue any likeneffe or correfpondencie, with any of the kindes of Dockes, that euer he had feene, read, or heard of, in face, or fhew of leaues, flowers, or feede; but efpecially in giuing milke. I haue you fee (and that not without iuft and euident caufe) giuen it a differing Latine name from Gerard, becaufe the *Afclepias* giueth no milke, but the *Periploca* or *Apocynum* doth; and therefore fitter to be referred to this then to that. And becaufe it fhould not want an Englifh name anfwerable to fome peculiar property thereof, I haue from the filken doune called it Virginian Silke: but I know there is another plant growing in Virginia, called Silke Graffe, which is much differing from this.

The Vertues.

I know not of any in our Land hath made any tryall of the properties hereof. Captaine Iohn Smith in his booke of the difcouery and defcription of Virginia, faith, that the Virginians vfe the rootes hereof (if his be the fame with this) being bruifed and applyed to cure their hurts & difeafes.

Chap. CXXV.

Liguftrum. Primme or Priuet.

Becaufe the vfe of this plant is fo much, and fo frequent throughout all this Land, although for no other purpofe but to make hedges or arbours in Gardens, &c. whereunto it is fo apt, that no other can be like vnto it, to bee cut, lead, and drawne into what forme one will, either of beafts, birds, or men armed, or otherwife: I could not forget it, although it be fo well knowne vnto all, to be an hedge bufh growing from a wooddy white roote, fpreading much within the ground, and bearing manie long, tough, and plyant fprigs and branches, whereon are fet long, narrow, and pointed fad greene leaues by couples at euery ioynt: at the tops whereof breake forth great tufts of fweete fmelling white flowers, which when they are fallen, turne into fmall blacke berries, hauing a purple iuyce within them, and fmall feede, flat on the one fide, with an hole or dent therein: this is feene in thofe branches that are not cut, but fuffered to beare out their flowers and fruit.

The Place.

This bufh groweth as plentifully in the Woods of our owne Couutrey, as in any other beyond the Seas.

The Time.

It flowreth fometimes in Iune, and in Iuly; the fruit is ripe in Auguft and September.

The Names.

There is great controuerfie among the moderne Writers concerning this plant, fome taking it to be χύπρ@ of Diofcorides, other to be *Phillyrea* of Diofcorides, which followeth next after *Cyprus*. Plinie maketh mention of *Cyprus* in two places; in the one he faith, *Cyprus* hath the leafe of *Ziziphus*, or the Iuiube tree: in the other he saith, that certain do affirme, that the *Cyprus* of the East Country, and the *Ligustrum* of Italy is one and the same plant: whereby you may plainly see, that our Priuet which is *Ligustrum*, cannot be that *Cyprus* of Plinie with Iuiube leaues: Besides, both Dioscorides & Plinie say, that *Cyprus* is a tree; but all know that *Ligustrum*, Priuet, is but an hedge bush: Againe, Dioscorides saith, that the leaues of *Cyprus* giue a red colour, but Priuet giueth none. Bellonius and Prosper Alpinus haue both recorded, that the true *Cyprus* of Dioscorides groweth plentifully in Egypt, Syria, and those Easterne Countries, and noursed vp also in Constantinople, and other parts of Greece, being a merchandise of much worth, in that they transport the leaues, and young branches dryed, which laid in water giue a yellow colour, wherewith the Turkish women colour the nailes of their hands, and some other parts of their bodies likewise, delighting much therein: and that it is not our *Ligustrum*, or Priuet, because *Cyprus* beareth round white seede, like Coriander seede, and the leaues abide greene alwaies vpon the tree, which groweth (if it bee not cut or pruined) to the height of the Pomegranet tree. I haue (I confesse) beyond the limits I set for this worke spoken concerning our Priuet, because I haue had the seede of the true *Cyprus* of Dioscorides sent mee, which was much differing from our Priuet, and although it sprang vp, yet would not abide any time, whereas if it had beene our Priuet, it would haue beene familiar enough to our Countrey.

The Vertues.

It is of small vse in physicke, yet some doe vse the leaues in Lotions, that serue to coole and dry fluxes or sores in diuers parts.

Chap. CXXVI.

Saluia variegata. Party coloured Sage. And
Maiorana versicolor siue aurea. Yellow or golden Marierome.

VNto all these flowers of beauty and rarity, I must adioyne two other plants, whose beauty consisteth in their leaues, and not in their flowers: as also to separate them from the others of their tribe, to place them here in one Chapter, before the sweete herbes that shall follow, as is fittest to furnish this our Garden of pleasure. This kinde of Sage groweth with branches and leaues, very like the ordinary Sage, but somewhat smaller, the chiefest difference consisteth in the colour of the leaues, being diuersly marked and spotted with white and red among the greene: for vpon one branch you shall haue the leaues seuerally marked one from another, as the one halfe of the leafe white, and the other halfe greene, with red shadowed ouer them both, or more white then greene, with some red in it, either parted or shadowed, or dasht here and there, or more greene then white, and red therein, eyther in the middle or end of the leafe, or more or lesse parted or striped with white and red in the greene, or else sometimes wholly greene the whole branch together, as nature listeth to play with such varieties: which manner of growing rising from one and the same plant, because it is the more variable, is the more delightfull and much respected.

There is another speckled Sage parted with white and greene, but it is nothing of that beauty to this, because this hath three colours euidently to bee discerned in euery leafe almost, the red adding a superaboundant grace to the rest.

Maiorana aurea siue versicolor. Yellow or golden Marierome.

This kinde of Marierome belongeth to that sort is called in Latine *Maiorana latifolia,*

lia, which Lobel fetteth forth for *Hyſſopus Græcorum genuina*: In Englifh Winter Marierome, or pot Marierome : for it hath broader and greater leaues then the fweete Marierome, and a different vmbell or tuft of flowers. The difference of this from that fet forth in the Kitchin Garden, confifteth chiefly in the leaues, which are in Summer wholly yellow in fome, or but a little greene, or parted with yellow and greene more or leffe, as nature lifteth to play : but in Winter they are of a darke or dead greene colour, yet recouering it felfe againe : the fent hereof is all one with the pot Marierome.

Wee haue another parted with white and greene, much after the manner with the former.

The Place, Time, Names, and Vertues of both thefe plants, fhall be declared where the others of their kindes are fpecified hereafter, and in the Kitchen Garden; for they differ not in properties.

CHAP. CXXVII.

Lauendula. Lauender Spike.

AFter all thefe faire and fweete flowers before fpecified, I muft needes adde a few fweete herbes, both to accomplifh this Garden, and to pleafe your fenfes, by placing them in your Nofegayes, or elfe where, as you lift. And although I bring them in the end or laft place, yet are they not of the leaft account.

1. *Lauendula maior.* Garden Lauender.

Our ordinary Garden Lauender rifeth vp with a hard wooddy ftemme aboue the ground, parted into many fmall branches, whereon are fet whitifh, long, and narrow leaues, by couples one againft another; from among which rifeth vp naked fquare ftalkes, with two leaues at a ioynt, and at the toppe diuers fmall huskes ftanding round about them, formed in long and round heads or fpikes, with purple gaping flowers fpringing out of each of them : the roote is wooddy, and fpreadeth in the ground : The whole plant is of a ftrong fweete fent, but the heads of flowers much more, and more piercing the fenfes, which are much vfed to bee put among linnen and apparrell.

There is a kinde hereof that beareth white flowers, and fomewhat broader leaues, *Flore albo.* but it is very rare, and feene but in few places with vs, becaufe it is more tender, and will not fo well endure our cold Winters.

2. *Lauendula minor feu Spica.* Small Lauender or Spike.

The Spike or fmall Lauender is very like vnto the former, but groweth not fo high, neither is the head or fpike fo great and long, but fhorter and fmaller, and of a more purplifh colour in the flower : the leaues alfo are a little harder, whiter, and fhorter then the former; the fent alfo is fomewhat fharper and ftronger. This is not fo frequent as the firft, and is nourifhed but in fome places that are warme, and where they delight in rare herbes and plants.

The Place.

Lauender groweth in Spaine aboundantly, in many places fo wilde, and little regarded, that many haue gone, and abiden there to diftill the oyle thereof whereof great quantity now commeth ouer from thence vnto vs : and alfo in Lanquedocke, and Prouence in France.

The Time.

It flowreth early in thofe hot Countries, but with vs not vntill Iune and Iuly. The

The Names.

It is called of some *Nardus Italica*, and *Lauendula*, the greater is called *Fæmina*, and the lesser *Mas*. We doe call them generally Lauender, or Lauender Spike, and the lesser Spike, without any other addition.

The Vertues.

Lauender is little vsed in inward physicke', but outwardly; the oyle for cold and benummed parts, and is almost wholly spent with vs, for to perfume linnen, apparrell, gloues, leather, &c. and the dryed flowers to comfort and dry vp the moisture of a cold braine.

Chap. CXXVIII.

Stæchas. Sticadoue, Cassidony, or French Lauender.

Cassidony that groweth in the Gardens of our Countrey, may peraduenture somewhat differ in colour, as well as in strength, from that which groweth in hotter Countries; but as it is with vs, it is more tender a great deale then Lauender, and groweth rather like an herbe then a bush or shrub, not aboue a foote and a halfe high, or thereabouts, hauing many narrow long greene leaues like Lauender, but softer and smaller, set at seuerall distances together about the stalkes, which spread abroad into branches: at the tops whereof stand long and round, and sometimes foure square heads, of a darke greenish purple colour, compact of many scales set together; from among which come forth the flowers, of a blewish purple colour, after which follow seede vessels, which are somewhat whitish when they are ripe, containing blackish browne seede within them: the roote is somewhat wooddy, and will hardly abide the iniuries of our cold Winters, except in some places onely, or before it haue flowred: The whole plant is somewhat sweete, but nothing so much as Lauender.

The Place.

Cassidony groweth in the Islands Stæchades, which are ouer against Marselles, and in Arabia also: we keep it with great care in our Gardens.

The Time.

It flowreth the next yeare after it is sowne, in the end of May, which is a moneth before any Lauender.

The Names.

It is called of some *Lauendula siluestris*, but most vsually *Stæchas*: in English, of some Stickadoue, or French Lauender; and in many parts of England, Cassidony.

The Vertues.

It is of much more vse in physicke then Lauender, and is much vsed for old paines in the head. It is also held to be good for to open obstructions, to expell melancholy, to cleanse and strengthen the liuer, and other inward parts, and to be a Pectorall also.

Chap. CXXIX.

Abrotanum fœmina siue Santolina. Lauender Cotton.

THis Lauender Cotton hath many wooddy, but brittle branches, hoary or of a whitish colour, whereon are set many leaues, which are little, long, and foure square, dented or notched on all edges, and whitish also : at the tops of these branches stand naked stalkes, bearing on euery one of them a larger yellow head or flower, then eyther Tansie or Maudeline, whereunto they are somewhat like, wherein is contained small darke coloured seede : the roote is hard, and spreadeth abroad with many fibres : the whole plant is of a strong sweete sent, but not vnpleasant, and is in many places planted in Gardens, to border knots with, for which it will abide to be cut into what forme you thinke best ; for it groweth thicke and bushy, very fit for such workes, besides the comely shew the plant it selfe thus wrought doth yeeld, being alwayes greene, and of a sweet sent ; but because it quickly groweth great, and will soon runne out of forme, it must be euery second or third yeare taken vp, and new planted.

The Place.

It is onely planted in Gardens with vs, for the vses aforesaid especially.

The Time.

It flowreth in Iuly, and standeth long in the hot time of the yeare in his colour, and so will doe, if it be gathered before it haue stood ouer long.

The Names.

Diuers doe call it as Matthiolus doth, *Abrotanum fœmina,* and *Santolina ;* and some call it *Chamæcyparissus,* because the leaues thereof, are somewhat like the leaues of the Cypresse tree : Wee call it in English generally Lauender Cotton.

The Vertues.

This is vsually put among other hot herbes, eyther into bathes, ointments, or other things, that are vsed for cold causes. The seede also is much vsed for the wormes.

Chap. CXXX.

Ocimum. Bassill.

BAssill is of two sorts (besides other kindes) for this our Garden, the one whereof is greater, the other lesse in euery part thereof, as shall be shewed.

1. *Ocimum Citratum.* Common Bassill.

Our ordinary Garden Bassill hath one stalke rising from the root, diuersly branched out, whereon are set two leaues alwayes at a ioynt, which are broad, somewhat round, and pointed, of a pale greene colour, but fresh, a little snipt or dented about the edges, and of a strong or heady sent, somewhat like a Pomecitron, as many haue compared it, and thereof call it *Citratum :* the flowers are small and white, standing at the tops of the branches, with two smal leaues at euery ioynt vnder them in some plants green, in o-

thers

thers browne vnder them : after which commeth blackifh feede : the roote perifheth at the firft approach of winter weather, and is to be new fowen euery yeare.

2. *Ocimum minimum fiue Gariophyllatum.* Bufh Bafill.

The bufh Bafill groweth not altogether fo high, but is thicker fpreade out into branches, whereon grow fmaller leaues, and thicker fet then the former, but of a more excellent and pleafant fmell by much : the flowers are white like the former, and the feede blacke alfo like it, and perifheth as fuddenly, or rather fooner then it, fo that it requireth more paines to get it, and more care to nourfe it, becaufe we feldome or neuer haue any feede of it.

Ocimum Indicum. Indian Bafill.

The Indian Bafill hath a fquare reddifh greene ftalke, a foote high or better, from the ioynts whereof fpreade out many branches, with broade fat leaues fet thereon, two alwayes together at the ioynt, one againft another, as other Bafils haue, but fomewhat deepely cut in on the edges, and oftentimes a little crumpled, ftanding vpon long reddifh footeftalkes, of a darke purple colour, fpotted with deeper purple fpots, in fome greater, in others leffer: the flowers ftand at the tops of the ftalkes fpike-fafhion, which are of a white colour, with reddifh ftripes and veines running through them, fet or placed in darke purple coloured hufkes : the feede is greater and rounder then the former, and fomewhat long withall : the roote perifheth in like manner as the other former doe. The whole plant fmelleth ftrong, like vnto the other Bafils.

The Place.

The two laft forts of Bafils are greater ftrangers in our Country then the firft which is frequent, and only fowen and planted in curious gardens. The laft came firft out of the Weft Indies.

The Time.

They all flower in Auguft, or Iuly at the fooneft, and that but by degrees, and not all at once.

The Names.

The firft is vfually called *Ocimum vulgare*, or *vulgatius*, and *Ocimum Citratum*. In Englifh, Common or Garden Bafill. The other is called *Ocimum minimum*, or *Gariophyllatum*, Cloue Bafill, or Bufh Bafill. The laft eyther of his place, or forme of his leaues, being fpotted and curled, or all, is called *Ocimum Indicum maculatum, latifolium & crifpum*. In Englifh according to the Latine, Indian Bafill, broade leafed Bafill, fpotted or curled Bafill, which you pleafe.

The Vertues.

The ordinary Bafill is in a manner wholly fpent to make fweet, or wafhing waters, among other fweet herbes, yet fometimes it is put into nofegayes. The Phyficall properties are, to procure a cheerefull and merry heart, wherunto the feede is chiefly vfed in pouder, &c. and is moft vfed to that, and to no other purpofe.

CAPK.

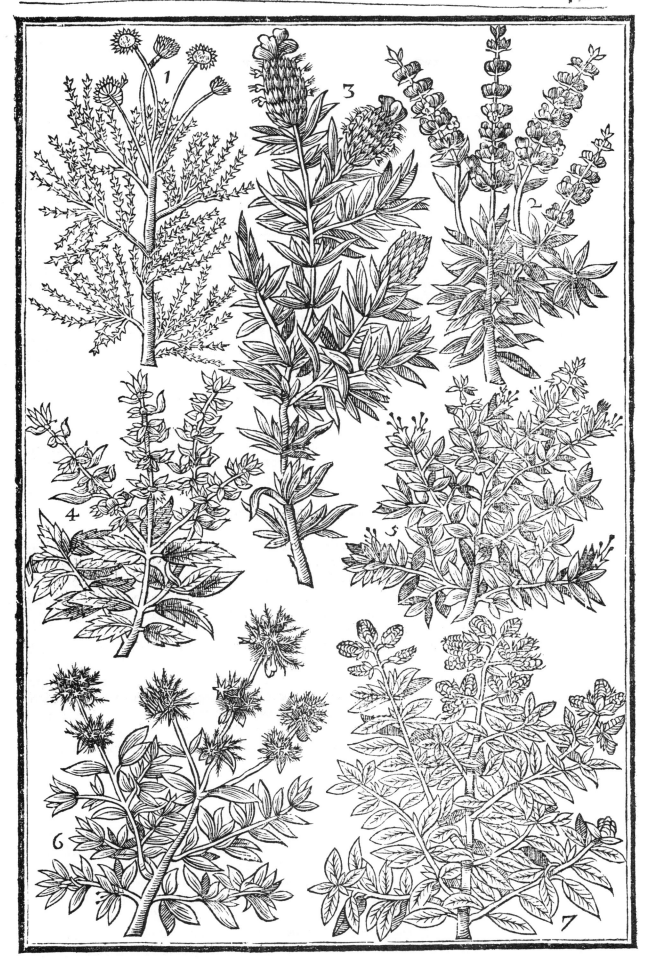

1 *Santolina*. Lauender Cotton. 2 *Lauendula*. Lauender Spike. 3 *Stœchas*. Caſſidony. 4 *Chamædrys*. Germander. 5 *Ocimum minus*. Fine Baſſill. 6 *Marum*. Herbe Maſticke. 7 *Maiorana*. Sweete Maricrome.

Chap. CXXXI.

Maiorana. Sweete Maricrome.

WEe haue many sorts of Maricrome ; some that are sweete, and but Summer plants ; others that are greater and not so sweet ; and some also that are wilde. Of all these I will onely select some of the choisest that are fit for this place, and leaue the other for the next garden, and the garden of simples, or a generall worke : yet hereunto I will adioyne another sweete plant called Masticke, as participating neerer with them then with Time, whereunto many doe referre it.

1. *Maiorana maior æstiua.* Common sweet Maricrome.

The sweet Maricrome that is most frequently sowen in our Country, is a low herbe little aboue a foote high when it is at the highest, full of branches, and small whitish soft roundish leaues, smelling very sweet : at the toppes of the branches stand diuers small scaly heads, like vnto knots, (and therefore of some called knotted Maricrome) of a whitish greene colour, out of which come here and there small white flowers, and afterwards small reddish seede : the roote is composed of many small threds or strings, which perish with the whole plant euery yeare.

2. *Maiorana tenuifolia.* Maricrome gentle.

This Maricrome hath likewise diuers small branches, growing low, and not higher then the former, but hauing finer and smaller leaues, hoary and soft, but much sweeter: the heads are like vnto the former, and so are the flowers and seede, and the whole plant abiding but a Summer in the like manner.

3. *Marum.* Herbe Masticke.

The neerer resemblance that this herbe hath with Maricrome then with Tyme (as I said before) hath made me place it next vnto the small sweet Maricrome. It riseth vp with a greater, and a more woody stalke then Maricrome, two foote high or better in some places, where it liketh the ground and ayre, branching out on all sides towards the vpper part, leauing the stemme bare below, if it bee old, otherwise being young, thinly furnishing the branches from the bottome with small greene leaues, bigger then the leaues of any Tyme, and comming neere vnto the bignesse and forme of the last recited finer Maricrome, but of a greener colour : at the toppes of the branches stand small white flowers on a head, which afterwards turne into a loose tuft of a long white hoary matter, like vnto soft doune, with some leaues vnderneath and about it, which abide not long on the stalkes, but are blowne away with the winde : the seede is so small if it haue any, that I haue not obserued it : the roote is threddy : the whole plant is of a sweete resinous sent, stronger then the Maricrome, and abideth our winters, if it be carefully planted and regarded.

The Place.

The sweete Maricromes grow naturally in hot Countreyes : the first in Spaine &c. the second is thought to come out of Syria, or Persia first into Italie, where they much esteeme it, and plant it curiously and carefully in pots, and set them in their windowes, beeing much delighted therewith for the sweet sent it hath. The first is vsually sowen euery yeare in most gardens with vs : but the second is very rare and daintie, and must as daintely be preserued, being more tender then the former. The herbe Masticke is thought to be first brought out of Candie, Clusius saith he found it in Spaine : It is planted by slippes, (and not sowen) in many gardens, and is much replanted
for

for increafe, but profpereth onely, or more frequently, in loamie or clay grounds then in any other foyle.

The Time.

The fweete Marieromes beare their knots or fcaly heads in the end of Iuly, or in Auguft. Herbe Mafticke in Iune many times, or in the beginning of Iuly.

The Names.

The firft of the two fweet Marieromes called *Maiorana* in Latine *à maiore cura*, is taken of moft writers to be the *Amaracus* or *Sampfuchum* of Diofcorides, Theophraftus and Plinie, although Galen doth feem a little to diffent therefrom. The other fweet Maricrome hath his name in his title as much as can be faid of it. The next is thought by the beft of the moderne Writers to be the true *Marum* that Galen preferreth for the excellent fweetneffe, before the former Maricrome in making the *Oleum*, or *vnguentum Amaricinum*, and feemeth to incline to their opinion that thought *Amaracus* was deriued from *Marum*. It is the fame alfo that Galen and others of the ancient Writers make mention of, to go into the compofition of the *Trochifci Hedychroi*, as well as *Amaracus* among the ingredients of the *Theriaca Andromachi*. In Englifh we call it Mafticke fimply, or Herbe Maftick, both to diftinguifh it from that Tyme that is called Mafticke Tyme, and from the Mafticke Tree, or Gum, fo called. Some of later times, and Clufius with them, haue thought this to be Diofcorides his *Tragoriganum*, which doth fomewhat refemble it : but there is another plant that Matthiolus fetteth forth for *Marum*, that in Lobels opinion and mine is the trueft *Tragoriganum*, and this the trueft *Marum*.

The Vertues.

The fweete Marieromes are not onely much vfed to pleafe the outward fenfes in nofegayes, and in the windowes of houfes, as alfo in fweete pouders, fweete bags, and fweete wafhing waters, but are alfo of much vfe in Phyficke, both to comfort the outward members, or parts of the body, and the inward alfo : to prouoke vrine being ftopped, and to eafe the paines thereof, and to caufe the feminine courfes. Herbe Mafticke is of greater force to helpe the ftopping of vrine, then the Maricrome, and is put into Antidotes, as a remedie againft the poyfon of venemous Beafts.

Chap. CXXXI.

Thymum. Tyme.

THere are many kindes of Tyme, as they are vfually called with vs, fome are called of the garden, and others wilde, which yet for their fweetneffe are brought into gardens, as Muske Tyme, and Lemon Tyme; and fome for their beauty, as embroidered or gold yellow Tyme, and white Tyme. But the true Tyme of the ancient Writers, called *Capitatum*, as a fpeciall note of diftinction from all other kindes of Tyme, is very rare to be feene with vs here in England, by reafon of the tenderneffe, that it will not abide our Winters. And all the other forts that with vs are called garden Tymes, are indeede but kindes of wilde Tyme, although in the defect or want of the true Tyme, they are vfed in the ftead of it. With the Tymes I muft doe as I did with the Marieromes in the Chapter before, that is, referue the moft common in vfe, for the common vfe of the Kitchen, and fhew you only thofe here, that are not put to that vfe : and firft with the true Tyme, becaufe it is knowne but to a few.

1, *Thymum*

1. *Thymum legitimum capitatum.* The true Tyme.

The true Tyme is a very tender plant, hauing hard and hoary brittle branches, spreading from a small wooddy stemme, about a foote and a halfe high, whereon are set at seuerall ioynts, and by spaces, many small, long, whitish, or hoary greene leaues, of a quicke sent and taste : at the tops of the branches stand small long whitish greene heads, somewhat like vnto the heads of *Stæchas*, made as it were of many leaues or scales, out of which start forth small purplish flowers (and in some white, as Bellonius saith) after which commeth small seede, that soone falleth out, and if it be not carefully gathered, is soone lost, which made (I thinke) Theophrastus to write, that this Tyme was to be sowne of the flowers, as not hauing any other seede : the root is small and wooddy. This holdeth not his leaues in Winter, no not about Seuill in Spaine, where it groweth aboundantly, as Clusius recordeth, finding it there naked or spoiled of leaues. And will not abide our Winters, but perisheth wholly, roote and all.

2. *Serpillum hortense siue maius.* Garden wilde Tyme.

The wilde Tyme that is cherished in gardens groweth vpright, but yet is lowe, with diuers slender branches, and small round greene leaues, somewhat like vnto small fine Marierome, and smelling somewhat like vnto it : the flowers growe in roundels at the toppes of the branches, of a purplish colour : And in another of this kinde they are of a pure white colour.

There is another also like hereunto, that smelleth somewhat like vnto Muske ; and therefore called Muske Tyme, whose greene leaues are not so small as the former, but larger and longer.

3. *Serpillum Citratum.* Lemon Tyme.

The wilde Tyme that smelleth like vnto a Pomecitron or Lemon, hath many weake branches trayling on the ground, like vnto the first described wilde Tyme, with small darke greene leaues, thinly or sparsedly set on them, and smelling like vnto a Lemon, with whitish flowers at the toppes in roundels or spikes.

4. *Serpillum aureum siue versicolor.* Guilded or embroidered Tyme.

This kinde of wilde Tyme hath small hard branches lying or leaning to the ground, with small party coloured leaues vpon them, diuided into stripes or edges, of a gold yellow colour, the rest of the leafe abiding greene, which for the variable mixture or placing of the yellow, hath caused it to be called embroidered or guilded Tyme.

The Place.

The first groweth as is said before, about Seuill in Spaine, in very great aboundance as Clusius saith; and as Bellonius saith, very plentifully on the mountaines through all Greece. The others growe some in this Country, and some in others : but wee preserue them with all the care wee can in our gardens, for the sweete and pleasant sents and varieties they yeeld.

The Time.

The first flowreth not vntill August; the rest in Iune and Iuly.

The Names.

Their names are seuerally set downe in their titles, as is sufficient to distinguish them ; and therefore I shall not neede to trouble you any further with them.

The

The Vertues.

The true Tyme is a speciall helpe to melancholicke and spleneticke diseases, as also to flatulent humours, either in the vpper or lower parts of the body. The oyle that is Chimically drawne out of ordinary Tyme, is vsed (as the whole herbe is, in the stead of the true) in pils for the head and stomach. It is also much vsed for the toothach, as many other such like hot oyles are.

Chap. CXXXII.

Hyssopus. Hyssope.

THere are many varieties of Hyssope, beside the common or ordinary, which I reserue for the Kitchen garden, and intend onely in this place to giue you the knowledge of some more rare: *viz.* of such as are nourfed vp by those that are curious, and fit for this garden: for there are some other, that must be remembred in the Physicke garden, or garden of Simples, or else in a generall worke.

1. *Hyssopus folijs niueis.* White Hyssope.

This white Hyssope is of the same kinde and smell with the common Hyssope; but differeth, in that this many times hath diuers leaues, that are wholly of a white colour, with part of the stalke also: others are parted, the one halfe white, the other halfe greene, and some are wholly greene, or with some spots or stripes of white within the greene, which makes it delightfull to most Gentlewomen.

2. *Hyssopus folijs cinereis.* Russet Hyssope.

As the last hath party coloured leaues, white and greene, so this hath his leaues of an ash-colour, which of some is called russet; and hath no other difference either in forme or smell.

3. *Hyssopus aureus.* Yellow or golden Hyssope.

All the leaues of this Hyssope are wholly yellow, or but a little greene in them, and are of so pleasant a colour, especially in Summer, that they prouoke many Gentlewomen to weare them in their heads, and on their armes, with as much delight as many fine flowers can giue: but in Winter their beautifull colour is much decayed, being of a whitish greene, yet recouer themselues againe the next Summer.

4. *Hyssopus surculis densis.* Double Hyssope.

As this kinde of Hyssope groweth lower then the former or ordinary kinde, so it hath more branches, slenderer, and not so wooddy, leaning somewhat downe toward the ground, so wonderfully thicke set with leaues, that are like vnto the other, but of a darker greene colour, and somewhat thicker withall, that it is the onely fine sweete herbe, that I know fittest (if any be minded to plant herbes) to set or border a knot of herbes or flowers, because it will well abide, and not growe too wooddy or great, nor be thinne of leaues in one part, when it is thicke in another, so that it may be kept with cutting as smooth and plaine as a table. If it be suffered to growe vp of it selfe alone, it riseth with leaues as before is specified, and flowreth as the common doth, and of the same sent also, not differing in any thing, but in the thicknesse of the leaues on the stalkes and branches, and the aptnesse to be ordered as the keeper pleaseth.

5. *Chamædrys*

Chamædrys. Germander.

Left Germander fhould be vtterly forgotten, as not worthy of our Garden, feeing many (as I faid in my treatife or introduction to this Garden) doe border knots therewith : let me at the leaft giue it a place, although the laft, being more vfed as a ftrewing herbe for the houfe, then for any other vfe. It is (I thinke) fufficiently knowne to haue many branches, with fmall and fomewhat round endented leaues on them, and purplifh gaping flowers : the rootes fpreading far abroad, and rifing vp againe in many places.

The Place.

Thefe Hyffopes haue beene moft of them nourfed vp of long time in our Englifh Gardens, but from whence their firft originall fhould be, is not well knowne. The Germander alfo is onely in Gardens, and not wilde.

The Time.

They flower in Iune and Iuly.

The Names.

The feuerall names whereby they are knowne to vs, are fet forth in their titles ; and therefore I neede not here fay more of them then onely this, that neyther they here fet downe, nor the common or ordinary fort, nor any of the reft not here expreffed, are any of them the true Hyffope of the ancient Greeke Writers, but *fuppofititia*, vfed in the ftead thereof. The Germander, from the forme of the leaues like vnto fmall oaken leaues, had the name *Chamædrys* giuen it, which fignifieth a dwarfe Oake.

The Vertues.

The common Hyffope is much vfed in all pectorall medicines, to cut fleagme, and to caufe it eafily to be auoided. It is vfed of many people in the Country, to be laid vnto cuts or frefh wounds, being bruifed, and applyed eyther alone, or with a little Sugar. It is much vfed as a fweet herbe, to be in the windowes of an houfe. I finde it much commended againft the Falling Sickneffe, efpecially being made into Pils after this manner : Of Hyffope, Horhound, and Caftor, of each halfe a dramme, of Peony rootes (the male kinde is onely fit to be vfed for this purpofe) two drams, of *Affa fætida* one fcruple : Let them be beaten, and made into pils with the iuyce of Hyffope ; which being taken for feuen dayes together at night going to bed, is held to be effectual to giue much eafe, if not thoroughly to cure thofe that are troubled with that difeafe. The vfe of Germander ordinarily is as Tyme, Hyffope, and other fuch herbes, to border a knot, whereunto it is often appropriate, and the rather, that it might be cut to ferue (as I faid) for a ftrewing herbe for the houfe among others. For the phyficall vfe it ferueth in difeafes of the fplene, and the ftopping of vrine, and to procure womens courfes.

Thus haue I led you through all my Garden of Pleafure, and fhewed you all the varieties of nature nourfed therein, pointing vnto them, and defcribing them one after another. And now laftly (according to the vfe of our old ancient Fathers) I bring you to reft on the Graffe, which yet fhall not be without fome delight, and that not the leaft of all the reft.

CHAP.

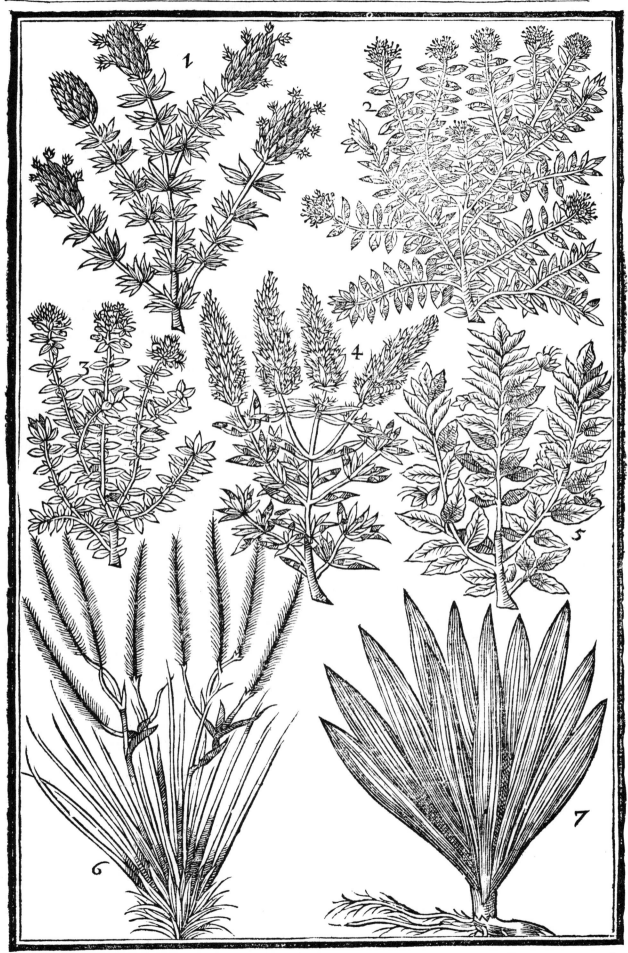

1 *Thymum legitimum.* The true Tyme. 2 *Serpillum maius hortense.* Garden wilde Tyme. 3 *Serpillum Citratum.* Lemon Tyme. 4 *Hyssopus versicolor siue aureus.* Golden Hyssope. 5 *Chamædrys.* Germander. 6 *Spartum Austriacum siue Gramen plumarium minus.* The lesser feather Grasse. 7 *Gramen striatum vel sulcatum.* Painted Grasse or Ladies Laces.

Chap. CXXXIII.

Gramina. Grasses.

THere are among an infinite number (as I may so say) of Grasses, a few onely which I thinke fit to be planted in this Garden, both for the rarity of them, and also for your delight, and the excellent beauty that is in them aboue many other plants. One of them hath long agoe bin respected, and cherished in the country gardens of many Gentlewomen, and others. The others are knowne but vnto a few.

1. *Gramen striatum.* Painted Grasse or Ladies laces.

This kinde of Grasse hath many stiffe, hard, round stalkes, full of ioynts, whereon are set at euery ioynt one long leafe, somewhat broad at the bottome, where it compasseth the stalke, and smaller to the end, where it is sharpe pointed, hard or rough in handling, and striped all the length of the leafe with white streakes or lines, that they seeme party coloured laces of white and greene: the tops of the stalkes are furnished with long spikie tufts, like vnto the tufts of Couch Grasse: the rootes are small, white, and threddy, like the rootes of other Grasses.

2. *Gramen Plumarium minus.* The lesser Feather-Grasse.

This lesser Feather-Grasse hath many small, round, and very long leaues or blades, growing in tufts, much finer and smaller then any other Grasse that I know, being almost like vnto haires, and of a fresh greene colour in Summer, but changing into gray, like old hay in Winter, being indeede all dead, and neuer reuiuing; yet hardly to be plucked away vntill the Spring, and then other greene leaues or rushes rise vp by them, and in their stead, and are aboue a foote in length: from the middle of these tufts come forth rounder and bigger rushes, which are the stalkes, and which haue a chaffie round eare about the middle thereof, which when it is full growne, is somewhat higher then the toppes of the leaues or rushes, opening it selfe (being before close) at the top, and shewing forth three or foure long ayles or beards, one aboue another, which bend themselues a little downewards (if they stand ouer long before they are gathered, and will fall off, and be blowne away with the winde) being so finely feathered on both sides, all the length of the beard, and of a pale or grayish colour, that no feather in the taile of the Bird of Paradise can be finer, or to be compared with them, hauing sticking at the end of euery one of them, within the eare, a small, long, whitish, round, hard, and very sharpe pointed graine, like vnto an oaten graine, that part of the stalke of the feather that is next vnder it, and aboue the seede for some two or three inches, being stiffe and hard, and twining or curling it selfe, if it be suffered to stand too long, or to fall away, otherwise being straight as the feather it selfe: the roote is composed of many long, hard, small threddy strings, which runne deepe and far, and will not willingly be remoued, in that it gaineth strength euery yeare by standing.

3. *Gramen Plumarium maius.* The greater Feather-Grasse.

The greater Feather-Grasse is like vnto the lesser, but that both the leaues and the feathers are greater, and nothing so fine, grosser also, and of lesse beauty and respect, though whiter then it; and therefore is not so much regarded: for I haue knowne, that many Gentlewomen haue vsed the former lesser kinde, being tyed in tufts, to set them in stead of feathers about their beds, where they haue lyen after childe-bearing, and at other times also, when as they haue been much admired of the Ladies and Gentles that haue come to visit them.

The Place.

The first of these Grasses, as Lobel saith, groweth naturally in the woods and hils of Sauoy. It hath long agoe beene receiued into our English gardens.

dens. The second, as Clufius faith, in Auftria, from whence alfo (as I take it) the greater came, and are both in the gardens of thofe, that are curious obferuers of thefe delights.

The Time.

The firft is in its pride for the leaues all the Spring and Summer, yeelding his bufh in Iune. The other giue their feather-like fprigs in Iuly and Auguft, and quickly (as I faid) are fhed, if they be not carefully gathered.

The Names.

The firft is called by Lobel *Gramen fulcatum*, or *ftriatum album*, of others *Gramen pictum*. The French call it *Aiguellettes d'armes*, of the fafhion that their Enfignes, Pennons, or Streamers vfed in wars were of, that is, like vnto a party coloured curtaine. In Englifh vfually Ladies laces, and Painted Graffe. The firft of the other two is called *Gramen plumarium* or *plumofum*, and *minus* is added for the diftinction of it. Clufius calleth it *Spartum Auftriacum*, of the likeneffe and place where he found it. The laft is called *Gramen plumarium*, or *plumofum maius*, The greater Feather-Graffe.

The Vertues.

Thefe kindes of Graffes are not in any time or place that I doe heare of applyed to any Phyficall vfe; and therefore of them I will fay no more: but here I will end the prime part of this worke.

THE

THE ORDERING
OF THE KITCHEN
GARDEN.

CHAP. I.

The situation of a Kitchen Garden, or Garden of Herbes, and what sort of
manure is fittest to helpe the decaying of the soyle thereof.

Auing giuen you the best rules and instructions that I can for your
flower Garden, and all the flowers that are fit to furnish it, I now
proceede to your herbe garden, which is not of the least respect
belonging to any mans house, nor vtterly to bee neglected for the
many vtilities are to be had from it, both for the Masters profit and
pleasure, and the meynies content and nourishment : all which if
I should here set down, I had a large field to wander in, and matter
sufficient to entreat of, but this worke permitteth not that libertie :
and I thinke there are but few but eyther know it already, or conceiue it sufficiently in
their minds. Passing therefore no further in such discourses, I come to the matter in
hand, which is to shew you where the fittest place is for an herbe garden. As before I
shewed you that the beautie of any worthy house is much the more commended for
the pleasant situation of the garden of flowers, or of pleasure, to be in the sight and full
prospect of all the chiefe and choisest roomes of the house; so contrariwise, your herbe
garden should bee on the one or other side of the house, and those best and choyse
roomes : for the many different sents that arise from the herbes, as Cabbages, Onions,
&c. are scarce well pleasing to perfume the lodgings of any house; and the many ouer-
tures and breaches as it were of many of the beds thereof, which must necessarily bee,
are also as little pleasant to the sight. But for priuate mens houses, who must like their
habitations as they fall vnto them, and cannot haue time or meanes to alter them, they
must make a vertue of necessity, and conuert their places to their best aduantage, by
making their profit their chiefest pleasure, and making one place serue for all vses. The
choyce of ground for this Garden, is (as I said before) where it is fat, fertill and good,
there needeth the lesse labour and cost : and contrariwise, where it is cold, wet, dry or
barren, there must bee the more helpes still added to keepe it in heart. For this Garden
by reason of the much and continuall stirring therein, the herbes and rootes drawing
out the substance of the fertilitie thereof more aboundantly then in the former, must
be continually holpen with soyle, or else few things of goodnesse or worth will come
forward therein. The stable soyle of horses is best and more proper for any colde
grounds, for being the hottest, it will cause any the seedes for this Garden to prosper
well, and be more forward then in any other ground that is not so holpen. The stable
soyle of Cattell is of a colder and moister nature, and is therefore more proper for

the

the hot fandy or grauelly grounds, and although it bee longer before it bee brought to mould then that of horfes, yet it will outlaft it more then twice fo long. Let euery one therefore take according to the nature of the ground fuch helpes as are moft fit and conuenient, as I haue here and before fhewed. But I doe here ingenuoufly confeffe my opinion of thefe forcings and helpings of ground, that howfoeuer it doth much good to fome particular things, which becaufe they delight in heate, and cannot be brought to perfection without it in this our Countrey, which is colder then their naturall from whence they are brought, muft therfore haue artificiall helpes to forward them ; yet for many other things the compoft doth much alter and abate the naturall vigour, and quickeneffe of tafte, that is perceiued in them that grow in a naturall fat or fandy foile that is not fo holpen.

CHAP. II.

The forme of a Garden of herbes for neceffary vfes, with the ordering thereof.

AS our former Garden of pleafure is wholly formable in euery part with fquares, trayles, and knots, and to bee ftill maintained in their due forme and beautie : fo on the contrary fide this Garden cannot long conferue any forme, for that euery part thereof is fubiect to mutation and alteration. For although it is conuenient that many herbes doe grow by themfelues on beds, caft out into fome proportion fit for them, as Tyme, Hiffope, Sage, &c. yet many others may bee fowen together on a plot of ground of that largeneffe that may ferue euery mans particular vfe as he fhall haue occafion to employ it, as Reddifh, Lettice and Onions, which after they are growne vp together may be drawne vp and taken away, as there is occafion to fpend them : but Carrots or Parfneps being fowen with others muft bee fuffered to grow laft, becaufe they require a longer time before they be fit to be taken vp. Other herbes require fome large compaffe of ground whereon they may grow of themfelues without any other herbes growing among them, as Artichokes, Cowcumbers, Melons, Pompions. And fome will doe fo with their Cabbages alfo, but the beft and moft frugall way now vfed, is to plant them round about the border of your plot or ground whereon you plant Cowcumbers, Pompions, or other things, in that by this meanes fo much ground will be well faued, and the other things be no whit hindered thereby, which elfe a great deale of ground muft be employed for them apart. So that by this that I haue here faid, you may perceiue the forme of this Garden is for the moft part, to bee ftill out of forme and order, in that the continuall taking vp of the herbes and rootes that are fowen and planted, caufeth the beds or parts of this Garden to lye broken, difmembered, and out of the order that at the firft it was put into. Remember herewithall that (as I faid before) this Garden requireth the continuall helpe of foyle to be brought into it, in that the plenty of thefe manner of herbes and rootes doe fo much wafte the fertilitie and fatneffe of the ground, that without continuall refrefhing it would quickly become fo poore and barren, that it would not yeelde the worth of the feede. The ordinary time to foyle a Garden, is to bring in manure or dung before Chriftmas, and eyther bury it fome fmall depth, not too deepe, or elfe to lay it vpon the ground that the winter froftes may pierce it, and then turne it fhallow into the ground to fow your feeds in the Spring.

Chap. III.

How to order diuers Garden herbes, both for their sowing,
spending, and gathering of the seede.

OVr chiefest and greatest Gardiners now adaies, doe so prouide for themselues
euery yeare, that from their owne grounds they gather the seede of many
herbes that they sowe againe: for hauing gained the best kind of diuers herbes,
they will be still furnished with the same, and be not to seeke euery yeare for new that
oftentimes will not yeelde them halfe the profit that their choyce seede will : I say of
many herbes, but not of all ; for the best of them all hath not ground sufficient for all
sorts, nor will our climate bring some to that perfection that other forraine doth, and
therefore the seede of some things are continually brought from beyond Sea vnto vs.
And againe although our chiefe Gardiners doe still prouide their owne seede of diuers
things from their owne ground, because as I said it is of the best kinde, yet you must vnderstand also, that good store of the same sortes of seeds are brought from beyond the
Seas, for that which is gathered in this Land is not sufficient to serue euery mans vse in
the whole Kingdome by many parts ; yet still it is true, that our English seede of many
things is better then any that commeth from beyond the Seas : as for example, Reddish, Lettice, Carrots, Parsneps, Turneps, Cabbages, and Leekes, of all which I intend to write in this place ; for these are by them so husbanded, that they doe not sow
their owne grounds with any other seede of these sorts but their owne : which that
you may know the manner how to doe, I will here set it downe, that euery one may
haue the best directions if they will follow them. Of Reddish there are two sorts, one
more early then the other : they vse therefore to sow their early Reddish first, that they
may haue the earliest profit of them, which is more worth in one fortnight, then in
a moneth after. And to effect this they haue some artificiall helps also, which are these:
They vse to digge vp a large plot of ground where they intend to sow their seede a little before or after Christmas, casting it into high balkes or ridges fiue or sixe foote a-
sunder, which they suffer to lye and take all the extreame frosts in Ianuary to mellow
the earth, and when the frostes are past, they then beginne to bring into it good store
of fresh stable dung, which they laye neyther too deepe nor too thicke, and couer it
with the mould a hand breadth thicknesse aboue the dung, which doth giue such a
warmth and comfort to whatsoeuer is sowen thereon, that it forceth it forward much
sooner then any other way can doe : And to preuent both the frostes, and the cold
bitter windes which often spoyle their seede new sprung vp, they vse to set great high
and large mattes made of reedes, tyed together, and fastened vnto strong stakes, thrust
into the ground to keepe them vp from falling, or being blowne down with the winde ;
which mattes they place on the North and East side to breake the force of these winds,
and are so sure and safe a defence, that a bricke wall cannot better defend any thing
vnder it, then this fence will. In this manner they doe euery yeare to bring forward
their seede to gaine the more by them, and they that will haue Reddish early, must
take the same course. The other sort of Reddish for the most part is sowen in Februarie, a fortnight after the other at the least, and likewise euery moneth after vnto September, that they may haue young continually. For the blacke Reddish, although many in many places doe sowe it in the same time, and in the same manner that the ordinary is sowen, yet the nature thereof is to runne vp to seede more speedily then the
other, if it haue so rich ground to grow vpon, and therefore the best time to sow it is
in August, that so it may abide all winter, wherein is the chiefest time for the spending
thereof, and to keepe it vntill the beginning of the next yeare from running vp to seed:
the gathering whereof, as also of the other sort, is all after one manner, that is, to be
pulled vp when the pods change whitish, and then hanged vpon bushes, pales, or such
other thing, vntill they bee thorough dry, and then beaten or thrashed out vpon a
smooth plancher, or vpon clothes, as euery ones store is, and their conueniencie. Lettice is sowen oftentimes with the early Reddish, in the same manner before said, that
they may haue Lettice likewise as early as the time of the year will permit them, which

every

they pull vp where they grow too thicke, spending them first, and so taking vp from time to time, vntill they stand two foote in sunder one from another, and beginne to spindle and shoote vp for seede. In this is vsed some arte to make the plants strong to giue the better seede without danger of rotting or spoyling with the wet, which often happeneth to those about whom this caution is not obserued : Before your Lettice is shot vp, marke out the choysest and strongest plantes which are fittest to grow for seede, and from those when they are a foote high, strippe away with your hand the leaues that grow lowest vpon the stalke next the ground, which might rot, spoyle or hinder them from bearing so good seede; which when it is neere to be ripe, the stalkes must be cut off about the middle, and layde vpon mats or clothes in the Sunne, that it may there fully ripen and be gathered ; for it would be blowne away with the winde if it should be suffered to abide on the stalkes long. Parsneps must be sowen on a deep trenched mellow ground, otherwise they may run to seede the first yeare, which then are nothing worth : or else the rootes will be small staruelings and short, and runne into many spires or branches, whereby they will not bee of halfe the worth. Some vse to sow them in August and September, that so they may bee well growne to serue to spend in Lent following, but their best time is in February, that the Summers growth may make them the fairer and greater. When they runne vp to seede, you shall take the principall or middle heades, for those carry the Master seede, which is the best, and will produce the fairest rootes againe. You shall hardly haue all the seede ripe at one instant, for vsually the chiefest heads will be fallen before the other are ripe : you must therefore still looke them ouer, and cut them as they ripen. Carrots are vsually sowen in March and Aprill, and if it chance that some of them doe runne vp for seede the same year, they are to be weeded out, for neyther the seed nor roots of them are good : You must likewise pull them vp when they are too thicke, if you will haue them grow fair, or for seed, that they may grow at the least three or foure foot in sunder : the stalkes of Carrots are limber, and fall downe to the ground ; they must therefore be sustained by poles layde acrosse on stalkes thrust into the ground, and tyed to the poles and stalkes to keepe them vp from rotting or spoyling vpon the ground : the seed hereof is not all ripe at once, but must be tended and gathered as it ripeneth, and layd to dry in some dry chamber or floore, and then beaten out with a stick, and winnowed from the refuse. Turneps are sowne by themselues vpon a good ground in the end of Iuly, and beginning of August, to haue their rootes best to spend in winter ; for it often happeneth that those seedes of Turneps that are sowen in the Spring, runne vp to seede the same yeare, and then it is not accounted good. Many doe vse to sow Turneps on those grounds from whence the same yeare they haue taken off Reddish and Lettice, to make the greater profit of the ground, by hauing two crops of increase in one yeare. The stalkes of Turneps will bend downe to the ground, as Carrots doe, but yet must not be bound or ordered in that manner, but suffered to grow without staking or binding, so as they grow of some good distance in sunder : when the seede beginneth to grow ripe, be very carefull to preserue it from the birds, which will be most busie to deuour them. You shall vnderstand likewise that many doe account the best way to haue the fairest and most principall seede from all these fore-recited herbes, that after they are sowen, and risen to a reasonable growth, they be transplanted into fresh ground. Cabbages also are not only sowen for the vse of their heads to spend for meat, but to gather their seede likewise, which howsoeuer some haue endeauoured to doe, yet few haue gained good seede, because our sharpe hard frostes in winter haue spoyled and rotted their stockes they preserued for the purpose ; but others haue found out a better and a more sure way, which is, to take vp your stocks that are fittest to be preserued, and bring them into the house, and there wrap them eyther in clothes, or other things to defend them from the cold, and hang them vp in a dry place, vntill the beginning of March following, then planting them in the ground, and a little defend them at the first with straw cast ouer them from the cold nights, thereby you may be sure to haue perfect good seede, if your kinde be of the best : Sowe your seed in the moneths of February or March, and transplant them in May where they may stand to grow for your vse, but be carefull to kill the wormes or Caterpillers that else will deuoure all your leaues, and be carefull also that none of the leaues bee broken in the planting, or otherwise rubbed, for that oftentimes hindereth the well closing of them. Leekes are

for

for the moſt part wholly nourſed vp from the ſeede that is here gathered; and becauſe there is not ſo much ſtore of them either ſowne or ſpent, as there is of Onions by the twentieth part, we are ſtill the more carefull to be prouided from our owne labours; yet there be diuers Gardiners in this Kingdome, that doe gather ſome ſmall quantity of Onion ſeede alſo for their owne or their priuate friends ſpending. The ſowing of them both is much about one time and manner, yet moſt vſually Leeks are ſowne later then Onions, and both before the end of March at the furtheſt; yet ſome ſowe Onions from the end of Iuly to the beginning of September, for their Winter prouiſion. Thoſe that are ſowne in the Spring, are to be taken vp and tranſplanted on a freſh bed prepared for the purpoſe, or elſe they will hardly abide a Winter; but hauing taken roote before Winter, they will beare good ſeede in the Summer following: You muſt ſtake both your Leekes and your Onion beds, and with poles laid a croſſe, binde your lopple headed ſtalkes vnto them, on high as well as belowe, or elſe the winde and their owne weight will beare them downe to the ground, and ſpoile your ſeede. You muſt thinne them, that is, pull vp continually after they are firſt ſprung vp thoſe that growe too thicke, as you doe with all the other herbes before ſpoken of, that they may haue the more roome to thriue. Of all theſe herbes and rootes before ſpoken of, you muſt take the likelieſt and faireſt to keepe for your ſeede; for if you ſhould not take the beſt, what hope of good ſeede can you expect? The time for the ſpending of theſe herbes and rootes, not particularly mentioned, is vntill they begin to runne vp for ſeede, or vntill they are to be tranſplanted for ſeede, or elſe vntill Winter, while they are good, as euery one ſhall ſee cauſe.

Chap. IIII.

How to order Artichokes, Melons, Cowcumbers, and Pompions.

THere are certaine other herbes to be ſpoken of, which are wholly nourſed vp for their fruit ſake, of whom I ſhall not need to ſay much, being they are ſo frequent in euery place. Artichokes being planted of faire and large ſlips, taken from the roote in September and October (yet not too late) will moſt of them beare fruit the next yeare, ſo that they be planted in well dunged ground, and the earth raiſed vp like vnto an Anthill round about each roote, to defend them the better from the extreame froſts in Winter. Others plant ſlips in March and Aprill, or ſooner, but although ſome of them will beare fruit the ſame yeare, yet all will not. And indeede many doe rather chooſe to plant in the ſpring then in the fall, for that oftentimes an extreame hard Winter following the new ſetting of ſlips, when they haue not taken ſufficient heart and roote in the ground, doth vtterly pierce and periſh them, when as they that are ſet in the Spring haue the whole Summers growth, to make them ſtrong before they feele any ſharpe froſts, which by that time they are the better able to beare. Muſke Melons haue beene begun to bee nourſed vp but of late dayes in this Land, wherein although many haue tryed and endeauoured to bring them to perfection, yet few haue attained vnto it: but thoſe rules and orders which the beſt and skilfulleſt haue vſed, I will here ſet downe, that who ſo will, may haue as good and ripe Melons as any other in this Land. The firſt thing you are to looke vnto, is to prouide you a peece of ground fit for the purpoſe, which is either a ſloping or ſheluing banke, lying open and oppoſite to the South Sunne, or ſome other fit place not ſheluing, and this ground alſo you muſt ſo prepare, that all the art you can vſe about it to make it rich is little enough; and therefore you muſt raiſe it with meere ſtable ſoyle, thorough rotten & well turned vp, that it may be at the leaſt three foote deepe thereof, which you muſt caſt alſo into high beds or balkes, with deepe trenches or furrowes betweene, ſo as the ridges may be at the leaſt a foot and a halfe higher then the furrowes; for otherwiſe it is not poſſible to haue good Melons growe ripe. The choiſe of your ſeede alſo is another thing of eſpeciall regard, and the beſt is held to be Spaniſh, and not French, which hauing once gained, be ſure to haue ſtill of the ſame while they laſt

good,

good, that you may haue the seede of your owne ripe Melons from them that haue eaten them, or saue some of the best your selfe for the purpose. I say while they last good; for many are of opinion, that no seede of Muske Melons gathered in England, will endure good to sowe againe here aboue the third yeare, but still they must be renewed from whence you had your choisest before. Then hauing prepared a hot bed of dung in Aprill, set your seedes therein to raise them vp, and couer them, and order them with as great care or greater then Cowcumbers, &c. are vsed, that when they are ready, they may be transplanted vpon the beds or balkes of that ground you had before prepared for them, and set them at the least two yards in sunder, euery one as it were in a hole, with a circle of dung about them, which vpon the setting being watered with water that hath stood in the Sunne a day or two, and so as often as neede is to water, couer them with strawe (some vse great hollow glasses like vnto bell heads) or some such other things, to defend them both from the cold euenings or dayes, and the heate of the Sunne, while they are young and new planted. There are some that take vpon them great skill, that mislike of the raising vp of Melons, as they doe also of Cowcumbers, on a hot bed of horse dung, but will put two or three seedes in a place in the very ground where they shall stand and growe, and thinke without that former manner of forcing them forwards, that this their manner of planting will bring them on fast and sure enough, in that they will plucke away some of the worst and weakest, if too many rise vp together in a place; but let them know for certaine, that howsoeuer for Cowcumbers their purpose and order may doe reasonable well, where the ground is rich and good, and where they striue not to haue them so early, as they that vse the other way, for Muske Melons, which are a more tender fruit, requiring greater care and trouble in the noursing, and greater and stronger heate for the ripening, they must in our cold climate haue all the art vsed vnto them that may be, to bring them on the more early, and haue the more comfort of the Sunne to ripen them kindly, or else they will not bee worth the labour and ground. After you haue planted them as aforesaid, some of good skill doe aduise, that you be carefull in any dry season, to giue them water twice or thrice euery weeke while they are young, but more afterward when they are more growne, and that in the morning especially, yea and when the fruit is growne somewhat great, to water the fruit it selfe with a watering pot in the heate of the day, is of so good effect, that it ripeneth them much faster, and will giue them the better taste and smell, as they say. To take likewise the fruit, and gather it at the full time of his ripenesse is no small art; for if it be gathered before his due time to be presently eaten, it will be hard and greene, and not eate kindly; and likewise if it be suffered too long, the whole goodnesse will be lost: You shall therefore know, that it is full time to gather them to spend presently, when they begin to looke a little yellowish on the outside, and doe smell full and strong; but if you be to send them farre off, or keepe them long vpon any occasion, you shall then gather them so much the earlier, that according to the time of the carriage and spending, they may ripen in the lying, being kept dry, and couered with woollen clothes: When you cut one to eate, you shall know it to be ripe and good, if the seede and pulpe about them in the middle be very waterish, and will easily be separated from the meate, and likewise if the meate looke yellow, and be mellow, and not hard or greene, and taste full and pleasant, and not waterish: The vsuall manner to eate them is with pepper and salt, being pared and sliced, and to drowne them in wine, for feare of doing more harme. Cowcumbers and Pompions, after they are noursed vp in the bed of hot dung, are to be seuerally transplanted, each of them on a large plot of ground, a good distance in sunder: but the Pompions more, because their branches take vp a great deale more ground, & besides, will require a great deale more watering, because the fruit is greater. And thus haue you the ordering of those fruits which are of much esteeme, especially the two former, with all the better sort of persons; and the third kinde is not wholly refused, of any, although it serueth most vsually for the meaner and poorer sort of people, after the first early ripe are spent.

CHAP. V.

The ordering of diuers sorts of herbes for the pot, for meate, and for the table.

TYme, Sauory, and Hyssope, are vsually sowne in the Spring on beds by themselues, euerie one a part; but they that make a gaine by selling to others the young rootes, to set the knots or borders of Gardens, doe for the most part sowe them in Iuly and August, that so being sprung vp before Winter, they will be the fitter to be taken vp in the Spring following, to serue any mans vse that wonld haue them. Sage, Lauender, and Rosemary, are altogether set in the Spring, by slipping the old stalkes, and taking the youngest and likeliest of them, thrusting them either twined or otherwise halfe a foote deepe into the ground, and well watered vpon the setting; if any seasonable weather doe follow, there is no doubt of their well thriuing: the hot Sunne and piercing drying Windes are the greatest hinderances to them; and therefore I doe aduise none to set too soone in the Spring, nor yet in Autumne, as many doe practise: for I could neuer see such come to good, for the extremity of the Winter comming vpon them so soone after their setting, will not suffer their young shootes to abide, not hauing taken sufficient strength in the ground, to maintain themselues against such violence, which doth often pierce the strongest plants. Marierome and Bassill are sowne in the Spring, yet not too early; for they are tender plants, and doe not spring vntill the weather bee somewhat warme: but Bassill would bee sowne dry, and not haue any water of two or three daies after the sowing, else the seede will turne to a gelly in the ground. Some vse to lowe the seed of Rosemary, but it seldome abideth the first Winter, because the young plants being small, and not of sufficient strength, cannot abide the sharpnesse of some Winters, notwithstanding the couering of them, which killeth many old plants; but the vsuall way is to slippe and set, and so they thriue well. Many doe vse to sowe all or the most sorts of Pot-herbes together on one plot of ground, that they neede not to goe farre to gather all the sorts they would vse. There are many sorts of them well knowne vnto all, yet few or none doe vse all sorts, but as euery one liketh, some vse those that others refuse, and some esteem those not to bee wholesome and of a good rellish, which others make no scruple of. The names of them are as followeth, and a short relation of their sowing or planting.

Rosemary, Tyme, and Sauorie are spoken of before, and Onions and Leekes.

Mints are to bee set with their rootes in some by-place, for that their rootes doe creepe so farre vnder ground, that they quickly fill vp the places neare adioyning, if they be not puld vp.

Clarie is to be sowne, and seedeth and dyeth the next yeare, the herbe is strong, and therefore a little thereof is sufficient.

Nep is sowne, and dyeth often after seeding, few doe vse it, and that but a little at a time: both it and Clarie are more vsed in Tansies then in Broths.

Costmarie is to be set of rootes, the leaues are vsed with some in their Broths, but with more in their Ale.

Pot Marierome is set of rootes, being separated in sunder.

Penniroyall is to be set of the small heads that haue rootes, it creepeth and spreadeth quickly.

Allisanders are to be sowne of seede, the tops of the rootes with the greene leaues are vsed in Lent especially.

Parsley is a common herbe, and is sowne of seede, it seedeth the next yeare and dyeth: the rootes are more vsed in broths then the leaues, and the leaues almost with all sorts of meates.

Fennell is sowne of seede, and abideth many yeares yeelding seede: the rootes also are vsed in broths, and the leaues more seldome, yet serue to trimme vp many fish meates.

Borage is sowne of seede, and dyeth the next yeare after, yet once being suffered to seede in a Garden, will still come of it owne shedding.

Buglosse

Buglosse commeth of seede, but abideth many yeares after it hath giuen seede, if it stand not in the coldest place of the Garden.

Marigolds are sowne of seede, and may be after transplanted, they abide two or three yeares, if they be not set in too cold a place : the leaues and flowers are both vsed.

Langedebeefe is sowne of seede, which shedding it selfe will hardly be destroyed in a Garden.

Arrach is to be sowne of seede, this likewise will rise euery yeare of it owne seed, if it be suffered to shed it selfe.

Beetes are sowne of seede, and abideth some yeares after, still giuing seede.

Blites are vsed but in some places ; for there is a generall opinion held of them, that they are naught for the eyes : they are sowne euery yeare of seede.

Bloodwort once sowne abideth many yeares, if the extremity of the frosts kill it not, and seedeth plentifully.

Patience is of the same nature, and vsed in the same manner.

French Mallowes are to be sowne of seede, and will come of it owne sowing, if it be suffered to shed it selfe.

Ciues are planted onely by parting the rootes ; for it neuer giueth any seede at all.

Garlicke is ordered in the same manner, by parting and planting the rootes euerie yeare.

These be all the sorts are vsed with vs for that purpose, whereas I said before, none vseth all, but euery one will vse those they like best : and so much shall suffice for pot-herbes.

Chap. VI.

The manner and ordering of many sorts of herbes and rootes for Sallets.

IF I should set downe all the sorts of herbes that are vsually gathered for Sallets, I should not onely speake of Garden herbes, but of many herbes, &c. that growe wilde in the fields, or else be but weedes in a Garden ; for the vsuall manner with many, is to take the young buds and leaues of euery thing almost that groweth, as well in the Garden as in the Fields, and put them all together, that the taste of the one may amend the rellish of the other : But I will only shew you those that are sown or planted in gardens for that purpose. Asparagus is a principall & delectable Sallet herbe, whose young shootes when they are a good handfull high aboue the ground, are cut an inch within the ground, which being boyled, are eaten with a little vinegar and butter, as a Sallet of great delight. Their ordering with the best Gardiners is on this wise : When you haue prouided seede of the best kinde, you must sowe it either before Christmas, as most doe, or before the end of February ; the later you sowe, the later and the more hardly will they spring : after they are growne vp, they are to be transplanted in Autumne on a bed well trenched in with dung ; for else they will not bee worth your labour, and set about a foote distance in sunder, and looke that the more carefull you are in the replanting of them, the better they will thriue, and the sooner growe great : after fiue or six yeares standing they vsually doe decay ; and therefore they that striue to haue continually faire and great heads, doe from seede raise vp young for their store. You must likewise see that you cut not your heads or young shoote too nigh, or too much, that is, to take away too many heads from a roote, but to leaue a sufficient number vncut, otherwise it will kill the heart of your rootes the sooner, causing them to dye, or to giue very small heads or shootes ; for you may well consider with your selfe, that if the roote haue not head enough left it aboue the ground to shoote greene this yeare, it will not, nor cannot prosper vnder ground to giue encrease the next yeare. The ordering of Lettice I haue spoken of before, and shall not neede here to repeate what hath beene already said, but referre you thereunto for the sowing, planting, &c. onely I will here shew you the manner of ordering them for Sallets. There are some sorts of Lettice that growe very great, and close their heads, which are called Cab-

bage

bage Lettice, both ordinary and extraordinary, and there are other forts of great Lettice that are open, and clofe not, or cabbage not at all, which yet are of an excellent kinde, if they be vfed after that efpeciall manner is fit for them, which is, That when they are planted (for after they are fowne, they muft be tranfplanted) of a reafonable diftance in funder, and growne to be of fome bigneffe, euery one of them muft bee tyed together with baft or thread toward the toppes of the leaues, that by this meanes all the inner leaues may growe whitifh, which then are to be cut vp and vfed : for the keeping of the leaues clofe doth make them tafte delicately, and to bee very tender. And thefe forts of Lettice for the moft part are fpent after Summer is paft, when other Lettice are not to be had. Lambes Lettice or Corne Sallet is an herbe, which abiding all Winter, is the firft Sallet herbe of the yeare that is vfed before any ordinarie Lettice is ready ; it is therefore vfually fowne in Auguft, when the feede thereof is ripe. Purflane is a Summer Sallet herbe, and is to be fowne in the Spring, yet fomewhat late, becaufe it is tender, and ioyeth in warmth ; and therefore diuers haue fowne it vpon thofe beddes of dung, whereon they nourfed vp their Cowcumbers, &c. after they are taken away, which being well and often watered, hath yeelded Sallet vntill the end of the yeare. Spinach is fowne in the Spring, of all for the moft part that vfe it, but yet if it be fowne in Summer it will abide greene all the Winter, and then feedeth quickly : it is a Sallet that hath little or no tafte at all therein, like as Lettice and Purflane ; and therefore Cookes know how to make many a good difh of meate with it, by putting Sugar and Spice thereto. Coleworts are of diuers kinds, and although fome of them are wholly fpent among the poorer fort of people, yet fome kindes of them may be dreffed and ordered as may delight a curious palate, which is, that being boyled tender, the middle ribs are taken cold, and laid in difhes, and vinegar and oyle poured thereon, and fo eaten. Coleflowers are to be had in this Countrey but very feldome, for that it is hard to meete with good feede : it muft bee fowne on beds of dung to force it forward, or elfe it would perifh with the froft before it had giuen his head of flowers, and tranfplanted into verie good and rich ground, left you lofe the benefit of your labours. Endiue is of two forts, the ordinary, and another that hath the edges of the leaues curld or crumpled ; it is to be whited, to make it the more dainty Sallet, which is vfually done in this manner : After they are grown to fome reafonable greatneffe (but in any cafe before they fhoote forth a ftalke in the midft for feede) they are to be taken vp, and the rootes being cut away, lay them to dry or wither for three or foure houres, and then bury them in fand, fo as none of them lye one vpon another, or if you can, one to touch another, which by this meanes will change whitifh, and thereby become verie tender, and is a Sallet both for Autumne and Winter. Succorie is vfed by fome in the fame manner, but becaufe it is more bitter then Endiue, it is not fo generally vfed, or rather vfed but of a verie few : and whereas Endiue will feede the fame yeare it is fowne, and then dye, Succorie abideth manie yeares, the bitterneffe thereof caufing it to be more Phyficall to open obftructions ; and therefore the flowers pickled vp, as diuers other flowers are vfed to be now adaies, make a delicate Sallet at all times when there is occafion to vfe them. Of red Beetes, the rootes are onely vfed both boyled and eaten cold with vinegar and oyle, and is alfo vfed to trimme vp or garnifh forth manie forts of difhes of meate : the feede of the beft kinde will not abide good with vs aboue three yeares, but will degenerate and growe worfe ; and therefore thofe that delight therein muft be curious, to be prouided from beyond Sea, that they may haue fuch as will giue delight. Sorrell is an herbe fo common, and the vfe fo well knowne, both for fawce, and to feafon broths and meates for the found as well as ficke perfons, that I fhall not neede to fay anie more thereof. Cheruill is a Sallet herbe of much vfe, both with French and Dutch, who doe much more delight in herbes of ftronger tafte then the Englifh doe : it is fowne early, and vfed but a while, becaufe it quickly runneth vp to feede. Sweete Cheruill, or as fome call it, Sweete Cis, is fo like in tafte vnto Anife feede, that it much delighteth the tafte among other herbes in a Sallet : the feede is long, thicke, blacke, and cornered, and muft be fowne in the end of Autumne, that it may lye in the ground all the Winter, and then it will fhoote out in the Spring or elfe if it be fowne in the Spring, it will not fpring vp that yeare vntill the next : the leaues (as I faid before) are vfed among other herbes : the rootes likewife are not onely cordiall, but alfo held to be preferuatiue againft the Plague, either greene, dryed, or preferued

R r   with

with sugar. Rampion rootes are a kinde of Sallet with a great many, being boyled tender, and eaten cold with vinegar and pepper. Cresses is an herbe of easie and quick growth, and while it is young eaten eyther alone, or with parsley and other herbes : it is of a strong taste to them that are not accustomed thereunto, but it is much vsed of strangers. Rocket is of the same nature and qualitie, but somewhat stronger in taste : they are both sowen in the Spring, and rise, seede and dye the same yeare. Tarragon is an herbe of as strong a taste as eyther Rocket or Cresses, it abideth and dyeth not euery yeare, nor yet giueth ripe seede (as far as euer could bee found with vs) any yeare, but maketh sufficient increase within the ground, spreading his roots all abroad a great way off. Mustard is a common sawce both with fish and flesh, and the seed thereof (and no part of the plant besides) is well knowne how to be vsed being grownded, as euery one I thinke knoweth. The rootes of horse Radish likewise beeing grownd like Mustard, is vsed both of strangers and our owne nation, as sawce for fish. Tansie is of great vse, almost with all manner of persons in the Spring of the yeare : it is more vsu-ally planted of the rootes then otherwise ; for in that the rootes spread far and neere they may be easily taken away, without any hurt to the rest of the rootes. Burnet, al-though it be more vsed in wine in the Summer time then any way else, yet it is likewise made a sallet herbe with many, to amend the harsh or weak rellish of some other herbs. Skirrets are better to be sowen of the seed then planted from the roots, and will come on more speedily, and be fairer rootes : they are as often eaten cold as a Sallet, being boyled and the pith taken out, as stewed with butter and eaten warme. Let not Parsley and Fenell be forgotten among your other Sallet herbes, wherof I haue spoken before, and therefore need say no more of them. The flowers of Marigolds pickt cleane from the heads, and pickled vp against winter, make an excellent Sallet when no flowers are to be had in a garden. Cloue Gilloflowers likewise preserued or pickled vp in the same manner (which is *stratum super stratum*, a lay of flowers, and then strawed ouer with fine dry and poudered Sugar, and so lay after lay strawed ouer, vntill the pot bee full you meane to keepe them in, and after filled vp or couered ouer with vinegar) make a Sallet now adayes in the highest esteeme with Gentles and Ladies of the greatest note : the planting and ordering of them both is spoken of seuerally in their proper places. Goates beard that groweth in Gardens only, as well as that which groweth wilde in Medowes, &c. bearing a yellow flower, are vsed as a Sallet, the rootes beeing boyled and pared are eaten cold with vinegar, oyle and pepper; or else stewed with butter and eaten warme as Skirrets, Parsneps &c. And thus haue you here set downe all those most vsuall Sallets are vsed in this Kingdome: I say the most vsuall, or that are noursed vp in Gardens; for I know there are some other wilde herbes and rootes, as Dandelion &c. but they are vsed onely of strangers, and of those whose curiositie searcheth out the whole worke of nature to satisfie their desires.

Chap. VII.

Of diuers Physicall herbes fit to be planted in Gardens, to serue
for the especiall vses of a familie.

Hauing thus shewed you all the herbes that are most vsually planted in Kitchen Gardens for ordinary vses, let mee also adde a few other that are also noursed vp by many in their Gardens, to preserue health, and helpe to cure such small diseases as are often within the compasse of the Gentlewo-mens skils, who, to helpe their owne family, and their poore neighbours that are farre remote from Physitians and Chirurgions, take much paines both to doe good vnto them, and to plant those herbes that are conducing to their desires. And although I doe recite some that are mentioned in other places, yet I thought it meete to remem-ber them altogether in one place. Angelica, the garden kinde, is so good an herbe, that there is no part thereof but is of much vse, and all cordiall and preseruatiue from infectious or contagious diseases, whether you will distill the water of the herbe, or preserue or candie the rootes or the greene stalkes, or vse the seede in pouder or in di-stillations, or decoctions with other things : it is sowen of seede, and will abide vntill

it

it giue seede, and then dyeth. Rue or Herbe grace is a strong herbe, yet vsed inwardly against the plague as an Antidote with Figs and Wall-nuts, and helpeth much against windy bodies : outwardly it is vsed to bee layde to the wrestes of the hands, to driue away agues : it is more vsually planted of slips then raised from seede, and abideth long if sharpe frostes kill it not. Dragons being distilled are held to be good to expell any euill thing from the heart : they are altogether planted of the rootes. Setwall, Valerian, or Capons tayle, the herbe often, but the roote much better, is vsed to prouoke sweating, thereby to expell euill vapours that might annoy the heart : it is only planted of the rootes when they are taken vp, and the young replanted. Asarabacca, the leaues are often vsed to procure vomiting being stamped, and the strained iuice to a little quantitie, put into a draught of ale and drunke, thereby to ease the stomacke of many euill and grosse humours that there lye and offend it ; diuers also take the leaues and rootes a little boyled in wine, with a little spice added thereunto, to expell both tertian and quartan agues : the rootes of our English growing is more auaileable for these purposes then any outlandish : it is planted by the roote ; for I could neuer see it spring of seede. Masterwort commeth somewhat neere in propertie vnto Angelica, and besides very effectuall to disperse winde in the bodie, whether of the collicke or otherwise ; as also very profitable to comfort in all cold causes : it yeeldeth seede, but yet is more vsually planted from the rootes being parted. Balme is a cordiall herbe both in smell and taste, and is wholly vsed for those purposes, that is, to comfort the heart being distilled into water either simple or compound, or the herbe dryed and vsed : it is set of the rootes being parted, because it giueth no seede that euer I could obserue. Camomill is a common herbe well knowne, and is planted of the rootes in alleyes, in walkes, and on bankes to sit on, for that the more it is troden on, and pressed downe in dry weather, the closer it groweth, and the better it will thriue : the vse thereof is very much, both to warme and comfort, and to ease paines being applyed outwardly after many fashions : the decoction also of the flowers prouoketh sweat, and they are much vsed against agues. Featherfew is an herbe of greater vse for women then for men, to dissolue flatulent or windy humours, which causeth the paines of the mother : some vse to take the iuice thereof in drinke for agues : it is as well sowen of the seede as planted of the rootes. Costmary is vsed among those herbes that are put ino ale to cause it haue a good rellish, and to be somewhat physicall in the moneth of May, and doth helpe to prouoke vrine : it is set of the rootes being parted. Maudlin is held to be a principall good herbe to open and cleanse the liuer, and for that purpose is vsed many wayes, as in ale, in tansies, and in broths &c. the seed also is vsed, and so is the herbe also sometimes, to kill the wormes in children : it is sowen of the seede, and planted also of the separated rootes. Cassidonie is a small kinde of Lauender, but differing both in forme and qualitie : it is much vsed for the head to ease paines thereof, as also put among other things to purge melancholicke diseases : it is sowen of seede, and abideth not a winter vnlesse it bee well defended, and yet hardly giueth ripe seede againe with vs. Smallage is a great opening herbe, and much more then eyther Parsley or Fenell, and the rootes of them all are often vsed together in medicines : it is sowen of seede, and will not bee wanting in a Garden if once you suffer it to sow it selfe. Cardus Benedictus, or the Blessed Thistle, is much vsed in the time of any infection or plague, as also to expell any euill symptome from the heart at all other times. It is vsed likewise to be boyled in posset drink, & giuen to them that haue an ague, to help to cure it by sweating or otherwise. It is vsually sowen of seed, and dyeth when it hath giuen seed. Winter Cherries are likewise nursed vp in diuers gardens, for that their propertie is to giue helpe to them that are troubled eyther with the stopping or heate of their vrine: the herbe and berries are often distilled, but the berries alone are more often vsed: after it is once planted in a garden it will runne vnder ground, & abide well enough. Celondine is held to bee good for the iaundise, it is much vsed for to cleere dim eyes, eyther the iuice or the water dropped into them : it is sowen of seede, and being once brought into a garden, will hardly be weeded out ; the seede that sheddeth will so sow it selfe, and therefore some corner in a garden is the fittest place for it. Tabacco is of two sorts, and both vsed to be planted in Gardens, yet the English kinde (as it is called) is more to be found in our Countrey Gardens then the Indian sort : the leaues of both sorts indifferently, that is, of eyther of which is next at hand, being stamped and boy-

led

led eyther by it felfe, or with other herbes in oyle or hogs fuet, doe make an excellent falue for greene wounds, and alfo to clenfe old vlcers or fores; the iuice of the greene leaues drunke in ale, or a dryed leafe fteeped in wine or ale for a night, and the wine or ale drunke in the morning, prouoketh to caft, but the dryed leafe much ftronger then the greene: they are fowen of feede, but the Indian kinde is more tender, and will not abide a winter with vs abroade. Spurge that vfually groweth in Gardens, is a violent purger, and therefore it is needfull to be very carefull how it is vfed: the feede is more ordinarily vfed then any other part of the plant, which purgeth by vomiting in fome, and both vpwards and downwards in many; the iuice of the herbe, but efpecially the milke thereof, is vfed to kill warres: it is fowen of feede, and when it doth once fhed it felfe, it will ftill continue fpringing of the fallen feede. Bearefoote is fowen of feed, and will hardly abide tranfplanting vnleffe it bee while it is young; yet abideth diuers yeares, if it ftand not in too cold a place. This I fpeake of the greater kinde; for the lower fmall wilde kind (which is the moft ordinary in this land) will neuer decay: the leaues are fometimes vfed greene, but moft vfually dryed and poudered, and giuen in drinke to them that haue the wormes: it purgeth melancholy, but efpecially the roots. In many Countries of this Land, and elfewhere, they vfe to thruft the ftalk of the great kinde through the eare or dewlap of Kine and Cattell, to cure them of many difeafes. Salomons Seale, or (as fome call it) Ladder to heauen, although it doth grow wilde in many places of this Land, yet is planted in Gardens: it is accounted an excellent wound herbe to confolidate, and binde, infomuch that many vfe it with good fucceffe to cure ruptures, and to ftay both the white and the red fluxe in women: it is planted altogether of the rootes, for I could neuer finde it fpring from the feede, it is fo ftrong. Comfry likewife is found growing wilde in many places by ditch fides, and in moift places, and therefore requireth fome moift places of the garden: it is wholly vfed for knitting, binding, and confolidating fluxes and wounds, to be applyed either inwardly or outwardly: The rootes are ftronger for thofe purpofes then any other parts of the plant. Licoris is much vfed now adaies to bee planted in great quantitie, euen to fill many acres of ground, whereof rifeth a great deale of profit to thofe that know how to order it, and haue fit grounds for it to thriue in; for euery ground will not be aduantagious: It will require a very rich, deepe and mellow ground, eyther naturall or artificiall; but for a priuate houfe where a fmall quantitie will ferue, there needeth not fo much curiofitie: it is vfually planted of the top heads, when the lower rootes (which are the Licoris that is vfed) and the runners are cut from them. Some vfe to make an ordinary drinke or beuerage of Licoris, boyled in water as our vfuall ale or beere is with malt, which fermented with barme in the fame manner, and tunned vp, ferueth in ftead thereof, as I am credibly informed: It is otherwife in a manner wholly fpent for colds, coughes and rheumes, to expectorate flegme, but vfed in diuers formes, as in iuice, in decoctions, fyrrups, roules, trochifces, and the greene or dryed roote of it felfe.

And thefe are the moft ordinary Phyficall herbes that are vfed to be planted in gardens for the vfe of any Country familie, that is (as I faid before) farre remote from Phyfitians or Chirurgions abidings, that they may vfe as occafion ferueth for themfelues or their neighbours, and by a little care and paines in the applying may doe a great deale of good, and fometimes to them that haue not wherewith to fpend on themfelues, much leffe on Phyfitians or Chirurgions, or if they haue, may oftentimes receiue leffe good at their hands then at others that are taught by experience in their owne families, to be the more able to giue helpe to others.

The

THE
KITCHEN
GARDEN.

THE SECOND PART,

Ontaining as well all forts of herbes, as rootes and fruits, that are vfually planted in Gardens, to ferue for the vfe of the Table whether of the poore or rich of our Countrey : but herein I intend not to bring any fruite bearing trees, fhrubbes, or bufhes ; for I referue them for my Orchard, wherin they fhal be fet forth. So that in thefe three parts, I fuppofe the exquifite ornament of any worthy houfe is confummate for the exteriour bounds, the benefit of their riches extending alfo to the furnifhing of the moft worthy inward parts thereof : but becaufe many take pleafure in the fight and knowledge of other herbes that are Phyficall, and much more in their properties and vertues, if vnto thefe three I fhould adde a Phyficke Garden, or Garden of Simples, there would be a quadripartite complement, of whatfoeuer arte or nature, neceffitie or delight could affect : which to effect (as many my friends haue intreated it at my hands) will require more paines and time then all this worke together : yet to fatisfie their defires and all others herein, that would bee enformed in the truth, and reformed of the many errours and flips fet forth and publifhed heretofore of plants by diuers, I fhall (God affifting and granting life)labour to performe, that it may fhew it felfe to the light in due conueniencie, if thefe bee well and gratefully accepted. And becaufe I ended with fome fweete herbes in the former part, I will in this part beginne with the reft, which I referued for this place, as fitter for the pot and kitchen then for the hand or bofome, and fo defcend to other herbes that are for meat or fallets : and after them to thofe rootes that are to be eaten, as meate or as fallets : and laftly the fruits that grow neere, or vpon the ground, or not much aboue it ; as the Artichoke, &c. in which I make a fhorter defcription then I did in the former, rather endeauouring to fhew what they are, and whereunto they are vfed, then the whole varietie or any exact declaration : which methode, although in fome fort it may bee fitting for this purpofe, yet it is not for an hiftory or herball : I fhall therefore require their good acceptance for whofe fake I doe it, not doubting, but that I, or others, if they write againe of this fubiect, may polifh and amende what formerly hath beene eyther mif fet, or not fo thoroughly expreffed, befides fome additions of new conceits; feeing I treade out a new path, and therefore thofe that follow may the eafilier fee the Meanders, and fo goe on in a direct line.

CHAP.

Chap. I.

Maiorana latifolia, siue maior Anglica. Winter, or pot Marierome.

Winter Marierome is a small bushie herbe like vnto sweete Marierome, being parted or diuided into many branches, whereon doe grow broader and greener leaues, set by couples, with some small leaues likewise at the seuerall ioynts all along the branches : at the tops whereof grow a number of small purplish white flowers set together in a tuft, which turne into small and round seed, bigger then sweet Marierome seede : the whole plant is of a small and fine sent, but much inferiour to the other, and is nothing so bitter as the sweete Marierome, and thereby both the fitter and more willingly vsed for meates : the roote is white and threddy, and perisheth not as the former, but abideth many yeares.

The Vse of winter Marierome.

The vse of this Marierome is more frequent in our Land then in others, being put among other pot-herbes and farsing (or faseting herbes as they are called) and may to good profit bee applyed in inward as well as outward griefes for to comfort the parts, although weaker in effect then sweete Marieromes.

Chap. II.

Thymum vulgatius siue durius. Ordinary Garden Tyme.

The ordinary Garden Tyme is a small low wooddy plant with brittle branches, and small hard greene leaues, as euery one knoweth, hauing small white purplish flowers, standing round about the tops of the stalkes : the seed is small and browne, darker then Marierome seed : the root is woody, and abideth well diuers Winters.

Thymum latifolium. Masticke Tyme.

This Tyme hath neyther so wooddy branches, nor so hard leaues, but groweth lower, more spreading, and with somewhat broader leaues : the flowers are of a purplish white colour, standing in roundles round about the stalkes, at the ioynts with leaues at them likewise. This Tyme endureth better and longer then the former, and by spreading it selfe more then the former, is the more apt to bee propagated by slipping, because it hath beene seldome seene to giue seede : It is not so quicke in sent or taste as the former, but is fitter to set any border or knot in a garden, and is for the most part wholly employed to such vses.

The Vse of Tyme.

To set downe all the particular vses whereunto Tyme is applyed, were to weary both the Writer and Reader; I will but only note out a few : for besides the physicall vses to many purposes, for the head, stomacke, spleene, &c. there is no herbe almost of more vse, in the houses both of high and low, rich and poore, both for inward and outward occasions ; outwardly for bathings among other hot herbes, and among other sweete herbes for strewings : inwardly in most sorts of broths, with Rosmary, as also with other faseting (or rather farsing) herbes, and to make sawce for diuers sorts both fish and flesh, as to stuffe the belly of a Goose to bee rosted, and after put into the sawce, and the pouder with breade to strew on meate when it

is

1 *Maioran mmior Anglica.* Pot Marierome. 2 *Thymum vulgatius.* Garden Tyme. 3 *Satureia.* Sauorie. 4 *Hyssopus.* Hyssope. 5 *Pulegium.* Penniroyall. 6 *Saluia maior.* Common Sage. 7 *Saluia minor primata.* Sage of vertue.

is rofted, and fo likewife on rofted or fryed fish. It is held by diuers to bee a fpeedy remedy againft the fting of a Bee, being bruifed and layd thereon.

Chap. III.

Satureia fiue Thymbra. Sauorie.

THere are two forts of of Sauory, the one called Summer, and the other Winter Sauorie : The Summer Sauory is a fmall tender herbe, growing not aboue a foote and a halfe high, or thereabouts, rifing vp with diuers brittle branches, flenderly or fparfedly fet with fmall long leaues, foft in handling, at euery ioynt a couple, one againft another, of a pleafant ftrong and quicke fent and tafte : the flowers are fmall and purplish, growing at the toppes of the ftalkes, with two fmall long leaues at the ioynts vnder them : the feede is fmall, and of a darke colour, bigger then Tyme feede by the halfe : the roote is wooddy, and hath many ftrings, perifhing euery yeare wholly, and muft bee new fowen againe, if any will haue it.

The Winter Sauorie is a fmall low bufhie herbe, very like vnto Hyffope, but not aboue a foote high, with diuers fmall hard branches, and hard darke green leaues thereon, thicker fet together then the former by much, and as thicke as common Hyffope, fometimes with foure leaues or more at a ioynt, of a reafonable ftrong fent, yet not fo ftrong or quicke as the former : the flowers are of a pale purplish colour, fet at feuerall diftances at the toppes of the ftalkes, with leaues at the ioynts alfo with them, like the former : the roote is woody, with diuers fmall ftrings thereat, and abideth all the winter with his greene leaues : it is more vfually encreafed by flipping or diuiding the roote, and new fetting it feuerally againe in the Spring, then by fowing the feed.

The Vfe of Sauorie.

The Summer Sauorie is vfed in other Countryes much more then with vs in their ordinary diets, as condiment or fawce to their meates, fometimes of it felfe, and fometimes with other herbes, and fometimes ftrewed or layde vpon the dishes as we doe Parfley, as alfo with beanes and peafe, rife and wheate ; and fometimes the dryed herbe boyled among peafe to make pottage.

The Winter Sauorie is one of the (farfing) fafeting herbes as they call them, and fo is the Summer Sauorie alfo fometimes. This is vfed alfo in the fame manner that the Summer Sauorie is, fet downe before, and to the fame purpofes : as alfo to put into puddings, fawfages, and fuch like kindes of meates. Some doe vfe the ponder of the herbe dryed (as I fayd before of Tyme) to mixe with grated bread, to breade their meate, be it fifh or flefh, to giue it the quicker rellifh. They are both effectuall to expell winde.

Chap. IIII.

Hyffopus. Hyffope.

GArden Hyffope is fo well knowne to all that haue beene in a Garden, that I fhall but *actum agere*, to beftow any time thereon, being a fmall bufhie plant, not rifing aboue two foote high, with many branches, woody below, and tender aboue, whereon are fet at certaine diftances, fundry fmall, long and narrow greene leaues : at the toppe of euery ftalke ftand blewifh purple gaping flowers, one aboue another in a long fpike or eare : after which followeth the feede, which is fmall and blackifh : the rootes are compofed of many threddy ftrings ; the whole plant is of a ftrong fweet fent.

The

The Vſe of Hyſſope.

Hyſſope is much vſed in Ptiſans and other drinkes, to help to expectorate flegme. It is many Countrey peoples medicine for a cut or greene wound, being bruiſed with ſugar and applyed. I finde it is alſo much commended againſt the falling ſickeneſſe, eſpecially being made into pils after the manner before rehearſed. It is accounted a ſpeciall remedy againſt the ſting or biting of an Adder, if the place be rubbed with Hyſſope, bruiſed and mixed with honey, ſalt and cummin ſeede. A decoction thereof with oyle, and annointed, taketh away the itching and tingling of the head, and vermine alſo breeding therein. An oyle made of the herbe and flowers, being annointed, doth comfort benummed ſinewes and ioynts.

Chap. V.

Pulegium. Pennyroyall.

Pennyroyall alſo is an herbe ſo well knowne, that I ſhall not neede to ſpend much time in the deſcription of it : hauing many weake round ſtalkes, diuided into ſundry branches, rather leaning or lying vpon the ground then ſtanding vpright, whereon are ſet at ſeuerall ioynts, ſmall roundiſh darke greene leaues : the flowers are purpliſh that grow in gardens, yet ſome that grow wilde are white, or more white then purple, ſet in roundles about the tops of the branches ; the ſtalkes ſhoote forth ſmall fibres or rootes at the ioynts, as it lyeth vpon the ground, thereby faſtening it ſelfe therein, and quickly increaſeth, and ouer-runneth any ground, eſpecially in the ſhade or any moiſt place, and is replanted by breaking the ſprouted ſtalkes, and ſo quickely groweth.

Other ſorts of Pennyroyall are fit for the Phyſicke Garden, or Garden of Simples.

The Vſe of Pennyroyall.

It is very good and wholeſome for the lunges, to expell cold thin flegme, and afterwards to warme and dry it vp : and is alſo of the like propertie as Mintes, to comfort the ſtomacke, and ſtay vomiting. It is alſo vſed in womens baths and waſhings : and in mens alſo to comfort the ſinewes. It is yet to this day, as it hath beene in former times, vſed to bee put into puddings, and ſuch like meates of all ſorts, and therefore in diuers places they know it by no other name then Pudding-graſſe.

The former age of our great Grandfathers, had all theſe hot herbes in much and familiar vſe, both for their meates and medicines, and therewith preſerued themſelues in long life and much health : but this delicate age of ours, which is not pleaſed with any thing almoſt, be it meat or medicine, that is not pleaſant to the palate, doth wholly refuſe theſe almoſt, and therefore cannot be partaker of the benefit of them.

Chap. VI.

Salvia. Sage.

There are two eſpeciall kindes of Sage nourſed vp in our Gardens, for our ordinary vſe, whereof I intend to write in this place, leauing the reſt to his fitter place. Our ordinary Sage is reckoned to bee of two ſorts, white and red,

both

both of them bearing many foure fquare wooddy ftalkes, in fome whiter, in others redder, as the leaues are alfo, ftanding by couples at the ioynts, being long, rough, and wrinkled, of a ftrong fweete fent : at the tops of the ftalkes come forth the flowers, fet at certaine fpaces one aboue another, which are long and gaping, like vnto the flowers of Clary, or dead Nettles, but of a blewifh purple colour ; after which come fmall round feede in the huske that bore the flower : the roote is wooddy, with diuers ftrings at it : It is more vfually planted of the flips, pricked in the Spring time into the ground, then of the feed.

Saluia minor fiue pinnata. Small Sage or Sage of vertue.

The leffer Sage is in all things like vnto the former white Sage, but that his branches are long and flender, and the leaues much fmaller, hauing for the moft part at the bottome of each fide of the leafe a peece of a leafe, which maketh it fhew like finns or eares : the flowers alfo are of a blewifh purple colour, but leffer. Of this kinde there is one that beareth white flowers.

The Vfe of Sage.

Sage is much vfed of many in the moneth of May fafting, with butter and Parfley, and is held of moft much to conduce to the health of mans body.

It is alfo much vfed among other good herbes to bee tund vp with Ale, which thereupon is termed Sage Ale, whereof many barrels full are made, and drunke in the faid moneth chiefly for the purpofe afore recited: and alfo for teeming women, to helpe them the better forward in their childebearing, if there be feare of abortion or mifcarrying.

It is alfo vfed to be boyled among other herbes, to make Gargles or waters to wafh fore mouths and throates : As alfo among other herbes, that ferue as bathings, to wafh mens legs or bodies in the Summer time, to comfort nature, and warme and ftrengthen aged cold finewes, and lengthen the ftrength of the younger.

The Kitchen vfe is either to boyle it with a Calues head, and being minced, to be put with the braines, vinegar and pepper, to ferue as an ordinary fawce thereunto : Or being beaten and iuyced (rather then minced as manie doe) is put to a rofted Pigges braines, with Currans for fawce thereunto. It is in fmall quantity (in regard of the ftrong tafte thereof) put among other fafting herbes, to ferue as fawce for peeces of Veale, when they are farfed or ftuffed therewith, and rofted, which they call Olliues.

For all the purpofes aforefaid, the fmall Sage is accounted to be of the more force and vertue.

Chap. VII.

Horminum fativum. Garden Clary.

THere is but one fort of Garden Clary, though many wilde, which hath foure fquares ftalks, with broad rough wrinkled whitifh leaues, fomewhat vneuenly cut in on the edges, and of a ftrong fweete fent, growing fome next the ground, & fome by couples vpon the ftalkes: the flowers growe at certaine diftances, with two fmall leaues at the ioynts vnder them, fomewhat like vnto the flowers of Sage, but leffer, and of a very whitifh or bleake blew colour : the feede is of a blackifh browne colour, fomewhat flat, and not fo round as the wilde : the rootes fpread not farre, and perifh euery yeare that they beare flowers and feede. It is altogether to bee fowne of feed in the Spring time, yet fometimes it will rife of it owne fowing.

The

The Vse of Clary.

The moſt frequent and common vſe of Clary, is for men or women that haue weake backes, to helpe to comfort and ſtrengthen the raines, being made into Tanſies and eaten, or otherwiſe. The ſeede is vſed of ſome to be put into the corner of the eye, if any mote or other thing haue happened into it: but aſſuredly although this may peraduenture doe ſome good, yet the ſeede of the wilde will doe much more. The leaues taken dry, and dipped into a batter made of the yolkes of egges, flower, and a little milke, and then fryed with butter vntill they be criſpe, ſerue for a diſh of meate accepted with manie, vnpleaſant to none.

Chap. VIII.

Nepeta. Nep.

ALthough thoſe that are Herbariſts do know three ſorts of Nep, a greater & two leſſer, yet becauſe the leſſer are not vſuall, but in the Gardens of thoſe that delight in natures varieties, I do not here ſhew you them. That which is vſuall (and called of manie Cat Mint) beareth ſquare ſtalkes, but not ſo great as Clarie, hauing two leaues at euery ioynt, ſomewhat like vnto Balme or Speare Mintes, but whiter, ſofter, and longer, and nicked about the edges, of a ſtrong ſent, but nothing ſo ſtrong as Clary: the flowers growe at the toppes of the ſtalkes, as it were in long ſpikes or heads, ſomewhat cloſe together, yet compaſſing the ſtalkes at certaine ioynts, of a whitiſh colour, for forme and bigneſſe like vnto Balme, or ſomewhat bigger: the rootes are compoſed of a number of ſtrings, which dye not, but keepe greene leaues vpon them all the Winter, and ſhoote anew in the Spring. It is propagated both by the ſeede, and by ſlipping the rootes.

The Vse of Nep.

Nep is much vſed of women either in baths or drinkes to procure their feminine courſes: as alſo with Clarie, being fryed into Tanſies, to ſtrengthen their backes. It is much commended of ſome, if the iuyce thereof be drunke with wine, to helpe thoſe that are bruiſed by ſome fall, or other accident. A decoction of Nep is auaileable to cure the ſcabbe in the head, or other places of the body.

Chap. IX.

Meliſſa. Baulme.

THe Garden Baulme which is of common knowne vſe, hath diuers ſquare blackiſh greene ſtalkes, and round, hard, darke, greene pointed leaues, growing thereon by couples, a little notched about the edges, of a pleaſant ſweete ſent, drawing neareſt to the ſent of a Lemon or Citron; and therefore of ſome called *Citrago*: the flowers growe about the toppes of the ſtalkes at certaine diſtances, being ſmall and gaping, of a pale carnation colour, almoſt white: the rootes faſten themſelues ſtrongly in the ground, and endure many yeares, and is encreaſed by diuiding the rootes; for the leaues dye downe to the ground euery yeare, leauing no ſhew of leafe or ſtalke in the Winter.

The

The Vſe of Baulme.

Baulme is often vſed among other hot and ſweete herbes, to make baths and waſhings for mens bodies or legges, in the Summer time, to warme and comfort the veines and ſinewes, to very good purpoſe and effect, and hath in former ages beene of much more vſe then now adaies. It is alſo vſed by diuers to be ſtilled, being ſteeped in Ale, to make a Baulme water, after the manner they haue beene taught, which they keepe by them, to vſe in the ſtead of *Aqua vitæ*, when they haue any occaſion for their owne or their neighbours Families, in ſuddaine qualmes or paſſions of the heart : but if they had a little better direction (for this is ſomewhat too rude) it would doe them more good that take it : For the herbe without all queſtion is an excellent helpe to comfort the heart, as the very ſmell may induce any ſo to beleeue. It is alſo good to heale greene wounds, being made into ſalues : and I verily thinke, that our forefathers hearing of the healing and comfortable properties of the true naturall Baulme, and finding this herbe to be ſo effectuall, gaue it the name of Baulme, in imitation of his properties and vertues. It is alſo an herbe wherein Bees doe much delight, as hath beene found by experience of thoſe that haue kept great ſtore ; if the Hiues bee rubbed on the inſide with ſome thereof, and as they thinke it draweth others by the ſmell thereof to reſort thither. Plinie ſaith, it is a preſent remedy againſt the ſtinging of Bees.

Chap. X.

Mentha. Mintes.

There are diuers ſorts of Mints, both of the garden, and wilde, of the woods, mountaines, and ſtanding pooles or waters : but I will onely in this place bring to your remembrance two or three ſorts of the moſt vſuall that are kept in gardens, for the vſes whereunto they are proper.

Red Mint or browne Mint hath ſquare browniſh ſtalkes, with ſomewhat long and round pointed leaues, nicked about the edges, of a darke greene colour, ſet by couples at euery ioynt, and of a reaſonable good ſent : the flowers of this kinde are reddiſh, ſtanding about the toppes of the ſtalkes at diſtances : the rootes runne creeping in the ground, and as the reſt, will hardly be cleared out of a garden, being once therein, in that the ſmalleſt peece thereof will growe and encreaſe apace.

Speare Mint hath a ſquare greene ſtalke, with longer and greener leaues then the former, ſet by couples, of a better and more comfortable ſent, and therefore of much more vſe then any other : the flowers hereof growe in long eares or ſpikes, of a pale red or bluſh colour : the rootes creepe in the ground like the other.

Party coloured or white Mint hath ſquare greene ſtalkes and leaues, ſomewhat larger then Speare Mint, and more nicked in the edges, whereof many are parted, halfe white and halfe greene, and ſome more white then greene, or more green then white, as nature liſteth : the flowers ſtand in long heads cloſe ſet together, of a bluſh colour : the rootes creepe as the reſt doe.

The Vſe of Mintes.

Mintes are oftentimes vſed in baths, with Baulme and other herbes, as a helpe to comfort and ſtrengthen the nerues and ſinewes.

It is much vſed either outwardly applyed, or inwardly drunke, to ſtrengthen and comfort weake ſtomackes, that are much giuen to caſting : as alſo for feminine fluxes. It is boyled in milke for thoſe whoſe ſtomackes are

apt

1 *Horminum sativum.* Garden Clary. 2 *Nepeta.* Nep. 3 *Melissa.* Baulme. 4 *Mentha sativa.* Garden Mintes.
5 *Balsamita mas, seu Costus hortorum.* Costmary. 6 *Ageratum.* Maudeline.

apt to caufe it to curdle. And applyed with falt, is a good helpe for the biting of a mad dogge.

It is vfed to be boyled with Mackarell, and other fifh.

Being dryed, is often and much vfed with Penniroyall, to bee put into
puddings : as alfo among peafe that are boyled for pottage.

Where Dockes are not ready at hand, they vfe to bruife Mintes, and
lay them vpon any place that is ftung with Bees, Wafpes, or fuch like, and
that to good purpofe.

<hr />

CHAP. XI.

Balfamita mas & femina, feu Coftus hortorum maior & minor.
Coftmary and Maudeline.

COftmary or Alecoaft is a fweet herbe, bearing many broad and long pale green
leaues, fnipped about the edges, euery one vpon a long foote-ftalke ; among
which rife vp many round greene ftalkes, with fuch like leaues on them, but
leffer vp to the toppe, where it fpreadeth it felfe into three or foure branches, euery
one bearing an vmbell or tuft of gold yellow flowers, fomewhat like vnto Tanfie
flowers, but leffer, which turne into fmall heads, containing fmall flat long feede : the
roote is fomewhat hard and ftringy, and being diuided, is replanted in the Spring of
the yeare for increafe.

Maudeline hath fomewhat long and narrow leaues, fnipt about the edges : the ftalks
are two foot high, bearing many yellow flowers on the tops of the branches, in an vmbell or tuft like vnto Tanfie : the whole herbe is fweete, and fomewhat bitter, and is
replanted by flipping.

The Vfe of Coftmary and Maudeline.

Coftmary is of efpeciall vfe in the Spring of the yeare, among other fuch
like herbes, to make Sage Ale, and thereupon I thinke it tooke the name of
Alecoaft.

It is alfo vfed to be put among other fweete herbes, to make fweete wafhing water, whereof there is great ftore fpent.

The leaues haue an efpeciall vertue to comfort both the ftomack and
heart, and to warme and dry a moift braine. The feede is much vfed in the
Country, to be giuen to children for the wormes, in the ftead of wormfeed,
and fo is the feede of Maudeline alfo.

Maudeline is much vfed with Coftmary and other fweet herbes, to make
fweete wafhing water : the flowers alfo are tyed vp with fmall bundels of
Lauender toppes, thefe being put in the middle of them, to lye vpon the
toppes of beds, preffes, &c. for the fweete fent and fauour it cafteth. It is
generally accounted of our Apothecaries to be the true *Eupatorium* of Auicen, and the true *Ageratum* of Diofcorides ; but Dodonæus feemeth to contradict both.

<hr />

CHAP. XII.

Tanacetum vulgare & crifpum. Tanfie.

OVr Garden Tanfie hath many hard greene leaues, or rather wings of leaues ;
for they are many fmall ones, fet one againft another all along a middle ribbe
or ftalke, and fnipt about the edges : in fome the leaues ftand clofer and thicker, and fomewhat crumpled, which hath caufed it to be called double or curld Tanfie,

sie, in others thinner and more sparsedly : It riseth vp with many hard stalks, whereon growe at the tops vpon the seuerall small branches gold yellow flowers like buttons, which being gathered in their prime, will hold the colour fresh a long time : the seede is small, and as it were chaffie : the roote creepeth vnder ground, and shooteth vp againe in diuers places : the whole herbe, both leaues and flowers, are of a sharpe, strong, bitter smell and taste, but yet pleasant, and well to be endured.

The Vse of Tansie.

The leaues of Tansie are vsed while they are young, either shred small with other herbes, or else the iuyce of it and other herbes fit for the purpose, beaten with egges, and fryed into cakes (in Lent and the Spring of the yeare) which are vsually called Tansies, and are often eaten, being taken to be very good for the stomack, to helpe to digest from thence bad humours that cleaue thereunto: As also for weak raines and kidneyes, when the vrine passeth away by drops : This is thought to be of more vse for men then for women. The seed is much commended against all sorts of wormes in children.

Chap. XII.

Pimpinella siue Sanguisorba. Burnet.

BVrnet hath many winged leaues lying vpon the ground, made of many small, round, yet pointed greene leaues, finely nicked on the edges, one set against another all along a middle ribbe, and one at the end thereof; from among which rise vp diuers round, and sometimes crested browne stalkes, with some few such like leaues on them as growe belowe, but smaller : at the toppes of the stalkes growe small browne heads or knaps, which shoote forth small purplish flowers, turning into long and brownish, but a little cornered seede : the roote groweth downe deepe, being small and brownish : the whole plant is of a stipticke or binding taste or quality, but of a fine quicke sent, almost like Baulme.

The Vse of Burnet.

The greatest vse that Burnet is commonly put vnto, is to put a few leaues into a cup with Claret wine, which is presently to be drunke, and giueth a pleasant quicke taste thereunto, very delightfull to the palate, and is accounted a helpe to make the heart merrie. It is sometimes also while it is young, put among other Sallet herbes, to giue a finer rellish thereunto. It is also vsed in vulnerary drinkes, and to stay fluxes and bleedings, for which purposes it is much commended. It hath beene also much commended in contagious and pestilentiall agues.

Chap. XIIII.

Hippolapathum satiuum, siue Rhabarbarum Monachorum. Monkes Rubarbe or Patience.

GArden Patience is a kinde of Docke in all the parts thereof, but that it is larger and taller then many others, with large and long greene leaues, a great, strong, and high stalke, with reddish or purplish flowers, and three square seede, like as all other Dockes haue : the roote is great and yellow, not hauing any shew of flesh coloured veines therein, no more then the other kinde with great round thin leaues, commonly called *Hippolapathum rotundifolium*, Baſtard Rubarbe, or Monkes Rubarbe, the properties of both which are of very weake effect : but I haue a kinde of round leafed Dock growing in my Garden, which was ſent me from beyond Sea by a worthy Gentleman, Mr. Dr. Matth. Liſter, one of the Kings Phyſitians, with this title, *Rhaponticum verum*, and firſt grew with me, before it was euer ſeen or known elſewhere in England, wch by proof I haue found to be ſo like vnto the true Rubarbe, or the Rha of Pontus, both for forme and colour, that I dare ſay it is the very true Rubarbe, our climate only making it leſſe ſtrong in working, leſſe heauy, and leſſe bitter in taſte: For this hath great and thicke rootes, as diuerſly diſcoloured with fleſh coloured veines as the true Rubarbe, as I haue to ſhew to any that are deſirous to ſee and know it ; and alſo other ſmaller ſprayes or branches of rootes, ſpreading from the maine great roote, which ſmaller branches may well be compared to the *Rhaponticum* which the Merchants haue brought vs, which we haue ſeene to be longer and ſlenderer then Rubarbe, but of the very ſame colour : this beareth ſo goodly large leaues, that it is a great beauty in a garden to behold them : for I haue meaſured the ſtalke of the leafe at the bottome next the roote to bee of the bigneſſe of any mans thumbe ; and from the roote to the leafe it ſelfe, to bee two foote in length, and ſometimes more ; and likewiſe the leafe it ſelfe, from the lower end where it is ioyned to the ſtalke, to the end or point thereof, to bee alſo two foote in length, and ſometimes more ; and alſo in the broadeſt part of the leafe, to be two foote or more ouer in breadth : it beareth whitiſh flowers, contrary to all other Dockes, and three ſquare browniſh ſeede as other Dockes doe, but bigger, and therefore aſſuredly it is a Docke, and the true Rubarbe of the Arabians, or at the leaſt the true *Rhaponticum* of the Ancients. The figure of the whole plant I haue cauſed to be cut, with a dryed roote as it grew in my garden by it ſelfe, and haue inſerted it here, both becauſe Matthiolus giueth a falſe figure of the true Rubarbe, and that this hath not been expreſſed and ſet forth by any before.

The Vſe of Patience, and of the Rubarbe.

The leaues of Patience are often, and of many vſed for a pot-herbe, and ſeldome to any other purpoſe : the roote is often vſed in Diet-beere, or ale, or in other drinkes made by decoction, to helpe to purge the liuer, and clenſe the blood. The other Rubarbe or *Rhaponticum*, wherof I make mention, and giue you here the figure, I haue tryed, and found by experience to purge gently, without that aſtriction that is in the true Rubarbe is brought vs from the Eaſt Indies, or China, and is alſo leſſe bitter in taſte ; whereby I coniecture it may bee vſed in hot and feaueriſh bodies more effectually, becauſe it doth not binde after the purging, as the Eaſt India Rubarbe doth : but this muſt bee giuen in double quantitie to the other, and then no doubt it will doe as well : The leaues haue a fine acide taſte : A ſyrrupe therefore made with the iuice and ſugar, cannot but be very effectuall in deiected appetites, and hot fits of agues; as alſo to helpe to open obſtructions of the liuer, as diuers haue often tryed, and found auaileable by experience.

CHAP. XV.

Lapathum ſanguineum. Blood-wort.

AMong the ſorts of pot-herbes Blood-worte hath alwayes beene accounted a principall one, although I doe not ſee any great reaſon therein, eſpecially ſeeing there is a greater efficacie of binding in this Docke, then in any of the other : but as common vſe hath receiued it, ſo I here ſet it downe. Blood-worte is one of the ſorts of Dockes, and hath long leaues like vnto the ſmaller yellow Docke, but ſtriped with red veines, and ouer-ſhadowed with red vpon the greene leafe, that it ſeemeth almoſt wholly red ſometimes : the ſtalke is reddiſh, bearing ſuch like leaues, but
ſmaller

1 *Tanacetum.* Tanſie. 2 *Pimpinella.* Burnet. 3 *Rhaponticum verum ſeu potius Rhabarbarum verum.* True Raponticke or rather true Rubarbe. 4 *Lapathum ſativum ſeu Patientia.* Monkes Rubarbe or Patience. 5 *Lapathum ſanguineum.* Bloudwort. 6 *Acetoſa.* Sorrell.

ſmaller vp to the toppe, where it is diuided into diuers ſmall branches, whereon grow purpliſh flowers, and three ſquare darke red ſeede, like vnto others : the roots are not great, but ſomewhat long, and very red, abiding many yeares, yet ſometimes ſpoiled with the extremitie of winter.

The Vſe of Blood-worte.

The whole and onely vſe of the herbe almoſt, ſerueth for the pot, among other herbes, and, as I ſaid before, is accounted a moſt eſpeciall one for that purpoſe. The ſeede therof is much commended for any fluxe in man or woman, to be inwardly taken, and ſo no doubt is the roote, being of a ſtipticke qualitie.

Chap. XVI.

Oxalis ſiue Acetoſa. Sorrell.

Sorrell muſt needes bee reckoned with the Dockes, for that it is ſo like vnto them in all things, and is of many called the ſower Docke. Of Sorrels there are many ſorts, but I ſhall not trouble you with any other in this place, then the common Garden Sorrell, which is moſt knowne, and of greateſt vſe with vs ; which hath tender greene long leaues full of iuice, broade, and bicorned as it were, next vnto the ſtalke, like as Arrach, Spinach, and our Engliſh Mercurie haue, of a ſharpe ſower taſte : the ſtalkes are ſlender, bearing purpliſh long heads, wherein lye three ſquare ſhining browne ſeede, like, but leſſer then the other : the root is ſmaller then any of the other Dockes, but browne, and full of ſtrings, and abideth without decaying, hauing greene leaues all the winter, except in the very extremitie thereof, which often taketh away all or moſt of his leaues.

The Vſe of Sorrell.

Sorrell is much vſed in ſawces, both for the whole, and the ſicke, cooling the hot liuers, and ſtomackes of the ſicke, and procuring vnto them an appetite vnto meate, when their ſpirits are almoſt ſpent with the violence of their furious or fierie fits ; and is alſo of a pleaſant relliſh for the whole, in quickning vp a dull ſtomacke that is ouer-loaden with euery daies plenty of diſhes. It is diuers waies dreſſed by Cooks, to pleaſe their Maſters ſtomacks.

Chap. XVII.

Bugloſſum luteum, ſiue Lingua Bouis. Langdebeefe.

Vnto this place may well bee referred our ordinary Borage and Bugloſſe, ſet forth in the former Booke, in regard of the properties whereunto they are much employed, that is, to ſerue the pot among other herbes, as is ſufficiently knowne vnto all. And yet I confeſſe, that this herbe (although it bee called *Bugloſſum luteum,* as if it were a kind of Bugloſſe) hath no correſpondency with Bugloſſe or Borage in any part, ſauing only a little in the leafe; & our Borage or Bugloſſe might more fitly, according to the Greeke name, bee called Oxe tongue or Langdebeefe; and this might in my iudgement more aptly be referred to the kinds of *Hieratium* Hawkeweed, whereunto it neereſt approacheth : but as it is commonly receiued, ſo take it in this place, vntill it come to receiue the place is proper for it. It hath diuers broad and long darke green leaues, lying vpon the ground, very rough in handling, full of ſmall haires or prickes, ready to enter into the hands of any that handle it ; among which riſeth

vp

1 *Lingua bouis siue Buglossum luteum.* Langdebeefe. 2 *Atriplex siue Olus aureum.* Arrach. 3 *Blitum.* Blites.
4 *Beta.* Beetes. 5 *Hipposelinum siue Olus atrum.* Allisanders. 6 *Selinum dulce.* Sweete Parsley.

vp a round greene hairy or prickly ſtalk, bearing at the toppe, among a few ſmall green leaues, diuers ſmall yellow flowers in rough heads, which turne into doune, containing within them browne yellowiſh ſmall long ſeedes, ſomewhat like vnto the ſeede of Hawkeweede : the roote is wooddy, which periſheth quickly after it hath borne ſeed; but is tender while it is young.

The Vſe of Langdebeefe.

The leaues are onely vſed in all places that I know, or euer could learne, for an herbe for the pot among others, and is thought to bee good to looſen the belly.

CHAP. XVIII.

Atriplex ſiue Olus Aureum. Arrach.

THere be diuers kindes of Arrach, or Orach, as ſome doe call them ; ſome of the Garden, whereof I meane to entreate in this place ; others wilde of the Fieldes, &c. and others of the Sea, which are not to bee ſpoken of in this worke, but referred to a generall hiſtorie. The white garden Arrach, or Orach, hath diuers leaues, ſtanding vpon their ſeuerall footeſtalkes, broade at the bottome, ending in two points like an arrow, with two feathers at the head, and ſmall pointed at the end of the leafe, of a whitiſh yellow greene colour, and as it were ſtrewed ouer with flower or meale, eſpecially while they are young : the ſtalke likewiſe is mealy, bearing many branches with ſmall yellow flowers on them, which turne into ſmall leafie ſeeds : the rooote groweth ſomewhat deepe in the ground, with many ſmall threds faſtened thereto : it quickly ſpringeth vp of the ſeede, groweth great, and fadeth away as ſoon as it hath borne ſeede.

The purple Arrach is in all things like vnto the white, ſauing onely in the colour of the leafe, ſtalke, ſeede, &c. which are all of a mealy duſty purpliſh colour.

The Vſe of Arrach.

Arrach is cold and moiſt, and of a lubricke or ſlippery qualitie, whereby it quickely paſſeth through the ſtomacke and belly, and maketh it ſoluble, and is of many vſed for that purpoſe, being boyled and buttered, or put among other herbes into the pot to make pottage.

There are many diſhes of meate made with them while they are young, for being almoſt without ſauour of themſelues, they are the more conuertible into what relliſh any one will make them with Sugar, Spice &c.

CHAP. XIX.

Blitum. Blites.

THere be diuers ſorts of Blites, ſome whereof I haue entreated in the former part of this worke, vnder the title of *Amaranthus*, Flower gentle : others that are nourſed vp in Gardens, I will ſet forth in this place, which are onely two, that haue come to my knowledge, that is, the white and the red, and are of a qualitie as neere vnto Arrach as vnto Beetes, participating of both, and therefore I haue placed them betwixt them. The white Blite hath leaues ſomewhat like vnto Beetes, but ſmaller, rounder, and of a whitiſh greene colour, euery one ſtanding vpon a ſmall long footeſtalke : the ſtalke riſeth vp two or three foote high, with many ſuch like leaues thereon : the flowers grow at the top in long round tufts or cluſters, wherein are contained

tained fmall round feede : the roote is very full of threds or ftrings.

The red Blite is in all things like the white, but that his leaues and tufted heades are exceeding red at the firft, and after turne more purplifh.

The Vfe of Blites.

Blites are vfed as Arrach, eyther boyled of it felfe or ftewed, which they call Loblolly, or among other herbes to bee put into the pot ; and yet fome doe vtterly refufe it, becaufe in diuers it prouoketh caftings. It is altogether infipide or without tafte, but yet by reafon of the moift flipperie qualitie it hath, it helpeth to loofen the belly. The vnfauorineffe whereof hath in many Countries growne into a prouerbe, or by-word, to call dull, flow, or lazie perfons by that name : They are accounted more hurtfull to the ftomacke, and fo to the head and eyes, then other herbes, and therefore they are the leffe vfed.

Chap. XX.

Beta. Beetes.

THere are many diuerfities of Beetes, fome growing naturally in our own Country, others brought from beyond Sea ; whereof fome are white, fome greene, fome yellow, fome red : the leaues of fome are of vfe only, and the root not vfed : others the roote is only vfed, and not the leaues : and fome againe, both roote and leafe. The ancient Authors, as by their workes appeare, knew but two forts, the white and the blacke Beete, whereof the white is fufficiently known, and was of them termed *Sicula*, of the later Phyfitians *Sicla*, becaufe it was thought firft to be brought from Sicilie : the blacke abideth fome controuerfie ; fome thinking that our common greene Beete, becaufe it is of a darke greene colour, was that they called the blacke Beete ; others that our fmall red Beete, which is of a darke red colour, was their black Beete, which in my opinion is the more likely : But to come to the matter in hand, and giue you the defcriptions of them which are in vfe with vs, and leaue controuerfies to fuch a worke as is fit for them, wherein all fuch matters may be difcuffed at large.

The common white Beete hath many great leaues next the ground (in fome hot Countries growing to be three foote long, and very broade, in our Countrey they are very large, but nothing neere that proportion) of a whitifh greene colour ; the ftalke is great, ftrong, and ribbed or crefted, bearing great ftore of leaues vpon it vp to the very toppe almoft : the flowers grow in very long tufts, fmall at the ends, and turning down their heads, which are fmall pale greenifh yellow burres, giuing cornered prickly feede : the roote is great, long and hard, when it hath giuen feede, of no vfe at all, but abideth a former winter with his leaues vpon it, as all other forts following doe.

The common red Beet differeth not from the white Beete, but only that it is not fo great, and both the leaues and rootes are fomewhat red : the leaues bee in fome more red then in others, which haue but red veines or ftrakes in them, in fome alfo of a frefh red, in others very darke red : the roote hereof is red, fpongy, and not vfed to bee eaten.

The common greene Beete is alfo like vnto the white Beete, but of a darke greene colour. This hath beene found neere the falt Marfhes by Rochefter, in the foote-way going from the Lady Levefons houfe thither, by a worthy, diligent and painefull obferuer and preferuer both of plants and all other natures varieties, often remembred before in this worke, called Iohn Tradefcante, who there finding it, gaue me the knowledge thereof, and I haue vpon his report fet it here down in this manner :

The Romane red Beete, called *Beta rapofa*, is both for leafe and roote the moft excellent Beete of all others : his rootes bee as great as the greateft Carrot, exceeding red both within and without, very fweete and good, fit to bee eaten : this Beete groweth higher then the laft red Beete, whofe rootes are not vfed to bee eaten : the leaues likewife

wife are better of tafte, and of as red a colour as the former red Beete : the roote is fometimes fhort like a Turnep, whereof it took the name of *Rapa* or *rapofa* ; and fometimes as I faid before, like a Carrot and long : the feede is all one with the leffer red Beete.

The Italian Beete is of much refpect, whofe faire greene leaues are very large and great, with great white ribbes and veines therein: the ftalke in the Summer time, when it is growen vp to any height, is fix fquare in fhew, and yellowifh withall, as the heades with feede vpon them feeme likewife.

The great red Beete that Mafter Lete a Merchant of London gaue vnto Mafter Gerrard, as he fetteth it downe in his Herball, feemeth to bee the red kinde of the laft remembred Beete, whofe great ribbes as he faith, are as great as the middle ribbe of the Cabbage leafe, and as good to bee eaten, whofe ftalke rofe with him to the height of eight cubits, and bore plenty of feede.

The Vfe of Beetes.

Beetes, both white, greene and red, are put into the pot among other herbes, to make pottage, as is commonly known vnto all, and are alfo boyled whole, both in France vfually with moft of their boyled meates, and in our Countrey, with diuers that delight in eating of herbes.

The Italian Beete, and fo likewife the laft red Beete with great ribbes, are boyled, and the ribbes eaten in fallets with oyle, vinegar and pepper, and is accounted a rare kinde of fallet, and very delicate.

The roote of the common red Beete with fome, but more efpecially the Romane red Beete, is of much vfe among Cookes to trimme or fet out their difhes of meate, being cut out into diuers formes and fafhions, and is grown of late dayes into a great cuftome of feruice, both for fifh and flefh.

The rootes of the Romane red Beete being boyled, are eaten of diuers while they are hot with a little oyle and vinegar, and is accounted a delicate fallet for the winter ; and being cold they are fo vfed and eaten likewife.

The leaues are much vfed to mollifie and open the belly, being vfed in the decoction of Glifters. The roote of the white kinde fcraped, and made vp with a little honey and falt, rubbed on and layd on the belly, prouoketh to the ftoole. The vfe of eating Beetes is likewife held to bee helpefull to fpleneticke perfons.

Chap. XXI.

Hippofelinum, fiue Olus atrum. Alifanders.

ALifanders hath beene in former times thought to be the true Macedonian Parfley, and in that errour many doe yet continue : but this place giueth not leaue to difcuffe that doubt : but I muft here only fhew you, what it is, and to what vfe it is put ordinarily for the Kitchen. The leaues of Alifanders are winged or cut into many parts, fomewhat refembling Smallage, but greater, broader, and more cut in about the edges : the ftalkes are round and great, two foote high or better, bearing diuers leaues on them, and at the toppe fpokie roundles of white flowers on feuerall fmall branches, which turne into blacke feede, fomewhat cornered or crefted, of an aromaticall bitter tafte : the roote is blacke without, and white within, and abideth well the firft year of the fowing, perifhing after it hath borne feed.

The Vfe of Alifanders.

The tops of the rootes, with the lower part of the ftalkes of Alifanders, are vfed in Lent efpecially, and Spring of the yeare, to make broth, which although it be a little bitter, yet it is both wholfome, and pleafing to a great many,

many, by reason of the aromaticall or spicie taste, warming and comforting the stomack, and helping it digest the many waterish and flegmaticke meates are in those times much eaten. The rootes also either rawe or boyled are often eaten with oyle and vinegar. The seede is more vsed physically then the roote, or any other part, and is effectuall to prouoke plenty of vrine in them that pisse by drops, or haue the Strangury : It helpeth womens courses, and warmeth their benummed bodies or members, that haue endured fierce cold daies and nights, being boyled and drunke.

Chap. XXII.

Selinum dulce. Sweete Parsley or sweete Smallage.

THis kinde of sweete Parsley or Smallage, which soeuer you please to call it, for it resembleth Smallage as well in the largenesse of the leaues, as in the taste, yet sweeter and pleasanter, is (as I take it) in this like vnto sweete Fennell (that hath his sweetnesse from his naturall soyle and clymate ; for howsoeuer it bee reasonable sweete the first yeare it is sowne with vs, yet it quickly doth degenerate, and becommeth no better then our ordinarie Fennell afterwards). The first yeare it is sowne and planted with vs (and the first that euer I saw, was in a Venetian Ambassadours Garden in the Spittle yard, neare Bishops gate streete) is so sweete and pleasant, especially while it is young, as if Sugar had beene mingled with it : but after it is growne vp high and large, it hath a stronger taste of Smalladge, and so likewise much more the next yeare ; that it groweth from the seed was gathered here : the leaues are many, spreading farre about the roote, broader and of a fresher greene colour then our ordinary Smalladge, and vpon longer stalkes : the seed is as plentifull as Parsly, being small and very like vnto it, but darker of colour.

The Vse of sweete Parsley.

The Venetians vse to prepare it for meate many waies, both the herbe and the roote eaten rawe, as many other herbes and rootes are, or boyled or fryed to be eaten with meate, or the dryed herbe poudered and strewed vpon meate ; but most vsually either whited, and so eaten rawe with pepper and oyle, as a dainty Sallet of it selfe, or a little boyled or stewed : the taste of the herbe being a little warming, but the seede much more, helpeth cold windy stomackes to digest their meate, and to expell winde.

Chap. XXIII.

Petrosolinum & Apium. Parsley and Smalledge.

WE haue three sorts of Parsley in our Gardens, and but one of Smalladge : Our common Parsley, Curld Parsley, and Virginia Parsley ; which last, although it be but of late knowne, yet it is now almost growne common, and of as good vse as the other with diuers. Our common Parsley is so well knowne, that it is almost needlesse to describe it, hauing diuers fresh greene leaues, three alwaies placed together on a stalke, and snipt about the edges, and three stalkes of leaues for the most part growing together : the stalkes growe three or foure foote high or better, bearing spikie heads of white flowers, which turne into small seede, somewhat sharpe and hot in taste : the roote is long and white.

Curld Parsley hath his leaues curled or crumpled on the edges, and therein is the onely difference from the former.

Virginia

Virginia Parſley is in his leafe altogether like vnto common Parſley for the forme, conſiſting of three leaues ſet together, but that the leaues are as large as Smallage leaues, but of a pale or whitiſh greene colour, and of the ſame taſte of our common Parſley : the ſeede hereof is as the leaues, twice if not thrice as bigge as the ordinary Parſley, and periſheth when it hath giuen ſeede, abiding vſually the firſt yeare of the ſowing.

Smallage is in forme ſomewhat like vnto Parſley, but greater and greener, and leſſe pleaſant, or rather more bitter in taſte : the ſeede is ſmaller, and the root more ſtringy.

The Vſe of Parſley.

Parſley is much vſed in all ſorts of meates, both boyled, roaſted, fryed, ſtewed, &c. and being greene it ſerueth to lay vpon ſundry meates, as alſo to draw meate withall. It is alſo ſhred and ſtopped into poudered beefe, as alſo into legges of Mutton, with a little beefe ſuet among it, &c.

The rootes are often vſed to be put into broth, to helpe to open obſtru-ctions of the liuer, reines, and other parts, helping much to procure vrine.

The rootes likewiſe boyled or ſtewed with a legge of Mutton, ſtopped with Parſley as aforeſaid, is very good meate, and of very good relliſh, as I haue proued by the taſte ; but the rootes muſt bee young, and of the firſt yeares growth, and they will haue their operation to cauſe vrine.

The ſeed alſo is vſed for the ſame cauſe, when any are troubled with the ſtone, or grauell, to open the paſſages of vrine.

Although Smallage groweth in many places wilde in moiſt grounds, yet it is alſo much planted in Gardens, and although his euill taſte and ſauour doth cauſe it not to be accepted into meates as Parſley, yet it is not without many ſpeciall good properties, both for outward and inward diſeaſes, to helpe to open obſtructions, and prouoke vrine. The iuyce cleanſeth vlcers ; and the leaues boyled with Hogs greaſe, healeth felons on the ioynts of the fingers.

Chap. XXIIII.

Fœniculum. Fenell.

THere are three ſorts of Fenell, whereof two are ſweete. The one of them is the ordinary ſweete Fenell, whoſe ſeedes are larger and yellower then the common, and which (as I ſaid before in the Chapter of ſweete Parſley) doth ſoone degenerate in this our Country into the common. The other ſweete Fenell is not much knowne, and called Cardus Fenell by thoſe that ſent it out of Italy, whoſe leaues are more thicke and buſhie then any of the other. Our common Fenell, whereof there is greene and red, hath many faire and large ſpread leaues, finely cut and diuided into many ſmall, long, greene, or reddiſh leaues, yet the thicker tufted the branches be, the ſhorter are the leaues : the ſtalkes are round, with diuers ioynts and leaues at them, growing fiue or ſix foot high, bearing at the top many ſpoakie rundels of yellow flowers : the Common, I meane, doth turne into a darke grayiſh flat ſeede, and the Sweete into larger and yellower : the roote is great, long, and white, and endureth diuers yeares.

The Vſe of Fenell.

Fenell is of great vſe to trimme vp, and ſtrowe vpon fiſh, as alſo to boyle or put among fiſh of diuers ſorts, Cowcumbers pickled, and other fruits, &c. The rootes are vſed with Parſley rootes, to be boyled in broths and drinkes to open obſtructions. The ſeed is of much vſe with other things to expell winde. The ſeede alſo is much vſed to be put into Pippin pies, and diuers

other

1 *Petroſoinum.* Parſley. 2 *Atium.* Smallage. 3 *Fæniculum.* Fenell. 4 *Anetham.* Dill. 5 *Myrrhis ſiue Cereſolium magnum.*
Sweete Chervill. 6 *Cereſolium vulgare.* Common Chervill.

Ff

other such baked fruits, as also into bread, to giue it the better rellish.

The sweete Cardus Fenell being sent by Sir Henry Wotton to Iohn Tradescante, had likewise a large direction with it how to dresse it; for they vse to white it after it hath been transplanted for their vses, which by reason of the sweetnesse by nature, and the tendernesse by art, causeth it to be the more delightfull to the taste, especially with them that are accustomed to feede on greene herbes.

Chap. XXV.

Anethum. Dill.

DIll doth much growe wilde, but because in many places it cannot be had, it is therefore sowne in Gardens for the vses whereunto it serueth. It is a smaller herbe then Fenell, but very like, hauing fine cut leaues, not so large, but shorter, smaller, and of a stronger and quicker taste: the stalke is smaller also, and with few ioynts and leaues on them, bearing spoakie tufts of yellow flowers, which turne into thinne, small, and flat seedes: the roote perisheth euery yeare, and riseth againe for the most part of it owne sowing.

The Vse of Dill.

The leaues of Dill are much vsed in some places with Fish, as they doe Fenell; but because it is so strong many doe refuse it.

It is also put among pickled Cowcumbers, wherewith it doth very well agree, giuing vnto the cold fruit a pretty spicie taste or rellish.

It being stronger then Fenell, is of the more force to expell winde in the body. Some vse to eate the seed to stay the Hickocke.

Chap. XXVI.

Myrrhis siue Cerefolium maius & vulgare.
Sweet Cheruill and ordinary Cheruill.

THe great or sweete Cheruill (which of some is called Sweete Cicely) hath diuers great and faire spread winged leaues, consisting of many leaues set together, deeply cut in the edges, and euery one also dented about, very like, and resembling tne leaues of Hemlockes, but of so pleasant a taste, that one would verily thinke, he chewed the leaues or seedes of Aniseedes in his mouth: The stalke is reasonable great, and somewhat cornered or crested about three or foure foote high, at the toppe whereof stand many white spoakie tufts of flowers, which change into browne long cornered great seede, two alwaies ioyned together: the roote is great, blackish on the outside, and white within, with diuers fibres annexed vnto it, and perisheth not, but abideth many yeares, and is of a sweete, pleasant, and spicie hot taste, delightfull vnto many.

The common Cheruill is a small herbe, with slender leaues, finely cut into long peeces, at the first of a pale yellowish greene colour, but when the stalke is growne vp to seede, both stalkes and leaues become of a darke red colour: the flowers are white, standing vpon scattered or thin spread tufts, which turne into small, long, round, and sharpe pointed seedes, of a brownish blacke colour: the roote is small, with diuers long slender white strings, and perisheth euery yeare.

The

The Vfes of thefe Cheruils.

The common Cheruill is much vfed of the French and Dutch people, to bee boyled or ftewed in a pipkin, eyther by it felfe, or with other herbes, whereof they make a Loblolly, and fo eate it. It is vfed as a pot-herbe with vs.

Sweete Cheruill, gathered while it is young, and put among other herbes for a fallet, addeth a meruellous good rellifh to all the reft. Some commend the greene feedes fliced and put in a fallet of herbes, and eaten with vinegar and oyle, to comfort the cold ftomacke of the aged. The roots are vfed by diuers, being boyled, and after eaten with oyle and vinegar, as an excellent fallet for the fame purpofe. The preferued or candid rootes are of fingular good vfe to warme and comfort a cold flegmaticke ftomack, and is thought to be a good preferuatiue in the time of the plague.

CHAP. XXVII.

Malua Crifpa. French Mallowes.

THe curld or French Mallow groweth vp with an vpright greene round ftalke, as high vfually as any man, whereon from all fides grow forth round whitifh greene leaues, curld or crumpled about the edges, like a ruffe, elfe very like vnto an ordinary great Mallow leafe : the flowers grow both vpon the ftalke, and on the other branches that fpring from them, being fmall and white; after which come fmall cafes with blacke feede like the other Mallowes : the roote perifheth when it hath borne feede, but abideth vfually the firft yeare, and the fecond runneth vp to flower and feede.

The Vfe of French Mallowes.

It is much vfed as a pot-herbe, efpecially when there is caufe to moue the belly downward, which by his flippery qualitie it doth helpe forward. It hath beene in times paft, and fo is to this day in fome places, vfed to be boyled or ftewed, eyther by it felfe with butter, or with other herbes, and fo eaten.

CHAP. XXVIII.

Intubum. Succorie and Endiue.

I Put both Succorie and Endiue into one chapter and defcription, becaufe they are both of one kindred; and although they differ a little the one from the other, yet they agree both in this, that they are eaten eyther greene or whited, of many. Endiue, the fmooth as well as the curld, beareth a longer and a larger leafe then Succorie, and abideth but one yeare, quickely running vp to ftalke and feede, and then perifheth: whereas Succorie abideth many years, and hath long and narrower leaues, fomewhat more cut in, or torne on the edges : both of them haue blew flowers, and the feede of the fmooth or ordinary Endiue is fo like vnto the Succorie, that it is very hard to diftinguifh them afunder by fight; but the curld Endiue giueth blackifh and flat feede, very like vnto blacke Lettice feede : the rootes of the Endiue perifh, but the Succorie abideth.

The Vfe of Succory and Endiue.

Although Succorie bee fomewhat more bitter in tafte then the Endiues,

T t 2   yet

yet it is oftentimes, and of many eaten greene, but more vſually being buried a while in ſand, that it may grow white, which cauſeth it to loſe both ſome part of the bitterneſſe, as alſo to bee the more tender in the eating ; and Horace ſheweth it to be vſed in his time, in the 32. Ode of his firſt Book, where he ſaith,

Me paſcunt Oliuæ, me Cithorea leueſ{que} Maluæ.

Endiue being whited in the ſame, or any other manner, is much vſed in winter, as a ſallet herbe with great delight ; but the curld Endiue is both farre the fairer, and the tenderer for that purpoſe.

Chap. XXIX.

Spinachia, ſiue Olus Hiſpanicum. Spinach.

SPinach or Spinage is of three ſorts (yet ſome doe reckon of foure, accounting that herbe that beareth no ſeede to be a ſort of it ſelfe, when it is but an accident of nature, as it falleth out in Hempe, Mercury, and diuers other herbes) two that bear prickly ſeed, the one much greater then the other : the third that beareth a ſmooth ſeede, which is more daintie, and nourſed vp but in few Gardens : The common Spinach which is the leſſer of the two prickly ſorts, hath long greene leaues, broad at the ſtalke, and rent, or torne as it were into foure corners, and ſharpe pointed at the ends : it quickly runneth vp to ſtalke, if it be ſowen in the Spring time ; but elſe, if at the end of Summer, it will abide all the winter green, and then ſuddenly in the very beginning of the Spring, runne vp to ſtalke, bearing many leaues both below and at the toppe, where there doth appeare many ſmal greeniſh flowers in cluſters, and after them prickly ſeede : The other greater ſort that hath prickly ſeede, is in all things like the former, but larger both in ſtalke, leafe and ſeede. The ſmooth Spinach hath broader, and a little rounder pointed leaues then the firſt, eſpecially the lower leaues ; for thoſe that grow vpwards vpon the ſtalke, are more pointed, and as it were three ſquare, of as darke a greene colour as the former : at the ſeuerall ioynts of the ſtalkes and branches, ſtand cluſtering many ſmall greeniſh flowers, which turne into cluſters of round whitiſh ſeede, without any prickles at all vpon them : the roote is long, white and ſmall, like vnto the other, with many fibres at it : If it be often cut, it will grow the thicker, or elſe ſpindle vp very thinly, and with but few leaues vpon the ſtalke.

The Vſe of Spinage.

Spinage is an herbe fit for ſallets, and for diuers other purpoſes for the table only ; for it is not knowne to bee vſed Phyſically at all. Many Engliſh that haue learned it of the Dutch people, doe ſtew the herbe in a pot or pipkin, without any other moiſture then it owne, and after the moiſture is a little preſſed from it, they put butter, and a little ſpice vnto it, and make therewith a diſh that many delight to eate of. It is vſed likewiſe to be made into Tartes, and many other varieties of diſhes, as Gentlewomen and their Cookes can better tell then my ſelfe ; vnto whom I leaue the further ordering of theſe herbes, and all other fruits and rootes of this Garden : For I intend only to giue you the knowledge of them, with ſome briefe notes for their vſe, and no more.

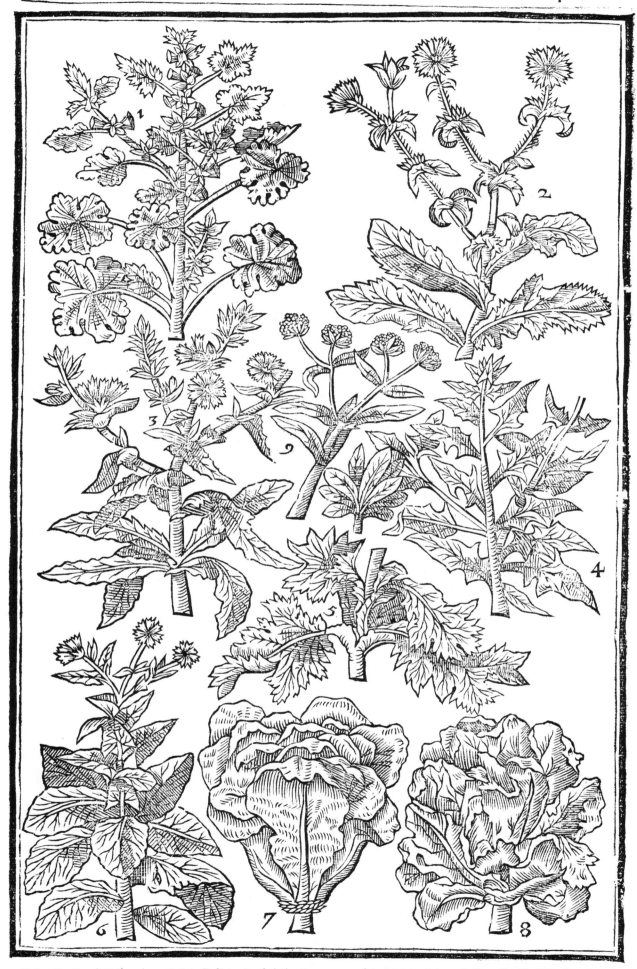

1 *Malua crispa.* French Mallowes. 2 *Endiuia.* Endiue. 3 *Cichorium.* Succory. 4 *Spinachia.* Spinach. 5 *Lactuca crispa.* Curld Lettice. 6 *Lactuca patula.* An open Lettice. 7 *Lactuca capitata vulgaris.* Ordinary cabbage Lettice. 8 *Lactuca capitata Romana.* The great Romane cabbage Lettice. 9 *Lactuca agnina.* Cornu Sallet or Lambes Lettice.

Tt 3

Chap. XXX.

Lactuca. Lettice.

THere are ſo many ſorts, and ſo great diuerſitie of Lettice, that I doubt I ſhall ſcarce be beleeued of a great many. For I doe in this Chapter reckon vp vnto you eleauen or twelue differing ſorts; ſome of little vſe, others of more, being more common and vulgar; and ſome that are of excellent vſe and ſeruice, which are more rare, and require more knowledge and care for the ordering of them, as alſo for their time of ſpending, as ſome in the ſpring, ſome in ſummer, others in autumne, and ſome being whited for the winter. For all theſe ſorts I ſhall not neede many deſcriptions, but only ſhew you which doe cabbage, and which are looſe, which of of them are great or ſmall, white, greene or red, and which of them beare white ſeeds, and which of them blacke. And laſtly I haue thought good to adde another Sallet herbe, which becauſe it is called Lambes Lettice of many, or Corne Sallet of others, is put in only to fill vp a number in this Chapter, and that I muſt ſpeake of it, and not that I thinke it to be any of the kindes of Lettice.

All ſorts of Lettice, after a while that they haue cloſed themſelues, if they bee of the Cabbage kindes, or otherwiſe being looſe, and neuer cloſing, ſend forth from among the middle of their leaues a round ſtalke (in ſome greater, in others leſſer, according to their kinde) full of leaues like vnto the lower, branching at the toppe into ſundry parts, whereon grow diuers ſmall ſtar-like flowers, of a pale yellowiſh colour; after which come ſeede, eyther white or blackiſh, as the plant yeeldeth, whereat hangeth ſome ſmall peece of a cottony doune, wherewith the whole head is ſtored, and is carried away with the winde, if it be not gathered in time: the roote is ſomewhat long and white, with ſome fibres at it, and periſheth quickely after the ſeede is ripe.

The Romane red Lettice is the beſt and greateſt of all the reſt. For Iohn Tradeſcante that firſt, as I thinke, brought it into England, and ſowed it, did write vnto mee, that after one of them had been bound and whited, when the refuſe was cut away, the reſt weighed ſeuenteene ounces: this hath blacke ſeede.

The white Romane Lettice is like vnto it, hauing long leaues like a Teaſell, it is in goodneſſe next vnto the red, but muſt be whited, that it may eate kindly: the ſeede hereof is white.

The Virginia Lettice hath ſingle and very broade reddiſh leaues, and is not of any great regard, and therefore is kept but of a few: it beareth blacke ſeede.

The common Lumbard Lettice that is looſe, and another kinde thereof that doth ſomewhat cabbage, haue both white ſeedes.

The Venice Lettice is an excellent Cabbage Lettice, and is beſt to bee ſowen after Midſummer for lateward Lettice; they be ſometimes as great as the crowne of a mans hatt: the ſeede hereof is white, and groweth to be of a meane height.

Our common Cabbage Lettice is well known, and beareth blacke ſeede.

The curld Lettice which is open, and differeth but little from Endiue, beareth black ſeede.

Another ſort of curld Lettice doth cabbage, and is called Flanders Cropers, or Cropers of Bruges; this groweth loweſt, and hath the ſmalleſt head, but very hard and round, and white while it groweth: the ſeed is blacke.

A kinde of Romane Lettice is of a darke green colour, growing as low as the Venice Lettice, and is an excellent kinde, bearing blacke ſeede.

And laſtly our winter Lettice is wonderfull hardy to endure our cold: It is but ſingle, and muſt be ſowen at Michaelmas, but will be very good, before any of the other good ſorts ſowen in the Spring, will be ready to be vſed, and beareth white ſeed.

To inſtruct a nouice (for I teach not a Gardiner of knowledge) how to gather his ſeede that it may be good, is in this manner: Let him marke out thoſe plants that hee meaneth ſhall run vp for ſeede, which muſt be the moſt likely; & after they haue begun to ſhoote forth ſtalkes, ſtrip away the lower leaues, for two or three hands breadth aboue the ground, that thereby in taking away the loweſt leaues, the ſtalke doe not rot, nor the ſeed be hindered in the ripening.

There

There are two manner of wayes to whiten Lettice to make them eate the more tender : the one is by rayfing vp earth like moale hils, round about the plants while they are growing, which will make them grow white : the other is by tying vp all the loofe leaues round together while it groweth, that fo the clofe tying may make it grow white, and thereby be the more tender.

Lambes Lettice or Corne Sallet is a fmall plant while it is young, growing clofe vpon the ground, with many whitifh greene, long and narrow, round pointed leaues, all the winter, and in the beginning of the fpring (if it bee fowen in autumne, as it is vfuall to ferue for an early fallet) rifeth vp with fmall round ftalkes, with two leaues at euery ioynt, branching forth at the toppe, and bearing tufts of fmall bleake blew flowers, which turne into fmall round whitifh feede : the roote is fmall and long, with fome fmall threds hanging thereat : the whole plant is of a waterifh tafte, almoft infipide.

The Vfe of Lettice.

All forts of Lettice are fpent in fallets, with oyle and vinegar, or as euery one pleafe, for the moft part, while they are frefh and greene, or whited, as is declared of fome of the forts before, to caufe them to eate the more delicate and tender. They are alfo boyled, to ferue for many forts of difhes of meate, as the Cookes know beft.

They all coole a hot and fainting ftomacke.

The iuice of Lettice applyed with oyle of Rofes to the foreheads of the ficke and weake wanting fleepe, procureth reft, and taketh away paines in the head : bound likewife to the cods, it helpeth thofe that are troubled with the Colts euill. If a little camphire be added, it reftraineth immoderate luft : but it is hurtfull to fuch as are troubled with the fhortneffe of breath.

Lambes Lettice is wholly fpent for fallets, in the beginning of the yeare, as I faid, before any almoft of the other forts of Lettice are to be had.

Chap. XXXI.

Portulaca. Purflane.

PVrflane hath many thicke round fhining red ftalkes, full of iuice, lying vpon the ground for the moft part ; whereon are fet diuers long, thicke, pale green leaues, fometimes alone by themfelues, and fometimes many fmall ones together with them ; among which grow fmall yellow flowers, which ftand in little greene huskes, containing blacke feede : the roote is fmall, and perifheth euery yeare, and muft be new fowen in Aprill, in the alleyes of the Garden betweene the beds, as fome haue heretofore vfed, where it may haue the more moifture, or, as I haue feene in fome Gardens, vpon thofe beds of dung that Gardiners haue vfed to nourfe vp their Cowcumbers, Melons, and Pompions, whereon after they haue beene taken away, they haue fowen Purflane, where if it be much watered, the warmth of the dung, and the water giuen it, the Purflane hath grown great and large, and continued vntill winter.

The Vfe of Purflane.

It is vfed as Lettice in fallets, to coole hot and faint ftomackes in the hot time of the yeare, but afterwards if only for delight, it is not good to bee too prodigall in the vfe thereof.

The feede of Purflane doth coole much any inflammation inward or outward, and doth a little binde withall.

CHAP. XXXII.

Dracoherba siue Tarchon & Dracunculus hortensis. Tarragon.

Tarragon hath long and narrow darke greene leaues, growing on slender and brittle round stalkes, two or three foote high, at the tops whereof grow forth long slender spikes of small yellowish flowers, which seldome giue any good seede, but a dustie or chaffie matter, which flieth away with the winde: the roote is white, and creepeth about vnder ground, whereby it much encreaseth : the whole herbe is of a hot and biting taste.

The Vse of Tarragon.

It is altogether vsed among other cold herbes, to temper their coldnesse, and they to temper its heate, so to giue the better rellish vnto the Sallet; but many doe not like the taste thereof, and so refuse it.

There are some Authors that haue held Tarragon not to be an herbe of it owne kinde, but that it was first produced, by putting the seede of Lin or Flaxe into the roote of an Onion, being opened and so set into the ground, which when it hath sprung, hath brought forth this herbe Tarragon, which absurd and idle opinion, Matthiolus by certaine experience saith, hath been found false.

CHAP. XXXIII.

Nasturtium hortense. Garden Cresses.

Garden Cresses growe vp to the height of two foote or thereabouts, hauing many small, whitish, broad, endented, torne leaues, set together vpon a middle ribbe next the ground, but those that growe higher vpon the stalkes are smaller and longer : the tops of the stalkes are stored with white flowers, which turne into flat pods or pouches, like vnto Shepheard purse, wherein is contained flat reddish seede : the roote perisheth euery yeare : the taste both of leaues and seedes are somewhat strong, hot, and bitter.

The Vse of Cresses.

The Dutchmen and others vse to eate Cresses familiarly with their butter and bread, as also stewed or boyled, either alone or with other herbes, whereof they make a Hotch potch, and so eate it. Wee doe eate it mixed among Lettice or Purslane, and sometimes with Tarragon or Rocket, with oyle and vinegar and a little salt, and in that manner it is very sauoury to some mens stomackes.

The vse of Cresses physically is, it helpeth to expectorate tough flegme, as also for the paines of the breast; and as it is thought taketh away spots, being laid to with vinegar. The seede is giuen of many to children for the wormes.

1 *Portulaca.* Purſlane. 2 *Dracho herba ſeu Tarchon.* Tarragon. 3 *Eruca ſatiua.* Garden Rocket. 4 *Naſturtium ſativum.* Garden Creſſes.
5 *Sinapi.* Muſtard. 6 *Aſparagus.* Aſparagus or Sperage.

Chap. XXXIIII.

Eruca sativa. Garden Rocket.

OVr Garden Rocket is but a wilde kinde brought into Gardens ; for the true Romane Rocket hath larger leaues ; this hath many long leaues , much torne or rent on the edges, smaller and narrower then the Romane kinde : the flowers hereof are of a pale yellowish colour, whereas the true is whitish, consisting of foure leaues : the seede of this is reddish, contained in smaller and longer pods then the true, which are shorter and thicker, and the seede of a whitish yellow colour : the rootes of both perish as soone as they haue giuen seede. Some haue taken one sort of the wilde kinde for Mustard, and haue vsed the seede for the same purpose.

The Vse of Rocket.

It is for the most part eaten with Lettice, Purslane, or such cold herbes, and not alone , because of its heate and strength ; but that with the white seede is milder. The seede of Rocket is good to prouoke vrine, and to stirre vp bodily lust.

The seede bruised, and mixed with a little vinegar, and of the gall of an Oxe , cleanseth the face of freckles, spots, and blew markes, that come by beatings, fals, or otherwaies.

Matthiolus saith, that the leaues boyled, and giuen with some Sugar to little children, cureth them of the cough.

The seede is held to be helpfull to spleneticke persons ; as also to kill the wormes of the belly.

Chap. XXXV.

Sinapi sativum. Garden Mustard.

THe Mustard that is most vsuall in this Country, howsoeuer diuers doe for their priuate vses sowe it in their Gardens or Orchards, in some conuenient corner, yet the same is found wilde also abroad in many places. It hath many rough long diuided leaues, of an ouerworne greene colour : the stalke is diuided at the toppe into diuers branches, whereon growe diuers pale yellow flowers, in a great length, which turne into small long pods , wherein is contained blackish seede, inclining to rednesse, of a fiery sharpe taste : the roote is tough and white, running deepe into the ground, with many small fibres at it.

The Vse of Mustard.

The seede hereof grownd between two stones, fitted for the purpose, and called a Querne, with some good vinegar added vnto it , to make it liquid and running , is that kinde of Mustard that is vsually made of all sorts , to serue as sawce both for fish and flesh.

The same liquid Mustard is of good vse, being fresh, for Epilepticke persons, to warme and quicken those dull spirits that are sopite and scarce appeare, if it be applyed both inwardly and outwardly.

It is with good successe also giuen to those that haue short breathes , and troubled with a cough in the lungs.

Chap. XXXVI.

Asparagus. Sperage or Asparagus.

ASparagus riseth vp at the first with diuers whitish greene scaly heads, very brittle or easie to breake while they are young, which afterwards rise vp into very long and slender greene stalkes, of the bignesse of an ordinary riding wand at the bottome of most, or bigger or lesser, as the rootes are of growth, on which are set diuers branches of greene leaues, shorter and smaller then Fennell vp to the toppe, at the ioynts whereof come forth small mossie yellowish flowers, which turne into round berries, greene at the first, and of an excellent red colour when they are ripe, shewing as if they were beades of Corrall, wherein are contained exceeding hard and blacke seede : the rootes are dispersed from a spongious head into many long, thicke, and round strings, whereby it sucketh much nourishment out of the ground, and encreaseth plentifully thereby.

We haue another kinde hereof that is of much greater account, because the shootes are larger, whiter, and being dressed taste more sweete and pleasant, without any other difference.

The Vse of Asparagus.

The first shootes or heads of Asparagus are a Sallet of as much esteeme with all sorts of persons, as any other whatsoeuer, being boyled tender, and eaten with butter, vinegar, and pepper, or oyle and vinegar, or as euery ones manner doth please ; and are almost wholly spent for the pleasure of the pallate. It is specially good to prouoke vrine, and for those that are troubled with the stone or grauell in the reines or kidneyes, because it doth a little open and cleanse those parts.

Chap. XXXVII.

Brassica. Cabbages and Coleworts.

THere is greater diuersity in the forme and colour of the leaues of this plant, then there is in any other that I know groweth vpon the ground. But this place requireth not the knowledge of all sorts which might be shewen, many of them being of no vse with vs for the table, but for delight, to behold the wonderfull variety of the workes of God herein. I will here therefore shew you onely those sorts that are ordinary in most Gardens, and some that are rare, receiued into some especiall Gardens : And first of Cabbages, and then of Coleworts.

Our ordinary Cabbage that closeth hard and round, hath at the first great large thicke leaues, of a grayish greene colour, with thicke great ribbes, and lye open most part of the Summer without closing, but toward the end of Summer, being growne to haue many leaues, it then beginneth to growe close and round in the middle, and as it closeth, the leaues growe white inward ; yet there be some kindes that will neuer be so close as these, but will remaine halfe open, which wee doe not account to be so good as the other : in the middle of this head, the next yeare after the sowing, in other Countries especially, and sometimes in ours, if the Winter be milde, as may be scene in diuers Gardens (but to preuent the danger of our Winter frosts, our Gardiners now doe vse to take vp diuers Cabbages with their rootes, and tying a cloth or some such thing about the rootes, doe hang them vp in their houses, where they may be defended from cold, and then set them againe after the frosts are past) and then there shooteth out a great thicke stalke, diuided at the toppe into many branches, bearing thereon diuers small flowers, sometime white, but most commonly yellow, made of foure leaues, which turne into long, round, and pointed pods, containing therein small
round

round feede, like vnto Turnep feede : the roote fpreadeth not farre nor deepe, and dyeth vfually in any great frofte ; for a fmall froft maketh the Cabbage eate the tenderer.

The red Cabbage is like vnto the white, laft fpoken of, but differing in colour and greatneffe ; for it is feldome found fo great as the white, and the colour of the leaues is very variable, as being in fome ftript with red, in others more red, or very deepe red or purple.

The fugar loafe Cabbage, fo called becaufe it is fmaller at the toppe then it is at the bottome, and is of two forts, the one white, the other greene.

The Sauoy Cabbadge, one is of a deepe greene coloured leafe, and curld when it is to be gathered ; the other is yellowifh : neyther of both thefe doe clofe fo well as the firft, but yet are vfed of fome, and accounted good.

The Cole flower is a kinde of Coleworte, whofe leaues are large, and like the Cabbage leaues, but fomewhat fmaller, and endented about the edges, in the middle wherof, fometimes in the beginning of Autumne, and fometimes much fooner, there appeareth a hard head of whitifh yellow tufts of flowers, clofely thruft together, but neuer open, nor fpreading much with vs, which then is fitteft to be vfed, the green leaues being cut away clofe to the head : this hath a much pleafanter tafte then eyther the Coleworte, or Cabbage of any kinde, and is therefore of the more regard and refpect at good mens tables.

The ordinary Coleworte is fufficiently knowne not to clofe or cabbage, and giueth feede plentifully enough.

The other Colewortes that are nourfed vp with thofe that delight in curiofities, befides the aforefaid ordinary greene, which is much vfed of Dutchmen, and other ftrangers, are thefe : The Curld Colewortte eyther wholly of a greene colour, or of diuers colours in one plant, as white, yellow, red, purple or crimfon, fo variably mixed, the leaues being curld on the edges, like a ruffe band, that it is very beautifull to behold.

There is alfo another curld Colewort of leffe beauty and refpect, being but a little curld on the edges, whofe leaues are white, edged with red, or green edged with white.

Two other there are, the one of a popingaye greene colour : the other of a fine deepe greene, like vnto the Sauoyes.

Then there is the Cole rape, which is alfo a kinde of Colewort, that beareth a white heade, or headed ftalke aboue the ground, as bigge as a reafonable Turnep, but longer, and from the toppe thereof fpringeth out diuers great leaues, like vnto Colewortes ; among which rife diuers ftalkes that beare yellow flowers, and feede in pods, almoft as fmall as Muftard feede : the roote is fomewhat long, and very bufhie with threds.

The Vfe of Cabbages and Colewortes.

They are moft vfually boyled in poudered beefe broth vntil they be tender, and then eaten with much fat put among them.

The great ribs of the Popingay, and deepe greene Colewortes, beeing boyled and layde into difhes, are ferued to the table with oyle and vinegar in the Lent time for very good fallets.

In the cold Countries of Ruffia and Mufcouia, they pouder vp a number of Cabbages, which ferue them, efpecially the poorer fort, for their moft ordinary foode in winter ; and although they ftinke moft grieuoufly, yet to them they are accounted good meate.

It is thought, that the vfe of them doth hinder the milke in Nurfes breafts, caufing it to dry vp quickely : but many women that haue giuen fucke to my knowledge haue denyed that affertion, affirming that they haue often eaten them, and found no fuch effect. How it might proue in more delicate bodies then theirs that thus faid, I cannot tell : but Matthiolus auerreth it to encreafe milke in Nurfes breaftes ; fo differing are the opinions of many. The feede groffely bruifed and boyled a little in flefh broth, is a prefent remedie for the Collicke ; the feede and the broth being taken together, eafing them that are troubled therewith of all griping paines : as alfo for the ftone in the kidneyes. A Lohoc or licking Electuary made of the pulpe of

the

1 *Brassica capitata.* Cole Cabbage. 2 *Brassica patula.* Open Cabbage. 3 *Brassica Sabaudica crispa.* Curld Sauoye Colewort. 4 *Caulis florida.* Cole flower. 5 *Caulis crispa.* Curld Colewort. 6 *Caulis crispa variata.* Changeable curld Colewort. 7 *Rapocaulis.* Cole rape.

the boyled ftalkes, and a little honey and Almond milke, is very profitable for fhortneffe of breath, and thofe that are entring into a Confumption of the lunges. It hath beene formerly held to be helpfull in all difeafes : for Crifippus, an ancient Phyfitian, wrote a whole Volume of the vertues, applying it to all the parts of the body : which thing neede not feeme wonderfull, in that it is recorded by writers, that the old Romanes hauing expelled Phyfitians out of their Common-wealth, did for many hundred of yeares maintaine their health by the vfe of Cabbages, taking them for euery difeafe.

Chap. XXXVIII.

Sifarum. Skirrets.

AFter all the herbes before rehearfed, fit for fallets, or otherwife to bee eaten, there muft follow fuch rootes as are vfed to the fame purpofe : and firft, Skirrets haue many leaues next the ground, compofed of many fmall fmooth green leaues, fet each againft other vpon a middle ribbe, and euery one fnipt about the edges: the ftalke rifeth vp two or three foote high, fet with the like leaues, hauing at the toppe fpoakie tufts of white flowers, which turne into fmall feede, fomewhat bigger and darker then Parfley feede : the rootes be many growing together at one head, beeing long, flender, & rugged or vneuen, of a whitifh colour on the outfide, and more white within, hauing in the middle of the roote a long fmall hard pith or ftring : thefe heads are vfually taken vp in February and March, or fooner if any fo pleafe, the greater number of them being broken off to bee vfed, the reft are planted againe after the heads are feparated, and hereby they are encreafed euery yeare by many ; but it is now adayes more fowen of the feed, which come forwards well enough if the ground be fat and good.

The Vfe of Skirrets.

The rootes being boyled, peeled and pithed, are ftewed with butter, pepper and falt, and fo eaten ; or as others vfe them, to roule them in flower, and fry them with butter, after they haue beene boyled, peeled and pithed: each way, or any way that men pleafe to vfe them, they may finde their tafte to be very pleafant, far beyond any Parfnep, as all agree that tafte them.

Some doe vfe alfo to eate them as a fallet, colde with vinegar, oyle, &c. being firft boyled and dreffed as before faid. They doe helpe to prouoke vrine, and as is thought, to procure bodily luft, in that they are a little windy.

Chap. XXXIX.

Paſtinaca ſatiua latifolia. Parfneps.

THe common garden Parfnep hath diuers large winged leaues lying vpon the ground, that is, many leaues fet one by another on both fides of a middle ftalk, fomewhat like as the Skirret hath, but much larger, and clofer fet: the ftalke rifeth vp great and tall, fiue or fix foot high fomtimes, with many fuch leaues thereon at feuerall ioynts ; the top whereof is fpread into diuers branches, whereon ftand fpoakie rundles of yellow flowers, which turne into brownifh flat feede : the root is long, great and white, very pleafant to bee eaten, and the more pleafant if it grow in a fat fandy foyle.

There is another fort of garden Parfnep, called the Pine Parfnep, that is not common in euery Garden, and differeth from the former in three notable parts. The root is not fo long, but thicker at the head and fmaller below ; the ftalke is neither fo bigge,

nor

1 *Sifarum*. Skirrits. 2 *Paftinaca latifolia*. Parfneps. 3 *Paftinaca tenuifolia*. Carrets. 4 *Rapum*. Turneps. 5 *Napus fatiuus*. Navewes.
6 *Raphanus niger*. Blacke Raddish. 7 *Raphanus vulgaris*. Common. Raddish.

nor so high ; and the seede is smaller : yet as Iohn Tradescante saith (who hath giuen me the relation of this, and many other of these garden plants, to whom euery one is a debtor) the roote hereof is not altogether so pleasant as the other.

Moreouer the wilde kinde, which groweth in many places of England (and whereof in some places there might be gathered a quarter sacke full of the seede) if it be sowen in Gardens, and there well ordered, will proue as good as the former kinde of Garden Parsneps.

The Vse of Parsneps.

The Parsnep root is a great nourisher, and is much more vsed in the time of Lent, being boyled and stewed with butter, then in any other time of the yeare ; yet it is very good all the winter long. The seede helpeth to dissolue winde, and to prouoke vrine.

Chap. XL.

Pastina satiua tenuifolia. Carrots.

THe Carrot hath many winged leaues, rising from the head of the roote, which are much cut and diuided into many other leaues, and they also cut and diuided into many parts, of a deepe greene colour, some whereof in Autumne will turne to be of a fine red or purple (the beautie whereof allureth many Gentlewomen oftentimes to gather the leaues, and sticke them in their hats or heads, or pin them on their armes in stead of feathers) : the stalke riseth vp among the leaues, bearing many likewise vpon it, but nothing so high as the Parsnep, being about three foote high, bearing many spoakie tufts of white flowers, which turne into small rough seede, as if it were hairy, smelling reasonable well if it bee rubbed : the roote is round and long, thicke aboue and small below, eyther red or yellow, eyther shorter or longer, according to his kinde ; for there is one kinde, whose roote is wholly red quite throughout ; another whose roote is red without for a pretty way inward, but the middle is yellow.

Then there is the yellow, which is of two sorts, both long and short : One of the long yellow sorts, which is of a pale yellow, hath the greatest and longest roote, and likewise the greatest head of greene, and is for the most part the worst, being spongy, and not firme.

The other is of a deepe gold yellow colour, and is the best, hauing a smaller head, or tuft of greene leaues vpon it.

The shorte rootes are likewise distinguished, into pale and deepe yellow colours.

The Vse of Carrots.

All these sorts being boyled in the broth of beefe, eyther fresh or salt, but more vsually of salted beefe, are eaten with great pleasure, because of the sweetenesse of them : but they nourish lesse then Parsneps or Skirrets.

I haue not often knowne the seede of this Garden kinde to bee vsed in Physicke : but the wilde kinde is often and much vsed to expell winde, &c.

Chap. XLI.

Rapum hortense. Turneps.

THere are diuers sorts of Turneps, as white, yellow, and red : the white are the most common, and they are of two kinds, the one much sweeter then the other.

The yellow and the red are more rare, and noursed vp only by those that are curious : as also the Navewe, which is seene but with very few.

The

The ordinary Garden Turnep hath many large, and long rough greene leaues, with deepe and vneuen gashes on both sides of them : the stalke riseth vp among the leaues about two foote high, spread at the toppe into many branches, bearing theron yellow flowers, which turne into long pods, with blackish round seede in them : the roote is round and white, some greater, some smaller; the best kinde is knowne to be flat, with a small pigges tale-like roote vnderneath it; the worser kinde which is more common in many places of this land, both North and West, is round, and not flat, with a greater pigges tayle-like roote vnderneath.

The yellow kinde doth often grow very great, it is hardly discerned from the ordinary kinde while it groweth, but by the greatnesse and spreading of the leaues beeing boyled, the roote changeth more yellow, somewhat neare the colour of a Carrot.

The red Turnep groweth vsually greater then any of the other, especially in a good ground, being of a faire red colour on the outside, but being pared, as white as any other on the inside. This, as Matthiolus saith, doth grow in the Countrey of Anania, where hee hath seene an infinite number of them that haue waighed fifty pound a peece, and in some places hee saith, a hundred pound a peece, both which we would thinke to be incredible, but that we see the kind is greatly giuen to grow, and in warme Countries they may so thriue, that the bulke or bignesse of the roote may so farre passe the growth of our Countrey, as that it may rise to that quantity aboue specified.

The Navew gentle is of two kindes, a smaller and a greater ; the smaller is vsually called in France, *Naveau de Cane*, the roote is somewhat long with the roundnesse; this kinde is twice as bigge as a mans thumbe, and many of them lesse : The other is long and great, almost as big as the short Carrot, but for the most part of an vneuen length, and roundnesse vnto the very end, where it spreadeth inte diuers small long fibres : neyther of them doth differ much from the Turnep, in leafe, flower or seed.

The Vse of Turneps.

Being boyled in salt broth, they all of them eate most kindly, and by reason of their sweetnesse are much esteemed, and often seene as a dish at good mens tables : but the greater quantitie of them are spent at poore mens feasts. They nourish much, and engender moist and loose flesh, and are very windy. The seede of the Navew gentle is (as I take it) called of Andromachus in the composition of his Treakle, *Bunias dulcis* : for Dioscorides and Plinie doe both say, that the seede of the tame Bunias or Napus is put into Antidotes, and not the seede of the wilde, which is more sharpe and bitter; neyther the seede of the Turnep, which is called in Greeke γογύλη, in Latine *Rapum*, becaule the seede is not sweete.

Chap. XLII.

Raphanus. Raddish.

There are two principall kindes of Garden Raddish, the one is blackish on the outside, and the other white ; and of both these there is some diuision againe, as shall be shewed. Dittander and horse Raddish be reckoned kinds thereof.

The ordinary Raddish hath long leaues, vneuenly gashed on both sides, the stalke riseth vp to the height of three or foure foote, bearing many purplish flowers at the top, made of foure leaues a peece, which turne into thicke and short pods, wherein are contained round seede, greater then Turnep or Coleworte seede, and of a pale reddish colour : the roote is long, white, and of a reddish purple colour on the outside toward the toppe of it, and of a sharpe biting taste.

There is a small kind of Raddish that commeth earlier then the former, that we haue had out of the low Countries, not differing in any thing else.

The blacke Raddish I haue had brought me out of the lowe Countries, where they sell them in some places by the pound, and is accounted with them a rare winter sallet:

the

the roote of the beſt kinde is blackiſh on the outſide (and yet the ſeede gathered from ſuch an one, hath after the ſowing againe, giuen rootes, whereof ſome haue beene blacke, but the moſt part white on the outſide) and white within, great and round at the head, almoſt like a Turnep, but ending ſhorter then a Raddiſh, and longer then a Turnep, almoſt peare-faſhion, of a firmer and harder ſubſtance then the ordinary Raddiſh, but no leſſe ſharpe and biting, and ſomewhat ſtrong withall; the leaues are ſomewhat ſmaller, and with deeper gaſhes, the flower and ſeede are like the former, but ſmaller.

Another ſort of blacke Raddiſh is like in leafe and ſeede to the former, but the flower is of a lighter purple colour : the roote is longer and ſmaller, and changeth alſo to bee white as the former doth, ſo that I thinke they haue both riſen from one kinde.

The Horſe Raddiſh is a kinde of wilde Raddiſh, but brought into Gardens for the vſe of it, and hath great large and long greene leaues, which are not ſo much diuided, but dented about the edges : the roote is long and great, much ſtronger in taſte then the former, and abideth diuers yeares, ſpreading with branches vnder ground.

Dittander is likewiſe a wilde kinde hereof, hauing long pointed blewiſh greene leaues, and a roote that creepeth much vnder ground : I confeſſe this might haue bin placed among the herbes, becauſe the leaues and not the rootes are vſed; but let it paſſe now with the kindes of Raddiſh.

The Vſe of theſe Raddiſhes.

Raddiſhes doe ſerue vſually as a *ſtimulum* before meat, giuing an appetite thereunto ; the poore eate them alone with bread and ſalt. Some that are early ſowen, are eaten in Aprill, or ſooner if the ſeaſon permit ; others come later ; and ſome are ſowen late to ſerue for the end of Summer : but (as of all things elſe) the earlier are the more accepted.

The blacke Raddiſhes are moſt vſed in the winter, (yet ſome in their naturall and not forc'd grounds, haue their rootes good moſt part of the Summer) and therefore muſt bee ſowen after Midſomer ; for if they ſhould bee ſowen earlier, they would preſently runne vp to ſtalke and ſeed, and ſo loſe the benefit of the roote. The Phyſicall propertie is, it is often vſed in medicines that helpe to breake the ſtone, and to auoyde grauell.

The Horſe Raddiſh is vſed Phyſically, very much in Melancholicke, Spleneticke and Scorbuticke diſeaſes. And ſome vſe to make a kinde of Muſtard with the rootes, and eate it with fiſh.

Dittander or Pepperworte is vſed of ſome cold churliſh ſtomackes, as a ſawce or ſallet ſometimes to their meate, but it is too hot, bitter and ſtrong for weake and tender ſtomackes.

Our Gardiners about London vſe great fences of reede tyed together, which ſeemeth to bee a mat ſet vpright, and is as good as a wall to defend the cold from thoſe things that would be defended, and to bring them forwards the earlier.

Chap. XLIII.

Cepæ. Onions.

Wee haue diuers ſorts of Onions, both white and red, flat, round and long, as ſhall be preſently ſhewed : but I will doe with theſe as I doe with the reſt, only giue you one deſcription for them all, and afterwards their ſeuerall names and varieties, as they are to be known by.

Our common Garden Onion hath diuers long greene hollow leaues, ſeeming halfe flat ; among which riſeth vp a great round hollow ſtalke, bigger in the middle then any where elſe, at the toppe whereof ſtandeth a cloſe round head, couered at the firſt with a thin skinne, which breaketh when the head is growne, and ſheweth forth a great vmbell

1 *Raphanus rusticanus.* Horse Raddish. 2 *Lepidium siue Piperitis.* Dittander. 3 *Cepæ rotundæ.* Round Onions. 4 *Cepæ longæ.* Long Onions. 5 *Porrum.* Leekes 6 *Allium.* Garlicke. 7 *Rapunculus.* Rampions. 8 *Tragopogon.* Goates beard.

bell of white flowers, which turne into blacke feede : but then the head is fo heauie that the ftalke cannot fuftaine it, but muft be vpheld from falling to the ground, left it rot and perifh : the roote as all know is round, in fome greater, in others leffer, or flat, in fome red on the outfide only, in others quite thorough out, in fome white, and very fharpe and ftrong, in others milder, and more pleafant, and fome fo pleafant that they may be eaten as an Apple : All thefe kindes of Onions, contrary to the nature of all other bulbous rootes, haue no off-fet, or other roote growing to it, but are euery one alone fingle by themfelues ; and therefore it feemeth, the Latines, as Columella recordeth, haue giuen it the name *Vnio*, and the French it fhould feeme following the Latine, and the Englifh the French, do call it *Oignon* and *Onion*, as an vnite, or as if they were but one and one, and dye euery yeare after feed bearing.

The red flat kinde is moft vfually with vs the ftrongeft of them all, yet I haue had a great red Onion brought mee from beyond Sea, that was as great almoft as two mens fiftes, flat and red quite thoroughout, and very pleafant both to fmell vnto, and to eate, but did quickly degenerate, fo that we plainly fee, that the foyle and climate doth giue great alteration to plants of all forts.

The long kinde wee call St. Omers Onions, and corruptly among the vulgar, St. Thomas Onions.

The other red kinde we call Strasborough Onions, whofe outfide onely is red, and are very fharpe and fierce.

The white Onions both long and flat, are like vnto Chalke-ftones lying vpon the ground, when they are ripe and fit to be gathered.

And laftly, there is the Spanifh Onion, both long and flat, very fweete, and eaten by many like an apple, but as Iohn Tradefcante faith, who hath beene in Spaine, that the Spaniards themfelues doe not eate them fo familiarly, as they doe thofe white Onions that come out of our owne Countrey, which they haue there more plentifully then their fweete Onions.

The Vfe of Onions.

Onions are vfed many wayes, as fliced and put into pottage, or boyled and peeled and layde in difhes for fallets at fupper, or fliced and put into water, for a fawce for mutton or oyfters, or into meate roafted being ftuffed with Parfly, and fo many waies that I cannot recount them, euery one pleafing themfelues, according to their order, manner or delight.

The iuice of Onions is much vfed to be applyed to any burnings with fire, or with Gun-pouder, or to any fcaldings with water or oyle, and is moft familiar for the Country, where vpon fuch fudden occafions they haue not a more fit or fpeedy remedie at hand : The ftrong fmell of Onions, and fo alfo of Garlicke and Leekes, is quite taken away from offending the head or eyes, by the eating of Parfley leaues after them.

Chap. XLIIII.

Porrum. Leekes.

THere be likewife fundry forts of Leekes, both great and fmall. Leekes are very like vnto Onions, hauing long green hollow-like leaues, flattifh on the one fide, and with a ridge or creft on the backe fide : if they bee fuffered to grow vncut, then in the fecond or third yeare after the fowing, they will fend forth a round and flender ftalke, euen quite thoroughout, and not fwollen or bigger in the middle like the Onion, bearing at the toppe a head of purplifh flowers, and blacke feede after them, very like vnto Onion feede, that it is hard to diftinguifh them : the root is long and white, with a great bufh of fibres hanging at it, which they call the beards.

The vnfet Leeke hath longer and flenderer roots then the other, which being tranf-planted, groweth thicker and greater.

The

The French Leeke, which is called the Vine Leeke, is the beſt of all others.

Our common kinde is of two ſorts, one greater then another.

Another ſort encreaſeth altogether by the roote, as Garlicke doth.

And then Ciues, which are the ſmalleſt, and encreaſe aboundantly only by the root.

Some doe account Scalions to be rather a kinde of Onions then Leekes, and call them *Cepa Aſcalonica,* or *Aſcalonitides,* which will quickly ſpend it ſelfe, if it be ſuffered to be vncut; but all Authors affirme, that there is no wilde kinde of Onion, vnleſſe they would haue it to be *Gethyum,* whereof Theophraſtus maketh mention, ſaying, that it hath a long necke (and ſo theſe Scalions haue) and was alſo of ſome called *Gethyllides,* which antiquity accounted to be dedicated to Latona, the mother of Apollo, becauſe when ſhe was bigge with childe of Apollo, ſhe longed for theſe Leekes.

The Vſe of Leekes.

The old World, as wee finde in Scripture, in the time of the children of Iſraels being in Egypt, and no doubt long before, fed much vpon Leekes, Onions, and Garlicke boyled with fleſh; and the antiquity of the Gentiles relate the ſame manner of feeding on them, to be in all Countries the like, which howſoeuer our dainty age now refuſeth wholly, in all ſorts except the pooreſt; yet Muſcouia and Ruſſia vſe them, and the Turkes to this day, (as Bellonius writeth) obſerue to haue them among their diſhes at their tables, yea although they be *Baſhas, Cades,* or *Vaiuodas,* that is to ſay, Lords, Iudges, or Gouernours of countries and places. They are vſed with vs alſo ſometimes in Lent to make pottage, and is a great and generall feeding in Wales with the vulgar Gentlemen.

Onions boyled or roſted vnder the embers, and mixed with ſugar and butter, are good for thoſe that are troubled with coughes, ſhortneſſe of breath, and wheeſing. An Onion made hollow at the bottome, and ſome good Treakle put into it, with a little iuyce of Citrons (or Lemons in the ſtead thereof) being well baked together vnder the embers, after the hole is ſtopped againe, and then ſtrained forth, and giuen to one that hath the plague, is very helpefull, ſo as hee be laid to ſweate vpon it.

Ciues are vſed as well to be ſhred among other herbes for the pot, as to be put into a Sallet among other herbs, to giue it a quicker relliſh.

Leekes are held to free the cheſt and lungs from much corruption and rotten flegme, that ſticketh faſt therein, and hard to be auoided, as alſo for them that through hoarſeneſſe haue loſt their voice, if they be eyther taken rawe, or boyled with broth of barley, or ſome ſuch other ſupping, fit and conducing thereunto. And baked vnder hot embers is a remedy againſt a ſurfeit of Muſhromes.

The greene blades of Leekes being boyled and applyed warme to the *Hemorrhoides* or piles, when they are ſwolne and painfull, giue a great deale of eaſe.

Chap. XLV.

Allium. Garlicke.

I Haue ſpoken of diuers ſorts of Garlicke called Moly, in the former booke : I ſhall neede in this place to ſhew onely thoſe kindes, that this Garden nourſeth vp, and leaue the reſt to his fit time and place.

Garlicke hath many long greene leaues, like vnto Onions, but much larger, and not hollow at all as Onions are : the ſtalke riſeth vp to be about three foote high, bearing ſuch a head at the toppe thereof as Onions and Leekes doe, with purpliſh flowers, and blacke ſeede like Leekes : the roote is white within, couered ouer with many purplish skins, and is diuided into many parts or cloues, which serue both to set againe for increase, and also to vse as neede shall require, and is of a very strong smell and taste, as euery one knoweth, passing either Onions or Leekes, but exceeding wholsome withall for them that can take it.

Allium Vrsinum. Ramsons.

Ramsons are another kinde of Garlicke, and hath two or three faire broad leaues, of a fresh or light greene colour, pointed at the end : the stalke groweth about an hand length high, bearing many small and pure white starre-like flowers at the toppe, and afterwards small, blacke, and smooth round seede : the roote is also diuided into many parts, whereby it is much encreased, and is much milder then the former, both in smell and taste.

The Vse of Garlicke.

It being well boyled in salt broth, is often eaten of them that haue strong stomackes, but will not brooke in a weake and tender stomacke.

It is accounted, and so called in diuers Countries, The poore mans Treakle, that is, a remedy for all diseases. It is neuer eaten rawe of any man that I know, as other of the rootes aforesaid, but sodden alwaies and so taken.

Ramsons are oftentimes eaten with bread and butter, and otherwise also, as euery mans affection and course of life leadeth him to vse.

Chap. XLVI.

Rapunculus siue Rapuntium. Rampions.

Garden Rampions are of two sorts, the one greater, the other lesser : the leaues of Rampions are in the one somewhat broad like a Beete, in the other somewhat long and narrow, and a little broader at the end, of a light greene colour, lying flat vpon the ground all the first winter, or yeare of the springing, and the next Spring shooteth forth stalkes two or three foote high, bearing at the toppe, in the bigger sort, a long slender spike of small horned or crooked flowers, which open their brimmes into foure leaues ; in the lesser many small purplish bels, standing vpon seuerall small foote-stalkes, which turne into heads, bearing small blackish seede : the root is white, branched into two or three rootes, of the bignesse and length of a mans finger or thumbe.

The Vse of Rampions.

The rootes of both are vsed for Sallets, being boyled, and then eaten with oyle and vinegar, a little salt and pepper.

Chap. XLVII.

Tragopogon. Goates beard.

Goates beard hath many long and narrow leaues, broader at the bottome, and sharper at the end, with a ridge downe the backe of the leafe, and of a pale greene colour ; among which riseth vp a stalke of two or three foote high, smooth and hollow, bearing thereon many such like leaues, but smaller and shorter, and at the toppe thereof on euery branch a great double yellow flower, like almost vnto the flower of a Dandelion, which turneth into a head, stored with doune, and long whitish seede therein, hauing on the head of euery one some part of the doune, and

and is carried away with the winde if it bee neglected : the roote is long and round, somewhat like vnto a Parfnep, but farre fmaller, blackifh on the outfide, and white within, yeelding a milkie iuyce being broken, as all the reft of the plant doth, and of a very good and pleafant tafte. This kinde, as alfo another with narrower leaues, almoft like graffe, growe wilde abroad in many places, but are brought into diuers Gardens. The other two kindes formerly defcribed in the firft part, the one with a purple flower, and the other with an afh-coloured, haue fuch rootes as thefe here defcribed, and may ferue alfo to the fame purpofe, being of equall goodneffe, if any will vfe them in the fame manner ; that is, while they are young, and of the firft yeares fowing, elfe they all growe hard, in running vp to feede.

The Vfe of Goates beard.

If the rootes of any of thefe kindes being young, be boyled and dreffed as a Parfnep, they make a pleafant difh of meate, farre paffing the Parfnep in many mens iudgements, and that with yellow flowers to be the beft.

They are of excellent vfe being in this manner prepared, or after any other fit and conuenient way, to ftrengthen thofe that are macilent, or growing into any confumption.

CHAP. XLVIII.

Carum. Carawayes.

CArawayes hath many very fine cut and diuided leaues lying on the ground, being alwaies greene, fomewhat refembling the leaues of Carrots, but thinner, and more finely cut, of a quicke, hot, and fpicie tafte: the ftalke rifeth not much higher then the Carrot ftalke, bearing fome leaues at the ioynts along the ftalke to the toppe, where it brancheth into three or foure parts, bearing fpoakie vmbels of white flowers, which turne into fmall blackifh feede, fmaller then Anifeede, and of a hotter and quicker tafte: the roote is whitifh, like vnto a Parfnep, but much fmaller, more fpreading vnder ground, and a little quicke in tafte, as all the reft of the plant is, and abideth long after it hath giuen feede.

The Vfe of Carawayes.

The rootes of Carawayes being boyled may be eaten as Carrots, and by reafon of the fpicie tafte doth warme and comfort a cold weake ftomacke, helping to diffolue winde (whereas Carrots engender it) and to prouoke vrine, and is a very welcome and delightfull difh to a great many, yet they are fomewhat ftronger in tafte then Parfneps.

The feede is much vfed to bee put among baked fruit, or into bread, cakes, &c. to giue them a rellifh, and to helpe to digeft winde in them are fubiect thereunto.

It is alfo made into Comfits, and put into *Trageas*, or as we call them in Englifh, Dredges, that are taken for the cold and winde in the body, as alfo are ferued to the table with fruit.

CHAP.

Chap. XLIX.

Pappas siue Battatas. Potatoes.

THree sorts of Potatoes are well knowne vnto vs, but the fourth I rest doubtfull of, and dare not affirme it vpon such termes as are giuen vnto it, vntill I may be better informed by mine owne sight.

The Spanish kinde hath (in the Islands where they growe, either naturally, or planted for increase, profit, and vse of the Spaniards that nourse them) many firme and verie sweete rootes, like in shape and forme vnto Asphodill rootes, but much greater and longer, of a pale browne on the outside, and white within, set together at one head ; from whence rise vp many long branches, which by reason of their weight and weaknesse, cannot stand of themselues, but traile on the ground a yard and a halfe in length at the least (I relate it, as it hath growne with vs, but in what other forme, for flower or fruit, we know not) whereon are set at seuerall distances, broad and in a manner three square leaues, somewhat like triangled Iuie leaues, of a darke greene colour, the two sides whereof are broad and round, and the middle pointed at the end, standing reasonable close together : thus much we haue seene growe with vs, and no more : the roote rather decaying then increasing in our country.

The Potatoes of Virginia, which some foolishly call the Apples of youth, is another kinde of plant, differing much from the former, sauing in the colour and taste of the roote, hauing many weake and somewhat flexible branches, leaning a little downwards, or easily borne downe with the winde or other thing, beset with many winged leaues, of a darke grayish greene colour, whereof diuers are smaller, and some greater then others : the flowers growe many together vpon a long stalke, comming forth from betweene the leaues and the great stalkes, euery one seuerally vpon a short footstalke, somewhat like the flower of Tabacco for the forme, being one whole leafe six cornered at the brimmes, but somewhat larger, and of a pale blewish purple colour, or pale doue colour, and in some almost white, with some red threads in the middle, standing about a thicke gold yellow pointell, tipped with greene at the end : after the flowers are past, there come vp in their places small round fruit, as bigge as a Damson or Bulleis, greene at the first, and somewhat whitish afterwards, with many white seedes therein, like vnto Nightshade : the rootes are rounder and much smaller then the former, and some much greater then others, dispersed vnder ground by many small threads or strings from the rootes, of the same light browne colour on the outside, and white within, as they, and neare of the same taste, but not altogether so pleasant.

The Potatos of Canada, (which hath diuers names giuen it by diuers men, as Bauhinus vpon Matthiolus calleth it, *Solanum tuberosum esculentum,* Pelleterius of Middleborough in his *Plantarum Synonimia, Heliotropium Indicum tuberosum,* Fabius Columna in the second part of his *Phytobasanos, Flos Solis Farnesianus, siue Aster Peruanus tuberosus :* We in England, from some ignorant and idle head, haue called them Artichokes of Ierusalem, only because the roote, being boyled, is in taste like the bottome of an Artichoke head : but they may most fitly be called, Potatos of Canada, because their rootes are in forme, colour and taste, like vnto the Potatos of Virginia, but greater, and the French brought them first from Canada into these parts) riseth vp with diuers stiffe, round stalkes, eight or tenne foote high in our Country, where they haue scarce shewed their flowers, whereas the very head of flowers in other Countries, as Fabius Columna expresseth it, being of a Pyramis or Sugar loafe fashion, broade spreading below, and smaller pointed vpwards towards the toppe, is neere of the same length, whereon are set large and broade rough greene leaues, very like vnto the leaues of the flower of the Sunne, but smaller, yet growing in the very same manner, round about the stalkes : at the very later end of Summer, or the beginning of Autumne, if the roote bee well planted and defended, it will giue a shew of a few small yellow flowers at the top, like vnto the flowers of *Aster* or Starre-worte, and much smaller then any flower of the Sunne, which come to no perfection with vs : the roote, while the plant

1 *Carum.* Carawayes. 2 *Battatas Hispanorum.* Spanish Potatoes. 3 *Papas seu Battatas Virginianrum.* Virginia Potatoes. 4 *Battatas de Canada.* Potatoes of Canada, or Artichokes of Ierusalem.

is growing aboue ground, encreaseth not to his full growth, but when the Summer is well spent, and the springing of the stalk is past, which is about the end of August, or in September, then the root is perceiued to be encreased in the earth, and will before Autumne be spent, that is, in October, swell like a mound or hillocke, round about the foote of the stalkes, and will not haue his rootes fit to be taken vp, vntill the stalkes be halfe withered at the soonest ; but after they be withered, and so all the winter long vntill the Spring againe, they are good, and fit to bee taken vp and vsed, which are a number of tuberous round rootes, growing close together ; so that it hath beene obserued, that from one roote, being set in the Spring, there hath been forty or more taken vp againe, and to haue ouer-filled a pecke measure, and are of a pleasant good taste as many haue tryed.

The Vse of all these Potato's.

The Spanish Potato's are roasted vnder the embers, and being pared or peeled and sliced, are put into sacke with a little sugar, or without, and is delicate to be eaten.

They are vsed to be baked with Marrow, Sugar, Spice, and other things in Pyes, which are a daintie and costly dish for the table.

The Comfit-makers preserue them, and candy them as diuers other things, and so ordered, is very delicate, fit to accompany such other banquetting dishes.

The Virginia Potato's being dressed after all these waies before specified, maketh almost as delicate meate as the former.

The Potato's of Canada are by reason of their great increasing, growne to be so common here with vs at London, that euen the most vulgar begin to despise them, whereas when they were first receiued among vs, they were dainties for a Queene.

Being put into seething water they are soone boyled tender, which after they bee peeled, sliced and stewed with butter, and a little wine, was a dish for a Queene, beeing as pleasant as the bottome of an Artichoke : but the too frequent vse, especially being so plentifull and cheape, hath rather bred a loathing then a liking of them.

Chap. L.

Cinara. Artichokes.

THe fruits that grow vpon or neere the ground, are next to be entreated of, and first of Artichokes, whereof there be diuers kindes, some accounted tame and of the Garden, others wilde and of late planted in Gardens, Orchards or Fieldes, of purpose to be meate for men.

The Artichoke hath diuers great, large, and long hollowed leaues, much cut in or torne on both edges, without any great shew of prickles on them, of a kinde of whitish greene, like vnto an ash colour, whereof it tooke the Latine name *Cinara* : the stalke is strong, thicke and round, with some skins as it were downe all the length of them, bearing at the toppe one scaly head, made at the first like a Pine-apple, but after growing greater, the scales are more separate, yet in the best kindes lying close, and not staring, as some other kindes doe, which are eyther of a reddish browne, whitish, or greenish colour, and in some broade at the ends, in others sharpe or prickly : after the head hath stood a great while, if it bee suffered, and the Summer proue hot and kindly, in some there will breake forth at the toppe thereof, a tuft of blewish purple thrumes or threds, vnder which grow the seede, wrapped in a great deale of dounie substance : but that roote that yeeldeth flowers will hardly abide the next winter ; but else being cut off when it is well growne, that dounie matter abideth close in the middle of the head, hauing the bottome thereof flat and round, which is that matter or substance that is vsed to be eaten : the roote spreadeth it selfe in the ground reasona-

ble

1 *Cinara satiua rubra.* The red Artichoke. 2 *Cinara satiua alba.* The white Artichoke. 3 *Cinara patula.* The French Artichoke. 4 *Cinara siluestris.* The Thistle Artichoke. 5 *Carduus esculentus.* The Chardon.

ble well, yeelding diuers heads of leaues or suckers, whereby it is increased.

The white Artichoke is in all things like the red, but that the head is of a whitish ashe colour, like the leaues, whereas the former is reddish.

We haue also another, whose head is greene, and very sharpe vpwards, and is common in many places.

Wee haue had also another kinde in former times that grew as high as any man, and branched into diuers stalkes, euery one bearing a head thereon, almost as bigge as the first.

There is another kinde, called the Muske Artichoke, which groweth like the French kinde, but is much better in spending, although it haue a lesser bottome.

The French Artichoke hath a white head, the scales whereof stand staring far asunder one from another at the ends, which are sharpe : this is well known by this qualitie, that while it is hot after it is boyled, it swelleth so strong, that one would verily thinke it had bin boyled in stinking water, which was brought ouer after a great froste that had well nigh consumed our best kindes, and are now almost cleane cast out again, none being willing to haue it take vp the roome of better.

There is a lowe kinde that groweth much about Paris, which the French esteeme more then any other, and is lower then the former French kinde, the head whereof as well as the leaues, is of a fresher greene colour, almost yellowish.

Then there is the Thistle Artichoke, which is almost a wilde kinde, and groweth smaller, with a more open and prickly head then any of the former.

And lastly, the Chardon as they call it, because it is almost of the forme and nature of a Thistle, or wilde Artichoke. This groweth high, and full of sharpe prickles, of a grayish colour. Iohn Tradescante assured mee, hee saw three acres of Land about Brussels planted with this kinde, which the owner whited like Endiue, and then sold them in the winter : Wee cannot yet finde the true manner of dressing them, that our Countrey may take delight therein.

All these kindes are encreased by slipping the young shootes from the root, which being replanted in February, March, or Aprill, haue the same yeare many times, but the next at the most, borne good heads.

Wee finde by dayly experience, that our English red Artichoke is in our Countrey the most delicate meate of any of the other, and therefore diuers thinking it to bee a seuerall kinde, haue sent them into Italie, France, and the Lowe Countries, where they haue not abode in their goodnesse aboue two yeare, but that they haue degenerated ; so that it seemeth, that our soyle and climate hath the preheminence to nourish vp this plant to his highest excellencie.

The Vse of Artichokes.

The manner of preparing them for the Table is well knowne to the youngest Housewife I thinke, to bee boyled in faire water, and a little salt, vntill they bee tender, and afterwardes a little vinegar and pepper, put to the butter, poured vpon them for the sawce, and so are serued to the Table.

They vse likewise to take the boyled bottomes to make Pyes, which is a delicate kinde of baked meate.

The Chardon is eaten rawe of diuers, with vinegar and oyle, pepper and salt, all of them, or some, as euery one liketh for their delight.

CHAP.

Chap. LI.

Fabæ & Phaseoli. Garden and French Beanes.

THe Garden Beane is of two colours, red or blacke, and white, yet both rife from one ; the fmall or fielde Beanes I make no mention of in this place ; but the French or Kidney Beane is almoft of infinite forts and colours : we doe not for all that intend to trouble you in this place, with the knowledge or relation of any more then is fit for a Garden of that nature, that I haue propounded it in the beginning.

Our ordinary Beanes, feruing for foode for the poorer fort for the moft part, are planted as well in fieldes as in gardens, becaufe the quantity of them that are fpent taketh vp many acres of land to be planted in, and rife vp with one, two or three ftalks, according to the fertilitie of the foyle, being fmooth and fquare, higher then any man oftentimes, whereon are fet at certaine diftances, from the very bottome almoft to the toppe, two long fmooth flefhy and thicke leaues almoft round, one ftanding by another at the end of a fmall footeftalke : betweene thefe leaues and the ftalke, come forth diuers flowers, all of them looking one way for the moft part, which are clofe a little turned vp at the brimmes, white and fpotted with a blackifh fpot in the middle of them, and fomwhat purplifh at the foot or bottome, of the forme almoft of Broome or Peafe flowers, many of which that grow vpward toward the toppe, doe feldome beare fruit, and therefore are gathered to diftill, and the toppes of the ftalkes cut off, to caufe the reft to thriue the better ; after which grow vp long great fmooth greene pods, greater then in any other kinde of Pulfe, which grow blacke when they are ripe, and containe within them two, three or foure Beanes, which are fomewhat flat and round, eyther white or reddifh, which being full ripe grow blackifh : the roote hath diuers fibres annexed vnto the maine roote, which dyeth euery yeare.

The French or Kidney Beane rifeth vp at the firft but with one ftalke, which afterwards diuideth it felfe into many armes or branches, euery one of them being fo weak, that without they be fuftained with ftickes or poles, whereon with their winding and clafpers they take hold, they would lye fruitleffe vpon the ground : vpon thefe branches grow forth at feuerall places long footeftalkes, with euery of them three broade, round and pointed greene leaues at the end of them, towards the tops whereof come forth diuers flowers, made like vnto Peafe bloffomes, of the fame colour for the moft part that the fruit will be or, that is to fay, eyther white, or yellow, or red, or blackifh, or of a deepe purple &c. but white is moft vfuall for our Garden ; after which come long and flender flat pods, fome crooked, and fome ftraight, with a ftring as it were running downe the backe thereof, wherein are contained flattifh round fruit, made to the fafhion of a kidney : the roote is long, and fpreadeth with many fibres annexed vnto it, perifhing euery yeare.

The Vfe of thefe Beanes.

The Garden Beanes ferue (as I faid before) more for the vfe of the poore then of the rich : I fhall therefore only fhew you the order the poore take with them, and leaue curiofity to them that will beftow time vpon them. They are only boyled in faire water and a little falt, and afterwards ftewed with fome butter, a little vinegar and pepper being put vnto them, and fo eaten : or elfe eaten alone after they are boyled without any other fawce. The water of the bloffomes diftilled, is vfed to take away fpots, and to cleer the skin. The water of the greene huskes or cods is good for the ftone.

The Kidney Beanes boyled in water huske and all, onely the ends cut off, and the ftring taken away, and ftewed with butter &c. are efteemed more fauory meate to many mens pallates, then the former, and are a difh more oftentimes at rich mens Tables then at the poore.

CHAP. LII.

Pifam. Peaſe.

THere is a very great variety of manured Peaſe known to vs, and I think more in our Country then in others , whereof ſome proſper better in one ground and country, and ſome in others : I ſhall giue you the deſcription of one alone for all the reſt, and recite vnto you the names of the reſt.

Garden Peaſe are for the moſt part the greateſt and ſweeteſt kinds, and are ſuſtained with ſtakes or buſhes. The Field Peaſe are not ſo vſed , but growe without any ſuch adoe. They ſpring vp with long, weake , hollow, and brittle (while they are young and greene) whitiſh greene ſtalkes , branched into diuers parts , and at euery ioynt where it parteth one broad round leafe compaſſing the ſtalke about , ſo that it commeth as it were thorough it : the leaues are winged, made of diuers ſmall leaues ſet to a middle ribbe , of a whitiſh greene colour, with claſpers at the ends of the leaues, whereby it taketh hold of whatſoeuer ſtandeth next vnto it : betweene the leaues and the ſtalkes come forth the flowers , ſtanding two or three together , euery one by it ſelfe on his owne ſeuerall ſtalke, which are either wholly white, or purple, or mixed white and purple, or purple and blew : the fruit are long, and ſomewhat round cods, whereof ſome are greater, others leſſer, ſome thicke and ſhort, ſome plaine and ſmooth, others a little crooked at the ends ; wherein alſo are contained diuers formes of fruit or peaſe ; ſome being round, others cornered, ſome ſmall, ſome great, ſome white, others gray, and ſome ſpotted : the roote is ſmall, and quickly periſheth.

The kindes of Peaſe are theſe :

The Rounciuall.	The gray Peaſe.
The greene Haſting.	The white Haſting.
The Sugar Peaſe.	The Peaſe without skins.
The ſpotted Peaſe.	

The Scottiſh or tufted Peaſe, which ſome call the Roſe Peaſe, is a good white Peaſe fit to be eaten.

The early or French Peaſe, which ſome call Fulham Peaſe, becauſe thoſe grounds thereabouts doe bring them ſooneſt forward for any quantity , although ſometimes they miſcarry by their haſte and earlineſſe.

Cicer Arietinum. Rams Ciches.

This is a kinde of Pulſe, ſo much vſed in Spaine, that it is vſually one of their daintie diſhes at all their feaſts : They are of two ſorts , white and red ; the white is onely vſed for meate, the other for medicine. It beareth many vpright branches with winged leaues, many ſet together, being ſmall, almoſt round, and dented about the edges: the flowers are either white or purple, according to the colour of the Peaſe which follow, and are ſomewhat round at the head, but cornered and pointed at the end, one or two at the moſt in a ſmall roundiſh cod.

The Vſe of Peaſe.

Peaſe of all or the moſt of theſe ſorts , are either vſed when they are greene, and be a diſh of meate for the table of the rich as well as the poore, yet euery one obſeruing his time, and the kinde : the faireſt, ſweeteſt, youngeſt, and earlieſt for the better ſort , the later and meaner kindes for the meaner, who doe not giue the deereſt price : Or

Being dry, they ſerue to boyle into a kinde of broth or pottage, wherein many doe put Tyme, Mints, Sauory, or ſome other ſuch hot herbes, to giue it the better relliſh , and is much vſed in Towne and Countrey in the Lent

time,

1 *Faba satina.* Garden Beanes. 2 *Phaseoli satiui.* French Beanes. 3 *Pisum vulgae.* Garden Pease. 4 *Pisum vmbellatum siue Roseum.* Rose Pease or Scottish Pease. 5 *Pisum Saccharatum.* Sugar Pease. 6 *Pisum maculatum.* Spotted Pease. 7 *Cicer Arietinum.* Rams Ciches or Cicers.

time, especially of the poorer sort of people.

It is much vsed likewise at Sea for them that goe long voyages, and is for change, because it is fresh, a welcome diet to most persons therein.

The Rams Ciches the Spaniards call *Grauancos*, and *Garauancillos*, and eate them boyled and stewed as the most dainty kinde of Pease that are, they are of a very good rellish, and doe nourish much; but yet are not without that windy quality that all sorts of Pulse are subiect vnto : they increase bodily lust much more then any other sorts, and as it is thought, doth helpe to encrease seede.

Chap. LIII.

Cucumer. The Cowcumber.

OF Cowcumbers there are diuers sorts, differing chiefly in the forme and colour of the fruit, and not in the forme of the plant; therefore one description shall serue in stead of all the rest.

The Cowcumber bringeth forth many trailing rough greene branches lying on the ground, all along whereof growe seuerall leaues, which are rough, broad, vneuen at the edges, and pointed at the ends, with long crooked tendrels comming forth at the same ioynt with the leafe, but on the other side therof: between the stalks & the leaues at the ioynts come forth the flowers seuerally, euery one standing on a short foot-stalke, opening it selfe into fiue leaues, of a yellowish colour, at the bottome whereof groweth the fruit, long and greene at the first, but when it is thorough ripe, a little yellowish, hauing many furrowes, and vneuen bunches all the length of it, wherein is a white firme substance next vnto the skin, and a cleare pulpe or watery substance, with white flat seede lying dispersed through it : the roote is long and white, with diuers fibres at it.

The kindes.

The first described is called, The long greene Cowcumber.

There is another is called, The short Cowcumber, being short, and of an equall bignesse in the body thereof, and of an vnequall bignesse at both ends.

The long Yellow, which is yellowish from the beginning, and more yellow when it is ripe, and hath beene measured to be thirteene inches long : but this is not that small long Cowcumber, called of the Latines, *Cucumis anguinus.*

Another kinde is early ripe, called The French kinde.

The Dantsicke kinde beareth but small fruit, growing on short branches or runners : the pickled Cowcumbers that are vsually sold are of this kind.

The Muscouie kinde is the smallest of all other, yet knowne, and beareth not aboue foure or fiue at the most on a roote, which are no bigger then small Lemons.

The Vse of Cowcumbers.

Some vse to cast a little salt on their sliced Cowcumbers, and let them stand halfe an houre or more in a dish, and then poure away the water that commeth from them by the salt, and after put vinegar, oyle, &c. thereon, as euery one liketh : this is done, to take away the ouermuch waterishnesse and coldnesse of the Cowcumbers.

In many countries they vse to eate Cowcumbers as wee doe Apples or Peares, paring and giuing slices of them, as we would to our friends of some dainty Apple or Peare.

The pickled Cowcumbers that come from beyond Sea, are much vsed

with

with vs for fawce to meate all the Winter long. Some haue ftriuen to equall them, by pickling vp our Cowcumbers at the later end of the yeare, when they are cheapeft, taking the little ones and fcalding them thoroughly well, which after they put in brine, with fome Dill or Fenell leaues and ftalkes: but thefe are nothing comparable to the former, wee either miffing of the right and orderly pickling of them, or the kinde it felfe differing much from ours (as I faid of the Dantficke kinde) for ours are neither fo tender and firme, nor fo fauoury as the other.

The rawe or greene Cowcumbers are fitteft for the hotter time of the yeare, and for hot ftomackes, and not to be vfed in colder weather or cold ftomackes, by reafon of the coldneffe, whereby many haue been ouertaken.

The feede is vfed phyfically in many medicines that ferue to coole, and a little to make the paffages of vrine flippery, and to giue eafe to hot difeafes.

CHAP. LIIII.

Melo. Milions or Muske Melons.

THere bee diuers forts of Melons found out at this day, differing much in the goodneffe of tafte one from another. This Countrey hath not had vntill of late yeares the skill to nourfe them vp kindly, but now there are many that are fo well experienced therein, and haue their ground fo well prepared, as that they will not miffe any yeare, if it be not too extreme vnkindly, to haue many ripe ones in a reafonable time: yet fome will be later then others alwayes.

The Melon is certainly a kinde of Cowcumber, it doth fo neare refemble it, both in the manner of his growing, hauing rough trailing branches, rough vneuen leaues, and yellow flowers: after which come the fruit, which is rounder, thicker, bigger, more rugged, and fpotted on the outfide then the Cowcumber, of a ruffet colour, and greene vnderneath, which when it groweth full ripe, will change a little yellowifh, being as deepe furrowed and ribbed as they, and befides hauing chaps or rifts in diuers places of the rinde: the inward hard fubftance is yellow, which onely is eaten: the feede which is bigger, and a little yellower then the Cowcumber, lying in the middle onely among the moifter pulpe: the fmell and changing of his colour, fore-fhew their ripeneffe to them that are experienced: the roote is long, with many fibres at it. The fruit requireth much watering in the hot time of the day, to caufe them to ripen the fooner, as I haue obferued by diuers of the beft skill therein.

The Vfe of the kindes of Melons.

The beft Melon feede doe come to vs out of Spaine, fome haue come out of Turkie, but they haue been nothing fo good and kindly.

Some are called Sugar Melons, others Peare Melons, and others Musk Melons.

They haue beene formerly only eaten by great perfonages, becaufe the fruit was not only delicate but rare; and therfore diuers were brought from France, and fince were nourfed vp by the Kings or Noblemens Gardiners onely, to ferue for their Mafters delight: but now diuers others that haue skill and conueniencie of ground for them, doe plant them and make them more common.

They paire away the outer rinde, and cut out the inward pulpe where the feede lyeth, flice the yellow firme inward rinde or fubftance, & fo eate it with falt and pepper (and good ftore of wine, or elfe it will hardly difgeft) for this is firmer, & hath not that moifture in it that the Cowcumbers haue. It is alfo more delicate, and of more worth, which recompenfeth the paine.

The feed of thefe Melons are vfed as Cowcumbers phyfically, and together with them moft vfually.

CHAP.

Chap. LV.

Pepo. Pompions.

WE haue but one kinde of Pompion (as I take it) in all our Gardens, notwithstanding the diuersities of bignesse and colour.

The Pompion or great Melon (or as some call it Milion) creepeth vpon the ground (if nothing bee by it whreeon it may take hold and climbe) with very great, ribbed, rough, and prickly branches, whereon are set very large rough leaues, cut in on the edges with deepe gashes, and dented besides, with many claspers also, which winde about euery thing they meete withall : the flowers are great and large, hollow and yellow, diuided at the brims into fiue parts, at the bottome of which, as it is in the rest, groweth the fruit, which is very great, sometimes of the bignesse of a mans body, and oftentimes lesse, in some ribbed or bunched, in others plaine, and either long or round, either green or yellow, or gray, as Nature listeth to shew her selfe; for it is but waste time, to recite all the formes and colours may be obserued in them : the inner rinde next vnto the outer is yellowish and firme : the seede is great, flat, and white, lying in the middle of the watery pulpe : the roote is of the bignesse of a mans thumbe or greater, dispersed vnder ground with many small fibres ioyned thereunto.

Gourds are kindes of Melons; but because wee haue no vse of them, wee leaue them vnto their fit place.

The Vse of Pompions.

They are boyled in faire water and salt, or in powdered beefe broth, or sometimes in milke, and so eaten, or else buttered. They vse likewise to take out the inner watery substance with the seedes, and fill vp the place with Pippins, and hauing laid on the couer which they cut off from the toppe, to take out the pulpe, they bake them together, and the poore of the Citie, as well as the Country people, doe eate thereof, as of a dainty dish.

The seede hereof, as well as of Cowcumbers and Melons, are cooling, and serue for emulsions in the like manner for Almond milkes, &c. for those are troubled with the stone.

Chap. LVI.

Fragaria. Strawberries.

THere be diuers sorts of Strawberries, whereof those that are noursed vp in Gardens or Orchards I intend to giue you the knowledge in this place, and leaue the other to a fitter; yet I must needs shew you of one of the wilde sorts, which for his strangenesse is worthy of this Garden : And I must also enforme you, that the wilde Strawberry that groweth in the Woods is our Garden Strawberry, but bettered by the soyle and transplanting.

The Strawberry hath his leaues closed together at the first springing vp, which afterwards spread themselues into three diuided parts or leaues, euery one standing vpon a small long foote-stalke, greene on the vpperside, grayish vnderneath, and snipped or dented about the edges; among which rise vp diuers small stalkes, bearing foure or fiue flowers at the tops, consisting of fiue white round pointed leaues, somewhat yellowish in the bottome, with some yellow threads therein; after which come the fruit, made of many small graines set together, like vnto a small Mulberry or Raspis, reddish when it is ripe, and of a pleasant winy taste, wherein is enclosed diuers small blackish seede : the roote is reddish and long, with diuers small threads at it, and sendeth

forth

1 *Cucumis vagus vulgaris.* The ordinary Cowcumber. 2 *Cucumis Hispanicus.* The long yellow Spanish Cowcumber. 3 *Melo vulgaris.* The ordinary Melon. 4 *Melo maximus optimus.* The greatest Muske Melon. 5 *Pepo.* The Pompion. 6 *Fraga vulgaris.* Common Strawberries. 7 *Fraga Bohemica maxima.* The great Bohemia Strawberries. 8 *Fraga aculeata.* The prickly Strawberry.

forth from the head therof long reddiſh ſtrings running vpon the ground, which ſhoot forth leaues in many places, whereby it is much encreaſed.

The white Strawberry differeth not from the red, but in the colour of the fruite, which is whiter then the former when it is thorough ripe, enclining to redneſſe.

The greene Strawberry likewiſe differeth not, but that the fruit is green on all ſides when it is ripe, ſaue on that ſide the Sun lyeth vpon it, and there it is ſomewhat red.

The Virginia Strawberry carryeth the greateſt leafe of any other, except the Bohemian, but ſcarce can one Strawberry be ſeene ripe among a number of plants; I thinke the reaſon therof to be the want of ſkill, or induſtry to order it aright. For the Bohemia, and all other Strawberries will not beare kindly, if you ſuffer them to grow with many ſtrings, and therefore they are ſtill cut away.

There is another very like vnto this, that Iohn Tradeſcante brought with him from Bruſſels long agoe, and in ſeuen yeares could neuer ſee one berry ripe on all ſides, but ſtill the better part rotten, although it would euery yeare flower abundantly, and beare very large leaues.

The Bohemia Strawberry hath beene with vs but of late dayes, but is the goodlieſt and greateſt, both for leafe next to the Virginian, and for beauty farre ſurpaſſing all; for ſome of the berries haue beene meaſured to bee neere fiue inches about. Maſter Queſter the Poſtmaſter firſt brought them ouer into our Country, as I vnderſtand, but I know no man ſo induſtrious in the carefull planting and bringing them to perfection in that plentifull maner, as Maſter Vincent Sion who dwelt on the Banck ſide, neer the old Paris garden ſtaires, who from ſeuen rootes, as hee affirmed to me, in one yeare and a halfe, planted halfe an acree of ground with the increaſe from them, beſides thoſe he gaue away to his friends, and with him I haue ſeene ſuch, and of that bigneſſe before mentioned.

One Strawberry more I promiſed to ſhew you, which although it be a wilde kinde, and of no vſe for meate, yet I would not let this diſcourſe paſſe, without giuing you the knowledge of it. It is in leafe much like vnto the ordinary, but differeth in that the flower, if it haue any, is greene, or rather it beareth a ſmall head of greene leaues, many ſet thicke together like vnto a double ruffe, in the midſt whereof ſtandeth the fruit, which when it is ripe, ſheweth to be ſoft and ſomwhat reddiſh, like vnto a Strawberry, but with many ſmall harmleſſe prickles on them, which may be eaten and chewed in the mouth without any maner of offence, and is ſomewhat pleaſant like a Strawberry : it is no great bearer, but thoſe it doth beare, are ſet at the toppes of the ſtalks cloſe together, pleaſant to behold, and fit for a Gentlewoman to weare on her arme, &c. as a raritie in ſtead of a flower.

The Vſe of Strawberries.

The leaues of Strawberries are alwaies vſed among other herbes in cooling drinkes, as alſo in lotions, and gargles for the mouth and throate : the rootes are ſometimes added to make it the more effectuall, and withall ſomwhat the more binding.

The berries themſelues are often brought to the Table as a reare ſeruice, whereunto claret wine, creame or milke is added with ſugar, as euery one liketh; as alſo at other times, both with the better and meaner ſort, and are a good cooling and pleaſant diſh in the hot Summer ſeaſon.

The water diſtilled of the berries, is good for the paſſions of the heart, cauſed by the perturbation of the ſpirits, being eyther drunke alone, or in wine; and maketh the heart merry.

Some doe hold that the water helpeth to clenſe the face from ſpots, and to adde ſome cleereneſſe to the ſkinne.

CHAP.

CHAP. LVII.

Angelica. Garden Angelica.

HAuing thus furnished you out a Kitchen Garden with all sorts of herbes, roots & fruits fit for it, and for any mans priuate vse, as I did at the first appropriate it; let me a little transcend, and for the profit & vse of Country Gentlewomen and others, furnish them with some few other herbes, of the most especiall vse for those shall need them, to be planted at hand in their Gardens, to spend as occasion shall serue, and first of Angelica.

Angelica hath great and long winged leaues, made of many broade greene ones, diuided one from another vpon the stalk, which is three foot long or better somtimes, among which rise vp great thicke and hollow stalkes with some few ioynts, whereat doth alwayes stand two long leaues compassing the stalke at the bottome, in some places at the ioynts spring out other stalkes or branches, bearing such like leaues but smaller, and at the tops very large vmbels of white flowers, that turne into whitish seede somewhat thicke : the roote groweth great with many branches at it, but quickly perisheth after it hath borne seede : to preserue the roote therefore the better, they vse to cut it often in the yeare, thereby to hinder the running vp to seede : the whole plant, both leafe, roote and seede, is of an excellent comfortable sent, sauour and taste.

The Vse of Angelica.

The distilled water of Angelica, eyther simple or compound, is of especiall vse *in deliquium animi, vel cordis tremores & passiones,* that is, swounings, when the spirits are ouercome and faint, or tremblings and passions of the heart, to expell any windy or noysome vapours from it. The green stalkes or the young rootes being preserued or candied, are very effectuall to comfort and warme a colde and weake stomacke : and in the time of infection is of excellent good vse to preserue the spirits and heart from infection. The dryed roote made into pouder, and taken in wine or other drinke, will abate the rage of lust in young persons, as I haue it related vnto me vpon credit : A Syrupe made thereof in this manner, is very profitable to expectorate flegme out of the chest and lunges, and to procure a sweete breath. Into the greene stalke of Angelica as it standeth growing, make a great gashe or incision, wherein put a quantitie of fine white Sugar, letting it there abide for three dayes, and after take it forth by cutting a hole at the next ioynt vnder the cut, where the Syrupe resteth, or cut off the stalke, and turne it downe, that the Syrupe may drayne forth ; which keepe for a most delicate medicine.

CHAP. LVIII.

Dracunculus hortensis siue Serpentaria. Dragons.

DRagons riseth out of the ground with a bare or naked round whitish stalke, spotted very much with purplish spots and strakes, bearing at the toppe therof a few greene leaues very much diuided on all sides, standing vpon long footestalkes, in the middle whereof (if the roote be old enough) commeth forth a great long huske or hose, green on the outside, and of a darke purplish colour on the inside, with a slender long reddish pestell or clapper in the middle : the roote is great, round, flat and whitish on the outside, and whiter within, very like vnto the rootes of *Arum,* or Wakerobin, and tasting somewhat sharpe like it.

The

The Vſe of Dragons.

The chiefe vſe whereunto Dragons are applyed, is, that according to an old receiued cuſtome and tradition (and not the iudgement of any learned Author) the diſtilled water is giuen with Mithridatum or Treakle to expell noyſome and peſtilentiall vapours from the heart.

Chap. LIX.

Ruta. Garden Rue, or Herbe Grace.

Garden Rue or Herbe Grace groweth vp with hard whitiſh wooddy ſtalkes, whereon are ſet diuers branches of leaues, being diuided into many ſmall ones, which are ſomewhat thicke and round pointed, of a blewiſh greene colour: the flowers ſtand at the tops of the ſtalkes conſiſting of foure ſmall yellow leaues, with a greene button in the middle, and diuers ſmall yellow threds about it, which growing ripe, containe within them ſmall blacke ſeede: the roote is white and wooddy, ſpreading farre in the ground.

The Vſe of Rue.

The many good properties whereunto Rue ſerueth, hath I thinke in former times cauſed the Engliſh name of Herbe Grace to be giuen vnto it. For without doubt it is a moſt wholeſome herbe, although bitter and ſtrong, and could our dainty ſtomackes brooke the vſe thereof, it would worke admirable effects being carefully and skilfully applyed, as time and occaſion did require: but not vndiſcreetly or hand ouer head, as many vſe to doe that haue no skill. Some doe rippe vp a beade rowle of the vertues of Rue, as Macer the Poet and others, in whom you ſhall finde them ſet downe, to bee good for the head, eyes, breaſt, liuer, heart, ſpleene, &c. In ſome places they vſe to boyle the leaues of Rue, and keep them in pickle, to eate them as Sampire for the helpe of weake eyes. It is very auaileable in gliſters or drinkes againſt the winde or the collicke, and to procure vrine that is ſtayed by the paines therof. The diſtilled water is often vſed for the ſame purpoſes aforeſaid: but beware of the too frequent or ouermuch vſe thereof, becauſe it heateth exceedingly, and waſteth nature mightily.

Chap. LX.

Carduus Benedictus. The Bleſſed Thiſtle.

Carduus benedictus or the bleſſed Thiſtle, hath many weake tender branches lying for the moſt part on the ground, whereon are ſet long and narrow leaues, much cut in or waued about the edges, hairy or rough in handling, yet without any hard or ſharpe thornes or prickles at all, that the tendereſt hand may touch them without harme: but thoſe that grow toward the toppes of the ſtalkes are ſomewhat more prickly, and the heads which grow on the tops of the ſeuerall branches are ſomewhat ſharpe, ſet with prickles like a Thiſtle: the flower is yellow, and the ſeede lying within the woolly or flocky doune like to all other thiſtles, are blackiſh, long and round, with a few haires on the head of them: the roote is white, and periſheth euery yeare after it hath giuen ſeede.

The Vſe of the bleſſed Thiſtle.

The diſtilled water hereof is much vſed to be drunke againſt agues of all ſortes, eyther peſtilentiall or humorall, of long continuance or of leſſe:

but

1 *Angellica.* Angellica. 2 *Dracunculus hortensis.* Dragons. 3 *Ruta hortensis.* Garden Rue, or Herbegrace. 4 *Carduus benedictus.* The bleſſed Thiſtle. 5 *Alkakengi ſiue Solanum Halicacabum & Veſicarium.* Winter Cherries. 6 *Aſarum.* Aſarabacca. 7 *Liqueritia.* Licoriſe.

but the decoction of the herbe giuen in due time, hath the more forcible operation : it helpeth to expell wormes, becaufe of the bitternefle, and is thereby alfo a friend to the ftomack ouercharged with chollar, and to clenfe the liuer : it prouoketh fweate and vrine, is helpefull to them are troubled with the ftone, and to eafe paines in the fides.

Chap. LXI.

Solanum veficarium, fiue Alkakengi. Winter Cherries.

THe Winter Cherry hath a running or creeping roote in the ground, of the big-neffe many times of ones little finger, fhooting forth at feuerall ioynts in feue-rall places, whereby it quickly fpreadeth a great compaffe of ground : the ftalke rifeth not aboue a yard high, whereon are fet many broade and long greene leaues, fomewhat like vnto the leaues of Nightfhade, but larger : at the ioynts where-of come forth whitifh flowers made of fiue leaues a peece, which after turne into green berries, inclofed with thin skins or bladders, which change to bee reddifh when they grow ripe, the berry likewife being reddifh, and as large as a Cherry, wherein are contained many flat and yellowifh feed lying within the pulpe : which being gathered and ftrung vp, are kept all the yeare to be vfed vpon occafion.

The Vfe of Winter Cherries.

The diftilled water of the herbe and fruit together, is often taken of them that are troubled with the fharpneffe or difficultie of vrine, and with the ftone in the kidneyes, or grauel in the bladder : but the berries themfelues ei-ther greene or dryed boyled eyther in broth, in wine, or in water, is much more effectuall : It is likewife conducing to open obftructions of the liuer, &c. and thereby to helpe the yellow Iaundife.

Chap. LXII.

Afarum. Afarabacca.

ASarabacca, from a fmall creeping roote fet with many fibres, fhooteth forth di-uers heads, and from euery of them fundry leaues, euery one ftanding vpon a long greene ftalke, which are round, thicke, and of a very fad or darke greene colour, and fhining withall : from the rootes likewife fpring vp fhort ftalkes, not fully foure fingers high, at the toppe of euery one of which ftandeth the flower, in fa-fhion very like the feede veffell of Henbane feede, of a greenifh purple colour, which changeth not his forme, but groweth in time to containe therein fmall cornered feed : the greene leaues abide all the winter many times, but vfually fheddeth them in winter, and recouereth frefh in the fpring.

The Vfe of Afarabacca.

The leaues are much and often vfed to procure vomits, fiue or feuen of them bruifed, and the iuice of them drunke in ale or wine. An extract made of the leaues with wine artificially performed, might bee kept all the yeare thorough, to bee vfed vpon any prefent occafion, the quantitie to bee pro-portioned according to the conftitution of the patient. The roote worketh not fo ftrongly by vomit, as the leaues, yet is often vfed for the fame pur-pofe, and befides is held auaileable to prouoke vrine, to open obftructions in the liuer and fpleene, and is put among diuers other fimples, both into Mithridatum and Andromachus Treakle, which is vfually called Venice Treakle. A dram of the dryed roots in pouder giuen in white wine a little before the fit of an ague, taketh away the fhaking fit, & therby caufe the hot fit to be the more remiffe, and in twice taking expell it quite.

CHAP.

CHAP. LXIII.

Glycyrrhiza siue Liqueritia. Licorice.

Although there are two sorts of Licorice set downe by diuers Authors, yet because this Land familiarly is acquainted but with one sort, I shall not neede for this Garden, to make any further relation of that is vnknowne, but onely of that sort which is sufficiently frequent with vs. It riseth vp with diuers wooddy stalks, whereon are set at seuerall distances many winged leaues, that is to say, many narrow long greene leaues set together on both sides of the stalke, and an odde one at the end, very well resembling a young Ashe tree sprung vp from the seede : this by many yeares continuance in a place without remouing, and not else, will bring forth flowers many standing together spike-fashion one aboue another vpon the stalkes, of the forme of Pease blossomes, but of a very pale or bleake blew colour, which turne into long somewhat flat and smooth cods, wherein is contained small round hard seede : the roote runneth downe exceeding deep into the ground, with diuers other smaller roots and fibres growing with them, and shoote out suckers from the maine rootes all about, whereby it is much encreased, of a brownish colour on the outside, and yellow within, of a farre more weake sweete taste, yet far more pleasing to vs then that Licorice that is brought vs from beyond Sea ; because that, being of a stronger sweet taste hath a bitternesse ioyned with it, which maketh it the lesse pleasing and acceptable to most.

The Vse of Licorice.

Our English Licorice is now adaies of more familiar vse (as I said before) then the outlandish, and is wholly spent and vsed to helpe to digest and expectorate flegme out of the chest and lunges, and doth allay the sharpenesse or saltnesse thereof. It is good also for those are troubled with shortnesse of breath, and for all sorts of coughes. The iuice of Licorice artificially made with Hyssope water, serueth very well for all the purposes aforesaid. It being dissolued with Gum Tragacanth in Rose water, is an excellent Lohoc or licking medicine to breake flegme, and to expectorate it, as also to avoyde thin frothy matter, or thin salt flegme, which often fretteth the lunges. It doth also lenifie exulcerated kidneyes, or the bladder, and helpeth to heale them. It is held also good for those that cannot make their water but by drops, or a small deale at a time.

The dryed root finely minced, is a speciall ingredient into all Trageas or Dredges, seruing for the purposes aforesaid, but the vse of them is almost wholly left now adaies with all sorts.

Thus haue I shewed you not only the herbes, rootes and fruites, nourced vp in this Garden, but such herbes as are of most necessary vses for the Country Gentlewomens houses : And now I will shew you the Orchard also.

The

THE ORDERING OF THE ORCHARD.

The third part, or ORCHARD.

CHAP. I.

The situation of an Orchard for fruit-bearing trees, and how to amend the defects of many grounds.

AS I haue done in the two former parts of this Treatise, so I meane to proceede in this ; first to set downe the situation of an Orchard, and then other things in order : And first, I hold that an Orchard which is, or should bee of some reasonable large extent, should be so placed, that the house should haue the Garden of flowers iust before it open vpon the South, and the Kitchen Garden on the one side thereof, should also haue the Orchard on the other side of the Garden of Pleasure, for many good reasons : First, for that the fruit trees being grown great and tall, will be a great shelter from the North and East windes, which may offend your chiefest Garden, and although that your Orchard stand a little bleake vpon the windes, yet trees rather endure these strong bitter blasts, then other smaller and more tender shrubs and herbes can doe. Secondly, if your Orchard should stand behinde your Garden of flowers more Southward, it would shadow too much of the Garden, and besides, would so binde in the North and East, and North and West windes vpon the Garden, that it would spoile many tender things therein, and so much abate the edge of your pleasure thereof, that you would willingly wish to haue no Orchard, rather then that it should so much annoy you by the so ill standing thereof. Thirdly, the falling leaues being still blowne with the winde so aboundantly into the Garden, would either spoile many things, or haue one daily and continuall attending thereon, to cleanse and sweepe them away. Or else to auoide these great inconueniences, appoint out an Orchard the farther off, and set a greater distance of ground betweene. For the ground or soile of the Orchard, what I haue spoken concerning the former Garden for the bettering of the seuerall grounds, may very well serue and be applyed to this purpose. But obserue this, that whereas your Gardens before spoken of may be turned vp, manured, and bettered with soile if they growe out of heart, your Orchard is not so easily done, but must abide many yeares without altering ; and therefore if the ground be barren, or not good, it had the more neede to bee amended, or wholly made good, before you make an Orchard of it ; yet some there be

that

that doe appoint, that where euery tree fhould bee fet, you onely digge that place to make it good : but you muft know, that the rootes of trees runne further after a little times ftanding, then the firft compaffe they are fet in ; and therefore a little compaffe of ground can maintaine them but a little while, and that when the rootes are runne beyond that fmall compaffe wherein they were firft fet, and that they are come to the barren or bad ground, they can thriue no better then if they had beene fet in that ground at the firft, and if you fhould afterwards digge beyond that compaffe, intending to make the ground better further off, you fhould much hurt the fpreading rootes, and put your trees in danger : the fituation of hils in many places is grauelly or chalky, which is not good for trees, becaufe they are both too ftonie, and lacke mellow earth, wherein a tree doth moft ioy and profper, and want moifture alfo (which is the life of all trees) becaufe of the quicke defcent of raine to the lower grounds : and befides all thefe inconueniences there is one more ; your trees planted either on hils or hill fides, are more fubiect to the fury and force of windes to be ouer-turned, then thofe that growe in the lower grounds ; for the ftrongeft and moft forci-ble windes come not vfually out of the North Eaft parts, where you prouide beft de-fence, but from the South and Weft, whence you looke for the beft comfort of the Sunne. To helpe therefore manie of the inconueniences of the hils fides, it were fit to caufe manie leauels to bee made thereon, by raifing the lower grounds with good earth, and fuftaining them with bricke or ftone wals, which although chargeable, will counteruaile your coft, befide the pleafure of the walkes, and profpect of fo worthy a worke. The plaine or leuell grounds as they are the moft frequent, fo they are the moft commendable for an Orchard, becaufe the moulds or earths are more rich, or may better and fooner be made fo ; and therefore the profits are the more may be rai-fed from them. A ftiffe clay doth nourifh trees well, by reafon it containeth moi-fture ; but in regard of the coldneffe thereof, it killeth for the moft part all tender and early things therein: fea-cole afhes therefore, bucke afhes, ftreete foyle, chaulke after it hath lyen abroad and been broken with many yeares frofts and raine, and fheepes dung, are the moft proper and fitteft manure to helpe this kinde of foyle. The dry fandy foile, and grauelly ground are on the contrary fide as bad, by reafon of too much heate and lacke of moifture : the dung of kine or cattell in good quantity beftowed thereon, will much helpe them. The amending or bettering of other forts of grounds is fet down toward the end of the firft Chapter of the firft part of this worke, where-vnto I will referre you, not willing to repeate againe the fame things there fet downe. The beft way to auoide and amend the inconueniences of high, boifterous, and cold windes, is to plant Walnut trees, Elmes, Oakes or Afhes, a good diftance without the compaffe of your Orchard, which after they are growne great, will bee a great fafe-guard thereunto, by breaking the violence of the windes from it. And if the foyle of your Orchard want moifture, the conueying of the finke of the houfe, as alfo any o-ther draine of water thereinto, if it may be, will much helpe it.

Chap. II.

The forme of an Orchard, both ordinary, and of more grace and rarity.

Accordingto the fituation of mens grounds, fo muft the plantation of them of neceffitie be alfo ; and if the ground be in forme, you fhall haue a formall Or-chard : if otherwife, it can haue little grace or forme. And indeed in the elder ages there was fmall care or heede taken for the formality ; for euery tree for the moft part was planted without order, euen where the mafter or keeper found a vacant place to plant them in, fo that oftentimes the ill placing of trees without fufficient fpace be-tweene them, and negligence in not looking to vphold them, procured more wafte and fpoile of fruit, then any accident of winde or weather could doe. Orchards in moft places haue not bricke or ftone wals to fecure them, becaufe the extent thereof being larger then of a Garden, would require more coſt, which euery one cannot vndergoe; and therefore mud wals, or at the beſt a quicke ſet hedge, is the ordinary and moſt vſuall defence it findeth almoſt in all places : but with thoſe that are of ability to compaſſe it with bricke or ſtone wals, the gaining of ground, and profit of the fruit trees planted there againſt, will in ſhort time recompenſe that charge. If you make a doubt how to be ſure that your Orchard wall ſhall haue ſufficient comfort of the Sunne to ripen the fruits, in regard the trees in the Orchard being ſo nigh thereunto, and ſo high withall, will ſo much ſhadow the wall, that nothing will ripen well, becauſe it will want the comfort of the Sunne : you may follow this rule and aduice, to remedy thoſe inconueniences. Hauing an Orchard containing one acre of ground, two, three, or more, or leſſe, walled about, you may ſo order it, by leauing a broad and large walke betweene the wall and it, containing twenty or twenty foure foote (or yards if you will) that the wall ſhall not be hindered of the Sun, but haue ſufficient comfort for your trees, notwithſtanding the height of them, the diſtance betweene them and the wall being a ſufficient ſpace for their ſhadow to fall into : and by compaſſing your Orchard on the inſide with a hedge

(wherein may bee planted all ſorts of low ſhrubs or buſhes, as Roſes, Cornellian Cherry trees plaſhed lowe, Gooſeberries, Curran trees, or the like) you may encloſe your walke, and keepe both it and your Orchard in better forme and manner, then if it lay open. For the placing of your trees in this Orchard, firſt for the wals : Thoſe ſides that lye open to the South & Southweſt Sunne, are fitteſt to bee planted with your tendereſt and earlieſt fruits, as Apricockes, Peaches, Nectarius, and May or early Cherries : the Eaſt, North and Weſt, for Plums and Quinces, as you ſhall like beſt to place them. And for the Orchard it ſelfe, the ordinary manner is to place them without regard of meaſure or difference, as Peares among Apples, and Plums among Cherries promiſcuouſly ; but ſome keepe both a diſtance and a diuiſion for euery ſort, without intermingling : yet the moſt gracefull Orchard containeth them all, with ſome others, ſo as they be placed that one doe not hinder or ſpoile another ; and therefore to deſcribe you the modell of an Orchard, both rare for comelineſſe in the proportion, and pleaſing for the profitableneſſe in the vſe, and alſo durable for continuance, regard this figure is here placed for your direction, where you muſt obſerue, that your trees are here ſet in ſuch an equall diſtance one from another euery way, & as is fitteſt for them, that when they are grown great, the greater branches ſhall not gall or rubbe one againſt another ; for which purpoſe twenty or ſixteene foot is the leaſt to be allowed for the diſtance euery way of your trees, & being ſet in rowes euery one in the middle diſtance, will be the moſt gracefull for the plantation, and beſides, giue you way ſufficient to paſſe through them, to pruine, loppe, or dreſſe them, as need ſhall require, and may alſo bee brought (if you pleaſe) to that gracefull delight, that euery alley or diſtance may be formed like an arch, the branches of either ſide meeting to be enterlaced together. Now for the ſeuerall ſorts of fruit trees that you ſhall place in this modell, your beſt direction is to ſet Damſons, Bulleis, and your taler growing Plums on the outſide, and your lower Plums, Cherries, and Apples on the inſide, hauing regard, that you place no Peare tree to the Sunward, of any other tree, leſt it ouer-ſhadow

shadow them : Let your Peare trees therefore be placed behinde, or on the one side of your lower trees, that they may be as it were a shelter or defence on the North & East side. Thus may you also plant Apples among Plums and Cherries, so as you suffer not one to ouer-growe or ouer-toppe another ; for by pruning, lopping, and shredding those that growe too fast for their fellowes, you may still keepe your trees in such a conformity, as may be both most comely for the sight, and most profitable for the yeelding of greater and better store of fruit. Other sorts of fruit trees you may mixe among these, if you please, as Filberds, Cornellian Cherries in standerds, and Medlers : but Seruice trees, Baye trees, and others of that high sort, must be set to guard the rest. Thus haue I giuen you the fairest forme could as yet be deuised ; and from this patterne, if you doe not follow it precisely, yet by it **you may** proportion your Orchard, be it large or little, be it walled or hedged.

Chap. III.

Of a nourſery for trees, both from ſowing the kernels, and planting fit ſtockes to graft vpon.

ALthough I know the greater sort (I meane the Nobility and better part of the Gentrie of this Land) doe not intend to keepe a Nursery, to raise vp those trees that they meane to plant their wals or Orchards withall, but to buy them already grafted to their hands of them that make their liuing of it : yet because many Gentlemen and others are much delighted to bestowe their paines in grafting themselues, and esteeme their owne labours and handie worke farre aboue other mens : for their incouragement and satisfaction, I will here set downe some conuenient directions, to enable them to raise an Orchard of all sorts of fruits quickly, both by sowing the kernels or stones of fruit, and by making choise of the best sorts of stockes to graft on : First therefore to begin with Cherries ; If you will make a Nursery, wherein you may bee stored with plenty of stockes in a little space, take what quantitie you thinke good of ordinarie wilde blacke Cherrie stones, cleansed from the berries, and sowe them, or pricke them in one by one on a peece of ground well turned vp, and large enough for the quantitie of stones you will bestowe thereon, from the midst of August vnto the end of September, which when they are two or three yeares old, according to their growth, you may remoue them, and set them anew in some orderly rowes, hauing pruned their tops and their rootes, which at the next yeares growth after the new planting in any good ground, or at the second, will be of sufficient bignesse to graft vpon in the bud what sorts of Cherries you thinke best : and it is fittest to graft them thus young, that pruning your stockes to raise them high, you may graft them at fiue or six foote high, or higher, or lower, as you shall see good, and being thus grafted in the bud, will both more speedily and safely bring forward your grafts, and with lesse danger of losing your stockes, then by grafting them in the stocke : for if the bud take not by inoculating the first yeare, yet your tree is not lost, nor put in any hazzard of losse ; but may be grafted anew the yeare following, if you will, in another place thereof, whereas if you graft in the stocke, and it doe not take, it is a great chance if the stocke dye not wholly, or at least be not so weakened both in strength and height, that it will not bee fit to bee grafted a yeare or two after. In the same manner as you doe with the blacke, you may deale with the ordinary English red Cherrie stones, or kernels, but they are not so apt to growe so straight and high, nor in so short a time as the blacke Cherrie stones are, and besides are subiect in time to bring out suckers from the rootes, to the hinderance of the stockes and grafts, or at the least to the deformitie of your Orchard, and more trouble to the Gardiner, to pull or digge them away. Plumme stones may bee ordered in this manner likewise, but you must make choise of your Plums ; for although euery Plumme is not so fit for this purpose, as the white Peare Plumme, because it groweth the goaleſt and freeſt, the barke being smooth and aptest to be raised, that they may be grafted vpon ; yet diuers other Plummes may be taken, if they be not at hand, or to be had, as the blacke and red Peare Plumme, the

white

white and red Wheate Plumme, becaufe they are neareft in goodneffe vnto it. Peach ſtones will be ſoone raiſed vp to graft other ſorts of Peaches or Nectorins vpon, but the nature of the Peach roote being ſpongie, is not to abide long. As for Almonds, they will be raiſed from their ſtones to be trees of themſelues; but they will hardly a-bide the remouing, and leſſe to bee grafted vpon. Apricocke ſtones are the worſt to deale withall of any ſort of ſtone fruit; for although the Apricocke branches are the fitteſt ſtockes to graft Nectorins of the beſt ſorts vpon, yet thoſe that are raiſed from the kernels or ſtones will neuer thriue to be brought on for this purpoſe; but will ſtarue and dye, or hardly grow in a long time to be a ſtraight and fit ſtocke to be grafted, if it be once remoued. Your Cornellian Cherrie trees are wholly, or for the moſt part rai-ſed from the ſtones or kernels; yet I know diuers doe increaſe them, by laying in their loweſt branches to take roote: and thus much for ſtone fruits. Now for Apples and Peares, to be dealt withall in the ſame manner as aforeſaid. They vſe to take the preſ-ſing of Crabs whereas Veriuyce is made, as alſo of Cidar and Perry where they are made, and ſowing them, doe raiſe vp great ſtore of ſtockes; for although the beating of the fruit doth ſpoile many kernels, yet there will bee enough left that were neuer toucht, and that will ſpring: the Crabbe ſtockes ſome preferre for the fitteſt, but I am ſure, that the better Apple and Peare kernels will growe fairer, ſtraighter, quicklier, and better to be grafted on. You muſt remember, that after two or three yeares you take vp theſe ſtockes, and when you haue pruned both toppe and roote, to ſet them a-gaine in a thinner and fitter order, to be afterwards grafted in the bud while they are young, as I ſhall ſhew you by and by, or in the ſtocke if you will ſuffer them to growe greater. Now likewiſe to know which are the fitteſt ſtockes of all ſorts to chooſe, thereon to graft euery of theſe ſorts of fruits, is a point of ſome ſkill indeede; and therefore obſerue them as I doe here ſet them downe: for bee you aſſured, that they are certaine rules, and knowne experiences, whereunto you may truſt without being deceiued. Your blacke Cherrie ſtockes (as I ſaid before) are the fitteſt and beſt for all ſorts of Cherries long to abide and proſper, and euen May or early Cherry will a-bide or liue longer, being grafted thereon, either in the budde or in the ſtocke, then on the ordinary red Cherry ſtocke; but the red Cherry ſtocke is in a manner the onely tree that moſt Nurſery men doe take to graft May Cherries on in the ſtocke (for it is but a late experience of many, to graft May Cherries in the bud) many alſo doe graft May Cherries on Gaſcoigne Cherry ſtockes, which doe not onely thriue well, but en-dure longer then vpon any ordinay Cherry ſtocke: For indeede the May Cherries that are grafted vpon ordinary red Cherrie ſtockes, will hardly hold aboue a dozen yeares bearing well, although they come forwarder at the firſt, that is, doe beare ſoo-ner then thoſe that are grafted on Gaſcoigne or blacke Cherry ſtockes; but as they are earlier in bearing, ſo they are ſooner ſpent, and the Gaſcoigne and blacke Cherry ſtockes that are longer in comming forward, will laſt twice or thrice their time; but many more grafts will miſſe in grafting of theſe, then of thoſe red Cherry ſtockes, and beſides, the natures of the Gaſcoigne and blacke Cherry ſtockes are to riſe higher, and make a goodlier tree then the ordinary red ſtocke will, which for the moſt part ſprea-deth wide, but riſeth not very high. The Engliſh red Cherry ſtocke will ſerue very well to graft any other ſort of Cherry vpon, and is vſed in moſt places of this Land, and I know no other greater inconuenience in it, then that it ſhooteth out many ſuckers from the roote, which yet by looking vnto may ſoone bee remoued from doing any harme, and that it will not laſt ſo long as the Gaſcoigne or blacke Cherry ſtocke will. May Cherries thus grafted lowe, doe moſt vſually ſerue to be planted againſt a wall, to bring on the fruit the earlier; yet ſome graft them high vpon ſtandards, although not many, and it is, I thinke, rather curioſity (if they that doe it haue any wals) then anie o-ther matter that cauſeth them thus to doe: for the fruit is naturally ſmall, though early, and the ſtandard Cherries are alwaies later then the wall Cherries, ſo that if they can ſpare any roome for them at their wals, they will not plant many in ſtandards. Now concerning Plummes (as I ſaid before) for the ſowing or ſetting of the ſtones, ſo I ſay here for their choiſe in grafting of them, either in the budde or ſtocke. The white Peare Plumme ſtocke, and the other there mentioned, but eſpecially the white Peare Plumme is the goodlieſt, freeſt, and fitteſt of all the reſt, as well to graft all ſort of Plummes vpon, as alſo to graft Apricockes, which can be handſomely, and to any

good

good purpose grafted vpon no other Plum stocke, to rise to bee worth the labour and paine. All sorts of Plums may be grafted in the stocke, and so may they also in the bud; for I know none of them that will refuse to be grafted in the bud, if a cunning hand performe it well; that is, to take off your bud cleanely and well, when you haue made choice of a fit cyon: for, as I shal shew you anon, it is no small peece of cunning to chuse your cyon that it may yeeld fit buds to graft withall, for euery plum is not of a like aptnes to yeeld them. But Apricocks cannot be grafted in the stock for any thing that euer I could heare or learne, but only in the bud, and therefore let your Plum stocke bee of a reasonable size for Apricockes especially, and not too small, that the graft ouergrow not the stocke, and that the stocke bee large enough to nourish the graft. As your Plum stockes serue to graft both Apricockes and Plummes, so doe they serue also very well to graft Peaches of all sorts; and although Peach stockes will serue to be grafted with Peaches againe, yet the Peach stocke (as I said before) will not endure so long as the Plumme stocke, and therefore serueth but for necessity if Plum stocks be not ready, or at hand, or for the present time, or that they afterwards may graft that sort of Peach on a Plumme stocke : for many might lose a good fruit, if when they meete with it, and haue not Plumme stockes ready to graft it on, they could not be assured that it would take vpon another Peach stocke or branch, or on the branch of an Apricocke eyther. Plumme stockes will serue likewise very well for some sorts of Nectorins; I say, for some sorts, and not for all : the greene and the yellow Nectorin will best thriue to be grafted immediately on a Plumme stocke; but the other two sorts of red Nectorins must not be immediately grafted on the Plumme stocke, but vpon a branch of an Apricocke that hath beene formerly grafted on a Plumme stocke, the nature of these Nectorins being found by experience to be so contrary to the Plum stocke, that it will sterue it, and both dye within a yeare, two or three at the most : Diuers haue tryed to graft these red Nectorins vpon Peach stockes, and they haue endured well a while; but seeing the Peach stocke will not last long it selfe, being ouerweake, how can it hold so strong a nature as these red Nectorins, which will (as I said before) sterue a Plum stocke that is sufficient durable for any other Plumme?

Apricocke stockes from the stones are hardly nursed vp, and worse to be remoued, and if a red Nectorin should be grafted on an Apricock raysed from the stone, and not remoued, I doubt it might happen with it as it doth with many other trees raised from stones or kernels, and not remoued, that they would hardly beare fruit : for the nature of most trees raised from stones or kernels, and not remoued, is to send great downeright rootes, and not to spread many forwards; so that if they be not cut away that others may spreade abroad, I haue seldome seene or known any of them to beare in any reasonable time; and therefore in remouing, these great downe-right rootes are alwayes shred away, and thereby made fit to shoote others forwards. Hereby you may perceiue, that these red Nectorins will not abide to bee grafted vpon any other stocke well, then vpon an Apricocke branch, although the green and the yellow (as I said before) will well endure and thriue vpon Plums. The suckers or shootes both of Plums and Cherries that rise from their rootes, eyther neare their stockes, or farther off, so that they bee taken with some small rootes to them, will serue to bee stockes, and will come forward quickly; but if the suckers haue no small roots whereby they may comprehend in the ground, it is almost impossible it should hold or abide. There is another way to rayse vp eyther stockes to graft on, or trees without grafting, which is, by circumcising a faire and fit branch in this manner : About Midsomer, when the sappe is thoroughly risen (or before if the yeare be forward) they vse to binde a good quantity of clay round about a faire and straight branch, of a reasonable good size or bignesse, with some conuenient bands, whether it be ropes of hey, or of any other thing, about an handfull aboue the ioynt, where the branch spreadeth from the tree, and cutting the barke thereof round about vnder the place where the clay is bound, the sap is hereby hindered from rising, or descending further then that place so circumcised, whereby it will shoote out small knubs and rootes into the clay, which they suffer so to abide vntill the beginning of winter, whenas with a fine Sawe they cut off that branch where it was circumcised, and afterwardes place it in the ground where they would haue it to grow, and stake it, and binde it fast, which will shoote forth rootes, and will become eyther a faire tree to beare fruite without grafting, or else a fit stocke to graft on according

ding

ding to the kinde: but oftentimes this kinde of propagation miſſeth, in that it ſendeth not forth rootes ſufficient to cauſe it to abide any long time. Let me yet before I leaue this narration of Plummes, giue you one admonition more, that vpon whatſoeuer Plumme ſtocke you doe graft, yet vpon a Damſon ſtocke that you neuer ſtriue to graft, for it (aboue all other ſorts of Plumme ſtockes) will neuer giue you a tree worth your labour. It remaineth only of ſtone fruit, that I ſpeake of Cornelles, which as yet I neuer ſaw grafted vpon any ſtocke, being as it ſhould ſeeme vtterly repugnant to the nature thereof, to abide grafting, but is wholly rayſed vp (as I ſaid before) eyther from the ſtones, or from the ſuckers or layers. For Peares and Apples your vſuall ſtockes to graft on are (as I ſaid before, ſpeaking of the nurſing vp of trees from the kernels) your Crabbe ſtockes, and they bee accepted in euery Countrey of this Land as they may conueniently be had, yet many doe take the ſtockes of better fruit, whether they bee ſuckers, or ſtockes rayſed from the kernels (and the moſt common and knowne way of grafting, is in the ſtocke for all ſorts of them, although ſome doe vſe whipping, packing on, or inciſing, as euery one liſt to call it: but now we doe in many places begin to deale with Peares and Apples as with other ſtone fruit, that is, graft them all in the bud, which is found the moſt compendious and ſafeſt way both to preſerue your ſtocke from periſhing, and to bring them the ſooner to couer the ſtock, as alſo to make the goodlier and ſtraighter tree, being grafted at what height you pleaſe:) for thoſe ſtockes that are rayſed from the kernels of good fruit (which are for the moſt part eaſily knowne from others, in that they want thoſe thornes or prickles the wilde kindes are armed withall:) I ſay for the moſt part; for I know that the kernels of ſome good fruite hath giuen ſtockes with prickles on them (which, as I thinke, was becauſe that good fruite was taken from a wilde ſtocke that had not beene long enough grafted to alter his wilde nature; for the longer a tree is grafted, the more ſtrength the fruite taketh from the graft, and the leſſe ſtill from the ſtocke) being ſmoother and fairer then the wilde kinds, muſt needes make a goodlier tree, and will not alter any whit the taſte of your fruit that is grafted thereon, but rather adde ſome better relliſh thereunto; for the Crabbe ſtockes yeelding harſh fruite, muſt giue part of their nature to the grafts are ſet thereon, and therefore the taſte or relliſh, as well as ſome other naturall properties of moſt fruits, are ſomewhat altered by the ſtocke. Another thing I would willingly giue you to vnderſtand concerning your fruits and ſtockes, that whereas diuers for curioſity and to try experiments haue grafted Cherries vpon Plumme ſtockes, or Plums on Cherry ſtockes, Apples vpon Peare ſtockes, and Peares vpon Apple ſtockes, ſome of theſe haue held the graft a yeare, two or three peraduenture, but I neuer knew that euer they held long, or to beare fruite, much leſſe to abide or doe well: beſtow not therefore your paines and time on ſuch contrary natures, vnleſſe it be for curioſitie, as others haue done: Yet I know that they that graft peares on a white thorne ſtocke haue had their grafts ſeeme to thriue well, and continue long, but I haue ſeldome ſeene the fruite thereof anſwerable to the naturall wilde Peare ſtocke; yet the Medlar is knowne to thriue beſt on a white thorne. And laſtly, whereas diuers doe affirme that they may haue not only good ſtockes to graft vpon, but alſo faire trees to bear ſtore of fruit from the kernels of Peares or Apples being prickt into the ground, and ſuffered to grow without remouing, and then eyther grafted or ſuffered to grow into great trees vngrafted; and for their bearing of fruite, aſſigne a dozen or twenty yeares from the firſt ſetting of the kernels, and abiding vngrafted, I haue not ſeene or heard that experience to hold certaine, or if it ſhould be ſo, yet it is too long time loſt, and too much fruit alſo, to waite twenty yeares for that profit may be gained in a great deale of leſſe time, and with more certainty. Vnto theſe inſtructions let mee adde alſo one more, which is not much known and vſed, and that is, to haue fruit within foure or fiue years from the firſt ſowing of your ſtones or kernels in this manner: After your ſtones or kernels are two or three yeares old, take the faireſt toppe or branch, and graft it as you would doe any other cyon taken from a bearing tree, and looke what rare fruite, eyther Peare or Apple, the kernell was of that you ſowed, or Peach or Plum &c. the ſtone was ſet, ſuch fruite ſhall you haue within two or three yeares at the moſt after the grafting, if it take, and the ſtocke be good. And thus may you ſee fruit in farre leſſe time then to ſtay vntill the tree from a kernell or ſtone beareth fruit of it ſelfe.

CHAP.

CHAP. IIII.

*The diuers manners of grafting all forts of fruits
vfed in our Land.*

THe moft vfuall manner of grafting in the ftocke is fo common and well known
in this Land to euery one that hath any thing to doe with trees or an Orchard,
that I think I fhall take vpon mee a needleffe worke to fet downe that is fo well
knowne to moft; yet how common foeuer it is, fome directions may profit euery one,
without which it is not eafily learned. And I doe not fo much fpend my time and
paines herein for their fakes that haue knowledge, but for fuch as not knowing would
faine be taught priuately, I meane, to reade the rules of the arte fet downe in priuate,
when they would refufe to learne of a Gardiner, or other by fight: and yet I difcom-
mend not that way vnto them to learne by fight; for one may fee more in an inftant by
fight, then he fhall learn by his own practice in a great while, efpecially if he be a little
practifed before he fee a cunning hand to doe it. There are many other kindes of grafting, which fhall be fpoken of hereafter, and peraduenture euen they that know it well,
may learne fomething they knew not before.

1. The grafting in the ftocke, is, to fet the fprigge of a good fruit into the body or
ftocke of another tree, bee it wilde or other, bee it young or old, to caufe that tree to
bring forth fuch fruit as the tree bore from whence you took the fprigge, and not fuch
as the ftocke or tree would haue borne, if it had not beene grafted, and is performed in
this manner : Looke what tree or ftocke you will chufe to graft on, you muft with a
fmall fine fawe and very fharpe, whip off, or cut off the head or toppe thereof at what
height you eyther thinke beft for your purpofe, or conuenient for the tree: for if you
graft a great tree, you cannot without endangering the whole, cut it downe fo low to
the ground, as you may without danger doe a fmall tree, or one that is of a reafonable
fize; and yet the lower or neerer the ground you graft a young tree, the fafer it is both
for your ftocke and graft, becaufe the fappe fhall not afcend high, but foone giue vigour to the graft to take and fhoote quickly : After you haue cut off the toppe of your
ftocke, cut or fmooth the head thereof with a fharpe knife, that it may be as plaine and
fmooth as you can, and then cleaue it with a hammer or mallet, and with a ftrong knife,
cleauer or cheffell, either in the middle of it if it be fmall, or of a reafonable fize, or on
the fides an inch or more within the barke, if it be great : into both fides of the cleft
put your grafts, or into one if the ftocke bee fmaller ; which grafts muft bee made
fit for the purpofe on this fafhion : Hauing made choife of your grafts from the toppe
branches efpecially, or from the fides of that tree wherof you would haue the fruit, and
that they be of a reafonable good fize, not too fmall or too great for your ftockes, and
of one or the fame yeares fhoote ; (and yet many doe cut an inch or more of the olde
wood with the fprigge of the laft yeares growth, and fo graft the old and young together (but both are good, and the old wood no better then the young) cut your graft not
too long, but with two, three or foure eyes or buds at the moft, which at the lower or
bigger end for an inch long or more (for the greater ftockes, and an inch or leffe for the
leffer fort) muft be fo cut, that it be very thin on the one fide from the fhoulders downward, and thicker on the other, and thin alfo at the end, that it may goe downe clofe into the cleft, and reft at the fhoulders on the head of the ftocke : but take heede that in
cutting your grafts your knife bee very fharpe that you doe not rayfe any of the barke,
eyther at the fides or the end, for feare of lofing both your paines and graft, and ftocke
too peraduenture ; and let not your grafts bee made long before you fet them, or elfe
put the ends of them in water to keepe them frefh and cleane : when you fet them you
muft open the cleft of your ftocke with a wedge or cheffell as moft doe, that the graft
may goe eafily into it, and that the barke of both graft and ftocke may ioyne clofe the
one to the other, which without ftirring or difplacing muft bee fo left in the cleft, and
the wedge or cheffell gently pulled forth; but becaufe in the doing hereof confifteth
in a manner the whole loffe or gaine of your paines, graft and ftocke, to preuent which
inconuenience I doe vfe an iron Inftrument, the forme whereof is fhowne in the following

lowing page, marked with the letter A, crooked at both ends, and broade like vnto a cheſſell, the one bigger, and the other leſſer, to fit all ſorts of ſtockes, and the iron handle ſomewhat long betweene them both, that being thruſt or knocked downe into the cleft, you may with your left hand open it as wide as is fit to let in your graft, without ſtrayning, which being placed, this iron may bee pulled or knocked vp againe without any mouing of your graft : when you haue thus done, you muſt lay a good handfull or more (according to the bigneſſe of your ſtocke) of ſoft and well moiſtned clay or loame, well tempered together with ſhort cut hey or horſe dung, vpon the head of your ſtocke, as lowe or ſomewhat lower then the cleft, to keepe out all winde, raine or ayre from your graft vntill Midſomer at the leaſt, that the graft be ſhot forth ſomewhat ſtrongly, which then if you pleaſe may be remoued, and the cleft at the head only filled with a little clay to keepe out earewigs, or other things that may hurt your graft.

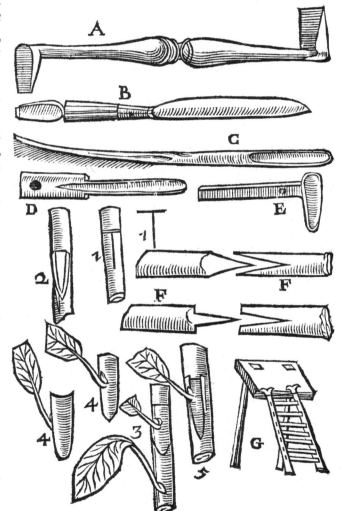

A. The Iron Inſtrument with cheſſels at each end, the one bigger and the other leſſer, to keepe the cleft of the Tree open vntill the graft bee placed in the ſtocke, which with a knock vpwards will be eaſily taken away.

B. The ſmall Penne-knife with a broad and thinne ended hafte, to raiſe the ſides both of the bud and the down-right ſlit in the body or arme of a Tree to be grafted in the bud.

C. A pen or quil cut halfe round to take off a bud from the branch.

D. An Iuory Inſtrument made to the ſame faſhion.

E. A ſhielde of braſſe made hollow before to be put into the ſlit, to keepe it open vntill the bud be put into its place.

F. The manner of grafting called inciſing or ſplicing.

G. A Ladder made with a ſtoole at the toppe, to ſerue both to graft higher or lower, and alſo to gather fruit without ſpoyling or hurting any buddes or branches of Trees.

1. The firſt ſlit in the body or arme of a Tree to be grafted in the bud with the croſſe cut at the head.

2. The ſame ſlit opened on both ſides, ready to receiue the budde ſhould be put therein : theſe ſmall peeces ſerue as well as trees to ſhew the manner and order of the grafting.

3. The branch of a Tree with one budde cut ready to be taken off, and another not yet touched.

4. The bud cleane taken off from the branch, both the foreſide and backſide.

5. The graft or bud now put into the ſtocke or tree you intend to be grafted : but the binding thereof is omitted.

2. Inarching is another manner of grafting in the ſtocke, and is more troubleſome, and more caſuall alſo then the former, and is rather a curioſity then any way of good ſpeede, certainety or profit, and therefore vſed but of a few. Yet to ſhew you, the man-

manner thereof, it is thus: Hauing a tree well growne, bee it high or low, yet the lower the better, with young branches well spread, they vse to set stockes round about it, or on the one side as you please ; into which stockes they ingraft the young branches of the well growne tree as they are growing (before they cut them from the tree) by bowing downe the branch they intend to graft, and putting it into the stocke, hauing first cut off the head thereof, and cut a notch in the middle of the head a little slope on both sides, wherein the branch must be fitted : let the branch be cut thinne on the vnderside, only of that length as may suffice to fit the notch in the stocke, leauing about halfe a yarde length of the branch, to rise aboue or beyond the stocke, which beeing bound on, and clayed ouer or couered with red or greene soft waxe, they let so abide, that if it take in the stocke they cut off the branch a little below the grafting place in Nouember following, and remouing the stocke, they haue thus gained a grafted and growne tree the first yeare : but it is vsually seene, that where one branch taketh, three doe misse : yet this manner of grafting was much in vse for May Cherries, when they were first known to vs, and the way thought to be a rare manner of grafting to encrease them, vntill a better way was found out, which now is so common and good also, that this is not now scarce thought vpon.

3. Another kinde of grafting in the stocke is called of some whipping, of some splicing, of others incising, and of others packing on (and as I heare, is much vsed in the West parts especially, and also in the North parts of this Land) and is performed in this manner : Take and slice the branch of a tree (so as the branch be not too bigge) or else a young tree of two, or three, or foure yeares growth at the most, quite off slope wise, about an inch and a halfe long or more, and cut a deep notch in the middle thereof, then fit into it a graft iust of that size or bignesse, cut on both sides with shoulders, and thin at the end, that it may ioyne close in the notch, and neyther bigger or lesser, but that the barke of the one may bee fitted iust to the barke of the other, the figure wherof is expressed at the letters E.F. which shew the one to be with a shoulder & the other without ; binde them gently together with bast, and put clay or waxe ouer the place, vntill it be taken : this is much vsed of late dayes for such young trees as are risen of stones or kernels after the second or third yeares growth, and thriue very well in that it not only saueth much time, but diuers checks by remouing and grafting.

4. Inoculating or grafting in the budde is another manner of grafting, which is the taking of a budde from one tree, and putting it into the barke of another tree, to the end, that thereby you may haue of the same kinde of fruit the tree bare from whence the budde was taken ; and although it bee sufficiently knowne in many places of this Land, yet as I vnderstand, good Gardiners in the North parts, and likewise in some other places, can scarce tell what it meaneth, or at the least how to doe it well. It is performed after a different fashion from the former, although they all tend vnto one end, which is the propagating of trees. You must for this purpose obserue, that for those trees you would graft, either with, or vpon, you choose a fit time in Summer, when the sappe is well risen, and your graft well shot, that the barke will rise easily and cleanly, both of stocke and graft, which time I cannot appoint, becaufe both the years doe differ in earlinesse, and the seuerall parts or countries of this Land likewise one from another, but most vsually in these Southerne parts, from the beginning of Iune vnto the end of it, or to the middle of Iuly, or either somewhat before or after. First (as I said) hauing taken the fittest time of the yeare, you must take especiall care, that your grafts be well growne, and of the same yeares shoote, and also that the buds or eyes haue but single leaues at them, as neare as you can : for I would vtterly refuse those buds that haue aboue two leaues as vnprofitable, either in Peaches or any other fruit ; and therefore see that your grafts or cyons bee taken from the chiefest place of the tree, that is, either from the toppe, or from a sunnie side thereof, and not from the contrarie side if you may otherwise, nor from any vnder-boughes ; for seeing your graft is so small a thing, you had neede take the more care that it be the best and fairest. You must to take off this eye or budde from the sprigge, haue a small sharpe pen-knife, the end of the haft being made flat and thinne, like a chessell or wedge, the figure whereof is set forth at the letter B, and a pen or goose quill cut, to be lesse then halfe round, and to be broad at the end, but not sharpe pointed like a penne, or else such a peece of bone or Iuorie made in that fashion as the quill is, to bee thinne, hollow, or

halfe

halfe round, the figures of both which are marked with the letters C, D. with your knife cut the barke of the bud (hauing firſt cut off the leafe, leauing onely the ſhort foote ſtalke thereof at the bud) about a ſtrawes breadth aboue the eye thereof halfe round, and then from that round or ouerthwart cut, with your knife cut it downe on both ſides of the eye, cloſe to the bud ſlopewiſe about an inch long or thereabouts, that it bee broad at the head aboue the eye, and pointing at the end like a ſheild or ſcutcheon; and then cutting away the reſt of the barke from about it, with the thinne flat end of the haft of your knife raiſe vp both ſides of your bud a little, and with your quill or bone put vnder the barke, raiſe your budde, and thruſt it quite off, beginning at the toppe or head of your eye; but ſee that you thruſt it off cloſe to the wood of the branch or ſprigge, and that you doe not leaue the eye of the budde behinde ſticking vpon the branch; for if that eye be left or loſt, your bud is worth nothing; you muſt caſt it away, and cut another that may haue that eye abiding within the budde on the inſide: you may perceiue if that eye be wanting, if you ſee an emptie hole in the place where the eye ſhould be, to fill it vp on the inſide thereof; thus hauing taken off your bud well and cleanly, which is ſet forth vnto you at the figures 3 and 4. preſently ſet it on the tree you would graft (for your ſmall bud can abide no delay, leſt by taking the ayre too long it become dry, and nothing worth) in this manner: Cut the barke of your tree you would graft in a ſmooth place, at what height you pleaſe, firſt aboue or ouerthwart, and then downe right in the middle thereof, more then an inch long, the figure whereof you ſhall haue at the figure 1. and then raiſe vp both ſides of the barke, firſt one, and then another, with the flat and thinne haft end of your knife, a prettie way inwards (for if the barke will not riſe eaſily, the ſtocke is not then fit to graft vpon) put in your budde into the cleft with the point downewards, holding the ſtalke of the leafe that is with the budde betweene your fingers of the one hand, and opening the cleft with the flat end of your knife with the other hand, that the head of your bud may be put cloſe vnder the ouerthwart cut in the ſtocke or tree (which muſt not be raiſed or ſtirred as the ſides are) & the eye of the bud ſtand iuſt in the middle of the ſlit that is downeright, and then cloſing the barke of the ſtocke or tree ſoftly vnto the bud thus put in with your fingers, let it be bound gently with a ſmall long peece of baſte, or other ſuch like ſoft thing, firſt aboue the eye, & then compaſſing it belowe as cloſe as you can, but not too hard in any caſe, vntil you haue bound it all ouer the ſlit you made, eſpecially the lower end, leſt any winde get in to dry and ſpoile it; and hauing tyed both ends thereof faſt, leaue it ſo for a fornight or ſomewhat more, in which ſpace it will take and hold, if it be well done, which you ſhall perceiue, if the bud abide green, and turne not blacke, when you haue vnlooſed the tying; for if it hold faſt to the tree, and be freſh and good, tye it vp gently againe, and ſo leaue it for a fortnight longer, or a moneth if you will, and then you may take away your binding cleane: this budde will (if no other miſchance happen vnto it) ſpring and ſhoote forth the next yeare, (and ſometimes the ſame yeare, but that is ſeldome) and therfore in the beginning of the yeare, cut off the head of the grafted tree about an handfull aboue the grafted place, vntill the graft be growne ſtrong, and then cut it off cloſe, that the head may be couered with the graft, and doe not ſuffer any buds to ſprout beſides the graft, either aboue or belowe it. If you graft diuers buds vpon one ſtocke (which is the beſt way) let that onely remaine and abide that ſhooteth beſt forth, and rubbe off, or take away the other: the ſeuerall parts of this grafting I haue cauſed to be expreſſed for your further information.

5. Grafting in the ſcutcheon is accounted another kinde of grafting, and differeth verie little from grafting in the budde: the difference chiefly conſiſteth in this, that in ſtead of the downe right ſlit, and that aboue ouerthwart, they take away iuſt ſo much barke of the great tree, as your bud is in bigneſſe, which vſually is a little larger then the former, and placing it therein, they binde it as formerly is ſaid: ſome vſe for this purpoſe a paire of compaſſes, to giue the true meaſure both of bud and ſtocke; this manner of grafting is moſt vſed vpon greater trees, whoſe young branches are too high to graft vpon in the former maner, and whoſe tops they cut off (for the moſt part) at the latter end of the next yeare after the bud is taken: both theſe waies were inuented to ſaue the loſſe of trees, which are more endangered by grafting in the ſtocke,

then

then any of thefe waies; and befides, by thefe waies you may graft at a farre grea
height without loffe.

Chap. V.

Of the manner of grafting and propagating all forts of Rofes.

HAuing now fpoken of the grafting of trees, let mee adioyne the properties of
Rofes, which although they better fit a Garden then an Orchard, yet I could
not in a fitter place expreffe them then here, both for the name and affinity of
grafting, & becaufe I do not expreffe it in the firft part. All forts of Rofes may be grafted (although all forts are not, fome feruing rather for ftockes for others to be grafted
on) as eafily as any other tree, & is only performed, by inoculating in the fame maner I
haue fet downe in the former Chapter of grafting trees in the bud; for both ftocke and
budde muft bee dealt with after the fame fafhion. And although fome haue boafted of
grafting Rofes by flicing or whipping, as they call it, or in the ftocke, after the firft
manner, fet downe in the former Chapter, yet I thinke it rather a bragge, not hauing
feene or heard any true effect proceede from that relation. The fweete Briar or Eglantine, the white and the Damaske Rofes, are the chiefeft ftockes to graft vpon. And if
you graft lowe or neare the ground, you may by laying downe that graft within the
ground, after it hath bin fhot out well, and of a years growth, by pinning it faft downe
with fhort ftickes, a thwart or acroffe, caufe that grafted branch, by taking roote, to
become a naturall Rofe, fuch as the graft was, which being feparated and tranfplanted
after it hath taken root wel, will profper as well as any naturall fucker. And in this maner, by laying downe branchese at length into the ground, if they be full of fpreading
fmall branches, you may increafe all forts of Rofes quickly and plentifully; for they
will fhoote forth rootes at the ioynt of euery branch: But as for the manner of grafting
white Rofes or Damaske vpon Broome ftalkes or Barbary bufhes, to caufe them to
bring forth double yellow Rofes, or vpon a Willowe, to beare greene Rofes, they
are all idle conceits, as impoffible to be effected, as other things, whereof I haue fpoken in the ninth Chapter of my firft part, concerning a Garden of flowers, vnto which
I referre you to be fatisfied with the reafons there alledged. And it is the more needleffe, becaufe we haue a naturall double yellow Rofe of it owne growing. The fowing
of the feedes of Rofes (which are fometimes found vpon moft forts of Rofes, although
not euery yeare, and in euerie place) hath bin formerly much vfed; but now the laying
downe of the young fhootes is a way for increafe fo much vfed, being fafe and verie
fpeedie to take, efpecially for thofe Rofes that are not fo apt to giue fuckers, that it
hath almoft taken quite away the vfe of fowing of the feedes of Rofes, which yet if
anie one bee difpofed to make the triall, they muft gather the feede out of the round
heads, from amongft the doune, wherein they lye verie like vnto the berries of the
Eglantine or fweete Briar bufh, and efpecially of thofe Rofes that bee of the more fingle kindes, which are more apt to giue berries for feed then the more double, although
fometimes the double Rofes yeeld the like heads or berries. Their time of fowing is
in the end of September (yet fome referue them vntill February) and their manner
of nourfing is to bee tranfplanted, after the firft or fecond yeares growth, and tended carefully, that while they are young they be not loft for want of moifture in the
dry time of Summer.

CHAP. VI.

Certaine rules and obseruations in and after grafting, not remembred in the former Chapter.

THe time of some manners of grafting being not mentioned before, must here be spoken of. For the grafting of all sorts of trees in the stocke, the most vsuall time is from the middle of February vntill the middle of March, as the yeare and the countrie is more forward or backward, with vs about London wee neuer passe midde March : but because the May Cherrie is first ripe, and therefore of a very forward nature, it doth require to be grafted somewhat sooner then others. The time of gathering likewise, or cutting your grafts for grafting in the stocke, is to be obserued, that they bee not long gathered before they bee grafted, for feare of being too dry, which I commend, howsoeuer diuers say, if they be long kept they are not the worse; and therefore if you be forced to haue your grafts from farre, or by some other chance to keepe them long, be carefull to keepe them moist, by keeping their ends stucke in moist clay; but if neare hand, neglect no time I say after the cutting of them for their grafting, but either the same, or the next day, or verie speedily after, in the meane time being put into the ground to keepe them fresh. The grafts taken from old trees, because they are stronger, and shoote forth sooner, are to bee sooner grafted then those that are taken from younger trees : of a good branch may bee made two, and sometimes three grafts sufficient for anie reasonable stocke. For whipping, the time is somewhat later then grafting in the stocke, because it is performed on younger trees, which (as I said before) doe not so early bud or shoote forth as the elder. Inarching likewise is performed much about the later end of the grafting time in the stocke; for being both kindes thereof they require the same time of the yeare. The times of the other manners of graftings are before expressed, to bee when they haue shot forth young branches, from whence your buds must be taken; and therefore need not here againe to be repeated. If a graft in the stocke doth happen not to shoote forth when others do(so as it holdeth green) it may perchance shoot out a moneth or two after,& do well, or else after Midsummer, when a second time of shooting, or the after Spring appeareth: but haue an especiall care, that you take not such a graft that shal haue nothing but buds for flowers vpon it, and not an eye or bud for leaues (which you must be carefull to distinguish) for such a graft after it hath shot out the flowers must of necessitie dye, not hauing wherewith to maintaine it selfe. Also if your good graft doe misse, and not take, it doth hazzard your stocke at the first time, yet manie stockes doe recouer to be grafted the second time; but twice to faile is deadly, which is not so in the inoculating of buds in the greene tree : for if you faile therein three, or three times three, yet euerie wound being small, and the tree still growing greene, will quickly recouer it, and not be afterwards seen. Some vse to graft in the stocke the same yeare they remoue the stocke, to saue time,& a second checke by grafting; but I like better both in grafting in the stocke, and in the bud also, that your trees might be planted in the places where you would haue them growe, for a yeare or two at the least before you graft them, that after grafting there should be no remouall, I neede not be tedious, nor yet I hope verie sollicitous to remember many other triuiall, or at the least common knowne things in this matter. First, for the time to remoue trees, young or old, grafted or vngrafted, to be from a fortnight after Michaelmas vntill Candlemas, or if neede be, somewhat after, yet the sooner your remoue is, the better your trees will thriue, except it be in a very moist ground. For the manner or way to set them : *viz.* in the high and dry grounds set them deeper, both to haue the more moisture, and to be the better defended from windes; and in the lower and moister grounds shallower, and that the earth be mellow, well turned vp, and that the finer earth bee put among the small rootes, wherein they may spread, and afterwards gently troden downe, that no hollownesse remaine among the rootes: as also that after setting (if the time be not ouermoist) there may be some water powred to the rootes, to moisten and fasten them the better; and in the dry time of Summer, after the setting, let them not want moisture, if you will

haue

haue them thriue and profper; for the want thereof at that time, hath often killed manie a likely tree.　To ftake and fence them alfo if neede bee after they are new fet,
and fo to continue for two or three yeares after, is verie expedient, left windes or other
cafualties fpoile your paines, and ouerthrow your hopes.　And likewife to defend
your grafts from birds lighting on them, to breake or difplace them, to fticke fome
prickes or fharpe pointed ftickes longer then your graft into your clay, that fo they
may be a fure defence of it: As alfo to tye fome woollen cloathes about the lower end
of your ftockes, or thruft in fome thornes into the ground about the rootes, to defend
them from hauing their barkes eaten by Conies, or hurt by fome other noifome vermine.

<hr>

Chap. VII.

Obferuations for the dreffing and well keeping of Trees and an
Orchard in good order.

THere are two manner of waies to dreffe and keepe trees in good order, that
they may bee both gracefull and fruitfull; the one is for wall trees, the o-
ther is for ftandards: for as their formes are different, fo is their keeping or
ordering.　Wall trees, becaufe they are grafted lowe, and that their branches muft
be plafht or tackt vnto the wall to faften them, are to be fo kept, that all their branches
may be fuffered to growe, that fhoote forth on either fide of the bodie, and led either
along the wall, or vpright, and one to lappe ouer or vnder another as is conuenient,
and ftill with peeces of lifts, parings of felt, peeces of foft leather, or other fuch like
foft thing compaffing the armes or branches, faftened with fmall or great nailes, as
neede requireth, to the wals, onely thofe buds or branches are to be nipped or cut off,
that fhoot forward, and will not fo handfomely be brought into conformity, as is fitting; yet if the branches growe too thicke, to hinder the good of the reft, or too high
for the wall, they may, nay they muft be cut away or lopped off: and if anie dead
branches alfo happen to be on the trees, they muft be cut away, that the reft may haue
the more libertie to thriue.　Diuers alfo by carefully nipping away the wafte and fuperfluous buds, doe keepe their trees in conformity, without much cutting.　The time
to pruine or plafh, or tye vp wall trees, is vfually from the fall of the leafe, to the beginning of the yeare, when they begin to bloffome, and moft efpecially a little before
or after Chriftmas: but in any cafe not too late, for feare of rubbing off their buds.
Some I know doe plafh and tye vp their wall trees after bearing time, while the leaues
are greene, and their reafon is, the buds are not fo eafie or apt to bee rubbed from the
branches at that time, as at Chriftmas, when they are more growne: but the leaues
muft needes be very cumberfome, to hinder much both the orderly placing, and clofe
faftening of them to the wall.　This labour you muft performe euery yeare in its due
time; for if you fhall neglect and iouerflip it, you fhall haue much more trouble, to
bring them into a fit order againe, then at the firft.　The ftandard trees in an Orchard
muft be kept in another order; for whereas the former are fuffered to fpread at large,
thefe muft be pruined both from fuperfluous branches that ouerload the trees, & make
them leffe fruitfull, as well as leffe fightly, and the vnder or water boughes likewife,
that drawe much nourifhment from the trees, and yet themfelues little the better for
it, I meane to giue fruit. If therefore your Orchard confift of young trees, with a little care and paines it may bee kept in that comely order and proportion it was firft de-
ftined vnto; but if it confift of old growne trees, they will not without a great deale
of care and paines be brought into fuch conformitie, as is befitting good and comely
trees: for the marke of thofe boughes or branches that are cut off from young trees,
will quickly be healed againe, the barke growing quickly ouer them, whereby they
are not worfe for their cutting; but an old tree if you cut off a bough, you muft cut it
clofe and cleanly, and lay a fearcloth of tallow, waxe, and a little pitch melted together vpon the place, to keepe off both the winde, funne, and raine, vntill the barke
haue couered it ouer againe: and in this manner you muft deale with all fuch fhort
ftumps of branches, as are either broken fhort off with the winde, or by carelefneffe or
want

want of skill, or else such armes or branches as are broken off close, or sliued from the body of the tree : for the raine beating and falling into such a place, will in short time rotte your tree, or put it in danger, besides the deformity. Some vse to fill vp such an hole with well tempered clay, and tacke a cloth or a peece of leather ouer it vntill it be recouered, and this is also not amisse. Your young trees, if they stand in anie good ground, will bee plentifull enough in shooting forth branches; bee carefull therefore if they growe too thicke, that you pruine away such as growe too close (and will, if they be suffered, spoile one another) as they may be best spared, that so the sunne, ayre, and raine may haue free accesse to all your branches, which will make them beare the more plentifully, and ripen them the sooner and the more kindly. If anie boughes growe at the toppe too high, cut them also away, that your trees may rather spread then growe too high. And so likewise for the vnder boughes, or anie other that by the weight of fruit fall or hang downe, cut them off at the halfe, and they will afterwards rise and shoote vpwards. You shall obserue, that at all those places where anie branches haue been cut away, the sappe will euer bee readie to put forth : if therefore you would haue no more branches rise from that place, rubbe off or nippe off such buddes as are not to your minde, when they are new shot : and thus you may keep your trees in good order with a little paines, after you haue thus pruined and dressed them. One other thing I would aduertise you of, and that is how to preserue a fainting or decaying tree which is readie to perish, if it be not gone too farre or past cure, take a good quantitie of oxe or horse bloud, mixe therewith a reasonable quantitie of sheepe or pigeons dung, which being laid to the roote, will by the often raines and much watering recouer it selfe, if there bee anie possibilitie; but this must bee done in Ianuarie or Februarie at the furthest.

Chap. VIII.

Diuers other obseruations to be remembred in the well keeping of an Orchard.

THere be diuers other things to be mentioned, whereof care must be had, either to doe or auoide, which I thinke fit in this Chapter promiscuously to set down, that there may be nothing wanting to furnish you with sufficient knowledge of the care, paines, and casualties that befall an Orchard : for it hath many enemies, and euery one laboureth as much as in them lye, to spoile you of your pleasure, or profit, or both, which must bee both speedily and carefully preuented and helped; and they are these : Mosse, Caterpillars, Ants, Earwigs, Snailes, Moales, and Birds. If Mosse begin to ouergrowe your trees, looke to it betimes, lest it make your trees barren: Some vse to hacke, and crossehacke, or cut the barke of the bodies of their trees, to cause it fall away; but I feare it may endanger your trees. Others do either rubbe it off with a haire cloth, or with a long peece of wood formed like a knife, at the end of a long sticke or pole, which if it bee vsed cautelously without hurting the buds, I like better. Caterpillars, some smoake them with burning wet strawe or hay, or such like stuffe vnder the trees; but I doe not greatly like of that way : others cut off the boughes whereon they breed, and tread them vnder their feete, but that will spoile too manie branches; and some kill them with their hands : but some doe vse a new deuised way, that is, a pompe made of lattin or tin, spout-fashion, which being set in a tubbe of water vnder or neare your trees, they will cause the water to rise through it with such a force, and through the branches, that it will wash them off quickly. To destroy Ants, that eate your fruit before and when it is ripe, some vse to annoint the bodies of their trees with tarre, that they may not creepe vp on the branches; but if that doe not helpe, or you will not vse it, you must be carefull to finde out their hill, and turne it vp, pouring in scalding water, either in Summer, but especially if you can in Winter, and that will surely destroy them. I haue spoken of Earwigs in the first part of this worke, entreating of the annoyances of Gilloflowers, and therefore I referre you thereunto : yet one way more I
will

will here relate which some doe vse, and that is with hollow canes of halfe a yard long or more, open at both ends for them to creepe in, and stucke or laid among the branches of your trees, will soone drawe into them many Earwigs, which you may soone kill, by knocking the cane a little vpon the ground, and treading on them with your foote. Snailes must be taken with your hands, and that euerie day, especially in the morning when they will be creeping abroad. Moales by running vnder your trees make them lesse fruitfull, and also put them in danger to be blowne downe, by leauing the ground hollow, that thereby the rootes haue not that strength in the ground, both to shoote and to hold, that otherwise they might haue. Some haue vsed to put Garlicke, and other such like things into their holes, thinking thereby to driue them away, but to no purpose : others haue tryed manie other waies; but no way doth auaile anie thing, but killing them either with a Moale spade, or a trappe made for the purpose as manie doe know : and they must bee watched at their principall hill, and trenched round, and so to be caught. Birds are another enemie both to your trees and fruit; for the Bullfinch will destroy all your stone fruit in the budde, before they flower, if you suffer them, and Crowes, &c. when your Cherries are ripe : for the smaller birds, Lime twigs set either neare your trees, or at the next water where they drinke, will helpe to catch them and destroy them. And for the greater birds, a stone bowe, a birding or fowling peece will helpe to lessen their number, and make the rest more quiet : or a mill with a clacke to scarre them away, vntill your fruit be gathered. Some other annoyances there are, as suckers that rise from the rootes of your trees, which must be taken away euerie yeare, and not suffered to growe anie thing great, for feare of robbing your trees of their liuelihood. Barke bound, is when a tree doth not shoote and encrease, by reason the barke is as it were drie, and will not suffer the sappe to passe vnto the branches : take a knife therefore, and slit the barke downe almost all the length of the tree in two or three places, and it will remedy that euill, and the tree will thriue and come forward the better after. Barke pilled is another euill that happeneth to some trees, as well young as old, either by reason of casuall hurts, or by the gnawing of beasts, howsoeuer it bee, if it bee anie great hurt, lay a plaister thereon made of tallow, tarre, and a little pitch, and binde it thereto, letting it so abide vntill the wound bee healed : yet some doe only apply a little clay or loame bound on with ropes of hay. The Canker is a shrewd disease when it happeneth to a tree; for it will eate the barke round, and so kill the very heart in a little space. It must be looked vnto in time before it hath runne too farre; most men doe wholly cut away as much as is fretted with the Canker, and then dresse it, or wet it with vinegar or Cowes pisse, or Cowes dung and vrine, &c. vntill it be destroyed, and after healed againe with your salue before appointed. There are yet some other enemies to an Orchard : for if your fence be not of bricke or stone, but either a mudde wall, or a quicke set or dead hedge, then looke to it the more carefully, and preuent the comming in of either horse, or kine, sheepe, goates, or deere, hare, or conie; for some of them will breake through or ouer to barke your trees, and the least hole almost in the hedge will giue admittance to hares and conies to doe the like. To preuent all which, your care must be continuall to watch them or auoide them, and to stoppe vp their entrance. A dogge is a good seruant for many such purposes, and so is a stone bowe, and a peece to make vse of as occasion shall serue. But if you will take that medicine for a Canker spoken of before, which is Cowes dung and vrine mixed together, and with a brush wash your trees often to a reasonable height, will keepe hares and conies from eating or barking your trees. Great and cold windes doe often make a great spoile in an Orchard, but great trees planted without the compasse thereof, as Wall-nuts, Oakes, Elmes, Ashes, and the like, will stand it in great stead, to defend it both early and late. Thus haue I shewed you most of the euils that may happen to an Orchard, and the meanes to helpe them, and because the number is great and daily growing, the care and paines must be continuall, the more earnest and diligent, lest you lose that in a moment that hath been growing many yeares, or at the least the profit or beauty of some yeares fruit.

C H A P.

CHAP. IX.

The manner and way how to plant, order, and keepe other trees that
beare greene leaues continually.

THe way to order thofe trees that beare their leaues greene continually, is differing from all others that doe not fo : for neyther are they to bee planted or
remoued at the time that all other trees are fet, nor doe they require that manner of dreffing, pruining and keeping, that others doe. And although many ignorant
perfons and Gardiners doe remoue Bay trees, and are fo likewife perfwaded that all
other trees of that nature, that is, that carry their greene leaues continually, may
bee remoued in Autumne or Winter, as well as all other trees may bee; yet it
is certaine it is a great chance if they doe thriue and profper that are fet at that
time, or rather it is found by experience, that fcarce one of ten profpereth well that
are fo ordered. Now in regard that there be diuers trees and fhrubs mentioned here in
this booke that beare euer greene leaues, wherein there is very great beauty, and many
take pleafure in them ; as the ordinary Bay, the Rofe Bay, and the Cherry Bay trees,
the Indian Figge, the Cypreffe, the Pine tree, the Mirtle and dwarfe Boxe, and many
others ; I will here fhew you how to plant and order them, as is fitteft for them. For
in that they doe not fhed their greene leaues in winter as other trees doe, you may in
reafon be perfwaded that they are of another nature; and fo they are indeede: for feeing they all grow naturally in warme Countries, and are from thence brought vnto vs,
we muft both plant them in a warmer place, and tranfplant them in a warmer time then
other trees be, or elfe it is a great hazzard if they doe not perifh and dye, the cold and
frofts in the winter being able to pierce them through, if they fhould bee tranfplanted
in winter, before they haue taken roote. You muft obferue and take this therefore for
a certaine rule, that you alwaies remoue fuch trees or fhrubbes as are euer greene in the
fpring of the yeare, and at no time elfe if you will doe well, that is, from the end of
March, or beginning of Aprill, vnto the middle or end of May, efpecially your more
dainty and tender plants, fhadowing them alfo for a while from the heate of the Sun,
and giuing them a little water vpon their planting or tranfplanting; but fuch water as
hath not prefently been drawn from a Well or Pumpe, for that will go neer to kill any
plant, but fuch water as hath ftood in the open ayre for a day at the leaft, if not two or
three. Yet for dwarfe Boxe I confeffe it may endure one moneth to be earlier planted
then the reft, becaufe it is both a more hardy and lowe plant, and thereby not fo much
fubiect to the extremitie of the colde : but if you fhould plant it before winter, the
frofts would raife it out of the ground, becaufe it cannot fo foone at that time of the
yeare take roote, aud thereby put it in danger to be loft. Moreouer all of them will
not abide the extremitie of our winter frofts, and therefore you muft of neceffity houfe
fome of them, as the Rofe Bay, Mirtle, and fome others, but the other forts being fet
where they may bee fomewhat defended from the cold windes, froftes, and fnow in
winter, with fome couering or fhelter for the time, will reafonably well endure and
beare their fruit, or the moft of them. If any be defirous to be furnifhed with ftore of
thefe kinds of trees that will be nourfed vp in our Country, he may by fowing the feed
of them in fquare or long woodden boxes or chefts made for that purpofe, gaine plenty
of them : but hee muft be carefull to couer them in winter with fome ftraw or fearne,
or beane hame, or fuch like thing layd vpon croffe fticks to beare it vp from the plants,
and after two or three yeares that they are growne fomewhat great and ftrong, they
may bee tranfplanted into fuch places you meane they fhall abide : yet it is not amiffe
to defend them the firft yeare after they are tranfplanted, for their more fecuritie : the
feedes that are moft vfually fowen with vs, are, the Cypreffe tree, the Pine tree, the
Baye, the Pyracantha or prickly Corall tree, and the Mirtle : the Rofe Bay I haue had
alfo rifen from the feede that was frefh, and brought me from Spaine. But as for Orenge
trees, becaufe they are fo hardly preferued in this our cold climate (vnleffe it bee with
fome that doe beftow the houfing of them, befides a great deale more of care and refpect vnto them) from the bitterneffe of our cold long winter weather (although their
kernels

kernels being put into the ground in the Spring or Summer, and if care bee had of them and conuenient keeping, will abide, and by grafting the good fruite on the crab stocke they may bee in time nurſed vp) I doe not make any other eſpeciall account of them, nor giue you any further relation of their ordering. Now for the ordering of theſe trees after they are eyther planted of young ſets, or tranſplanted from the ſeede, it is thus : Firſt for Bay trees, the moſt vſuall way is to let them grow vp high to bee trees, and many plant them on the North or Eaſt ſide of their houſes that they may not bee ſcorched with the Sunne; but the bitter winters which we often haue, doe pinch them ſhrewdly, inſomuch that it killeth euen well growne trees ſometimes downe to the roote : but ſome doe make a hedge of them being planted in order, and keep them low by lopping of them continually, which will make them buſh and ſpread. The Cypreſſe tree is neuer lopped, but ſuffered to grow with all the branches from a foote a-boue the ground, if it may be, ſtraight vpright; for that is his natiue grace and greateſt beautie, and therefore the more branches doe dye that they muſt bee cut away, the more you deforme his propertie. The Pine tree may be vſed in the ſame manner, but yet it wil better endure to ſuſtaine pruining then the Cypreſſe, without any ſuch deformitie. The Lauroceraſus or Cherry Bay may be diuerſly formed, that is, it may be either made to grow into a tall tree by ſhredding ſtill away the vnder branches, or elſe by ſuffering all the branches to grow to be a low or hedge buſh, & both by the ſuckers and by laying downe the lower branches into the earth, you may ſoone haue much increaſe ; but this way will cauſe it to bee the longer before it beare anie fruit. The Roſe Baye will verie hardlie bee encreaſed either by ſuckers or by layers, but muſt bee ſuffered to grow without lopping, topping or cutting. The Pyracantha or Prickly Corall tree may bee made to grow into a reaſonable tall tree by ſhredding away the lower branches, or it may be ſuffered to grow lowe into an hedge buſh, by ſuffering all the branches to grow continually, you may alſo propagate it by the ſuckers, or by laying downe the lower branches. The Myrtle of all ſorts abideth a low buſh ſpreading his branches full of ſweete leaues and flowers, without anie great encreaſe of it ſelfe, yet ſometimes it giueth ſuckers or ſhootes from the rootes : but for the more ſpeedie propagating of them, ſome doe put the cuttings of them into the earth, and thereby increaſe them. There are ſome other trees that are not of any great reſpect, as the Yew tree, and the Savine buſh, both which may be encreaſed by the cuttings, and therefore I need not make any further relation or amplification of them, and to ſay thus much of them all, is (I thinke) ſufficient for this Worke.

Chap. X.

The ordering, curing, and propagating Vines of all ſorts.

IN moſt places of this countrie there is ſmall care or paines taken about the ordering of Vines : it ſufficeth for the moſt part with them that haue anie, to make a frame for it to ſpread vpon aboue a mans height, or to tacke it to a wall or window, &c. and ſo to let it hang downe with the branches and fruit, vntill the weight thereof, and the force of windes doe teare it downe oftentimes, and ſpoile the grapes : and this way doth ſomewhat reſemble that courſe that the Vineyard keepers obſerue in the hot countries of Syria, Spaine, and Italy, and in the furtheſt parts of France as I hear likewiſe : for in moſt of theſe hot countries they vſe to plant an Oliue betweene two Vines, and let them runne thereupon. But manie of the other parts of France, &c. doe not ſuffer anie trees to growe among their Vines ; and therefore they plant them thicke, and pruine them much and often, and keepe them lowe in compariſon of the other way, faſtening them to pearches or poles to hold them vp. And according to that faſhion many haue aduentured to make Vineyards in England, not onely in theſe later daies, but in ancient times, as may wel witneſſe the ſundrie places in this Land, entituled by the name of Vineyards; and I haue read, that manie Monaſteries in this Kingdome hauing Vineyards, had as much wine made therefrom, as ſufficed their couents yeare by yeare : but long ſince they haue been deſtroyed, and the knowledge how to order a Vineyard is alſo vtterly periſhed with them. For although diuers, both No-
bles

bles and Gentlemen, haue in thefe later times endeauoured to plant and make Vine-yards, and to that purpofe haue caufed French men, being skilfull in keeping and dref-fing of Vines, to be brought ouer to performe it, yet either their skill failed them, or their Vines were not good, or (the moft likely) the foile was not fitting, for they could neuer make anie wine that was worth the drinking, being fo fmall and heartleffe, that they foone gaue ouer their practice. And indeede the foile is a maine matter to bee chiefly confidered to feate a Vineyard vpon: for euen in France and other hot coun-tries, according to the nature of the foile, fo is the rellifh, ftrength, and durabilitie of the wine. Now although I think it a fruitleffe labour for any man to ftriue in thefe daies to make a good Vineyard in England, in regard not only of the want of knowledge, to make choife of the fitteft ground for fuch Vines as you would plant therupon, but alfo of the true maner of ordering them in our country; but moft chiefly & aboue all others, that our years in thefe times do not fal out to be fo kindly and hot, to ripen the grapes, to make anie good wine as formerly they haue done ; yet I thinke it not amiffe, to giue you inftructions how to order fuch Vines as you may nourfe vp for the pleafure of the fruit, to eate the grapes being ripe, or to preferue and keepe them to bee eaten almoft all the winter following : And this may be done without any great or extraordinarie paines. Some doe make a lowe wall, and plant their Vines againft it, and keepe them much about the height thereof, not fuffering them to rife much higher : but if the high bricke or ftone wals of your Garden or Orchard haue buttreffes thereat, or if you caufe fuch to bee made, that they bee fomewhat broade forwards, you may the more conueniently plant Vines of diuers forts at them, and by fticking down a couple of good ftakes at euery buttreffe, of eight or ten foot high aboue ground, tacking a few lathes acroffe vpon thofe ftakes, you may therunto tye your Vines, & carry them ther-on at your pleafure : but you muft be carefull to cut them euery year, but not too late, and fo keepe them downe, and from farre fpreading, that they neuer runne much be-yond the frame which you fet at the buttreffes : as alfo in your cutting you neuer leaue too many ioynts, nor yet too few, but at the third or fourth ioint at the moft cut them off. I doe aduife you to thefe frames made with ftakes and lathes, for the better ripe-ning of your grapes : for in the blooming time, if the branches of your vines bee too neare the wall, the reflection of the Sunne in the day time, and the colde in the night, doe oftentimes fpoile a great deale of fruit, by piercing and withering the tender foot-ftalkes of the grapes, before they are formed, whereas when the bloffomes are paft, and the fruit growing of fome bigneffe, then all the heate and reflection you can giue them is fit, and therefore cut away fome of the branches with the leaues, to admit the more Sunne to ripen the fruit. For the diuers forts of grapes I haue fet them downe in the Booke following, with briefe notes vpon euerie of them, whether white or blacke, fmall or great, early or late ripe; fo that I neede not here make the fame relation again. There doth happen fome difeafes to Vines fometimes, which that you may helpe, I thinke it conuenient to informe you what they are, and how to remedy them when you fhall be troubled with any fuch. The firft is a luxurious fpreading of branches and but little or no fruit : for remedie whereof, cut the branches fomewhat more neere then vfuall, and bare the roote, but take heed of wounding or hurting it, and in the hole put either fome good old rotten ftable dung of Horfes, or elfe fome Oxe blood new taken from the beafts, and that in the middle of Ianuarie or beginning of Febru-arie, which being well tempered and turned in with the earth, let it fo abide, which no doubt, when the comfort of the blood or dung is well foaked to the bottome by the raines that fall thereon, will caufe your Vine to fructifie againe. Another fault is, when a Vine doth not bring the fruit to ripeneffe, but either it withereth before it be growne of any bigneffe, or prefently after the blooming : the place or the earth where fuch a Vine ftandeth, affuredly is too cold, and therefore if the fault bee not in the place, which cannot bee helped without remouing to a better, digge out a good quantity of that earth, and put into the place thereof fome good frefh ground well heartned with dung, and fome fand mixed therewith (but not falt or falt water, as fome doe aduife, nor yet vrine, as others would haue) and this will hearten and ftrengthen your Vine to beare out the frut vnto maturitie. When the leaues of a Vine in the end of Summer or in Autumne, vntimely doe turne either yellow or red, it is a great figne the earth is

too

too hot and drie ; you muſt therefore in ſtead of dung and ſand, as in the former defect is ſaid, put in ſome freſh loame or ſhort clay, well mixed together with ſome of
the earth, and ſo let them abide, that the froſts may mellow them. And laſtly, a Vine
ſometimes beareth ſome ſtore of grapes, but they are too many for it to bring to ripeneſſe ; you ſhall therefore helpe ſuch a Vine (which no doubt is of ſome excellent
kinde, for they are moſt vſually ſubiect to this fault) by nipping away the bloſſomes
from the branches, and leauing but one or two bunches at the moſt vpon a branch, vntill the Vine be growne older, and thereby ſtronger, and by this meane inured to beare
out all the grapes to ripeneſſe. Theſe be all the diſeaſes I know doe happen to Vines :
for the bleeding of a Vine it ſeldome happeneth of it ſelfe, but commeth either by
cutting it vntimely, that is, too late in the yeare, (for after Ianuarie, if you will be well
aduiſed, cut not any Vine) or by ſome caſuall or wilfull breaking of an arme or a
branch. This bleeding in ſome is vnto death, in others it ſtayeth after a certaine ſpace
of it ſelfe : To helpe this inconuenience, ſome haue ſeared the place where it bleedeth
with an hot iron, which in many haue done but a little good ; others haue bound the
barke cloſe with packe-thred to ſtay it ; and ſome haue tied ouer the place, being firſt
dried as well as may bee, a plaiſter made with waxe roſſen and turpentine while it is
warme. Now for the propagating of them : You muſt take the faireſt and goaleſt ſhot
branches of one yeares growth, and cut them off with a peece of the old wood vnto it,
and theſe being put into the ground before the end of Ianuarie at the furtheſt, will
ſhoote forth, and take roote, and ſo become Vines of the ſame kinde from whence
you tooke them. This is the moſt ſpeedy way to haue increaſe : for the laying downe
of branches to take roote, doth not yeelde ſuch ſtore ſo plentifully, nor doe ſuckers
riſe from the rootes ſo aboundantly ; yet both theſe waies doe yeelde Vines, that being taken from the old ſtockes will become young plants, fit to bee diſpoſed of as any
ſhall thinke meete.

Chap. XI.

The way to order and preſerue grapes, fit to be eaten almoſt all the Winter long, and ſometimes vnto the Spring.

ALthough it bee common and vſuall in the parts beyond the Sea to dry their
grapes in the Sunne, thereby to preſerue them all the year, as the Raiſins of the
Sunne are, which cannot bee done in our Countrie for the want of ſufficient
heate thereof at that time : or otherwiſe to ſcald them in hot water (as I heare) and
afterwards to dry them, and ſo keepe them all the yeare, as our Malaga Raiſins are prepared that are packed vp into Frayles : yet I doe intend to ſhew you ſome other waies
to preſerue the grapes of our Countrie freſh, that they may be eaten in the winter both
before and after Chriſtmas with as much delight and pleaſure almoſt, as when they
were new gathered. One way is, when you haue gathered your grapes you intend to
keepe, which muſt be in a dry time, and that all the ſhrunke, dried, or euill grapes in e-
uery bunch be picked away, and hauing prouided a veſſell to hold them, be it of wood
or ſtone which you will, and a ſufficient quantitie of faire and cleane drie ſand ; make
ſtratum ſuper ſtratum of your grapes and the ſand, that is, a lay of ſand in the bottome
firſt, and a lay of grapes vpon them, and a lay or ſtrowing againe of ſand vpon thoſe
grapes, ſo that the ſand may couer euery lay of grapes a fingers breadth in thickneſſe,
which being done one vpon another vntill the veſſell be full, and a lay of ſand vppermoſt, let the veſſell be ſtopped cloſe, and ſet by vntill you pleaſe to ſpend them, being
kept in ſome drie place and in no ſellar : let them bee waſhed cleane in faire water to
take away the ſand from ſo many you will ſpend at a time. Another way is (which Camerarius ſetteth downe he was informed the Turkes vſe to keepe grapes all the winter
vnto the next ſummer) to take ſo much meale of Muſtard ſeede, as will ſerue to ſtrow
vpon grapes, vntill they haue filled their veſſels, whereon afterwards they poure new
wine before it hath boiled, to fill vp their veſſels therwith, and being ſtopped vp cloſe,
they keepe them a certaine time, and ſelling them with their liquour to them that will

vſe them, they doe waſh the ſeedes or meale from them when they vſe them. Another way is, that hauing gathered the faireſt ripe grapes, they are to be caſt vpon threds or ſtrings that are faſtened at both ends to the ſide walks of a chamber, neere vnto the ſeeling thereof, that no one bunch touch another, which will bee ſo kept a great while, yet the chamber muſt be well defended from the froſts, and cold windes that pierce in at the windowes, leſt they periſh the ſooner : and ſome will dippe the ends of the branches they hang vp firſt in molten pitch, thinking by ſearing vp the ends to keepe the bunches the better; but I doe not ſee any great likelihood therein. Your chamber or cloſet you appoint out for this purpoſe muſt alſo bee kept ſomewhat warme, but eſpecially in the more cold and froſtie time of the yeare, leſt it ſpoile all your coſt and paines, and fruſtrate you of all your hopes : but although the froſts ſhould pierce and ſpoile ſome of the grapes on a bunch, yet if you be carefull to keepe the place warme, the fewer will be ſpoiled. And thus haue I ſhewed you the beſt directions to order this Orchard rightly, and all the waies I know are vſed in our Countrie to keep grapes good anie long time after the gathering, in regard wee haue not that comfort of a hotter Sun to preſerue them by its heate.

The fruits themſelues ſhall follow euerie one in their order; the lower ſhrubbes or buſhes firſt, and the greater afterwards.

Aaa 2   The

THE THIRD PART
CALLED
THE ORCHARD,

Ontaining all forts of trees bearing fruit for mans vfe to eate, proper and fit for to plant an Orchard in our climate and countrie : I bound it with this limitation, becaufe both Dates, Oliues, and other fruits, are planted in the Orchards of Spaine, Italy, and other hot countries, which will not abide in ours. Yet herein I will declare whatfoeuer Art, ftriuing with Nature, can caufe to profper with vs, that whofoeuer will, may fee what can bee effected in our countrie. And firft to begin with the lower fhrubbes or bufhes, and after afcend to the higher trees.

CHAP. I.

Rubus Idæus. Rafpis.

THe Rafpis berrie is of two forts, white and red, not differing in the forme either of bufh, leafe, or berry, but onely in the colour and tafte of the fruit. The Rafpis bufh hath tender whitifh ftemmes, with reddifh fmall prickes like haires fet round about them, efpecially at the firft when they are young ; but when they grow old they become more wooddy and firme, without any fhew of thornes or prickles vpon them, and hath onely a little hairineffe that couereth them : the leaues are fomewhat rough or rugged, and wrinkled, ftanding three or fiue vpon a ftalke, fomewhat like vnto Rofes, but greater, and of a grayer greene colour : the flowers are fmall, made of fine whitifh round leaues, with a dafh as it were of blufh caft ouer them, many ftanding together, yet euery one vpon his owne ftalke, at the tops of the branches; after which come vp fmall berries, fomewhat bigger then Strawberries, and longer, either red or white, made of many graines, more eminent then in the Strawberry, with a kinde of douineffe caft ouer them, of a pleafant tafte, yet fomewhat fowre, and nothing fo pleafant as the Strawberrie. The white Rafpis is a little more pleafant then the red, wherein there is fmall feede inclofed : the rootes creepe vnder ground verie farre, and fhoote vp againe in many places, much encreafing thereby.

There is another whofe ftemme and branches are wholly without prickles : the fruit is red, and fomewhat longer, and a little more fharpe.

The Vfe of Rafpis.

The leaues of Rafpis may be vfed for want of Bramble leaues in gargles, and other decoctions that are cooling and drying, although not fully to that effect.

The

The Conſerue or Syrupe made of the berries, is effectuall to coole an hot ſtomacke, helping to refreſh and quicken vp thoſe that are ouercome with faintneſſe.

The berries are eaten in the Summer time, as an afternoones diſh, to pleaſe the taſte of the ſicke as well as the ſound.

The iuyce and the diſtilled water of the berries are verie comfortable and cordiall.

It is generally held of many, but how true I know not, that the red wine that is vſually ſold at the Vintners, is made of the berries of Raſpis that grow in colder countries, which giueth it a kinde of harſhneſſe : And alſo that of the ſame berries growing in hotter climates, which giueth vnto the wine a more pleaſant ſweetneſſe, is made that wine which the Vintners call **Alligant** : but we haue a Vine or Grape come to vs vnder the name of the **Alligant** Grape, as you ſhall finde it ſet downe hereafter among the Grapes; and therefore it is likely to be but an opinion, and no truth in this, as it may be alſo in the other.

Chap. II.

Ribes rubra, alba, nigra. Currans red, white, and blacke.

THe buſhes that beare thoſe berries, which are vſually called red Currans, are not thoſe Currans either blew or red, that are ſold at the Grocers, nor any kind thereof ; for that they are the grapes of a certaine Vine, as ſhall be ſhewed by and by : but a farre differing kinde of berry, whereof there are three ſorts, red, white, and blacke.

The red Curran buſh is of two ſorts, and groweth to the height of a man, hauing ſometimes a ſtemme of two inches thickneſſe, and diuers armes and branches, couered with a ſmooth, darke, browniſh barke, without anie pricke or thorne at all vpon anie part thereof, whereon doe growe large cornered blackiſh greene leaues, cut in on the edges, ſeeming to be made of fiue parts, almoſt like a Vine leafe, the ends a little pointing out, and ſtanding one aboue another on both ſides of the branches : the flowers are little and hollow, comming forth at the ioynts of the leaues, growing many together on a long ſtalke, hanging downe aboue a fingers length, and of an herbie colour : after which come ſmall round fruit or berries, greene at the firſt, and red as a Cherry when they are ripe, of a pleaſant and tart taſte : the other differeth not in anie other thing then in the berries, being twice as bigge as the former : the roote is wooddy, and ſpreadeth diuerſly.

The white Curran buſh riſeth vſually both higher then the red, and ſtraighter or more vpright, bigger alſo in the ſtemme, and couered with a whiter barke : the leaues are cornered, ſomewhat like the former, but not ſo large : the flowers are ſmall and hollow like the other, hanging downe in the ſame manner on long ſtalkes, being of a whiter colour : the berries likewiſe growe on the long ſtalkes, ſomewhat thicker ſet together, and of a cleare white colour, with a little blacke head, ſo tranſparent that the ſeedes may be eaſily ſeene thorough them, and of a more pleaſant winie taſte then the red by much.

The blacke Curran buſh riſeth higher then the white, with more plentifull branches, and more pliant and twiggie : the ſtemme and the elder branches being couered with a browniſh barke, and the younger with a paler : the flowers are alſo like vnto little bottles as the others be, of a greeniſh purple colour, which turne into blacke berries, of the bigneſſe of the ſmaller red Currans : the leaues are ſomewhat like vnto the leaues of the red Currans, but not ſo large : both branches, leaues, and fruit haue a kind of ſtinking ſent with them, yet they are not vnwholſome, but the berries are eaten of many, without offending either taſte or ſmell.

The Vſe of Currans.

The red Currans are vſually eaten when they are ripe, as a refreſhing to an
hot

1 *Rubus Idæus.* The Raſpis. 2 *Ribes fructu rubro vel albo.* White or red Currants. 3 *Groſſularia vulgaris.* The ordinary Gooſeberry
4 *Groſſularia fructu rubro.* The great red Gooſeberry. 5 *Groſſularia aculeata.* The prickly Gooſeberry. 6 *Oxyacantha ſeu Berberis.* The
Barbary buſh. 7 *Auellana Byzantina.* The Filberd of Conſtantinople. 8 *Auellana rubra noſtras.* The beſt red Filberd.

hot ſtomacke in the heate of the yeare, which by the tartneſſe is much delighted. Some preſerue them, and conſerue them alſo as other fruits, and ſpend them at neede.

The white Currans, by reaſon of the more pleaſant winie taſte, are more accepted and deſired, as alſo becauſe they are more daintie, and leſſe common.

Some vſe both the leaues and berries of the blacke Currans in ſawces, and other meates, and are well pleaſed both with the ſauour and taſte thereof, although many miſlike it.

CHAP. III.

Vva Criſpa ſiue Groſſularia. Gooſeberries or Feaberries.

WEe haue diuers ſorts of Gooſeberries, beſides the common kinde, which is of three ſorts, ſmall, great, and long.   For wee haue three red Gooſeberries, a blew and a greene.

The common Gooſeberrie, or Feaberrie buſh, as it is called in diuers Countries of England, hath oftentimes a great ſtemme, couered with a ſmooth darke coloured bark, without anie thorne thereon, but the elder branches haue here and there ſome on them, and the younger are whitiſh, armed with verie ſharpe and cruell crooked thorns, which no mans hand can well auoide that doth handle them, whereon are ſet verie greene and ſmall cornered leaues cut in, of the faſhion almoſt of Smallage, or Hawthorne leaues, but broad at the ſtalke: the flowers come forth ſingle, at euerie ioynt of the leafe one or two, of a purpliſh greene colour, hollow and turning vp the brims a little: the berries follow, bearing the flowers on the heads of them, which are of a pale greene at the firſt, and of a greeniſh yellow colour when they are ripe, ſtriped in diuers places, and cleare, almoſt tranſparent, in which the ſeede lyeth. In ſome theſe berries are ſmall and round; in others much greater; a third is great, but longer then the other: all of them haue a pleaſant winie taſte, acceptable to the ſtomacke of anie (but the long kinde hath both the thicker skin, and the worſer taſte of the other) and none haue been diſtempered by the eating of them, that euer I could heare of.

The firſt of the red Gooſeberries is better knowne I thinke then the reſt, and by reaſon of the ſmall bearing not much regarded; the ſtemme is ſomewhat bigge, and couered with a ſmooth darke coloured barke, the younger branches are whiter, and without anie thorne or pricke at all, ſo long, weake, ſmall, and ſlender, that they lye vpon the ground, and will there roote againe: the leaues are like vnto the former Gooſeberries, but larger: the flowers and berries ſtand ſingle, and not manie to bee found anie yeare vpon them, but are ſomewhat long, and are as great as the ordinarie Gooſeberry, of a darke browniſh red colour, almoſt blackiſh when they are ripe, and of a ſweetiſh taſte, but without any great delight.

The ſecond red Gooſeberry riſeth vp with a more ſtraight ſtemme, couered with a browniſh barke; the young branches are ſtraight likewiſe, and whitiſh, and grow not ſo thicke vpon it as the former red kinde, and without any thorne alſo vpon them: the leaues are like vnto the former red, but ſmaller: the berries ſtand ſingly at the leaues as Gooſeberries doe, and are of a fine red colour when they are ripe, but change with ſtanding to be of a darker red colour, of the bigneſſe of the ſmall ordinary Gooſeberry, of a pretty tart taſte, and ſomewhat ſweete withall.

The third red Gooſeberry which is the greateſt, and knowne but vnto few, is ſo like vnto the common great Gooſeberry, that it is hardly diſtinguiſhed: the fruit or berries grow as plentifully on the branches as the ordinary, and are as great & round as the great ordinary kinde, but reddiſh, and ſome of them paler, with red ſtripes.

The blew Gooſeberry riſeth vp to bee a buſh like vnto the red Curran, and of the ſame bigneſſe and height, with broader and redder leaues at the firſt ſhooting out, then the ſecond red Gooſeberry: the berries are more ſparingly ſet on the branches, then on the ſmall red, and much about the ſame bigneſſe, or rather leſſer, of the colour of a Damſon, with an ouerſhadowing of a blewiſh colour vpon them, as the Damſon hath, before it be handled or wiped away.

The greene prickly Gooseberry is very like vnto the ordinary Gooseberry in stemme and branches, but that they are not stored with so many sharpe prickles; but the young shootes are more plentifull in small prickles about, and the greene leafe is a little smaller: the flowers are alike, and so are the berries, being of a middle size, and not very great, greene when they are thorough ripe as well as before, but mellower, and hauing a few small short prickles, like small short haires vpon them, which are harmlesse, and without danger to anie the most dainty and tender palate that is, and of a verie good pleasant taste. The seede hereof hath produced bushes bearing berries, hauing few or no prickles vpon them.

The Vse of Gooseberries.

The berries of the ordinary Gooseberries, while they are small, greene, and hard, are much vsed to bee boyled or scalded to make sawce, both for fish and flesh of diuers sorts, for the sicke sometimes as well as the sound, as also before they be neere ripe, to bake into tarts, or otherwise, after manie fashions, as the cunning of the Cooke, or the pleasure of his commanders will appoint. They are a fit dish for women with childe to stay their longings, and to procure an appetite vnto meate.

The other sorts are not vsed in Cookery that I know, but serue to bee eaten at pleasure; but in regard they are not so tart before maturity as the former, they are not put to those vses they be.

Chap. IIII.

Oxyacantha, sed potius Berberis. Barberries.

THe Barberry bush groweth oftentimes with very high stemmes, almost two mens height, but vsually somewhat lower, with manie shootes from the roote, couered with a whitish rinde or barke, and yellow vnderneath, the wood being white and pithy in the middle: the leaues are small, long, and very greene, nicked or finely dented about the edges, with three small white sharpe thornes, for the most part set together at the setting on of the leaues: the flowers doe growe vpon long clustering stalkes, small, round, and yellow, sweete in smell while they are fresh, which turne into small, long, and round berries, white at the first, and very red when they are ripe, of a sharpe sowre taste, fit to set their teeth on edge that eate them: the roote is yellow, spreading far vnder the vpper part of the ground, but not very deepe.

There is (as it is thought) another kinde, whose berries are thrice as bigge as the former, which I confesse I haue not seene, and know not whether it be true or no: for it may peraduenture be but the same, the goodnesse of the ground and ayre where they growe, and the youngnesse of the bushes causing that largenesse, as I haue obserued in the same kinde, to yeeld greater berries.

There is said to be also another kinde, whose berries should be without stones or seede within them, not differing else in anie thing from the former: but because I haue long heard of it, and cannot vnderstand by all the inquirie I haue made, that any hath seene such a fruit, I rest doubtfull of it.

The Vse of Barberries.

Some doe vse the leaues of Barberries in the stead of Sorrell, to make sawce for meate, and by reason of their sowrenesse are of the same quality.

The berries are vsed to be pickled, to serue to trimme or set out dishes of fish and flesh in broth, or otherwise, as also sometime to bee boyled in the broth, to giue it a sharpe rellish, and many other wayes, as a Master Cooke can better tell then my selfe.

The

The berries are preserued and conserued to giue to sicke bodies, to helpe to coole any heate in the stomacke or mouth, and quicken the appetite.

The depurate iuyce is a fine menstrue to dissolue many things, and to verie good purpose, if it be cunningly handled by an Artist.

The yellow inner barke of the branches, or of the rootes, are vsed to be boyled in Ale, or other drinkes, to be giuen to those that haue the yellow iaundise: As also for them that haue anie fluxes of choller, to helpe to stay and binde.

Clusius setteth downe a secret that hee had of a friend, of a cleane differing propertie, which was, that if the yellow barke were laid in steepe in white wine for the space of three houres, and afterwards drunke, it would purge one very wonderfully.

Chap. V.

Nux Auellana. The Filberd.

THe Filberd tree that is planted in Orchards, is very like vnto the Hasell nut tree that groweth wilde in the woods, growing vpright, parted into many boughes and tough plyable twigges, without knots, couered with a brownish, speckled, smooth, thinne rinde, and greene vnderneath: the leaues are broad, large, wrinkled, and full of veines, cut in on the edges into deepe dents, but not into any gashes, of a darke greene colour on the vpperside, and of a grayish ash colour vnderneath: it hath small and long catkins in stead of flowers, that come forth in the Winter, when as they are firme and close, and in the Spring open themselues somewhat more, growing longer, and of a brownish yellow colour: the nuts come not vpon those stalkes that bore those catkins, but by themselues, and are wholly inclosed in long, thicke, rough huskes, bearded as it were at the vpper ends, or cut into diuers long iagges, much more then the wood nut: the nut hath a thinne and somewhat hard shell, but not so thicke and hard as the wood nut, in some longer then in other, and in the long kinde, one hath the skinne white that couereth the kernels, and another red.

There is another sort of the round kinde that came from Constantinople, whose huske is more cut, torne, or iagged, both aboue and belowe, then any of our country; the barke also is whiter, and more rugged then ours, and the leaues somewhat larger.

We haue had from Virginia Hasell nuts, that haue beene smaller, rounder, browner, thinner sheld, and more pointed at the end then ours: I know not if any hath planted of them, or if they differ in leafe or any thing else.

The Vse of Filberds.

Filberds are eaten as the best kinde of Hasell nuts, at bankets among other dainty fruits, according to the season of the yeare, or otherwise, as euery one please: But Macer hath a Verse, expressing prettily the nature of these nuts, which is,

Ex minimis nucibus nulli datur esca salubris.

that is, There is no wholsome food or nourishment had from these small kinde of nuts.

Yet they are vsed sometime physically to be rosted, and made into a Lohoc or Electuary, that is vsed for the cough or cold. And it is thought of some, that Mithridates meant the kernels of these nuts, to be vsed with Figs and Rue for his Antidote, and not of Walnuts.

Chap. VI.

Vitis. The Vine.

THere is fo great diuerfities of Grapes, and fo confequently of Vines that bear them, that I cannot giue you names to all that here grow with vs : for Iohn Tradefcante my verie good friend, fo often before remembred, hath affured me, that he hath twentie forts growing with him, that hee neuer knew how or by what name to call them. One defcription therefore fhall ferue (as I vfe to doe in fuch varieties) for all the reft, with the names afterwards, of as many as we can giue, and the feuerall formes, colours and proportions of the grapes.

The manured Vine, in the places where it hath abiden long time, groweth to haue a great bodie, ftemme or trunke, fometimes of the bigneffe of a mans arme, fleeue and all, fpreading branches if it bee fuffered without end or meafure, but vfually ftored with many armes or branches, both old and new, but weake, and therefore muft bee fuftained ; whereof the old are couered with a thin fcaly rinde, which will often chap and peele off of it felfe ; the youngeft being of a reddifh colour, fmooth and firme, with a hollowneffe or pith in the middle : from the ioints of the young branches, and fometimes from the bodie of the elder, break out on euerie fide broade greene leaues, cut on the edges into fiue diuifions for the moft part, and befides notched or dented about : right againft the leafe, and likewife at other ioynts of the branches, come forth long twining or clafping tendrels, winding themfelues about any thing ftandeth next vnto them : at the bottome of thefe leaues come forth clufters of fmall greenifh yellow bloomes or flowers, and after them the berries, growing in the fame manner in clufters, but of diuers formes, colours, taftes and greatneffe. For fome grapes are great, others leffe, fome very fmall (as the Currans that the Grocers fell) fome white, fome red, blew, blacke, or partie-coloured, fome are are as it were fquare, others round : fome the clufters are clofe, others open, fome are fweete, others fower or harfh, or of fome other mixed tafte ; euerie one differing from others, verie notably either in tafte, colour or forme ; within euerie one of which grapes, (and yet there is a grape without ftones) are contained one, two, or more kernels or ftones, fome of them being fmal, others greater : the rootes fpread far and deepe. They that keepe their Vines in the beft order, doe cut them low, not fuffering them to grow high, or with too many branches, whereby they grow the better, take vp the leffer roome, and bring their grapes fairer and fweeter.

The kinds of Vines and Grapes.

Our ordinarie Grape both white and red, which excelleth Crabs for veriuice, and is not fit for wine with vs.

The white Mufcadine Grape is a verie great Grape, fweete and firme, fome of the bunches haue weighed fixe pound, and fome of the grapes halfe an ounce.

The redde Mufcadine is as great as the white, and chiefly differeth in colour.

The Burlet is a very great white Grape, but fitter for veriuice then wine for the moft part ; yet when a hot yeare happeneth fit for it, the Grape is pleafant.

The little blacke Grape that is ripe very early.

The Raifin of the Sunne Grape is a very great Grape, and very great clufters, of a reddifh colour when it is ripe with vs, yet in an extraordinarie hot yeare, it hath got a little blewneffe caft ouer it by the heat : but naturally verie blew.

The Curran Grape (or the Grape of Corinth) is the leaft Grape of all, and beareth both few, and verie feldome with vs, but in reafonable great clufters, and of a blackifh blew colour, when they are ripe with vs, and very

fweet

ſweete. There is another ſort of them that are red or browne, and of a ſower taſte, nothing ſo ſweete.

The Greeke wine Grape is a blackiſh Grape, and very ſweete.

The Frontignack is a white Grape, of a verie ſweete and delicate taſte, as the wine declareth, that ſmelleth as it were of Muske.

The ſquare Grape is reported to beare a Grape not fully round, but ſided, or as it were ſquare, whereby it became ſo called.

The Damaſco Grape is a great white grape, very ſweete, and is the true *Vvs Zibeba,* that the Apothecaries ſhould vſe in the *Trochiſc: Ciphi:* and ſuch wee haue had in former times come ouer vnto vs in great, long and round white boxes, containing halfe an hundred weight a peece.

The Ruſſet Grape is a reaſonable faire grape, exceeding ſweet and whitiſh, with a thicke skinne, cruſted ouer with a ſhew of aſh colour.

The white long Grape is like vnto a Pigeons egge, or as it were pointed pendent like a Pearle.

The partie-coloured Grape is a reaſonable great Grape, and diſcoloured when it is ripe, ſometimes the whole bunches, and ſometimes but ſome of the grapes being parted whitiſh, and blacke halfe through, verie variably.

The Rheniſh wine Grape is a white Grape, and endureth the cold of winter when it commeth earely, more then the Muſcadine before ſet downe, and is nothing ſo ſweete.

The White wine Grape is verie like vnto the Rhine Grape, the ſoile only and climate adding more ſweetneſſe vnto the one then to the other.

The Claret wine Grape is altogether like the white Grape, but that it is not white, but of a reddiſh colour, which lying bruiſed vpon the skins before they are preſſed, giue that Claret tincture to the wine.

The Teint is a Grape of a deeper or darker colour, whoſe iuice is of ſo deepe a colour, that it ſerueth to colour other wine.

The Burſarobe is a faire ſweete white Grape of much eſteeme about Paris.

The Alligant is a verie ſweete Grape, giuing ſo deep and liuely a coloured red wine, that no other whatſoeuer is comparable to it, and therfore vſually called Spaniards blood.

The blew or blacke Grape of Orleans is another blacke Grape, giuing a darke coloured ſweete wine much commended in thoſe parts.

The Grape without ſtones is alſo a kinde by it ſelfe, and groweth naturally neere Aſcalon, as Brochard affirmeth, the wine whereof is redde, and of a good taſte.

The Virginia Vine, whereof I muſt needes make mention among other Vines, beareth ſmall Grapes without any great ſtore of iuice therein, and the ſtone within it bigger then in any other Grape: naturally it runneth on the ground, and beareth little.

The Vſe of Vines, Grapes, and other parts that come of them.

The greene leaues of the Vine are cooling and binding, and therefore good to put among other herbes that make gargles and lotions for ſore mouthes.

And alſo to put into the broths and drinke of thoſe that haue hot burning feauers, or any other inflammation.

They may (as it is held for true) womens longings, if they be either taken inwardly, or applyed outwardly.

Wine is vſually taken both for drinke and medicine, and is often put into ſawces, broths, cawdles, and gellies that are giuen to the ſicke. As alſo into diuers Phyſicall drinkes, to be as a *vehiculum* for the properties of the ingredients.

It is diſtilled likewiſe after diuers manners, with diuers things, for diuers & ſundry waters to drinke, & for diuers purpoſes both inward and outward.

As

1 *Vuæ nigræ minores.* The small blacke Grape. 2 *Vuæ cæruleæ maiores.* The great blew Grape. 3 *Vuæ Moschatellinæ.* The Muscadine Grape. 4 *Vuæ Buratenses.* The Burlet Grape. 5 *Vuæ insolatæ.* The Raysins of the sunne Grape. 6 *Ficus.* The Figge tree.

Also diſtilled of it ſelfe, is called Spirit of wine, which ſerueth to diſſolue, and to draw out the tincture of diuers things, and for many other purpoſes.

The iuice or veriuice that is made of greene hard grapes, before they be ripe, is vſed of the Apothecaries to be made into a Syrupe, that is very good to coole and refreſh a faint ſtomacke.

And being made of the riper grapes is the beſt veriuice, farre exceeding that which is made of crabs, to be kept all the yeare, to be put both into meates and medicines.

The grapes of the beſt ſorts of Vines are preſſed into wine by ſome in theſe dayes with vs, and much more as I verily beleeue in times paſt, as by the name of Vineyard giuen to many places in this Kingdome, eſpecially where Abbies and Monaſteries ſtood, may bee coniectured: but the wine of late made hath beene but ſmall, and not durable, like that which commeth from beyond Sea, whether our vnkindly yeares, or the want of skill, or a conuenient place for a Vineyard be the cauſe, I cannot well tell you.

Grapes of all ſorts are familiarly eaten when they are ripe, of the ſicke ſometimes as well as the ſound.

The dryed grapes which we call great Rayſins, and the Currans which we call ſmall Rayſins, are much vſed both for meates, broths, and ſawces, in diuers manners, as this Countrey in generall aboue any other, wherein many thouſands of Frailes full, Pipes, Hogs-heads, and Buts full are ſpent yearly, that it breedeth a wonder in them of thoſe parts where they growe and prouide them, how we could ſpend ſo many.

The Rayſins of the Sunne are the beſt dryed grapes, next vnto the Damaſco, and are very wholſome to eate faſting, both to nouriſh, and to helpe to looſen the belly.

The dryed Lees of wine called Argoll or Tartar, is put to the vſe of the Goldſmith, Dyer, and Apothecary, who doe all vſe it in ſeuerall manners, uery one in his art.

Of it the Apothecaries make *Cremor Tartari,* a fine medicine to bee vſed, as the Phyſitian can beſt appoint, and doth helpe to purge humours by the ſtoole.

Thereof likewiſe they make a kinde of water or oyle, fit to bee vſed, to take away freckles, ſpots, or any ſuch deformities of the face or skinne, and to make it ſmooth. It cauſeth likewiſe haire to growe more aboundantly in thoſe places where it naturally ſhould growe.

The liquor of the Vine that runneth forth when it is cut, is commended to be good againſt the ſtone whereſoeuer it be; but that liquor that is taken from the end of the branches when they are burnt, is moſt effectuall to take away ſpots and markes, ring-wormes and tetters in any place.

Chap. VII.

Ficus. The Figge tree.

THe Figge trees that are nourſed vp in our country are of three ſorts, whereof two are high; the one bearing againſt a wall goodly ſweete and delicate Figs, called Figs of Algarua, and is blewiſh when it is ripe: the other tall kinde is nothing ſo good, neither doth beare ripe Figges ſo kindly and well, and peraduenture may be the white ordinary kinde that commeth from Spaine. The third is a dwarfe kinde of Figge tree, not growing much higher then to a mans body or ſhoulders, bearing excellent good Figges and blew, but not ſo large as the firſt kinde.

The Figge trees of all theſe three kindes are in leaues and growing one like vnto another, ſauing for their height, colour, and ſweetneſſe of the fruit, hauing many armes or branches, hollow or pithy in the middle, bearing very large leaues, and ſomewhat thicke, diuided ſometimes into three, but vſually into fiue ſections, of a darke greene colour on the vpperſide, and whitiſh vnderneath, yeelding a milkie iuyce when it is broken,

broken, as the branches also or the figges when they are greene : the fruit breaketh out from the branches without anie bloſſome, contrary to all other trees of our Orchard, being round and long, faſhioned very like vnto a ſmall Peare, full of ſmall white grains or kernels within it, of a very ſweete taſte when it is ripe, and very mellow or ſoft, that it can hardly be carried farre without bruiſing.

The other two ſorts you may eaſily know and vnderſtand, by ſo much as hath been ſaid of them. Take only this more of the Figge tree, That if you plant it not againſt a bricke wall, or the wall of an houſe, &c. it will not ripen ſo kindly. The dwarfe Figge tree is more tender, and is therefore planted in great ſquare tubs, to be remoued into the ſunne in the Summer time, and into the houſe in Winter.

The Vſe of Figges.

Figges are ſerued to the table with Rayſins of the Sunne, and blanched Almonds, for a Lenten diſh.

The Figs that growe with vs when they are ripe, and freſh gathered, are eaten of diuers with a little ſalt and pepper, as a dainty banquet to entertaine a freind, which ſeldome paſſeth without a cup of wine to waſh them downe.

In Italy (as I haue beene enformed by diuers Gentlemen that haue liued there to ſtudy phyſicke) they eate them in the ſame manner, but dare not eate many for feare of a feuer to follow, they doe account them to be ſuch breeders of bloud, and heaters of it likewiſe.

The Figges that are brought vs from Spaine, are vſed to make Ptiſan drinkes, and diuers other things, that are giuen them that haue coughes or colds.

It is one of the ingredients alſo with Nuts and Rice, into Mithridates counterpoiſon.

The ſmall Figges that growe with vs, and will not ripen, are preſerued by the Comfitmakers, and candid alſo, to ſerue as other moiſt or candid banquetting ſtuffe.

Chap. VIII.

Sorbus. The Seruice tree.

THere are two kindes of Seruice trees that are planted in Orchards with vs, and there is alſo a wilde kinde like vnto the later of them, with Aſhen leaues, found in the woods growing of it ſelfe, whoſe fruit is not gathered, nor vſed to bee eaten of any but birds. And there is another kinde alſo growing wilde abroad in many places, taken by the Country people where it groweth, to be a Seruice tree, and is called in Latine, *Aria Theophraſti,* whoſe leaues are large, ſomewhat like Nut tree leaues, but greene aboue, and grayiſh vnderneath : ſome doe vſe the fruit as Seruices, and for the ſame purpoſes to good effect, yet both of theſe wilde kindes wee leaue for another worke, and here declare vnto you onely thoſe two ſorts are nourſed vp in our Orchards.

The more common or ordinary Seruice tree with vs, is a reaſonable great tree, couered with a ſmooth barke, ſpread into many great armes, whereon are ſet large leaues, very much cut in on the edges, almoſt like vnto a Vine leafe, or rather like vnto that kind of Maple, that is vſually called the Sycomore tree with vs : the flowers are white, and growe many cluſtering together, which after bring forth ſmall browne berries when they are ripe, of the bigneſſe almoſt of Haſell nuts, with a ſmall tuft, as if it were a crowne on the head, wherein are ſmall blacke kernels.

The other kinde, which is more rare with vs, and brought into this Land by Iohn Tradeſcante, heretofore often remembred, hath diuers winged leaues, many ſet together like vnto an Aſhen leafe, but ſmaller, and euery one endented about the edges : the flowers growe in long cluſters, but nothing ſo many, or ſo cloſe ſet as the wilde kinde : the fruit of this tree is in ſome round like an Apple, and in others a little longer

like

like a Peare, but of a more pleafant tafte then the ordinarie kinde, when they are ripe and mellowed, as they vfe to doe with both thefe kindes, and with Medlars.

The Vfe of Seruices.

They are gathered when they growe to be neare ripe (and that is neuer before they haue felt fome frofts) and being tyed together, are either hung vp in fome warme roome, to ripen them thoroughly, that they may bee eaten, or (as fome vfe to doe) lay them in ftrawe, chaffe, or branne, to ripen them.

They are binding, fit to be taken of them that haue any fcouring or laske, to helpe to ftay the fluxe; but take heed, left if you binde too much, more paine and danger may come thereof then of the fcouring.

Chap. IX.

Mefpilus. The Medlar tree.

THere are three forts of Medlers: The greater and the leffer Englifh, and the Neapolitan.

The great and the fmall Englifh Medlar differ not one from the other in any thing, but in the fize of the fruit, except that the fmall kinde hath fome prickes or thornes vpon it, which the great one hath not, bearing diuers boughes or armes, from whence breake forth diuers branches, whereon are fet long and fomewhat narrow leaues, many ftanding together; in the middle whereof, at the end of the branch, commeth the flower, which is great and white, made of fiue leaues, broad at the ends, with a nicke in the middle of euery one; after which commeth the fruit, being round, and of a pale brownifh colour, bearing a crowne of thofe fmall leaues at the toppe, which were the huske of the flower before, the middle thereof being fomewhat hollow, and is harfh, able to choake any that fhall eate it before it be made mellow, wherein there are certaine flat and hard kernels.

The Medlar of Naples groweth likewife to bee a reafonable great tree, fpreading forth armes and branches, whereon are fet many gafhed leaues, fomewhat like vnto Hawthorne leaues, but greater, and likewife diuers thornes in many places: the flowers are of an herbie greene colour, and fmall, which turne into fmaller fruit then the former, and rounder alfo, but with a fmall head or crowne at the toppe like vnto it, and is of a more fweete and pleafant tafte then the other, with three feeds only therein ordinarily.

The Vfe of Medlars.

Medlars are vfed in the fame manner that Seruices are, that is, to be eaten when they are mellowed, and are for the fame purpofes to binde the body when there is a caufe: yet they as well as the Seruices, are often eaten by them that haue no neede of binding, and but onely for the pleafant fweetneffe of them when they are made mellow, and fometimes come as a difh of ripe fruit at their fit feafon, to be ferued with other forts to the table.

Chap. X.

Lotus. The Lote or Nettle tree.

THe firft kinde of Lote tree, whereof Diofcorides maketh mention, is but of one kinde; but there are fome other trees fpoken of by Theophraftus, that may be referred thereunto, which may bee accounted as baftard kindes thereof, of which I meane to entreate in this Chapter, hauing giuen you before the defcription

of

1 *Sorbus legitima.* The true Seruice tree. 2 *Sorbus vulgaris siue Torminalis.* The ordinary Seruice tree. 3 *Mespilus vulgaris.* The common Mespilus tree. 4 *Mespilus Aronia.* The Medlar of Naples. 5 *Lotus arbor.* The Nettle tree. 6 *Lotus Virginiana.* The Pishamin or Virginia Plumme. 7 *Cornus mas.* The Cornell Cherry tree.

Bbb 3

of another kinde hereof (by the opinion of good Authors) vnder the name of *Lauro-cerasus.*

The first or true Lote tree groweth to be a tree of a great height, whose bodie and elder branches are couered with a smooth darke greene barke, the leaues are somewhat rough in handling, of a darke greene colour, long pointed, and somewhat deepe dented about the edges, somewhat like vnto a Nettle leafe, and oftentimes growe yellow toward Autumne : the flowers stand here and there scattered vpon the branches; after which come round berries like vnto Cherries, hanging downewards vpon long foot-stalkes, greene at the first, and whitish afterwards; but when they are ripe they become reddish, and if they be suffered to hang too long on the branches, they grow blackish, of a pleasant austere taste, not to be misliked, wherein is a hard round stone.

The second, which is a bastard kinde, and called *Guaiacum Patauinum*, groweth to bee a faire tree, with a smooth darke greene barke, shooting out many faire great boughes, and also slender greene branches, beset with faire broad greene leaues, almost like vnto the leaues of the Cornell tree, but larger : the flowers growe along the branches close vnto them, without any or with a very short foote-stalke consisting of foure greene leaues, which are as the huske, containing within it a purplish flower, made of foure leaues somewhat reddish : the fruit standeth in the middle of the green huske, greene at the first, and very harsh, but red and round when it is ripe, and somewhat like a Plumme, with a small point or pricke at the head thereof, and of a reasonable pleasant taste or rellish, wherein are contained flat and thicke browne seeds or kernels, like vnto the kernels of *Cassia Fistula*, somewhat hard, and not so stonie, but that it may somewhat easily be cut with a knife.

The third is called in Virginia *Pishamin*, The Virginia Plumme (if it be not all one with the former Guaiacana, whereof I am more then halfe perswaded) hath growne with vs of the kernels that were sent out of Virginia, into great trees, whose wood is very hard and brittle, and somewhat white withall : the branches are many, and grow slender to the end, couered with a very thinne greenish bark, whereon doe grow many faire broad greene leaues, without dent or notch on the edges, and so like vnto the former *Guaiacum*, that I verily thinke it (as I before said) to bee the same. It hath not yet borne flower or fruit in our Countrey that I can vnderstand : but the fruit, as it was sent to vs, is in forme and bignesse like vnto a Date, couered with a blackish skinne, set in a huske of foure hard leaues, very firme like vnto a Date, and almost as sweete, with great flat and thicke kernels within them, very like vnto the former, but larger.

The Vse of these Lote trees.

The first sort is eaten as an helper to coole and binde the body : the last, as Captaine Smith relateth in the discouery of Virginia, if the fruit be eaten while it is greene, and not ripe, is able by the harsh and binding taste and quality to draw ones mouth awry (euen as it is said of the former Guaiacana) but when it is thorough ripe it is pleasant, as I said before.

Chap. XI.

Cornus mas. The Cornell tree.

THe Cornell tree that is planted in Orchards, being the male (for the female is an hedge bush) is of two sorts, the one bearing red, the other whiter berries, which is very rare yet in our country, and not differing else.

It groweth to a reasonable bignesse and height, yet neuer to any great tree, the wood whereof is very hard, like vnto horne, and thereof it obtained the name : the body and branches are couered with a rugged barke, and spreadeth reasonable well, hauing somewhat smooth leaues, full of veines, plaine, and not dented on the edges: the flowers are many small yellow tufts, as it were of short haires or threads set together, which come forth before any leafe, and fall away likewise before any leafe bee much open : the fruit are long and round berries, of the bignesse of small Oliues, with an

hard

hard round ſtone within them, like vnto an Oliue ſtone, and are of a yellowiſh red when they are ripe, of a reaſonable pleaſant taſte, yet ſomewhat auſtere withall.

The white (as I ſaid) is like vnto the red, but onely that his fruit is more white when it is ripe.

The Vſe of the Cornelles.

They helpe to binde the body, and to ſtay laskes, and by reaſon of the pleaſantneſſe in them when they are ripe, they are much deſired.

They are alſo preſerued and eaten, both for rarity and delight, and for the purpoſe aforeſaid.

Chap. XII.

Ceraſus. The Cherry tree.

THere are ſo many varieties and differences of Cherries, that I know not well how to expreſſe them vnto you, without a large relation of their ſeuerall formes. I will therefore endeauour after one generall deſcription (as my cuſtome is in many other the like variable fruits) to giue as briefe and ſhort notes vpon all the reſt, as I can both for leafe and fruit, that ſo you may the better know what the fruit is, when you haue the name.

The Engliſh Cherrie tree groweth in time to be of a reaſonable bigneſſe and height, ſpreading great armes, and alſo ſmall twiggy branches plentifully ; the leaues whereof are not verie large or long, but nicked or dented about the edges : the flowers come forth two or three or foure at the moſt together, at a knot or ioynt, euerie one by it ſelfe, vpon his owne ſmall and long footeſtalke, conſiſting of fiue white leaues, with ſome threds in the middle ; after which come round berries, greene at the firſt, and red when they are through ripe, of a meane bigneſſe, and of a pleaſant ſweete taſte, ſomewhat tart withall, with a hard white ſtone within it, whoſe kernell is ſomewhat bitter, but not vnpleaſant.

The Flanders Cherrie differeth not from the Engliſh, but that it is ſomewhat larger, and the Cherry ſomewhat greater and ſweeter, and not ſo ſower.

The early Flanders Cherry is more rathe or early ripe, almoſt as ſoone as the May Cherry, eſpecially planted againſt a wall, and of many falſe knaues or Gardiners are ſold for May Cherrie trees.

The May Cherrie in a ſtandard beareth ripe fruite later then planted againſt a wall, where the berries will be red in the verie beginning of May ſometimes.

The Arch-Dukes Cherrie is one of the faireſt and beſt cherries wee haue, being of a very red colour when it is ripe, and a little long more then round, and ſomewhat pointed at the end, of the beſt relliſh of any Cherrie whatſoeuer, and of a firme ſubſtance; ſcarce one of twentie of our Nurſerie men doe ſell the right, but giue one for another: for it is an inherent qualitie almoſt hereditarie with moſt of them, to ſell any man an ordinary fruit for whatſoeuer rare fruit he ſhall aske for : ſo little they are to be truſted.

The ounce Cherrie hath the greateſt and broadeſt leafe of any other cherrie, but beareth the ſmalleſt ſtore of cherries euerie yeare that any doth, and yet bloſſometh well : the fruit alſo is nothing anſwerable to the name being not verie great, of a pale yellowiſh red, neere the colour of Amber, and therefore ſome haue called it, the Amber Cherrie.

The great leafed Cherrie is thought of diuers to bee the Ounce Cherrie, becauſe it hath almoſt as great a leafe as the former : but the fruit of this alſo doth not anſwer the expectation of ſo great a leafe, being but of a meane bigneſſe, and a ſmall bearer, yet of a pale reddiſh colour.

The true Gaſcoign Cherry is known but to a few; for our Nurſery men do ſo change the names of moſt fruits they ſell, that they deliuer but very few true names to any : In former times before our wilde blacke Cherrie was found to grow plentifully in our owne woods in many places of this Land, the French continually ſtored vs with wilde ſtockes to graft vpon, which then were called Gaſcoigne ſtocks, but ſince they haue ſo

termed

termed another red Cherrie, and obtruded it vpon their cuftomers: but the true is one of our late ripe white Cherries, euen as Gerard faith, it is a great cherrie and fpotted: and this is that Cherrie I fo commend to be a fit ftocke to graft May cherries vpon.

The Morello Cherrie is of a reafonable bigneffe, of a darke red colour when they are full ripe, and hang long on, of a fweetifh fower tafte, the pulpe or fubftance is red, and fomewhat firme : if they be dryed they will haue a fine fharpe or fower tafte very delectable.

The Hartlippe Cherrie is fo called of the place where the beft of this kinde is nourfed vp, being betweene Sittingbourne and Chattam in Kent, and is the biggeft of our Englifh kindes.

The fmaller Lacure or Hart Cherrie is a reafonable faire Cherrie, full aboue, and a little pointing downward, after the fashion of an heart, as it is vfually painted, blackifh when it is full ripe, and leffer then the next.

The great Lacure or Hart Cherrie differeth not in forme, but in greatneffe, being vfually twice as great as the former, and of a reddifh blacke colour alfo : both of them are of a firme fubftance, and reafonable fweete. Some doe call the white cherrie, the White hart cherrie.

The Luke Wardes Cherrie hath a reafonable large leafe, and a larger flower then many other : the cherries grow with long ftalkes, and a ftone of a meane fize within them, of a darke reddifh colour when they are full ripe, of a reafonable good rellifh, and beareth well.

The Corone Cherrie hath a leafe little differing from the Luke Wardes cherrie, the fruit when it is ripe, is of a faire deepe red colour, of a good bigneffe, and of a verie good tafte, neither verie fweete or fower: the pulpe or iuice will ftaine the hands.

The Vrinall Cherrie in a moft fruitfull yeare is a fmall bearer, hauing many yeares none, and the beft but a few ; yet doth bloffome plentifully euery yeare for the moft part : the cherrie is long and round, like vnto an Vrinall, from whence it tooke his name ; reddifh when it is full ripe, and of an indifferent fweete rellifh.

The Agriot Cherrie is but a fmall Cherrie, of a deepe redde colour when it is ripe, which is late ; of a fine fharpe tafte, moft pleafant and wholfome to the ftomacke of all other cherries, as well while they are frefh as being dryed, which manner they much vfe in France, and keepe them for the vfe both of the ficke and found at all times.

The Biguarre Cherrie is a fair cherrie, much fpotted with white fpots vpon the pale red berry, and fometimes difcoloured halfe white and halfe reddifh, of a reafonable good rellifh.

The Morocco Cherrie hath a large white bloffome, and an indifferent big berrie, long and round, with a long ftalke of a darke reddifh purple colour, a little tending to a blew when it is full ripe, of a firme fubftance : the iuice is of a blackifh red, difcolouring the hands or lips, and of a pleafant tafte : Some doe thinke that this and the Morello be both one.

The Naples Cherrie is alfo thought to bee all one with the Morello or Morocco.

The white Spanifh Cherrie is an indifferent good bearer, the leafe and bloffome fomewhat large, and like the Luke Wardes cherrie : the cherries are reafonable faire berries, with long ftalkes and great ftones, white on the outfide, with fome redneffe, on the one fide of a firme fubftance, and reafonable fweet, but with a little aciditie, and is one of the late ripe ones : But there is another late ripe white Cherry, which fome call the Gafcoigne, before remembred.

The Flanders clufter Cherrie is of two forts, one greater then another : the greater kinde hath an indifferent large leafe ; the bloffomes haue many threds within them, fhewing as it were many parts, which after turne into clufters of berries, foure, fiue or fixe together, and but with one ftalke vnder them, as if they grew one out of another, and fometimes they will beare but two or three, and moft of them but one cherry on a ftalke, which are red when they are ripe, very tender, and waterifh fweete in eating.

The leffer is in all things like the greater, but fmaller, which maketh the difference.

The wilde clufter or birds clufter Cherry beareth many bloffomes fet all along the ftalkes, and cherries after them in the fame maner, like a long thinne bunch of grapes, and therefore called of fome the Grape cherry : there are of them both red and blacke.

The

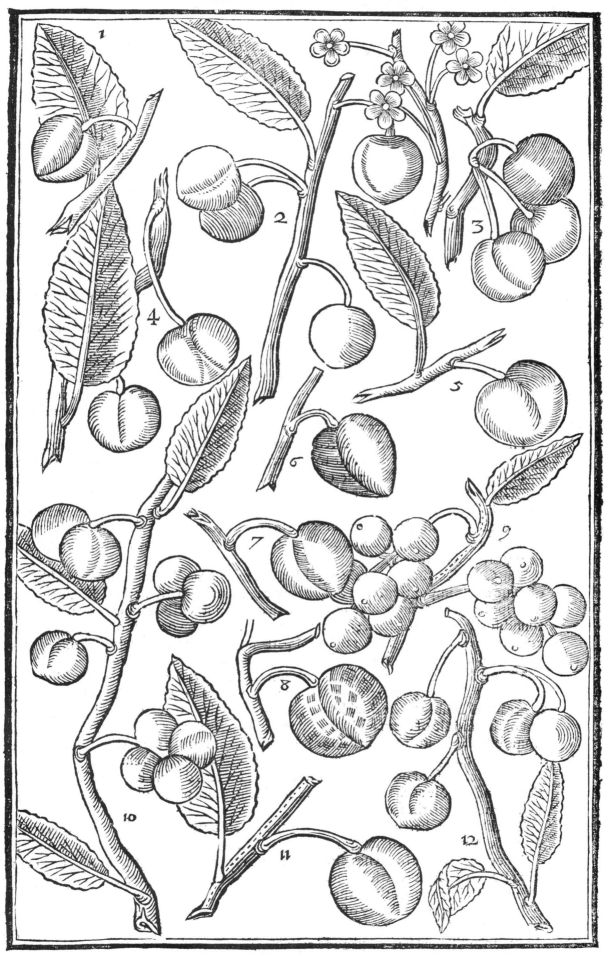

1 *Cerasus præcox.* The May Cherry. 2 *Cerasus Batauica.* The Flanders Cherry. 3 *Cerasus Hispanica siue alba.* The white Cherry. 4 *Cerasus plate-phyllos.* The great leafed Cherry. 5 *Cerasus Luca Wardi.* Luke Wards Cherry. 6 *Cerasus Neapolitana.* The Naples Cherry. 7 *Cerasus Cordata.* The Heart Cherry. 8 *Cerasus maculata.* The bignarre or spotted Cherry. 9 *Cerasus auium racemosa.* The wilde cluster Cherry. 10 *Cerasus Corymbifera.* The Flanders cluster Cherry. 11 *Cerasus Archiducis.* The Archdukes Cherry. 12 *Chamæcerasus.* The dwarfe Cherry.

The soft sheld Cherrie is a small red cherrie when it is ripe, hauing the stone within it so soft and tender, that it may easily be broken in the eating of the cherrie.

Iohn Tradescantes Cherrie is most vsually sold by our Nursery Gardiners, for the Archdukes cherrie, because they haue more plenty thereof, and will better be increased, and because it is so faire and good a cherrie that it may be obtruded without much discontent : it is a reasonable good bearer, a faire great berrie, deepe coloured, and a little pointed.

The Baccalaos or New-found-land Cherrie hath a shining long leafe, most like vnto a Peach leafe, the blossomes come very many together as it were in an vmbell, which is such a cluster as is neither like the Flanders cluster, nor the wilde cluster cherrie blossome : it bringeth forth berries standing in the same manner euerie one vpon his own footestalke, being no bigger then the largest berrie of the red Curran tree or bush, of a pale or waterish red colour when it is ripe.

The strange long cluster Cherrie, or *Padus Theophrasti Dalechampio* is reckoned by the Author of that great Herball that goeth vnder his name, among the sorts of cherries ; and so must I vntill a fitter place be found for it. It groweth in time to be a great tree, with a sad coloured barke both on the bodie and branches, whereon doe grow many leaues, somewhat broade, shorter, harder, and a little more crumpled then any cherrie leafe : the blossomes are very small, and of a pale or whitish colour, smelling very sweete and strong, or rather heady, like Orenge flowers, growing on small long branches, very like the toppe of flowers vpon the Laburnum or Beane trefoile trees : after which come small blacke berries, growing together all along the long stalke, like vnto the wilde cluster or birds cherrie mentioned before, but not much bigger then tares, with small stones within them, and little or no sustance vpon them : the French call the tree *Putier*, because the wood thereof stinketh, and make it to be wonderfull that the blossomes of the tree should be so sweete, and the wood so stinking.

The Cullen Cherrie is a darke red cherrie like the Agriot, which they of those parts neere Cullen and Vtrecht &c. vse to put into their drinke, to giue it the deeper colour.

The great Hungarian Cherrie of Zwerts is like both in leafe and fruite vnto the Morello cherrie, but much greater and fairer, and a far better bearer : for from a small branch hath beene gathered a pound of cherries, and this is vsuall continually, and not accidentally, most of them foure inches in compasse about, and very many of them more of a faire deepe red colour, and very sweete, excelling the Arch-Dukes cherry, or any other whatsoeuer.

The Cameleon or strange changeable Cherry deseruedly hath this name, although of mine owne imposition, not only because it beareth vsually both blossomes, greene and ripe fruit at one time thereupon, but that the fruit will be of many formes ; some round, some as it were square, and some bunched forth on one side or another, abiding constant in no fashion, but for the most part shewing forth all these diuersities euerie yeare growing vpon it : the fruit is of a very red colour, and good taste.

The great Rose Cherry, or double blossomd Cherry differeth not in any thing from the English Cherrie, but only in the blossomes, which are very thicke of white leaues, as great and double as the double white Crowfoote, before remembred, and somtimes out of the middle of them will spring another smaller flower, but double also ; this seldome beareth fruit, but when it doth I suppose it commeth from those blossomes are the least double, and is red, no bigger then our ordinary English cherrie.

The lesser Rose or double blossomd Cherrie beareth double flowers also, but not so thicke and double as the former ; but beareth fruit more plentifully, of the same colour and bignesse with the former.

The Dwarfe Cherrie is of two sorts ; one whose branches fall downe low, round about the body of it, with small greene leaues, and fruit as small, of a deep red colour.

The other, whose branches, although small, grow more vpright, hauing greener shining leaues : the fruit is little bigger then the former, red also when it is ripe, with a little point at the end : both of them of a sweetish rellish, but more sower.

The great bearing Cherry of Master Millen is a reasonable great red cherry, bearing very plentifully, although it bee planted against a North wall, yet it will bee late ripe, but of an indifferent sweet and good rellish.

The long finger Cherry is another small long red one, being long & round like a finger, wherof it took the name : this is not the Vrinall cherry before, but differing from it.

The

The Vſe of Cherries.

All theſe ſorts of Cherries ſerue wholly to pleaſe the palate, and are eaten at all times, both before and after meales.

All Cherries are cold, yet the ſower more then the ſweete; and although the ſweete doe moſt pleaſe, yet the ſower are more wholſome, if there bee regard taken in the vſing.

The Agriot or ſower Cherries are in France much vſed to bee dryed (as is ſaid before) as Pruines are, and ſo ſerue to miniſtred to be the ſick in all hot diſeaſes, as feuers &c. being both boyled in their drinkes, and taken now and then of themſelues, which by reaſon of their tartneſſe, doe pleaſe the ſtomacke paſſing well.

The Gum of the Cherrie tree is commended to bee good for thoſe are troubled with the grauell or ſtone. It is alſo good for the cough being diſſolued in liquour, and ſtirreth vp an appetite. The diſtilled water of the blacke Cherries, the ſtones being broken among them, is vſed for the ſame purpoſe, for the grauell, ſtone, and winde.

Chap. XIII.

Prunus. The Plumme tree.

THere are many more varieties of Plummes then of Cherries, ſo that I muſt follow the ſame order with theſe that I did with them, euen giue you their names apart, with briefe notes vpon them, and one deſcription to ſerue for all the reſt. And in this recitall I ſhall leaue out the Apricockes which are certainly a kind of Plum, of an eſpeciall difference, and not of a Peach, as Galen and ſome others haue thought, and ſet them in a chapter by themſelues, and only in this ſet down thoſe fruits are vſually called Plums.

The Plum tree (eſpecially diuers of them) riſeth in time to bee a reaſonable tall and great tree, whoſe bodie and greater armes are couered with a more rugged barke, yet in ſome more or leſſe, the younger branches being ſmooth in all, the leaues are ſomewhat rounder then thoſe of the Cherrie tree, and much differing among themſelues, ſome being longer, or larger, or rounder then others, and many that are exerciſed herein, can tell by the leafe what Plum the tree beareth (I ſpeake this of many, not of all) as in many Cherries they can doe the like: the flowers are white, conſiſting of fiue leaues: the fruit is as variable in forme, as in taſte or colour, ſome being ovall, or Peare faſhion or Almond like, or ſphericall or round, ſome firme, ſome ſoft and wateriſh, ſome ſweete, ſome ſower or harſh, or differing from all theſe taſtes: and ſome white, others blacke, ſome red, others yellow, ſome purple, others blew, as they ſhall bee briefly ſet downe vnto you in the following lines, where I meane not to inſert any the wilde or hedge fruit, but thoſe only are fit for an Orchard, to be ſtored with good fruit: and of all which ſorts, the choyſeſt for goodneſſe, and rareſt for knowledge, are to be had of my very good friend Maſter Iohn Tradeſcante, who hath wonderfully laboured to obtaine all the rareſt fruits hee can heare off in any place of Chriſtendome, Turky, yea or the whole world; as alſo with Maſter Iohn Millen, dwelling in Olde ſtreete, who from Iohn Tradeſcante and all others that haue had good fruit, hath ſtored himſelfe with the beſt only, and he can ſufficiently furniſh any.

The Amber Primordian Plumme is an indifferent faire Plumme, early ripe, of a pale yellowiſh colour, and of a wateriſh taſte, not pleaſing.

The red Primordian Plumme is of a reaſonable ſize, long and round, reddiſh on the outſide, of a more dry taſte, and ripe with the firſt ſorts in the beginning of Auguſt.

The blew Primordian is a ſmall plumme, almoſt like the Damaſcene, and is ſubiect to drop off from the tree before it be ripe.

The white Date Plum is no very good plum.

The

The red Date plumme is a great long red pointed plumme, and late ripe, little better then the white.

The blacke Muffell plumme is a good plumme, reafonable drye, and tafteth well.

The red Muffell Plumme is fomewhat flat as well as round, of a very good tafte, and is ripe about the middle of Auguft.

The white Muffell plumme is like the redde, but fomewhat fmaller, and of a whitifh greene colour, but not fo well tafted.

The Imperiall plum is a great long reddifh plum, very waterifh, and ripeneth fomewhat late.

The Gaunt plum is a great round reddifh plum, ripe fomewhat late, and eateth waterifh.

The red Pefcod plum is a reafonable good plum.

The white Pefcod plum is a reafonable good rellifhed plumme, but fomewhat waterifh.

The greene Pefcod plum is a reafonable big and long pointed plum, and ripe in the beginning of September.

The Orenge plum is a yellowifh plum, moift, and fomewhat fweetifh.

The Morocco plumme is blacke like a Damfon, well tafted, and fomewhat drye in eating.

The Dine plum is a late ripe plum, great and whitifh, fpeckled all ouer.

The Turkie plum is a large long blackifh plum, and fomewhat flat like the Muffell plum, a well rellifhed dry plum.

The Nutmeg plumme is no bigger then a Damfon, and is of a greenifh yellow colour when it is ripe, which is with vs about Bartholmew tide, and is a good plum.

The Perdigon plumme is a dainty good plumme, early blackifh, and well rellifhed.

The Verdoch plum is a great fine greene fhining plum fit to preferue.

The Ienua plum is the white Date plum, before remembred.

The Barberry plum is a great early blacke plum, and well tafted.

The Pruneola plum is a fmall white plum, of a fine tart tafte : it was wont to bee vfually brought ouer in fmall round boxes, and fold moft commonly at the Comfitmakers, (cut in twaine, the ftone caft away) at a very deere rate: the tree groweth and beareth well with vs.

The Shepway Bulleis is of a darke blewifh brown colour, of a larger fize then the ordinary, and of a fharpe tafte, but not fo good as the common.

The white and the blacke Bulleis are common in moft Countries, being fmall round plums, leffer then Damfons, fharper in tafte, and later ripe.

The Flufhing Bulleis groweth with his fruite thicke cluftring together like grapes.

The Winter Creke is the lateft ripe plum of all forts, it groweth plentifully about Bifhops Hatfield.

The white Peare plum early ripe, is of a pale yellowifh greene colour.

The late ripe white Peare plum is a greater and longer plum, greenifh white, and is not ripe vntill it be neere the end of September, both waterifh plums.

The blacke Peare plum is like vnto the white Peare plumme, but that the colour is blackifh when it is ripe, and is of a very good rellifh, more firme and drye then the other.

The red Peare plumme is of the fame fafhion and goodneffe, but is the worft of the three.

The white Wheate plum is a waterifh fulfome plum.

The red Wheate plum is like the other for tafte.

The Bowle plum is flat and round, yet flatter on the one fide then on the other, which caufed the name, and is a very good rellifhed blacke plum.

The Friars plumme is a very good plum, well tafted, and comming cleane from the ftone, being blacke when it is ripe, and fome whitifh fpots vpon it.

The Catalonia plum is a very good plum.

The don Alteza is alfo a very good plum.

The Mufcadine plum, fome call the Queene mother plumme, and fome the Cherry plum, is a faire red plum, of a reafonable bigneffe, and ripe about Bartholmew tide.

The Chriftian plum, called alfo the Nutmeg plum ; the tree groweth very fhrubby,

and

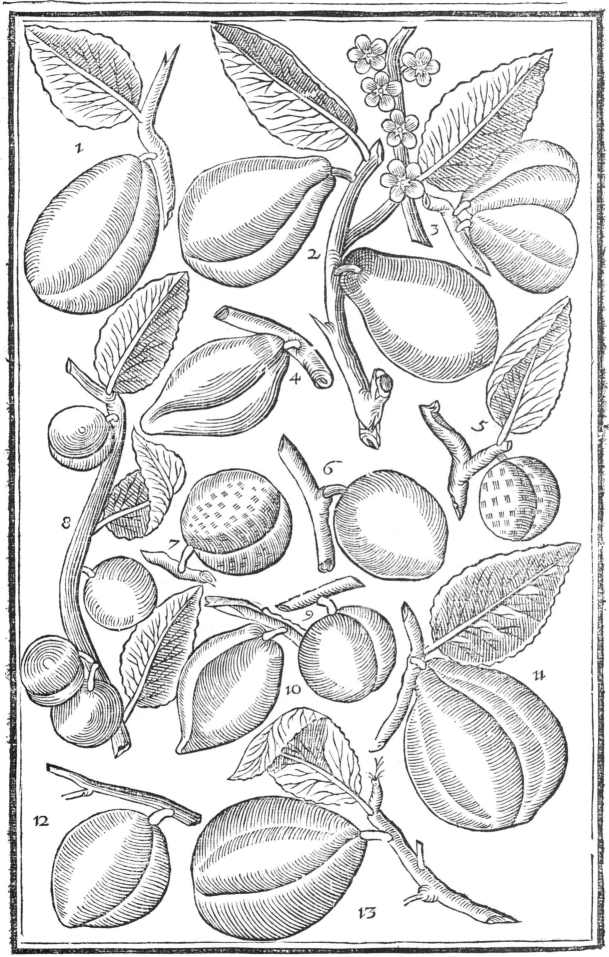

1 *Prunum Imperiale.* The Imperiall Plum. 2 *Prunum Turcicum.* The Turkey Plum. 3 *Prunum præcox rubrum.* The red Primordian Plum. 4 *Prunum Mytellinum.* The Mussell Plum. 5 *Prunum Ambarinum.* The Amber Plum. 6 *Prunum Reginenm.* The Queen mother Plum. 7 *Prunum viride.* The green Oysterly Plum. 8 *Prunum Arantiacum.* The Orenge Plum. 9 *Prunum Myristicum.* The Nutmeg Plum. 10 *Prunum Siliquosum.* The Pescod Plum. 11 *Prunum Gaudenense.* The Gauat Plum. 12 *Prunum Dactylites.* The Date Plum. 13 *Prunum Pyrinum præcox.* The early Peare Plum.

and will abide good for six weekes at the least after it is gathered, and after all other plums are spent.

The Cherry plum remembred before, speaking of the Muscadine plum, is a very good plum, but small.

The Amber plum is a round plum, as yellow on the outside almost as yellow waxe, of a sowre vnpleasant taste that which I tasted, but I thinke it was not the right; for I haue seene and tasted another of the same bignesse, of a paler colour, farre better relished, and a firmer substance, comming cleane from the stone like an Apricocke.

The Apricocke plum is a good plum when it is in its perfection, but that is seldome; for it doth most vsually cracke, thereby diminishing much of its goodnesse, and besides yeeldeth gumme at the crackes.

The Eason plum is a little red plum, but very good in taste.

The Violet plum is a small and long blackish blew plum, ripe about Bartholmew tide, a very good dry eating fruit.

The Grape plum is the Flushing Bulleis before remembred

The Dennie plum is called also the Cheston, or the Friars plum before remembred.

The Damaske Violet plum, or Queen mother plum spoken of before.

The blacke Damascene plum is a very good dry plum, and of a darke blew colour when it is ripe.

The white Damson is nothing so well rellished as the other.

The great Damson or Damaske plum is greater then the ordinary Damson, and sweeter in taste.

The blew Damson well knowne, a good fruit.

The Coferers plum is flat, like vnto a Peare plum, it is early ripe and blacke, of a very good rellish.

The Margate plum the worst of an hundred.

The green Oysterly plum is a reasonable great plum, of a whitish green colour when it is ripe, of a moist and sweete taste, reasonable good.

The red Mirobalane plum groweth to be a great tree quickly, spreading very thicke and farre, very like the blacke Thorne or Sloe bush: the fruit is red, earlier ripe, and of a better taste then the white.

The white Mirobalane plum is in most things like the former red, but the fruit is of a whitish yellow colour, and very pleasant, especially if it be not ouer ripe: both these had need to be plashed against a wall, or else they will hardly beare ripe fruit.

The Oliue plum is very like a greene Oliue, both for colour and bignesse, and groweth lowe on a small bushing tree, and ripeneth late, but is the best of all the sorts of greene plums.

The white diapred plum of Malta, scarce knowne to any in our Land but Iohn Tradescante, is a very good plum, and striped all ouer like diaper, and thereby so called.

The blacke diapred plum is like the Damascene plum, being blacke with spots, as small as pins points vpon it, of a very good rellish.

The Peake plum is a long whitish plum, and very good.

The Pishamin or Virginia plum is called a plum, but vtterly differeth from all sorts of plums, the description whereof may truely enforme you, as it is set downe in the tenth Chapter going before, whereunto I referre you.

The Vse of Plums.

The great Damaske or Damson Plummes are dryed in France in great quantities, and brought ouer vnto vs in Hogs-heads, and other great vessels, and are those Prunes that are vsually sold at the Grocers, vnder the name of Damaske Prunes: the blacke Bulleis also are those (being dryed in the same manner) that they call French Prunes, and by their tartnesse are thought to binde, as the other, being sweet, to loosen the body.

The Bruneola Plumme, by reason of his pleasant tartnesse, is much accounted of, and being dryed, the stones taken from them, are brought ouer to vs in small boxes, and sold deere at the Comfitmakers, where they very often accompany all other sorts of banquetting stuffes.

Some

Some of these Plums, becaufe of their firmneffe, are vndoubtedly more wholfome then others that are fweete and waterifh, and caufe leffe offence in their ftomackes that eate them ; and therefore are preferued with Sugar, to be kept all the yeare. None of them all is vfed in medicines fo much as the great Damfon or Damaske Prune, although all of them for the moft part doe coole, lenifie, and draw forth choller, and thereby are fitteft to be vfed of fuch as haue chollericke Agues.

CHAP. XIIII.

Mala Armeniaca fiue Præcocia. Apricockes.

THe Apricocke (as I faid) is without queftion a kinde of Plumme, rather then a Peach, both the flower being white, and the ftone of the fruit fmooth alfo, like a Plumme, and yet becaufe of the excellencie of the fruit, and the difference therein from all other Plummes, I haue thought it meete to entreate thereof by it felfe, and fhew you the varieties haue been obferued in thefe times.

The Apricocke tree rifeth vp to a very great height, either ftanding by it felfe (where it beareth not fo kindly, and very little in our country) or planted againft a wall, as it is moft vfuall, hauing a great ftemme or body, and likewife many great armes or branches, couered with a fmooth barke : the leaues are large, broad, and almoft round, but pointed at the ends, and finely dented about the edges : the flowers are white, as the Plumme tree bloffomes, but fomewhat larger, and rounder fet : the fruit is round, with a cleft on the one fide, fomewhat like vnto a Peach, being of a yellowifh colour as well on the infide as outfide, of a firme or faft fubftance, and dry, not ouermoift in the eating, and very pleafant in tafte, containing within it a broad and flat ftone, fomewhat round and fmooth, not rugged as the Peach ftone, with a pleafant fweete kernell (yet fome haue reported, that there is fuch as haue their kernels bitter, which I did neuer fee or know) and is ripe almoft with our firft or earlieft Plummes, and thereof it tooke the name of *Præcox* ; and it may bee was the earlieft of all others was then knowne, when that name was giuen.

The great Apricocke, which fome call the long Apricocke, is the greateft and faireft of all the reft.

The fmaller Apricocke, which fome call the fmall round Apricocke, is thought to be fmall, becaufe it firft fprang from a ftone : but that is not fo ; for the kinde it felfe being inoculated, will bee alwaies fmall, and neuer halfe fo faire and great as the former.

The white Apricocke hath his leaues more folded together, as if it were halfe double : it beareth but feldome, and very few, which differ not from the ordinary, but in being more white, without any red when it is ripe.

The Mafcoline Apricocke hath a finer greene leafe, and thinner then the former, and beareth very feldome any ftore of fruit, which differeth in nothing from the firft, but that it is a little more delicate.

The long Mafcoline Apricocke hath his fruit growing a little longer then the former, and differeth in nothing elfe.

The Argier Apricocke is a fmaller fruit then any of the other, and yellow, but as fweete and delicate as any of them, hauing a blackifh ftone within it, little bigger then a Lacure Cherry ftone : this with many other forts Iohn Tradefcante brought with him returning from the Argier voyage, whither hee went voluntary with the Fleete, that went againft the Pyrates in the yeare 1620.

The Vfe of Apricockes.

Apricockes are eaten oftentimes in the fame manner that other dainty Plummes are, betweene meales of themfelues, or among other fruit at banquets.

They

They are also preserued and candid, as it pleaseth Gentlewomen to be-stowe their time and charge, or the Comfitmaker to sort among other can-did fruits.

Some likewise dry them, like vnto Peares, Apples, Damsons, and other Plummes.

Matthiolus doth wonderfully commend the oyle drawne from the ker-nels of the stones, to annoint the inflamed *hæmorrhoides* or piles, the swel-lings of vlcers, the roughnesse of the tongue and throate, and likewise the paines of the eares.

CHAP. XV.

Mala Persica. Peaches.

AS I ordered the Cherries and Plummes, so I intend to deale with Peaches, be-cause their varieties are many, and more knowne in these dayes then in former times: but because the Nectorin is a differing kinde of Peach, I must deale with it as I did with the Apricocke among the Plummes, that is, place it in a Chapter by it selfe.

The Peach tree of it selfe groweth not vsually altogether so great, or high as the A-pricocke, because it is lesse durable, but yet spreadeth with faire great branches, from whence spring smaller and slenderer reddish twigges, whereon are set long narrow greene leaues, dented about the edges: the blossomes are greater then of any Plumme, of a deepe blush or light purple colour: after which commeth the fruit, which is round, and sometimes as great as a reasonable Apple or Pippin (I speake of some sorts; for there be some kindes that are much smaller) with a furrow or cleft on the one side, and couered with a freese or cotton on the outside, of colour either russet, or red, or yel-low, or of a blackish red colour; of differing substances and tastes also, some being firme, others waterish, some cleauing fast to the stone on the inside, others parting from it more or lesse easily, one excelling another very farre, wherein is contained a rugged stone, with many chinkes or clefts in it, the kernell whereof is bitter: the roots growe neither deepe nor farre; and therefore are subiect to the winds, standing alone, and not against a wall. It sooner waxeth old and decayeth, being sprung of a stone, then being inoculated on a Plumme stocke, whereby it is more durable.

The great white Peach is white on the outside as the meate is also, and is a good well rellished fruit.

The small white Peach is all one with the greater, but differeth in size.

The Carnation Peach is of three sorts, two are round, and the third long; they are all of a whitish colour, shadowed ouer with red, and more red on the side is next the sunne: the lesser round is the more common, and the later ripe.

The grand Carnation Peach is like the former round Peach, but greater, and is as late ripe, that is, in the beginning of September.

The red Peach is an exceeding well rellished fruit.

The russet Peach is one of the most ordinary Peaches in the Kingdome, being of a russet colour on the outside, and but of a reasonable rellish, farre meaner then many other.

The Island Peach is a faire Peach, and of a very good rellish.

The Newington Peach is a very good Peach, and of an excellent good rellish, being of a whitish greene colour on the outside, yet halfe reddish, and is ripe about Barthol-mew tide.

The yellow Peach is of a deepe yellow colour; there be hereof diuers sorts, some good and some bad.

The St. Iames Peach is the same with the Queenes Peach, here belowe set downe, although some would make them differing.

The Melocotone Peach is a yellow faire Peach, but differing from the former yel-low both in forme and taste, in that this hath a small crooked end or point for the most part, it is ripe before them, and better rellished then any of them.

The

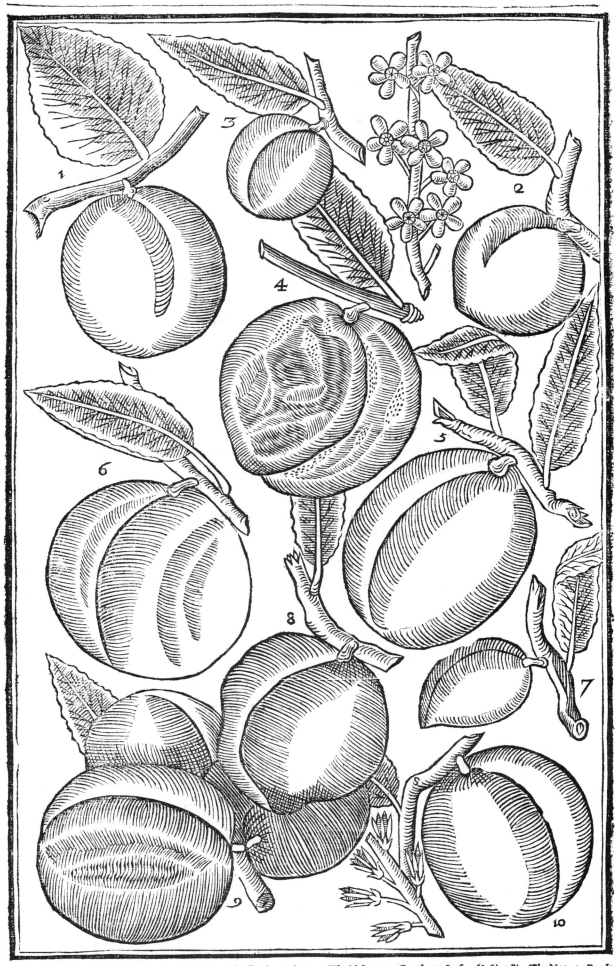

1 *Malus Armeniaca siue Præcocia*. The Apricocke. 2 *Malus Persica Melocotonea*. The Melocotone Peach. 3 *Persica Moschatellina*. The Nutmeg Peach. 4 *Persica nigra*. The blacke Peach. 5 *Persica Carnea longa*. The long Carnation Peach. 6 *Persica Reginea*. The Queenes Peach. 7 *Amygdalus*. The Almond. 8 *Persica du Troas*. The Peach du Troas. 9 *Nucipersica rubra optima*. The best Romane red Nectorin. 10. *Nucipersica rubra altera*. The bastard red Nectorin with a pricking blossome.

The Peach *du Troas* is a long and great whitifh yellow Peach, red on the outfide, early ripe, and is another kinde of Nutmeg Peach.

The Queenes Peach is a faire great yellowifh browne Peach, fhadowed as it were ouer with deepe red, and is ripe at Bartholmew tide, of a very pleafant good tafte.

The Romane Peach is a very good Peach, and well rellifhed.

The Durafine or Spanifh Peach is of a darke yellowifh red colour on the outfide, and white within.

The blacke Peach is a great large Peach, of a very darke browne colour on the outfide, it is of a waterifh tafte, and late ripe.

The Alberza Peach is late ripe, and of a reafonable good tafte.

The Almond Peach, fo called, becaufe the kernell of the ftone is fweete, like the Almond, and the fruit alfo fomewhat pointed like the Almond in the huske; it is early ripe, and like the Newington Peach, but leffer.

The Man Peach is of two forts, the one longer then the other, both of them are good Peaches, but the fhorter is the better rellifhed.

The Cherry Peach is a fmall Peach, but well tafted.

The Nutmeg Peach is of two forts, one that will be hard when it is ripe, and eateth not fo pleafantly as the other, which will bee foft and mellow; they are both fmall Peaches, hauing very little or no refemblance at all to a Nutmeg, except in being a little longer then round, and are early ripe.

Many other forts of Peaches there are, whereunto wee can giue no efpeciall name; and therefore I paffe them ouer in filence.

The Vfe of Peaches.

Thofe Peaches that are very moift and waterifh (as many of them are) and not firme, doe foone putrefie in the ftomacke, caufing furfeits oftentimes; and therefore euery one had neede bee carefull, what and in what manner they eate them: yet they are much and often well accepted with all the Gentry of the Kingdome.

The leaues, becaufe of their bitterneffe, ferue well being boyled in Ale or Milke, to be giuen vnto children that haue wormes, to help to kill them and doe gently open the belly, if there be a fufficient quantity vfed.

The flowers haue the like operation, that is, to purge the body fomewhat more forceably then Damaske Rofes; a Syrupe therefore made of the flowers is very good.

The kernels of the Peach ftones are oftentimes vfed to be giuen to them that cannot well make water, or are troubled with the ftone; for it openeth the ftoppings of the vritory paffages, whereby much eafe enfueth.

Chap. XVI.

Nuciperfica. Nectorins.

I Prefume that the name *Nuciperfica* doth moft rightly belong vnto that kinde of Peach, which we call Nectorins, and although they haue beene with vs not many yeares, yet haue they beene knowne both in Italy to Matthiolus, and others before him, who it feemeth knew no other then the yellow Nectorin, as Dalechampius alfo: But we at this day doe know fiue feuerall forts of Nectorins, as they fhall be prefently fet downe; and as in the former fruits, fo in this, I will giue you the defcription of one, and briefe notes of the reft.

The Nectorin is a tree of no great bigneffe, moft vfually leffer then the Peach tree, his body and elder boughes being whitifh, the younger branches very red, whereon grow narrow long greene leaues, fo like vnto Peach leaues, that none can well diftinguifh them, vnleffe it be in this, that they are fomewhat leffer: the bloffomes are all reddifh, as the Peach, but one of a differing fafhion from all the other, as I fhall fhew you by and by: the fruit that followeth is fmaller, rounder, and fmoother then Peaches, without any cleft on the fide, and without any douny cotton or freeze at all; and

herein

herein is like vnto the outer greene rinde of the Wallnut, whereof as I am perfwaded it tooke the name, of a faft and firme meate, and very delicate in tafte, efpecially the beft kindes, with a rugged ftone within it, and a bitter kernell.

The Muske Nectorin, fo called, becaufe it being a kinde of the beft red Nectorins, both fmelleth and eateth as if the fruit were fteeped in Muske : fome thinke that this and the next Romane Nectorin are all one.

The Romane red Nectorin, or clufter Nectorin, hath a large or great purplifh bloffome, like vnto a Peach, reddifh at the bottome on the outfide, and greenifh within : the fruit is of a fine red colour on the outfide, and groweth in clufters, two or three at a ioynt together, of an excellent good tafte.

The baftard red Nectorin hath a fmaller or pincking bloffome, more like threads then leaues, neither fo large nor open as the former, and yellowifh within at the bottome : the fruit is red on the outfide, and groweth neuer but one at a ioynt; it is a good fruit, but eateth a little more rawifh then the other, euen when it is full ripe.

The yellow Nectorin is of two forts, the one an excellent fruit, mellow, and of a very good rellifh; the other hard, and no way comparable to it.

The greene Nectorin, great and fmall; for fuch I haue feene abiding conftant, although both planted in one ground : they are both of one goodneffe, and accounted with moft to be the beft rellifhed Nectorin of all others.

The white Nectorin is faid to bee differing from the other, in that it will bee more white on the outfide when it is ripe, then either the yellow or greene : but I haue not yet feene it.

The Vfe of Nectorins.

The fruit is more firme then the Peach, and more delectable in tafte; and is therefore of more efteeme, and that worthily.

Chap. XVII.

Amygdala. Almonds.

THe Almond alfo may be reckoned vnto the ftock or kindred of the Peaches, it is fo like both in leafe and bloffome, and fomewhat alfo in the fruit, for the outward forme, although it hath onely a dry skinne, and no pulpe or meate to bee eaten : but the kernell of the ftone or fhell, which is called the Almond, maketh recompenfe of that defect, whereof fome are fweete, fome bitter, fome great, fome fmall, fome long, and fome fhort.

The Almond tree groweth vpright, higher and greater then any Peach; and is therefore vfually planted by it felfe, and not againft a wall, whofe body fometime exceedeth any mans fadome, whereby it fheweth to be of longer continuance, bearing large armes, and fmaller branches alfo, but brittle, whereon are fet long and narrow leaues, like vnto the Peach tree : the bloffomes are purplifh, like vnto Peach bloffoms, but paler : the fruit is fomewhat like a Peach for the forme of the skinne or outfide, which is rough, but not with any fuch cleft therein, or with any pulpe or meate fit to bee eaten, but is a thicke dry skinne when it is ripe, couering the ftone or fhell, which is fmooth and not rugged, and is either long and great, or fmall, or thicke and fhort, according as the nut or kernell within it is, which is fweete both in the greater and fmaller, and onely one fmaller kinde which is bitter: yet this I haue obferued, that all the Almond trees that I haue feene growe in England, both of the fweete and bitter kindes, beare Almonds thicke and fhort, and not long, as that fort which is called the Iorden Almond.

The Vfe of Almonds.

They are vfed many wayes, and for many purpofes, either eaten alone with Figges, or Rayfins of the Sunne, or made into pafte with Sugar and Rofewater for Marchpanes, or put among Floure, Egges, and Sugar, to

make

make Mackerons, or crusted ouer with Sugar, to make Comfits, or mixed with Rosewater and Sugar, to make Butter, or with Barley water, to make Milke, and many other waies, as euery one list, that hath skill in such things.

The oyle also of Almonds is vsed many waies, both inwardly and outwardly, for many purposes ; as the oyle of sweete Almonds mixt with poudered white Sugar Candy, for coughes and hoarsenesse, and to be drunk alone, or with some other thing (as the Syrupe of Marsh Mallowes) for the stone, to open and lenifie the passages, and make them slipperie, that the stone may passe the easier. And also for women in Child bed after their sore trauell. And outwardly either by it selfe, or with oyle of Tartar to make a creame, to lenifie the skin, parched with the winde or otherwise, or to annoint the stomacke either alone, or with other things to helpe a cold.

The oyle of bitter Almonds is much vsed to be dropped into their eares that are hard of hearing, to helpe to open them. And as it is thought, doth more scoure and cleanse the skin then the sweet oyle doth, and is therefore more vsed of many for that purpose, as the Almonds themselues are.

Chap. XVIII.

Mala Arantia. Orenges.

I Bring here to your consideration, as you see, the Orenge tree alone, without mentioning the Citron or Lemmon trees, in regard of the experience we haue seen made of them in diuers places : For the Orenge tree hath abiden with some extraordinary looking and tending of it, when as neither of the other would by any meanes be preserued any long time. If therefore any be desirous to keepe this tree, he must so prouide for it, that it be preserued from any cold, either in the winter or spring, and exposed to the comfort of the sunne in summer. And for that purpose some keepe them in great square boxes, and lift them to and fro by iron hooks on the sides, or cause them to be rowled by trundels, or small wheeles vnder them, to place them in an house, or close gallerie for the winter time : others plant them against a bricke wall in the ground, and defend them by a shed of boardes, couered ouer with seare-cloth in the winter, and by the warmth of a stoue, or other such thing, giue them some comfort in the colder times : but no tent or meane prouision will preserue them.

The Orenge tree in the warme Countries groweth very high, but with vs (or else it is a dwarfe kinde thereof) riseth not very high : the barke of the elder stemmes being of a darke colour, and the young branches very greene, whereon grow here and there some few thornes : the leaues are faire, large, and very greene, in forme almost like a Bay leafe, but that it hath a small eare, or peece of a leafe, fashioned like vnto an heart vnder euery one of them, with many small holes to be seene in them, if you hold them vp betweene you and the light, of a sweet but strong smell, naturally not falling away, but alwaies abiding on, or vntill new be come vp, bearing greene leaues continually : the flowers are whitish, of a very strong and heady sent ; after which come small round fruit, greene at the first, while they are small, and not neere maturitie, but being grown and ripe, are (as all men know) red on the out side, some more pale then others, and some kindes of a deeper yellowish red, according to the climate, and as it receiueth the heate of the sunne, wherein is contained sower or sweete iuice, and thicke white kernels among it : it beareth in the warme Countries both blossomes and greene fruit continually vpon it, and ripe fruit also with them for the best part of the yeare, but especially in Autumne and Winter.

The Vse of Orenges.

Orenges are vsed as sawce for many sorts of meates, in respect of their sweete sowernesse, giuing a rellish of delight, whereinsoeuer they are vsed.

The inner pulpe or iuice doth serue in agues and hot diseases, and in Summer to coole the heate of deiected stomackes, or fainting spirits.

The

1 *Malus Arantia*. The Orenge tree. 2 *Malus*. The Apple tree. 3 *Malum Carbonarium*. The Pomewater. 4 *Malum Curtipendulum*. The golden Pippin.
5 *Melapium*. The Pearemaine. 6 *Malum Reginoum*. The Queene Apple. 7 *Malum primò maturum*. The Genneting. 8 *Malum Regale*. The pound Royall. 9 *Malum Kentij ad feruescendum*. The Kentish Codlin. 10 *Malum Regineum spurium*. The Bardfield Quining.

The dryed rinde, by reaſon of the ſweete and ſtrong ſent, ſerueth to bee put among other things to make ſweet pouthers.

The outer rindes, when they are clenſed from all the inner pulpe and skins, are preſerued in Sugar, after the bitterneſſe by often ſteepings hath been taken away, & do ſerue either as Succots, and banquetting ſtuffes, or as ornaments to ſet out diſhes for the table, or to giue a relliſh vnto meats, whether baked or boyled : Phyſically they helpe to warme a cold ſtomack, and to digeſt or breake winde therein : or they are candid with Sugar, and ſerue with other dryed Iunquets.

The water of Orange flowers is oftentimes vſed as a great perfume for glones, to waſhe them, or in ſtead of Roſe-water to mixe with other things.

It is vſed to bee drunke by ſome, to preuent or to helpe any peſtilentiall feuer.

The oyntment that is made of the flowers, is very comfortable both for the ſtomache, againſt the could or cough, or for the head, for paines and diſineſſe.

The kernels or ſeede beeing caſt into the ground in the ſpring time, will quickely grow vp, (but will not abide the winter with vs, to bee kept for growing trees) and when they are of a finger length high, being pluckt vp, and put among ſallats, will giue them a maruellous fine aromaticke or ſpicy taſte, very acceptable.

The ſeed or kernels are a little cordiall, although nothing ſo much as the kernels of the Pomecitron.

CHAP. XIX.

Poma. Apples.

THe ſorts of Apples are ſo many, and infinite almoſt as I may ſay, that I cannot giue you the names of all, though I haue endeauoured to giue a great many, and I thinke it almoſt impoſſible for any one, to attaine to the full perfection of knowledge herein, not onely in regard of the multiplicitie of faſhions, colours and taſtes, but in that ſome are more familiar to one Countrey then to another, being of a better or worſe taſte in one place then in another, and therefore diuerſly called : I will therefore as I haue done before, giue you the deſcription of the Tree in generall, as alſo of the Paradiſe or dwarfe Apple, becauſe of ſome eſpeciall difference, and afterwards the names of as many, with their faſhions, as haue come to my knowledge, either by ſight or relation : for I doe confeſſe I haue not ſeene all that I here ſet downe, but vſe the helpe of ſome friends, and therefore if it happen that the ſeuerall names doe not anſwer vnto ſeuerall ſorts, but that the ſame fruit may bee called by one name in one Country, that is called by another elſewhere, excuſe it I pray you ; for in ſuch a number, ſuch a fault may eſcape vnknowne.

The Apple tree for the moſt part is neyther very high, great or ſtraight, but rather vſually boweth and ſpreadeth (although in ſome places it groweth fairer and ſtraighter then in others) hauing long and great armes or boughes, and from them ſmaller branches, whereon doe grow ſomewhat broade, and long greene leaues, nicked about the edges : the flowers are large and white, with bluſh coloured ſides, conſiſting of fiue leaues : the fruit (as I ſaid) is of diuers formes, colours and taſtes, and likewiſe of a very variable durabilitie; for ſome muſt be eaten preſently after they are gathered, and they are for the moſt part the earlieſt ripe; others will abide longer vpon the trees, before they bee fit to be gathered; ſome alſo will be ſo hard when others are gathered, that they will not be fit to be eaten, for one, two or three months after they bee gathered; and ſome will abide good but one, two or three moneths, and no more; and ſome will be beſt, after a quarter or halfe a yeares lying, vnto the end of that yeare or the next.

The Paradiſe or dwarfe Apple tree groweth nothing ſo high as the former, and many times not much higher then a man may reach, hauing leaues and flowers altogether like the other, the fruit is a faire yellow Apple, and reaſonable great, but very light and ſpongy or looſe, and of a bitteriſh ſweet taſte, nothing pleaſant. And theſe faults alſo-so are incident vnto this tree, that both bodie and branches are much subiect vnto cancker, which will quickely eate it round, and kill it ; besides it will haue many bunches, or tuberous swellings in many places, which grow as it were scabby or rough, and will soone cause it to perish : the roote sendeth forth many shootes and suckers, whereby it may be much increased. But this benefit may be had of it, to recompence the former faults, That being a dwarfe Tree, whatsoeuer fruit shall bee grafted on it, will keepe the graft low like vnto it selfe, and yet beare fruit reasonable well. And this is a pretty way to haue Pippins, Pomewaters, or any other sort of Apples (as I haue had my selfe, and also seene with others) growing low, that if any will, they may make a hedge rowe of these low fruits, planted in an Orchard all along by a walke side : but take this Caueat, if you will auoide the danger of the cancker and knots, which spoile the tree, to graft it hard vnto the ground, that therby you may giue as little of the nature of the stock thereunto as possibly you can, which wil vndoubtedly help it very much.

The kindes or sorts of Apples.

The Summer pippin is a very good apple first ripe, and therefore to bee first spent, because it will not abide so long as the other.

The French pippin is also a good fruit and yellow.

The Golding pippin is the greatest and best of all sorts of pippins.

The Russet pippin is as good an apple as most of the other sorts of pippins.

The spotted pippin is the most durable pippin of all the other sorts.

The ordinary yellow pippin is like the other, and as good; for indeed I know no sort of pippins but are excellent good well rellished fruites.

The great pearemaine differeth little either in taste or durabilitie from the pippin, and therefore next vnto it is accounted the best of all apples.

The summer pearemaine is of equall goodnesse with the former, or rather a little more pleasing, especially for the time of its eating, which will not bee so long lasting, but is spent and gone when the other beginneth to be good to eate.

The Russetting is also a firme and a very good apple, not so waterish as the pippin or pearemaine, and will last the best part of the year, but will be very mellow at the last, or rather halfe dryed.

The Broading is a very good apple.

The Pomewater is an excellent good and great whitish apple, full of sap or moisture, somewhat pleasant sharpe, but a little bitter withall : it will not last long, the winter frosts soone causing it to rot, and perish.

The Flower of Kent is a faire yellowish greene apple both good and great.

The Gilloflower apple is a fine apple, and finely spotted.

The Marligo is the same, that is called the Marigold apple, it is a middle sized apple, very yellow on the outside, shadowed ouer as it were with red, and more red on one side, a reasonable well rellished fruit.

The Blandrill is a good apple.

The Dauie Gentle is a very good apple

The Gruntlin is somewhat a long apple, smaller at the crowne then at the stalke, and is a reasonable good apple.

The gray Costerd is a good great apple, somewhat whitish on the outside, and abideth the winter.

The greene Costerd is like the other, but greener on the outside continually.

The Haruy apple is a faire great goodly apple, and very well rellished.

The Dowse apple is a sweetish apple not much accounted of.

The Pome-paris is a very good apple.

The Belle boon of two sorts winter and summer, both of them good apples, and fair fruit to look on, being yellow and of a meane bignesse.

The pound Royall is a very great apple, of a very good and sharpe taste.

The Doues Bill a small apple.

The Deusan or apple Iohn is a delicate fine fruit, well rellished when it beginneth to be fit to be eaten, and endureth good longer then any other apple.

The Master William is greater then a pippin, but of no very good rellish.

The Master Iohn is a better tasted apple then the other by much.

The

The Spicing is a well tasted fruite.

Pome de Rambures
Pome de Capanda } all faire and good apples brought from France.
Pome de Calual

The Queene apple is of two sorts, both of them great faire red apples, and well relished, but the greater is the best.

The Bastard Queene apple is like the other for forme and colour, but not so good in taste : some call this the bardfield Queening.

The Boughton or greening is a very good and well tasted apple.

The Leathercoate apple is a good winter apple, of no great bignesse, but of a very good and sharpe taste.

The Pot apple is a plaine Country apple.

The Cowsnout is no very good fruit.

The Gildiling apple is a yellow one, not much accounted.

The Cats head apple tooke the name of the likenesse, and is a reasonable good apple and great.

The Kentish Codlin is a faire great greenish apple, very good to eate when it is ripe; but the best to coddle of all other apples.

The Stoken apple is a reasonable good apple.

The Geneting apple is a very pleasant and good apple.

The Worcester apple is a very good apple, as bigge as a Pomewater.

Dorime Couadis is a French apple, and of a good rellish.

The French Goodwin is a very good apple.

The old wife is a very good, and well rellished apple.

The towne Crab is an hard apple, not so good to be eaten rawe as roasted, but excellent to make Cider.

The Virgilling apple is a reasonable good apple.

The Crowes egge is no good rellished fruit, but nourced vp in some places of the common people.

The Sugar apple is so called of the sweetnesse.

Sops in wine is so named both of the pleasantnesse of the fruit, and beautie of the apple.

The womans breast apple is a great apple.

The blacke apple or pippin is a very good eating apple, and very like a Pearemaine, both for forme and bignesse, but of a blacke sooty colour.

Tweenty sorts of Sweetings and none good.

The Peare apple is a small fruit, but well rellished being ripe, and is for shape very like vnto a small short Peare, and greene.

The Paradise apple is a faire goodly yellow apple, but light and spongy, and of a bitterish sweet taste, not to be commended.

The apple without blossome, so called becaue although it haue a small shew of a blossome, yet they are but small threds rather than leaues, neuer shewing to bee like a flower, and therefore termed without blossome : the apple is neyther good eating nor baking fruit.

Wildings and Crabs are without number or vse in our Orchard, being to be had out of the woods, fields and hedges rather then any where else.

The Vse of Apples.

The best sorts of Apples serue at the last course for the table, in most mens houses of account, where, if there grow any rare or excellent fruit, it is then set forth to be seene and tasted.

Diuers other sorts serue to bake, either for the Masters Table, or the meynes sustenance, either in pyes or pans, or else stewed in dishes with Rosewater and Sugar, and Cinamon or Ginger cast vpon.

Some kinds are fittest to roast in the winter time, to warme a cup of wine, ale or beere ; or to be eaten alone, for the nature of some fruit is neuer so good, or worth the eating, as when they are roasted.

Some

Some forts are fitteft to fcald for Codlins, and are taken to coole the ftomacke, as well as to pleafe the tafte, hauing Rofewater and Sugar put to them.

Some forts are beft to make Cider of, as in the Weft Countrey of England great quantities, yea many Hogfheads and Tunnes full are made, efpecially to bee carried to the Sea in long voyages, and is found by experience to bee of excellent vfe, to mixe with water for beuerage. It is vfually feene that thofe fruits that are neither fit to eate raw, roafted, nor baked, are fitteft for Cider, and make the beft.

The iuice of Apples likewife, as of pippins, and pearemaines, is of very good vfe in Melancholicke difeafes, helping to procure mirth, and to expell heauineffe.

The diftilled water of the fame Apples is of the like effect.

There is a fine fweet oyntment made of Apples called *Pomatum*, which is much vfed to helpe chapt lips, or hands, or for the face, or any other part of the skinne that is rough with winde, or any other accident, to fupple them, and make them fmooth.

CHAP. XX.

Cydonia. Quinces.

WEe haue fome diuerfities of Quinces, although not many, yet more then our elder times were acquainted with, which fhall be here expreffed.

The Quince tree groweth oftentimes to the height and bigneffe of a good Apple tree, but more vfually lower, with crooked and fpreading armes and branches farre abroad, the leaues are fomewhat round, and like the leaues of the Apple tree, but thicker, harder, fuller of veines, and white on the vnderfide: the bloffomes or flowers are white, now and then dafht ouer with blufh, being large and open, like vnto a fingle Rofe: the fruit followeth, which when it is ripe is yellow, and couered with a white cotton or freeze, which in the younger is thicker and more plentifull, but waxeth leffe and leffe, as the fruit ripeneth, being bunched out many times in feuerall places, and round, efpecially about the head, fome greater, others fmaller, fome round like an Apple, others long like a Peare, of a ftrong heady fent, accounted not wholfome or long to be endured, and of no durabilitie to keepe, in the middle whereof is a core, with many blackifh feedes or kernels therein, lying clofe together in cels, and compaffed with a kinde of cleare gelly, which is eafier feene in the fcalded fruit, then in the raw.

The Englifh Quince is the ordinarie Apple Quince, fet downe before, and is of fo harfh a tafte being greene, that no man can endure to eate it rawe, but eyther boyled, ftewed, roafted or baked; all which waies it is very good.

The Portingall Apple Quince is a great yellow Quince, feldome comming to bee whole and faire without chapping; this is fo pleafant being frefh gathered, that it may be eaten like vnto an Apple without offence.

The Portingall Peare Quince is not fit to be eaten rawe like the former, but muft be vfed after fome of the waies the Englifh Quince is appointed, and fo it will make more dainty difhes then the Englifh, becaufe it is leffe harfh, will bee more tender, and take leffe fugar for the ordering then the Englifh kinde.

The Barbary Quince is like in goodneffe vnto the Portingall Quince laft fpoken of, but leffer in bigneffe.

The Lyons Quince.

The Brunfwicke Quince.

The Vfe of Quinces.

There is no fruit growing in this Land that is of fo many excellent vfes as this, feruing as well to make many difhes of meate for the table, as for

ban-

banquets, and much more for the Phyſicall vertues, whereof to write at large is neither conuenient for mee, nor for this worke : I will onely briefly recite ſome, as it were to giue you a taſte of that plenty remaineth therein, to bee conuerted into ſundry formes : as firſt for the table, while they are freſh (and all the yeare long after being pickled vp) to be baked, as a dainty diſh, being well and orderly cookt. And being preſerued whole in Sugar, either white or red, ſerue likewiſe, not onely as an after diſh to cloſe vp the ſtomacke, but is placed among other Preſerues by Ladies and Gentlewomen, and beſtowed on their friends to entertaine them, and among other ſorts of Preſerues at Banquets. Codiniacke alſo and Marmilade, Ielly and Paſte, are all made of Quinces, chiefly for delight and pleaſure, although they haue alſo with them ſome phyſicall properties.

We haue for the vſe of phyſicke, both Iuyce and Syrupe, both Conſerue and Condite, both binding and looſening medicines, both inward and outward, and all made of Quinces.

The Ielly or Muccilage of the ſeedes, is often vſed to be laid vpon womens breaſts, to heale them being ſore or rawe, by their childrens default giuing them ſucke.

Athenæus reciteth in his third booke, that one Philarchus found, that the ſmell of Quinces tooke away the ſtrength of a certaine poiſon, called *Phariacum*. And the Spaniards haue alſo found, that the ſtrength of the iuyce of white Ellebor (which the Hunters vſe as a poyſon to dippe their arrow heads in, that they ſhoote at wilde beaſts to kill them) is quite taken away, if it ſtand within the compaſſe of the ſmell of Quinces. And alſo that Grapes, being hung vp to bee kept, and ſpent in Winter, doe quickly rot with the ſmell of a Quince.

Chap. XXI.

Pyra. Peares.

THe variety of peares is as much or more then of apples, and I thinke it is as hard in this, as before in apples, for any to be ſo exquiſite, as that hee could number vp all the ſorts that are to be had : for wee haue in our country ſo manie, as I ſhall giue you the names of by and by, and are hitherto come to our knowledge : but I verily beleeue that there be many, both in our country, and in others, that we haue not yet knowne or heard of ; for euery yeare almoſt wee attaine to the knowledge of ſome, we knew not of before. Take therefore, according to the manner before held, the deſcription of one, with the ſeuerall names of the reſt, vntill a more exact diſcourſe be had of them, euery one apart.

The Peare tree groweth more ſlowly, but higher, and more vpright then the apple tree, and not leſſe in the bulke of the body : his branches ſpread not ſo farre or wide, but growe vprighter and cloſer : the leaues are ſomewhat broader and rounder, greene aboue, and whiter vnderneath then thoſe of the apple tree : the flowers are whiter and greater : the fruit is longer then round for the moſt part, ſmaller at the ſtalke, and greater at the head, of ſo many differing formes, colours, and taſtes, that hardly can one diſtinguiſh rightly between them, the times alſo being as variable in the gathering and ſpending of them, as in apples : the roote groweth deeper then the apple tree, and therefore abideth longer, and giueth a faſter, cloſer, & ſmoother gentle wood, eaſie to be wrought vpon.

The kindes of Peares.

The Summer bon Chretien is ſomewhat a long peare, with a greene and yellow ruſſetiſh coate, and will haue ſometimes red ſides ; it is ripe at Michaelmas : ſome vſe to dry them as they doe Prunes, and keepe them all the yeare after. I haue not ſeene or heard any more Summer kindes hereof then this one, and needeth no wall to nourſe it as the other.

The

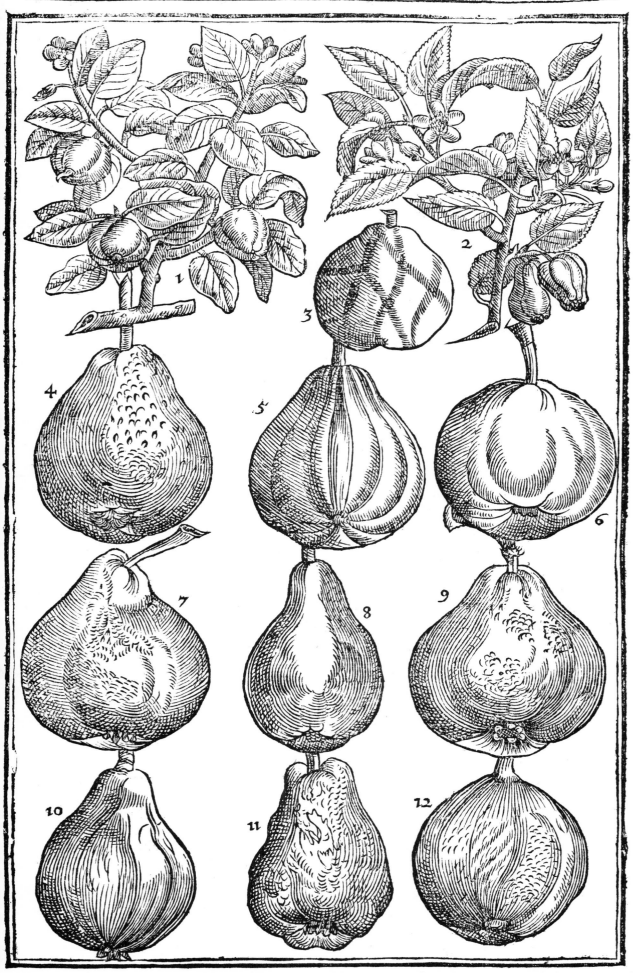

1 *Malus Cotonea.* The Quince tree. 2 *Cydonium Lusitanicum.* The Portingall Quince. 3 *Pyrus.* The Peare tree. 4 *Pyrum Pompeianum, siue Cucumerinum hyemale.* The Winter Bon Chretien. 5 *Pyrum pictum vel striatum.* The painted or striped Peare of Ierusalem. 6 *Pyrum Palatinal.* The Burgomot Peare. 7 *Pyrum Cucumerinum siue Pompeianum æstiuum.* The Summer Bon Chretien. 8 *Pyrum Volemum.* The best Warden. 9 *Pyrum Librale.* The pound Peare. 10 *Pyrum Windsorianum.* The Windfor Peare. 11 *Pyrum Cucumerinum.* The Gratiola Peare. 12 *Pyrum Caryophyllatum.* The Gilloflower Peare.

The Winter bon Chretien is of many forts, fome greater, others leffer, and all good; but the greateft and beft is that kinde that groweth at Syon: All the kinds of this Winter fruit muft be planted againft a wall, or elfe they will both feldome beare, and bring fewer alfo to ripeneffe, comparable to the wall fruit : the kindes alfo are according to their lafting ; for fome will endure good much longer then others.

The Summer Bergomot is an excellent well relliſhed peare, flattiſh, & ſhort, not long like others, of a meane bigneffe, and of a darke yellowiſh greene colour on the outfide.

The Winter Bergomot is of two or three forts, being all of them small fruit, fomewhat greener on the outfide then the Summer kindes; all of them very delicate and good in their due time : for fome will not be fit to bee eaten when others are will-nigh fpent, euery of them outlafting another by a moneth or more.

The Diego peare is but a fmall peare, but an excellent well rellifhed fruit, tafting as if Muske had been put among it; many of them growe together, as it were in clufters.

The Duetete or double headed peare, fo called of the forme, is a very good peare, not very great, of a ruffettifh browne colour on the outfide.

The Primating peare is a good moift peare, and early ripe.

The Geneting peare is a very good early ripe peare.

The greene Chefill is a delicate mellow peare, euen melting as it were in the mouth of the eater, although greeniſh on the outfide.

The Catherine peare is knowne to all I thinke to be a yellow red fided peare, of a full waterifh fweete tafte, and ripe with the foremoft.

The King Catherine is greater then the other, and of the fame goodneffe, or rather better.

The Ruffet Catherine is a very good middle fized peare.

The Windfor peare is an excellent good peare, well knowne to moft perfons, and of a reafonable greatneffe : it will beare fruit fome times twice in a yeare (and as it is faid) three times in fome places.

The Norwich peare is of two forts, Summer and Winter, both of them good fruit, each in their feafon.

The Worfter peare is blackiſh, a farre better peare to bake (when as it will be like a Warden, and as good) then to eate rawe ; yet fo it is not to be mifliked.

The Muske peare is like vnto a Catherine peare for bigneffe, colour, and forme; but farre more excellent in tafte, as the very name importeth.

The Rofewater peare is a goodly faire peare, and of a delicate tafte.

The Sugar peare is an early peare, very fweete, but waterifh.

The Summer Popperin ⎱ both of them are very good firme dry peares, fomewhat
The Winter Popperin ⎰ fpotted, and browniſh on the outfide.

The greene Popperin is a winter fruit, of equall goodneffe with the former.

The Soueraingne peare, that which I haue feene and tafted, and fo termed vnto me, was a fmall browniſh yellow peare, but of a moft dainty tafte ; but fome doe take a kind of Bon Chretien, called the Elizabeth peare, to be the Soueraigne peare ; how truely let others iudge.

The Kings peare is a very good and well tafted peare.

The peare Royall is a great peare, and of a good rellifh.

The Warwicke peare is a reafonable faire and good peare.

The Greenfield peare is a very good peare, of a middle fize.

The Lewes peare is a browniſh greene peare, ripe about the end of September, a reafonable well rellifhed fruit, and very moift.

The Biſhop peare is a middle fized peare, of a reafonable good tafte, not very waterifh ; but this property is oftentimes feene in it, that before the fruit is gathered, (but more vfually thofe that fall of themfelues, and the reft within a while after they are gathered) it will be rotten at the core, when there wil not be a fpot or blemiſh to be feene on the outfide, or in all the peare, vntill you come neare the core.

The Wilford peare is a good and a faire peare.

The Bell peare a very good greene peare.

The Portingall peare is a great peare, but more goodly in ſhew then good indeed.

The Gratiola peare is a kinde of Bon Chretien, called the Cowcumber peare, or Spinola's peare.

The Rowling peare is a good peare, but hard, and not good before it bee a little rowled or bruifed, to make it eate the more mellow.

The

The Pimpe peare is as great as the Windſor peare, but rounder, and of a very good rellifh.

The Turnep peare is a hard winter peare, not ſo good to eate rawe, as it is to bake.

The Arundell peare is moſt plentifull in Suffolke, and there commended to be a verie good peare.

The Berry peare is a Summer peare, reaſonable faire and great, and of ſo good and wholſome a taſte, that few or none take harme by eating neuer ſo many of them.

The Sand peare is a reaſonable good peare, but ſmall.

The Morley peare is a very good peare, like in forme and colour vnto the Windſor, but ſomewhat grayer.

The peare pricke is very like vnto the Greenfield peare, being both faire, great, and good.

The good Rewell is a reaſonable great peare, as good to bake as to eate rawe, and both wayes it is a good fruit.

The Hawkes bill peare is of a middle ſize, ſomewhat like vnto the Rowling peare.

The Petworth peare is a winter peare, and is great, ſomewhat long, faire, and good.

The Slipper peare is a reaſonable good peare.

The Robert peare is a very good peare, plentifull in Suffolke and Norfolke.

The pound peare is a reaſonable good peare, both to eate rawe, and to bake.

The ten pound peare, or the hundred pound peare, the trueſt and beſt, is the beſt Bon Chretien of Syon, ſo called, becauſe the grafts coſt the Maſter ſo much the fetching by the meſſengers expences, when he brought nothing elſe.

The Gilloflower peare is a winter peare, faire in ſhew, but hard, and not fit to bee eaten rawe, but very good to bake.

The peare Couteau is neither good one way nor other.

The Binſce peare is a reaſonable good winter peare, of a ruſſetiſh colour, and a ſmall fruit: but will abide good a long while.

The Pucell is a greene peare, of an indifferent good taſte.

The blacke Sorrell is a reaſonable great long peare, of a darke red colour on the outſide.

The red Sorrell is of a redder colour, elſe like the other.

The Surrine is no very good peare.

The Summer Haſting is a little greene peare, of an indifferent good rellifh.

Peare Gergonell is an early peare, ſomewhat long, and of a very pleaſant taſte.

The white Genneting is a reaſonable good peare, yet not equall to the other.

The Sweater is ſomewhat like the Windſor for colour and bigneſſe, but nothing neare of ſo good a taſte.

The bloud red peare is of a darke red colour on the outſide, but piercing very little into the inner pulpe.

The Hony peare is a long greene Summer peare.

The Winter peare is of many ſorts, but this is onely ſo called, to bee diſtinguiſhed from all other Winter peares, which haue ſeuerall names giuen them, and is a very good peare.

The Warden or Luke Wards peare of two ſorts, both white and red, both great and ſmall.

The Spaniſh Warden is greater then either of both the former, and better alſo.

The peare of Ieruſalem, or the ſtript peare, whoſe barke while it is young, is as plainly ſeene to be ſtript with greene, red, and yellow, as the fruit it ſelfe is alſo, and is of a very good taſte: being baked alſo, it is as red as the beſt Warden, whereof Maſter William Ward of Eſſex hath aſſured mee, who is the chiefe keeper of the Kings Granary at Whitehall.

Hereof likewiſe there is a wilde kinde no bigger then ones thumbe, and ſtriped in the like manner, but much more.

The Choke peares, and other wilde peares, both great and ſmall, as they are not to furniſh our Orchard, but the Woods, Forreſts, Fields, and Hedges, ſo wee leaue them to their naturall places, and to them that keep them, and make good vſe of them.

The Vſe of Peares.

The moſt excellent ſorts of Peares, ſerue (as I ſaid before of Apples) to make an after-courfe for their mafters table, where the goodneffe of his Orchard is tryed. They are dryed alfo, and fo are an excellent repafte, if they be of the beft kindes, fit for the purpofe.

They are eaten familiarly of all forts of people, of fome for delight, and of others for nourifhment, being baked, ftewed, or fcalded.

The red Warden and the Spanifh Warden are reckoned among the moft excellent of Peares, either to bake or to roaft, for the ficke or for the found: And indeede, the Quince and the Warden are the two onely fruits are permitted to the ficke, to eate at any time.

Perry, which is the iuyce of Peares preffed out, is a drinke much efteemed as well as Cyder, to be both drunke at home, and carried to the Sea, and found to be of good vfe in long voyages.

The Perry made of Choke Peares, notwithftanding the harfhneffe, and euill tafte, both of the fruit when it is greene, as alfo of the iuyce when it is new made, doth yet after a few moneths become as milde and pleafant as wine, and will hardly bee knowne by the fight or tafte from it : this hath beene found true by often experience; and therefore wee may admire the goodneffe of God, that hath giuen fuch facility to fo wilde fruits, altogether thought vfeleffe, to become vfefull, and apply the benefit thereof both to the comfort of our foules and bodies.

For the Phyficall properties, if we doe as Galen teacheth vs, *in fecundo Alimentorum*, referre the qualities of Peares to their feuerall taftes, as before he had done in Apples, we fhall not neede to make a new worke; thofe that are harfh and fowre doe coole and binde, fweet do nourifh and warme, and thofe betweene thefe, to haue middle vertues, anfwerable to their temperatures, &c.

Much more might be faid, both of this and the other kinds of fruits; but let this fuffice for this place and worke, vntill a more exact be accomplifhed.

Chap. XXII.

Nux Iuglans. The Wallnut.

ALthough the Wallnut tree bee often planted in the middle of great Courtyards, where by reafon of his great fpreading armes it taketh vp a great deale of roome, his fhadow reaching farre, fo that fcarce any thing can well grow neare it ; yet becaufe it is likewife planted in fit places or corners of Orchards, and that it beareth fruit or nuts, often brought to the table, efpecially while they are frefheft, fweeteft, and fitteft to be eaten, let not my Orchard want his company, or you the knowledge of it. Some doe thinke that there are many forts of them, becaufe fome are much greater then others, and fome longer then others, and fome haue a more frangible fhell then others; but I am certainly perfwaded, that the foyle and climate where they grow, are the whole and onely caufe of the varieties and differences. Indeed Virginia hath fent vnto vs two forts of Wallnuts, the one blacke, the other white, whereof as yet wee haue no further knowledge. And I know that Clufius reporteth, he tooke vp at a banquet a long Wallnut, differing in forme and tenderneffe of fhell from others, which being fet, grew and bore farre tenderer leaues then the other, and a little fnipt about the edges, which (as I faid) might alter with the foyle and climate: and befides you may obferue, that many of Clufius differences are very nice, and fo I leaue it.

The Wallnut tree groweth very high and great, with a large and thicke body or trunke, couered with a thicke clouen whitifh greene barke, tending to an afh-colour; the armes are great, and fpread farre, breaking out into fmaller branches, whereon doe grow long & large leaues, fiue or feuen fet together one againft another, with an odde one at the end, fomewhat like vnto Afhen leaues, but farre larger, and not fo many on a ftalke, fmooth, and fomewhat reddifh at the firft fpringing, and tender alfo, of a reafonable good fent, but more ftrong and headie when they growe old: the fruit or nut is great and round, growing clofe to the ftalkes of the leaues, either by couples or by

three

three fet together, couered with a double fhell, that is to fay, with a greene thicke and foft outer rinde, and an inner hard fhell, within which the white kernell is contained, couered with a thinne yellow rinde or peeling, which is more eafily peeled away while it is greene then afterwards, and is as it were parted into foure quarters, with a thinne wooddy peece parting it at the head, very fweete and pleafant while it is frefh, and for a while after the gathering; but the elder they growe, the harder and more oily: the catkins or blowings are long and yellow, made of many fcaly leaues fet clofe together, which come forth early in the Spring, and when they open and fall away, vpon their ftalkes arife certaine fmall flowers, which turne into fo many nuts.

The Vfe of Wallnuts.

They are often ferued to the table with other fruits while they abide frefh and fweete; and therefore many to keepe them frefh a long time haue deuifed many wayes, as to put them into great pots, and bury them in the ground, and fo take them out as they fpend them, which is a very good way, and will keepe them long.

The fmall young nuts while they are tender, being preferued or candid, are vfed among other forts of candid fruits, that ferue at banquets.

The iuyce of the outer greene huskes are held to be a foueraigne remedy againft either poyfon, or plague, or peftilentiall feuer.

The diftilled water of the huskes drunke with a little vinegar, if the fits growe hot and tedious, is an approued remedy for the fame.

The water diftilled from the leaues, is effectuall to be applyed to fluent or running vlcers, to dry and binde the humours.

Some haue vfed the pouder of the catkins in white wine, for the fuffocation or ftrangling of the mother.

The oyle of Wallnuts is vfed to varnifh Ioyners workes. As alfo is accounted farre to excell Linfeede oyle, to mixe a white colour withall, that the colour bee not dimmed. It is of excellent vfe for the coldneffe, hardneffe and contracting of the finewes and ioynts, to warme, fupple, and to extend them.

Chap. XXIII.

Caftanea Equina. The Horfe Chefnut.

ALthough the ordinary Chefnut is not a tree planted in Orchards, but left to Woods, Parkes, and other fuch like places; yet wee haue another fort which wee haue nourfed vp from the nuts fent vs from Turky, of a greater and more pleafant afpect for the faire leaues, and of as good vfe for the fruit. It groweth in time to be a great tree, fpreading with great armes and branches, whereon are fet at feuerall diftances goodly faire great greene leaues, diuided into fix, feuen, or nine parts or leaues, euery one of them nicked about the edges, very like vnto the leaues of *Ricnus,* or *Palma Chrifti,* and almoft as great: it beareth at the ends of the branches many flowers fet together vpon a long ftalke, confifting of foure white leaues a peece, with many threads in the middle, which afterwards turne into nuts, like vnto the ordinary Chefnuts, but fet in rougher and more prickly huskes: the nuts themfelues being rounder and blacker, with a white fpot at the head of each, formed fomewhat like an heart, and of a little fweeter tafte.

The Vfe of this Chefnut.

It ferueth to binde and ftop any maner of fluxe, be it of bloud or humours, either of the belly or ftomacke; as alfo the much fpitting of bloud. They are roafted and eaten as the ordinary fort, to make them tafte the better.

They are vfually in Turkie giuen to horfes in their prouender, to cure them of coughes, and helpe them being broken winded.

Chap.

Chap. XXIIII.

Morus. The Mulberrie.

There are two forts of Mulberries fufficiently known to moſt, the blackiſh and the white : but wee haue had brought vs from Virginia another ſort, which is of greater reſpect then eyther of the other two, not onely in regard of the raritie, but of the vſe, as you ſhall preſently vnderſtand.

1. *Morus nigra.* The blacke Mulberrie.

The blacke Mulberrie tree groweth oftentimes tall and great, and oftentimes alſo crooked, and ſpreading abroade, rather then high; for it is ſubiect to abide what forme you will conforme it vnto : if by ſuffering it to grow, it will mount vp, and if you will binde it, or plaſh the boughes, they will ſo abide, and be carried ouer arbours, or other things as you will haue it. The bodie groweth in time to bee very great, couered with a rugged or thicke barke, the armes or branches being ſmoother, whereon doe grow round thicke leaues pointed at the ends, and nicked about the edges, and in ſome there are to be ſeene deep gaſhes, making it ſeeme ſomewhat like the Vine leafe: the flowers are certaine ſhort dounie catkings, which turne into greene berries at the firſt, afterwards red, and when they are full ripe blacke, made of many graines ſet together, like vnto the blacke berrie, but longer and greater : before they are ripe, they haue an auſtere and harſh taſte, but when they are full ripe, they are more ſweete and pleaſant ; the iuice whereof is ſo red, that it will ſtaine the hands of them that handle and eate them.

2. *Morus alba.* The white Mulberrie.

The white Mulberrie tree groweth not with vs to that greatneſſe or bulke of bodie that the blacke doth, but runneth vp higher, ſlenderer, more knotty, hard and brittle, with thinner ſpreade armes and branches : the leaues are like the former, but not ſo thicke ſet on the branches, nor ſo hard in handling, a little paler alſo, hauing ſomewhat longer ſtalkes: the fruit is ſmaller and cloſer ſet together, greene, and ſomewhat harſh before they be ripe, but of a wonderfull ſweetneſſe, almoſt ready to procure loathing when they are thorough ripe, and white, with ſuch like ſeede in them as in the former, but ſmaller.

3. *Morus Virginiana.* The Virginia Mulberrie.

The Virginia Mulberry tree groweth quickely with vs to be a very great tree, ſpreading many armes and branches, whereon grow faire great leaues, very like vnto the leaues of the white Mulberrie tree : the berry or fruit is longer and redder then either of the other, and of a very pleaſant taſte.

The Vſe of Mulberries.

The greateſt and moſt eſpeciall vſe of the planting of white Mulberries, is for the feeding of Silke wormes, for which purpoſe all the Eaſterne Countries, as Perſia, Syria, Armenia, Arabia &c. and alſo the hither part of Turkie, Spaine alſo and Italie, and many other hot Countries doe nouriſh them, becauſe it is beſt for that purpoſe, the wormes feeding thereon, giuing the fineſt and beſt ſilke ; yet ſome are confident that the leaues of the blacke will doe as much good as the white : but that reſpect muſt be had to change your ſeede, becauſe therein lyeth the greateſt myſterie. But there is a Booke or Tractate printed, declaring the whole vſe of whatſoeuer can belong vnto them : I will therefore referre them thereunto, that

would

1 *Nux Inglans.* The Wallnut. 2 *Castanea equina.* The horſe Cheſnut. 3 *Morus nigra vel alba.* The Mulberry. 4 *Morus Virginiana.* The Virginia Mulberry. 5 *Laurus vulgaris.* The ordinary Bay tree. 6 *Laurea Cerasus Virginiana.* The Virginia Cherry Bay.

would further vnderſtand of that matter.

Mulberries are not much deſired to be eaten, although they be ſomewhat pleaſant, both for that they ſtaine their fingers and lips that eate them, and doe quickly putreſie in the ſtomacke, if they bee not taken before meate.

They haue yet a Phyſicall vſe, which is by reaſon of the aſtringent quality while they are red, and before they bee ripe, for ſore mouthes and throats, or the like, whereunto alſo the Syrup, called Diamoron, is effectuall.

Corollarium.
A COROLLARIE
To this Orchard.

Here are certaine other trees that beare no fruit fit to bee eaten, which yet are often ſeene planted in Orchards, and other fit and conuenient places bout an houſe, whereof ſome are of eſpeciall vſe, as the Bay tree &c. others for their beauty and ſhadow are fit for walkes or arbours; ſome being euer green are moſt fit for hedge-rowes; and ſome others more for their raritie then for any other great vſe, wherof I thought good to entreat apart by themſelues, and bring them after the fruit trees of this Orchard, as an ornament to accompliſh the ſame.

1. *Laurus.* The Bay tree.

THere are to bee reckoned vp fiue kindes of Bay trees, three whereof haue been entreated of in the firſt part, a fourth wee will only bring hereto your conſideration, which is that kinde that is vſually planted in euery mans yard or orchard, for their vſe throughout the whole land, the other we will leaue to bee conſidered of in that place is fit for it.

The Bay tree riſeth vp oftentimes to carry the face of a tree of a meane bigneſſe in our Countrey (although much greater in the hoter) and oftentimes ſhooteth vp with many ſuckers from the roote, ſhewing it ſelfe more like to a tall ſhrubbe or hedgebuſh, then a tree, hauing many branches, the young ones whereof are ſometimes reddiſh, but moſt vſually of a light or freſh greene colour, when the ſtemme and elder boughes are couered with a darke greene barke : the leaues are ſomewhat broad, and long pointed as it were at both the ends, hard and ſometimes crumpled on the edges, of a darke greene colour aboue, and of a yellowiſh greene vnderneath, in ſmell ſweet, in taſte bitter, and abiding euer greene : the flowers are yellow and moſſie, which turne into berries that are a little long as well as round, whoſe ſhell or outermoſt peele is greene at the firſt, and blacke when it is ripe; wherein is contained an hard bitter kernell, which cleaueth in two parts.

The Vſe of Bayes.

The Bay leaues are of as neceſſary vſe as any other in Garden or Orchard; for they ſerue both for pleaſure and profit, both for ornament and for vſe, both for honeſt Ciuill vſes, and for Phyſicke, yea both for the ſicke and for the ſound, both for the liuing and for the dead : And ſo much might be ſaid of this one tree, that if it were all told, would as well weary the Reader, as the Relater : but to explaine my ſelfe ; It ſerueth to adorne the houſe of God as well as of man : to procure warmth, comfort and ſtrength to the limmes of men and women, by bathings and annoyntings outward, and by drinkes &c. inward to the ſtomacke, and other parts : to ſeaſon veſſels &c. wherein are preſerued our meates, as well as our drinkes : to crowne or en-
circle

circle as with a garland, the heads of the liuing, and to fticke and decke forth the bodies of the dead : fo that from the cradle to the graue we haue ftill vfe of it, we haue ftill neede of it.

The berries likewife ferue for ftitches inward, and for paines outward, that come of cold eyther in the ioynts, finewes, or other places.

---

2. *Laurea Cerafus, fiue Laurus Virginiana.* The Virginian Bay, or Cherry Baye.

THis Virginian (whether you will call it a Baye, or a Cherrie, or a Cherrie Bay, I leaue it to euery ones free will and iudgement, but yet I thinke I may as well call it a Bay as others a Cherrie, neither of them being anfwerable to the tree, which neyther beareth fuch berries as are like Cherries, neither beareth euer greene leaues like the Bay : if it may therefore bee called the Virginia Cherry Bay, for a diftinction from the former Bay Cherry that beareth faire blacke Cherries, it will more fitly agree thereunto, vntill a more proper may be impofed) rifeth vp to be a tree of a reafonable height, the ftemme or bodie thereof being almoft as great as a mans legge, fpreading forth into diuers armes or boughes, and they againe into diuers fmall branches, whereon are fet without order diuers faire broade greene leaues, fomewhat like vnto the former Bay leaues, but more limber and gentle, and not fo hard in handling, broader alfo, and for the moft part ending in a point, but in many fomewhat round pointed, very finely notched or toothed about the edges, of a bitter tafte, very neere refembling the tafte of the Bay leafe, but of little or no fent at all, either greene or dryed, which fall away euery autumne, and fpring afrefh euery yeare : the bloffomes are fmall and white, many growing together vpon a long ftalke, fomewhat like the Bird Cherry bloffomes, but fmaller, and come forth at the ends of the young branches, which after turne into fmall berries, euery one fet in a fmall cup or huske, greene at the firft, and blacke when they are ripe, of the bigneffe of a fmall peafe, of a ftrong bitter tafte, and fomewhat aromaticall withall, but without any flefhy fubftance like a Cherry at all vpon it ; for it is altogether like a berry.

The Vfe of this Virginia Cherry Bay.

Being a ftranger in our Land, and poffeffed but of a very few, I doe not heare that there hath beene any triall made thereof what properties are in it : let this therefore fuffice for this prefent, to haue fhewed you the defcription and forme thereof, vntill we can learne further of his vfes.

---

3. *Pinus.* The Pine tree.

MY purpofe in this place is not to fhew you all the diuerfities of Pine trees, or of the reft that follow, but of that one kinde is planted in many places of our Land for ornament and delight, and there doth reafonably well abide : take it therefore into this Orchard, for the raritie and beautie of it, though we haue little other vfe of it.

The Pine tree groweth with vs, though flowely, to a very great height in many places, with a great ftraight bodie, couered with a grayifh greene barke, the younger branches are fet round about, with very narrow long whitifh greene leaues, which fall away from the elder, but abide on the younger, being both winter and fummer alwaies greene. It hath growing in fundry places on the branches, certaine great hard wooddy clogs (called of fome apples, of others nuts) compofed of many hard wooddy fcales, or tuberous knobs, which abide for the moft part alwaies greene in our Countrey, and hardly become brownifh, as in other Countries, where they haue more heat and comfort of the Sun, and where the fcales open themfelues ; wherein are contained white long and round kernels, very fweete while they are frefh, but quickely growing oylely and rancide.

The

The Vse of the Pine apples and kernels.

The Cones or Apples are vsed of diuers Vintners in this City, being painted, to expresse a bunch of grapes, whereunto they are very like, and are hung vp in their bushes, as also to fasten keyes vnto them, as is seene in many places.

The kernels within the hard shels, while they are fresh or newly taken out, are vsed many waies, both with Apothecaries, Comfit-makers, and Cookes : for of them are made medicines, good to lenifie the pipes and passages of the lungs and throate, when it is hoarse. Of them are made Comfits, Pastes, Marchpanes, and diuers other such like : And with them a cunning Cooke can make diuers Keck shofes for his Masters table.

Matthiolus commendeth the water of the greene apples distilled, to take away the wrinkles in the face, to abate the ouer-swelling breasts of Maidens, by fomenting them after with linnen clothes, wet in the water; and to restore such as are rauisht into better termes.

4. *Abies.* The Firre tree.

THe Firre tree groweth naturally higher then any other tree in these parts of Christendome where no Cedars grow, and euen equalling or ouer-topping the Pine : the stemme or bodie is bare without branches for a great height, if they bee elder trees, and then branching forth at one place of the bodie foure wayes in manner of a crosse, those boughes againe hauing two branches at euery ioynt, on which are set on all sides very thicke together many small narrow long hard whitish greene leaues, and while they are young tending to yellownesse, but nothing so long or hard or sharpe pointed as the Pine tree leaues, growing smaller and shorter to the end of the branches : the bloomings are certaine small long scaly catkins, of a yellowish colour, comming forth at the ioynts of the branches, which fall away : the cones are smaller and longer then of the Pine tree, wherein are small three square seede contained, not halfe so big as the Pine kernels.

The Vse of the Firre tree.

The vse of this tree is growne with vs of late daies to bee more frequent for the building of houses then euer before : for hereof (namely of Deale timber and Deale boords) are framed many houses, and their floores, without the helpe of any other timber or boord of any other tree almost ; as also for many other workes and purposes. The yellow Rossen that is vsed as well to make salues as for many other common vses, is taken from this tree, as the Pitch is both from the Pitch and Pine trees, and is boyled to make it to bee hard, but was at the first a yellow thin cleere Turpentine, and is that best sort of common Turpentine is altogether in vse with vs, as also another more thicke, whitish, and troubled, both which are vsed in salues, both for man and beast (but not inwardly as the cleere white Venice Turpentine is) and serueth both to draw, cleanse and heale. Dodonæus seemeth to say, that the cleere white Turpentine, called Venice Turpentine, is drawn from the Firre : but Matthiolus confuteth that opinion, which Fulsius also held before him.

5. *Ilex arbor.* The euer-greene Oake.

THe *Ilex* or euer-greene Oake riseth in time to be a very great tree, but very long and slow in growing (as is to be seene in the Kings priuy Garden at Whitehall, growing iust against the backe gate that openeth into the way going to Westminster, and in some other places) spreading many fair large great armes and branches, whereon are set small and hard greene leaues, somewhat endented or cornered, and prickly

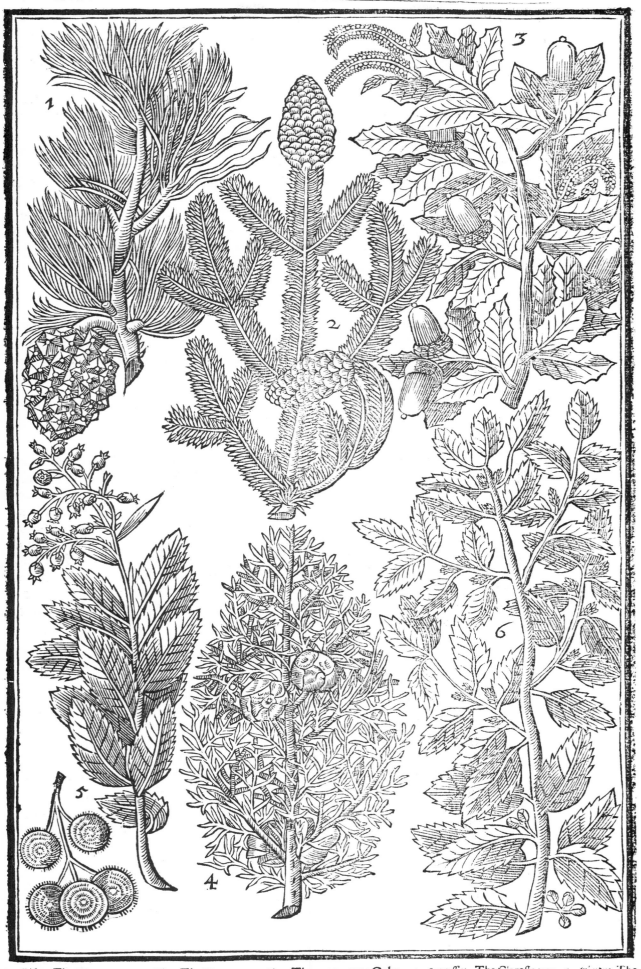

1 *Pinus* The Pine tree. 2 *Abies.* The Firre tree. 3 *Ilex.* The euer greene Oake. 4 *Cupressus,* The Ciprosse tree. 5 *Arbutus.* The Strawberry tree. 6 *Alaternus.* The euer greene Priuet.

prickly on the edges, especially in the young trees, and sometimes on those branches that are young and newly sprung forth from the elder rootes, but else in a manner all smooth in the elder growne, abiding greene all the winter as well as summer, and are of a grayish greene on the vnderside. It beareth in the spring time certaine slender long branches (like as other Okes doe) with small yellowish mossie flowers on them, which fall away, and are vnprofitable, the acornes not growing from those places, but from others which are like vnto those of our ordinary Oake, but smaller and blacker, and set in a more rugged huske or cuppe. This and no other kinde of *Ilex* doe I know to grow in all our land in any Garden or Orchard: for that kind with long and narrower leaues, and not prickly, growing so plentifully as Matthiolus saith in Tuscane, I haue not seen: and it is very probable to bee the same that Plinie remembreth to haue the leafe of an Oliue ; but not as some would haue it, that *Smilax* Theophrastus maketh mention of in his third Booke and sixteenth Chapter of his Historie of Plants, which the Arcadians so called, and had the leafe of the *Ilex*, but not prickly : for Theophrastus saith, the timber of *Smilax* is smooth and soft, and this of the *Ilex* is harder, and stronger then an Oake.

The Vse of the *Ilex* or euer-greene Oake.

Seeing this is to be accounted among the kindes of Oake (and all Oakes by Dioscorides his opinion are binding) it is also of the same qualitie, but a little weaker, and may serue to strengthen weake members. The young tops and leaues are also vsed in gargles for the mouth and throate.

6 *Cupressus*. The Cypresse tree.

THe Cypresse tree that is nourſed vp by vs, in our Country, doth grow in those places where it hath beene long planted, to a very great height, whose bodie and boughes are couered with a reddish ash-coloured bark ; the branches grow not spreading, but vpright close vnto the bodie, bushing thicke below, and small vpwards, spire fashion, those below reaching neere halfe the way to them aboue, whereon doe grow euer greene leaues, small, long and flat, of a resinous sweete smell, and strong taste, somewhat bitter : the fruit, which are called nuts, grow here and there among the boughes, sticking close vnto them, which are small, and clouen into diuers parts, but close while they are young, of a russetish browne colour ; wherein are contained small browne seede, but not so small as motes in the Sunne, as Matthiolus and others make them to be.

The Vse of the Cypresse tree.

For the goodly proportion this tree beareth, as also for his euer-greene head, it is and hath beene of great account with all Princes, both beyond, and on this side of the Sea, to plant them in rowes on both sides of some spatious walke, which by reason of their high growing, and little spreading, must be planted the thicker together, and so they giue a goodly, pleasant and sweet shadow : or else alone, if they haue not many, in the middle of some quarter, or as they thinke meete. The wood thereof is firme and durable, or neuer decaying, of a brown yellow colour, and of a strong sweete smell, whereof Chests or Boxes are made to keepe apparell, linnen, furres, and other things, to preserue them from moths, and to giue them a good smell.

Many Physicall properties, both wood, leaues and nuts haue, which here is not my purpose to vnfold, but only to tell you, that the leaues being boyled in wine, and drunke, helpe the difficultie of making vrine, and that the nuts are binding, fit to bee vsed to stay fluxes or laskes, and good also for ruptures.

7. *Arbutus*

7. *Arbutus*. The Strawberry tree.

THe Strawberry tree groweth but flowly, and rifeth not to the height of any great tree, no not in France, Italy, or Spaine : and with vs the coldneffe of our country doth the more abate his vigour, fo that it feldome rifeth to the height of a man : the barke of the body is rough, and fmooth in the younger branches : the leaues are faire and greene, very like vnto Baye leaues, finely dented or fnipped about the edges, abiding alwayes greene thereon both Winter and Summer : the flowers come forth at the end of the branches vpon long ftalkes, not cluftering thicke together, but in long bunches, and are fmall, white, and hollow, like a little bottle, or the flower of Lilly Conually, which after turne into rough or rugged berries, moft like vnto Strawberries (which hath giuen the name to the tree) fomewhat reddifh when they are ripe, of a harfh tafte, nothing pleafant, wherein are contained many fmall feedes : It hardly bringeth his fruit to ripeneffe in our countrey ; for in their naturall places they ripen not vntill Winter, which there is much milder then with vs.

The Vfe of the Strawberry tree.

Amatus Lufitanus I thinke is the firft that euer recorded, that the water diftilled from the leaues and flowers hereof, fhould bee very powerfull againft the plague and poyfons : for all the ancient Writers doe report, that the fruit hereof being eaten, is an enemy to the ftomacke and head. And Clufius likewife fetteth downe, that at Lifhbone, and other places in Portingall where they are frequent, they are chiefly eaten, but of the poorer fort, women and boyes. They are fomewhat aftringent or binding, and therefore may well ferue for fluxes. It is chiefly nourfed with vs for the beauty and rareneffe of the tree; for that it beareth his leaues alwayes green.

8. *Alaternus*. The euer greene Priuet.

THe tree which we haue growing in our country called *Alaternus*, groweth not to be a tree of any height ; but abiding lowe, fpreadeth forth many branches, whereon are fet diuers fmall and hard greene leaues, fomewhat round for the forme, and endented a little by the edges : it beareth many fmall whitifh greene flowers at the ioynts of the ftalkes, and fetting on of the lower leaues cluftering thicke together, which after turne into fmall blacke berries, wherein are contained many fmall graines or feedes : the beauty and verdure of thefe leaues abiding fo frefh all the yeare, doth caufe it to be of the greater refpect ; and therefore findeth place in their Gardens onely, that are curious conferuers of all natures beauties.

The Vfe of the euer greene Priuet.

It is feldome vfed for any Phyficall property, neither with vs, nor in the places where it is naturall and plentifull : but as Clufius reporteth, hee learned that the Portingall Fifhermen do dye their nets red with the decoction of the barke hereof, and that the Dyers in thofe parts doe vfe the fmall peeces of the wood to ftrike a blackifh blew colour.

9. *Celaftrus Theophrafti Clufio*. Clufius his Celaftrus.

ALthough the Collectour (who is thought to be Ioannes Molineus of the great Herball or Hiftory of plants, and generally bearing Dalefchampius name, becaufe the finding and relation of diuers herbes therein expreffed, is appropiate to him, and printed at Lyons) of all our moderne Writers doth firft of all others appoint the *Celaftrus*, whereof Theophraftus onely among all the ancient Writers of

plants

plants maketh mention, to be the first *Alaternus* that Clusius hath set forth in his History of rarer plants : yet I finde, that Clusius himselfe before his death doth appropiate that *Celastrus* of Theophrastus to another plant, growing in the Garden at Leyden, which formerly of diuers had beene taken to be a kinde of *Laurus Tinus*, or the wilde Baye; but he impugning that opinion for diuers respects, decyphreth out that Leyden tree in the same manner that I doe: and because it is not onely faire, in bearing his leaues alwayes greene, but rare also, being noursed vp in our Land in very few places, but principally with a good old Lady, the widow of Sir Iohn Leuson, dwelling neere Rochester in Kent; I thought it fit to commend it for an ornament, to adorne this our Garden and Orchard. It groweth vp to the height of a reasonable tree, the body whereof is couered with a darke coloured barke, as the elder branches are in like manner; the younger branches being greene, whereon are set diuers leaues thicke together, two alwayes at a ioynt, one against another, of a sad but faire greene colour on the vpperside, and paler vnderneath, which are little or nothing at all snipped about the edges, as large as the leaues of the *Laurus Tinus*, or wilde Baye tree: at the end of the young branches breake forth between the leaues diuers small stalkes, with foure or fiue flowers on each of them, of a yellowish greene colour, which turne into small berries, of the bignesse of blacke Cherries, greene at the first, and red when they begin to be ripe, but growing blacke if they hang too long vpon the branches, wherein is contained a hard shell, and a white hard kernell within it, couered with a yellowish skin. This abideth (as I said before) with greene leaues as well Winter as Summer; and therefore fittest to be planted among other of the same nature, to make an euer greene hedge.

The Vse of Clusius his Celastrus.

Being so great a stranger in this part of the Christian world, I know none hath made tryall of what property it is, but that the taste of the leaues is somewhat bitter.

10. *Pyracantha.* The euer greene Hawthorne, or prickly Corall tree.

THis euer greene shrubbe is so fine an ornament to a Garden or Orchard, either to be noursed vp into a small tree by it selfe, by pruining and taking away the suckers and vnder branches, or by suffering it to grow with suckers, thicke and plashing the branches into a hedge, for that it is plyable to be ordered either way; that I could not but giue you the knowledge thereof, with the description in this manner. The younger branches are couered with a smooth darke blewish greene barke, and the elder with a more ash coloured, thicke set with leaues without order, some greater and others smaller, somewhat like both in forme and bignesse vnto the leaues of the Barberry tree, but somewhat larger, and more snipt about the edges, of a deeper greene colour also, and with small long thornes scattered here & there vpon the branches: the flowers come forth as well at the ends of the branches, as at diuers places at the ioynts of the leaues, standing thicke together, of a pale whitish colour, a little dasht ouer with a shew of blush, consisting of fiue leaues a peece, with some small threads in the middle, which turne into berries, very like vnto Hawthorne berries, but much redder and dryer, almost like polished Corall, wherein are contained foure or fiue small yellowish white three square seede, somewhat shining. It is thought to be the *Oxyacantha* of Dioscorides; but seeing Dioscorides doth explaine the forme of the leafe in his Chapter of Medlars, which he concealed in the Chapter of *Oxyacantha*, it cannot be the same : for *Mespilus Anthedon* of Theophrastus, or *Aronia* of Dioscorides, hath the leafe of *Oxyacantha*, as Dioscorides saith, or of Smalladge, as Theophrastus, which cannot agree to this Thorne; but doth most liuely delineate out our white Thorne or Hawthorne, that now there is no doubt, but that *Oxyacantha* of Dioscorides is the Hawthorne tree or bush.

The Vse of this Corall tree.

Although Lobel maketh mention of this tree to grow both in Italy, and

1 *Celastrus Theophrasti Clusio.* Clusius his Celastrus. 2 *Pyracantha.* The euer green prickly Corall tree; 3 *Taxus.* The Yewe tree. 4 *Buxus arbor.* The Boxe tree 5 *Buxus humilis.* The lowe or dwarfe Boxe. 6 *Sabina.* The Sauine tree. 7 *Paliurus.* Christs thorne. 8 *Larix.* The Larch tree.

Prouence in France, in fome of their hedges, yet he faith it is neglected in the naturall places, and to be of no vfe with them : neither doe I heare, that it is applyed to any Phyficall vfe with vs , but (as I before faid) it is preferued with diuers as an ornament to a Garden or Orchard, by reafon of his euer greene leaues, and red berries among them , being a pleafant fpectacle, and fit to be brought into the forme of an hedge, as one pleafe to lead it.

---

11. *Taxus*. The Yewe tree.

THe Yewe tree groweth with vs in many places to bee a reafonable great tree, but in hoter countries much bigger, couered with a reddifh gray fcaly barke ; the younger branches are reddifh likewife, whereon grow many winged leaues, that is, many narrow long darke greene leaues, fet on both fides of a long ftalke or branch, neuer dying or falling away, but abiding on perpetually, except it be on the elder boughes : the flowers are fmall, growing by the leaues , which turne into round red berries, like vnto red Afparagus berries, in tafte fweetifh , with a little bitterneffe, and caufing no harme to them for any thing hath been knowne in our country,

The Vfe of the Yewe tree.

It is found planted both in the corners of Orchards, and againft the windowes of Houfes, to be both a fhadow and an ornament , in being alwayes greene, and to decke vp Houfes in Winter : but ancient Writers haue euer reckoned it to be dangerous at the leaft, if not deadly.

---

12. *Buxus*. The Boxe tree.

THe Boxe tree in fome places is a reafonable tall tree , yet growing flowly ; the trunke or body whereof is of the bigneffe of a mans thigh, which is the biggeft that euer I faw : but fometimes, and in other places it groweth much lower, vfually not aboue a yard, or a yard and a halfe high , on the backe fides of many Houfes, and in the Orchards likewife : the leaues are fmall, thicke and hard, and ftill the greater or leffer the tree is. the greater or leffer are the leaues, round pointed, and of a frefh fhining greene colour : the flowers are fmall and greenifh, which turne into heads or berries, with foure hornes, whittifh on the outfide, and with reddifh feede within them.

Buxus aureus.
Gilded Boxe. There is another kinde hereof but lately come to our knowledge, which differeth not in any thing from the former, but onely that all the leaues haue a yellow lift or gard about the edge of them on the vpperfide, and none on the lower, which maketh it feeme very beautifull , and is therefore called gilded Boxe.

Buxus humilis.
Dwarfe Boxe. We haue yet another kinde of Boxe, growing fmall and lowe, not aboue halfe a foote, or a foote high at the moft, vnleffe it be neglected , which then doth grow a little more fhrubby, bearing the like leaues, but fmaller, according to the growth, and of a deeper greene colour : I could neuer know that this kinde euer bore flower or feede, but is propagated by flipping the roote, which encreafeth very much.

The Vfe of Boxe.

The wood of the Boxe tree is vfed in many kindes of fmall works among Turners, becaufe it is hard, clofe, and firme, and as fome haue faid, the roots much more , in regard of the diuers waues and crooked veines running through it. It hath no Phyficall vfe among the moft and beft Phyfitians, although fome haue reported it to ftay fluxes, and to be as good as the wood of *Guaiacum*, or *Lignum vitæ* for the French difeafe. The leaues and branches ferue both Summer and Winter to decke vp houfes ; and are many times giuen to horfes for the bots.

The lowe or dwarfe Boxe is of excellent vfe to border vp a knot, or the
                                                                                    lon

long beds in a Garden, being a maruailous fine ornament thereunto, in regard it both groweth lowe, is euer greene, and by cutting may bee kept in what maner euery one pleafe, as I haue before fpoken more largely.

13. *Sabina.* The Sauine tree or bufh.

THe Sauine tree or bufh that is moft vfuall in our country, is a fmall lowe bufh, not fo high as a man in any place, nor fo bigge in the ftemme or trunke as a mans arme, with many crooked bending boughes and branches, whereon are fet many fmall, fhort, hard, and prickly leaues, of a darke green colour, frefh and green both Winter and Summer: it is reported, that in the naturall places it beareth fmall blacke berries, like vnto Iuniper, but with vs it was neuer knowne to beare any.

The Vfe of Sauine.

It is planted in out-yards, backfides, or voide places of Orchards, as well to caft clothes thereon to dry, as for medicines both for men and horfes: being made into an oyle, it is good to annoint childrens bellies for to kill the Wormes: and the powder thereof mixed with Hogs greafe, to annoint the running fores or fcabs in their heads; but beware how you giue it inwardly to men, women, or children. It is often put into horfes drenches, to helpe to cure them of the bots, and other difeafes.

14. *Paliurus.* Chrifts thorne.

THis thorny fhrubbe (wherewith as it is thought, our Sauiour Chrift was crowned, becaufe as thofe that haue trauelled through Paleftina and Iudæa, doe report no other thorne doth grow therein fo frequent, or fo apt to be writhed) rifeth in fome places to a reafonable height, but in our country feldome exceedeth the height of a man, bearing many flender branches, full of leaues, fet on either fide thereof one by one, which are fomewhat broad and round, yet pointed, and full of veines, thicke fet alfo with fmall thornes, euen at the foote of euery branch, and at the foote of euery leafe one or two, fome ftanding vpright, others a little bending downe: the flowers are fmall and yellow, ftanding for the moft part at the end of the branches, many growing vpon a long ftalke, which after turne into round, flat, and hard fhelly fruit, yet couered with a foft flefhy skinne, within which are included two or three hard, fmall, and browne flat feeds, lying in feuerall partitions. The leaues hereof fall away euery yeare, and fpring forth afrefh againe the next May following. The rarity and beauty of this fhrubbe, but chiefly (as I thinke) the name hath caufed this to be much accounted of with all louers of plants.

The Vfe of Chrifts thorne.

Wee haue fo few of thefe fhrubbes growing in our country, and thofe that are, doe, for any thing I can vnderftand, neuer beare fruit with vs; that there is no other vfe made hereof then to delight the owners: but this is certainly receiued for the *Paliurus* of Diofcorides and Theophraftus, and thought alfo by Matthiolus to be the very true *Rhamnus tertius* of Diofcorides. Matthiolus alfo feemeth to contradict the opinion is held by the Phyfitians of Mompelier, and others, that it cannot be the *Paliurus* of Theophraftus. It is held to be effectuall to helpe to breake the ftone, both in the bladder, reines, and kidneyes: the leaues and young branches haue an aftringent quality, and good againft poyfons and the bitings of ferpents.

15. *Larix.*

15. *Larix*. The Larch tree.

THe Larch tree, where it naturally groweth, rifeth vp to be as tall as the Pine or Firre tree, but in our Land being rare, and nourfed vp but with a few, and thofe onely louers of rarities, it groweth both flowly, and becommeth not high : the barke hereof is very rugged and thicke, the boughes and branches grow one aboue another in a very comely order, hauing diuers fmall yellowifh knobs or bunches fet thereon at feuerall diftances ; from whence doe yearely fhoote forth many fmall, long, and narrow fmooth leaues together, both fhorter and fmaller, and not fo hard or fharpe pointed as either the Pine or Firre tree leaues, which doe not abide the Winter as they doe, but fall away euery yeare, as other trees which fhed their leaues, and gaine frefh euery Spring : the bloffomes are very beautifull and delectable, being of an excellent fine crimfon colour, which ftanding among the greene leaues, allure the eyes of the beholders to regard it with the more defire : it alfo beareth in the naturall places (but not in our Land that I could heare) fmall foft cones or fruit, fomewhat like vnto Cypreffe nuts, when they are greene and clofe.

The Vfe of the Larch tree.

The coles of the wood hereof (becaufe it is fo hard and durable as none more) is held to be of moft force being fired, to caufe the Iron oare to melt, which none other would doe fo well. Matthiolus contefteth againft Fuchfius, for deeming the Venice Turpentine to be the liquid Roffen of the Firre tree, which he affureth vpon his owne experience and certaine knowledge, to be drawne from this Larch tree, and none other ; which cleere Turpintine is altogether vfed inwardly, and no other, except that of the true Turpintine tree, and is very effectuall to cleanfe the reines, kidneyes, and bladder, both of grauell and the ftone, and to prouoke vrine : it is alfo of efpeciall property for the *gonorrhea*, or running of the reines, as it is called, with fome powder of white Amber mixed therewith, taken for certaine dayes together. Taken alfo in an Electuary, it is fingular good for to expectorate rotten flegme, and to helpe the confumption of the lungs. It is vfed in plaifters and falues, as the beft fort of Turpintine. The Agaricke that is vfed in phyficke, is taken from the bodies and armes of this tree. And Matthiolus doth much infift againft Brafauolus, that thought other trees had produced Agaricke, affirming them to be hard *Fungi*, or Mufhroms (fuch as wee call Touch-wood) wherwith many vfe to take fire, ftrooke thereinto from fteele.

16. *Tilia*. The Line or Linden tree.

THere are two forts of Line trees, the male and the female ; but becaufe the male is rare to be feene, and the female is more familiar, I will onely giue you the defcription of the female, and leaue the other.
The female Line tree groweth exceeding high and great, like vnto an Elme, with many large fpreading boughes, couered with a fmooth barke, the innermoft being very plyant and bending from whence come fmaller branches, all of them fo plyable, that they may bee led or carried into any forme you pleafe : the leaues thereon are very faire, broad, and round, fomewhat like vnto Elme leaues, but fairer, fmoother, and of a frefher greene colour, dented finely about the edges, and ending in a fharpe point : the flowers are white, and of a good fmell, many ftanding together at the top of a ftalke, which runneth all along the middle ribbe of a fmall long whitifh leafe ; after which come fmall round berries, wherein is contained fmall blackifh feede : this tree is wholly neglected by thofe that haue them, or dwell neere them, becaufe they fuppofe it to be fruitleffe, in regard it beareth chaffie huskes, which in many places fall away, without giuing ripe feede.

1 *Tilia fœmina.* The Line or Linden tree. 2 *Tamariscus.* The Tamariske tree. 3 *Acer maius latifolium.* The Sycomore tree. 4 *Staphy-lodendron.* The bladder nut. 5 *Rhus Myrtifolia.* The Mirtle leafed Sumach. 6 *Rhus Virginiana.* The Bucks horne tree. 7 *Vitis seu Potius Hedera Virginensis.* The Virginia Vine or rather Iuie.

The Vse of the Line tree.

It is planted both to make goodly Arbours, and Summer banquetting houfes, either belowe vpon the ground, the boughes feruing very handfomely to plafh round about it, or vp higher, for a fecond aboue it, and a third alfo : for the more it is depreffed, the better it will grow. And I haue feene at Cobham in Kent, a tall or great bodied Line tree, bare withont boughes for eight foote high, and then the branches were fpread round about fo orderly, as if it were done by art, and brought to compaffe that middle Arbour : And from thofe boughes the body was bare againe for eight or nine foote (wherein might bee placed halfe an hundred men at the leaft, as there might be likewife in that vnderneath this)& then another rowe of branches to encompaffe a third Arbour, with ftayres made for the purpofe to this and that vnderneath it : vpon the boughes were laid boards to tread vpon, which was the goodlieft fpectacle mine eyes euer beheld for one tree to carry.

The coles of the wood are the beft to make Gunpowder. And being kindled, and quenched in vinegar, are good to diffolue clotted bloud in thofe that are bruifed with a fall. The inner barke being fteeped in water yeeldeth a flimie iuyce, which is found by experience, to be very profitable for them that haue been burnt with fire.

17. *Tamarix.* Tamariske tree.

THe Tamariske tree that is common in our country, although in fome places it doth not grow great, yet I haue feene it in fome other, to be as great as a great apple tree in the body, bearing great arms; from whofe fmaller branches fpring forth young flender red fhootes, fet with many very fine, fmall, and fhort leaues, a little crifped, like vnto the leaues of Sauine, not hard or rough, but foft and greene : the flowers be white moffie threads, which turne into dounie feede, that is carried away with the winde.

Tamarifcus folijs ablidis. White Tamariske. There is another kinde hereof very beautifull and rare, not to be feene in this Land I thinke, but with Mr. William Ward, the Kings feruant in his Granary, before remembred, who brought me a fmall twigge to fee from his houfe at Boram in Effex, whofe branches are all red while they are young, and all the leaues white, abiding fo all the Summer long, without changing into any fhew of greene like the other, and fo abideth conftant yeare after yeare, yet fhedding the leaues in Winter like the other.

The Vse of Tamariske.

The greateft vfe of Tamariske is for fpleneticke difeafes, either the leaues or the barke made into drinkes; or the wood made into fmall Cans or Cups to drinke in.

18. *Acer maius latifolium.* The great Maple or Sycomore tree.

THe Sycomore tree, as we vfually call it (and is the greateft kind of Maple, cherifhed in our Land onely in Orchards, or elfewhere for fhade and walkes, both here in England, and in fome other countries alfo) groweth quickly to bee a faire fpreading great tree, with many boughes and branches, whofe barke is fomewhat fmooth : the leaues are very great, large, and fmooth, cut into foure or fiue diuifions, and ending into fo many corners, euery one ftanding on a long reddifh ftalke: the bloomings are of a yellowifh greene colour, growing many together on each fide of a long ftalke, which after turne into long and broad winged feede, two alwaies ftanding together on a ftalke, and bunched out in the middle, where the feed or kernell lyeth, very like vnto the common Maple growing wilde abroad, but many more together, and larger.

The

The Vse of the Sycomore tree.

It is altogether planted for fhady walkes, and hath no other vfe with vs that I know.

19. *Nux Veſicaria.* The bladder Nut.

THis tree groweth not very high, but is of a meane ſtature, when it is preſerued and pruined to grow vpright, or elſe it ſhooteth forth many twigges from the rootes, and ſo is fit to plant in a hedge rowe, as it is vſed in ſome places : the body and armes are couered with a whitiſh greene barke : the branches and leaues on them are like vnto the Elder, hauing three or fiue leaues ſet one againſt another, with one of them at the end, each whereof is nicked or dented about the edges: the flowers are ſweete and white, many growing together on a long ſtalke, hanging downeward, in forme reſembling a ſmall Daffodill, hauing a ſmall round cup in the middle, and leaues about it : after which come the fruit, incloſed in ruſſetiſh greene bladders, containing one or two browniſh nuts, leſſer then Haſell nuts, whoſe outer ſhell is not hard and woody, like the ſhell of a nut, but tough, and hard withall, not eaſie to breake, within which is a greene kernell, ſweetiſh at the firſt, but lothſome afterwards, ready to procure caſting, and yet liked of ſome people, who can well endure to eate them.

The Vse of the Bladder Nut.

The greateſt vſe that I know the tree or his fruit is put vnto, is, that it is receiued into an Orchard, either for the rarity of the kinde, being ſuffered to grow into a tree, or (as I ſaid before) to make an hedge, being let grow into ſuckers.

Some Quackſaluers haue vſed theſe nuts as a medicine of rare vertue for the ſtone, but what good they haue done, I neuer yet could learne.

20. *Rhus Myrtifolia.* The Mirtle leafed Sumach.

THis lowe ſhrubbe groweth ſeldome to the height of a man, hauing many ſlender branches, and long winged leaues ſet thereon, euery one whereof is of the bigneſſe of the broad or large Mirtle leafe, and ſet by couples all the length of the ribbe, running through the middle of them. It beareth diuers flowers at the tops of the branches, made of many purple threads, which turne into ſmall blacke berries, wherein are contained ſmall, white, and rough ſeed, ſomewhat like vnto Grape kernels or ſtones. This vſeth to dye down to the ground in my Garden euery Winter, and riſe vp again euery Spring, whether the nature thereof were ſo, or the coldneſſe of our climate the cauſe therof, I am not well aſſured. It is alſo rare, and to be ſeen but with a few.

The Vse of this Sumach.

It is vſed to thicken or tanne leather or hides, in the ſame manner that the ordinary Sumach doth ; as alſo to ſtay fluxes both in men and women.

21. *Rhus Virginiana.* The Virginia Sumach, or Buckes horne tree of Virginia.

THis ſtrange tree becommeth in ſome places to bee of a reaſonable height and bigneſſe, the wood whereof is white, ſoft, and pithy in the middle, like vnto an Elder, couered with a darke coloured barke, ſomewhat ſmooth : the young branches that are of the laſt yeares growth are ſomewhat reddiſh or browne, very ſoft and

and fmooth in handling, and fo like vnto the Veluet head of a Deere, that if one were cut off from the tree, and fhewed by it felfe, it might foone deceiue a right good Woodman, and as they grow feeme moft like thereunto, yeelding a yellowifh milke when it is broken, which in a fmall time becommeth thicke like a gumme : the leaues grow without order on the branches, but are themfelues fet in a feemly order on each fide of a middle ribbe, feuen, nine, ten, or more on a fide, and one at the end, each whereof are fomewhat broad and long, of a darke greene colour on the vpperfide, and paler greene vnderneath, finely fnipped or toothed round about the edges : at the ends of the branches come forth long and thicke browne tufts, very foft, and as it were woolly in handling, made all of fhort threads or thrums ; from among which appeare many fmall flowers, much more red or crimfon then the tufts, which turne into a very fmall feede : the roote fhooteth forth young fuckers farre away, and round about, whereby it is mightily encreafed.

The Vfe of this Sumach.

It is onely kept as a rarity and ornament to a Garden or Orchard, no bo-die, that I can heare of, hauing made any tryall of the Phyficall properties.

---

22. *Vitis, feu potius Hedera Virginenfis.* The Virginia Vine, or rather Iuie.

THis flender, but tall climing Virginia Vine (as it was firft called ; but Iuie, as it doth better refemble) rifeth out of the ground with diuers ftems, none much bigger then a mans thumbe, many leffe ; from whence fhoote forth many long weake branches, not able to ftand vpright, vnleffe they be fuftained: yet planted neere vnto a wall or pale, the branches at feuerall diftances of the leaues will fhoote forth fmall fhort tendrels, not twining themfelues about any thing, but ending into foure, fiue, or fix, or more fmall fhort and fomewhat broad clawes, which will faften like a hand with fingers fo clofe thereunto, that it will bring part of the wall, morter, or board away with it, if it be pulled from it, and thereby ftay it felfe, to climbe vp to the toppe of the higheft chimney of a houfe, being planted thereat : the leaues are crumpled, or rather folded together at the firft comming forth, and very red, which after growing forth, are very faire, large, and greene, diuided into foure, fiue, fix, or feuen leaues, ftanding together vpon a fmall foote-ftalke, fet without order on the branches, at the ends whereof, as alfo at other places fometime, come forth diuers fhort tufts of buds for flowers ; but we could neuer fee them open themfelues, to fhew what manner of flower it would be, or what fruit would follow in our country : the roote fpreadeth here and there, and not very deepe.

The Vfe of this Virginian.

We know of no other vfe, but to furnifh a Garden, and to encreafe the number of rarities.

And thus haue I finifhed this worke, and furnifhed it with whatfoeuer Art and Nature concurring, could effect to bring delight to thofe that liue in our Climate, and take pleafure in fuch things ; which how well or ill done, I muft abide euery ones cenfure : the iudicious and courteous I onely refpect, let Momus bite his lips, and eate his heart ; and fo Farewell.

FINIS.

Index omnium ſtirpium

quæ in hoc opere continentur.

Fff   Bellis

Fff 2   Gnaphalium

Index.

INDEX.

A

A Table of the English names of such Plants as are contained in this Booke.

The

Roſarubie

THE

A Table of the Vertues and Properties of the Hearbes contained in this Booke.

Ggg

Faults efcaped in fome Copies.

FOlio 8. line 14. for own reade home. f.12.l.27. for trouble reade treble. f.42. l.5. reade, like vnto that of a Lilly f.66.l.42. for χφς read χρίνε or λείεςς. f.73. l.37. for top of the flower, read cup. f.134.l.36. for compofed reade compaffed. f.150.l.4. for hath, reade haue, and line 5. for is are. f.173.l.12. put out thefe wordes, the infide, in the beginning of the line. f.189.l.38. reade *Biniflorum ordinibus.* f.218.l.19. reade goulons, and line 28 pratenfis. f.272. line 36. read Pothos. f.276 l.12. Chelidonia. f.281.l.37. for hath, haue. and l.28. Maftuerzo. f.284 l.15. Vicenza. f.287.l.39. Citrina. f.290.l.39. reade prouoke, and, helpe. f.329.l.37. for Melancholicke, reade Flegmaticke. f.330.331.333. reade Eryngium in all places. f.336.l.8. reade, and not very flat. f.356.l.31. Americanum. f.357.l.26. Cervicaria. f.358. l.45. reade, before it can haue. f.372.l.9. blot out, except it. f.389. for fpockes, reade fmockes. f.393.l.3. in the margent for cæruleo, read pleno. f.397.l.10. reade dwarfe. f.424.l.45. Hirculus. f.428.l.10. Tarentina. f.431.l.10. Cyprium. l.19. Amomum. f.438.l.17. for Diofcorides, reade Theophraftus. f.442.l.3. for caftings reade purgings. f.509.l.35. reade ρηγγύλη. f.513.l.24. transferre all that claufe of Onions vnto the other fide, vnder the vfe of Onions. f.516.l.37. transferre thefe words, [Bauhinus vpon Matthiolus calleth it *Solanum tuberofum efculentum*] vnto the former Potatoes of Virginia. f.520.l.13. for fwelleth, read fmelleth. f.541.l.51. reade, after your ftockes rayfed from ftones. f.566.l.20. for as, read and. and l.29. euery one. f.567.l.24. for Rice, read Rue. f.575 l.8. reade ferue to be miniftred to the ficke. f.588 l.3. Capandu. f.594.l.18. for facility, read faculty. f.595. l.39. reade Ricinus. f.600.l.4. Fuchfius

LONDON,

Printed by HVMFREY LOWNES *and* ROBERT YOVNG
at the figne of the Starre *on* Bread-ftreet hill.
1629.